MCA

Microsoft Certified Associate Azure® Data Engineer

Study Guide

MCA

Microsoft Certified Associate Azure® Data Engineer

Study Guide

Exam DP-203

Benjamin Perkins

Published by John Wiley & Sons, Inc., Hoboken, New Jersey.
Published simultaneously in Canada and the United Kingdom.

ISBNs: 9781119885429 (paperback), 9781119885443 (ePDF), 9781119885436 (ePub)

For general information on our other products and services or for technical support, please contact our Customer Care Department within the United States at (800) 762-2974, outside the United States at (317) 572-3993 or fax (317) 572-4002.

Wiley also publishes its books in a variety of electronic formats. Some content that appears in print may not be available in electronic formats. For more information about Wiley products, visit our web site at www.wiley.com.

Library of Congress Control Number: 2023941199

Cover image: © Jeremy Woodhouse/Getty Images
Cover design: Wiley

SKY10051302_071423

Acknowledgments

Creating a book starts first as an idea, which then iterates through many versions, until it takes the form of something consumable. Many people helped to progress this book from idea to final product. Here is a list of those who played a significant role in the creation of this book and the organization of its content:

- Ken Brown, senior acquisitions editor
- Robyn Alvarez, project manager
- Heini Ilmarinen, technical editor
- John Sleeva, copyeditor
- Nancy Carrasco, proofreader

Writing this book—and writing in general—has become something I enjoy. Writing gives me the opportunity to share some of my technical knowledge and experiences so that others can gain some knowledge and insights. In addition to sharing my words, I gain an even greater understanding of the topic, as I structure the content, conduct research, and create hands-on exercises. Writing a book requires a huge effort, but there are many reasons to do it. I'd like to thank my family for their support while I was writing this book. I know it took hours away from them. Thanks, Andrea, Lea, and Noa. You are the reason and my purpose.

About the Author

Benjamin Perkins is currently employed at Microsoft in Munich, Germany, as a Senior Escalation Engineer on the Azure team. He has been working professionally in the IT industry for close to three decades. He started computer programming with QBasic at the age of 11 on an Atari 1200XL desktop computer. He takes pleasure in the challenges that troubleshooting technical issues have to offer and savors in the rewards of a well-written program. After completing high school, he joined the United States Army. After successfully completing his military service, he attended Texas A&M University in College Station, Texas, where he received a Bachelor of Business Administration in Management Information Systems. He also received a Master of Business Administration from the European University.

His roles in the IT industry have spanned the entire spectrum, including programmer, system architect, technical support engineer, team leader, and mid-level manager. While employed at Hewlett-Packard and Compaq Computer Corporation, he received numerous awards, degrees, and certifications. He has a passion for technology and customer service and looks forward to troubleshooting and writing more world-class technical solutions: "My approach is to write code with support in mind, and to write it once correctly and completely so we do not have to come back to it again, except to enhance it."

Benjamin has written numerous magazine articles and training courses and is an active blogger. His catalog of books covers C# programming, IIS, NHibernate, and Microsoft Azure.

Benjamin is married to Andrea and has two wonderful children, Lea and Noa.

About the Technical Editor

Heini Ilmarinen is a data enthusiast with a passion for architecture and DevOps. Heini currently works as Azure Lead and DevOps Consultant at Polar Squad, helping customers bring their data platforms to life in Azure.

Heini initially studied to become a mathematics teacher, graduating from Helsinki University with a Master of Science. After graduating, she transitioned to the IT industry, leveraging her skills for problem-solving and making complex topics easy to understand. In IT, Heini started her career working in infrastructure architecture development projects in hybrid environments. With architecture as a starting point, her career developed from working with Azure to getting deeper into data projects to topics related to DevOps.

Over the years, Heini has worked in a multitude of Azure projects, from application development to data projects, gaining a broad understanding of the requirements for creating functional, production-ready solutions. For the past two years, she has also engaged in community events and public speaking, gaining the Data Platform MVP award.

Heini can be often found riding her snowboard and enjoying the fresh air, or riding up and down hills on her mountain bike.

Contents at a Glance

Contents

Table of Exercises

Introduction

A long time ago, I was sitting at my desk happily coding my Active Server Page (ASP) and COM component, when someone approached me and asked if I knew anything about databases. Without even a pause, I answered a confident yes, most people in IT know "something" about databases, right? Well, it turned out that a big project was starting, and they needed someone to create and manage a database. I acquired a server, installed a relational database management system (RDMBS), and executed `CREATE DATABASE dbName; GO`. And the rest is history. I like to call that out because these days, most of the data storage architecture already exists when you start the job. You must learn what someone else created. You experience problems but do not know why, because a lot happened before you started.

The new emerging technology called *big data* is providing a rare opportunity, kind of like the one I had. The opportunity is to build and/or be involved in creating an IT data analytics solution from the beginning. Being the person or the team who builds the framework and foundation of what could become a system that shapes the future of a company is career-altering. The experience is a differentiator that stays with you for the rest of your career, as it has in mine. But it could also be a catastrophe for numerous reasons, such as not being able to scale, being too hard to make changes, and not being reliable.

I must admit that during the early stages I re-created that database numerous times, dropping and re-creating tables, removing primary and foreign keys, changing indexes, reconfiguring triggers, and tuning stored procedures. I knew this was necessary in numerous scenarios because I made all the configurations myself and felt it was easier to start over than it was to troubleshoot further or make a questionable configuration that could have harsh consequences later. As the project matured, it became much more difficult and impactful to make changes; the design could no longer be changed; it was go time, do or die, succeed or fail.

Building the foundation of a project is great, though it can be a bit overwhelming, and at times you might feel you are guessing or simply bulldozing full speed ahead. Those feelings are normal, and some can end up defining you, destroying you, or making you stronger. The data analytics system you design must be able to scale, change, and provide dependable data on request; anything else will ultimately fail. This book can help you learn about scalability, flexibility, and reliability, which are areas that ultimately determine the success of a data analytics solution.

Who This Book Is For

This book is for anyone who wants to learn about Microsoft Azure products and features and, ultimately, to attain the Azure Data Engineer Associate certification. This book is not intended for absolute beginners, although beginners may gain some greater insights into Azure and how to consume and configure its products and services. Gaining the Azure Data

Engineer Associate certification means that you can design, develop, implement, monitor, and optimize data solutions using the following:

- Azure Synapse Analytics
- Azure Data Factory (ADF)
- Azure Databricks
- Azure Data Lake Storage (ADLS)
- Azure Storage
- Azure SQL
- Azure Cosmos DB
- Apache Spark
- HDInsight
- Azure Stream Analytics
- Azure Event Hubs / IoT Hub
- Azure Batch

In addition understanding these Azure data products, you need to have some additional knowledge and experience with the following and many other related and dependent Azure products:

- Microsoft Purview
- Azure Virtual Machines
- Azure Functions
- Azure App Service
- Azure DevOps
- Azure Key Vault
- Azure Policy
- Azure Active Directory
- Azure Managed Identity
- Azure Monitor
- Azure Migrate
- Azure Virtual Network

That is a very broad range of topics, and the number of possible scenarios in which to apply them is equally as great. This book will provide insights into each of those topics, plus numerous others, but you are expected to have some basic, preexisting experience with them.

What This Book Covers

This book covers everything you need to know to greatly increase the probability of passing the Azure Data Engineer Associate exam. Of most importance, however, this book will help you design, implement, and support the ingestion, preparation, analysis, and presentation of data. Which of those two scenarios is most important to you? Hopefully both, because that is the goal and purpose of this book. You will learn about many Azure products and features, including Azure Synapse Analytics, Azure SQL, Azure Databricks, Azure Data Factory, Azure security, Azure networking, Azure compute, Azure datastores and storage, Azure messaging services, Azure migration tools, Azure monitoring tools and Azure recovery tools. In addition to learning about what these products and features are and do, you will perform some real-world exercises to implement and use many of them.

How This Book Is Structured

Good design really is everything. Unless you plan before doing it, it is highly probable that the result will not quite measure up to the expectations. In many instances, even with good planning and thought, the result might not measure up or even be successful. There are many priorities and areas to be concerned with when planning a big project. The same is true when you are migrating existing on-premises workloads to Azure or creating new applications and infrastructure directly on Azure. In both scenarios, security, networking, compute, and data storage all come into focus. The chapters in this book are provided in the order of priority. When planning your migration or deployments, make sure to include each of the phases. The order in which those IT components are analyzed, designed, and implemented is important and is the reason the book is constructed in this way.

- Part I: Azure Data Engineer Certification and Azure Products
- Part II: Design and Implement Data Storage
- Part III: Develop Data Processing
- Part IV: Secure, Monitor, and Optimize Data Storage and Data Processing

Security is by far the most important point of concentration. The network needs to be secured before you place your workloads into it. Then your data, compliance and governance, messaging concepts, development concepts, initial application deployment, and updates cannot be ignored or missed. Once your application is deployed, its lifecycle is really just the beginning. Monitoring it and having a failover and disaster recovery plan designed and tested are necessities for production IT solutions.

Following the design pattern laid out by the chapter flow will help you become a great Azure Data Engineer. Note that when you take the Data Engineering on Microsoft Azure exam, you sign a nondisclosure agreement (NDA) stating that you will not discuss the questions or any of the content of the exam. That is very important so that the integrity and value of the credential you gain when passing the exam maintains its prestige. This book will help you learn the skills and gain the experience an Azure Data Engineer should have. By learning and exercising the techniques in this book, your probability of passing the exam will be greatly increased. The point is, the book is geared towards building your experience and skill set on the Azure platform, which will then enable you to gain the certification.

Chapter 1: Gaining the Azure Data Engineer Associate Certification Chapter 1 provides an overview of what it takes to attain the Azure Data Engineer Associate certification. It begins with a quick overview of all Microsoft data-related certifications, such as the Azure Data Scientist and Azure Data Analytics certifications. This way you get good insights into the specific expectations regarding the Azure Data Engineer Associate certification. Comparing different certifications helps you gain a more precise set of Azure Data Engineer skills. You might also consider taking the AZ-900 exam, which is an introduction to Azure certification, and/or the DP-900 exam, which is an introduction to the Azure data service products. Both certifications will benefit your learning progressions in this field, but they are optional and not required for the DP-203 exam. You will also find some tips on how to pass the DP-203 exam, followed by an introduction to many Azure products and features. Although the DP-203 exam focuses on data services such as Azure Synapse Analytics, Azure Data Factory, and Azure Databricks, you must have some knowledge of other Azure products, including Azure Active Directory, Azure Key Vault, Azure Managed Identity, and Azure Stream Analytics, to name a few.

Chapter 2: CREATE DATABASE dbName; GO The first few chapters of a book are usually meant to get the reader into the right mindset so that the content in the succeeding chapters can be digested more easily. In this case, however, buckle your seatbelt and get ready to hit the ground running, because there is no time to waste. Chapter 2 briefly introduces the world of data but then dives right into some rather sophisticated data structures, types, and concepts an Azure Data Engineer Associate must know. To some extent, the discussion on those topics should be a refresher for an experienced data engineer who intends on taking the Azure Data Engineer Associate exam. The chapter then proceeds to explain some details about Azure *software development kits (SDKs)* that target Azure data products, data querying languages, and some relevant programming language and techniques. Chapter 2 concludes with a discussion of the different stages of big data processing on the Azure platform.

Chapter 3: Data Sources and Ingestion At this point you will have gained ample knowledge of data structures, mid-level to advanced Data Manipulation Language (DML) operations, DataFrame capabilities, big data stages, and analytical types. All of what you have learned up to now has been theoretical; now it is time to put some of that knowledge into practice. Chapter 3 focuses on the numerous data sources that can contribute to an enterprise-scale data analytics solution. You will learn how to ingest data into a datastore on Azure, securely and in a location where it is ready to enter the next stage of processing. You will provision an Azure Data Lake Storage container, an Azure Synapse Analytics workspace, an Azure Data Factory, and much more.

Chapter 4: The Storage of Data Azure Storage, Azure SQL, Azure Cosmos DB, Azure Databricks, and numerous other data analytics products provide features across the numerous big data processing stages. Data—and its ingestion onto the Azure platform, no matter which product transforms it—requires a place to be stored. Data typically arrives in its raw state and in its defined format, such as JSON, Parquet, XML, etc. The data at this stage from all your data sources and producers is stored in a data lake. In Chapter 4 you will learn some techniques and best practices for storing data at the ingestion stage. You will also implement physical and logical data storage structures and a serving layer.

Chapter 5: Transform, Manage, and Prepare Data Your journey is far from over. Although you have now successfully ingested data onto the Azure platform, there is still much more to do. The data at this stage can be in two separate states. The first state is related to streaming in that the data is in transit, stored briefly, transformed very little, and passed on to a data consumer in almost real time. The other state is one that lends itself to a more extended lifecycle of transformation. The transformation of data often requires more than a single column update or data type conversion. More complicated activities like joins, merges, or purges are performed in predefined sequences along a pipeline. As each transformation activity occurs through these often interdependent activities, it becomes obvious that preparations and management of these activities are paramount. In Chapter 5 you will transform the data in your data lake from a raw state to a more refined and business-ready state.

Chapter 6: Create and Manage Batch Processing and Pipelines In Chapter 6 you really get your hands on some of the core features required to perform big data analytics on Azure. There is extensive focus on Azure Batch, a high-performance computing platform with massive amounts of CPU and memory available on demand. You will find enough computational power using Azure Batch for any big data workload. You will create numerous Azure Synapse Analytics pipelines that include multiple activities that transform data into a form that delivers data insights. Should you trigger a pipeline using a scheduled, tumbling, storage, or customer trigger? After reading this chapter, you will know. Solutions for handling missing, duplicate, and late-arriving data are provided in the form of hands-on exercises, with follow-up textual discussions about what you accomplished and how it works. After reading Chapter 6, you will have a solid working knowledge of concepts like upserting, batch job interdependencies, Jupyter notebooks, and data regressions.

Chapter 7: Design and Implement a Data Stream Processing Solution Chapter 7 is where all the work you have done in the previous chapters comes together. The sample data has been ingested and transformed, and the necessary insights have been discovered through exploratory data analysis. Those findings are used to create an Azure Stream Analytics query that analyzes brain wave readings in real time and determines the scenario in which they were taken. The brain wave readings are streamed to an event hub endpoint, processed by the Azure Stream Analytics job, and sent to a Power BI workspace that displays the results in real time. All the steps required to implement that solution are provided through the exercises in this chapter. If you do not have a brain interface, don't worry. There is an application and test data you can use to simulate that activity. You also learn how to optimize a data stream using partition keys, which results in massive parallelization of stream processing capability. Chapter 7 provides hands-on experience implementing the data insights learned from a big data analytics solution.

Chapter 8: Keeping Data Safe and Secure Keeping the data that is ingested, transformed, and consumed through the data analytics processes secure is the number one priority. Whether the data is at rest or in transit, it must be protected from bad actors with malicious intent. The first step to securing the data is to understand what kind of data you have, which is where Microsoft Purview can help. Then you need to set the sensitivity levels of the data, which helps you determine the kind of security to apply. Data that can be made public should have a different level of security than data that is highly confidential and personally identifiable. Row- and column-level security as well as data encryption are useful methods for protecting data at the lowest level. Protecting access to your data using firewalls, network security groups (NSGs), and private endpoints should be first and foremost in your mind. Additional security measures include role-based access control (RBAC) and access control lists (ACLs), which control who can access your data and what permissions they have with it. Auditing capabilities provide another layer of security, helping to identify and then restrict someone who is accessing data with high sensitivity levels. Microsoft Defender for Cloud is also a relevant toolset for monitoring and prevents activities that have malicious intentions. Chapter 8 discusses all these concepts and includes many hands-on exercises to help you gain deeper insights.

Chapter 9: Monitoring Azure Data Storage and Processing Once you're here, for all intents and purposes, you have achieved what most people do not. You now have a functional data analytics application running on the Azure platform. Whether you migrated it or created it from scratch, your application is secure; you have optimized your compute and data consumption; and you are certain to be compliant with all regulations in the countries where your company operates. Take a second to reflect and celebrate your accomplishments, but only for a second, and then recognize that you are not quite finished. Although you have done a lot, you need to ensure that the solutions you have running on Azure continue to work properly. If they stop running, you need to quickly gather logs to determine why. In Chapter 9 you will learn about the monitoring capabilities of each Azure data analytics product. You will also examine the execution of an Azure Synapse Analytics pipeline run and drill down into the performance details of each activity contained within it.

Chapter 10: Troubleshoot Data Storage Processing In Chapter 10 you will learn how to interpret monitor logs and use them to create action plans for resolving and improving performance issues. The chapter also provides tips that can be useful for improving data analytics performance in general, like compacting files, managing skewed data, and tuning queries. Once you finish this chapter and implement the performance enhancements, your data analytics pipelines will perform at the fastest speed possible. You will also learn how to troubleshoot Azure Synapse Analytics pipeline runs and Apache Spark jobs. Once your pipelines and/or Spark jobs are deployed to a production environment, they should handle unexpected scenarios without crashing. Examples on how to manage exceptions in Azure Batch, Azure Stream Analytics, and pipelines are covered here in detail.

What You Need to Use This Book

The following items are necessary to realize all the benefits of this book and to complete the exercises:

- A computer/workstation
- Internet access
- An Azure subscription
- Visual Studio 2022 Community (free) or Visual Studio Code
- Azure DevOps account
- Power BI Enterprise subscription

Many of the exercises require you to consume Azure resources, which has an associated financial cost. Make sure in all cases that you understand the costs you may incur when creating and consuming Azure products. After completing an exercise that requires the creation of an Azure product, you should remove the product. However, in many cases throughout the book, you rely on the Azure products created in previous exercises to complete the current exercise. Those scenarios are called out as much as possible.

Interactive Online Learning Environment and TestBank

Studying the material in the *MCA Microsoft Certified Associate Azure Data Engineer Study Guide* is an important part of preparing for the Data Engineering on Microsoft Azure certification exam, but we provide additional tools to help you prepare. The online TestBank will help you understand the types of questions that will appear on the certification exam.

- The Practice Tests in the TestBank include all the questions in each chapter as well as the questions from the Assessment test. *In addition,* there is one practice exam with 65 questions. You can use these tests to evaluate your understanding and identify areas that may require additional study.
- The Flashcards in the TestBank will push the limits of what you should know for the certification exam. There are 100 questions in digital format. Each flashcard has one question and one correct answer.
- The online Glossary is a searchable list of key terms introduced in this exam guide that you should know for the Data Engineering on Microsoft Azure certification exam.

To start using these to study for the Data Engineering on Microsoft Azure Certification exam, go to `www.wiley.com/go/sybextestprep` and register your book to receive your unique PIN. Once you have the PIN, return to `www.wiley.com/go/sybextestprep`, find your book, and click Register or Login and follow the link to register a new account or add this book to an existing account.

Like all exams, the Azure Data Engineer Associate certification from MCA is updated periodically and may eventually be retired or replaced. At some point after MCA is no longer offering this exam, the old editions of our books and online tools will be retired. If you have purchased this book after the exam was retired, or are attempting to register in the Sybex online learning environment after the exam was retired, please know that we make no guarantees that this exam's online Sybex tools will be available once the exam is no longer available.

DP-203 Exam Objectives

MCA Azure Data Engineer Study Guide: Exam DP-203 has been written to cover every DP-203 exam objective at a level appropriate to its exam weighting. The following table provides a breakdown of this book's exam coverage, showing you where each objective or subobjective is covered:

Exam Objective	Chapters
Design and implement data storage	
Implement a partition strategy	
▪ Implement a partition strategy for files	3, 4
▪ Implement a partition strategy for analytical workloads	3, 4
▪ Implement a partition strategy for streaming workloads	4
▪ Implement a partition strategy for Azure Synapse Analytics	3, 4
▪ Identify when partitioning is needed in Azure Data Lake Storage Gen2	3
Design and implement the data exploration layer	
▪ Create and execute queries by using a compute solution that leverages SQL serverless and Spark cluster	4
▪ Recommend and implement Azure Synapse Analytics database templates	4
▪ Push new or updated data lineage to Microsoft Purview	8

Exam Objective	Chapters
▪ Browse and search metadata in Microsoft Purview Data Catalog	8
Develop data processing	
Ingest and transform data	
▪ Design and implement incremental loads	6
▪ Transform data by using Apache Spark	5
▪ Transform data by using Transact-SQL (T-SQL)	5
▪ Ingest and transform data by using Azure Synapse Pipelines or Azure Data Factory	5
▪ Transform data by using Azure Stream Analytics	5
▪ Cleanse data	5
▪ Handle duplicate data	6
▪ Handle missing data	6
▪ Handle late-arriving data	6
▪ Split data	5
▪ Shred JSON	5
▪ Encode and decode data	5
▪ Configure error handling for a transformation	5
▪ Normalize and denormalize data	5
▪ Perform data exploratory analysis	5
Develop a batch processing solution	
▪ Develop batch processing solutions by using Azure Data Lake Storage, Azure Databricks, Azure Synapse Analytics, and Azure Data Factory	6
▪ Use PolyBase to load data to a SQL pool	6
▪ Implement Azure Synapse Link and query the replicated data	6
▪ Create data pipelines	6
▪ Scale resources	6, 10
▪ Configure the batch size	6
▪ Create tests for data pipelines	9
▪ Integrate Jupyter or Python notebooks into a data pipeline	6

Exam Objective	Chapters
▪ Upsert data	6
▪ Revert data to a previous state	6
▪ Configure exception handling	6, 9, 10
▪ Configure batch retention	10
▪ Read from and write to a delta lake	6
Develop a stream processing solution	
▪ Create a stream processing solution by using Stream Analytics and Azure Event Hubs	7
▪ Process data by using Spark structured streaming	7
▪ Create windowed aggregates	7
▪ Handle schema drift	7
▪ Process time series data	7
▪ Process data across partitions	7
▪ Process within one partition	7
▪ Configure checkpoints and watermarking during processing	7
▪ Scale resources	7, 10
▪ Create tests for data pipelines	7, 9
▪ Optimize pipelines for analytical or transactional purposes	7, 10
▪ Handle interruptions	7, 10
▪ Configure exception handling	10
▪ Upsert data	6
▪ Replay archived stream data	7
Manage batches and pipelines	
▪ Trigger batches	6
▪ Handle failed batch loads	6, 10
▪ Validate batch loads	6
▪ Manage data pipelines in Azure Data Factory or Azure Synapse Pipelines	6
▪ Schedule data pipelines in Data Factory or Azure Synapse Pipelines	6

Exam Objective	Chapters
▪ Implement version control for pipeline artifacts	6
▪ Manage Spark jobs in a pipeline	6
Secure, monitor, and optimize data storage and data processing	
Implement data security	
▪ Implement data masking	8
▪ Encrypt data at rest and in motion	8
▪ Implement row-level and column-level security	8
▪ Implement Azure role-based access control (RBAC)	8
▪ Implement POSIX-like access control lists (ACLs) for Data Lake Storage Gen2	8
▪ Implement a data retention policy	8
▪ Implement secure endpoints (private and public)	8
▪ Implement resource tokens in Azure Databricks	8
▪ Load a DataFrame with sensitive information	8
▪ Write encrypted data to tables or Parquet files	8
▪ Manage sensitive information	8
Monitor data storage and data processing	
▪ Implement logging used by Azure Monitor	9
▪ Configure monitoring services	9
▪ Monitor stream processing	9
▪ Measure performance of data movement	9
▪ Monitor and update statistics about data across a system	9
▪ Monitor data pipeline performance	9
▪ Measure query performance	9
▪ Schedule and monitor pipeline tests	9
▪ Interpret Azure Monitor metrics and logs	9
▪ Implement a pipeline alert strategy	9

Exam Objective	Chapters
Optimize and troubleshoot data storage and data processing	
▪ Compact small files	10
▪ Handle skew in data	10
▪ Handle data spill	10
▪ Optimize resource management	10
▪ Tune queries by using indexers	10
▪ Tune queries by using cache	10
▪ Troubleshoot a failed Spark job	10
▪ Troubleshoot a failed pipeline run, including activities executed in external services	10

Reader Support for This Book

Source Code

The source code for this book can be found on GitHub at `https://github.com/benperk/ADE`.

How to Contact the Author

Connect with Benjamin on LinkedIn: `www.linkedin.com/in/csharpguitar`.

Follow Benjamin on Twitter `@csharpguitar`: `https://twitter.com/csharpguitar`.

Read Benjamin's blog: `www.thebestcsharpprogrammerintheworld.com`.

Visit Benjamin on GitHub: `https://github.com/benperk`.

How to Contact the Publisher

If you believe you have found a mistake in this book, please bring it to our attention. At John Wiley & Sons, we understand how important it is to provide our customers with accurate content, but even with our best efforts an error may occur.

In order to submit your possible errata, please email it to our Customer Service Team at `wileysupport@wiley.com`, with the subject line "Possible Book Errata Submission."

Assessment Test

1. Which Azure products are related to data management?
   - **A.** Azure Key Vault
   - **B.** Azure Synapse Analytics
   - **C.** Azure Data Lake Storage
   - **D.** Azure Active Directory
2. Which of the following datastores are both open source and available on Azure?
   - **A.** Oracle
   - **B.** Cosmos DB
   - **C.** Databricks
   - **D.** HDInsight
3. Which Azure products assist in managing and governing your Azure resources?
   - **A.** Azure Monitor
   - **B.** Azure Virtual Networks
   - **C.** Azure Event Hubs
   - **D.** Microsoft Purview
4. At which level can RBAC permissions be applied?
   - **A.** Subscription
   - **B.** Resource group
   - **C.** Database row
   - **D.** File, read, write, execute
5. Which of the following data structures are most valid for analytics?
   - **A.** Structured
   - **B.** Semi-structured
   - **C.** Unstructured
   - **D.** Object-oriented
6. Which of the following statements about data sharding are true?
   - **A.** Dedicated SQL pools rely on the Data Management Service (DMS) to realize benefits.
   - **B.** It distributes data across machines.
   - **C.** It is a useful approach for managing an amount of data too large to fit within a single database.
   - **D.** It is a storage technique used with small amounts of data.

7. What of the following statements about partitioning are true?
   - A. The data is divided by a numeric key generated by the platform.
   - B. A partition is commonly hosted on a single node and distribution.
   - C. Partitioning involves splitting data into smaller datasets.
   - D. Data can be divided by any logical grouping.
8. Which file types are optimized for WORM (write once, read many) operations?
   - A. Parquet
   - B. JSON
   - C. ORC
   - D. AVRO
9. Which type of policy can be used to archive data stored on an ADLS (Azure Data Lake Storage) container?
   - A. Data landing zone (DLZ)
   - B. Lifecycle management
   - C. Time to live (TTL)
   - D. Data archiving migration
10. Which of the following file formats supports the Zip Deflate (`.zip`) codec?
    - A. Parquet
    - B. XML
    - C. ORC
    - D. AVRO
11. Which Azure Storage access tier is the most expensive in terms of cost?
    - A. Archive
    - B. Hot
    - C. Premium
    - D. Cold
12. What distribution model is typically recommended as the most optimal for dimension tables, taking into consideration their unique characteristics and requirements?
    - A. Replicated
    - B. Round-robin
    - C. Heap
    - D. Partitioned columnstore

13. When your dedicated SQL pool performance level expands to 10 nodes, what is the recommended or optimal number of files to load?
    - A. 6
    - B. 60
    - C. 600
    - D. 300
14. What does the *E* in ETL stand for?
    - A. Elicit
    - B. Evacuate
    - C. Extract
    - D. Excerpt
15. Which options are useful for performing `UPSERT`s (`UPDATE` or `INSERT`) operations?
    - A. `WHEN NOT MATCHED THEN INSERT`
    - B. `MERGE INTO`
    - C. `WHEN MATCHED THEN UPDATE`
    - D. Hashed column
16. Which Azure product is typically used for running batch jobs as part of an Azure Synapse Analytics Custom activity?
    - A. Azure Virtual Machine
    - B. Azure Functions
    - C. Azure App Services WebJob
    - D. Azure Batch
17. Which of the following languages are supported in Azure Stream Analytics?
    - A. SQL
    - B. JavaScript
    - C. C#
    - D. Python
18. Why are partition keys significant when streaming data through Azure Stream Analytics?
    - A. Partitions are only important on datastores, not data streams.
    - B. The number of inbound partitions must equal the number of outbound partitions.
    - C. They optimize OLAP operations.
    - D. They enable parallelism and concurrency.

19. Which of the following are examples of an applied data mask?

    A. ****@**********.net

    B. (###) ###-7592

    C. 123-45-6789

    D. 11/11/2011

20. Which dynamic management view (DMV) offers insights into the resources and operations that are causing waits or delays within the system?

    A. `sys.dm_pdw_diag_processing_stats`

    B. `sys.dm_pdw_wait_stats`

    C. `sys.dm_pdw_request_steps`

    D. `sys.dm_tran_active_transactions`

21. Which dynamic management view (DMV) provides information about the steps executed within a query or request in Azure Synapse Analytics?

    A. `sys.dm_pdw_diag_processing_stats`

    B. `sys.dm_pdw_wait_stats`

    C. `sys.dm_pdw_request_steps`

    D. `sys.dm_tran_active_transactions`

22. Which default monitoring capabilities are typically available for most Azure products?

    A. Diagnostics settings

    B. Metrics

    C. Alerts

    D. Snapshot

23. What information is displayed as output when you execute the `PDW_SHOWSPACEUSED` command?

    A. The number of rows on each table for each distribution

    B. The amount of physical space used for the table on each distribution

    C. The amount of data read from cache for the given table per distribution

    D. The amount of remaining space in the distribution

24. What distinguishes a Failure dependency from a Fail activity?

    A. When a Fail activity is executed without error, the pipeline status is set to Success.

    B. When an activity bound to a Failure dependency is successful, the pipeline status is set to Success.

    C. Fail activities always result in a Failed pipeline run status.

    D. Failure dependencies are useful for cleaning up failed activities so the issue can be avoided when triggered again.

25. Which of the following data file format offers the highest performance and flexibility for data analytics?
   - **A.** Yet Another Markup Language (YAML)
   - **B.** Extensible Markup Language (XML)
   - **C.** Apache Parquet
   - **D.** JavaScript Object Notation (JSON)

26. Which statement accurately describes a Type 3 slowly changing dimension (SCD) table?
   - **A.** It contains the features of both a Type 1 table and a Type 2 SCD table.
   - **B.** It contains a version of the previous value(s) only.
   - **C.** It uses a surrogate key.
   - **D.** It provides the complete data change history.

27. Which of the following are columns typically found in a Type 3 slowly changing dimension (SCD) table?
   - **A.** A surrogate key
   - **B.** `COUNTER` (a value containing the number of times the row has been changed)
   - **C.** `IS_CURRENT` (a column with a flag that identifies the current version of the row)
   - **D.** A column containing the original value

28. Which of the following options can provide valuable data for optimizing data shuffling latency?
   - **A.** `sys.dm_pdw_nodes_db_partition_stats`
   - **B.** `df.shuffleOptimizer(true)`
   - **C.** `UPDATE STATISTICS`
   - **D.** `PDW_SHOWSPACEUSED`

29. Which of the following dynamic management views (DMVs) provides information about locked requests?
   - **A.** `sys.dm_pdw_waits_lock`
   - **B.** `sys.dm_pdw_lock_waits`
   - **C.** `sys.dm_pdw_resource_waits`
   - **D.** `sys.dm_pdw_node_status`

30. Which of the following networking security options are highly recommended for enhancing data security?
   - **A.** Firewall
   - **B.** OSI level 4 Azure Firewall
   - **C.** Azure Gateway
   - **D.** Private endpoints

Answers to Assessment Test

1. B, C. Only options B and C are Azure data products. The Azure products related to data management are Azure Data Lake Storage and Azure Synapse Analytics. Azure Data Lake Storage is designed for storing and analyzing big data, whereas Azure Synapse Analytics provides a unified analytics service for big data and data warehousing. Azure Key Vault is primarily used for storing secrets, keys, and certificates, and Azure Active Directory focuses on authentication and authorization.

2. B, C, D. Among the given options, HDInsight, Databricks, and Cosmos DB are available on Azure and leverage open-source technology. Oracle is not an open source datastore.

3. A, D. Among the provided options, Microsoft Purview and Azure Monitor are particularly helpful for managing and governing Azure resources. Azure Virtual Networks and Azure Event Hubs also play important roles in managing and monitoring Azure resources, but they are not specifically focused on governance.

4. A, B. RBAC permissions can be set at the subscription level, allowing users to manage resources within that subscription. RBAC permissions can also be assigned at the resource group level, allowing users to manage resources within that specific group. The other two options are not supported by RBAC.

5. A, B, C. Structured data refers to data that is organized in a fixed format, typically in tables with predefined schemas. It follows a well-defined model, making it easily analyzable. Semi-structured data lies somewhere between structured and unstructured data. It has some organization or metadata associated with it. The data does not adhere strictly to a predefined schema. Examples of semi-structured data include JSON files and XML documents. Unstructured data does not have a predefined format or organization. It can include text, images, videos, social media posts, and other forms of data that don't fit into traditional structured formats. Analyzing unstructured data requires specialized techniques. Object-oriented data structures, such as those used in programming languages like Java or Python, are not directly related to the concept of data structures for analytics. Object-oriented programming focuses on encapsulating data and behavior into objects, which is different from the structural organization of data for analytics purposes.

6. A, B, C. Dedicated SQL pools, also known as SQL data warehouses, may rely on the Data Management Service (DMS) to realize benefits such as efficient data movement, workload management, and query optimization. However, this statement is not directly related to data sharding, which focuses on data distribution rather than specific services or technologies. Data sharding involves distributing data across multiple machines. This helps improve scalability and performance by allowing parallel processing and reducing the load on individual machines. Data sharding is an approach commonly used for managing large amounts of data that cannot fit within a single database. By dividing the data into smaller subsets (shards), it becomes more manageable and easier to process.

7. B, C, D. A partition is commonly hosted on a single node and distributed across multiple nodes or servers. Each partition can be stored and processed independently, allowing for

parallelism and scalability. Partitioning involves splitting data into smaller datasets or subsets. This helps in managing and processing large volumes of data by dividing it into more manageable chunks. Data can be divided by any logical grouping based on specific criteria, such as range, hash value, or specific attributes. This logical grouping enables efficient data organization and retrieval based on the partitioning strategy chosen. Option A is not necessarily true for all partitioning techniques. While some partitioning approaches may use numeric keys, others may employ different methods, such as hashing or range-based partitioning. The choice of partitioning method depends on the specific requirements and characteristics of the data and the platform being used.

8. A, C. Parquet is a columnar storage file format designed for high-performance analytics. It is well suited for WORM operations due to its efficient compression, encoding, and columnar layout, which enable fast reads while minimizing data writes. Optimized Row Columnar (ORC) is another columnar storage file format commonly used for big data processing. It supports WORM operations by providing high compression rates, advanced predicate pushdown, and lightweight indexing, enabling efficient read operations.

9. B. Azure storage accounts have a feature named lifecycle management policy. Lifecycle management policies provide a mechanism to automatically manage the lifecycle of data stored in an ADLS container. These policies define rules and actions to be taken based on specified criteria, such as file age, file size, or custom metadata. With a lifecycle management policy, data can be seamlessly transitioned to archival storage tiers, such as Azure Blob Storage Archive or Azure Blob Storage Cool, to reduce costs while still retaining accessibility when needed.

10. B. XML files can be compressed using the Zip Deflate codec, which is commonly used to reduce file size and improve storage efficiency. The Zip Deflate codec is a widely supported compression algorithm, and XML files can be zipped using this codec to create compressed archives. The Parquet, ORC, and AVRO file formats do not natively support the Zip Deflate codec. These file formats typically have their own compression mechanisms optimized for columnar storage and efficient data processing. However, it's worth noting that the contents of these file formats can still be zipped using the Zip Deflate codec if needed, but the compression is applied to the resulting archive file rather than the file format itself.

11. B. There is no Premium access tier in this context. The Archive access tier is the least expensive among the options but has the longest retrieval times, making it suitable for infrequently accessed data with long-term retention needs. The Cold access tier offers a balance between cost and access latency, whereas the Hot access tier provides the highest availability and fastest access but at a slightly higher cost than the Cold tier.

12. A. Replicated distribution is generally preferred for dimension tables. In this distribution model, the entire dimension table is replicated across all compute nodes or shards in the data warehouse or database. Replication ensures that each compute node has a complete copy of the dimension table, allowing for efficient join operations and improved query performance. Replicated distribution is suitable for dimension tables, as they are usually smaller in size compared to fact tables and are frequently used in queries for filtering and grouping purposes.

13. C. 600 / 10 = 60, which abides by the law of 60. By default, a dedicated SQL pool has 60 distributions per node, so 600 files can all run in parallel, concurrently, on these 10 nodes. As the performance level of the dedicated SQL pool expands to 10 nodes, it is generally recommended to load around 600 files. Distributing the data across a sufficient number of files allows for parallel processing and optimal utilization of the available resources within the SQL pool, resulting in improved performance and query execution times.

14. C. ETL stands for extract, transform, and load.

15. A, B, C. Although hashed columns can have various applications in data management and optimization, they are not directly related to performing `UPSERT` operations. Hashed columns typically refer to columns that are processed or indexed using a hash function for improved performance or distribution.

16. D. Azure Batch is a cloud-based job scheduling service that allows you to run large-scale parallel and high-performance computing (HPC) batch jobs. It provides a platform for executing compute-intensive workloads across a pool of virtual machines, making it an ideal choice for running batch jobs as part of a Custom activity in Azure Synapse Analytics.

17. A, B. Table 7.1 in Chapter 7 describes the languages supported in Azure Stream Analytics.

18. B, D. Partition keys are essential in Azure Stream Analytics because they enable parallelism and concurrency during data processing. By partitioning the incoming data stream based on specific keys, Azure Stream Analytics can distribute the workload across multiple processing resources or nodes, allowing for simultaneous processing of data in parallel. This parallelism enhances the overall throughput and performance of the streaming pipeline.

19. A, B. A data mask is a technique or process used to obfuscate or modify sensitive data in order to protect its confidentiality while still allowing the data to be used for certain purposes, such as testing, development, or analytics. Data masking is commonly applied to personally identifiable information (PII) or other sensitive data elements to prevent unauthorized access or exposure.

20. B. See Table 9.2 in Chapter 9 for a description of each DMV.

21. C. See Table 9.2 in Chapter 9 for a description of each DMV.

22. A, B, C. Azure products provide built-in alerting mechanisms that allow you to set up notifications based on specific conditions or thresholds. Metrics provide insights into resource usage, availability, and health. Diagnostic settings allow you to collect and store diagnostic logs and telemetry data. There is no default snapshot capability for Azure products.

23. A, B, D. Executing the `PDW_SHOWSPACEUSED` command in Azure Synapse Analytics provides information on the physical space used by tables on each distribution and the number of rows in each table. It primarily focuses on the storage aspects of tables rather than cache utilization or remaining space in the distribution.

24. B, C, D. Fail activities are designed to generate a Failed pipeline run status. If a Fail activity is executed, it will always lead to the pipeline being marked as failed, regardless of whether any errors or exceptions occurred during its execution. Therefore, option A is incorrect, and the others are correct.

25. C. Apache Parquet is specifically designed for big data processing and analytics. JSON, XML, and YAML are less performant and less optimized for data analytics compared to Apache Parquet. These formats are typically more suitable for data interchange and human readability rather than high-performance analytics processing.

26. B. A Type 3 SCD table combines the features of both Type 1 and Type 2 SCD tables, storing a limited history by retaining a version of the previous value(s) for selected attributes. However, it does not provide the complete data change history associated with Type 2 SCD tables. There is no surrogate key, and a complete data change history is not stored.

27. D. Of the options, a Type 3 SCD table typically only contains a column with the original value, as shown in Figure 3.17 in Chapter 3.

28. A, C, D. `sys.dm_pdw_nodes_db_partition_stats` offers insights into how data is distributed and can be useful for identifying potential bottlenecks and optimizing data shuffling operations. `PDW_SHOWSPACEUSED` is a command used to display information about the space usage of a table in Azure Synapse Analytics. `UPDATE STATISTICS` is a command used to update the query optimizer's statistical information about the distribution and density of data in tables or indexes. `df.shuffleOptimizer(true)` is neither an option nor a command in the context of optimizing data shuffling latency.

29. B. See Table 9.2 in Chapter 9 for a description of each DMV. The `sys.dm_pdw_waits_lock` DMV does not exist. The `sys.dm_pdw_lock_waits` DMV in Azure Synapse Analytics provides insights into the lock waits occurring within the system. It specifically focuses on capturing information related to locked requests, allowing users to identify and analyze processes that are waiting for locks during their execution.

30. A, D. Firewalls are essential components of network security that monitor and control incoming and outgoing network traffic based on predetermined security rules. Private endpoints enable secure access to Azure services over a private network connection. They enable you to connect to Azure resources, such as storage accounts or Azure SQL Database, via a private IP address within your virtual network.

Azure Data Engineer Certification and Azure Products

Chapter 1

Gaining the Azure Data Engineer Associate Certification

WHAT YOU WILL LEARN IN THIS CHAPTER:

- ✓ The journey to certification
- ✓ How to pass Exam DP-203
- ✓ Azure product name recognition

The Azure Data Engineer Associate certification is one of several data-related accreditations offered by Microsoft. When compared to other available data-oriented certifications, as seen in Table 1.1, the Azure Data Engineer Associate certification is more complex. The primary reason for the added complexity relates to the dependencies a data scientist and a data analyst have on an Azure data engineer.

One primary responsibility of an Azure data engineer is to design a companywide platform on which data scientists or data analysts perform their experiments and analyses. For them to run these experiments and perform such analyses, the data needs to be hosted in a compliant, secured, performant, organized, and reliant manner. Although an Azure data scientist and an Azure data analyst are expected to understand and implement suitable analytical workloads, an Azure data engineer is expected to have a much broader range of responsibilities and reach.

TABLE 1.1 Azure certifications

Azure certification	Description
Azure Data Fundamentals	DP-900: Microsoft Data Fundamentals; basic knowledge of data concepts and Azure data products
Azure Data Scientist Associate	DP-100: Designing and Implementing a Data Science Solution on Azure; knowledge of predictive models and machine learning
Azure Data Analyst Associate	DA-100: Analyzing Data with Microsoft Power BI; proficiency to clean and transform data, provide data visualizations
Azure Data Engineer Associate	DP-203: Data Engineering on Microsoft Azure; design and support the platform for data scientists and data analysts to achieve their objectives
Azure Database Administrator Associate	DP-300: Administering Relational Databases on Microsoft Azure; ability to administer SQL Server database on-premises and in the cloud

I'm not suggesting that the other certifications are easy; my intention is to point out how the certifications link together. To better explain the expectations and responsibilities for each role, begin by reviewing Figure 1.1.

FIGURE 1.1 Comparing the Azure data scientist and analyst roles

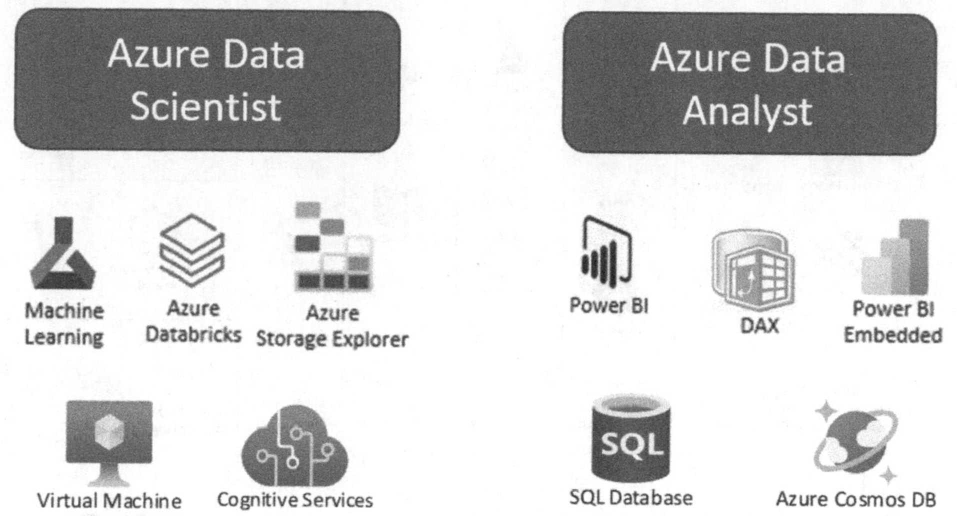

Notice that an Azure data scientist primarily focuses on Azure products that concentrate on the preparation, training, and experimentation of data, whereas an Azure data analyst focuses on making proper connections to data sources, extracting data from those sources, and then creating easy-to-comprehend data visualizations. It is certainly true that some individuals who have either of those job titles perform duties and have responsibilities other than these. In general, however, both roles focus heavily on the data and not so much on the end-to-end platform used for placing, accessing, manipulating, and consuming the data. That end-to-end responsibility falls to the Azure data engineer; the scope of that role is partially illustrated in Figure 1.2.

Considering all the products and features within the scope of responsibility of an Azure data engineer, it is clear that this role exceeds, in both scale and scope, that of data management, preparation, and analysis. In addition to those responsibilities typically given to an Azure data scientist and an Azure data analyst, the Azure data engineer role expands into aspects of the provisioning, securing, and management of a company's data services solution.

FIGURE 1.2 The Azure data engineer role

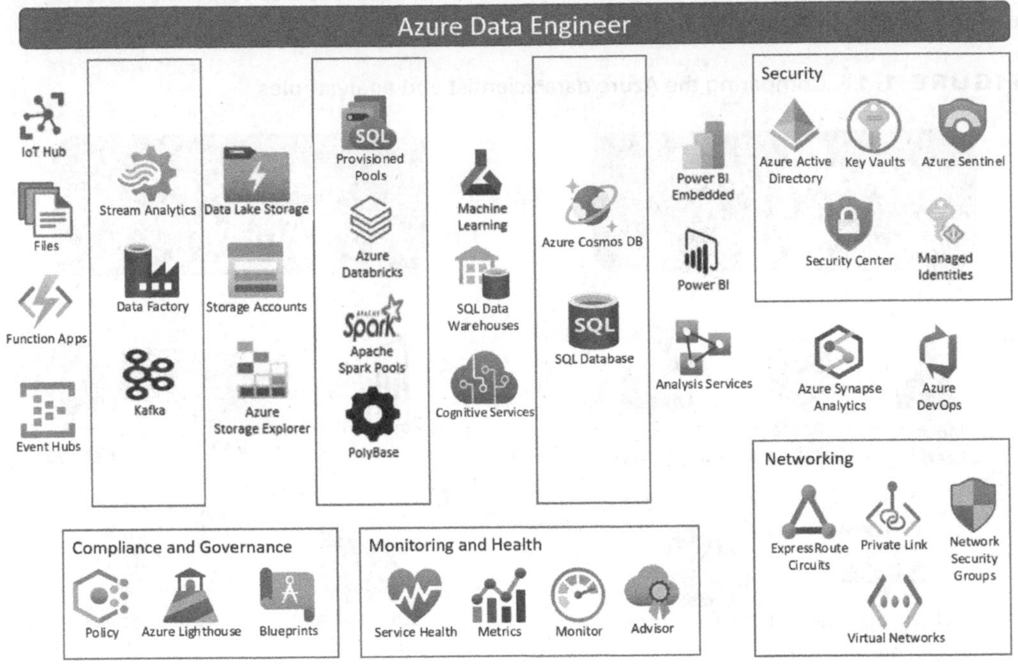

At this point in your career, many of the products in Figure 1.2 should already be somewhat familiar. You will be learning in more depth what these Azure products do, how they work together, and in what scenarios to use them. Understanding these topics is necessary to pass the Data Engineering on Microsoft Azure exam and become a great Azure data engineer.

Before moving on, there is one more certification we need to review: the Azure Database Administrator Associate certification. Figure 1.3 shows the context of the role and responsibilities.

This role focuses on *Structured Query Language (SQL)* Server and other Azure data-related products and services. There are many different implementations and operational aspects of running SQL Server solutions, such as on-premises, in the cloud, or using a hybrid model. It should be without any doubt that performing Big Data analytics running the SQL Server *relational database management system (RDBMS)* is possible and the resulting insights realize great value. Those who have been using SQL to *create, read, update, and delete (CRUD)* data stored in relational data structures will find this certification valuable. However, remaining isolated in the context of structured, or "relational," data would reduce and possibly prevent the realization of what other products and concepts can offer. *Not Only SQL (NoSQL)*, or "unstructured" or "nonrelational," data is not necessarily the substitute but rather a technique that must be added to anyone working in the *information technology (IT)* data management field. NoSQL and the tools commonly used in this discipline are part of a skillset that is no longer optional.

FIGURE 1.3 The Azure database administrator associate role

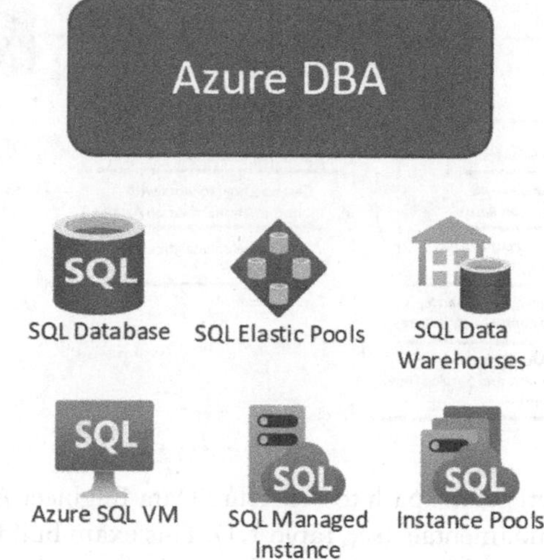

The Journey to Certification

When you set a goal—in this case, to attain the Azure Data Engineer Associate certification—make sure to take a moment to acknowledge the journey. Although the objective of this book is to help you earn a passing score on the test, the effort you make and the knowledge you retain are the critical components involved in performing the role. The certification is a validation of what you have learned. What you will learn in this book will not only help you study for the exam, but will provide you with opportunities to apply and use what you learn. Then you can take that skillset into your daily job.

Unlike numerous other Microsoft Azure certifications, there is no prerequisite to take the DP-203: Data Engineering on Microsoft Azure exam, but this doesn't mean you shouldn't consider preparing for and procuring some additional exam experience. Figure 1.4 provides a viable path to gradually build confidence and pertinent knowledge before taking the exam.

The first recommended exam on the path toward Azure Data Engineer Associate certification is AZ-900, Azure Fundamentals. This exam will help you understand basic cloud concepts, Azure product descriptions, and use case scenarios of core Azure products, features, and services. AZ-900 also covers Azure security, identity, networking, privacy, and governance constructs, as well as the products used for applying them. I will cover each of those concepts in this book, so if you choose not to pursue AZ-900, you will still learn enough about all those products to pass the exam. If you do prepare and pass the AZ-900, then most of what you read in this book about those topics will be a review, but with perhaps a different approach and context.

FIGURE 1.4 A path to the Azure Data Engineer Associate certification

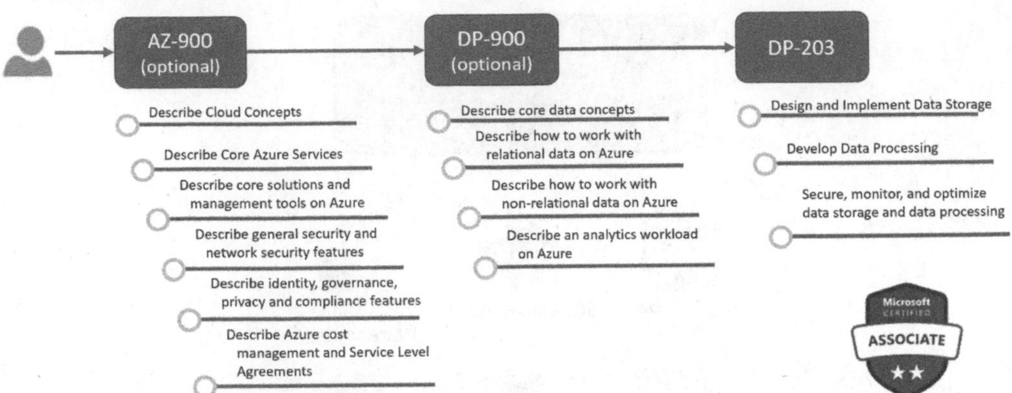

The other optional exam on the path to the Azure Data Engineer Associate certification is DP-900, Azure Data Fundamentals (see Table 1.1). This exam builds on the AZ-900, as it assumes you know the basics of Azure and therefore focuses mostly on data-oriented Azure products and concepts. If you are reading this book and have a zero cognizant comparative description between relational and nonrelational data structures, then you might want to take a step back and seriously consider the DP-900 before proceeding further. Those two concepts are covered in detail in this book, but you should be familiar with those two terms. The DP-900 also introduces the concept of data analytics, which should render a visualization of the Azure Synapse Analytics product into your brain. If it doesn't, then that is another reason to consider DP-900.

Remember that the journey, the acquired skillset, and the experience you gain along the way will make you successful in your career and job. The certification is only one endorsement of your skills. So, two things you should know before moving on: First, consider preparing for and taking both the AZ-900 and DP-900 exams before DP-203. The knowledge you gain is 100 percent related to the DP-203 exam and your job. Second, feel confident that although those two exams are recommended yet optional, the content in this book will be enough for you to be successful in obtaining the Azure Data Engineer Associate certification.

How to Pass Exam DP-203

There is no secret process or shortcut for passing the exam, at least using publicly available sources. You must invest the time and effort necessary to learn the required content to be successful. Consider this book as a source to guide you along that process. The following list contains ways to help you learn the required information and gain the skills for passing the Data Engineering on Microsoft Azure exam:

- Have a clear understanding of the exam expectations and requirements.
- Use Azure daily.

- Read articles on Azure to stay current.
- Understand all Azure products.

Before proceeding, it is important to note that before attempting any Microsoft certification exam, you must commit to a *nondisclosure agreement (NDA)*. In other words, you agree not to capture and/or share notes concerning the content contained within the actual exam. To protect the integrity of the exam and the Azure Data Engineer Associate certification itself, I will make no references to any actual question found within the exam. When you pass the exam using the content of this book, it is because you have learned the required information and can therefore wear the badge and share the credential with true pride.

Understanding the Exam Expectations and Requirements

It doesn't take much imagination to realize that it is helpful to know what an exam is testing before you take it. The more you know about the tested topics, the higher probability you have of passing it. There is a list of the skills measured on the DP-203 exam on the Microsoft certification website; go to `https://aka.ms/certification` and search for **data engineer**. Click the Exam DP-203: Data Engineering on Microsoft Azure link and then click the Download Exam Skills Outline link toward the middle/bottom of the page. In the skills outline, it clearly states that it is neither a definitive nor a complete list, but it is a helpful summary for setting boundaries of knowledge expectations. Take particular note of the four primary categories of skill expectations. This division of skills is how this book is organized, beginning with Chapter 3, "Data Sources and Ingestion":

- Part II: Design and Implement Data Storage
- Part III: Develop Data Processing
- Part IV: Secure, Monitor, and Optimize Data Storage and Data Processing

If you currently have the same amount of knowledge and experience for each of the four topics, your exam preparation should match the percentage of the exam the topic represents. If this is not the case, then use your own best judgment to decide which areas you need to focus most on.

Design and Implement Data Storage

The first topic is *Design and Implement Data Storage*, which as its name implies, involves designing a data storage solution and then implementing that solution in Azure. This topic covers 15 – 20% of the exam content. This topic mostly focuses on the formats in which data can be stored, which kind of storage product is best for each format, and how you place and manage the data on that storage product. Data is stored in many formats, such as documents, blobs, parquet, and relational databases. Some relevant, in-scope services might be *Azure Data Lake Storage (ADLS)*, Azure Blob Storage, or Azure Cosmos DB. Finally, some related terms are *schema*, *changing dimensions*, *temporal data*, and *incremental loading*.

Don't worry if you aren't familiar with any of these formats, products, or concepts. Part II will cover everything you need to know.

Develop Data Processing

The next section is *Develop Data Processing*, which covers 40 - 45% of the exam making it the largest part of the exam. Here, the primary focus is on the transformation of the data that has been ingested and/or stored either on the Azure platform or on-premises. An important term relating to data management is *extract, transform, and load (ETL)*, as illustrated in Figure 1.5.

FIGURE 1.5 The extract, transform, and load (ETL) approach

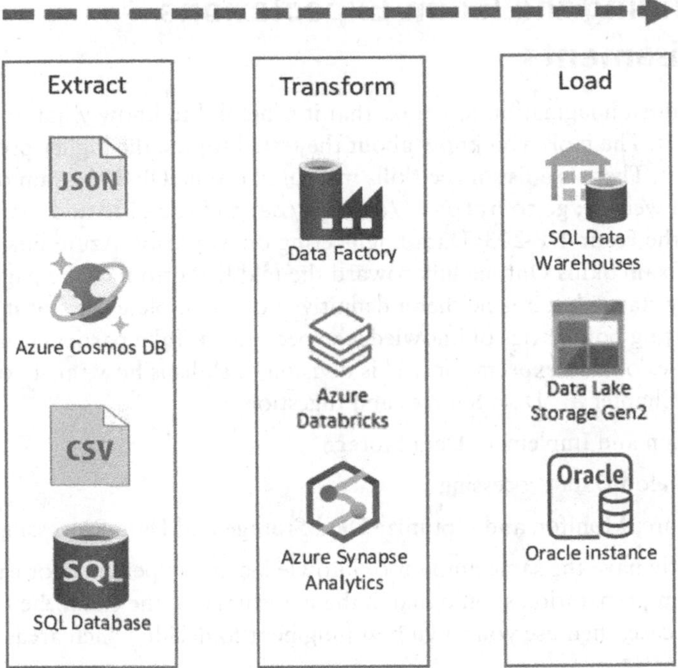

Data used for analytics is extracted from numerous sources. Each source has a unique format, for example, *JavaScript Object Notation (JSON)* or *comma-separated values (CSV)*. The transformation process occurs when data in different formats are changed from their original source format to a standard destination format. This data transformation is necessary so that intelligence can be gathered from a single location using a standard method, such as *Transact Structured Query Language (T-SQL)*.

There are numerous methods for transforming data. The most common methods occur during either *batching* or *streaming*. A simple definition of *batching* is the incremental processing of an existing set of data, in bulk. The "batch job" performs, for example, filtering, sorting, aggregation, and deduplication, all of which are based on business requirements. The batch processing logic must reflect the format of the data at the source, the format in which the destination is expecting it, and how to convert the data between the two formats.

The batch processing can occur in near real time, which means the data is transformed very shortly after it is generated, or it can be processed periodically, such as every hour, day, or month. Again, the schedule depends on the purpose of the data and business requirements. This is by no means an easy exercise, and data transformation is most often a distinct scenario for each person or company performing the processing. Azure products like *Azure Data Factory (ADF)*, *Azure Databricks*, and *Azure Synapse Analytics* are useful for handling batch processing of data.

The illustrations in this chapter are meant to introduce you to the relevant Azure data products. The intention is for you to get comfortable with the products and begin to visualize where they fit into an Azure data services solution and strategy. More product details, how the products work together, and their roles are described in detail in the remainder of this book.

Streaming, on the other hand, is not static (Figure 1.6). The data is not processed in bulk and is not pulled from an existing set of data. If you visualize a stream, you most likely think of flowing water moving effortlessly from a source to a destination. The same visualization applies for data streaming in that data is being generated from a source, such as via a *brain computer interface (BCI)*, a weather monitor, or a location tracker. Streamed data is received and transformed, in real time, then stored. That data could be reprocessed again offline via batching, or depending on the streaming logic, the data might be ready for loading into a destination data source for intelligence gathering. *Apache Kafka for HDInsight*, *Azure Stream Analytics*, *Azure Event Hubs*, and *Azure Databricks* are useful products for implementing a highly available and performant streaming solution.

Secure, Monitor, and Optimize Data Storage and Data Processing

Secure, monitor, and optimize data storage and data processing covers —30–35% of the exam. Protecting the data you store on the Azure platform is of extreme importance. That statement is generally accepted but should be acknowledged often so that it remains front and center of all Azure data service project deployments. In many cases, the unintentional exposure of sensitive data has a catastrophic impact on both the company and on the individuals to whom the data belongs. The recovery from such an exposure will be costly, so it is something that must avoided. You can approach the security aspects of Azure from these four perspectives:

- The Azure management portal
- Accessing and securing data

- Protecting passwords and identities
- Privacy and governance

FIGURE 1.6 A data streaming pipeline

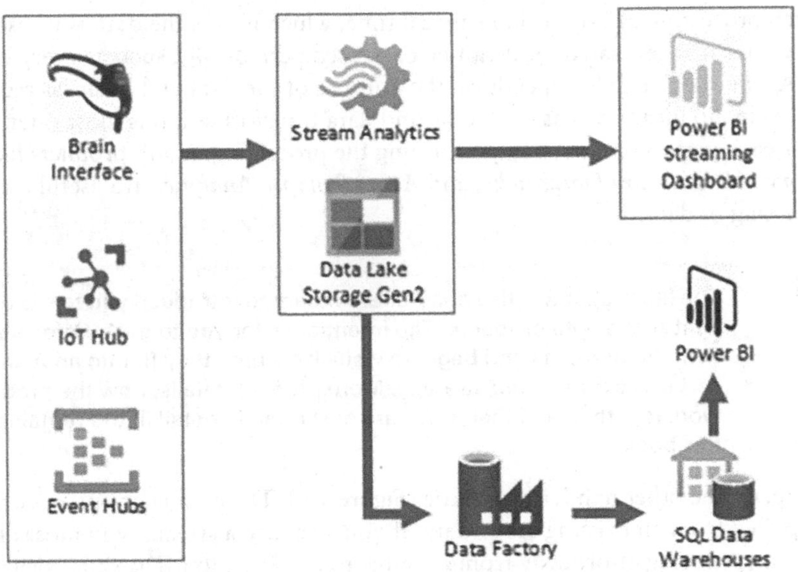

The Azure management portal (`https://portal.azure.com`) is where subscription owners, administrators, and contributors build and manage their applications. There are numerous roles and responsibilities within a team that contribute to an IT solution running on the Azure platform. Not all of those roles require access to the cost reports or need the ability to delete an Azure SQL database. *Role-based access control (RBAC)* limits individual access to portal-related and resource management activities. There are numerous components to this concept, as shown in Figure 1.7. A crucial product to achieve this aspect of security is *Azure Active Directory (Azure AD)*.

FIGURE 1.7 Azure portal security product and feature security hierarchy

The Azure AD is where access credentials, group affiliations, and permission information are stored. The privilege to administer the Azure AD should be limited and tightly controlled.

Anyone with administrator access to your company's Azure AD will have access to all your Azure assets contained with it, including access to all user, group, and application information in the Azure AD, plus management rights to some Microsoft 365 services. By default, they will not have access to Azure resources, but any global admin in Azure AD can elevate themselves to the User Access Administrator role. That way, they gain visibility to all Azure resources in subscriptions that are linked to that Azure AD and can then elevate themselves to any role in any of these subscriptions. Protect this privilege by all means necessary.

Azure data products tend to provide more management capabilities via the Azure portal when compared to other compute resources. This means you may need to spend extra time defining what tasks each person on your team requires and then map them to the RBAC roles provided by the Azure data product in the portal. For example, does a single person need access to both the Synapse Apache Spark Administrator role and the Synapse SQL Administrator role? Perhaps, perhaps not, but that decision needs to be made based on requirements.

Once the Azure resources are provisioned and configured, accessing and manipulating that data comes into focus. There are two primary methods used to gain access to data. The first one is through an application. In Figure 1.8, an Azure app service, a function app, and Power BI are attempting to access resources that store data. Some products to help secure access are *private links*, *virtual network (VNet)*, and *network security groups (NSGs)*. Many Azure products have a global discoverable endpoint enabled by default. For example, an Azure Cosmos DB has a *Uniform Resource Identifier (URI)* of `https://*.documents.azure.com`, where * is the name of the Azure Cosmos DB account. This might not be a desired scenario; in that case, the solution is to implement a private link that results in the endpoint no longer being globally discoverable. Additionally, implementing a VNet allows you to control the ports and protocols used for accessing the resource that houses your data via NSGs.

The second means of accessing data is illustrated toward the bottom of Figure 1.8. The diagram shows how users, via the Azure portal, can access the resources and the data residing on those resources. This is related to the previous RBAC topic. Two additional concepts that relate to this type of data access are *access control lists (ACLs)* and data encryption. ACLs are used to control access to files existing in a hierarchical directory structure. ACLs are applied within the context of ADLS. Data encryption is focused on how the data is stored and transferred: data-at-rest or data-in-transit. By default, all data on Azure storage products are encrypted by the data-at-rest feature. There are some additional details about how to implement data-in-transit which I'll discuss later in this book, but the main concept with data-in-transit has to do with *Transport Layer Security (TLS)*.

Next, consider the requirements around managing passwords and identities. It is considered bad practice to store user IDs, passwords, and connection strings in application configuration files because anyone who has access to the application code has access to the data. Instead, you store sensitive credentials in an *Azure Key Vault (AKV)*, which can be accessed at runtime to retrieve the necessary credentials to access a database. The identity used to access AKV is known as a *Managed Identity (MI)*. Consider that from an end-user perspective, user identities are managed via Azure AD; however, there is also the concept of a *service principle.* A service principal, also called MI, is an account that is assigned to a service instead of a human and can only be used with an Azure resource. Figure 1.9 describes the flow where an application is assigned an MI, which is then used to get a connection string from Azure Key Vault, which in turn is used to connect to a datastore.

FIGURE 1.8 An Azure data security diagram with products and features

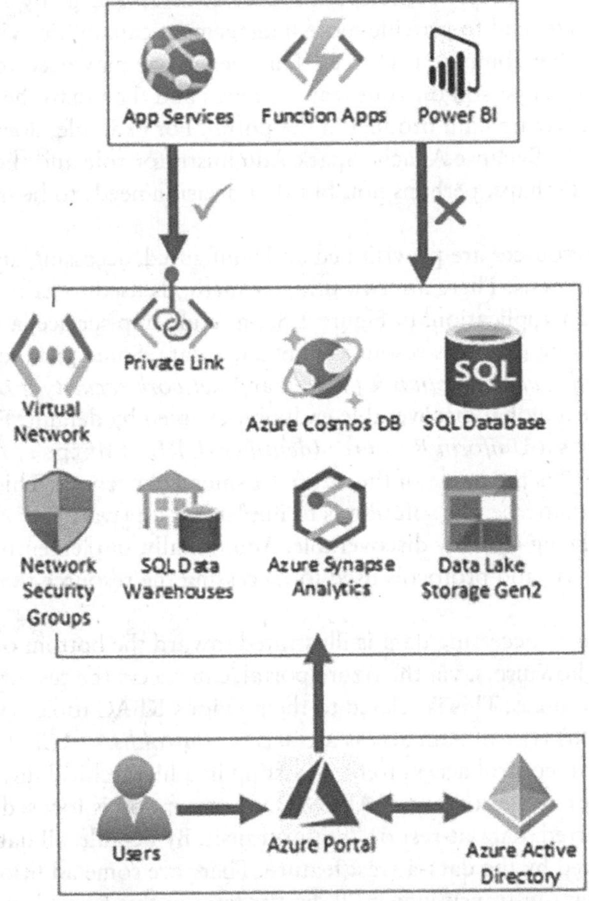

The last remaining topic for this portion of the exam has to do with privacy and governance. Azure has some of the best tools for complying with industry standards, some of which are shown in Figure 1.10.

FIGURE 1.9 Using Azure Key Vault and MI

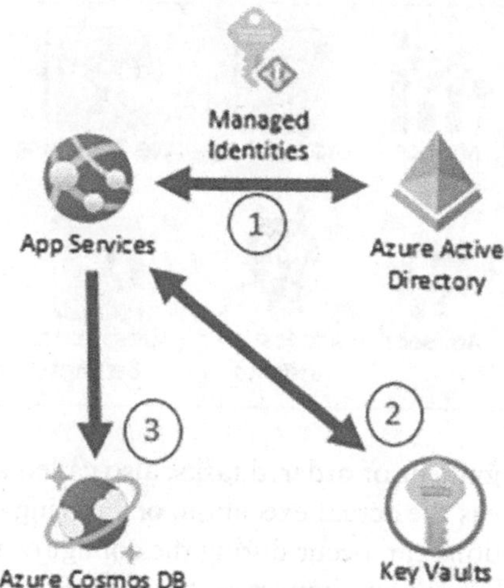

FIGURE 1.10 Azure privacy and governance products

These tools help a company manage the provisioning of Azure products so that they conform to a certain level of security; for example, making sure that any resource with a globally discoverable endpoint prohibits access via an unsecured channel. The privacy and governance features can also walk you through the process of marking the sensitivity levels of your data. Then, you can restrict data based on those levels and monitor who is accessing that data, when, and how often. Companies often overlook this aspect of managing an application running in the cloud. In some cases, there can be legal ramifications and potential loss of a contract if certain criteria are not met. You must be able to identify and use the tools and features available to adhere to these privacy and governance requirements in order to pass the exam. Monitoring and optimizing data storage and data processing are concerned with monitoring, performance tuning, and debugging failed pipeline executions or jobs. Numerous products are available for monitoring the health of your data analytics products, some of which are shown in Figure 1.11. The Azure product listed most prominently in the online skill requirements for the Azure Data Engineer Associate certification is *Azure Monitor*. Without a logging capability of some kind, you'd have trouble identifying the source and extent of compromise in the event of an incident.

FIGURE 1.11 Azure health and monitoring products

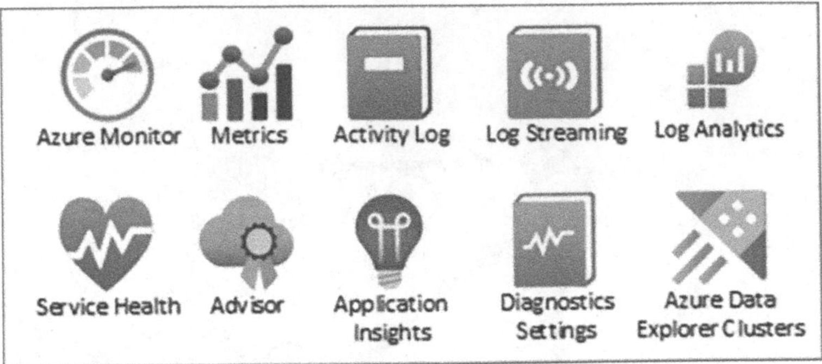

The configuration and alignment of ordered tasks, also called a *pipeline*, is an administrative activity, whereas the actual execution, or carrying out of those tasks, is what manipulates the data. Exceptions can occur during the configuration of a pipeline, but those exceptions wouldn't normally have any impact on the data. Pipeline tasks that manipulate data by performing inserts, updates, and deletes can result in data corruption, exceptions, or failures. For that reason, it is important to have information about the success and failure of each task throughout the pipeline run. That information should be logged into Azure Monitor. These logs are useful for identifying the specific task that caused the unexpected outcome. Using that information, you can review that specific task to find out what happened and implement a fix to prevent it in the future.

Scenarios consisting of failures and exceptions are not the only kind of problem you might face. A pipeline may simply hang, stop unexpectedly, or perform very slow. Capturing and analyzing performance metrics also help to pin down the causes for latent behavior.

Performance metrics, once analyzed, are useful for improving the performance of, for example, *Apache Spark Pools* or *SQL Pools* running within Azure Synapse Analytics (Figure 1.12). Partitioning, indexing, caching, and *user-defined function (UDF)* optimizations can be used to improve the performance of the pipeline or job. Keep in mind that the longer the job runs, the greater the incurred cost since the compute pool is consumed for longer periods of time. Therefore, it is prudent to get the jobs and pipelines to run as quickly and efficiently as possible.

FIGURE 1.12 Azure Synapse pools, performance, and debugging

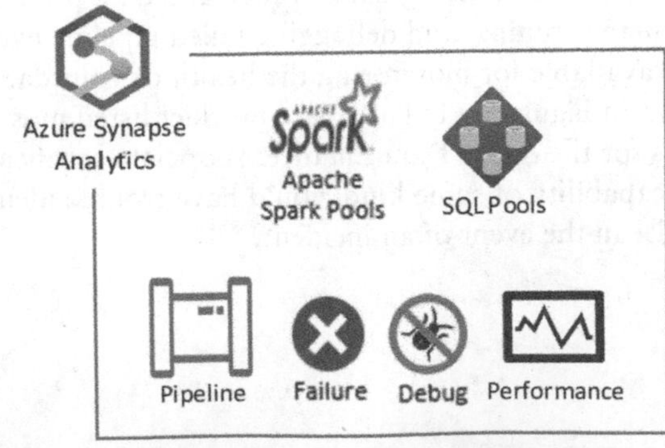

Having a solid skillset and some applicable experience relating to monitoring, gathering logs, and analyzing performance data and troubleshooting failed Azure Spark jobs and SQL Pool pipeline runs is a necessity to pass the exam. This is achieved by provisioning, consuming, and experiencing the Azure data service products. In this book you will gain this experience through detailed descriptions and extensive discussions covering each key Azure data product and feature. Now that you know the sections of the exam, read on for more tips about not only passing the exam, but how to become a great Azure data engineer.

Use Azure Daily

If you do not have an Azure subscription, this is the first action you need to take. Navigate to `https://azure.microsoft.com` and open a free account. The subscription currently offers $200 of free credits and many other free services for the first 12 months. If you have Azure but you are not actively using it, consider increasing your consumption and exposure to it immediately. You need to have a good understanding of how products and features are organized in the Azure portal. You need significant exposure to the many Azure data services, such as analytics, databases, and storage. The more of those services you regularly work with and the more often you work with them, the better.

The best-case scenario for gaining the Azure Data Engineer Associate certification is that you are already working on a solution running on Azure. Perhaps you were part of the design team that implemented a data solution for your company, or perhaps you are using an existing set of tools to perform analytics. Either way, your chances of passing the exam are increased the more you use the product. There is a term, *catch-22*, that describes a dilemma of being trapped between mutual conflicting circumstances. This can come into play here because what happens if you are motivated to earn this certification to gain the experience but you need the experience to gain the certification? There exists a similar scenario when you're looking for a job that requires three years of experience, but you need a job to get that experience. What you will learn in this book will be helpful in getting you out of the catch-22. Read the chapter contents and perform the exercises to gain some hands-on experience, which is how you learn the most.

Read Azure Articles to Stay Current

To write that the amount and velocity of change in the IT industry is "moving rapidly" would greatly understate reality. The fact is, change is happening constantly in real time. Companies are now able to serve customers 24 hours a day, 7 days a week thanks to, for the most part, globalization. It is always daytime someplace on Earth, and that fact allows a company to strategically place subsidiaries around the globe. With global processes in place, a single task can be passed from location to location and effectively worked on, from beginning to end, without any pause.

The cloud computing sector is no exception and is where most of the change is happening. This is due to two main reasons:

- Cloud computing is "relatively" new.
- Competition for customers is fierce.

Although cloud computing has been around for a few decades, it has only started to kick into high gear in the last few years. Originally, running IT operations in the "cloud" was focused very much on *infrastructure as a service (IaaS)* product offerings. IaaS offers the compute power for running IT operations without having to pay for, set up, or administer the networking or datacenter architecture. Table 1.2 lists popular cloud service offerings.

TABLE 1.2 Popular cloud service offerings

Cloud Service	Acronym	Description
Infrastructure as a service	IaaS	Not responsible for network or datacenter; complete control of the operating system.
Platform as a service	PaaS	IaaS but without control of the operating system
Software as a service	SaaS	Online, subscription-based software
Function as a service	FaaS	PaaS while platform manages compute scaling
Database as a service	DBaaS	PaaS while platform provides DB software, backups, and management
Data analytics as a service	AaaS	SaaS but platform provides infrastructure, storage, and compute for Big Data analytics

The volume and velocity of change in cloud computing has a lot to do with its relative newness. There is so much to create and the demand for it so intense that customers often choose a cloud provider solely based on which one brings a single feature to market first. The cost a company can realize by no longer needing to manage a datacenter drives the consumption of cloud supplier resources and the extinction of the concept of on-premises IT. Here are some ideas you should consider to speed up enhancements and changes within the context of the Azure data engineer associate role and scope.

Consider making it a habit to review official Azure feature updates at `https://azure.microsoft.com/updates`. Filter on product categories such as Analytics, Databases, and Storage. Additionally, as seen on Figure 1.13, restrict the article results to new or updated features only.

There is another very nice tool, Azure Heat Map (`https://aka.ms/azheatmap`), which is an online graphical representation of all Azure products, features, and much more.

FIGURE 1.13 Azure feature updates

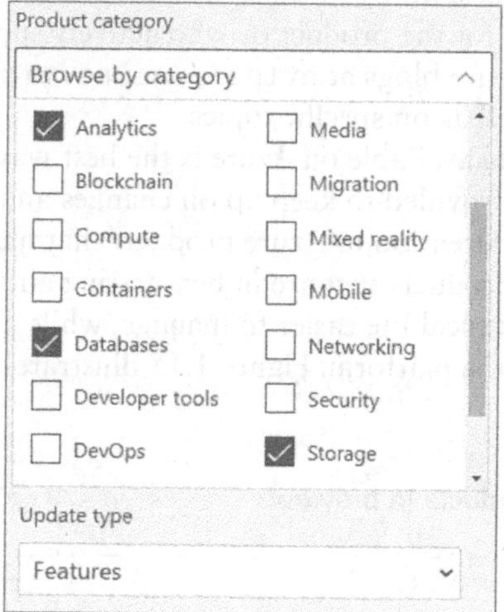

There is also a massive amount of Azure product documentation available here: `https://docs.microsoft.com/azure`. You can search for a specific term or navigate to a product grouping, like `https://docs.microsoft.com/azure/?product=analytics`, which displays all Azure products related to analytics (see Figure 1.14).

FIGURE 1.14 Azure Analytics product documentation

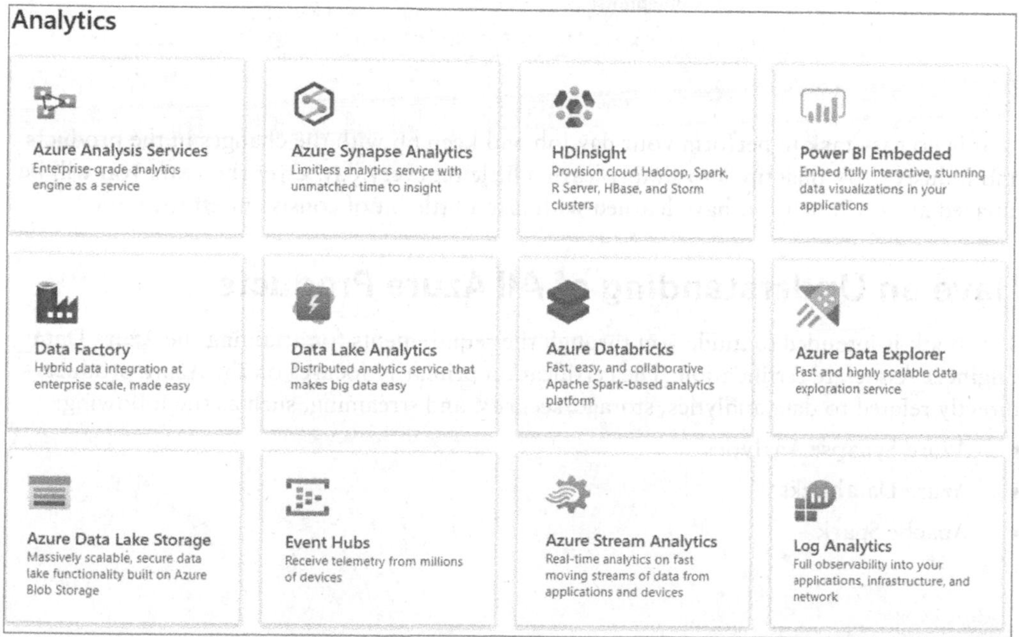

There are also many skilled and experienced Microsoft employees who post blogs about technical concepts and practices. Many of those who contribute to the Azure blog site are the ones who wrote the code for the product or who actively support the customers of the product. Access the public Azure blogs at `https://azure.microsoft.com/blog`, where you can filter on a date as well as on specific topics.

Actively using the products available on Azure is the best way to stay current with what is happening. Use the tips just provided to keep up on changes and updates to the products you use. Consider paying special attention to Azure products that have the word PREVIEW next to the name. These are new products that are in beta testing and usually contain new features that can make your technical life easier to manage, while also growing the capabilities of your solution running on the platform. Figure 1.15 illustrates how PREVIEW products may appear online.

FIGURE 1.15 Azure products in preview

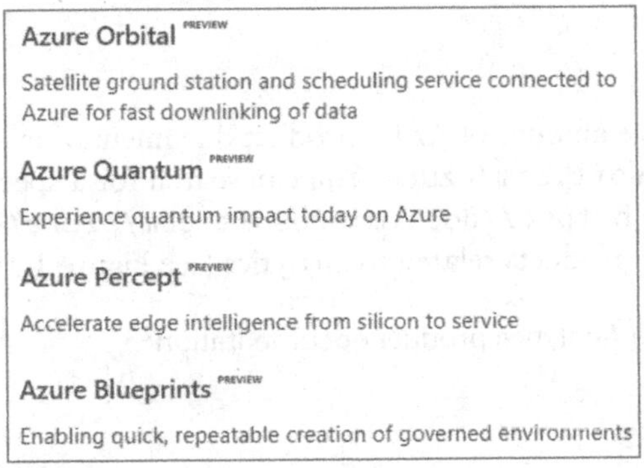

Azure Orbital PREVIEW
Satellite ground station and scheduling service connected to Azure for fast downlinking of data

Azure Quantum PREVIEW
Experience quantum impact today on Azure

Azure Percept PREVIEW
Accelerate edge intelligence from silicon to service

Azure Blueprints PREVIEW
Enabling quick, repeatable creation of governed environments

It is no easy task to perform your day job and keep up with the changes in the products and industry. My final tip is to simply learn a little bit every day. Over the years you will be amazed at how much you have learned with just a little bit of consistent effort.

Have an Understanding of All Azure Products

This book is intended to guide you through the requirements for attaining the Azure Data Engineer Associate certification. The certification primarily focuses on the Azure products directly related to data analytics, storage, security, and streaming, such as the following:

- Azure Synapse Analytics
- Azure Databricks
- Apache Spark

- Azure Data Factory
- Azure Data Lake Storage
- Azure Active Directory
- Azure Key Vault
- Azure Managed Identity
- Azure Stream Analytics
- Azure Event Hubs

You should develop a deep level of knowledge and experience for these products; otherwise, you have a limited chance of passing the exam. However, the exam does sometimes expand into other Azure products from an integration point of view. These products are not directly related to data analytics; rather they are products that are required to implement a data analytics solution on Azure. Given that, you should expand your knowledge of Azure products to include a large majority of them. You do not need to know the technical complexities, in depth, of all Azure products, but you should have a general idea of what the products are used for. Read on for an introduction to many Azure products, all of which you must know to pass the exam.

Azure Product Name Recognition

There are currently over 200 Azure products. Thankfully they are categorized into approximately 20 different categories, which makes it easier to locate products directly related to the solution you need. Analytics, Compute, Databases, Networking, Management and Governance, Security, and Storage are a few of the most popular and most relevant categories. You can find the complete list here: `https://azure.microsoft.com/services`.

The following content provides product summaries and use cases of many Azure products. Products that the exam targets heavily will have additional content in upcoming chapters. The content includes product hands-on exercises and additional descriptions of specific capabilities and limitations in more detail.

Let's get right to it and summarize the Azure products anyone with a desire to become a world-class Azure data engineer should know. Review Table 1.3 for terms and their associated definitions, which are referred to in the following sections. You may need to return to this table if you come across an unfamiliar term.

TABLE 1.3 Technical terms and definitions

Term	Definition
Data lake	A repository of datastored in its natural, unformatted, unmodified, or raw form. Additionally, cleaned and enriched data. Can include structured, semi-structured, unstructured, and binary data. A successor to data mart or data warehouse.
Cluster, pool	Two or more compute machines bound together to collaborate on a shared compute task. See *orchestrator*.
Container	An isolated package of software that contains all application dependencies.
DataFrame	An in-memory compendium of data organized into specified columns. Commonly referred to in the context of Apache Spark.
Data model	An organization of elements in a standardized form. A data model may define a brainwave, which has elements such as frequency and channel. Also called *semantic model*.
Engine, runtime	A combination of source code and compute power that manages the transformation of data.
Ingest	A stage in the data analytics process where data is received from the originating source.
Job, batch job	A unit of work, often executed offline due to its high compute requirements.
Node	A compute machine that performs computations by following coded instructions. Also called *Worker node*.
Notebook	An organizational unit focused on unifying processes, experiments, and deployments. Contains visualizations and runnable commands.
Model and Serve	A stage in the data analytics process where conflated data is stored for the gathering of data intelligence.
Orchestrator	One compute machine, part of the cluster, provisioned to administer the worker nodes also contained in the cluster. See *node*.
Pipeline	A series of tasks that occur in serial succession from beginning to end.
Prep and Train	A stage in the data analytics process where data is pulled from numerous sources. Computer algorithms are then run on the data with the intention of merging the data into a single source.
Workspace	A web page or user interface containing quick, easy access to relevant tools, experiments, and information.

Azure Data Analytics

The products in this section are ones that you absolutely must know and have experience with to pass the exam. Consider the following content an introduction, just so you can get your head around what these products can do. Upcoming chapters provide more product details and hands-on exercises.

An important point to keep in mind as you read through these Azure data analytics services is that Azure Databricks, Azure HDInsight, and Azure Analysis Services are cloud-based implementations of Databricks, HDInsight, and Analysis Services. The latter three products are very popular data analytics services that run in on-premises datacenters. Therefore, if you are currently using one of them already and you want to migrate to the cloud, you can choose the one that you are already using and easily move your existing workloads to the cloud. Remember that when you move your workload to the cloud, you are outsourcing the infrastructure and platform management to the cloud service provider. This means you can focus all your efforts on data analytics, business insights, and *business intelligence (BI)* gathering.

It is important to know which of these objectives are in scope so that you can choose the correct Azure data analytics product:

- You want to create a new data analytics project that will run on Azure.
- You want to redesign an existing on-premises data analytics project and run it on Azure.
- You want to migrate an existing data analytics project to Azure.

If your objective is either of the first two, then those projects should target Azure Synapse Analytics. This workspace is where Microsoft is building connectivity and configuration capabilities to the other popular data analytics products. Otherwise, the Azure platform supports an implementation of the most popular data analytics frameworks. As you read through these first descriptions, how best to target a creation or migration will become clearer because you will learn which features are provided by each product.

Azure Synapse Analytics

There is a term used to describe projects that fit nicely into the use case for Azure Synapse Analytics (ASA). The term is *greenfield*. A *greenfield project* means exactly what you might visualize if you close your eyes and think of a green field of grass. It's open, no fences, no constraints, a foundation that will support any idea, bound only by the limits of your imagination. Bringing it back into context, Azure Synapse Analytics is the workspace you need when you are starting a new project that will run on Azure. This isn't to say you can't migrate existing data analytics projects; it depends on the size, scale, and maturity of the project. Preexisting analytics solutions with limited complexity and already existing solutions with relatively small datasets might also be a good fit for Azure Synapse Analytics. Note that Azure Synapse Analytics is the product Microsoft wants all new data analytics customers to use. You should therefore expect many questions about it on the exam.

Azure Synapse Analytics includes a workspace management console as well as other Azure data service offerings, including pipelines and SQL pools. Figure 1.16 illustrates some of those services. Azure Synapse Analytics can also be integrated with many other Azure data services like Cosmos DB and Azure SQL. A very important feature is that you can run your analytics on either SQL pools or Apache Spark pools using Azure Synapse Analytics.

FIGURE 1.16 Azure Synapse Analytics services

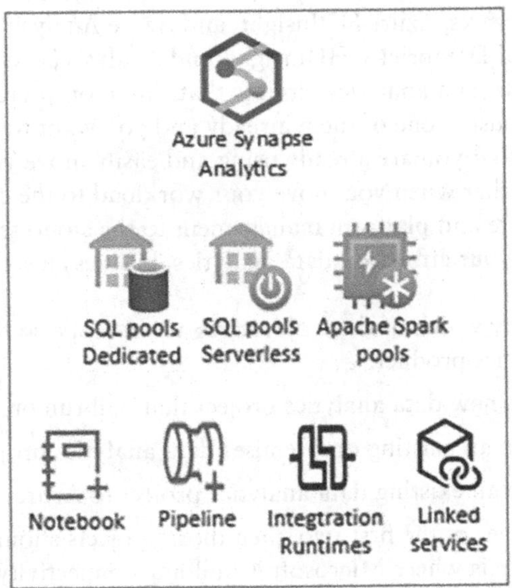

If you need to perform analytics with SQL-based analytics, then use a SQL pool. If Scala, PySpark, or Spark SQL is required, then an Apache Spark pool would be your choice. The next several sections will introduce these and other important terms related to Azure Synapse Analytics.

SQL Pool

For individuals or companies that typically run SQL Server or other relational database solutions, the SQL pool makes the most sense. This pool provides two options: serverless and dedicated. A serverless SQL pool ensures that enough compute resources (CPU and memory) will be available, as required, on-demand, in real time. Once that compute is no longer required, it is deallocated so that the cost is optimized, and you are billed for only what you use. The other option is a dedicated SQL pool. Although there is scaling, you typically choose a compute size targeting a predetermined number of CPUs and memory. When more capacity is required, another instance (aka node) of that same size of compute (the same number of CPUs and amount of memory) is added to the pool and used.

Apache Spark Pool

Apache Spark is explored in the context of both Azure Databricks and Azure HDInsight in the next two sections. One benefit of running Apache Spark pools via Azure Synapse Analytics is that this approach uses Azure Data Lake Storage Gen2 as the primary filesystem, whereas the other products mentioned here do not fully support Gen2 in that capacity. Some of the frameworks provided by default are Spark SQL, GraphX, MLlib, Anaconda, and Apache Livy. There are numerous others; additional frameworks are added on a regular basis. It is the intent that all capabilities found in other Azure data analytics products that offer Apache Spark have the same features and capabilities in Azure Synapse Analytics. If there are any notable missing features, they will be called out in later chapters.

Pipelines

Table 1.3 offered a brief definition of a pipeline. From an Azure Synapse Analytics perspective, the definition is the same in that a pipeline groups activities together to perform a task. The most common type of pipeline in this context has to do with data integration. Data integration involves pulling data from numerous sources, manipulating it into a similar form, and storing that final data in a place for intelligence gathering or machine learning. A few related terms here are SQL scripts, Notebook, and Apache Spark job. Those terms are units where logic is organized and strung together to perform specific activities that execute during a pipeline run.

Integration Runtimes

There is also a brief description of a runtime in Table 1.3. In the context of integration runtimes (IRs), it is simply some provisioned compute power to manage and perform tasks and activities configured within a pipeline. There are three types of integration runtimes: Azure, self-hosted, and Azure-SSIS (SQL Server Integration Services). Only Azure and self-hosted are currently supported in Azure Synapse Analytics. If you require Azure-SSIS, then you need to use Azure Data Factory (ADF) discussed later in this book. The Azure integration runtime uses compute resources that exist on Azure, whereas self-hosted compute would come from hardware hosted on-premises. Think of the integration runtime as a compute machine that manages the movement of data between datastores that may exist either on Azure or within an on-premises private network. Another responsibility of the IR is to trigger and monitor the status of data transformations that run on your provisioned SQL or Apache Spark pools.

Linked Services

A *linked service* allows you to connect to several external sources using a connection string. This is necessary if you want to pull the data from those sources and integrate it into your data model. This feature is accessible from the Manage menu in the Synapse Studio, as shown in Figure 1.17.

FIGURE 1.17 Azure Synapse Analytics Studio

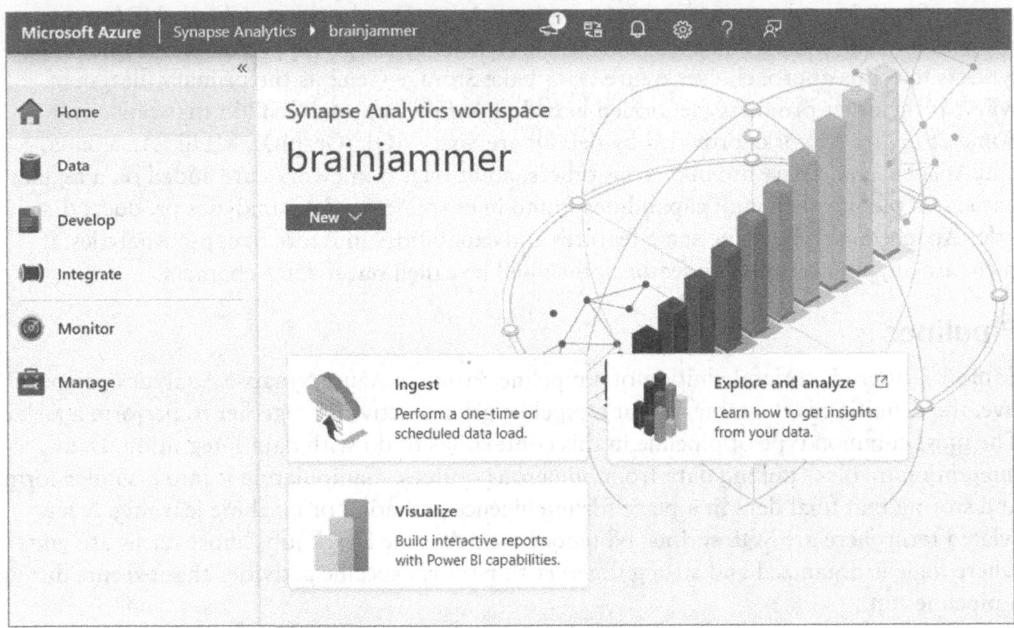

Examples of the kinds of resource that can be configured using this service are Azure Cosmos DB, Azure Data Explorer, Azure SQL Database, Azure Blob Storage, and resources hosted at competing cloud service providers like Amazon. There are well over 30 possibilities, with more being added regularly.

Azure Databricks

Azure Databricks is an implementation of the Databricks data analytics platform optimized to run on the Azure platform. If your organization is currently using Databricks to perform data analytics on-premises and is considering migrating that workload to the cloud, this is the place to begin your investigation. A significant benefit of using Azure Databricks is the elimination of complexities required to manage the infrastructure necessary to operate an on-premises version of Databricks. Azure Databricks abstracts away that complexity, which frees up technical resources, thus allowing them to focus on data analytics instead of infrastructure management. Although the Azure Databricks platform can be useful for managing all phases of the data analytics process, its most foremost effect concerns the Prep and Train phase.

The Azure Databricks offering is divided into three environments:

- Databricks Data Science and Engineering
- Databricks Machine Learning
- Databricks SQL

The default workspace environment is Data Science and Engineering, as shown in Figure 1.18. The workspace provides access to common tasks such as creating notebooks, clusters, jobs, and tables as well as seamless integration with Azure storage and security products.

The most popular technologies commonly associated with Databricks that are integrated with Azure Databricks are the following:

- Apache Spark
- Delta Lake
- MLflow
- PyTorch

They consist of a runtime, a datastore, and frameworks that are not limited to only Azure Databricks. These products can stand alone and be used from a multitude of workspaces and products.

FIGURE 1.18 Azure Databricks workspace

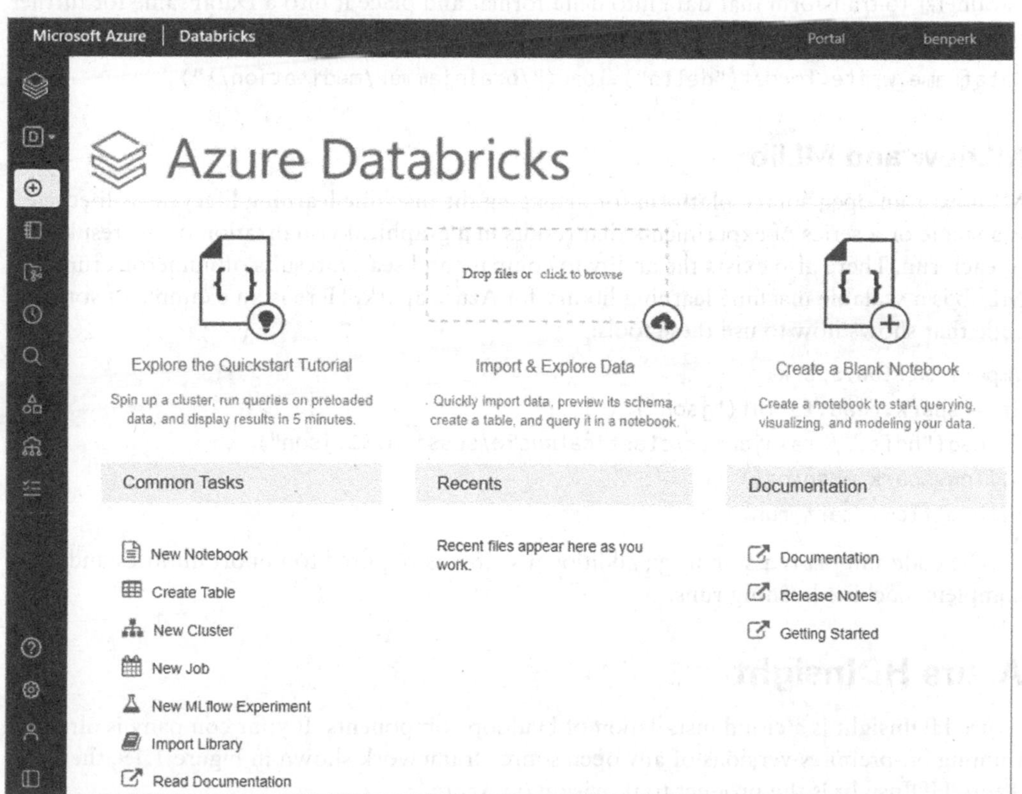

Apache Spark

A runtime is where the work happens; it is where the compute power is used the most. Azure Synapse Analytics Apache Spark pools represent a cluster of computers ready to perform the task at hand. The task is the merging of data stored in different locations and formats into a single construct. The merged data is then placed in a datastore for gaining insights in real time or later. The feature that sets Apache Spark apart from other similar products is the support for in-memory data processing. Performing high amounts of I/O, such as writing to disk, incurs unnecessary latency. Instead, the data is stored in-memory using a *DataFrame*.

Delta Lake

Delta Lake is a layer of capabilities, accessible using languages such as Python, R, Scala, or SQL to query and manipulate data pulled from your data lake. Delta lake tables are built on top of the *Azure Databricks File System (DBFS)*, which is useful for versioning data, managing indexes, and capturing statistics. Using that information, Delta Lake can deliver those capabilities in a highly performant, reliable, and secure manner. Consider a scenario in which data in your Data Lake is in both JSON and CSV formats. You can use a Delta Lake parameter to transform that data into delta format and place it into a DataFrame for further refining and aggregation. The following code snippet illustrates how to achieve that:

```
dataframe.write.format("delta").load("/brainjammer/meditation/*")
```

MLflow and MLlib

MLflow is an open source platform for managing the machine learning lifecycle. A lifecycle is a single or a series of experiments that results in a graphical visualization of the result of each run. There also exists the ability to compare and search results of numerous runs. MLlib is a scalable machine learning library for Azure Spark. Here is an example of some code that shows how to use these tools:

```
import mlflow.spark
df = spark.read.format("json") \
 .load("hdfs://brainjammer/classicalmusic/session101.json")
mlflow.spark.autolog()
with mlflow.start_run()
```

The code snippet is a summary; additional syntax is required to import libraries and complete machine learning runs.

Azure HDInsight

Azure HDInsight is a cloud installation of Hadoop components. If your company is already running on-premises versions of any open source framework shown in Figure 1.19, then Azure HDInsight is the product to provision on Azure.

FIGURE 1.19 Azure HDInsight most popular supported open source frameworks

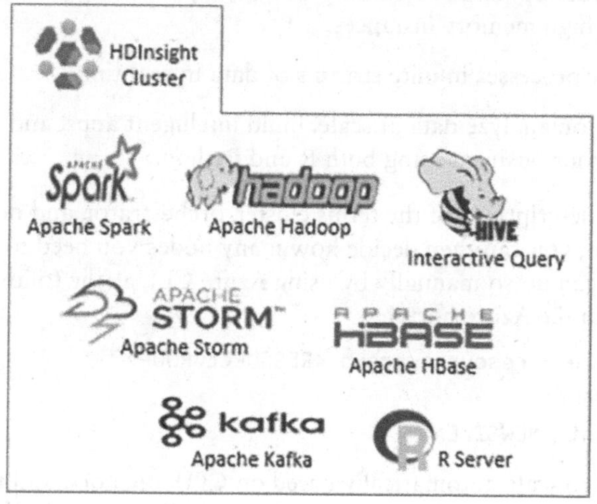

The benefits of migrating your on-premises workloads to the cloud include scaling and outsourcing infrastructure management. Here are a few additional benefits you can expect from running your Hadoop component on Azure:

- HDInsight provides an end-to-end *service level agreement (SLA)*.
- Data engineers and scientists can use popular notebooks such as Jupyter and Zeppelin.
- Supported development tools include Visual Studio, Visual Studio Code, Eclipse, and .NET, IntelliJ, Java, R, and Python.
- There is seamless integration with Azure Monitor, Azure Active Directory, and Azure Virtual Networks.

The provisioning of these frameworks was achieved by first creating an HDInsight cluster. This can be performed using the Azure portal or Azure Data Factory and managed using Azure CLI, the .NET SDK, or PowerShell. Part of the process of creating a HDInsight cluster is selecting the cluster type. The various types of clusters are described in the following subsections and use the descriptions provided in the Azure portal.

Hadoop Petabyte-scale processing with Hadoop components like MapReduce, Hive (SQL on Hadoop), Pig, Sqoop, and Oozie.

Spark Fast data analytics and cluster computing using in-memory processing.

Kafka Lets you build a high throughput, low-latency, real-time streaming platform using a fast, scalable, durable, and fault-tolerant publish-subscribe messaging system. The Azure alternative to this is Azure Stream Analytics, discussed later in this chapter.

HBase Fast and scalable NoSQL database. Available with both standard and premium (SSD) storage options.

Interactive Query Build enterprise data warehouses with in-memory analytics using Hive (SQL on Hadoop) and low-latency analytical processing (LLAP). Note that this feature requires high memory instances.

Storm Reliably processes infinite streams of data in real time.

R Server Lets you analyze data at scale, build intelligent apps, and discover valuable insights across your business using both R and Python.

See Table 1.3 for descriptions of the terms cluster, orchestrator, and nodes. Once the cluster is provisioned, you can then decide how many nodes you need to perform the required work. You can do so manually by using Azure CLI, as the following snippet illustrates, or from within the Azure portal:

```
az hdinsight resize --resource-group <RESOURCEGROUP>`
 --name <CLUSTERNAME>`
 --workernode-count <NEWSIZE>
```

It is also possible to scale automatically based on CPU, memory, and number of containers on a node. Autoscaling is the most effective and efficient means for running your cluster. When the code in your container requires more compute, the platform adds more compute power to scale out. When that compute power is no longer needed, it scales in, which results in you being charged only for the compute power required to run your workloads.

Azure Analysis Services

For a company that already has an on-premises installation of SQL Server Analysis Services, Azure Analysis Services is the cloud implementation of this. Azure Analysis Services provides access to all the data you have in your on-premises databases and data warehouses, using a gateway, as well as any data source running on Azure. Figure 1.20 illustrates how the access is realized.

Azure Analysis Services is a PaaS cloud service offering, which means the magical aspect of this product is its scalability. As with most PaaS offerings, the product delivers numerous tiers to meet your needs based on *query processing units (QPU)* and memory. The tiers range from the Developer tier, which offers 20 QPUs and 3 GB of memory, up to over 1,000 QPUs and hundreds of gigabytes of memory. A QPU is the means for measuring how much query and data processing is used for performing computations. Instead of binding your compute requirements to a *central processing unit (CPU)*, which is a common approach, the QPU approach focuses more on the data processing needs versus the need to know how many CPUs are required to perform the work. Additionally, running on PaaS means that as your data grows you do not have to be concerned about buying, installing, configuring, and supporting extra hardware to store it; all of that comes at part of the PaaS offering.

FIGURE 1.20 Azure Analysis Services

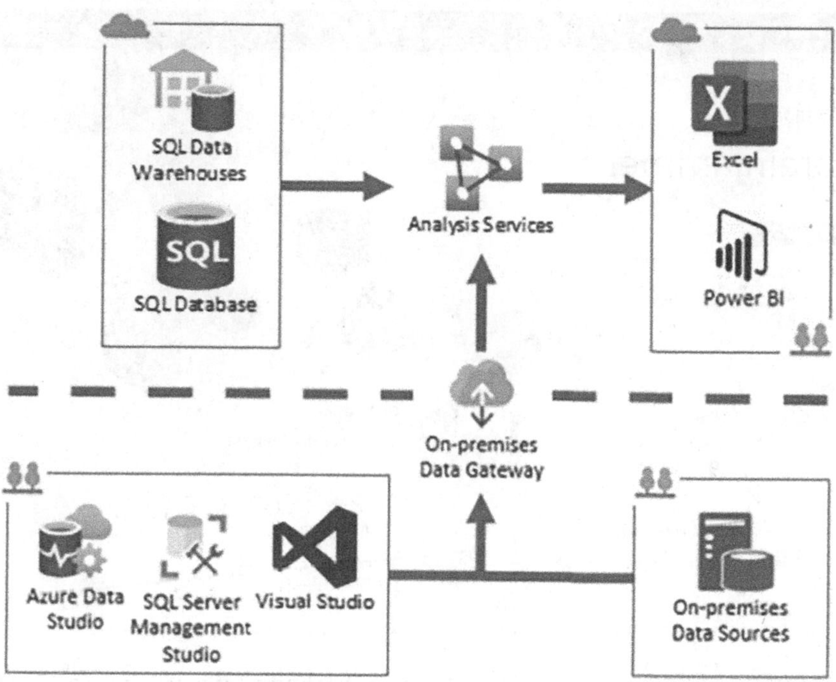

From a usability perspective *SQL Server Management Studio (SSMS)*, *SQL Server Data Tools (SSDT)*, Microsoft Excel, and Power BI all function the same as you would expect them to when working with SQL Server Analysis Services. From a performance perspective, Azure Analysis Services improves the performance of queries with an in-memory caching feature. This means that instead of making a call all the way to the data source again and again, the result of like queries can be stored in a cache, which reduces cost and latency. Another benefit of Azure Analysis Services is that you can continue using the existing business knowledge, business models, and business logic that you have invested much time and energy into tuning and perfecting. You can deploy these models to Azure using Visual Studio, for example, by changing the data source from your on-premises to Azure and choosing Deploy from the Solution pop-up menu.

Azure Data Factory

Azure Data Factory (ADF) is a data integration service accessible via Azure Data Factory Studio. Figure 1.21 shows an example of how that looks. You might recognize some similarities between it and Azure Synapse Analytics Studio, discussed earlier and shown in Figure 1.17.

FIGURE 1.21 Azure Data Factory Studio

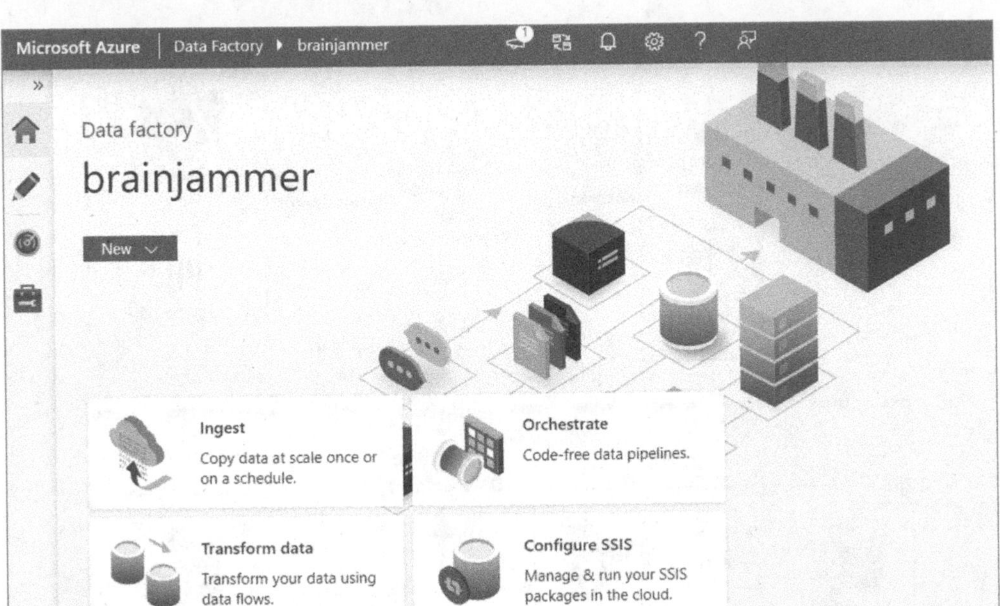

As you saw in the earlier section "Azure Synapse Analytics," it is the service you should use if you are building new data analytic projects and workspaces on Azure. Azure Data Factory existed prior to ASA and there are many customers who currently use ADF. Many of the features of ASA are similar to those in ADF, such as integration runtimes, linked services, and pipelines, although there are some differences in the process of creating those features between the two studios. This will become more obvious later in this chapter when you work through the exercises and see for yourself.

ADF contains mainly integration capabilities, though Dataflows has expanded it a bit more to the analytics side. ASA includes these capabilities (except Azure-SSIS IR, as mentioned later) and also full analytics capabilities with SQL pools and Apache Spark pools. ADF corresponds to the pipeline capability and associated components of ASA, plus improved integrations with several data services like Cosmos DB and Azure SQL.

ADF does not have integration with SQL or Apache Spark pools and therefore no notebooks, no Spark job definitions, and SQL pool stored procedure activities. Keep in mind these two important points:

- New features will be released to ASA Studio, meaning that ADF will slowly (over many years) decline into oblivion. If you are using ADF, consider moving your workspaces to ASA as soon as possible.
- Azure-SSIS integration runtimes currently only exist in ADF, and there hasn't been any mention about whether this capability will be ported to ASA.

Let's take a closer look at Azure-SSIS.

Azure-SSIS

SQL Service Integrated Services (SSIS) is described in greater detail later in the "Azure Databases" section. You can apply similarities to an SSIS package as you can to a pipeline. A package, like a pipeline, contains a series of steps, tasks, and activities that perform copying, transforming, and storing of the modeled data. An Azure-SSIS is an IR, which means that it is a compute machine that is allocated a CPU and memory. Azure-SSIS lets customers lift and shift existing SSIS packages onto Azure compute resources.

Azure Event Hubs

Azure Event Hubs is an endpoint for ingesting data at high-scale frequencies. There are numerous ways to move data into a datastore, such as by creating a connection to a database via code running on a website or within a client application. The problem with that approach is that databases typically have a limit on the number of concurrent connections that can be opened. When that limit is hit, clients that need a connection must wait, and the wait period has a timeout value. If the timeout is breached, then the connection is broken and the data possibly lost. The scenario in which a client connects directly to a database to store data is called a *coupled* or *real-time* solution. The alternative to a coupled solution is a *decoupled* solution.

Placing a service—for example, Azure Event Hubs—between a client and the database decouples the transaction involving those two entities. Think of Azure Event Hubs as a messaging queue, where the information that the client would normally send directly to a database instead places it into a queue. Once the message is in the queue, the client no longer has a connection and can continue with other work. The insertion into the queue (aka a *trigger*) notifies another resource, such as an Azure Function, to pull that data from the queue and perform the processing and insertion into the database. This decoupling reduces the chance of losing data and lowers the chance of experiencing an overload on the datastore side. Azure Event Hub is designed primarily for Big Data streaming scenarios that load billions of requests—for example, logging every stock trade happening globally per day. Event Hubs are also commonly used as a decoupler for Azure Databricks, Stream Analytics, Azure Data Lake Storage, or HDInsight products that are used to process the data to gather intelligence.

IoT Hub

IoT Hub is like Event Hub in that it is used to ingest large amounts of data with high reliability and low latency but the target data producers are Internet of Things (IoT) devices, such as weather readers, automobile trackers, brain–computer interfaces (BCIs), or streetlamps, to name a few. One option that is available via IoT Hub is the ability to send notifications to the IoT device in addition to receiving data from it. Consider the streetlamp that needs to be turned on at a certain time of day. IoT Hub can be configured to send that signal to the lamp at a certain time per day. The technology to achieve cloud-to-device messaging is called *WebSockets*. The primary difference between Event Hub and IoT Hub has to do with the number of messages received within a given time frame and the kind of message producer sending the message.

Azure Stream Analytics

Azure Stream Analytics can be used to analyze data flowing in from an IoT device or from any other numerous kinds of message producers. Event Hubs and IoT Hubs are what you use to ingest those messages at scale. Those messages are placed into a queue and then processed by a consumer that has subscribed to the hub. In other words, a binding exists between the queue where the messages arrive and the consumer that will process that message. When the message arrives at the queue, a notification that includes metadata is sent to the consumer. Then the consumer takes an action on that message. As you can see in Figure 1.22, a binding can exist between either an Event Hub or an IoT Hub and Azure Stream Analytics.

FIGURE 1.22 Azure Stream Analytics data flow

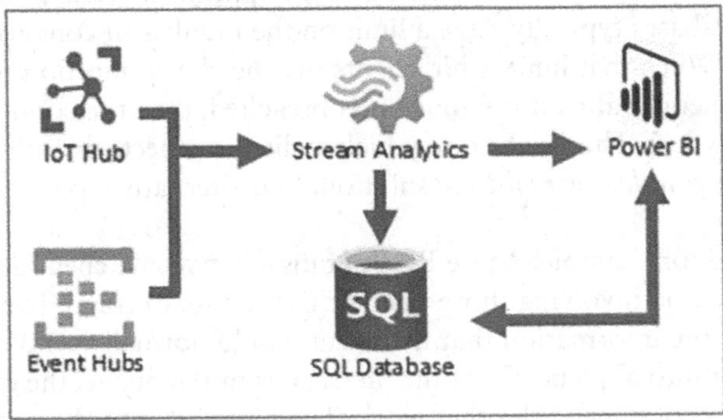

Azure Stream Analytics uses SQL query syntax to perform analysis of the streaming data, something like the following:

```
SELECT *
INTO Output
FROM Input
WHERE AF3Alpha BETWEEN 11 AND 15
```

Once the data is transformed, it can be streamed in real time to a Power BI dashboard or to a SQL Server database for offline or near-real-time reporting. Remember that ASA has the word "stream" in its name. If your solution requires a product to perform analytics on a stream of data in real time, this is the product you would choose. Alternatively, if your solution is event-driven or timer-based, then consider choosing Azure Functions or Logic Apps instead.

Other Products

There are other products related to data analytics that are available on the Azure platform. It is possible that the exam will ask a question about these products, but don't expect many. Regardless, if your desire is to be the best Azure data engineer possible, then the more you know, the better.

Anomaly Detector

Anomaly Detector is an *application programming interface (API)* used to find irregularities in data. Consider that a normal reading of an alpha brain wave is typically between 5.311 and 12.541 Hz. That range is determined by running data analytics on very large sets of recordings. If there is a reading outside of that range, it can be highlighted as an anomaly. Highlighting it ensures that the person who monitors such activities will be notified and take appropriate actions. Anomaly Detector can be used in real time, offline, or near real time.

Data Science Virtual Machines

A *Data Science Virtual Machine (DSVM)* is an Azure VM that comes preconfigured with lots of standard data sciences–related products. Instead of provisioning a default Azure VM, which would have nothing but the operating system on it, you would find the following, and more, installed by default:

- CUDA, Horovod, PyTorch, TensorFlow
- Python, R, C#, Node, Java
- Visual Studio, RStudio, PyCharm
- H2O, LightGBM, Rattle
- Apache Spark, SQL Server
- Azure CLI, AzCopy, Azure Storage Explorer

Azure Data Lake Analytics

Azure Data Lake Analytics is used to run on-demand data analytic jobs in parallel. The parallelism is achieved using Microsoft Dryad, which can compute data represented in *directed acyclic graphs (DAGs)*. A DAG is a model helpful in the calculation of the "traveling salesman" scenario, in which there can be sequential proposed directions that never form a complete loop. Behind the scenes, there is an implementation of Apache Hadoop, which uses Apache YARN to manage the resources across clusters. Azure Data Lake Analytics also support the U-SQL syntax, which combines SQL with C#. An example of U-SQL is shown in the following snippet:

```
@alphareading =
 EXTRACT
 AF3Alpha     decimal,
 T7Alpha      decimal,
```

```
 PzAlpha      decimal,
 T8Alpha      decimal,
 AF4Alpha     decimal
 FROM "/brainjammer/playingguitar/reading001.tsv"
 USING Extractors.Tsv();
OUTPUT @alphareading
 TO "/output/brainjammer/playingguitar.csv"
 USING Outputters.csv();
```

Note also that Azure Data Lake Analytics requires the Gen1 version of Azure Data Lake Storage; Gen2 is the most current one. If you need these options, then choose this product; otherwise, choose Azure Synapse Analytics to perform your data analytics on Azure since Azure Data Lake Analytics is retiring in the near future.

Power BI/Power BI Embedded

Power BI is a tool used to visualize data. The Power BI desktop application supports connecting to numerous datastores. Once connected, many visualizations can then be applied to the data. The following is a list of a few of the built-in visualizations:

- Area charts
- Stacked column charts
- Maps
- Matrices
- Key performance indicators

The data accessed from Power BI has typically already been through the data analytics and data modeling process. The result of those activities is then visualized using this product. Reporting and the creation of dashboards are also common uses for Power BI.

Power BI Embedded is an online SaaS service and is a means of delivering customer-facing analytics, reports, and dashboards via a web application or website. The benefit is that everyone who wants or needs to consume the results of your data analytics solutions is not required to have a Power BI license. Instead, the results can be placed online and accessed without any software installation requirements.

Azure Storage Products

Azure Storage is a group of products that provide a secure, scalable, and highly available solution for storing your data. This product grouping offers numerous capabilities and also serves as a place to store blobs and files rather than storing rows and columns of data into a *database management system (DBMS)*. An Azure Storage account provides a NoSQL store and a messaging queue, both of which have higher scale alternatives. Read on to learn about each Azure Storage feature and its purpose and possible alternatives.

Azure Data Lake Storage

Azure Data Lake Storage (ADLS) is a fundamental piece of most enterprise data analytics solutions running on Azure. This product is optimized for Big Data analytics workloads. ADLS accomplishes this by providing storage capacity of up to multiple exabytes of data and supplying access to that data at a throughput of hundreds of gigabytes per second. ADLS Gen2 supports the open source platforms described in Table 1.4.

TABLE 1.4 ADLS-supported platforms

Platform	Supported version
Azure Databricks	5.1+
Cloudera	6.1+
Hadoop	3.2+
HDInsight	3.6+
Hortonworks	3.1.x+

ADLS Gen2 can also be easily integrated with many Azure products, such as Azure Data Factory, Azure Event Hub, Azure Machine Learning, Azure Stream Analytics, IoT Hub, Power BI, and Azure SQL databases. Additional information and capabilities include the following:

- Gen1 vs. Gen2
- Hadoop Distributed File System (HDFS)
- ACL and POSIX security model
- Hierarchical namespaces

Gen1 vs. Gen2

ADLS Gen1 will be retired as of February 29, 2024. Therefore, we don't recommended that you build any new solutions on that version. As mentioned earlier, Azure Data Lake Analytics uses Gen1; therefore, we also don't recommended building new data analytics solutions with that product either. ADLS Gen2 supports all the capabilities that exist in ADLS Gen1. The significant change is that Gen2 is now aligned with and built on Azure Blob

Storage. Building on top of Azure Blob Storage (described later) makes ADLS Gen2 more cost effective and provides diagnostic logging capabilities and access tiers.

Hadoop Distributed File System

If you have used HDFS in the past, you can expect the same experience when using ADLS. This has to do with how you and the operating system interact with data files. Reading, writing, copying, renaming, and deleting are most of the activities you would expect to be able to perform. The *Azure Blob Filesystem (ABFS) driver* is available on all Apache Hadoop environments such as Azure Synapse Analytics, Azure Databricks, and Azure HDInsight. ABFS has some major performance improvements over the previous *Windows Azure Storage Blob (WASB) driver* when it comes to renaming and deleting files. Examples of HDFS commands to create a directory, to copy data from local storage to a cluster, and to list the contents of a directory are shown here:

```
hdfs dfs -mkdir /brainjammer/
hdfs dfs -copyFromLocal meditation.json /brainjammer/
hdfs dfs -ls /brainjammer/
```

ACL and POSIX Security Model

When you're securing files and folders, the access permission level (aka Access ACL) is critical. The access permission level has to do with what actions a person or entity can perform on those files or folders. Table 1.5 describes those permissions.

TABLE 1.5 File/folder access permission levels

Permission	File permission	Directory permission
Execute (X)	No meaning in ADLS Gen2	Required to navigate child items in directory
Read (R)	Read contents of a file	R and X required to list directory contents
Write (W)	Write or append to a file	W and X required to create directory items

There is another kind of access control that pertains to ACLs and ADLS Gen2 called *Default ACLs*. An important distinction between Access ACLs and Default ACLs is that Default ACLs are associated with directories, not files. When you set an ACL on a directory, new files created within it take on the permission granted to the directory. A very important point to note is that if you change the Default ACL, it does not change the permissions on the files within it. The new ACL is only applied to files and directories created after the change. An additional step is required to apply those changes recursively.

Some tools you can use to set ACL permissions on files and directories hosted in ADLS Gen2 are

- Azure Storage Explorer
- Azure Portal
- Azure CLI, PowerShell
- Python, Java, .NET SDKs

Most distributions of Linux support *portable operating system interface (POSIX)* ACLs, which is a means for setting permissions on files and directories on that OS type. That activity is typically performed through a command window; the following code snippet shows a command and the result:

```
$ mkdir brainjammer
$ ls -la brainjammer
$ drwxr-xr-x 3 csharpguitar root 60 2022-05-02 16:19 ..
$ drwxr-xr-x 2 csharpguitar user 80 2022-05-02 16:52 brainjammer
$ -rw-r--r-- 1 csharpguitar user 131 2022-05-02 18:07 playingguitar.json
```

A directory named `brainjammer` is created using the `mkdir` command. The `ls` command lists the attributes of the directory and any other object within it. Notice that user `csharpguitar` has full access to the directory `brainjammer` and the groups `root` and `user` have read, execute, and read, respectively. Access can be further clarified by reading the contents in this list. We will break down the fourth line of the snippet `drwxr-xr-x` into its parts:

- `d` stands for directory.
- `rwx` means the user and group have read (r), write (w), and execute (x) permissions on that directory.
- `r-x` means the user and group have read (r) and execute (x) permissions.
- `r--` means "other" entities that are neither that user nor a user in that group.

Hierarchical Namespace

Hierarchical namespaces organize directories and blob files the same way the filesystem does on your personal computer. There exists a nested hierarchy of directories, each of which can include a file of some type. Hierarchical namespace keeps your data logically structured and by doing so renders better storage and retrieval performance. The following is an example of a hierarchical namespace on a filesystem:

```
brainjammer\
brainjammer\sessionjson\
brainjammer\sessionjson\metalmusic\
brainjammer\sessionjson\metalmusic\pow\
brainjammer\sessionjson\metalmusic\pow\brainjammer-pow-0904.json
brainjammer\sessionjson\worknoemail\pow\brainjammer-pow-1855.json
```

Object stores are typically flat, which results in less efficient behavior when moving, renaming, or deleting directories. Stating that a flat file structure is less efficient is understating a bit; it is actually quite dramatic. When it comes to performing data analytics, it is common for part of the analysis process to copy, move, create, and delete files. In many cases, the time required to achieve such actions using flat structures can take longer than the analysis process itself. Running on Azure, you are charged by the amount of time you consume the product, so if this time can be reduced because your files are stored more optimally, then you save money. Using the hierarchical namespaces provided via ADLS Gen2 reduces the latency and therefore reduces costs.

Azure Storage

Azure Storage is a suite of modern storage solutions, all of which are massively scalable, secure, reliant, and accessible. When you need one of the offered Azure Storage services, you create what is called an Azure Storage Account. The storage account is where you can choose certain attributes that apply to all the services within it—for example, performance and redundancy details.

Performance

An Azure Storage Account has two performance options:

- *Standard* is recommended for most scenarios and is referred to as a general-purpose v2 account. When you visualize storage, a hard drive might pop into your mind. What you have in mind is likely a *hard disk drive (HDD)*. The speed of data access via an HDD is impacted by its proximity to the consumer and the magnetic heads reading from and writing to the platters. This is very fast and acceptable for most use cases, and it is what you get when you provision a Standard Azure Storage Account.
- *Premium* results in the provisioning of solid-state drives (SSDs), which are very low latency. Instead of physically aligning magnetic nibbles on a platter, the data is loaded into a memory chip, making it instantly accessible. If any of the following scenarios meet your requirements, then you should choose Premium which, is supported by a general-purpose v2 account:
  - Artificial intelligence/machine learning (AI/ML) processing
  - IoT or streaming scenarios
  - Data transformation solutions that require constant editing or modification that needs to be reflected immediately
  - Real-time applications that must write data quickly

Storage Redundancy

It is important to have your data stored in more than one place. For example, if you have your data in one datacenter and the datacenter loses power, you are out of business until the power is restored. If a storm destroys the datacenter and everything within it, then you are likely out of business for good if that is the only place you have stored your data.

Azure Storage provides six options for storing your data into different Azure datacenters. They are described in Table 1.6.

TABLE 1.6 Azure storage redundancy

Option	Acronym	Description
Locally redundant storage	LRS	Replicated 3 times within a single datacenter
Zone-redundant storage	ZRS	Replicated to 3 datacenters in the same region
Geo-redundant storage	GRS	LRS + replicated to another region
Geo-zone-redundant storage	GZRS	ZRS + replicated to another region
Read-access GRS	RA-GRS	Read access GRS
Read-access GZRS	RA-GZRS	Read access GZRS

LRS is straightforward in that you get three isolated copies of your data within a single datacenter. If there is any issue with a copy, Azure will take care that access is redirected to another copy. Most of the time, the redirection happens so fast you won't even notice. With ZRS, instead of having three copies of your data in the same datacenter, your three copies are in three different locations, but in the same region. A region may be an area like West Europe, South Central US, or UK South. Within each region, there are numerous datacenters (typically three) that service Azure customers, and those multiple datacenters are referred to as *zones*. Each region also has what is sometimes referred to as a *paired region*. For example, West Europe's paired region is North Europe, and South Central US is paired with North Central US. The regions exist in the same geography (or geo). GRS copies three times in one local datacenter, like LRS, and stores another copy in a different geographical location. With GZRS your data is copied into three datacenters in the first region and zones (ZRS) and then copied three times to one datacenter in another region. The read-access option means that only the primary copy of your data is writable and the other copies are read only.

Blob Storage

If you need to store files such as JSON, XML, DOCX, MP3, PDF, or any other kind of file, then use Blob Storage. Blob Storage implements a flat namespace for organizing data, in contrast to the hierarchical namespace organization that comes with ADLS Gen2. Although you can create folders and place files within them when using Blob Storage, renaming files or deleting them must be performed on each file. In other words, you cannot use wildcard syntax, which involves performing a command on all the files within a directory using a single command. This isn't possible with Blob Storage; you must instead execute one command per file. Therefore, ADLS is more performant when running data analytics.

Table Storage

Azure Table Storage is a key-value pair database product that stores nonrelational structured data. This product is very efficient if you have a large set of data objects or records that are retrievable using a key. The Azure Cosmos DB Table API is built on top of Azure Table Storage. The additional feature you get when using the Azure Cosmos DB Table API is that your data can be distributed to all supported Azure regions, which is currently around 30+, whereas with Azure Table Storage, your data is confined to a single region with an optional read-only version in another. Refer to Table 1.6 for additional details.

Azure Files

The Azure Files feature provides the same functionality as mapping a drive using Windows Explorer or mounting a drive to a network file share. Instead of the network share being on a server within your private network, the share is in the cloud. Azure Files supports both the *Server Message Block (SMB)* and *Network Files System (NFS)* protocols.

Storage Queues

Azure has three messaging services: Azure Service Bus, Azure Event Hubs, and Azure Storage Queues. Each can receive a short text message, store it for a short period of time, and notify a subscribed system that a message has arrived. Once notified, the system can retrieve the message and perform whatever the system has been programmed to do. Storage Queue messages have a size limit of 64 KB. Compared to the other two messaging services, Azure Storage Queues are the most cost-effective for most IT solutions that need to decouple transactions. Azure Service Bus provides *first in, first out (FIFO)* capabilities, and Azure Event Hubs are for high-frequency data streaming scenarios.

Azure Disks

An Azure Disk, also called an Azure managed disk, is a hard drive that can be mounted to an Azure VM that you provision. There are data disks that come in large sizes, up to around 32,767 GB. If you needed a place to store data that is used by a process running on an Azure VM, then this is the kind of disk you should select. Alternatively, there is an OS disk where you would store and configure the operating system. The cool thing about the OS disk is that you can make numerous copies of it and mount it to multiple Azure VMs, which means you can have multiple identical servers with minimal effort.

Other Products

Here are some additional storage products that may be included on the exam. Even if they do not appear on the exam, it is good practice to know most of the Azure products, what they do, and why you would use them.

Azure Data Explorer

Azure Data Explorer (ADE) has been referred to often as a Kusto cluster, which is a datastore, typically an RDBMS, that is query-able using Kusto Query Language (KQL) syntax, which is very similar to SQL. There is tight integration between Azure Data Explorer and Azure Monitor logs and Application Insights. Therefore, if you enable those features and place the data into the Kusto cluster, you can analyze the logs using KQL. ADE can also be hooked into a data analytics process, where you can learn behaviors and find opportunities that exist using the logs generated by your applications.

Azure Storage Explorer

Azure Storage Explorer is a graphical user interface (GUI) that provides features for managing your Azure Storage features like Blob Storage, Azure Files, Storage Queues, and Table Storage. You can also set ACLs on files within your ADLS Gen2 container.

Azure Data Share

This product lets you pull data from numerous sources, create a dataset, and then share that dataset with partners or suppliers. Supported datastores include the following:

- Azure Blob Storage
- Azure Data Lake Storage Gen1 and Gen2
- Azure SQL Database
- Azure Synapse Analytics

Once your datasets are added to the Azure Data Share, you then set up a snapshot schedule. The snapshot schedule will update the datasets with the most current data on the scheduled frequency. A Data Share Invitation is sent to the data consumer, which must be accepted to access the data. The invite contains the agreed terms and conditions of how the data can be used.

Azure Databases

Azure has data service products that support most of the popular RDBMS and NoSQL databases. There are many of them, and you need to know details about each. Read on to learn more.

Azure Cosmos DB

Azure Cosmos DB is a database administration feature. It will automatically administer DBMS updates and patching, storage capacity management, and autoscaling capabilities. From a storage perspective, the scale happens automatically and elastically. *Elastically* means that when the database needs more storage space, it gets allocated, and when it is no longer needed, it gets deallocated. That is a very cost-effective approach where only what is needed is provided and paid for. In this scenario, capacity scaling has more to do than increasing the size or number of compute instances the database runs on. It means that the instances can be scaled into different Azure regions, globally. Then, not only do you have built-in isolated data failover capabilities spread worldwide, you can also get the data as close as possible to those who produce or consume it. The closer the data is to those who require or produce it, the faster the data can be retrieved and manipulated.

Another great feature is the ability to have write capabilities in different regions. In most multi-instance data service scenarios, there is a single-source database, often called the *single version of the truth*. The other instances are copies of that source database, are read only, and get updated on a scheduled basis. However, Azure Cosmos DB will support multiregion writes and will manage the synchronization of data among all the instances.

If Azure Cosmos DB is a data administration tool, where is the data stored? When you provision an Azure Cosmos DB account, the first step is to select which data storage service API you require. The list of possible APIs is shown in Figure 1.23.

FIGURE 1.23 Azure Cosmos DB and supported APIs

See Table 1.7 for a quick overview of the APIs.

TABLE 1.7 Azure Cosmos DB APIs

API	Data model	Container item
Core (SQL)	Document database	Document
Azure Cosmos DB API for MongoDB	Document database	Document
Cassandra	Relations (Apache/CQL)	Row
Table	Key/value pair	Item
Gremlin	Graph database	Node or edge

Core (SQL)

Choose this native API if you need to work with documents, especially when the documents are JSON. Using the familiar SQL query language supports searching the content within the document itself. Additionally, there is a very feature-rich Azure Cosmos DB SDK that lets you interface and query the data source using .NET, Python, JavaScript, and Java.

Azure Cosmos DB API for MongoDB

If you already have an existing on-premises version of MongoDB, then choose this API when moving the workload to Azure. It uses the SQL query language and the Azure Cosmos DB SDK, which supports several programming languages, such as Rust, Golang, Xamarin, .NET, and Python.

Apache Cassandra

If you have an on-premises NoSQL Cassandra database and want to migrate to the Azure platform, choose this service. When you migrate to Azure, you no longer need to manage nodes, clusters, or the OS. All of that is outsourced to Azure. Data is queried using the *Cassandra Query Language (CQL)*, and you can use the client drivers you are already familiar with for accessing via code.

Table API

The Azure Cosmos DB Table API is the same concept as an Azure Table, where it stores keys and their values. You can store a massive number of these pairs, and querying them is also very fast. There is a guarantee of <10 ms latency for reads and writes, 10 million operations per second, and the global distribution you would expect from an Azure Cosmos DB API. None of those mentioned features is available using the standard Azure Table feature found in the Azure Storage account. If you want those features, then it is easy to migrate between an Azure Table and an Azure Cosmos DB Table API.

Gremlin (Graph)

Gremlin is a graph database service useful for storing data as it appears in the real world. Using the Gremlin query language, based on Apache TinkerPop project, you can access and manipulate data. The Gremlin API on Azure Cosmos DB is recommended for new workloads you want to run on the Azure platform. A graph database represents data at the storage layer instead of at a table layer. For example, if you had a relational database and wanted to store information about people, the accounts they have, and their location, you would probably create three tables and link them together with primary and foreign keys. With a graph database, each of those three would be represented by a node, and the relationship is bound between nodes and not between the data that exists within them.

Azure SQL Server Products

Microsoft SQL Server has been around for some time. It is a RDBMS created by Microsoft and uses SQL queries to manage the data stored within it. All the common concepts that go along with an RDBMS apply, like primary/foreign keys, triggers, indexes, and stored procedures. There are a lot of customers who run very large workloads on this RDBMS on Azure and in private datacenters. Numerous SQL Server offerings are available on Azure. Azure SQL is a group of products that use the SQL Server database engine in the cloud. Each of the products is described in more detail next.

SQL Server on Virtual Machines

Running this product is identical to running a full version of Microsoft SQL Server in your private datacenter. When you migrate that to Azure, though, you no longer need to manage the hardware and networking aspects. Since an Azure VM is an IaaS cloud service, you are still required to manage updates to the operating system (both Windows and Linux are supported) and SQL Server version and patches. It is still a very cost-effective solution and a vast variety of VM sizes and locations are available to run your data service on.

Azure SQL Database

This product is on the other side of the cloud service spectrum when compared to SQL Server on Azure VMs. An Azure SQL Database (SQL DB) is a relational DBaaS that offers not only the outsourcing of network and hardware infrastructure, but also operating system and DBMS responsibilities. All you need to worry about is the data and innovation. There is also a serverless (i.e., elastic) version of this product, which means your compute and storage expands and contracts on demand. Notice that the name of this product is singular, meaning it is a single database. You can have numerous Azure SQL Databases running on Azure, but they are isolated from each other.

Azure SQL Managed Instances (SQL MI)

Azure SQL Managed Instances (SQL MI) is most relevant when you want to migrate an existing SQL Server workload from a private datacenter to Azure. It is optimized for lift-and-shift scenarios. It is a PaaS service offering and supports a collection of databases manageable from a single management console.

Additional Azure Databases

Here are a few other Azure databases that are not part of the Azure Cosmos DB suite or Azure SQL Server offerings.

MariaDB MariaDB is a relational database running on Azure based on the MariaDB community edition. You can choose to run this database as either IaaS or PaaS.

MySQL MySQL is a relational database running on Azure based on the MySQL Community Edition. You can choose to run this database as either IaaS or PaaS.

PostgreSQL PostgreSQL is a relational database running on Azure based on the PostgreSQL Community Edition. You can choose either the IaaS or PaaS offering.

Other Products

The following are database-related Azure products that play an important role. They might not be on the exam, but they are good to know about nonetheless.

Azure Migrate This is the recommended tool to use for planning migrations to Azure. Azure Migrate will analyze all your on-premises servers, data, applications, and infrastructure to assess the effort and complexities of the migration.

Azure Database Migration Service You can use Azure Database Migration Service (DMS) to migrate data from multiple on-premises database sources, with minimal downtime to Azure data services.

Azure Data Box Azure Data Box helps you migrate large amounts of data to Azure. This service is optimized for data larger than 40 TB, with a maximum of 80 TB. Moving that kind of data across a network of any kind would not be possible. You place your data on a secure storage device, ship it to an Azure datacenter, and someone loads the data onto a storage point.

SQL Server Integrated Services This tool is useful for building data transformation and data integration solutions. You might notice some similarities between SSIS and Azure Data Factory or Azure Synapse Analytics as you work through your exam prep. SSIS is useful for pulling data from numerous datastores, transforming the data, and storing it on a central datastore for analysis. The central datastore historically is a data warehouse.

SQL Server Management Studio SSMS is a GUI that provides tools and features for creating and managing SQL Server databases. It supports the editing and execution of queries, performing complex administrative tasks, security management, and vulnerability assessments. Using SSMS, a database administrator (DBA) can perform most tasks required to maintain a database. SSMS can be used on SQL Server databases running on the Azure platform as well as on-premises. This GUI runs only on Windows.

Azure Data Studio This product is a more feature-limited version of SSMS. It can be run cross-platform, meaning it can run on Windows, Linux, and macOS. It is useful for creating and running SQL queries but not useful if deep administrative actions are necessary. However, many admin actions can be performed through an integrated terminal using PowerShell or sqlcmd.

Azure Security

Security is the most important aspect of IT. Networks, compute machines, data storage, and so on are important, but a data breach is almost, if not worse, than losing all your data. Knowing about the security products, features, and services that exist on Azure is an absolute must. Although your job as an Azure data engineer might not make you responsible for implementing a security model, it is very important that you can see when something is not secure and know how to approach fixing it.

Azure Active Directory

There are numerous approaches when it comes to signing up for an Azure subscription. When you sign up for an Azure subscription, you must provide the name of your organization. That name becomes what is called an Azure Active Directory *tenant*. The tenant is assigned a Tenant ID, which is a unique GUID, and a directory endpoint in the format of `*.onmicrosoft.com`, where `*` is the tenant name. When you code applications to authenticate against the Azure Active Directory for your subscription, then that is the URL you use—for example, `csharpguitar.onmicrosoft.com`. Figure 1.24 illustrates how the Azure Active Directory blade renders in the Azure portal.

FIGURE 1.24 Azure Active Directory portal

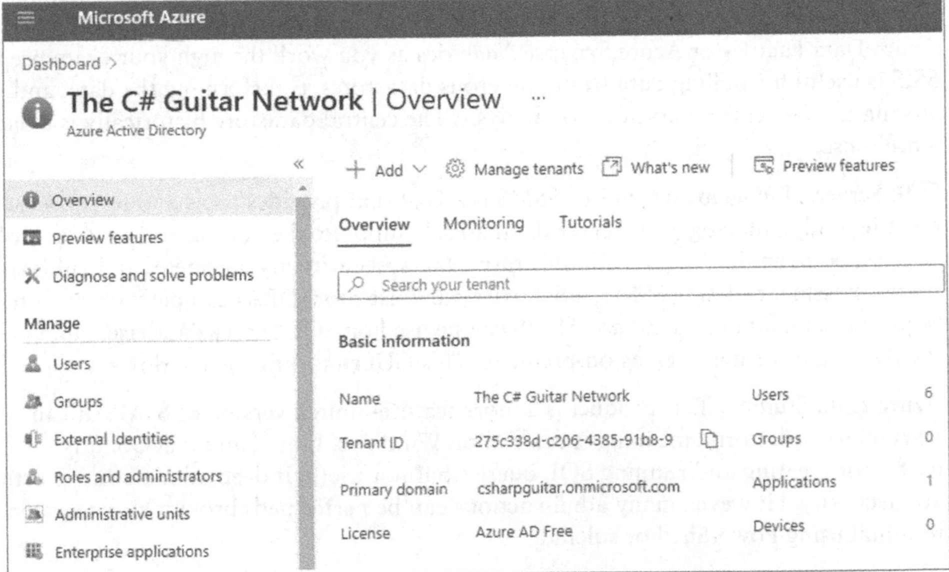

Azure Active Directory offers many features, and we'll discuss them in the following subsections.

Remember that this chapter is an introduction and the information about many of these products have been summaries. There are many exercises in the following chapters where you will get hands-on exposure and gain more insight into the products.

Users and Groups

The most common types of accounts are the user account and the service principal. The first, as you might expect, is linked to a human being. A user account has properties like first name, last name, email address, telephone number, and most importantly, a user ID and password. The user ID and password represent the credentials and are used to confirm the user's identity. This is known as *authentication.* A service principal is also used for authentication reasons; however, this account type is not linked to a human but to a resource. A resource can be a server, a workstation, an application, or perhaps a mobile device. The point is a service principal is not linked to a person. A common reason for using a service principal is when you want to grant access to a database. Instead of using an account linked to a person, you use an account linked to the resource that needs access to the database. Then all requests from that resource to the database are rightly authenticated.

User accounts and service principals can be added to a group. It takes less administration to grant a group access to a resource versus individual accounts. The process is to create a group, then add accounts to the group. You then grant that group access to the resource and certain permissions, like read, write, and delete. If you need to add or remove someone's access to that resource, then you remove them from the group, instead of changing the properties in an individual account. If you need to remove the delete permission from everyone, then you make the change on the group, instead of on each account. When an account is used to authenticate against a resource, the permissions assigned to the group is what gets used to verify *authorization.* Since the identity has already been authenticated, which means they are who they say they are, the account is granted certain permissions that define what they are allowed to do, known as authorization.

Multifactor Authentication

Using only user IDs and passwords to protect a resource is no longer considered secure. People have a habit of using the same set of credentials on numerous locations, so if one location is compromised, then all of them are. This is where multifactor authentication (MFA) can help. User IDs and passwords are something a person knows, but when you implement MFA, it requires an object that a person has. This object is typically a mobile device, but it can also be a fingerprint, retina, thumb drive, or RFID card. When configuring your Azure Active Directory security policies, you enable this by simply selecting a check box; the platform does the rest for you.

Conditional Access

In addition to restricting access to your resources based on an authenticated identity or group affiliation, you can control access on the following common signals:

- IP location
- Device

In most corporate scenarios, you know where your employees will be connecting to your network from. Keep in mind that the context here is not a scenario where you have a website on the Internet being accessed all over the world; rather, the context is to an intranet or internal/private network. In this case you know all your users because they would have an account in the Azure AD. Every device connected to a network has an IP address, and IP addresses are grouped by country. Therefore, you can easily identify a range of IP addresses that would be requesting access to your resources, monitor them, and trigger an alert or action when not within the range. Many organizations also enforce which devices can connect to their networks. If the device is not recognized, again, an alert can be sent and an action taken.

If access is attempted and fails one or more of the conditions, you can configure the Azure AD to deny access by default. That is a bit restrictive, however, so you can instead apply an additional authentication step, such as MFA. If a user tried to authenticate from an unknown location or an unknown device, it makes sense not to, by default, deny their access. Instead, have Azure AD act on that information and ask for some additional information, like a code sent to a mobile device or email account. Once that information is successfully entered, the user can access as expected.

Azure Managed Identity

An Azure Managed Identity (MI) is the Azure AD implementation of a service principal. MI is an account that can be granted access to your Azure resources or any application that supports Azure AD authentication. It is like a service principal, but instead of using an account linked to a human, the account is linked to a resource.

Reporting and Monitoring

Since Azure AD is the place where most of your authentication and authorization activities will happen, it is very important to have some tools to make sure all is working. If you see in the audit logs that many of your employees are failing to be authenticated because of IP location, you might want to perform some analysis to find that IP range and consider changing the Conditional Access rule. Reporting and monitoring is also important to check if there have been any malicious attempts to exploit your directory. There are two reports that might come in handy here, which are available with an Azure AD Premium P2 license:

- The first is "user flagged for risk," which highlights an account that may have been compromised. It is possible for a person to lose a device that isn't protected by a PIN, and someone who finds the device can use a cached user ID and password to access the application without having to enter those credentials. The Azure platform captures telemetry and can flag and alert security anomalies that might not be obvious to individuals. This report can help surface such events.

- The other report is called "risky sign-ins" or "risky users," which is similar to the first but instead targets compromised credentials versus a lost device. Either way, knowing what is going on in your Azure AD is extremely important.

Role-Based Access Control

RBAC is a feature that is used to control access to Azure resources in the Azure portal, Azure PowerShell, or Azure CLI. For example, you can grant someone the authority to provision and configure Azure VMs and at the same time deny them the authority to provision networking and data services. You can also grant some the authority to provision an Azure Synapse Analytics workspace and deny them authority to provision an Azure Cognitive service. It is very flexible, so you can come up with your scenarios, and they are likely supported using RBAC. There are two fundamental concepts you need to know about RBAC:

- Role definitions
- Scope

Role Definitions

Consider, for example, a role named Synapse User. When you think about that role, imagine what kind of permissions such a role would require. Does a person assigned that role need access to Azure Arc or the Azure Active Directory? Probably not. Would that role need access to Azure Synapse Analytics? That is very likely. This is what RBAC provides—it lets you define roles that have specific permissions to perform specific tasks on specific Azure resources. There are two important things to keep in mind:

- First, no permissions are granted by default, which is a good thing. It is best practice to grant a role the absolute minimum permissions required to perform their tasks.
- Second, assign a role to a group and not an individual. If you have a large organization, it is much more feasible to assign permissions to a group versus an individual. Then, if you need to change permissions, then you change it on a single group instead of potentially thousands of individual user accounts.

The following snippet illustrates an example Synapse User role in JSON format:

```
{
 "Name": "Synapse User",
 "Id": null,
 "IsCustom": true,
 "Description": "Read Synapse Analytics resources and create support cases",
 "Actions": [
               "Microsoft.Synapse/workspaces/read",
               "Microsoft.Synapse/workspaces/bigDataPools/read",
```

```
                "Microsoft.Synapse/workspaces/sqlPools/read",
                "Microsoft.Synapse/workspaces/integrationruntimes/read",
                "Microsoft.Support/*"
 ],
 "NotActions": [ ],
 "DataActions": [ ],
 "NotDataActions": [ ],
 "AssignableScopes": [
 "/subscriptions/#######-####-####-####-#########"
 ]
}
```

The first entry seen in the `Actions` property of the previous snippet is `Microsoft.Synapse/workspaces/read`, which gives the person the ability to read Azure Synapse Analytics workspaces. Notice that there is no ability to create or delete. Adding something like `Microsoft.Synapse/workspaces/*` would grant all permissions to the workspaces. The next three actions grant read access to Spark pools, SQL pools, and integration runtimes. The final entry is not part of the built-in Synapse User role but is added to allow the individual to create support cases with Microsoft, if required. This additional permission calls out the fact that if a built-in RBAC role doesn't match your needs, it is possible to create custom roles. Notice that the `IsCustom` attribute is `true`. To see a list of all built-in Azure Synapse Analytics roles, visit `https://docs.microsoft.com/en-us/azure/synapse-analytics/security/synapse-workspace-synapse-rbac-roles`.

Scope

The next concept that is important to RBAC is scope. Notice the hierarchical structure illustrated in Figure 1.25.

FIGURE 1.25 Role-based access control scope

A management group is the top level, and it can be used to define different departments within a company—for example, IT, Finance, HR, and Accounting. Each of those may be responsible for managing their own spending and therefore would want to have control over all the subscriptions for which they receive the bill. A subscription is the second level and is the bill unit; it is the place where Azure resources are provisioned into. When you provision any Azure product or feature, you must provide the associated subscription. You might imagine that a company would have numerous ongoing projects that require a set of different products and features. If you were to put them all directly into the subscription bucket, it would be hard to visually group each product into their respective projects. This is where resource groups come in. You can name a resource group based on a project and then place those resources into that group. It is an organizational unit that helps structure and categorize your Azure resources. Keep in mind that a resource can only be assigned to a single resource group.

So, what does all that have to do with scope? Well, when you place an individual into a group and then grant that group a role, the next step is to give that group access to Azure resources. You can do that at any level, as shown in Figure 1.25. Two locations are likely inefficient, such as at the top management group and at the bottom to a specific resource. Granting access at the top would give the group access to all Azure resources in all Azure subscriptions. Granting access at the resource level gives access to a specific resource and all members are constrained to only that resource. The other two, subscription or resource group, make the most sense. It depends on the role and the expectations the Azure administrator has of that role. Granting access at the subscription level gives the group access to all the included resource groups and all resources within them. Granting access to the resource group gives permissions on all the resources only within the resource group.

Attribute-Based Access Control

Attribute-based access control (ABAC) is in `PREVIEW` (or beta) as of this writing. ABAC builds on RBAC and uses an additional check based on attributes. For example, say you have provisioned an ADLS Gen2 and have loaded up thousands of files. Some of those files are highly confidential, whereas others are public. If you grant a group read access on that ADLS container, it means they can read all the files, regardless of sensitivity level. Instead, you can set an attribute on each file and add an ABAC condition to the permission based on that sensitivity attribute.

Azure Key Vault

It is unfortunately very common to store passwords and connection strings within application code. Sometimes they are stored in a configuration file along with the coded application. Even if the password or connection string is encrypted, it can still be compromised. This is because anyone with administrative access to the machine that decrypts the credential can also decrypt it. The solution to this is Azure Key Vault (AKV), which is a place to store secrets, keys, and certificates.

A secret is the place to store things like tokens, passwords, or API keys. A key is a tool that can generate and store highly sophisticated encryption keys used for encrypting your data. Certificates are *Transport Layer Security/Secure Sockets Layer (TLS/SSL)* certificates for use with your Azure web-accessible hosted resources. The most common and most secure procedure for attaining access to the information stored within the AKV is by using an MI. An application that historically used a connection string existing within a configuration file would have code that accesses and uses the value in that file. That code would need to be changed to access an AKV instead. The resource running the code—for example an Azure Function, Azure App Services Web App, or an Azure VM—would need an MI that is authenticated and authorized against the AKV. Notice in Figure 1.26 that there is a system-assigned identity configured for an Azure App Service. A user-assigned identity can be used across multiple resources, whereas a system-assigned identity is restricted to a single resource.

FIGURE 1.26 Azure App Service Managed Identity

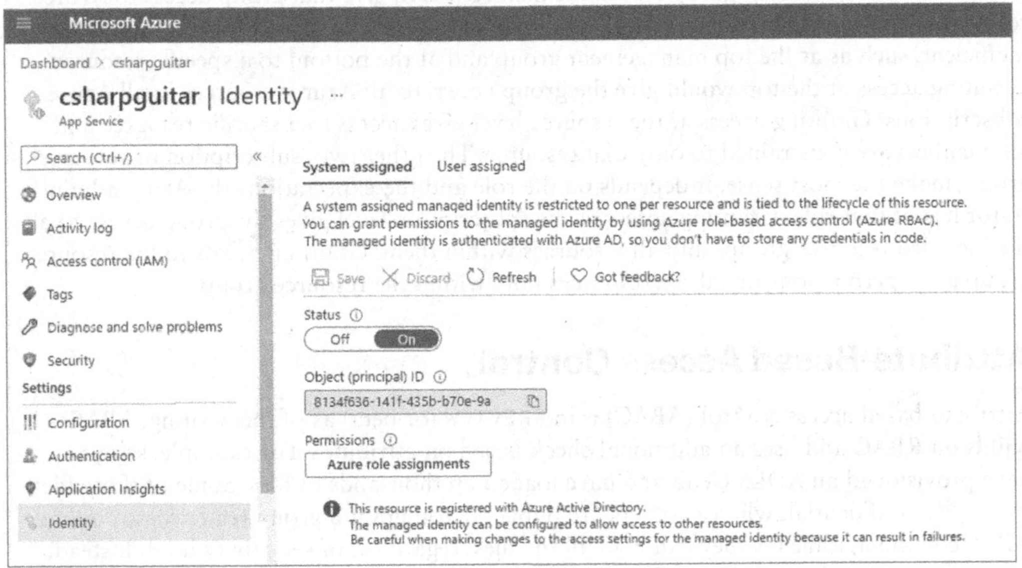

Figure 1.27 illustrates the application resource in Azure Active Directory. You would see the same on the Enterprise applications blade.

And finally, Figure 1.28 shows the granted permission to an AKV for the MI.

AKV is the go-forward solution for storing secrets, keys, and certificates. You should know this product very well.

FIGURE 1.27 Azure Managed Identity in Azure Active Directory

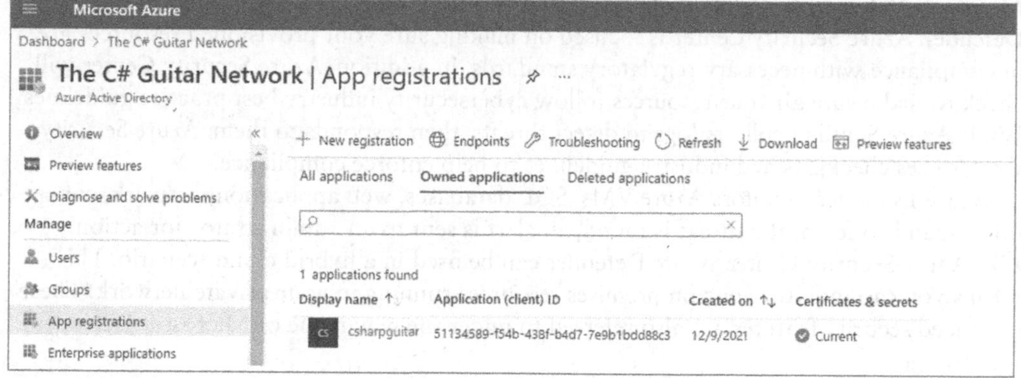

FIGURE 1.28 Azure Managed Identity in Azure Key Vault

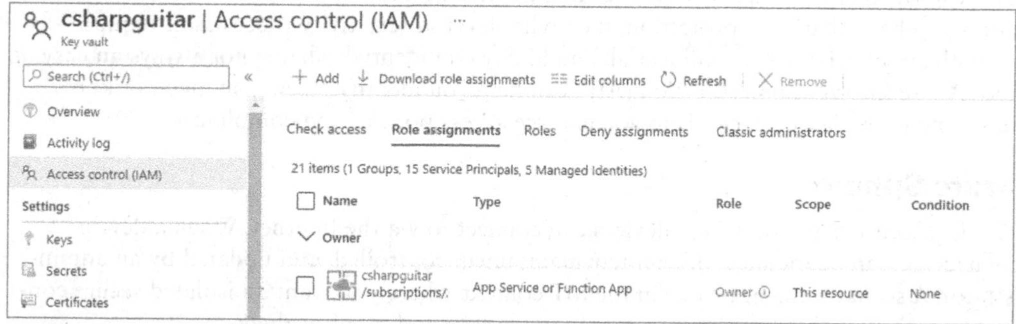

Other Products

Security is very important. Here are some additional security-related Azure products and features you should know about.

Azure Sentinel

For those responsible for implementing a security solution, Azure Sentinel is the place to start, and it's helpful to become an expert at it. This product is an industry-leading *security information event management (SIEM)* and *security orchestration automated response (SOAR)* solution. In addition to data collections and analysis capabilities, Azure Sentinel has threat intelligence, detection, and hunting features. Founded on a collecting, detecting, investigating, and responding philosophy, Azure Sentinel protects not only all your cloud resources, but your on-premises, private resources as well.

Microsoft Defender for Cloud

Microsoft Defender for Cloud consists of two features: Azure Security Center and Azure Defender. Azure Security Center is focused on making sure your provisioned resources are in compliance with necessary regulatory standards. In addition, Azure Security Center will check to make sure all your resources follow cybersecurity industry best practice guidelines. While Azure Sentinel collects logs to detect threats, then responds to them, Azure Security Center uses checklists and industry guidelines to help enforce compliance.

Azure Defender monitors Azure VMs, SQL databases, web application, network, containers, and so forth. If a threat is found, an alert is sent to an administrator for action. Like Azure Security Center, Azure Defender can be used in a hybrid cloud scenario. This means you can monitor your on-premises resources running in your private network. These enhanced security features are also referred to under the new name of Microsoft Defender for Storage.

Azure Information Protection

If you want to have a chance at privacy and governance, the first step is to identify what assets you have that need protection, then what level of sensitivity those assets require—for example, public, internal, confidential, and highly confidential. That is not always an easy task. Azure Information Protection (AIP) can help you identify assets you may not know exist, and once classified, can help you enforce access policies and compliance.

Azure Sphere

This is a secure platform where devices can connect to via the Internet. When a device connects, it can be monitored, remotely maintained, controlled, and updated by an administrator. A scenario might be one in the IoT context where you want an isolated secure connection point for the devices and a means to manage and monitor them.

Azure Networking

The networking capabilities in Azure are in most cases abstracted away from customers. The Azure network capabilities that link the Azure resources within a datacenter and between datacenters is owned, operated, and administrated by Microsoft. However, there are some networking products and features that let customers use and configure virtual aspects of the Azure infrastructure to meet their specific requirements.

Virtual Networks

There are two scenarios you should visualize when you attempt to understand how VNets work on Azure. The first concerns IaaS, aka Azure VMs, which cannot be created without a VNet. In that case, consider that an Azure VM exists within the VNet. There are other products like Azure Data Lake Storage, Azure SQL, and Azure Cosmos DBs that can be created without a VNet and then integrated with a VNet later. This means that the product is not created within the VNet; rather it can be bound to it and use some of its features. When you create a product without connecting it to a VNet, in most cases it means the product has a globally discoverable endpoint—that is, a public IP. That is not a security issue because the endpoint is protected, but some companies simply want to have that endpoint private. Changing an endpoint from public to private can be accomplished by binding the product to a VNet, then using the features of the VNet to control access. The most important features are as follows:

- Routing
- Network security group
- Peering
- Azure private link/endpoint
- Service endpoints
- Service tags

Routing

Once a product is connected to a VNet, you can force all outbound traffic into the VNet. Then you can use a *user-defined route (UDR)* to force that traffic wherever you would like. This is often referred to as *tunneling*. For example, many companies have on-premises software that tracks all outbound connections coming from within their networks. You can use a forced tunneling via UDRs to force the touring of traffic from Azure into your local networks and then out to the Internet via your company's network devices. Terms such as address prefix and next hop type are common in this context.

Network Security Group

A network security group (NSG) consists of numerous properties like protocol, action, direction, and port number. For example, if you wanted to allow only secured outbound Internet connectivity from machines within your VNet, you would create a rule that contains the properties shown in Table 1.8.

TABLE 1.8 NSG example

Property	Value	Possible values
Action	Allows	Allow or deny
Port	443	$1 - 2^{16}$
Direction	Outbound	Inbound or Outbound
Protocol	HTTPS	TCP, UDP, HTTP, or Any

It is also possible to allow or deny access based on the IP address of the machines. Classless Inter-Domain Routing (CIDR) is used to identify a group of allowed or denied IP address ranges. CIDR looks something like `10.0.0.0/24`.

Peering

This is a relatively easy concept to grasp. It means that you can connect two or more VNets together. Resources in VNet A can have access to resources in VNet B. You can make the access between the two VNets the same, or perhaps you wouldn't want resources in VNet B to have any or limited access to resources in VNet A.

Azure Private Link/Endpoint

So far, you have read about what is referred to as a global discoverable endpoint. Many Azure products are allocated these by default when provisioned. Here is an example of a few, where * represents the name of the provisioned product, which must be unique.

- `*.documents.azure.com`
- `*.azuresynapse.net`
- `*.azuredatabricks.net`
- `*.blob.core.windows.net`

To make the endpoint private, which means it is not visible on the Internet, you need to provision an Azure Private Link Service. Then, you can bind any of the endpoints shown in the list to that service, and it makes them invisible to anyone excluding the services you configure to allow discoverability. Keep in mind that this is different from simply configuring a firewall or IP restrictions. Those two actions restrict what can pass through to the resources, but the endpoint remains visible on the Internet. A private endpoint makes the endpoint invisible and then secured using a firewall or IP restriction.

Service Endpoints

This feature existed before Azure Private Links, but you should use Azure Private Links instead of Service Endpoints. If you use Service Endpoints, the global endpoint remains discoverable, but only resources that exist in the integrated VNet are allowed to access the bound resource, and vice versa. For example, if you have an Azure VM residing in a VNet and integrate an Azure App Service with the VNet, then enable Service Endpoints, that would mean that the Azure VM within the VNet can access the Azure App Service and nothing else. Of course, you have control over that—you could allow more or less access. The beauty of this product is the elevated level of security with very low configuration complexity.

Service Tags

A difficulty when setting up security that uses IP addresses is finding out which ones need to be allowed and which ones denied. When setting up these kinds of restrictions on Azure, instead of setting a restriction based on IP, you use a *service tag*, which will give all machines that run a specific service access to your protected service. For example, `AzureKeyVault`, `AzureMonitor`, `Sql`, and `Storage` are service tags that give access to those services to your Azure resource instead of restricting to a single IP or range of IPs.

Other Products

Let's look at other networking-related Azure products you should be familiar with.

Azure Bastion

It is common practice to make a remote desktop connection to a Windows machine using the *Remote Desktop Protocol (RDP)*. The port is 3389. RDP may not be supported in some company scenarios due to security restrictions. Instead, you can use Azure Bastion to connect over port 443 from within the Azure portal. The connection between you and the Azure VM is confined to the Microsoft Azure internal network and does not traverse the Internet.

Azure ExpressRoute

Making a secured connection between your private datacenter and Azure requires a connection of some kind. You might be able to simply expose an endpoint on your local firewall and allow traffic into your intranet. This might not be the most secure approach, but it is possible. Another approach is a *virtual private network (VPN)*, which is a more secure connection between two entities across the public Internet. A VPN does have capacity constraints and the traffic does travers the Internet. An Azure ExpressRoute is useful for enterprises that need a secure, high-capacity connection from their private datacenters to the Azure platform that does not traverse the Internet.

Azure Compute

Renting computers was the original cloud service offering. The ability to provision a computer when you need it and then decommission it when it's no longer needed is very cost effective. Also, no longer having to worry about the networking and datacenter security is a very attractive part of running IT operations in the cloud.

Azure Virtual Machines

An Azure virtual machine (Azure VM) is an allocation of a CPU and memory from a larger host machine. This is the IaaS service offering from Azure. There is a great variety of sizes that are optimized for high CPU or high memory compute requirements.

Azure Virtual Machine Scale Sets

Once upon a time, it took some effort to scale out instances of Azure VMs. Historically, when you chose IaaS as your cloud solution, the code running on it was expected to run on a single instance. As time changes, so do expectations. Azure Virtual Machine Scale Sets (VMSS) is a solution that simplifies the scaling out of identical instances of a single Azure VM when required.

Azure App Service Web Apps

Azure App Service Web Apps is a PaaS cloud service offering. This product offers web application and website hosting services. The beauty of this is the scalability. When you need to add an additional server to run your code, click a button and it will be added and online within a few moments. This is also a great place to host REST APIs for your customers or partners to consume. Lastly, there is a service named WebJobs that supports the scheduling and execution of small- to middle-scale batch jobs.

Azure Functions

An Azure Function is a FaaS, aka serverless cloud service, offering on Azure. This product is useful for event-driven IT solutions, such as monitoring and processing messages that enter a messaging queue. The code that is executed is typically small, consisting of a single method or snippet of code. This product scales to the capacity that is required to perform the work automatically.

Azure Batch

Azure Batch is focused on large-scale batch execution workloads. The machines that can be selected are tuned for CPU- or memory-intensive activities. The ability to schedule and create dependencies between a sequence of jobs is also supported.

Azure Management and Governance

Once you have decided to run your workloads on Azure and identified the products you need, you should consider management and governance. Make sure you have control over spending, who can provision products, who can access data, and of course, how the products you use are performing. You also need to consider certifications like ISO, GDPR, and PCI DSS and what kind of compliance is necessary to fulfill those requirements.

Azure Monitor

You must log information about the performance, availability, and use of your workloads running on the Azure platform. This is admittedly an often overlooked aspect from IT organizations in general, not just of those that run some of their solutions in the cloud. Azure Monitor is shown in Figure 1.29.

FIGURE 1.29 Azure Monitor

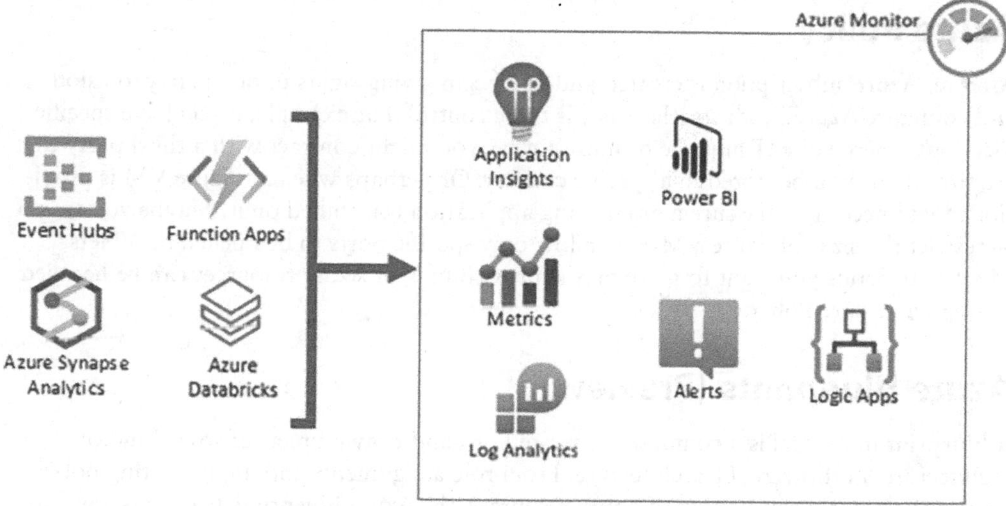

One aspect that jumps out when looking at Figure 1.29 is that Azure Monitor groups together other logging and tracing products. Azure Monitor is a management console that helps you integrate and create a monitoring solution. Notice that many Azure products can integrate with Azure Monitor, like Event Hubs, Azure Functions, Azure Synapse Analytics, and Azure Databricks. The logs are stored in a datastore that can be analyzed by Azure Synapse Analytics, Metrics, and Log Analytics. The data can be visualized with Power BI, and if you find some data that is not as expected, it is possible to send alerts or trigger a Logic App so that the anomaly is surfaced.

Azure Purview

Use Azure Purview to help manage and govern your data landscape. You can use this tool with on-premises, SaaS, Azure, and other cloud service providers. Being able to identify sensitive data and where data has come from, and discovering new data sources are all features of Azure Purview. This tool is focused on your data real estate hosted on Azure. Data

Map, Data Catalog, and Data Insights are all capabilities you get via the Azure Purview Studio console.

Your company may have many datastores and databases that need to be monitored not only from an access perspective, but based on what kind of data is stored in each. Azure Purview provides an administrative overview of your data sources. Defining the reason for the data's existence, what the data's intended purpose is, the sensitivity classification of the data, and who can access are "need to know" pieces of information. Governance and manageability of your data sources is what this product is all about.

Azure Policy

After an Azure subscription is created and you begin giving rights to others to provision and configure Azure products, there needs to be control. For example, if you have specific locations where your IT must be or must not be, you might contract with a third party that requires their data be stored in a specific country. Or perhaps when an Azure VM is provisioned you need to make sure a monitoring application is installed on it. Maybe you want to restrict the sizes of Azure VMs and allow only specific ports to be opened on VNets. Most restrictions you want to place on the provisioning of Azure resources can be handled through an Azure Policy.

Azure Blueprints (Preview)

A blueprint in general is a computer-generated or hand-drawn image of some kind of architecture, in this case, IT architecture. From role assignments and implementing policies to the actual provisioning of Azure resources, the Azure Blueprints feature is a way to orchestrate the deployment of each declaratively.

Azure Lighthouse

There are many customers who run solutions on Azure that are used and/or resold by other companies. Azure Lighthouse supplies tools for governing, controlling scale, and automating the many tasks for managing such an offering.

Azure Cost Management and Billing

There are products on Azure that are very costly. Even having them provisioned for a single day, sitting idle, can cost hundreds or even thousands of dollars. The way you can manage this is by using Azure Cost Management. This toolset lets you set budgets and spending limits and configure alerts when spending is approaching that limit. You can create reports that identify which products are generating the most costs, which can help you control cash flow. One additional feature of this tool is the ability to report the cost on a group of products and features that make up a specific project. This helps you isolate and get more clarity on cost and profits on a per-project basis.

Other Products

Here are a few additional products and features that are good to know about.

Tags

When you provision an Azure resource in the Azure portal, one common step is requesting tags (see Figure 1.30). This gives you the option to add a query-able identifier to the resource. For example, you can mark it as production, test, or development, or perhaps identify a contact person for the given resource. Regardless, this is a valuable concept you might consider implementing to manage your Azure resources as your footprint grows.

FIGURE 1.30 Tags for Azure products

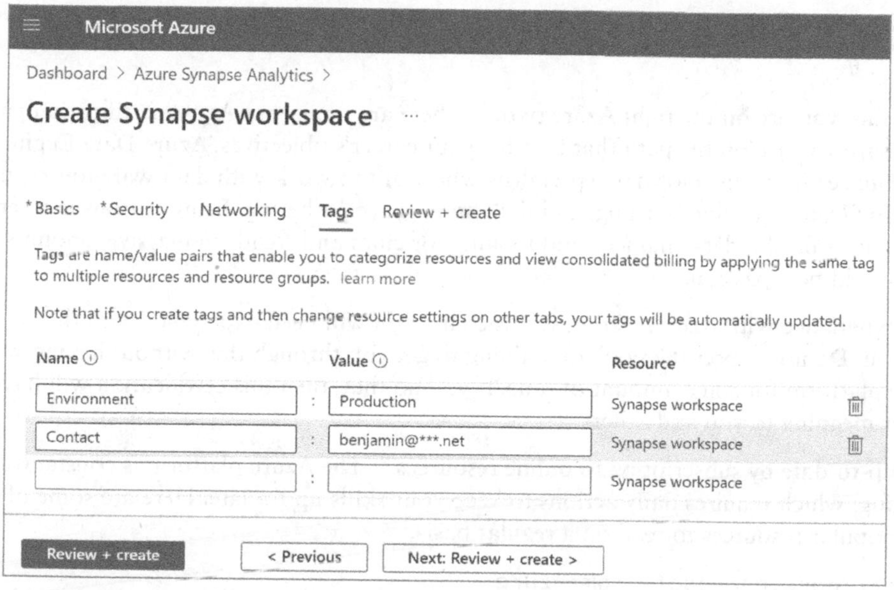

Azure DevOps

This product is based on application source code and the development process. A company's application source code is stored in Azure Repos that store history. Azure Pipelines can be configured to automatically perform a release into production when source code is checked in. That process is commonly referred to as *continuous integration/continuous deployment (CI/CD)*. Azure Boards and Azure Test plans are helpful in linking source code changes to specific work items and making sure the change works and meets the expectations of the requested work.

Summary

This chapter provided tips on preparing for the Data Engineering on Microsoft Azure exam. You learned about the importance of staying current and that you should make sure to work with Azure often, especially with Azure data service products. Working with these tools will keep the information fresh in your head and will make it much easier to pass the exam. Finally, this chapter introduced you to a large number of Azure products. Some of them you must know in great depth, whereas others you only need to know a little bit and the rest not so much. The point is that you know, or have at least some idea of, what most Azure products are and when you would use them.

Exam Essentials

Make sure you are on the right Azure path. There are numerous Azure certification paths. Make sure you are on the path that best fits your career's objectives. Azure Data Engineer Associate certification is for data specialists who want to work with data warehouses, data lakes, Big Data, machine learning, and data intelligence gathering. Being curious is a very important trait of a data engineer, and looking for clues and trends in massive amounts of data should be a passion.

Gain experience with Azure. To pass this exam, you will need experience with the platform. Do not expect the book or training to get you through this without having worked on the platform for some amount of time. If you do that, then this certification will have greater meaning to you and others.

Keep up-to-date by subscripting to online resources. The Azure platform is constantly changing, which requires daily actions to keep your skills up-to-date. Here are some of the most popular resources to read on a regular basis.

`https://docs.microsoft.com/azure`

`https://azure.microsoft.com/updates`

`https://aka.ms/azheatmap`

`https://azure.microsoft.com/services`

`https://docs.microsoft.com/azure/?product=analytics`

Know what products exist in Azure. Sometimes, possible answers to exam questions mention products that are not real Azure products. They read or sound like they are, but they are not. Knowing what really is available on the platform will help you remove at least one possible answer to a few questions.

Gain deep, some and base knowledge. No one knows everything, but you can be an expert in one or two Azure products and features. Those products and features usually have a connection or dependency to other Azure features, which you could then learn some internals about. There are some products and features that are not related to any other directly. For example, there is no direct relationship between Azure Cognitive Services and a VNet. It would be good to have at least a base knowledge of what benefits they can provide.

Focus on certain products. The Azure Data Engineer Associate exam is heavy on Azure Synapse Analytics, SQL Pools, Azure Databricks, Azure Data Factory, Azure Active Directory, Azure Key Vault, and Stream Analytics products. Make sure you have a very good understanding of these products, their features, and their limits, as well as DataFrames, advanced SQL querying, clusters, and *slowly changing dimensions (SCDs)*. This knowledge gives you the best chance of passing the exam.

Review Questions

Many questions can have more than a single answer. Please select all choices that are true.

1. Which of the following are pools available in Azure Synapse Analytics?
   - A. SQL pools
   - B. Spark pools
   - C. Azure Cosmos DB pools
   - D. Integration runtime (IR) pools
2. Which of the following are components of Azure Synapse Analytics?
   - A. SQL Pools and Apache Spark Pools
   - B. Integration runtimes (IRs)
   - C. Pipelines
   - D. Linked Services
3. What is the *best* definition of a data lake?
   - A. A place where data that is no longer needed gets stored
   - B. A place to store data that has not yet been transformed
   - C. A logical grouping of all your data
   - D. The location where transformed data is stored
4. Why would a customer choose to use Azure HDInsight?
   - A. The solution must run on Apache Spark pools.
   - B. The solution requires the Linux operating system.
   - C. Their solution is dependent on Kafka.
   - D. The on-premises solution already runs HDInsight.
5. What is a common use of Azure Stream Analytics?
   - A. To analyze data existing on an ADLS Gen1 datastore
   - B. To analyze data streams and identify anomalies
   - C. To transform data existing on an Azure Cosmos DB
   - D. To update Power BI with real-time analytics
6. Which of the following are Azure SQL database offerings?
   - A. SQL Server on Virtual Machines
   - B. SQL on Elastic Pools (SQL EP)
   - C. Azure SQL Managed Instance (SQL MI)
   - D. Azure SQL Database (SQL DB)

7. What is the purpose of role-based access controls (RBACs)?
   - **A.** Defines the permissions for a group of individuals
   - **B.** Prevents users from deleting data from a database
   - **C.** Can enforce sensitivity level data access
   - **D.** Assigns the scope of permissions
8. An Azure Managed Identity is which of the following?
   - **A.** Similar to a service principal
   - **B.** An identity of a provisioned Azure resource
   - **C.** Can be either user- or system-defined identities
   - **D.** A permission constrained account for guests
9. Which of the following are features of a VNet?
   - **A.** A subnet
   - **B.** Azure Virtual Machine
   - **C.** Network security group (NSG)
   - **D.** Azure Firewall
10. Which tool is responsible for monitoring your Azure resources?
    - **A.** Azure Lighthouse
    - **B.** Azure Purview
    - **C.** Azure Monitor
    - **D.** Azure Sphere

Chapter

2

CREATE DATABASE dbName; GO

If you think about it, without data there really isn't a need for a computer. It does somewhat depend on your definition of what data is, but consider why we access websites from a computer or open apps on our mobile devices. It is done to consume data in one form or another, like a newsfeed, a music stream, a video stream; to send/receive text messages; or to read emails. All those actions require that data already exists and is stored in a place where it can be easily retrieved. When you consume any kind of data, you are in fact generating access and usage data yourself, which is collected and stored. The consumption and collection of data cannot be achieved without having it stored in some accessible location. It all requires a database, which is created using the syntax `CREATE DATABASE dbName; GO`.

Even if you are creating a database using an API or via the Azure portal, somewhere there is a command to the database management system (DBMS) that invokes a create method. From that point you have a blank canvas to design, deploy, configure, and optimize your data structure. Whether it is relational, semi-structured, or unstructured, we all start from the same empty place. How you design a successful data storage and retrieval solution has many dependencies. For example, what kind of data will you store and what format is it in? Then there are numerous other questions, like where is the data coming from—what is generating the data, from how many locations will the data be generated, who or what will access the data, and where are those consumers physically located? And very importantly, what is the purpose of or use case for the data? Read on and you will gain some insights that will help you better answer those questions and perhaps also learn why those questions are important at all.

The Brainjammer

The data used for this book has come from my own brain. I have used an Emotiv Insight to capture approximately 20 sessions per scenario, over a two-month period in eight different scenarios, for approximately two minutes per session. An Emotiv Insight has five electrodes: `AF3`, `AF4`, `T7`, `T8`, and `Pz`. Each of those electrodes collect five different frequencies: `THETA`, `ALPHA`, `BETA_L`, `BETA_H`, and `GAMMA`. Through much scientific analysis of brain waves, those frequencies have been attributed to certain human characteristics, which are described in the following list:

- `THETA` = Creativity
- `ALPHA` = Relaxation

- BETA_L = Problem Solving
- BETA_H = Concentration
- GAMMA = Learning

Frequencies are measurable and distinguishable signals that the brain interface can capture and convert into a decimal number. If you are performing an activity that requires a lot of creativity, you would expect that the values captured for THETA would be greatest and farthest away from, perhaps, ALPHA. We can assume that if values for THETA are a high number, when compared to the other frequency values in the same scenario, then we must be doing something creative. The same goes for BETA_H: we must have been concentrating hard. The different scenarios performed are in the following list:

- Listing to classical music
- Reading through a FlipChart newsfeed
- Meditating
- Listening to metal music
- Playing my guitar
- Flipping through TikTok
- Attending a meeting at work, remotely
- Working, not reading email, really working

It is possible to make some preliminary conclusions and assumptions about which of those scenarios would exhibit the most powerful frequency. Should working have high BETA_L and should meditation have high ALPHA? It seems like they should, but maybe the brain works differently than we assume. Some would say data doesn't lie, but it can depend on how the data is captured, manipulated, and interpreted. The data for this book was collected in two formats, JSON and CSV, which are all downloadable in the BrainwaveData directory on GitHub here: `https://github.com/benperk/ADE`. The Emotiv Insight captures two kinds of signals, electroencephalography (EEG) and power (POW), which have both been collected and stored on GitHub. In the next chapter I'll walk you through downloading them from GitHub and then uploading the files to an Azure Data Lake Storage (ADLS) container, which you will also provision.

It is kind of exciting looking forward to what we can find through the analysis of this data using some Azure data analytics products and features. The approach you take while analyzing this data can be applied for any type of data or use case. I just didn't want to use the same ol' taxicab, Twitter, or sales forecasting scenarios, which are valid but . . . well, boring.

A Historical Look at Data

Humans have been collecting and storing data for thousands of years. The earliest example is a tally stick, which was a bone that people scratched lines into when counting supplies or tracking business activities of some kind. You have probably also heard of an abacus, which was the first dedicated device created for the purpose of performing calculations and storing data. There were many iterations of data storage mechanisms between the tally stick and what exists now on cloud platforms. Two events that have had the most profound impact on data storage and data creation were the mass adoption of the Internet and the establishment of social platforms.

Early on, the Internet was a place to get information. There were very few websites, and most data was being shared on a Usenet. The Usenet was simply a group of interconnected servers that users could dial into and then post, read, and comment on messages. It was similar to Twitter or Discord platforms, but the Usenet was a console application and totally text-based. The data on the Usenet was archived and searchable. Those were the early days when computers were not on every desktop, so primarily professionals used them for work-related activities. Then came along affordable home computers, and Netscape and Yahoo, which changed everything. Initially, once people could afford a personal computer and make a connection to the Internet, there was no user-friendly software to access data on public servers. There also was no global Internet address registry, which meant you needed to know the data address in advance to access it. The Netscape browser filled the gap for a user-friendly application to "surf the web" and Yahoo became the platform where you could discover the locations of different kinds of data information.

Once the ease of using the Internet increased and the number of people accessing it grew, companies began doing business commerce on it. Amazon, of course, was one of the first and most successful examples of companies doing business on the Internet. Companies that did business on the Internet needed to capture and store information about the people they transacted with. That makes sense, especially when there are financial transactions that take place. Internet commerce is a primary contributor to the beginning of data capturing and storage of personal information. The amount of data being collected and generated has continually increased to the point where an entire virtual private network (VPN) industry was conceived to conceal the identity and activity of individuals using the Internet. Without a VPN, your location, the kind of device you are accessing from, the operating system version on the device, and the application you are accessing with can all be detected and stored while traversing the Internet. Companies have come up with some very interesting uses for that kind of data. You could probably come up with some uses for this data too if that data was in front of you in Azure Synapse Analytics, and you had some moments of inspirations.

Most people have an Internet-connected device with them, 24/7. They willingly (sometimes unwittingly) share almost every aspect of their life with the numerous companies whose apps they have installed. Many of those apps are social apps like Facebook, Google Maps, and TikTok, each of which has greatly contributed to data generation and storage. The combination of Internet commerce and the constant generation and storage of data from Internet-connected devices and social apps contributed to the emergence of the term *Big Data*. To better understand what Big Data means, see Figure 2.1, then read on to learn about its three characteristics: variety, velocity, and volume.

FIGURE 2.1 Big Data characteristics

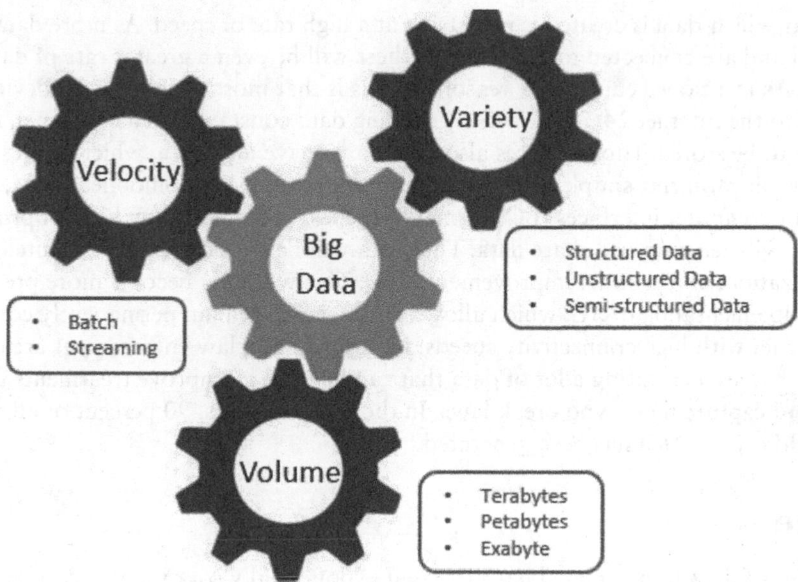

Variety

Data comes not only in different formats but also from different sources. The kind of data shared and stored on the Usenet was typically text, but as usage progressed, the Internet needed to be able to share many different types of files. For example, Amazon needed to show pictures of their products. Pictures are typically in PNG, JPEG, BMP, or GIF format. Music streaming services, such as Napster, emerged. Most files downloaded or shared on Napster were MP3 or WAV files. Sharing movie or video files, which were typically in MP4 or MOV format, over the Internet wasn't very popular early on because the speed was slow a decade or so ago. People who worked with web-based applications used HTML, ASPX, PHP, and JS files. And of course, there are the familiar DOC, TXT, PPT, and PDF files. Finally, some of the more popular data formats are JSON, YAML, XML, CSV, and Apache Parquet. Data created from a mobile device might be in image form or even JSON files, which can send location to a consumer on the Internet. Web servers may expose an API, which expects the file format to be in XML, which is common with *Windows Communication Foundation (WCF)* interfaces. The point is that there are many different types of data being stored and created and many require a different approach for optimally storing and transferring them.

Velocity

The pace at which data is created is increasing at a high rate of speed. As more data streams get created and are connected to the Internet, there will be even a greater rate of data being generated. As mentioned earlier, one reason for this is that most people have a device that is connected to the Internet 24/7 and is likely sending data constantly to a consumer, and that data needs to be stored. Those devices also commonly have a camera, which makes capturing sharable moments simple. From an industry perspective, automobiles, ships, running shoes, brain-computer interfaces (BCIs), smart watches, and almost any kind of product imaginable will generate and share data. That data will be stored for business intelligence, self-optimization, and product improvement ideas. This will only become more prevalent with the implementation of 5G, which allows the device to remain permanently connected to the Internet with high connectivity speeds. Healthcare and law enforcement are other industries that are generating a lot of data that can be used to improve treatments for rare illnesses and capture those who break laws. In the last two years, 90 percent of all the data in the world ever created has been generated.

Volume

The amount of data being created has increased exponentially over the last decade and continues to do so. Two decades ago the typical amount of storage on a computer was measured in megabytes. Today, a few terabytes aren't uncommon, especially when you recognize that there are approximately 2.5 quintillion bytes of data created each day. That is approximately 2 MB of data created per second, for every person on Earth. A quintillion is a 1 followed by 18 zeros: 1,000,000,000,000,000,000. As the velocity of data generation increases due to more devices and improved technology, the volume of data will increase respectively. That means the volume will continue to increase on a daily basis. Consider the kind of infrastructure required to handle even 1 percent of that amount of data. The management of even a small percentage of that amount of data is not something individuals or small companies could ever scale large enough to handle. Therefore, the creation of the cloud to provide the solution for such scenarios obviously didn't happen by chance. Rather, the cloud service originated to address the need for a cost-effective solution to manage the growth of data volume.

Data Locations

Companies and individuals have not always had a global perspective, and many still do not. The location of customers who want access to your data or the location of data producers does matter. A company's customers can be local, regional, national, and/or global. If that is the case, you want to have the data they use as close to them as possible. It is simply too slow to have a customer in India access a database in Texas. If that is the case, you would lose your customers in India. To save them, you would place a database in India. Decades ago, that would be a very costly and time-consuming activity. However today, cloud service providers have datacenters in almost every country and can be provisioned and brought online in minutes.

Devices that produce data may be stationary, move a short distance, or perhaps move around the globe. A lamppost is not going to move; therefore, you could theoretically have a database of lampposts in the same city, which would be very effective. However, if you have a logistics company that moves goods nationwide, then the distance between the truck (i.e., the data producer) and the datastore might result in some data loss. The same goes for moving goods internationally using a ship or an airplane. Knowing where these vehicles are and perhaps their speed is valuable data, especially in the logistics industry that runs on *just-in-time (JIT)* delivery modes. Again, the existence of cloud service provider datacenters in most countries around the world helps you gain this piece of business intelligence and data reliability.

Data File Formats

Data comes in numerous forms, as stated earlier. The most common types and the types that are important to know about and be comfortable with for the exam are as follows:

- JavaScript Object Notation (JSON)
- Apache Parquet file format
- Optimized Row Columnar (ORC)
- Extensible Markup Language (XML)
- Yet Another Markup Language (YAML)
- Comma-separated values (CSV)

Let's take a closer look at each of those formats, beginning with the most common, JSON.

JavaScript Object Notation

The JavaScript Object Notation (JSON) file format is very useful for capturing and storing data. In addition to that, JSON is often used for configuration files, which are loaded into process memory at runtime. JSON is also the default file structure for data transmissions between a client and a REST API. Take a look at the following example of a JSON file:

```
{"Session": {
    "Scenario": "TikTok",
    "POWReading": [
      {
        "ReadingDate": "2021-07-30T09:40:25.6635",
        "Counter": 0,
        "AF3": [
```

```
    {
      "THETA": 9.681,
      "ALPHA": 3.849,
      "BETA_L": 2.582,
      "BETA_H": 0.959,
      "GAMMA": 0.738
    }]}]}
}
```


The JSON snippet is an example of a single reading of a brainwave from a brain computer interface IoT device. It was captured while viewing TikTok. This is only a small snippet of the actual reading, as it reflects only the waves from the `AF3` electrode of the BCI. There are four other electrodes on the BCI: `AF4`, `T7`, `T8`, and `Pz`, so five in total. The `AF3` electrode, like the others tracks, the `THETA`, `ALPHA`, `BETA` and `GAMMA` values.

A common difficulty of working with JSON files has to do with getting all the opening and closing curly brackets `{ }`, square brackets `[ ]`, quotes `""`, and commas to work out symmetrically. As you can see just in this small snippet, there is an abundance of each. If you want to see how this file was created, take a look at the C# code in the `Chapter02/Source Code` directory on GitHub: `https://github.com/benperk/ADE`. One benefit of JSON-formatted files is that they are rather easy to read through and get an idea of what they contain. Additionally, the number of unnecessary characters are limited, which reduces the size of the file. Finally, there are many libraries that help efficiently parse the file, such as `System.Text.Json` and `Netwtonsoft.Json`. The best uses of JSON files include the following:

- Large, complex datasets
- When you are already working with JavaScript
- When you are communicating between systems over the Internet

Apache Parquet File Format

Apache Parquet files are used in the Hadoop ecosystem. JSON, CSV, and XML are useful when it comes to sharing data between applications, whereas parquet files perform better for temporarily storing intermediate data between different stages in an application. To get an idea of how to work with this file type, consider the following code snippet:

```
data = [('TikTok', '5', 'AF3', 'THETA', '9.681'),
        ('TikTok', '5', 'AF3', 'ALPHA', '3.849'),
         ('TikTok', '5', 'AF3', 'GAMMA', '0.738')]
columns = ['Scenario', 'Counter', 'Electrode', 'Frequency', 'Value']
df = spark.createDataFrame(data, columns)
df.write.parquet('/tmp/output/brainjammer/tiktok.parquet')
```

That code snippet creates a `DataFrame`, which is a location in memory for storing data in the context of Apache Spark and Azure Databricks. Then the data can be written to disk in parquet format using the `DataFrame write()` method, passing the location to write the file as a parameter. Using the `spark.sql()` method, you could then create an in-memory view, named `BRAIN` in our example, and then query it:

```
spark.sql("CREATE VIEW BRAIN USING parquet OPTIONS ('/tmp/output/
brainjammer/*')")
spark.sql('SELECT * FROM BRAINWAVE').show()
```

The output would look like the following table:

```
+----------+----------+-----------+-----------+-------+
| Session  | Counter  | Electrode | Frequency | Value |
+----------+----------+-----------+-----------+-------+
| TikTok   | 5        | AF3       | THETA     | 9.681 |
| TikTok   | 5        | AF3       | ALPHA     | 3.849 |
| TikTok   | 5        | AF3       | GAMMA     | 0.738 |
+----------+----------+-----------+-----------+-------+
```

Here are a few additional benefits of the parquet file format:

- Partitioning
- Compression
- Columnar format
- Support for complex types

Partitioning will be described in more detail later, but for now know that it is a method for grouping certain types of data together so that it's more efficiently stored and therefore more efficient to query. The following snippet first creates a partition on the `Wave` column and then queries for all `Waves` that have a value of `GAMMA`. Calling the `show()` method would create a table like the previous one, but with only rows where `Wave` equals `GAMMA`.

```
df.write.partitionBy('Frequency').mode('overwrite') \
      .parquet('/tmp/output/brainjammer/tiktoFrequency.parquet')
data = spark.read \
      .parquet('/tmp/output/brainjammer/tiktokFrequency.parquet/
Frequency=GAMMA')
data.show()
```

Working with a file or partition that contains only the data you require is smaller and therefore more efficient. Parquet files have an advantage when it comes to compression due to their columnar format.

Compression should not be a new term; it means that the data within a file is compacted and reorganized in a way that it requires less storage space. From a relational perspective, we typically think of data in rows, but a parquet file is focused on columns—that is, columnar format. Think about performing a query from a vertical perspective versus a horizontal one, and you should be able to visualize how this would result in less data. There is a term called projection, which is used to limit the columns that are returned from a SQL query of a row. Columnar format is a default SQL projection feature.

CSV and JSON files are typically used for basic data storing, like strings, Booleans, and basic numbers. Parquet files can be used to store more complex data structures like structs, arrays, and even maps, where a map would resemble something like the following:

```
DESCRIBE BRAIN
+-----------+--------------------+
| name      | type               |
+-----------+--------------------+
| Electrode | string             |
| Frequency | map<string,value>  |
+-----------+--------------------+
```

Then, when you perform a query on datastored in the `BRAIN` table, the following could be realized:

```
+-----------+----------+----------+
| Electrode | key      | value    |
+-----------+----------+----------+
| AF3       | THETA    | 9.681    |
| AF3       | ALPHA    | 3.849    |
| AF3       | GAMMA    | 0.738    |
+-----------+----------+----------+
```

Parquet files are one of the best formats for working with Big Data. The best uses of parquet files include the following:

- When you are using Hadoop
- Working with read-heavy analytical applications
- *Write once, read many (WORM)*

Optimized Row Columnar

This file format is a columnar format used in the Hadoop ecosystem, like parquet files. Both ORC and parquet files are often referred to as self-describing, which means the information that describes the data in the file is contained within the file itself. Metadata typically accompanies the file. For example, in Windows, when you right-click a file in Windows Explorer and select Properties, you will see information about the file. That is considered metadata; that information would instead be within the ORC or parquet file itself, making the file self-describing.

Facebook was the company that came up with the ORC file format. ORC is supported on Apache Hive and Apache Pig, which is optimized for *Hadoop Distributed File System (HDFS)* read operations. Parquet, on the other hand, works best with Apache Spark and is its default format for reading and writing data on that architecture. When it comes to ORC files, there is a concept known as a *stripe*. You might think of a zebra with vertical black and white stripes, and that is exactly what it is. Since the context here is columnar, which is vertical as compared to a row that is horizontal, then perhaps it is easier to comprehend.

Data structures are conceptual but are physically stored in memory or on disk. Therefore, the memory addresses at which they are stored and the drive sectors on which they are placed have a significant impact on latency. The closer the addresses are together and the closer the sectors are, the faster all the data is retrieved. It has been proven that taking this vertical approach has a speed advantage over a horizontal approach.

Working with an ORC file is very similar to working with a parquet file. Assume that you have already loaded the data into a `DataFrame`. The first line of the PySpark code snippet saves the data in `df` to an ORC file. The lines of code that follow show how to write an ORC file, create a table view, and then display the contents of the ORC file:

```
df.write.format('orc').save('/temp/orc/brainjammer/tiktok.orc')
spark.sql("CREATE VIEW BRAIN USING parquet OPTIONS ('/tmp/output/
brainjammer/*') ")
spark.sql('SELECT * FROM BRAINWAVE').show()

+----------+----------+-----------+-----------+----------+
| Session  | Counter  | Electrode | Frequency | Measure  |
+----------+----------+-----------+-----------+----------+
| TikTok   | 5        | AF3       | THETA     | 9.681    |
| TikTok   | 5        | AF3       | ALPHA     | 3.849    |
| TikTok   | 5        | AF3       | GAMMA     | 0.738    |
+----------+----------+-----------+-----------+----------+
```

Partitioning and querying of the data in an ORC file is the same as previously shown in the parquet section. If you are going to use Apache Hive, then you would want to use the ORC file format to get the best performance. The best uses of ORC include the following:

- When working with read-heavy analytical applications
- When working with Apache Hive

Extensible Markup Language

The Extensible Markup Language (XML) file format has been around for many years. It was a very nice advancement coming from its predecessors like CSV or TXT files. What XML has that CSV and TXT files do not is the ability to strongly type the contents of the file. For example, numbers can be represented as either integers or strings, based on the code that is going to interpret it. An XML Document Type Definition (DTD) or XML Schema Definition (XSD) file would be used in combination with the XML that identified the types. For example, here is an example of a `brainwave.dtd` file:

```
<xs:element name="brainwave">
<xs:complexType>
  <xs:sequence>
    <xs:element name="Scenario" type="xs:string"/>
    <xs:element name="Counter" type="xs:int"/>
    <xs:element name="Electrode" type="xs:string"/>
```

```
    <xs:element name="THETA" type="xs:decimal"/>
    <xs:element name="ALPHA" type="xs:decimal"/>
    <xs:element name="GAMMA" type="xs:decimal"/>
  </xs:sequence>
</xs:complexType>
</xs:element>
```

Additionally, XML supports building arrays and objects from the file structure, which isn't optimal or even possible when receiving rows of comma- or semicolon-delimited data in CSV or TXT files. Here is an example of an XML file that references the XML DTD file:

```
<!DOCTYPE brainwave SYSTEM "brainwave.dtd">
<Session>
  <Scenario>TikTok</Scenario>
  <Counter>5</Counter>
  <Electrode>AF3</Electrode>
  <THETA>9.681</THETA>
  <ALPHA>3.849</ALPHA>
  <GAMMA>0.738</GAMMA>
</Session>
```

You can save the XML content into a file using the classes and methods found in the `System.Xml` namespace. The following C# syntax illustrates how to achieve this:

```
public class Brainwave
{
  public string Scenario;
  public int Counter;
  public string Electrode;
  public decimal THETA;
  public decimal ALPHA;
  public decimal GAMMA;
}
public static WriteXML()
{
  Brainwave brainwave = new Brainwave();
  System.Xml.Serialization.XmlSerializer writer =
    new System.Xml.Serialization.XmlSerializer(typeof(Brainwave));
  System.IO.FileStream file = System.IO.File.Create("brainwave.xml");
  writer.Serialize(file, brainwave);
  file.Close();
}
```

Once the files are written, the files can be used and sent to other applications, which can parse and use the data within it. Although this format is not the most effective for Big Data analytics, due to the historical significance of this format there are likely many systems that use this file format as a basis for their solution. Therefore, it is a valid format to know and understand, but do not use it when designing a new data analytics solution. The best uses of XML include the following:

- When the data requires validation
- When the file contains a mixture of content
- When working with WCF

Yet Another Markup Language

Yet Another Markup Language (YAML) is one of the newest file formats. You will find it permanently in the context of Docker container configuration and deployments. That approach is commonly referred to as *infrastructure as code* and is often used to define pipelines with Azure DevOps and GitHub Actions, also for deployments. However, YAML can also be used to store data in the same way, similar to JSON. Here is an example of YAML syntax:

```
Session:
  # This is a comment
  Scenario: TikTok
  Counter: 5
  Electrode: AF3
  THETA: 9.681
  ALPHA: 3.849
  GAMMA: 0.738
```

One benefit of this format, which you might see immediately, is that there are no more curly or square brackets. YAML can be considered a superset of JSON with a few extra features such as comments, anchoring, and aliasing. Simply precede a line in the file with a # character and it is considered a comment. Anchoring and aliasing has to do with removing the necessity to duplicate data throughout the file. Also, the alias simplifies updates to an attribute, where the change needs to only happen in a single place, instead of multiple ones.

```
Session:
  # This is a comment
  Scenario: &scenario TikTok
    Counter: 5
    Electrode: AF3
    THETA: 9.681
    ALPHA: 3.849
    GAMMA: 0.738
```

```
Scenario: *scenario
  Counter: 6
  Electrode: Pz
  THETA: 8.392
  ALPHA: 4.142
  GAMMA: 1.106
```

Notice that the first instance of `Scenario:` is followed by an ampersand, &, then the name of the identifier followed by the value. In all future locations where this same value is needed, enter the identifier preceded with a star instead of placing the actual value. YAML isn't prime time yet and not the primary choice for doing Big Data analytics. But it is up and coming and worthy of being called out. The best uses of YAML include when you have been using JSON but want the additional features available in YAML.

Comma-Separated Values

A comma-separated values (CSV) file is just that, a CVS file that contains data values separated by commas. Sometimes, the first row in a CVS file identifies the column names:

```
Scenario,Counter,Electrode,THETA,ALPHA,GAMMA
TikTok,5,AF3,9.681,3.849,0.738
TikTok,6,Pz,8.392,4.142,1.106
```

Loading that file into memory using Python would look something like the following. First you import the CVS library, then open the file and load it in memory via the `reader` object. Each value in each row is accessible through the enumerable `row`.

```
import csv

with open('brainjammer.csv') as f:
    reader = csv.reader(f)
    for row in reader:
        #load each row into database
```

The best uses for CVS files include the following:

- Small datasets
- If you want a simple solution for importing and exporting data
- If you are working with Microsoft Excel

Count on the data used within a large-scale data analytics solution to come in lots of different formats. We've covered six different types along with some insights about their use cases and the way in which you can access the data using code. See Table 2.1 for a comparison overview of these file formats.

TABLE 2.1 File comparison

	JSON	Parquet	ORC	XML	YAML	CSV
Columnar	No	Yes	Yes	No	No	No
Complex structure	Yes	Yes	Yes	Yes	Yes	No
Compressible	Yes	Yes	Yes	Yes	Yes	Yes
Human readable	Yes	No	No	Yes	Yes	Yes
Simplicity	Simple	Complex	Complex	Simple	Simple	Simple
Write	Fast	Slow	Slow	Slow	Fast	Fastest
Read	Fast	Fastest	Fastest	Slow	Fast	Fast
Dataset size	Small	Large	Large	Small	Small	Small

There are many other formats, but the ingestion of those formats into your data warehouse or data lake is just a matter of first identifying the existing format. Then you need to identify the end format and develop the code to make the transformation.

Data Structures, Types, and Concepts

Now it is time to delve a bit deeper into some data concepts. Up to now you may have noticed that the chapter content has been introductory and perhaps not so much about data. In this section, we will focus on data structures, data types, and some general, yet complex, data concepts. You will need to know many of these concepts to pass the exam, and you will see them again in action in later chapters.

Data Structures

Data can be classified in three different ways: structured, semi-structured, and unstructured. Here you will learn about each one.

Structured

This classification of data arrangement is synonymous with relational data structures. It is found within relational DBMS (RDBMS) systems like SQL Server, MySQL, and Oracle. On Azure, any of the Azure SQL products is where you will find the solution for storing, managing, and analyzing structured data. Figure 2.2 illustrates an example of numerous tables contained within a relational database.

FIGURE 2.2 Tables in a relational database

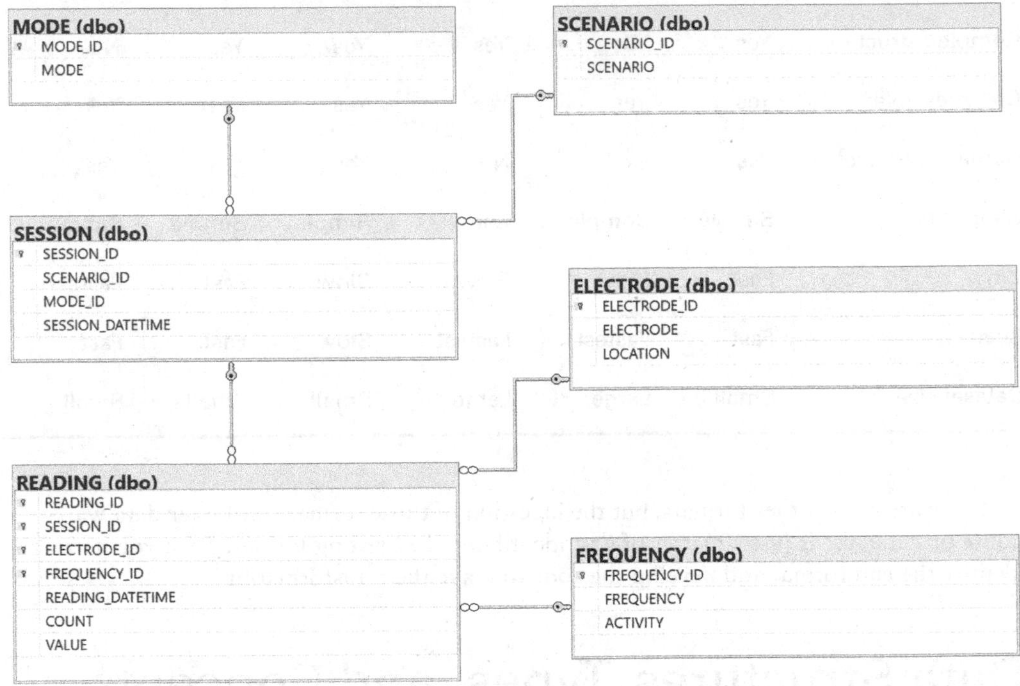

Notice that there are many relationships between the data in the table that contains a reading from a single electrode of a BCI. The data in the related tables are linked by what is called a *foreign key*. For example, `ELECTRODE_ID`, which is the *primary key* on the `ELECTRODE` table, is the foreign key on the `READING` table. This relational structure is helpful in two ways: querying to answer questions and data normalization. With this structure you can query the data to answer any question imaginable. For example, how long did one session take, what is the average value of all `ALPHA` readings per scenario, or what is the maximum `GAMMA` value from electrode `T8`?

Data normalization is most practiced in the context of a relational database. Normal form attempts to maintain data integrity and minimize data redundancy. Data integrity has to do with the usefulness of data over the long term. Over time, data is updated and deleted, and if you are not careful, you can lose the meaning and purpose of the data. One way of maintaining data integrity is to enforce primary and foreign key referential integrity. For example, consider a SCENARIO table that looks like this:

```
+---------------+-----------------+
| SCENARIO_ID   | SCENARIO        |
+---------------+-----------------+
| 1             | ClassicalMusic  |
| 2             | FlipChart       |
| 3             | Meditation      |
+---------------+-----------------+
```

SCENARIO_ID is the primary key for this table and is used as part of the foreign key on the SESSION table. If the SCENARIO_ID of 1 is added to the SESSION table, this means you would no longer be able to delete that row with a primary key of 1 from the SCENARIO table. This is because there is now a referential integrity constraint between the SCENARIO and the SESSION table. Imagine if you were able to delete the SCENARIO row with the primary key of 1. If, after you deleted it, you wanted to check which scenario the SESSION was linked to, it would no longer be possible since the value of 1 is included in the SESSION table instead of ClassicalMusic. Essentially, without knowing the scenario in which it was collected, the data is worthless.

An alternative to creating relationships between numerous tables and building relationships between them is to simply create a single table. You could then dump all the data into that table. The table would very likely end up with a huge number of columns and a large amount of redundant data. Consider the fact that it would be expected to have numerous sessions for each type of scenario. If you placed all that data into a single table, you would end up with having ClassicalMusic, FlipChart, Meditation, and so forth duplicated many times in the Scenario column instead of a single numeric value. This results in less space and less duplication of the same data, even if it is not useful.

To get some better insights and experience with a relational database, complete Exercise 2.1, where you create an Azure SQL database and tables and load it with data.

EXERCISE 2.1

Create an Azure SQL DB

1. Log into the Azure portal at https://portal.azure.com. Enter **Azure SQL** in the top middle search box, click Azure SQL, and then click the + Create button to display the Select SQL Deployment Option blade in Figure 2.3. Click the Create button under SQL Databases and leave Single Database as Resource Type.

EXERCISE 2.1 *(continued)*

FIGURE 2.3 The Select SQL Deployment Option blade

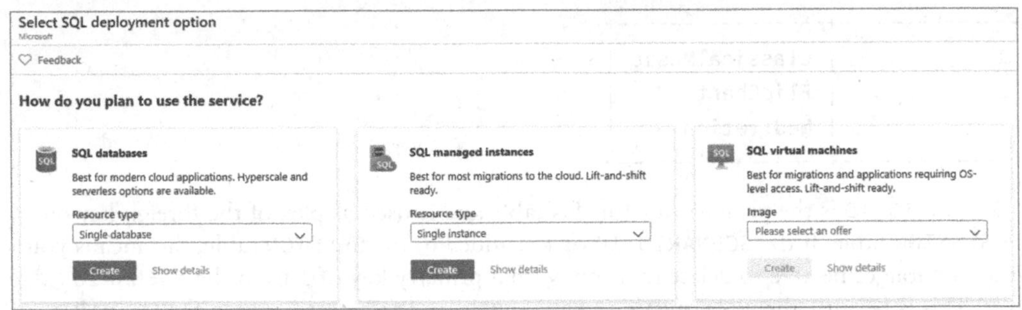

2. Select the subscriptions and resource group where you want the database to reside. Enter a database name (I used **`brainjammer`**). Under the Server drop-down box, click the Create New link to create a database server. Enter the server name (I used **`csharpguitar`**), and enter a server admin login and password. Confirm the password and select the location of the server. I recommend placing it in the same location as your resource group, but doing so is not required. Click OK.
3. Select the Locally Redundant Backup Storage radio button. This is the cheapest solution. For a production environment, you would want to have ZRS or GRS, click Review + Create, and click Create.
4. Navigate to the Azure SQL database (`brainjammer` in my case). Click the Connection Strings link in the navigation menu and you will see different tabs that provide examples of connection strings.
5. Navigate back to the Overview blade. Click the Set Server Firewall link. Notice that the Allow Azure Services And Resources To Access This Server is defaulted to ON. Also notice there is a link named + Add Client IP; click that link and then click Save.
6. From the Connect With drop-down, select Azure Data Studio. Click the New Connection link and enter the connection details for your database (Figure 2.4). Click Connect.

FIGURE 2.4 Azure Data Studio

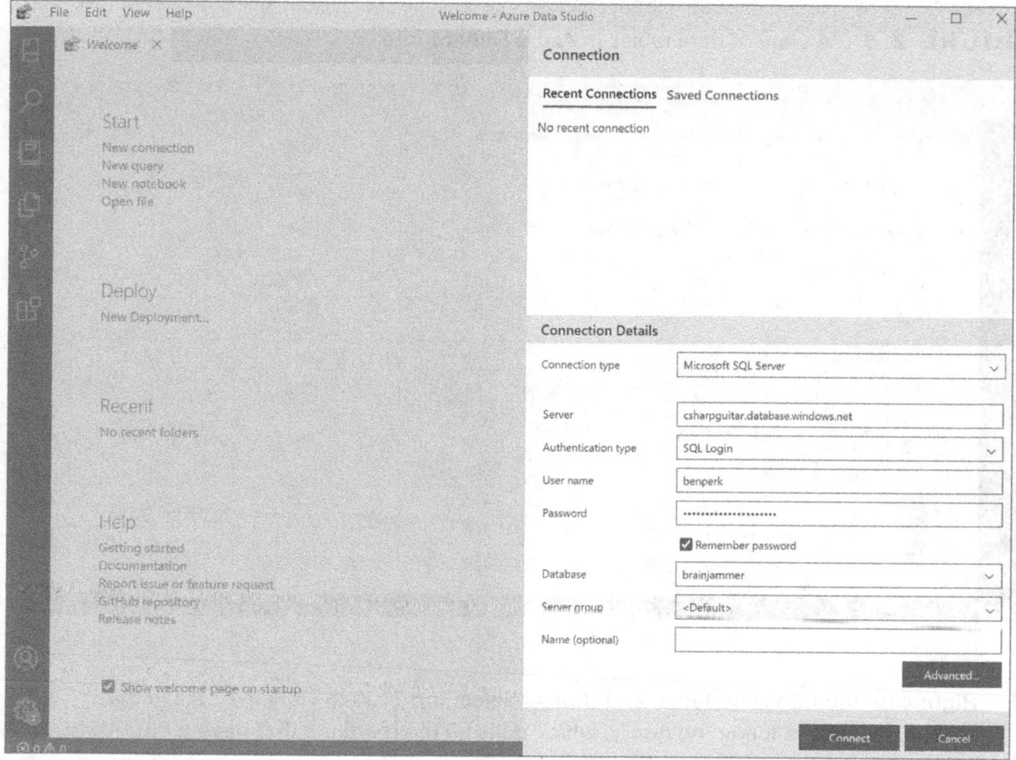

7. Select New Query and download/open the `brainjammer.sql` file, located in the folder `Chapter02/Ch02Ex01` at this location: `https://github.com/benperk/ADE`. Create the tables and insert the data after successfully running the SQL script, then click the Refresh button to see the window in Figure 2.5.

EXERCISE 2.1 ***(continued)***

FIGURE 2.5 A view of data tables in Azure Data Studio

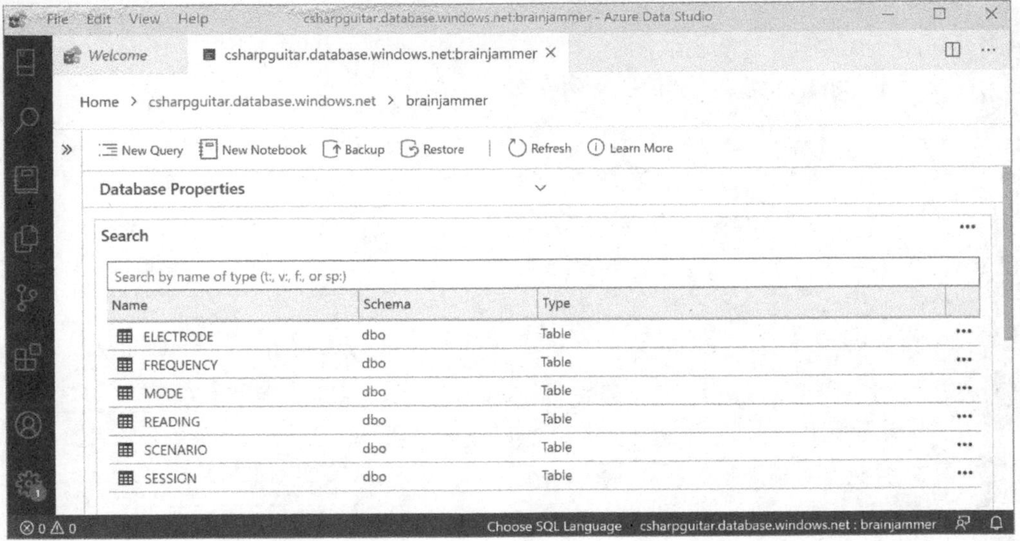

8. Right-click the READING table, and choose Select Top 1000 to view the data in that table. Execute the following query, which pulls all the readings that have a FREQUENCY of 1 that is THETA:

```
SELECT F.FREQUENCY, R.VALUE
FROM READING R JOIN FREQUENCY F
ON R.FREQUENCY_ID = F.FREQUENCY_ID
WHERE R.FREQUENCY_ID = 1
```

There will be more opportunities to execute queries against this database in the "Querying Data" section later in this chapter, but there are other data structures we need to discuss first.

Semi-Structured

Two problems that have come up regarding relational databases over the years have to do with the complexity of SQL queries and the difficulty of representing objects. The simple structured database you created in the previous exercise contains six tables. Creating a query to join three, four, or even five of those tables together would be long and complex.

Further, there is a concept, *object relational models (ORMs)*, that libraries like NHibernate, Hibernate, and Entity Framework work with. However, relational databases do not work optimally with ORMs. Semi-structured databases, also called NoSQL databases, can resolve both of those situations. Semi-structured data APIs such as Azure Table, Gremlin (Graph), and Core (SQL) on Azure can be found within an Azure Cosmos DB account.

Azure Table: Key-Value Database

Key-value databases store values in pairs. This makes for fast querying using `GET`, `PUT`, and `DELETE` commands instead of SQL-like queries. Most use cases for key-value pair databases will have millions if not billions of rows. This scale and the speed at which you can work with data that big is where a lot of the value of this kind of database is found. Take the following table, for example, which illustrates a key-value pair database:

```
+-----+----------------+
| KEY | VALUE          |
+-----+----------------+
| 1   | ClassicalMusic |
| 2   | FlipChart      |
| 3   | Meditation     |
| 4   | MetalMusic     |
| 5   | PlayingGuitar  |
| 6   | TikTok         |
| 7   | WorkMeeting    |
| 8   | WorkNoEmail    |
+-----+----------------+
```

Retrieving data from such a table is commonly performed using REST APIs that are HTTP-based. HTTP endpoints require an address that is provided when you provision an Azure Cosmos DB Table API. To retrieve, insert, and delete a row of data, you would use the following syntax. Replace `*` shown in the following endpoint address with the name of your Azure Cosmos DB Table API address. Replace *`scenario`* with the name of your table.

```
GET *.table.cosmos.azure.com/scenario/keys/5
PUT *.table.cosmos.azure.com/scenario/keys/9/?value=Sleeping
DELETE *.table.cosmos.azure.com/scenario/keys/5
```

Gremlin: Graph Database

Graph databases consist of nodes that contain records that point to other nodes. The relational aspect of a graph database exists between the nodes instead of within a node. This improves query times.

Core (SQL): Document Database

The Core (SQL) API is the main and native API in Cosmos DB. Data in this document database is stored using a markup language like JSON, YAML, or XML. This means you can store any data you need in any format. Instead of using table column names to identify data like you would in the relational context, tags are used to define the data and the hierarchy. To learn more about semi-structured document databases, perform Exercise 2.2.

EXERCISE 2.2

Create an Azure Cosmos DB

1. Log in to the Azure portal at `https://portal.azure.com`. Click the menu button in the top-left corner of the main page, and click + Create A Resource. Select Databases and click Azure Cosmos DB. Then, click the Create button under (Core) SQL, as shown in Figure 2.6.

FIGURE 2.6 Azure Cosmos DB APIs

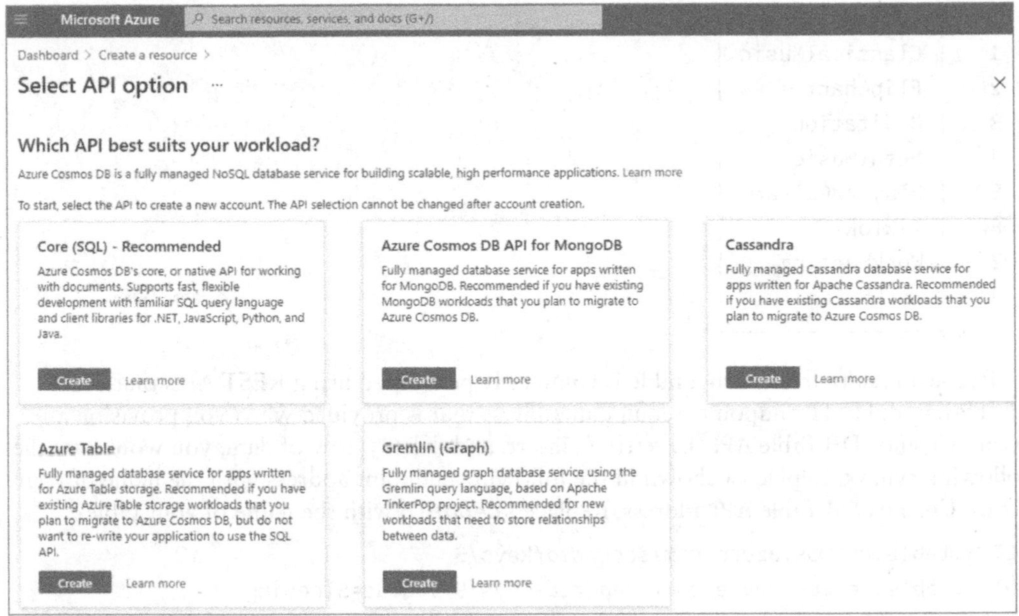

2. Select the subscription and resource group where you want to place the Azure Cosmos DB. Enter an account name (I used **`csharpguitar`**) and select a location. Select the Serverless Capacity mode. Leave all other default settings and click the Review + Create button and then the Create button.

3. After the provision is complete, navigate to the resource and from the Features menu select Azure Synapse Link and click Enable.

4. Navigate to the Overview blade of the Azure Cosmos DB. Click + Add Container, add a database ID (I used **brainjammer**), add a container ID (I used **sessions**), and change the partition key (I used **/pk**). Click the On radio button for Analytical Store and click OK.
5. Navigate to the folder `Chapter02/Ch02Ex02/brainjammer-cosmos` at `https://github.com/benperk/ADE` to check out some C# code that you can use to upload a JSON file to the database and container. There are also two JSON files that you can use.
6. Choose Data Explorer from the Azure Cosmos DB navigation menu and expand the database (in my example, `brainjammer`). Expand the container ID (in my example, `sessions`), then click Items. You will see the contents of the file you selected, similar to Figure 2.7. Notice that there is also an Upload Item button where you can click to manually upload one of the provided JSON files.

FIGURE 2.7 Azure Cosmos Data Explorer

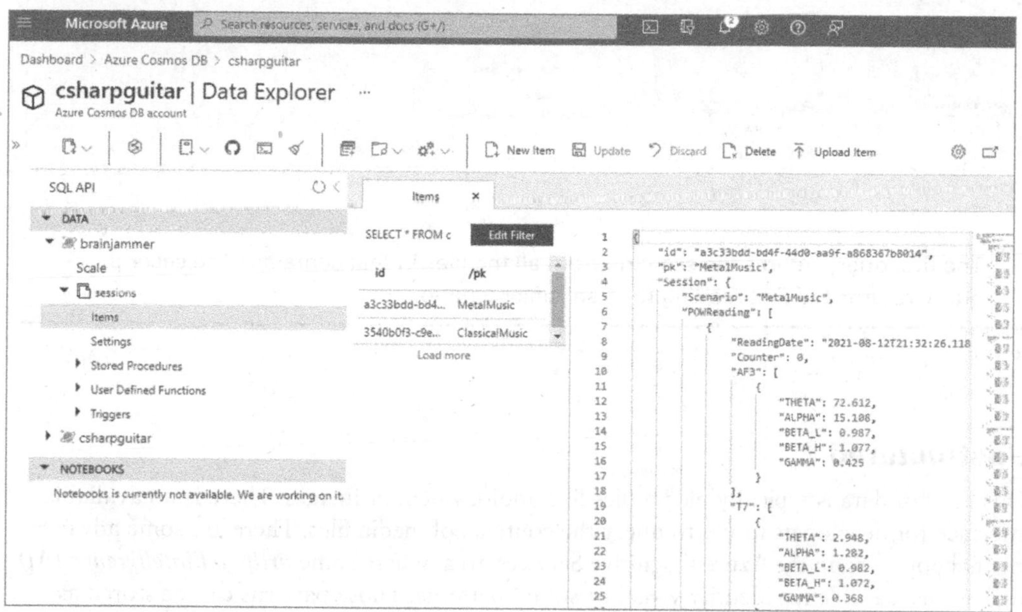

7. Try running a few queries; the output of the first is shown in Figure 2.8.

```
SELECT sessions.Session.Scenario FROM sessions
SELECT s.pk, s.Session.POWReading[0]
FROM sessions s
WHERE s.pk = "MetalMusic"
```

EXERCISE 2.2 *(continued)*

FIGURE 2.8 Azure Cosmos Data Explorer SQL query

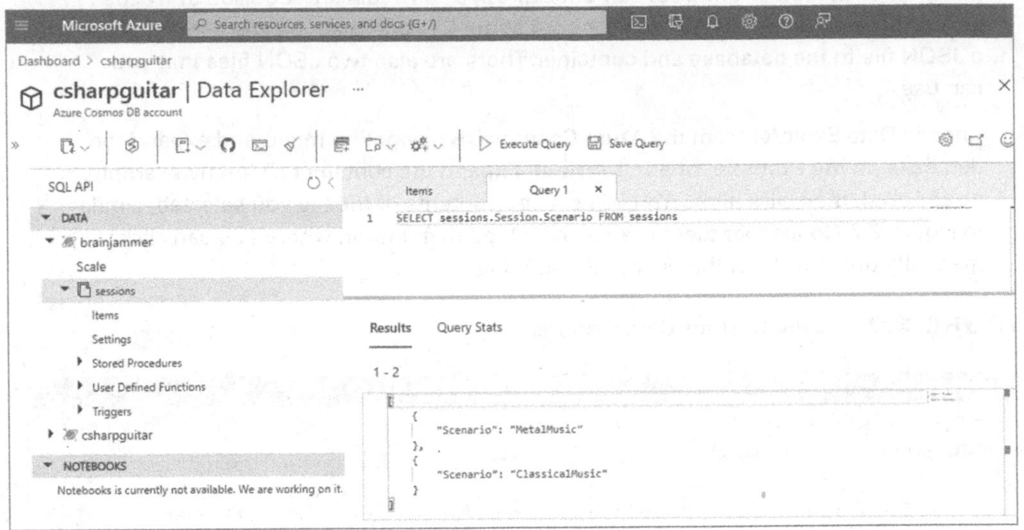

The first query returns the scenario from all the files in that container. The second query returns the first reading for a specific scenario.

Unstructured

This kind of data is typically media files like audio, video, or images. There is no available interface for developers to use to query the contents of media files. There are some advancements happening in the Azure Cognitive Services area, where some *artificial intelligence (AI)* algorithms are able the identify visual or sound patterns. Those patterns can be stored as metadata and used to compare with known patterns to determine the contents of the media file. This is a new area you could pursue if you find it interesting.

Data Types and Management

It is important to know in depth the different kinds of data you will work with and store for analysis. Is the piece of data you use in a `WHERE` clause an integer, GUID, or string? It makes a difference in not only the column definitions, if used, but also the size of the value and the way in which you make reference to them. Notice the different ways in which you reference those different types in the following snippet:

```
WHERE count = 1
WHERE name = "Benjamin Perkins"
WHERE id = '081EBD8A-6032-4B99-976B-D59215B2BB2A'
```

You can also see how different the lengths of each are. The sizes of the values are significant when you are working with huge amounts of data. A GUID takes up a lot more space than the integer. Storage space is required to store the data on disk and then in memory when loaded from disk for manipulation or analysis.

Data Types

Table 2.2 contains a list of the most common data types.

TABLE 2.2 Common data types

Type	Example	Description
`binary`	1–8,000	Values between 1 and 8,000
`bit`	1 or 0	Either a 1 or 0; `nulls` can also be stored
`blob`	`goodvibes.mp3`	An un/semi/structured file
`bool`	true or false	Used to compare values
`array`	`{'1', '2', '3'}`	A group of elements
`char`	a	A single number, letter, symbol, or space
`datetime`	2022-05-02 08:02:00	A date and time value; YYYY-MM-DD HH:MM:SS
`decimal`	1.5	~ $\pm 1.0 \times 10^{-28}$ to $\pm 7.9 \times 10^{28}$ with 28–29 digits
`double`	1.5	~ $\pm 5.0 \times 10^{-324}$ to $\pm 1.7 \times 10^{38}$ with 15–16 digits
`float`	3.14	~ $\pm 1.5 \times 10^{-45}$ to $\pm 3.4 \times 10^{38}$ with 7 digits
`image`	brainmap.png	An image of some kind, such as PNG, BMP, GIF
`int`	100	A whole number, ±2,147,483,648

TABLE 2.2 Common data types *(continued)*

Type	Example	Description
`json`	`{ "brain" : "ben" }`	Used to store JSON data
`money`	€100	Currency values
`nchar`	Now is the time for...	Fixed length up to 4,000 characters
`nvarchar`	To no one will we...	Variable length up to 4,000 characters
`nvarchar (max)`	In the beginning...	Variable length up to maximum
`string`	`csharpguitar`	An array of characters
`uniqueidentifier`	081EBD8A-6032-...	16-byte GUID
`varchar`	30-65-EC-6F-C4-58	Use for fixed-length data, e.g., SSN or MAC
`xml`	`<brain>ben</brain>`	Store XML data

There are a few more than this, but the table represents the most common data types for a database. There are three important items you should note. First, you might notice that the value is the same for a decimal and a double. The difference between the two, however, is in the description. A decimal can contain ~29 digits to the right of the decimal, which makes it more precise than a double, which can contain ~16. Second, `VARCHAR` and `NVARCHAR` let you specify a specific length, such as `VARCHAR(100)` or `NVARCHAR(125)`. You should do this if you know the maximum length of the data that can be added to that column. Specifying the length value will save space compared to using `VARCHAR(MAX)` or `NVARCHAR(MAX)` to save space on your database. Lastly, use `VARCHAR` unless there is a specific need for `NVARCHAR` that you need to store or work with foreign language special characters.

Data Management

Don't confuse *data* management with *database* management, where the focus is on the mechanics of the DBMS. When you choose to run your database on the Azure platform and select a PaaS product, then the management of that database is no longer your or your company's responsibility. Instead, the focus here is the management of the data, such as where the data is stored, who has access to the data, what the meaning and use cases are for the data, how long the data is useful, and how long the data should be retained. You can apply *Time To Live (TTL)* configuration to data that can help managing data lifetime. Many of these topics have been touched on already in this chapter, and will likely be covered again, but they are important concepts that pertain to data management. The data needs to be as close to those who consume or produce it so that latency and potential data loss can be minimized. There may be some constraints on the location in which the data can be stored based on industry and governmental regulations.

From a data privacy and governance perspective, you need to know the sensitivity level each column, node, or file has in your datastore. You also need to control access. You must know who has access, who is accessing the data, and how often. If you consider the data being used in this book, brainwave data, the validity of the data is likely determined on the sophistication of the device that captured it. Once there are better devices, the data that has been captured today is no longer as useful as what can be collected with a better BCI. Which leads to the question: how long should the data be retained?

There are numerous reasons to retain data. For one, being able to revisit historical data to show the path of forward progression from beginning to end might add some value. For example, if all things remain equal, the trend will continue in that direction. Further, if there is ever some kind of investigation required to uncover reasons for missing projections or beating projections, historical data is a place to find out some reasons for the outcome. This kind of data analytics is called *predictive analytics*. There are also reasons for expiring data, such as legal obligations, costs, and data staleness. There is a very popular privacy framework named *General Data Protection Regulation (GDPR)* that contains some guidelines for the retention of data for given circumstances. One general example is for bookkeeping documents where the retention period is seven years, after which the data should be permanently deleted. The retention period also depends on the type of data it is. For example, if it contains information that can identify an individual human, then it should be deleted as quickly as possible.

Data retention also comes with a cost. Consider the cost of storage space on ADLS Gen2, which currently starts at $0.00099 per gigabyte in an archived state, up to $0.15 per gigabyte when running in Premium mode. If you are storing massive amounts of data, which is common in the Big Data context, you can do the math and determine how much storing a terabyte or even a petabyte of data costs; it is significant. Finally, at some point data become less relevant. For example, consider that the `AF3`/`AF4` electrodes on a BCI have a 10 percent margin of error. When a new BCI device is created with a margin of error at 2.5 percent, then the old data collected with a 10 percent margin of error is mostly useless. There is no real reason to store that data any longer. Delete it and save the money for the new, more precise data collections.

Data Concepts

There are many concepts you must be aware, comfortable, and competent with to manage data efficiently. This section covers many data concepts that will not only help you pass the Data Engineering on Microsoft Azure exam, but also help you do the job in the real world. Keep in mind that when discussing relational structure or tables, the context is generally focused on Azure SQL or Azure Synapse Analytics SQL pools. In contrast, `DataFrames` lean toward Azure Synapse Analytics Spark pools. Much of the following is about Azure Synapse Analytics SQL pools. When this is not the case, the context will be specifically called out.

Sharding

This is a technique used primarily to store large amounts of data that is too big to fit on a single database. Sharding is also useful for separating data within a database into faster, smaller, easier-to-manage shards. Shards distribute data across different machines, aka nodes. Figure 2.9 illustrates how data might be sharded across numerous database instances.

FIGURE 2.9 Azure Synapse Analytics Sharding example

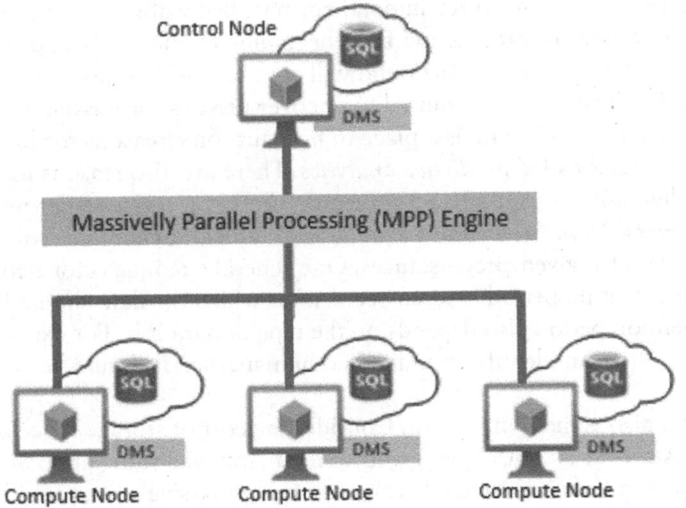

There are two features in Figure 2.9 that need some explanation, beginning with the *Data Movement Service (DMS)*. DMS is responsible for moving data across the nodes when necessary for executing queries and returning the results. This is a platform-level feature and is configured by the way your table distributions are implemented. Table distributions will be discussed in a later section. The other feature is the *massively parallel processing (MPP) Engine*, which is shown as a layer between the control node and the compute nodes. MPP manages and coordinates the processing of queries across all the SQL dedicated compute nodes in the cluster. DMS moves the data while MPP manages the state and optimizes queries that are running in parallel—in other words, at the same time. Numerous clients or users can connect to the control node and execute queries at the same time. Running the queries one after another (i.e., sequentially) is not optimal. MPP will manage the query executions and run them as quickly and efficiently as possible.

Symmetric Multiprocessing (SMP)

You will find the MMP design in Azure Synapse Analytics and Symmetric Multiprocessing (SMP) design in Azure SQL Database. MMP processors (i.e., CPUs) are allocated with dedicated compute resources like memory, while SMP shares those compute resources. Consider the fact that the retrieval of datastored in memory is less latent than when stored on disk. In the shared resource SMP architecture, it is possible for datasets to be cached in memory and reused, but with MMP this is not possible. You must find the best solution for your requirements.

Partition

Partitions are like shards, but instead of moving data to different databases on different nodes, the data is instead split across the same machine. Note that a machine and node are the same thing. Recall from Exercise 2.2 where you created an Azure Cosmos DB, that part of the provisioning required a partition key. The partition key name was `/pk` with a value of the `Session.Scenario`, for example, `ClassicalMusic`, `FlipChart`, `Meditation`. The data is divided into logical, queryable datasets using the value in the identified column as the basis for the split. Splitting, or partitioning, the data into smaller sets improves performance. Consider a scenario where you have collected brainwaves for millions of sessions. Retrieving the session information that has the scenario of `Meditation` is faster if the query is executed on a partition that contains only that scenario. In contrast, if there was no partition, the query would have to parse through the entire table of all sessions and pick only the records that match the desired scenario.

The following is an example of how you might create a table in Azure Synapse Analytics on a SQL pool named `READING` with a partition on a `SCENARIO_ID`:

```
CREATE TABLE [dbo].[READING] (
    [READING_ID]      INT            NOT NULL IDENTITY(1,1),
    [SCENARIO_ID]     INT            NOT NULL,
    [ELECTRODE_ID]    INT            NOT NULL,
    [FREQUENCY_ID]    INT            NOT NULL,
    [VALUE]             DECIMAL(7,3)  NOT NULL)
WITH
(   CLUSTERED COLUMNSTORE INDEX,
    DISTRIBUTION = HASH([SCENARIO_ID]),
    PARTITION (
       [SCENARIO_ID] RANGE RIGHT FOR VALUES
                     (1, 2, 3, 4, 5, 6, 7, 8)));
);
```

Both INDEX and DISTRIBUTION are discussed in the next sections. Since there are only eight captured scenarios, it is possible to specifically identify the values used to identify them—for example, SCENARIO_ID = 1 is ClassicalMusic and SCENARIO_ID = 2 is FlipChart. You should know the values from the database you built in Exercise 2.1 and the SCENARIO table you loaded with data.

The PARTITION option contains arguments that can be provided with it. In the previous example, you see RANGE RIGHT and FOR VALUES. RANGE LEFT is the default, which means that the boundary values belong to the partition on the left (lower values), where the boundary values are, in the example (1, 2, 3, 4, 5, 6, 7, 8). The opposite is true for RANGE RIGHT in that the boundary values belong to the partition on the right (higher values). If there is a value in the tables that is less than 1 or greater than 8, this is how it is determined onto which partition the data is placed. If you provide only a single boundary value—for example, a 4—two partitions are created, one for values lower than the value and one for values that are higher. If the data changes and you need to adjust the partitions, there are ways to do this using partition splitting, merging, and switching functions. Splitting comes into play, for example, when that partition gets too big and warrants breaking it down into more partitions. Perhaps you need to split the partition using the ELECTRODE_ID as well. Merging, on the other hand, is the opposite of splitting. Since the objective of partitions is to enhance performance and utilization, if some partitions are taking more time to return than others, level out the workloads. You can level them out by combining two or more existing partitions into one, for example. Lastly, switching has to do with changing the table to which the partition targets. Perhaps a need arises to create a table named READING2 that is loaded with fresh data. It is possible to switch one or more of the partitions to point to data on READING2 instead of the original table READING. Other partitions that are not switched continue targeting the original data on the READING table. All three partition functions (splitting, merging, and switching) are executed using the ALTER TABLE SQL statement. One additional option available supported with the ALTER TABLE command is the TRUNCATE_TARGET option. When this is used, as seen here, the data on the partition is overwritten with new data:

```
ALTER TABLE [dbo].[READING_NEW] SWITCH PARTITION 2
TO [dbo].[READING] PARTITION 2 WITH (TRUNCATE_TARGET = ON);
```

It is possible to partition data when running on a Spark pool:

```
df = spark.read.json('abfss://*@*.dfs.core.windows.net/brainjammer.json')
df.write.partitionBy('Scenario').mode('overwrite').json('/tmp/brainwaves/
scenario')
```

This would result in eight directories being created on ADLS and files containing the data of different scenarios within the directories. You can use df.repartition(8), which will create eight partitions in memory instead of writing the data to files and directories.

Index

In its most common use, an index is the place you look for a key term to find a page number for the detailed explanation of that term. You will find an index at the end of this book.

If you look for the term Index, you will find this page referencing it. An index in the database world is a technique used to speed up queries. Typically, you create an index on the pattern of most common WHERE clauses. Just in case you are not clear on how a standard SQL statement looks, here is an example:

```
SELECT VALUE from READING WHERE ELECTRODE_ID = 2 AND FREQUENCY_ID = 5
```

Without an index, the query would scan the entire table looking for rows of data that match the WHERE clause. However, if you create an index using the following snippet, then the query would perform much faster because the DBMS would already know where those rows are, just like an index in a book:

```
CREATE INDEX idx_electrode_frequency
ON READING (ELECTRODE_ID, FREQUENCY_ID)
```

If you do not create any indexes in your Azure Synapse Analytics dedicated SQL pool, then a *Clustered Columnstore Index (CCI)* is created for you. Recall the CLUSTERED COLUMNSTORE INDEX statement from the previous section, which illustrated the creation of a READING table. A CCI is the format in which data is physically stored on a disk. There are two indexing aspects you should know: logical and physical storage. The logical aspect is the way in which you can approach interfacing with the data using SQL queries, C#, or Python code to filter, retrieve, and analyze it. Physically, however, the data that you are accessing is stored in a file that exists on a storage drive. The CCI instructs the DBMS how to store the data in the physical file so that both an increase in performance and a decrease in storage capacity are achieved. The DBMS is then able to decipher the commands you send and apply them onto the datastored in the file and retrieve the result as quickly as possible. There are two other types of indexes: heap and clustered. Replacing CLUSTERED COLUMNSTORE INDEX with either HEAP or CLUSTERED INDEX results in those kinds of indexing.

A HEAP index and a CLUSTERED INDEX both store the data by row instead of by column as with a CLUSTERED COLUMNSTORE INDEX. The difference between the two is that a HEAP index stores the data without any underlying order, whereas the CLUSTERED INDEX does. Data stored with a HEAP will perform faster when queried, but a CLUSTERED INDEX will perform faster when manipulating data with INSERT, UPDATE, and DELETE commands. If you want to create an index when using a Spark pool, there is a library named Hyperspace. You can create an index for a Spark pool using the following syntax:

```
from hyperspace import hyperspace
hs = Hyperspace(spark)
df = spark.read.json('abfss://<*.dfs.core.windows.net>/brainjammer.json')
hs.createIndex(df, IndexConfig('ELECTRODE_ID', ['FREQUENCY_ID'], ['VALUE'])
```

This command will create files in an index folder on your ADLS container. This will incur more cost for storage but less cost on the compute side because the queries will run more quickly and require less compute power. At the moment, Hyperspace does not provide an in-memory capability, so the indexed data must be written to and read from disk.

Tables

A table is something that was referred to earlier in Figure 2.2. It is a structure that contains data organized in rows and columns. When running queries on Azure Synapse Analytics SQL pools, there are many considerations that pertain to how a table is created and how the data is stored within it. Again, keep in mind that when focusing on Spark pools, queries are often performed on data loaded into memory. They are primarily semi-structured, loaded from a file and not relational.

Distributed Tables

Introduced in Chapter 1, "Gaining the Azure Data Engineer Associate Certification," there are two options when it comes to Azure Synapse Analytics SQL pools: serverless and dedicated. When you run in serverless, there is no need to be overly concerned about database table structures because you are querying data that already exists in other sources. Those sources should already be optimized for performance. If that is not the case, then you need to be concerned about tables. However, when running on a dedicated SQL pool architecture, you do need to understand a bit more about the table and data structure. You need to know this for the exam as well.

Azure Synapse Analytics dedicated SQL pools were previously named Azure SQL Data Warehouses.

Distributed tables is a feature found in Azure Synapse Analytics dedicated SQL pools. When running a dedicated SQL pool, your data is partitioned and distributed to 60 database nodes. Having your data rightly shared, partitioned, and indexed helps get your data efficiently placed across these nodes. Data is spread out across these nodes, with the help of the DMS to provide optimal MPP opportunities. Note that a `COLUMNSTORE INDEX` is not optimal for tables with fewer than 60 million rows. This is because the data is distributed to 60 database nodes and a performance enhancement is not gained unless there are over 1 million rows per distribution. There are three methods in which dedicated SQL pools distribute data:

- Round-robin (default)
- Hash
- Replicated

ROUND-ROBIN

This term is common and is used in many scenarios. It has a lot do to with load balancing. Imagine that you have 60 nodes that are running behind a controller. Requests to execute a query are sent to the controller, which then must choose a node to forward that request to. If many requests are incoming at the same time or in short sequence, then it makes a lot of sense not to send all the requests to only one of the 60 nodes. That would likely overload that node, leaving all the others idle. Round-robin is an algorithm that keeps track of which nodes have been forwarded a request to execute and attempts to distribute the incoming requests equally and sequentially across all the nodes in the pool. Round-robin is the default distribution method, so if you leave out the `DISTRIBUTION = ROUND_ROBIN` argument from your table definition, that is what distribution you get.

Round-robin delivers the fastest performance when it comes to the loading data onto a node; what data is loaded on what node is random. The data is loaded evenly across the nodes. The fact that there is no optimization regarding the location of data on the nodes means that query performance might be slower when compared to a hash table distribution.

HASH

This distribution model uses a function to make the distribution, as shown in Figure 2.10. For large table sizes, this distribution model delivers the highest query performance. Consider the following snippet, which can be added to the script that creates the `READING` table:

```
DISTRIBUTION = HASH([ELECTRODE_ID])
```

This results in the data being deterministically distributed across the nodes based on the electrode type (i.e., `AF3`, `AF4`, `T7`, `T8`, or `Pz`) that captured the brainwave reading. A query that contains `AF3` in the `WHERE` clause would be executed on the compute node that contains the data where `ELECTRODE_ID = 1`—that is, `AF3`. The column name parameter sent to the `HASH` function is known as the distribution key or distribution column.

FIGURE 2.10 Azure Synapse Analytics hash table distribution

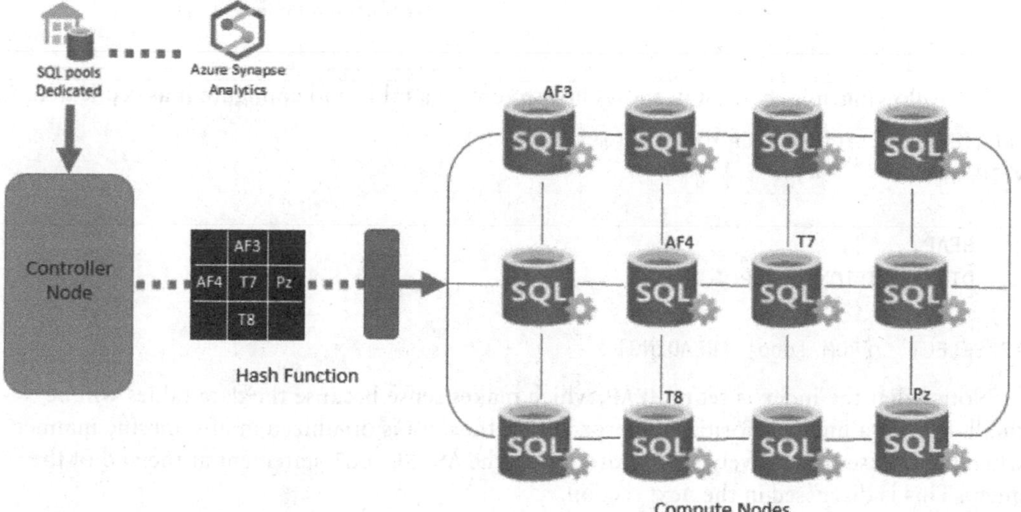

REPLICATED

This approach copies all the data from the entire table to each node. This mode delivers the best query performance for small tables. Figure 2.11 illustrates the copying of a table to the SQL pool nodes. As you might expect, the requirement for additional storage is necessary to store the multiple copies of the data on each node. Again, this is another reason when using this mode is best for small tables.

FIGURE 2.11 Azure Synapse Analytics replicated table distribution

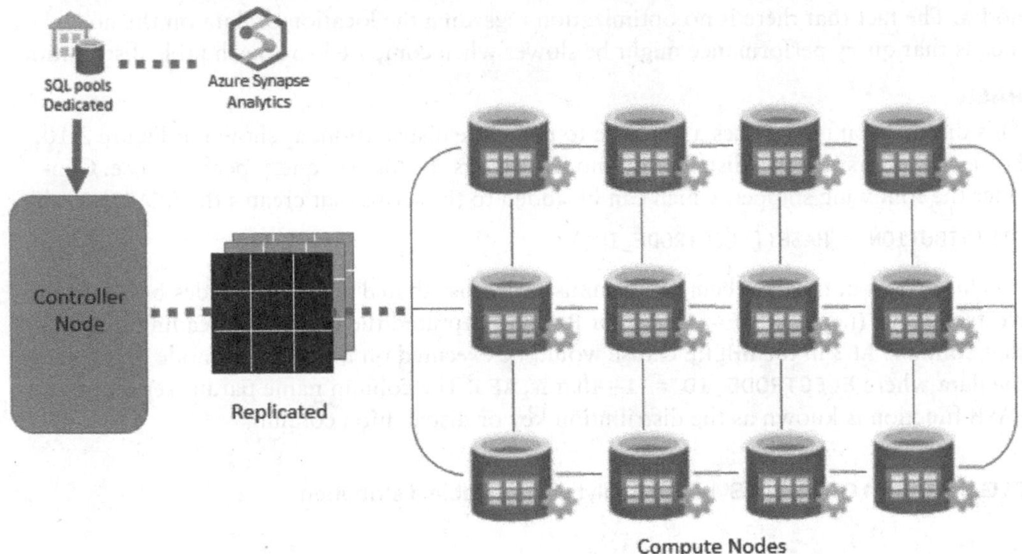

The following snippet of SQL shows how to create a table and configure it as replicated:

```
CREATE TABLE [dbo].[READING_REPLICATE]
WITH
  (
    HEAP,
    DISTRIBUTION = REPLICATE
  )
AS SELECT * FROM [dbo].[READING]
```

Notice that the index is set to HEAP, which makes sense because the data tables will be small. It's not a highly prioritized approach that the data is organized in any specific manner when the dataset is relatively small. Also notice the AS SELECT statement at the end of the query. This is discussed in the next section.

Create Table as Select

A *Create Table as Select (CTAS)* statement is one that generates a table using the output of a SELECT statement. CTAS is a very powerful command that can be used for, but not limited to, changing the distribution mode and indexes. A very primitive approach to achieving a similar output of a CTAS command is using the INTO statement. The following statement creates a new table called READING_NEW, identical to the READING table, and copies all the data into READING_NEW:

```
SELECT * INTO READING_NEW FROM READING
```

That is the most direct way to get a copy of a table. If you wanted to change DISTRIBUTION, INDEX, or even a PARTITION, you could perform the following:

```
CREATE TABLE [dbo].[READING_NEW]
WITH
(
  DISTRIBUTION = ROUND_ROBIN,
  HEAP,
  PARTITION (
   [ELECTRODE_ID] RANGE RIGHT FOR VALUES
     (1, 2, 3, 4, 5))
)
AS
SELECT  *
FROM    [dbo].[READING];
```

If you recall from an earlier example in the "Partition" section, the READING table was created with a CLUSTERED COLUMNSTORE INDEX, a HASH distributed table on SCENARIO_ID and a partition on the eight different scenarios. This new table, READING_NEW, changed the distribution model, index, and partition, as you can see. Not only is the table structure replicated on the new table, but the data is copied as well. You can execute the following SQL commands to replace the existing table with the new one:

```
RENAME OBJECT READING TO READING_OLD
RENAME OBJECT READING_NEW TO READING
DROP TABLE READING_OLD
```

The first command renames the existing table by adding a suffix of _OLD. Then the new table, READING_NEW, is renamed to READING. Once you are sure that all worked as expected, you no longer need the old table, so you execute a DROP TABLE command to delete it.

Table Categories

You might be wondering which distribution model you should use. The answer has to do with the table category to which the table you are creating belongs; see Table 2.3.

TABLE 2.3 Table category distribution matrix

Category	Distribution model
Staging	ROUND_ROBIN
Fact	HASH
Dimension (small table)	REPLICATED
Dimension (large table)	HASH

STAGING TABLE

A *staging table* can also be referred to as an integration table. The purpose or use for this kind of table is in the name itself. This is an intermediate table where you store data that won't be used for production purposes. Perhaps you store some brainwave readings from a different BCI in a staging table. You can then run some transformation queries on the table so that it gets into a desired format. A desired format would be structured in a way that the same existing intelligence gathering logic can be used on data coming from multiple BCIs after transformation.

FACT TABLE

There has long been the concept of a transactional database. This database is one that is used to accept incoming `INSERT`, `UPDATE`, and `DELETE` statements. It did not take long to realize that performing reporting or data analysis on the transactional database caused resource constraints and the latent processing of transactions. The reporting and analysis queries took a long time to render results as well, due to the live transactions. You do not want your analysis of data to impact the gathering and storage of data. This is the purpose of a fact table. A *fact table* is one that is loaded into an Azure Synapse Analytics dedicated SQL pool with a copy of data from a transactional database. Once the data is loaded, that is the place where your intelligence gathering takes place.

Online transactional processing (OLTP) is a transactional database that captures and maintains data in real time. *Online analytical processing (OLAP)* is a database that stores historical data for analysis and intelligence gathering. *Hybrid transaction/analytical processing (HTAP)* is a mixture of both OLTP and OLAP.

DIMENSION TABLE

A *dimension table* is one that contains data that doesn't change very often. Suppose you have a fact table that is very large and you want to reduce its size. You could remove parts of the data that do not change much and place that data into a dimension table. For example, the type of electrodes used to capture brainwaves will not change often (i.e., `AF3`, `AF4`, `T7`,

T8, or Pz); therefore, you could remove that information from the fact table and store it in a dimension table. The same goes for the frequencies (i.e., THETA, ALPHA, BETA_L, BETA_H, and GAMMA). Pulling this information out of the fact table would also reduce the fact table size. The information between the dimension and fact tables would be maintained using an ID and combined using a JOIN statement. You executed a JOIN operation in Exercise 2.1, and there is more on this operation later in this chapter.

Temporary Table

A temporary table is one that is intended to be used only for a given session. For example, if you create a normal table, you expect the table to remain persisted on the database until you purposefully remove it. Each time you log in, you expect that the table is available and queryable. This isn't the case with a temporary table. You create this kind of table using syntax like the following snippet. Notice the hash tag before the table name; this is what identifies the table as temporary.

```
CREATE TABLE #MODE
(
  [MODE_ID]  INT            NOT NULL,
  [MODE]     NVARCHAR (50)  NOT NULL
)
```

Temporary tables are only visible to the session owner. No one else will be able to query the contents of the table. Use this type of table to hold data that is in an intermediate transformation stage.

Sink Table

A *sink table* is often also referred to as a *data sink*. Again, the name itself can be used to describe its purpose. Like an ordinary sink, you normally have water running in it, but sometimes you stop the outflow and sometimes you stop the inflow. Instead of water flowing in and out, it is data. Consider a sink table as one that can store data as you copy it into your data lake or data warehouse. It is similar to a temporary table; however, the main difference is that the data is stored in a storage account like ADLS instead of a SQL table.

Create External Table as Select

You have already learned what a CTAS is, and it is very similar to *Create External Table as Select (CETAS)*. Instead of a regular table, which is created with CTAS, an external table can be created using the SELECT statement. You simply need to add the key word EXTERNAL to the SQL command and configure a few specific attributes. The following is an example of a CETAS statement. Note that you can also create an external table without the SELECT statement, just as you would a typical database table.

```
CREATE EXTERNAL TABLE Meditation
WITH
(
  LOCATION      = 'SessionCSV/Meditation/POW',
```

```
  DATA_SOURCE = Meditation_Source,
  FILE_FORMAT = BrainwaveCSVFormat
)
AS
SELECT  *
FROM    'abfss://<uid>@<accountName>.dfs.core.windows.net'
```

A CETAS statement is a way to copy data from a file into a table so that you can run SQL queries against the data. While we're at it, here is another way to copy some data from a file stored in an Azure Storage account container into a table for querying using the `COPY INTO` SQL statement:

```
COPY INTO [dbo][.READING]
FROM 'https://<accountName>.blob.core.windows.net/SessionCSV/Meditation/POW'
WITH
(
  FILE_TYPE = 'CSV',
  FIELD_TERMINATOR = ','
)
```

The arguments described in the previous snippet are fully discussed in the next section on external tables.

External Table

External tables provide the ability to perform SQL queries on sources stored on many different data storage products. For example, from a dedicated SQL pool, you could query data originally stored on Hadoop or ADLS. Querying data from IBM DB2, SAP Hana, Azure Cosmos DB, and Oracle datastores is also possible after the data has been placed into external tables. The feature that facilitates the connectivity between Azure Synapse Analytics and those other data sources is called *PolyBase*. The SQL syntax later in this section, where you create the external table, the data source, and file format, automatically implements and uses PolyBase. PolyBase is a feature that works behind the scenes without getting much recognition and visibility of the significant capability it provides. An overview of the external table concept is illustrated in Figure 2.12.

Before you can query data from those other sources, you need to set up the external data source, the external file format, and the external table. Keep in mind that this is performed in Azure Synapse Analytics. Consider the following an introduction; hands-on exercises are offered later in this book. The syntax to create a data source is illustrated with the following syntax:

```
CREATE EXTERNAL DATA SOURCE Meditation_Source
WITH (LOCATION = 'https://<accountName>.dfs.core.windows.net/<container>/
<path>',
      TYPE = HADOOP);
```

FIGURE 2.12 Azure Synapse Analytics external tables

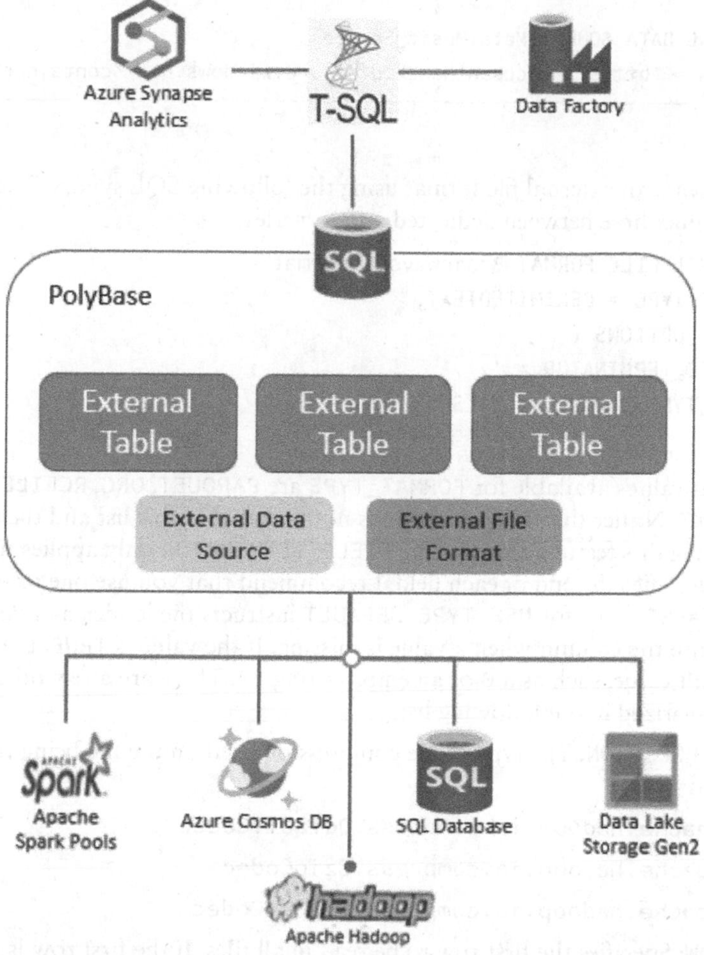

This SQL command creates a data source named `Meditation_Source` using data files hosted on an ADLS file share. When `TYPE` is set to `HADOOP`, it instructs the platform to use the Java-based technology to access the files.

Feature Availability

Hadoop external tables, created using the previous SQL syntax, are only available when using dedicated SQL pools and support CSV, parquet, and ORC file types. Notice in the following SQL syntax that there is no TYPE argument. The result of not identifying a TYPE is supported only on serverless SQL pools, with CSV and Parquet the supported file types. When there is no TYPE, the table is referred to as a *native external table*.

```
CREATE EXTERNAL DATA SOURCE MetalMusic_Source
WITH (LOCATION = 'https://<accountName>.dfs.core.windows.net/<container>/<path>')
```

Next, you create an external file format using the following SQL syntax. There is no difference in syntax here between dedicated and serverless:

```
CREATE EXTERNAL FILE FORMAT BrainwaveCSVFormat
WITH ( FORMAT_TYPE = DELIMITEDTEXT,
       FORMAT_OPTIONS (
         FIELD_TERMINATOR = ',',
         USE_TYPE_DEFAULT = FALSE
       ))
```

The different values available for FORMAT_TYPE are PARQUET, ORC, RCFILE, and DELIMITEDTEXT. Notice that JSON or YAML is not included in this list and therefore cannot be managed using this feature directly. The FIELD_TERMINATOR only applies to delimited text files and identifies the end of each field. I recommend that you use one or more ASCII characters. A FALSE value for USE_TYPE_DEFAULT instructs the loader, aka PolyBase, to insert a NULL into the column when a value is missing. If the value is TRUE, then you can provide a default value, such as a 0 or an empty string "". There are a few other options, which are summarized in the following list:

- DATA_COMPRESSION: The type of file compression used on the file being processed, if compressed
  - org.apache.hadoop.io.compress.DefaultCodec
  - org.apache.hadoop.io.compress.GzipCodec
  - org.apache.hadoop.io.compress.SnappyCodec
- FIRST_ROW: Specifies the first row to be read in all files. If the first row is a header, then set this value to 2.
- DATE_FORMAT: The date can come in a wide range of formats; use this to make sure it gets transferred as expected.
- ENCODING: UTF8 or UTF16.

Now it is time to create the table itself. You can use the following syntax as an example, similar to that shown in Figure 2.13 and in the following code snippet

```
CREATE EXTERNAL TABLE MetalMusic
(
  [C1]  DATETIME,
  [C2]  DECIMAL(7,3),
  [C3]  DECIMAL(7,3),
```

```
    [C4]  DECIMAL(7,3),
    [C5]  DECIMAL(7,3),
    [C6]  DECIMAL(7,3)
)
WITH (
        LOCATION = 'SessionCSV/MetalMusic/POW',
        DATA_SOURCE = MetalMusic_Source,
        FILE_FORMAT = BrainwaveCSVFormat )
```

FIGURE 2.13 Azure Synapse Analytics external tables example

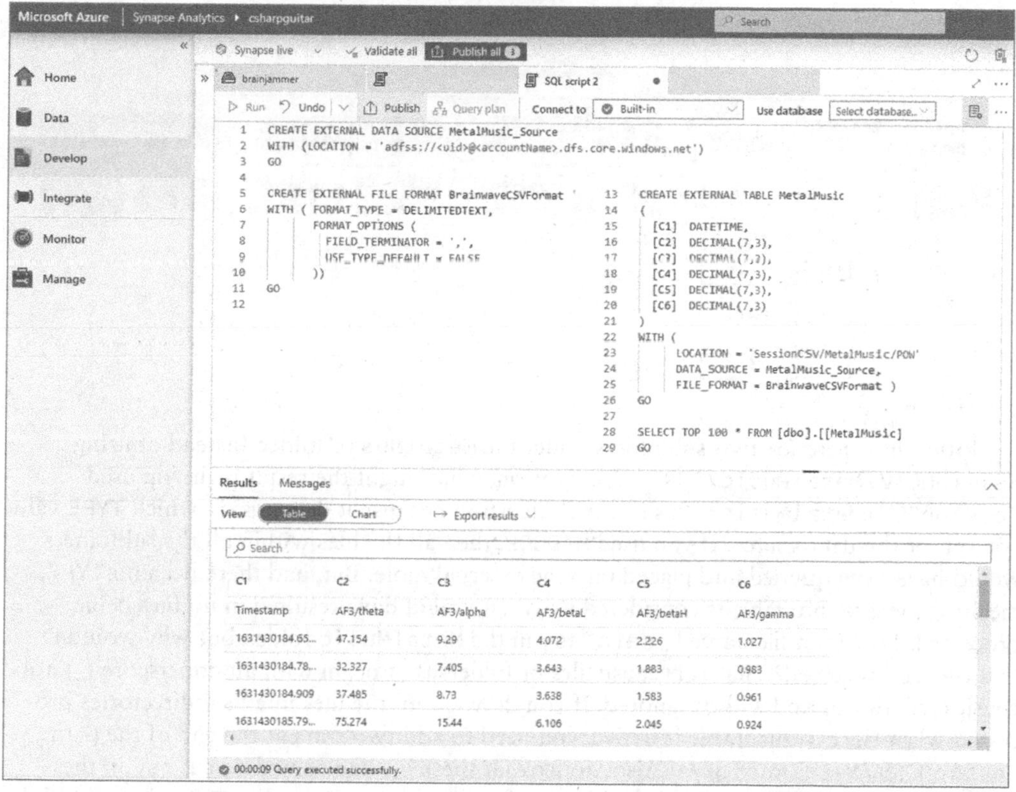

The LOCATION argument needs some additional clarification. While DATA_SOURCE and FILE_FORMAT are clear since they were created and named in the two SQL commands prior to the creation of the external table seen previously, the LOCATION argument identifies the location—in this case, of a group of files to load into the external table. The location value of SessionCSV/MetalMusic/POW results in all the files within the POW directory being included during the import process that brings the data within those files into the external table. Figure 2.14 illustrates a data directory hierarchy that is stored in an ADLS container named `brainjammer`.

FIGURE 2.14 ADLS directory hierarchy example

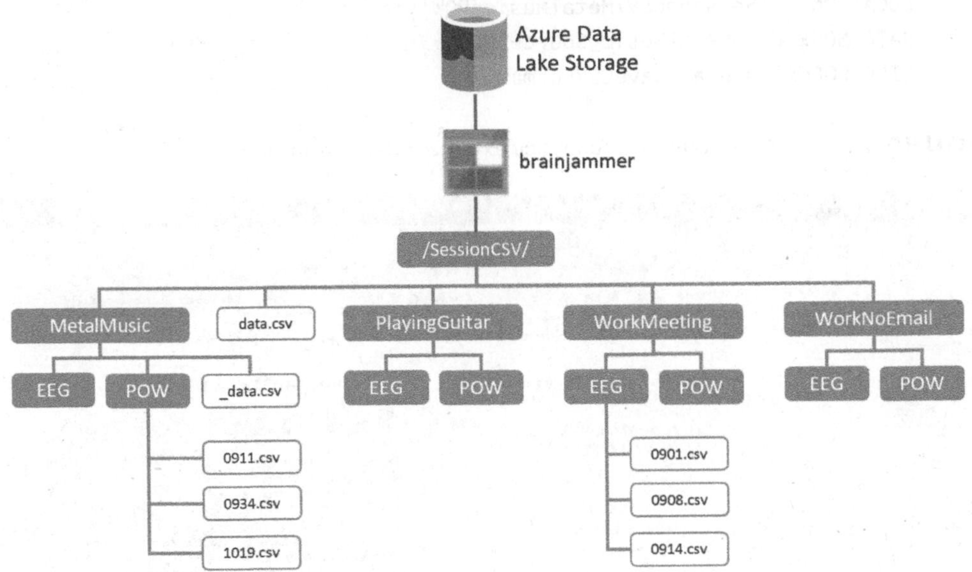

Notice that there are two subfolders under the `MetalMusic` folder. Instead of using `SessionCSV/MetalMusic/POW` as the location, what might the result be if you used `SessionCSV/MetalMusic`? This is a trick question because it depends on which `TYPE` value you set for the data source. If you used `HADOOP`, then all the files within all the subfolders would have been queried and placed into the external table. But, had there been no `TYPE`, meaning the external table is considered native, it would have resulted in no files being processed. There is a file named `_data.csv` in the `MetalMusic` folder, but why wouldn't that one be processed? That is because files or folders that begin with an underscore (_) are considered hidden and will be ignored. If you do want all the files in all subdirectories processed when the external table is native, you need to add two stars at the end of the path: `SessionCSV/MetalMusic/**`. Also, notice that there is a file named `data.csv` in the `SessionCSV` root directory. Had the location been set to only `SessionCSV`, what would the outcome be for both Hadoop and native external tables? Think about it first and then read on. The Hadoop external table would include all files from all the subfolders, excluding any file or folder that is hidden, whereas the native external table would have loaded only the `data.csv` file.

There are characters known as *wildcards* that can be used to set the location. Read through Table 2.4 to gain more knowledge about the types of wildcard characters that can be used to search folder, file paths, or filenames.

TABLE 2.4 Wildcard location examples

Symbol	Example	Description
*	/MetalMusic/POW/*.csv	Gets all CSV files in the POW directory
**	/MetalMusic/**/*.csv	Gets all CSV files under MetalMusic
?	*/*/POW/?901.csv	Gets all CSV files in all POW directories where the filename has one character before a 901
[]	*/*/POW/[09].csv	Gets all CSV files in all POW directories that begin with 09

When you set a location using a wildcard path, it will search through the entire storage directory looking for pattern matches. This is a very powerful feature. You will do some of this wildcard searching in later chapters. A few other external table arguments are worthy of some additional explanation:

- REJECT_TYPE
- REJECT_VALUE
- REJECT_SAMPLE_VALUE
- REJECTED_ROW_LOCATION

These arguments are used to instruct PolyBase when to abort the query and data transport process. REJECT_TYPE can be either a value or a percentage. If REJECT_TYPE is set to value and REJECT_VALUE is set to 5, if PolyBase rejects five rows of data, the query will fail. Remember that when you created the external table you defined the column data types. A reason why a row may fail (i.e., be rejected) is because the column in the source does not match the destination column data type. If REJECT_TYPE is set to percentage, then PolyBase will keep a running tally of the ratio between success and failure. The query will fail if the failure rate breaches the set percentage threshold. If the threshold is 30, and 31 of 100 rows have failed to migrate, the query stops. How often would you like PolyBase to calculate the percentage? You set this using the REJECT_SAMPLE_VALUE. If set to 1000, then after 1,000 migrated rows, PolyBase will check the success/failure percentage rate and take appropriate actions. PolyBase can create a log and store the rows that have failed to migrate in the location placed into REJECTED_ROW_LOCATION. By default, a folder named _rejectedrows is created in that location and the logs and data are written into it.

Unsupported PolyBase Data Types

When you're working with external tables, the following data types are not supported:

- Geography
- Geometry
- Hierarchyid
- Image
- Text
- nText
- XML
- Any user-defined type

Unsupported Table Features

Here is a list of unsupported Azure Synapse Analytics dedicated SQL pool features:

- User-defined types
- Unique indexes
- Triggers
- Synonyms
- Sparse columns
- Sequence
- Indexed views
- Computed columns

Schema

A *schema* is an organization feature found in a database. Imagine a large relational database where you have over a thousand tables. You would hope that there is great documentation that can help you discover and understand what tables exist and how to interpret the data that is in them. It would be even better if there was a way to group similar tables together, and there is—it's called a schema. The default schema in Azure SQL is `[dbo]`, which you have seen already in numerous places so far. You create a schema using the following syntax.

```
CREATE SCHEMA views
AUTHORIZATION dbo
```

That syntax created a schema named `views` and granted user `dbo` access to it. As you can see in Figure 2.15, there are tables that are prefixed with schema `dbo` and `views` that are prefixed with the schema name. Both schemas have granted access to the `dbo` user, which is the default user account.

FIGURE 2.15 Schemas, views, and users as seen in SSMS

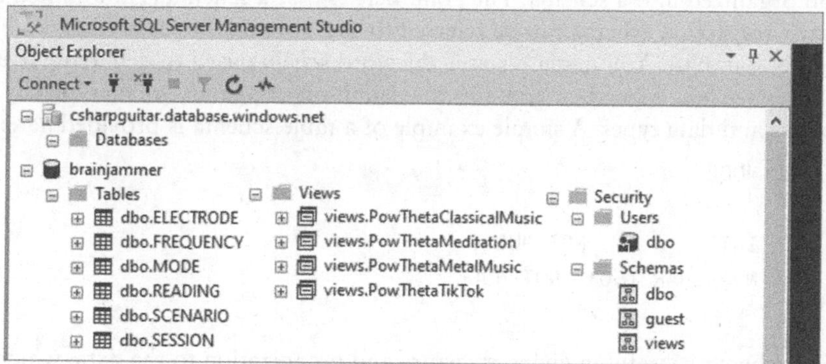

Note that you can also create a schema using PySpark with this syntax. The following snippet running in a Notebook attached to a Spark pool within Azure Synapse Analytics Studio will create a schema. The schema in the context of PySpark is a little different than with a SQL schema. In this context the schema is concerned with the structure and type of data, instead of being a logical unit of control to isolate tables as it is with a SQL schema. This will become clearer as you read through the next few sections.

```
%%pyspark
data ='abfss://<uid>@<accountName>.dfs.core.windows.net/SessionCSV/
MetalMusic/POW'
df = spark.read.format('csv').option('inferSchema', True).load(data)
df = spark.createDataFrame(data, schema=skema)
```

Once the schema is created, the output of `df.printSchema()` results in the following. The CSV files have 26 columns and therefore there are 26 total columns in the output, shown summarized for brevity, followed by the summarized output of `df.show(2)`.

```
root
 |-- _c0: string (nullable = true)
 |-- _c1: string (nullable = true)
 |-- _c2: string (nullable = true)
 |-- _c3: string (nullable = true)
 |-- _c4: string (nullable = true)
 ...

+------------+-----------+-----------+-----------+-----------+----------+
| Timestamp   | AF3/theta | AF3/alpha | AF3/betaL | AF3/betaH | AF3/gamma |...
| 1627801...  | 110.994   | 25.473    | 3.987     | 0.483     | 0.242     |...
| 1627801...  | 108.518   | 22.73     | 3.625     | 0.468     | 0.264     |...
...
```

Stored procedures, data types, views, primary and foreign keys, and so forth can also be created and organized into a schema. The point here is that a schema is not limited to tables only. In many respects, a schema can be referred to as a container of related data objects within a larger database. You might also see the word *schema* used to define the structure of a table. A *table schema* is one that contains the definition of a table, which typically includes column names and data types. A simple example of a table schema is provided here:

```
CREATE TABLE MODE
(
  [MODE_ID]  INT             NOT NULL,
  [MODE]     NVARCHAR (50)  NOT NULL
)
```

Mostly, a schema is useful in giving structure and organization to the data, which is contained on your data platform, whether it be structured or semi-structured. Schemas can help give a little order to the data management activities.

Static Schema

The word *static* has numerous meanings, and the one that applies is dependent on the context in which it is used. In the database context, the meaning is that once a schema is defined and created, it will not change. You find *static schemas* in relational (aka structured) databases. If you recall from the previous section, you notice the SQL command used to create the schema is quite simple—just two statements. However, the construction of the contents that lives within the schema takes much design, planning, and management. That leads again into the context of a database table as those existing within a database schema. In the relational database context, there is a concept known as *schema on write*, which is represented by the following steps:

- Create the table.
- Load the table with data.
- Query the table.

Assume that the amount of data loaded was very large and continues to grow. Assume that you need to change the data type of an existing column or add a new column. This is a very time-consuming action because performing an ALTER command on the table to make this change will not work. It doesn't support such activities without some additional actions. Consider the following SQL syntax. If any values in that column are greater than 25, then the ALTER command will fail.

```
ALTER TABLE MODE
  ALTER COLUMN MODE NVARCHAR(25)
```

The only way to make this kind of change is to remove the data in the column before changing it or drop and re-create the table. For small datasets this might be acceptable, but for large datasets, it is not, due to the time required to execute those commands and actions, not to mention the risk of data loss.

Dynamic Schema

The opposite of a static schema is a *dynamic* one. This kind of schema is most prevalent in nonrelational databases. If you recall from the content in the "Schema" section earlier, you can see that the table schema is inferred when the data is loaded into the `DataFrame`. If a schema is not defined when the `DataFrame` is loaded with data, Spark will do its best to infer the data types based on the row values. Here is an example of a schema definition using PySpark followed by the loading of the data from a data source like ADLS, referencing the schema:

```
schema = StructType([
    StructField('Timestamp', TimeStampType(), False),
    StructField('AF3/theta', DecimalType(), False),
    StructField('AF3/alpha', DecimalType(), False),
    ...
])
df = spark.createDataFrame(data, schema)
```

What this means is that the table schema can be modified prior to loading the data from its source. The schema is interpreted as the data is being loaded into the `DataFrame`. If the data type for a given column changes, then you can change it in the schema definition before you load the data. Recognize the fact that how an Azure data engineer approaches and consumes data occurs from many different vectors, where a vector is relational, nonrelational, and so forth. How you consume this data and the constraints within you must operate are significantly different. The point is, someone who has more experience with relational databases typically expects structure and the concepts in a structured environment don't always align with the concepts in a dynamic environment. When you are using a Spark pool on Azure Synapse Analytics, you would typically pull data from a nonrelational source and load it into memory for transformation and modeling, whereas in a SQL pool the data is most likely coming from a structured relational source, and it is expected to be in a defined table. Therefore, numerous kinds of table schemas and methods must exist for loading data because there are numerous kinds of data storage structures. Lastly, I used the words *typically* and *likely* in my previous comments on purpose. This is because, although Spark pools have historically worked well with nonrelational data and SQL pools with relational data, it does not mean that either cannot be used in both scenarios.

Star Schema

A *star schema* is a fact table surrounded by multiple dimension tables. When visualized, the shape the table makes resembles that of a star, something similar to Figure 2.16.

FIGURE 2.16 A star schema example

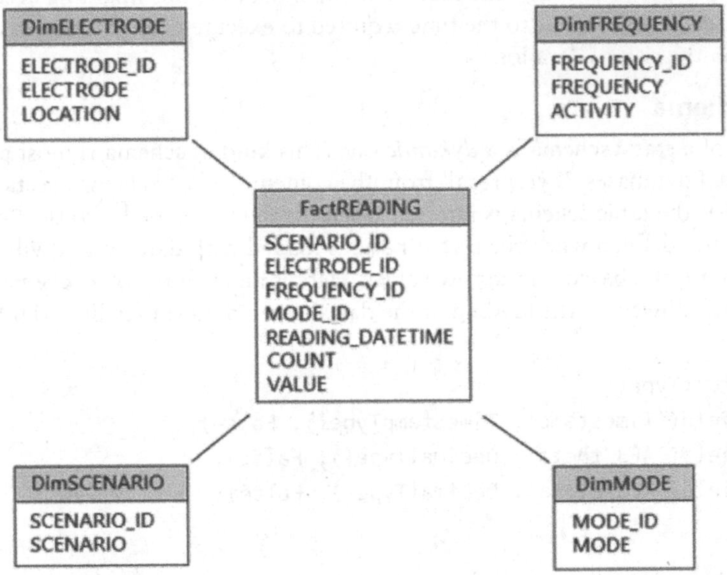

DimELECTRODE
ELECTRODE_ID
ELECTRODE
LOCATION

DimFREQUENCY
FREQUENCY_ID
FREQUENCY
ACTIVITY

FactREADING
SCENARIO_ID
ELECTRODE_ID
FREQUENCY_ID
MODE_ID
READING_DATETIME
COUNT
VALUE

DimSCENARIO
SCENARIO_ID
SCENARIO

DimMODE
MODE_ID
MODE

Do you remember what table distribution type you use for a fact table and what type you use for a dimension table? You might consider reading back over that section to confirm this. It might start to make a bit more sense now that you see this diagram. The reason you might use a HASH distribution for the fact table is because that is the one you will query most. When you configure the `HASH` you also provide the argument used as the key to distribute data across the nodes, known as the *distribution key* or distribution column. The dimension tables, which rarely if ever change, have a REPLICATED distribution, meaning the content of the tables is copied to each node. You might also notice in Figure 2.16 that there are no database layer–enforced primary or foreign key relationships between the fact and the dimension tables. This is the case when you're running on SQL pools in Azure Synapse Analytics but is *not* the case when you're running a database in Azure SQL. See Figure 2.2 for a reminder of how primary and foreign keys are displayed visually.

Snowflake Schema

A *snowflake schema* is what typically exists before a normalization of dimension tables into the state you see in Figure 2.16. With some imagination, Figure 2.16 looks like a star, but consider a scenario where there were additional dimension tables, aka *subdimension tables*, which needed to be transformed—in other words, normalized into the dimension tables that are directly linking to the fact table. Figure 2.17 illustrates what a simple snowflake schema might look like.

FIGURE 2.17 A snowflake schema example

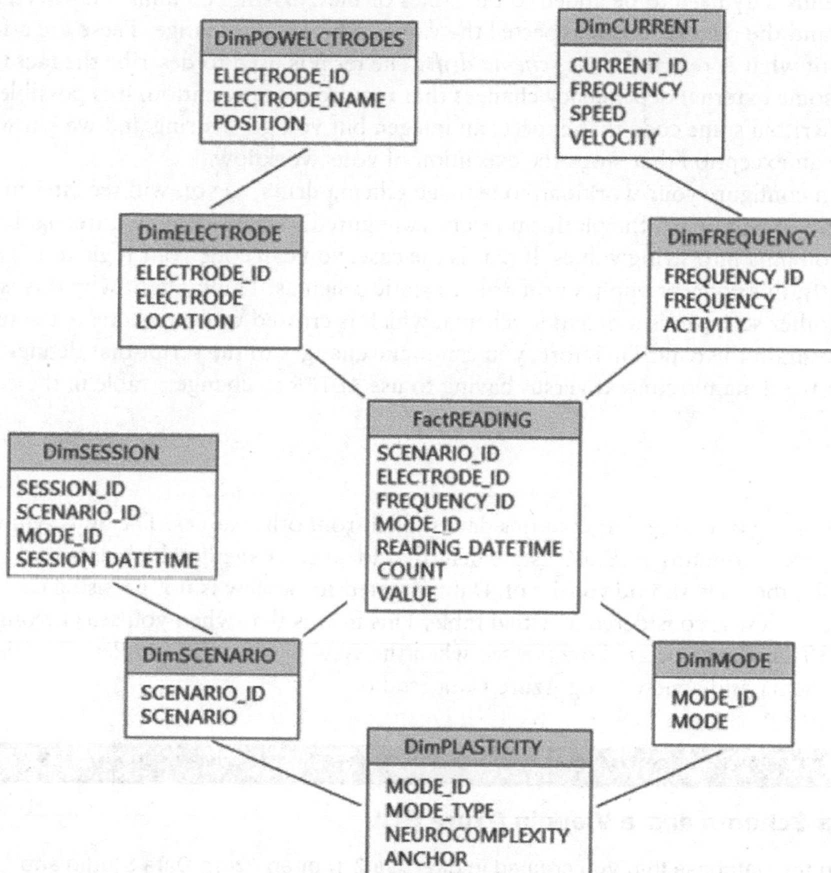

When you compare this to a star schema, you can see many similar tables. Those extra tables moving from the snowflake schema to the star schema took place because the data was transformed and moved into other dimension tables. That transformation is also referred to as *normalization*, which results in a star schema.

Schema Drift

You have now read and learned about the many kinds of schemas and all the different kinds of tables. Those concepts help you as an Azure data engineer to better understand the kind of data structures you could be working with. You need to know something about the data to normalize it and query to gather intelligence from. In the real world, due to the quantity of data and the speed and velocity in which things move, change happens a lot. Therefore, the tables and schemas your data analytics solution depends on will likely change too. New columns may need to be added to the tables or files, existing columns may need to be removed, and the data type you expected the value to be in may change. These are a few examples of what is referred to as *schema drift*. The term is used to describe the fact that there are some external dependency changes that require some attention. It is possible that you have written some code that expects an integer, but you get a string and we know that will cause an exception that stops the execution of your workflow.

You can configure your workload to manage schema drifts, as you will see later in Exercise 2.3. In summary, the platform can be configured to transform all unrecognized fields or columns into string values. If that is the case, you can code your logic to expect the same. Lastly, this concept applies primarily to static schemas. Think about why this is the case. The other scenario is a dynamic schema, which is created when you create the table that will contain the data. Therefore, you can make changes to the script that defines the schema in the dynamic context versus having to use `ALTER` to change a table in the context of static.

View

A *database view* is a table that contains data pulled from other tables. The SQL syntax to create a view contains a `SELECT` statement that identifies exactly which data and from which tables the view should consist of. Data targeted for a view is not persisted or cached by default; a view is considered a virtual table. This means that when you select from a view, the DBMS runs the associated query used when the view is created. Complete Exercise 2.3 to create a schema and a view using Azure Data Studio.

EXERCISE 2.3

Create a Schema and a View in Azure SQL

1. Using the database that you created in Exercise 2.1, open Azure Data Studio and connect to the Azure SQL database you created in Exercise 2.1. See Figure 2.4 as a reminder of what the connection details look like.
2. After successfully connecting to the database, expand the `Security` folder, which is below the Server endpoint URL in the Servers menu. Expand the `Schemas` folder and view the list of existing schemas.
3. Right-click the server endpoint URL in the Server menu, select New Query, and execute the following SQL syntax:

```
CREATE SCHEMA views
AUTHORIZATION dbo
```

4. Refresh the list of schemas to see the new schema named `views`. Execute the following SQL syntax from the Query window to create a view:

```
CREATE VIEW [views].[PowThetaClassicalMusic]
AS SELECT RE.READING_DATETIME, RE.[COUNT], RE.[VALUE]
FROM [SESSION] SE, READING RE
WHERE SE.MODE_ID = 2 AND SE.SCENARIO_ID = 1 AND RE.FREQUENCY_ID = 1
```

5. Expand the `Views` folder to confirm the successful creation of the view. Then execute the following SQL syntax to count the total number of rows, and 10 rows from the database view the output will resemble that shown in Figure 2.18.

```
SELECT COUNT(*) FROM [views].[PowThetaClassicalMusic]
SELECT TOP 10 * FROM [views].[PowThetaClassicalMusic]
```

FIGURE 2.18 SQL Query from view table and new schema

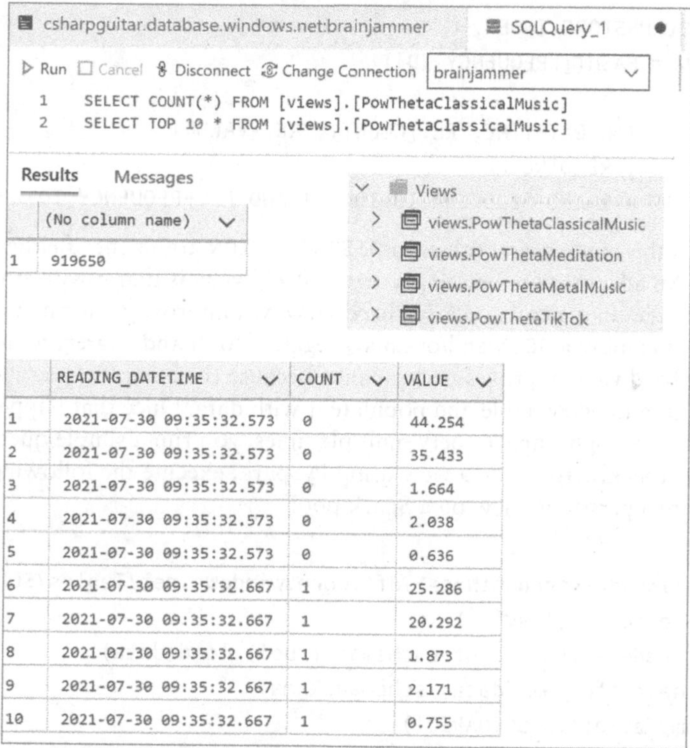

You will notice in Figure 2.18 that there are a few more views and some additional data. Both the database and the queries to create the schema and view in Exercise 2.3 plus the additional views are downloadable from GitHub in the `Chapter02/Ch02Ex03` folder in this repository: `https://github.com/benperk/ADE`. The SQL Server Authentication password for the compressed BACPAC (database backup) file is `AzureDataEngineer2022` and the user ID is `benperk`. You can import the database by selecting Import Database on the SQL Server blade in the Azure portal.

You might be wondering why you are working with an Azure SQL database instead of a SQL pool in Azure Synapse Analytics. The reason is that you built this and the Azure Cosmos DB so that you have something to import and copy data from later, after you get through all these necessary terms and concepts. You need to know these basic things before you start building, configuring, and consuming data using those Big Data analytics tools.

In Azure Synapse Analytics there is a special kind of view called a *materialized view*. You create it using the following SQL syntax:

```
CREATE MATERIALIZED VIEW [views].[mPowThetaClassicalMusic]
WITH
(
  CLUSTERED COLUMNSTORE INDEX,
  DISTRIBUTION = HASH([FREQUENCY_ID])
)
AS SELECT RE.READING_DATETIME, RE.[COUNT], RE.[VALUE]
FROM [SESSION] SE, READING RE
WHERE SE.MODE_ID = 2 AND SE.SCENARIO_ID = 1 AND RE.FREQUENCY_ID = 1
```

Notice that in this context you can set a `DISTRIBUTION` argument of either `HASH` or `ROUND-ROBIN`. An advantage to creating a materialized view is that it will be persisted, unlike a default view. In general, a materialized view will improve performance of complex queries, ones that employ a `JOIN` and/or an aggregate. (`JOIN` and aggregates are discussed later.) A materialized view improves performance because the complex query was used beforehand to build the view table and populate it with data. Once that happens, instead of running the complex, high-impact query multiple times, you run a simple query on the view to get the results quickly. To create a view using PySpark, execute the following. Note that you cannot create a persistent view on a Spark pool.

```
%%pyspark
data ='abfss://<uid>@<accountName>.dfs.core.windows.net/Tables/SCENARIO.csv'
df = spark.read.format('csv') \
    .options(header='true', inferSchema='true').load(data)
df = spark.createDataFrame(data, schema=skema)
df.registerTempTable('tmpSCENARIO')

%%sql
spark.sql('CREATE VIEW tmpPowThetaClassicalMusic AS SELECT ...')
spark.table('tmpPowThetaClassicalMusic').printSchema
spart.sql('SELECT * FROM tmpPowThetaClassicalMusic').show()
```

The last concept we'll examine in this context has to do with something called *pruning*.

Pruning

If you already know what the term *projection* means, then you can use that as a basis for the meaning of *pruning*. You can also use the literal meaning of the word, which involves trimming branches of a tree or a bush. Also, many times there are some stems that simply come out of nowhere and make the entire bush look awkward, so that one gets cut away. Implementing projection is rather simple. You would not execute a global query like the following:

```
SELECT * FROM READING
```

Instead, you can project that query by adding a WHERE clause, which will reduce the amount of data returned:

```
SELECT * FROM READING WHERE ELECTRODE_ID = 1
```

Both projection and pruning will reduce the amount of time required to perform the query, but for different reasons. In many of the examples so far where HASH distribution tables have been created, you notice there has been either ELECTRODE_ID or FREQUENCY_ID used as the distribution key of the partition. Rightly assume that there are five electrodes. If you perform a query that is looking for data WHERE ELECTRODE_ID = 1, then the partitions that contain ELECTRODE_ID IN (2, 3, 4, 5) will not be searched, since that data will not exist on those nodes. Nodes are used here in place of partitions because it is common, when using huge datasets, that a partition is placed on its own node. An optimizer, which is typically part of the DBMS, is what implements such query execution plans. There is also a term called explain plan. Both topics are discussed in Part IV, "Secure, Monitor, and Optimize Data Storage and Data Processing."

Data Shuffling

The *data shuffling* concept is typically applied to tables with a DISTRIBUTION value of HASH. Shuffling (or reshuffling when shuffling has taken place once already) is a data movement operation that results in the transfer of data from one node to another. This is an expensive operation and is likely to increase query execution latency. Shuffling cannot be avoided 100 percent of the time; it is often inevitable. However, knowing some reasons shuffling can happen is valuable. There are two primary reasons: The first is due to joining two tables that have different distributions. For example, if you have configured the READING table to be HASH distributed and SCENARIO to be ROUND_ROBIN, it is possible that the data on the node that is selected to execute the query does not have the SCENARIO data, which then requires the data to be transferred.

The other example to watch out for is like the first but has to do with joining two tables, both of which are HASH, but with different distribution keys. If you think about that for a second, you can probably already visualize why this might cause a data shuffle. For example, a READING table with a HASH distribution key of ELECTRODE_ID and another table READING_TMP with a HASH distribution key of FREQUENCY_ID can cause a data shuffle. If you executed a query that joined those two tables together, the data may not exist on the same node. In that case, the data from one would need to be moved/shuffled to the one on which the query is executed. JOINs and aggregates have not been fully explained up to now but are covered later in this chapter in the Querying data section. Skip ahead if you want to learn about them now, and then come back here.

Data Skew

When data is *skewed*, it means that one category is represented more often when compared to the other data categories in a given dataset. Take Figure 2.19, which represents a right/positive skew, no skew, and a left/negative skew for the BCI electrodes. You might notice that the graph in the middle, with no skew, is symmetrical.

FIGURE 2.19 A data skew example

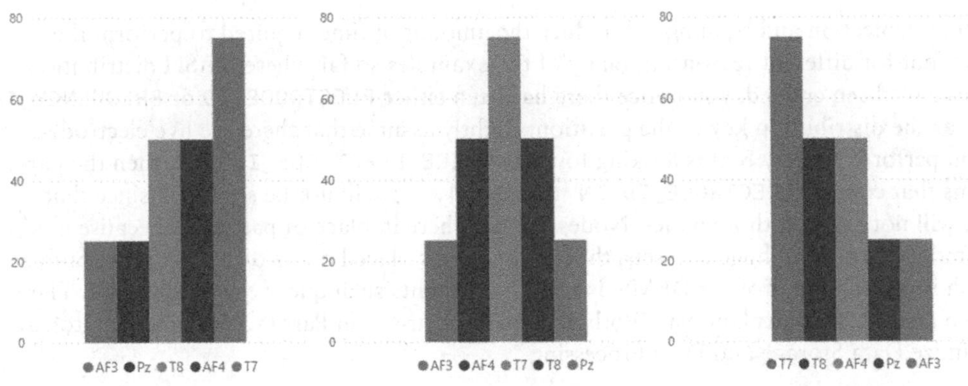

Uneven distribution of data across the nodes is known to cause latency in data query executions. You might remember the numerous examples of creating the `READING` table, one of which used a `HASH` with a distribution key of `ELECTRODE_ID`. In Figure 2.19 you can see that there is much more data relating to electrode `T7` than any other. This would cause queries that include `T7` as part of the query parameter to perform more slowly than others. This is because there is more `T7` data. When you see a *data skew* like this, you need to reevaluate whether you have chosen the correct distribution key. Perhaps distributing the data onto the nodes using `FREQUENCY_ID` would result in a more even distribution of data across the nodes.

Processing Skew

The term *processing skew* has a lot to do with data skew. Basically, the more data that exists on a node, the more compute power required to retrieve it. Assume that all nodes in the SQL or Spark pool have the same number of CPUs and the same speed and amount of memory. A query run on a node with more data to parse would perform more slowly than when running that same query on a node with less data. Where data skew has the role of getting equal amounts of data onto each node, processing skew has to do with the compute power required to process such data.

Recursive SQL

A *recursion* is a term you will find not only in SQL but also in programming languages. Recursion in general is when an object refers to itself. In the context of *recursive SQL*, it means a SQL query that refers back to itself. The most efficient way to create a recursive query is by using *common table expressions (CTEs)*, the structure of which is shown here:

```
WITH POW_CTE (SESSION_ID, ELECTRODE_ID, FREQUENCY_ID)
AS
(
  SELECT SESSION_ID, ELECTRODE_ID, FREQUENCY_ID
  FROM READING
  WHERE READING_DATETIME > (SELECT dateadd(week, -1, getdate()))
)
SELECT ELECTRODE_ID, FREQUENCY_ID, VALUE
FROM POW_CTE
GROUP BY ELECTRODE_ID, FREQUENCY_ID
ORDER BY ELECTRODE_ID
```

Notice the `WITH` clause, which is a sure sign that some recursion is coming up. Be sure to watch out when using recursion because you can get into trouble and end up in an infinite loop. To avoid such possibilities, use the option `MAXRECURSION`, which you can set to a number of allowed recursion levels. The deeper you go, the more latent the query will become, so be careful and design precisely.

Explode Arrays

The concept of exploding arrays is related to Apache Spark pools and the programming language PySpark. The command to explode an array resembles the following:

```
%%pyspark
from pyspark.sql.functions import explode
df = spark.read.json('abfss://<endpoint>/brainjammer.json')
dfe = df.select('Session.Scenario', explode('Session.POWReading.AF3'))
dfe.show(2, truncate=False, vertical=True)
```

The first line of the code snippet is what is referred to as a *magic command*. The magic command is preceded with two percent signs and is what identifies the language in which the following code is written. The languages are listed in Table 2.5.

TABLE 2.5 Spark pool magic commands

Magic command	Language
%%pyspark	Python
%%spark	Scala
%%sql	SparkSQL
%%csharp	C#

The next line of code imports the `explode` method, and then a JSON file is loaded into a `DataFrame` named `df`. Next, a `select` query is performed on the `DataFrame` to retrieve the brain reading scenario and then explodes the readings held within the `AF3` electrode array and displays two results by using the `show()` method. The snippet of the data that is loaded into the `DataFrame`—the contents of the `brainjammer.json` file—is shown here. The snippet constitutes the first brain reading in that file, which is a `ClassicalMusic` session for one of the five electrodes, in this case `AF3`. Each electrode captures five different brainwave frequencies.

```
{"Session": {
    "Scenario": "ClassicalMusic",
    "POWReading": [
      {
        "ReadingDate": " 2021-09-12T09:00:18.492",
        "Counter": 0,
        "AF3": [
          {
            "THETA": 15.585,
            "ALPHA": 5.892,
            "BETA_L": 3.415,
            "BETA_H": 1.195,
            "GAMMA": 0.836
          }]}]}
}
```

The output of the exploded `AF3` array resembles the following. Notice that `Session.Scenario` equals the expected value of `ClassicalMusic`. The second column is named `col` and contains a single reading of all five frequencies from the `AF3` electrode. Because we passed a 2 to the `show()` method, two records are returned.

```
-RECORD 0-------------------------------------------------
 Session.Scenario | ClassicalMusic
 col              | [[5.892, 1.195, 3.415, 0.836, 15.585]]
```

```
-RECORD 1-----------------------------------------------
 Session.Scenario | ClassicalMusic
 col              | [[5.871, 1.331, 3.56, 0.799, 26.864]]
```

Without using the `explode()` method, if you instead select the entire content of the `AF3` electrode array as in the following snippet, you end up with two columns:

```
dfe = df.select('Session.Scenario', 'Session.POWReading.AF3')
```

The first column is the scenario, as expected, and the second is every `AF3` reading contained within the `brainjammer.json` file. A snippet of the output is shown here. A given session lasts about two minutes and the number of readings in this file is close to 1,200, which is a lot of data—and remember, this is only for a single electrode.

```
Scenario | ClassicalMusic
AF3      | [[[5.892, 1.195, 3.415, 0.836, 15.585]], [[5.871, 1.331, 3.56,
0.799, 26.864]], [[6.969, 1.479, 3.61, 0.749, 47.282]], [[9.287, 1.624, 3.58,
0.7, 75.78]], [[12.231, 1.736, 3.5, 0.658, 104.216]], [[14.652, 1.792, 3.389,
0.621, 124.413]], [[15.983, 1.805, 3.259, 0.587, 131.456]], ...
```

So, what the `explode()` method provides is a way to format the data in a more presentable, human-friendly, and interpretable manner. You might also find that the output helps build the basis for further queries—for example, searching for an average, max, or min value for this specific electrode. When you create an Azure Synapse Analytics workspace, provision a Spark pool, and create a Notebook (described in Chapters 3, "The Sources and Ingestion of Data," and 4, "The Storage of Data"), you will be able to execute this code and certainly learn more about the data. The nature of gathering intelligence from data has a lot to do with the creativity and curiosity of the person performing the data analysis.

Data Programming and Querying for Data Engineers

To perform the duties of an Azure data engineer, you will need to write some code. Perhaps you will not need to have a great understanding of encapsulation, asynchronous patterns, or parallel LINQ queries, but some coding skill is necessary. Up to this point you have been exposed primarily to SQL syntax and PySpark, which targets the Python programming language. Going forward you might see a bit of C# code, but SQL and PySpark will be the primary syntax used in examples. There are, however, a few examples of data manipulation code in C# in the `/Chapter02/Source Code` directory here: `https://github.com/benperk/ADE`. Take a look at those code examples if you have not already done so.

Please note that there are many books that focus specifically on programming languages like Python, R, Scala, C#, and the SQL syntax, and there are also books dedicated specifically to database structures and data storage theory and concepts. This book helps improve your knowledge and experience in all those areas; however, the focus is to make sure you get the knowledge required to become a great Azure data engineer, which then will lead to becoming accredited by passing the DP-203 exam.

Data Programming

The coding you will do in the context of the DP-203 exam will take place primarily within an Azure Synapse Analytics Notebook. I haven't covered *notebooks* in detail yet, but I will in the coming chapters. Other places where you might find yourself coding is in Azure Databricks, Azure Data Factory, or Azure HDInsight. What you learn in this section relating to PySpark and SparkSQL will work across all those products. As you'll see later, C# (dotnet) will work in each of these scenarios in some capacity as well.

PySpark/Spark

You might have noticed the usage of the magic command `%%pyspark` and `spark` when loading a `DataFrame` or manipulating data. Table 2.6 compares PySpark and Spark, which can help clarify your understanding.

TABLE 2.6 PySpark vs. Spark

PySpark	Spark
An API that allows Python to work with Spark	A computational platform that works with Big Data
Requires Python, Big Data, and Spark knowledge	Requires Scala and database knowledge
Uses Py4j library written in Python	Written in Scala

For more complete details, visit these sites:

- PySpark: `https://spark.apache.org/docs/latest/api/python/index.html`
- Spark: `https://spark.apache.org/docs/latest/index.html`
- Scala: `https://scala-lang.org`

The remainder of this section will focus on PySpark example syntax that you might see while taking the DP-203 exam. It would, however, be prudent to have a look at the official documentation sites to get a complete view of the syntax, language, and capabilities. You might also consider a book on those specific languages.

Data Sources

There are many locations where you can retrieve data. In this section you will see how to read and write JSON, CSV, and parquet files using PySpark. You have already been introduced to a `DataFrame` in some capacity. Reading and writing data can happen totally within the context of a file, or the data can be read from a file and loaded into a `DataFrame` for in-memory manipulation. Here are some common JSON PySpark examples:

```
df = spark.read.json('path/brainwaves.json')
df = spark.read.json('path/*.json')
df = spark.read.json(['AF3/THETA.json', 'T8/ALPHA.json'])
df = spark.read.format('json').load('path/')
df = spark.read.option('multiline', 'true').json('pathToJsonFile')
df = spark.read.schema('schemaStructure').json('path/brainwaves.json')
df.write.json('path/brainwave.json')
dr.write.mode('overwrite').json('path/brainwave.json')
```

Reading a JSON file and loading it into a `DataFrame` in the previous code snippet is performed in a variety of approaches. The first example is loading a single JSON file, which is identified using the path and the filename, `path/brainwaves.json`. The next example uses a wildcard that results in all JSON files in the described location being loaded into a `DataFrame`, `path/*.json`. The next line illustrates that individual files, located in different locations, can be loaded into the same `DataFrame`. As you can see, instead of using the `json()` method, you can use the `format()` method in combination with the `load()` method to load a JSON file into a `DataFrame`.

When you're working with JSON files, it is common that the file is written on multiple lines, like the following code snippet. If the format of your JSON file is spread across multiple lines, you need to use the `option()` method and set the multiline option to `true`; it is `false` by default.

```
{"Session": {
    "Scenario": "TikTok",
    "POWReading": [
      {
        "ReadingDate": "2021-07-30T09:40:25.6635",
        "Counter": 0,
        "AF3": [
          {
            "THETA": 9.681,
            "ALPHA": 3.849,
            "BETA_L": 2.582,
            "BETA_H": 0.959,
            "GAMMA": 0.738
          }]}]}
}
```

The alternative to this is a single line, like the next code snippet. Single lines are a bit harder to read, which is why the previous multiline example is very common with JSON files. However, if the data producer is aware that no human will look at these files, consider making JSON files in a single line.

```
{"Session":{"Scenario":"TikTok","POWReading":[{"ReadingDate": "2021-07
-30T09:40:25.6635","Counter":0,"AF3":[{"THETA": 9.681,"ALPHA": 3.849,
"BETA_L": 2.582,"BETA_H": 0.959,"GAMMA": 0.738}]}]}}
```

You should already have an understanding of what a schema is; it is a definition of or a container for your data. An example schema for a JSON file might resemble the following. The format for the `StructField()` method is column name, data type, and nullable option. If you do not provide a schema, the runtime will attempt to infer a schema itself. This is not the case with CSV, where everything is returned as a `String` data type.

```
schema = StructType([
         StructField('Scenario', StringType(), True),
         StructField('ReadindDate', DateTimeType(), True),
         StructField('Counter', IntegerType(), False),
         StructField('THETA', DecimalType(), True)])
```

Once you have defined the schema of the data within the JSON file, you can read it into a `DataFrame`. Use the `df.printSchema()` method to see the result of your schema definition. After you have loaded a JSON into a `DataFrame` and done some manipulation, you might want to write it back to a file. You can do so using the write capability. Notice that there is something shown as `mode` in one of the write code snippets, which is set to `overwrite`. This means if a file of that name already exists, replace that one with the one being written now. Other `mode` options are as follows:

- Using `append` will add the new data to the end of an existing file with the same name identified in the `write` command.
- The `ignore` option will not perform the write if a file with the same filename already exists in the given location.
- The `errorifexists` means that the file will not be written and that an error will be thrown.

Take a look at the following code snippets related to CSV files. They are very similar, but there are a few syntactical differences.

```
df = spark.read.csv('path/brainwaves.csv')
df = spark.read.csv('path/')
df = spark.read.csv('AF3/THETA.csv, 'T8/ALPHA.csv)
df = spark.read.format('csv').load('path/')
df = spark.read.option('header', True).csv('pathToCsvFile')
df = spark.read.format('csv') \
          .option('header', True) \
          .schema('schemaStructure').load('path/brainwaves.csv')
df.write.option('header', True).csv('path/brainwave.csv')
dr.write.format(csv).mode('error').save('path/brainwave.csv')
```

How to read from a CSV file—for example, reading a specific file, reading all the files in a directory, and reading one or more specific files—is illustrated with the first three lines of code. There are a few more options when working with CSV files than with JSON—for example, `delimiter`, `inferSchema`, `header`, `quotes`, `nullValues`, and `dateFormat`. Notice in the following two lines of code the different approaches for adding an option or options:

```
df = spark.read.options(inferSchema='True', delimiter=',').csv('path/
wave.csv')

df = spark.read.option('inferSchema', True).option('delimeter', ',')
.csv('T7.csv')
```

Since CSV stands for comma-separated values, the default delimiter is a comma. However, a pipe (|), a tab (\t), or a space can also be used as a delimiter. If your CSV file does not use a comma, then you need to set the `delimiter` in the option. The `inferSchema` option, which is `False` by default, will notify the runtime that it should attempt to identify the data type of the columns itself. When the option is `False`, all columns will be data typed as a `string`. The top or first line of a CSV file commonly contains the header names of the data included per column. The `header` option will instruct the runtime to use the first row as column names. The `header` default is `False` and will therefore be a `string` if not set to `True`. The syntax for building a schema with a CSV file is shown here:

```
schema = StructType().add('Scenario', StringType(), True) \
                     .add('ReadindDate', DateTimeType(), True) \
                     .add('Counter', IntegerType(), False) \
                     .add('THETA', DecimalType(), True)
```

If the data within the CSV file can have quotes, use the `quote` option to notify the runtime; the same goes for `nullValues`. If there can be `null` values for columns, you can instruct the runtime to use a specific value in the place of a `null`. For example, you can use `1900-01-01` if a date column is `null` in the CSV file. Dates can come in many formats. If you need to instruct how the date will be received, use the `dateFormat` option. The available values for `mode` are the same for CSV: `overwrite`, `append`, `ignore`, and `error` have the same meaning and use case as JSON. Finally, review the following snippets, which work with parquet files:

```
df = spark.read.parquet('path/brainwaves.parquet')
df = spark.read.format('parquet').load('path/')
df.write.parquet('path/brainwave.parquet')
dr.write.mode('append').parquet('path/brainwave.parquet')
```

Parquet, CSV, and JSON files have very similar capabilities, so there is not much more to discuss about them here. Parquet files maintain the schema, which is used in the processing of the file; therefore, using a schema to read the files is not as important when compared to CSV or JSON. The options for `mode` are the same for all three file formats discussed here. It is also possible to manage ORC files in the same way:

```
df = spark.read.orc('path\brain*.orc')
spark.write.format('orc').mode('overwrite').save('path/brainwave.orc')
```

However, there will not be many examples using this file format in this book. That file format has some great use cases and can add great value, but more detail in that area is outside of the scope of the DP-203 exam.

DataFrame

Up to this point you have seen examples that created a `DataFrame`, typically identified as `df` from a `spark.read.*` method:

```
df = spark.read.csv('/tmp/output/brainjammer/reading.csv')
```

Instead of passing the data to load into a `DataFrame` as a path via the `read.*` method, you could load the data into an object, named `data`, for example:

```
data ='abfss://<uid>@<accountName>.dfs.core.windows.net/reading.csv'
```

Once you have the reference point set to the `data` variable, you can load the data into a `DataFrame` using the `createDataFrame()` method. The `createDataFrame()` method also takes a `schema` parameter:

```
df = spark.createDataFrame(data, schema)
```

Once the data has been read into a `DataFrame`, many actions are available that you can take on that data. Remember that a `DataFrame` is a container that holds a copy of the immutable data loaded into it. This data can be structured like a table, having columns and rows with an associated schema and casted data types. The distribution of a `DataFrame` onto the nodes in the Spark pool, for example, is handled by the platform, using its own optimizers to determine the best placement and distribution model. Let's take a closer look at a few of the most important functions that you should know when working with a `DataFrame`. In practice, these methods are prefixed with `df.`, such as `df.show()`.

SHOW()

This method returns rows to an output console, for example:

```
df.show(5, truncate=False, vertical=True)
```

The following parameters are supported:

n Identifies the number of rows to return; if no value, up to 20 rows are rendered.

truncate `True` by default. Only the first 20 characters of the column are rendered. If set to `False`, then the entire column value is rendered.

vertical `False` by default. If set to `True`, rows and columns are listed one after another from top to bottom, instead of the common left-to-right row column alignment.

JOIN()

The concept of a `JOIN` hasn't been fully covered yet; it is later in this chapter. In summary, `JOIN` is the means for combining data, based on given criteria, from two `DataFrames` into one.

```
dfSession = spark.read.csv('path/session.csv')

+------------+-------------+---------+-------------------+
| SESSION_ID | SCENARIO_ID | MODE_ID | SESSION_DATETIME |
+------------+-------------+---------+-------------------+
| 1          | 1           | 2       | 2021-07-30 09:35 |
| 2          | 1           | 2       | 2021-07-31 10:15 |
| 3          | 2           | 2       | 2021-07-30 12:49 |
| ...        | ...         | ...     | ...              |
+------------+-------------+---------+-------------------+

dfScenario = spark.read.csv('path/scenario.csv')

+-------------+-----------------+
| SCENARIO_ID | SCENARIO        |
+-------------+-----------------+
| 1           | ClassicalMusic  |
| 2           | FlipChart       |
| ...         | ...             |
+-------------+-----------------+

dfSession.join(dfScenario, dfSession.SCENARIO_ID == dfScenario.SCENARIO_ID)

+------------+----------+---------+------------------+----------+-----------------+
| SESSION_ID | SCEN*_ID | MODE_ID | SESSION_DATETIME | SCEN*_ID | SCENARIO        |
+------------+----------+---------+------------------+----------+-----------------|
| 1          | 1        | 2       | 2021-07-30 09:35 | 1        | ClassicalMusic  |
| 2          | 1        | 2       | 2021-07-31 10:15 | 1        | ClassicalMusic  |
| 3          | 2        | 2       | 2021-07-30 12:49 | 2        | FlipChart       |
| ...        | ...      | ...     | ...              | ...      | ...             |
+------------+----------+---------+------------------+----------+-----------------+
```

The default join type is `inner`, which means the information that matches is combined, and data that has no match is not added to the result. You can find a summary of all `DataFrame` methods in the Apache Spark documentation website at `https://spark.apache.org`. There are numerous methods that provide some very powerful capabilities.

GROUPBY()

This method provides the ability to run aggregation, which is the gathering, summary, and presentation of data in an easily consumable format. The `groupBy()` method provides several aggregate functions; here are the most common:

avg() Returns the average of grouped columns

count() Returns the number of rows in that identified group

max() Returns the largest value in the group

mean() Returns the mean value of the group

min() Returns the smallest value in the group

sum() Returns the total value of the group

You can again either append a `show()` or add the result to a new `DataFrame`:

```
df.groupBy('frequency_id').avg('value').show()
df2 = df.groupBy('session_id').count()
df.groupBy('frequency_id').max('value').show()
df.groupBy('frequency_id').mean('value').show()
df.groupBy('frequency_id').min('value').show()
df2 = df.groupBy('frequency_id').sum('value').where(col('value') > 2.254)
```

The last line of the preceding code snippet uses the `where()` method to place a projection onto the resulting data.

WHERE() AND *FILTER()*

The `where()` method is an alias for `filter()`. These methods provide the same capabilities, which include accepting a condition and returning the rows that match the condition. You can render the result into a console or load the result into a new `DataFrame`.

```
df.filter(df.electrode_id == 2).show()
df2 = df.filter(df.electrode_id == 2)
```

ORDERBY() AND *SORT()*

The `sort()` method performs the same manipulation as `orderby()`. Passing one or more column names to the method results in the output of the data being rendered in ascending order—in other words, from smallest to largest. Sorting in descending order is also supported, which results in the output being rendered largest to smallest.

```
df.orderBy(df.electrode_id.asc(), df.frequency_id.asc()).show()
df.sort(col('AF3/theta').desc()).show()
df2 = df.sort(col('AF3/alpha').desc())
```

As seen in the first line, you can identify which column to sort or order by referencing the element name in the `DataFrame`. Also notice in the first line that it is possible to sort and order by multiple columns. In that case, the data is sorted by the first parameter, then by the second. It is also possible to provide the name of the column as a string and pass it to the method. Finally, rendering the data to the console for review or into another `DataFrame` for further transformation is a typical activity.

SELECT()

This method returns only the columns identified and provides the ability to reduce the amount of rendered data. Either append a `show()` at the end to render the value in a console or load a `DataFrame` with the result. Adding `'*'` to the `select()` method results in all columns being returned.

```
df.select('AF3/theta', 'AF3/alpha').show()
df.select('*')
df2 = df.select('AF3/theta', 'AF3/alpha')
```

WITHCOLUMN()

This method provides one way to rename or add a column of data that will be loaded into a `DataFrame`:

```
df2 = df.withColumn('AF3 THETA', col('AF3/theta')) \
        .withColumn('AF3 ALPHA', col('AF3/alpha')) \
        .printSchema()

root
 |-- AF3 THETA: decimal (nullable = true)
 |-- AF3 ALPHA: decimal (nullable = true)
```

You may have a need to rename a column for some reason. For example, the existing column name may not represent the data well, or perhaps a downstream system that cannot be changed needs the column to be a different name. The `withColumn()` method is a way for you to change the column names for data to be loaded into a `DataFrame`.

The following `DataFrame` methods create a table or a view that gives you the ability to execute queries on the data using SQL syntax. A `DataFrame` should already be loaded with data. Using SQL syntax is an alternative to using the `select()` method covered earlier.

CREATEGLOBALTEMPVIEW()

This method creates a temporary view, which has a lifetime of the Spark application. If a view with the same name already exists, then an exception is thrown.

```
df.createGlobalTempView('Brainwaves')
df2 = spark.sql('SELECT Session.POWReading.AF3[0].THETA FROM Brainwaves')
```

Notice that the argument following `FROM` is the name of the view created in the previous line of code.

CREATEORREPLACEGLOBALTEMPVIEW()

This method does the same as the previous method, but if the view already exists, it will not be re-created. Instead, the data in the current view will be replaced (i.e., overwritten) by the new data. This avoids the invocation of an exception if it already exists.

```
df.createOrReplaceGlobalTempView('Brainwaves')
df2 = df.filter(Session.POWReading.Counter > 5)
```

```
df2.createOrReplaceGlobalTempView('Brainwaves')
df3 = spark.sql('SELECT Session.POWReading.AF3[0].THETA FROM Brainwaves')
```

This code snippet calls the `createOrReplaceGlobalTempView()` method twice: once to initialize the view and then again after the data is filtered using the `filter()` method. Finally, the data you wanted is extracted using SQL syntax.

When an object has application scope, it means anyone who has access to that application has access to that object. Multiple users can have access to an object with application scope. An object with session scope is accessible only to the user who instantiated that object.

CREATETEMPVIEW()

This method creates a view that has a lifespan of the Spark session. If the name of the view already exists, an exception is thrown.

```
df.createTempView('Brainwaves')
df2 = spark.sql('SELECT Session.POWReading.AF3[0].THETA FROM Brainwaves')
```

CREATEORREPLACETEMPVIEW()

You can probably guess how this one differs from the previous. This method does the same as the previous method, but if the view already exists, then it will not be created; it will instead be replaced. This avoids the invocation of an exception if it already exists.

```
df.createOrReplaceTempView('Brainwaves')
df2 = df.filter(Session.POWReading.Counter > 5)
df2.createOrReplaceTempView('Brainwaves')
df3 = spark.sql('SELECT Session.POWReading.AF3[0].THETA FROM Brainwaves')
```

PySpark Functions

In addition to what you just read regarding the methods associated to a `DataFrame`, there are many built-in PySpark functions. These functions are useful for manipulation of data outside of the `DataFrame` context. There are numerous functions; a summary of the most common is provided here. You'll find official PySpark documentation at `https://spark.apache.org` along with complete language documentation.

EXPLODE()

There was a section about this method earlier, "Explode Arrays." Review that section if you don't remember specifically what this method does. I'm covering it here again because you might be asked about it on the exam. The important thing to note is that this method parses an array and places each component in the array into its own column. Recall how to use `explode()`:

```
dfe = df.select('Session.Scenario', explode('Session.POWReading.AF3'))
```

This code snippet is from the previous example, which results in the frequency values of an AF3 electrode to be placed into individual columns.

SUBSTRING()

It is common to find yourself working with strings when coding. One scenario involves getting a specific part of the string. It is useful for parsing out a date, for example.

```
data = [(1, '2021-07-30'), (2, '2021-07-31')]
columns = ['id', 'session_date']
df = spark.createDataFrame(data, columns)
df.withColumn('year', substring('session_date', 1, 4) \
  .withColumn('month', substring('session_date', 6, 2) \
  .withColumn('day', substring('session_date', 9, 2)
df.show()

+----+--------------+------+-------+-----+
| id | session_date | year | month | day |
+----+--------------+------+-------+-----+
| 1  | 2021-07-30   | 2021 | 07    | 30  |
| 2  | 2021-07-31   | 2021 | 07    | 31  |
+----+--------------+------+-------+-----+
```

Notice that the `substring()` method is not preceded with a `df.`, which illustrates that this method is not part of the `DataFrame`; rather it's part of the PySpark programming language. Notice the `withColumn()` method and recall from the previous section where it states that this method is used for renaming columns. It is also useful for adding columns. The following example uses the `select()` method with the `substring()` method. The result is the same.

```
df.select('session_date', substring('session_date', 1, 4).alias('year'), \
                          substring('session_date', 6, 2).alias('month'), \
                          substring('session_date', 9, 2).alias('day'))
```

Instead of using the `withColumn()` method to add the column, the `alias()` method is used.

TO_DATE() AND *TO_TIMESTAMP()*

There can be many challenges when working with dates and datetimes. In many scenarios a date is stored as a `string`. That means if you want to perform any calculation with it, the date value stored in the string needs to be converted to the date data type. Additionally, the date format is often specific to the platform or stack with which you are working, which results in some complexities and requires some additional troubleshooting. In general, you can find descriptions online to help you work through it, and the error messages are helpful. Getting a date into the format you require may be challenging at times but it's doable.

```
data = [(1, '2021-07-30 09:35:00'), (2, '2021-07-31 10:15:00')]
columns = ['id', 'session_date']
df = spark.createDataFrame(data, columns)
df.withColumn('date', to_date(col('session_date'))) \
  .withColumn('timestamp', to_timestamp(col('session_date'))) \
  .show()

+----+---------------------+------------+--------------------+
| id | session_date        | date       | timestamp          |
+----+---------------------+------------+--------------------+
| 1  | 2021-07-30 09:35:00 | 2021-07-30 | 2021-07-30 09:35:00 |
| 2  | 2021-07-31 10:15:00 | 2021-07-31 | 2021-07-31 10:15:00 |
+----+---------------------+------------+--------------------+
```

The value in the `session_date` column is a `string`, but the other two columns, `date` and `timestamp`, are not `strings` because they were cast into the `date` and `timestamp` data types. Review the following to gain a better understanding:

```
df.select(col('date'), current_date().alias('today'),
datediff(current_date(), to_date(col('date')).alias('date_diff'))).show()

+------------+------------+-----------+
| date       | today      | date_diff |
+----+--------------------+-----------+
| 2021-07-30 | 2021-11-29 | 123       |
| 2021-07-31 | 2021-11-29 | 122       |
+------------+------------+-----------+
```

Notice the PySpark method `current_date()`, which returns the current date on the machine where the method is executed—that is, the system clock. The `datediff()` method compares two dates and returns the number of days in between them. This method requires that the inputs be of type `date`; it would not work with `strings`. There is another date-related method, `months_between()`, which as its name implies, returns the number of months that exist between two dates.

```
df.select(col('date'), current_date().alias('today'),
          months_between(current_date(),
          to_date(col('date')).alias('month_diff'))).show()

+------------+------------+------------+
| date       | today      | month_diff |
+----+--------------------+------------+
| 2021-07-30 | 2021-11-29 | 3.933      |
| 2021-07-31 | 2021-11-29 | 3.966      |
+------------+------------+------------+
```

Again, the values cannot be strings. The date content in a string must be converted to a supported date type format for the date methods to run without exception.

WHEN()

This method is used when you want to apply some conditions on the data in a DataFrame. It is similar to an if then else statement in Python or C#, or CASE WHEN cond1 THEN result ELSE result in SQL syntax. The when() method is commonly used in conjunction with otherwise(). The otherwise() method is useful for setting a default if the data does not match any of the when() method's conditions.

```
df2 = df.withColumn("new_scenario",
                    when(df.Scenario == "ClassicalMusic", "Music") \
                     .when(df.Scenario == "FlipChart", "News") \
                     .otherwise(df.Scenario)
```

Assume that df was loaded with the SCENARIO table. Running the previous code snippet on the data would result in the following:

```
+------------+-----------------+-------------+
| SCENARIO_ID + SCENARIO        | new_scenario |
+------------+-----------------+-------------+
| 1          + ClassicalMusic  + Music       +
| 2          + FlipChart       + News        +
| 3          + Meditation      + Meditation  +
| 4          + MetalMusic      + MetalMusic  +
| ...        + ...             + ...         +
+------------+-----------------+-------------+
```

Using the withColumn() method results in the creation of a column with the provided name. The column is populated with the results of the when() and otherwise() methods. If there is no match with the when() condition, the original Scenario is applied; otherwise, the new value is added to the column.

Spark Streaming

The previous chapter introduced you to both Azure Stream Analytics/Event Hubs and Apache Spark/Apache Kafka. Those products are what you use to implement a data streaming solution, as illustrated in Figure 2.20. Notice the various kinds of data producers that can feed into Kafka. Any device that has permission and that can send correctly formatted data to the Kafka Topic works. Note that the Kafka distribution includes a producer shell, which you can use for testing. The Apache Spark is a consumer of the data being sent to Kafka. Apache Spark can then store the stream to files, store the data in memory, or make the data available to an application. Before you begin reading the stream from your Apache Spark instance, you need a subscription to a Kafka Topic. When you subscribe to a topic, when data arrives a notification is sent to you. The notification contains either the data or the metadata, which can then be used by the consumer to pull the data from Kafka.

FIGURE 2.20 Data streaming solution using Apache Kafka and Apache Spark

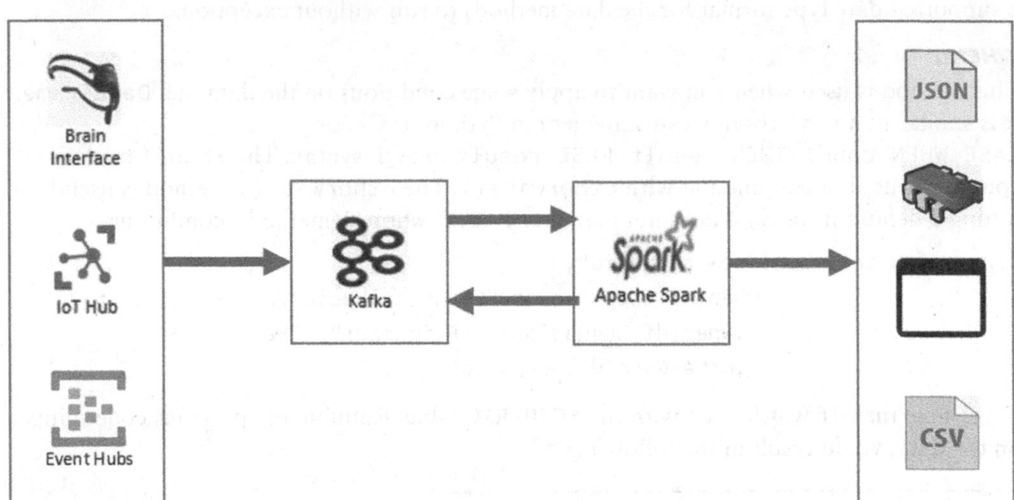

As the data enters your Apache Spark cluster, you can process and store the data. The data can be stored in many formats, such as JSON, TXT, or CSV files. It is also possible to store the data in memory or dump it out into a command console. To read a JSON-formatted stream of data from a Kafka Topic you would use the `spark.readStream()` method:

```
val df = spark.readStream.format("kafka") \
            .option("<serverName>","<IP:PORT>") \
            .option("subscribe","brainwave_topic") \
            .option("startingOffsets","latest").load()
```

This code snippet first identifies that the stream is intended to come from Kafka. An `option()` method follows that contains the pointer to the Kafka server and IP address. The next `option()` method is where you notify Kafka which topic you want to subscribe to. The default value for `startingOffsets` is `latest`, which means that the `readStream()` method only gets data it has not already received. The alternative is `earliest`, which means that when that code snippet is executed, all the data is requested. Once the data is read, you can write the stream to any of the numerous datastores or to a console. The following code snippet illustrates how to write the stream to a console:

```
df.writeStream.format("console").outputMode("append").start()
  .awaitTermination()
```

You can use a wide range of formats; the most common are file types (`json`, `parquet`, `csv`, etc.), `console`, and `memory`. When the `format()` method is a file type, the only supported `outputMode` is `append`. Other formats support `update` or `complete` modes. The `start()` method begins the write process and will continue writing until the session is terminated. Here are a few additional examples of writing the stream of data:

```
df.writeStream.format("json").option("path", "/path/to/brainwaves")
df.writeStream.format("memory").queryName("Brainwaves").start()
```

C# and .NET

It goes without saying that many if not most people who work with Big Data use programming languages like Python, R, and Scala, etc. It also goes without saying that when you work with Microsoft products, you will run into C# and .NET at some point. Having options is good for a company because they can choose the language based on the skills of their staff. It is also good for Microsoft because the door is no longer closed to people who know, use, and prefer open source technologies. In this section you will learn about a few C#-compatible *software development kits (SDKs)* that exist for Azure Data Solution development.

The *integrated development environment (IDE)* that is commonly used for coding C# is Visual Studio. There is also a popular Microsoft IDE named Visual Studio Code, which is a lightweight but feature-rich version of the full Visual Studio edition. The content that follows will target Visual Studio. Notice in Figure 2.21 that there are some data-oriented workloads available with the IDE.

FIGURE 2.21 Visual Studio data workloads

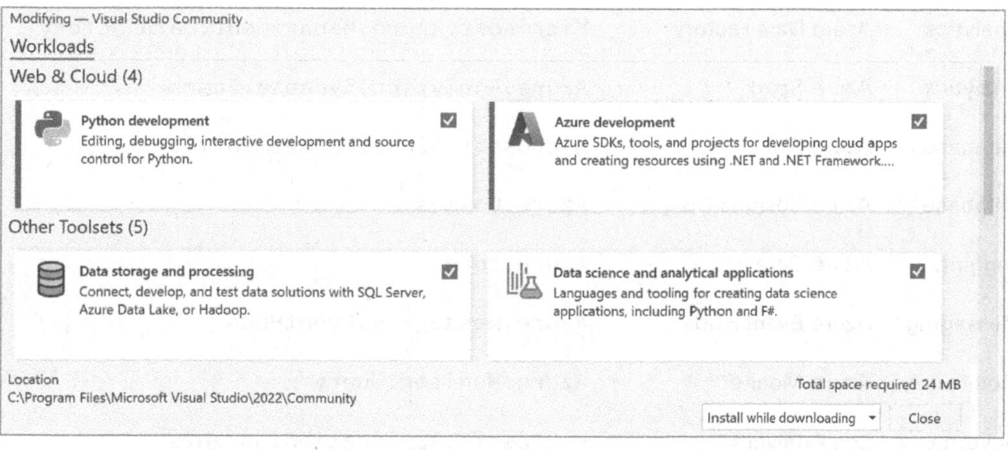

When you install these workloads, templates for those kinds of projects are installed and can be helpful for getting started. They are helpful because when you create those projects, such as a SQL Server database project, you get a list of the types of items you can add into the project and build upon, such as External Table, External Data Source, Inline Functions, Tables, and Views. These templates and workloads exist so that you do not have to start from scratch, which is very beneficial, especially if you are not highly skilled in the area or have a tight deadline. An SDK is similar to templates in that you do not need to write all the code to perform common tasks, like making a connection to a database. Using an SDK, you can accomplish that in less than five lines of code. Imagine if you needed to perform that without the SDK—you would be talking hundreds of lines of code. Thank goodness for SDKs.

SDKs

Coding, especially with C#, is not a big part of the DP-203 exam, but knowing about the available SDKs might come up. Table 2.7 provides an overview of the most relevant SDKs in the scope of the DP-203 exam. A complete list of all Azure SDKs for .NET can be found at `https://docs.microsoft.com/dotnet/azure/sdk/packages`.

TABLE 2.7 Azure SDKs packages

Category	Product	NuGet package
Analytics	Azure Synapse Analytics	`Azure.Analytics.Synapse.Artifacts`
Analytics	Azure Databricks	`Microsoft.Azure.Databricks.Client`
Analytics	Azure HDInsight	`Microsoft.Azure.HDInsight.Job`
Analytics	Azure Analysis Services	`Microsoft.Azure.Management.Analysis`
Analytics	Azure Data Factory	`Microsoft.Azure.Management.DataFactory`
Analytics	Azure Spark	`Azure.Analytics.Synapse.Spark`
Database	Azure SQL	`Microsoft.Azure.Management.Sql`
Database	Azure Cosmos DB	`Azure.Cosmos`
Logging	Azure Core	`Azure.Core`
Messaging	Azure Event Hubs	`Azure.Messaging.EventHubs`
Monitoring	Azure Monitor	`Azure.Monitor.Query`
Governance	Log Analytics	`Microsoft.ApplicationInsights .TraceListner`
Security	Azure Active Directory	`Microsoft.Azure.Services .AppAuthentication`
Security	Azure Identity	`Azure.Identity`
Storage	Azure Data Lake Storage	`Azure.Storage.Files.DataLake`
Storage	Azure Storage	`Azure.Storage`
Streaming	Azure Stream Analytics	`Microsoft.Azure.Management .StreamAnalytics`

All of the SDKs are open source and available on GitHub, which can help you figure out what capabilities exist in these assemblies (SDKs). It is often the case that new technologies, features, and capabilities have limited documentation. Therefore, you need to be creative and curious about finding out how to properly use and discover the capabilities. Here is an example of the way to find out what you can do with these assemblies using the `Azure.Analytics.Synapse.Artifacts` assembly. The first action is to install the assembly into a Visual Studio Console App project using the following command:

```
Install-Package Azure.Analytics.Synapse.Artifacts
```

That command is executed within the Package Manager Console in Visual Studio. Then choose the Class View menu option, which displays the classes and methods contained in the assembly. If there are no examples of what you need to code, you must proceed with trial and error until you get something that works. Figure 2.22 illustrates the previously described scenario.

FIGURE 2.22 Visual Studio C# code example

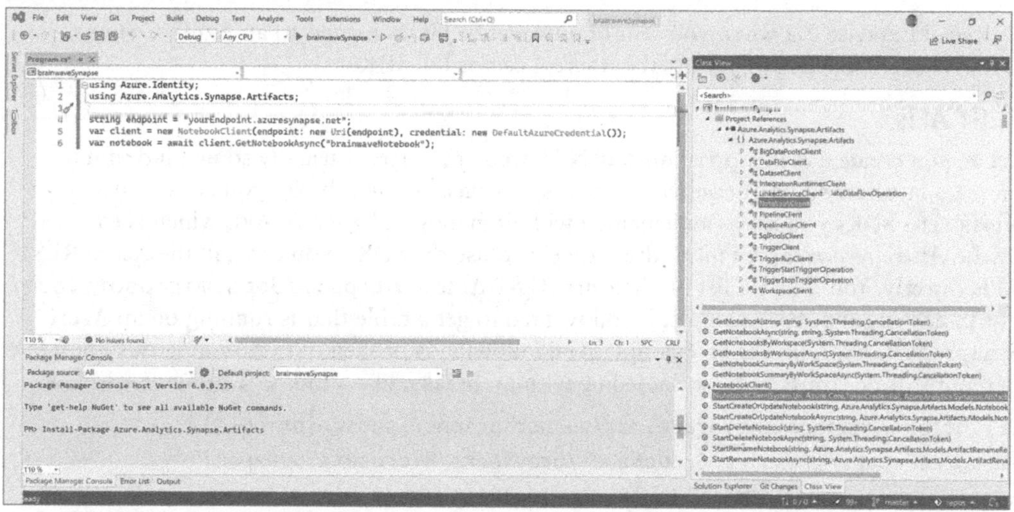

It might be a bit difficult to visualize where to use an SDK, or where to execute the code that runs the application that implemented the SDK logic. As seen in Figure 2.23, there are two places where applications that use SDKs can run: on a client device or on a server. In Visual Studio, if you created a Console app or a Windows Presentation Foundation (WPF) app, then once it's compiled, you can run it on a workstation. In that scenario, the code needs to be deployed to numerous client machines, once for each person who uses it. Alternatively, you can create an ASP.NET web app that runs on a web server such as an Azure web app. When you run the SDK on an Azure web app, the code is deployed only to a single machine and typically accessed using a browser.

FIGURE 2.23 Where to implement and use an SDK

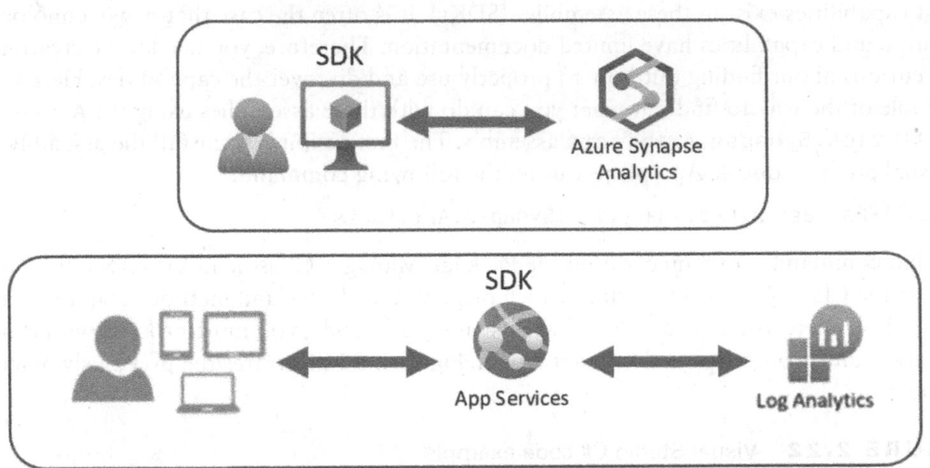

Recall Exercise 2.2 when you sent brainwaves in JSON format to an Azure Cosmos DB. You accomplished this using the Azure Cosmos DB SDK.

REST APIs

When you create a WPF app or an ASP.NET web app, there is usually some kind of interface. An interface (a GUI) consists of menus, buttons, and text boxes you click to perform a task. The SDKs you have implemented will ultimately call a REST API, which is exposed by the *Azure resource provider*. Alternatively, to use the SDKs, you can call the Azure REST APIs directly. You'll find a list of all Azure REST APIs at `https://docs.microsoft.com/rest/api/azure`. For example, if you wanted to get a table that is running on an Azure Synapse SQL pool, here is an example. The following is broken out into numerous lines, but in reality all this must be on a single line with no breaks, like a link in a browser window:

```
GET https://management.azure.com/subscriptions/{subscriptionId}/
resourceGroups/{resourceGroupName}/providers/Microsoft.Synapse/
workspaces/{workspaceName}/sqlPools/{sqlPoolName}/
schemas/{schemaName}/tables/{tableName}?api-version=2021-06-01
```

The result provides a context to the requested table, which you could then use to perform further actions on. The benefit to using an SDK is that you have classes and methods that can guide you through the implementation of the Azure product features and capabilities. If you want the most flexibility or find some feature in a REST API that has not yet been implemented in the SDK, then you might get a bit ahead of the game.

Querying Data

Data is not very useful without some way to look at it, search through it, and manipulate it—in other words, querying. You have seen many examples of managing and manipulating data from both structured and semi-structured data sources. In this section, you'll learn many ways to analyze the data in your data lake, data warehouse, or any supported data source store.

SQL, T-SQL, and SparkSQL

What is it with all these SQL acronym variants? *Structured Query Language (SQL)* was originally called *SEQUEL* but was later renamed to *SQL*. So when you refer to or see a reference to SQL, it means the common structured query language for RDBMS products. Other variants of SQL, like T-SQL, PL/SQL, and SparkSQL, to name a few, use the SQL base to extend the language. *Transact-SQL (T-SQL)* is found in the context of Microsoft SQL Server and Azure SQL. *Procedural Language/Structured Query Language (PL/SQL)* is an extension of the base SQL language for Oracle databases, and SparkSQL is, of course, an extension of SQL on Apache Spark. Take a look at the following snippet. Notice that the results would be the same for each line of code, but the first line is default SQL and the second is T-SQL. In many cases the differences have to do with syntax.

```
SELECT * FROM [READINGS] ORDER BY [VALUE] LIMIT 10;
SELECT TOP 10 (*) FROM [READINGS] ORDER BY [VALUE];
```

There are, for certain, numerous technical and implementation differences between the different SQL libraries as well. T-SQL, PL/SQL, and SparkSQL all have some tuning, feature, and management capabilities that are specific to the targeted RDBMSs. To learn more about each of those SQL libraries, visit

- `https://docs.microsoft.com/sql/t-sql`
- `https://docs.oracle.com/en/database/oracle/oracle-database/19/lnpls/index.html`
- `https://spark.apache.org/docs/latest/sql-ref.html`

More on this topic is not in the scope for this book, but it is an important area to understand if you plan on working a lot with data. It wouldn't be a stretch to assume your work scope could span across many different types of data sources that use different SQL implementations. Being well-versed in such views can help progress projects along much faster.

Database Console Commands

Database Console Command (DBCC) statements are useful for maintaining and analyzing the performance and state of an Azure SQL or Azure Synapse Analytics SQL pool instance. These commands do not run on a Spark pool. If you are experiencing any unexpected latency that you cannot attribute to a change in the velocity or variety of data flowing into your data solution, you might want to look at the database itself. Using these commands can help you gather insights into how the DBMS itself is performing and if the data is optimally stored and structured. There are many commands, so the following is a summary of some of the most important ones.

DBCC DROPRESULTSETCACHE

To enable caching for a session on an Azure Synapse Analytics SQL pool, you would execute the following command. Caching is `OFF` by default.

```
SET RESULT_SET_CACHING ON
```

The first time a query is executed, the results are stored in cache. The next time the same query is run, instead of parsing through all the data on disk, the result is pulled from cache. Cache is stored in memory, which is faster than performing I/O operations. However, the cache in a pool can fill up and may need to be reset. This command will clear the cache so that new or different data can be stored in memory cache. The platform itself will remove the cache after 48 hours for result sets that have not been accessed during that time.

DBCC PDW_SHOWEXECUTIONPLAN

When you run complex queries on a data source, the DBMS needs to perform some analysis to find the most efficient way to execute the query. That plan is called an *execution plan*. You can run the command shown in the following snippet:

```
DBCC PDW_SHOWEXECUTIONPLAN (distribution_id, session_id)
```

You can find the `distribution_id` using the `PDW_SHOWSPACEUSED` command illustrated in Figure 2.24. This operation is not supported on the serverless SQL pool, but only on dedicated. The `session_id` is an integer, which can found by executing this statement:

```
SELECT SESSION_ID()
```

The execution plan will show the template for how your SQL query is executed. You can review it to find the points of contention that can help you tune and optimize its performance.

DBCC PDW_SHOWPARTITIONSTATS

This command will show you the number of rows and space used for a given partition. The following will show those values for the `READING` table:

```
DBCC PDW_SHOWPARTITIONSTATS ("dbo.READING")
```

DBCC PDW_SHOWMATERIALIZEDVIEWOVERHEAD

To refresh your memory, review the earlier section "View" where we discussed materialized views. When you run this command, passing it the schema and name of the view, it returns a ratio between the view base rows and total rows. For example, if base rows = 10 and total rows = 30, then the ratio is 3. As the ratio increases, the query uses the persisted data less and less, which results in poor query performance. You should monitor this value and identify a ratio that works for your scenario. Once the ratio breaks your threshold, you can rebuild the materialized view, which would reset the ratio to 0.

FIGURE 2.24 Output of running the PDW_SHOWSPACEUSED command

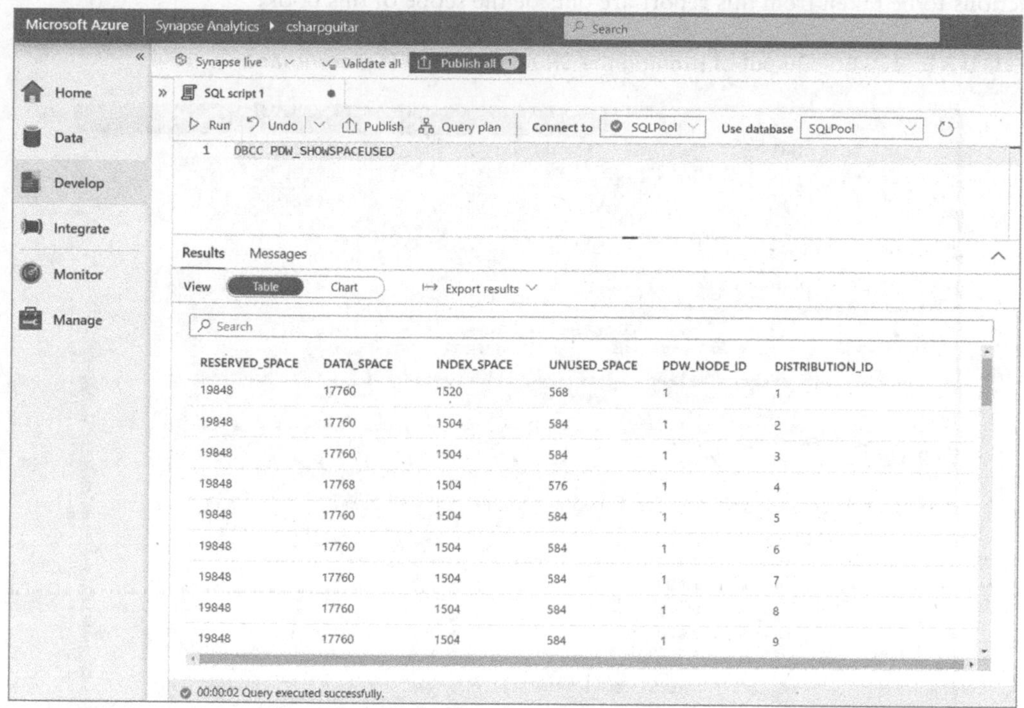

DBCC PDW_SHOWSPACEUSED

As illustrated in Figure 2.24, the amount of reserved disk space, space used for data, the amount of space taken for indexing, free space, and the node and distribution ID can be accessed using this command.

This information is useful for making sure you have enough space to run your data solution workloads.

DBCC SHOW_STATISTICS

This command will display the current optimization statistics for a table or view. Before you can show the statistics, you first need to create them. The following snippet illustrates how this is done. Provide a statistics name, the table (e.g., READING), and the column (e.g., VALUE) for which you want to capture statistics:

```
CREATE STATISTICS ReadingValue ON READING ([VALUE]) WITH SAMPLE 5 PERCENT
```

Once complete, execute the following command with a reference to the table and statistics name:

```
DBCC SHOW_STATISTICS ("READING", "ReadingValue")
```

The result is illustrated in Figure 2.25. A discussion of the interpretations, meaning, and actions to be taken from this report are outside the scope of this book.

FIGURE 2.25 Output of running the SHOW_STATISTICS command

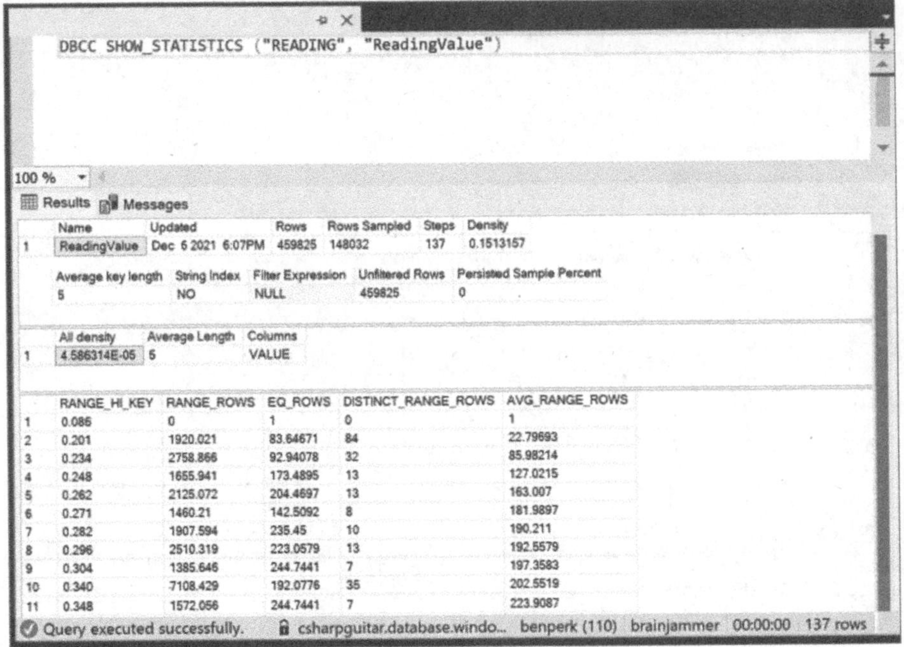

	Name	Updated	Rows	Rows Sampled	Steps	Density
1	ReadingValue	Dec 6 2021 6:07PM	459825	148032	137	0.1513157

Average key length	String Index	Filter Expression	Unfiltered Rows	Persisted Sample Percent
5	NO	NULL	459825	0

	All density	Average Length	Columns
1	4.586314E-05	5	VALUE

	RANGE_HI_KEY	RANGE_ROWS	EQ_ROWS	DISTINCT_RANGE_ROWS	AVG_RANGE_ROWS
1	0.086	0	1	0	1
2	0.201	1920.021	83.64671	84	22.79693
3	0.234	2758.866	92.94078	32	85.98214
4	0.248	1655.941	173.4895	13	127.0215
5	0.262	2125.072	204.4697	13	163.007
6	0.271	1460.21	142.5092	8	181.9897
7	0.282	1907.594	235.45	10	190.211
8	0.296	2510.319	223.0579	13	192.5579
9	0.304	1385.646	244.7441	7	197.3583
10	0.340	7108.429	192.0776	35	202.5519
11	0.348	1572.056	244.7441	7	223.9087

DBCC SHOWRESULTCACHESPACEUSED

Like the PDW_SHOWSPACEUSED command, this command shows the storage consumed by the data stored in cache. This command is not supported when running on an Azure Synapse serverless SQL pool.

Data Definition Language

Data Definition Language (DDL) SQL commands like CREATE, ALTER, TRUNCATE, and RENAME are considered part of the *Data Definition Language (DDL)*. There are lots of SQL commands, so grouping them into different categories is helpful when learning about managing databases. DDL commands are used to define, configure, and remove data structures, like tables, views, schema, indexes, and the database itself. You typically do not run DDL commands to work directly with data. Instead, use these commands perform required actions at the table level or higher. DDL commands have great impact, especially when considering the power of the DROP command.

```
DROP TABLE READING
DROP DATABASE brainjammer
```

Remember from Exercise 2.1 where you created an Azure SQL database. If you execute those DROP commands, the referenced table and database will be deleted. Unlike when you are working in Windows, you are not asked to confirm if you really want to delete the database. If you execute the command, the database is deleted without question. There are many reasons to perform backups of your database; this is one such example. Here are a few other DDL SQL commands that may be useful.

DESCRIBE

The command is not supported on either Azure SQL or Azure Synapse Analytics SQL pool. It is supported only when using a Spark pool. You use this command to show the details of a table. Execute the DESCRIBE command on a Spark pool in Azure Synapse Analytics using the following SparkSQL syntax:

```
%%sql
DESCRIBE TABLENAME
```

The alternative to DESCRIBE on Azure SQL or a SQL pool is the following:

```
exec sp_columns TABLENAME
```

EXPLAIN

This command is useful for discovering the query plan of a SQL statement run on Azure Synapse Analytics. This command is not supported by the serverless SQL pool, but only on dedicated SQL pools. This is similar to an explain plan, which I mentioned earlier, and will be covered more in Part IV of this book. Here is an example:

```
EXPLAIN WITH_RECOMMENDATIONS
SELECT SESSION.SESSION_DATETIME, SCENARIO.SCENARIO
FROM   SESSION
INNER  JOIN SCENARIO ON SESSION.SCENARIO_ID = SCENARIO.SCENARIO_ID
```

The result is an XML-formatted report explaining how the query would execute. The details can provide some insights into bottlenecks and location of latency.

Data Manipulation Language

The Data Manipulation Language (DML) category of SQL commands are the ones most used when querying, modifying, and managing data. DML operations are typically executed on rows, columns, and tables. The *Data Manipulation Language (DML)* consists of the most well-known SQL commands, like INSERT, UPDATE, DELETE, SELECT, WHERE, SET, and FROM. There are many DML commands, so not all of them are covered in depth in this chapter. Note that you are expected to know the basic DML commands already; therefore, we won't discuss them. But here is a list just so you know what the basic DML commands are: AND, AS, BETWEEN, COMMIT, DELETE, FROM, GROUP BY, IN, INSERT, INTO, LIKE, MERGE, OR, ORDER BY, PARSE, ROLLBACK, SELECT, SET, UPDATE, and WHERE.

You do need to know both basic and advanced DML commands and SQL functions for the DP-203 exam. Some of the more complicated and relevant DML commands are mentioned in this book. The command statements and functions covered here are enough to know for the exam and enough to get you skilled up to a level where you can create and perform some very sophisticated data analysis. Read on to learn many of the more complex DML command statements and functions.

Command Statements and Functions

There are different groupings of SQL syntax, some of which you have already read about, like DBCC, DDL, and DML. When you directly query data, the syntax you use would typically fall into the DML category of commands—for example, `BULK INSERT`, `CASE`, and `CROSS APPLY`. When you want to perform some calculation or transformation during the execution of the query, you would then use a function—for example, `AVG`, `COALESCE`, `CAST`, `DATEDIFF`, `MAX`, `OPENJSON`, and `COUNT`. There are numerous groupings of functions; two of the most common are *aggregate functions* and *Windows functions*. Aggregate functions are those you are probably most familiar with, such as `AVG`, `MAX`, `MIN`, and `SUM`. You can use them along with `GROUP BY`, as in the following example:

```
SELECT CONVERT(VARCHAR(50), [READING_DATETIME], 23) AS READINGDATE,
       AVG([VALUE]) AS Average, MAX([VALUE]) AS Maximum,
       MIN([VALUE]) AS Minimum, SUM([VALUE]) AS Sum, COUNT(*) AS COUNT
FROM  [dbo].[READING]
WHERE [ELECTRODE_ID] = 1 AND [FREQUENCY_ID] = 1
GROUP BY [SESSION_ID], CONVERT(VARCHAR(50), [READING_DATETIME], 23)
ORDER BY CONVERT(VARCHAR(50), [READING_DATETIME], 23)
```

That query calculates the average, maximum, minimum, and total brainwave values per session, by reading date, for electrode `AF3` and frequency `THETA`. `CONVERT` is discussed in more detail later. The following table illustrates the output of the aggregate function query.

```
+------------+---------+---------+---------+-----------+-------+
| READINGDATE | Average | Maximum | Minimum | Sum       | COUNT |
+------------+---------+---------+---------+-----------+-------+
| 2021-07-29  | 6.86226 | 213.940 | 0.465   | 8824.872  | 1286  |
| 2021-07-29  | 71.6606 | 427.917 | 0.842   | 104839.58 | 1463  |
| 2021-07-29  | 63.5138 | 262.267 | 1.168   | 64403.058 | 1014  |
| 2021-07-30  | 58.8885 | 180.377 | 0.763   | 64188.516 | 1090  |
| 2021-07-30  | 45.8514 | 4205.59 | 0.772   | 43971.521 | 959   |
| 2021-07-30  | 45.0759 | 189.511 | 0.820   | 45391.499 | 1007  |
| 2021-08-01  | 104.214 | 386.386 | 0.434   | 120471.73 | 1156  |
| ...         | ...     | ...     | ...     | ...       | ...   |
+------------+---------+---------+---------+-----------+-------+
```

Converting the aggregate function into a Windows function requires the implementation of the OVER clause. The following query illustrates how this is achieved, followed by the results:

```
SELECT  CONVERT(VARCHAR(50), [READING_DATETIME], 23) AS READINGDATE, [VALUE],
 AVG([VALUE]) OVER (PARTITION BY [SESSION_ID], CONVERT(VARCHAR(50),
                    [READING_DATETIME], 23)) AS Average,
 MAX([VALUE]) OVER (PARTITION BY [SESSION_ID], CONVERT(VARCHAR(50),
                    [READING_DATETIME], 23)) AS Maximum,
 MIN([VALUE]) OVER (PARTITION BY [SESSION_ID], CONVERT(VARCHAR(50),
                    [READING_DATETIME], 23)) AS Minimum,
 SUM([VALUE]) OVER (PARTITION BY [SESSION_ID], CONVERT(VARCHAR(50),
                    [READING_DATETIME], 23)) AS Total
FROM  [dbo].[READING]
WHERE [ELECTRODE_ID] = 1 AND [FREQUENCY_ID] = 1
ORDER BY CONVERT(VARCHAR(50), [READING_DATETIME], 23)
```

READINGDATE	VALUE	Average	Maximum	Minimum	Total
2021-07-29	114.687	6.86226	213.940	0.465	8824.872
2021-07-29	79.648	6.86226	213.940	0.465	8824.872
2021-07-29	51.234	6.86226	213.940	0.763	63939.72
...	...	...	...	...	...
2021-07-30	44.254	58.8885	180.377	0.763	64188.51
2021-07-30	25.286	58.8885	180.377	0.763	64188.51
2021-07-30	15.232	58.8885	180.377	0.763	64188.51
...	...	...	...	...	...
2021-08-01	6.112	104.214	386.386	0.434	120471.7
2021-08-01	7.772	104.214	386.386	0.434	120471.7
...	...	...	...	...	...

As you can see in the first table, the aggregate function performed the calculations using values based on the GROUP BY clause. A Windows function does not employ a GROUP BY—it instead calculates the values for each row based on the parameters used with OVER and PARTITION BY. Notice that the parameters that come after PARTITION BY for the Windows function are the same as the GROUP BY clause used in the aggregate function. Windows functions employ what is called a *window frame*. Each row rendered using a Windows function has an associated frame that provides the capacity to perform ranking, aggregation, and analytics on each row value based on a group of rows. The remaining content in this section provides some information about many of the common mid- to advanced level SQL command statements and SQL functions. You'll learn more about the OVER clause and Windows functions in the section "Data Manipulation Language (DML)," later in this chapter.

AVG, MAX, MIN, SUM, COUNT

These are some of the most common aggregate SQL functions. You saw them in the previous section. You can use these functions to calculate average, maximum, minimum, and total of numeric column values on one or more tables. The COUNT function returns the number of rows that match the SQL statement criteria. Note that after loading all brainwave readings into an Azure SQL database, executing the following function resulted in 459,825 rows:

```
SELECT COUNT(*) FROM READING
```

The code to upload the JSON readings is located on GitHub at https://github.com/benperk/ADE in the Chapter02/Source Code/brainjammer-cosmos directory. The actual brainwave reading data is located in the BrainwaveData directory. Finally, these are some basic aggregate functions you likely already know pretty well. Since the examples in the previous section covered these aggregate functions, no further explanation is necessary.

BULK INSERT

This can be used to load data from a file existing on an Azure Data Lake Storage container. You first need to create an external data source, using the following syntax:

```
CREATE EXTERNAL DATA SOURCE PlayingGuitarPOW
WITH ( TYPE = BLOB_STORAGE,
       LOCATION = 'https://<account>.blob.core.windows.net/<container>/<path>'
);
```

Then identify the specific file and the table into which the data should be loaded:

```
BULK INSERT [dbo].[READINGCSV]
FROM 'csharpguitar-brainjammer-pow-PlayingGuitar-0911.csv'
WITH (DATA_SOURCE = 'PlayingGuitarPOW',
      FIRSTROW = 2,
      FIELDTERMINATOR = ',',
      ROWTERMINATOR = '0x0a');
```

The columns in the CSV file must match the table that will receive the data contained in the file. You might encounter this command more in the context of Azure SQL. In the Azure Synapse Analytics SQL pool scenario, it is more common to use the COPY TO command, which is explained later.

CASE

In the "Data Programming" section earlier, you learned about the PySpark `when()` method. A SQL `CASE` command results in the same outcome:

```
SELECT SESSION_ID, ELECTRODE =
   CASE ELECTRODE_ID
      WHEN 1 THEN 'AF3'
      WHEN 2 THEN 'AF4'
      WHEN 3 THEN 'T7'
      WHEN 4 THEN 'T8'
      WHEN 5 THEN 'Pz'
      ELSE 'Invalid'
   END,
  Value
FROM [dbo].[READING]
ORDER BY READING_DATETIME
```

In the `READING` table `ELECTRODE_ID` is an integer. This statement would make the output more user friendly by converting those integers to the name of the electrode.

COALESCE

This SQL function is helpful in managing data columns that may contain a `NULL` value. Instead of returning `NULL` or an empty string, you can use `COALESCE` to perform some evaluations and return an alternative value. The following snippet will evaluate the content of the `VALUE` column. If the content is `NULL`, then it returns `0`; if not, the command returns the value stored on the database.

```
COALESCE(VALUE, 0)
```

You will find this function typically embedded within a `SELECT` statement, as follows:

```
SELECT READING_DATETIME, ELECTRODE_ID, FREQUENCY_ID, COALESCE(VALUE, 0)
FROM READING
```

CONVERT and *CAST*

`CONVERT` and `CAST` are essentially the same—there is no difference between their capabilities or performance. They both exist solely for historical reasons, not for any functional ones. As long as you understand that both of these SQL functions are used to change the data type of data stored in a table, you have this one 99 percent covered. In case you want to review something about data types, take a look back at Table 2.2, which describes some of the more common data types.

In the following snippet:

```
SELECT TIMESTAMP,
       DATEADD(S, CAST([TIMESTAMP] AS DECIMAL(14, 4)) , '19700101') AS
Timestamp2,
       AF3gamma,
        CONVERT(VARBINARY(8), CAST(AF3gamma AS DECIMAL(14, 4))) AS AF3GammaHex
FROM READINGCSV
```

the CAST function in the second line changes the string contained in the TIMESTAMP column to a DECIMAL and then converts it to a DATETIME, as you can see in Figure 2.26. The value in the original TIMESTAMP column is in Epoch time format. Converting the Epoch time format into a format most people are used to seeing requires some special handling, as you can see in the previous snippet. You need to use the DATEADD() function, passing it the interval, in this case S for seconds, followed by the amount to add to the date, which is provided as the last parameter.

FIGURE 2.26 Using CONVERT and CAST SQL commands

TIMESTAMP	Timestamp2	AF3gamma	AF3GammaHex
1631430707.5535	2021-09-12 07:11:47.000	4.508	0x0E04000118B00000
1631430707.6794	2021-09-12 07:11:47.000	4.896	0x0E04000140BF0000
1631430707.8058	2021-09-12 07:11:47.000	5.124	0x0E04000128C80000
1631430707.932	2021-09-12 07:11:47.000	5.075	0x0E0400013EC60000
1631430708.0583	2021-09-12 07:11:48.000	4.752	0x0E040001A0B90000
1631430708.1841	2021-09-12 07:11:48.000	4.276	0x0E04000108A70000
1631430708.3102	2021-09-12 07:11:48.000	3.818	0x0E04000124950000
1631430708.4362	2021-09-12 07:11:48.000	3.514	0x0E04000144890000
1631430708.5623	2021-09-12 07:11:48.000	3.409	0x0E0400012A850000
1631430708.6884	2021-09-12 07:11:48.000	3.463	0x0E04000146870000

In the fourth line, CONVERT changes the data type in the AF3Gamma column, after it is cast to a DECIMAL, into HEX, just for fun.

COS, COT, LOG, SIN, STDEV, TAN, VAR

This group of functions consists of both aggregate (STDEV and VAR) and mathematical (COS, COT, LOG, SIN, and TAN) functions. Look at the following SQL query:

```
SELECT m.MODE, sc.SCENARIO, e.ELECTRODE, f.FREQUENCY, AVG([VALUE]) AS Average,
       SUM([VALUE]) AS Total, STDEV([VALUE]) AS Deviation,
       VAR([VALUE]) AS Variance,
       TAN(AVG([VALUE])) AS TANGENTAVG, TAN(SUM([VALUE])) AS TANGENTSUM,
       LOG(AVG([VALUE])) AS LOGARITHMAVG, LOG(SUM([VALUE])) AS LOGARITHMASUM,
       COS(AVG([VALUE])) AS COSINEMAVG, COS(SUM([VALUE])) AS COSINESUM,
       SIN(AVG([VALUE])) AS SINEMAVG, SIN(SUM([VALUE])) AS SINEASUM,
```

```
    COT(AVG([VALUE])) AS COTANGENTAVG, COT(SUM([VALUE])) AS COTANGENTASUM
FROM MODE m, SCENARIO sc, [SESSION] s, ELECTRODE e, FREQUENCY f, READING r
WHERE m.MODE_ID = s.MODE_ID
   AND sc.SCENARIO_ID = s.SCENARIO_ID
   AND s.SESSION_ID = r.SESSION_ID
   AND e.ELECTRODE_ID = r.ELECTRODE_ID
   AND f.FREQUENCY_ID = r.FREQUENCY_ID
GROUP BY m.MODE, sc.SCENARIO, e.ELECTRODE, f.FREQUENCY
```

This query is experimental only. There may or may not be any significance of the cosine or sine value, for example, of the sum or average brainwave value based on the MODE, SCENARIO, ELECTRODE, and FREQUENCY. However, if there is some kind of trend that can be identified, then it can perhaps be used for driving the predictability of the scenario in which the brainwave is being captured in real time. Table 2.8 describes the functions implemented in the previous query in more detail.

TABLE 2.8 Aggregate and mathematical functions

Function	Description
COS	Returns the trigonometric cosine of a provided value as a float data type
COT	Returns the trigonometric cotangent of a value as a float data type
LOG	Returns the logarithm of a given numeric value
SIN	Returns the trigonometric sine of a value as a float data type
STDEV	Returns the statistical standard deviation of all values in the defined expression
TAN	Returns the tangent of a provided value
VAR	Returns the statistical variance of all values in the defined expression

There are a great deal of SQL functions that can be run against data. They are often bound to the specific type of DBMS. Oracle, SQL Server, and MySQL all have proprietary functions available only for the given DBMS.

CORR

This function returns the coefficient of correlation when passed a pair of numbers. CORR will determine if a relationship exists between the pair of values it receives. The result is a range from −1 to 1 where either ±1 means there is a correlation between the two numbers, and a 0 means there is no correlation. An interesting check using the brainwave data might be to determine if there is correlation between reading values for given scenarios. Note that there is no CORR support on SQL pools; therefore, you must run this on a Spark pool using SparkSQL. This table contains data for all electrodes and the frequency of BETA_H in columns based on the scenario.

```
+---------------+--------------+------------+------------+--------+
| ClassicalMusic | WorkMeeting  | Meditation | MetalMusic | TikTok |
+---------------+--------------+------------+------------+--------+
| 1.688          | 2.084        | 1.129      | 2.725      | 0.758  |
| 1.544          | 1.898        | 0.974      | 2.706      | 0.945  |
| 1.829          | 0.99         | 0.575      | 1.781      | 1.139  |
| ...            | ...          | ...        | ...        | ...    |
+---------------+--------------+------------+------------+--------+
```

To make some sense of the results, it would help to know that the BETA_H frequency is linked to scenarios that require concentration. Looking at the output you might conclude relative to ClassicalMusic, watching TikTok perhaps does not take as much concentration. That conclusion can be made because the values are higher for ClassicalMusic than for TikTok. However, there is not enough rendered data to make a real conclusion; it is just a first impression. To check to see if there is a correlation between any two of those columns, you can use CORR, as in the following example:

```
%%sql
SELECT CORR(_c1, _c5) AS Correlation FROM BETA_H
```

The BETA_H frequency correlation coefficient between ClassicalMusic and TiKTok is 0.03299257. The CORR clause returns the Pearson correlation coefficient, and how to interpret this output is worthy of a book in itself. However, it is safe to say that there is a small positive correlation between the two scenarios.

CROSS APPLY

Use this command to make a cross-reference to rows from a subquery. CROSS APPLY is the equivalent to a LATERAL JOIN. The following code snippet illustrates the implementation of CROSS APPLY. You can identify a subquery by the existence of multiple SELECT statements.

```
SELECT
  S.SESSION_ID AS SESSION_ID, AGE_IN_YEARS,
  DATEADD(year, (AGE_IN_YEARS + 1), SESSION_DATETIME) AS NEXT_ANNIVERSARY,
  DATEDIFF(day, GETDATE(), DATEADD(year, (AGE_IN_YEARS + 1),
           SESSION_DATETIME)) AS DAYS_TO_NEXT_ANNIVERSARY
FROM [SESSION] S
CROSS APPLY
(SELECT FLOOR(DATEDIFF(week, S.SESSION_DATETIME,
       GETDATE()) / 52.177457) AS AGE_IN_YEARS
) AS T
ORDER BY SESSION_ID
```

This query uses the SESSION_DATETIME value, which exists on the SESSION table to determine how old the session is in years. Notice that the AGE_IN_YEARS is produced in the subquery, but it is referenced from the main query. This is the power of CROSS APPLY because results from the subquery can be used in the main query during its execution. You might notice the DATEDIFF() function, which will return the number of days between two dates. You can pass year, quarter, month, day, week, and so on as the first parameter and DATEDIFF() will return the number of years, months, weeks, whatever you passed it back. FLOOR() returns the integer part of the number that is passed to it as a parameter; basically, it rounds the number down to the nearest integer. You will see CROSS APPLY again later when we discuss OPENROWSET, which is commonly used when working with JSON files.

COPY INTO

This command is similar to BULK INSERT, but COPY INTO is optimized and only supported on Azure Synapse Analytics. It is supported on dedicated SQL pools; you cannot run COPY INTO on the built-in serverless SQL instance at this time. Here's the simplest example of using this SQL command:

```
COPY INTO READINGCSV
FROM 'https://?.blob.core.windows.net/brainjammer/<path>'
WITH ( FIRSTROW = 2 )
```

This command assumes there is a table named READINGCSV that has a schema that matches the content of the CSV file. You can view the SQL for the READINGCSV table in the BrainwaveTable folder on GitHub here: https://github.com/benperk/ADE. Once the data is loaded, you can execute the SQL queries required to perform your analysis.

DISTINCT

Using the DISTINCT command eliminates duplicate records from your SQL queries. The following query will return all rows from the SESSION table. Assume that the SCENARIO_ID of 1, which is the ClassicalMusic scenario, exists multiple times. In that case all rows are returned, in addition to all other SCENARIO_IDs.

```
SELECT [SCENARIO_ID] FROM [dbo].[SESSION]
```

If you wanted to return only a single occurrence of each SCENARIO_ID, you'd use the following syntax:

```
SELECT DISTINCT [SCENARIO_ID] FROM [dbo].[SESSION]
```

Do this if you want to check whether sessions exist for all scenarios, quickly and easily.

EXCEPT and *INTERSECT*

These commands are useful for querying data from two different tables and either excluding or including the matches. This first query, which uses EXCEPT, results in distinct values from the first query, which are not found in the query after EXCEPT.

```
SELECT [SESSION_ID]
FROM [dbo].[READING]
EXCEPT
SELECT [SESSION_ID]
FROM [dbo].[SESSION]
```

To use INTERSECT, you can execute the following. The query returns distinct values, which are found in the results of both queries.

```
SELECT [SESSION_ID]
FROM [dbo].[READING]
INTERSECT
SELECT [SESSION_ID]
FROM [dbo].[SESSION]
ORDER BY [SESSION_ID]
```

You could also include an ORDER BY to make the result render in ascending order.

EXISTS and *IN*

Use either of these predicate functions, which are semantically equivalent, as part of a WHERE clause. Here is an example of a query using the EXISTS predicate:

```
SELECT m.MODE FROM MODE AS m
WHERE EXISTS
(SELECT * FROM [SESSION] AS s WHERE m.MODE_ID = s.MODE_ID)
```

Here is an example using the IN predicate function:

```
SELECT m.MODE FROM MODE AS m
WHERE m.MODE IN
(SELECT m.MODE FROM [SESSION] AS s WHERE m.MODE_ID = s.MODE_ID)
```

Both the EXISTS and IN predicate functions return the same results in this example. Both CONTAINS and LIKE are considered predicate functions as well and are useful in similar scenarios where you want to filter data.

FIRST_VALUE and *LAST_VALUE*

Use the FIRST_VALUE to return the first value in an ordered set of values. The following SQL query returns the first READING_DATETIME value for a given brainwave VALUE. The query is projected to return only brainwaves collected from the AF3 electrode.

```
SELECT READING_DATETIME, [VALUE],
FIRST_VALUE(READING_DATETIME) OVER (ORDER BY [VALUE] ASC) AS AF3DATE
FROM READING
WHERE ELECTRODE_ID = 1
```

For example, if VALUE has two rows with a reading of 0.141, the READING_DATETIME of the first occurrence of 0.141 will be placed into the AF3DATE column. Here is an example of using LAST_VALUE, followed by Figure 2.27, which compares the output of the two queries.

```
SELECT READING_DATETIME, [VALUE],
LAST_VALUE(READING_DATETIME) OVER (ORDER BY [VALUE] ASC) AS AF3DATE
FROM READING
WHERE ELECTRODE_ID = 1
```

FIGURE 2.27 SQL query output from FIRST_VALUE and LAST_VALUE

FIRST_VALUE

READING_DATETIME	VALUE	AF3DATE
2021-08-01 09:06:05.613	0.141	2021-08-01 09:06:05.613
2021-07-31 10:16:41.000	0.141	2021-08-01 09:06:05.613

LAST_VALUE

READING_DATETIME	VALUE	AF3DATE
2021-08-01 09:06:05.613	0.141	2021-07-31 10:16:41.000
2021-07-31 10:16:41.000	0.141	2021-07-31 10:16:41.000

HAVING

Use this command to apply a search condition to a GROUP BY clause:

```
SELECT SCENARIO_ID, MODE_ID FROM [SESSION]
GROUP BY SCENARIO_ID, MODE_ID
HAVING COUNT(SCENARIO_ID) > 5
```

The query results in rendering rows for scenarios with more than five sessions.

JOIN

This is a relational structure-oriented concept that has to do with querying data that exists in two or more tables using a single query. It is possible to use JOINs on NoSQL data, but the nature of nonstructured or semi-structured means it won't be a very performant experience. If the JOIN on non- or unstructured data will not happen often, it might be useful, but not on huge datasets. If you find yourself needing a JOIN, you might consider restructuring the data to be relational. There are four kinds of JOINs as seen in Figure 2.28: INNER, LEFT, RIGHT, and FULL. The light shading shows the rows that will be returned.

Table 2.9 provides a summary of the various types of JOINs.

FIGURE 2.28 Representation of SQL JOINs

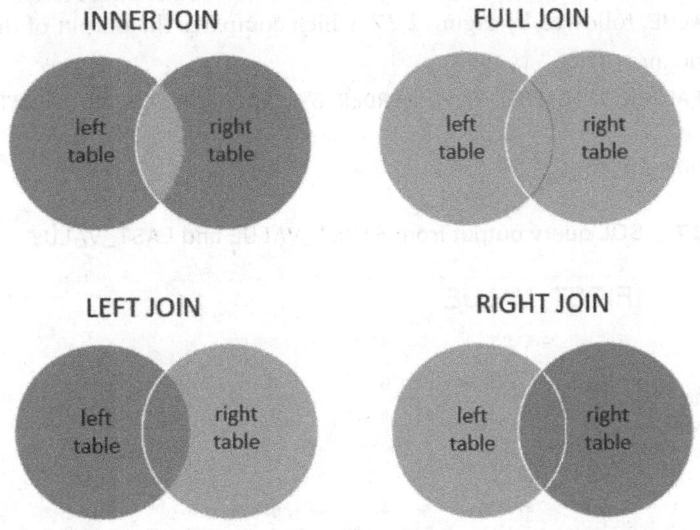

TABLE 2.9 JOIN types

Type	Description
`INNER JOIN`	Returns all rows if joined column is matched
`FULL JOIN`	Returns all rows on all tables even if no matches found
`LEFT JOIN`	Returns all rows from the left table and matches on the right
`RIGHT JOIN`	Returns all rows from the right table and matches on the left

Here is an example of each join using the `brainjammer` database created in Exercise 2.1, starting with an `INNER JOIN`. An `INNER JOIN` selects all the rows that match the `ON` clause. Rows that do not match are not included. This query shows the session datetime and its associated scenario:

```
SELECT SESSION.SESSION_DATETIME, SCENARIO.SCENARIO
FROM   SESSION
```

```
INNER  JOIN SCENARIO ON SESSION.SCENARIO_ID = SCENARIO.SCENARIO_ID

+-------------------------+----------------+
| SESSION_DATETIME        | SCENARIO       |
+-------------------------+----------------+
| 2021-07-30 08:00:00.000 | TikTok         |
| 2021-08-31 09:30:00.000 | ClassicalMusic |
| 2021-09-30 09:35:00.000 | PlayingGuitar  |
+-------------------------+----------------+
```

A LEFT JOIN resembles the following. The READING table is considered left and any result that is NULL means that there is no matching session in the SESSION table. There are no matches on the right table and therefore nothing is returned for the SESSION_DATETIME, but since all readings have a READING_DATETIME, all readings are returned.

```
SELECT READING.READING_DATETIME, [SESSION].[SESSION_DATETIME]
FROM READING
LEFT JOIN [SESSION]
ON [SESSION].[SESSION_DATETIME] = READING.READING_DATETIME

+-------------------------+------------------+
| READING_DATETIME        | SESSION_DATETIME |
+-------------------------+------------------+
| 2021-07-30 08:02:49.687 | NULL             |
| 2021-07-30 08:02:49.687 | NULL             |
| 2021-07-30 08:02:49.687 | NULL             |
| 2021-07-30 08:02:49.687 | NULL             |
| 2021-07-30 08:02:49.687 | NULL             |
| 2021-08-31 09:34:53.687 | NULL             |
| ...                     | ...              |
+-------------------------+------------------+
```

A RIGHT JOIN provides the opposite of the LEFT JOIN. Instead of returning data from the left table, the data on the right table is returned as well as anything matching on the left. Three sessions are loaded into the database, all of which have a SESSION_DATETIME, but none of them match the READING_DATETIME on the READING table.

```
SELECT [SESSION].[SESSION_DATETIME], READING.READING_DATETIME
FROM READING
RIGHT JOIN [SESSION]
ON [SESSION].[SESSION_DATETIME] = READING.READING_DATETIME
```

```
+-------------------------+------------------+
| SESSION_DATETIME        | READING_DATETIME |
+-------------------------+------------------+
| 2021-07-30 08:02:49.687 | NULL             |
| 2021-08-31 09:34:53.687 | NULL             |
| 2021-09-30 09:37:18.557 | NULL             |
+-------------------------+------------------+
```

A FULL JOIN returns all the records from both tables regardless of a match. A word of caution: This query can return a lot of results, potentially two tables' worth of data.

```
SELECT [SESSION].[SESSION_DATETIME], READING.READING_DATETIME
FROM READING
FULL JOIN [SESSION]
ON [SESSION].[SESSION_DATETIME] = READING.READING_DATETIME
```

```
+-------------------------+-------------------------+
| SESSION_DATETIME        | READING_DATETIME        |
+-------------------------+-------------------------+
| 2021-07-30 08:02:49.687 | NULL                    |
| 2021-08-31 09:34:53.687 | NULL                    |
| 2021-09-30 09:37:18.557 | NULL                    |
| NULL                    | 2021-07-30 08:02:49.687 |
| NULL                    | 2021-07-30 08:02:49.687 |
| NULL                    | 2021-07-30 08:02:49.687 |
| ...                     | ...                     |
+-------------------------+-------------------------+
```

These kinds of queries are helpful to find sessions that don't have any readings or readings that do not have any sessions. Because the database has referential integrity, some scenarios for which a JOIN comes in handy may not add great results. However, for many databases that were created without such constraints and that have grown too large to implement such an enforcement, this kind of command is very useful.

CARTESIAN *JOIN*

A *Cartesian JOIN*, or a CROSS JOIN, renders a Cartesian product, which is a record set of two or more joined tables. The following snippet is an example of a CROSS JOIN:

```
SELECT [ELECTRODE], [FREQUENCY]
FROM [ELECTRODE], [FREQUENCY]
ORDER BY ELECTRODE
```

Notice that there is no JOIN condition, which results in each row in the ELECTRODE table being paired with each row in the FREQUENCY table. The output resembles the following:

```
+-----------+-----------+
| ELECTRODE | FREQUENCY |
+-----------+-----------+
| AF3       | THETA     |
| AF3       | ALPHA     |
| ...       | ...       |
| Pz        | BETA_L    |
| ...       | ...       |
| T8        | BETA_H    |
| T8        | GAMMA     |
+-----------+-----------+
```

The result is a table containing all electrodes with their associated frequencies.

INCOMPATIBLE *JOIN*

This concept is in reference to performance bottlenecks that occur with distributed tables on Azure Synapse Analytics. Remember from earlier where you learned about distributed tables and data shuffling. You learned that when tables are created you need to decide the distribution type for a table. Distribution types can be ROUND-ROBIN, HASH, or REPLICATED, which determine how the data is placed onto the different compute nodes. You learned that shuffling happens when a query running on nodeA needs some data that is stored on nodeB, which requires the data to be moved to nodeA. The reason for that shuffle is an *incompatible JOIN*. Consider the following EXPLAIN query:

```
EXPLAIN
SELECT SESSION.SESSION_DATETIME, SCENARIO.SCENARIO
FROM   SESSION
INNER REDISTRIBUTE JOIN SCENARIO ON SESSION.SCENARIO_ID = SCENARIO.SCENARIO_ID
```

In this code snippet, SCENARIO_ID is the distribution key for the SESSION table but not for the SCENARIO table. Adding the REDISTRIBUTE hint in the query forces a shuffle, which prevents latent query behaviors. Explaining to the SQL optimizer that this is an incompatible JOIN results in the data being shuffled in the most efficient way possible. The same behavior can be experienced when executing aggregate functions, which is referred to as *incompatible aggregations*. The difference as you can infer is that this happens when aggregate functions are used that cause the shuffle instead of commands.

MEDIAN

There is no MEDIAN function in T-SQL, but using a rather complex query makes it possible. You have the luxury of using the PERCENTILE function in SparkSQL, which is one of numerous options. The median is different from the average in that the values at the highest and lowest spectrum of data values are removed. Those large values can have a dramatic effect on the rendered value. Consider the following SparkSQL query and result:

```
%%sql
SELECT AVG(_c1) AS Average, PERCENTILE(_c1, 0.5) AS Median FROM BETA_H

+---------+---------
| Average | Median |
+---------+--------+
| 1.55598 | 1.3375 |
+---------+--------+
```

The data that this query was run against was the brainwave value for all electrodes, the BETA_H frequency, and the ClassicalMusic scenario.

OPENROWSET

Use this function when you want to perform some ad hoc queries from a remote data source. OPENROWSET can perform SELECT, INSERT, UPDATE, and DELETE statements. The following snippet illustrates how to use this command:

```
SELECT Scenario, details
FROM OPENROWSET('CosmosDb',
                'Account=csharpguitar;Database=brainjammer;Key=sMxCN...xyQ==',
                sessions)
WITH (
     Scenario varchar(max) '$.Session.Scenario',
     details varchar(max) '$.Session') AS Sessions
```

Notice that the first parameter is a reference to the provider. A provider is the driver, or the coded assembly, that contains the code to make a connection to the targeted data source. In this case it is a reference to the Azure Cosmos DB you created earlier in Exercise 2.2. The value, CosmosDb, is an alias to an Azure Synapse Linked Service, which is configured with a connection string. (You have not created that connection yet, but you will in the following chapters.) Notice that the values for Account and Database match the example names provided in Exercise 2.2 as well. The third parameter, sessions, is the container ID. The WITH clause is similar to the CROSS APPLY command in that it provides the reference to an object outside the scope of the SQL query but uses it in the final rendered result set. This is a very useful command, especially when you're working with JSON files.

OPENJSON

This function is used in combination with OPENROWSET and instructs the runtime about the format of the content being retrieved. In addition to OPENJSON, we can use OPENXML and OPENQUERY, which are used in the same context but on different file formats or to run SQL queries directly against a database. The following query illustrates how to implement the OPENJSON function:

```
SELECT TOP (5) Cntr, ReadingDate, AF3ALPHA, T7ALPHA, PzALPHA, T8ALPHA,
               AF4ALPHA,
               Scenario, details, ScenarioReadings.[key] as ScenarioReading
FROM OPENROWSET('CosmosDb',
'Account=csharpguitar;Database=brainjammer;Key=sMxCN...
xyQ==',           sessions)
    WITH (
          Scenario varchar(max) '$.Session.Scenario',
          details varchar(max) '$.Session.POWReading') AS Sessions
    CROSS APPLY OPENJSON(Sessions.details) AS ScenarioReadings
    CROSS APPLY OPENJSON(ScenarioReadings.[value])
    WITH (
          Cntr int '$.Counter', ReadingDate varchar(50) '$.ReadingDate',
          AF3ALPHA decimal(7,3) '$.AF3[0].ALPHA',
          T7ALPHA decimal(7,3) '$.T7[0].ALPHA',
          PzALPHA decimal(7,3) '$.Pz[0].ALPHA',
          T8ALPHA decimal(7,3) '$.T8[0].ALPHA',
          AF4ALPHA decimal(7,3) '$.AF4[0].ALPHA') AS ScenarioDetails
```

The first few lines you know from the previous subsection. There is a function named TOP that, when passed a number, returns only that number of rows. Notice as well the utilization of the CROSS APPLY command. Remember that the data in the Azure Cosmos DB are JSON files, which represent a brainwave session. Executing the previous query results in something similar to that shown in Figure 2.29.

A very powerful and useful implementation of this would be to use it as input to the creation of a view or table using the CREATE AS command. For example, you can place the following four words in front of the previous code snippet:

```
CREATE VIEW READINGSTMP AS
```

Once the code executed, the referenced JSON files stored on the Azure Cosmos DB will be parsed and the data within them is placed into a view for further transformation or analysis. That is a truly simple and amazing feature. I hope you agree.

OVER

The OVER clause is used in the context of SQL Windows functions. OVER is used to perform calculations on a group of records, similar to GROUP BY. The difference is that GROUP BY collapses the dataset, making it impossible to then reference a single row in that same dataset. The following SparkSQL query is executed using a Spark pool on a table containing brainwaves collected in CSV format:

```
%%sql
SELECT DISTINCT from_unixtime(_c0, 'yyyy-MM-dd HH:mm:ss') AS TIMESTAMP,
AVG(_c1) OVER(PARTITION BY from_unixtime(_c0, 'yyyy-MM-dd HH:mm:ss')) AS Average,
MAX(_c1) OVER(PARTITION BY from_unixtime(_c0, 'yyyy-MM-dd HH:mm:ss')) AS Maximum,
MIN(_c1) OVER(PARTITION BY from_unixtime(_c0, 'yyyy-MM-dd HH:mm:ss')) AS Minimum,
SUM(_c1) OVER(PARTITION BY from_unixtime(_c0, 'yyyy-MM-dd HH:mm:ss')) AS Total
  FROM MEDITATION
  ORDER BY TIMESTAMP
```

FIGURE 2.29 OPENJSON query

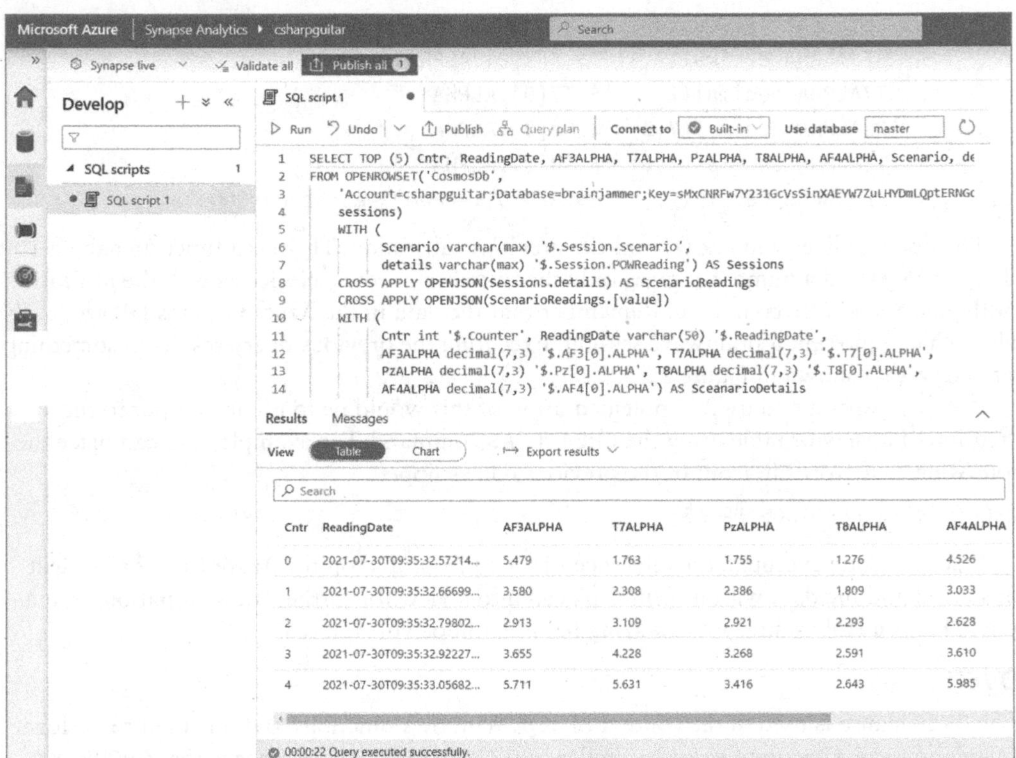

As you can see, this kind of query can be executed on both types of pools. The OVER clause supports three arguments: PARTITION BY, ORDER BY, and ROWS/RANGE. You have seen the first one in both scenarios and how it breaks the result into partitions. In this case, the partition is a timestamp. Therefore, the output would look similar to the result of a GROUP BY on the same timestamp, which is what makes OVER and Windows frames so useful. ORDER BY will logically order the results within each partition. Here's an example of how that looks:

```
SUM(_c1) OVER(PARTITION BY TimeStamp ORDER BY SCENARIO ) AS Total
```

The ROWS/RANGE arguments give you the ability to specify row number start and end points or a range of rows for displaying a result of data.

UNION

The UNION command combines the data from two or more tables without adding any additional rows. This is best understood visually, so consider the following SQL statement:

```
SELECT SESSION_ID AS ID, CONVERT(VARCHAR(50),
       SESSION_DATETIME, 127) AS DATE_SCENARIO
FROM [SESSION]
UNION
SELECT SCENARIO_ID, SCENARIO
FROM SCENARIO
```

The result would be something similar to the following. Notice that the rendered output is a single table with the two columns combined.

```
+------------+--------------------+
| ID         | DATE_SCENARIO      |
+------------|--------------------+
| 1          | 2021-07-30T09:35:00 |
| 1          | ClassicalMusic     |
| 2          | FlipChart          |
| 3          | Meditation         |
| 4          | 2021-07-31T10:15:00 |
| 4          | MetalMusic         |
| 5          | 2021-07-31T18:25:00 |
| ...        | ...                |
+------------+--------------------+
```

It means that there exists a SCENARIO_ID on the SESSION table that equals 1 and a SCENARIO_ID on the SCENARIO table that also equals 1. That is why you see the first two rows in the previous table illustration. The same is the case when SCENARIO_ID is 4, which exists on both tables. A UNION is often bundled into the same category of commands as

JOIN, EXCEPT, and INTERSECT in that they all provide the means or interface for working with more than a single table. If you add an ALL command directly after the UNION, the result will include duplicates from both tables. Without ALL, duplicates are excluded. Look at the previous table. Although there is a duplicate ID on both tables, there isn't a duplicate for DATE_SCENARIO as well. Had there been, then without the use of ALL, that row would have been excluded.

VAR and *STDEV*

Both VAR and STDEV have been introduced already, so this section will provide only a brief summary of what these aggregate functions do, without going too deep into the field of statistics. VAR is used to show how varied the data being analyzed is, known as *variance*. You can capture the variance between two groups (scenarios)—for example, TikTok and MetalMusic. The assessment will help determine how similar or different the two scenarios are from each other. STDEV returns the standard deviation, a value that represents its distance from the mean, or the average. Data interpretation is not part of the DP-203 exam.

WITH

You've seen the WITH clause already but let's discuss it in greater depth. As a data engineer you will be confronted with complicated questions that will require you to query a database to answer. Sometimes these questions and the queries you come up with are either extremely complicated or not even possible. Extremely complicated queries are those that would contain numerous subqueries, which make them hard to understand. Take warning that some DBMSs have a maximum number of allowed subqueries, so in some cases a single query is not possible. An alternative to subqueries might be to use CTAS to create a table based on the query, then write another query to query that table. You can create the flow of table creations and querying those tables into as many steps as required to get the answer. Although these options are valid approaches, you might instead consider trying to get the answer using the WITH clause when you find yourself taking such actions. The following code snippet is long but legible to someone with a skilled eye. It illustrates the implementation of the WITH clause:

```
WITH GETSTATS AS
(
        SELECT AVG([AVG]) AS AF3_BETA_L_AVG
        FROM READINGSTATS
        WHERE ELECTRODE = 'AF3' and FREQUENCY = 'BETA_L'
        GROUP BY ELECTRODE, FREQUENCY
)
SELECT r.MODE, r.SCENARIO, r.ELECTRODE, r.FREQUENCY,
     r.[AVG] AS AVERAGE_PROBLEM_SOLVING
FROM READINGSTATS r, GETSTATS
WHERE GETSTATS.AF3_BETA_L_AVG > r.[AVG]
     AND ELECTRODE = 'AF3' and FREQUENCY = 'BETA_L'
```

```
GROUP BY r.MODE, r.SCENARIO, r.ELECTRODE, r.FREQUENCY, r.[AVG]
ORDER BY AVERAGE_PROBLEM_SOLVING DESC
```

Because a `WHERE` clause cannot include an aggregate function, a possible solution is to capture that value using `WITH`. The query captures the average of the averages of brainwave readings for a given electrode and frequency, for all scenarios. Then, that value is used to render scenarios that have a higher average reading value for the given electrode and frequency. Since the `BETA_L` frequency is linked to scenarios where problem-solving stimulation is happening, you can partially assume that listening to `ClassicalMusic`, being the most above average, stimulates this kind of brainwave. Only a single electrode is used here; all five electrodes capture all five frequencies, so a more sophisticated query needs to be written. This is a step in the right direction, however.

```
+------+----------------+-----------+-----------+-------------------------+
| MODE | SCENARIO       | ELECTRODE | FREQUENCY | AVERAGE_PROBLEM_SOLVING |
+------+----------------+-----------+-----------+-------------------------+
| POW  | ClassicalMusic | AF3       | BETA_L    | 2.854088                |
| POW  | TikTok         | AF3       | BETA_L    | 2.629033                |
| POW  | WorkMeeting    | AF3       | BETA_L    | 2.522477                |
| POW  | MetalMusic     | AF3       | BETA_L    | 2.192918                |
+------+----------------+-----------+-----------+-------------------------+
```

It is interesting to see that TikTok resulted in such a high `BETA_L`. This is exactly the point of data analysis and analytics in that you run queries and analyze the output, which you can then relate to what you think should happen in the real world. The event of the data not representing the world as you perceive it either changes you and your mindset or makes you want to dig more deeply into the data source, the data analytics, and try to find out if there is a flaw and prove you are right after all.

Stored Procedures

When you write code or a query, you typically do so on a workstation on your desk or via a browser. If the code needs to make a connection to a database to retrieve and parse some data, it is important to decide where the parsing should take place. There are two places where the data parsing can happen. The first is on your workstation or on the server responding to the browser. Keep in mind that processing data requires compute power—that is, CPU and memory resource—as well as networking capacity to send and receive the requested dataset. The other location where the data can be parsed is on the database server itself. When you parse data on the database server, you use a stored procedure. A *stored procedure* is SQL query syntax executed on the database server itself; any of the previous examples can be used. This snippet is an example of how to run a stored procedure:

```
EXECUTE [dbo].[GetMeditationScenarios]
```

The `GetMeditationScenarios` stored procedure would contain the SQL syntax to return exactly what the name implies. This not only makes it much easier for others to consume but also provides consistency in what you get in return when triggering the stored procedure. In contrast, any developer who wanted to get that data would have to write their own query that might miss some data, or they might misunderstand the entire meaning of the data. That would result in bad results and therefore wrong conclusions and wrong decisions. Not only do stored procedures improve performance and reduce networking latency, but they also make sure the data is easily accessible and interpreted correctly.

User-Defined Functions

Functions are small snippets of code that get executed when you reference to the function name. You have been exposed to numerous functions that can be identified by open and closed parentheses (). Between the parentheses you can send parameters that the code within the function will use to flow through the code path execution. The functions you have read about so far are system or built-in functions. It is possible to create your own function called a *user-defined function (UDF)*. The process has a great deal to do with which operating system, language, platform, and programming language you choose. With T-SQL you can use the following syntax:

```
CREATE FUNCTION ValuesByFrequency (@frequencyid)
RETURNS TABLE
AS
RETURN
(
  SELECT TOP 10 sc.SCENARIO, e.ELECTRODE, f.FREQUENCY, r.[VALUE]
  FROM SCENARIO sc, [SESSION] s, ELECTRODE e, FREQUENCY f, READING r
  WHERE sc.SCENARIO_ID = s.SCENARIO_ID
    AND s.SESSION_ID = r.SESSION_ID
    AND e.ELECTRODE_ID = r.ELECTRODE_ID
    AND f.FREQUENCY_ID = r.FREQUENCY_ID
    AND f.FREQUENCY_ID = @frequencyid
)
```

Instead of writing the query multiple times, you can retrieve the data by executing this statement:

```
SELECT * FROM ValuesByFrequency(1)
```

This will return all brainwaves values for all readings.

Understanding Big Data Processing

The previous sections covered much of the mid-level data theory required to be a great Azure data engineer and give you a good chance of passing the exam. Now it's time to learn a bit about the processing of Big Data across the various data management stages. You will also learn about some different types of analytics and Big Data layers. After reading this section you will be in good shape to begin provisioning some Azure products and performing hands-on exercises.

Big Data Stages

In general, it makes a lot of sense to break complicated solutions, scenarios, and activities into smaller, less difficult steps. Doing this permits you to focus on a single task, specialize on it, dissect it, master it, and then move on to the next. In the end you end up providing a highly sophisticated solution with high-quality output in less time. This approach has been applied in the management of Big Data, which the industry has mostly standardized into the stages provided in Table 2.10.

TABLE 2.10 Big Data processing stages

Name	Description
Ingest	The act of receiving the data from producers
Prepare	Transforms the data into queryable datasets
Train	Analyzes and uses the data for intelligence
Store	Places final state data in a protected but accessible location
Serve	Exposes the data to authorized consumers

Figure 2.30 illustrates the sequence of each stage and shows which products are useful for each. In addition, Table 2.11 provides a written list of Azure products and their associated Big Data stage. Each product contributes to one or more stages through the Big Data architecture solution pipeline.

FIGURE 2.30 Big Data stages and Azure products

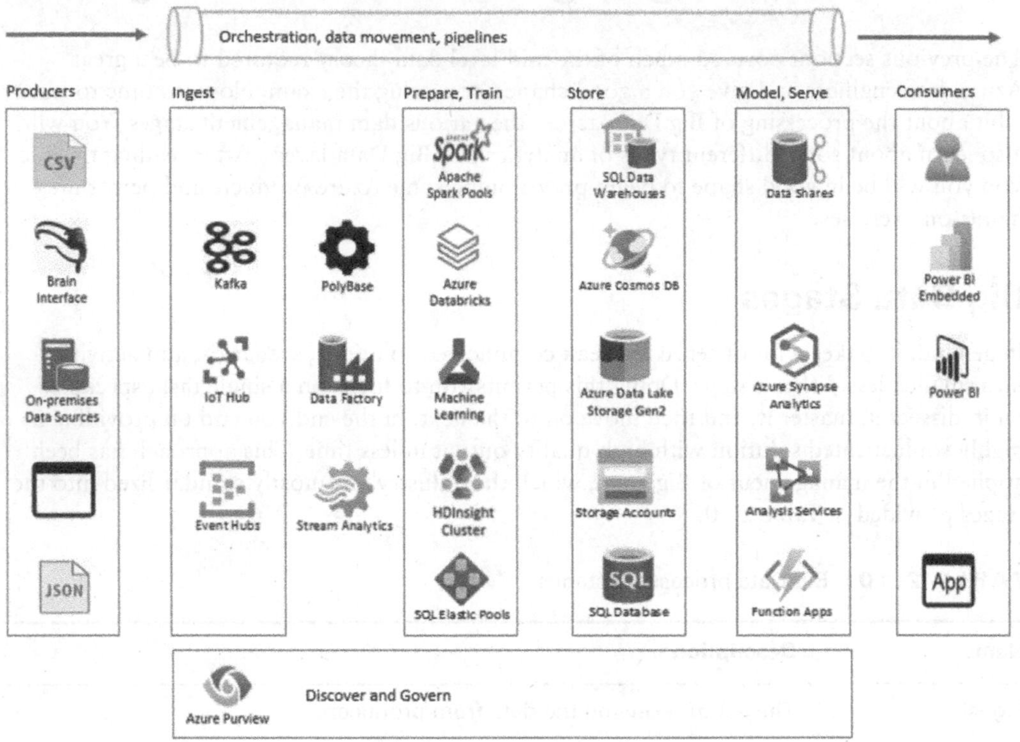

TABLE 2.11 Azure products and Big Data stages

Product	Stage
Apache Spark	Prepare, Train
Apache Kafka	Ingest
Azure Analysis Services	Model, Serve
Azure Cosmos DB	Store
Azure Databricks	Prepare, Train
Azure Data Factory	Ingest, Prepare
Azure Data Lake Storage	Store
Azure Data Share	Serve

Product	Stage
Azure Event / IoT Hub	Ingest
Azure HDInsight	Prepare, Train
Azure Purview	Governance
Azure SQL	Store
Azure Stream Analytics	Ingest, Prepare
Azure Storage	Store
Azure Synapse Analytics	Model
PolyBase	Ingest, Prepare
Power BI	Consume

Some Azure products in Table 2.11 can span several stages—for example, Azure Data Factory, Azure Stream Analytics, and even Azure Databricks in some scenarios. These overlaps are often influenced by the data type, data format, platform, stack, or industry in which you are working. As you work with these products in real life and later in this book, the use cases should become clearer. For instance, one influencer of the Azure products you choose is the source from which the data is retrieved, such as the following:

- Nonstructured data sources
- Relational databases
- Semi-structured data sources
- Streaming

Remember that nonstructured data commonly comes in the form of images, videos, or audio files. Since these file types are usually on the large size, real-time ingestion is most likely the best option. Otherwise, the ingestion would involve simply using a tool like Azure Storage Explorer to upload them to ADLS. Apache Spark has some great features, like PySpark and MLlib, for working with these kinds of data. Once the data is transformed, you can use Azure Machine Learning or the Azure Cognitive service to enrich the data to discover additional business insights. Relational data can be ingested in real time, but perhaps not as frequently as streaming from IoT devices. Nonetheless, you ingest the data from either devices or from, for example, an on-premises OLTP database and then store the data on ADLS. Finally, in a majority of cases, the most business-friendly way to deliver, or serve, Big Data results is through Power BI. Read on to learn more about each of those stages in more detail.

Ingest

This stage begins the process of the Big Data pipeline solution. Consider this the interface for data producers to send their raw data to. The data is then included and contributes to the overall business insights gathering and process establishment. In addition to receiving data for ingestion, it is possible to write a program to retrieve data from a source for ingestion.

SQL Server Integration Services

Introduced in Chapter 1, SQL Server Integration Services (SSIS) is useful for pulling data from numerous datastores, transforming the data, and storing it in a central datastore for analysis. Ingestion can be initiated by pulling data from existing sources instead, which is in contrast to data producers pushing data into the pipeline.

Bulk Copy Program

There are scenarios in which you have numerous files you want to load to Azure once or occasionally and not on a regular schedule. In those cases, there is no need to create a process since that kind of activity is typically done manually. In this case, using a *bulk copy program (BCP)* to upload the data is a good option. Azure Storage Explorer, which uses a popular application called AzCopy under the covers, is a solid tool for uploading files from a local source to an Azure Data Lake Storage container.

Streaming

Data streaming implies that there is a producer creating data all the time and sending it to an endpoint. That endpoint can be numerous products like Apache Kafka, Azure IoT Hub, or Azure Event Hub, which are designed to handle and temporarily store data at extremely high incoming frequencies. Those products are not intended to be stored for long periods of time; instead, when data is received, those products notify subscribers that data is present. Then those subscribers take an action that is dependent on their requirements and use of the data.

Prepare, Transform, Process

Once the raw data is ingested, whether via streaming, bulk, pulling from a data source, or using PolyBase, it then needs to be transformed. The data can come from numerous data sources and be in many different formats. Transforming this data into a standard format results in a larger set of shared queries and commands being run against it. If you needed to run a unique query against data from each data source, using all the data wouldn't lead to the optimal conclusion. Instead, merge and transform all the data into a single source and format, then run a single set of queries or commands against it. The result will be much more encompassing thanks to the wider set of data diversity. The movement and transformation of data in this stage has much to do with *data flow*.

Data Flows and Pipelines

Data flow is the means by which you manage the flow of your data through a transformative process. As you can see in Figure 2.31, data is retrieved, transformed, stored into a staging environment, and placed into an Azure SQL database using an Azure function. Notice the notebook; this is where you can run all the queries and commands you have learned in this chapter. Once you have the query, commands, or code you need to perform the transformation, save them and they will run as a pipeline that includes a data flow transformation activity. This explanation is only an introduction, and you will get some hands-on experience with this later in this book.

FIGURE 2.31 Pipeline data flow Azure Synapse transform stage

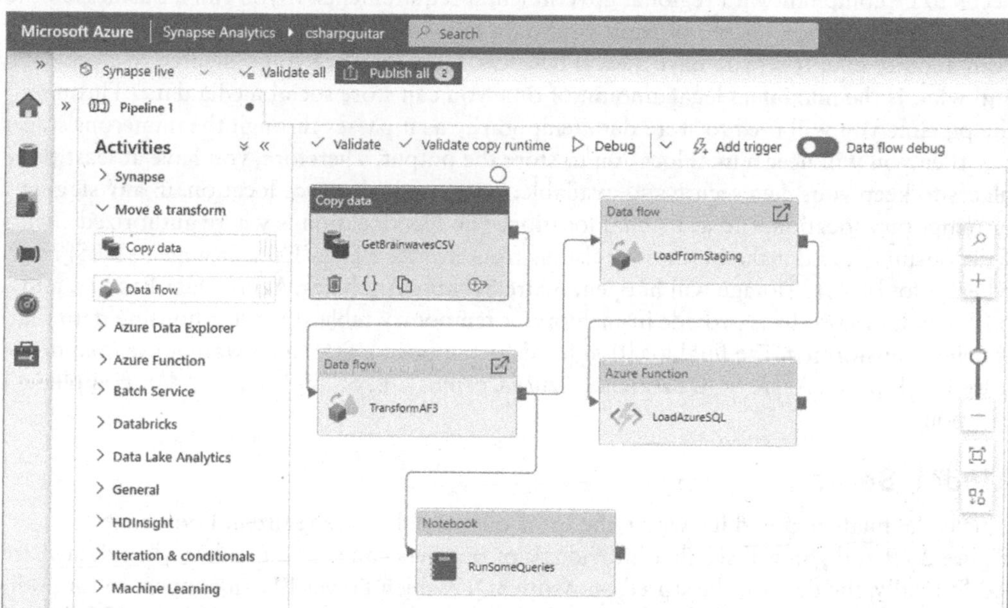

This data flow activity is available in both Azure Synapse analytics and Azure Data Factory. Figure 2.31 represents what is commonly referred to as *mapping data flows*. An alternative is called *wrangling data flows*, which is currently only available in Azure Data Factory, as is the *Power Query Online* mashup editor. The primary difference between the two flows is that mapping data flows has a focus on visually representing the flow between sources, transformations, and sinks, whereas wrangling data flows provides more visualization on the data, giving you quick visibility on what the end dataset will look like. Both do not require any coding to perform the data transformation.

Training and Enrichment

The training and enrichment of data typically happens by making improvements to the data quality or invoking Azure Machine Learning models, which can be later consumed by Azure Cognitive Services. The invoke can take place within a pipeline or manually. Azure Machine

Learning models can be used to predict future outcomes based on historical trends identified in the data. Azure Cognitive Services can be used to analyze audio files, images, and videos, which might result in findings that can be logged as data to be used later in queries. There is more about this phase of the Big Data pipeline in Chapter 5, "Transform, Manage, and Prepare Data."

Store

Where is the data stored? Rule number one is that it needs to be in a secure place. It also needs to be compliant with regional governmental requirements. If you run a business in the European Union, you might not want your data to be stored physically in another region or even another country if you have a local business. How long are you obligated to store data and what is the maximum legal amount of time you can store social media data? Through the pipeline you will need to store data temporarily as it passes through the numerous stages, and then you will need a final location to store the output. Therefore, you have at least three places to keep your data secure and available: at its original source location, in any staging or temporary location, and at its final location. The final location is where authorized clients will consume it and make business decisions from it. Azure Data Lake Storage (ADLS) is where a lot of your storage will happen. Azure Synapse Analytics, Azure Data Factory, and other analytics products provide in-memory or temporary table stores for housing data that is being transformed. The final location for data can be in a SQL data warehouse (aka dedicated SQL pool), Azure SQL database, Azure Cosmos DB, or any secure and/or compliant location.

Model, Serve

This is the final stage and it's where the fruits of your labor are realized. Look back at Figure 2.29 and you will see that individuals or partners can access the data via a data share. Additionally, the data can be stored on Azure SQL, which Power BI can connect to for additional modeling and manipulation. Or the data can be sent to or exposed via an API and accessed by authorized computer applications.

ETL, ELT, ELTL

Both *extract, transform, and load (ETL)* and *extract, load, and transform (ELT)* are processes that take raw data from a data source and place it into a data target. Those processes overlap the Big Data stages described earlier. They do, however, influence the order in which the stages occur. Both ETL and ELT are technical jargon that helps better describe the approach you are taking to implement your data analytics solution. The ETL process is best applied to relational data sources, whereas ELT has some better features to handle unstructured data. ELT will perform faster because it does not need to worry about managing any constraints found in a relational data model. You get faster speed of data transformation, but the data can be jumbled, and the process might fail at some point for numerous reasons, like an unexpected data type. If speed is critical and datasets are large and frequently updated, then ELT is the best option. ETL is most useful when pulling data from numerous sources that need to be pooled and stored into a single, queryable location. The extract part comes first, then if datasets are large, unstructured, and frequent, you load it and then transform it. Otherwise, if the data is structured and changes less frequently, then after extraction, you transform the data and then load it onto a place for consumption.

There is a newer concept making some headway called *extract, load, transform, and load (ELTL)*, which is likely self-explanatory. Based on the first three letters, you know the scenario consists of unstructured and large datasets that change frequently. The addition of the load at the end indicates that the data can ultimately be stored, analyzed, and consumed in the same manner as relational data.

Analytics Types

There are numerous types of data analytics, all of which are supported by Azure products, specifically Azure Synapse Analytics. In most cases, the name of the analytics type is enough to determine its meaning and purpose. However, here are the most common analytics types and a brief summary of each.

Descriptive

The descriptive analytic type explains, visualizes, and describes what is happening for a given scenario. For example, questions like "what is my brain doing?" or "how is my business going?" can be answered using this kind of data analytics. It is considered the first stage of business analytics.

Diagnostic

Diagnostics determine why something happened. Why did my brain act like it did, or why is my business performing so fantastic?

Predictive

Use historical data to determine what will happen in the future in each scenario. Using previous patterns and trends, if you assume the same constraints will exist in the future, you might be able to predict the future outcome. This is considered the second stage of business analytics.

Preemptive

Preemptive means to take an action based on an action that is expected to happen at some point in the future. It is like predictive in that you need to have some sense of what is going to happen. The preemptive part is knowing what action to take based on that foreseen event so that the result matches your desire.

Prescriptive

The prescriptive method uses descriptive and predictive results and then applies computational science and mathematical algorithms to take advantage of data analytics findings. This is considered the third stage of business analytics. Once you know what is going on and have some idea of what might happen in the future, this type provides some ideas on what to do to optimize, enrich, or enhance the desired outcome.

Big Data Layers

The term *layer* exists in numerous technical contexts. For example, TCP/IP consists of seven layers known as the OSI model. There is an operating system layer and an application layer. There are a machine code, assembly, native, and managed coding layers. In Big Data there are also layers. They align closely with stages but are worthy of being called out.

Data Source Layer

The data source layer describes where the data comes from: not only the data location, but also the kind of data, like monitor data, purchase order data, brainwave data, GPS data, and so forth. The source can also mean its format, like relational, semi-, or nonstructured, and which DBMS or system the data is managed on.

Data Storage Layer

There are many methods to store data, many of which you have already read about, such as ADLS, Azure Cosmos DB, Azure SQL, and Apache Hadoop. Knowing some details about the platform on which the data is stored will help you determine what is needed to connect to and retrieve the data. Take special note that this location must be very secure because lots of sensitive information can be stored in data files. You do not want to make the data storage layer publicly available, and you want to govern authorized connections and actions by monitoring and logging them.

Data Processing/Analysis Layer

This is where the data is prepared, transformed, and temporarily stored. Azure Data Factory, Azure Databricks, Azure HDInsight, Apache Spark, and Azure Synapse Analytics are considered part of the data processing and analysis layer.

Data Output/Serving/Consumption Layer

This is where you place the final dataset. The data provided at this layer is in its final state, ready to be presented through a web-based report or application. The data can also be in a state that allows additional queries or commands to be run against it, which supports even more granularity and flexibility. That flexibility is something that Power BI is great at doing and visualizing.

Summary

There was a lot covered in this chapter, starting with the description of the first data storage device up to real-time data analysis and intelligence gathering. You learned about the different file formats, like JSON, CSV, and Parquet. You learned about the different ways in which data can be stored, like structured, semi-structured, and nonstructured. You learned about the many types of data, such as characters and numbers, and data storage concepts like sharding, indexes, and partitions. Data shuffling, data skew, distributed tables, schemas, and table views should all have a place in your mind now.

There are numerous methods for interfacing with data on the Azure platform. When using an Apache Spark pool, you can use PySpark and `DataFrames` to manipulate and store data. SparkSQL is a familiar syntax for those who are more comfortable with T-SQL or other SQL variants. You learned about the DBCC and DDL capabilities and a lot about some mid-level complex DML commands, clauses, and functions. Syntax such as `COPY INTO`, `CROSS APPLY`, `OVER`, `INTERSECT`, `OPENJSON`, and `WITH` should be tightly bound into your data analysis repertoire. And finally, you learned some introductory concepts and theory regarding Big Data processing stages, analytical types, and layers. Ingest, transform, train, store, and serve are the primary Big Data stages. You should have a good understanding of which Azure products are used for each of those stages.

Exam Essentials

Know how data is structured. Relational databases, document databases, and blob storage are ways to store the three primary data structure types. Azure SQL is useful for structured, relational data. Azure Cosmos DB is useful for semi-structured document data, and blob storage is useful for nonstructured data. Remember that ADLS is built on top of blob storage and is most useful for data analytic solutions.

Describe the various kinds of distributed tables. Distributed tables in Azure Synapse Analytics come in three varieties: round-robin, hash, and replicated. Round-robin is the default and means that data is randomly placed across the nodes in your cluster. Hash means that the data is placed across the nodes based on a key that groups similar kinds of data together. Replicated means that all the data is placed onto all the nodes. This type will consume the most amount of storage space.

Be able to name the table categories. Staging tables, fact tables, dimension tables, temporary tables, sink tables, and external tables are all necessary to run an enterprise-level data analytics process.

Understand how to use PySpark, `DataFrames`, and SparkSQL. Although there is no coding exercise on the exam, you will need to review code snippets and determine which one is the most optimal. There might even be small syntactical mistakes that are hard to recognize. Perform the exercises in this book and read through the examples provided in this chapter so that you can recognize common coding and SQL syntax for running data analytics on Apache Spark.

Know how to use DBCC, DDL, and DML. An Azure data engineer needs to know SQL syntax. You must understand the basics as well as the mid-level and advanced commands, clauses, and functions. You will need to know the less common, yet very powerful, SQL syntax for performing sophisticated analytics. SQL syntax is much more advanced than beginner.

Be able to define Big Data. Know the stages, the Azure products, and the analytics types (descriptive, predictive, and prescriptive). Although data layers overlap the stages, they are still used in many data analytics solutions, and therefore, you need to know them well.

Review Questions

Many questions can have more than a single answer. Please select all choices which are true.

1. Which of the following are common data file formats?
   A. JSON
   B. ORC
   C. PHP
   D. XML

2. Which of the following are common data structures?
   A. Structured
   B. Nonstructured
   C. Relational
   D. Organizational

3. Which distributed table copies data to all nodes in the cluster?
   A. Round-robin
   B. Hash
   C. Replicated
   D. All

4. Which kind of table should you use to store data that does not change often?
   A. Dimension
   B. External
   C. Fact
   D. Sink

5. What is PolyBase?
   A. An API for building a DBMS
   B. A tool used for data type conversions
   C. Glue that binds data sources together
   D. A migration utility

6. Which of the following is a data subset from other tables?
   A. View
   B. Index
   C. Schema
   D. Partition

7. Which of the following are valid `DataFrame`, PySpark syntax? (Choose all that apply.)
   A. `df.show(5, truncate=False, vertical=True)`
   B. `df.select('*')`
   C. `df.groupBy('frequency_id').max('value').show()`
   D. `df.createOrReplaceTemporaryView("Brainwaves")`
8. What kind of SQL syntax is considered aggregate functions?
   A. `AVG`
   B. `MIN`
   C. `SUM`
   D. `MAX`
9. Which SQL syntax can you use to work with JSON files?
   A. `OPENROWSET`
   B. `PARSEJSON`
   C. `CLOSEJSON`
   D. `OPENJSON`
10. Which of the following is not a big data stage?
    A. Digest
    B. Store
    C. Serve
    D. Transform

Design and Implement Data Storage

PART II

Chapter 3

Data Sources and Ingestion

EXAM DP-203 OBJECTIVES COVERED IN THIS CHAPTER:

- ✓ Implement a partition strategy
- ✓ Design and implement the data exploration layer
- ✓ Ingest and transform data

WHAT YOU WILL LEARN IN THIS CHAPTER:

- ✓ Where data comes from
- ✓ Ingesting data into a pipeline
- ✓ Migrating and moving data

The data analytics solution you design, implement, monitor, and maintain depends very much on your given scenario or context. But one thing that all data analytics solutions have in common is that they require data. The data can be pushed to your ingestion endpoint, or you can automate some kind of scheduled retrieval process to pull it in. As shown in Figure 3.1, data can be produced by devices, application logs, data files, or on-premises datastores. Each of those data producers and their associated datastore scenarios typically need a different kind of ingestion mechanism.

FIGUER 3.1 Data producers and processing services

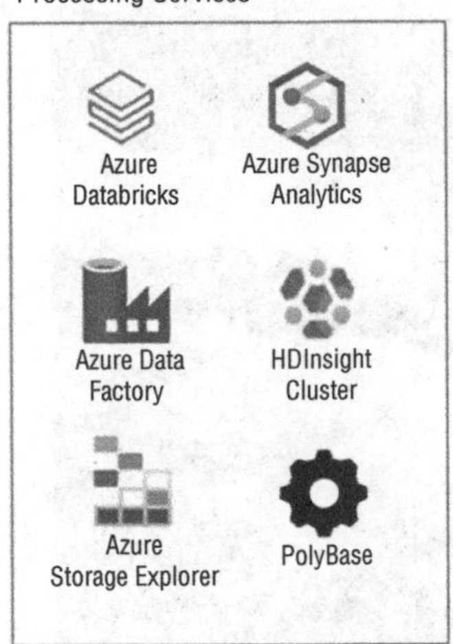

The data source and state dictate the Azure products necessary to ingest the data. The state of data refers to whether the data is streaming or is infrequently or frequently scheduled for ingestion. Table 3.1 provides an overview of Azure products that are useful for ingesting data onto the Azure platform. The "Ingestion type" column identifies the source of the data, and the "Processing and ingesting services" column contains the recommended Azure product to use for its ingestion.

TABLE 3.1 Types and tools for ingestion

Ingestion type	Processing and ingesting services
Ad hoc	Azure Storage Explorer, AzCopy, Azure PowerShell, Azure CLI, Azure Portal
Hadoop clusters	Azure Synapse Analytics, Azure Data Factory, Azure Data Box, Apache DistCp
HDInsight clusters	Azure Synapse Analytics, Azure Data Factory, AzCopy, Apache DistCp
Large datasets	Azure ExpressRoute
Relational data	Azure Synapse Analytics, Azure Data Factory
Streaming data	Azure Stream Analytics, Apache Kafka, HDInsight Storm, Azure Event Hubs, Azure IoT Hub
Web server logs	Azure Data Factory, Azure SDKs, Azure PowerShell, Azure CLI

You need to ingest (aka capture) data and store it before you can progress through the subsequent stages of the Big Data pipeline. It makes sense then that data ingestion is the first stage, but where does all this data come from?

Where Does Data Come From?

Chapter 2, "CREATE DATABASE dbName; GO," discussed the variety, velocity, and volume characteristics of data. You learned that the velocity and volume of data are increasing exponentially and that those two characteristics are the reason running data analytics in the cloud became necessary. Most companies cannot afford to purchase and maintain the compute and storage resources required to handle data at that scale. The variety of data, however, is where your expertise as an Azure Data Engineer becomes most valuable.

After passing the DP-203 exam, you will be expected to be able to provision and configure the necessary Azure products for your data analytics solution. Given a set of requirements, you would know if you needed Azure Stream Analytics, Apache Kafka, Azure Data Factory, Azure Synapse Analytics Spark, or SQL pool (serverless or dedicated), etc. This would be expected from all certified Azure Data Engineer Associates. What is not tested is your ability to know your data and to know the questions you need to answer with it. This is not tested due to the variety of scenarios in which data exists, not only in form and location but also in its meaning. Consider the following scenarios of where data can come from, how it might look, and what you might be able to learn from it:

- Sales forecasting
- Stock trading
- Social media
- Application logs
- IoT devices like a Brain Computer Interface (BCI)

If you want to predict what your company will realize in annual sales for the current year and in the next quarter, what kind of data would you need? Two ideas come into mind. First, the sales trend of over the last few years and quarterly sales comparisons. Consider the following dataset:

```
+------+----------+----------+----------+----------+
| YEAR | SALES Q1 | SALES Q2 | SALES Q3 | SALES Q4 |
+------+----------+----------+----------+----------+
| 2020 | 1000     | 1100     | 1650     | 2900     |
| 2021 | 3050     | 3355     | 5000     | 8750     |
| 2022 | 9200     | ??       |          |          |
+------+----------+----------+----------+----------+
```

Over the past two years you can see a consistent increase in sales. In 2020 total sales were 6,650, and in 2021 total sales were 20,155, which is a little over 300% growth year to year. Using that data, you can predict expected total sales by multiplying the total sales for 2021 by 300%. You might also notice that sales in Q2 have consistently been 10% more than Q1; therefore, it might be safe to predict a sales target of 10,120 in Q2 of 2022. This is a simple example that ignores many elements that can influence predictions. However, as your data analytics become more sophisticated, you can apply algorithms that assess the factors that influence the sales predictions. Then use those assessments to make a sales prediction more precisely and reliably. The data itself may be hosted in a relational database, where you can perform a simple query, or it may be ingested into your pipeline as a CSV file.

People generally invest in the stock market to make money—by buying low and selling high. Some investors try to use historical prices as a basis to predict future prices, instead of looking at a company profit and loss statement or a balance sheet. You can download historical stock prices from many places on the Internet. The data might look something like the following Microsoft stock history:

```
Date,Open,High,Low,Close,Adj Close,Volume
2021-12-21,323.290009,327.730011,319.799988,327.290009,327.290009,24740600
2021-12-22,328.299988,333.609985,325.750000,333.200012,333.200012,24831500
2021-12-23,332.750000,336.390015,332.730011,334.690002,334.690002,19617800
2021-12-27,335.459991,342.480011,335.429993,342.450012,342.450012,19947000
2021-12-28,343.149994,343.809998,340.320007,341.250000,341.250000,15661500
2021-12-29,341.299988,344.299988,339.679993,341.950012,341.950012,15042000
2021-12-30,341.910004,343.130005,338.820007,339.320007,339.320007,15994500
```

Using a similar approach as with the sales prediction example, you can find the direction of the price trend by comparing the daily or quarterly average closing prices. If the price is trending upwards, you might want to buy it; if not, then not. There are numerous properties and elements to employ when analyzing stock prices in hopes of finding the one that makes you wealthy. That is exactly the point. Although you have the data, the data alone will not be enough to gather insights from. Using the data in isolation or in collaboration with a massive number of other sources and data types can still result in unexpected results. The magic sauce typically comes from the individual (you) performing the data analytics, because in many cases that individual also has the experience with that specific type or variety of data.

Data also can come from social media outlets in the form of comments or ratings. An Azure Cognitive Service called the *Language Understanding Intelligent Service (LUIS)* can help you understand the meaning of comments. LUIS converts a comment into a meaning using something called an *intent*. If the comments contain words such as "bad," "angry," "hard," or "upset," then LUIS returns an intent equal to something like "negative." If the comments contain words like "happy," "love," "friends," or "good," then the result would be "positive." On platforms like Twitter, Instagram, and Facebook, where there are billions of messages daily, you might be able to gauge the societal sentiment for a given day. With more focused analytics, you might be able to narrow down society's opinion on a specific current issue. Data can be uploaded to LUIS in bulk in the following format:

```
Business is good
Can you recommend a good restaurant?
That smells bad
Have a good trip
That person is a very good student
That's too bad
I feel good
There is a restaurant over there, but I don't think it's very good
I'm happy
```

Each row represents a comment, with a line break symbolizing the end of the phrase. The response to each phrase is a rating in JSON format, similar to the following. The `score` is a measurement of how probable the `intent` is true; a 1 would represent a 100 percent certainty that the `intent` of the sentence is positive.

```
{
 "query": "Business is good",
 "topScoringIntent":
 {
 "intent": "positive",
 "score": "0.856282966"
 }
}
```

Monitoring the availability and performance of an application requires activity logs. The frequency and utilization of the application is the leading factor when it comes to the volume and velocity of data generated—that, and the verbose level of logging, which is configured in the monitored application. Verbosity has to do with if you want information-level logs or just the critical error log. Information logs occur much more often than critical errors—at least you hope that is the case. When the application is coded to generate logs, you can decide to store them and analyze them offline, or you can monitor them in real time and trigger alerts that immediately notify someone who can take an action, depending on the level and criticality the application has on the business. The format in which these logs are written is totally open and up to the team who codes the logic into the application. Log files are typically text-based and may resemble the following:

```
Date time s-sitename cs-method sc-status sc-substatus sc-bytes time-taken
2022-05-02 12:01 CSHARPGUITAR POST 500 0 2395146 44373
2022-05-02 12:01 CSHARPGUITAR POST 404 14 11118 783
2022-05-02 12:02 CSHARPGUITAR POST 403 6 8640 1055
2022-05-02 12:04 CSHARPGUITAR POST 503 1 32911 104437
2022-05-02 12:04 CSHARPGUITAR POST 200 0 32911 95
```

Sometimes the log files will contain an error message, or sometimes the log only contains the error number, which requires additional analysis to understand. Here is another example of an application log:

```
Date time cs-version cs-method sc-status s-siteid s-reason s-queuename
2022-11-09 08:15 HTTP/1.1 GET 503 2 Disabled csharpguitar
2022-11-09 08:16 HTTP/1.1 GET 403 1 Forbidden brainjammer
2022-11-09 08:16 HTTP/1.1 GET 400 1 BadRequest brainjammer
2022-11-09 08:19 HTTP/1.1 HEAD 400 2 Hostname csharpguitar
2022-11-09 08:20 HTTP/1.1 POST 411 1 LengthRequired brainjammer
```

On-premises application logs are typically written to a file on the machine where the application runs. In that scenario you would need to pull them at scheduled intervals and ingest them into your data analytics pipeline. The Azure platform includes numerous products to provide this kind of analysis and alerting, such as Application Insights, Log Analytics, and Azure Monitor.

Relatively new sources of data producers are IoT devices. Humidity trackers, light bulbs, automobiles, alarm clocks, and brain computer interfaces (BCIs) are all examples of IoT devices. The examples of data analytics for the remainder of this book will have to do with the BCI that was described in Chapter 2. You have already seen many examples of the data generated from the BCI that was captured and stored on a local workstation, then uploaded ad hoc to the Azure platform. The same data could have been saved to an Azure Cosmos DB as a JSON file or into an Azure SQL database in real time. An objective for this analysis is to stream the brain data and determine in real time what activity (aka scenario) the person is performing. The following is an example of a brain wave reading in JSON format:


```
{"Session": {
 "Scenario": "ClassicalMusic",
 "POWReading": [
 {
 "ReadingDate": " 2021-09-12T09:00:18.492",
 "Counter": 0,
 "AF3": [
 {
 "THETA": 15.585,
 "ALPHA": 5.892,
 "BETA_L": 3.415,
 "BETA_H": 1.195,
 "GAMMA": 0.836
 }]}]}
}
```


And the following is a similar reading is CSV format:


```
Scenario,Counter,Sensor,THETA,ALPHA,GAMMA
TikTok,5,AF3,9.681,3.849,0.738
TikTok,6,Pz,8.392,4.142,1.106
```


Data comes in a large variety of formats and from many different sources, and it can have very diverse interpretations and use cases. This section attempted to show this by discussing a few different scenarios where you would benefit from provisioning some Azure data analytics products. Your greatest contribution and impact lies in your ability to ingest relevant data from numerous sources and formats, then run it through the pipeline and find business insights from it. The "running it through the pipeline" part requires some coding—PySpark, DML, or C#—and an understanding of what the data means and what questions you are trying to answer.

Design a Data Storage Structure

In this chapter you will provision numerous Azure data analytics products. By doing so, you will begin to understand more about the products and their features, which can help you create and choose the best tool for your given solution requirements. Choosing a proper service for a scenario results in having a solid design. Table 3.2 reviews the mapping between Azure datastores and the data model supported within them.

TABLE 3.2 Analytical datastores

Datastore	Data model
Azure Analysis Services	Tabular semantic
Azure Cosmos DB	Document, graph, key-value, wide column store
Azure Data Explorer	Relational, telemetry, time series
Azure Data Lake Storage	File storage
Azure Synapse Spark pool	Wide column store
Azure Synapse SQL pool	Relational with columnar
Hive on HDInsight	In-memory
SQL Database	Relational

Throughout the numerous Big Data stages, storage is required. As data is ingested, it needs to be stored before moving to the next stage. Each stage requires a place to store the transformed data, and once the transformation is complete, the final version also needs to be stored. An Azure product that plays a central role in the entire Big Data analytics solution is Azure Data Lake Storage (ADLS).

Design an Azure Data Lake Solution

A data lake is defined as a repository of data stored in its natural, unformatted, unmodified, or raw form. Can include structured, semi-structured, unstructured, and binary data. A successor to data mart or data warehouse, a data lake is a collection of your datastores and the data within them. On Azure these datastores are products like ADLS, Azure SQL, and Azure Cosmos DB. Continue reading this book to learn about the numerous Azure products and how they all work together to provide a data lake. You have already provisioned, configured, and used an Azure SQL database and an Azure Cosmos DB. Another Azure product that plays a significant role in your data lake is an ADLS container.

Complete Exercise 3.1 to provision an Azure storage account and an ADLS container.

EXERCISE 3.1

Create an Azure Data Lake Storage Container

1. Log in to the Azure portal at `https://portal.azure.com` ➢ click the menu button on the top left of the browser ➢ click + Create a Resource ➢ click Storage ➢ click Storage Account; if not found, search for Storage Account ➢ select it ➢ and then click Create.
2. Select the subscription and resource group where you want the storage account to reside ➢ enter a storage account name (I used **csharpguitar**) ➢ enter a location (should be the same as a resource group location but is not required) ➢ and then select Locally Redundant Storage (LRS) from the Replication drop-down. Leave all the remaining options as the defaults.
3. Click the Next: Advanced > button ➢ check the Enable Hierarchical Namespace check box in the Data Lake Storage Gen2 section ➢ check the Enable Network File System v3 check box in the Blob Storage section (if this is grayed out, leave it as default); feel free to navigate through the other tabs but leave everything else as default ➢ on the Review + Create tab ➢ and then click Create.
4. Once the provision is complete, navigate to the Overview blade of the storage account. In the center of the blade, you will see something similar to Figure 3.2.

FIGUER 3.2 An Azure storage account Overview blade

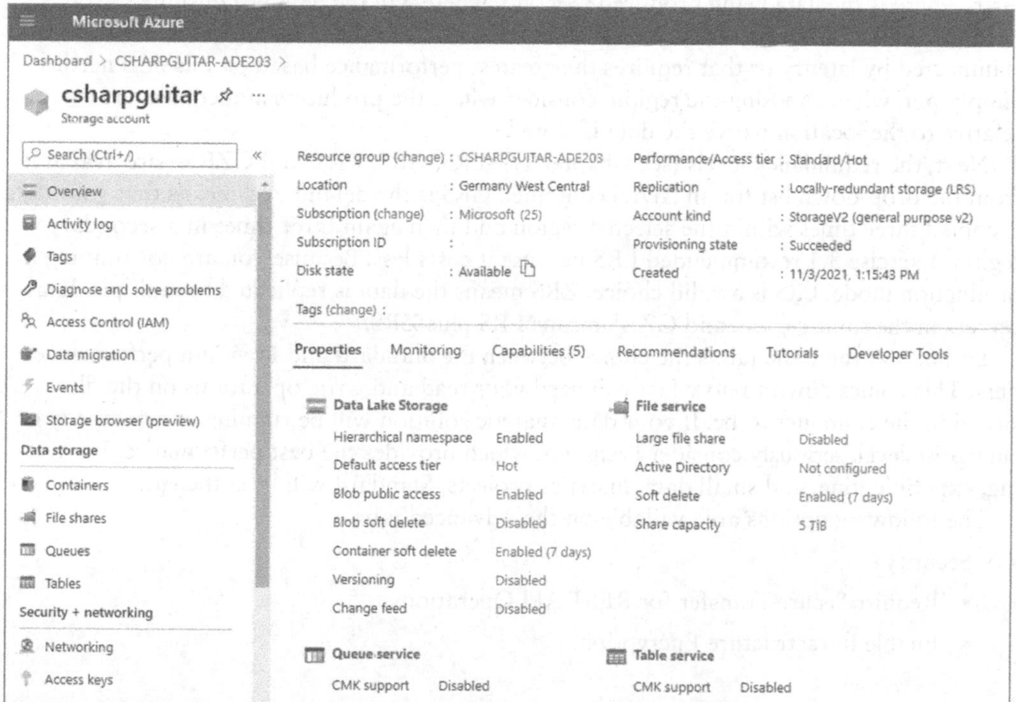

EXERCISE 3.1 *(continued)*

5. Click the Data Lake Storage link on the Overview blade or Containers from the navigation menu ➢ click + Container ➢ enter a Name (I used **brainjammer**) ➢ and then click Create.

Exercise 3.1 walked you through provisioning an ADLS container. You encountered numerous options, beginning with the first items selected, the subscription and resource group. Remember that an Azure subscription is the location where billing happens. It is a grouping of all provisioned Azure products. You can have multiple subscriptions within what is called a *management group*. Similarly, you can have multiple resource groups. A resource group logically groups together resources within a subscription and is where you would typically create all the provisioned Azure resources for a given project, thereby providing better visibility of the costs on a project basis. Having all the related Azure products grouped together is also helpful. The hierarchy, management group ➢ subscription ➢ resource group, is also the place where you typically enforce role-based access control (RBAC) restrictions. Granting access and privileges to groups of individuals (not to individuals themselves) is recommended at the resource group level. See Chapter 1, "Gaining the Azure Data Engineer Associate Certification," for a review of RBAC.

When selecting the region (aka datacenter location), you need to consider two things. First, where is the data being produced? Second, where will the data be consumed? You need to choose a location that is closest to both—closest to the most critical entity that is impacted by latency or that requires the greatest performance based on business need. Simply put, when choosing the region, consider where the producers and consumers are relative to the location where the data is stored.

Next, the redundancy levels (see Chapter 1)—LRS, GRS, ZRS, and GZRS—are available from the drop-down list for an ADLS container. GRS is the default and means that your data is copied three times within the selected region and then again three times in a secondary region. Exercise 3.1 recommended LRS because it costs less. Because you are not running in production mode, LRS is a valid choice. ZRS means the data is replicated to multiple datacenters in the same region, and GZRS means LRS plus ZRS.

Ending out the Basic tab is the choice between the Standard and Premium performance tiers. This comes down to how fast you need your read and write operations on the files stored in the container to be. If your data analytic solution will be running at a company or enterprise level, seriously consider Premium, which provides the best performance. For testing, experimenting, and small data analytics projects, Standard will be sufficient.

The following options are available on the Advanced tab:

- Security
  - Require Secure Transfer for REST API Operations.
  - Enable Infrastructure Encryption.

- Enable Blob Public Access.
- Enable Storage Account Key Access.
- Default to Azure Active Directory Authorization in the Azure Portal.
- Minimum TLS Version.

- Data Lake Storage Gen2
  - Enable Hierarchical Namespace.
- SSH File Transfer Protocol (SFTP)
  - Enable SFTP.
- Blob Storage
  - Enable Network File System v3.
  - Allow Cross-tenant Replication.

Begining with the selections you made during the provisioning of ADLS in Exercise 3.1, start with Enable Hierarchical Namespaces. If you do not select this, instead of getting an ADLS container, you get a general-purpose v2-based blob container. As discussed in Chapter 1, blob containers are flat and do not support wildcard syntax; they also do not perform well when files are renamed or deleted. A hierarchical namespace renders better performance when storing and retrieving files when compared to a flat file hierarchical structure. The hierarchical namespace structure also aligns well with the implementation of access control lists (ACLs), which are used to control access to files.

The other option selected during Exercise 3.1 was Enable Network File System v3. This option can only be set during provision and cannot be changed, and it is required for many products to be configured as a Linked Service in Azure Synapse Analytics. This option allows files to be shared across the network; if the Enable Network File System v3 option is not enabled, the data cannot be shared. This means that you would have to provision an Azure storage account to enable this, which may or may not have serious implications. For example, if you have already transferred a large amount of data to the Azure storage account and now must move it to a new account, the transfer can be both costly and time-consuming.

You learned about endpoints in Chapter 1. Most Azure products have a globally discoverable address accessible over HTTP. Requiring secure transfer for REST API operations enforces that the protocol is HTTPS and disallows access using HTTP only. By default, the data you place into an Azure storage account is encrypted. This is known as *encrypted at rest*. When you enable infrastructure encryption, your data is encrypted twice: once at the default service level and then again at the infrastructure level. Enabling blob public access allows clients to access the blob over the public endpoint; both anonymous access or authenticated access options are available. If blob public access is disabled, then anonymous access to the files stored in the container is allowed but not the default. You can still apply ACLs on the container to restrict access, even though access is initially anonymous.

Clients typically connect to an Azure storage account over HTTPS. The Enable Storage Account Key Access option creates a key to append at the end of the endpoint URL and used to authenticate the client. This is a valid approach, but in most cases using a managed identity or Azure AD is a more secure, recommended, and long-term approach. The storage account keys could become compromised or be re-created. In both cases the ability to connect to the Azure storage account would be impacted for some time. In mission critical scenarios, this could be a catastrophe. It is possible to access the contents in your ADLS container via the Azure Portal. To protect the ADLS contents using Azure AD, enable the Default to Azure Active Directory Authorization in Azure Portal the option. HTTPS has historically used Secure Sockets Layer (SSL), the latest version of which is 3.0. There is now Transport Layer Security (TLS), with the most widely supported and secure version being TLS 1.2. To enforce the use of only the most secure version of encryption over HTTPS, select Version 1.2 from the Minimum TLS Version drop-down box. Be warned, however, that many client machines do not support this version. If you enforce TLS 1.2, it will cause all client machines that do not support that version to fail when connecting.

If you have a business need to open access to an FTP client, you can enable the Enable SFTP option. Recall from Chapter 1 where you were introduced to Azure Active Directory and that it is bound to a tenant. By default, you are not able to replicate content in your container to another Azure AD tenant. If this is necessary, enable the Allow Cross-tenant Replication option. Azure Files, Tables and Queues are not in scope here, so the final two options are not discussed; you have enough on your plate already, but the option name itself is enough to gather its purpose.

Finally, when creating the ADLS container in Exercise 3.1, you might have noticed the Public Access Level drop-down, which contained Private (no anonymous access), Blob (anonymous read access for blobs only), and Container (anonymous read access for containers and blobs). If you select Private, then the client must have an authorized credential to access the container, which means the client must be configured to send this along with the request for files. If you select Blob, then all blobs in the container can be accessed from any client without authentication. By selecting Container, not only are the blobs accessible, but the client has the ability to list the contents of the container and discover its contents.

Some Azure products generate costs even when not actively used, whereas others do not. An empty ADLS container does not incur any costs, but one that consumes space does. You should remove resources that are no longer being used. Make sure to perform due diligence when provisioning Azure products, as you will be required to pay for them when consumed.

The next tab, Networking, provides options to configure how the Azure storage account is accessed using network-level constraints. The Network Connectivity section includes an option named Connectivity Method, where you will find the following possible values:

- Public Endpoint (All Networks)
- Public Endpoint (Selected Networks)
- Private Endpoint

The default is Public Endpoint (All Networks), which means the globally discoverable URL is available via the Internet. This does not mean anyone can access the content in the Azure storage account; it simply means the endpoint is "pingable." If you select Public Endpoint (Selected Networks), you are prompted to select an existing virtual network (VNet) or create a new one. Once the network is configured, only resources existing in the VNET can access the Azure storage account. The connection protection is from inbound traffic only, and the global endpoint is still visible. The Private Endpoint option will remove the global endpoint from Internet discoverability and requires the binding with a VNET.

The Network Routing section includes an option named Routing Preferences with the following possible values:

- Microsoft Network Routing
- Internet Routing

When you select Microsoft Network Routing, traffic to your Azure Storage Account will enter the Microsoft network as quickly as possible. The Internet Routing option routes the traffic to the Azure network closest to where the Azure Storage Account is hosted. For example, if your ADLS container is in the western United States and the client wanting access is in the eastern United States, and if Microsoft Network Routing is enabled, the traffic will enter the Microsoft network from the eastern US datacenter. Then all traffic between the client and the ADLS container would flow primarily within the Microsoft network. If Internet Routing is selected, the traffic from the eastern US would traverse the Internet to the western US and enter the Microsoft network there. That would mean that most of the traffic between the client and the endpoint would be transmitted over the Internet instead of within the Microsoft network.

The last tab, Data Protection, enables you to configure some recovery, tracking, and access controls. Many of these options are disabled when ADLS Gen2 is the targeted storage container type. This is because many of the options have a great impact on performance and can cause latency when enabled. Data protection options are different between blob and ADLS containers; options that are not available are grayed out and will be disabled in the Azure Portal. The following list contains all available Azure Storage container options:

- Recovery
  - Enable Point-in-time Restore for Containers.
  - Enable Soft Delete for Blobs.
  - Enable Soft Delete for Containers.
  - Enable Soft Delete for Shares.
- Tracking
  - Enable Versioning for Blobs.
  - Enable Blob Change Feed.
- Access Control
  - Enable Version-level Immutability Support.

If the data in your container becomes corrupt or gets deleted, having the Enabled Point-in-time Restore for Containers option configured means that regular backups have been performed, so you would not lose everything. You could then roll back to a specific time where you know the data was in a valid state and then recover from that backup. This option is not yet supported when you are using hierarchical namespaces. When the option Enable Soft Delete for Blobs is selected, files that were deleted are stored for 7 days by default, just in case you want to recover the deletion. The same goes for the Enable Soft Delete for Containers and Enable Soft Delete for Shares options, where deletions are stored for a default of 7 days before being permanently deleted. Tracking changes and version control of your blobs in the container is important for monitoring what is changed and by whom. Both Enable Versioning for Blobs and Enable Blob Change Feed provide the features to achieve that. You might have a requirement that necessitates the retention of complete historical versions of any updated file. Instead of performing a change and updating the version metadata for that file, a new file is created with the update and the old one is maintained for historical reference. To achieve that, check the Enable Version-level Immutability Support check box.

While you are in the ADLS mindset, complete Exercise 3.2 to load some brain wave data to an ADLS container.

EXERCISE 3.2

Upload Data to an ADLS Container

1. Access the GitHub repository located at `https://github.com/benperk/ADE`. Click the <> Code button, and then select Download ZIP from the drop-down list. The compressed download, `ADE-main.zip`, is approximately 200 MB. Navigate to the downloaded file. The `BrainwaveData` directory includes folders named `SessionCSV` and `SessionJson`. Decompress the contents of those two folders.
2. Download and install Azure Storage Explorer at `https://azure.microsoft.com/features/storage-explorer`. Note that Azure Storage Explorer uses AzCopy.
3. Once logged in, expand the subscription where you provisioned the ADLS container in Exercise 3.1 ➢ expand the Storage Accounts group and then Blob Containers ➢ select the ADLS container where you want to add the brain wave files (in my example, `brainwaves`) ➢ click Upload ➢ select Upload Folder ➢ navigate to the location where you saved the uncompressed files ➢ and then select the `SessionCSV` folder. Leave the Destination directory as default. Figure 3.3 illustrates the Upload Folder window. Click Upload.

FIGUER 3.3 The Upload folder in Azure Storage Explorer

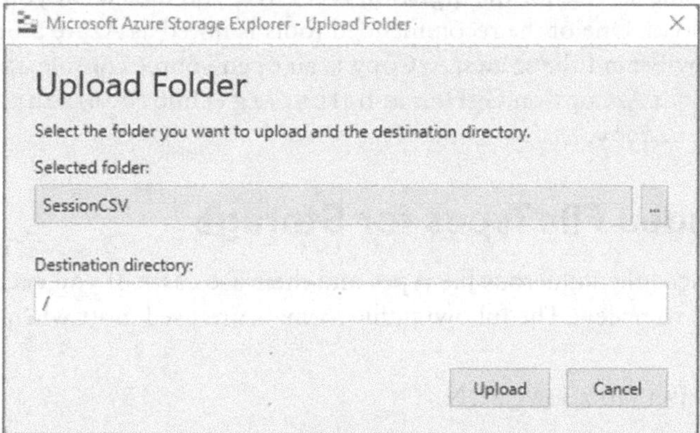

4. Once the upload is complete, perform the same upload procedure with the `SessionJson` folder. Once both uploads are complete, you should see something similar to Figure 3.4.

FIGUER 3.4 Files uploaded to ADLS using Azure Storage Explorer

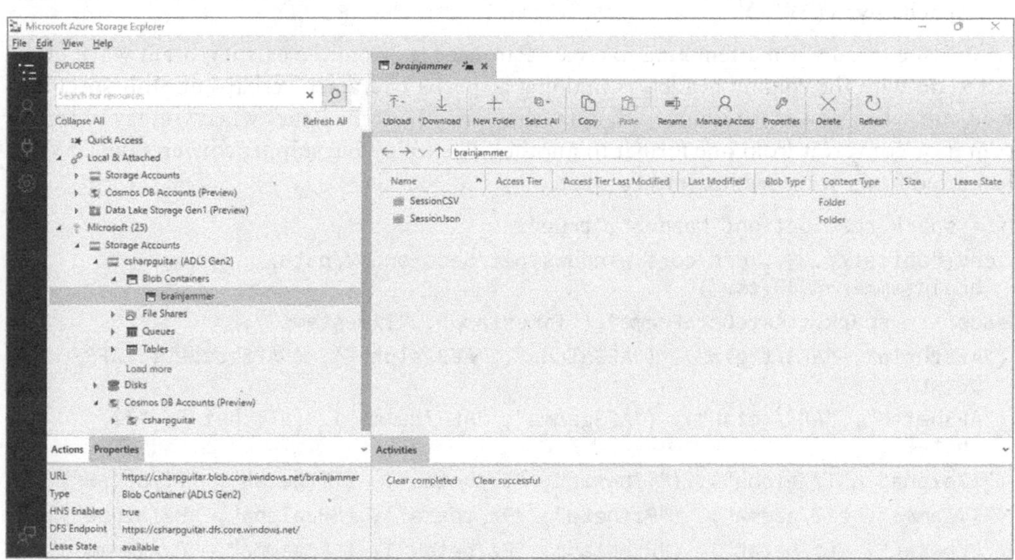

5. Navigate through the different directories to get comfortable with the structure and contents.

Refer to Table 3.1 and try to determine what kind of ingestion this was. Did you use the correct processing service for the ingestion type? Yes, you did. What you just performed was an ad hoc upload. One of the recommended tools is noted as Azure Storage Explorer, which uses AzCopy behind the scenes. AzCopy is an open-source console application. You can learn more about AzCopy on GitHub at `https://github.com/Azure/azure-storage-azcopy`.

Recommended File Types for Storage

Chapter 2 introduced the numerous file types and their use cases. If you need a refresher, go back to Chapter 2 to review. The following file formats are used most when working in the Big Data context:

- JavaScript Object Notation (JSON)
- Apache Parquet
- Optimized Row Columnar (ORC)
- Extensible Markup Language (XML)
- Yet Another Markup Language (YAML)
- Comma-separated values (CSV)
- Apache Avro (AVRO)

An issue faced when attempting to create Parquet files from the existing brain wave files had to do with the column headers containing a special character. Perhaps not this specific issue, but when you are working with data, there may be some issues when you try to transform it or convert it from one format to another. The following snippet converts the CSV formatted brain wave session into Parquet:

```
df = spark.read.option("header","true")
 .csv("abfss://..@...dfs.core.windows.net/SessionCSV/path/
   brainjammer-0900.csv")
headers = spark.createDataFrame([("Timestamp", "Timestamp"),
 ("AF3theta", "AF3/theta"), ("AF3alpha", "AF3/alpha"), ("AF3betaL", "AF3/
   betaL"),
 ("AF3betaH", "AF3/betaH"), ("AF3gamma", "AF3/gamma"), ("T7theta", "T7/
   theta"),
 ("T7alpha", "T7/alpha"), ("T7betaL", "T7/betaL"), ("T7betaH", "T7/betaH"),
 ("T7gamma", "T7/gamma"), ("Pztheta", "Pz/theta"), ("Pzalpha", "Pz/alpha"),
 ("PzbetaL", "Pz/betaL"), ("PzbetaH", "Pz/betaH"), ("Pzgamma", "Pz/gamma"),
 ("T8theta", "T8/theta"), ("T8alpha", "T8/alpha"), ("T8betaL", "T8/betaL"),
 ("T8betaH", "T8/betaH"), ("T8gamma", "T8/gamma"), ("AF4theta", "AF4/theta"),
 ("AF4alpha", "AF4/alpha"), ("AF4betaL", "AF4/betaL"), ("AF4betaH", "AF4/
   betaH"),
 ("AF4/gamma", "AF4/gamma")],['newHeader','oldHeader'])
```

```
newHeaders = headers.sort('oldHeader').select('newHeader').rdd
 .flatMap(lambda x: x).collect()
dfh = df.toDF(*newHeaders)
dfh.write.mode("overwrite").parquet("brainjammer-0900.parquet")
dfp = spark.read.parquet("brainjammer-0900.parquet")
dfp.select("*").show(5)
```

This code loads an existing session into a `DataFrame` and then creates a new `DataFrame` to contain the old and new headers. The new headers replace the old ones in the original `DataFrame` named `df` and then are placed into another `DataFrame` named `dfh`. That `DataFrame`, `dfh`, is then written to the `/user/trusted-service-user` directory on the originally referenced ADLS container in the first line of code. Then the new Parquet file is loaded into a new `DataFrame` named `dfp` and queried. Figure 3.5 illustrates how the Parquet files are stored in the Storage browser blade in the Azure Portal.

FIGUER 3.5 Storing Parquet files in an ADLS container

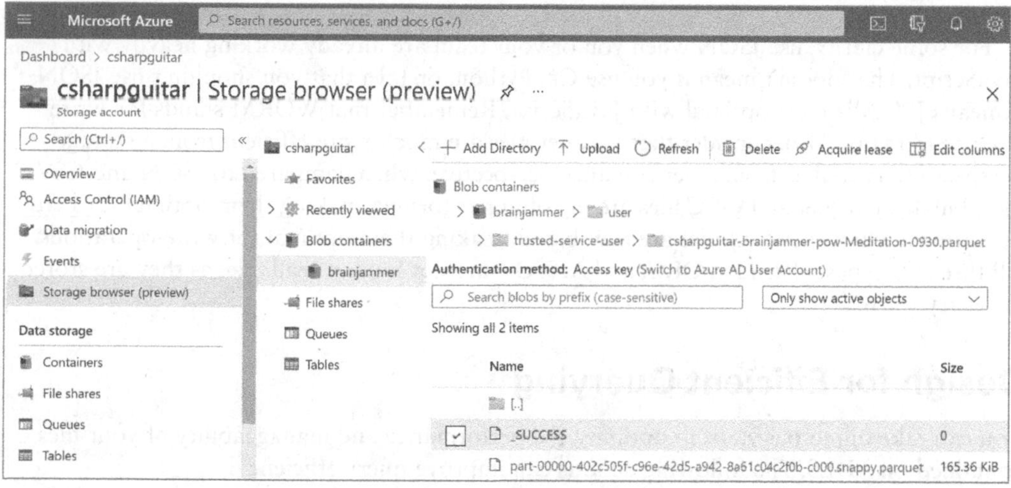

Similar views of these files—and all files in your ADLS container—are possible from numerous sources. Azure Synapse Analytics has a feature to navigate through the ADLS content, as does Azure Storage Explorer. Note that Azure Storage Explorer has a handy Download feature.

Recommended File Types for Analytical Queries

Table 3.3 provides a refresher on when to use which file types.

TABLE 3.3 File type use cases

File type	Synapse pool type	Use case
JSON	SQL and Spark	Large complex datasets, using JavaScript
Parquet	Spark	WORM operations with Hadoop or Spark
ORC	Spark	Apache Hive, WORM operations
XML	SQL and Spark	Data validation with content variety
YAML	N/A	Primarily for configurations, not data
CSV	SQL and Spark	Small datasets, simple, using Excel
AVRO	Spark	Write heavy, I/O operations, optimal for batch processing

For some clarity, use JSON when you or your team are already working heavily with JavaScript. That doesn't mean if you use C#, Python, or Java that you shouldn't use JSON; it means JSON is most optimal with JavaScript. Remember that WORM stands for write once, read many. Also, consider that Parquet files are much more efficient from a storage perspective, as well as from a performance perspective, when compared to JSON and CSV files. Finally, Parquet and ORC files are in columnar format, making them optimal for read operations, whereas AVRO files are row-based, making them optimal for write operations. All three file types—Parquet, ORC, and ARVO—are not human readable, as they are stored in binary form.

Design for Efficient Querying

You can take numerous steps to optimize the performance and manageability of your files contained on ADLS. The following actions can improve query efficiency:

- File size, type, and quantity
- Directory structure
- Partitioning
- Designing for read operations

Use this information as a basis for the design of your storage structure.

File Size, Type, and Quantity

The more data contained within a file, the larger it is and the longer it takes to parse it. The most efficient size of file has a lot to do with the platform on which you will perform your analytics, i.e., SQL or Spark pools. Some characteristics impact both:

- Many small files can negatively impact performance.
- File should be at least 4 MB due to ADLS transaction costs. Read and write procedures are charged in 4 MB increments. If the operation takes place on a file 4 KB in size, you still get charged for 4 MB.

Other characteristics are pool specific:

- SQL pool
  - A file size between 100 MB and 10 GB is optimal.
  - Convert large CSV or JSON files to Parque.
  - When using `OPENROWSET`, have equally sized files.
- Spark pool
  - A file size between 256 MB and 100 GB is optimal.
  - Use Parquet files as often as possible.

The snippet shown earlier that converts a CSV file to Parquet might be useful for managing file size. Instead of loading only a single file into a `DataFrame`, load 10 or 20 files, and then write all that data to a single Parquet file. That single file would then be the size of all the others combined.

Directory Structure

The structuring of your files into directories has an impact on both manageability and performance. Figure 3.6 illustrates the folder structure for the brainjammer data. The directory is structured in a way that makes it relatively intuitive where data is located. If you want CSV, JSON, or Parquet files, or if you want `MetalMusic` brain wave sessions in JSON format, they are easy to find. This means that anyone can find the desired files without documentation or training, making the directory structure manageable and well designed.

FIGURER 3.6 The brainjammer directory structure

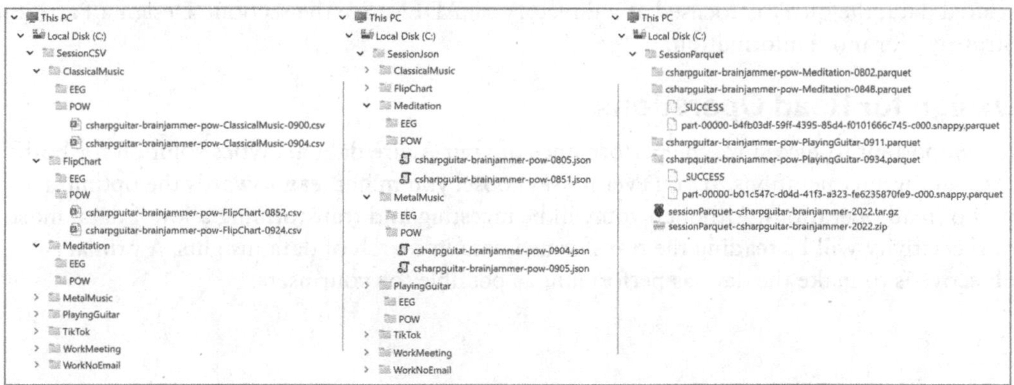

From a performance perspective, note that the file names contain the MODE (EEG or POW) and the SCENARIO. Notice, also, that the JSON-formatted files do not contain the SCENARIO. Assume that all JSON data files, instead of being stored into a well-designed directory structure, are placed into a single folder. You would then need to query all the files to find which were related to a specific SCENARIO. That would not be as performant as querying a smaller group of files that are grouped logically together. An alternative and very common directory structure for managing files contains dates. Consider the following directory template:

```
{location}/{subject}/{direction}/{yyyy}/{mm}/{dd}/{hh}/*
```

Here are a few examples of how this might look:

```
EMEA/brainjammer/in/2022/01/07/09/
NA/brainjammer/out/2022/01/07/10/
```

The {location} identifies the physical location of the data, followed by an identifier or {subject} of what the data is. The {direction} folder can help identify the state of the data. For example, {in} might symbolize that the data is raw and needs to be read and processed, whereas {out} means the data has been processed at least once. The folders that identify the file ingestion, {yyyy}/{mm}/{dd}/{hh}, give you a well-designed directory structure. Being able to query data in a constrained context, such as year, month, day, and hour, improves performance when compared to parsing all files for a given year and month.

Partitioning

As discussed in Chapter 2, partitioning is a way to logically structure data. The closer queried data physically exists together, the faster the query will render results. What you learned in Chapter 2 related to PolyBase and CTAS, where you added a PARTITION argument to the WITH clause; therefore, the data was allocated properly across the node pools. In this context, however, the focus is on files and directory structures on ADLS. In the same way you learned about partitions previously, partitions in this context are created by the directory structures themselves. Instead of a query being constrained to a node that contains all the related data, the query is focused at a directory on ADLS.. See the section "Design a Partition Strategy" for more information.

Design for Read Operations

It is important to maximize the performance of your Azure data analytics solution for both read and write operations. If you ever must choose, you might lean towards the optimization of read operations. Although you will be ingesting and transforming a lot of data, most of the activity will be reading the transformed data in search of data insights. A primary objective is to make the data as performant as possible for your users.

Design for Data Pruning

Consider the word *pruning* to mean the same as *elimination* or *deletion*. Removing unnecessary data from your data lake, from a table, or from a file, or removing an entire file, will improve query performance. The less data needing querying means less time required to query. Managing data will also prevent your data lake from becoming a *data swamp*. Removing unnecessary data means that what remains is relevant and valuable, which is not the case in a data swamp. A data swamp contains large amounts of duplicated and/or irrelevant data, which can negatively influence performance, insights, and costs. Storing excessive, unneeded, or irrelevant data will increase costs, since you pay for storage space. Pruning data is not only a performance-related activity but also a cost-reduction and data-integrity maneuver.

Files generally have some associated metadata that includes a creation and/or update timestamp. You can use this to determine if the content within the file is still valid. Data storage duration can depend on the kind of data. For example, if the data is application or performance logging, it probably doesn't make sense to keep that for years and years. You might need to save data for some extended timeframe due to governance and compliance reasons, but application logs are not as important as, for example, financial or customer order history. Having your files in the aforementioned directory structure would also be helpful for identifying the age and relevance of your data.

Removing data from a file itself typically requires a parameter that identifies the state of the row or column, perhaps at timestamp. You could query files based on that timestamp, write new files that match the query result, and then purge or archive the old files. Finally, there is also a term called *time to live (TTL)* that can be applied to data. This setting is mostly related to datastores like SQL Server, Azure Cosmos DB, and MongoDB, but knowing it is available in those scenarios is worth mentioning. TTL is a metadata setting that determines how long the associated data is considered relevant.

Design a Folder Structure That Represents the Levels of Data Transformation

Once data is ingested and initially stored into what is commonly referred to as a *data landing zone (DLZ)*, the data will flow through the other Big Data stages. More, in-depth detail about the Big Data transformation stage is covered in Part III, "Develop Data Processing." For now, only the file structure to support data transformation is important. The data is stored in the Raw File zone immediately after ingestion. Data in the Raw File zone means it is neither in a state necessary for data analysis and insights gathering nor does it have an enforced schema. The data in a raw state might not even be in a state that is queryable at all. Table 3.4 describes the data landing zones.

TABLE 3.4 Data landing zones

Zone name	Description
Raw File, raw, bronze	Data is in its original state after initial ingestion.
Cleansed Data, enriched, silver	Data is in a queryable state.
Business Data, workspace, gold	Data is ready for analytics and insights gathering.

You might notice that there are numerous names for each zone. There is no universal industry guideline for the zone names, so there are a few. The point is that you give each zone a name that identifies the state of the data. Figure 3.7 shows an example of how raw files might end up in an ADLS container. This data could be pushed by an authorized client or pulled from a data source using an Azure function, for example.

FIGUER 3.7 The brainjammer `raw-files` directory

Note in Figure 3.7 the variety of file formats in which brainjammer sessions and modes (i.e., EEG and POW) are captured and stored. In addition to the file format variety, notice the directory structure and names. Simply by looking at the directory structure, you can make some conclusions about the state of the data within it. The next iteration of transformation might look like something in Figure 3.8.

FIGUER 3.8 The brainjammer `cleansed-data` directory

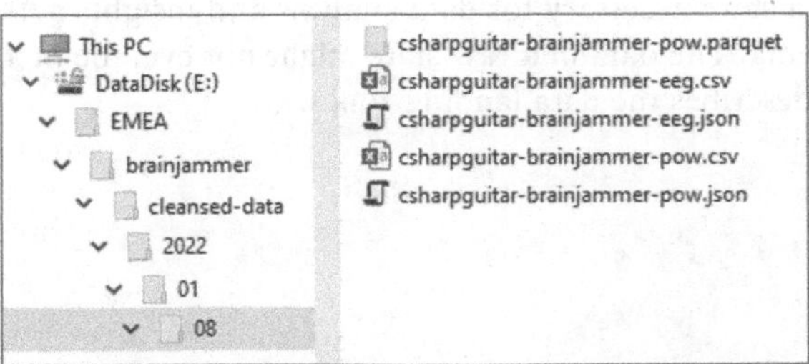

Notice that there are fewer files. It is safe to conclude that a process or procedure took place that analyzed all the files in the `raw-files` directory. The procedure likely grouped and sorted the data, by file format type, into single files. This can be a very complicated activity, functionally speaking; this step requires not only technical knowledge but also significant experience with the data being transformed. It is outside the scope of this book to attempt a conversion from EEG brain waves to POW brain waves. In order to make that conversion, you would need to have an in-depth understanding of the device that captured the brain waves as well as standard brain functions. That is why, in this example, those files were not merged. Once the process completes, the transformed files are stored in the `cleansed-data` directory and are now considered query ready. The final step in the workflow (aka data flow) would be to get the data files into the most optimal form for performing data analytics and business insights gathering (Figure 3.9).

FIGUER 3.9 The brainjammer `business-data` directory

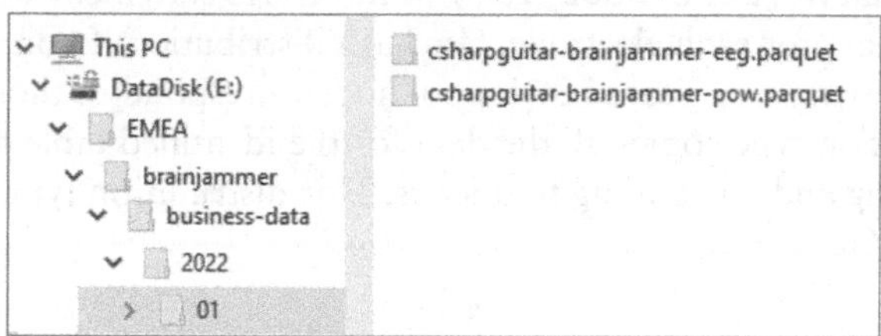

Notice again that there are fewer files in the `business-data` directory—in this case, a single file per brain wave mode. Keep in mind that the number of files depends on file type and analytics stack on which the analysis will be performed. Since these files are in Parquet format, it means they will be analyzed using a Spark pool, which has a recommended file size of between 256 MB and 100 GB. You would create as many or as few files that work best in your scenario. Data in this DLZ is considered ready for reporting. A final point is that some large enterprise implementations would place each DLZ into a different ADLS container or even different Azure storage accounts. This would be done for better isolation, redundancy, to manage growth, to better align with team roles and responsibilities, or for compliance reasons. Just keep in mind that your design is not confined to a single ADLS container in a single location.

Design a Distribution Strategy

When running your Big Data workloads using Azure Synapse Analytics dedicated SQL pools, how you distribute your data is worthy of meticulous consideration. To summarize, distribution is concerned with the way data is loaded onto the numerous nodes (aka compute machine) running your data analytics queries. When you execute a query, the platform chooses a node to perform the execution on. That node may or may not locally contain the data required to complete the query. If the node contains all the data for the query, you would expect a faster query time when compared to a query run on a node that must pull the data from another location before executing the query. There are three different distribution techniques for data in this context:

- Round-robin
- Hash
- Replicated

Round-robin is the default distribution type. The distribution of data across the nodes (you get a maximum of 60) is random. In a scenario where you need to frequently load or refresh data, this would be a good choice for distribution. A hash distribution type spreads data across nodes based on an identified key. For example, if you are analyzing brain waves, you can place all readings with an `ELECTRODE = 1` onto a specific node. All queries where this data selection is requested will be routed to the specific node that contains the data. Consider that there are five electrodes. Adding the snippet `DISTRIBUTION = HASH([ELECTRODE_ID])` to the CTAS statement would result in five nodes receiving the data for each electrode. Use hash distribution if your dataset is large enough to warrant having a dedicated SQL pool node to respond to those kinds of queries. A replicated distribution type copies all the data for the identified table to all provisioned nodes that are running and responding to queries. This distribution type is best for small datasets (less than 2 GB).

Design a Data Archiving Solution

Make sure to differentiate between purging (deleting) and archiving data. The former means you completely remove the data from any existing datastore within your control. Purging is becoming more important from the perspective of security, privacy, governance, and compliance. There is simply no longer any reason to persist collected data permanently; it should be completely deleted at some point. (See Part IV, "Secure, Monitor, and Optimize Data Storage and Data Processing," for more information.) Archiving data means moving data to a less frequently accessed datastore from a production environment due to its relevance and need. Changes in business objectives, age of data, changes in regulations, or changes in customer behaviors could make the data collected over a given time unnecessary. If those things happen, you might not want to delete the data immediately but keep it for some time before making that decision. But in all cases, you would want to remove the irrelevant data from the tables or directories so that it no longer influences your data analytics and business insights gathering activities. You would also do this because you can save some cost.

Azure storage accounts offer lifecycle management policies. A *lifecycle management policy* enables you to automatically move data between the different blob storage access tiers, such as Hot, Cool, and Archive. You can configure a rule to move data from Hot to Cool or Archive, or from Cool to Archive, or even to delete the data. The decision point for when the access tier changes can be based on days from creation date or time since last modification. You can also manually change the access tier from the Azure portal, by selecting the file and clicking the Change Tier button, as shown in Figure 3.10.

FIGUER 3.10 Changing the access tier of files in an ADLS container

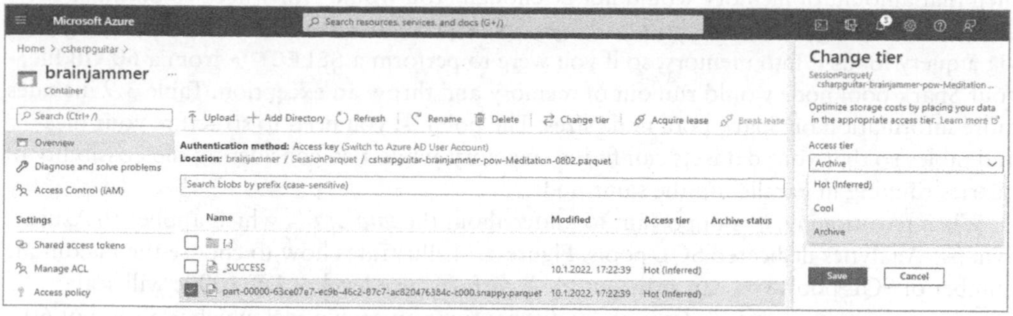

If your data is stored in folders named for the date and time ({yyyy}/{mm}/{dd}/{hh}), then you could write an automated batch process to remove data within certain folders based on age. When working with data stored on tables, the approach is a bit different. Files have metadata, such as created and updated date, while rows and columns do not have that metadata easily accessible. If you need to implement some archiving on tables, you might consider adding a column that identifies the last time the data was accessed, updated, and/or originally inserted. You could use those column values as the basis for identifying relevant and irrelevant data. If the data is deemed irrelevant, due to age or access, it can either be moved to a different schema or deleted. You could consider such a data archive process as part of a pipeline operation, which you will create in the next chapter. You might also consider creating a copy of the table and append the word *archive* to it.

Design a Partition Strategy

A core objective of your data analytics solution is to have queries return results within an acceptable amount of time. If the dataset on which a query executes is huge, then you might experience unacceptable latency. In this context, "dataset" refers to a single database table or file. As the volume of data increases, you must find a solution for making the queries more performant. The solution is partitioning. Consider, for example, that you have one file that is 60 GB. When you run a query on that file, the entire contents of the file must be parsed. It might be less latent if the 60 GB file were broken into two 30 GB files instead. The same goes for a data table that has 60,000,000 rows. It makes sense that a query on a partitioned table of 1,000,000 rows would perform faster than on a single 60,000,000 row table. This, of course, assumes you can effectively and logically split the data into multiple files or partitions. To summarize, the more data you query at once, the longer it takes.

The partitioning strategy should also consider how the data is to be distributed across your SQL pool or Spark pool nodes. Partitions themselves can become too big for the selected node sizes, which have limits on CPU and memory. If you only have a single user or limited scheduled parallel pipeline executions, then perhaps a small Spark pool node with

32 GB of memory is enough. However, if you run numerous jobs, in parallel on big datasets, then that amount of memory would not be enough. You would either need to optimize the distribution configuration or choose a larger Spark pool node size. Note that data retrieved via a query loads it into memory, so if you were to perform a `SELECT *` from a 60 GB file, your Spark pool node would run out of memory and throw an exception. Table 3.9 includes more information on Spark pool node sizes. The point is, you need to structure your files and tables so that your datasets can fit into memory, while also considering the possibility of queries running in parallel on the same node.

When partitioning, it is important to know about the *law of 60*, which applies to Azure Synapse Analytics dedicated SQL pools. Figure 3.11 illustrates how to choose the maximum number of SQL pools you can scale out to. A performance level of DW1000c will scale out to a maximum of two nodes with 30 distributions on each node, which is a total of 60 distributions. The largest performance level is currently DW30000c, which can scale out to 60 nodes that contain a single distribution on each node, again totaling 60 distributions. Each time the platform determines that you need a new node, the defined table distribution for the workflow will be copied to the new node in the ratio bound to the selected performance level.

FIGUER 3.11 Configuring a new dedicated SQL pool

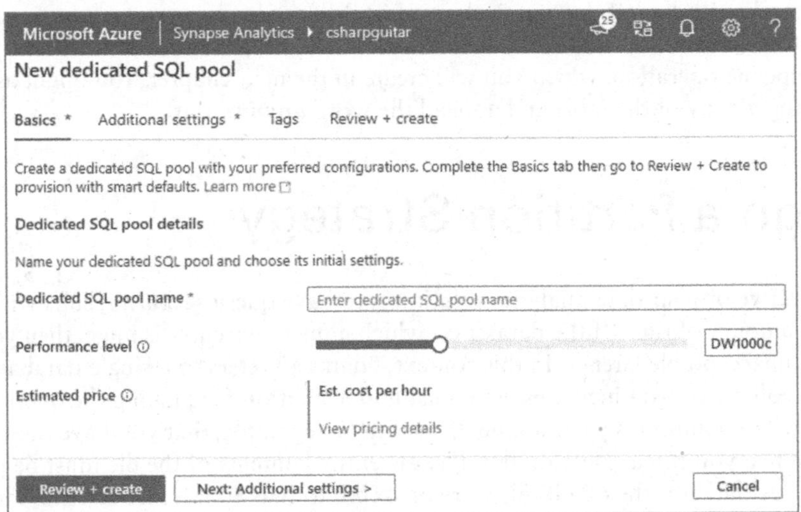

If your table has 60,000,000 rows and two nodes, then 30,000,000 rows will be copied to each node, assuming you are using the default distribution method, round-robin. Your distribution must be greater than 1,000,000 rows per node to benefit from compressed column store indexing. This is where the law of 60 comes into play again, in that if you choose the highest performance level, which has 60 nodes, then your table needs to be at least 60,000,000 rows to meet the 1,000,000-row requirement for caching.

Design a Partition Strategy for Files

Having an intuitive directory structure for the ingestion of data is a prequel to implementing the partitioning strategy. You may not know how the received files will be formatted in all scenarios; therefore, analysis and preliminary transformation is often required before any major actions like partitioning happens. A directory structure similar to the following is optimal:

```
{location}/{subject}/{direction}/{yyyy}/{mm}/{dd}/{hh}/*
```

where `{direction}` of `in` contains raw data that can then be partitioned using the `partitionBy()` method. Once the partitioning is completed, the files can be placed in the `out` directory folder. The following code snippets select data based on the columns within the `DataFrame`:

```
df.write.partitionBy('SCENARIO').mode('overwrite')
 .parquet('/EMEA/brainjammer/out/2022/01/12/15/SCENARIO.parquet')
df.write.partitionBy('ELECTRODE').mode('overwrite')
 .parquet('/EMEA/brainjammer/out/2022/01/12/15/ELECTRODE.parquet')
df.write.partitionBy('FREQUENCY').mode('overwrite')
 .parquet('/EMEA/brainjammer/out/2022/01/12/15/FREQUENCY.parquet')
```

Figure 3.12 shows the results. When the data was loaded into the `DataFrame`, there was a single large file. As you can infer from Figure 3.12, the data is now split into many smaller files.

FIGUER 3.12 Partitioning files

The following snippets perform a query on the partitioned data and display 10 rows:

```
data = spark.read
 .parquet('/EMEA/brainjammer/out/2022/01/12/15/ELECTRODE.parquet/
   ELECTRODE=AF3')
data.show(10)
```

Consider the following recommendations:

- The fewer the number of files that need parsing, the faster the query renders.
- The partitioning of large data files improves performance by limiting the amount data searched.

Design a Partition Strategy for Analytical Workloads

Before you can design a partition strategy for an analytical workload, you need to have a description of what an analytical workload is. In your job or school, your workload is probably very high. What do you do to manage your own workload? One method is to make a list of all the work tasks and prioritize them. Then, you can identify an amount of time required to complete each task and add them all together, which results at some point in the future all the work being completed. Is the timeframe to complete the work acceptable? If not, you need to look a bit further into the details of each task and perhaps find a way to optimize the required actions so that they are completed more quickly.

The same principle is applied to an analytical workload. Your data analytics solution, which runs in a pipeline, performs specific tasks. If it does not perform fast enough or needs to be optimized for cost, then consider whether any of task would benefit from creating or optimizing (aka tuning) existing partitions. Data can change in format, relevance, and volume, so reviewing existing partitions on a regular basis is beneficial. The following are questions to consider and recommendations for designing analytical workloads. Each has been discussed in previous sections or chapters.

- Which analytical stack or pool will you use?
- Is your data from relational, semi-, or nonstructured sources?
- If data storage is file-based
  - Use Parquet files and partition them.
  - Determine the optimal balance between file size and number of files for your given set of requirements.
- If data storage is table-based
  - Keep the law of 60 in scope.
  - Confirm that the table distribution type is still the most valid.

Design a Partition Strategy for Efficiency and Performance

Both efficiency and performance were discussed in earlier sections pertaining to the design of a partition strategy. An efficient query is one in which the time required to execute it is well used. That means the query should not be waiting on data shuffling or querying irrelevant data. The most efficient query would be one that has a table or file that contains only the data that the query requires. In the grand scale of things, this is not efficient, but in principle it is. It is because that means the data is partitioned to a point that is most optimal. Remember previously where you saw how the brain waves were partitioned on `ELECTRODE`. If you need all the data for a given electrode, then this would be a very efficient partition. However, if you want only the `THETA` frequency for a given electrode, then the query would need to parse out all frequencies not equal to `THETA`.

The amount and size of data parsed when a query is run have a significant impact on performance. Decreasing the size via partitioning can have benefits as well as detriments. The benefits are that the data being queried will be smaller and more efficient. The files will be smaller because the rows in the tables will be fewer. However, if partitioning results in the rows in a table falling below the level necessary to enable column store indexing, then you will experience more latency. Too many partitions, in other words, too many files, often results in an increase in latency, so again, you need to find the optimal balance for your scenario. On a final note, the compute power you provision for your data analytics can overcome many performance-related problems. If you have significant funding that lets you provision larger machines, this might be your best, easiest, and quickest option, because the cost and risk of making changes also have a price, which could be catastrophic.

Design a Partition Strategy for Azure Synapse Analytics

The reason you partition your data is to improve the efficiency and performance of loading, querying, and deleting it. As previously mentioned, partitioning data improves those activities because it reduces size of the data by grouping together similar data. The smaller the set of data you perform an action on, the faster the action will complete, *ceteris paribus*. You also know that Azure Synapse Analytics features two pool types: SQL and Spark. In the SQL pool context, it is most common to approach partitioning from a table perspective. The following code snippet is an example of creating a partition:

```
CREATE TABLE [dbo].[READING] (
 [READING_ID]      INT           NOT NULL IDENTITY(1,1),
 [SCENARIO_ID]     INT           NOT NULL,
 [ELECTRODE_ID]    INT           NOT NULL,
 [FREQUENCY_ID]    INT           NOT NULL,
 [VALUE]           DECIMAL(7,3) NOT NULL)
WITH
( CLUSTERED COLUMNSTORE INDEX,
```

```
DISTRIBUTION = HASH([SCENARIO_ID]),
PARTITION (
[SCENARIO_ID] RANGE RIGHT FOR VALUES
(1, 2, 3, 4, 5, 6, 7, 8)));
);
```

This code snippet creates a partition using the hash distribution type based on the brainjammer scenarios (for example, `PlayingGuitar`, `Meditation`, etc.). Although you can create persisted tables on a Spark pool, working with and querying Parquet files are most common and most likely to be questioned on the exam. As shown in Figure 3.12, you can use the `partitionBy()` method to partition your files.

```
df.write.partitionBy('SCENARIO').mode('overwrite')
 .parquet('/EMEA/brainjammer/out/2022/01/12/15/SCENARIO.parquet')
```

Identify When Partitioning Is Needed in Azure Data Lake Storage Gen2

The following are reasons to consider partitioning:

- You have never implemented any partitioning.
- The file sizes are no longer within the recommended size for optimal performance.
- The partitions are skewed.
- Some partitions have more than 1,000,000 rows, while some do not.
- You notice excessive data shuffling.
- There has been a great influx of data.
- You have too many partitions.

If you have never performed any analysis on your datasets to see if they would benefit from partitioning, by all means do that. You should now have the skill set to ask those basic questions. The recommended file size depends on the pool type: SQL is between 100 MB and 10 GB, and Spark is between 256 MB and 100 GB. The number of files as well as their size impact performance, so finding the best ratio for the given context requires testing and tuning. Over time, the amount of data for a specific partition might get much larger than the other. That means that those queries would run more slowly than others. Perhaps most brainjammer scenarios uploaded over the past few months were of a single type. If that's the case, then a partition would be larger than the others, so you might want to find a new way to partition, perhaps on session datetime.

When rows of data exceed 1,000,000 in a partition, the compression improves; therefore, performance increases. You need to keep an eye on that number and make sure the row number is optional on all partitions. You can monitor shuffling on a SQL pool by running an Execution plan that will show the amount of shuffling for a given query. Queries that suffer from shuffling are ones that contain `JOIN`s that include data that is not present on the chosen node that executes the query. To manage shuffling on a Spark pool, you can make a configuration change using the `spark.conf.set("spark.sql.shuffle`

`.partitions",200)` method. This is typically handled by the runtime, but you can set the default value if you already know there should be more or less than the 200 default. A large influx of data can cause your data to skew. Review the state and size of the partitions regularly.

Finally, having too many partitions can cause shuffling. It is important to get the number of partitions right for the given context. The `sys.partitions` and `sys.dm_db_partition_stats` tables provide the necessary information on a SQL pool, while `print(df.rdd.getNumPartitions())` will show the partitions on a Spark pool.

Design the Serving/Data Exploration Layer

What is a *serving/data exploration layer*? Don't confuse it with something called the servicing layer, which is common in a *service-oriented architecture (SOA)*. For an illustration of the serving layer, see Figure 3.13. The serving layer is one component of a larger architecture that includes a speed layer and batch layer. The Big Data architecture pattern shown in Figure 3.13 is called *lambda architecture*. The purpose of the serving layer is to boost transformation of data so that consumers can query it in near real time or as fast as technically possible. It enables consumers to query data ingested through both a hot and cold path simultaneously.

FIGUER 3.13 The lambda architecture serving layer

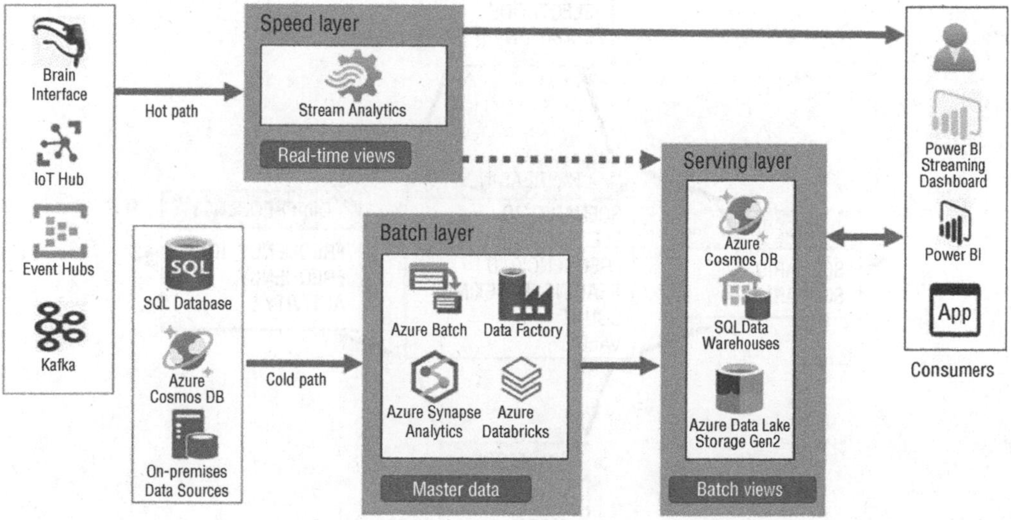

Notice that the Azure products Azure Cosmos DB, SQL Data Warehouse, and ADLS are represented as datastores in the serving layer. Data provided through the serving layer requires a place to be stored, and those are some relevant products to store them on. It is important, however, to recognize that the data stored in those products, in this context, is not canonical data. That means the data is not in its final state. Data in its final state would be of the highest formal quality necessary for complex analytic processing. The data in this state has a context bound to a specific purpose and can be deleted and regenerated at any time. The purpose again is to get the data from ingestion to a state of consumption quickly.

A new alternative to the lambda architecture is called *kappa architecture*. When you implement the lambda architecture, you will find some duplication of effort. The coded logic that transforms and moves data through the cold and hot path is often duplicated. In most cases, the coded logic in these two paths is not 100 percent identical, which means you must perform changes and testing on more than a single set of code. The kappa architecture removes the necessity of the serving layer altogether. It combines the cold and hot path into one and focuses on the real-time views and master data for providing the optimized transformation of data from producers to consumers.

Design Star Schemas

A star schema is a fact table that is surrounded by multiple dimension tables. It resembles a star shape, as shown in Figure 3.14.

FIGUER 3.14 A relational star schema

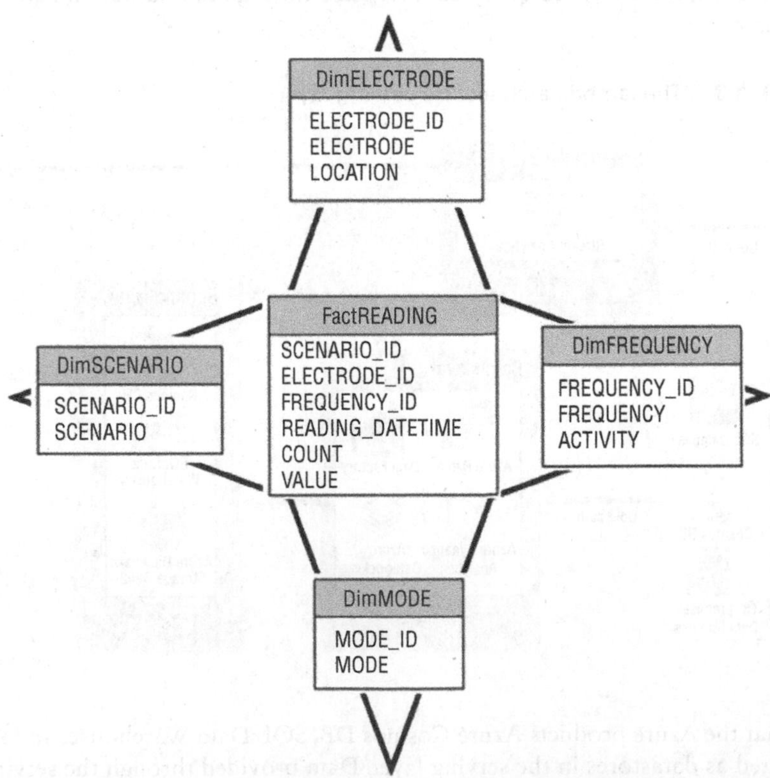

A fact table is a table that holds the data that is used for your data analytics work. The table is specifically and optimally designed for read operations, in contrast to supporting write operations—for example, INSERT, UPDATE, and DELETE. A fact table is the opposite of a table you would find in an OLTP, OLAP, or HTAP environment, as those are optimized for write operations. The data stored on the FactREADING table would change when new data is added from other data sources. The frequency would be dictated by the business need.

Tables that have data that does not change often are called dimension tables. The data in the DimELECTRODE table, for example, would seldom change. That table contains data that represents a physical BCI and cannot be modified. The other Dim tables might change, but the expectation is that dimension tables, in general, contain data that will not change often. Data in a dimension table can also be used to filter data—for example, if you want to capture only data for a given electrode. You can use the data on the dimension table to find the value used to filter the data on the fact table.

Design Slowly Changing Dimensions

Managing changes to the data stored on dimension tables over time is an important factor to consider and be handled by designing *slowly changing dimensions (SCD)*. Recognize that the data on the fact table will contain a large amount of data. Making an update to data on that scale is not a prudent approach to manage changes that happen while running a business. Perhaps the model of BCI changes, or either the ELECTRODE name or its LOCATION on your head changes. How would you manage the dimension table data if the AF3 electrode were renamed to AF3i and its location were changed from Front Left to Top Left? Because it might not be feasible to update all the data in the fact table, you could instead keep track of the changes—for example, by adding two columns to the DimELECTRODE table. The first column would store the date when initially inserted, and the second column would store when the data has been modified—something like the following:

```
+---------------+
| DimELECTRODE  |
+---------------+
| ELECTRODE_ID  |
| ELECTRODE     |
| LOCATION      |
| INSERT_DATE   |
| MODIFIED_DATE |
+---------------+
```

You might be wondering what happens when the data in the ELECTRODE and LOCATION data is changed. Do you lose that data? How would you then know that before AF3i and Top Left, existed AF3 and Front Left? This is accomplished by choosing which slowly changing dimension type is required for the given scenario (see Table 3.5).

TABLE 3.5 Slowly changing dimension types

Type	Description
Type 1 SCD	Reflects latest values, overwrites historical data
Type 2 SCD	Performs versioning of dimensional data
Type 3 SCD	Stores both current and original data in separate columns
Type 4 SCD	Creates a new table to store dimensional table data history
Type 5 SCD	A combination ofType 1 and 4
Type 6 SCD	A combination ofType 1, 2, and 3

The most common SCD types are 1, 2, 3, and 6.

Type 1 SCD

The two tables in Figure 3.15 represent the change in data in a Type 1 SCD scenario. Notice the values on the top table—specifically, `ELECTRODE` and `LOCATION`—which are the values that change in the update. Also note the values in the `INSERT_DATE` and `MODIFIED_DATE` columns. They are the same, which means there has been no change to these values.

FIGUER 3.15 Type 1 SCD

ELECTRODE_ID	ELECTRODE	LOCATION	INSERT_DATE	MODIFIED_DATE
1	**AF3**	**Front Left**	2022-01-18	**2022-01-18**
2	AF4	Front Right	2022-01-18	2022-01-18
3	T7	Ear Left	2022-01-18	2022-01-18
4	T8	Ear Right	2022-01-18	2022-01-18
5	Pz	Center Back	2022-01-18	2022-01-18

ELECTRODE_ID	ELECTRODE	LOCATION	INSERT_DATE	MODIFIED_DATE
1	**AF3i**	**Top Left**	2022-01-18	**2022-02-29**
2	AF4	Front Right	2022-01-18	2022-01-18
3	T7	Ear Left	2022-01-18	2022-01-18
4	T8	Ear Right	2022-01-18	2022-01-18
5	Pz	Center Back	2022-01-18	2022-01-18

In the second table, note that the ELECTRODE and LOCATION values have changed, and the MODIFIED_DATE has been updated with a new date. You can see that there is no history of what the value was before the update. If you do not need this history in your scenario, then use this type. In the brainjammer scenario, is it important to know what the electrode was named before it got changed? Not really, from an analytics perspective.

Type 2 SCD

This SCD type provides a means for viewing historical records of the value prior to an update. This is commonly called versioning. Notice the columns in the top dimension table of Figure 3.16. The SK_ID column is a surrogate key, which is an internal key that identifies the version history of a unique dimensional member. START_DATE and END_DATE describe when the given value was the current one. Note that many database management systems consider the value of 9999-12-31 in a DateTime data type column to mean empty or none, so rows that contain that value in the END_DATE column would be considered the current version of the value.

FIGUER 3.16 Type 2 SCD

ELECTRODE_ID	SK_ID	ELECTRODE	LOCATION	START_DATE	END_DATE	IS_CURRENT
1	101	**AF3**	**Front Left**	2022-01-18	**9999-12-31**	**True**
2	102	AF4	Front Right	2022-01-18	9999-12-31	True
3	103	T7	Ear Left	2022-01-18	9999-12-31	True
4	104	T8	Ear Right	2022-01-18	9999-12-31	True
5	105	Pz	Center Back	2022-01-18	9999-12-31	True

ELECTRODE_ID	SK_ID	ELECTRODE	LOCATION	START_DATE	END_DATE	IS_CURRENT
1	101	AF3	Front Left	2022-01-18	**2022-02-29**	**False**
2	102	AF4	Front Right	2022-01-18	9999-12-31	True
3	103	T7	Ear Left	2022-01-18	9999-12-31	True
4	104	T8	Ear Right	2022-01-18	9999-12-31	True
5	105	Pz	Center Back	2022-01-18	9999-12-31	True
6	**101**	**AF3i**	**Top Left**	**2022-03-01**	**9999-12-31**	**True**

The addition of the IS_CURRENT column provides an easier way to find the most current version. Instead of retrieving all the rows where SK_ID = 101 and comparing the date range with the current date, you can instead retrieve the rows and filter the data using the IS_CURRENT value.

Type 3 SCD

The Type 2 SCD supports an infinite amount of change history. If you instead need only to track the previous value, then you should choose Type 3. Figure 3.17 shows the additional columns, ORIGINAL_ELECTRODE and ORIGINAL_LOCATION.

FIGUER 3.17 Type 3 SCD

ELECTRODE_ID	ELECTRODE	ORIGINAL_ELECTRODE	LOCATION	ORIGINAL_LOCATION	INSERT_DATE	MODIFIED_DATE
1	AF3	AF3	**Front Left**	Front Left	2022-01-18	**2022-01-18**
2	AF4	AF4	Front Right	Front Right	2022-01-18	2022-01-18
3	T7	T7	Ear Left	Ear Left	2022-01-18	2022-01-18
4	T8	T8	Ear Right	Ear Right	2022-01-18	2022-01-18
5	Pz	Pz	Center Back	Center Back	2022-01-18	2022-01-18

ELECTRODE_ID	ELECTRODE	ORIGINAL_ELECTRODE	LOCATION	ORIGINAL_LOCATION	INSERT_DATE	MODIFIED_DATE
1	**AF3i**	AF3	**Top Left**	Front Left	2022-01-18	**2022-02-29**
2	AF4	AF4	Front Right	Front Right	2022-01-18	2022-01-18
3	T7	T7	Ear Left	Ear Left	2022-01-18	2022-01-18
4	T8	T8	Ear Right	Ear Right	2022-01-18	2022-01-18
5	Pz	Pz	Center Back	Center Back	2022-01-18	2022-01-18

When either of those column values need to be changed, for example, the electrode name, the current value in the ELECTRODE column is placed into the ORIGINAL_ELECTRODE column. Then the new value is stored in the ELECTRODE column. The MODIFIED_DATE is also updated to identify when the last update was performed.

Type 6 SCD

Type 6 SCD is a combination of the previous three SCD types: 1, 2, and 3 (in the same way that 1 + 2 + 3 = 6). Notice in Figure 3.18 that the SK_ID, START_DATE, END_DATE, and IS_CURRENT columns come from Type 2 SCD. The columns prefixed with ORIGINAL_ (which store the original values) come from the Type 3 SCD. Being able to update the actual value with a corresponding modified date is representative of Type 1 SCD. The date stored in the END_DATE column is also the modified date.

Type 6 SCD provides both versioning and the most recent noncurrent value. Therefore, if you have a scenario where you want simple and quick access to the current version, perhaps sometimes the last version and rarely a later version, then this SCD type would be optimal.

FIGUER 3.18 Type 6 SCD

ELECTRODE_ID	SK_ID	ELECTRODE	ORIGINAL_ELECTRODE	LOCATION	ORIGINAL_LOCATION	START_DATE	END_DATE	IS_CURRENT
1	101	AF3	AF3	Front Left	Front Left	2022-01-18	9999-12-31	True
2	102	AF4	AF4	Front Right	Front Right	2022-01-18	9999-12-31	True
3	103	T7	T7	Ear Left	Ear Left	2022-01-18	9999-12-31	True
4	104	T8	T8	Ear Right	Ear Right	2022-01-18	9999-12-31	True
5	105	Pz	Pz	Center Back	Center Back	2022-01-18	9999-12-31	True

ELECTRODE_ID	SK_ID	ELECTRODE	ORIGINAL_ELECTRODE	LOCATION	ORIGINAL_LOCATION	START_DATE	END_DATE	IS_CURRENT
1	101	AF3i	AF3	Top Left	Front Left	2022-01-18	2022-02-29	False
2	102	AF4	AF4	Front Right	Front Right	2022-01-18	9999-12-31	True
3	103	T7	T7	Ear Left	Ear Left	2022-01-18	9999-12-31	True
4	104	T8	T8	Ear Right	Ear Right	2022-01-18	9999-12-31	True
5	105	Pz	Pz	Center Back	Center Back	2022-01-18	9999-12-31	True
6	106	AF3i	AF3i	Top Left	Top Left	2022-03-01	9999-12-31	True

Design a Dimensional Hierarchy

A dimensional hierarchy is set of related data tables that align to different levels (see Figure 3.19). The tables commonly have one-to-many or many-to-one relationships with each other.

FIGUER 3.19 A dimensional hierarchy

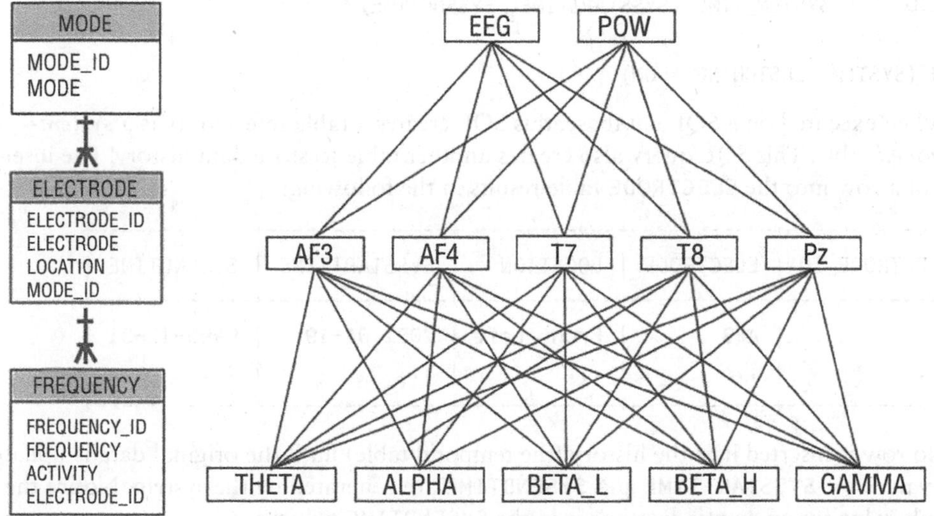

The hierarchy shown in Figure 3.19 could be named the "brainjammer dimension." The frequencies roll up to electrodes, and the electrodes roll up to modes. This hierarchical representation of data provides two benefits. The first benefit is that it reduces the complexity of a fact table. If the mode, electrode, and frequency of the reading were all stored on a single fact table, it would be difficult to deduce the relationship between those columns. When represented by the dimensional hierarchy, this is not the case. The second benefit is the hierarchy provides the means for drilling up and down into the data, where drilling up renders summarized data and drilling down renders more details. If you want to see which mode a reading or group of readings is generated from, you can drill up to find that.

Design a Solution for Temporal Data

The concept of temporal data is structured around the need to know the data stored in a table within a specific timeframe, instead of what is stored in the table now. Explained in another way, if you want to know the value stored in the `LOCATION` column on `2021-01-19`, a date in the past, you can use a temporal data solution. The following snippet shows how to create a temporal table:

```
CREATE TABLE [dbo].[ELECTRODE]
(
 [ELECTRODE_ID]      INT           NOT NULL IDENTITY(1,1) PRIMARY KEY CLUSTERED,
 [ELECTRODE]         NVARCHAR (50) NOT NULL,
 [LOCATION]          NVARCHAR (50) NOT NULL,
 [SYSSTARTTIME] DATETIME2 GENERATED ALWAYS AS ROW START NOT NULL,
 [SYSENDTIME] DATETIME2 GENERATED ALWAYS AS ROW END NOT NULL,
 PERIOD FOR SYSTEM_TIME (SYSSTARTTIME, SYSENDTIME)
)
WITH (SYSTEM_VERSIONING = ON)
```

When executed on a SQL database, this SQL creates a table referred to as a *system-versioned* table. This SQL query also creates another table to store data history. The insertion of a row into the `ELECTRODE` table results in the following:

```
+--------------+-----------+------------+--------------+------------+
| ELECTRODE_ID | ELECTRODE | LOCATION   | SYSSTARTTIME | SYSENDTIME |
+--------------+-----------+------------+--------------+------------+
| 1            | AF3       | Front Left | 2022-01-19   | 9999-12-31 |
| ...          | ...       | ...        | ...          | ...        |
+--------------+-----------+------------+--------------+------------+
```

No row is inserted into the history (the temporal table) until the original data is updated. The values for `SYSSTARTTIME` and `SYSENDTIME` are generated by the system. Notice the default value for an empty datetime is in the `SYSENDTIME` column.

The following SQL query updates the AF3 electrode:

```
UPDATE ELECTRODE
 SET ELECTRODE = 'AF3i', LOCATION = 'Top Left'
 WHERE ELECTRODE_ID = 1
```

This query results in the updating of the data on the ELECTRODE table, which is system-versioned, as expected. The value in the SYSENDTIME column remains empty, as the row contains the most current data.

```
+--------------+-----------+------------+--------------+------------+
| ELECTRODE_ID | ELECTRODE | LOCATION   | SYSSTARTTIME | SYSENDTIME |
+--------------+-----------+------------+--------------+------------+
| 1            | AF3i      | Top Left   | 2022-01-19   | 9999-12-31 |
+--------------+-----------+------------+--------------+------------+
```

Performing a SELECT query on the temporal table results in the following:

```
+--------------+-----------+------------+--------------+------------+
| ELECTRODE_ID | ELECTRODE | LOCATION   | SYSSTARTTIME | SYSENDTIME |
+--------------+-----------+------------+--------------+------------+
| 1            | AF3       | Front Left | 2022-01-19   | 2022-01-19 |
+--------------+-----------+------------+--------------+------------+
```

Figure 3.20 illustrates how the table looks when you use Azure Data Studio to query the database.

FIGUER 3.20 A temporal table

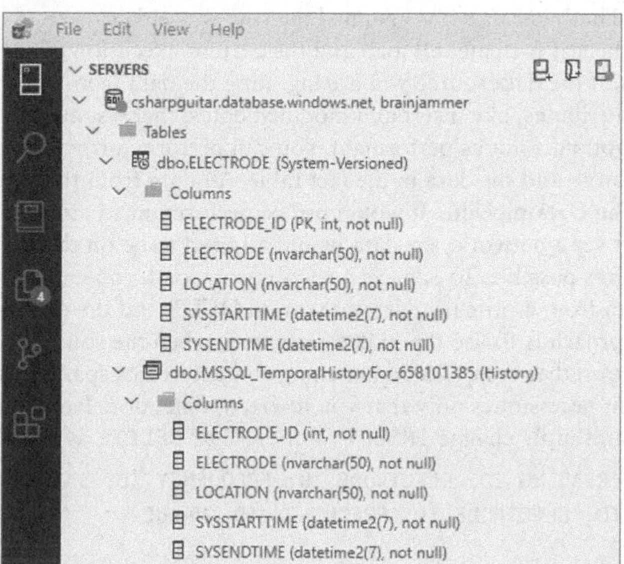

Each time a row is updated, the system generates a row in the history table to show its previous values. At any time you are required to perform historical analysis, then you have a place to retrieve the values (the dimensional values) that were current at a given time.

Design for Incremental Loading

Data is ingested in many forms and from a variety of different sources. From a streaming perspective, the data is being generated, sent to a subscriber, and ingested in real time. There is no incremental loading context in the streaming scenario when the data is coming directly from the data producer. Data that is captured and stored into an on-premises or any other datastore and later sent to or retrieved by your data analytics solution is a scenario when incremental loading makes sense. *Incremental loading* is the opposite of a full data load. As you begin designing and building your data analytics solution, the amount of data being initially extracted and migrated from data sources can be vast. But after the initial phases of the migration and the ingestion of that data, future data loads wouldn't be as large, because instead of loading all the data from the datastores again, you would only load the changes, i.e., the delta. So when you set up the extraction logic of the ETL process, it would need to include the feature to extract and ingest only the changes from the last time a data load was performed.

To achieve the ETL, all you need to do is look over the previous few sections in this chapter. Temporal tables and SCD types provide some guidance for determining what has changed and when. In simple terms, if your data at the source has an insert date (created date) and/or a modified date, then part of the extraction process would be to check those values. You need to first establish the last time the extraction process ran and compare the last run date to the insert or update date for each data row. If the last run date is less than the insert or update date for the selected row, that row should be extracted as part of the incremental load. That's because it is assumed the row was either inserted or updated between the time of the last incremental load and the current execution of the incremental extraction process. If the data source you are ingesting the data from doesn't contain such change detection attributes, like insert and modified dates, there is another option.

Although this option is not as performant, you can perform a row-by-row comparison of the source datastore and the data in the fact table. All data from the source must first be ingested into the Big Data pipeline. It would not be performant to attempt a comparison of two datastores over a network; the data would all need to be on the same machine or as close to each other as possible. To achieve a row-by-row load, you can use two approaches to synchronize data from a primary datastore (or an OLTP) and the one used for data analytics. The first approach is to use the `MERGE` statement when the source and destination have a diverse mixture of rather complicated matching characteristics spanning numerous tables. If your requirement necessitates only that you insert, update, or delete data between two like tables, then you can simply change `INSERT` to `UPDATE` or `DELETE` as required.

```
INSERT READING (READING_ID, ELECTRODE_ID, FREQUENCY_ID, VALUE)
SELECT READING_ID, ELECTRODE_ID, FREQUENCY_ID, VALUE
FROM READING_TMP
```

```
WHERE NOT EXISTS (SELECT READING_ID, ELECTRODE_ID, FREQUENCY_ID, VALUE
 FROM READING R WHERE R.READING_ID = READING_TMP.READING_ID)
```

In this SQL query `READING` is the fact table, and `READING_TMP` is the table into which you ingested all the source data.

The other method is to use hashing. This technique, again, is not as performant as one that includes data versioning. This is implemented by selecting all the data in a row and then hashing it and storing that hash in a column on the row. Your migration process would select a row, perform the same hash technique, and compare it to the stored hash. If the hash is the same, then the data is the same for that row. If the hash is not the same, something has changed and therefore needs to be part of the incremental load.

Design Analytical Stores

Before reading any further, ask yourself what an analytical store is. If you struggle for the answer, refer to Table 3.2, which provides the analytical datastores available in Azure, as well as the data model that works optimally with those products. Table 3.1 provides a list of different ingestion types mapped to the most suitable Azure data analytics product. The reason to call attention to the information in Table 3.1, which is focused on ingestion, is that you will notice that many of the same analytical datastores in Table 3.2 are also optimal for certain types of ingestion. Combine those two tables with Table 3.3, and you can narrow down which Azure data analytics product to use in your scenario.

Consider a few additional scenarios using the information you have learned in this chapter. For example, does your data analytics solution need to supply data to a hot path serving layer? Or does your solution require massively parallel processing (MPP)? Table 3.6 provides some information about these options, which, when used in addition to the other tables, should be very helpful in picking the necessary analytical store for your solution.

TABLE 3.6 Hot path serving layer and MPP products

Product	Hot path serving	Massively parallel processing (MPP)
Azure Synapse SQL pool	Yes	Yes
Azure Synapse Spark pool	Yes	Yes
Azure Data Explorer	Yes	Yes
Azure Cosmos DB	Yes	No
Azure Analysis Services	No	Yes

An analytical store is a place where you store data used by your data analytics solutions, from end to end. An analytical store houses data regardless of the Big Data stage (as illustrated by Figure 2.30) and regardless of the data landing zone (as identified in Table 3.4).

Design Metastores in Azure Synapse Analytics and Azure Databricks

A metastore is a place to store metadata. Earlier in this chapter you learned about the metadata associated with files, such as creation date, size, and update date. Metadata is also available for the objects stored within a database, for example, views, relationships, schemas, and tables. You can access the metadata for your database objects in the metastore. There are numerous tools that will graphically illustrate the objects in a database, including Azure Data Studio and Microsoft SQL Server Management Studio. However, not all DBMSs or analytical datastores have such features. Querying the metastore is the only means for discovering the existence and structure of tables. Metastores also help you begin to visualize database details that help you figure out what is contained in the database and how the data can be used. Remember that data is simply organized characters in a flat file, managed by a DBMS. Without any means for analyzing the data and the structure of the data in a file, it would be hard to get value from it. Queries such as `select * from sys.tables` or `describe formatted <tableName>` will render table and schema information on a SQL database.

Since Apache Spark workloads are most often concentrated on data files, there needs to be some kind of mechanism for creating virtual databases and tables on top of your file data. The product that stores metadata and creates this virtualization is called Apache Hive. The database and table listings shown in Figure 3.21 are made possible by the metadata stored in Hive. Azure Databricks, for example, uses Hive to build the content for the Data menu item, as shown in Figure 3.21.

FIGUER 3.21 A Hive metadata metastore

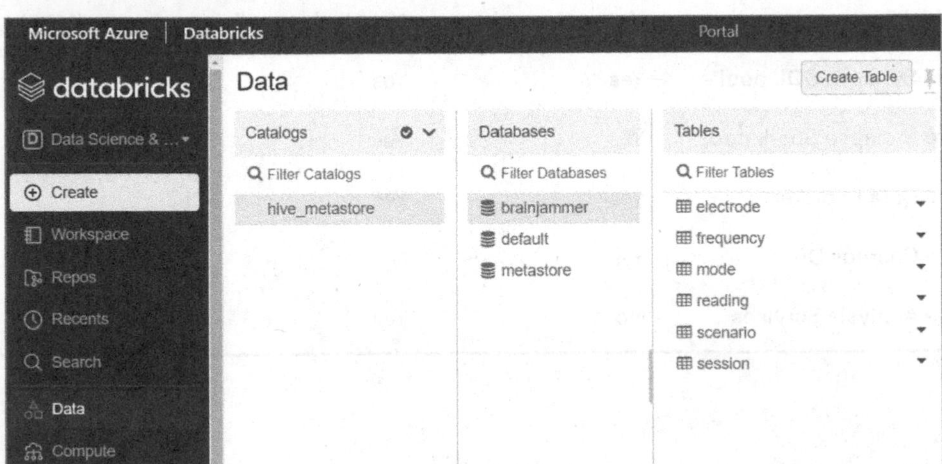

The list of databases and tables are retrieved from the default file-based Hive metastore loaded on a data share. See the next section for more about this Hive metastore using Azure Databricks.

Azure Databricks

Azure Databricks generates a metastore by default with the provisioning of a cluster. After creating a cluster, you can query the metastore. Doing so produces a visualization of any table. Figure 3.22 illustrates the retrieval from the metastore using the `show tables in <databaseName>` command. Executing the command lists all the tables in the targeted database.

FIGUER 3.22 A Hive metadata metastore database

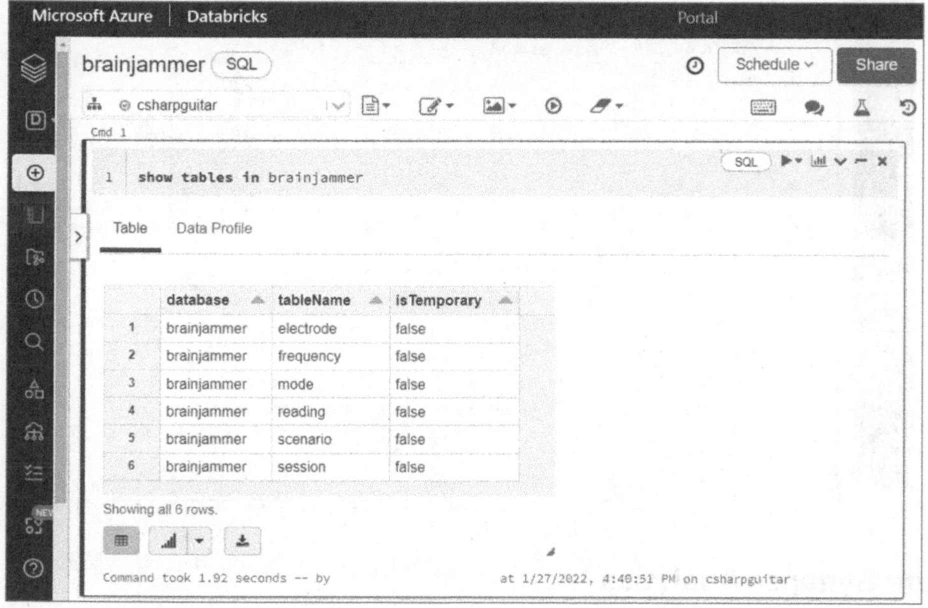

To show the details of a table, use the command `describe formatted <databaseName>.<tableName>`, as shown in Figure 3.23. Notice that the table column names and data types are rendered as well as other metadata, such as the location, owner, and provider.

The metastore is file-based by default and accessible during and from your Azure Databricks session. Other individuals who use the same workspace will not have access by default. The default Hive metastore is not optimal for team or enterprise Big Data analytics. Instead, you should create an external metastore that runs in a database such as Azure SQL or an Azure Database for MySQL. This way, other team members can discover these tables and use them in their analytics efforts. Creating an external Apache Hive metastore makes its contents more discoverable and scalable for large data analytics workloads.

FIGUER 3.23 A Hive metadata metastore table

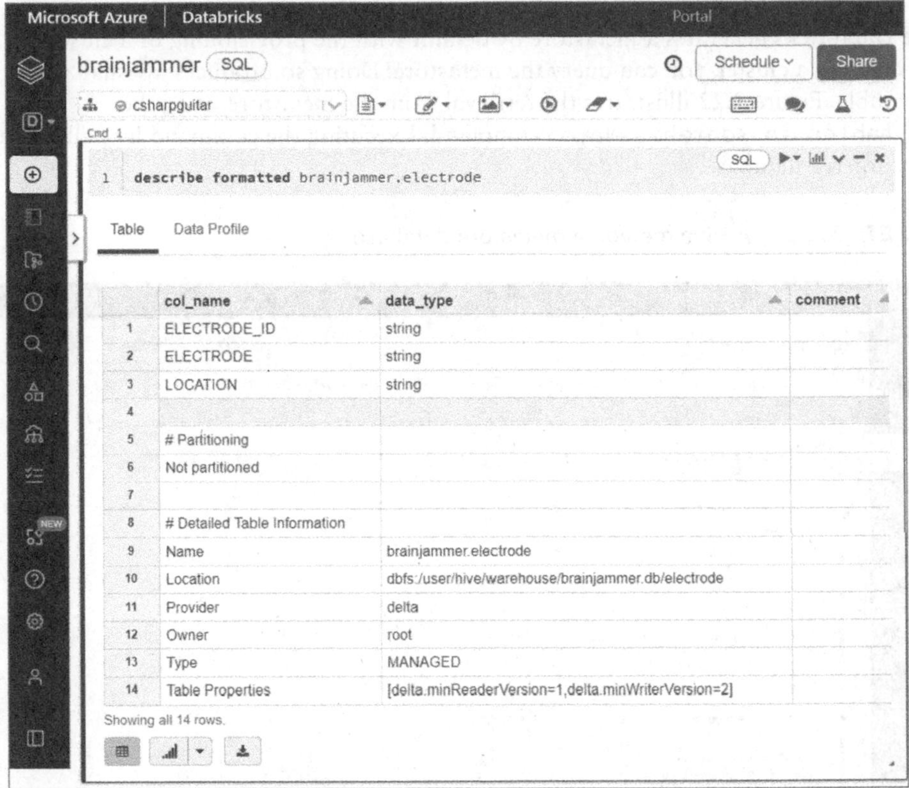

Azure Synapse Analytics

Azure Synapse Analytics includes support for accessing an Apache Hive metastore. You can access a Hive metastore by using a Spark pool.

Spark Pool

After learning in Exercise 3.4 how to configure a linked service, you will be able to execute the query shown in Figure 3.24.

The `spark.sql` queries are similar to those shown in the previous figures concerning metastores. The output of the queries renders the list of databases found in the namespace and the tables within the targeted database.

FIGUER 3.24 A Hive metadata metastore spark pool

```
spark.sql("show databases").show()
spark.sql("show tables in brainjammer ").show()

+-----------+
|  namespace|
+-----------+
|brainjammer|
|    default|
|  metastore|
+-----------+

+-----------+---------+-----------+
|   database|tableName|isTemporary|
+-----------+---------+-----------+
|brainjammer|electrode|      false|
|brainjammer|frequency|      false|
|brainjammer|     mode|      false|
|brainjammer|  reading|      false|
|brainjammer| scenario|      false|
|brainjammer|  session|      false|
+-----------+---------+-----------+
```

The metastore in your chosen external database must exist before you can perform queries on it. Create the external metastore first, and then you can access it from the Spark pool.

The metadata is retrieved from the same data source when running on an Azure Synapse Analytics Spark pool as when running on an Azure Databricks cluster. This is true when both the Azure Databricks cluster and the Spark pool have been configured to do so. This will become clearer after you complete Exercise 3.4 and Exercise 3.14.

SQL Pool

You also can query metadata in a SQL database, as shown in Figure 3.25.

You can discover which tables are available on a targeted database by selecting the list of databases and tables from the sys schema. It is possible to query files on a SQL pool; however, this most likely will not be on the exam, because that kind of analytics is mostly approached using Spark pools.

FIGUER 3.25 Querying metadata in a SQL database

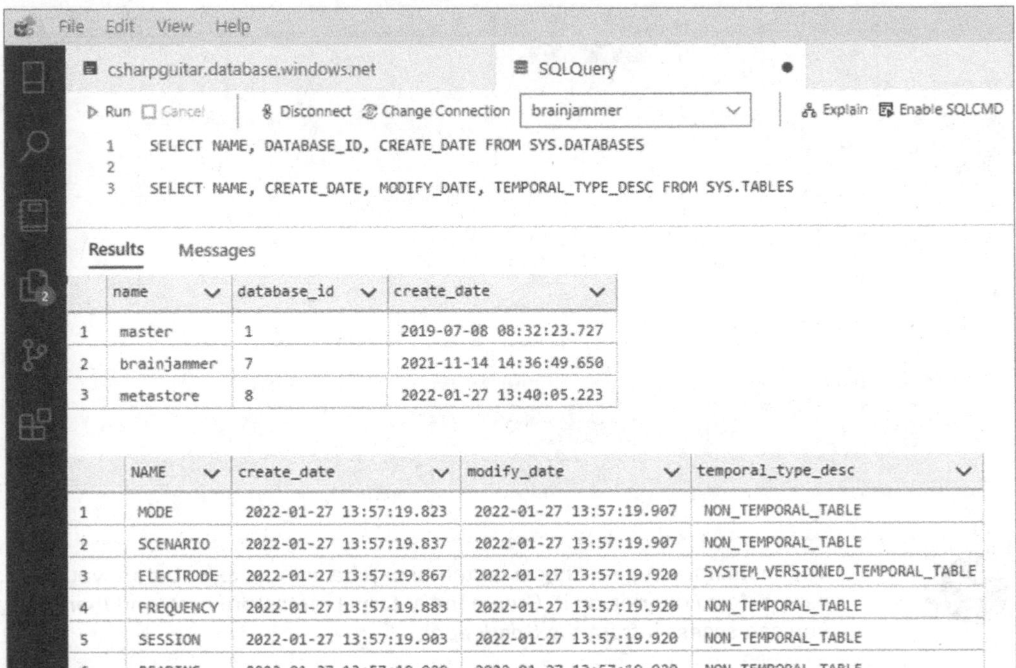

The Ingestion of Data into a Pipeline

The Big Data pipeline has been touched on numerous times; if you need a refresher, refer to Figure 2.30. Data ingestion is the first phase of that pipeline (refer to Figure 3.1). The pipeline itself is a series of purposefully sequenced activities. The activities can and often do span all the Big Data stages, from ingestion to serving. But sometimes you can have pipelines that perform activities that perform tasks within a single stage, for example, ingestion. You learned which Azure products are useful for ingestion (refer to Table 3.1). Now it is time to provision some of these products, which will help you better learn their constraints, capabilities, and features.

Azure Synapse Analytics

What Azure Synapse Analytics is and what it is used for should be no surprise at this point. This is the Big Data analytics product that Microsoft is driving customers toward. This is the product you need to know the most about when preparing for the exam. As shown in Figure 3.26, an Azure Synapse Analytics pipeline is useful for ingesting data that can be stored onto an ADLS container.

FIGUER 3.26 An overview of Azure Synapse Analytics

Depending on your requirements, transformation and analytics can be performed using the numerous types of compute pools. The best way to learn about this product is to use it. Begin by provisioning Azure Synapse Analytics and then opening Synapse Studio.

EXERCISE 3.3

Create an Azure Synapse Analytics Workspace

1. Log in to the Azure portal at `https://portal.azure.com` ➢ enter **Azure Synapse Analytics** in the search box ➢ click Azure Synapse Analytics ➢ click the + Create button ➢ select the subscription ➢ select or create a new resource group ➢ provide a workspace name ➢ select the region ➢ leave the From Subscription radio button selected ➢ select the storage account and ADLS container that you provisioned in Exercise 3.1 ➢ and then click the Next: Security button.
2. Review the options ➢ click the Next: Networking button ➢ select Enable Managed Virtual Network ➢ review the options, leaving the defaults ➢ click the Review + Create button ➢ review the configuration ➢ and then click Create.
3. Once provisioned, navigate to the Azure Synapse Analytics Overview blade ➢ click the Open link in the Open Synapse Studio box ➢ and then select the Manage hub item. You should see something similar to Figure 3.27.

EXERCISE 3.3 ***(continued)***

FIGUER 3.27 The Azure Synapse Analytics Manage hub

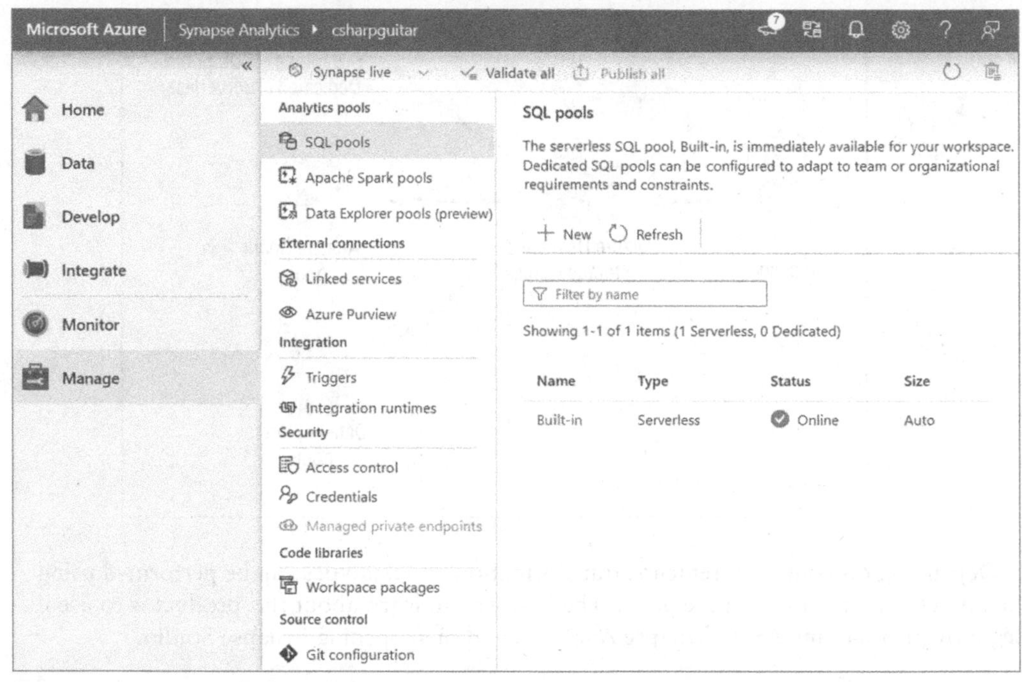

If you receive a message like "The Azure Synapse resource provider (`Microsoft.Synapse`) needs to be registered with the selected subscription" while attempting to provision, you need to add the `Microsoft.Synapse` resource provider to the subscription.

During the provisioning process in Exercise 3.3, you may have noticed that you skipped over some features and left them with the default values. On the Basic tab, for example, you left the Managed resource group . This is an optional resource group that is used for storing additional resources that are created by Azure Synapse Analytics for your workspace. Remember that access restrictions can be applied at the Resource group level using RBAC. There may be scenarios where you want to give users access to specific workspace resources instead of all of them. The Managed resource group is a means for achieving such a security implementation.

On the Security tab you are prompted to create a password for the `sqladminuser`. This password is used for administrator access to the SQL pools in your workspace. You can create a password or let the system generate it. You can change the password later if you need it to be a specific value. The ADLS account you created earlier is not restricted or configured with a VNet, as the scenarios that surround such a configuration are various and complicated. This is discussed in later chapters where security is the focus. Had the ADLS container been configured with a VNet and protected by some networking rules, checking the Allow Network Access to Data Lake Storage Gen2 Account box would have been necessary. Otherwise, connectivity would have been likely blocked by a network security group (NSG). Workspace encryption was introduced earlier but referred to as infrastructure encryption. Remember that the data you place into an Azure storage account is encrypted, known as encrypted-at-rest. When you enable infrastructure encryption, your data is encrypted twice: once at the default service level and again at the infrastructure level. Networking capabilities increase the complexities of a solution significantly. Note that the exam does not include many questions about this. However, be sure to read Chapter 8, "Keeping Data Safe and Secure," as these networking capabilities play a big part in keeping your data secure.

On the Networking tab you are offered the option of configuring a managed VNet. When you implement this, the connectivity to your workspace becomes restricted. That means you will need to manually approve and allow which resources have access to the workspace. There is also an option to control outbound connectivity. If you choose to configure this, you need two kinds of information: which resources need access to your workspace and which resources your workspace needs access to. Once you have those, configure the Managed virtual network settings for your Azure Synapse Analytics workspace, then circle back to the networking portion and modify the firewalls to allow the necessary inbound and outbound traffic. Some of this will be discussed in later chapters, but most of those configurations are outside the scope of this book. Refer to Figure 3.27 for a list of features presented on the Manage hub within Azure Synapse Analytics Studio. The following sections describe those features in greater detail.

Manage

The Manage hub includes the enablers to provision, configure, and connect many Azure Synapse Analytics features to other products. From the creation of SQL pools to the configuration of GitHub, read on to learn about each possibility.

Analytics Pools

When you run a SQL script in Azure Synapse Analytics Studio, some form of compute machine is required to perform its execution. Those machines are called *pools* and come in two forms: SQL and Spark. You should provision a SQL pool if you are working primarily with relational databases, and a Spark pool if you are working primarily with files. It is perfectly reasonable that your data analytics solution span across both of those scenarios, i.e., relational databases and files. If this is the case, you can provision both types of pools and use them as required to transform, analyze, and store data. You will need to find the optimal configuration for your given scenario.

SQL POOLS

By default, when you provision Azure Synapse Analytics, a serverless SQL pool is provided. Creating a dedicated SQL pool is rather simple: Click the + New link (refer to Figure 3.27) and provide the necessary information, as shown in Figure 3.28. Remember that dedicated SQL pools were previously referred to as Azure SQL data warehouses.

FIGUER 3.28 Creating an Azure Synapse Analytics dedicated SQL pool

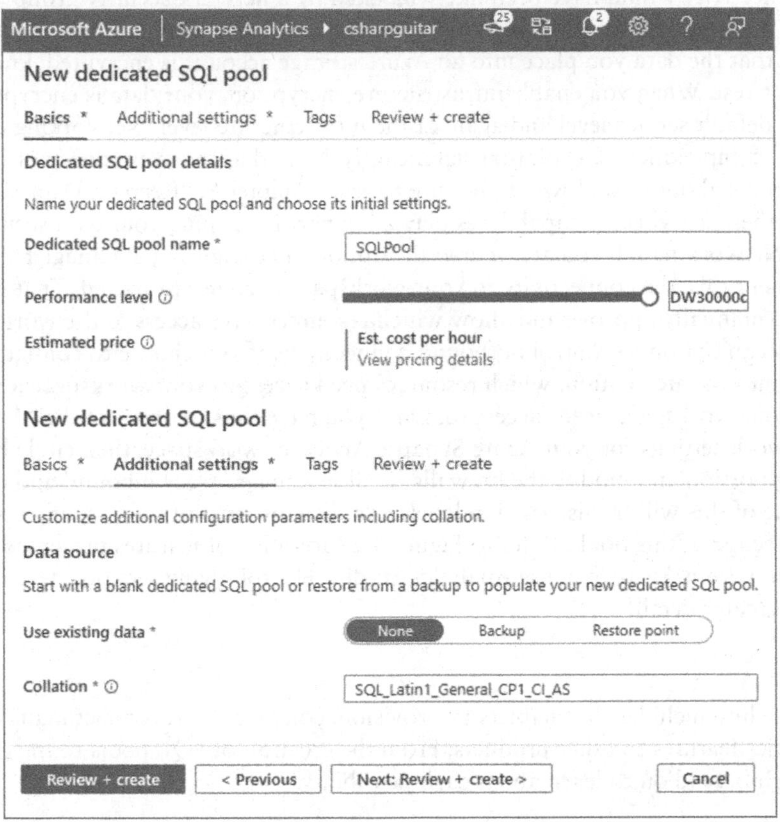

Table 3.7 summarizes the numerous differences between dedicated and serverless SQL pools.

TABLE 3.7 Dedicated vs. serverless SQL pools

Capability	Dedicated SQL pool	Serverless SQL pool
Database tables	Yes	No
External tables (CETAS)	Yes	Yes
Triggers	Yes	No
Materialized views	Yes	No

Capability	Dedicated SQL pool	Serverless SQL pool
DDL statements	Yes	Views and security only
DML statements	Yes	No
Azure AD integration	Yes	Yes
Views	Yes	Yes
Stored procedures	Yes	Yes
Select performance level	Yes	No
Max query duration	No	Yes, 30 minutes

The most obvious constraint when running on a serverless SQL pool is that you cannot create tables to store data on. When using a serverless pool, you should instead consider using external tables. In Chapter 2 you learned how to create an external table. That process requires the creation of a data source, using `CREATE EXTERNAL DATA SOURCE`, that identifies the file(s) containing the data you want to query. Then you identify the file format using `CREATE EXTERNAL FILE FORMAT`. Finally, you use the data source and the file format as parameters in the `WITH` clause of the `CREATE EXTERNAL TABLE` statement. So, in reality you are creating a pointer to the file that is mapped to a table structure that is queryable. It acts like a table, but it is not the same as a table created on a dedicated SQL pool. The other capability to call out is the Max query duration. Unlike dedicated SQL pools, which allow you to choose the performance level of the node, as shown in Table 3.8, serverless SQL pools manage the scaling for you. Cost management for serverless pools is managed by limiting the amount of data queried daily, weekly, and/or monthly. This is in contrast to dedicated pools, where you pay for the selected performance level.

TABLE 3.8 Dedicated SQL pool performance level

Performance Level	Maximum nodes	Distributions	Memory
DW100c	1	60	60 GB
DW300c	1	60	180 GB
DW500c	1	60	300 GB
DW1000c	2	30	600 GB
DW1500c	3	20	900 GB

TABLE 3.8 Dedicated SQL pool performance level *(continued)*

Performance Level	Maximum nodes	Distributions	Memory
DW2500c	5	12	1,500 GB
DW5000c	10	6	3,000 GB
DW7500c	15	4	4,500 GB
DW10000c	20	3	6,000 GB
DW15000c	30	2	9,000 GB
DW30000c	60	1	18,000 GB

Notice in Table 3.8 that the ratios between maximum nodes and distributions conform to the law of 60. Using this table together with the knowledge of number of data rows can help you determine the optimal size. Remember that you need 1,000,000 rows of data per node to meet the requirement for performance boosting caching to kick in. If your distribution were 10,000,000 rows of data, which performance level would you choose? The maximum would be DW5000c, because you want to have 1,000,000 distributed across the nodes. Perhaps DW1500c or DW2500c are better choices to be certain you breach the threshold. But, like with all decisions, the choice is based on the scenario and how compute-intense your queries are.

APACHE SPARK POOLS

An Apache Spark pool is the compute node that will execute the queries you write to pull data from, for example, Parquet files. You can provision a Spark pool from numerous locations. One such place is from the Manage page in Azure Synapse Analytics Studio. After clicking the Manage hub option, select Apache Spark pools. The Basics tab is rendered, as shown in Figure 3.29.

This is where you can name the Spark pool, choose the node size, configure autoscaling, and more. Currently, the only selectable value from the Node Size Family drop-down is Memory Optimized. Perhaps Compute Optimized is coming at some point in the future. The options found in the Node Size drop-down are provided in Table 3.9.

TABLE 3.9 Spark pool node sizes

Size	vCores	Memory
Small	4	32 GB
Medium	8	64 GB
Large	16	128 GB
XLarge	32	256 GB
XXLarge	64	432 GB

FIGUER 3.29 Azure Synapse Analytics Apache Spark pool Basics tab

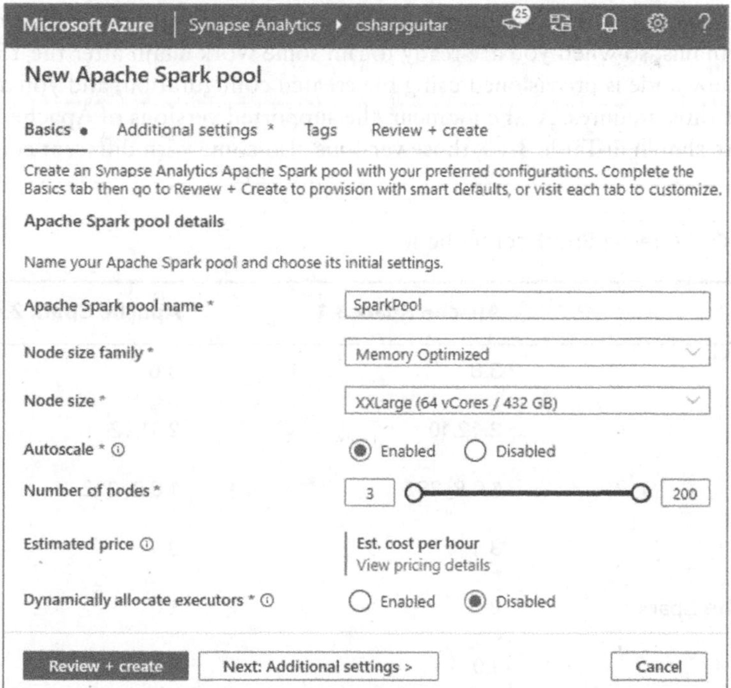

The great part about autoscaling is that the logic and algorithms that determine when the processing of data analytic queries require more compute is provided to you. You do not need to worry about it. Scaling is targeted toward CPU and memory consumption, but there are other proprietary checks that make scaling work very well. In addition to provisioning more nodes when required, autoscaling also decommissions nodes when they are no longer required. This saves you a lot of money, because you are allocated only the compute power you need and not more. It used to be that you needed to purchase your own hardware to manage queries, and those servers often were idle, which was not an optimal use of resources. This is one reason running Big Data analysis in the cloud is so popular. Provisioning required compute power on demand and then decommissioning it when complete is very cost effective. You might want to limit the maximum number of nodes that the Spark pool expands to. This can help control costs. The ability to dynamically allocate executors lets you scale in and out across the different stages of the Spark jobs you run on the node.

Next, you can navigate to the Additional Settings tab (Figure 3.30). It is a good idea to enable Automatic Pausing and then set the Number of Minutes Idle, which is used to shut down the node. This will save you money, as you are charged while the node is provisioned even if it is not doing anything. The default is to have Automatic Pausing enabled in 15 minutes. That means if you do not use the node in 15 minutes, it is shut down. The configuration of the node remains, so when you are ready to run some work again after the 15-minute timeframe, a new node is provisioned using the created configuration, and you are ready to go in about three minutes. At the moment, the supported versions of Apache Spark are 3.1 and 2.4. As shown in Table 3.10, those versions also come with different component versions.

TABLE 3.10 Apache Spark components

Component	Apache Spark 3.1	Apache Spark 2.4
Python	3.8	3.6
Scala	2.12.10	2.11.12
Java	1.0.8_282	1.8.0_272
.NET Core	3.1	3.1
.NET for Apache Spark	2.0	1.0
Delta Lake	1.0	0.6

FIGUER 3.30 Azure Synapse Analytics Apache Spark pool Additional Settings tab

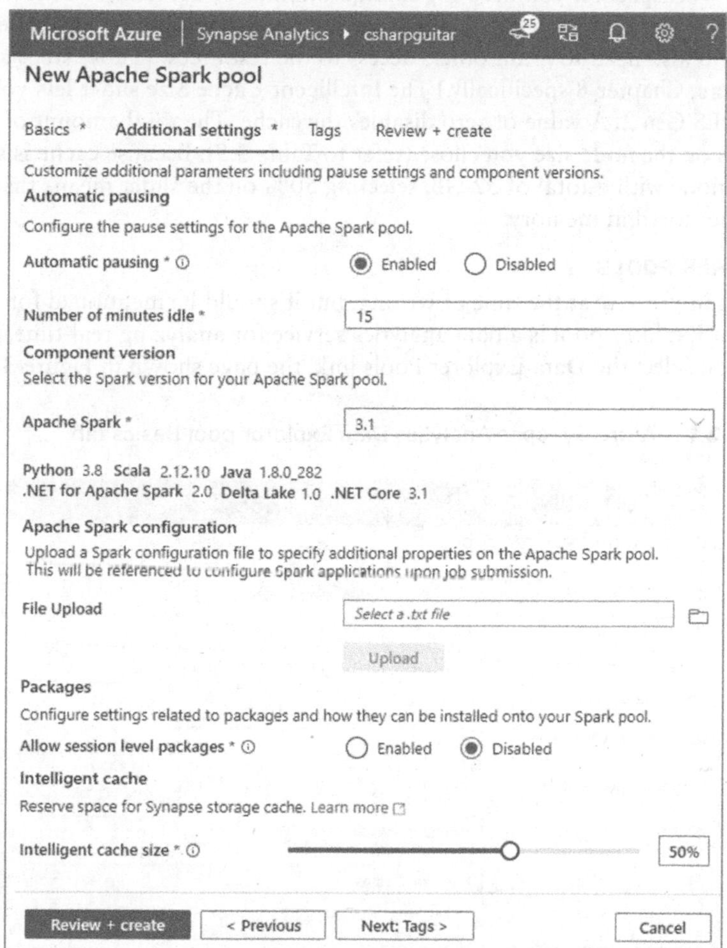

If you need to perform any Spark configurations on the nodes at startup (while booting), the Apache Spark Configuration section is the place to add them. For example, you can add the required configuration to create or bind to an external Hive metastore. Save the necessary configurations to a `.txt` file and upload it. If you need to install packages or code libraries at the session level, select the Enabled radio button in the Allow Session Level Packages section. Remember that your sessions have a context isolated to the work you are specifically doing in Azure Synapse Analytics Studio. The session is terminated when you log out of the workspace. If you need the configuration to be accessible to more people and remain static even after you log off, then use the configuration option in the File Upload option. You will also need to grant others access to the resources. (Those steps are coming in later chapters, Chapter 8 specifically.) The Intelligent Cache Size slider lets you cache files read from ADLS Gen 2. A value of zero disables the cache. The total amount of storage for cache depends on the node size you chose (refer to Table 3.9). Because cache is stored in memory, in a node with a total of 32 GB, selecting 50% on the slider means that 16 GB of file data can be stored in memory.

DATA EXPLORER POOLS

This feature is in preview at the time of writing, but it should be mentioned for future reference. A Data Explorer pool is a data analytics service for analyzing real-time, large-scale data. When you select the Data Explorer Pools link, the page shown in Figure 3.31 appears.

FIGUER 3.31 Azure Synapse Analytics Data Explorer pool Basics tab

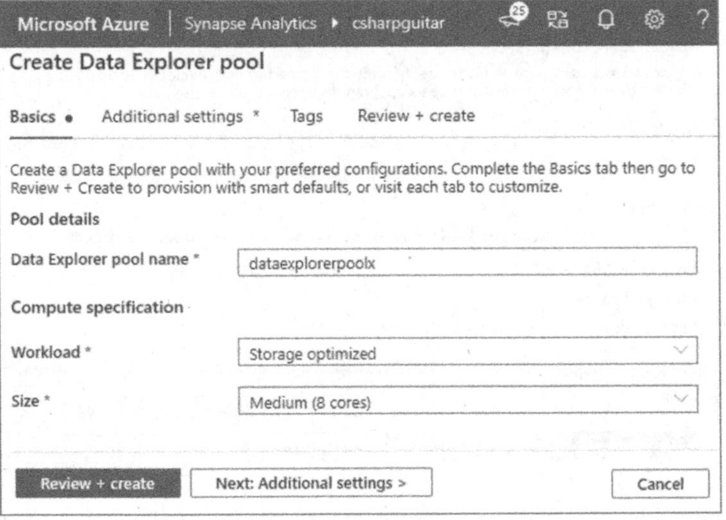

As shown in Table 3.11, there are two selectable workloads and four possible sizes.

The Additional Settings page contains scaling and configuration options, as shown in Figure 3.32. Autoscaling helps you use compute resources optimally. The platform provides more instances when required and deallocates them when no longer required. When the scaling happens it is a proprietary algorithm, but it has to do with CPU and memory consumption. Scaling also saves you money, as you do not have unused resources allocated.

TABLE 3.11 Data Explorer pool workload size

Size	Storage optimized	Compute optimized
Extra Small (2 cores)	No	Yes
Small (4 cores)	No	Yes
Medium (8 cores)	Yes	Yes
Large (16 cores)	Yes	Yes

FIGUER 3.32 Azure Synapse Analytics Data Explorer pool Additional Settings tab

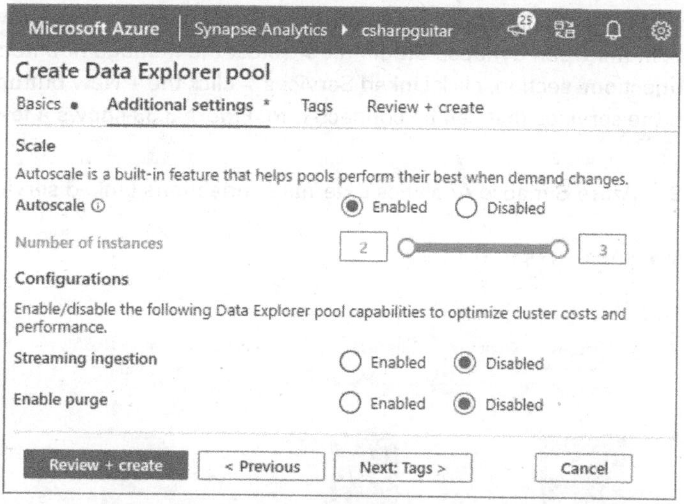

A Data Explorer pool is designed to integrate with Azure Data Explorer. Azure Data Explorer is a datastore from which you use the Kusto Query Language (KQL) to extract data. Azure Data Explorer is also the product used behind the scenes to store Application Insights data. If you enable streaming ingestion, you also need to configure your linked Azure Data Explorer cluster to expect it. You can ingest Event Hubs or IoT Hub messages, or you can create a custom client, using the Azure Data Explorer SDK to program what you need. Setting the Enable Purge option to Enabled allows you to remove data from the Azure Data Explorer cluster using the `.purge` command. Enabling this option will help you conform to the numerous privacy and governance requirements for the storage, archival, and removal of data.

External Connections

You can ingest data into your pipeline by making an external connection to it. At the moment more than 100 endpoints can be connected to, for example, an Amazon RDS, Azure Cognitive Services, Azure Database for MySQL, DB2, Google Big Query, Oracle Service Cloud, and much more.

LINKED SERVICES

A linked service seems to be very similar to a *data source name (DSN)*. A DSN enables you to store connection information for a data source that can be referenced in source code or a configuration by a name. Attributes of a DSN include a connection driver, a name, and the name of the server where the data source is stored. If you have ever worked with a DSN, you might notice the similarities it has with a linked service. In Exercise 3.4 you will create a linked service that connects to the Azure SQL database from Exercise 2.1. After creating the linked service, you will provision a Spark pool, configure it to connect to an external Hive metastore, and query it.

EXERCISE 3.4

Create an Azure Synapse Analytics Linked Service

1. Log in to the Azure portal at `https://portal.azure.com` ➢ navigate to the Azure Synapse Analytics workspace you created in Exercise 3.3 ➢on the Overview blade, click the Open link in the Open Synapse Studio tile ➢ select the Manage hub item ➢ in the External Connections section, click Linked Services ➢ click the + New button ➢ and then look through the services that can be connected to. Figure 3.33 shows a few options.

FIGUER 3.33 Azure Synapse Analytics External connections Linked services

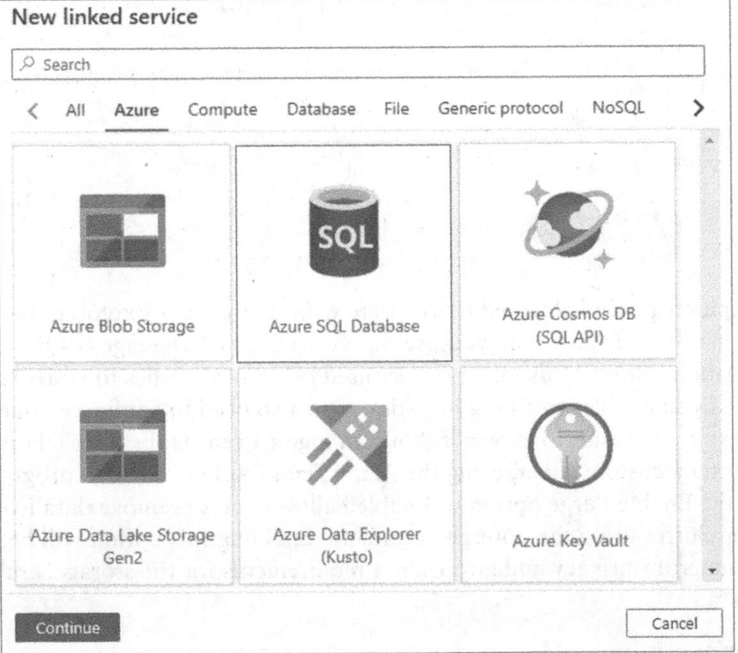

2. Select Azure SQL Database ➢ click Continue ➢ use the database you created in Exercise 2.1 ➢ provide a name (I used **BrainjammerAzureSQL**) ➢ add a description ➢ hover over the information icon next to the Interactive Authoring Disabled message ➢ click the Edit Interactive Authoring link ➢ enable interactive authoring ➢ select the Azure subscription where the Azure SQL database is linked to ➢ select the server name and database name ➢ leave SQL authentication as the authentication type ➢ and then enter the user name and password. The configuration should resemble Figure 3.34.

FIGUER 3.34 Azure Synapse Analytics Linked Azure SQL Database

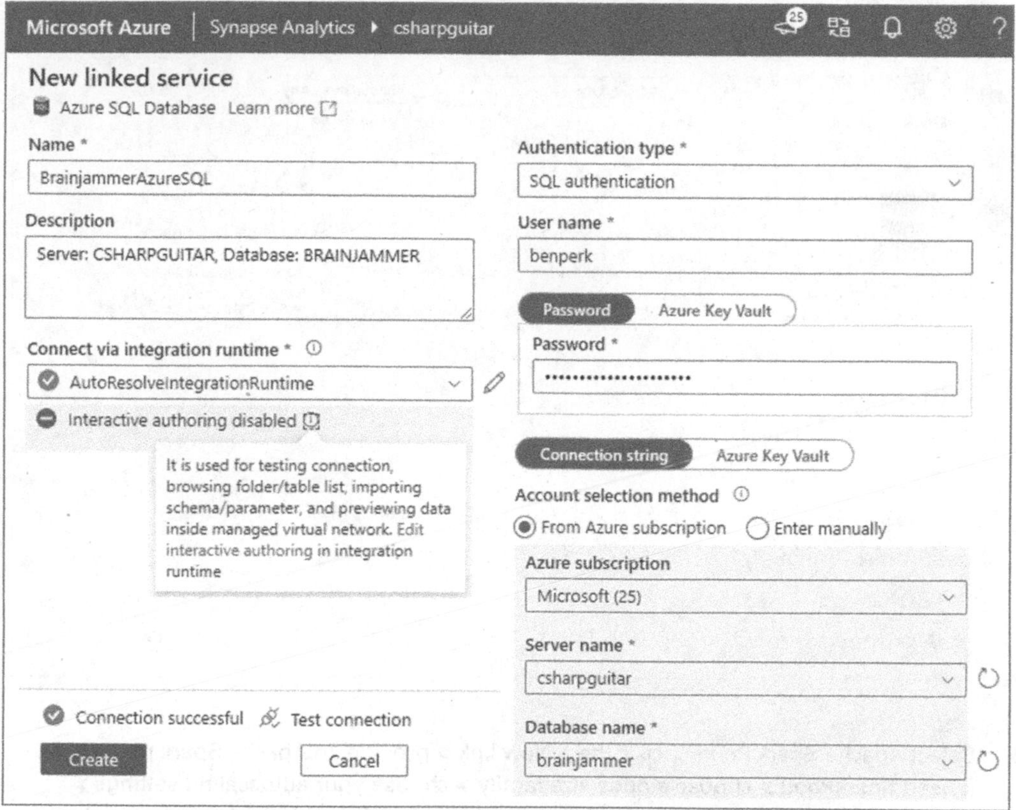

3. Click the Test Connection link, and then click Create. Once enabled, you will see something like Figure 3.25.

EXERCISE 3.4 *(continued)*

FIGUER 3.35 Azure Synapse Analytics linked services

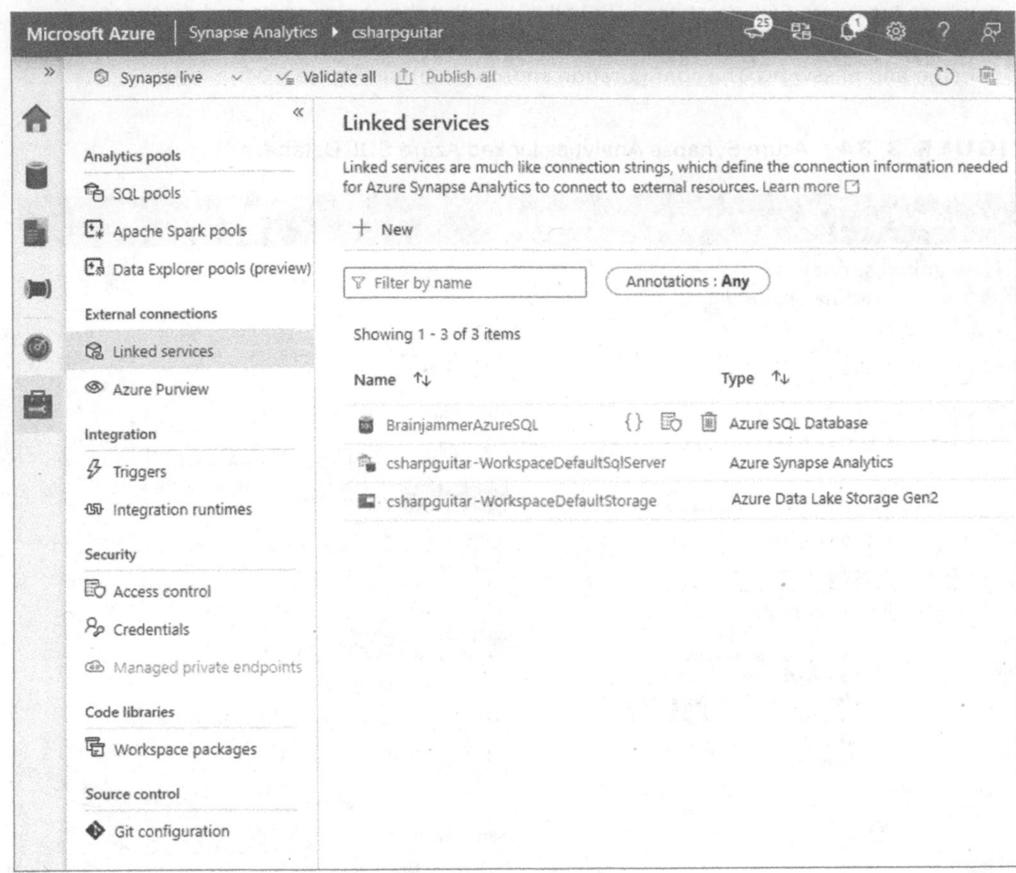

4. Select Apache Spark Pools ➢ click the + New link ➢ provide an Apache Spark pool name (I used **SparkPool**) ➢ choose a node size family ➢ choose your autoscaling settings ➢ click Next: Additional Settings ➢ and then create a `.txt` file with the following content:

```
spark.sql.hive.metastore.version 0.13
spark.hadoop.hive.synapse.externalmetastore.linkedservice.name BrainjammerAzureSQL
spark.sql.hive.metastore.jars /opt/hive-metastore/lib-0.13/*:/usr/hdp/current/
hadoop-client/lib/*
```

Upload the file using the File Upload text box in the Apache Spark configuration section, and then click Upload. Note that there must be only three lines in the code snippet. The third line might break due to formatting. A file example named `metastore.txt` can be downloaded from the `Chapter03/Ch03Ex04` directory on GitHub at `https://github.com/benperk/ADE`.

5. Click the Review + Create button, and then click Create.
6. Once provisioned, select Develop from the navigation menu ➢ click the + ➢ select Notebook ➢ in the Attach To drop-down, select the Spark pool you created in step 4 ➢ enter the following commands into the cell ➢ and then run the following commands. The output will be like that shown previously in Figure 3.24.

```
spark.sql("show databases").show()
spark.sql("show tables in brainjammer").show()
```

When you navigate to the Additional Settings tab, you will see a page that resembles Figure 3.30.

If you have problems with the previous exercise, it might be because you have not yet instantiated the Hive metastore itself. You can achieve this in numerous ways, one of which is described in Exercise 3.14.

Notice that you used the linked service name you created in step 2 of the previous exercise as part of the `.txt` file as the Apache Spark configuration file. Passing that to the startup process loads the linked service configuration into memory and uses its contents to make the connection. In addition to a configuration file, you might see this linked service name used as the value for `DATA_SOURCE` when in the context of `COPY`, `CREATE EXTERNAL TABLES` and `BULK INSERT` SQL command statements. Review those commands in Chapter 2 as a refresher, as necessary.

AZURE PURVIEW

Azure Purview was introduced in Chapter 1. Azure Purview is very useful for governance, data discovery, and exploration. Keeping tabs on the data sources you have and what they contain is key to being able to securely manage them. There will be more on this in Chapter 8, which discusses data security and governance. When you click the Purview link, you are prompted to create an Azure Purview account or connect to one that you already have. You will do this later, at a more appropriate time.

Integration

The Triggers and the Integrated runtime features are directly related to pipelines, which is discussed in the section "Integrate," which covers the features available when you select the Integrate hub option (refer to Figure 3.27).

You need a few things to make a pipeline work: something to trigger (invoke/execute) the pipeline and some compute to process the pipeline activity. Both of those needs are found in the Integration section on the Manage hub.

TRIGGERS

There are two ways to trigger a pipeline. You can do it manually, or you can schedule it. To manually trigger the pipeline in the Azure Synapse Analytics Studio (shown later), you can use REST API or Azure PowerShell. If you need the pipeline to run at scheduled intervals, for example, every hour, click the Triggers menu item followed by + New. If you have a Copy activity in your pipeline that ingests data from an ADLS container each hour, then you would want to schedule that here. Figure 3.36 shows an example of how that scheduled trigger configuration might look.

FIGUER 3.36 Azure Synapse Analytics integration triggers

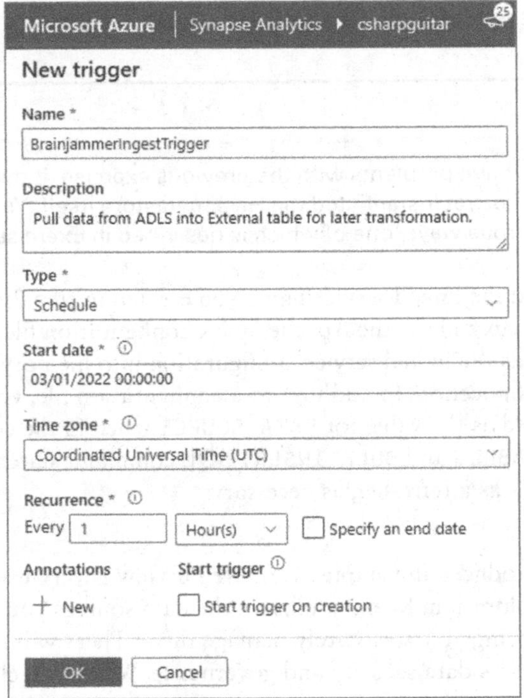

There are four different types of triggers:

- Schedule triggers
- Tumbling window triggers
- Storage event triggers
- Custom event triggers

A tumbling window trigger has a few advantages over a scheduled trigger. For example, when you use a tumbling window trigger, you can run scheduled pipelines for past dates. This is not possible with scheduled triggers, which can only be run currently or at a future time. Failed pipeline runs triggered by a tumbling window trigger will be retried, whereas scheduled will not. Finally, tumbling window triggers can be bound only to a single pipeline, while a single scheduled trigger can invoke multiple pipelines, or multiple pipelines can be invoked by a single scheduled trigger. The storage event trigger is invoked when a blob is either created or deleted in the configured Azure Storage container. A custom event trigger provides the interface to subscribe to an *Event Grid* topic. An Event Grid is a product that acts as a middle tier between a message producer or a message queue and subscribers who want to receive those messages.

INTEGRATION RUNTIMES

An integration runtime (IR) is the compute infrastructure used to run the work configured in your pipeline. Activities such as data flow management, SSIS package execution, data movement, and the monitoring of transformation activities are performed by the IR. There are three types of integration runtimes, which were introduced in Chapter 1.

- Azure
- Self-hosted
- Azure-SSIS

Azure is the default IR named `AutoResolveIntegrationRuntime`. A self-hosted IR lets you use some external compute instead of the Azure Synapse Analytics compute offering. The Azure-SSIS IR is currently only available with Azure Data Factory but is in preview in Azure Synapse Analytics at the time of writing. This IR supports the execution of SSIS execution packages. When you select the Integration Runtimes menu item, you will first see the default, Azure IR. When you click the + New button, you are prompted to choose create either an Azure, self-hosted, or Azure-SSIS IR, as shown in Figure 3.37.

FIGUER 3.37 Choosing an Azure Synapse Analytics integration runtime

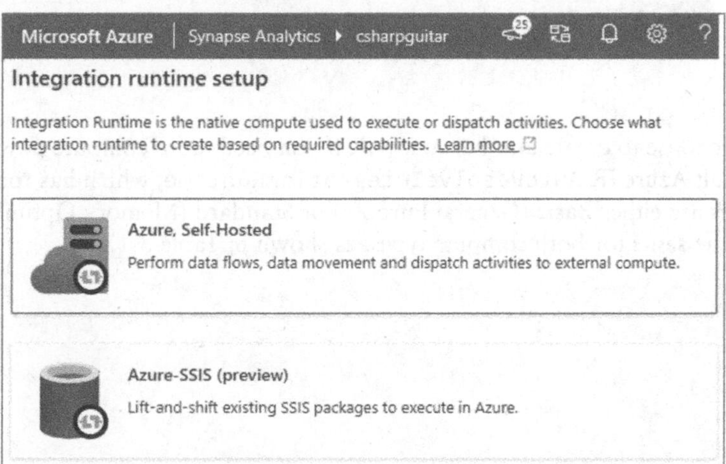

The data ingested in your scenario may exist in numerous locations around the country, continent, or globe. In most cases you want the IR to be as close to the data source as possible. You can achieve this by selecting Auto Resolve from the Region drop-down, or you can select the region in which you created the Azure Synapse Analytics workspace. When you expand the Data Flow Run Time item, the Compute Type, Core Count, and Time to Live options are rendered, as shown in Figure 3.38.

FIGUER 3.38 Creating an Azure Synapse Analytics integration runtime

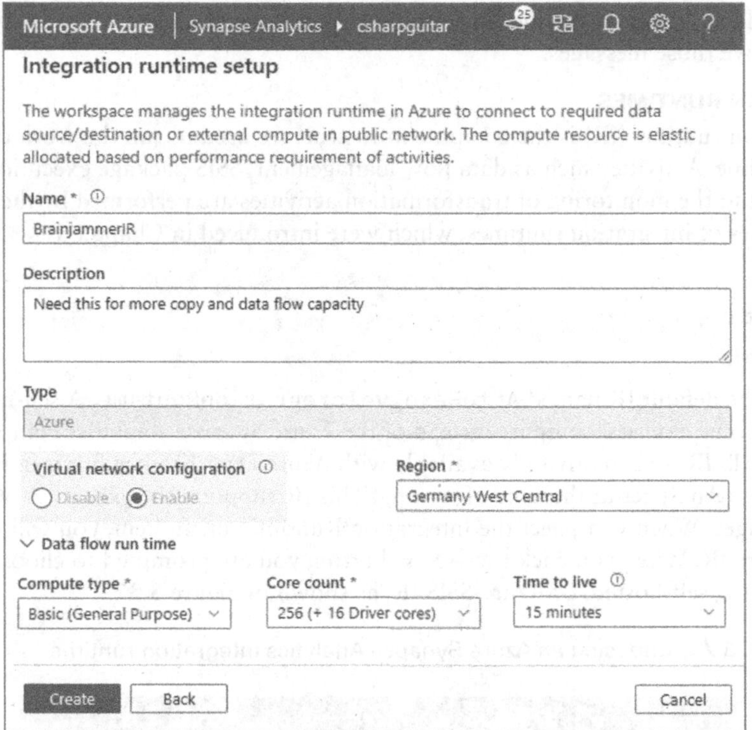

You might choose to create another Azure IR if you need more compute power than the provided default Azure IR `AutoResolveIntegrationRuntime`, which has four cores. Compute types are either Basic (General Purpose) or Standard (Memory Optimized). The core count is the same for both compute types, as shown in Table 3.12.

TABLE 3.12 Integration runtimes core count

Basic (General Purpose)	Standard (Memory Optimized)
4 (+ 4 driver cores)	4 (+ 4 driver cores)
8 (+ 8 driver cores)	8 (+ 8 driver cores)
16 (+ 16 driver cores)	16 (+ 16 driver cores)
32 (+ 32 driver cores)	32 (+ 32 driver cores)
64 (+ 64 driver cores)	64 (+ 64 driver cores)
128 (+ 128 driver cores)	128 (+ 128 driver cores)
256 (+ 256 driver cores)	256 (+ 256 driver cores)

The Time to Live option allows you to set a time when the IR will shut down when idle. Setting this value will result in lower costs, as you are charged while the instance is allocated to you.

Security

After attaining the Azure Data Engineer Associate certification, you will be expected to know how to configure a secure data analytics solution. You will also be expected to know which products and features are necessary to achieve such security. Beyond those two expectations, it is important to approach security as a top priority. Always highly consider engaging a security specialist to perform a security review of the design as early in the process as possible.

ACCESS CONTROL

This feature enables you to grant individuals access to either the Azure Synapse Analytics workspace or a single workspace item. When you initially access the Access Control page, you will see something similar to Figure 3.39.

The Access Control page lists the user accounts grouped by Synapse RBAC roles, the type of account, the role, and the scope. Only users who have an account configured into the Azure Active Directory tenant where the Azure Synapse Analytics workspace was provisioned can be granted access. That means user accounts or service principal accounts that meet that requirement will render in the Select User search box, as shown in Figure 3.40. Synapse RBAC roles were introduced in Chapter 1, but you can see some examples such as Synapse Administrator, Synapse SQL Administrator, and Synapse Compute Operator. Each of those roles has a different level of resource permissions, such as reading, writing, or deleting data, making configurations to compute pools, or provisioning new workspace resources. There is a link to all the Synapse roles in Chapter 1.

FIGUER 3.39 The Access Control page in Azure Synapse Analytics

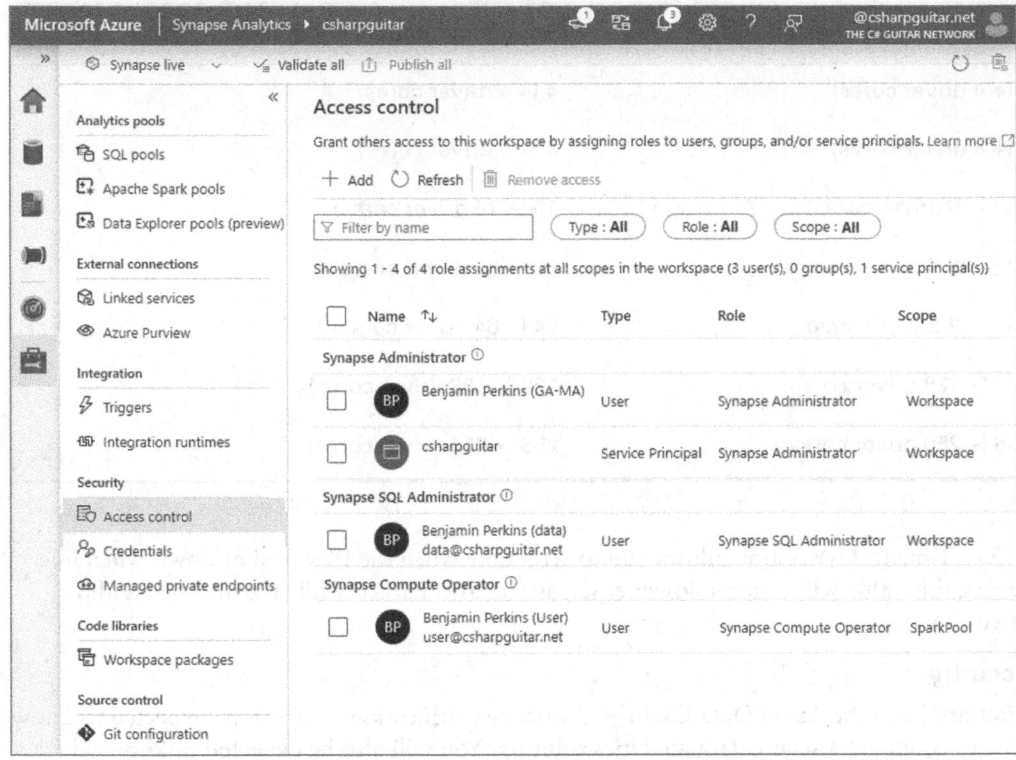

FIGUER 3.40 Adding a role assignment in Azure Synapse Analytics

The different user types can be either a user, a group, or a service principle. Notice that there is a service principle with the same name as the Azure Synapse Analytics workspace. That identity is what is used to grant the workspace access to other Azure resources. For example, in the Azure portal navigate to the ADLS account that you configured when provisioning the Azure Synapse Analytics workspace in Exercise 3.3. Click the Access Control (IAM) link in the navigation menu, and then click the Role Assignments tab. You will see that service principle has been granted access. The service principle is part of the Storage Blob Data Container role. The data in the Scope column, in Synapse Studio, identifies whether the user or service principal account has access to the workspace or a specific item within the workspace. Most of Chapter 8 has to do with security, so if you are interested in that topic now, consider skipping forward (but do come back).

CREDENTIALS

As of this writing, the features available from the Credentials menu item are in preview. This feature has to do with managed identities. As mentioned in the previous section, the Azure Synapse Analytics workspace generates a service principal account, which is used for gaining access to other Azure resources. This feature provides the interface to grant user-assigned, systems-assigned managed identities and service principals permission to access the workspace. There is a twist, though. This identity is used in collaboration with resources configured in the Linked Services area. For other resources in the workspace, you can use the capabilities provided via Access Control.

MANAGED PRIVATE ENDPOINTS

In Exercise 3.3 you enabled managed virtual networking during the provisioning of the Azure Synapse Analytics workspace. This feature enables you to configure outbound workspace connectivity with products, applications, and other services that exist outside of the managed virtual network. When you click the Managed Private Endpoints link, you will see some existing private endpoints. As shown in Figure 3.41, the managed VNet contains data flow, integration runtimes, Spark pools, and those private endpoints.

Private endpoints provide connectivity not only with Azure products but also with on-premises applications and services offered by other cloud hosting providers. Another conclusion you can get from Figure 3.41 is that both serverless and dedicated SQL pools have globally accessible endpoints, whereas Spark pools do not. That means client applications and consumers like Power BI can make a direct connection to the SQL pools to extract data but cannot do so from a Spark pool. Azure Synapse compute pools have access to the ADLS, which is configured when you first provision the Azure Synapse Analytics workspace. The Spark pool uses a private endpoint to make the connection, while the SQL pools use an ADLS endpoint, similar to the following.

- abfss://container@account.dfs.core.windows.net
- `https://account.blob.core.windows.net/container`

Finally, the ADLS can and should have a firewall configured to restrict access to the data contained within it. Especially for production and/or private data, consider having a firewall. Chapter 8 discusses firewalls in more detail.

FIGUER 3.41 Azure Synapse Analytics private endpoints

Code Libraries

By default, Azure Synapse Spark pools come with numerous components and code libraries. As shown in Figure 3.30, components like Java 1.8.0_282, .NET Core 3.1, Python 3.8, and many others are preinstalled on the pool instance(s) for usage in your data analysis and transformation procedures. In addition, you can use more than 100 preinstalled libraries—for example, numpy 1.19.4, pandas 1.2.3, and tensorflow 2.8.0. If you find that a library is missing, you can upload the code package to the platform and use it. In addition to using third-party packages, you can code your own set of data transformation logic, build the package, upload it to the platform, and use it.

There are three scopes where you can make packages available: session, pool, and workspace. At least one is required. When you add a new package to your environment without testing, you are taking a risk. The new package may have some impact on the current ongoing processing pipeline workflows. If you do not have another testing-oriented environment for determining the impact of changes, then consider constraining an uploaded package to a session, instead of the pool or workspace. When you give the code package (aka library) the scope of pool, it means all the instances of that provisioned pool will include the package, while a package with the workspace scope applies the code library on all pools in the Azure Synapse Analytics workspace. Read more about workspace packages in the next section.

WORKSPACE PACKAGES

The best way to learn more about workspace packages is by performing an exercise. In Exercise 3.5 you will upload a simple Python package to the Azure Synapse Analytics workspace and execute it. The source code for the package can be found in the `Chapter03/Ch03Ex05/csharpguitar` directory on GitHub here at `https://github.com/benperk/ADE`.

EXERCISE 3.5

Configure an Azure Synapse Analytics Workspace Package

1. Log in to the Azure portal at `https://portal.azure.com` ➢ navigate to the Azure Synapse Analytics workspace you created in Exercise 3.3 ➢ on the Overview blade click the Open link in the Open Synapse Studio tile ➢ select the Manage hub item ➢ click Upload in the Workspace Packages section ➢ upload the `brainjammer*.whl` file downloadable from the `Chapter03/Ch03Ex05` directory on GitHub at `https://github.com/benperk/ADE` ➢ choose the Apache Spark Pools menu item ➢ hover over the Spark pool you created earlier ➢ select the ellipse (. . .) ➢ select Packages ➢ select the Enable radio button under the Allow Session Level Packages section ➢ in the Workspace Packages section, click + Select from Workspace Packages ➢ check the box next to the `brainjammer*.whl` package (if the package is not there, wait; it is likely still being applied) ➢ be patient ➢ click again on the ellipse (. . .) ➢ once the `.whl` file is visible (see Figure 3,42), also consider clicking the notification bell at the top of the page and look for a Successfully Applied Settings notification.

FIGUER 3.42 Adding a workspace package in Azure Synapse Analytics

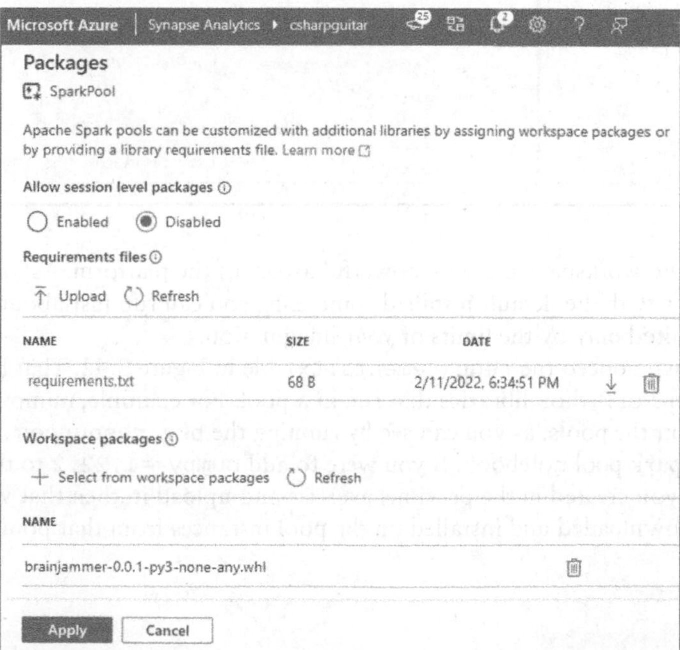

EXERCISE 3.5 *(continued)*

2. Select the Develop hub link ➢ click the + ➢ select Notebook ➢ in the Attach To drop-down box, select your Spark pool ➢ enter the following code snippet into the command window ➢ run the command:

```
import pkg_resources
for d in pkg_resources.working_set:
 print(d)
```

3. The results show `brainjammer 0.0.1` in the list of packages available on that instance. Enter the following snippet to execute the code in the `csharpguitarpkg` package. Figure 3.43 shows the output.

```
from csharpguitarpkg.brainjammer import brainjammer
brainjammer()
```

FIGUER 3.43 Consuming a workspace package in Azure Synapse Analytics

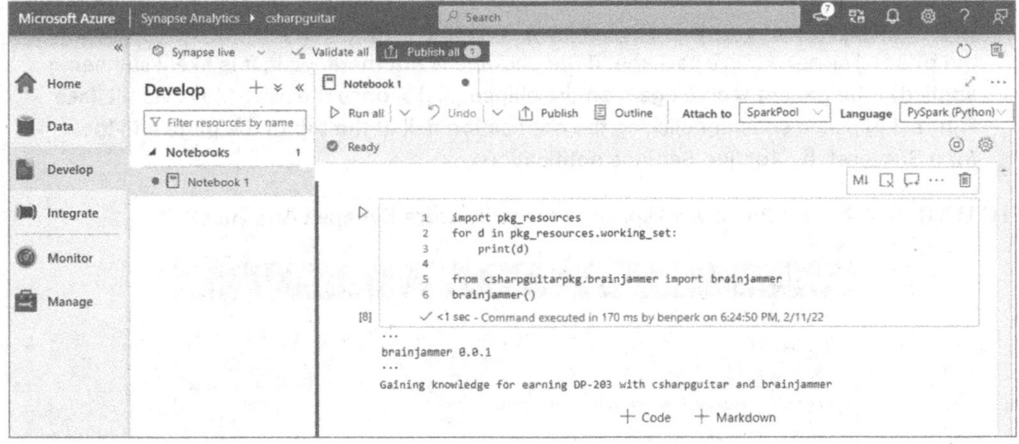

Configuring the workspace is a very powerful aspect of the platform. As long as your custom code runs with the default installed comments, you can run just about any computation. You are limited only by the limits of your imagination.

You might have noticed the `requirements.txt` file in Figure 3.42. That file is useful for managing versions of Python libraries that run in a pool. For example, numpy 1.19.4 is currently installed on the pools, as you can see by running the `pkg_resources.working_set` method in the Spark pool notebook. If you were to add `numpy==1.22.2` to the `requirements.txt` file you created in the previous exercise and upload it, then that version of the library will be downloaded and installed on the pool instances from that point on. You can confirm this by running `pkg_resources.working_set` again after the change has successfully been applied.

Source Control

If you will be writing code or queries to manage your data analytics solution running on Azure Synapse Analytics, you should consider storing them in a repository. Source repositories like Azure DevOps and GitHub provide features like protection of losing the code, storage of change history and branching. After spending hours, days, and sometimes precious weekends creating the code to find insights in your data, the last thing you want is to misplace the code, accidentally delete it, or have your workstation crash and lose the code or queries. If the code is not stored safely, you must create it again. Avoid that by using a source code repository. Having some version history of your code helps debugging issues that might occur after a new version is released. Looking back to see how the code execution path was before the change can help you determine the problem and possible solutions.

Branching enables you to work on different requirements that may have different complexities and delivery dates in parallel. Once the code on these branches is ready for testing, they can be merged back into the main/master branch and flow through the deployment process toward production. Teamwork and security are two additional benefits that can come from having your code stored in a source code repository. If the code is located on a single workstation, then the person who owns that workstation is the only person who can make changes to the code. If it is stored on a central location, then others can get a copy, make changes, make commits, and, after testing, merge those changes into the main production branch. Source code repositories also provide authentication and authorization mechanisms to control who has access to the code and what kind of access they have—for example, read vs. write and whether or not the person can approve the merging of two or more branches. Azure Synapse Analytics provides an interface to connect your workspace with a source control. This is accessible by clicking on the Git configuration link via the Manage hub within the Source Control section. As shown in Figure 3.44, it is also accessible from the Data, Develop, Integrate, and Manage hubs.

FIGUER 3.44 Setting up a code repository in Azure Synapse Analytics

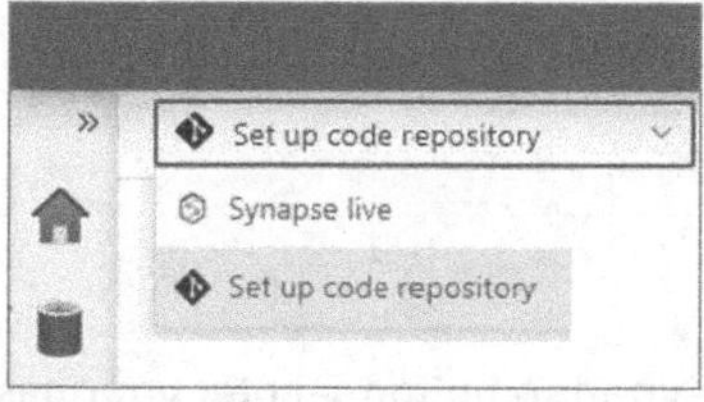

In Chapter 9, "Monitoring Azure Data Storage and Processing," you will get the opportunity to configure source and version control for your pipeline artifacts. Until then, continue

to the next section, where you will configure the connection between your Azure Synapse Analytics and GitHub.

GIT CONFIGURATION

Git is a software application used to track changes to files. It is used most commonly by developers who want to collaborate on the creation of code with others. A common location where developers share their source and let others contribute to it is GitHub. Exercise 3.6 walks you through the steps of connecting your Azure Synapse Analytics workspace with GitHub. You must have a GitHub account in order to complete this exercise.

EXERCISE 3.6

Configure an Azure Synapse Analytics Workspace with GitHub

1. Log in to the Azure portal at `https://portal.azure.com` ➢ navigate to the Azure Synapse Analytics workspace you created in Exercise 3.3 ➢ on the Overview blade, click the Open link in the Open Synapse Studio box ➢ select the Manage hub item ➢ click Git Configuration in the Source Control section ➢ click Configure (it is assumed you do not have an existing configuration) ➢ select GitHub from the drop-down menu (notice that Azure DevOps Git is also available) ➢ and then enter your GitHub user name. Once the configuration resembles Figure 3.45, click Continue.

FIGUER 3.45 Azure Synapse Analytics configure GitHub

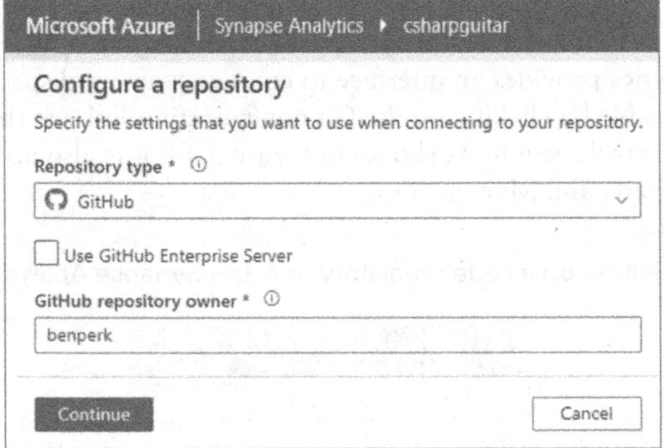

2. Click the Authorize `azuresynapse` button ➢ enter your password ➢ click the Select Repository radio button ➢ choose a name for the repository where you will store your code and/or configurations ➢ choose the Collaboration branch ➢ and then choose the Import Resources into This Branch value. Leave the other values as default. Figure 3.46 represents how this might look. Click Apply.

FIGUER 3.46 Azure Synapse Analytics configure GitHub repository

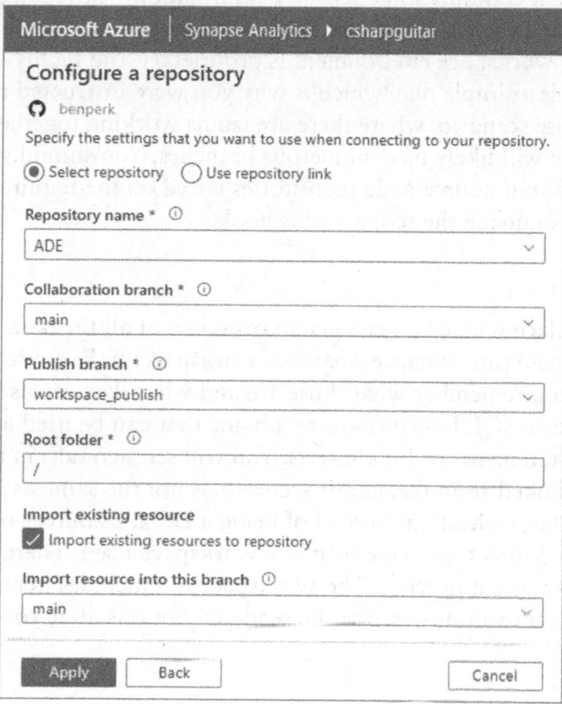

3. Select the Use Existing radio button on the Set Working Branch window ➢ leave the default value of Main ➢ and then click Save. Once the configuration is complete, you should see something like Figure 3.47.

FIGUER 3.47 Azure Synapse Analytics configure GitHub saved

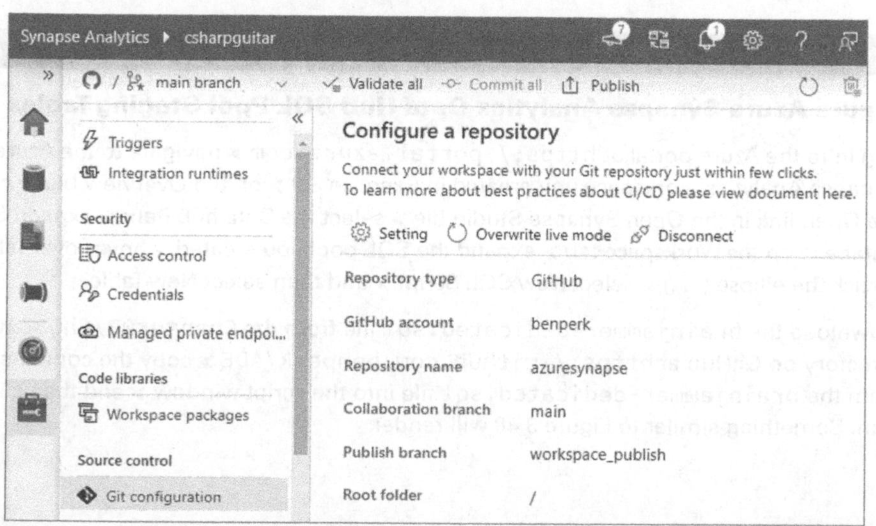

You should not make public the repository where you store the Azure Synapse Analytics content, because it contains some sensitive information—for example, your Azure subscription number and the general configuration of your workspace. In many scenarios the configuration of your workspace environment is proprietary and highly confidential. Additionally, this scenario is a simple one, which is why you were instructed to choose the main branch. In an enterprise scenario, where there are teams working together to build the data analytics solution, you will likely have numerous branches. You should spend some time building the design of your source code repositories based on the requirements of your organization. Doing that is outside the scope of this book.

Data

The Data hub is the place where you can get an overview of all the data sources that are directly available to the Azure Synapse Analytics workspace. In Exercise 3.4 you created a linked service. Do you remember what those are and what they are used for? Remember that you gave that Azure SQL linked resource a name that can be used as a parameter in scenarios like CTAS statements or bulk inserts. You will see two tabs in the Data hub: Workspace and Linked. A linked resource, in this scenario, is not the same as a linked service; the similar name is a bit misleading. Instead of being a DSN, resources on the Linked tab support navigation and direct querying from the workspace itself. There are a few exercises later where you will see the difference. The Workspace tab includes items like dedicated SQL pools. The following subsections describe the rendered options after you click the + icon to the right of Data.

SQL Database

Take a moment to review the discussion around Figure 3.28 dealing with the process for provisioning a dedicated SQL pool. Follow the process and provision one yourself. Once the pool is provisioned, it will appear on the Workspace tab of the Data hub. Once you see the dedicated SQL pool, complete the Exercise 3.7, where you will create and query a staging table on a dedicated SQL pool in Azure Synapse Analytics.

EXERCISE 3.7

Configure Azure Synapse Analytics Data Hub SQL Pool Staging Tables

1. Log in to the Azure portal at `https://portal.azure.com` ➢ navigate to the Azure Synapse Analytics workspace you created in Exercise 3.3 ➢ on the Overview blade click the Open link in the Open Synapse Studio tile ➢ select the Data hub item ➢ expand SQL Database on the Workspace tab ➢ expand the SQL pool you created ➢ hover over Tables ➢ click the ellipse (. . .) ➢ select New SQL Script ➢ and then select New Table.

2. Download the `brainjammer-dedicated.sql` file from the `Chapter03/Ch03Ex07` directory on GitHub at `https://github.com/benperk/ADE` ➢ copy the contents from the `brainjammer-dedicated.sql` file into the script window ➢ and then click Run. Something similar to Figure 3.48 will render.

FIGUER 3.48 Azure Synapse Analytics Data SQL database

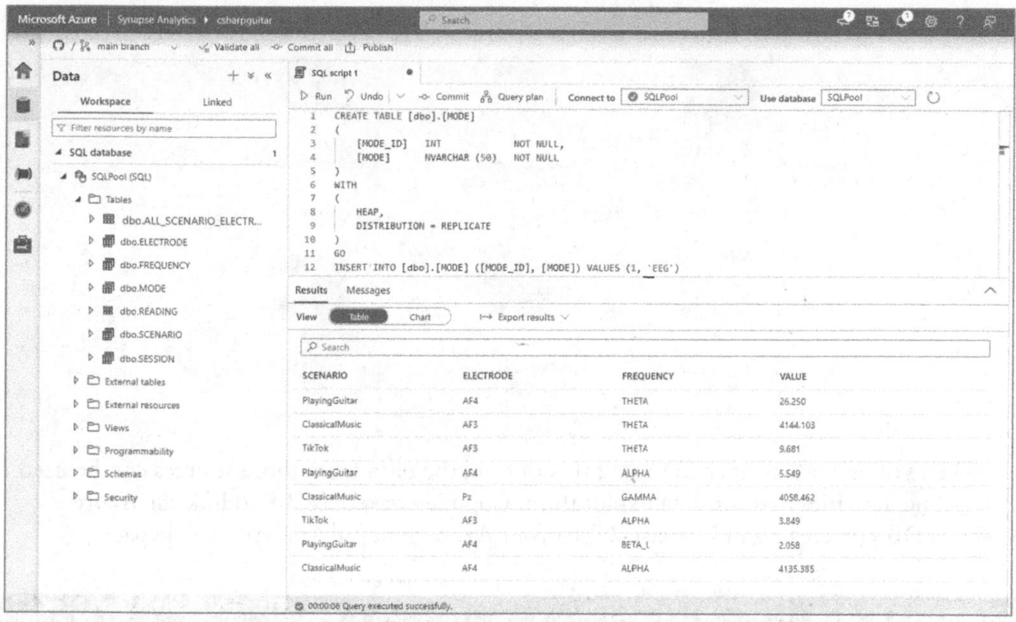

In addition to creating tables, you can also create external tables, external resources, views, stored procedures, and schemas, and implement security. All the features and capabilities of an Azure SQL database or a dedicated SQL pool are found. These kinds of database incur costs when idle; consider pausing it via the Pause button in the Manage hub.

Lake Database (Preview)

At the time of writing, lake databases are in preview. Preview features are unlikely to be included in the exam; furthermore, many features can change during this phase. Lake databases are intended to provide an overview of the vast variety of data stored in your data lake. Data can come from many sources, be in many formats, and might also be unrelated to each other. Lake databases can help you analyze and organize the data in your data lake so that you can better understand how it is structured and how to use it effectively.

Data Explorer Database (Preview)

Data Explorer databases are also in preview. Like SQL databases and lake databases, Data Explorer databases provide an interface to interact directly with the data on your Data Explorer pool. Options include direct querying, data discovery, and performance metrics.

Connect to External Data

When you select the Connect to External Data option from the Data hub menu, you will see the option to add a connection to numerous Azure products, some of which are shown in Figure 3.49.

FIGUER 3.49 Azure Synapse Analytics Data external data

When you make a connection using this option, the data from those sources can be used in pipeline activities and for data exploration. Copmlete Exercise 3.8 to link the Azure Cosmos DB you created in Exercise 2.2 to your Azure Synapse Analytics workspace.

EXERCISE 3.8

Configure Azure Synapse Analytics Data Hub with Azure Cosmos DB

1. Log in to the Azure portal at `https://portal.azure.com` ➢ navigate to the Azure Synapse Analytics workspace you created in Exercise 3.3. On the Overview blade click the Open link in the Open Synapse Studio tile ➢ select the Data hub item ➢ select the Workspace tab ➢ click the + to the right of Data ➢ select Connect to External Data ➢ select Azure Cosmos DB (SQL API) ➢ and then click Continue.
2. Name the connection ➢ provide a description ➢ enable interactive authoring by hovering over the information icon next to the item ➢ select Edit Interactive Authoring ➢ enable it ➢ click Apply ➢ and then choose the Azure Cosmos DB by selecting the subscription, Azure Cosmos DB account, and database name. Leave everything else. The configuration should be similar to Figure 3.50. Click Commit.

FIGUER 3.50 Azure Synapse Analytics Data connect Azure Cosmos DB

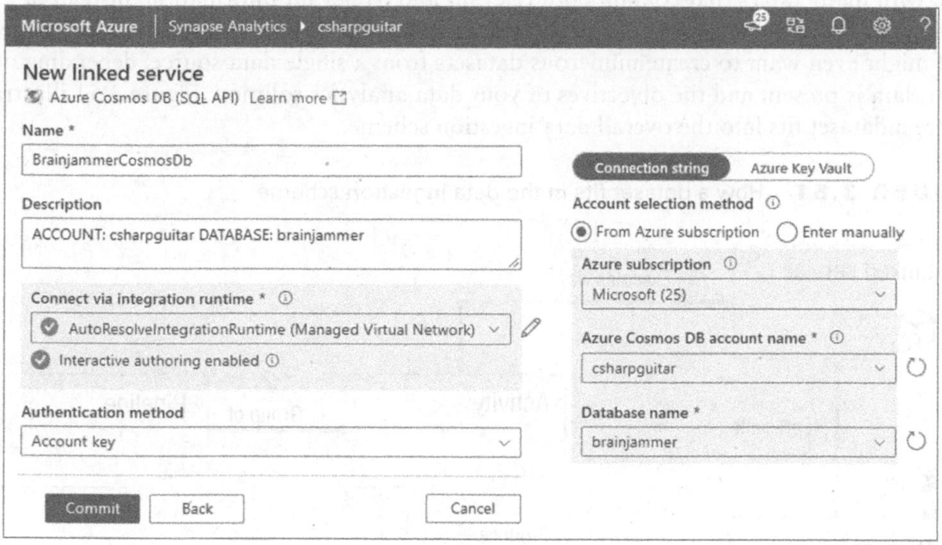

3. Once the connection is rendered on the Linked tab, expand Azure Cosmos DB ➢ expand the connection you just created ➢ hover over the Container (in this case, `sessions`) ➢ click the ellipse (. . .) ➢ select New SQL Script ➢ click Select TOP 100 Rows ➢ consider opening another browser tab and navigate to your Azure Cosmos DB in the Azure Portal ➢ choose the Keys navigation menu option ➢ copy the `PRIMARY KEY` ➢ use this key as the `SECRET` ➢ use the Azure Cosmos DB account name as the `SERVER_CREDENTIAL` (it is prepopulated in the system generated SQL query) ➢ and then place the following snippet at the top of the generated SQL so that it runs first:

```
CREATE CREDENTIAL <SERVER_CREDENTIAL>
WITH IDENTITY = 'SHARED ACCESS SIGNATURE', SECRET = '<PRIMARY KEY>'
GO
```

4. Click Run. The selected results are rendered into the Results window.

You can use this feature to try out queries and discover what data you have in the container. Then use those findings to perform data transformations or gather business insights.

Integration Dataset

The purpose of integration datasets is in its name. Integration datasets provide an interface to easily integrate existing datasets into the Azure Synapse Analytics workspace. Once the data is placed onto a node accessible on the workspace by the IR, computations can be performed on it. A dataset is a collection of data. Consider that you have a relational database with many tables that contain both relevant and irrelevant information. Instead of copying over the entire database, you can extract a dataset of just the information you need. You might even want to create numerous datasets from a single data source, depending on what data is present and the objectives of your data analytics solution. Figure 3.51 illustrates where a dataset fits into the overall data ingestion scheme.

FIGUER 3.51 How a dataset fits in the data ingestion scheme

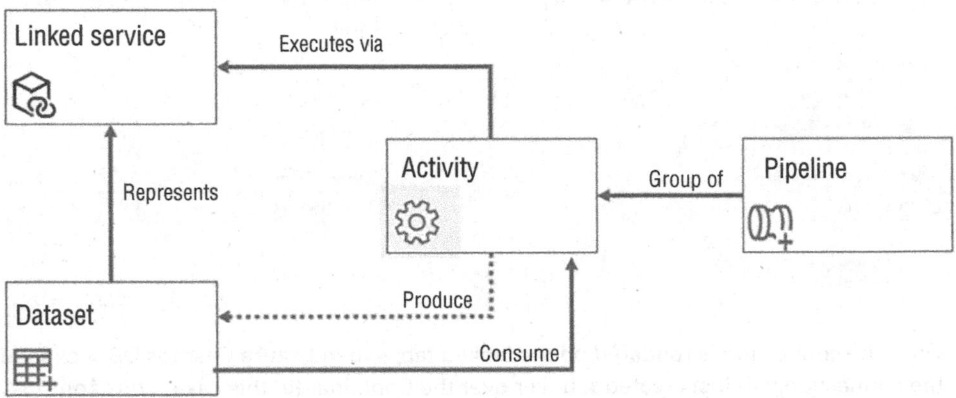

A linked service is required to extract data from a storage container to populate the dataset when instantiated. The dataset is a representation of a collection of data located on the targeted linked service. A dataset is not concrete, in that it is a representation of data collected from a file, table, or view, for example. A pipeline consists of a group of activities, where an activity can be the execution of a stored procedure, a copy/move process, or the triggering of a batch process, to name a few. As shown in Figure 3.51, the activity is gathering the data from the linked service, placing it into the dataset, and then performing any additional activity on it, as required. To learn more about the configuration of an integration dataset, complete Exercise 3.9.

EXERCISE 3.9

Configure an Azure Synapse Analytics Integrated Dataset

1. Log in to the Azure portal at `https://portal.azure.com` ➢ navigate to the storage account you created in Exercise 3.1 ➢ click the File Shares link in the navigation menu ➢ click the + File Share link on the File Shares blade ➢ provide a name (I used **brainjammer**) ➢ select Hot as the Tier (to save some costs) ➢ and then click Create. You just provisioned an Azure Files share.

2. Download the `ALL_SCENARIO_ELECTRODE_FREQUENCY_VALUE.zip` file from the `Chapter03/Ch03Ex09` directory on GitHub at `https://github.com/benperk/ADE` ➢ decompress the zipped file ➢ navigate to the file share you just created ➢ click the + Add directory link ➢ enter a name (I used **brainwaves**) ➢ click OK ➢ navigate into the directory you just created ➢ click Upload ➢ upload both `ALL_SCENARIO_ELECTRODE_FREQUENCY_VALUE` files (`.csv` and `.xlsx`) ➢ and then click Upload.
3. Navigate to the Azure Synapse Analytics workspace you created in Exercise 3.3. On the Overview blade click the Open link in the Open Synapse Studio tile ➢ select the Data hub item ➢ select the Workspace tab ➢ click the + to the right of Data ➢ select Integration Dataset ➢ choose Azure File Storage from the options ➢ consider filtering the data by selecting the Azure tab ➢ click Continue ➢ select the `DelimitedText` format (notice the different supported format shown in Figure 3.52) ➢ and then click Continue.

FIGUER 3.52 Azure Synapse Analytics data integration dataset formats

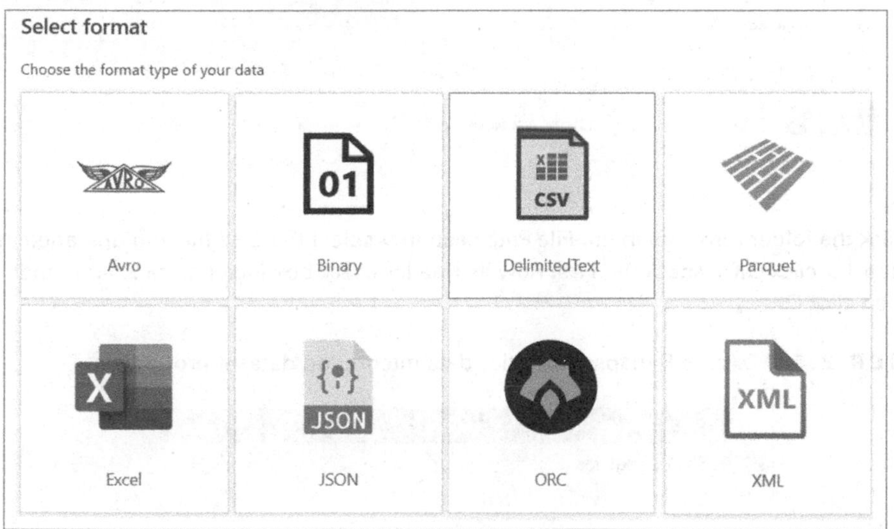

4. Provide a name (I used **brainjammerReadingsCSV**) ➢ expand the Linked Service drop-down ➢ select + New ➢ enter a name ➢ enter a description ➢ enable Interactive Authoring ➢ hover over the information icon next to the Interactive Authoring Disabled message ➢ click Edit Interactive Authoring under the Interactive Authoring heading ➢ click the Enable radio button ➢ click Apply ➢ wait a moment ➢ choose the subscription, storage account name, and file share you created in step 1 (the configuration should resemble Figure 3.53) ➢ click the Test Connection link ➢ and then click Commit.

EXERCISE 3.9 (continued)

FIGUER 3.53 Azure Synapse Analytics data integration dataset linked service

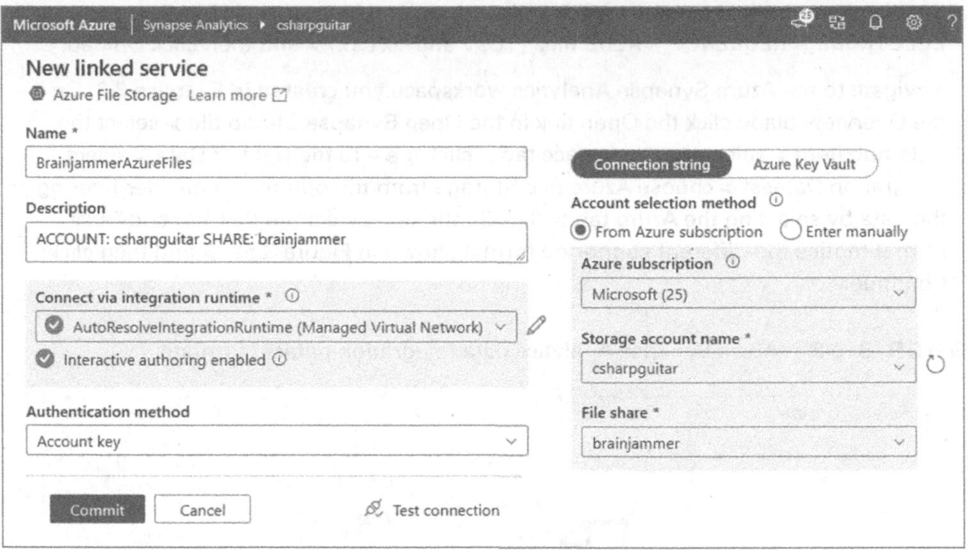

5. Click the folder (browse) in the File Path section ➢ select the CSV file you uploaded in step 1 ➢ click OK ➢ check the First Row as Header check box (see Figure 3.54) ➢ and then click OK.

FIGUER 3.54 Azure Synapse Analytics data integration dataset properties

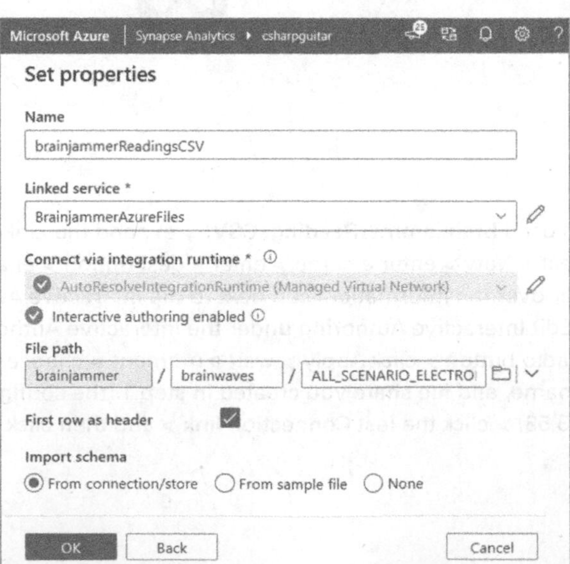

6. Take a look through the Connection, Schema, and Parameters ➤ click the Commit button ➤ click the Linked tab ➤ and then expand Integration Datasets. The dataset is created and accessible.

Nothing in this exercise should be new to you, except perhaps Azure Files. For now, the provisioning of these Azure Synapse Analytics hub components is as far as you will go. Creating and learning about these components now enables you to build upon them in later exercises. As you progress through this book, you should begin to visualize your own paths to take, from learning about each component to designing and implementing an entire enterprise data analytics solution.

Browse Gallery

The Data, Develop, and Integrate hubs each have a link to the Gallery. When you click the Browse Gallery link after clicking the + to the right of either hub, you will see something similar to Figure 3.55.

FIGURE 3.55 The Azure Synapse Analytics Browse Gallery

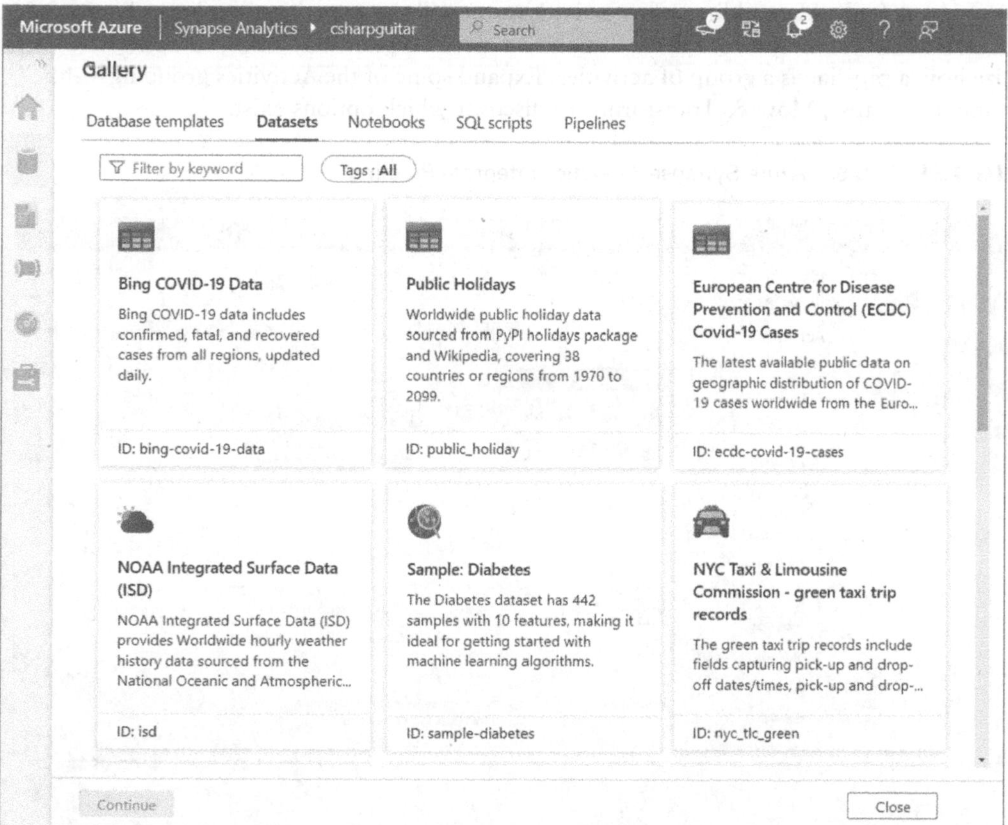

This page includes templates for databases, datasets, notebooks, SQL scripts, and pipelines. This isn't only a great place to get some tips on how to begin building your data analytics solution; there are some useful preconfigured datasets with data that you might find helpful. For example, the Public Holidays dataset includes data that identifies different holidays from around the world. With a simple click of a button, you can have the dataset in your workspace and ready to be queried and used with your solution.

Integrate

It is correct to refer to the integration of data as part of the ingestion stage. The features found on the Integrate hub provide the means for bringing data from numerous data sources into the Azure Synapse Analytics workspace so that later transformations and analytics can be performed. A few of the most powerful Azure Synapse Analytics ingestion and data transformation capabilities are found on the Integrate hub. Other than working within the Develop hub, which is discussed in Chapter 4, "The Storage of Data," you will find that your time is spent most within the Integrate hub.

Pipeline

When you open the Integrate hub, click the + on the right, and then click Pipelines, which is empty by default. After adding a few activities, you will see something similar to Figure 3.56. This first item you may notice is the Activities pane. This pane may help you better visualize how a pipeline is a group of activities. Expand some of the Activities groupings—for example, Synapse, Move & Transform—to discover which options exist.

FIGUER 3.56 Azure Synapse Analytics Integrate Pipeline

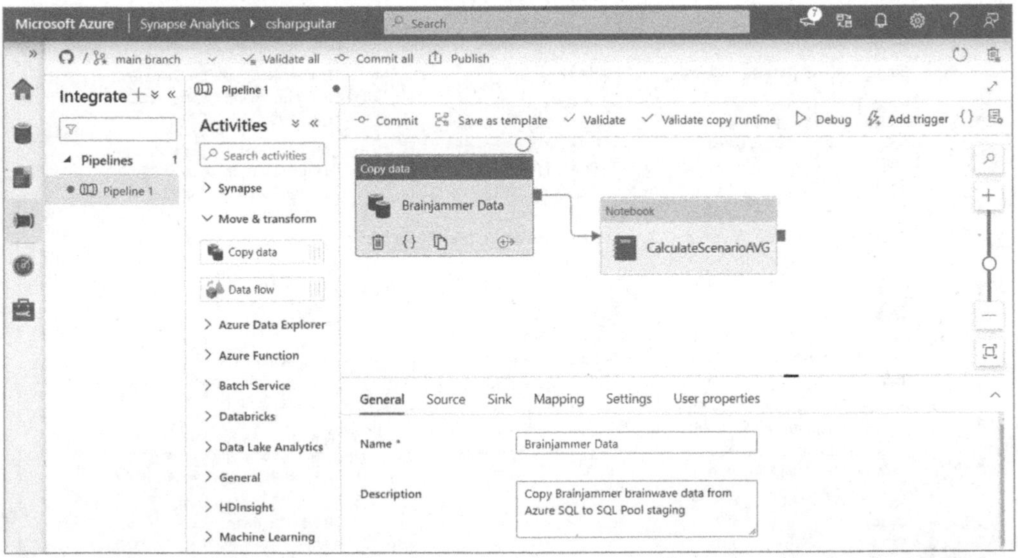

The pipeline presented in Figure 3.56 contains two activities. The first activity is responsible for copying data from a source selected from the Source tab. The Data Source list is populated from the datasets that exist on the integration dataset—specifically, the one you created in Exercise 3.9. The destination is an Azure Synapse Analytics workspace that contains a linked service targeting a database table, for example. Once the data is copied to the database, some code within the notebook is triggered on the data. The code may either complete the data transformation process or simply progress the data one step closer to its business-ready (i.e., gold) state.

A number of options are available when you click the General, Source, Sink, Mapping, Settings, and User Properties tabs. The options that contain configurations that require some extra attention and are likely the most interesting are Source, Sink, and Mapping. They include many of the concepts that have been discussed until now, but here is where you can actually configure and implement them.

SOURCE

When you drag a Copy activity into the pipeline editor canvas, you will see the properties of that activity. Then, when you click the Source tab, you will see something similar to Figure 3.57. Notice that the value shown in the Source Dataset drop-down box is the one you created in Exercise 3.9.

FIGUER 3.57 Azure Synapse Analytics Pipeline Copy data Source tab

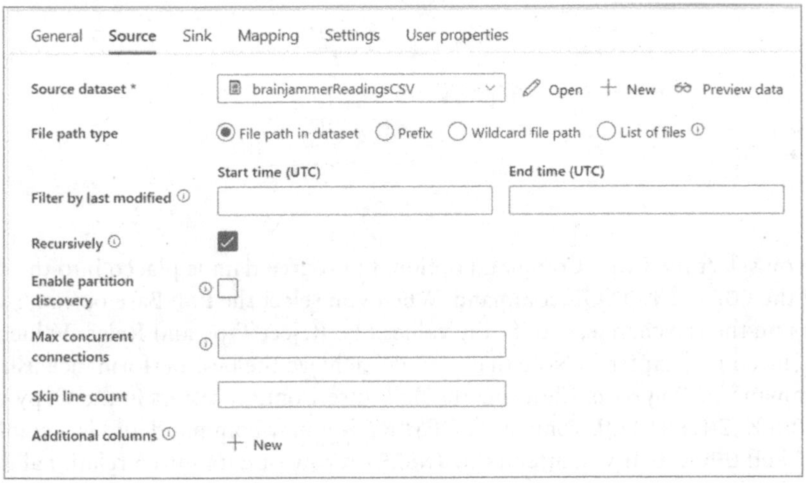

Clicking the Preview Data link will open a window that contains 10 rows from the targeted data source of the integration dataset. To view the details of the `brainjammerReadingsCSV` integrated dataset, select the Open link. This integration dataset is mapped to a CSV file residing on an Azure Files share. In Exercise 3.9 you were instructed to target a specific file, but as you see in Figure 3.57, it is also possible to pull from that share based on the file prefix or a wildcard path, or select a list of files.

SINK

Chapter 2 introduced sink tables. A sink table is a table that can store data as you copy it into your data lake or data warehouse.

You have not completed an exercise for the integrated dataset you see in the sink dataset shown in Figure 3.58. The integration dataset is of type Azure Synapse dedicated SQL pool and targets the `ALL_SCENARIO_ELECTRODE_FREQUENCY_VALUE` table you created in Exercise 3.7. The support file `BrainjammerSqlPoolTable_support_GitHub.zip` for this integration dataset is located in the `Chapter03` directory on GitHub at `https://github.com/benperk/ADE`. The most interesting part of the Sink tab is the Copy method options: Copy Command, PolyBase, Bulk Insert, and Upsert. Support files are discussed in the upcoming sections.

FIGUER 3.58 Azure Synapse Analytics Pipeline Copy data Sink tab

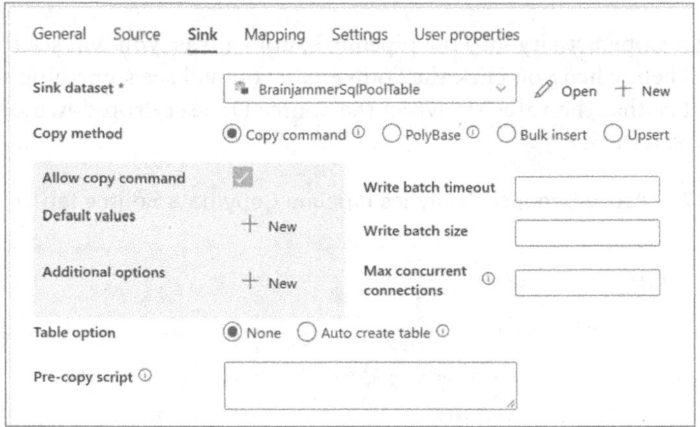

When you select the Copy Command option, the source data is placed into the destination using the `COPY INTO` SQL command. When you select the PolyBase option, some of the parameters on the tab change, specifically values like Reject Type and Reject Value, which were introduced in Chapter 2. Note that you will achieve the best performance using either Copy Command or PolyBase. Choosing the Bulk Insert option results in the Copy command using the `BULK INSERT` SQL command. *UPSERT* is a new command and is a combination of `INSERT` and `UPDATE`. If you attempt to `INSERT` a row of data into a relational database table that already has a row matching the primary key, an error is rendered. In the same manner, if you attempt to `UPDATE` a row and the primary key or matching where criteria do not exist, an error will be rendered. To avoid such errors, use the `UPSERT` statement, which will perform an `INSERT` if the row does not already exist and an `UPDATE` if it does.

MAPPING

The Mapping tab, as shown in Figure 3.59, provides a comparison of the source data to the target data structure.

FIGUER 3.59 Azure Synapse Analytics Pipeline Copy data Mapping tab

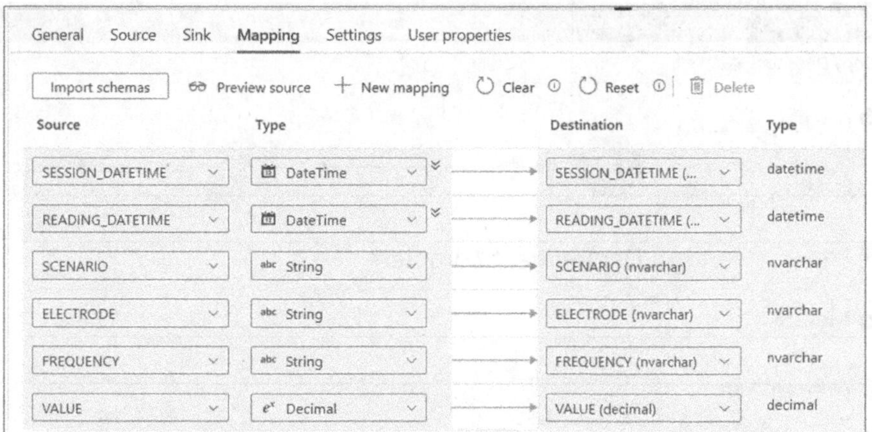

You have the option to change the data order, the column name, and the data type. This is a very powerful feature that can prevent or reduce issues when performing a copy—for example, having extra or missing columns and wrong data type mapping, or trying to place a string into a numeric or datetime column.

Copy Data Tool

The Copy Data tool is a wizard that walks you through the configuration and scheduling of a process to copy data into your workspace. The first window offers numerous scheduling capabilities like Run Once Now, Schedule, and Tumbling. The Run Once Now option does exactly what its name implies. The Schedule option offers the configuration of a start date, a recurrence, like hourly, daily, weekly, etc., and an optional end date. Tumbling, like the similar option discussed previously regarding triggers, has some advanced capabilities like retry policies, concurrency capabilities, and delaying the start of a run.

The copy retrieves data from a datastore connection from the set of integration datasets configured for the workspace. The destination can be, for example, a SQL pool running on the Azure Synapse Analytics workspace. Before the Copy Data tool configuration is executed, you might see something similar to Figure 3.60.

There is a step called Mapping where the wizard analyzes the source data schema and attempts to map it to the destination data schema. If there are any errors, you are prompted to repair them, which is quite a powerful and helpful feature.

Import Resources from Support File

You can find an example of a support file (`BrainjammerSqlPoolTable_support_GitHub.zip`) in the `Chapter03` folder on GitHub at `https://github.com/benperk/ADE`. This compressed file contains information about the configuration of an integration dataset. If you want to include this configuration in your Azure Synapse Analytics workspace, you would use this feature to import it. Note that the configuration contains some sensitive information, so do not make this support file public. The example on GitHub has been modified to remove the sensitive information.

FIGUER 3.60 Azure Synapse Analytics Copy Data tool

Import from Pipeline Template

You may have noticed the Save As Template option in Figure 3.56. There is also an Export Template option. Export templates are accessible by clicking the ellipse (. . .) on the right side of the page, which renders a drop-down menu. If your Azure Synapse workspace is configured with a source control, like what you did in Exercise 3.6, then each time you click the Commit button, the configuration is saved or updated into that repository. Any time you want to import that pipeline template, you can download it from your source control, or you can use an exported or saved template from another source.

Azure Data Factory

It is the near to midterm objective of Microsoft to merge as many features as possible from all existing data analytics offerings into Azure Synapse Analytics. Looking back at Figure 1.17 and Figure 1.21, you can the similarities between Azure Synapse Analytics and Azure Data Factory. Both products use the same procedures, configuration, and requirements for creating linked services, integration datasets, and pipelines. Two primary differences between Azure Synapse Analytics and Azure Data Factory concern SSIS packages and the term Power Query. Azure Data Factory now fully supports importing and running existing SSIS packages—refer to Figure 3.37, which shows the capability as Azure-SSIS preview. The feature is currently in the Azure Synapse Analytics workspace but not yet fully supported. Until it is fully supported in Azure Synapse Analytics and no longer in preview mode, I recommended using the SSIS capability of Azure Data Factory for production workloads. Complete Exercise 3.10 to provision an Azure data factory.

EXERCISE 3.10

Create an Azure Data Factory

1. Log in to the Azure portal at `https://portal.azure.com` ➢ enter **Data Factories** in the search box ➢ click Data Factories ➢ click the + Create button ➢ select the subscription ➢ select or create a new resource group ➢ select the region ➢ name the data factory ➢ and then click the Next: Git configuration button.
2. Select the Configure Git Later check box ➢ click the Next: Networking button ➢ check the Enable Managed Virtual Network check box ➢ leave the Public Endpoint radio button selected ➢ click the Next: Advanced button ➢ review the options, leaving the default settings ➢ click the Review + Create button ➢ review the selections ➢ and then click Create.
3. Once the data factory is provisioned, navigate to it, and then click the Open link on the Overview blade in the Open Azure Data Factory Studio tile.

The provisioning of an Azure data factory is straightforward. The one item you have not seen before was on the Advanced tab: the Enable Encryption Using a Customer Managed Key check box. As you might have read in the text on that tab, the data stored in Azure Data Factory is encrypted by default using a Microsoft managed encryption key. If you wanted some additional control over the encryption of the blobs and files stored in Azure Data Factory, you can supply your own managed keys. The key must be stored in Azure Key Vault in order to be used. Clicking the check box results in the rendering of a text box for providing the Azure Key Vault endpoint and a drop-down text box to select managed identity used for accessing the key stored in the identified vault.

When you access Azure Data Factory Studio, you might notice is how similar the look and feel is as compared to Azure Synapse Analytics Studio. Azure Synapse Studio is the recommended place to perform ingestion from now, but since Azure Data Factory was the predecessor to Azure Synapse, customers have provisioned Azure Data Factory and are dependent on it; therefore, the product remains. New features will be added to Azure Synapse Analytics, and the capabilities that exist in Azure Data Factory will be migrated to Azure Synapse Analytics, until the point where there is likely no visible difference between the two.

You will find three hubs in Azure Data Factory Studio: Manage, Author, and Monitor. The first two are covered here, and Monitor is covered in Chapter 9. Before heading into the hubs, notice on the Home page that there is a tile named Ingest. When you click it, you might notice the same thing shown in Figure 3.60: the Copy Data tool. The Orchestrate tile is the pipeline capability you saw in Figure 3.56, and Transform navigates you to the Data Flows page. Data flows are covered in detail later in this chapter. Many of the features found in Azure Data Factory were already covered in the previous section, so you will find only summaries of the duplicates. Features that are not in Azure Synapse Analytics will be discussed in a bit more detail.

Manage

The Manage hub is the place for creating linked services, IRs, triggers, configuring Git, credentials, and managed endpoints. This is the place to visit to configure the dependencies Azure Data Factory requires to ingest, copy, and transform data.

Connections

This section contains the interface to configure linked services, IRs, and Azure Purview.

LINKED SERVICES

This is a configuration that contains the necessary parameters to make a connection to a data source. You name the linked service and choose the IR performing the actions that require compute power and the connection information. Perform Exercise 3.11 to create a linked service in Azure Data Factory.

EXERCISE 3.11

Create a Linked Service in Azure Data Factory

1. Navigate to the Azure data factory you created in Exercise 3.10, and then click the Open link on the Overview blade in the Open Azure Data Factory Studio tile.
2. Select the Manage hub ➢ select Linked Services ➢ select + New ➢ select Azure File Storage ➢ click Continue ➢ provide a name ➢ provide a description ➢ enable interactive authoring (hover over the information icon for instructions) ➢ select the subscription where you provisioned the Azure storage account in Exercise 3.1, which also contains the Azure file share from Exercise 3.9 ➢ select the storage account name from Exercise 3.1 ➢ select the file share from Exercise 3.9 ➢ click the Test Connection link at the bottom of the window ➢ and then click Create.

A linked service is used as a basis for the creation of a dataset.

INTEGRATION RUNTIMES

Some activities, such as testing a linked service or dataset connection or pulling resources from a data source using the Preview Data option, require some compute power. This compute power is provided by IRs and comes with an associated cost.

AZURE PURVIEW

Azure Purview, introduced in Chapter 1, is very useful for governance, data discovery, and exploration. Keeping tabs on your data sources and what they contain is key to being able to securely manage them. There will be more on this in Chapter 8, which discusses data security and governance. If you click the link, you will be prompted to create an Azure Purview account or connect to one that you already have. You will do this later, at a more appropriate time.

Source Control

When working as a team, you need to have a central location to store source code and configurations. Working alone, it is a very good idea to store your code in a place other than your workstation, since workstations have been known to crash and never return. Take precautions, perform due diligence, and put your work in a safe location, like GitHub or Azure DevOps.

GIT CONFIGURATION

This feature walks you through the configuration of a Git repository. You can integrate with either GitHub or Azure DevOps. A GitHub repository named `azuredatafactory` can be similar to that shown in Figure 3.61.

FIGUER 3.61 Azure Data Factory Manage Git configuration example

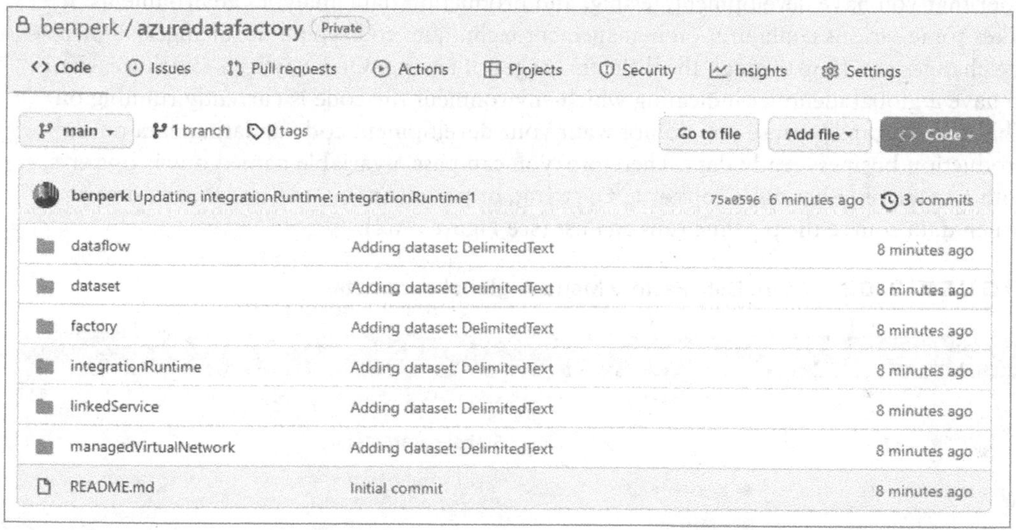

When you navigate to any of the folders, you will find JSON files that contain the configuration details for the features, services, and dependencies for your Azure Data Factory workspace.

ARM TEMPLATE

The Azure Resource Manager (ARM) exposes many capabilities you can use to work with the Azure platform. One such capability is an API that allows client systems to send ARM templates to API.These ARM templates contain JSON-structured configurations that instruct the ARM API to provision and configure Azure products, features, and services. Instead of performing the provisioning and configuration using the Azure portal, you could instead use an ARM template sent to the ARM API. The main page includes an Export ARM Template tile. Consider exporting the ARM template and take a look at the JSON files. You can easily deploy the same configuration into a different region with minimal changes to the exported ARM template.

Author

The Author hub contains two features: triggers and global parameters.

TRIGGERS

Triggers are a means for starting the orchestration and execution of your pipelines. As in Azure Synapse Analytics, there are four types of triggers: scheduled, tumbling window, storage events, and customer events.

GLOBAL PARAMETERS

Global parameters enable you to pass parameters between different steps in a pipeline. Consider that you have development, testing, and production data analytics environments. It takes some serious configuration management techniques to keep all the changes aligned so the changes can flow through the different stages of testing. One way to make this easier is to have a global identifier indicating which environment the code is currently running on. This is important because you do not want your development code updating data on the production business-ready data. Therefore, you can pass a variable named `environment`, with a value of either `development`, `testing`, or `production`, and use that to determine which data source the pipeline runs against (see Figure 3.62).

FIGUER 3.62 Azure Data Factory Manage global parameters

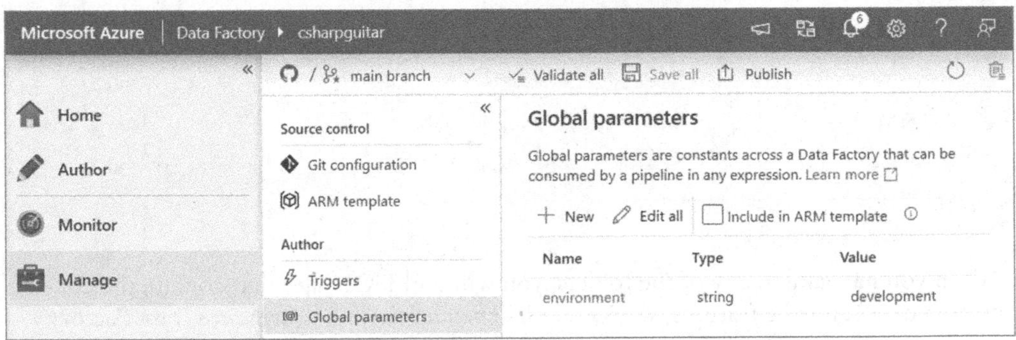

Access the environment variable using the following code clicking via the JSON configuration file for the given pipeline:

```
@pipeline().globalparameters.evironment
```

You can modify the JSON configuration by selecting the braces ({}) on the right side of the Pipeline page.

Security

Security, as always, should be your top priority. Consider consulting an experienced security expert to help you determine the best solution for your scenario.

CUSTOMER MANAGED KEY

The customer managed key was mentioned shortly after Exercise 3.10 regarding the Enable Encryption Using a Customer Managed Key check box. Had you provided an Azure Key Vault key and managed identity, they would have appeared here. If you change your mind and want to add a managed key after the initial provision, you can do so on this page.

CREDENTIALS

The Credentials page enables you to create either a service principle or a user-assigned managed identity. These are credentials that give the Azure product an identity that can be used for granting access to other resources.

MANAGED PRIVATE ENDPOINTS.JS

Private endpoints were discussed in the "Managed Private Endpoints" subsection of the "Azure Synapse Analytics" section. Review that section, as the concept is applicable in this context as well.

Author

Authoring in this context is another word for developing and is where you will find some tools for data ingestion and transformation.

Dataset

A dataset in Azure Data Factory is the same as in Azure Synapse Analytics. In ADF or ASA is where you specifically identify the data format, which linked service to use, and the actual set of data to be ingested. Perform Exercise 3.12 to create a dataset in Azure Data Factory.

EXERCISE 3.12

Create a Dataset in Azure Data Factory

1. Navigate to the Azure Data Factory you created in Exercise 3.10, and then click the Open link on the Overview blade in the Open Azure Data Factory Studio tile.
2. Select the Author hub ➢ hover over Dataset and click the ellipse (. . .) ➢ click New Dataset ➢ select Azure File Storage ➢ select Excel ➢ click Continue ➢ enter a name ➢ select the linked service you created in Exercise 3.11 ➢ click the folder icon at the end of File path ➢ navigate to and select the `ALL_SCENARIO_ELECTRODE_FREQUENCY_VALUE.xlsx` file you uploaded in Exercise 3.9 ➢ click OK ➢ select `READINGS` from the Sheet Name drop-down box ➢ check the First Row as Header check box ➢ select the None radio button ➢ and then click OK.

EXERCISE 3.12 *(continued)*

3. Click the Test Connection link on the Dataset page, and then click the Preview Data link, which renders something similar to Figure 3.63.

FIGUER 3.63 Azure Data Factory Author dataset

Preview data

Linked service: AzureFileStorage

Object: ALL_SCENARIO_ELECTRODE_FREQUENCY_VALUE.xlsx

SESSION_DATETIME	READING_DATETIME	SCENARIO	ELECTRODE	FREQUENCY	VALUE
1899-12-31 00:35:00.0000000	1899-12-31 00:35:32.6000000	ClassicalMusic	AF3	THETA	44.254
1899-12-31 00:35:00.0000000	1899-12-31 00:35:32.6000000	ClassicalMusic	AF3	ALPHA	5.479
1899-12-31 00:35:00.0000000	1899-12-31 00:35:32.6000000	ClassicalMusic	AF3	BETA_L	1.911
1899-12-31 00:35:00.0000000	1899-12-31 00:35:32.6000000	ClassicalMusic	AF3	BETA_H	1.688
1899-12-31 00:35:00.0000000	1899-12-31 00:35:32.6000000	ClassicalMusic	AF3	GAMMA	0.259
1899-12-31 00:35:00.0000000	1899-12-31 00:35:32.6000000	ClassicalMusic	AF4	THETA	35.433
1899-12-31 00:35:00.0000000	1899-12-31 00:35:32.6000000	ClassicalMusic	AF4	ALPHA	4.526
1899-12-31 00:35:00.0000000	1899-12-31 00:35:32.6000000	ClassicalMusic	AF4	BETA_L	3.824

A dataset is used as parameters for the source and sink configuration in a pipeline that contains a Copy Data activity.

Pipeline

The Azure Data Factory pipeline user interface is almost identical to the one in Azure Synapse Analytics. Pipelines are groups of activities that can ingest and transform data from many sources and formats. A dataset is required as an input for both the source and sink (destination) of the data. In Exercise 3.13, you use the dataset created in Exercise 3.12 to convert the data stored in XLSX into Parquet using the Copy data activity in a pipeline.

EXERCISE 3.13

Create a Pipeline to Convert XLSX to Parquet

1. Navigate to the Azure Data Factory you created in Exercise 3.10, and then click the Open link on the Overview blade in the Open Azure Data Factory Studio tile.

2. Select the Author hub ➢ hover over Pipeline and click the ellipse (. . .) ➢ click new pipeline ➢ expand the Move & Transform group ➢ drag and drop Copy Data into the workspace ➢ on the General tab, provide a name ➢ select the Source tab ➢ select the dataset you created in Exercise 3.12 from the Source Dataset drop-down box ➢ and then click the Sink tab.

3. Click + New next to the Sink Dataset drop-down box ➢ select Azure Data Lake Storage Gen2 ➢ click Continue ➢ select Parquet ➢ click Continue ➢ provide a name ➢ select + New from the Linked Service drop-down ➢ create a linked service to the ADLS container you created in Exercise 3.1 ➢ in the Set Properties window, select the folder icon in the File Path section (interactive authoring must be enabled and running) ➢ select the path where you want to store the file ➢ do not select a file ➢ enter a file name into the text box that contains File (I used **ALL_SCENARIO_ELECTRODE_FREQUENCY_VALUE.parquet**) ➢ select the None radio button ➢ and then click OK.

4. Click the Debug button at the top of the workspace window ➢ wait ➢ watch the Status value on the Output tab until you see Succeeded ➢ and then navigate to the ADLS container in the Azure portal. You will see the Parquet file.

Power Query

This option bears a great resemblance to what you might find in Power BI. The same engine that runs Power BI likely runs the Power Query plug-in. The feature provides an interface for viewing the data from a selected dataset. You can then run through some transformation ideas and see how the data will look once the change is applied. When you are happy with the outcome, you can use the Power Query feature as an activity in the pipeline.

Azure Databricks

Databricks is the most used Big Data analytics platform currently available for extract, transform, and load (ETL) or extract, load, and transform (ELT) transformations and insights gathering. Since Databricks is based on open-source principles, companies like Microsoft can branch the product and make their own version of it. That version is Azure Databricks. Databricks itself is based on the Apache Spark ecosystem, which is made up of four primary components: Spark SQL + DataFrames, Streaming, Machine Learning (MLlib), and Graph Computation. The platform also supports languages like R, SQL, Python, Scale, and Java. Azure Databricks provides an interface for provisioning, configuring, and

FIGUER 3.64 The Azure Databricks platform

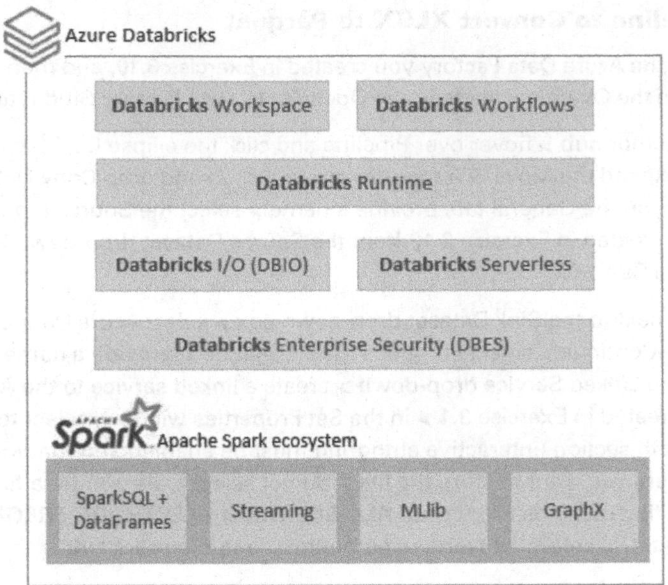

executing your data analytics on a mega scale. Figure 3.64 illustrates the Azure Databricks platform.

As previously mentioned, a workspace is a place where you and your team perform the actions required to create and maintain a data analytics solution. A Databricks workflow is like a pipeline, in that it has numerous activities to ingest and transform data. The Databricks runtime is the code and process that manages the health and execution of the workflows. Runtimes are the brains or the guts of a platform—where the magic happens. The *Databricks I/O (DBIO)* is a system driver that optimizes the reading and writing of files to disk. For example, when you use the `createDataFrame()` method along with the *Databricks File System (DBFS)*, DBIO will be engaged to help perform the loading and any writing of the data file. From a Databricks Serverless perspective, you know how the power of scaling increases performance and controls costs. It is possible to scale out to as many as 2,000 nodes (aka instances) to execute your data ingestion and transformations. This would only be possible in the cloud because the cost of having 2,000 servers, often sitting idle, is not cost-effective. Instead, serverless allows you to provision compute power when you need it, pay for that, and then deprovision the servers when not needed. You do not pay for compute that is not used. Encryption, identity management, RBAC, compliance, and governance are all components of *Databricks Enterprise Security (DBES)*. As you work through Exercise 3.14 and the following section, attempt to discover the security-related options, which are part of DBES.

EXERCISE 3.14

Create an Azure Databricks Workspace with an External Hive Metastore

1. Log in to the Azure portal at `https://portal.azure.com` ➢ enter **Azure Databricks** in the search box ➢ click Azure Databricks ➢ click the + Create button ➢ select the subscription ➢ select or create a new resource group ➢ name the Azure Databricks workspace (I used **brainjammer**) ➢ select the region ➢ select Pricing Tier Premium (consider using the trial version) ➢ click the Next: Networking button ➢ leave the default setting ➢ click the Next: Advanced button ➢ leave the default setting ➢ click the Review + create button ➢ and then click Create.

2. Once the Azure Databricks workspace is provisioned, navigate to it ➢ click the Open link on the Overview blade in the Launch Workspace tile ➢ choose the Compute menu item ➢ click Create Cluster ➢ name the cluster (I used **csharpguitar**) ➢ choose a worker type (consider a low spec one like Standard_D3_v2) ➢ change Min Workers to 1 and Max Workers to 2, to save costs ➢ expand the Advanced options ➢ and then add the following seven lines of text into the Spark config text box:

```
datanucleus.schema.autoCreateTables true
spark.hadoop.javax.jdo.option.ConnectionUserName userid@servername
datanucleus.fixedDatastore false
spark.hadoop.javax.jdo.option.ConnectionURL jdbc:sqlserver://*:1433;data
base=dbname
spark.hadoop.javax.jdo.option.ConnectionPassword *************
spark.hadoop.javax.jdo.option.ConnectionDriverName
com.microsoft.sqlserver.jdbc.SQLServerDriver
```

The text is located in the `Chapter03/Ch03Ex14` directory on GitHub at `https://github.com/benperk/ADE`. The file is named `AzureDatabricksAdvancedOptions.txt`. Update the text with your details, as described in the next step.

3. To find the values for `ConnectionUserName`, `ConnectionsURL`, and `ConnectionPassword`, navigate to the Azure SQL database you created in Exercise 2.1 ➢ choose the Connection String navigation menu item ➢ and then select the JDBC tab. The required data is provided in the necessary format in the rendered connection string.

4. Still on the Azure SQL database, select the Overview navigation menu item ➢ select the Set Server Firewall link ➢ set Allow Azure Services and Resources to Access This Server to Yes ➢ enter a rule name (I used **All**) ➢ enter **0.0.0.0** as the Start IP and **255.255.255.255** as the End IP ➢ and then click Save.

5. Navigate back to the Azure Databricks workspace ➢ place the contents of your updated `AzureDatabricksAdvancedOptions` into the Spark config text box ➢ and then click Create Cluster. The configuration should resemble Figure 3.65.

EXERCISE 3.14 *(continued)*

FIGUER 3.65 An Azure Databrick cluster

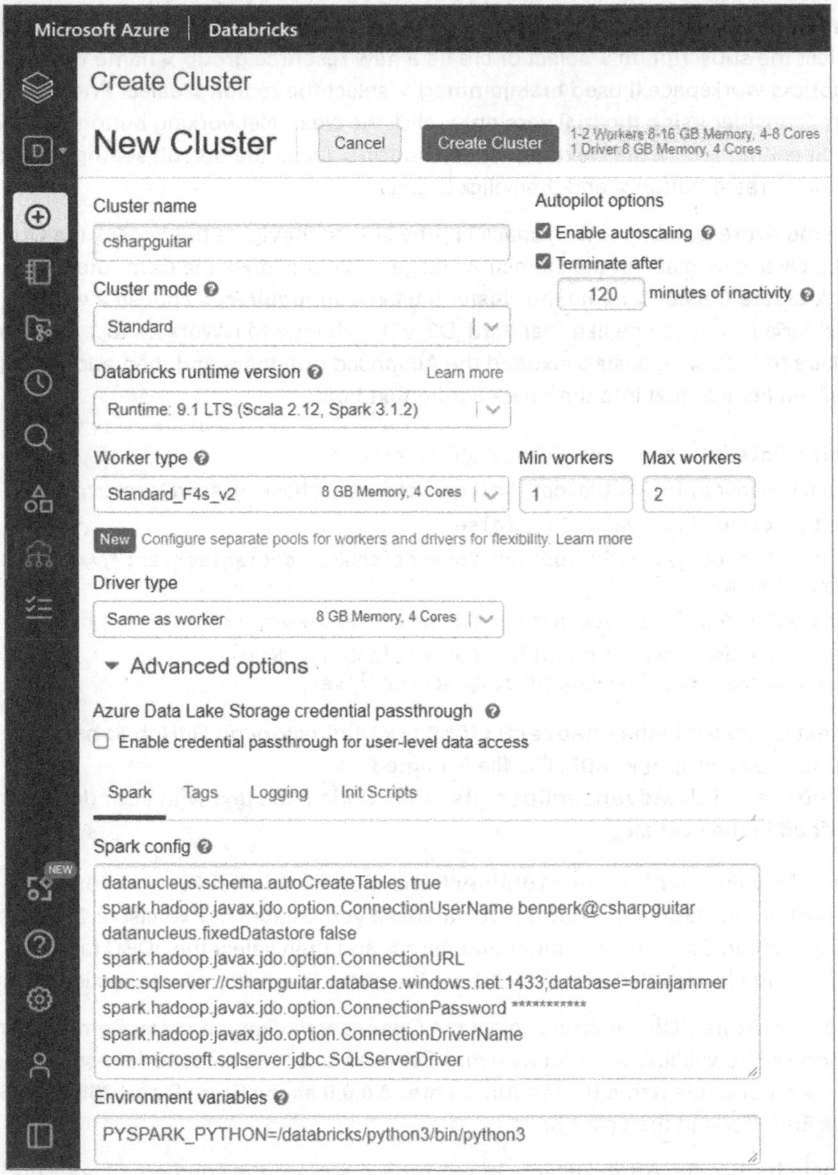

6. Choose the + Create menu item ➢ click Notebook ➢ enter a name (I used **brainjammer**) ➢ set the default language as SQL ➢ and then click Create, as illustrated in Figure 3.66.

FIGUER 3.66 An Azure Databrick notebook

Create Notebook

Name

brainjammer

Default Language

SQL

Cluster

csharpguitar

Cancel Create

7. Enter the following syntax into the command window, and then press the Run button or Shift + Enter to execute the command. If you used the BACPAC file to set up the `brainjammer` database, be sure to ensure that the name of the database matches the configuration you provided in the options file; otherwise, you might receive a SQLServerException error.

```
create database metastore
```

8. When the code snippet is successful, an OK result will appear, as shown in Figure 3.67. Consider running show `databases` or show `tables from <database>`, replacing `<database>` with your database name from Exercise 2.1.

FIGUER 3.67 Azure Databricks Notebook command

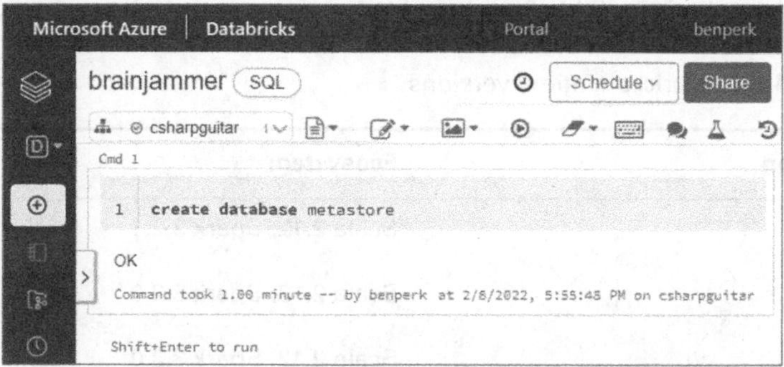

Refer to Figure 3.65, specifically the Cluster Mode drop-down. Table 3.13 describes the options available.

TABLE 3.13 Azure Databricks cluster modes

Mode	Description
High Concurrency	Optimized to run concurrent SQL, Python, and R workloads. Does not support Scala.
Standard	Recommended for single-user clusters. Can run SQL, Python, R, and Scala workloads.
Single Node	Spark clusters with no workers. Recommended for single-user clusters computing on small data volumes.

If your data analytics requirements necessitate a lot of computation and transformation resources, then choose the High Concurrency cluster. This mode provides the greatest resource capacity and reduces query latencies. Scala does not support running user code in separate processes, but this is the way that the High Concurrency cluster achieves massive scale. SQL, Python, and R do support running user code in separate processes. A process, in this context, is synonymous with a program or executable. When processes are spun up by the operating system kernel, they are allocated protected memory address ranges, load dependencies, and spawn threads to execute code. It is a relatively complicated feat to make cross-process application calls, and the code must support it. If you need Scala or do not need such massive compute resources, then choose the Standard mode. Standard mode requires at least one cluster to perform data computations. If you are developing or testing some small transformations, then choose the Single Node mode. When you provision Azure Databricks, a driver node is provisioned to help perform small tasks. No cluster is required with Single Node; instead, the small computations are executed on the driver node.

Numerous Azure Databricks runtime versions are selectable from the Databricks Runtime Version drop-down list box. Table 3.14 lists the options.

TABLE 3.14 Databricks runtime versions

Runtime version	Ecosystem
10.3 and 10.4	Scala 2.12, Spark 3.2.1
10.2	Scala 2.12, Spark 3.2.0
10.1	Scala 2.12, Spark 3.2.0
10.0	Scala 2.12, Spark 3.2.0
9.1 LTS	Scala 2.12, Spark 3.1.2

Runtime version	Ecosystem
7.3 LTS	Scala 2.12, Spark 3.0.1
6.4 Extended Support	Scala 2.11, Spark 2.4.5

The Enable Autoscaling check box uses the values provided in the Min Workers and Max Workers fields to manage autoscaling. If you uncheck Enable Autoscaling, those two options change into a text box named Workers, which allows you to set a static number of workers to be available at all times. It makes sense to enable the Terminate After # Minutes of Inactivity check box to save costs. After the amount of configured time has elapsed without the cluster being used, perhaps 15 minutes, the platform will terminate the workers/cluster and the charging will stop.

There is a wide variety of worker types and many different and changing resource allocations. Table 3.15 lists only the types of workers and not all possible resource allocations. A *hybrid hard drive (HHD)* is one that melds the performance, capacity, and cost of physical storage with that of the speed attained by a *solid state drive (SSD)*.

TABLE 3.15 Azure Databricks worker types

Type	Description
General Purpose	For normal workloads
General Purpose (HHD)	For workloads that need faster storage access
Memory Optimized (remote HHD)	For workloads that store data remotely rather than locally
Memory Optimized	For applications that need a lot of memory
Memory Optimized (Delta cached accelerated)	For applications that need a lot of memory for working with Delta Lake
Storage Optimized (Delta cached accelerated)	For workloads that require large amounts of local storage and use Delta Lake
Compute Optimized	For workloads that require large amounts of CPU
GPU Accelerated	For applications that can harvest the benefits of GPU processors

The next drop-down list in Figure 3.65 provides the option to select the driver type. As mentioned earlier, when you choose Single Node cluster mode, your computations are performed on the driver node. The selection defaults to Same as Worker; however, if your requirements compel a need to scale to a very large number of nodes, then you may need a more powerful driver to manage that.

In step 4 of Exercise 3.14 you created a rule that allowed all IP addresses. This is not recommended for production or any environment. In order to get the actual IP address range, you need to download this document and find it based on your location.

`www.microsoft.com/en-us/download/details.aspx?id=56519`

When you expand Advanced Options, you first see the check box to Enable Credential Passthrough for User-level Data Access (refer to Figure 3.65) and only allow Python and SQL commands, as well as four tabs: Spark, Tags, Logging, and Init Scripts. If you check the box, it means that Spark automatically uses the user's Azure AD credentials to access data on ADLS without being prompted for credentials. The Spark tab has a Spark Config text box, which is where you placed the Hive metastore configuration. That information is loaded into the process when the cluster starts. The Environment Variables are values you set that are accessible via code running on the worker. For example, a variable like `ENVIRONMENT=Testing` might be used to distinguish which release phase the code should run in. Your code can access this value and choose the data sources based on that. Tags are for tracking some attributes concerning the cluster instances, like who created it, the kind of resource, or any custom value you would want to see when you look at the details of the cluster, such as creation date or component dependencies. If you integrate logging into your application, the Logging tab enables you to configure the location of the logs. The platform itself generates diagnostic logs, which can also be written into this configured location—for example, `dbfs:/cluster-logs`. The Init Scripts tab gives you the option to add scripts that need to be run when a node is brought online (aka instantiated). For example, you might want to synchronize the system date and time at start up, which you can do by adding something like `sudo service ntp restart` to a file named `ntp.sh` and configuring it into the Init Script console.

Environments

There are three Azure Databricks environments, as listed in Table 3.16.

TABLE 3.16 Azure Databricks environments

Environment	Description
SQL	A platform optimized for those who typically run SQL queries to create dashboards and explore data
Data Science & Engineering	Used for collaborative Big Data pipeline initiatives
Machine Learning	An end-to-end ML for modeling, experimenting, and serving

The Data Science & Engineering environment is the one that is in focus, as it pertains most to the DP-203 exam. Data engineers, machine learning engineers, and data scientists would collaborate, consume, and contribute to the data analytics solution here. Figure 3.21 shows some of the options you will find while working in the Data Science & Engineering environment. The following section provides some additional information about those features.

Create

This section provides features to create notebooks, tables, clusters, and jobs.

Notebook

In step 6 of Exercise 3.14 you created a notebook to run code to create a metastore and then query it (refer to Figure 3.67). A few concepts surrounding the Azure Databricks notebook are discussed in the following subsections.

ACCESS CONTROL

Access control is only available with the Azure Databricks Premium Plan; you may remember that the option from the Pricing Tier drop-down. The option was Premium (+ Role-based access control). By default, all users who have been granted access to the workspace can create and modify everything contained within it. This includes models, notebooks, folders, and experiments. You can view who has access to the workspace and their permissions via the Settings ➢ Admin Console ➢ Users page, which is discussed later but illustrated in Figure 3.68.

If you want to provide a specific user access to a notebook, click Workspace ➢ Users ➢ the account that created the notebook ➢ the drop-down menu arrow next to the notebook name ➢ and then Permissions. As shown in Figure 3.69, you have the option to select the user and the permission for that specific notebook.

The permission options include Can Read, Can Run, Can Edit, and Can Manage. Adding permissions per user is a valid approach only for very small teams; if you have a larger team, consider using groups as the basis for assigning permissions.

FIGUER 3.68 Azure Databricks Settings Admins Console Users

Microsoft Azure | Databricks

Portal ga@csharpguitar.net

Admin Console

Users Groups Global Init Scripts Workspace Settings

+ Add User

Username	Name	Admin	Workspace access	Databricks SQL access	Allow unrestricted cluster creation
user@csharpguitar.net					
ga@csharpguitar.net	Benjamin Perkins				
data@csharpguitar.net					
developer@csharpguitar.net					

FIGUER 3.69 Azure Databricks Workspace User notebook Permission

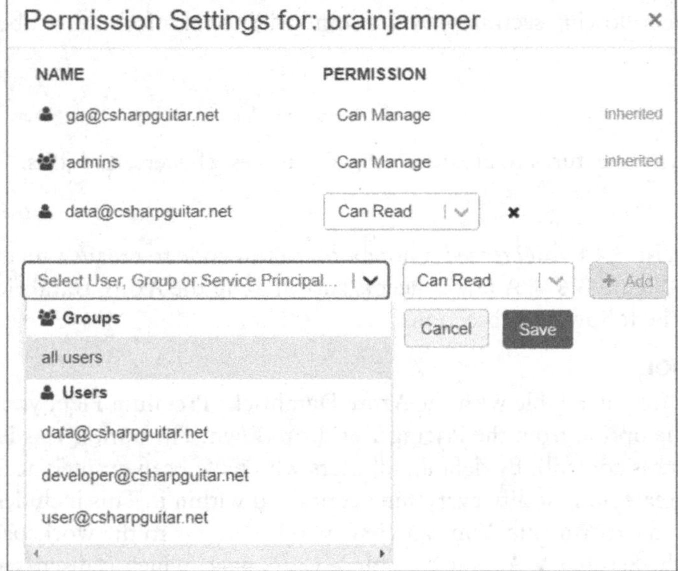

NOTEBOOK DISTRIBUTION

If you want to share a notebook with someone who does not have access to the workspace in which it exists, the Export can help. Within the File drop-down menu, with the notebook in focus, the Export option expands out with four options: DBC Archive, Source File, iPython Notebook, and HTML. There is an example of an exported Azure Databricks Notebook named `brainjammer.html` in the `Chapter03` folder on GitHub at `https://github.com/benperk/ADE`. To import the notebook, click Workspace ➢ Users ➢ the drop-down arrow next to the user who wants it ➢ and then Import. Once the notebook has been imported, you can execute and modify it as desired, assuming you have access to the data it references.

VERSION CONTROL

As you create the logic that runs within your notebook, the revision history is automatically stored. Figure 3.70 illustrates the output of the change history.

FIGUER 3.70 Azure Databricks Workspace User notebook revision history

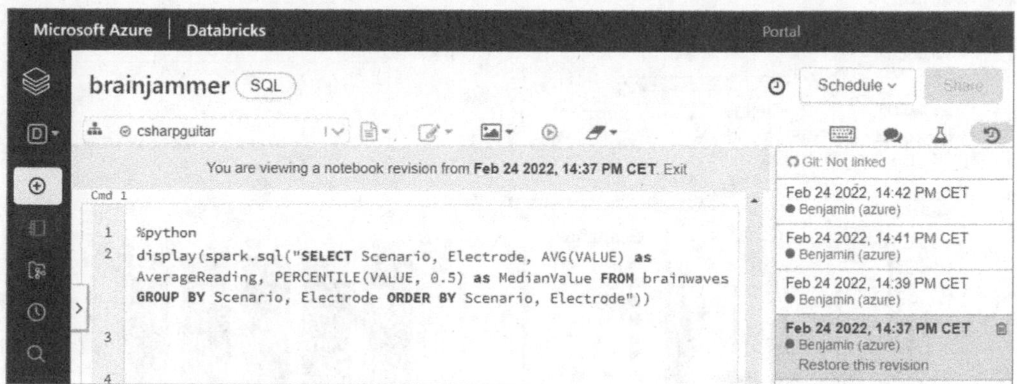

You can navigate through the list and restore back to a given point of time. This is helpful if you work yourself into a bug that you cannot seem to resolve. Simply revert back to a revision that you know was working and start again.

DASHBOARDS

Azure Databricks has some nice dashboards that are useful for visualizing data. When working with a notebook, you might find that you have a lot of cells that extract data using different queries. Scrolling through them and looking at them one by one is not the best option. Instead, create a dashboard by expanding the View menu item and selecting + New Dashboard, which adds the query results from each cell into a single consumable unit, as shown in Figure 3.71.

You might find it is much easier to make assumptions about the data when looking at a chart versus looking at the numbers in columns. Using a dashboard is very helpful toward achieving greater insights into your data.

Table

When you navigate to the Create New Table page, you will see three tabs: Upload File, DBFS, and Other Data Sources. The Upload File feature supports users uploading files directly onto the platform, which is a very common scenario when using Azure Databricks. This feature supports that through dragging and dropping a file onto the page or browsing for it using a file picker window. The file must be in a supported format, and you will need to select a running cluster to perform the creation and preview. If you want to place the file into a folder other than the `/FileStore/tables/` folder, then you have the option to define that in the DBFS Target Directory text box. When a table is created in this manner, it is placed into a database named `default`.

FIGUER 3.71 Azure Databricks brain wave charting example

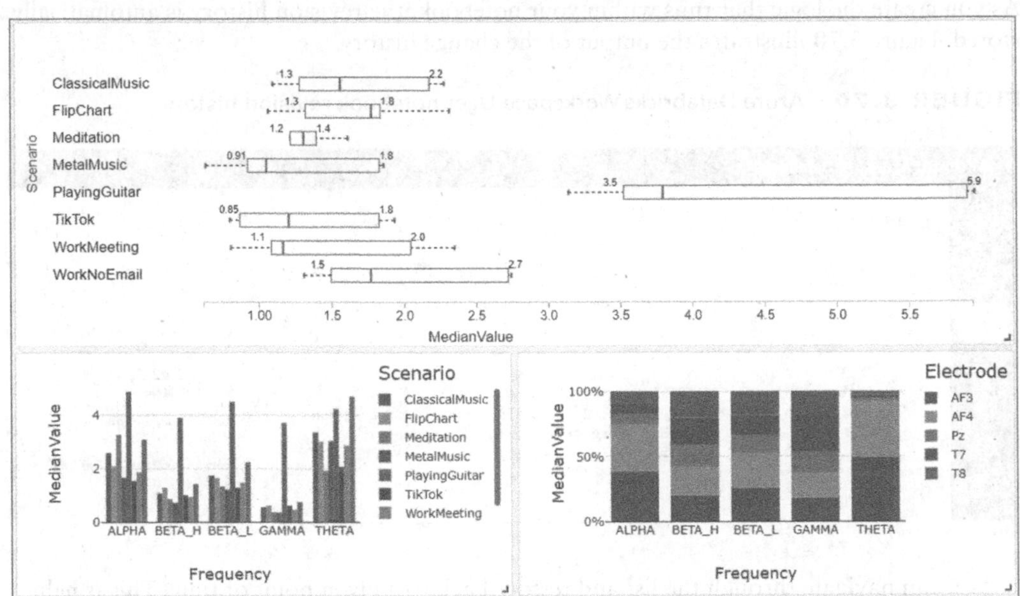

The DBFS tab provides a navigation feature that allows you to traverse the contents found within the /FileStore/* and other folders. This is similar to Windows File Explorer, for example, but the feature is in the browser. Clicking files in the folder gives you a direct path for creating tables for them to be queried from. The remaining tab, Other Data Sources, provides a list of connectors that Azure Databricks can retrieve data from. Examples of connectors include Azure Blob Storage, ADLS, Kafka, JDBC, Cassandra, and Redis. Selecting a connector and clicking Create Table in Notebook will result in a template that walks you through the connection being rendered. Follow the instructions and then perform your ingestion, transformation, and/or analytics.

Cluster

The Create Cluster page was illustrated in Figure 3.65. All the attributes and configurations found on this page have been called out already after Exercise 3.14.

Job

A job is similar to an activity that is part of a pipeline. There are numerous types of jobs, which are selectable from the drop-down text box shown in Figure 3.72.

FIGUER 3.72 Azure Databricks workspace jobs

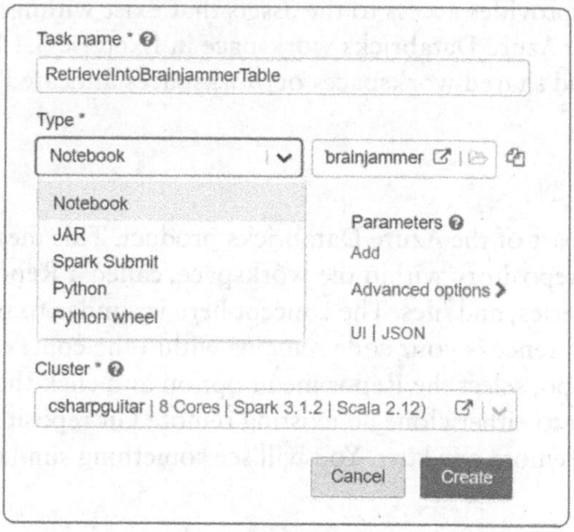

Table 3.17 describes the possible types of jobs.

TABLE 3.17 Azure Databricks job types

Type	Description
Notebook	Runs a sequence of instructions that can be executed on a data source
JAR	Executes and passes data parameters to JAR components
Spark Submit	Runs a script in the Spark `/bin` directory
Python	Runs the code within a targeted Python file
Delta Live Tables	Executes Delta pipeline activities
Python Wheel	Executes a function within a `.whl` package

After configuring the job, you can run it immediately or use the built-in platform scheduling capabilities to run it later.

Workspace

The Workspace section provides access to the assets that exist within the workspace. For example, you created an Azure Databricks workspace in Exercise 3.14. Depending on your permissions, you can find shared workspaces or workspaces allocated directly to you or other users.

Repos

Repository-level Git is part of the Azure Databricks product. This means you can create a local source code repository within the workspace, called a Repo, to store a copy of your source code, queries, and files. The concept here is similar to that of GitHub or Azure DevOps. The difference is your code remains within the context of your workspace. To create a local Git Repo, select the Repos menu option and click the Add Repo button. A window prompts you to either clone an existing remote Git repository or create a local empty one and clone a remote one later. You will see something similar to that shown in Figure 3.73.

FIGUER 3.73 Azure Databricks Repos

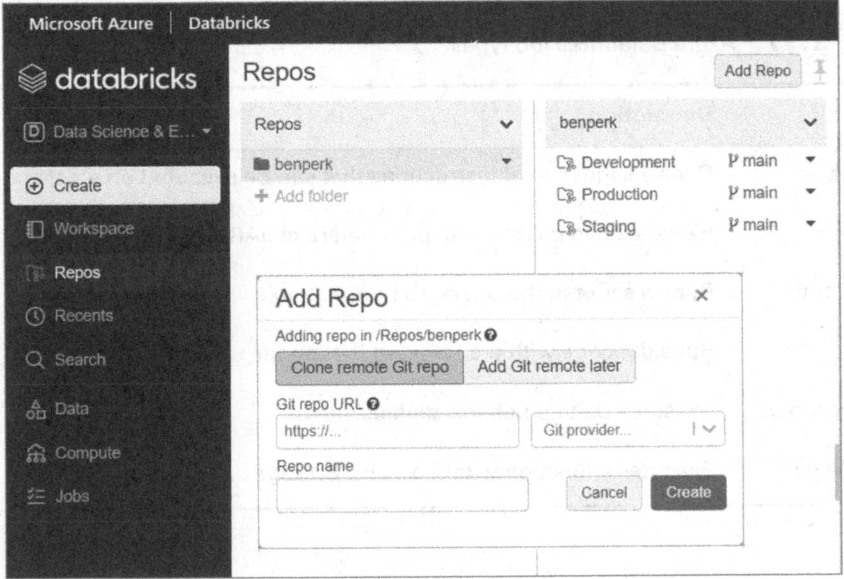

Notice that Figure 3.73 shows three Repos, one for each stage of the release process. This is only an example of the numerous approaches for building a configuration and release management process. Remember that this kind of source code management process requires thought, a design, management, security, and control.

Data

The Data section provides features for creating, managing, and viewing the structure of the data stored in the workspace. When you click the Data section, a pop-out menu will render that contains a navigation hierarchy between catalogs, databases, and tables.

Catalogs

A catalog is the top-level logical container and consists of metadata definitions of the databases and tables contained within it. Catalogs enable you to organize and structure your data into more logical groupings. You gain the same benefits from this kind of organization as you realize with Management Groups ➢ Subscriptions ➢ Resource Groups in Azure. For example, if you happen to be working on projects from different companies but are using the same workspace, you might consider separating the data at the highest possible logical level.

Databases

When you click an existing catalog (for example, `hive_metastore`), the list of databases consisting within it are rendered. Multiple databases can exist in a catalog, as shown previously in Figure 3.21. This is another level of separation that is helpful for managing the logical organization of data. Consider an example where you work on the analysis of brain waves that use an assortment of different devices. An option for organizing the data could be to place different device-bound brain waves into different databases.

Tables

The final grouping in the pop-out menu contains a list of all the tables within the selected database. When you select the table, it will render the details (aka metadata) for the table, similar to Figure 3.23.

Compute

The capabilities found in the Compute section provide the means for creating, listing, and configuring all-purpose clusters, job clusters, pools, and cluster policies.

Clusters

In Exercise 3.14 you created an all-purpose cluster. The attributes and configuration details were covered in the discussion following the exercise. In most cases an all-purpose cluster and a job cluster are the same. The use case for the two are that you use an all-purpose cluster to analyze data via notebooks. This analysis can be collaborative and interactive with a team. A job cluster is one allocated to the execution of automated and scheduled jobs. When your ingestion and analysis are complete, you move the final version of the notebook to be executed on a job cluster. Each cluster type provides the CPU and memory required to provide a performant platform. Azure Databricks has two types of clusters: interactive and automated. You use interactive clusters to analyze data collaboratively with interactive notebooks. You use automated clusters to run fast and robust automated jobs.

Pools

The concept of a pool spans across many scenarios and has the same purpose. A pool is a number of objects waiting to serve their intended purpose. Consider connection pools or thread pools, for example. It takes milliseconds to seconds to instantiate a database connection or a thread to perform the expected activity. Whereas a connection in a connection pool is waiting to be used as the means for the manipulation or retrieval of data, a thread in a thread pool is on standby, waiting to be instructed by the kernel to perform some execution of code. The same applies to a pool of nodes. If you want to improve the performance and start up times of the workloads running on Azure Databricks, then you can create a pool of nodes. These nodes will be provisioned and on standby, ready to execute the instructed code algorithms. This is in contrast to the time required to provision and configure a node before running the code. That provisioning and configuration can take minutes, in some cases, to come online and be ready to contribute to the compute needs. To avoid this delay, you create a pool of nodes, which are already online waiting for work allocations. Keep in mind, however, that you pay for these nodes, so you need to take actions to manage them as optimally as possible.

Cluster Policies

Controlling cost, security, and permissions is important. Azure includes a feature called *Azure Policy* that gives the subscription owner the means to control how products are configured from security and cost perspective. The cluster policies feature provides the same capability, in that it provides the means for controlling the size and the allowed cluster configurations, meaning you can control which components must or must not be existing on the cluster and/or the maximum supported worker size.

Jobs

The Jobs section provides an interface for viewing and managing the existing jobs on the workspace. The page renders details such as the name of the job, the ID of the job, who created the job, the task, and the cluster that is bound to the job. You can also delete a job or execute a job manually, as shown in Figure 3.74.

When you click the job name, the details of the selected job will appear. Notice that the allocated cluster is all-purpose. If you click the Swap button, you are given the opportunity to switch it to a job cluster. You also can view the history of the execution of the jobs by selecting the Job Runs tab. The content on the Job Runs tab gives you the interface to drill down into each run to view logs, metrics, and the output of the job.

Settings

The Settings section contains three subsections: User Settings, Access Tokens, and Manage Account. The Manage Account subsection links you back into the Azure Portal to the provisioned instance of your Azure Databricks Service.

FIGUER 3.74 Azure Databricks Jobs

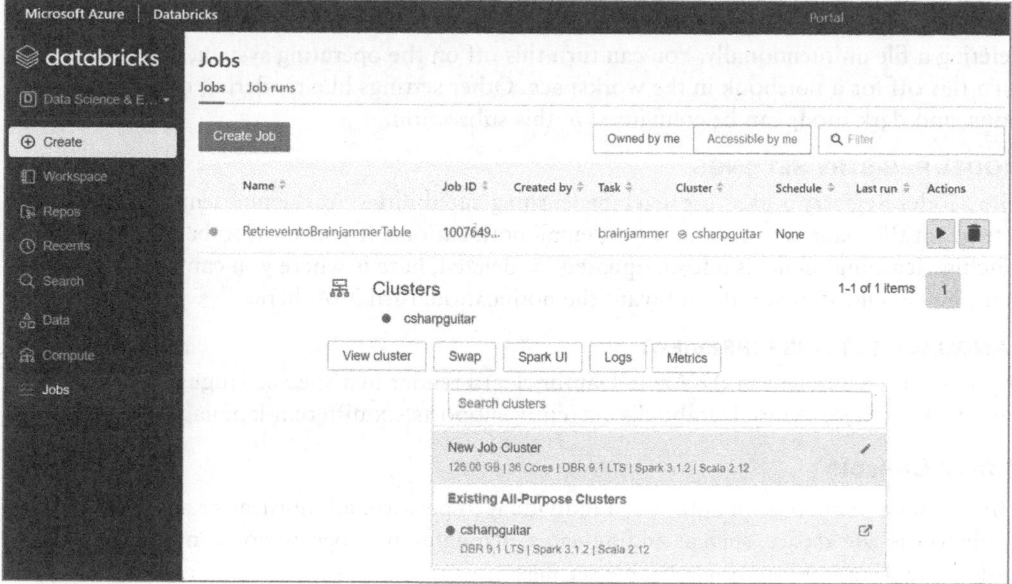

User Settings

The User Settings subsection provides access to workspace settings specific to the logged-in user or settings accessible to the logged-in user but applied workspace wide.

ACCESS TOKENS

An access token is a string of characters used as an encrypted message. A client entity sends this token along with a request for some resource to a server. The server decrypts and authenticates the client and, if successful, returns the requested resource. Additionally, the token can be used to provide access to features within Azure Databricks. Azure Databricks exposes an API that supports the triggering of a job, for example. If this is required, you could use the Azure Databricks SDK and code the ability to trigger a job from another application. To make this secure, you would generate a token, then use this token, along with the SDK, to ensure that the client is authorized to perform this action.

GIT INTEGRATION

Storing your notebooks in a Git repository provides version control, the ability to collaborate with others, and a backup of the source code. Azure Databricks provides seamless integration with many Git providers. Click the drop-down list of Git providers to see them all. To integrate your Azure Databricks workspace with GitHub, you must provide the email address linked to your GitHub account and a personal access token with read/write permissions.

NOTEBOOK SETTINGS

When you try to delete something on most operating systems, you are often prompted with an "Are you sure?" message. Sometimes this is annoying, but sometimes it saves you from deleting a file unintentionally. You can turn this off on the operating system, and you can turn this off for a notebook in the workspace. Other settings like rendering tips, notifications, and dark mode can be configured in this subsection.

MODEL REGISTRY SETTINGS

The Model Registry is used for machine learning capabilities. At the moment the only setting on this page is to turn on or off email notifications. If you want to be notified when a machine learning model is added, updated, or deleted, here is where you can achieve that. It is on by default, so if you do not want the notification, turn it off here.

LANGUAGE SETTINGS (PREVIEW)

If you want the content in the Azure Databricks to render in a specific language, then you can change it here. Azure Databricks currently supports six different languages.

Admin Console

This subsection enables an authorized individual to perform administrative activities that apply to the workspace, such as adding users, managing user permissions, managing groups, and configuring workspace-applicable settings.

USERS

The Users page provides a list of users who have access to the workspace. The role and permissions of each user are rendered as well. Table 3.18 describes the permissions (i.e., entitlements).

TABLE 3.18 Azure Databricks user entitlements

Entitlement	Description
Workspace access	The user is allowed access to workspace environments, excluding Databricks SQL.
Databricks SQL access	The user is allowed access to the Databricks SQL environment.
Allow unrestricted cluster creation	The user can create clusters.
Allow-instance-pool-create	The user can create cluster pools.

Figure 3.68 shows how the user list and their permissions appear in the workspace.

GROUPS

It is best to grant permissions to groups instead of individuals, especially if you have many users who will have access to the workspace. The grouping concept is also useful to help discover and control who is working on a specific project. This assumes that you have a scenario in which you have multiple projects running on the same workspace. Users, other groups, and service principles can all be added to a group. You need to watch out that you do not have the same users in multiple groups. If you do, then users will get the maximum allowed permission when summed across all groups in which the user account is added. For example, if a user is in one group that does not allow access to the Databricks SQL environment and another group that does, then the user will get access to the Databricks SQL environment.

GLOBAL INIT SCRIPTS

A global init script is similar to a cluster policy. They are the same in principle, but when you use a global init script, the scope is across all clusters in the workspace, versus a single cluster. Global init scripts enable you to enforce organization-wide library installations, security configurations, and security-monitoring scripts.

WORKSPACE SETTINGS

This subsection provides custom settings applied to the entire workspace. Therefore, changes to the settings in this subsection impact all users who have access to the workspace. The kinds of configurations include the following:

- Access control
- Storage and purging
- Jobs
- Cluster
- Repos
- Advanced

Many options are available. Spend some time looking into them to become more familiar with them.

Data Ingestion

Figure 3.75 shows how data is ingested into Azure Databricks.

There are numerous ways to ingest data, including by streaming via Event Hubs, Stream Analytics, or Kafka, or by copying data from a remote source using Azure Data Factory. You also can stream data directly from an IoT device and store it into a datastore. The ingested data may be stored, initially in a raw format, on an ADLS container. A technology called *Delta Lake* is built into Azure Databricks. Delta Lake is a software library that sits on top of your data lake to help manage activities performed on the data. It is especially helpful in terms of data landing zones (DLZ), which concern the classifications of data into bronze, silver, and gold data zone categories. The features and capabilities described in this section concerning Azure Databricks are then used to transform the data from its initial raw state into something that can be analyzed, studied, and used for making business or scientific decisions. The model illustrated in Figure 3.75 is often referred to as *medallion architecture*.

FIGUER 3.75 Azure Databricks data ingestion

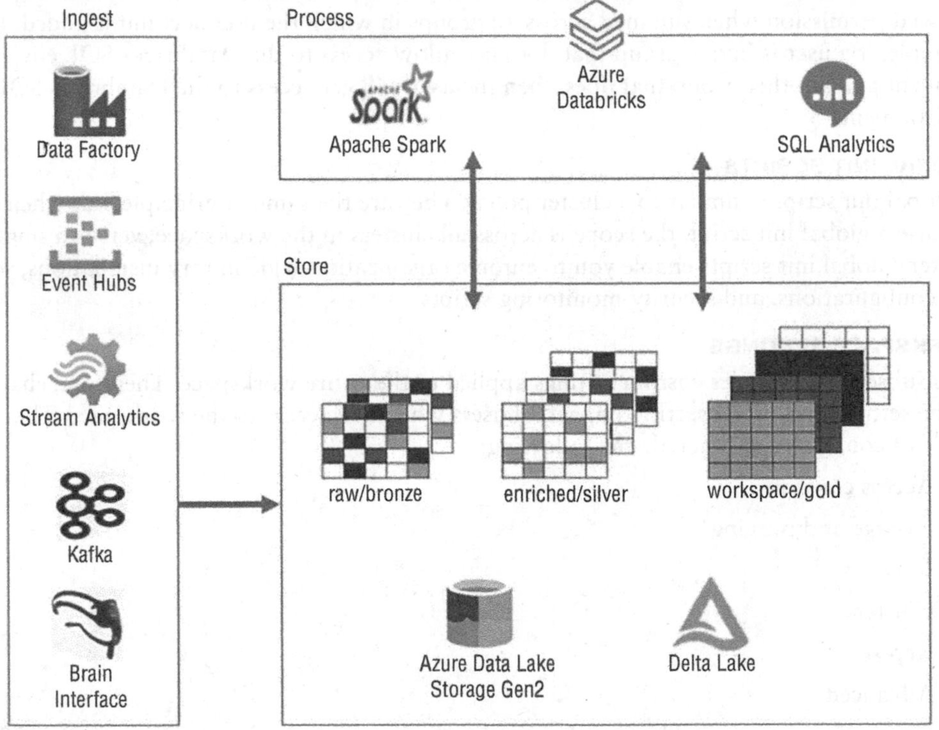

Delta Lake on Databricks

Delta Lake is a storage and management software layer that provides numerous benefits for working with your data lake over the default features of Azure Databricks. A data lake is illustrated in Figure 3.76.

Data comes from many different sources. A data lake is a single location to store all this varied data into. You might consider the *data quality level (DQL)* in the data lake as cleansed data, or bronze. From that state, you implement something like the lambda architecture (refer to Figure 3.13) or use the capabilities in Delta Lake to progress the data's transformation to business level, or gold, quality data. Some of the benefits you gain by implementing Delta Lake are the following:

- ACID transactions
- Streaming and batch unification

- Time travel
- Upserts and deletes

FIGUER 3.76 A data lake

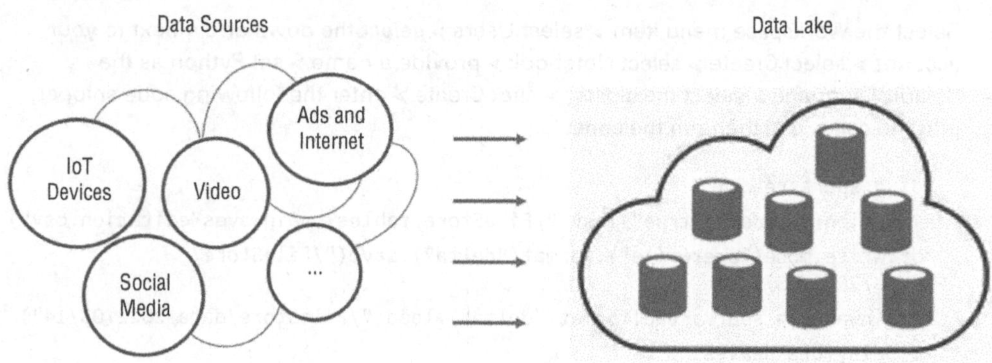

Before proceeding to the details of those features, complete Exercise 3.15, where you will perform some activities with Delta Lake on the Azure Databricks service you created in Exercise 3.14. Delta Lake version 1.0.0 is installed by default with the Databricks runtime version 9.1 LTS. Version 9.1 LTS is currently the default version and should be the one in which you provisioned the cluster in Exercise 3.14.

EXERCISE 3.15

Configure Delta Lake

1. Log in to the Azure portal at `https://portal.azure.com` > navigate to the Azure Databricks service you created in Exercise 3.14 > click the Launch Workspace button on the Overview blade > choose the Compute menu item > and then select the cluster you created previously. If the cluster is not running, start it by selecting it from the list and clicking Start.
2. Download and decompress the file `brainwavesMeditationAndPlayingGuitar.zip` located in the `Chapter03/Ch03Ex15` directory on GitHub at `https://github.com/benperk/ADE` > choose the Data menu item and select Create Table > drag and drop the `brainwavesMeditation.csv` file onto the Upload File tab > click the Create Table with UI button > select the cluster from the Cluster drop-down box > click the Preview Table button > click the First Row Is Header check box and change `STRING` to `DOUBLE` from the drop-down text box under the `VALUE` heading > and then click Create Table.

EXERCISE 3.15 *(continued)*

3. Select the Data menu item ➢ click the database you placed the table into ➢ click Create Table ➢ click the DBFS tab ➢ and then click `FileStore`. Notice the file that you just uploaded.

4. Select the Workspace menu item ➢ select Users ➢ select the down arrow next to your account ➢ select Create ➢ select Notebook ➢ provide a name ➢ set Python as the default Language ➢ select the cluster ➢ click Create ➢ enter the following code snippet into the cell ➢ and then run the code.

```
df = spark.read \
 .option("header","true").csv("/FileStore/tables/brainwavesMeditation.csv")
df.write.mode("overwrite").format("delta").save("/FileStore/
data/2022/03/14")
brainwaves = spark.read.format("delta").load("/FileStore/data/2022/03/14")
display(brainwaves)
print(brainwaves.count())
```

5. Run the following code snippet:

```
display(spark.sql("DROP TABLE IF EXISTS BRAINWAVES"))
display(spark \
 .sql("CREATE TABLE BRAINWAVES USING DELTA LOCATION '/FileStore/
data/2022/03/14'"))
display(spark.table("BRAINWAVES").select("*").show(10))
print(spark.table("BRAINWAVES").select("*").count())
```

6. Upload the `brainwavesPlayingGuitar.csv` file using the same process performed in step 2 ➢ navigate back to the workspace ➢open the previous notebook ➢ and then execute the following code snippet:

```
df = spark.read \
 .option("header","true").csv("/FileStore/tables/brainwaves
PlayingGuitar.csv")
df.write.mode("append").format("delta").save("/FileStore/data/2022/03/14/")
brainwaves = spark.read.format("delta").load("/FileStore/data/2022/03/14")
print(brainwaves.count())
display(spark.sql("DROP TABLE IF EXISTS BRAINWAVES"))
display(spark \
 .sql("CREATE TABLE BRAINWAVES USING DELTA LOCATION '/FileStore/
data/2022/03/14'"))
print(spark.table("BRAINWAVES").select("*").count())
```

7. **Consider running the following code snippet, then perform some experiments with charting:**

```
display(spark.sql("SELECT SCENARIO, ELECTRODE, CAST(AVG(VALUE) AS
DECIMAL(7,3)) as AverageReading, PERCENTILE(VALUE, 0.5) as MedianValue FROM
brainwaves GROUP BY SCENARIO, ELECTRODE"))
```

The code snippets and importable notebook are available in the folder `Chapter03/Ch03Ex15` on GitHub at `https://github.com/benperk/ADE`.

When you first uploaded the CSV file and created a table, it was not a Delta Lake table. That means the benefits, which you will read about later, would not be realized while performing your data transformations and analytics. The first code snippet in Exercise 3.15 loaded the data from the Spark table into a `DataFrame`, then converted it into the delta-supported format. The conversion was achieved by using the `.format("delta")` method. The second code snippet used the Parquet file created by the first code snippet to create a delta table, then queried the table and counted the number of total rows. In a real-world example, it would be expected to receive files at different intervals, which is what the third code snippet attempts to represent. That code snippet loads another CSV file containing brain waves, converts it to delta format, and appends it to the existing dataset. The append is achieved by using the `.mode("append")` method, instead of, for example, the `.mode("overwrite")` method. The existing table is dropped, then re-created using the appended delta-compliant file, then queried again. The final code snippet performs some high-level review of the brain wave data.

In an effort to transpose this exercise onto a DLZ or DQL architecture flow, consider the CSV files and their associated Spark tables as raw or bronze. Consider the two actions that converted the data into delta format and appended the multiple files as pipeline work necessary to get the data from bronze into a more enriched state like silver. The final code snippet is an example of some preliminary analytics that help confirm the data is in a decent state to begin its final stage into a gold, business-ready state. This process could and should be automated using a scheduled job once the process is finalized and happens consistently. Remember that you can configure a job to run the contents of a notebook, so once the data is flowing into the defined location, create the job and you have a pipeline that is performing ingestion and transformation from bronze to silver. There are two missing parts to the entire process here. First is the automated ingestion; remember that you manually placed the data onto the platform. The second is the transformation to gold and the serving of the data to consumers. This final process is what this book is attempting to accomplish; remember, you are still in the ingestion chapter, so there is much more to come regarding this.

ACID Transactions

Anyone who has worked with computers, even for a short amount of time, knows that unexpected events happen. You can track this down all the way to the 3.3V of electricity required to flip a transistor to true. Everything from there has fault tolerance built in to manage these unexpected events in the best way possible. Exceptions happen all the time, but because of the layers of technologies that exist between the transistors and you, those exceptions are concealed. Most of the time you do not even know they happened, because they get handled and self-healed. One such technology that abstracts and isolates exceptions from users and processes is *atomicity, consistency, isolation, and durability (ACID)* transaction enforcement.

Apache Spark, which Azure Databricks runs as the compute node, is not ACID-compliant. The feature is found in Delta Lake; therefore, if you use Delta Lake on Azure Databricks, you can achieve ACID compliance. Consider the following scenarios in which ACID compliance makes a difference:

- Failed appends or overwrites
- Concurrent reading and writing of data

Atomicity means that the transaction is completely successful; otherwise, it is rolled back. Consider the execution of the code snippet `df.write.mode("append")` and assume an exception happened before all the data was appended to the file. Since Apache Spark does not support atomic transaction, you can end up with missing and lost data. When you execute the code `df.write.mode("overwrite")`, it results in the existing file being deleted and a new one created. This can fail the *consistency* test because if the method fails, data can be lost. The rule of consistency states that data must always be in a valid state, and with this process, there is a time when there is no data. This can also result in the noncompliance to *durability*, which states that once data is committed, it is never lost. Delta Lake has built-in capabilities to manage these noncompliant ACID capabilities that Apache Spark is missing.

In a majority of enterprise production scenarios, data sources are simultaneously written to by more than a single individual or program. When the volume of changes to the data source is high, the frequency of data changes is also high. That means that a program that retrieves and processes data from the source could receive a different result when compared to another program a few seconds later. This is where *isolation* comes into play. To be compliant, an operation must be isolated from other concurrent operations so that other concurrent operations do not impact the current one. Just imagine what happens if someone executes `df.write.mode("overwrite")`, which takes a minute to complete, and another program attempts to read that file 10 seconds after the overwrite started. The overwrite does impact the rule of isolation. Many DBMS products provide the option to provide an isolation level to data, which includes read uncommitted, read committed, repeatable read, and serializable. Since Apache Spark does not provide this, you can use Delta Lake to find options to make your Azure Databricks data analytics solution ACID-compliant.

Streaming and Batch Unification

Streaming, batching, and querying data are all very performant and reliable activities when using delta tables. This means if your data analytics solution requires streaming or batching, the approach for ingesting, transforming, and serving is the same.

Time Travel

When you create a delta table, which is the default on Azure Databricks from version 8.0, any table you create will result in the table being stored in the Hive metastore with the added advancements. To confirm which version of the Azure Databricks runtime you are on, execute the following snippet:

```
spark.conf.get("spark.databricks.clusterUsageTags.sparkVersion")
```

Having a delta table provides version control, which allows you to query past versions of the data. This is a very useful capability, because it gives you access to several historical versions of your data useful for analyzing changes over time. Additionally, if the queries worked on previous versions of the data but are for some reason no longer working, you can get them working by pointing them to an older version. Then, once they are working, you can debug the queries and get them working on the current data as quickly as possible. You can determine the different available versions of the table by using the following SQL command, which is followed by its output:

```
DESCRIBE HISTORY default.BRAINWAVES;

+--------+-------------------------------+-------+----------+----------+-----+
| version | timestamp                    | userId | userName | operation | ... |
+--------+-------------------------------+-------+----------+----------+-----+
| 1      | 2022-03-15T09:06:05.000+0000 | 33515  | benperk  | WRITE     | ... |
| 0      | 2022-03-15T09:02:13.000+0000 | 33515  | benperk  | WRITE     | ... |
+--------+-------------------------------+-------+----------+----------+-----+
```

Using the timestamp as a parameter of your query, you can target the execution of the command on that version of the data, as follows:

```
SELECT COUNT(1) FROM default.BRAINWAVES
TIMESTAMP AS OF '2022-03-15T09:06:05.000+0000';
```

You can achieve the same thing using Python with the following version of the `versionAsOf` option:

```
brainwaves = spark.read.format("delta") \
 .option("versionAsOf", 0).load("/FileStore/data/2022/03/14")
print(brainwaves.count())
```

Both the timestamp and version query options are available in all languages supported by Apache Spark.

By passing the `version` value shown in the aforementioned results of the `DESCRIBE HISTORY` command (in this example, a `0`), you can identify the `version` on which the `count()` method is executed. If you change the `0` to `1`, you will get different results, as expected. This capability not only gives you the opportunity to debug, but you can also use this technique to roll back to a previous version or create a new, permanent table with a version of the old data. It is important to note that the history is not stored indefinitely; therefore, if you need a copy of a previous version, you need to make that copy permanent by inserting the historical data into another delta table.

Upserts and Deletes

The example of combining multiple data files into a single table for analysis in Exercise 3.15 simply appended one file onto the next. This required you to remove and re-create the table. Instead of dropping and re-creating the table, you could also use UPDATE, MERGE, or DELETE capabilities to modify the data on a delta table. Performing an update is the same as with other SQL-based datastores. The following syntax illustrates how to achieve this and is followed by the output:

```
UPDATE BRAINWAVES SET SCENARIO = 'Flipboard' WHERE SCENARIO = 'FlipChart';

+--------------------+
| num_affected_rows |
+--------------------+
| 23975             |
+--------------------+
```

The MERGE SQL command looks something like the following. This command is often referred to as an upsert activity. An upsert is useful for retrieving rows from a view, a source table, or a DataFrame, and then placing them into a target delta table.

```
MERGE INTO BRAINWAVES
USING BRAINWAVESUPDATES
ON BRAINWAVES.ID = BRAINWAVESUPDATES.ID
WHEN MATCHED THEN
 UPDATE SET
 ID = BRAINWAVESUPDATES.ID,
 SESSION_DATETIME = BRAINWAVESUPDATES.SESSION_DATETIME,
 READING_DATETIME = BRAINWAVESUPDATES.READING_DATETIME,
 SCENARIO = BRAINWAVESUPDATES.SCENARIO,
 ELECTRODE = BRAINWAVESUPDATES.ELECTRODE,
 FREQUENCY = BRAINWAVESUPDATES.FREQUENCY,
 VALUE = BRAINWAVESUPDATES.VALUE
WHEN NOT MATCHED THEN
 INSERT (
 ID, SESSION_DATETIME, READING_DATETIME, SCENARIO, ELECTRODE, FREQUENCY, VALUE
 )
 VALUES (
 BRAINWAVESUPDATES.ID,
 BRAINWAVESUPDATES.SESSION_DATETIME,
 BRAINWAVESUPDATES.READING_DATETIME,
 BRAINWAVESUPDATES.SCENARIO,
 BRAINWAVESUPDATES.ELECTRODE,
 BRAINWAVESUPDATES.FREQUENCY,
 BRAINWAVESUPDATES.VALUE
 )
```

The target delta table, BRAINWAVES, follows the INTO syntax, with the source table following USING. The criteria used to check for a match follows the ON syntax. The matching behavior resembles what you might find in the relational database context, where a primary key exists. As there is no referential integrity built into these tables, it is possible to make a match and perform an update that is not expected. For example, what if the IDs on the update table get reset? You would end up unintentionally overwriting existing data. Thank goodness for the history logs if this ever happens. Next, there is some code logic that uses WHEN and THEN to determine whether the row already exists. If there are matching IDs, then the data is updated; if there are no matching IDs for the given row, then the data is inserted.

You can remove rows from the delta table as follows, which is the same as with many other datastores:

```
DELETE FROM BRAINWAVES WHERE READING_DATETIME < '2022-01-01 00:00:00'
```

The DELETE SQL command will remove all the data that matches the WHERE clause. Again, this being a delta table, you have the ability to recover or query the table after this delete being performed.

Event Hubs and IoT Hub

Both Event Hubs and IoT Hub were introduced in Chapter 1 but are discussed in greater detail here, as they are both key contributors for data ingestion. Refer to Figure 1.22 to see how their deployment into the ingestion stage of your Big Data solution might look. IoT Hub is built on top of Event Hubs, so all capabilities found on Event Hubs are also available with IoT Hub, but not vice versa. Table 3.19 compares the two products. You can use this to determine which product you need for your ingestion scenario.

TABLE 3.19 Event Hubs vs. IoT Hub

Feature	Event Hubs	IoT Hub
Send messages to the cloud from devices.	Yes	Yes
HTTPS, AMQP over WebSockets, AMQP.	Yes	Yes
MQTT over WebSockets, MQTT.	No	Yes
Unique identity per device.	No	Yes
Send messages from devices to the cloud.	No	Yes
Support for more than 5,000 concurrent connections.	No	Yes

IoT Hub supports a very useful option: bidirectional communications between the device and the cloud. This outbound message capability is focused more on an IoT solution than on a Big Data solution. The data capturing from devices in the cloud is more aligned with data analytics, although this feature allows tight integration with both, if your requirements necessitate it. IoT Hub also gives you the option to uniquely authenticate each IoT device with its own security credential, whereas Event Hubs authenticates using a *shared access signature (SAS)* token. A SAS token is a shared key used for authenticating a connection and resembles the following:

`yCLIBBB76NKSLlQAOe64g8O2JyKMgqkZL91NsxKBLEI=`

There are some security concerns around using a shared token for authentication. For example, it needs to be used from each device that needs access to the hub. It is also necessary to ensure that the credential does not become compromised. Using Azure Key Vault, for example, can help with this. IoT Hub supports managed identity, while Event Hubs does not currently support it. The last point to know is that IoT hubs costs much more than event hubs. Prior to provisioning an IoT hub, check the prices, as they can cost thousands of US dollars per month, even while idle.

Perform Exercise 3.16 to provision an Azure Event Hub.

EXERCISE 3.16

Create an Azure Event Namespace and Hub

1. Log in to the Azure portal at `https://portal.azure.com` ➢ enter **Event Hubs** in the search box ➢ click Event Hubs ➢ click the + Create link ➢ select a subscription ➢ select a resource group ➢ provide a namespace name (I used **brainjammer**) ➢ select a location ➢ select the Basic Pricing tier (since this is not production) ➢ leave the default value of 1 forThroughput Units ➢ click the Review + Create button ➢ and then click Create.
2. Once provisioned, navigate to the Event Hub Namespace Overview blade ➢ select the + Event Hubs link ➢ name the event hub (I used **brainwaves**) ➢ leave the default of 2 for Partition Count ➢ and then click Create.
3. Choose the Shared Access Policies navigation menu item, and then click `RootManageSharedAccessKey`. Note the primary keys, secondary keys, and connection string.

It is possible to create an additional policy with fewer rights. The `RootManageSharedAccessKey` policy has full access. You might consider creating a policy with the minimum access necessary, perhaps Send Only. It depends on your requirements, but it is good practice to provide the minimum amount of access required to achieve the work, in all cases. This event hub will be used for numerous other examples in the coming chapters. To extrapolate a bit on Figure 1.22 and to expand a bit into the Event Hubs internals, take a look at Figure 3.77.

FIGUER 3.77 Event Hubs data ingestion

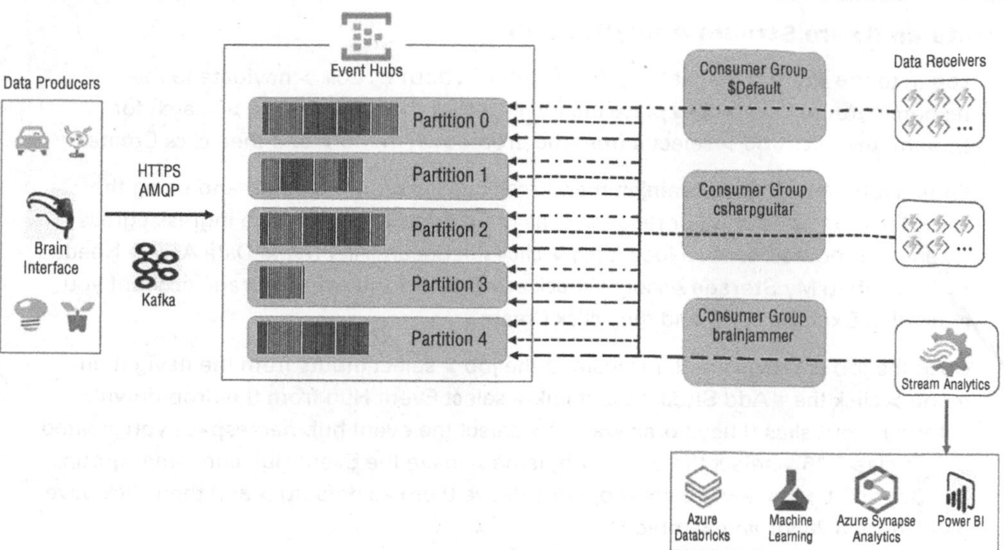

When you implement the Event Hubs namespace and hub in a later chapter, Chapter 7, "Design and Implement a Data Stream Processing Solution," you will be exposed to some of the concepts shown in Figure 3.77. The first item you might notice in the figure is Kafka. Note that it is possible to redirect data producers to send data to an event hub instead of being required to manage an Apache Kafka cluster. This can happen without any code changes on the Kafka-focused devices. When you provision an event hub, you select the number of partitions it will have. Partitions enable great parallelism, which translates into the capability to handle great levels of velocity and volumes of incoming data. The incoming data is load balanced across the partitions. Each subscriber to a consumer group will have access to the data at least once. That means the incoming data stream can be consumed by more than a single program or client. One such program is Azure Stream Analytics, which can perform real-time analytics on the incoming data. The conclusion made by Azure Stream Analytics can then be forwarded or stored in numerous other Azure products. Learn from the data using Azure Machine Learning and store the data in Azure Synapse Analytics or Azure Databricks, for further transformation, or Power BI, for real-time visualizations.

Azure Stream Analytics

To begin this section, complete Exercise 3.17, which walks you through the provisioning of an Azure Stream Analytics job.

EXERCISE 3.17

Create an Azure Stream Analytics Job

1. Log in to the Azure portal at `https://portal.azure.com` ➢ navigate to the resource group you want to place the job in ➢ click the + Create link ➢ search for Stream Analytics Job ➢ select it from the drop-down menu ➢ and then click Create.
2. Enter a job name (I used **brainjammer**) ➢ select a location (I recommend using the same location as your other resources, as there are charges for data ingress/egress when data moves between locations) ➢ click the Secure All Private Data Assets Needed by This Job in My Storage Account check box ➢ select the Azure storage account you created in Exercise 3.1 ➢ and then click Create.
3. Once the job is provisioned, navigate to the job ➢ select Inputs from the navigation menu ➢ click the + Add Stream Input link ➢ select Event Hub from the drop-down ➢ enter an input alias (I used **brainwaves**) ➢ select the event hub namespace you created in Exercise 3.16 ➢ select the event hub name ➢ leave the Event Hub consumer group as `$Default` ➢ review the other options (leave them as default) ➢ and then click Save. See Figure 3.78 for an example.

FIGUER 3.78 Provisioning an Azure Stream Analytics job

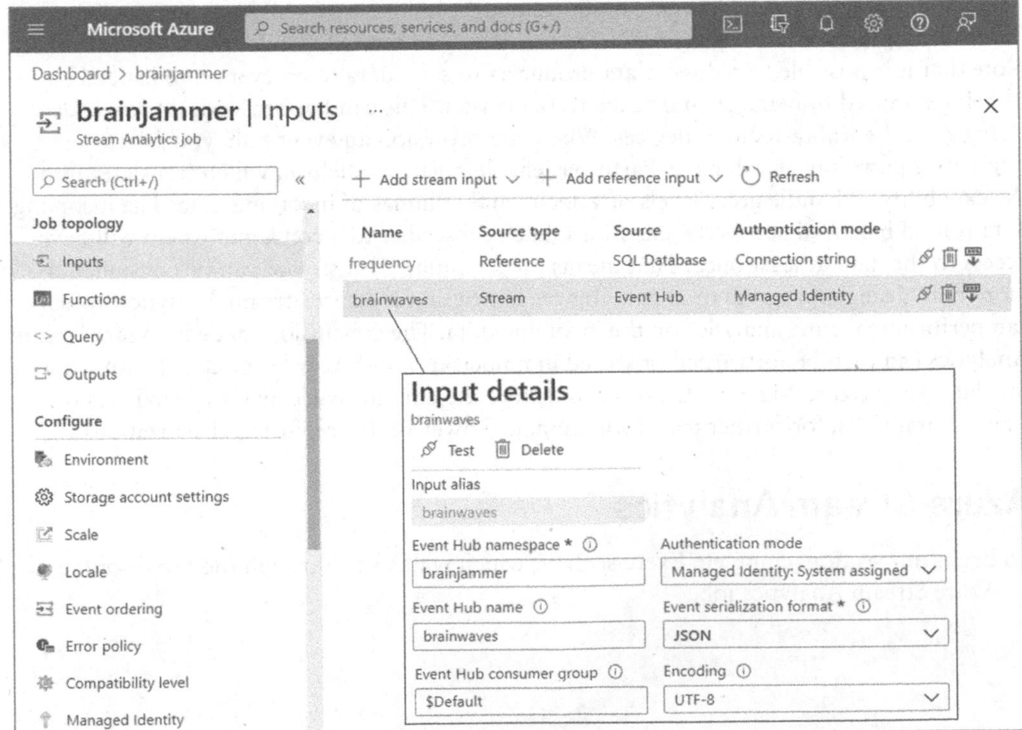

Consider testing the connection from the Azure Stream Analytics job and the event hub by pressing the Test menu option on the Input blade. The configuration of this input resulted in this job becoming a data receiver, also called a subscriber, just like the illustration in Figure 3.77. It is important to point out that at this point it is not known which query will be used to analyze the streaming brainjammer data. The data analytics project is still at the ingestion stage. Working through the streaming, transformation, and analysis of the data, in the coming chapters, it is hopeful that data patterns, attributes, or values that can uniquely identify scenarios will be discovered. The findings will be used as the basis for the query. This is the reason Exercise 3.17 stopped with the configuration of the input and did not continue to the query or outputs job topology configuration. You can find the completion of this configuration in Chapter 7.

Job Topology

The word *topology* is common in IT. The concept is often experienced in the context of a network topology. It is simply the arrangement of interrelated parts that constitute the whole. The same definition can be applied to a job topology, which combines inputs, functions, queries, and outputs.

Inputs

There are two types of inputs: stream and reference. A stream input, which you created in Exercise 3.17, can be either blob/ADLS, an event hub, or an IoT hub. The configuration for each type is very similar and results in whatever is added to either of those ingestion products being processed by the Azure Stream Analytics job. A reference input can be either blob/ADLS or a SQL database. This kind of input is useful for job query scenarios that need reference data, for example, a dimensional or a temporal table. Consider the following query:

```
SELECT b.VALUE, b.READING_DATETIME, f.FREQUENCY
FROM brainwaves b TIMESTAMP BY READING_DATETIME
JOIN frequency f
ON b.FREQUENCY_ID = f.FREQUENCY_ID
WHERE f.FREQUENCY_ID = 1
```

An input stream with the name of `brainwaves` is joined to a reference input named `frequency`. Note that part of the configuration of the reference input includes a SQL query to retrieve and store a local copy of that table, for example.

```
SELECT FREQUENCY_ID, FREQUENCY, ACTIVITY
FROM FREQUENCY
```

The values for `b.VALUE` and `b.READING_DATETIME` would be captured from the message stream sent via the event hub, whereas the value for `f.FREQUENCY` would be pulled from the reference input source table.

Functions

Chapter 2 introduced user-defined functions (UDFs). Azure Stream Analytics supports UDFs, which enable you to extend existing capabilities through custom code. The following function types are currently supported:

- Azure ML Service
- Azure ML Studio
- JavaScript UDA
- JavaScript UDF

Consider that you have a JavaScript UDF you created via the Azure Portal IDE and which resembles the following code snippet:

```
function squareRoot(n) {
 return Math.sqrt(n);
}
```

You can then reference the UDF via your input stream named `brainwaves` using the following query syntax:

```
SELECT
      SCENARIO,
      ELECTRODE,
      FREQUENCY,
      VALUE,
      UDF.squareRoot(VALUE) as VALUESQUAREROOT
INTO
      powerBI
FROM
      brainwaves
```

The result would be stored into the configured output location named, for example, `powerBI`.

Query

The query executed on each piece of streamed data into the Azure Stream Analytics input stream is the beginning of the magic. This is where you analyze the stream data and perform storage, transformation, computation, and/or alerting activities. Figure 3.79 shows an example of how the Query blade might look.

Azure Stream Analytics offers extensive support for queries. The available syntax is a subset of T-SQL and is more than enough to meet even the most demanding requirements. If by chance it does not, you can implement a UDF to fill the gap. The querying capabilities are split into the following categories, most of which you will find familiar. All of the capabilities are not called out—only the ones that are most likely to be on the DP-203 exam.

FIGUER 3.79 An Azure Stream Analytics job query

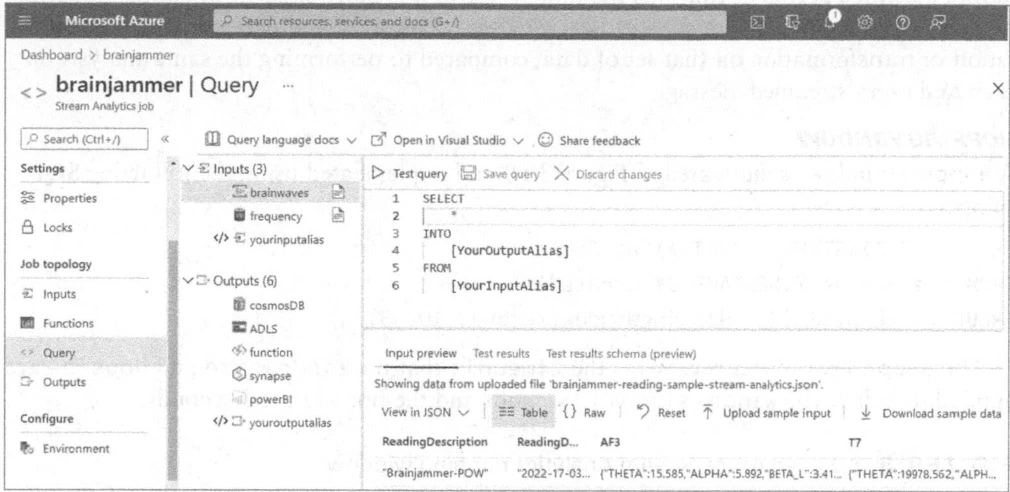

BUILT-IN FUNCTIONS

As shown in Table 3.20, the built-in functions are further categorized into groups such as aggregate, analytic, conversion, date, mathematical, and windowing.

TABLE 3.20 Azure Stream Analytics built-in functions

Type	Functions
Aggregate	AVG, COUNT, MIN, MAX, STDEV, SUM, VAR, TopOne
Analytic	ISFIRST, LAG, LAST
Conversion	CAST, GetType, TRY_CAST
Date	DATEADD, DATEDIFF, DATEPART
Mathematical	CEILING, FLOOR, POWER, ROUND, SIGN, SQUARE, SQRT
Windowing	Hopping, session, sliding, snapshot, tumbling

The most interesting, powerful, and complex function group in Table 3.20 is the windowing category. Chapter 2 introduced windows functions in the context of the OVER clause. Do not confuse a *windows* function with a *windowing* function. A windows function is used to execute aggregate functions on a complete dataset and return the computation as part of the result, whereas a windowing function is focused on the analysis of a data stream that arrived during a defined period of time, i.e. the time window. It is more efficient to perform queries on data that streamed over a span of, say, the past 10 seconds, and perform some computation or transformation on that set of data, compared to performing the same analysis on each and every streamed message.

HOPPING WINDOW

A hopping window is illustrated in Figure 3.80 and implemented using the following SQL snippet:

```
SELECT READINGTYPE, COUNT(*) as Count
FROM brainwaves TIMESTAMP BY CreatedAt
GROUP BY READINGTYPE, HoppingWindow(second, 10, 5)
```

The `second` parameter represents the `timeunit` that the `windowsize` and `hopsize` are applied to, where the `windowsize` is 10 seconds and the `hopsize` is 5 seconds.

FIGUER 3.80 An Azure Stream Analytics hopping window

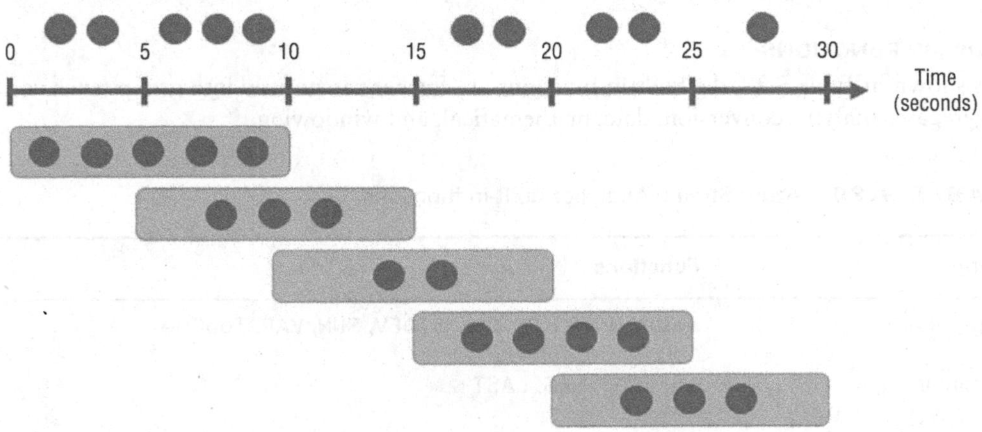

The query results in a count of the `READINGTYPE` every 5 seconds over the last 10 seconds.

SESSION WINDOW

A session window is illustrated in Figure 3.81 and implemented using the following SQL snippet:

```
SELECT READINGTYPE, COUNT(*) as Count
FROM brainwaves TIMESTAMP BY CreatedAt
GROUP BY READINGTYPE, SessionWindow(minute, 5, 10)
```

The `minute` parameter represents the `timeunit` that the `windowsize` and `maxdurationsize` are applied to, where the `windowsize` is 5 minutes and the `maxduration` is 10 minutes.

FIGUER 3.81 An Azure Stream Analytics session window

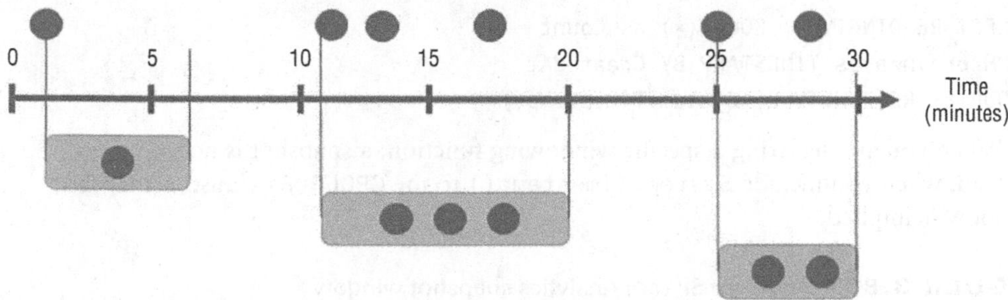

The query results in a count of `READINGTYPE` every 5 minutes when data exists in the 10-minute timeframe.

SLIDING WINDOW

A sliding window is illustrated in Figure 3.82 and implemented using the following SQL snippet:

```
SELECT READINGTYPE, COUNT(*) as Count
FROM brainwaves TIMESTAMP BY CreatedAt
GROUP BY READINGTYPE, SlidingWindow(second, 10)
HAVING COUNT(*) > 3
```

The `second` parameter represents the `timeunit` that the `windowsize` is applied to, where the `windowsize` is 10 seconds.

FIGUER 3.82 An Azure Stream Analytics sliding window

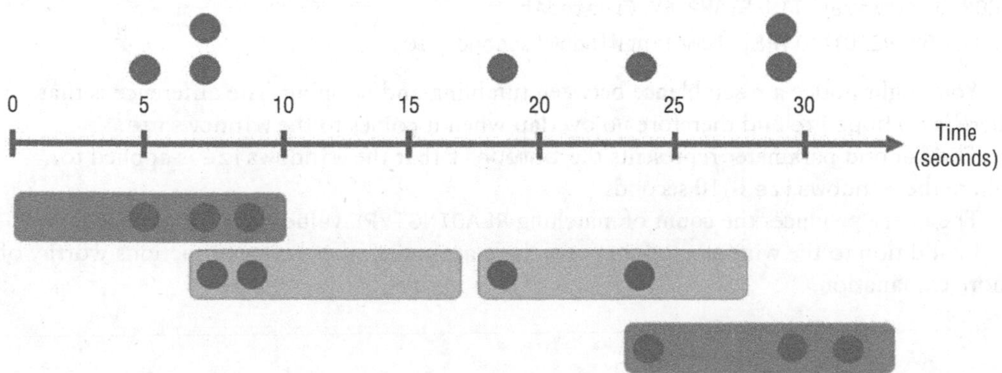

The query produces a data record when the count of the same READINGTYPE occurs more than 3 times in under 10 seconds. The darker timeline bars in Figure 3.82 illustrate.

SNAPSHOT WINDOW

A snapshot window is illustrated in Figure 3.83 and implemented using the following SQL snippet:

```
SELECT READINGTYPE, COUNT(*) as Count
FROM brainwaves TIMESTAMP BY CreatedAt
GROUP BY READINGTYPE, System.Timestamp()
```

When you are declaring a specific windowing function, a snapshot is not required; instead, when you include System.Timestamp() to the GROUP BY clause, a snapshot window is implied.

FIGUER 3.83 An Azure Stream Analytics snapshot window

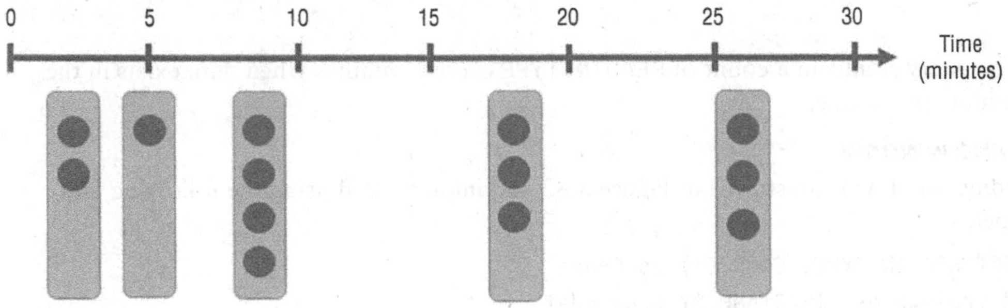

The query produces the count of like READINGTYPE values that have the same timestamp.

TUMBLING WINDOW

A tumbling window is illustrated in Figure 3.84 and implemented using the following SQL snippet:

```
SELECT READINGTYPE, COUNT(*) as Count
FROM brainwaves TIMESTAMP BY CreatedAt
GROUP BY READINGTYPE, TumblingWindow(second, 10)
```

You might notice a resemblance between tumbling and hopping. The difference is that there is no hopsize and therefore no overlap when it comes to the windowsize.

The second parameter represents the timeunit that the windowsize is applied to, where the windowsize is 10 seconds.

The query produces the count of matching READINGTYPE values every 10 seconds.

In addition to the windowing functions, there are some other built-in functions worthy of more explanation.

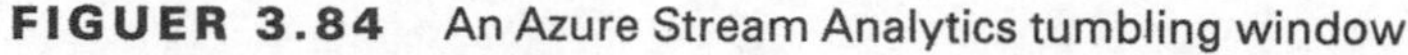
FIGUER 3.84 An Azure Stream Analytics tumbling window

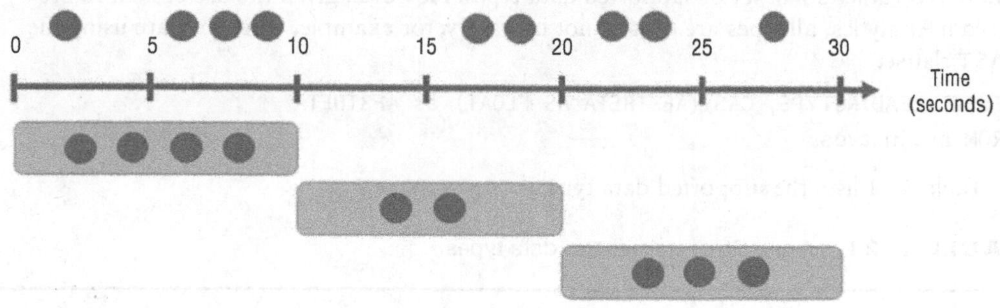

TOPONE

The TopOne aggregate function returns a single record, the first record that matches the group of selected data.

```
SELECT
 TopOne() OVER (ORDER BY READINGTIMESTAMP) as newestBrainwave
FROM brainwaves
GROUP BY TumblingWindow(second, 10)
```

Only `bigint`, `float`, and `datetime` data types are supported with the `ORDER BY` clause.

ISFIRST, LAG, AND LAST

The `ISFIRST` analytic function returns a `1` if the event is the first event in the stream for the defined interval; otherwise, it returns `0`. The implementation of the tumbling window function is performed as default. The following is the syntax to achieve this, followed by some example output:

```
SELECT
 READINGTYPE, READINGTIMESTAMP, ISFIRST(second, 10) as FIRST
FROM brainwaves
+--------------------------+------------------+-------+
| READINGTYPE              | READINGTIMESTAMP | FIRST |
+--------------------------+------------------+-------|
| 2022-03-17T14:00:01.2006 | Brainjammer-POW  | 1     |
| 2022-03-17T14:00:02.0209 | Brainjammer-POW  | 0     |
| 2022-03-17T14:00:03.2011 | Brainjammer-POW  | 0     |
| 2022-03-17T14:00:09.1212 | Brainjammer-POW  | 0     |
+--------------------------+------------------+-------+
```

The `LAG` analytic function enables you to retrieve the previous event in the data stream. `LAST` enables you to look up the most recent event in the stream for a given time window.

DATA TYPES

There is a rather small set of supported data types. However, given the use case of Azure Stream Analytics, all types are usually not necessary, for example, when you are using the CAST clause.

```
SELECT READINGTYPE, CAST(AF3THETA AS FLOAT) as AF3THETA
FROM brainwaves
```

Table 3.21 lists the supported data types.

TABLE 3.21 Azure Stream Analytics data types

Data type	Description
array	Ordered collection of values; values must be supported data type.
bigint	Integers between -2^{63} and 2^{63-1}.
bit	Integer with a value of either 1, 0, or NULL.
datetime	A date that is combined with a time of day.
float	Values: -1.79E+308 to -2.23E-308, 0, and 2.23E-308 to 1.79E+308.
nvarchar(max)	Text values.
record	Set of name-value pairs; values must be a supported data type.

There is also a SQL clause, TRY_CAST, as shown in the following SQL snippet:

```
SELECT READINGTYPE, CAST(AF3THETA AS FLOAT) as AF3THETA
FROM brainwaves
WHERE TRY_CAST(READINGTIMESTAMP AS datetime) IS NOT NULL
```

The TRY_CAST clause returns the data value if the CAST succeeds; otherwise, it returns a NULL.

QUERY LANGUAGE ELEMENTS

The supported query language clauses and commands in Azure Stream Analytics are some of the more powerful ones. The more complicated ones are covered in Chapter 2. SQL commands and clauses like GROUP BY, HAVING, INTO, JOIN, OVER, UNION, and WITH are all supported. They should be enough to provide access to all the data being streamed to your Azure Stream Analytics job.

TIME MANAGEMENT

There are many scenarios where the timestamp of a message/event is critical to the success of an application or business process. Consider a banking transaction that applies credits and debits to an account in the order they are performed. Also consider scenarios where you would need to implement first in, first out (FIFO) or last in, last out (LIFO) operations. From a streaming perspective, knowing the timeframe in which a stream event was received is useful for aggregations and comparing data between two streams. Azure Stream Analytics provides two options to handle time: the `System.Timestamp()` property and the `TIMESTAMP BY` clause.

As an event enters the stream and passes through Azure Stream Analytics, a timestamp is associated with it at every stage. This is the case for both event and IoT hub events. Consider the following query, followed by sample output:

```
SELECT READINGTIMESTAMP, READINGTYPE, System.Timestamp() t
FROM brainwaves
+--------------------------+-----------------+------------------------------+
| READINGTIMESTAMP         | READINGTYPE     | t                            |
+--------------------------+-----------------+------------------------------+
| 2022-03-17T14:00:00.0000 | Brainjammer-POW | 2022-03-17T14:00:01.9019671Z |
| 2022-03-17T15:01:15.0000 | Brainjammer-POW | 2022-03-17T15:01:17.9176555Z |
| ...                      | ...             | ...                          |
+--------------------------+-----------------+------------------------------+
```

Notice in the data result that there is a small difference between the two timestamps. You need to determine which of the timestamps is most important in your solution: the time in which the event was generated on source or when the event arrived at the Azure Stream Analytics stream. The other option is to use the `TIMESTAMP BY` clause, similar to the following:

```
SELECT READINGTIMESTAMP, READINGTYPE, System.Timestamp()
FROM brainwaves
TIMESTAMP BY DATEADD(millisecond, READINGTIMESTAMP, '1970-01-01T00:00:00Z')
```

The impact of this is that the platform uses the datetime value existing within the `READINGTIMESTAMP` as the event timestamp instead of the `System.Timestamp()` value. The point here is that the platform will do its best to process the streamed data events in the order they are received using the default event timestamp. If your requirements call for something different from that, you have these two options to change the default behavior.

Outputs

The inputs are where the data streams are coming from, and the outputs are where the data is to be stored after the query is performed on it. Figure 3.79 shows a few examples of the different Azure products that the data can be placed onto. If the data needs to be transformed more before it is ready for serving and consumption, a good location would be Azure Synapse Analytics. If the data is ready for consumption, then it can be streamed real time to a Power BI workspace. There will be more on this in later chapters, Chapter 7.

Apache Kafka for HDInsight

For customers who have an existing solution based on Apache Kafka for HDInsight and want to move it to Azure, this is the product of choice. From a Microsoft perspective, the same solution can be achieved using Event Hubs and IoT Hub with Azure Stream Analytics. Each of these product pairings can ingest streaming data from streaming sources on an unprecedented volume, velocity, and varied scale. Chapter 1 introduced Apache Kafka, and Chapter 2 provided more in-depth detail, which should be enough to respond to any questions you might get on the exam. The primary focus for the exam is on the Microsoft streaming products; however, you might see a reference to Apache Kafka for HDInsight. When you provision an HDInsight cluster on Azure, you must select the cluster type (see Figure 3.85). Refer to Chapter 1 for more about cluster types.

FIGUER 3.85 Choosing an Apache Kafka for HDInsight cluster type

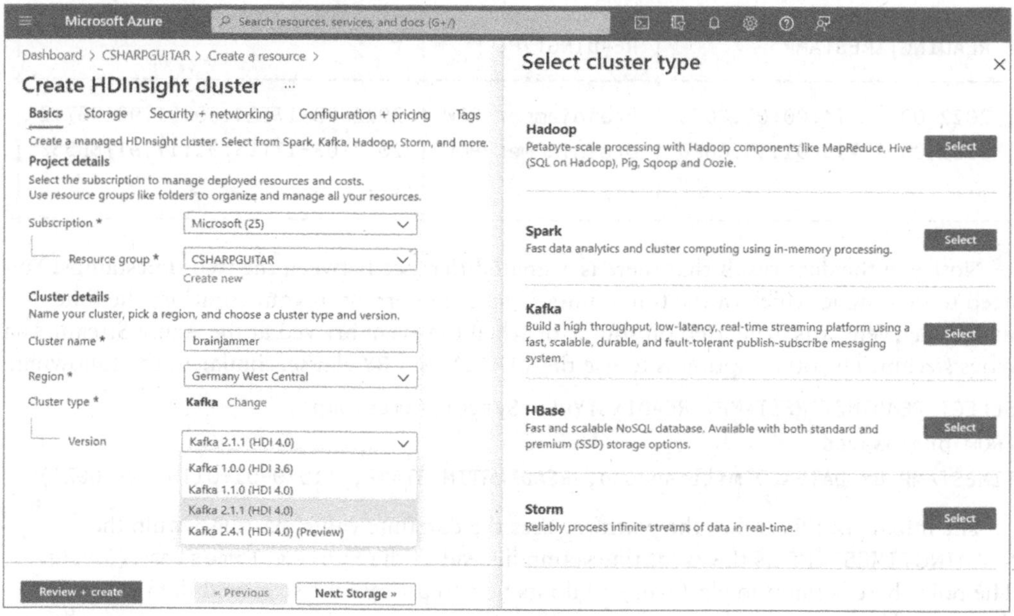

The required nodes to run Apache Kafka for HDInsight consist of head, Zookeeper, and worker nodes. As shown in Figure 3.86, there is a requirement for storage per worker node.

The head node is the node you can *Secure Shell (SSH)* into to manually execute applications and that will run across the HDInsight cluster. Processes that manage the execution and management of the HDInsight cluster run on the head node as well. The Zookeeper node is software that monitors and keeps track of the names, configuration, synchronization, topics, partitions, consumer group, and much more relating to Kafka. The Zookeeper node is a required component to run Kafka on HDInsight, and the head node is required for all HDInsight cluster types. Worker nodes provide the compute resource, CPU, and memory to perform the custom code and data processing required by the application. You might have noticed some similar terminology between Apache Kafka and Event Hubs, as shown in Table 3.22.

TABLE 3.22 Apache Kafka vs. Event Hubs terminology

Kafka	Event Hubs
Cluster	Namespace
Topic	Event Hub
Partition	Partition
Consumer group	Consumer group
Offset	Offset

FIGUER 3.86 Apache Kafka for HDInsight Kafka nodes

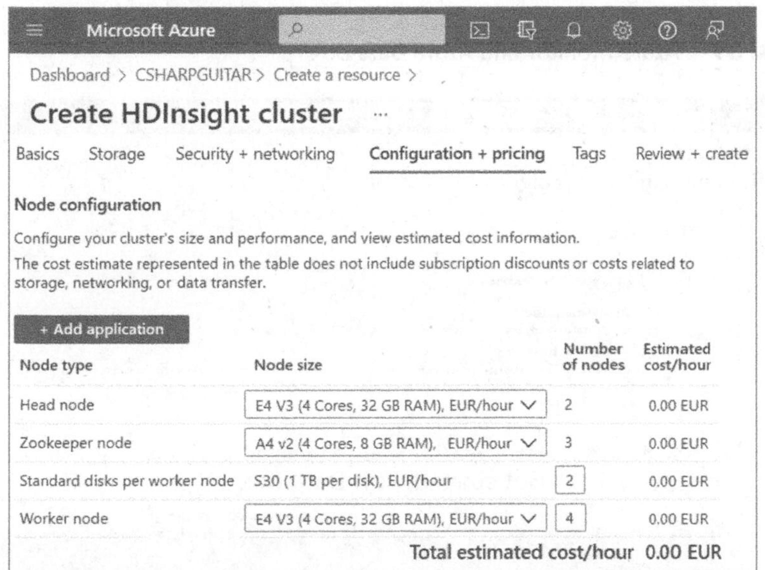

The only term in Table 3.22 that has not been explained yet is offset. The offset is a way to uniquely identify an event message within a partition. If you need to stop and restart the processing of events for a given partition, you can use the offset to determine where you need to start from.

Migrating and Moving Data

The persistent batching, incremental loading, streaming, inserting, or updating of data increases the amount of data over time. If you want to move your in-house data consisting of many gigabytes, terabytes, or petabytes of data to the cloud, then you need to use special migration products. Using FTP, copying a database backup over the network, or writing some custom code to move data to Azure are not optimal options. You need to use products like Azure Migrate, Azure Data Box, and Azure Database Migration Service to migrate and move large data sources from on-premises to the Azure platform. All three products were introduced in Chapter 1. As shown in Figure 3.87, Azure Migrate provides not only database migration features but also VMs, web apps, and *virtual desktop infrastructure (VDI)* migration. Azure Data Box is also available from the Azure Monitor blade and asks for information like whether the transfer is inbound to Azure or outbound from Azure. Also, it is necessary to identify the target or source subscription, resource group, the location of the data source, and the target data location.

FIGUER 3.87 Azure Monitor and Azure Data Box

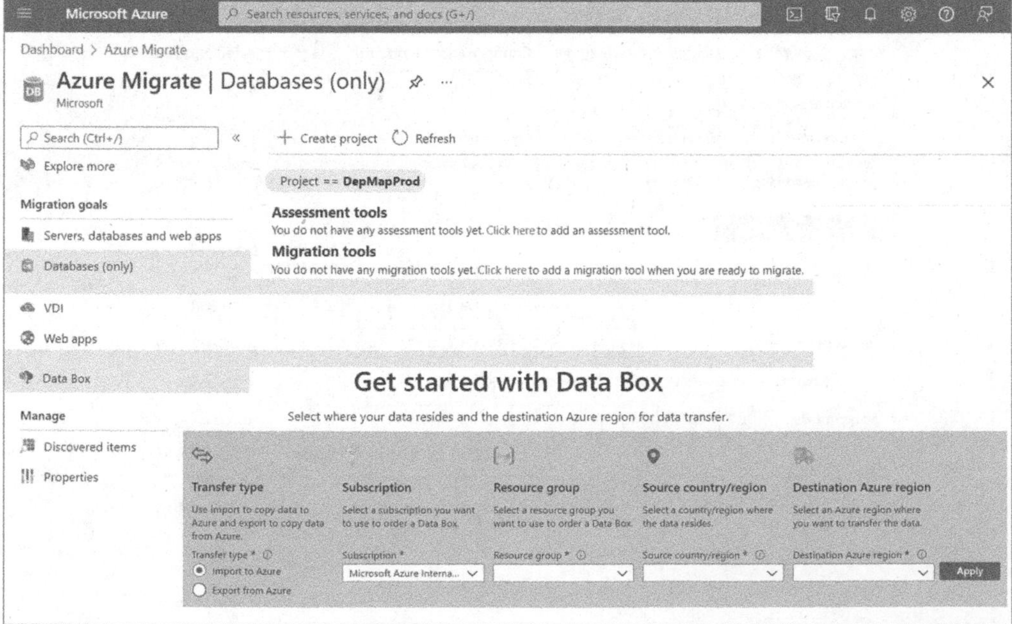

Azure Database Migration Service supports many different databases, including MySQL, PostgreSQL, MongoDB, and Azure Cosmos DB. If you are primarily focused on SQL Server, you can install an Azure SQL Migration extension into Azure Data Studio that will walk you through the steps necessary to migrate an existing database to Azure. Remember that copying large amounts of data over the Internet is risky, as it can fail, and can be costly. If you choose to move large data sources from your on-premises datastores onto Azure or vice versa, consider setting up an ExpressRoute connection. This is a private connection and a direct link between your network and the Azure network. Not only will this improve the performance and stability, but it also will be more secure.

Summary

This chapter covered the sources of data and the volume, variety, and velocity of ingestion. Azure Synapse Analytics contains ample features to manage the ingestion at Big Data scale. If you currently either have an HDInsight cluster or run your ingestion with Databricks, then Azure provides the service for you to run these at scale. There are also many different Azure products designed to house the ingested data. The product of choice depends on the variety of data ingested, like blobs, files, documents, or relational data. Managing the data size, managing age and retention, pruning data, archiving data, and properly storing it so that those management activities can be monitored are necessary so that appropriate actions can be taken.

Properly partitioning data results in optimized query performance. You learned to partition files by using the `df.write.partitionBy()` function and distributions like round-robin, hash, and replicated. Another partition-like approach for managing files is to store them in a directory structure by date and time, `YYYY/MM/DD/HH`. You learned about star schemas, which are made up of dimension and fact tables, managing dimension tables with SCD types, and using temporal tables for historical analysis. The concepts of an analytical store, a metastore, and a data lake should also be clear in your head.

In the final portion of this chapter, you provisioned a lot of Azure products, like Azure Synapse Analytics, Azure Data Factory, and Azure Databricks. You also learned about some streaming techniques and products like Event Hubs, IoT Hub, Kafka, and Azure Stream Analytics. After completing the exercises in this chapter, your knowledge regarding each of these products should be at a respectable skill level.

Exam Essentials

Design a data storage structure. Azure Data Lake Storage (ADLS) is the centerpiece of a Big Data solution running on Azure. Numerous other products can help in this capacity as well, like Azure Cosmos DB and Azure SQL. Each product is targeted for a specific type of data structure, files, documents, and relational data. Managing the ingestion of data is ongoing, and actions like pruning and archiving are necessary to keep this stage of the Big Data process in a healthy and performant state.

Design a partition strategy. A partition is a method for organizing your data in a way that results in better management, data discovery, and query performance. Optimizing the size of partitions based on groupings like arrival date and time or a hash distribution also makes for more performant ingestion and management. Monitoring the skew of your data and then reshuffling the data for better performance is something you must perform diligently.

Design a serving layer. The serving layer is one part of the lambda architecture. A hot and cold data path can provide real-time or near real-time access to data. To support such a process, you learned the concepts of a star schema; slowly changing dimension (SDC) tables of Type 1, 2, 3, and 6; and temporal tables.

Data ingestion. Azure provides numerous products designed for the ingestion of data. Azure Synapse Analytics is the one Microsoft is driving customers toward and the product they are adding new features to. Azure Data Factory provides ingestion capabilities; however, most of the existing capabilities are, or will soon be, found in Azure Synapse Analytics. Customers who use Databricks and Apache Spark can migrate their existing workloads to Azure. Azure Databricks is a Microsoft deployment of the open-source version of Databricks.

Data streaming. Two Azure product groupings are optimized to support a streaming solution on Azure. Event Hubs/IoT Hub and Azure Stream Analytics are recommended to customers who want to use Microsoft products in the cloud. Customers who currently have an existing streaming solution based on Kafka and Apache Spark can provision and manage that workstream on Azure.

Review Questions

Many questions can have more than a single answer. Please select all choices that are true.

1. What is a data lake?
   - **A.** The location where business-ready data for reporting is stored
   - **B.** A store of all your data in its various forms
   - **C.** A relational database with transactional data
   - **D.** An Azure Data Lake Storage container
2. Which data format is not supported on Azure Synapse Analytics?
   - **A.** Parquet
   - **B.** CSV
   - **C.** EXE
   - **D.** XML
3. Which of the following file types are most performant and recommended for running file-based data analytics?
   - **A.** JSON
   - **B.** YAML
   - **C.** XML
   - **D.** Parquet
4. Which of the following are useful for partitioning files?
   - **A.** df.write.partitionBy('. . .').
   - **B.** Store files in an initiative directory structure like YYYY/MM/DD.
   - **C.** Split the data into the smallest possible files as possible.
   - **D.** Merge all files into a single file.
5. Which of the following scenarios would identify a need to partition your data?
   - **A.** There is excessive data shuffling.
   - **B.** The data is skewed.
   - **C.** There has been a large increase in the amount of incoming data.
   - **D.** Your data is not partitioned.
6. Which of the following are true concerning dimension tables and fact tables?
   - **A.** The data on a dimension table changes often.
   - **B.** The data on a fact table changes often.
   - **C.** The data on a dimension table does not change often.
   - **D.** The data on a fact table does not change often.

7. Which of the following is true concerning a Type 3 SCD table?
   - **A.** It contains the features of both Type 1 and Type 2 tables.
   - **B.** It uses a surrogate key.
   - **C.** It contains a version of the previous value(s) only.
   - **D.** It provides the complete data change history.

8. Which of the following columns are included in a Type 6 SCD table?
   - **A.** A surrogate key
   - **B.** A Boolean column that identifies the current value
   - **C.** A start and end date
   - **D.** A foreign key to a parent reference table

9. Microsoft recommends all new data analytics projects target Azure Data Factory to perform all stages of big data analytics.
   - **A.** True
   - **B.** False

10. Which of the following product pairings can support all or a portion of a streaming solution?
    - **A.** HDInsight and Kafka
    - **B.** HDInsight and Azure Stream Analytics
    - **C.** IoT Hub and Azure Stream Analytics
    - **D.** Kafka and Event Hubs

The Storage of Data

EXAM DP-203 OBJECTIVES COVERED IN THIS CHAPTER:

- ✓ Implement a partition strategy
- ✓ Design and implement the data exploration layer

WHAT YOU WILL LEARN IN THIS CHAPTER:

- ✓ Storing raw data in Azure Databricks for transformation
- ✓ Storing data using Azure HDInsight
- ✓ Storing prepared, trained, and modeled data

The primary objective of Chapter 3, "Data Sources and Ingestion," was to explain the sources of data and the Azure products for ingesting it. As soon as the data exists, it is stored somewhere. The data can be on an IoT device, on a flash drive, in memory, or on the wire someplace between where it was created and where it is going. The ingestion products discussed in Chapter 3 are the entry point for that data onto the Azure platform. Azure Synapse Analytics, Azure Data Factory, Event Hubs, IoT Hub, and Kafka are products optimized for ingestions. Azure products that are optimized for the storage of the just ingested data are products like ADLS, Azure SQL, Azure Cosmos DB, Azure HDInsight, and Azure Databricks. This chapter discusses the techniques for optimally storing a potentially vast variety and volume of incoming data.

Implement Physical Data Storage Structures

When you think of something that is physical, it usually means the object is something you can touch with your hands. The same is true when it comes to physical data storage. A physical data storage device is a disk drive connected to or mapped from a computer. The data structures placed onto the physical disk are the directory patterns in which the files containing your data are stored.

Implement Compression

Processing large files can cause networking bottlenecks and increase the number of I/O operations. Compression reduces the size of files and can therefore have a positive impact on network and I/O latencies. Knowing that a company is charged by the amount of occupied storage space and ingress/egress data transfers, it makes sense to use as little of those as possible. Data compression makes the file in which it is stored smaller; decompression reverts the data to its original form and size and is required before the content within the file can be queried. The approach for performing the compressions/decompression of data, also known as encoding/decoding, begins with choosing the *codec*. Complete Exercise 4.1 to implement compression and learn more about what a codec is.

EXERCISE 4.1

Implement Compression

1. Log in to the Azure portal at `https://portal.azure.com` ➢ navigate to the storage account you created in Exercise 3.1 ➢ choose the Containers menu item ➢ select a directory ➢ upload the two GZ and ZIP compressed CSV-formatted data files located in the `Chapter04/Ch04Ex01` directory on GitHub at `https://github.com/benperk/ADE` ➢ navigate to the Azure Synapse Analytics workspace you created in Exercise 3.3 ➢ on the Overview blade, click the Open link in the Open Synapse Studio tile ➢ select the Data hub ➢ follow the instructions from Exercise 3.9 to create an integration dataset ➢ after completing the dataset, select one of the two compressed `brainjammer` reading files ➢ check the First Row as Header check box ➢ and then select the None radio box for Import Schema. Figure 4.1 illustrates how this might look.

FIGURE 4.1 Azure Synapse Analytics compression

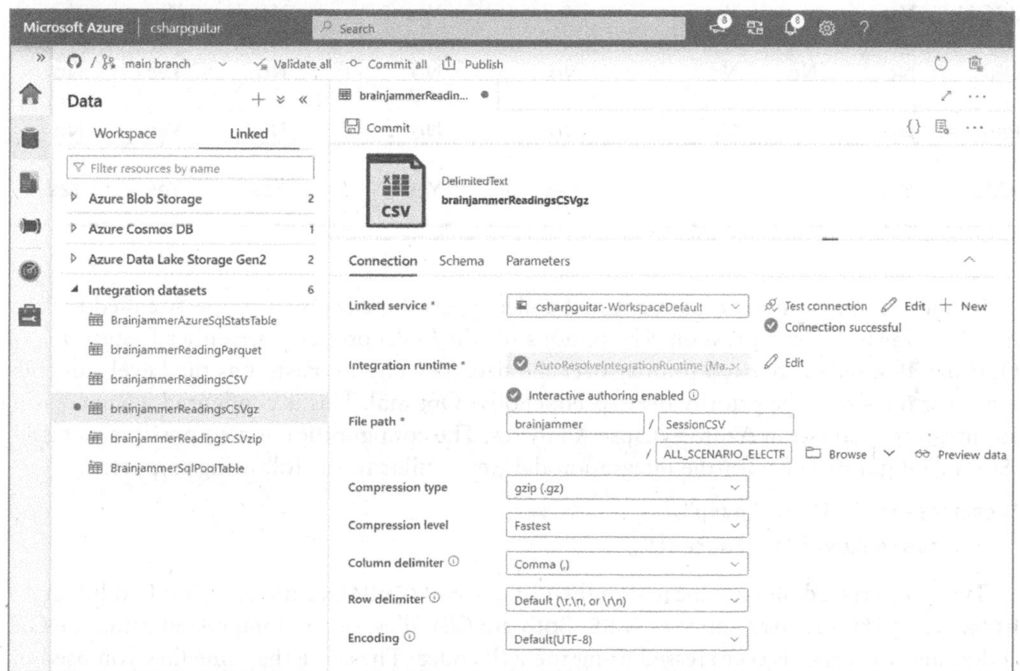

2. Click the Compression Type drop-down box ➢ select either `gzip (.gz)` or `ZipDeflate (.zip)`, depending on the file you uploaded ➢ click the Test Connection link ➢ click the Preview Data link ➢ click the Commit button ➢ and then click the brackets {} on the top right of Figure 4.1, which expose the JSON configuration for the integration dataset. Notice the `compressionCodec` and `compressionLevel` properties.

Table 4.1 shows the Azure Synapse Analytics file formats and their supported codecs.

TABLE 4.1 Supported codecs by file format

Format	bzip2 (.bz2)	gzip (.gz)	Deflate (.deflate)	ZipDeflate (.zip)	TarGZip (.tar/.tar.gz)	TAR (.tar)	Snappy	lz4
Avro	No	No	Yes	No	No	No	Yes	No
Binary	Yes	Yes	Yes	Yes	Yes	Yes	No	No
Delimited	Yes	Yes	Yes	Yes	Yes	Yes	Yes	Yes
Excel	Yes	Yes	Yes	Yes	Yes	Yes	Yes	Yes
JSON	Yes	Yes	Yes	Yes	Yes	Yes	Yes	Yes
ORC	No	No	No	No	No	No	Yes	No
Parquet	No	Yes	No	No	No	No	Yes	No
XML	Yes	Yes	Yes	Yes	Yes	Yes	Yes	Yes

In addition to the numerous supported codec types, there is also a property called Level that pertains to file compression. The options for the Level property are either Fastest or Optimal. If speed is your top priority over file size, then choose Fastest as the Level value. If a smaller file size is the priority over speed, choose Optimal. This is configured when creating an integrated dataset in Azure Synapse Analytics. The configuration is also possible using a JSON configuration file for the integration dataset, similar to the following snippet:

```
"compressionCodec": "gzip",
"compressionLevel": "Fastest",
```

Two compressed files are located in the `Chapter04/Ch04Ex1` directory on GitHub at `https://github.com/benperk/ADE`. Both are CSV files; one is compressed using the GZ codec, and the other is compressed using the ZIP codec. These are the same files you used in some of the previous exercises and is over 20 MB in a decompressed state. The compressed files are just over 2 MB, which represents a reduction of size on the scale of 10 to 1. Therefore, compressing your data files in this manner would also result in a tenfold cost savings.

Implement Partitioning

There are two primary reasons to implement partitioning: manageability and performance. From a manageability perspective, your tables are organized into a structure that makes their content discoverable. That makes it possible to deduce the content of the data on a table by its name, for example. If the variety of data in a table is too great, then it is harder to determine how to use the data and what purpose it has. Splitting the data from one large table in a logical manner into a smaller subset of tables can help you understand and manage the data more efficiently. Figure 4.2 illustrates how you might partition a large table into smaller ones. This is often referred to as *vertical partitioning*.

FIGURE 4.2 Azure Synapse Analytics SQL partitioning

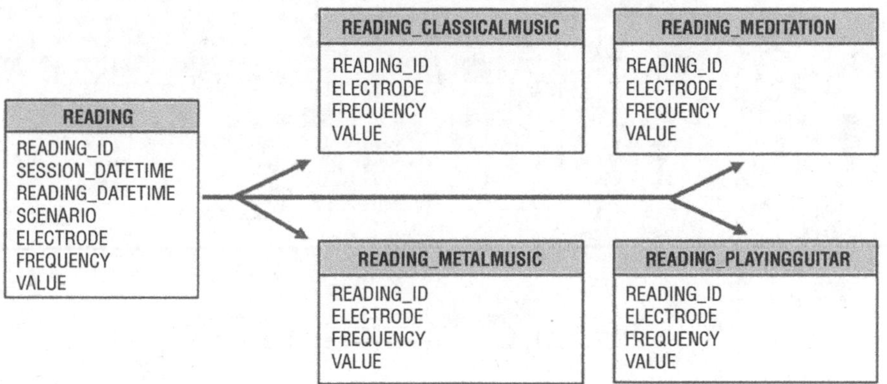

The other reason to implement partitioning is for performance. Consider that the `READING` table in Figure 4.2 contains millions of rows for all brainjammer scenarios. If you want to retrieve data for only a single scenario, then the execution could take some time. To improve performance in that scenario, you can create tables based on the scenario in which the reading took place.

Foreign keys are not supported in dedicated SQL pools on Azure Synapse Analytics. Both a primary key and a unique constraint are supported but only when the `NOT ENFORCED` clause is used. A primary key also requires the `NONCLUSTERED` clause.

You can implement partitioning using a Spark pool by running the following commands, which you learned a bit about in Chapter 3:

```
%%pyspark
df = spark.read \
```

```
    .load('abfss://.@..dfs.core.windows.net/SessionCSV/*_FREQUENCY_VALUE
.csv', \
          format='csv', header=True)
df.write \
    .partitionBy('SCENARIO').mode('overwrite') \
    .csv('/SessionCSV/ScenarioPartitions')
```

The partition is created on the same ADLS the loaded data file is retrieved from and loaded into a DataFrame. The result of the partitioning resembles Figure 4.3.

FIGURE 4.3 Azure Synapse Analytics Spark partitioning from Storage explorer

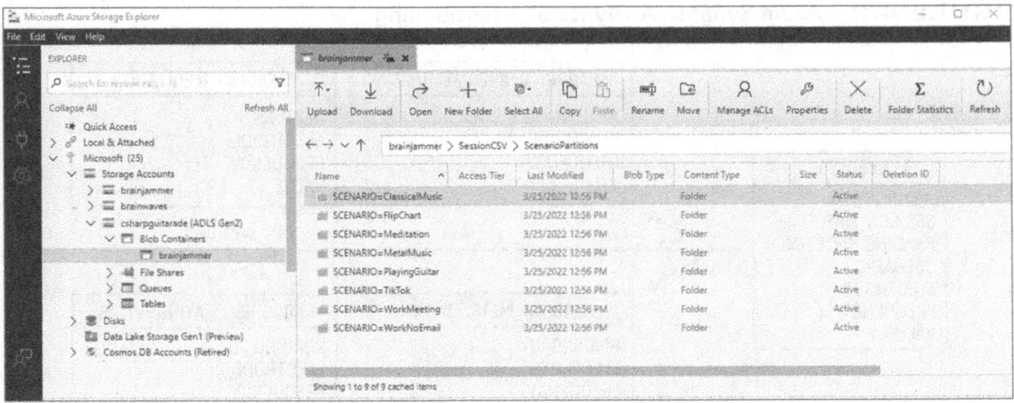

When you query the specific partition using the following code snippet, the result contains only readings from the Meditation scenario. This is in contrast to loading and querying the CSV file for the readings.

```
data = spark.read.csv('/SessionCSV/ScenarioPartitions/SCENARIO=Meditation')
data.show(5)
```

To gain some hands-on experience for these concepts, complete Exercise 4.2.

EXERCISE 4.2

Implement Partitioning

1. Log in to the Azure portal at `https://portal.azure.com` ➢ navigate to the Azure Synapse Analytics workspace you created in Exercise 3.3 ➢ on the Overview blade, click the Open link in the Open Synapse Studio tile ➢ select the Data hub ➢ expand the SQL database menu ➢ expand the dedicated SQL pool you created for Exercise 3.7 ➢ hover over the Schemas folder ➢ click the ellipse (. . .) ➢ click New SQL Script ➢ click New schema ➢ execute the `CREATE SCHEMA` SQL command after providing a name (I used **reading**).

2. Execute the SQL syntax located in the `Chapter04/Ch04Ex02` directory on GitHub at `https://github.com/benperk/ADE`. In the `partitionSQL.txt` file, view the newly created tables by refreshing the Tables folder.
3. Select the Linked tab within the Data hub ➢ expand Azure Data Lake Storage Gen2 ➢ navigate to the `ALL_SCENARIO_ELECTRODE_FREQUENCY_VALUE.csv` file, which you uploaded earlier, or download it from the `Chapter03/Ch03Ex09` folder on GitHub ➢ navigate to the file via the Linked service ➢ choose the New Notebook drop-down menu ➢ click Load to DataFrame ➢ attach the Spark pool you created in Exercise 3.4 from the Attach To drop-down ➢ and then enter the following code snippet (adjust the paths accordingly):

```
%%pyspark
df = spark.read \
  .load('abfss://.@..dfs.core.windows.net/SessionCSV/...ODE_FREQUENCY_VALUE.csv', \
        format='csv', header=True)
df.write \
  .partitionBy('SCENARIO').mode('overwrite').csv('/SessionCSV/ScenarioPartitions')
data = spark.read.csv('/SessionCSV/ScenarioPartitions/SCENARIO=PlayingGuitar')
data.show(5)
```

The code snippet is available in the `Chapter04/Ch04Ex02` directory on GitHub, in a file named `partitionSpark.txt`. The output resembles Figure 4.4.

FIGURE 4.4 Azure Synapse Analytics Spark partitioning

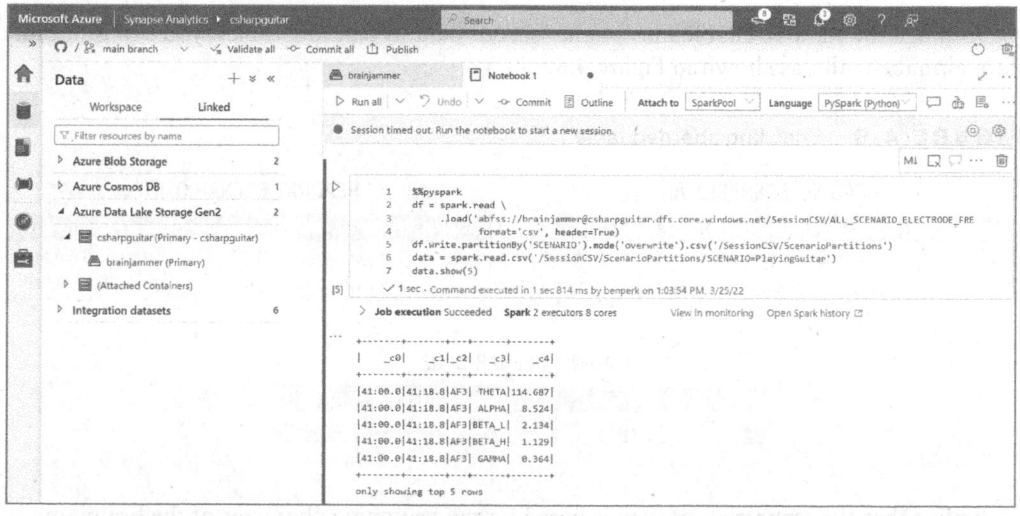

Implement Sharding

Sharding is a form of data partitioning, sometimes referred to as *horizontal partitioning*. Both sharding and partitioning are concerned with reducing the size of a dataset. The primary difference is that sharding implies that the data partitions will be spread across multiple nodes (i.e., computers). Vertical partitioning can also be spread across multiple nodes, though more commonly just across tables or databases. A partition concerns the grouping of data that will run within a single database instance. There is a lot of overlapping terminology relative to these two concepts, including the terms vertical and horizontal. In some scenarios vertical and horizontal partitioning can be applied to both partitioning and sharding. For now, you can learn the basics here and then, as you progress, you can dig deeper into the complexities that drive your choice in your given context. Consider the `READING` table shown in Figure 4.5.

FIGURE 4.5 Sharding original table

Original Table (READING)

READING_ID	SESSION_DATETIME	READING_DATETIME	SCENARIO	ELECTRODE	FREQUENCY	VALUE
1	2022-03-25 14:55:32	2022-03-25 14:57:16	ClassicalMusic	AF3	THETA	92.687
2	2022-03-25 15:31:11	2022-03-25 15:33:23	FlipChart	AF4	BETA_L	2.397
3	2022-03-25 15:49:22	2022-03-25 15:49:22	MetalMusic	T7	GAMMA	0.461
4	2022-03-25 16:41:54	2022-03-25 16:41:54	TikTok	Pz	GAMMA	0.235
5	2022-03-25 17:28:21	2022-03-25 17:28:21	PlayingGuitar	AF4	ALPHA	6.843

To shard the `READING` table into smaller sets of data in separate tables, you can group the data alphabetically, as shown in Figure 4.6.

FIGURE 4.6 Sharding sharded table

READING_SCENARIO_AH

READING_ID	SCENARIO	ELECTRODE	FREQUENCY	VALUE
1	ClassicalMusic	AF3	THETA	92.687
2	FlipChart	AF4	BETA_L	2.397

READING_SCENARIO_IP

READING_ID	SCENARIO	ELECTRODE	FREQUENCY	VALUE
3	MetalMusic	T7	GAMMA	0.461
5	PlayingGuitar	AF4	ALPHA	6.843

READING_SCENARIO_QZ

READING_ID	SCENARIO	ELECTRODE	FREQUENCY	VALUE
4	TikTok	Pz	GAMMA	0.235

Notice that the separation of data is based on the beginning character of the brainjammer scenario. The way you shard data requires some analysis of the original table. Notice that the tables are appended with characters `_AH`, `_IP`, and `_QZ`. This indicates that scenarios beginning with the letters *A* through *H* are placed into the READING_SCENARIO_AH table; scenarios beginning with *I* through *P* are placed into their own table; and so on. The point is, you need to balance the data so that you have a similar number of rows per sharded table. A table containing *A–H* might not be the best solution in a different situation, so you need to analyze the data in the original table to determine the best way to shard your data. You should perform analysis periodically to make sure the tables remain comparable in size. If you receive a lot of a scenarios that start with the letters *I* through *P*, you may need to reshuffle and reevaluate the shards.

When you need to retrieve data for a specific scenario, you will know that the data is sharded by scenario name. Your queries can therefore target the appropriate tables based on that knowledge. There is a file named shardingSQL.txt in the Chapter04 directory on GitHub at https://github.com/benperk/ADE. Consider performing the steps in Exercise 4.2 but using the sharding SQL script instead. Note that the READING table will already exist from previous exercises; just remove that part of the SQL statement, if it causes problems.

Implement Different Table Geometries with Azure Synapse Analytics Pools

To effectively use the massively parallel processing (MPP) architecture with a SQL pool, you need to understand table geometries. Table geometries specify how data is sharded into distributions on your existing compute nodes. These table geometries optimize the performance of the queries that run on them and are defined as you create the table. There are three types, which you already know about.

- Round-robin is optimal for staging/temporary tables (default).
- Hash is optimal for fact and large dimensional tables.
- Replicated is optimal for small dimensional tables in a star schema.

To implement a round-robin distributed table, execute the following SQL statement. The result is an even distribution of rows from the table across randomly selected compute nodes.

```
CREATE TABLE [staging].[PlayingGuitar]
(
  [SESSION_DATETIME]     DATETIME          NOT NULL,
  [READING_DATETIME]     DATETIME          NOT NULL,
  [SCENARIO]             NVARCHAR (100)    NOT NULL,
  [ELECTRODE]            NVARCHAR (50)     NOT NULL,
  [FREQUENCY]            NVARCHAR (50)     NOT NULL,
  [VALUE]                DECIMAL(7,3)      NOT NULL
)
WITH
```

```
(
  CLUSTERED COLUMNSTORE INDEX,
  DISTRIBUTION = ROUND_ROBIN
)
```

In Exercise 3.7 you created a hash-distributed table, which resembled the following SQL statement. This results in all the data from the table being distributed to different nodes per the column identified in the hash. In this case the value is the FREQUENCY, but it could also be ELECTRODE or SCENARIO. Because this table contains all the readings from all scenarios and sessions, it is the largest one; therefore, it is a good candidate for this distribution type, so it is broken down into smaller, queryable datasets. Tables that require JOIN or aggregation command statements can also realize performance gains using the hash distribution model.

```
CREATE TABLE [brainwaves].[FactREADING]
(
  [SESSION_DATETIME]   DATETIME          NOT NULL,
  [READING_DATETIME]   DATETIME          NOT NULL,
  [SCENARIO]            NVARCHAR (100)   NOT NULL,
  [ELECTRODE]           NVARCHAR (50)    NOT NULL,
  [FREQUENCY]           NVARCHAR (50)    NOT NULL,
  [VALUE]               DECIMAL(7,3)     NOT NULL
)
WITH
(
  CLUSTERED COLUMNSTORE INDEX,
  DISTRIBUTION = HASH ([FREQUENCY]
)
```

A replicated distribution places a copy of the table data on each node in the cluster. This provides optimal performance for small tables.

```
CREATE TABLE [brainwaves].[DimFREQUENCY]
(
  [FREQUENCY_ID]      INT                NOT NULL,
  [FREQUENCY]         NVARCHAR (50)      NOT NULL,
  [ACTIVITY]          NVARCHAR (100)     NOT NULL
)
WITH
(
  CLUSTERED COLUMNSTORE INDEX,
  DISTRIBUTION = REPLICATE
)
```

There is a file named tableGeometries.txt in the Chapter04 directory on GitHub at https://github.com/benperk/ADE. Consider performing the steps in Exercise 4.2 but instead using the table geometries distribution SQL script. Note the new schemas and be sure to create them as well.

Implement Data Redundancy

When something is redundant, it means that the item is not needed. In many scenarios the redundant object is never needed again. In other circumstances, however, it might not be needed at the moment but may be in the future. Having a copy of a database, for example, may be redundant, but if the primary database is harmed, having this redundancy will be very helpful. Data redundancy can be important in cases where a user executes an unintended update, truncate, or delete that impacts a massive amount of data. Another possibility is for resiliency in case of a problem at the datacenter where your data exists.

Human Error

Unintentional actions happen, such as deleting files, dropping a table, or truncating data. Hopefully none of those happen very often, but if they do, there are actions you can take to recover. P*oint-in-time restore (PITR)* can be helpful in scenarios where data has been deleted or modified in a way that is not easily recoverable. PITR is dependent on something called a snapshot, which is an action that creates a restore point. So, what needs to happen is that when a human error causes data loss or corruption, you can restore the data by using a snapshot taken before the corruption. From an Azure Synapse Analytics dedicated SQL pool perspective, snapshots are a built-in feature. PITR follows an eight-hour *recovery point objective (RPO)*, which means when your data gets into an unwanted state, the maximum time to get recovered should be 8 hours. RPO defines how much data can be lost at maximum, meaning that you can lose up to 8 hours of data. To view the most recent dedicated SQL pool snapshot in Azure Synapse Analytics, execute the following query in a SQL script:

```
SELECT   TOP 1 *
FROM     sys.pdw_loader_backup_runs
ORDER BY run_id DESC
```

Notice the results, as shown in Figure 4.7, and what can be concluded from them.

You can infer from the query results information like when the snapshot took place, when it was completed, how long it took, the type, the mode, the status, and the progress.

FIGURE 4.7 Data redundancy snapshots

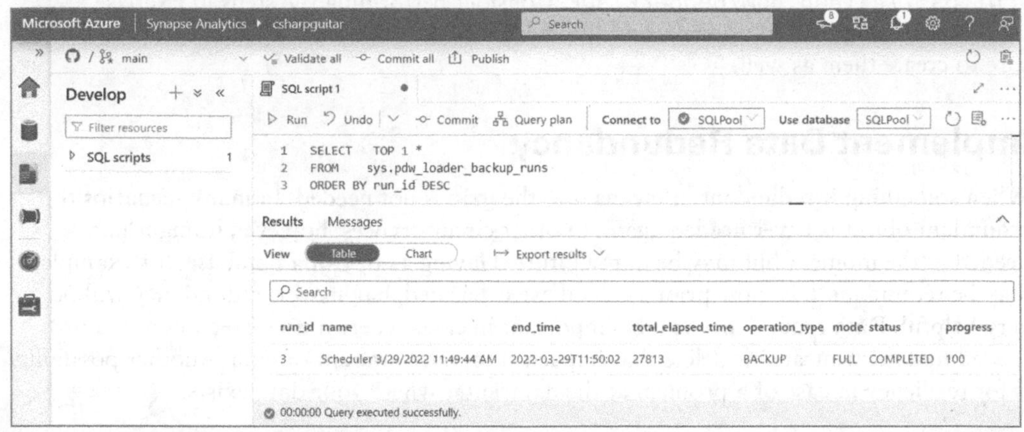

EXERCISE 4.3

Implement Data Redundancy

1. Log in to the Azure portal at `https://portal.azure.com` > navigate to the Azure Synapse Analytics workspace you created in Exercise 3.3 > choose the SQL Pools link from the left navigation menu in the Analytics Pools section > and then select the dedicated SQL pool you created for Exercise 3.7. Something similar to Figure 4.8 is rendered.

FIGURE 4.8 Data redundancy dedicated SQL pool

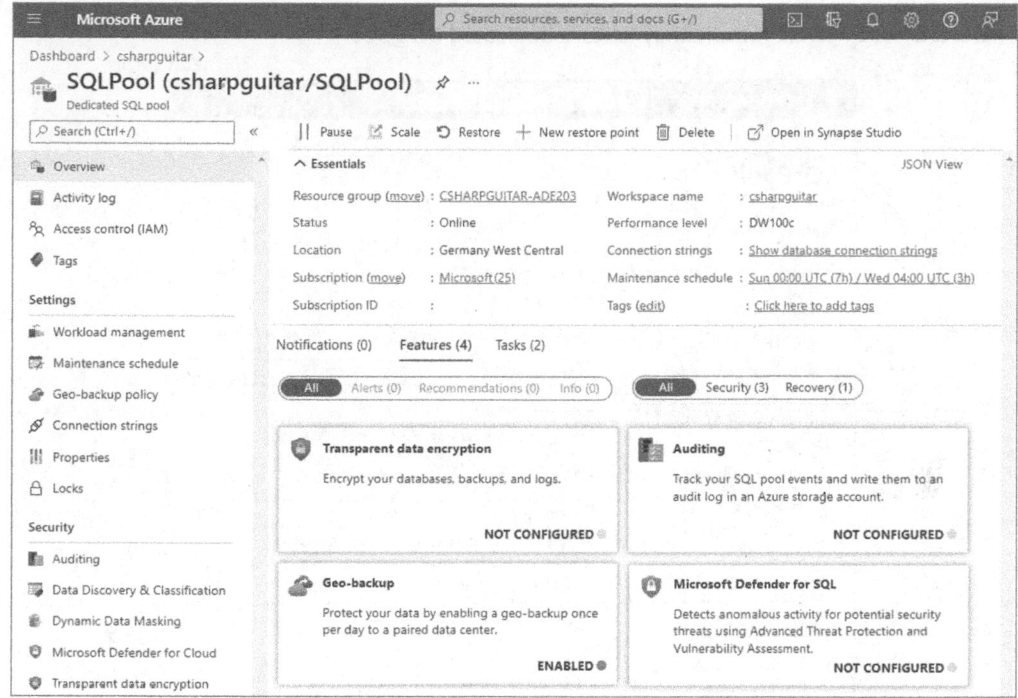

2. Choose the Restore menu option on the SQL Pool blade (see Figure 4.8) ➢ enter a dedicated SQL pool name to apply the snapshot to (see Figure 4.9) ➢ select the Review + Restore button ➢ review the details ➢ and then click Create.

EXERCISE 4.3 *(continued)*

FIGURE 4.9 Data redundancy restore dedicated SQL pool

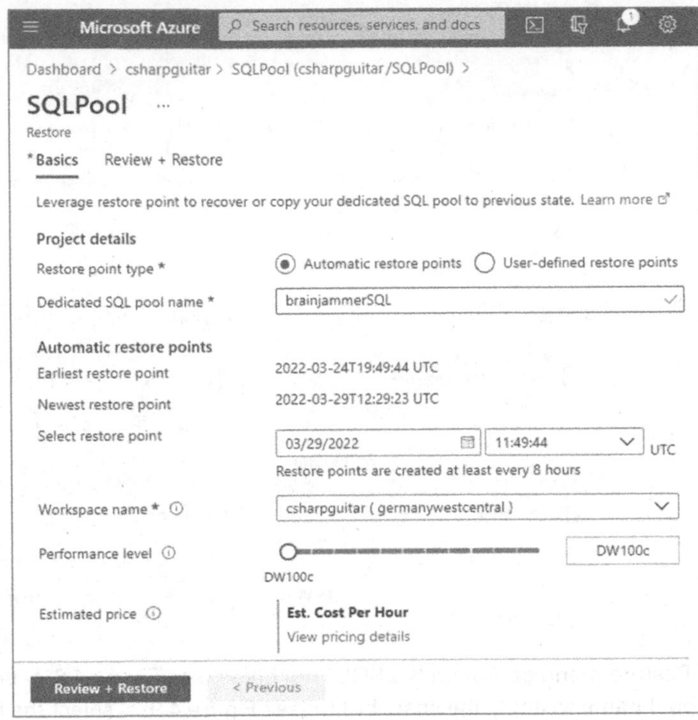

The first option was to select either the Automatic Restore Points or User-defined Restore Points radio button. Notice that the Newest Restore Point datetime in Figure 4.9 is the same as the one shown via the SQL query just provided and shown in Figure 4.7. So, you know there is a link between what you see when running the SQL query and the snapshot to be applied if this option is selected. It is also possible to select a previous snapshot and restore it from the portal blade shown in Figure 4.9. In addition to applying the newest snapshot (the default) or an older one, had you created a user-defined snapshot, it would show in a drop-down list box when the User-defined Restore Points radio button is selected. To create a user-defined restore point, simply choose the + New Restore Point menu item, shown in Figure 4.8, enter a name, and then click Apply. One last point is that the snapshot must be applied to a new dedicated SQL pool; it cannot be applied to the one it was taken from. This is a platform restriction and not something you can change.

There is also a similar capability available with ADLS where your data files are stored. By default, a feature called Enable Soft Delete for Blobs is enabled. It is configurable from the Data Protection blade for the Azure storage account, as shown in Figure 4.10.

FIGURE 4.10 Data redundancy restore ADLS

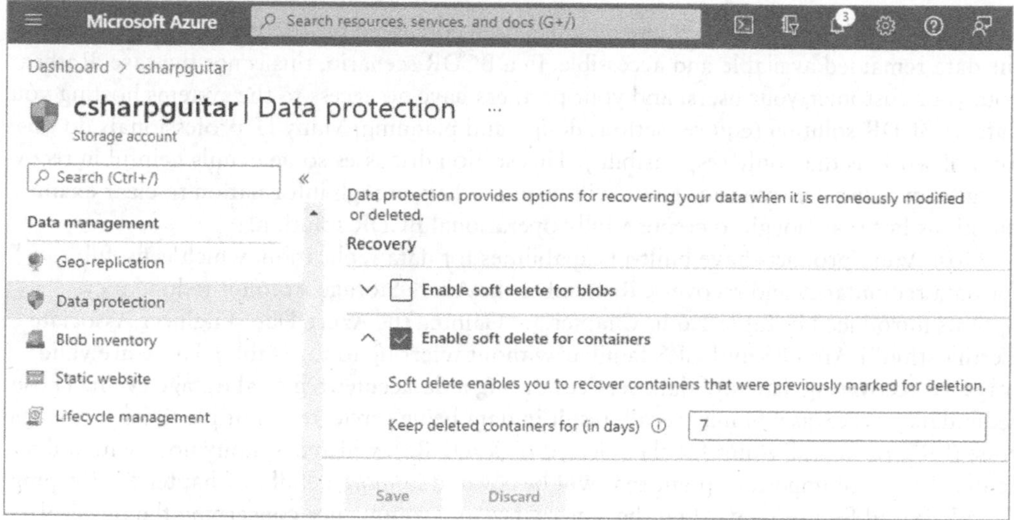

At the time of writing, it is not possible to recover a single file, only an entire container. When a container is deleted, it is considered a soft delete. That means it can be recovered up to the number of days configured, which is 7 by default. After that time expires, the container and its contents are permanently removed and cannot be recovered. To recover a container that has been deleted, toggle the Show Deleted Containers switch, as shown in Figure 4.11.

FIGURE 4.11 Data redundancy restore ADLS container

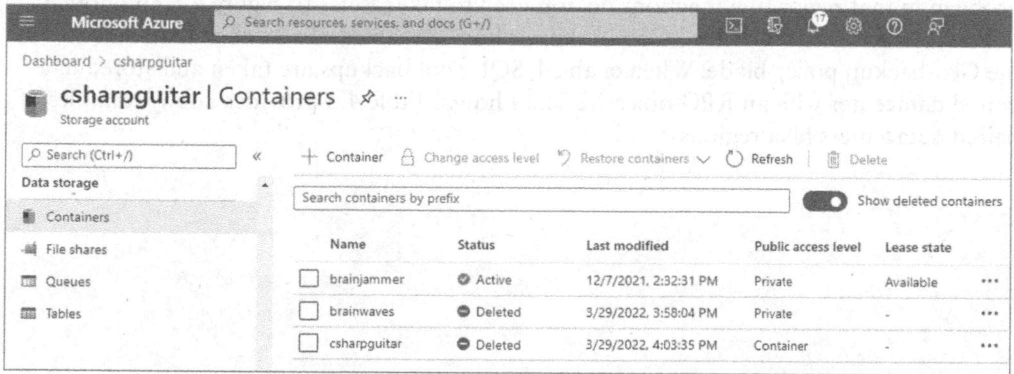

To recover a container, click it and, in the next blade, click Undelete. The container and all the files are then recovered and ready for use. There is ongoing work to make this work on a file basis. Until then, you may consider implementing a *business continuity and disaster recovery (BCDR)* solution.

Business Continuity and Disaster Recovery

In the scenario just discussed, where data has been corrupted or deleted, the system hosting the data remained available and accessible. In a BCDR scenario, this is not the case. Rather, you, your customer, your users, and your partners have no access to the systems hosting your data. A BCDR solution requires serious design and planning. Many IT professionals do this kind of work as their only responsibility. This section discusses some details helpful in recovering from a disaster scenario. There will be more than enough information to clear exam questions but not enough to create a fully operational BCDR solution.

Most Azure products have built-in capabilities for data replication, which is useful for data redundancy and recovery. Remember the Azure Storage Account redundancy options introduced in Table 1.6 in Chapter 1, "Gaining the Azure Data Engineer Associate Certification"? Are LRS and ZRS familiar without referring to that table? Those are valid ways for recovering data and data services during a datacenter/regional outage event. Those redundancy types, as you may recall, result in data being replicated multiple times in a single zone (LRS) or into all zones for the selected region (ZRS), which is synonymous with a datacenter. This is an important point that will be covered in more detail in Chapter 8, "Keeping Data Safe and Secure," regarding the governance and compliance concerning the physical location of your data. Consider the other storage redundancy types, such as GRS, GZRS, and their read-only equivalents. In those scenarios data is replicated outside of the primary region, to what is called a paired region, which is usually on the same continent but not always the same country. So, if your data has restrictions on where it can be stored, this is an important consideration.

Azure Synapse Analytics and ADLS

When you provision an Azure Synapse Analytics workspace, you choose a region to place it into. The associated ADLS storage container, although recommended to be in the same region, does not have to be, but in most cases it is. The point is, when there is an access problem in that region, what actions do you need to take? Refer to Figure 4.8 and notice, toward the bottom, a tile called Geo-backup, which is enabled. If you click that, it routes to the Geo-backup policy blade. When enabled, SQL pool backups are taken and stored in a paired datacenter with an RPO objective of 24 hours. Table 4.2 provides a few examples of paired datacenters (aka regions).

TABLE 4.2 Cross-region replication pairings, paired datacenters

Geography	Region A	Region B
Asia-Pacific	East Asia (Hong Kong)	Southeast Asia (Singapore)
Australia	Australia East	Australia Southeast
Canada	Canada Central	Canada East
China	China North	China East
Europe	North Europe (Ireland)	West Europe (Netherlands)
India	Central India	South India
North America	East US	West US
South Africa	South Africa North	South Africa West
UK	UK West	UK South
United Arab Emirates	UAE North	UAE Central

If you are placing your Azure Synapse Analytics workspace in West Europe and perform a backup, as you learned in Exercise 4.2, it is also stored in North Europe. The Geo-backup policy blade enables you to disable this feature. Disabling it results in backups being stored only within the single region chosen during provisioning. This makes your data vulnerable in a BCDR scenario, since you then have no means for recovery yourself. Therefore, it is not recommended to disable it, unless your data privacy restrictions require it. The recovery process when you have backups available in another region is to have available or provision a second Azure Synapse Analytics workspace in the paired region and recover in that secondary region. The recovery is performed by provisioning a new dedicated SQL pool in the new workspace and using the most recent backup to populate it. Refer to Figure 3.28 and look at the Use Existing Data option on the Additional settings tab. There is an option to select a backup. When selected, and after a successful provision, the data will be available on that dedicated SQL pool in that new region.

There is a tight dependency between Azure Synapse Analytics and ADLS, especially when you are working with files. Recall Exercise 3.1, where you provisioned an Azure storage account and created an ADLS container. The chosen replication option was LRS, which means the platform is not making copies to another region or zone. As shown in Figure 4.12, it is possible to change this from LRS to either GRS or RA-GRS.

FIGURE 4.12 Data redundancy ADLS replication options

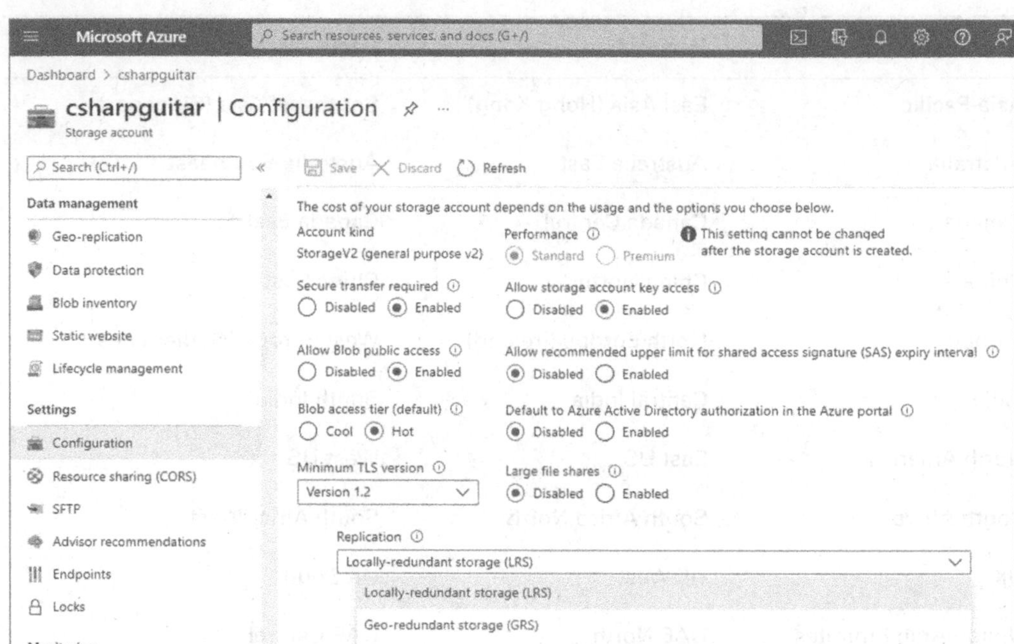

You cannot make this change when the region is having any kind of outage. This replication needs some time to complete its tasks and must be configured prior to its need, which is the definition of being redundant. LRS is recommended for testing purposes only; for production use, choose the one that conforms to your data residency requirements. But it is important to have at least one additional copy.

When you begin to provision your resources for running your data analytics on Azure, keep data redundancy in mind. Consider two Azure Synapse Analytics. The first model isolates data to different Azure storage accounts and ADLS containers per data landing zone (DLZ) stage (see Table 3.4). Figure 4.13 illustrates what this might look like. The Azure Synapse Analytics workspace on the far right illustrates the fact that multiple workspaces can point to the same ADLS container.

Each Azure storage account and its corresponding ADLS container can be in different regions too. These ADLS containers that contains your data could act as backups for each other by using tools like AzCopy or Azure Data Explorer to preemptively copy or move data manually. When one of the regions is having some problems, provision a new workspace in the region where the backup exists and point the workspace to the backed up data in that ADLS container.

FIGURE 4.13 Data redundancy backups Azure Synapse Analytics regional redundancy per DLZ stage model

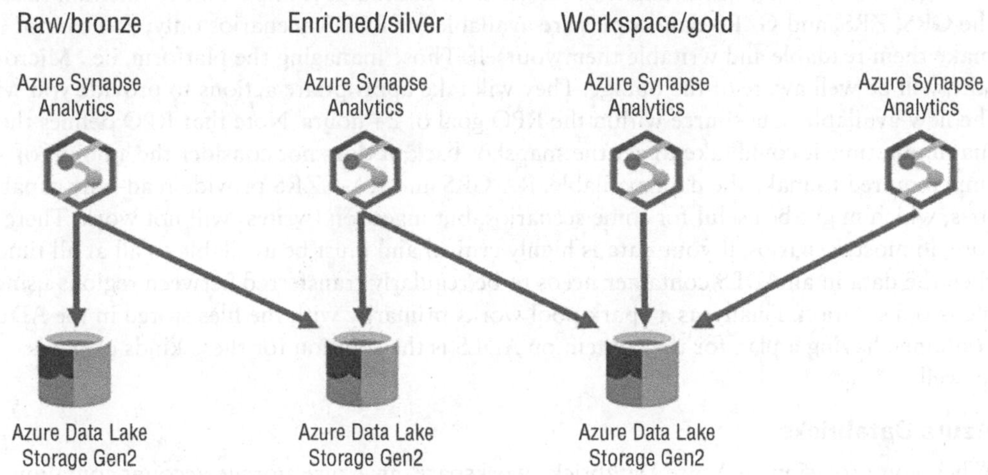

In the second model you store all DLZ stages in a single Azure storage account with an ADLS container per DLZ stage and point all workspaces to the appropriate one, as shown in Figure 4.14.

FIGURE 4.14 Data redundancy Azure Synapse Analytics single redundancy model containing all DLZs

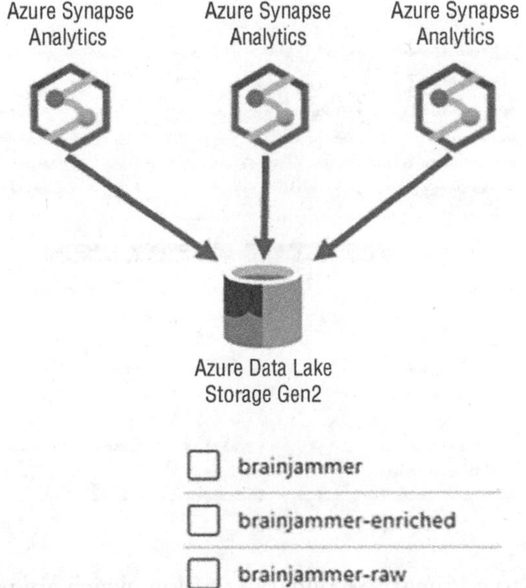

This model, if configured with something other than LRS replication, will result in the data being copied into another region or zone. In this BCDR scenario, recognize that the RPO goal is 24 hours, which might be longer than desired. It is important to mention that the GRS, ZRS, and GZRS data copies are available for BCDR scenarios only; you cannot make them readable and writable them yourself. Those managing the platform, i.e., Microsoft, will be well aware of the outage. They will take appropriate actions to provide you with the new available data source within the RPO goal of 24 hours. Note that RPO defines the maximum time it could take to get the snapshot back; it does not consider the amount of time required to make the data available. RA-GRS and RA-GZRS provide read-only capabilities, which might be useful for some scenarios, but ingestion (writes) will not work. Therefore, in most scenarios, if your data is highly critical and must be available to all at all times, then the data in an ADLS container needs to be regularly transferred between regions using a custom solution. Finally, as a Spark pool works primarily with the files stored in the ADLS container, having a plan for the content on ADLS is the solution for these kinds of pools as well.

Azure Databricks

When you provision an Azure Databricks workspace, an Azure storage account containing an Azure blob container used for storing your data is also provisioned. Figure 4.15 shows the details of the Azure storage account and the blob container service.

FIGURE 4.15 Data redundancy storage account for Azure Databricks

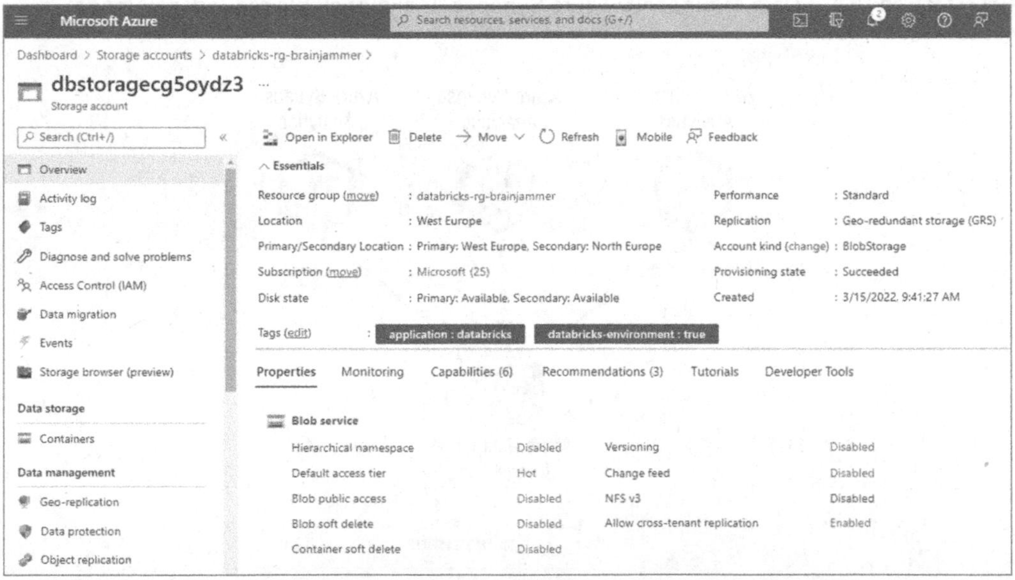

Notice the reference to a Primary/Secondary Location, which are paired regions (see Table 4.2). Additionally, notice the Disk State and the Replication setting of Geo-redundant

Storage (GRS). If, for example, there is an outage in West Europe, the people working on the issue will make the data on the GRS replicated drive available for access. Then, you must provision a new Azure Databricks workspace in North Europe (the paired region), using the replicated Azure storage account and Azure blob container.

Implement Distributions

Table distributions are an important concept. The different table distribution types are round-robin, hash, and replicated. Perform Exercise 4.4 to implement each of these table distribution types.

EXERCISE 4.4

Implement Distributions

1. Log in to the Azure portal at `https://portal.azure.com` ➤ navigate to the Azure Synapse Analytics workspace you created in Exercise 3.3 ➤ on the Overview blade, click the Open link in the Open Synapse Studio tile ➤ select the Data hub ➤ expand the SQL database menu ➤ expand the dedicated SQL pool you created for Exercise 3.7 ➤ hover over the Tables folder ➤ click the ellipse (`...`) ➤ click New SQL Script ➤ click New table ➤ and then execute the SQL found on GitHub at `https://github.com/benperk/ADE`, in the `Chapter04/Ch04Ex03` directory; the file is named `distributionSQL.txt`.
2. Execute the SQL syntax located in the `Chapter04/Ch04Ex03` directory on GitHub at `https://github.com/benperk/ADE`, in the filed named `checkDistribution.txt` ➤ view the tables and their associated distribution type. An example is illustrated in Figure 4.16.

FIGURE 4.16 Implementing table distributions

Results Messages

View Table Chart ↦ Export results

Search

schemaName	tableName	object_id	distribution_policy	distribution_policy_desc
brainwaves	DimMODE	782625831	3	REPLICATE
brainwaves	DimSCENARIO	798625888	3	REPLICATE
brainwaves	DimELECTRODE	814625945	3	REPLICATE
brainwaves	DimFREQUENCY	830626002	3	REPLICATE
brainwaves	TmpREADING	862626116	4	ROUND_ROBIN
brainwaves	FactREADING	878626173	2	HASH

00:00:00 Query executed successfully.

For more information about distribution types, refer to the section "Design a Distribution Strategy" in Chapter 3. See also the section "Implement Different Table Geometries with Azure Synapse Analytics Pools" earlier in this chapter.

Implement Data Archiving

Archiving data saves costs, improves performance, and may be necessary due to data privacy compliance. Cost savings are realized because you are charged by the amount of storage space required by your data. Removing the unnecessary data or changing the storage access tier from Hot to Archive for long-term retention reduces cost. Performance is improved because the less data your queries are required to parse, the faster the result set is returned. Consider that a specific type of data in your data lake is no longer valid after a given age. If the date of validity is, for example, after 2022-03-31, then selecting that data and using it in your data analytics solution could have a negative impact on your conclusions. Instead of expecting all developers and consumers of the data to know to exclude this from their queries, you should consider archiving or purging this data from your data lake completely. From a data compliance perspective, not only is the location where the data is saved important, but so is the duration in which it is stored. Based on the data compliance requirements of the policy you are mandating, consider whether you are allowed to store the data over a year, month, day, or even at all. A common lifetime data retention amount is 7 years.

Archiving Data on Azure Synapse Analytics

A common and efficient technique for archiving data when it comes to a dedicated SQL pool running in your Azure Synapse Analytics workspace is by using a datetime stamp. A typical scenario is one where you do not want to remove the data completely but instead remove it from the primary locations where the retrieval and analysis are happening. You want to avoid your consumers and users executing queries that select all the data from tables, when much of the old data is no longer relevant. The performance of such queries would be considered latent. A method for archiving the data is to create another table that holds older data. What is considered old depends on your data and your requirements. The following snippet retrieves brain wave readings from the `READING` table that are over 5 years old and copies the rows into a table named `READING_HISTORY`, which resides on a schema named `archive`:

```
SELECT * INTO [archive].[READING_HISTORY]
FROM READING WHERE DATEDIFF(YEAR, READING_DATETIME, GetDate()) > 5
```

Next, the following SQL statement removes the same data from the `READING` table:

```
DELETE FROM READING WHERE DATEDIFF(YEAR, READING_DATETIME, GetDate()) > 5
```

Deleing the rows that are older than 5 years reduces the table's size and would increase the performance of a query that retrieves all records from the `READING` table. If a user needs older brain waves, they can be retrieved from the READING_HISTORY table. I also recommend that you create a backup or snapshot prior to deleting a large amount of data. This can be achieved using the Restore feature for a given dedicated SQL pool and selecting the User-defined Restore Points option. Finally, not all tables will have a datetime stamp. If this is the case, consider adding one as part of the pipeline transformation processing.

Archiving Files on ADLS

From an ADLS perspective there are a few options for data archiving, such as those described in Table 4.3. These actions are components of the built-in lifecycle management policy feature of your Azure storage account.

TABLE 4.3 ADLS archiving actions

Action	Action name	Blob type	Snapshot
Move to Cool tier	tierToCool	blockBlob	Yes
Move to Archive tier	tierToArchive	blockBlob	Yes
Delete	Delete	block/appendBlob	Yes
Move to Hot from Cool	enableAutoTierToHotFromCool	blockBlob	No

The most expensive access tier for a blob is Hot. Therefore, if the data in a given blob, which in this context is synonymous with a data file, is not accessed, then in order to save costs, you can move it to a less expensive tier. Complete Exercise 4.5, where you will implement data archiving for ADLS.

EXERCISE 4.5

Implement Data Archiving

1. Log in to the Azure portal at `https://portal.azure.com` ➢ navigate to the Azure Data Lake storage container you created in Exercise 3.1 ➢ and then navigate to a directory within the container that contains some files. Notice the current access tier and blob type, similar to Figure 4.17.

EXERCISE 4.5 *(continued)*

FIGURE 4.17 Implement data archiving access tier

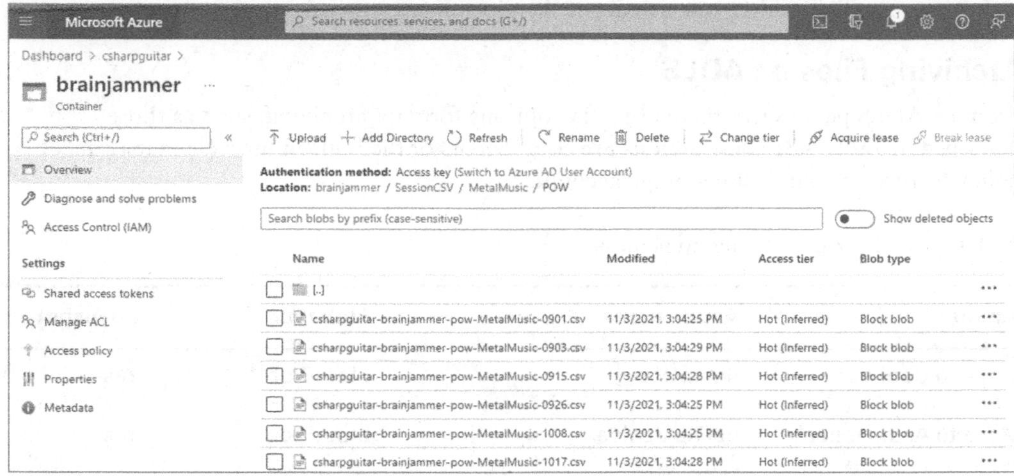

2. Navigate back to the Container blade ➢ select the Lifecycle Management link in the navigation menu at the storage account level ➢ place a check in the Enable Access Tracking check box ➢ click the + Add a Rule link ➢ enter a rule name (I used **moveToCold**) ➢ click Next ➢ select the Last Accessed radio button ➢ enter a value into the More Than (Days Ago) text box (I used **180**) ➢ select Move to Cool Storage and Move Back If Accessed from the Then drop-down text box ➢ review the other options ➢ and then click Add.
3. Select the + Add rule link ➢ enter a rule name (I used **moveToArchive**) ➢ click Next ➢ enter a value into the More Than (Days Ago) text box (I used **365**) ➢ select Move to Archive Storage from the Then drop-down text box ➢ and then click Add.
4. View the created Lifecycle management rules, and then select the Code View tab. Notice that the rules are stored in the JSON file format. The file is available in the `Chapter04/Ch04Ex04` directory on GitHub at `https://github.com/benperk/ADE`.

The `moveToCold` lifecycle management policy moves any file that has not been accessed for more than 180 days to the Cold access tier. If the file is accessed after being moved to the Cold access tier, it will be moved back to Hot; this is what `enableAutoTierToHotFromCool` refers to in Table 4.3. If the file has not been modified in 365 days, then the file is moved to the Archive access tier. Finally, as shown in Figure 4.18, if the file has not been accessed in 730 days, it is deleted (and has been disabled in this example).

FIGURE 4.18 Implement data archiving lifecycle management

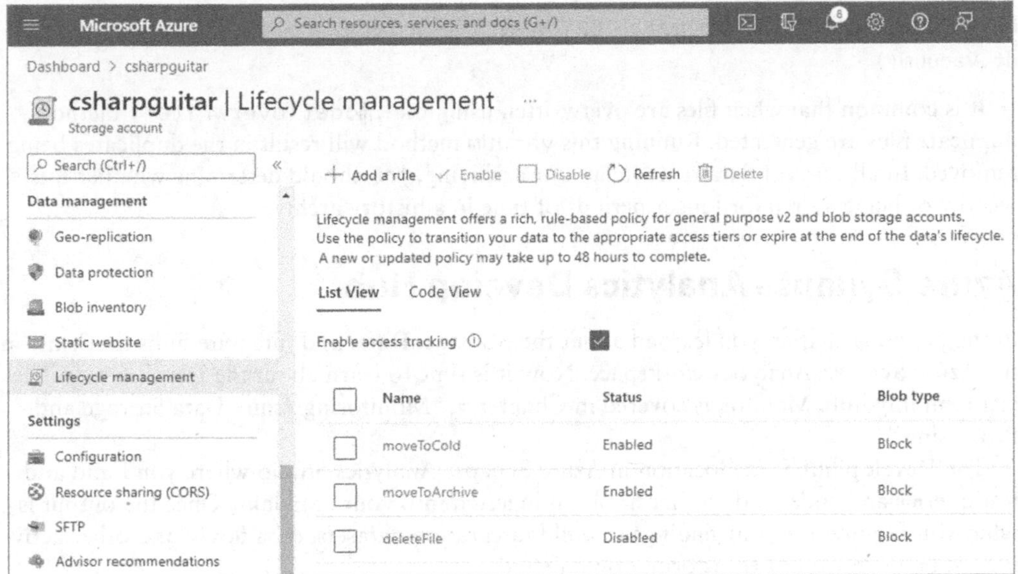

The rules created in Exercise 4.5 would also apply to the directories that adhere to a common directory naming convention (`{yyyy}/{mm}/{dd}/{hh}`), that is, so long as the directory and files are stored in the Azure storage account where the lifecycle management policy is applied.

Azure Databricks

Your Azure Databricks workspace includes an associated Azure storage account and blob container. Two lifecycle management policies that delete temporary and log files are created by default. You can view the rule details via the Code View tab on the Lifecycle Management blade in the Azure portal. Temporary files are removed after 7 days of no modification, and log files after 30.

Azure Databricks and Azure Delta Lake provide some helpful features for data archiving. The aforementioned approach about removing data based on a datetime stamp is valid in this context as well. For example, the following SQL syntax will remove brain wave readings from a table named `BRAINWAVES` that are over 1,825 days (5 years) old. You could also consider creating history tables, as described earlier.

```
%sql
DELETE FROM BRAINWAVES WHERE DATEDIFF(current_date(), READING_DATETIME) > 1825
```

Another approach is to use a Delta Lake method called `vacuum`. This method, by default, removes data files that are no longer referenced by any data table and that are greater than 7 days old. Use the following code snippet to remove unnecessary files:

```
%python
from delta.tables import *
dt = DeltaTable.forName(spark, 'BRAINWAVES')
dt.vacuum()
```

It is common that when files are overwritten using the `.mode('overwrite')` method, duplicate files are generated. Running this `vacuum` method will result in the duplicates being removed. In all cases of data removal and/or archiving, you should determine whether it is worthy of being stored for longer periods of time in a history archive.

Azure Synapse Analytics Develop Hub

In the previous chapter you learned about the Manage, Data, and Integrate hubs that exist in the Azure Synapse Analytics workspace. Now it is time to learn about the Develop hub. The last remining hub, Monitor, is covered in Chapter 9, "Monitoring Azure Data Storage and Processing."

The Develop hub is the location in Azure Synapse Analytics Studio where you build and test queries and code on data that has been ingested into your data lake. Once the output is what you require, use your findings to build integration datasets, data flows, and other activities to be included in a transformation pipeline.

SQL Scripts

When your data analytics needs to run T-SQL, like queries using either a serverless or dedicated SQL pool, start with SQL Scripts. The Develop Hub is also the location where you can access tables and execute stored procedures and UDFs residing on your dedicated SQL pool. Complete Exercise 4.6, where you will create and execute some syntax using the SQL scripts feature.

EXERCISE 4.6

Azure Synapse Analytics Data Hub SQL Script

1. Either log in to the Azure portal at `https://portal.azure.com` and navigate to the Azure Data Lake storage container you created in Exercise 3.1 or use Microsoft Azure Storage Explorer and navigate to the same ADLS container ➢ and then create the following directory structure:

   ```
   EMEA/brainjammer/in/2022/04/01/18
   ```

2. Download the file `brainjammer_brainwaves_20220401.zip` from `Chapter04/Ch04Ex05` directory on GitHub ➢ extract the files from the compressed file ➢ and then upload them to the directory you just created. Your folder should resemble Figure 4.19.

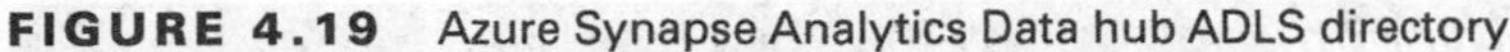

FIGURE 4.19 Azure Synapse Analytics Data hub ADLS directory

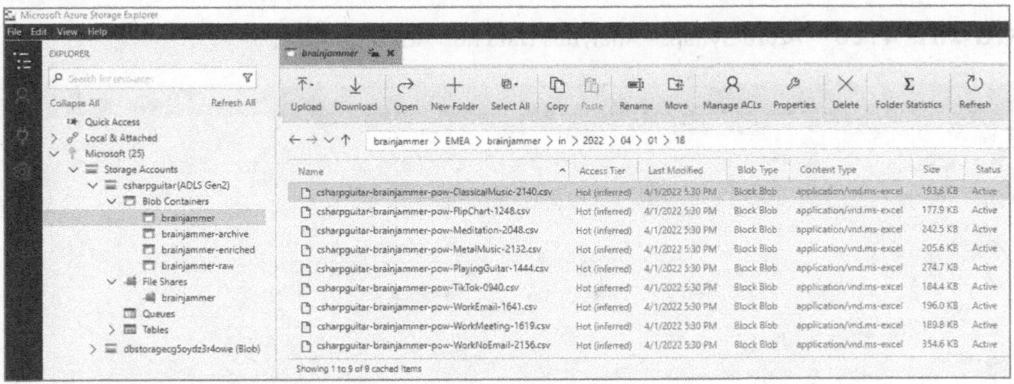

3. Navigate to the Azure Synapse Analytics workspace you created in Exercise 3.3 ➢ on the Overview blade, click the Open link in the Open Synapse Studio tile ➢ select the Develop hub ➢ click the + to the right of the Develop text ➢ and then click SQL Script and enter the following script:

```
SELECT
  TOP 100 *
FROM
  OPENROWSET(
    BULK (
      'https://*.dfs.core.windows.net/./EMEA/brainjammer/in/2022/04/01/
18/*.csv'
    ),
    FORMAT = 'CSV',
    PARSER_VERSION = '2.0',
    HEADER_ROW = TRUE
  ) AS [result]
```

4. Make sure to update the HTTPS address to point to your ADLS container, and then run the query. The output resembles Figure 4.20. Consider renaming the SQL script ➢ hover over the value in the Develop SQL Scripts group ➢ click the ellipse (. . .) ➢ select Rename ➢ provide a useful name (for example, **Ch04Ex05**) ➢ and then click the Commit button, which will place the file on the GitHub you configured in Exercise 3.6.

EXERCISE 4.6 *(continued)*

FIGURE 4.20 Azure Synapse Analytics Data hub ADLS directory

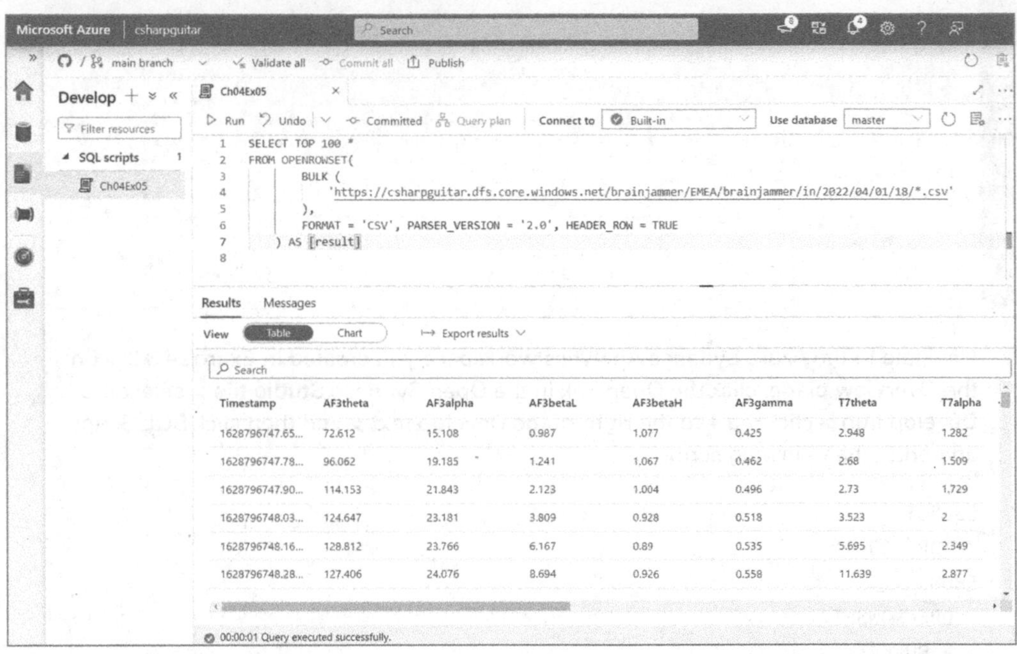

Notice in Figure 4.20 that the SQL pool running this query is the serverless one, i.e., built-in. Remember that in the context of a serverless SQL pool, you can create only external tables. At the time of this writing, external table support is in preview regarding dedicated SQL pools, which can only be used with Parquet files. The benefit external tables have over managed tables is that the data remains in your data lake. An external table is a logical representation of that data, so when or if the external table is dropped, the data remains in the data lake. However, if you drop a managed table, then the data within it is also removed and lost.

KQL Script

When working with Data Explorer pools, this is the feature to choose. KQL scripts enable you to execute Kusto-like queries on your Azure Data Explorer clusters. At the time of this writing, Data Explorer pools are in preview. They were covered in the previous chapter and introduced in Chapter 1.

Notebook

Choose the Notebook menu item to execute PySpark (Python), Spark (Scala), .NET Spark (C#) or Spark SQL code. Complete Exercise 4.6 prior to Exercise 4.7, as the files used to convert to Parquet in Exercise 4.7 are the ones you uploaded in Exercise 4.6.

EXERCISE 4.7

Azure Synapse Analytics Develop Hub Notebook

1. Log in to the Azure portal at `https://portal.azure.com` ➢ navigate to the Azure Synapse Analytics workspace you created in Exercise 3.3 ➢ on the Overview blade, click the Open link in the Open Synapse Studio tile ➢ select the Develop hub ➢ click the + to the right of the Develop text ➢ and then click Notebook.
2. Select the Apache Spark pool you created in Exercise 3.4 from the Attach to drop-down text box ➢ and then enter the following syntax into the code cell, replacing `*@*` in the endpoint with your `containderName@accountName`:

```
%%pyspark
df = spark.read.option("header","true") \
  .csv('abfss://*@*.dfs.core.windows.net/EMEA/brainjammer/in/2022/04/01/18/*')
display(df.limit(10))
```

3. Run the code. The first time you run the code in a cell, it can take up to 3 minutes for the Spark pool to instantiate. Be patient. The result should resemble Figure 4.21.

FIGURE 4.21 Azure Synapse Analytics Develop hub load Notebook

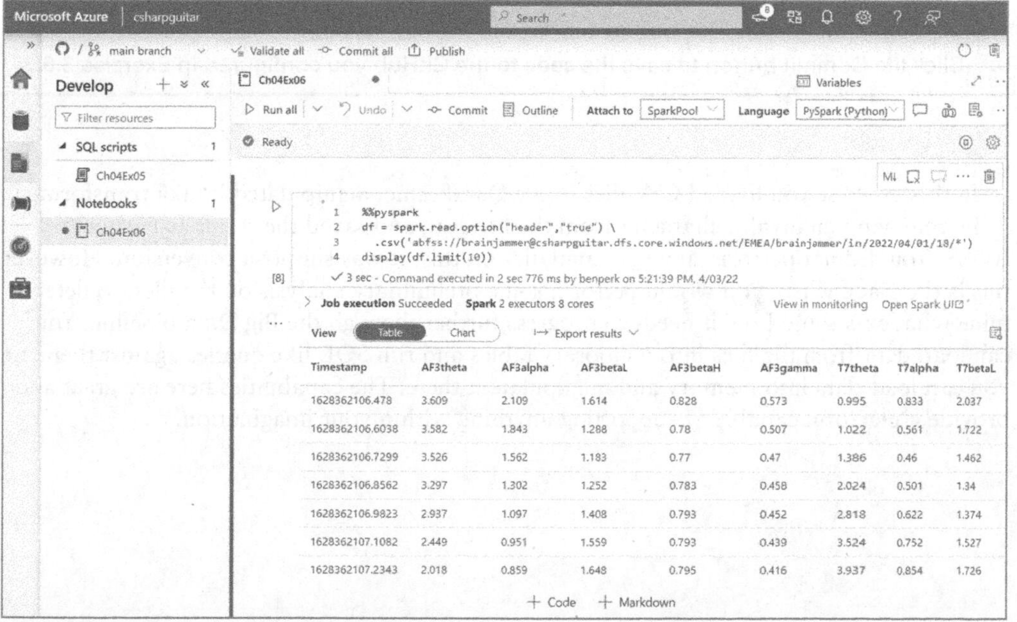

EXERCISE 4.7 *(continued)*

4. Use either Microsoft Azure Storage Explorer or the Azure Portal at `https://portal.azure.com` and navigate to the Azure Data Lake storage container you created in Exercise 3.1 ➢ navigate to the same ADLS container as you did in Exercise 4.6 ➢ and then create the following directory structure:

```
EMEA/brainjammer/out/2022/04/03/17
```

5. Access the file `saveBrainwavesAsParquet.txt` from GitHub at `https://github.com/benperk/ADE`, in the `Chapter04/Ch04Ex6` directory ➢ place the syntax into the cell ➢ and then run the code. Parquet files, similar to those shown in Figure 4.22, are created and stored.

FIGURE 4.22 Azure Synapse Analytics Develop hub write Notebook Parquet files

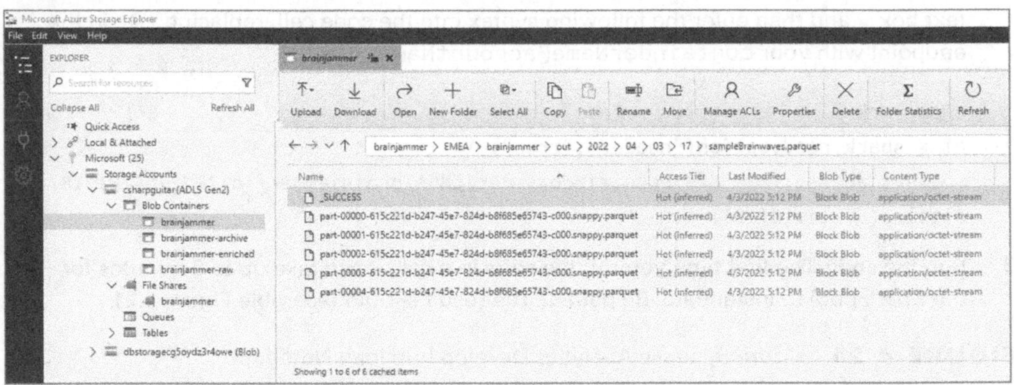

6. Click the Commit button to save the code to the GitHub you configured in Exercise 3.6.

In this exercise you loaded CSV files into a DataFrame, manipulated it (aka transformed it) by removing an invalid character from the headers, and saved the result as Parquet to ADLS. You did not perform any data analytics on this; it was simply a conversion. However, this is the place where you would perform some preliminary analysis on the files, to determine what exists and how it needs to progress further through the Big Data pipeline. You can load data from the files into temporary tables and run SQL-like queries against them, or you can load data into memory and manipulate it there. The capabilities here are great and provide a platform capable of supporting anything within your imagination.

Data Flow

You can think of a data flow as an activity that will become part of a pipeline. The capabilities available on the Data flow blade are similar to the Power Query capability found in Azure Data Factory (ADF), in that it is a place to load some data from your data lake, perform some work on it, and once you like the output, you can save it and include is as part of your overall Big Data solution. There are a lot of capabilities in the Data Flow context. Complete Exercise 4.8 to get some hands-on experience.

EXERCISE 4.8

Azure Synapse Analytics Develop Hub Data Flow

1. Log in to the Azure portal at `https://portal.azure.com` > navigate to the Azure Synapse Analytics workspace you created in Exercise 3.3 > on the Overview blade, click the Open link in the Open Synapse Studio tile > select the Develop hub item > click the + to the right of the Develop text > click Data Flow > and then slide the toggle button next to Data Flow Debug on the top bar, which starts the session. Be patient.
2. In the graph area click the Add Source tile in the graph area > in the configuration panel with the Source Settings tab in focus, provide an output stream name (I used **Brainwaves**) > select Integration Dataset for the Source type > click the + New button to the right of the Dataset drop-down list box > and then create a new integration dataset (ADLS and Parquet) that points to the `sampleBrainwaves.parquet` directory created in Exercise 4.7. (Choose only the directory, not the files.)

   ```
   EMEA/brainjammer/out/2022/04/03/17/sampleBrainwaves.parquet
   ```

3. Name the new integration dataset (I used **sampleBrainwavesParquet**) > select the From Connection/Store radio button > click OK > return to the data flow > click the Data Preview tab > and then view the data. Notice the `Timestamp` column is in Epoch format.
4. Select the + to the lower right of the Source tile > select Derived Column > enter an output stream name (I used **EpochConversion**) > the incoming stream should be prepopulated with the source created in step 2 (`Brainwaves`) > click the Open Expression Builder link > enter a column name (I used **ReadingTimestamp**) > enter the following into the Expression text box. The expression is available in `Chapter04/Ch04Ex07` directory on GitHub at `https://github.com/benperk/ADE`. Note that `1000l` begins with the number *1* and ends with a lowercase *L*.

   ```
   toTimestamp(toLong(toDecimal(Timestamp, 14, 4) * (1000l)))
   ```

5. Click the Save and Finish button > press the Data Preview tab (see Figure 4.23) > and then click the Commit button to save the data flow.

EXERCISE 4.8 *(continued)*

FIGURE 4.23 Azure Synapse Analytics data flow

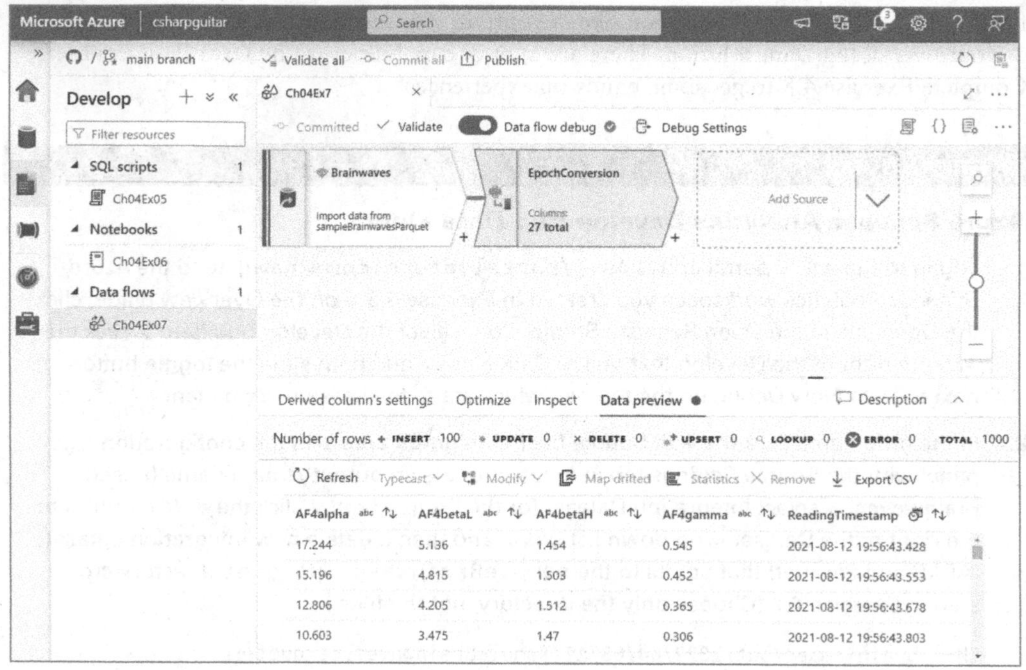

In Exercise 4.8 you used some knowledge you learned on how to create an integration dataset. You will be using these concepts and product features more frequently. You also only completed the first phase of this data flow; the final phase is to store the transformed data into a sink. This chapter focuses on the ingestion phase of the Big Data pipeline stages, so that action is saved for later. Before this data flow can be used in a pipeline, a sink (output) must be added to it. See if you can figure it out now, add a sink, configure it, and store it. Note Figure 4.24, which contains all the data flow transformation capabilities, as described in Table 4.4 and Table 4.5.

As you may have noticed, the first item added to the graph canvas is a source. The source is what is configured to retrieve data that will be transformed through the following transformation logic. The items in Figure 4.24 are called transformations. You can see the list of available transformations by clicking the + sign on an existing transformation. When you add a transformation to the data flow graph, an associated configuration panel provides an interface to configure its details.

FIGURE 4.24 Azure Synapse Analytics data flow transformations

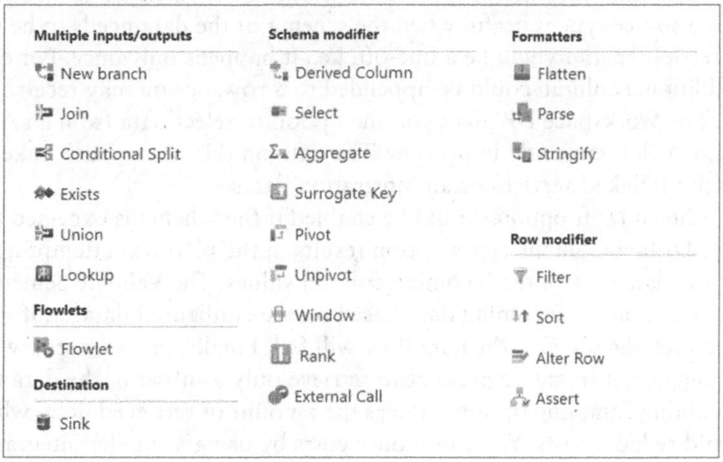

Multiple inputs/outputs
- New branch
- Join
- Conditional Split
- Exists
- Union
- Lookup

Flowlets
- Flowlet

Destination
- Sink

Schema modifier
- Derived Column
- Select
- Aggregate
- Surrogate Key
- Pivot
- Unpivot
- Window
- Rank
- External Call

Formatters
- Flatten
- Parse
- Stringify

Row modifier
- Filter
- Sort
- Alter Row
- Assert

Source

When you select the Source item, six tabs are rendered in the configuration panel: Source Settings, Source Options, Projection, Optimize, Inspect, and Data Preview. Figure 4.25 shows the Source Settings configuration tab.

FIGURE 4.25 Azure Synapse Analytics Develop hub, data flow Source Settings tab

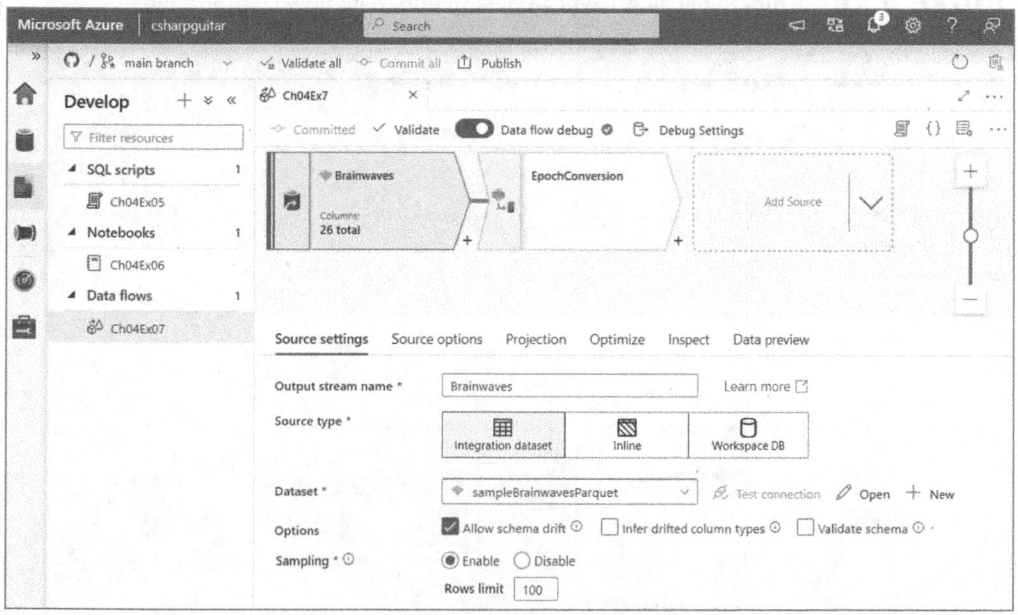

You can choose three types of sources. The first is an integration dataset, which is a preconfigured object that identifies a specific set of data to be retrieved from a designated source. An inline source type is useful when the schema of the data needs to be flexible, or the data flow retrieval activity will be a one-off, i.e., it happens only once. For example, on occasion an additional column could be appended to a row, or you may receive a one-time dump of data. The Workspace DB gives you the option to select data from an Azure Data Lake database, which is currently in preview. The data on this Azure Data Lake database can be accessed without linked services or an integration dataset.

The Allow Schema Drift option should be enabled if the schema is expected to change often. The Infer Drifted Column Types option results in the platform attempting to identify and apply the data type of the incoming column values. The Validate Schema option imposes a restriction on the incoming data based on the configured dataset. If the incoming data does not match the schema, the data flow will fail. Finally, in a scenario where you are testing and debugging, it might be prudent to retrieve only a subset of the data from the source. The Enabling Sampling option reduces the amount of retrieved data, which improves performance and reduces costs. You can reduce costs by using a smaller integration runtime machine to complete the testing. You might also be able to debug more quickly due to there being less data to analyze.

The next tab of interest is Optimize, as shown in Figure 4.26. This first setting you might notice is Partition Type. You see where you can visually configure the distribution method in the Azure Synapse Analytics workspace. Since you know the data being loaded, because you configured and provisioned the integration dataset, you can make the judgment as to which distribution is best for this data flow.

FIGURE 4.26 Azure Synapse Analytics Develop hub, data flow Optimize tab

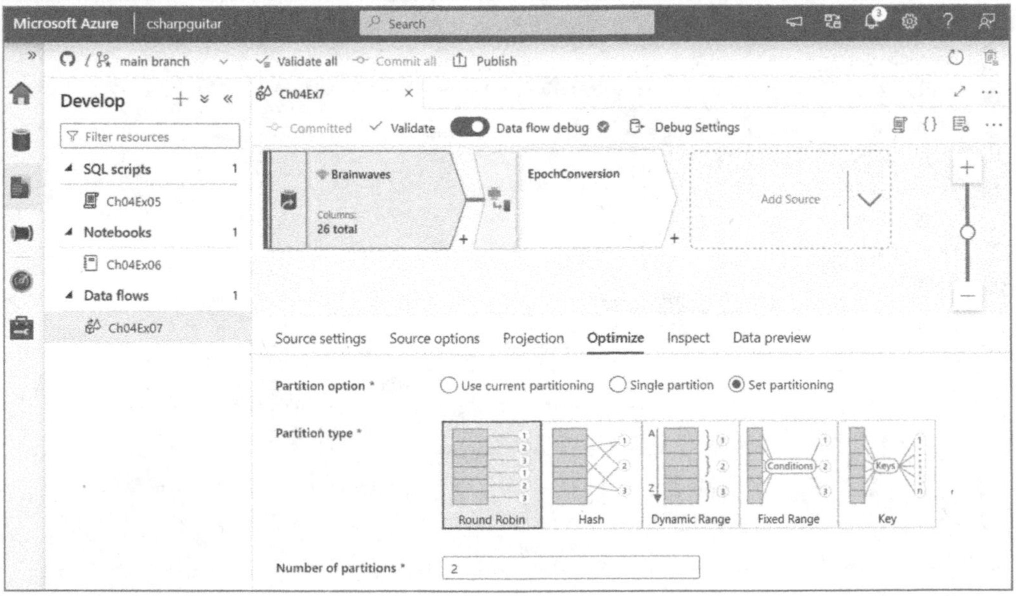

The Data Preview tab renders the data from the data source configured on the Source Settings tab. In addition to this Source section, there are numerous options to discuss, for example, the Schema Modifier.

Schema Modifier

Consider adding a few additional transformations and viewing the configuration details. Add an Aggregate schema modifier or a Window schema modifier and see how they can be used to transform the sample data. An Aggregate schema modifier, as you know, enables you to use SQL aggregations like `SUM`, `AVG`, `MIN`, `MAX`, `LAST`, or `FIRST`. A Window Schema modifier simulates the `OVER` SQL statement. This is commonly used with Window frames for making a calculation from a subset of data to produce a result relevant to a single row. For a summary of all schema modifier transformations, see Table 4.4.

TABLE 4.4 Data flow schema modifiers

Modifier	Description
Aggregate	Enables the usage of `SUM`, `MIN`, `MAX`, `COUNT`, etc.
Derived Column	Creates new columns using the data flow expression language.
External Call	Calls external endpoints, one row at a time.
Pivot	An expansion of data from multiple rows and their single column to multiple columns. Groups the rows by a defined value using aggregation.
Rank	Orders rows based on a sort condition.
Select	Streams names and alias columns; reorders or drops columns.
Surrogate Key	Adds a non-business incrementing arbitrary key value.
Unpivot	Transforms a row with multiple columns to multiple rows with a single column.
Window	Uses window-based aggregation of columns with a data stream.

In Exercise 4.8 you used a Derived Column schema identifier, as shown in Figure 4.27.

FIGURE 4.27 Azure Synapse Analytics Develop hub, data flow Derived Column schema modifier

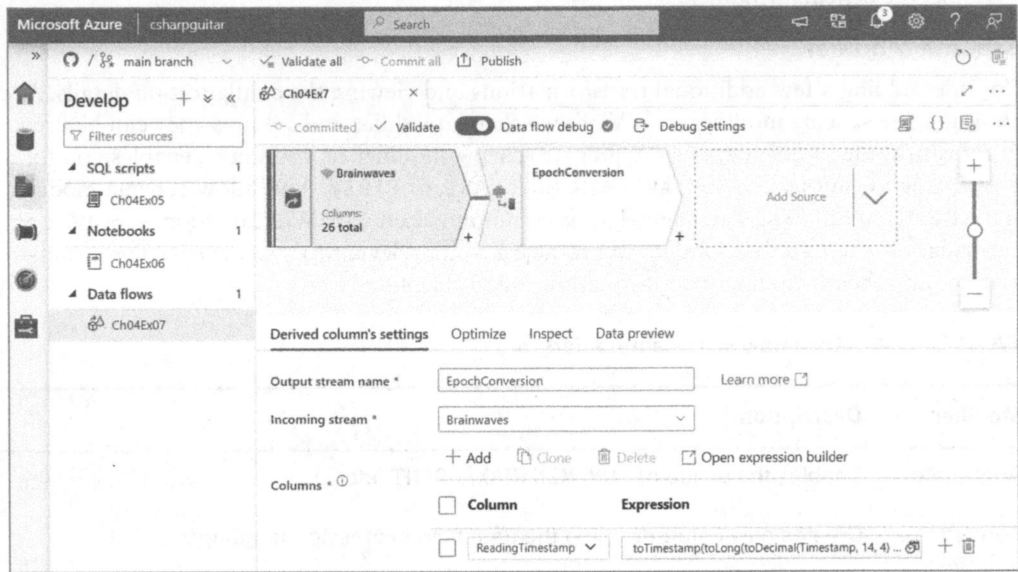

The Incoming Stream is the name of the previous source transformation. Notice the Open Expression Builder link. That link is used for creating, testing, and debugging the code snippet placed into the Expression text box. Click the Open Expression Builder link to view the capabilities on that blade (see Figure 4.28).

The Optimize tab provides the same capabilities as shown previously in Figure 4.26. In this case, however, the kind of data distribution is applied to the result of the additional column constructed by the execution of the code snippet in the Expression text box.

Flowlets

A *flowlet* is a container that holds reusable activities. Consider the activity you created in Exercise 4.8, which retrieves brain wave data and converts the epoch date into a more human-readable format. You can now place those transformations into a flowlet. Then, if you ever need that same set of transformations, you can use the flowlet instead of duplicating the configuration and the code within the Derived Column. In many cases the code and transformations that take place will be much more complicated. Being able to group sets of transformation activities into a container and then reuse that container has benefits. If something in the pipeline changes and requires a modification, then you would need to modify it in only a single place, instead of everywhere. To create a new data flow flowlet containing the transformations, right-click the transformation in the location where you want the flowlet to stop, and then select Create a New Flowlet. This flowlet can now be used in other data flows.

FIGURE 4.28 Azure Synapse Analytics Develop hub, Visual Expression Builder

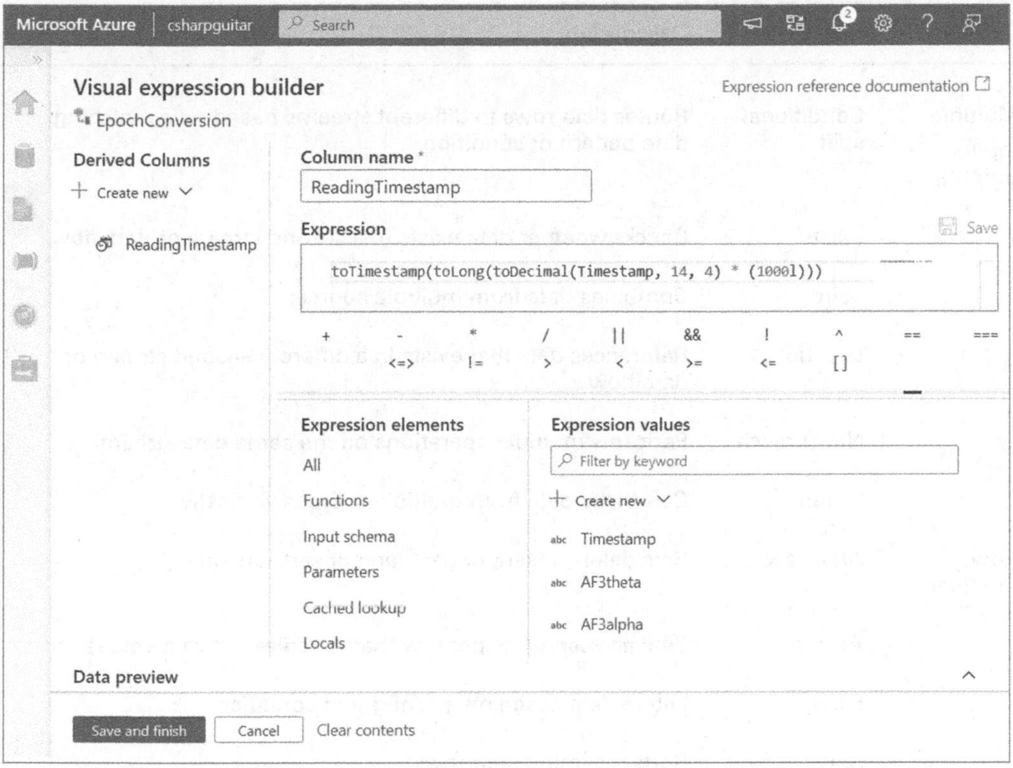

Destination

The sink is the location you intend to store the data once the transformation has been performed. Where and how you store the transformed data has much to do with the kind of data and the DLZ stage of the transformation. Should the data be stored back in an ADLS container or in an Azure SQL relational database? Perhaps the output is a JSON document that needs to be immediately available globally, making Azure Cosmos DB a valid option. Table 4.5 provides some additional information about data flow transformation features.

TABLE 4.5 Data flow transformation features

Category	Name	Description
Formatters	Flatten	Converts hierarchical files like JSON and unrolls them into individual rows
	Parse	Parses data from the incoming stream
	Stringify	Converts complex data types to a string

TABLE 4.5 Data flow transformation features *(continued)*

Category	Name	Description
Multiple inputs/ outputs	Conditional split	Routes data rows to different streams based on a matching data pattern or condition
	Exists	Checks whether data exists in a second stream or data flow
	Join	Combines data from multiple sources
	Lookup	References data that exists in a different second stream or data flow
	New branch	Performs multiple operations on the same data stream
	Union	Combines data from multiple sources vertically
Row modifier	Alter row	Sets delete, insert, update, and upsert row policy
	Assert	Sets an assert rule per row that specifies allowed values
	Filter	Filters data based on a configured condition
	Sort	Sorts incoming data rows

In summary, a data flow consists of a source, a sink, and one or more transformations, as described in Table 4.4 and Table 4.5. You can construct a flowlet from a subset of transformations within a data flow for reuse in other data flows. As you will soon learn, one or more data flows are considered activities that are added to a pipeline. The pipeline is responsible for initiating, executing, monitoring, and completing all the activities within it.

Apache Spark Job Definition

The Apache Spark job definition feature enables you to execute code snippets using PySpark (Python), Spark (Scala) or .NET Spark (C#, F#).

The first text box is requesting a main definition file. The type of file is based on the selected language. For example, PySpark is expecting a PY file; .NET Spark can be either a DLL or EXE file; and when using Scala, a JAR file is expected. The value placed into that text box represents the location of the code file, for example, stored on an ADLS container. It may look something like this:

```
abfss://*@*.dfs.core.windows.net/EMEA/brainjammer/archiveData.py
```

The next text box, Command Line Arguments, gives you the options to pass arguments to the code. The values in Figure 4.29 are `in 2022 04 01` and could be used to identify the path to be archived. The following code example uses these arguments and archives the data. The full `archiveData.py` program file can be found on GitHub at `https://github.com/benperk/ADE`, in the `Chapter04` directory.

```
sc._jsc.hadoopConfiguration() \
  .set('fs.defaultFS', 'abfss://*@*.dfs.core.windows.net/EMEA/brainjammer/')
endpoint = hadoop_config.get('fs.defaultFS')
path = sys.argv[1] + "/" + sys.argv[2] + "/" + sys.argv[3] + "/" + sys.argv[4]
if (fs.exists(sc._jvm.org.apache.hadoop.fs.Path(endpoint + path))):
  fs.delete(sc._jvm.org.apache.hadoop.fs.Path(endpoint + path), True)
```

FIGURE 4.29 Azure Synapse Analytics Develop hub, Apache Spark job definition

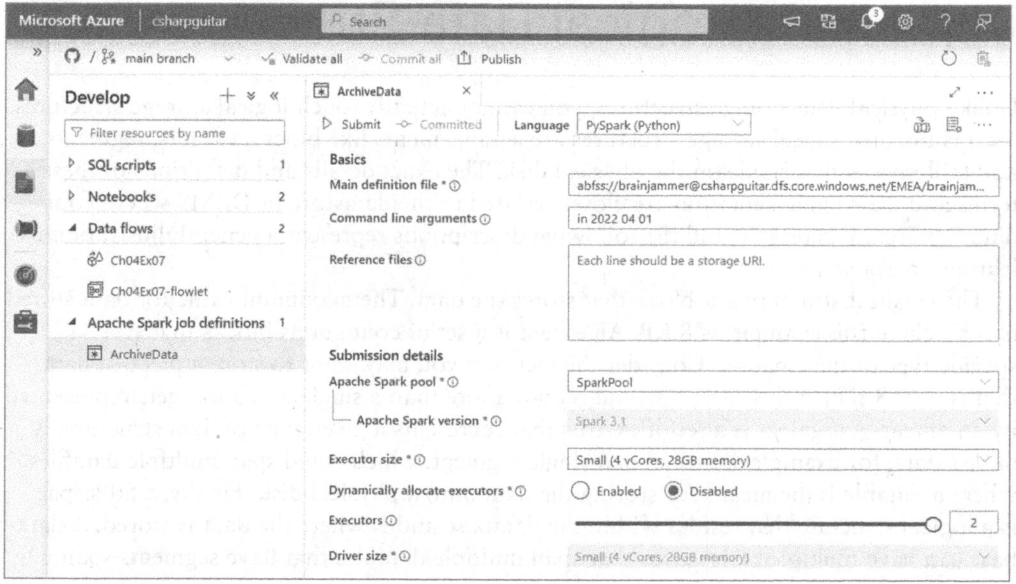

The command-line arguments are optional and can instead be passed to the job via a pipeline that is used to execute it. That means the path that contains files that are no longer needed can be different with each execution of the pipeline that archives/deletes the unnecessary data. It would also be good practice to send the ADLS endpoint as an argument as well. This was done for simplicity reasons; in general, it is not good practice to hard code any values within source code.

Browse Gallery

This feature was introduced in Chapter 3. It is the same content from the Develop hub as exists in the Data and Integrate hubs. Figure 3.55 illustrates how this looks, in case you want to see it and read its description again.

Import

SQL scripts, KQL scripts, notebooks, and Apache Spark job definitions all have the option to export the configuration. For example, when you hover over a notebook, click the ellipse (. . .), and select Export, you will see that you can export the configuration as a notebook (`.ipynb`), HTML (`.html`), Python (`.py`), or LaTeX (`.tex`) file. Then, you can use the Import feature to share the configuration or import it into another Azure Synapse Analytics workspace.

Implement Logical Data Structures

Unlike physical data storage structures, you cannot actually touch logical storage structures. That is because logical storage structures are arrangements like blocks, extents, segments, and tablespaces that reside on the physical disk. The exact details and definitions of these terms and their implementation are closely related to the datastore or DBMS where your data is stored. Figure 4.30 and the following descriptions represent a general illustration for learning purposes.

The smallest structure is a block that stores the data. The maximum value for data stored in a block, in this example, is 8 KB. An extent is a set of contiguous blocks that store a specific type of information. Consider the fact that you may want to store a piece of data that is over 8 KB; in this case, it would require more than a single block but gets represented by an extent. A segment is a set of extents that represents a given type of data structure. A table's data, for example, is stored in a single segment, which could span multiple datafiles, where a datafile is the means for storing the data onto a physical disk. Finally, a tablespace is a logical structure that resides within the database and is where the data is stored. A database can have multiple tablespaces that span multiple datafiles that have segments spanning across them.

FIGURE 4.30 Logical data structure

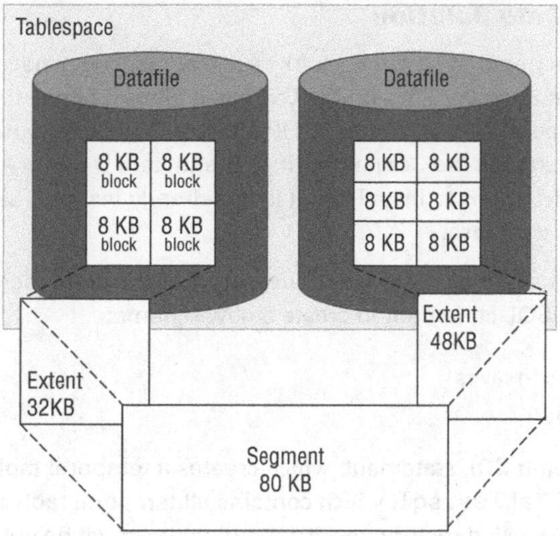

Generally, logical data structures do not include datasets. Instead, the purpose of a logical data structure is to improve the ease of locating data and to improve performance by having an efficient retrieval process. This book is a good example of the difference between physical and logical data storage structures. The content printed onto the pages of this book is physically stored there. The way the book is structured is logical. For example, Parts, Chapters, Sections, and Pages help you navigate and quickly find the information you are looking for. The logical components are contextual information that exist in the book, but they are not part of the provided learnings contained within the book itself. Also consider the index at the end of the book and how looking through it helps you quickly find exactly what you want. An index in the database sense performs the same function with very similar benefits.

Build a Temporal Data Solution

Chapter 3 discussed the design and details of a temporal table (refer to Figure 3.20). In summary, a temporal table is one that keeps a history of CRUD operations performed on the rows contained within it. Begin with Exercise 4.9, where you will build and implement a temporal data solution. As of this writing, temporal tables are not supported in Azure Synapse Analytics. Therefore, the exercise is performed on the Azure SQL database you provisioned in Exercise 2.1.

EXERCISE 4.9

Build a Temporal Data Solution

1. Log in to the Azure portal at `https://portal.azure.com` ➢ navigate to the Azure SQL you created in Exercise 2.1 ➢ on the Overview blade, choose the Set Server Firewall menu item ➢ confirm that your client IP address is allowed ➢ navigate back to the Overview blade ➢ choose the Connect with. . . menu item ➢ select Azure Data Studio and follow the instructions to install it, if it is not already installed ➢ and then connect to your Azure SQL database.

2. Right-click the connection ➢ select New Query from the pop-up menu ➢ and then execute the following SQL statement to create a new schema:

```
CREATE SCHEMA brainwaves
AUTHORIZATION dbo
```

3. Execute the following SQL statement, which creates a temporal table. A file named `createTemporalTables.sql`, which contains all temporal tables, is located in the `Chapter04/Ch04Ex08` directory on GitHub. All tables must be created; only one statement is provided for brevity.

```
CREATE TABLE [brainwaves].[DimMODE] (
  [MODE_ID]       INT        NOT NULL IDENTITY(1,1) PRIMARY KEY CLUSTERED,
  [MODE]              NVARCHAR (50)  NOT NULL,
  [SYSSTARTTIME]    DATETIME2 GENERATED ALWAYS AS ROW START NOT NULL,
  [SYSENDTIME]      DATETIME2 GENERATED ALWAYS AS ROW END NOT NULL,
  PERIOD FOR SYSTEM_TIME (SYSSTARTTIME, SYSENDTIME)
)
WITH (SYSTEM_VERSIONING = ON)
```

4. Populate the temporal tables using the `INSERT` commands in the file `populateTemporalTables.sql` in the `Chapter04/Ch04Ex08` directory on GitHub ➢ and then execute the following SQL queries to observe the inserted data. The next two sets of queries are in the file `selectTemporalData.sql`.

```
SELECT * FROM [brainwaves].[DimMODE]
SELECT * FROM [brainwaves].[DimSCENARIO]
SELECT * FROM [brainwaves].[DimELECTRODE]
SELECT * FROM [brainwaves].[DimFREQUENCY]
SELECT * FROM [brainwaves].[DimSESSION]
```

5. Execute the following SQL statements to view the contents of the history table. Note the unique numbers at the end of the history tables. Replace the `##########` with

your numbers, which you can find by expanding the temporal table, as shown in Figure 4.31. Since there have not been changes, the history tables are empty.

```
SELECT * FROM [brainwaves].[MSSQL_TemporalHistoryFor_#########] --DimMODE
SELECT * FROM [brainwaves].[MSSQL_TemporalHistoryFor_#########] --DimSCENARIO
SELECT * FROM [brainwaves].[MSSQL_TemporalHistoryFor_#########] --DimELECTRODE
SELECT * FROM [brainwaves].[MSSQL_TemporalHistoryFor_#########] --DimFREQUENCY
SELECT * FROM [brainwaves].[MSSQL_TemporalHistoryFor_#########] --DimSESSION
```

FIGURE 4.31 Finding the history table

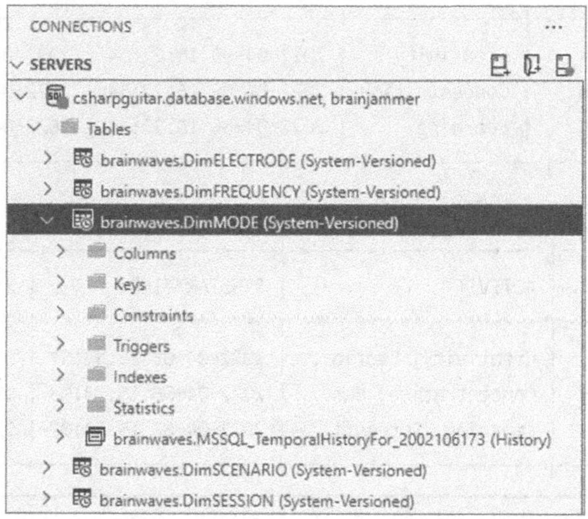

6. Note the current time, and then execute updates to the temporal tables. For more `UPDATE` statements, see the file `modifyTemporalTable.sql`, which includes some examples for you to use, located in the `Chapter04/Ch04Ex08` directory on GitHub at `https://github.com/benperk/ADE`. Then query the history tables again, as you did in step 5:

```
UPDATE [brainwaves].[DimSCENARIO] SET SCENARIO = 'Flipboard'
WHERE SCENARIO_ID = 2
```

7. Using the time that you executed the `UPDATE` statement in step 6 as a reference ➢ execute the following SQL statements. The first `SELECT` uses a timestamp before you executed the `UPDATE` queries, and the second `SELECT` is a time after the queries were executed. The queries and the result are shown in the following text:

EXERCISE 4.9 ***(continued)***

```
SELECT *
  FROM [brainwaves].[DimFREQUENCY] FOR SYSTEM_TIME AS OF '2022-04-06 15:58:56'
SELECT *
  FROM [brainwaves].[DimFREQUENCY] FOR SYSTEM_TIME AS OF '2022-04-06 16:00:00'
RESULT #1
+------+-------------|---------------|--------------------+--------------------+
| ..._ID | FREQUENCY | ACTIVITY      | SYSSTARTTIME        | SYSENDTIME          |
+------+-------------|---------------|--------------------+--------------------+
| 1      | THETA     | Creativity    | 2022-04-06 15:22:54 | 2022-04-06 15:58:57 |
| 4      | BETA_H    | Concentration | 2022-04-06 15:22:54 | 2022-04-06 15:59:03 |
| 5      | GAMMA     | Learning      | 2022-04-06 15:22:54 | 2022-04-06 15:59:07 |
+------+-----------|---------------|--------------------+--------------------+
RESULT #2
+--------+---------|----------------------|--------------------+--------------------+
| ..._ID | FREQ... | ACTIVITY              | SYSSTARTTIME        | SYSENDTIME          |
+------+-----------|----------------------|--------------------+--------------------+
| 1      | THETA   | Creativity, Emotio... | 2022-04-06 15:58:57 | 9999-12-31 23:59:59 |
| 4      | BETA_H  | Concentration, Mem... | 2022-04-06 15:59:03 | 9999-12-31 23:59:59 |
| 5      | GAMMA   | Learning, Percepti... | 2022-04-06 15:59:07 | 9999-12-31 23:59:59 |
+------+-----------|----------------------|--------------------+--------------------+
```

The differences between creating and working with a normal table versus a temporal table solution on Azure SQL, as shown in Figure 4.32, have to do primarily with two characteristics.

First, when you create the table itself, bear in mind that a temporal table needs to be versioned and include the required SQL clauses, for example, a start and end date with a data type of `DATETIME2` and a `PERIOD FOR SYSTEM_TIME` SQL statement. The datetimes are passed as parameters to determine the period for system time. The other characteristic is the querying of the history table, which requires a datetime passed to the `FOR SYSTEM_TIME AS OF` SQL statement. No changes are required for performing regular `CRUD` activities on a temporal table, and the versioning happens without requiring any action as well. As you learned, there is no history created with an `INSERT`, because the one initially created is always most current. Only with an `UPDATE` or `DELETE` will a row be written to the history table. The action required to add the versioning data to the history table is performed by the DBMS.

FIGURE 4.32 A temporal data solution

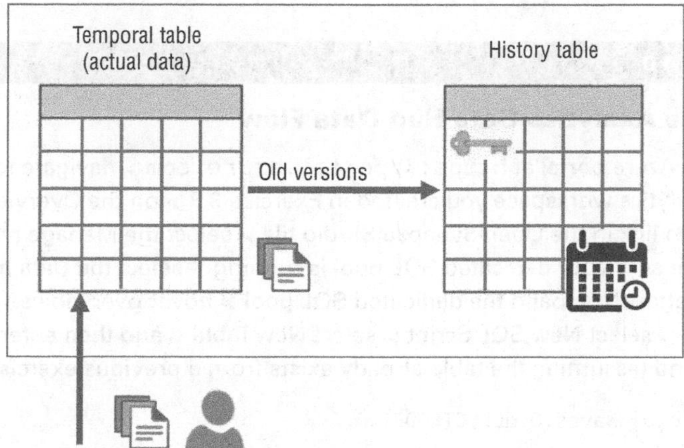

Build a Slowly Changing Dimension

If you think that temporal tables seem a bit like slowly changing dimension (SCD) tables, you are right. Both table types are intended to provide a history of changes that happen on tables that do not change very often. And as you learned in Chapter 3, there are numerous types of SCD tables, which provide different historical information. Table 4.6 summarizes the different SCD types. This is a very important concept, and you can expect questions on the exam about this.

TABLE 4.6 Slowly changing dimension types

Type	Figure	Description
1	3.15	No record of historical value, only current state
2	3.16	Historical records using active dates, surrogate key, and flags
3	3.17	Previous historical value only with inserted and modified dates
4	4.32	Actual data on the temporal table, historical data on another
6	3.18	Combines capabilities of Types 1, 2, and 3

In Exercise 4.10 you implement a slowly changing dimension table. As you work through the exercise, try to determine which type is being implemented.

EXERCISE 4.10

Azure Synapse Analytics Data Hub Data Flow

1. Log in to the Azure portal at `https://portal.azure.com` ➢ navigate to the Azure Synapse Analytics workspace you created in Exercise 3.3 ➢ on the Overview blade, click the Open link in the Open Synapse Studio tile ➢ select the Manage hub ➢ click SQL Pools ➢ make sure your dedicated SQL pool is running ➢ select the Data hub ➢ expand the SQL Database ➢ expand the dedicated SQL pool ➢ hover over Tables ➢ click the ellipse (`...`) ➢ select New SQL Script ➢ select New Table ➢ and then enter the following SQL command (assuming the table already exists from a previous exercise):

```
DROP TABLE brainwaves.DimELECTRODE
```

2. Create an SCD table, and then execute the following SQL script, which is located in the folder `Chapter04/Ch04Ex09` on GitHub at `https://github.com/benperk/ADE` and named `createSlowlyChangingDimensionTable.sql`:

```
 CREATE TABLE [brainwaves].[DimELECTRODE] (
  [ELECTRODE_ID]       INT                       NOT NULL IDENTITY(1,1),
  [SK_ID]              NVARCHAR (50)             NOT NULL,
  [ELECTRODE]          NVARCHAR (50)             NOT NULL,
  [LOCATION]           NVARCHAR (50)             NOT NULL,
  [START_DATE]         DATETIME2                 NOT NULL,
  [END_DATE]           DATETIME2,
  [IS_CURRENT]         INT                       NOT NULL
)
WITH
(
  CLUSTERED COLUMNSTORE INDEX,
  DISTRIBUTION = REPLICATE
)
```

3. Populate the SCD table with data, and then execute the `INSERT` statements from the file `insertSlowlyChangingDimensionTable.sql`, which is in the folder `Chapter04/Ch04Ex09` on GitHub:

```
DECLARE @SK_ID AS VARCHAR(10)
DECLARE @START_DATE AS DATETIME2 = GETDATE()
SELECT @SK_ID = CONCAT('E', COUNT(*) + 1) FROM brainwaves.DimELECTRODE
INSERT INTO [brainwaves].[DimELECTRODE]
```

```
([SK_ID], [ELECTRODE], [LOCATION], [START_DATE], [END_DATE], [IS_CURRENT])
VALUES (@SK_ID, 'AF3', 'Front Left', @START_DATE, '9999-12-31 23:59:59', 1)
```

4. **Select the inserted data using the following SQL command:**

```
SELECT * FROM brainwaves.DimELECTRODE

+--------+-------+-----------+-------------+------------+------------+------------+
| EL..ID | SK_ID | ELECTRODE | LOCATION    | START_DATE | END_DATE   | IS_CURRENT |
+--------+-------+-----------+-------------+------------+------------+------------+
| 5      | E3    | T7        | Ear Left    | 2022-04-07 | 9999-12-31 | 1          |
| 16     | E1    | AF3       | Front Left  | 2022-04-07 | 9999-12-31 | 1          |
| 28     | E5    | Pz        | Center Back | 2022-04-07 | 9999-12-31 | 1          |
| 38     | E4    | T8        | Ear Right   | 2022-04-07 | 9999-12-31 | 1          |
| 59     | E2    | AF4       | Front Right | 2022-04-07 | 9999-12-31 | 1          |
+--------+-------+-----------+-------------+------------+------------+------------+
```

5. **Wait some time ➢ perform an `UPDATE` by executing the SQL code in the file named `updateSlowlyChangingDimensionTable.sql` (available in folder `Chapter04/Ch04Ex09` on GitHub) ➢ and then execute another `SELECT` statement:**

```
SELECT * FROM brainwaves.DimELECTRODE

+--------+-------+-----------+-------------+------------+------------+------------+
| EL..ID | SK_ID | ELECTRODE | LOCATION    | START_DATE | END_DATE   | IS_CURRENT |
+--------+-------+-----------+-------------+------------+------------+------------+
| 5      | E3    | T7        | Ear Left    | 2022-04-07 | 9999-12-31 | 1          |
| 12     | E1    | AF3i      | Top Left    | 2022-04-08 | 9999-12-31 | 1          |
| 16     | E1    | AF3       | Front Left  | 2022-04-07 | 2022-04-08 | 0          |
| 28     | E5    | Pz        | Center Back | 2022-04-07 | 9999-12-31 | 1          |
| 38     | E4    | T8        | Ear Right   | 2022-04-07 | 9999-12-31 | 1          |
| 59     | E2    | AF4       | Front Right | 2022-04-07 | 9999-12-31 | 1          |
+--------+-------+-----------+-------------+------------+------------+------------+
```

The query that creates the table is like any dimension table, albeit with some additional columns. Those columns are a surrogate key, a start date, an end date, and a flag that identifies whether the row is the current one. These columns are required for which SCD type? The `INSERT` statements did contain some syntax that was leaning a bit toward coding and away from vanilla SQL. The `INSERT` statements required a surrogate key, which is identified by the variable `@SK_ID`. The value for this variable is captured by selecting the total number of rows on the table, increasing it by 1, and prefixing it with an `E`. See step 4 in the previous exercise if this is not clear. That variable is then used as part of the `INSERT` statement. The other variable is the current date, which is captured by executing the `GETDATE()` method and storing the result in @START_DATE. The END_DATE is one that is recognized as no date, and IS_CURRENT is set to 1, which means it is the current row.

The UPDATE logic is a bit more complicated. The code first declares two variables, @SK_ID and @START_DATE, and then checks the table being updated to see if the row already exists. If it does, then an UPDATE is necessary; however, if the row does not exist, then the code performs an INSERT. This is what many refer to as an UPSERT. When an UPDATE occurs, there is also an INSERT, which adds a new row to the table. The new row contains the same SK_ID as the one being updated, along with the new values: the new value for @START_DATE and the IS_CURRENT set to 1. The UPDATE sets the END_DATE column to the @START_DATE value and sets IS_CURRENT to 0. In case you have not already realized it, this is a Type 2 SCD table.

There are many approaches for implementing SCD tables. The approach in Exercise 4.10 is a manual one and is helpful for you to get a good understanding of how this works. Another approach could be something like the following.

1. You have one staging table and one target table.
2. Data is loaded into the staging table.
3. Tables are joined to find matches.
4. If the record exists in both the staging table and the target table, the record is updated on the target table.
5. If the record exists only in the staging table and not in the target table, the record is inserted into the target table.

That scenario is the one in which you would employ the MERGE SQL command. (Refer to Chapter 3.) Both of these approaches are fully supported using DataFrames and tables using a Spark pool or Azure Databricks.

Build a Logical Folder Structure

No single folder structure fits every solution; what is considered a logically designed folder structure is relative. You have seen the following folder structures:

- EMEA/brainjammer/in/2022/04/01/18
- EMEA/brainjammer/out/2022/04/01/19
- EMEA/brainjammer/raw-files/2022/04/08/18
- EMEA/brainjammer/cleansed-data/2022/04/08
- EMEA/brainjammer/business-data/2022/04

Those folders are well suited for ingesting data. The structure supports either allowing systems to send the data to those directories or writing a process to retrieve and store the data there. You can also see the data landing zone (DLZ) pattern, which progresses along the Big Data pipeline data transformation processing stages. Another example of a logical folder structure is the way the brainjammer brainwave files are organized:

- brainjammer/SessionCSV/ClassicalMusic/EEG
- brainjammer/SessionCSV/MetalMusic/POW
- brainjammer/SessionCSV/Meditation/EEG
- brainjammer/SessionJSON/TikTok/POW
- brainjammer/SessionJSON/PlayingGuitar/POW

The ultimate objective of a folder structure is to organize your files. They need to be arranged in a way that anyone looking for a specific kind of data can find it easily. The directory path name and even file names also can be very helpful for discovering data. The brainjammer brain waves provide that intuitive understanding from the structure and type of data stored within those folders. Folder structures can exist in an ADLS container, on Azure Files, on an FTP site, on your workstation, or via a network SMB share.

Build External Tables

An external table is one that targets data located, for example, on ADLS or an Azure Blob Storage container. Once you create the table from the data stored in those containers, you can perform T-SQL–like queries against the data. This is a powerful feature. You can make a few configurations and then perform SQL queries against a file without moving it from your data lake. This is the magic of PolyBase, which is working behind the scenes to make this happen. The approach to create an external table depends on which type of SQL pool you are targeting. For a serverless SQL pool, you would create an external table using the `CREATE EXTERNAL TABLE AS SELECT` (CETAS) statement. When targeting a dedicated SQL pool, you would use the `CREATE TABLE AS SELECT` (CTAS) command. CETAS is also supported (more about this later). Recall the following example from Chapter 2, "CREATE DATABASE dbName; GO," noting the value for `TYPE`:

```
CREATE EXTERNAL DATA SOURCE Meditation_Source
WITH (LOCATION = 'abfss://<uid>@<accountName>.dfs.core.windows.net',
      TYPE = HADOOP);
```

A Hadoop table type is only available for dedicated SQL pools. The table type used for serverless SQL pools is referred to as native and is considered to be more performant versus dedicated. Therefore, it is currently recommended to use CTAS for dedicated pools until the native type is "completely" supported by dedicated. "Completely" is in quotes because at the time of writing, the native table type is partially supported for dedicated SQL pools—but only for Parquet files, and that is in preview. So, you can use CETAS for dedicated SQL pools, but because it is not currently supported while in preview, the only option you have when targeting a dedicated SQL pool in production is to use the Hadoop table type. Complete Exercise 4.11, where you will build an external table on a serverless SQL pool in Azure Synapse Analytics.

EXERCISE 4.11

Build External Tables on a Serverless SQL Pool

1. Log in to the Azure portal at `https://portal.azure.com` ➢ navigate to the Azure Synapse Analytics workspace you created in Exercise 3.3 ➢ on the Overview blade, click the Open link in the Open Synapse Studio tile ➢ select the Develop hub ➢ click the + to the right of Develop ➢ select SQL Script from the pop-up menu ➢ ensure that Built-in is selected from the Connect To drop-down list box ➢ and then execute the following SQL syntax:

```
CREATE DATABASE BRAINJAMMER
COLLATE Latin1_General_100_BIN2_UTF8
```

2. Ensure that the database you just created (`BRAINJAMMER`) is selected from the Use Database drop-down list box ➢ enter the following SQL syntax, which creates an external data source ➢ reference the Parquet file you created in Exercise 4.7 ➢ and then change * in the URI to your endpoint details.

```
CREATE EXTERNAL DATA SOURCE SampleBrainwavesSource
WITH (LOCATION = 'abfss://*@*.dfs.core.windows.net')
```

3. Execute the following SQL syntax, which creates the external file format:

```
CREATE EXTERNAL FILE FORMAT SampleBrainwavesParquet
WITH  (FORMAT_TYPE = PARQUET)
```

4. Execute the SQL syntax required to create the external table. The file `createExternalTables.sql`, in the folder `Chapter04/Ch04Ex10`, on GitHub at `https://github.com/benperk/ADE`, contains the SQL to perform all these activities.

```
CREATE EXTERNAL TABLE SampleBrainwaves
(
 [Timestamp] NVARCHAR(50),
 [AF3theta] NVARCHAR(50),
 [AF3alpha] NVARCHAR(50),
 [AF3betaL] NVARCHAR(50),
...
)
WITH
(
 LOCATION = 'EMEA/brainjammer/out/2022/04/03/*/*.parquet/*',
 DATA_SOURCE = SampleBrainwavesSource,
 FILE_FORMAT = SampleBrainwavesParquet
)
```

5. Select the data stored in Parquet format on ADLS using the following SQL command:

```
SELECT TOP 10 * FROM SampleBrainwaves
```

6. After retrieving some data, navigate to the Data hub > expand SQL Database > expand the database you created in step 1 > and then look into all the additional folders. You should see something similar to Figure 4.33.

FIGURE 4.33 Building an external table

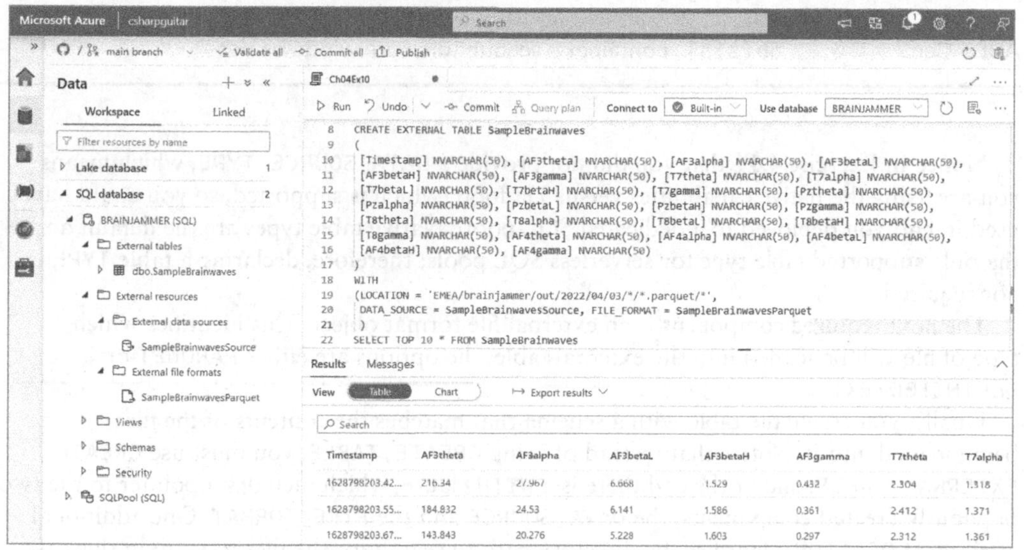

7. Consider renaming the SQL script, and then commit it to your GitHub repository.

You might have noticed when you created the database that there was another line of SQL using the `COLLATE` command. This command is very important, as it instructs the DBMS how to compare and sort character data. Note that `Latin1_General_100_BIN2_UTF8` is the collation that renders optimal performance for reading Parquet files and from Azure Cosmos DB. After creating the database on the serverless built-in SQL pool, you need three components to build an external table. The first component is the external data source that provides, in this example, a pointer to the ADLS endpoint. Table 4.7 describes the supported location settings.

TABLE 4.7 External location endpoints and protocols

External data source	Prefix	Path
Azure Blob Storage	`wasb[s]`	container@account.blob.core.windows.net
Azure Blob Storage	`http[s]`	`account.blob.windows.net/containerfolders`
ADLS Gen2	`http[s]`	`account.dfs.core.windows.net/container/folder`
ADLS Gen2	`abfs[s]`	container@account.dfs.core.windows.net

Notice in Exercise 4.11 that you did not provide a `DATA SOURCE TYPE`, which means you are using the native capabilities versus Hadoop (which is supported, so you could have used it, had you deployed to a dedicated SQL pool). Native table types are the default and the only supported table type for serverless SQL pools; therefore, declaring a table `TYPE` is not required.

The next required component is an external file format object. This identifies which type of file will be loaded into the external table; the options are either `PARQUET` or `DELIMITEDTEXT`.

Finally, you create the table with a schema that matches the contents of the files being loaded into it. Notice that instead of using `CREATE TABLE`, you must use `CREATE EXTERNAL TABLE`, and at the end there is a `WITH` clause, which includes a pointer to the two previously created components, the `DATA_SOURCE` and the `FILE_FORMAT`. One additional attribute, `LOCATION`, identifies the directory path to search for the files to load; in this case, the following snippet was configured. The wildcard search loads all Parquet files uploaded to the path on March 3, 2022.

```
LOCATION = 'EMEA/brainjammer/out/2022/04/03/*/*.parquet/*'
```

When you are working with a Spark pool, the closest object to an external table is realized using the `saveAsTable(tableName)` method. After creating the table and populating it with data, you can perform SQL commands against the table using Spark SQL, like the following code snippet:

```
Spark.sql('select * from tableName').show()
```

Implement File and Folder Structures for Efficient Querying and Data Pruning

The actions you can take to make your file and folder structures most efficient for querying and pruning are based primarily on two notions. First, organize the data files in a way that intuitively specifies enough information to know what is contained within them. You should be able to get a good idea about its content simply by looking at the folder structure and/or filename. The other idea is to partition the file into a structure that is optimal for the kinds of queries that will be run against the data file. For example, if you or your users query based on a given timeframe, it makes sense to partition the data based on the year, month, and day when the data was created and ingested. To implement such a file and folder structure, complete Exercise 4.12, where you will convert a CSV file to Parquet, partition it, move it to a more intuitive directory, and query it.

EXERCISE 4.12

Implement Efficient File and Folder Structures

1. Decompress the `ALL_SCENARIO_ELECTRODE_FREQUENCY_VALUE.zip` file from Exercise 4.1 and upload it to the directory structure you created in Exercise 4.7, for example as follows. (Consider choosing year, month, and date folder names that align with your timeframe.)

```
EMEA/brainjammer/in/2022/04/10/10
```

2. Create another directory that will contain the converted file, for example:

```
EMEA/brainjammer/out/2022/04/10/11
```

3. Log in to tho Azuro portal at `https://portal.azure.com` ➢ navigate to the Azure Synapse Analytics workspace you created in Exercise 3.3 ➢ on the Overview blade, click the Open link in the Open Synapse Studio tile ➢ select the Develop hub ➢ click the + to the right of Develop ➢ select Notebook from the pop-up menu ➢ ensure that your Spark pool is selected from the Attach To drop-down list box ➢ and then execute the following code snippet, which is available on GitHub in the `Chapter04/Ch04Ex11` directory:

```
%%pyspark
df = spark.read.load('abfss://*@*.dfs.core.windows.net/in-path/file.csv',
     format='csv', header=True)
df.write.mode("overwrite") \
     .parquet('abfss://*@*.dfs.core.windows.net/out-path/file.parquet')
```

4. Check your ADLS container to confirm that the Parquet file was successfully written, and then execute the following code snippet:

```
%%pyspark
df = spark.read.load('abfss://*@*.dfs.core.windows.net/out-path/file.parquet',
     format='parquet', header=True)
print(df.count())
```

5. Create the following folder structure in your ADLS container. (Consider choosing year, month, and date folder names that align with your timeframe.)

```
EMEA/brainjammer/cleansed-data/2022/04/10
```

EXERCISE 4.12 *(continued)*

6. Execute the following code snippet, which loads the Parquet file from the out path into a DataFrame and creates partitions for year and month:

```
%%pyspark
from pyspark.sql.functions import year, month, col
df = spark.read \
  .load('abfss://*@*.dfs.core.windows.net/out-path/file.parquet',
  format='parquet', header=True)
df_year_month_day = (df.withColumn("year", year(col("SESSION_DATETIME")))) \
  .withColumn("month", month(col("SESSION_DATETIME")))
```

7. Execute the following code snippet, which writes the files into the partitioned directories. The output files should resemble Figure 4.34.

```
%%pyspark
from pyspark.sql.functions import year, month, col
df_year_month_day.write \
  .partitionBy("year", "month").mode("overwrite") \
  .parquet('abfss://*@*.dfs.core.windows.net/EMEA/brainjammer/cleansed-data/
2022/04/10')
```

FIGURE 4.34 An efficient file and folder structure

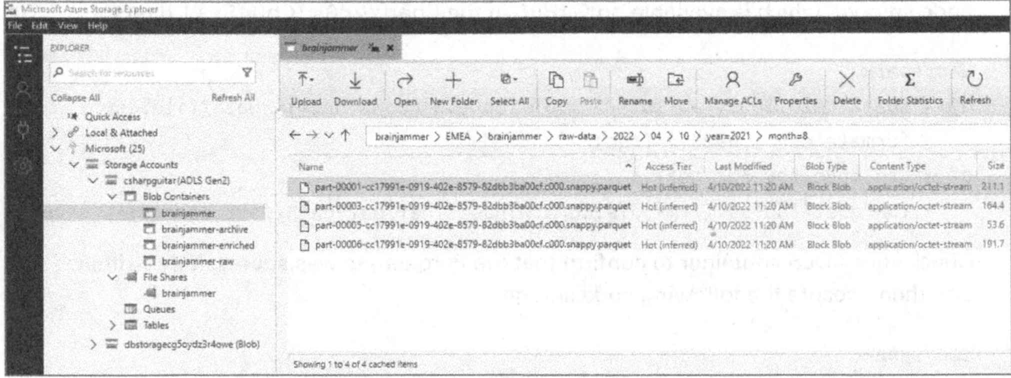

8. Query the data files on a specific partition as follows, replacing the * with your endpoint details:

```
%%pyspark
df = spark.read \
```

```
.load('abfss://*@*.dfs.core.windows.net/path/year=2021/month=7',
format='parquet', header=True)
print(df.count())
display(df.limit(10))
```

9. Consider committing your notebook to GitHub.

The folder from which the data files are retrieved and to which they are written are intuitive in the following ways. The original file is located within the file path that identifies the region, the ingestion direction, and a date. Looking at the following path, you can conclude the data is coming from EMEA and is brainjammer data sent/received on the date in the path:

```
EMEA/brainjammer/in/2022/04/10/10
```

The original data file format is ingested as CSV and converted to Parquet, which is a more efficient file format for querying. The converted data file is placed into an `out` directory, which signifies that some kind of ingestion operation was performed on it, and it is now ready for further transformation or optimization. One way to make querying more efficient is to partition the data file, like you did in steps 5 and 6 in the Exercise 4.12. You stored the partitioned files in a folder named `cleansed-data`, which represents a phase of the data landing zone (DLZ). Recall this from Figure 3.8 in the previous chapter.

```
EMEA/brainjammer/cleansed-data/2022/04/10
```

In all three of the actions, there is a timeframe that is closely related to the location where the files are stored. Additionally, the data itself is also stored in folder structures based on dates like year and month. This storage structure makes the removal, i.e., pruning, of the data more efficient because it is easier to locate and determine if it is still relevant. If it is determined that the data is no longer relevant, especially the data in the `in` and `out` directories, then the data can be removed. Partitioning data results in the files being smaller, which makes removing portions of the file or the entire file itself less latent.

Implement a Partition Strategy

Chapter 3 discussed designing partition strategies. Remember the two primary reasons for partitioning data. The first reason is to improve the speed at which a query for data responds with the dataset. When data is partitioned, it means that it is organized into smaller groups bound together by some common attribute. For example, if there was a partition based on the scenario from which a brain wave was captured, a query would return more quickly if there was a partition that included all readings from the PlayingGuitar scenario than if there was a partition that included all scenarios.

The second reason has to do with a combination of size and retention. Executing a query on a partition with 1 billion rows will take longer than running the same query on a partition with 1 million rows. Consider that you partition data using a datetime stamp on a table that contains 1 billion rows. In this hypothetical situation, partitioning based on a datetime stamp would reduce the queryable data considerably, thus reducing the size of data being queried. This partitioning approach also enables the deletion of data once it is no longer relevant. For example, once the datetime stamp is over 30 days old, it can be removed or archived, again reducing the size and amount of data being queried.

The following sections provide some additional insights into data partitioning for specific scenarios. In most cases, the implementation of these scenarios comes in later chapters and exercises, as noted.

Implement a Partition Strategy for Files

You implemented a partition strategy for a CSV and a Parquet file in Exercise 4.2 and Exercise 4.12, respectively. In Exercise 4.2 you applied the partitioning strategy to a CSV file and scenario, as shown in the following code snippet:

```
%%pyspark
df = spark.read \
  .load('abfss://.@..dfs.core.windows.net/SessionCSV/...ODE_FREQUENCY_VALUE.csv', \
        format='csv', header=True)
df.write \
  .partitionBy('SCENARIO').mode('overwrite').csv('/SessionCSV/
ScenarioPartitions')
data = spark.read.csv('/SessionCSV/ScenarioPartitions/SCENARIO=PlayingGuitar')
```

The first line loaded the CSV file containing brain waves readings taken in different scenarios into a DataFrame. The second line of code used the `partitionBy()` method to separate the CSV file into partitions based on the scenarios contained in the file. The third line of code loaded the data that exists in the `PlayingGuitar` partition. It would be easily agreed that if the original CSV file that contained all scenarios had 1 billion rows, a query against it would take longer than simply loading only the ones matching a specific scenario on an independent partition.

In Exercise 4.12, you used a year and month as the basis for your file partitioning. The following code snippet is an example of how partitioning was performed using the year and month in a Parquet file:

```
%%pyspark
df = spark.read \
  .load('abfss://*@*.dfs.core.windows.net/out-path/file.parquet',
  format='parquet', header=True)
df_year_month_day = (df.withColumn("year", year(col("SESSION_DATETIME")))) \
```

```
  .withColumn("month", month(col("SESSION_DATETIME")))
df_year_month_day.write \
  .partitionBy("year", "month").mode("overwrite") \
  .parquet('abfss://*@*.dfs.core.windows.net/EMEA/brainjammer/
    cleansed-data/2022/04/10')
df = spark.read \
  .load('abfss://*@*.dfs.core.windows.net/path/year=2021/month=7',
format='parquet', header=True)
print(df.count())
display(df.limit(10))
```

The data is first loaded into a DataFrame and is then loaded into a new DataFrame with the addition of a year and month column. The data is then partitioned using the `partitionBy()` method and retrieved using the following parameters passed to the `load()` method:

```
year=2021/month=7
```

The results are then counted and rendered to the console using the `display()` method.

Implement a Partition Strategy for Analytical Workloads

When you begin to brainstorm the storage of data for an analytical workload, terms such as hybrid transaction/analytical processing (HTAP) and online analytical processing (OLAP) might come to mind. Both of those data processing types are useful for analytical workloads. HTAP is a hybrid mechanism that combines OLAP and online transactional processing (OLTP). That means your data storage resource can efficiently respond to real-time transactions and data analytics processes, where transactions are inserts, updates, and deletes, and data analytics are selects and reporting. Chapter 6, "Create and Manage Batch Processing and Pipelines," discusses how to implement an HTAP solution in Azure Synapse Analytics using something called change data capture (CDC). CDC is a feature that captures transaction logs and transfers them in near real time so that data analytics can be run against them. This behavior would be similar to the serving layer in the lambda architecture, which is fed by the speed layer, meaning that you can analyze your transactional data and gather insights from it in near real time.

Some other important elements to consider when creating a partition strategy for analytical workloads are the stack, the datastore, the optimal balance between file size and the number of files, table distribution, and the law of 60. Determining whether your analytical workloads require a Spark cluster or a serverless or dedicated SQL pool is an important consideration. For example, if you want to (or must) use delta tables, then you will need to use a Spark cluster. The datastore is determined by the format of your data, for example, relational, semi-, or non-structured. Different products are necessary for optimizing the storage of data based on the data format. In Chapter 10, "Optimize and Troubleshoot Data Storage Processing," you perform an exercise in which you optimize the ratio between file size and the number of files. For example, if your queries must load a large number of small files, you need to consider the latency of the I/O transaction required to load each one. As discussed in Chapter 10, there is an optimal balance between the number of files and the size of files, which needs to be found for optimally partitioning analytical workload data. Chapter 10 also discusses table distribution (round-robin, hash, and replicated), which you implemented in Exercise 4.4. Finally, the law of 60 was first introduced in Chapter 2 and is discussed in numerous other chapters, including extensively in Chapter 10, and is implemented in Exercise 5.6.

Implement a Partition Strategy for Streaming Workloads

Chapter 7, "Design and Implement a Data Stream Processing Solution," discusses partitioning data within one partition and across partitions. Exercise 7.5 features the hands-on implementation of partitioning streaming workloads. Partitioning in the streaming sense has a lot to do with the allocation of datasets onto worker nodes, where a worker node is a virtual machine configured to process your data stream. Partitioning the streamed data improves execution times and efficiency by processing all data grouped together by a similar key on the same machine. Processing all the like data on a single node removes the necessity of splitting datasets and then merging them back together after processing is complete. How you achieve this will become clearer in Chapter 7, but the keyword for this grouping is *windowing*, which enables you to group together like data for a given time window and then process the data stream once that time window is realized.

Using partitions effectively in a streaming workload will result in the parallel processing of your data stream. This is achieved when you have multiple nodes that process these partition-based datasets concurrently. Whether the input stream and the output stream support partitions and number the same are important considerations to achieve parallelism. Not all streaming products support partitions explicitly (see Table 7.6). Some products create a partition key for you if one is not supplied, whereas other products do not. Some products like Power BI do not support partitions at all, which is important to know because it means if you plan on using Power BI as an output binding, you cannot achieve parallelism. Parallelism cannot be achieved in this scenario because the number of partitions configured for your input binding must be equal to the number of output partitions. There will always be one. See Figure 7.31 and Figure 7.37 for a visualization of parallelism using multiple partition keys.

Implement a Partition Strategy for Azure Synapse Analytics

Figure 2.10 showed the best example of partitioning in Azure Synapse Analytics. On a dedicated SQL pool, you can use the hash distribution key to group related data, which is processed on multiple nodes in parallel. For example, the following SQL snippet:

```
DISTRIBUTION = HASH([ELECTRODE_ID])
```

You implemented partitioning in Exercise 3.7 and Exercise 4.4.

Design and Implement the Data Exploration Layer

The serving layer is a component of the lambda architecture (refer to Figure 3.13). The serving layer is the place into which both the speed layer, which processes data incrementally, and the batch layer, which has more refined data, feed. Data stored in the serving layer is then accessed by other applications, individuals, or Power BI, for example. Therefore, to implement a serving layer, you would need to know the details about how those two preceding dependent layers (i.e., speed and batch) are forwarding the data. In other words, what are the format and schema of the data being ingested and likely transformed onto the serving layer? Remember that the speed layer receives data along the hot path, which typically flows from an IoT device through products like Event Hubs, IoT Hub, Stream Analytics, or Kafka. That streaming data is processed incrementally and can be transformed, but just a little in real time, before it is either sent live to a consumer or placed into a datastore like ADLS, an SQL pool, or an Azure Cosmos DB. The data being ingested to the batch layer is not streaming and flows along a cold path into an ingestion product like Azure Data Factory, Azure Databricks, or Azure Synapse Analytics. Once ingested and stored, that data can then be transformed and moved to the serving layer. Chapter 6 includes in-depth coverage of batching and batch processing, and Chapter 7 discusses stream processing.

Deliver Data in a Relational Star Schema

When you implement the serving layer portion of a lambda architecture along the cold path, consider storing data in a star schema. (Refer to Figure 3.14 for an illustration of a star schema.) Remember that the benefit expected from data flowing through the batch layer and onto the serving layer along the cold path is that the querying is most efficient. That is, querying data that has flowed through the batch layer to the serving layer will render better performance and be less raw than data flowing through the speed layer onto the serving layer. Complete Exercise 4.13, where you will retrieve data from an Azure SQL database, transform it a bit, and then store it for consumption on a serving layer (i.e., a dedicated SQL pool).

EXERCISE 4.13

Implement a Serving Layer with a Star Schema

1. Log in to the Azure portal at `https://portal.azure.com` > navigate to the Azure Synapse Analytics workspace you created in Exercise 3.3 > on the Overview blade, click the Open link in the Open Synapse Studio tile > select the Develop hub > click the + to the right Develop > click SQL Script > select your dedicated SQL pool from the Connect To drop-down list box > and then execute the SQL syntax in the file `createAlterStarSchemaTables.sql`, in the `Chapter04/Ch04Ex12` directory on GitHub.

EXERCISE 4.13 *(continued)*

After you execute the syntax, the tables in Figure 4.35 will be created. Notice the different icons next to the table names to identify their different distribution types.

FIGURE 4.35 Serving layer using star schema distribution types

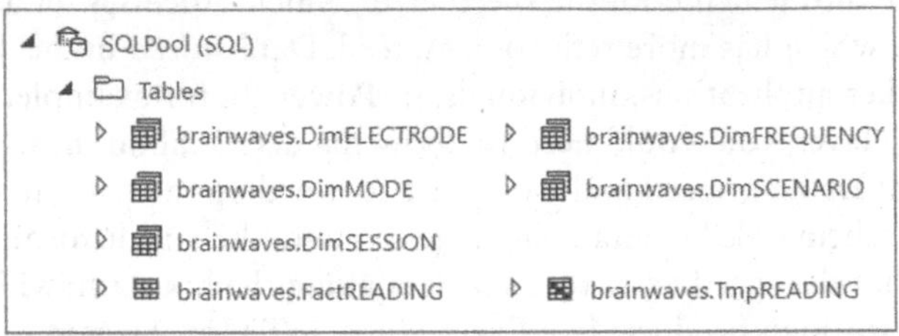

2. Using the Azure SQL database you created in Exercise 2.1 (`brainjammer`) and the Linked service you created in Exercise 3.4 (`BrainjammerAzureSQL`), create an integration dataset that represents the `[dbo].[READING]` table. Additional data for the table `[dbo].[READING]` is available, in CSV format, in the file `READING.zip` in the `BrainwaveData/Tables` directory, on GitHub at `https://github.com/benperk/ADE`. The integration dataset should resemble Figure 4.36.

FIGURE 4.36 Serving layer using star schema integration dataset

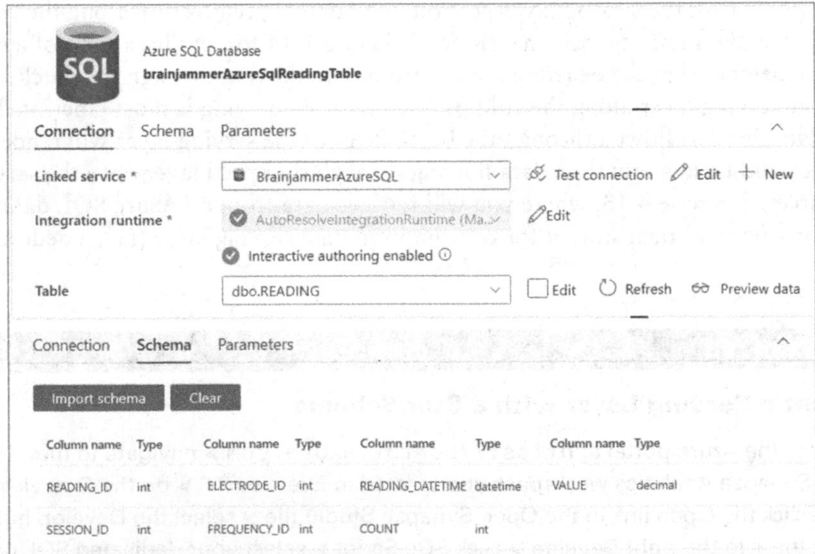

3. Load the star schema with data using the following bulk load COPY INTO command. You can find all the CSV table data in the BrainwaveData/Tables directory on GitHub. See the file copyIntoDimStarTables.sql, in the directory Chapter04/Ch04Ex12, for all the COPY INTO statements.

```
COPY INTO [brainwaves].[DimMODE]
FROM 'https://*.blob.core.windows.net/brainjammer/Tables/MODE.csv'
WITH (
    FILE_TYPE='CSV',
    FIRSTROW = 2
)
GO
COPY INTO [brainwaves].[DimSCENARIO]
FROM 'https://*.blob.core.windows.net/brainjammer/Tables/SCENARIO.csv'
WITH (
    FILE_TYPE='CSV',
    FIRSTROW = 2
)
...
```

4. Select the Develop hub ➢ click the + symbol to the right of the Develop title ➢ select Data Flow ➢ click the Add Source activity in the editor canvas ➢ provide the output stream name (I used **BrainwavesReading**) ➢ select the Integration Dataset as the Source type ➢ use the integration dataset you created in step 2 ➢ click the Open item next to the selected dataset ➢ enable Interactive Authoring ➢ navigate back to the data flow ➢ enable Data Flow Debug by selecting the toggle switch ➢ wait until enabling completes ➢ and then select the Enable radio button for Sampling.

5. Select the + on the lower right of the Source activity ➢ select Sink ➢ enter an output stream name (I used **brainjammerTmpReading**) ➢ set the incoming stream to the source you configured in step 4 ➢ select Integration Dataset as the Sink type ➢ create a new dataset by clicking the + New button next to the Dataset drop-down list box ➢ select Azure Synapse Analytics ➢ press Continue ➢ enter a name (I used **brainjammerSynapseTmpReading**) ➢ select the *WorkspaceDefaultSqlServer from the Linked service drop-down list box ➢ click the Refresh icon to the right of the Table Name drop-down list box ➢ enter the name of your dedicated SQL pool (I used **SQLPool**) ➢ click the OK button ➢ and then select the [brainwaves].[tmpREADING] table you created in step 1. The configuration should resemble Figure 4.37.

EXERCISE 4.13 *(continued)*

FIGURE 4.37 Serving layer using star schema tmp integration dataset

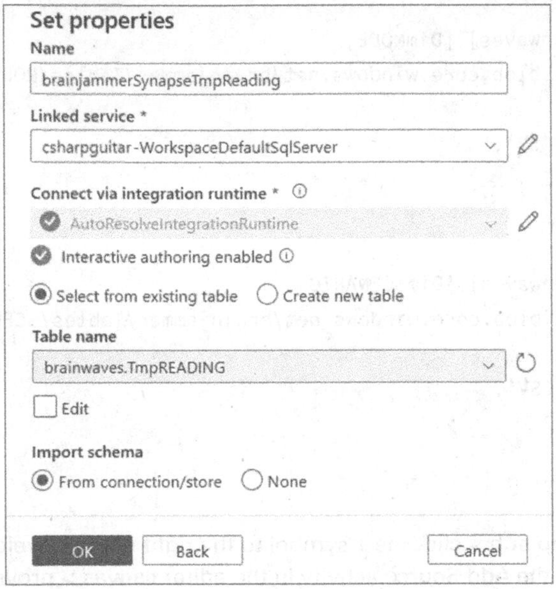

Set properties
Name
brainjammerSynapseTmpReading
Linked service *
csharpguitar-WorkspaceDefaultSqlServer
Connect via integration runtime *
AutoResolveIntegrationRuntime
Interactive authoring enabled
Select from existing table
Create new table
Table name
brainwaves.TmpREADING
Edit
Import schema
From connection/store
None
OK
Back
Cancel

6. Click the OK button ➢ look through the remaining tabs on the data flow configuration panel ➢ consider renaming the data flow ➢ and then click the Commit button to save the data flow to your GitHub repository. Figure 4.38 illustrates the configuration.

FIGURE 4.38 Serving layer using star schema data flow

Microsoft Azure
csharpguitar
Search
main branch
Validate all
Commit all
Publish
Data
Workspace
Linked
Filter resources by name
Azure Blob Storage 2
Azure Cosmos DB 1
Azure Data Lake Storage Gen2 2
Integration datasets 10
Ch04Ex12
Committed
Validate
Data flow debug
Debug Settings
BrainwavesReading
Import data from brainjammerAzureSqlReadingTable
brainjammerTmpRea...
Columns:
7 total
Sink
Settings
Mapping
Optimize
Inspect
Data preview
Description
Output stream name *
brainjammerTmpReading
Learn more
Incoming stream *
BrainwavesReading
Sink type *
Integration dataset
Inline
Workspace DB
Cache
Dataset *
brainjammerSynapseTmpReading
Test connection
Open
New
Connection successful
Options
Allow schema drift
Validate schema

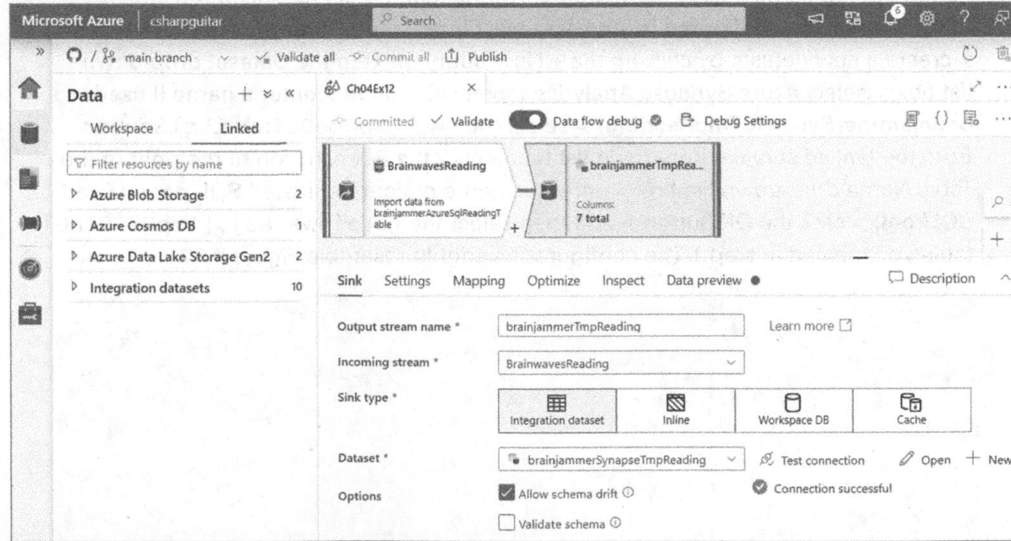

7. Navigate to the Integrate hub ➢ click the + to the right of the Integrate text ➢ select Pipeline in the Properties window ➢ enter a name (I used **IngestTmpReading**) ➢ expand the Move & Transform group from within the Activity pane ➢ drag and drop a data flow into the graph ➢ on the General tab, enter a name (I used **MoveToTmpReading**) ➢ on the Settings tab, select the data flow completed in step 5 from the Data Flow drop-down list box ➢ select your `WorkspaceDefaultStorage` from the Staging Linked Service drop-down list box ➢ click the Browse button next to the Staging Storage Folder text boxes ➢ and then choose a stage location for PolyBase. Figure 4.39 resembles how the configuration appears.

FIGURE 4.39 Serving layer using star schema pipeline

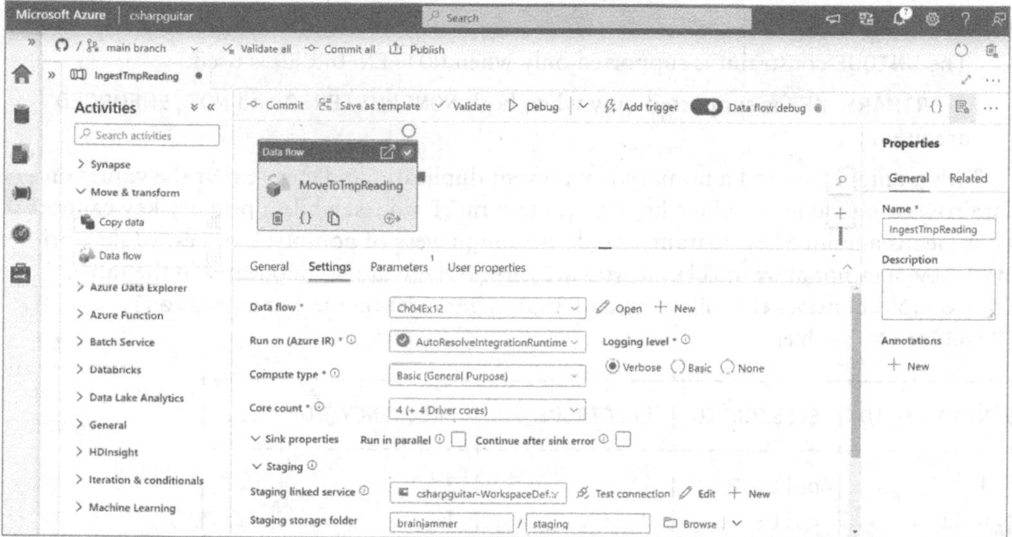

8. Click the Validate button ➢ click the Debug button ➢ and then execute the following SQL query. Notice the count of rows copied into the `[brainwaves].[tmpREADING]` table equals the Rows Limit Sampling number configured in step 4.

```
SELECT COUNT(*) FROM [brainwaves].[tmpREADING]
SELECT TOP (10) * FROM [brainwaves].[tmpREADING]
DELETE FROM [brainwaves].[tmpREADING]
```

9. Disable sampling in the data flow you created in step 4 ➢ commit the data flow to your source code repository ➢ navigate back to the pipeline ➢ commit the pipeline artifacts to your GitHub repository ➢ choose the Publish menu item ➢ review the pending changes ➢ click the OK button ➢ after the publishing has completed (be patient; view the status using the Notifications task bar item), select the Add Trigger menu drop-down ➢ select Trigger Now ➢ click the OK button ➢ click the Monitor hub ➢ click the Pipeline Runs link in the Integration section to monitor the status ➢ once complete (be patient), rerun the SQL queries from step 8.

Congratulations on creating your first Azure Synapse Analytics pipeline. Reflect a bit on all the features it relied on and how much you have learned about them so far. You have come a long way, but there is still much more to do and learn, beginning with the creation of the tables in step 1. You should already understand the purpose and differences between dimension tables and fact tables. In the SQL syntax that created them, they are prefixed with their associated table category. There are a few new concepts that have not yet been thoroughly discussed: `ALTER`, `PRIMARY KEY`, and `UNIQUE` SQL statements and an integration/staging/temporary table. The `ALTER` command is used to make a change to a database object—in this case, a table. The change to the table is to add a primary key constraint, which is similar in principle to, but not the same, as a relational database. Dedicated SQL pools do not support the concept of a foreign key, and therefore relationships between tables cannot be enforced. The following table constraints related to a dedicated SQL pool are also true.

- The `UNIQUE` constraint is supported only when `NOT ENFORCED` is used.
- A `PRIMARY KEY` is supported only when both `NONCLUSTERED` and `NOT ENFORCED` are used.

Both a unique key and a primary key prevent duplicates and ensure that the values on data rows are unique. A unique key can contain `null` values, while a primary key cannot. That means a unique key guarantees only the uniqueness of non-`null` values, while a primary key does not allow `nulls`, so you are certain there are no duplicates in the table. For example, consider the following data that might exist on the `[brainwaves].[TmpREADING]` table:

```
+------------+------------+--------------+------------------+-----+
| READING_ID | SESSION_ID | ELECTRODE_ID | FREQUENCY_ID     | ... |
+------------+------------+--------------+------------------+-----+
| 1          | null       | 1            | 3                | ... |
| null       | null       | 2            | 1                | ... |
| null       | 1          | 3            | 2                | ... |
| null       | null       | 2            | 1                | ... |
| 2          | 2          | 4            | 5                | ... |
+------------+------------+--------------+------------------+-----+
```

The `[brainwaves].[TmpREADING]` table, as you might recall, has a unique key on the `READING_ID` and the `SESSION_ID`. That means that either of those columns, or both at the same time, can contain `null` values. There cannot be another `1` in the `READING_ID` column or another set of 2s in both the `READING_ID` and `SESSION_ID` in the table. However, there can be numerous rows where both `READING_ID` and `SESSION_ID` are `null`. This behavior would not be supported had the `READING_ID` and `SESSION_ID` been a primary key. The foremost reason for choosing `UNIQUE` vs. `PRIMARY KEY` is based on whether you expect `nulls` in columns that help identify rows of data in a table uniquely. Finally, the `[brainwaves].[TmpREADING]` table is a staging table—that is, a table used to temporarily store data so that it can be transformed later. This table would reside in the batch layer of the lambda architecture. Once the data is transformed and placed into the `[brainwaves]`

.[FactREADING] table, it would then be on the serving layer. In Chapter 5, "Transform, Manage, and Prepare Data," you will continue with this pipeline and transform the data, then move it to a place along the DLZ stages where additional analysis can be performed.

The movement of the data employs two different approaches. The first approach uses the COPY INTO SQL statement, which is not as performant when compared to PolyBase but has much more flexibility. The flexibility comes in the form of storing error files in a custom location and having more supported datetime formats, additional wildcard search parameters, and automatic schema discovery. The second approach, which copies data from an Azure SQL database to the SQL pool, uses a data flow that employs PolyBase behind the scenes when you are using an Azure Synapse Analytics source or sink. PolyBase is a very fast and efficient way to copy and move around data from many source types, and in many formats, to a different source in a different format.

Deliver Data in Parquet Files

In Exercise 4.7 you performed a conversion of brain waves stored in multiple CSV files using the following PySpark code snippet:

```
%%pyspark
df = spark.read.option("header","true") \
  .csv('abfss://*@*.dfs.core.windows.net/EMEA/brainjammer/in/2022/04/01/18/*')
display(df.limit(10))
```

Then you wrote that data, loaded in a DataFrame, to Parquet format using the following code syntax:

```
df.write.mode("overwrite") \
  .parquet('/EMEA/brainjammer/out/2022/04/03/17/sampleBrainwaves.parquet')
```

The data source does not have to be from another file; it can also come from a database table. By using Spark SQL, you can retrieve that data from the table and then write the data to a Parquet file, as follows:

```
df = spark.sql('SELECT * FROM FactREADING')
```

You can perform calculations using aggregates or filter the data by using either Spark SQL or the methods available in the DataFrame.

```
df = spark.sql("SELECT * FROM FactREADING WHERE FREQUENCY == 'GAMMA'")
dfSceanrio = df.where("FREQUENCY == 'GAMMA'")
```

Delivering files in Parquet format means that you have placed your data into the most performant format. Querying the data source, parsing it, compressing it, and then moving it to a location for further processing through the next stages of Big Data are tasks you have already done and will do again.

Maintain Metadata

Metadata is information that exists for the purpose of explaining what the data is. Metadata is data about data; the better your metadata is, the more useful your data is. Files contain names, creation dates, and sizes, while databases have table relationships and schemas that represent metadata. Chapter 3 discussed metadata extensively, specifically Exercise 3.4 and Exercise 3.14, which walk you through the creation of an external Hive metastore.

The discipline known as *master data management (MDM)* focuses on the accuracy, accountability, and consistency of an enterprise's data assets. This requires a skill set that itself is worthy of a career. Consider an example where you have a DBMS, or better yet a database, running on a dedicated SQL pool in Azure Synapse Analytics. The database has numerous tables, view, schemas, stored procedures, etc., with data flows, jobs, activities, and pipelines running at random intervals. If something stops working, where should you look? Perhaps you would check to see if a table has been modified or dropped. You would do this by looking at the database metadata. For example, the following SQL query can identify when a table was modified:

```
SELECT OBJECT_SCHEMA_NAME(object_id) schemaName, OBJECT_NAME(object_id)
       tableName, modify_date
FROM sys.tables
```

This query will not identify whether a table has been dropped. There are some third-party tools, however, that can take an inventory of your metadata. Capture and store a document that contains your current data inventory. Companies with a low data requirement have been known to add and update metadata into Excel manually. If there is ever a problem that might be related to the database structure, you can compare the historical data inventory to the current metadata. However, this approach, commonly called fire-fighting mode, is not optimal for the enterprise. You need to have a formal process for managing and implementing changes that includes a step for updating your metadata-tracking documentation and programs. In addition to Excel, there are some companies that specialize in this area, like Informatica and Collibra. Finally, having solid metadata is a must for implementing a solution with Azure Purview, which provides data discovery and governance support.

Implement a Dimensional Hierarchy

Refer to Figure 3.19 to see a visual representation of a dimensional hierarchy. Perform Exercise 4.14 to implement a dimensional hierarchy on an Azure Synapse Analytics dedicated SQL pool.

EXERCISE 4.14

Implement a Dimensional Hierarchy

1. Log in to the Azure portal at `https://portal.azure.com` ➢ navigate to the Azure Synapse Analytics workspace you created in Exercise 3.3 ➢ on the Overview blade, click the Open link in the Open Synapse Studio tile ➢ select the Develop hub ➢ click the + to the right Develop ➢ click SQL Script ➢ select your dedicated SQL pool

from the ConnectTo drop-down list box ➢ and then execute the SQL syntax in file `createDimensionalHierarchy.sql`, which creates and populates the tables. You can find the syntax in the `Chapter04/Ch04Ex13` directory on GitHub.

2. Execute the SQL queries in file `queryDimensionalHierarchy.sql`, located in the `Chapter04/Ch04Ex13` directory on GitHub—for example:

```
--MODE
SELECT * FROM [dimensional].[MODE] WHERE [MODE_ID] = 2

+---------+------+
| MODE_ID | MODE |
+---------+------+
| 2       | POW  |
+---------+------+

--ELECTRODE
SELECT * FROM [dimensional].[ELECTRODE] WHERE [MODE_ID] = 2

+--------------+-----------+-------------+---------+
| ELECTRODE_ID | ELECTRODE | LOCATION    | MODE_ID |
+--------------+-----------+-------------+---------+
| 6            | AF3       | Front Left  | 2       |
| 7            | AF4       | Front Right | 2       |
| 8            | T7        | Ear Left    | 2       |
| 9            | T8        | Ear Right   | 2       |
| 10           | Pz        | Center Back | 2       |
+--------------+-----------+-------------+---------+

--FREQUENCY
SELECT * FROM [dimensional].[FREQUENCY] WHERE [ELECTRODE_ID] = 8

+--------------+-----------+-----------------+--------------+
| FREQUENCY_ID | FREQUENCY | ACTIVITY        | ELECTRODE_ID |
+--------------+-----------+-----------------+--------------+
| 36           | THETA     | Creativity      | 8            |
| 37           | ALPHA     | Relaxation      | 8            |
| 38           | BETA_L    | Problem Solving | 8            |
| 39           | BETA_H    | Concentration   | 8            |
| 40           | GAMMA     | Learning        | 8            |
+--------------+-----------+-----------------+--------------+
```

Approaching the data discovery from the top down would indicate a desire to understand which mode is connected to which frequencies. Because there is no direct relationship between a mode and frequency, the navigation through the dimensional hierarchy must flow through the `ELECTRODE` table. Working from the bottom up, you would be able to determine which frequency is linked to which mode, by navigating through the `ELECTRODE` table. For example, if you wanted to find out the mode, electrode, and frequency of a specific brain wave reading, you could use a query like the following:

```
SELECT M.MODE, E.ELECTRODE, F.FREQUENCY
FROM [dimensional].[MODE] M,
     [dimensional].[ELECTRODE] E,
     [dimensional].[FREQUENCY] F
WHERE M.MODE_ID = E.MODE_ID AND
      E.ELECTRODE_ID = F.ELECTRODE_ID AND
      M.MODE_ID = 2 AND E.ELECTRODE_ID = 8 AND F.FREQUENCY_ID = 37

+------+-----------+-----------+
| MODE | ELECTRODE | FREQUENCY |
+------+-----------+-----------+
| POW  | T7        | ALPHA     |
+------+-----------+-----------+
```

This kind of navigation and data discovery is useful when you have some data anomalies and want to find out where that value came from. Perhaps in this example that specific electrode is faulty or the code that is capturing the `POW` mode readings has a bug.

Create and Execute Queries by Using a Compute Solution That Leverages SQL Serverless and Spark Cluster

When you select Built-in from the Connect To drop-down list box, as shown in Figure 4.20, it means that you are targeting a serverless SQL pool. When you are running workloads on a serverless SQL pool, as you did in Exercise 4.6 and Exercise 4.11, the required CPU and memory are allocated as needed. Both serverless SQL pools and Apache Spark pools were introduced in detail in Chapter 3. Table 3.7 describes the differences between dedicated and serverless SQL pools, and Table 3.9 contains some different node sizes available for Apache Spark pools. In Exercise 3.4, you created an Apache Spark cluster and used it in Exercise 4.2, Exercise 4.7, and Exercise 4.12.

Recommend Azure Synapse Analytics Database Templates

One of the features of Azure Synapse Analytics is that it enables you to use database templates to quickly create new databases with predefined schemas and data structures. Database templates in Synapse Analytics are prebuilt databases that you can use as a starting point for your own database projects. These templates contain preconfigured tables, views, stored procedures, and other database objects that are designed to support specific business scenarios, such as sales analysis, customer data management, or financial reporting. Using a database template in Synapse Analytics can save you time and effort by providing you with a prebuilt structure that you can customize and expand to meet your specific needs. Some of the benefits of using database templates include the following:

- **Best practices:** Templates are designed to follow best practices and industry standards, which can help you ensure the reliability and performance of your database.
- **Accelerated development:** By starting with a prebuilt database structure, you can avoid the time-consuming process of designing and creating database objects from scratch.
- **Cost savings:** Templates can help reduce costs by eliminating the need for additional development and maintenance resources.

The database templates cover a wide range of business scenarios, including financial services, retail, health care, and more. You can also create your own custom templates based on your organization's specific needs.

Implement Azure Synapse Analytics Database Templates

To use a database template in Synapse Analytics, you can simply select the template from the Azure portal and follow the prompts to customize it for your own use. Alternatively, you can use Azure Synapse Studio to create a new database based on a template and customize it from there. The following are some tips to keep in mind while implementing Azure Synapse Analytics database templates:

- **Choose the right template:** Make sure to select a template that best matches your business scenario and data needs. Synapse Analytics provides a wide range of templates, so take the time to review the available options and select the template that's best suited for your use case.
- **Customize the template:** Although the templates provide a great starting point, it's important to customize the database objects to meet your specific needs. Be sure to review and modify the tables, views, stored procedures, and other objects, as needed, to ensure that they align with your data requirements.

- **Test the database:** Before deploying the database to production, thoroughly test it to ensure that it's working as expected. Use test data to validate the accuracy and performance of the database, and make any necessary adjustments before going live.
- **Secure the database:** As with any database implementation, security is critical. Take the time to configure appropriate security settings, including access controls, firewalls, and encryption, to protect your data from unauthorized access.
- **Monitor performance:** Use Azure Synapse Analytics monitoring and alerting features to track database performance and identify any issues that may arise. This can help you proactively address any performance or reliability concerns and ensure that your database is operating smoothly.
- **Stay up-to-date:** As your business needs evolve and new features are added to Synapse Analytics, be sure to review and update your database templates, as needed. Regular maintenance and updates can help ensure that your database remains optimized and aligned with your business goals.

By following these tips, you can implement Azure Synapse Analytics database templates effectively and create a reliable and efficient database that meets your organization's data needs.

Additional Data Storage Topics

This section will help you increase your knowledge of two of Azure open-source products and features, as well as provide a summary of the storage of data along the Big Data stages.

Storing Raw Data in Azure Databricks for Transformation

Data landing zones (DLZ) are categorized into Raw Files, cleansed data, and business data, and their equal terms of bronze, silver, and gold are synonymous. So far in this book, how data is stored on Azure Databricks behind the scenes might not be completely clear. There is an Azure storage account that contains numerous provisioned blob storage containers, along with your Azure Databricks service. The workspace uses the blob storage containers to store logs, jobs, meta, and the root container where your data is stored. Some restrictions are placed on the container to keep people from accessing the containers and any file or directory contained within them, most likely to keep curious people from accidentally changing something that may have negative or unintentional consequences for the workspace and the analytics performed on it. There is no way then to add files, for example, to that blob container and then access them from the Azure Databricks workspace. You can instead mount a different ADLS container to the Databricks File System (DBFS) and access your data stored on it. This capability aligns well with the DLZ stage alignment possibilities into multiple regions, as shown previously in Figure 4.13.

There are numerous ways to access data on your ADLS container. One method is to mount a DBFS path to it by using the following snippet:

```
dbutils.fs.mount
(
  source = "wasbs://<container>@<account>.blob.core.windows.net",
  mount_point = "/mnt/<mount-name>",
  extra_configs =
   {
     "fs.azure.account.key.<account>.blob.core.windows.net":dbutils.secrets
         .get(scope = "<scope-name>", key = "<key-name>")
   }
)
```

The mounting procedure requires an Azure Key Vault (AKV) secret. AKV was introduced in Chapter 1 and will be covered in detail in Chapter 8.

The other way to access your data on ADLS is to use the following snippet, which stores the Azure Storage Access key in the Spark configuration file. This isn't something you might feel comfortable doing, but it might be helpful during development activities. You can avoid doing this with AKV, which is the recommended approach.

```
spark.conf.set("fs.azure.account.key.<account>.blob.core.windows.net",
               "4jRwk0Ho7LB+KHS9WevW7yuZP+AKrr1FbWbQ==")
```

Note that the previous snippet should not have a line break, and the random characters are the Azure Storage account Access key.

The last approach discussed here is to add the following snippet to your Advanced options ➢ Spark configuration, like you did in Exercise 3.14. Doing this will apply the endpoint and credentials to the cluster at startup, making it available with no manual intervention.

```
fs.azure.account.key.<account>.blob.core.windows.net <access-key>
```

Then you can access the content as follows. Figure 4.40 shows the results.

```
df = spark.read. \
  parquet("wasbs://<container>@<account>.blob.core.windows
.net/<directory-name>")
print(df.count())
display(df.limit(10))
```

This flexibility means that you can directly access any ADLS container that contains raw files. Once the Raw Files are transformed, you can then store them in cleansed data or business data directories, containers, or storage accounts.

FIGURE 4.40 Storing raw data in Azure Databricks

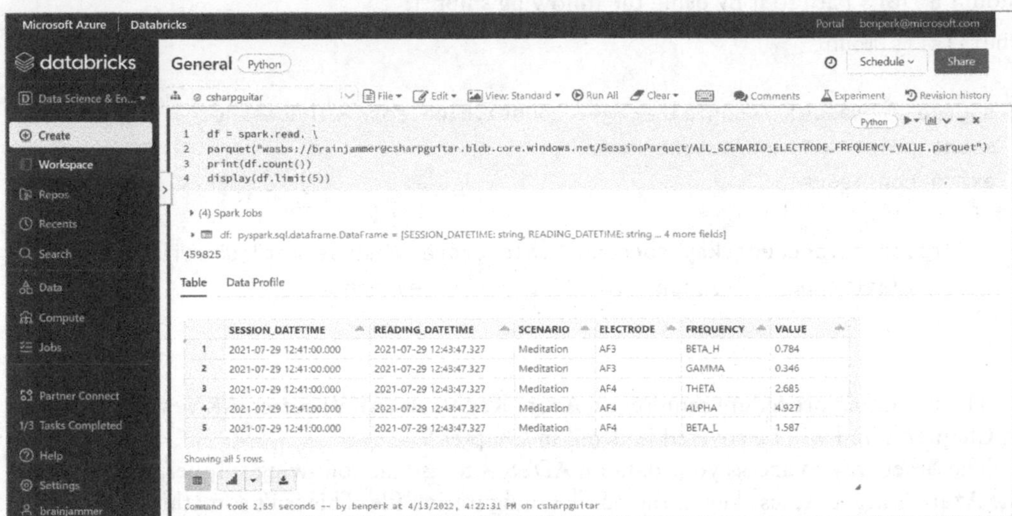

Storing Data Using Azure HDInsight

Like most other Azure Big Data analytics products, an Azure Storage account is provisioned along with the compute nodes and platform. Azure HDInsight is no different in this respect. When you provision an Azure HDInsight cluster, the selected Azure storage account contains the default filesystem. The storage account defaults to LRS and is intended for storing job history and logs, does not support the Premium tier (only up to Standard), and is not recommended for storing business data. That storing business data on the default filesystem is not recommended means you need an alternative solution. The recommended solution is to create a separate container or storage account. There are three options for storing and accessing data from an Azure HDInsight cluster (see Figure 4.41).

The data stored on an Azure Storage account created along with the provisioning of the Azure HDInsight cluster is accessible from both the head and worker nodes. When you `ssh` onto a node, the filesystem that is a container on the default storage account is accessible using the following URI:

```
hdfs://<nodename>/<path>
```

Any additional container, which exists within the default storage account, is accessible using the following syntax. This same syntax is used for accessing publicly accessible storage endpoints. Azure Storage endpoints that are publicly accessible would allow anonymous listing of containers and reading of the blobs contained within them. This scenario is reflected in Figure 4.41 as "unlinked." The first snippet is for accessing blob data, and the second is for accessing an account that is supporting a hierarchical namespace like ADLS.

```
wasbs://<container>@<account>.blob.core.windows.net/<path>
abfs://<container>@<account>.dfs.core.windows.net/<path>
```

FIGURE 4.41 Storing data using Azure HDInsight

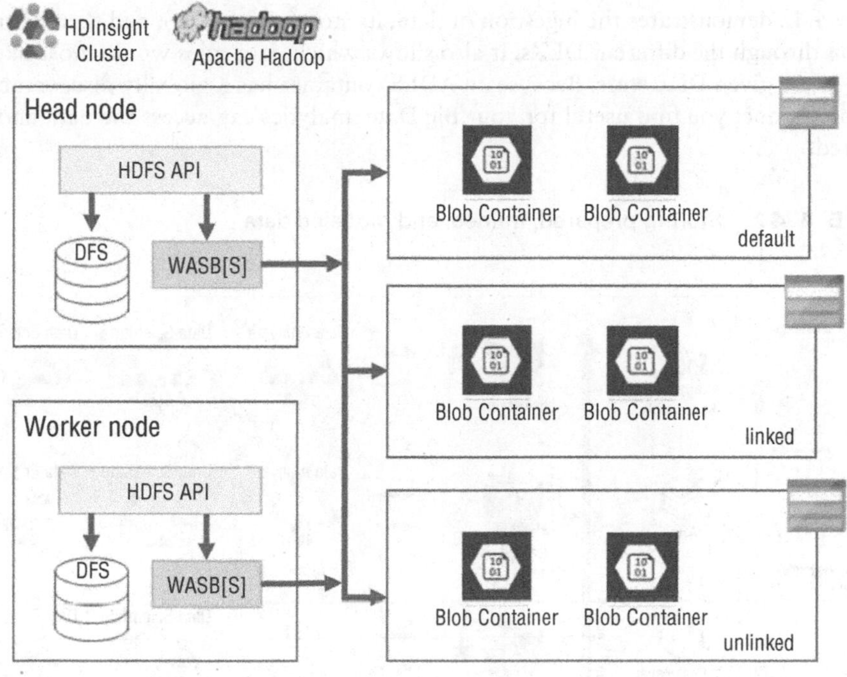

It is possible to access an additional Azure storage account secured by a SAS key or managed identities (MI), although the details of how to configure this aspect of an Azure HDInsight cluster are outside the scope of this book. However, it is very similar to the configuration required for an Azure Databricks cluster, in that you need to add a key-value pair to the configuration of the Azure HDInsight cluster—something like the following syntax, which uses a SAS key:

```
fs.azure.sas.<container>.<account>.blob.core.windows.net <SAS-key>
```

There are many options for storing data securely, including redundancy and aligning the storage structure with DLZ staging principles. Keep in mind that it is important to keep the storage accounts in the same region as the cluster to reduce costs and that the Azure storage account can be modified to use GRS or RA-GRS replication. Note, also, the associated costs of this replication and make sure your business requirements justify the potentially significant amount.

Storing Prepared, Trained, and Modeled Data

All data, regardless of the Big Data stage it is in, must be stored. The data not yet ingested into the pipeline is stored someplace too, but not yet on Azure. You can use Azure products like Azure Stream Analytics, Event Hubs, Apache Spark, Azure Databricks, and Azure Synapse Analytics to handle the ingestion of data onto the Azure platform. As the data is passed through any of those products, it finds its way into your data lake, which is most commonly an ADLS container.

Figure 4.42 demonstrates the ingestion of data, its storage on ADLS, and then its transformation through the different DLZs. It also shows which data roles would most likely use the data in the given DLZ state. Because an ADLS container has a globally discoverable endpoint, any product you find useful for your Big Data analytics can access the data and use it as required.

FIGURE 4.42 Storing prepared, trained, and modeled data

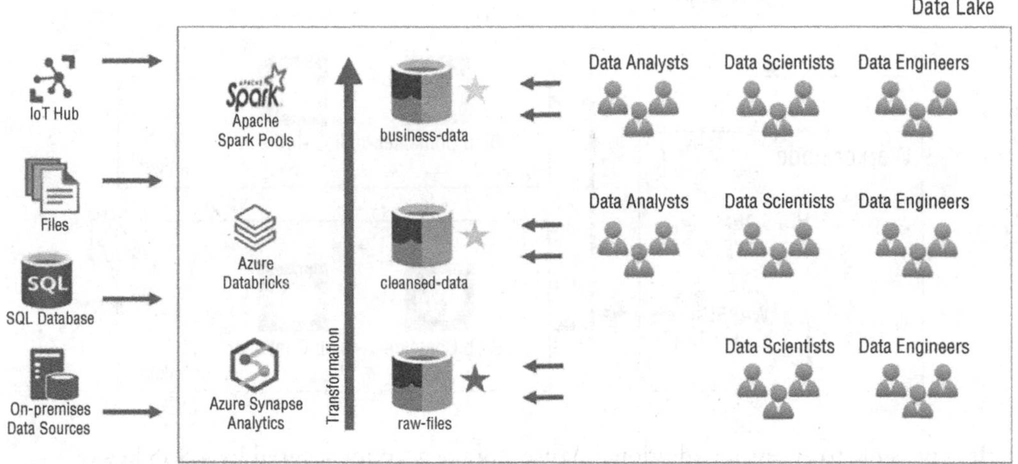

Summary

In this chapter you learned about the difference between physical and logical data storage structures, including concepts such as compression, partitioning, and sharding, which help to improve performance. Adhering to privacy compliance and reducing storage costs were also discussed. You loaded a lot of data into an ADLS container and ingested it into an Azure Synapse Analytics workspace. Then you manipulated the data using the Develop hub, SQL pools, and Spark pools. One of the highlights is that you created your first Azure Synapse pipeline and loaded data from an Azure SQL into the raw DLZ of your ADLS container. Slowly changing dimension (SCD) tables, fact tables, and external tables should all be very clear in their purpose, constructs, and use cases.

The serving layer is one of the three components of the lambda architecture, the other two being the batch layer, which is discussed in Chapter 6, and the streaming layer, which is discussed in Chapter 7. You learned that the serving layer receives data from both the cold path (i.e., the streaming layer) and the hot path (i.e., the batch layer), and both are available to data consumers who have different expectations of the data's state. Finally, you read about how data can be stored and accessed across DLZs from Azure Databricks and Azure HDInsight. Because all Azure storage products have a globally identifiable endpoint, any product you use for performing data analytics can access, read, and process the data stored on it.

Exam Essentials

Physical vs. logical storage. The difference between physical and logical storage is that the former involves objects you can touch, while the latter is of virtual construct. Physical storage structures include objects like a hard disk or a tape containing a backup. Logical storage structures include extents, segments, and tablespaces, which reside on the physical disk.

Compression, partitioning, and sharding. The amount of storage consumed on Azure is what drives the cost. Therefore, the less storage you consume, the less you pay. Compression is an effective way to reduce size and cost. The most common codecs include ZIP, TAR, and GZ. *Partitioning* refers to vertical partitioning, whereas *sharding* refers to horizontal partitioning. Breaking a table into many tables based on an attribute like the sequential value of `READING_ID` is an example of vertical partitioning, whereas breaking it into `SCENARIO` is an example of horizontal partitioning. Vertical partitions contain a subset of fields that horizontal partitions split into rows, from one table into different tables.

Slowly changing dimension. Slowly changing dimension (SCD) tables enable you to maintain a history of the changes to your data. As you progress along types 1, 2, 3 and 6, the greater amount of data history is available. Type 6 SCD is a combination of all capabilities found in types 1, 2, and 3. Temporal tables are supported on Azure SQL and SQL server but not on a SQL pool in Azure Synapse Analytics. Temporal tables target the Type 4 SCD pattern.

The serving layer and the star schema. The serving layer is where consumers retrieve data. It is fed by both the batch and streaming layers, which together make up the lambda architecture. The transformation that happens in and around the serving layer requires reference tables, which are referred to as dimension tables in the Big Data context. The star schema can be visualized by a fact table, which is surrounded by and references four to five dimension tables. The table relationships appear in a star pattern.

Metadata. Without a way to organize and structure data, it is difficult, if not impossible, to find value in it. A data file that contains a bunch of numbers or a database table that has a generic name or generic column names has little to no value. Many define metadata as data about data. Valid table names, schemas, views, file names, and file directory structures all provide some insights into what the data within them means.

Review Questions

Many questions can have more than a single answer. Please select all choices that are true.

1. Which codecs are supported on Azure data analytics products?
   - A. ZIP
   - B. Parquet
   - C. TAR
   - D. TAR.JZ
2. Which of the following statements about data partitioning are true?
   - A. It decreases query performance.
   - B. It improves query performance.
   - C. It reduces storage cost.
   - D. It improves data discoverability.
3. You can make data stored on ADLS redundant across two regions by doing which of the following?
   - A. Enabling LRS on your ADLS container
   - B. Enabling GRS on your Azure storage account
   - C. Enabling GRS on your ADLS container
   - D. Enabling ZRS on your Azure storage account
4. Which of the following is a table distribution type?
   - A. Hash
   - B. Round-robin
   - C. Dedicated
   - D. Replicated
5. Which of the following statements about temporal tables are true?
   - A. They are fully supported when you are using a dedicated SQL pool.
   - B. They are fully supported when you are using a Spark pool.
   - C. They have columns in the main table that store change history.
   - D. None of the above.
6. A Type 1 SCD table contains which of the following columns?
   - A. `INSERT_DATE`
   - B. `IS_CURRENT` (a column with a flag that identifies the current version of the row)
   - C. A surrogate key
   - D. `MODIFIED_DATE`

7. A Type 3 SCD table contains which of the following columns?
   - **A.** A surrogate key
   - **B.** A column containing the original value
   - **C.** `IS_CURRENT` (a column with a flag that identifies the current version of the row)
   - **D.** `COUNTER` (a value containing the number of times the row has been changed)

8. Which of the following statements concerning external tables are true?
   - **A.** Use CETAS when targeting a serverless SQL pool.
   - **B.** CTAS is recommended when targeting a dedicated SQL pool.
   - **C.** They are most useful for loading data contained in a file into a table, which can then be queried using SQL syntax.
   - **D.** They are most useful for loading data contained in a database into a Parquet file, which can then be queried using a DataFrame.

9. What is metadata?
   - **A.** A small dataset that represents the entire data content
   - **B.** A virtual reality 3D imaging of big data
   - **C.** Data about the data
   - **D.** A file's name, creation date, modified date, size, and extension

10. Which of the following are common data landing zones (DLZ)?
    - **A.** Raw
    - **B.** Bronze
    - **C.** Nickel
    - **D.** Consumable

PART III

Develop Data Processing

Transform, Manage, and Prepare Data

EXAM DP-203 OBJECTIVES COVERED IN THIS CHAPTER:

- ✓ Ingest and transform data

WHAT YOU WILL LEARN IN THIS CHAPTER:

- ✓ Transformation and data management concepts
- ✓ Data modeling and usage

Ingesting data and then storing it successfully, as complicated as it is, is only the beginning stage of a Big Data solution. The variety, volume, and velocity of that incoming data and its ingestion are manageable using the techniques and products discussed so far in this book. Now what? The different file types, their different content, and the various ingress frequencies are scenarios that now must be managed and transformed. The transformation into a small set of data segments, or even better, a single dataset used for gaining business insights, is the ultimate objective. Getting from that raw mass of varied data to your objective requires great knowledge, creativity, and some very sophisticated tools. But above all else, you need a plan and a defined process.

Ingest and Transform Data

Before diving into the process, which you have already seen in Figure 2.30, first you need a definition of transformation. A few examples of transformation that you have experienced so far were in Exercise 4.7 and Exercise 4.8. In Exercise 4.7 you changed the structure of brain wave readings from CSV into Parquet format. In Exercise 4.8 you converted a `DateTime` data type value from epoch to a more human readable format. Other types of transformation, covered later, have to do with cleansing, splitting, shredding, encoding, decoding, normalizing, and denormalizing data. Any activity you perform on the data in your data lake or any other datastore that results in a change is considered a transformation. Transformations may be big, small, low impact, or high impact. In some scenarios, you might receive data that is already in great form and requires minimal to no transformations. In that case, all you need to do is validate it and move it to the next DLZ. In other cases, the data you process may contain unexpected or partial data types, or be corrupted, which often requires manual interventions, like requesting a new file, manually modifying the file or data column, and retriggering the pipeline.

From a transformation process perspective, it is important to cover the different stages of the Big Data pipeline. There are many descriptions of what constitutes the different stages of the Big Data pipeline. Terms like produce, capture, acquire, ingest, store, process, prepare, manipulate, train, model, analyze, explore, extract, serve, visualize, present, report, use, and monetize are all valid for describing different Big Data stages. There are three important points to consider when choosing the terminology for describing your process. The first point is to describe what your definition of each stage means in totality. It must be described to the point where others understand what your intention is and what the inputs, actions, and results of the stage comprise. For example, serve, visualize, and report are very similar and, in many cases, can be used interchangeably. However, you could also consider them totally different stages based on your definition. You have great freedom in defining this process, so long as you abide by the second point.

The second point is that some of the stages need to flow in a certain order. For example, you cannot perform data modeling or visualization before the ingestion stage. There is, however, the storage stage, which is a bit challenging to represent because it is required and is referenced from many other stages; so, where does it go in your process diagram? Again, you have the liberty of choosing that, but make sure to remember the first point as you make that decision. You do need to consider the fact that after each stage the data is most likely enriched or transformed, some of which you might want to illustrate and call out specifically in your process.

Finally, the third point is to determine which products and tools you will use to perform each stage of the Big Data pipeline. At this point you should have a good idea of available data analytics tools and what they can do. You should also know that some features overlap among the available products and features. As you design your process and define what happens within your chosen stages, locate a product that contains all the features necessary to fulfill the objectives of that stage. It makes sense to have as few products, libraries, operating systems, languages, and datastores as possible. Why? Because it's easier that way. It is challenging, but not impossible to know Java, Scala, C#, and Python or Azure HDInsight, Azure Databricks, and Azure Synapse Analytics. But if you can specialize in a specific group of technologies, you have a greater chance of long-term success.

Figure 5.1 shows one possible Big Data pipeline stage process.

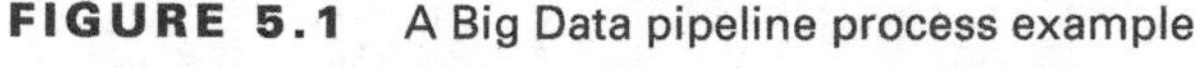

FIGURE 5.1 A Big Data pipeline process example

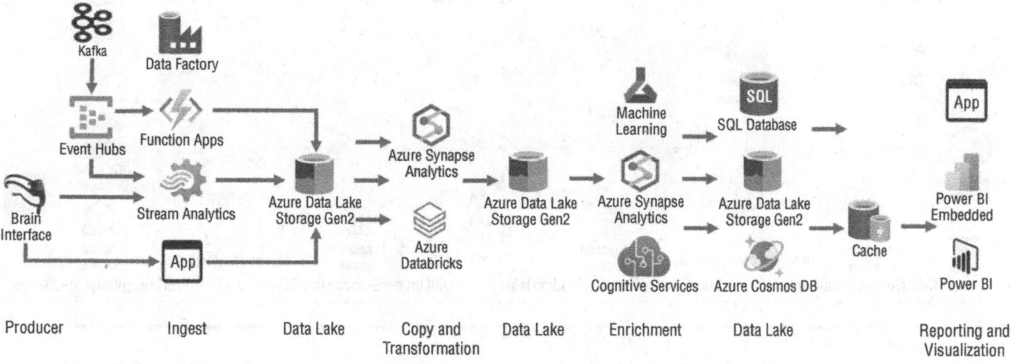

The illustration attempts to clarify the point that there is no single definition of what a Big Data pipeline process looks like. The design is completely up to your requirements; the sequence and products you choose are the key to a successful solution. As you proceed into the following sections, know that the transformation of your data can take place using numerous Azure products. It is up to you to decide which ones to use for your given circumstances.

Transform Data Using Azure Synapse Pipelines

It does provide some benefit to understand the structure of the data you must ingest, transform, and progress through the other Big Data pipeline stages. It is helpful to know because as you make decisions or conclusions about why data is stored in a certain way or what a column value is, knowing how the data was formed gives you a basis for coming to your conclusion. The data used in many examples up to now has been brain waves, which were captured from a BCI manufactured by SDK and stored as both JSON and CSV files on a local workstation. You can find the code that captured and stored that data on GitHub at `https://github.com/benperk/ADE`, in the `Chapter02/Source Code` directory, in a file named `BrainReadingToJSON.cs`. The JSON-formatted brainjammer brain waves were then uploaded into an Azure SQL database, like the one you created in Exercise 2.1. The code that performed that action is located in the same location as the previous source code file but is named `JSONToAzureSQL.cs`. The result of the storage in Azure SQL resulted in a relational data structure like the one shown in Figure 2.2.

The brain wave readings were ingested in Chapter 4, "The Storage of Data," specifically in Exercise 4.13. For reference, Figure 5.2 illustrates that ingestion. Note that although the data existed in a relational Azure SQL database, the data source could have existed in any location and in any format. The objective of ingestion in this scenario was to retrieve it from its current location and pull it into Synapse Analytics and the data lake for transformation. As you may recall, no transformation of the data took place in this set of pipeline activities.

FIGURE 5.2 Azure Synapse Analytics—ingesting Brainjammer brain waves

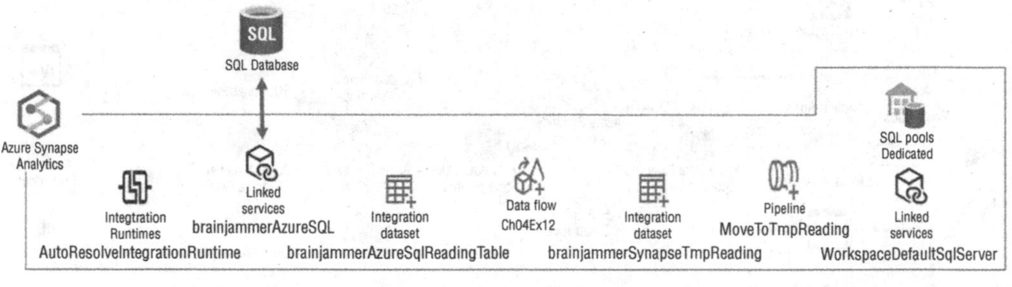

This activity could have also been considered preparing the data for transformation, i.e., a prepare or preparation stage. The term *ingestion* often implies a streaming scenario. In a streaming scenario the data is being ingested continuously in real time, in contrast to this scenario, where data already exists in some external datastore and gets pulled, pushed, moved, or copied into a data lake on the Azure platform. Again, it depends on how you define your process.

The way the data is initially captured and stored has a lot to do with the complexity and effort required to transform it. But you also need to know how the data should look after the transformation, which is sometimes difficult to define at the early stages. When you are doing a transformation on a dataset for the first time, you should expect to need numerous iterations and progress through numerous versions of your transformation logic. The final data structure needs to be in a state where business insights can be learned from it. Consider the way the brainjammer brain waves were stored on the Azure SQL database. They were stored in a classic data relational model, with primary and foreign keys between numerous reference tables. And after much thought, the final data format, which at the time seems to give the best chance of learning from it, is what you will see and implement in Exercise 5.1. The transformation is only a single SQL query and CTAS statement, so it is not an extensive transformation. However, you will certainly come across some very complicated scenarios. Those scenarios are the reason for the many schema modifiers (refer to Table 4.4) and data flow transformation features (refer to Table 4.5) available for managing and performing such transformations. After this initial transformation, when some exploratory analysis takes place, you might uncover some new angle to approach and transform the data, to get even more benefit from it. For starters, complete the Exercise 5.1.

EXERCISE 5.1

Transform Data Using Azure Synapse Pipeline

1. Log in to the Azure portal at `https://portal.azure.com` ➢ navigate to the Azure Synapse Analytics workspace you created in Exercise 3.3 ➢ on the Overview blade, click the Open link in the Open Synapse Studio tile ➢ select the Manage hub ➢ select SQL Pools from the menu list ➢ start the dedicated SQL pool ➢ select the Data hub ➢ expand the SQL database ➢ expand the dedicated SQL pool ➢ expand the Tables folder ➢ and then confirm that the dimension tables you created and populated in Exercise 4.13 are present. Refer to Figure 4.35 for the list.

2. Select the Develop hub ➢ hover over SQL Scripts ➢ click the ellipse (. . .) ➢ select New SQL Script ➢ select your dedicated SQL pool from the Connect To drop-down list box ➢ and then remove the `[brainwaves].[FactREADING]` table by adding and executing the following SQL command to the SQL script window:

```
DROP TABLE [brainwaves].[FactREADING]
```

3. Create a stored procedure named `uspCreateAndPopulateFactReading` (the syntax is in the directory `Chapter05/Ch05Ex01` on GitHub here at `https://github.com/benperk/ADE`) ➢ place the SQL syntax into the SQL script window ➢ click the Run button ➢ name the SQL script (I used **Ch05Ex01**) ➢ and then click the Commit button to save the SQL script to the GitHub repository you linked to in Exercise 3.6.

EXERCISE 5.1 ***(continued)***

4. Select the Data hub ➢ select the Workspace tab ➢ expand the SQL Database folder ➢ expand your dedicated SQL pool ➢ expand the Programmability folder ➢ expand the Stored Procedures folder (you should see the just created stored procedure) ➢ right-click the stored procedure ➢ select Add to Pipeline ➢ select Existing Pipeline ➢ click the pipeline you created in step 8 of Exercise 4.13 (`IngestTmpReading`) ➢ click the Add button ➢ on the General tab enter a name for the SQL pool Stored Procedure activity (I used **CreatePopulateFactReading**) ➢ and then select the Setting tab and review the configuration.

5. Notice the small rectangle on the right middle of the `MoveToTmpReading` Data Flow activity ➢ click, hold, and drag it over to the `CreatePopulateFactReading` SQL pool Stored Procedure activity ➢ release the mouse button ➢ and then click Commit to save your changes. The pipeline should resemble Figure 5.3.

FIGURE 5.3 Azure Synapse Analytics—transformating Brainjammer brain waves

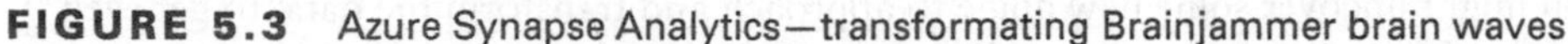

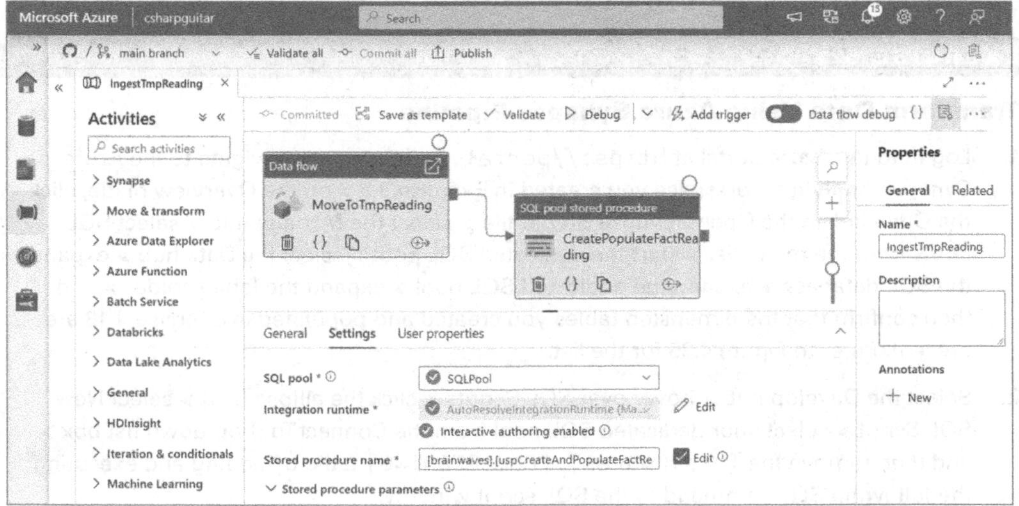

6. Click the Validate button ➢ click the Publish button ➢ review the proposed changes ➢ click OK ➢ click the Add Trigger button ➢ select Trigger Now ➢ click OK ➢ select the Monitor hub ➢ select the Pipeline Runs menu item ➢ and then view the progress. You will see something similar to Figure 5.4. Note that you might need to click the Refresh button to see the changes.

7. Execute the following queries, and then confirm the data was ingested, transformed, and moved as expected:

FIGURE 5.4 Azure Synapse Analytics—monitoring Brainjammer brain wave transformations

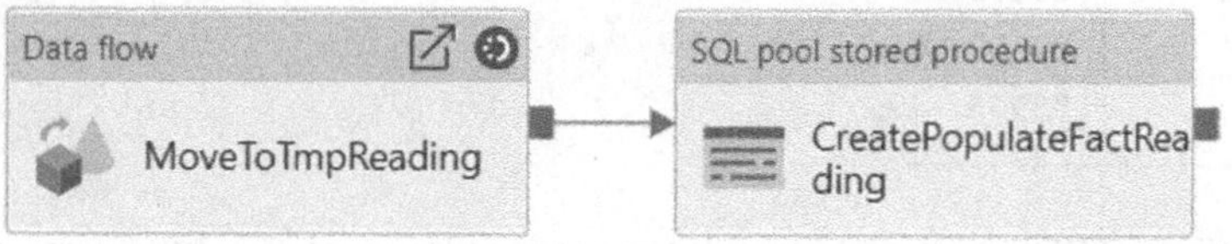

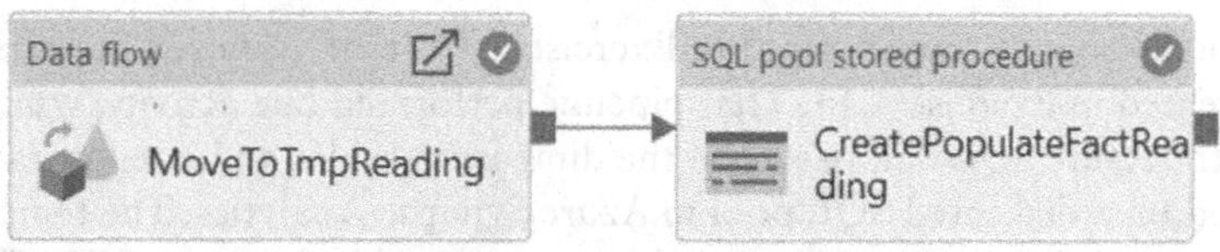


```
SELECT COUNT(*) AS [COUNT] FROM [brainwaves].[FactREADING]

+--------+
| COUNT  |
+--------+
| 459825 |
+--------+

SELECT COUNT(*) AS [COUNT] FROM [brainwaves].[TmpREADING]

+--------+
| COUNT  |
+--------+
| 459825 |
+--------+

SELECT SCENARIO, COUNT(*) AS [COUNT] FROM [brainwaves].[FactREADING]
GROUP BY SCENARIO
ORDER BY [COUNT] DESC

+----------------+--------+
| SCENARIO       | COUNT  |
+----------------+--------+
| ClassicalMusic | 264600 |
| PlayingGuitar  | 36575  |
| Meditation     | 32150  |
| WorkNoEmail    | 27200  |
| WorkMeeting    | 25350  |
```

EXERCISE 5.1 *(continued)*

```
| MetalMusic      | 25175  |
| TikTok          | 24800  |
| FlipChart       | 23975  |
+----------------+--------+
```

8. Pause the dedicated SQL pool and consider renaming the pipeline with a more appropriate name (for example, `IngestTransformBrainwaveReadings`).

One action you may have noticed in Exercise 5.1 is that you used the existing pipeline that you created in Exercise 4.13. That pipeline performed one activity, which was to copy data from the Azure SQL database into the dimension tables and a temporary table that were created on a dedicated SQL pool in Azure Synapse Analytics. The temporary table `tmpREADING` had the same structure as the `READING` table on Azure SQL. The objective now is to get the data on the `tmpREADING` table to map into the `FactREADING` table. This was achieved by adding a SQL pool stored procedure to the pipeline that ran after a successful data copy. Note that there also exists a Stored Procedure activity in the General folder that is not the same as a SQL pool stored procedure. Figure 5.5 shows the difference.

FIGURE 5.5 Azure Synapse Analytics—SQL pool vs. a linked service stored procedure

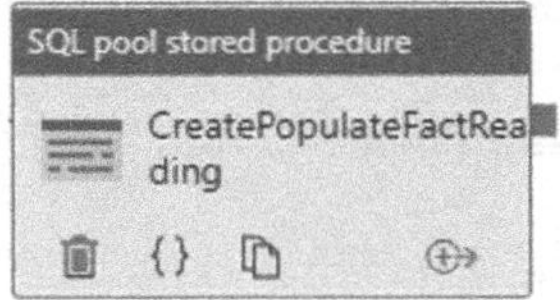

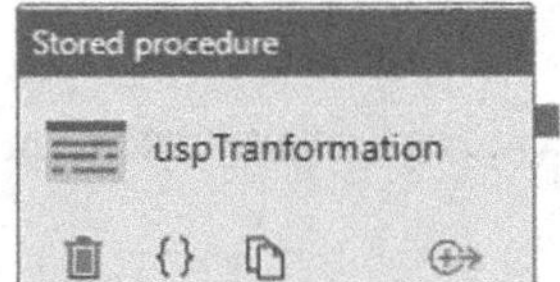

The primary difference between the two is that the SQL pool stored procedure targets a dedicated SQL pool directly, whereas the other requires a linked service. Here is what the stored procedure code looks like:

```
CREATE PROCEDURE brainwaves.uspCreateAndPopulateFactReading
AS
 CREATE TABLE [brainwaves].[FactREADING]
 WITH
 (
  CLUSTERED COLUMNSTORE INDEX,
  DISTRIBUTION = HASH ([FREQUENCY])
 )
 AS
```

```
SELECT  se.SESSION_DATETIME, r.READING_DATETIME,
        s.SCENARIO, e.ELECTRODE, f.FREQUENCY, r.[VALUE]
FROM    [brainwaves].[DimSESSION] se, [brainwaves].[TmpREADING] r,
        [brainwaves].[DimSCENARIO] s, [brainwaves].[DimELECTRODE] e,
        [brainwaves].[DimFREQUENCY] f
WHERE   r.SESSION_ID = se.SESSION_ID AND se.SCENARIO_ID = s.SCENARIO_ID
        AND r.ELECTRODE_ID = e.ELECTRODE_ID AND r.FREQUENCY_ID =
            f.FREQUENCY_ID;
```

The stored procedure code creates a fact table with a hash distribution type on the frequency column. Remember that the values of frequencies can be `THETA`, `ALPHA`, `BETA_L`, `BETA_H`, and `GAMMA`. The CTAS SQL statement uses the dimension tables to convert the numeric representations of the scenario, electrode, and frequency into their actual friendly, easily identifiable names.

It is possible to learn from even the simple queries you ran in step 7 of the Exercise 5.1. The two queries that selected the count from the `tmpREADING` and `FactREADING` tables are useful to make sure the query that populated them includes the expected values. In this scenario you would expect the number of rows in each table to be the same. The second query was unexpected and triggered some actions to determine why there were so many more brainjammer brain wave readings for the `ClassicalMusic` scenario versus the others. The data was skewed in the direction of that specific scenario, and the reason for this skew must be found. Recall from Figure 2.19 how a skew is generally illustrated. The following SQL query resulted in the reason for the skew:

```
SELECT s.SCENARIO, COUNT(*) AS [COUNT]
FROM [brainwaves].[DimSESSION] se, [brainwaves].[DimSCENARIO] s
WHERE se.SCENARIO_ID = s.SCENARIO_ID
GROUP BY SCENARIO
ORDER BY [COUNT] DESC

+----------------+--------+
| SCENARIO       | COUNT  |
+----------------+--------+
| ClassicalMusic | 10     |
| PlayingGuitar  | 1      |
| Meditation     | 1      |
| WorkNoEmail    | 1      |
| WorkMeeting    | 1      |
| MetalMusic     | 1      |
| TikTok         | 1      |
| FlipChart      | 1      |
+----------------+--------+
```

It turns out the brainjammer brain wave data stored in the JSON files had not been completely parsed and loaded into the Azure SQL database. Missing sessions turn out to be the cause of the skew leaning heavily toward the `ClassicalMusic` scenario. You can see that there are 10 sessions for the `ClassicalMusic` scenario and only one for the others. In this case the data owner responsible for the data loading procedure was contacted, and the complete set of data was uploaded. Perform the same exercise using all the data available from all the sessions.

If you could not upload all the JSON files using the source code in file `JSONToAzureSQL.cs`, located in the `Chapter02/Source Code` directory, you can instead download the compressed database backup from the `BrainwaveData/bacpac` directory on GitHub at `https://github.com/benperk/ADE`.

You can download the ZIP file, extract the `.bacpac` file, and then import it into your own Azure SQL server. The credentials for the database backup are `benperk` for the server admin login and `bra!njamm3r` for the password. After importing the `.bacpac` file, consider rerunning Exercise 5.1.

Transform Data Using Azure Data Factory

The capabilities for achieving most activities in Azure Data Factory (ADF) are also available in Azure Synapse Analytics. Unless you have a need or requirement to use ADF, you should use the go-forward tool Azure Synapse Analytics instead. In any case, the current DP-203 exam has a requirement for this scenario. Therefore, perform Exercise 5.2, where you will extract data from an Azure Synapse Analytics SQL pool and transform the data structure into CSV and Parquet files.

EXERCISE 5.2

Transform Data Using Azure Data Factory

1. Log in to the Azure portal at `https://portal.azure.com` ➢ navigate to the Azure Data Factory Studio you created in Exercise 3.10 ➢ on the Overview blade, click the Open link in the Open Azure Data Factory Studio tile ➢ select the Manage hub ➢ select the Linked Services menu item ➢ select the + New link ➢ create a linked service (in my example, `BrainjammerAzureSynapse`) for your Azure Synapse Analytics dedicated SQL pool (make sure it is running) ➢ and then, if required, review Exercise 3.11, where you created a linked service in ADF. The configuration should resemble Figure 5.6.

FIGURE 5.6 Azure Data Factory Synapse—linked service

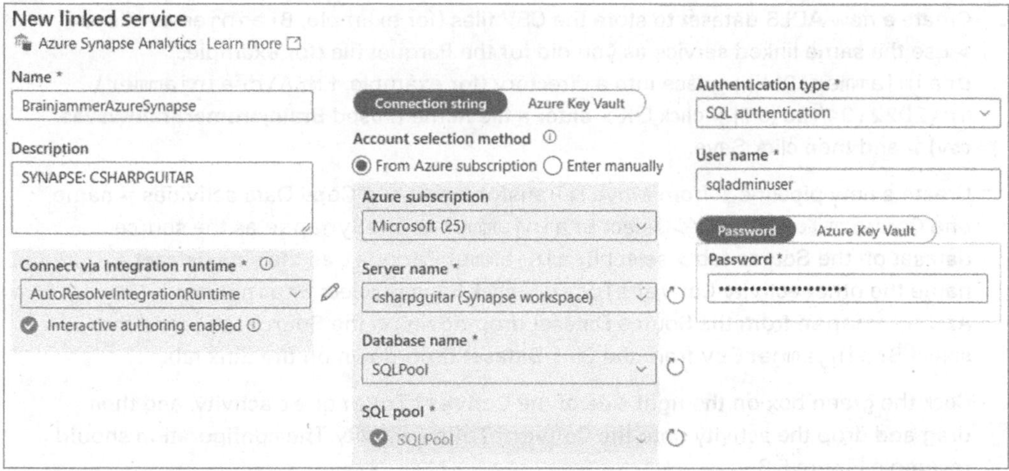

2. Create another linked service (for example, `BrainjammerADLS`) to the Azure storage account that contains the ADLS container you created in Exercise 3.1.
3. Select the Author hub ➢ create a new ADLS dataset to store the Parquet files (for example, `BrainjammerParquet`) ➢ use the just created linked service (for example, `BrainjammerADLS`) ➢ select a path to store the files (for example, `EMEA\brainjammer\in\2022\04\26\17`) ➢ click OK ➢ enter a file name (I used **BrainjammerBrainwaves.parquet**) ➢ and then create a new Azure Synapse dataset that retrieves data from the `[brainwaves].[FactREADING]` table (for example, `BrainjammerAzureSynapse`). The configuration should resemble Figure 5.7.

FIGURE 5.7 Azure Data Factory—Synapse dataset

EXERCISE 5.2 *(continued)*

4. Create a new ADLS dataset to store the CSV files (for example, `BrainjammerCsv`) ➢ use the same linked service as you did for the Parquet file (for example, `BrainjammerADLS`) ➢ place into a directory (for example, `EMEA\brainjammer\in\2022\04\26\17`) ➢ click OK ➢ enter a file name (I used **BrainjammerBrainwaves.csv**) ➢ and then click Save.

5. Create a new pipeline ➢ from Move & Transform add two Copy Data activities ➢ name one `ConvertToParquet` ➢ select `BrainjammerAzureSynapse` as the source dataset on the Source tab ➢ select `BrainjammerParquet` as the sink dataset ➢ name the other activity `ConvertToCsv` ➢ click Save ➢ select `BrainjammerAzureSynapse` from the Source Dataset drop-down on the Source tab ➢ and then select `BrainjammerCsv` from the Sink Dataset drop-down on the Sink tab.

6. Click the green box on the right side of the `ConvertToParquet` activity, and then drag and drop the activity onto the `ConvertToCsv` activity. The configuration should resemble Figure 5.8.

FIGURE 5.8 Azure Data Factory—Synapse pipeline

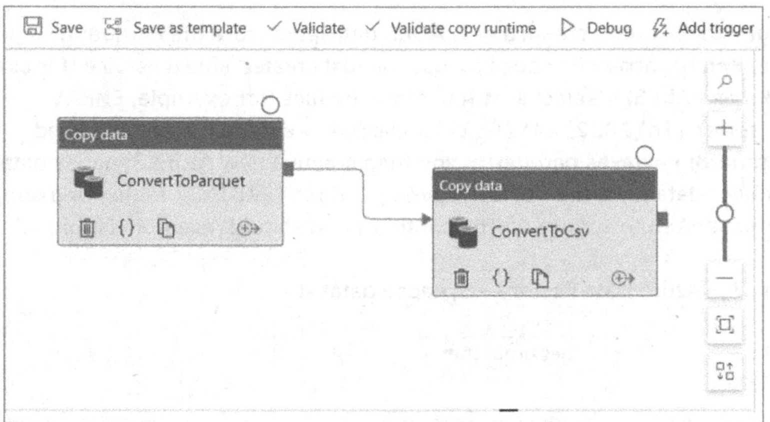

7. Click the Save All button to store your changes on the linked GitHub repository ➢ click the Publish button ➢ click the Add Trigger button ➢ select Trigger Now ➢ select the Monitor hub ➢ select Pipeline Runs to view the status ➢ view the files in the ADLS container directory ➢ and then stop the dedicated SQL pool.

Figure 5.9 shows a more elaborate illustration of what you just implemented. You created a linked service to an Azure Synapse SQL pool, which is used by a dataset as the source of the data to be transformed. The data retrieval exists in the `[brainwaves].[FactREADING]` table on the dedicated SQL pool. You also created two datasets for output sinks: one in the Parquet format and another in CSV-delimited text. Those two datasets use the linked service bound to your ADLS container.

FIGURE 5.9 Azure Data Factory Synapse—pipeline transformation

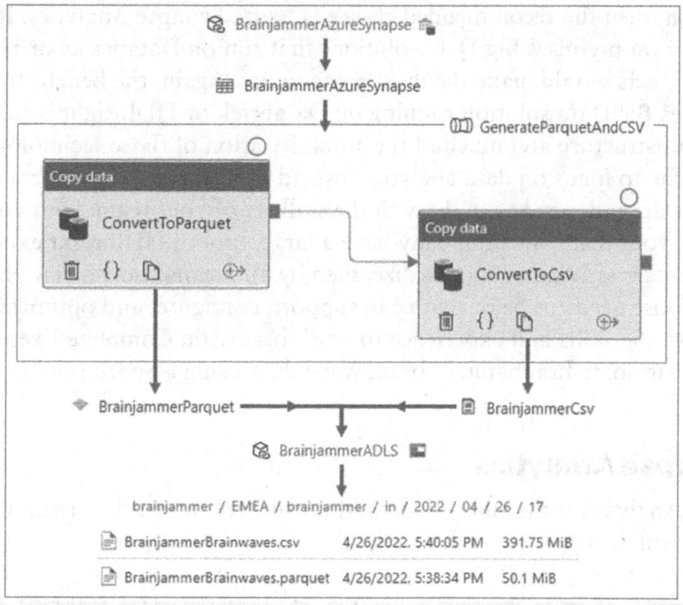

The ADLS container contains a directory that is useful in terms of storing data logically, in that you can conclude information from the names of the file and folders. This logical structure helps with archiving unnecessary data and data content discovery. To execute the transformation, you created a pipeline that contained two activities. The first activity pulls data from the source, performs the transformation, and places it into the sink in the configured Parquet format. The second activity performs the same but formats the output into CSV format. Saving, publishing, and triggering the pipeline results in the files being written to the expected location in your ADLS container data lake. You might notice that the resulting files are large, which could be because there are more than 4.5 million rows in the `[brainwaves].[FactREADING]` table, which are extracted and stored into the files. There is quite a difference between the size of Parquet and CSV files, even though they both contain the same data. Remember that a dedicated SQL pool runs most optimally when file sizes are between 100 MB and 10 GB; therefore, in this case the size is in the zone. However, it is recommended to use Parquet versus CSV in all possible cases. Processing files on a Spark pool has an optimal file range between 256 MB and 100 GB, so from a CSV perspective it is good. But from the recommended Parquet file format perspective, the data is on the small side, even with 4.5 million rows.

Transform Data Using Apache Spark

Apache Spark can be used in a few products running on Azure: Azure Synapse Analytics Spark pools, Azure Databrick Spark clusters, Azure HDInsight Spark clusters, and Azure Data Factory. The one you choose to work with depends on many things, but the two most important are the following. First, what is the current state of your Big Data solution? If you are starting fresh, then the recommended choice is Azure Synapse Analytics. If you already do some existing on-premises Big Data solutions that run on Databricks or HDInsight, then those Azure products would make the most sense to use. Again, the benefit from moving your on-premises Big Data solution running on Databrick or HDInsight is that Microsoft provides the infrastructure and much of the administration of those technologies, allowing you more time to focus on data analytics instead of keeping the platform running. The other important dependency has to do with the skill set of your team, your company, and yourself. If you, your team, and company have a large pool of HDInsight experience, or it is something you are striving to standardize, then by all means choose that platform. The product you choose needs to be one you can support, configure, and optimize, so choose the one you have the skills and experience to work best with. Complete Exercise 5.3, where you will transform some brainjammer brain wave data using a Spark pool in Azure Synapse Analytics.

Azure Synapse Analytics

Azure Synapse Analytics is the suite of tools Microsoft recommends for running Big Data on the Azure platform.

EXERCISE 5.3

Transform Data Using Apache Spark—Azure Synapse Analytics

1. Log in to the Azure portal at `https://portal.azure.com` ➢ navigate to the Azure Synapse Analytics workspace you created in Exercise 3.3 ➢ on the Overview blade, click the Open link in the Open Synapse Studio tile ➢ select the Manage hub ➢ select Apache Spark Pools from the menu list ➢ review the node size family ➢ review the size ➢ select the Develop hub ➢ hover over Data Flows ➢ click the ellipse (. . .) ➢ select New Data Flow ➢ enter an output stream name (I used **BrainwavesReading**) ➢ and then select the dataset you created earlier that retrieves data from the `[dbo].[READING]` table on your Azure SQL database. Review Exercise 4.13 and Figure 4.36 for further details of a similar dataset.

2. To add a sink, click the + on the lower-right corner of the Source module ➢ select Sink ➢ enter an output stream name (I used **brainjammerTmpReading**) ➢ select the + New link to the right of the Dataset drop-down list box ➢ choose ADLS ➢ choose Parquet ➢ enter a name (I used **BrainjammerBrainwavesTmpParquet**) ➢ select `WorkspaceDefaultStorage` from the Linked Service drop-down text box ➢ enable Interactive Authoring, if not already enabled ➢ select the folder icon to the right of the

File Path text boxes ➢ and then navigate to the location where you want to store the Parquet file, for example:

```
EMEA\brainjammer\in\2022\04\28\16
```

3. Leave the defaults ➢ click the OK button ➢ consider renaming the data flow (for example, Ch05Ex3) ➢ click the Commit button ➢ select the Integrate hub ➢ hover over the Pipelines group ➢ click the ellipse (. . .) ➢ select New Pipeline ➢ drag and drop a Data Flow activity from the Move & Transform Activities list ➢ on the General tab enter a name (I used **MoveToTmpReading**) ➢ select the Setting tab ➢ select the data flow you just created from the Data Flow drop-down list box ➢ consider renaming the pipeline (I used **IngestTransformBrainwaveReadingsSpark**) ➢ click the Commit button ➢ click the Validate button ➢ and then click Publish.
4. Select the Develop hub ➢ hover over Notebooks ➢ click the ellipse (. . .) ➢ select New Notebook ➢ select the Spark pool from the Attach To drop-down box ➢ and then enter the following PySpark code syntax:

```
%%pyspark
df = spark.read \
   .load('abfss://*@*.dfs.core.windows.net/../in/2022/04/28/16/*.parquet',
   format='parquet')
print("Total brainwave readings: " + str(df.distinct().count()))
df.createOrReplaceTempView("TmpREADING")
```

5. The complete PySpark syntax is in a file named `transformApacheSpark.txt`, in the directory `Chapter05/Ch05Ex03`, on GitHub at `https://github.com/benperk/ADE`. Enter the following snippet to load five reference tables required for transformation; these CSV files are from Exercise 4.13; see the directory `Chapter04/Ch04Ex12` on GitHub for instructions on how to get them.

```
dfMODE = spark.read \
  .load('abfss://*@*.dfs.core.windows.net/Tables/MODE.csv',
  format='csv', header=True)
dfMODE.createOrReplaceTempView("MODE")
dfELECTRODE = spark.read \
  .load('abfss://*@*.dfs.core.windows.net/Tables/ELECTRODE.csv',
  format='csv', header=True)
dfELECTRODE.createOrReplaceTempView("ELECTRODE")
dfFREQUENCY = spark.read \
  .load('abfss://*@*.dfs.core.windows.net/Tables/FREQUENCY.csv',
  format='csv', header=True)
dfFREQUENCY.createOrReplaceTempView("FREQUENCY")
dfSCENARIO = spark.read \
```

EXERCISE 5.3 ***(continued)***

```
  .load('abfss://*@*.dfs.core.windows.net/Tables/SCENARIO.csv',
  format='csv', header=True)
dfSCENARIO.createOrReplaceTempView("SCENARIO")
dfSESSION = spark.read \
  .load('abfss://*@*.dfs.core.windows.net/Tables/SESSIONALL.csv',
  format='csv', header=True)
dfSESSION.createOrReplaceTempView("SESSION")
```

6. Enter the following PySpark SQL syntax to transform the data into the preferred format:

```
dfREADING = sqlContext.sql("""
    SELECT  se.SESSION_DATETIME, r.READING_DATETIME,
            s.SCENARIO, e.ELECTRODE, f.FREQUENCY, r.VALUE
    FROM    SESSION se, TmpREADING r, SCENARIO s,
            ELECTRODE e, FREQUENCY f
    WHERE   r.SESSION_ID = se.SESSION_ID AND se.SCENARIO_ID = s.SCENARIO_ID
            AND r.ELECTRODE_ID = e.ELECTRODE_ID AND r.FREQUENCY_ID =
                f.FREQUENCY_ID
""")
```

7. Write the results to your ADLS data lake using the following snippet as an example. Note that there should be no line break in the path; it is broken for readability only.

```
dfREADING.write \
  .parquet(
    'abfss://*@*.dfs.core.windows.net/EMEA/brainjammer/out
                                                  /2022/04/28/17
                                                /BrainjammerBrainwavesSpark.parquet')
```

8. Consider renaming the notebook (for example, `Ch05Ex03`) ➢ click the Commit button ➢ click the Publish button ➢ select the Integrate Hub ➢ open the pipeline you created in step 3 (`IngestTransformBrainwaveReadingsSpark`) ➢ drag and drop a notebook from the Synapse group in the Activities pane onto the canvas ➢ provide a name (I used **TranformReadingsParquet**) ➢ on the Settings tab select the notebook you just created (`Ch05Ex03`) ➢ select your Spark pool ➢ click the square on the middle-right edge of the Data flow activity ➢ and then drag and drop it onto the Notebook activity. Figure 5.10 illustrates the pipeline configuration.

FIGURE 5.10 Transforming data using an Apache Spark Azure Synapse Spark pool

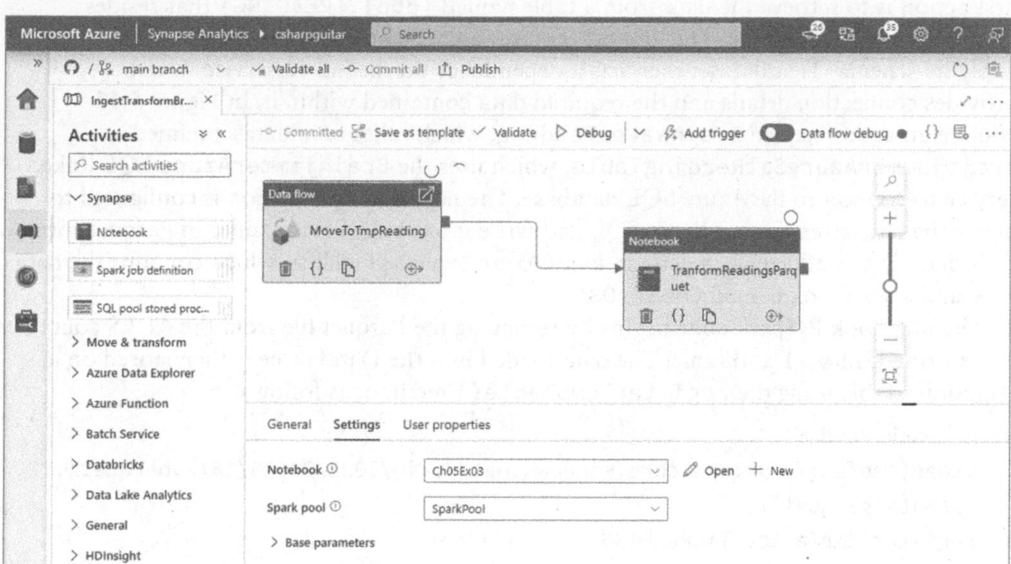

9. Click the Commit button ➢ click the Publish button ➢ select the Add Trigger menu option ➢ and then select Trigger Now. Once complete the publishing view the Parquet files in your ADLS data lake.

That was a long and complicated exercise, so congratulations if you got it all going. Figure 5.11 illustrates how what you just did all links together. After reviewing it, read on to further understand those steps, the features, and the code added to the notebook.

FIGURE 5.11 Transforming data using Apache Spark Azure Synapse Analytics

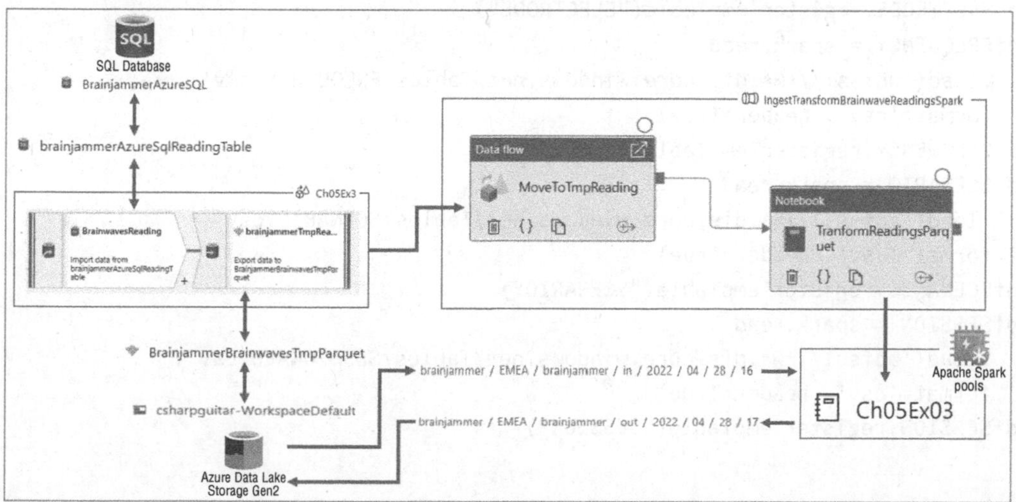

Exercise 5.3 begins with the creation of a data flow that performs two actions. The first action is to retrieve the data from a table named `[dbo].[READING]` that resides on an Azure SQL database. This import requires a dataset to hold the data and to apply its schema. That dataset then has a dependency on the linked service, which provides connection details and the required data contained within it. In Figure 5.11 you see an action named `BrainwavesReading`, which relies on a dataset named `brainjammerAzureSqlReadingTable`, which uses the `BrainjammerAzure` SQL linked service to connect to the Azure SQL database. The next data flow action is configured to ingest the data stream from Azure SQL and write it to an ADLS container in Parquet format. This data flow is added as an activity in an Azure Synapse Pipeline, which contains the data flow and a notebook named `Ch05Ex03`.

The notebook PySpark code begins by retrieving the Parquet file from the ADLS container and storing it into a DataFrame. The data loaded into the DataFrame is then stored on a temporary table using the `registerTempTable()` method, as follows:

```
df = spark.read \
   .load('abfss://*@*.dfs.core.windows.net/../in/2022/04/28/16/*.parquet',
   format='parquet')
df.registerTempTable("TmpREADING")
```

Reference tables are required to transform the data on the `TmpReading` table and are loaded into a DataFrame and then stored into temporary tables. The CSV files need to be uploaded to your ADLS container prior to successfully running that code.

```
dfMODE = spark.read \
  .load('abfss://*@*.dfs.core.windows.net/Tables/MODE.csv',
  format='csv', header=True)
dfMODE.registerTempTable("MODE")
dfELECTRODE = spark.read \
  .load('abfss://*@*.dfs.core.windows.net/Tables/ELECTRODE.csv',
  format='csv', header=True)
dfELECTRODE.registerTempTable("ELECTRODE")
dfFREQUENCY = spark.read \
  .load('abfss://*@*.dfs.core.windows.net/Tables/FREQUENCY.csv',
  format='csv', header=True)
dfFREQUENCY.registerTempTable("FREQUENCY")
dfSCENARIO = spark.read \
  .load('abfss://*@*.dfs.core.windows.net/Tables/SCENARIO.csv',
  format='csv', header=True)
dfSCENARIO.registerTempTable("SCENARIO")
dfSESSION = spark.read \
  .load('abfss://*@*.dfs.core.windows.net/Tables/SESSIONALL.csv',
  format='csv', header=True)
dfSESSION.registerTempTable("SESSION")
```

The next step is to perform a query that transforms the data on the `TmpReading` table into the format that has been assumed to be most optimal for querying and insight gathering.

```
dfREADING = sqlContext.sql("""
   SELECT  se.SESSION_DATETIME, r.READING_DATETIME,
           s.SCENARIO, e.ELECTRODE, f.FREQUENCY, r.VALUE
   FROM    SESSION se, TmpREADING r, SCENARIO s,
           ELECTRODE e, FREQUENCY f
   WHERE   r.SESSION_ID = se.SESSION_ID AND se.SCENARIO_ID = s.SCENARIO_ID
           AND r.ELECTRODE_ID = e.ELECTRODE_ID AND r.FREQUENCY_ID =
               f.FREQUENCY_ID
""")
```

The final step is to store the results of that query, in Parquet format, into the ADLS container data lake by using the following code snippet, for example:

```
dfREADING.write \
  .parquet('abfss://*@*.dfs.core.windows.net/EMEA/brainjammer/out
                                                 /2022/04/28/17
                                                 /BrainjammerBrainwavesSpark
                                                 .parquet')
```

The data ends up being in a format like the following:

```
Total brainwave readings: 4539221
+-----------------+--------------------+-------------+---------+---------+------+
| SESSION_DATETIME|    READING_DATETIME|     SCENARIO|ELECTRODE|FREQUENCY| VALUE|
+-----------------+--------------------+-------------+---------+---------+------+
|2021-07-30 09:3..|2021-07-30 09:35:...|ClassicalMusic|      AF3|    THETA|44.254|
|2021-07-30 09:3..|2021-07-30 09:35:...|ClassicalMusic|      AF3|    ALPHA| 5.479|
|2021-07-30 09:3..|2021-07-30 09:35:...|ClassicalMusic|      AF3|   BETA_L| 1.911|
|2021-07-30 09:3..|2021-07-30 09:35:...|ClassicalMusic|      AF3|   BETA_H| 1.688|
|2021-07-30 09:3..|2021-07-30 09:35:...|ClassicalMusic|      AF3|    GAMMA| 0.259|
+-----------------+--------------------+-------------+---------+---------+------+
```

Use `df.distinct().count()` and `df.show(10)` to render the total number of rows in the DataFrame and a summary of what the data looks like, respectively. These files are available in the `BrainwaveData/Tables` directory at `https://github.com/benperk/ADE`.

Azure Databricks

If you already have a large solution that utilizes Databricks and want to outsource the management of the platform to Azure, you can migrate your solution to Azure. Azure Databricks is the product offering to individuals and corporations that want to run their Big Data analytics on the Azure platform. Complete Exercise 5.4, where you will transform data using

Azure Databricks. It is assumed that you have completed the previous exercises and have the Parquet file that is an extract of the `[dbo].[Reading]` table existing on the Azure SQL database. If you did not perform Exercise 5.3, you can download the Parquet file from the `BrainwaveData/dbo.Reading` directory at `https://github.com/benperk/ADE`. The file is approximately 43 MB.

EXERCISE 5.4

Transform Data Using Apache Spark—Azure Databricks

1. Log in to the Azure portal at `https://portal.azure.com` ➢ navigate to the Azure Databricks workspace you created in Exercise 3.14 ➢ click the Launch Workspace button in the middle of the Overview blade ➢ select the Compute menu item ➢ select the cluster you also created in Exercise 3.14 ➢ click the Start button ➢ select the + Create menu item ➢ select Notebook ➢ enter a name (I used **brainjammer**) ➢ select Scala from the Default Language drop-down list box ➢ select the cluster you just started from the drop-down list box ➢ and then click Create.

2. Add the following configuration into the Advanced Options of the Apache Spark cluster:

```
fs.azure.account.key.<account>.blob.core.windows.net <access-key>
```

3. Add the following Scala syntax code, which loads the Parquet brainjammer brain wave reading data ➢ and then run the code snippet in the cell:

```
val rawReadings = "wasbs://*@*.blob.core.windows.net/*.parquet"
val rawReadingsDF = spark.read.option("header","true").parquet(rawReadings)
rawReadingsDF.createOrReplaceTempView("TmpREADING")
spark.sql("SELECT * FROM TmpREADING").limit(5).show()

+----------+----------+------------+------------+--------------------+-----+------+
|READING_ID|SESSION_ID|ELECTRODE_ID|FREQUENCY_ID|    READING_DATETIME|COUNT| VALUE|
+----------+----------+------------+------------+--------------------+-----+------+
|         1|         1|           1|           1|2021-07-30 09:35:...|    0|44.254|
|         2|         1|           1|           2|2021-07-30 09:35:...|    0| 5.479|
|         3|         1|           1|           3|2021-07-30 09:35:...|    0| 1.911|
|         4|         1|           1|           4|2021-07-30 09:35:...|    0| 1.688|
|         5|         1|           1|           5|2021-07-30 09:35:...|    0| 0.259|
+----------+----------+------------+------------+--------------------+-----+------+
```

4. Add a new cell ➢ click the + that is rendered when hovering over the lower line of the default cell ➢ and then load the required reference data into DataFrames and temporary tables using the following syntax:

```
val MODE = "wasbs://*@*.blob.core.windows.net/MODE.csv"
val ELECRODE = "wasbs://*@*.blob.core.windows.net/ELECTRODE.csv"
val FREQUENCY = "wasbs://*@*.blob.core.windows.net/FREQUENCY.csv"
```

```
val SCENARIO = "wasbs://*@*.blob.core.windows.net/SCENARIO.csv"
val SESSION = "wasbs://*@*.blob.core.windows.net/SESSIONALL.csv"

val MODEDF = spark.read.option("header","true").csv(MODE)
val ELECRODEDF = spark.read.option("header","true").csv(ELECRODE)
val FREQUENCYDF = spark.read.option("header","true").csv(FREQUENCY)
val SCENARIODF = spark.read.option("header","true").csv(SCENARIO)
val SESSIONDF = spark.read.option("header","true").csv(SESSION)

MODEDF.createOrReplaceTempView("MODE")
ELECRODEDF.createOrReplaceTempView("ELECTRODE")
FREQUENCYDF.createOrReplaceTempView("FREQUENCY")
SCENARIODF.createOrReplaceTempView("SCENARIO")
SESSIONDF.createOrReplaceTempView("SESSION")
spark.sql("SELECT COUNT(*) AS numSessions FROM SESSION").limit(5).show()
spark.sql("SELECT * FROM ELECTRODE").limit(5).show()

+-----------+
|numSessions|
+-----------+
|        150|
+-----------+

+------------+---------+-----------+
|ELECTRODE_ID|ELECTRODE|   LOCATION|
+------------+---------+-----------+
|           1|      AF3| Front Left|
|           2|      AF4|Front Right|
|           3|       T7|   Ear Left|
|           4|       T8|  Ear Right|
|           5|       Pz|Center Back|
+------------+---------+-----------+
```

5. Add a new cell, and then add the following Scala syntax, which transforms the raw brainjammer brain wave data:

```
val BrainwavesDF = spark.sql("""
    SELECT  se.SESSION_DATETIME, r.READING_DATETIME,
            s.SCENARIO, e.ELECTRODE, f.FREQUENCY, r.VALUE
    FROM    SESSION se, TmpREADING r, SCENARIO s,
            ELECTRODE e, FREQUENCY f
    WHERE   r.SESSION_ID = se.SESSION_ID AND se.SCENARIO_ID = s.SCENARIO_ID
            AND r.ELECTRODE_ID = e.ELECTRODE_ID AND r.FREQUENCY_ID =
               f.FREQUENCY_ID
""")
```

EXERCISE 5.4 *(continued)*

```
BrainwavesDF.select("SCENARIO", "ELECTRODE", "FREQUENCY", "VALUE").show(5)

+--------------+---------+---------+------+
|      SCENARIO|ELECTRODE|FREQUENCY| VALUE|
+--------------+---------+---------+------+
|ClassicalMusic|      AF3|    THETA|44.254|
|ClassicalMusic|      AF3|    ALPHA| 5.479|
|ClassicalMusic|      AF3|   BETA_L| 1.911|
|ClassicalMusic|      AF3|   BETA_H| 1.688|
|ClassicalMusic|      AF3|    GAMMA| 0.259|
+--------------+---------+---------+------+
```

6. Add a new cell, and then save the result to a delta file using the following syntax:

```
val BrainwavesPath = "/FileStore/business-data/2022/04/30"
BrainwavesDF.write.format("delta").mode(overwrite").save(BrainwavesPath)
val BrainwavesDeltaPath = "/FileStore/business-data/2022/04/30"
val BrainwavesDeltaDF = spark.read.format("delta").load(BrainwavesDeltaPath)
print(BrainwavesDeltaDF.count())
BrainwavesDeltaDF.select("SCENARIO", "ELECTRODE",
                         "FREQUENCY", "VALUE").orderBy($"SCENARIO"
                            .desc).show(5)

4539223

+-----------+---------+---------+------+
|   SCENARIO|ELECTRODE|FREQUENCY| VALUE|
+-----------+---------+---------+------+
|WorkNoEmail|      AF3|    THETA|33.904|
|WorkNoEmail|      AF4|    THETA|27.799|
|WorkNoEmail|      AF3|    ALPHA| 9.419|
|WorkNoEmail|      AF3|   BETA_L| 3.299|
|WorkNoEmail|      AF3|   BETA_H| 3.074|
+-----------+---------+---------+------+
```

The Azure Databricks workspace should resemble Figure 5.12.

FIGURE 5.12 Transforming data using an Apache Spark Azure Databricks workspace

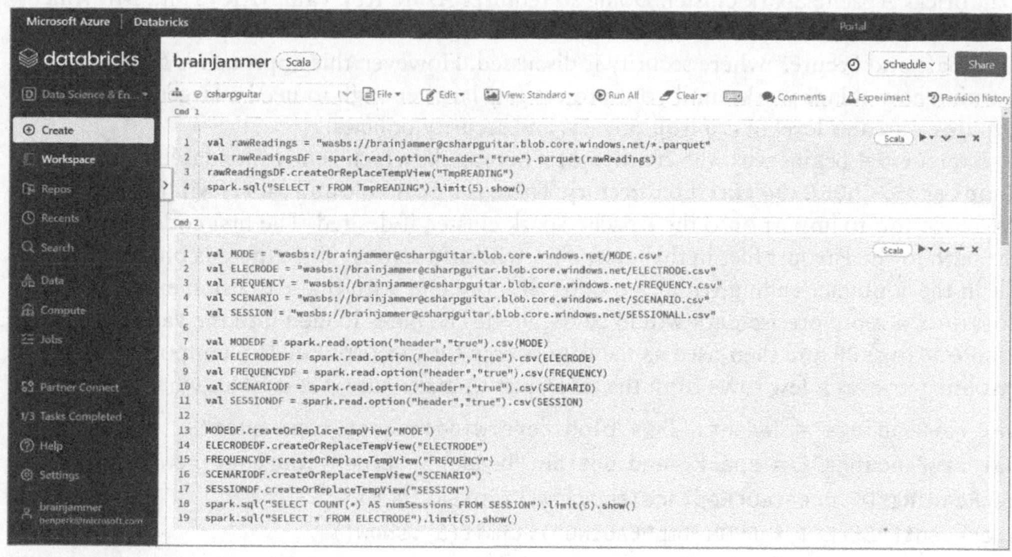

The first important point for Exercise 5.4 has to do with the location of the Parquet file that contains the raw reading data. The file in this exercise is hosted in a blob container and in a different Azure storage account from the one that contains your ADLS container. You might overlook that aspect of this exercise and get stuck. You can see this in the value of the Spark configuration setting in step 2. Notice that it contains `blob.core.windows.net` and not the `dfs.core.windows.net` endpoint address that exists for ADLS containers.

```
fs.azure.account.key.<account>.blob.core.windows.net <access-key>
```

To make sure this is clear, Figure 5.13 illustrates this transformation configuration. A notebook named brainjammer is running on an Apache Spark cluster in Azure Databricks. The Scala code within the notebook retrieves a Parquet file from an Azure blob storage container using the `wasbs` protocol. The data in the file is transformed and then saved into a Delta Lake.

FIGURE 5.13 Transforming data using Apache Spark Azure Databricks configuration

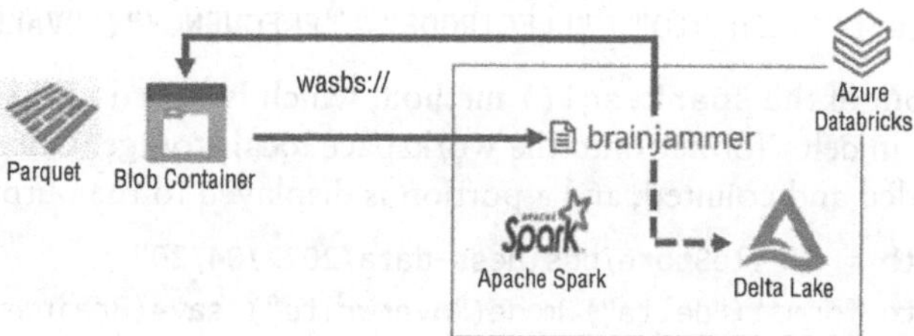

Note that it is possible to make a connection to an ADLS container from an Azure Databricks Apache Spark cluster. Doing so requires Azure Key Vault (AKV) and MI, which have not been covered yet. You will do another exercise with this in Chapter 8, "Keeping Data Safe and Secure," where security is discussed. However, this approach is sufficient for learning how things work, until your project gets large enough to need a larger team that requires a greater level of control, privacy, and security policies.

Exercise 5.4 begins with the creation of a notebook, which is downloadable from the `Chapter05/Ch05Ex04` GitHub directory. There is a Scala file and an HTML file for your reference and to import onto the Apache Spark cluster, if desired. The first code snippet sets the path to the Parquet file; in this case, it's a wildcard setting, since there is only a single file in the container ending with `.parquet`. If more files with that extension existed in the container, a more precise path would be required. The file is loaded into the variable named `rawReadingsDF` and then used as the data source for the `TmpREADING` temporary view. The last line retrieves a few rows from the table, just to make sure it resembles what is expected.

```
val rawReadings = "wasbs://*@*.blob.core.windows.net/*.parquet"
val rawReadingsDF = spark.read.option("header","true").parquet(rawReadings)
rawReadingsDF.createOrReplaceTempView("TmpREADING")
spark.sql("SELECT * FROM TmpREADING").limit(5).show()
```

The next notebook cell that included the Scala code loaded the path to all necessary reference data. The path was then used to load CSV files from a blob storage container and to use them to populate reference table data. A few `SELECT` queries on those tables made sure everything loaded as expected. The next cell in the notebook is where the transformation happens, using the `spark.sql()` method and passing it a query that joins together the reading and reference data resulting in output in a more usable form. That output is rendered to the output window for proofing purposes.

```
val BrainwavesDF = spark.sql("""
    SELECT  se.SESSION_DATETIME, r.READING_DATETIME,
            s.SCENARIO, e.ELECTRODE, f.FREQUENCY, r.VALUE
    FROM    SESSION se, TmpREADING r, SCENARIO s,
            ELECTRODE e, FREQUENCY f
    WHERE   r.SESSION_ID = se.SESSION_ID AND se.SCENARIO_ID = s.SCENARIO_ID
            AND r.ELECTRODE_ID = e.ELECTRODE_ID AND r.FREQUENCY_ID =
               f.FREQUENCY_ID
""")
BrainwavesDF.select("SCENARIO", "ELECTRODE", "FREQUENCY", "VALUE").show(5)
```

Finally, the output of the `spark.sql()` method, which is stored in the `BrainwavesDF` variable, is written in delta format onto the workspace local storage. Once stored, the file in delta format is loaded and counted, and a portion is displayed to the output page for review.

```
val BrainwavesPath = "/FileStore/business-data/2022/04/30"
BrainwavesDF.write.format("delta").mode("overwrite").save(BrainwavesPath)
```

```
val BrainwavesDeltaPath = "/FileStore/business-data/2022/04/30"
val BrainwavesDeltaDF = spark.read.format("delta").load(BrainwavesDeltaPath)
print(BrainwavesDeltaDF.count())
BrainwavesDeltaDF.select("SCENARIO", "ELECTRODE",
                         "FREQUENCY", "VALUE").orderBy($"SCENARIO".desc).show(5)
```

The transformation successfully transformed data from the following form:

```
+----------+----------+------------+------------+--------------------+-----+------+
|READING_ID|SESSION_ID|ELECTRODE_ID|FREQUENCY_ID|    READING_DATETIME|COUNT| VALUE|
+----------+----------+------------+------------+--------------------+-----+------+
|         1|         1|           1|           1|2021-07-30 09:35:...|    0|44.254|
|         2|         1|           1|           2|2021-07-30 09:35:...|    0| 5.479|
|         3|         1|           1|           3|2021-07-30 09:35:...|    0| 1.911|
|         4|         1|           1|           4|2021-07-30 09:35:...|    0| 1.688|
|         5|         1|           1|           5|2021-07-30 09:35:...|    0| 0.259|
+----------+----------+------------+------------+--------------------+-----+------+
```

into the following queryable and more understandable format:

```
+-----------+---------+---------+------+
|   SCENARIO|ELECTRODE|FREQUENCY| VALUE|
+-----------+---------+---------+------+
|WorkNoEmail|      AF3|    THETA|33.904|
|WorkNoEmail|      AF4|    THETA|27.799|
|WorkNoEmail|      AF3|    ALPHA| 9.419|
|WorkNoEmail|      AF3|   BETA_L| 3.299|
|WorkNoEmail|      AF3|   BETA_H| 3.074|
+-----------+---------+---------+------+
```

Jupyter Notebooks

Throughout the exercises in this book, you have created numerous notebooks. The notebooks are web-based and consist of a series of ordered cells that can contain code. The code within these cells is what you use to ingest, transform, enrich, and store the data you are preparing for gathering insights. The notebooks are based on what was formally named IPython Notebook but is now referred to as Jupyter Notebook. The "py" in the name is intended to give recognition to its preceding name and the Python programming language. Behind the browser-based shell exists a JSON document that contains schema information with a file extension of `.ipynb`. You will find support importing and exporting Jupyter notebooks in many places throughout the Azure platform. The following sections discuss many of them.

Azure Synapse Analytics

In Exercise 5.3 you created a notebook that targeted the PySpark language. When you hover over that notebook in Azure Synapse Analytics and click the ellipse (`...`), you will see the option to Export the Notebook. The supported formats are HTML (`.html`), Python (`.py`), LaTeX (`.tex`), and Notebook (`.ipynb`). The Jupyter notebook for Exercise 5.3 is in the `Chapter05` directory on GitHub at `https://github.com/benperk/ADE`. There was a small change to the published Jupyter notebook versus the one you created in Exercise 5.3. The change was to break the code out from a single cell into three cells. Breaking the code into smaller snippets that are focused on a specific part of the ingestion, transformation, and storage is helpful because you can run each cell independently while testing.

Azure Databricks

You experienced the creation of numerous cells in Exercise 5.4, where you successfully transformed brainjammer brain wave data in Azure Databricks. The logic and approach you used in Exercise 5.4 was similar to what you did in Exercise 5.3. The target language for Exercise 5.4 was Scala, for learning purposes, but had there not been a difference, you could have imported the `.ipynb` file from Exercise 5.3 into Azure Databricks. As shown in Figure 5.14, you start by navigating towards adding a new resource in the workspace, which ultimately renders a pop-up menu. The pop-up menu contains the Import option.

FIGURE 5.14 Jupyter notebooks—Azure Databricks Import option

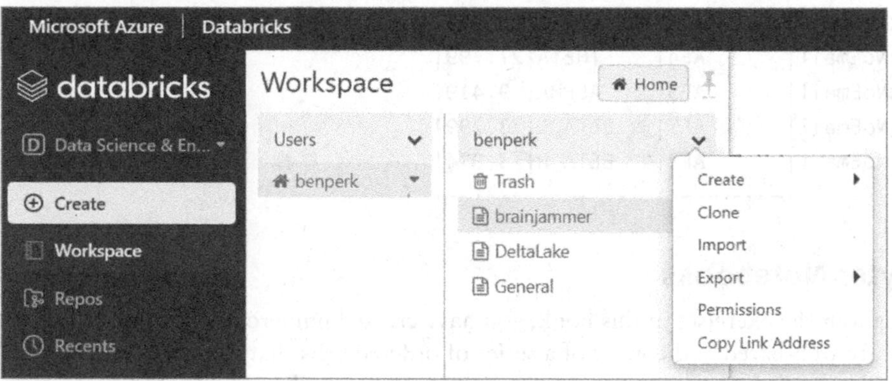

Once the notebook is imported, you see the exact same code in the numerous cells as you created in Azure Synapse Analytics, as shown in Figure 5.15.

Some steps will be required to make the imported notebook run. For example, if the configuration that allows access to the storage has not been enabled on the Apache Spark cluster, then the notebook would fail to run.

FIGURE 5.15 Jupyter notebooks—Azure Databricks imported

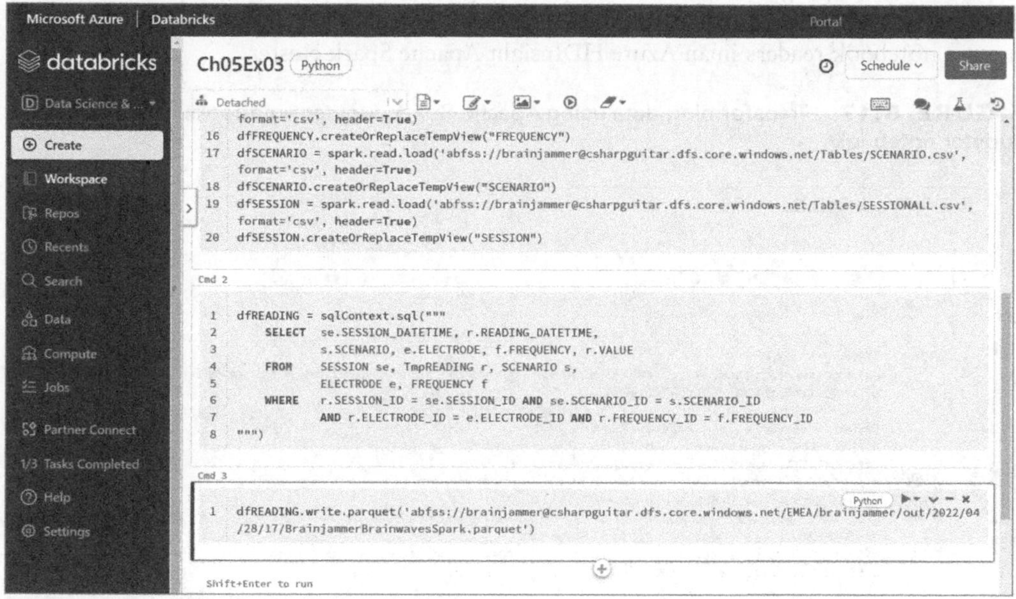

Azure HDInsight

If you provision an Azure HDInsight Apache Spark cluster, there exists a Jupyter notebook interactive environment. The Jupyter notebook environment is accessible by URL. If your HDInsight cluster is named `brainjammer`, for example, the Jupyter notebook environment is accessible at a web address similar to the following:

```
https://brainjammer.azurehdinsight.net/jupyter
```

Once you access the web-based environment, you can upload an existing notebook or create a new Jupyter notebook. The default page resembles Figure 5.16.

FIGURE 5.16 Transforming data using Apache Spark Jupyter notebooks Azure HDInsight default

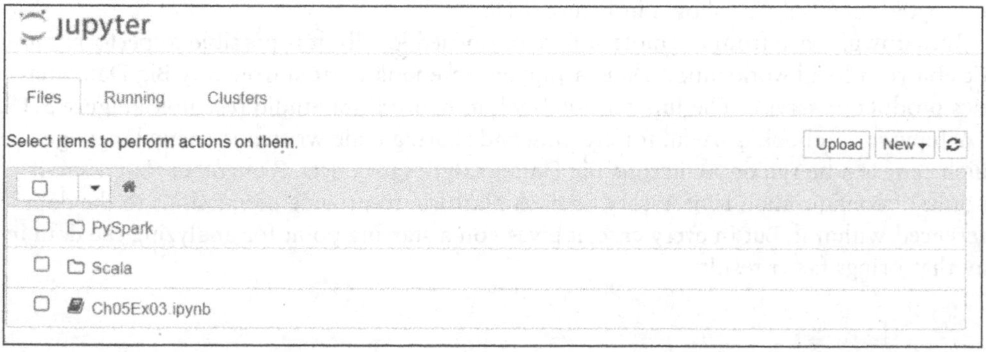

Notice that the exported notebook from Exercise 5.3 has already been uploaded. This is achieved by clicking the Upload button, selecting the exported Azure Synapse Analytics notebook (`Ch05Ex03.ipynb`), and uploading it. Figure 5.17 illustrates how the uploaded Jupyter notebook renders in an Azure HDInsight Apache Spark cluster.

FIGURE 5.17 Transforming data using Apache Spark Jupyter notebooks Azure HDInsight Jupyter notebook

Azure Data Studio

There is a Jupyter Extension for Azure Data Studio that enables you to work with Jupyter notebooks hosted on a public repository. After installing the extension, you can add and create Jupyter notebooks, as shown in Figure 5.18.

Once downloaded from a remote source or opened locally, it is possible to perform analytics on your local workstation using a Jupyter notebook created from any Big Data analytics product or service. The Jupyter notebook in Azure Data Studio resembles Figure 5.19.

A Jupyter notebook is useful for creating and sharing code written in many languages, which can then be run on numerous Big Data analytics products. Remember that a small amount of configuration is necessary on each platform to provide permissions to the data referenced within it. But in every case, it gives you a starting point for analyzing the data in a way that brings faster results.

FIGURE 5.18 Transforming data using Apache Spark Jupyter notebooks Azure Data Studio open Jupyter notebook

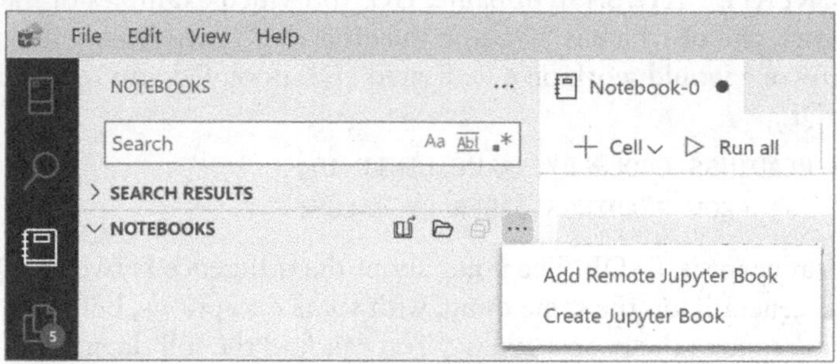

FIGURE 5.19 Transforming data using Apache Spark Jupyter notebooks Azure Data Studio Jupyter notebook

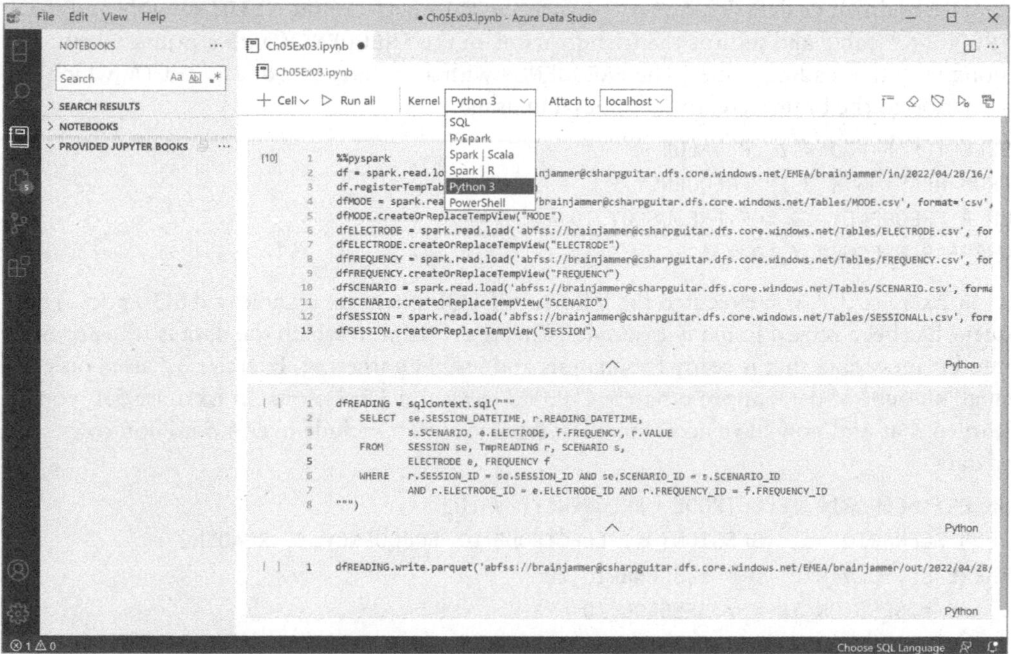

Transform Data Using Transact-SQL

Transact-SQL (T-SQL), as mentioned previously, is an extension of the SQL language developed by Microsoft. In this chapter and preceding chapters, you have read about and used T-SQL statements, functions, and commands. Any time you ran queries against a dedicated or serverless SQL pool, you were using T-SQL. In many of those scenarios, you transformed data, so you have already experienced hands-on activities concerning the transformation of data using T-SQL. This section will review and expand on what you have already learned.

Chapter 2 "CREATE DATABASE dbBame; GO," provided examples of the following two SELECT statements, one of which is SQL and the other T-SQL. Although they result in the same output, only one would work on a dedicated SQL pool. Do you remember which statement is T-SQL?

```
SELECT * FROM READINGS ORDER BY VALUE LIMIT 10;
SELECT TOP 10 (*) FROM READINGS ORDER BY VALUE;
```

The second statement is T-SQL. The point about the difference between SQL and T-SQL is that they both generally do the same thing, with some exceptions, but achieving the desired outcomes requires the proper syntax. You can find the full documentation for T-SQL at https://docs.microsoft.com/sql/t-sql, which also includes content about some of the important DBCC, DDL, and DML topics for the exam.

In Exercise 2.1, you executed the following T-SQL query against an Azure SQL database. This was one of your first exposures in this book to an Azure database and to the brain-jammer brain wave data. This query performs a JOIN between the READING table and the FREQUENCY table and returns the friendly name of the FREQUENCY with a primary key of 1, along with the reading values. The FREQUENCY with a primary key of 1 is THETA, which has a relation to the brain's creative abilities and usage.

```
SELECT F.FREQUENCY, R.VALUE
FROM READING R JOIN FREQUENCY F
ON R.FREQUENCY_ID = F.FREQUENCY_ID
WHERE R.FREQUENCY_ID = 1
```

In Exercise 3.7, you executed the following T-SQL query on a dedicated SQL pool. This query has been reused in many examples. This is the form in which the data is transformed into business data that is ready for analysis and insight gathering. Exercise 3.7 used only a small amount of data, approximately 450,000 rows and 15 sessions. In Exercise 5.1, you learned that and now have access to all 150 sessions that include over 4.5 million rows of data.

```
SELECT SCENARIO, ELECTRODE, FREQUENCY, VALUE
FROM SCENARIO sc, [SESSION] s, ELECTRODE e, FREQUENCY f, READING r
WHERE sc.SCENARIO_ID = s.SCENARIO_ID
  AND s.SESSION_ID = r.SESSION_ID
  AND e.ELECTRODE_ID = r.ELECTRODE_ID
  AND f.FREQUENCY_ID = r.FREQUENCY_ID
```

In Exercise 4.8, you added the first line of code syntax to a Derived Column transformation as part of a data flow. The first row is not T-SQL, but the second line is. Both lines of sample syntax result in the same output when transforming an epoch timestamp to T-SQL timestamp. This example shows some different approaches to achieving the same outcome and points out the need for different syntactical structure.

```
toTimestamp(toLong(toDecimal(Timestamp, 14, 4) * (1000l)))
DATEADD(S, CAST([TIMESTAMP] AS DECIMAL(14, 4)) , '19700101') AS Timestamp
```

Most recently, you created a dedicated SQL pool stored procedure that created a fact table by using a CTAS statement. The following is the T-SQL statement that performed the transformation from the raw `TmpREADING` table to the `FactREADING` table:

```
SELECT  se.SESSION_DATETIME, r.READING_DATETIME,
          s.SCENARIO, e.ELECTRODE, f.FREQUENCY, r.[VALUE]
   FROM   [brainwaves].[DimSESSION] se, [brainwaves].[TmpREADING] r,
          [brainwaves].[DimSCENARIO] s, [brainwaves].[DimELECTRODE] e,
          [brainwaves].[DimFREQUENCY] f
   WHERE  r.SESSION_ID = se.SESSION_ID AND se.SCENARIO_ID = s.SCENARIO_ID
          AND r.ELECTRODE_ID = e.ELECTRODE_ID
          AND r.FREQUENCY_ID = f.FREQUENCY_ID;
```

The point is that when you are working with dedicated SQL pools in Azure Synapse Analytics (previously called Azure SQL Data Warehouse), you are using T-SQL to CRUD data. The same is true with data stored on serverless SQL pools.

Transform Data Using Stream Analytics

Remember, as you begin this section, that Chapter 7, "Design and Implement a Data Stream Processing Solution," is devoted to data streaming. The content in this section will therefore target the Azure Stream Analytics feature that performs data transformation. Consider reviewing Exercise 3.17, where you provisioned an Azure Stream Analytics job. That exercise is followed by a thorough overview of the capabilities and features of Azure Stream Analytics. Also review Exercise 3.16, where you provisioned an Azure Event Hub. You will use that Azure Event Hub to manage the stream input into the Azure Stream Analytics job.

When you look at the existing brainjammer brain wave data, you will notice that the session—for example, `ClassicalMusic`—in which it was collected is included in the file. The objective of the data analysis on these 4.5 million rows of collected data is to determine which session the individual sending the brain waves is doing, in real time or near real time. Therefore, the structure of the data will resemble the following, to not include any session information. A sample JSON document that contains a single reading is available on GitHub at `https://github.com/benperk/ADE`, in the `BrainwaveData/SessionJson` directory. The JSON document named `POWReading.json` is structured in the following summarized format:

```
{
  "ReadingDate": "2021-07-30T09:26:25.54",
  "Counter": 0,
  "AF3":
```

```
  {
    "THETA": 17.368,
    "ALPHA": 2.809,
    "BETA_L": 2.72,
    "BETA_H": 2.725,
    "GAMMA": 1.014
  },
  "T7":
  {
    ... },...
```

Figure 5.20 illustrates an example of a Azure Stream Analytics query. The query will transform the JSON document, which contains a brain wave reading, in real time, from an event hub and pass it to Azure Synapse Analytics.

FIGURE 5.20 Transforming data using Azure Stream Analytics JSON

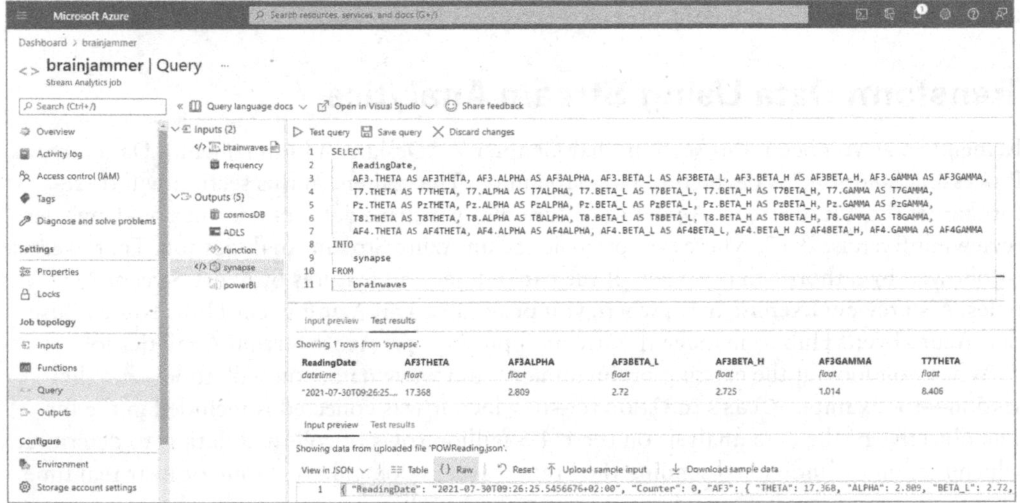

What is and is not considered a transformation is in the eye of the beholder. The JSON document includes a Counter attribute which is not passed along to Azure Synapse. As you learned in Chapter 3, "Data Sources and Ingestion," the Azure Stream Analytics query language has many capabilities that can be useful in additional transformations, such as aggregate functions (e.g., AVG, SUM, and VAR), conversion functions (e.g., CAST and TRY_CAST), and windowing functions (e.g., tumbling and sliding). At this moment, it is not clear what the final query here will be, as the brainjammer brain wave data has yet to be analyzed thoroughly. It is getting close to that point, as you have learned how to ingest it and then transform it into a structure that is amenable to insight gathering and pattern recognition.

Cleanse Data

In addition to managing the platform the analysis of your data happens on, you must manage the data itself. There can be scenarios where portions of your data are missing, there is unnecessary or corrupted data, or even the whole data file or table is no longer available. The point is that it takes more time than you might expect to make sure the data used for gathering business insights is and remains valid. If the data itself has lost its integrity, then any analytics performed, and the resulting findings, could lead to making wrong decisions. Perform Exercise 5.5 to cleanse some brain wave data.

EXERCISE 5.5

Cleanse Data

1. Log in to the Azure portal at `https://portal.azure.com` ➢ navigate to the Azure Synapse Analytics workspace you created in Exercise 3.3 ➢ on the Overview blade click the Open link in the Open Synapse Studio tile ➢ select the Develop hub ➢ hover over the Notebook folder ➢ click the ellipse (`...`) ➢ select New Notebook ➢ select your Apache Spark pool from the Attach To drop-down list box ➢ download the `BRAINWAVES_WITH_NULLS.csv` file from the `Chapter05/Ch05Ex0C` directory ➢ upload the file into your data lake (aka the ADLS container you created in Exercise 3.1) ➢ execute the following PySpark syntax to load the data file into a DataFrame and identify rows with `null` values ➢ and then replace the * with your container and ADLS endpoint URL:

```
%%pyspark
df = spark.read \
  .load('abfss://*@*.dfs.core.windows.net/SessionCSV/BRAINWAVES_WITH_
   NULLS.csv',
  format='csv', header=True)

df.filter(df.SESSION_DATETIME.isNull() | df.READING_DATETIME.isNull() \
   | df.SCENARIO.isNull() | df.ELECTRODE.isNull() | df.FREQUENCY.isNull() \
   | df.VALUE.isNull()).show()
```

```
+-----------------+-----------------+-------------+-----------+----------+-------+
| SESSION_DATETIME| READING_DATETIME| SCENARIO    | ELECTRODE | FREQUENCY | VALUE |
+-----------------+-----------------+-------------+-----------+----------+-------+
| null            | 7/30/2021 9:35  | Classica ... | AF3      | ALPHA     | 5.479 |
| 7/30/2021 12:49 | null            | FlipChart    | AF3      | BETA_H    | 1.061 |
| 7/30/2021 9:26  | 7/30/2021 9:26  | null         | AF3      | BETA_L    | 2.72  |
| 7/29/2021 14:44 | 7/29/2021 14:44 | PlayingG ... | null     | BETA_H    | 3.867 |
| 7/29/2021 14:44 | 7/29/2021 14:44 | PlayingG ... | T7       | null      | 2.237 |
| 7/30/2021 9:40  | 7/30/2021 9:40  | TikTok       | T8       | ALPHA     | null  |
+-----------------+-----------------+-------------+-----------+----------+-------+
```

EXERCISE 5.5 *(continued)*

2. Execute the following syntax, and then check the total number of rows and columns that are loaded into the Dataframe:

```
print((df.count(), len(df.columns)))

(35, 8)
```

3. Remove the rows that contain columns with `null` values ➤ execute the following code snippet ➤ and then check the number of rows and columns again:

```
df = df.na.drop("any")
print((df.count(), len(df.columns)))
df.show()

(24, 6)

+------------------+--------------------+------------+----------+----------+--------+
| SESSION_DATETIME | READING_DATETIME   | SCENARIO   |ELECTRODE | FREQUENCY| VALUE  |
+------------------+--------------------+------------+----------+----------+--------+
| 7/30/2021 12:49  | 7/30/2021 12:49    | Flip€hart  | AF3      | THETA    | 2X.nn6 |
| 7/29/2021 12:41  | 7/40/2021 12:41... | Meditati...| AF3      | BETA_H   | 1.129  |
| 7/30/2021 9:26   | 7/30/2021 9:26     | MetalMus...| AF3      | THETA    | 4.c1.. |
| ...              | ...                | ...        | ...      | ...      | ...    |
+------------------+--------------------+------------+----------+----------+--------+
```

4. Remove the data rows with corrupt data by executing the following code snippet:

```
df = df.filter(df.VALUE != '2X.n66').filter(df.VALUE != '4.c1..') \
    .filter(df.READING_DATETIME != '7/40/2021  12:41:00 PM')
print((df.count(), len(df.columns)))

(21, 6)
```

5. Remove the `SESSION_DATETIME` and `READING_DATETIME` columns, as follows:

```
df = df.drop(df.SESSION_DATETIME, df.READING_DATETIME)
print((df.count(), len(df.columns)))

(21, 4)
```

6. Rename the notebook to a friendly name (for example, `Ch05Ex05`), and then commit the code to your GitHub repository. The source code is located on GitHub at `https://github.com/benperk/ADE`, in the `Chapter05/Ch05Ex05` directory.

The final action to take after cleansing the data is to perhaps save it to a temporary table, using the `saveAsTable(tableName)` method, or into the Parquet file format. When you are ready perform your analytics on this data, you know the data is clean, with no compromises, which means the conclusions made from the data will be valid.

When a column that contains no data is loaded into a DataFrame, the result is `null`. To find those occurrences, the first action taken was to search the content loaded into the DataFrame for `nulls` and display that to the output window. Filtering the rows that had any column that contained a `null` was then performed and resulted in the removal of nine rows. The `drop()` method was passed a parameter of `any`, which means that the row is dropped when any of the columns have a `null` value. There is also an `all` parameter, which will remove the row when all columns on the row contain `null`. The next action was to remove some corrupt data. There are certainly more sophisticated techniques for validating and removing corrupt or even missing data, but this example was to show one approach and to point out that you need to know the data in order to determine whether or not the data is correct. For example, if you know that the value in `VALUE` must be a decimal, you could attempt a `try_cast()` conversion on each column in each row; if the conversion fails, then you would then filter it out. The same goes for any timestamp: Attempt to cast it, if it fails, then filter it out. That might not be feasible for massive amounts of data, but in this scenario figuring out how to implement something like that may be worthwhile.

Finally, the last action was to remove two columns from the DataFrame. It is likely that you would use the same data in different formats to gain numerous insights. Some of those transformations might need all the data from the data source, like a CSV file, while other analyses might not need a few columns. In that case it makes sense to remove unnecessary data from the final dataset used for gathering business insights. Again, you can use the `drop()` method, but this time passing the column names as the parameters results in the column being removed from the DataFrame.

Split Data

If you have not yet completed Exercise 5.2, consider doing so, as you will need the 391 MB CSV file that was created there in order to perform Exercise 5.6. The data in the `Chapter04/Ch04Ex01` directory on GitHub contains data in the same format as the one created in Exercise 5.2, but there is much less data in it. When you have a large file that needs to be loaded into a table on a dedicated SQL pool, it is more efficient to split the file into multiple files. The most efficient number of files is based on the selected performance level of your dedicated SQL pool. Table 5.1 summarizes the recommended splits based on performance level size, which is based on the amount of *data warehouse units (DWUs)*. A DWU is a combination of CPU, memory, and I/O resources allocated to a machine that processes your data queries and movements.

Notice in Table 5.1 the presence of the law of 60, where the number of files divided by the maximum number of nodes for the given DWU size is 60. Complete Exercise 5.6, where you will split the single 391 MB file into 60 separate files.

TABLE 5.1 Data file split recommendation

DWU	Number of Files	Maximum Nodes
DW100c	60	1
DW300c	60	1
DW500c	60	1
DW1000c	120	2
DW1500c	180	3
DW2500c	300	5
DW5000c	600	10
DW7500c	900	15
DW10000c	1,200	20
DW15000c	1,800	30
DW30000c	3,600	60

EXERCISE 5.6

Split Data

1. Log in to the Azure portal at `https://portal.azure.com` > navigate to the Azure Synapse Analytics workspace you created in Exercise 3.3 > on the Overview blade, click the Open link in the Open Synapse Studio tile > select the Develop hub > hover over the Data Flows group > click the ellipse (. . .) > select New Data Flow > and then click the Add Source box in the canvas.
2. On the Source Setting tab, provide an output stream name (I used **BrainjammerBrainwavesCSV**) > select the + New button to the right of the Dataset drop-down text box > choose ADLS > choose DelimitedText > enter a name (I used **BrainjammerBrainwavesCSV**) > select `WorkspaceDefaultStorage` from the Linked Service drop-down text box > enable interactive authoring > select the folder icon to the right of the File Path text boxes > and then navigate to and select the CSV file you created in Exercise 5.2, for example:

```
EMEA\brainjammer\in\2022\04\26\17\BrainjammerBrainwaves.csv
```

3. There is no header in this file, so leave the First Row as Header check box unchecked ➢ click the OK button ➢ select the Projection tab and make updates so that it resembles Figure 5.21. Note: Hover over the drop-down text box where you selected decimal ➢ click the Edit link ➢ enter a value of **8** for Precision ➢ enter a value of **3** for Scale ➢ and then click OK.

FIGURE 5.21 Splitting the data source—Projection tab

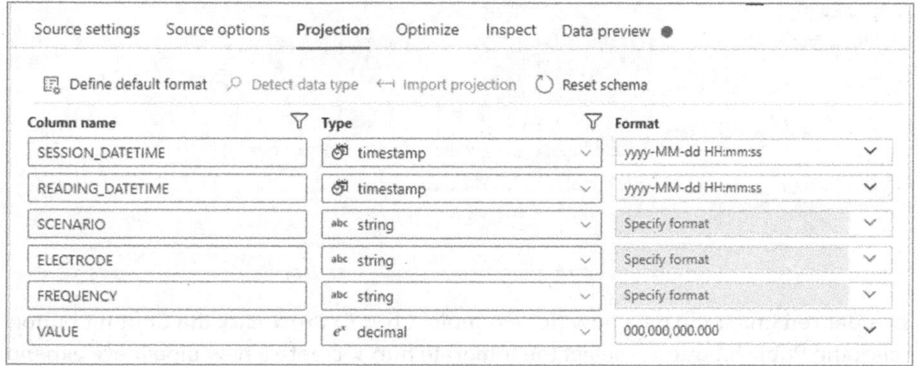

4. To add a sink transformation to the data flow, click the + at the lower right of the Source activity ➢ select Sink from the pop-up menu ➢ enter a name for the output stream (I used **BrainjammerBrainwavesSplitCSV**) ➢ click the + New button to the right of the Dataset drop-down list box ➢ choose ADLS ➢ choose DelimitedText ➢ enter a name (I used **BrainjammerBrainwavesSplitCSV**) ➢ select `WorkspaceDefaultStorage` from the Linked Service drop-down text box ➢ enable interactive authoring, if not already enabled ➢ select the folder icon to the right of the File Path text boxes ➢ and then navigate to the location where you want to store the split CSV files, for example:

```
EMEA\brainjammer\out\2022\04\28\12
```

5. Leave the defaults ➢ click the OK button ➢ select the Set Partitioning Radio button on the Optimize tab ➢ select Round Robin ➢ and then enter **60** into the Number of Partitions text box so that it resembles Figure 5.22.

EXERCISE 5.6 *(continued)*

FIGURE 5.22 Splitting the data sink—Optimize tab

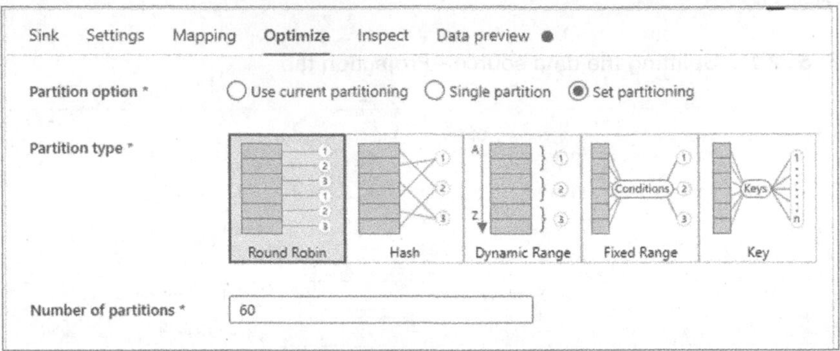

6. Consider renaming the data flow (for example, Ch05Ex06) ➢ click the Commit button ➢ click the Publish button ➢ select the Integrate hub ➢ create a new pipeline ➢ expand Move & Transfer ➢ drag and drop a Data Flow activity to the canvas pane ➢ provide a name (I used **SplitBrainjammerBrainwavesCSV**) ➢ select the just created data flow from the Data Flow drop-down textbox on the Settings tab ➢ click the Validate button ➢ consider renaming the pipeline ➢ click the Commit button ➢ click the Publish button ➢ click the Add Trigger button ➢ select the Trigger Now option ➢ be patient ➢ and then navigate to the output directory in your data lake, where you will find the 60 files.

In Exercise 5.6 you created a data flow that contains a source to import a large CSV file from ADLS. The data flow also contains a sink that splits the large CSV file into 60 smaller files and then exports it to the same ADLS container, but in another directory. Both the source and the sink require datasets and linked services to complete their work. As you saw in Table 5.1, the optimal number of files is 60 when your performance level is DW100c, DW300c, or DW500c. Having this many files is optimal when using the COPY statement to import data into a dedicated SQL pool. This is because having multiple files allows the platform to load more of them all at once and process them in parallel. This is in contrast to a single large file, which would be loaded and processed once. In this specific context, the 60 files turned out to be just under 5 MB each. This is an acceptable size; the smallest you would want is 4 MB, as this is the minimum size at which you are charged transaction costs on ADLS. In a larger data scenario, the best cases are between 100 MB and 10 GB for SQL pools, and 256 MB and 100 GB for Spark pools. Finally, when using Parquet or ORC files, you do not need to split them, as the COPY command will split them for you in this case.

Shred JSON

When you shred something, the object being shredded is torn into small pieces. In many respects, it means that the pieces that result from being torn are in the smallest possible size. In this scenario the object in question is a JSON document or file, and the result of shredding it fulfills two primary objectives. The first objective is the flattening of arrays, which are very common JSON constructs, where the common JSON construct is one with square brackets (`[]`) that hold arrays separated by a comma, and where curly braces (`{}`) hold name-value pairs. When you look through the brain waves JSON files, you will see a structure similar to the following. Also refer to Figure 2.7 to recall how this looks in an Azure Cosmos DB.

```
{ "Session":
 {
  "Scenario": "ClassicalMusic",
  "POWReading": [
  {
   "AF3":
   [
    {
      "THETA": 44.254,
      "ALPHA": 5.479,
      "BETA_L": 1.911,
      "BETA_H": 1.688,
      "GAMMA": 0.259
    }
   ],
   "T7":
   [
    {
      "THETA": 1.664,
      "ALPHA": 1.763,
      "BETA_L": 3.806,
      "BETA_H": 1.829,
      "GAMMA": 0.867
    }
   ],
   ...}]}}
```

If you want to shred that JSON file, you would do so with the objective of capturing the scenario, the electrode, the frequency, and the value. You might remember the term "exploding arrays" from Chapter 2, which has the same meaning and purpose as shredding; it is simply a different term. The second objective of shredding is done once the data you require is captured, i.e., pulled from the file into memory. Once the data is in memory, you can arrange the data into a format that can be easily queried using SQL-like syntax or DataFrame logic. In this state, you are then able to add `INSERT`, `UPDATE`, `UPSERT`, or `DELETE` statements directly into the file. Additionally, this gives you the facility to store the extracted data in a traditional relational database structure, if desired. The following sections offer specific information about shredding JSON files, as it pertains to different Azure products.

Azure Cosmos DB/SQL Pool

Azure Cosmos DB was formerly named Azure Document DB, at least the SQL API part of it. So, from its name alone you would think it is a good place to store documents like JSON files. In addition, Azure Cosmos DB can be scaled globally in a matter of minutes, with data synchronizations between the instances happening, by default, behind the scenes. You can find more about Azure Cosmos DB in Chapter 1 "Gaining the Azure Data Engineer Associate Certification." Complete Exercise 5.7, where you will configure an Azure Cosmos DB linked service and shred some JSON.

EXERCISE 5.7

Azure Cosmos DB—Shred JSON

1. Log in to the Azure portal at `https://portal.azure.com` ➢ navigate to the Azure Synapse Analytics workspace you created in Exercise 3.3 ➢ and then, on the Overview blade, click the Open link in the Open Synapse Studio. If you have already completed Exercise 3.8, skip to step 4; otherwise, continue to step 2.

2. Select the Manage Hub ➢ select Linked Services found within the External Connections section ➢ click the + New button (or reuse the linked service from Exercise 3.8) ➢ select Azure Cosmos DB (SQL API) from the New Linked Service window ➢ and then click Continue.

3. Enter a name (I used **BrainjammerCosmosDb**) ➢ add a description ➢ choose Account Key from the Authentication Type drop-down list box ➢ select Connection String ➢ select the From Azure Subscription radio button ➢ select the Azure subscription into which you provisioned the Azure Cosmos DB in Exercise 2.2 ➢ select the Azure Cosmos DB account name ➢ select the database name ➢ and then click Commit. Refer to Figure 3.50 for an example of how the configuration should look.

4. Select the Develop hub ➢ hover over SQL Scripts, click the ellipse (. . .) and select New SQL Script ➢ and then enter the syntax available in the `shredJSON.txt` file on GitHub, in the `Chapter05/Ch05Ex07` directory. The result looks something similar to Figure 5.23.

FIGURE 5.23 Shredding JSON with Azure Cosmos DB

Results Messages

View Table Chart ↦ Export results

Search

Scenario	ReadingDate	AF3THETA	AF3ALPHA	AF3BETA_L	AF3BETA_H	AF3GAMMA	AF4THETA	AF4ALPHA	AF4BETA_L	AF4BETA_H	T7GAMMA	T7THETA
ClassicalMusic	2021-07-30T09:...	44.254	5.479	1.911	1.688	0.259	35.433	4.526	3.824	1.544	0.259	1.664
ClassicalMusic	2021-07-30T09:...	25.286	3.580	2.264	1.573	0.244	20.292	3.033	4.976	1.539	0.244	1.873
ClassicalMusic	2021-07-30T09:...	15.232	2.913	2.595	1.488	0.239	12.563	2.628	5.948	1.554	0.239	2.095
ClassicalMusic	2021-07-30T09:...	16.011	3.655	2.883	1.445	0.241	13.611	3.610	6.562	1.558	0.241	2.290
ClassicalMusic	2021-07-30T09:...	24.615	5.711	3.095	1.444	0.246	20.789	5.985	6.699	1.521	0.246	2.422
MetalMusic	2021-08-01T09:...	1.961	1.991	2.607	0.850	0.270	2.157	1.812	2.140	1.180	0.270	6.186
MetalMusic	2021-08-01T09:...	1.635	1.755	2.567	0.851	0.303	1.842	1.617	1.819	1.150	0.303	5.737
MetalMusic	2021-08-01T09:...	1.392	1.664	2.578	0.828	0.338	1.660	1.574	1.652	1.054	0.338	5.324
MetalMusic	2021-08-01T09:...	1.313	1.700	2.532	0.780	0.367	1.651	1.659	1.592	0.907	0.367	5.319
MetalMusic	2021-08-01T09:...	1.406	1.789	2.326	0.717	0.386	1.799	1.789	1.540	0.742	0.386	6.016

5. **Rename, save, and commit the SQL script to your GitHub repository.**

The query you executed in step 4 begins with a `SELECT`, which is followed by the `OPENROWSET` that contains information about the `PROVIDER`, `CONNECTION`, and `OBJECT`.

```
SELECT TOP 10 Scenario, ReadingDate, AF3THETA, ...
FROM OPENROWSET(PROVIDER = 'CosmosDB',
    CONNECTION = 'Account=csharpguitar;Database=brainjammer;Key=sMxCN...
       ko7cJxyQ==',
    OBJECT = 'sessions')
```

The `PROVIDER` is `CosmosDB`, which the platform uses to load the necessary code and drivers to make a connection with an Azure Cosmos DB. The `CONNECTION` contains the details for making the connection, like endpoint and credentials, and the `OBJECT` is the container ID within the Azure Cosmos DB. The `WITH` clause provides a window to perform a query within a query, which relies on the `CROSS APPLY` statements that follow it.

```
WITH ( Scenario varchar(max) '$.Session.Scenario',
       POWReading varchar(max) '$.Session.POWReading') AS readings
CROSS APPLY OPENJSON(readings.POWReading) AS reading
CROSS APPLY OPENJSON(reading.[value])
```

Notice the result of the `WITH` clause is defined with the name `readings`. The first `CROSS APPLY` uses the `readings` object to reference the array of brain wave readings within the `POWReading` array. That `POWReading` array also contains an array of electrodes, frequencies, and reading values, which are references to again using a second

CROSS APPLY. Finally, the last WITH clause provides a reference to the reading.[value] property, which then links into the electrode array and each of its captured frequency's value.

```
WITH (
   ReadingDate varchar(50),
   AF3THETA decimal(7,3) '$.AF3[0].THETA',
   AF3ALPHA decimal(7,3) '$.AF3[0].ALPHA',
   AF3BETA_L decimal(7,3) '$.AF3[0].BETA_L',
   ...
) AS brainwave
```

Once the JSON document is in this format, i.e., shredded, you can load it into a temporary table, save it to a file, or transform it again into a relational database or star schema. Shredding a JSON document is likely something you have seen before, especially if you have worked with data in this format. Perhaps you have just never heard of it called shredding specifically, but you might remember from Chapter 2, where this kind of activity was discussed in the context of the explode() method. If you want to review what was covered in this book related to this, reread Chapter 2, specifically around Figure 2.29. Then read on to get some hands-on experience with the explode() method in the context of a DataFrame and an Azure Spark pool.

ADLS/Apache Spark Pool

When working in the context of an Azure Synapse Analytics Spark pool, it is common to work with files residing in your ADLS container. In Exercise 5.8 you will flatten, explode, and shred a JSON file loaded into a DataFrame using PySpark.

EXERCISE 5.8

Flatten, Explode, and Shred JSON

1. Log in to the Azure portal at https://portal.azure.com > navigate to the Azure Synapse Analytics workspace you created in Exercise 3.3 > on the Overview blade, click the Open link in the Open Synapse Studio tile > select the Develop hub > hover over Notebooks > click the ellipse (. . .) > select Notebook > and then load one of the brain wave JSON files from a previous exercise (for example, by using a similar syntax to the following, replacing the * with your ADLS container and account, and by replacing the directory path and filename):

```
%%pyspark
from pyspark.sql.functions import explode, col
df = spark.read.option('multiline', 'true') \
    .json('abfss://*@*.dfs.core.windows.net/Json/PlayingGuitar/POW/*-0914
      .json')
flatten = df.select('Session')
```

```
flatten.show()
```

```
+--------------------+
|             Session|
+--------------------+
|{[[[{9.441, 4.12,...|
+--------------------+
```

2. Add the following code to the notebook. This gets you a little bit deeper into the structure of the JSON document and closer to the data you need.

```
flatten = df.select('Session', 'Session.Scenario',
                    'Session.POWReading', 'Session.POWReading')
flatten.show()
```

```
+--------------------+-------------+--------------------+--------------------+
|             Session|     Scenario|         ReadingDate|          POWReading|
+--------------------+-------------+--------------------+--------------------+
|{[[[{9.441, 4.12,...|PlayingGuitar|[2021-09-12T09:11...|[{[[{9.441, 4.12,...|
+--------------------+-------------+--------------------+--------------------+
```

3. Add the following code, which uses the `explode()` method on the `POWReading` array, to the notebook. Consider also adding the `printSchema()` method to see the structure of the data loaded into the DataFrame.

```
exploded = df.select(col('Session.Scenario').alias('SCENARIO'),
                     explode('Session.POWReading').alias('READING'))
exploded.printSchema()
exploded.show(5)
```

```
+-------------+--------------------+
|     SCENARIO|             READING|
+-------------+--------------------+
|PlayingGuitar|{[[{9.441, 4.12, 4...|
|PlayingGuitar|{[[{8.103, 4.82, 4...|
|PlayingGuitar|{[[{8.058, 5.304, ...|
|PlayingGuitar|{[[{8.39, 5.383, 5...|
|PlayingGuitar|{[[{8.686, 5.062, ...|
+-------------+--------------------+
```

4. To shred to JSON so that the result resembles the same structure as you achieved in Exercise 5.7, add and execute the following syntax. You can find all the queries in the `pysparkFlattenExplodeShred.txt` file on GitHub, in the directory `Chapter05/Ch05Ex08`.

```
shredded = exploded.select('SCENARIO',
    col('READING.AF3.THETA').alias('AF3THETA'),
```

EXERCISE 5.8 *(continued)*

```
    col('READING.AF3.ALPHA').alias('AF3ALPHA'),
    col('READING.AF3.BETA_L').alias('AF3BETA_L'),
    col('READING.AF3.BETA_H').alias('AF3BETA_H'),
    col('READING.AF3.GAMMA').alias('AF34GAMMA'),
    col('READING.AF4.THETA').alias('AF4THETA'),
    col('READING.AF4.ALPHA').alias('AF4ALPHA'))
shredded.show(5)
```

```
+-------------+--------+--------+---------+---------+---------+--------+--------+
|     SCENARIO|AF3THETA|AF3ALPHA|AF3BETA_L|AF3BETA_H|AF34GAMMA|AF4THETA|AF4ALPHA|
+-------------+--------+--------+---------+---------+---------+--------+--------+
|PlayingGuitar|[10.841]| [9.441]|  [4.712]|   [4.12]|  [4.508]| [6.014]| [8.826]|
|PlayingGuitar| [4.685]| [8.103]|  [4.704]|   [4.82]|  [4.896]| [2.959]| [7.901]|
|PlayingGuitar| [3.122]| [8.058]|  [5.168]|  [5.304]|  [5.124]| [2.181]| [7.614]|
|PlayingGuitar| [2.854]|  [8.39]|  [5.864]|  [5.383]|  [5.075]| [2.033]| [7.534]|
|PlayingGuitar| [2.854]| [8.686]|  [6.548]|  [5.062]|  [4.752]| [2.088]| [7.515]|
+-------------+--------+--------+---------+---------+---------+--------+--------+
```

5. Rename, save, and commit the notebook to your GitHub repository.

The first snippet of code imports the `explode()` and `col()` methods from the `pyspark.sql.functions` class. Then the JSON file is loaded into a DataFrame with an option stipulating that the file is multiline as opposed to a single line. The top-level property in the JSON document, `Session`, is selected and shown. You might consider passing the `truncate=False` parameter to the `show()` method, if you want to see the entire file. By default, the first 20 characters of the data are rendered to the result window. The following snippet of code illustrates how you can access the different properties and fields within the JSON document:

```
flatten = df.select('Session', 'Session.Scenario',
                    'Session.POWReading.ReadingDate', 'Session.POWReading')
```

Both the `Session` and `Session.POWReading` properties are entities that contain data within them, i.e., they have no direct value. `Session.Scenario` and `Session.POWReading.ReadingDate` do return a value when referenced from the `select()` method. You should notice that when reviewing the results of the query. The third code snippet is where you see the `explode()` method, which breaks out each reading that contains all electrodes and all their associated frequencies. At this point the data you are after is getting very close to the structure you can use to further analyze it.

```
exploded = df.select(col('Session.Scenario').alias('SCENARIO'),
                     explode('Session.POWReading').alias('READING'))
exploded.printSchema()
```

This might be a good place to review the structure of the data that is currently loaded into the DataFrame. This is done by calling the `printSchema()` method on the DataFrame, as follows:

```
root
 |-- SCENARIO: string (nullable = true)
 |-- READING: struct (nullable = true)
 |    |-- AF3: array (nullable = true)
 |    |    |-- element: struct (containsNull = true)
 |    |    |    |-- ALPHA: double (nullable = true)
 |    |    |    |-- BETA_H: double (nullable = true)
 |    |    |    |-- BETA_L: double (nullable = true)
 |    |    |    |-- GAMMA: double (nullable = true)
 |    |    |    |-- THETA: double (nullable = true)
 |    |-- AF4: array (nullable = true)
 |    |    |-- element: struct (containsNull = true)
 |    |    |    |-- ALPHA: double (nullable = true)
 |    |    |    |-- BETA_H: double (nullable = true)
...
```

The schema gives you a map to navigate the data. For example, by reviewing the schema, you can see how to retrieve the `ALPHA` frequency value from the `AF4` electrode. This is done by using dot notation like `READING.AF4.ALPHA`, which results in the value for that field being returned. The final code snippet of Exercise 5.8 used that approach to develop the syntax that resulted in the JSON shredding. Remember that shredding occurs when you have transformed the data from a valid JSON-structured document into a new form. The shredded form can be stored on a Spark table or view (for example, `df.createOrReplaceTempView()`), stored in Parquet format, or placed into a relational database for further transformation or data analytics.

Encode and Decode Data

There is a lot of history surrounding the encoding and decoding of data. Fundamentally, this concept revolves around how to store and render letter characters. As you know, all things that are computed must be constructed from either a 0 or a 1—a bit. Then you build sequences of those two numbers into, most commonly, 8-bit bytes, which can then be used to represent a character. You also likely know that the maximum possible unique bytes you can have using 8-bits is 256 (2^8), a number you will see in a lot of places. Early on in the era of computing, the mapping to characters was focused on English characters. Using ASCII or HEX, a character string like `brainjammer` can be converted into a set of numeric values. Then those values can be further converted into binary.

```
brainjammer

62 72 61 69 6e 6a 61 6d 6d 65 72

00110110 00110010 00100000 00110111 00110010 00100000 00110110 00110001
00100000 00110110 00111001 00100000 00110110 01100101 00100000 00110110
01100001 00100000 00110110 00110001 00100000 00110110 01100100 00100000
00110110 00110101 00100000 00110111 00110010
```

It was decided to map all English characters to ASCII using the numbers between 32 and 127 within the available 256. Moving forward a few decades, it turns out that as the world began to open up, it was learned that many written languages have more than 256 characters and require more space than an 8-bit byte. An attempt was made to double the number of bytes, which would effectively deliver 16 bits, which is 65,536 (2^{16}) possible characters. This character recognition approach is referred to as Unicode, and on the Windows operating system, you can see this in a tool named `charmap`. When you enter `charmap` into a command prompt, the result resembles Figure 5.24. Following Figure 5.24 you see the conversion of brainjammer into Unicode.

FIGURE 5.24 Encoding and decoding data Unicode

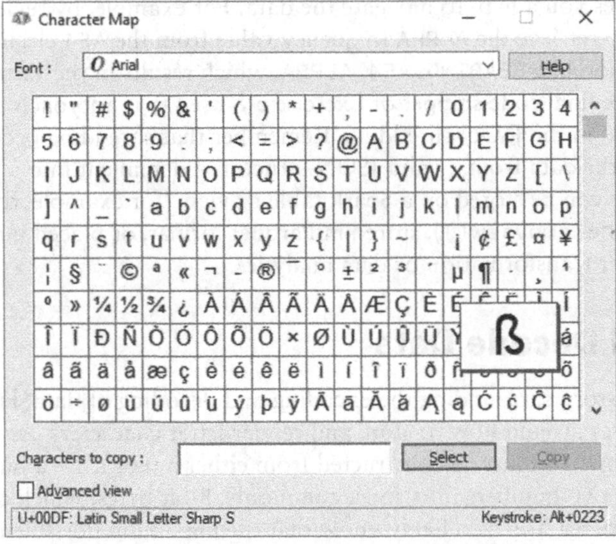


```
U+0062 U+0072 U+0061 U+0069 U+006e U+006a U+0061 U+006d U+006d U+0065 U+0072
```

There were some concerns about Unicode having to do with its size and some questionable internal technical techniques for converting bits to characters. Those concerns were enough to drive the invention of encodings and the concept of UTF-8. The introduction of

UTF-8 resulted in the ability to store Unicode in code points between 0 and 127 into a single byte, while all code points above 127 could be stored into two, three, or more bytes. First, a code point is a theoretical term used to describe how a letter is represented in memory. Second, the two, three, or more bytes that UTF-8 supports are for characters in languages that have greater than what can fit in a single byte, i.e., 256. Therefore, in addition to the encoding concept evolving around how to store and render letter characters, it is mostly concerned with the proper rendering of non-English character sets.

If you remember from Exercise 4.11, where you built a set of external tables, you ran the following `COLLATE` command along with the `CREATE DATABASE` command. The `COLLATE` command, along with its collation, sets the character encoding rules used for storing data into the database. The rules include locale, sort order, and character sensitivity conventions for character-based data types. This is not a supported collation type for a dedicated SQL pool, and the collation type cannot be changed after the database is created. Both are possible when creating external tables on a serverless SQL pool.

```
COLLATE Latin1_General_100_BIN2_UTF8
```

To work around the lack of UTF-8 support with dedicated SQL pools, you need to know about `VARCHAR` and `NVARCHAR` data types. A data type identifies what kind of value a data column contains. Simply, a `VARCHAR` data type stores ASCII values, and a `NVARCHAR` data type stores Unicode. You read previously that ASCII maps characters to numeric values between 32 and 127, which means there is limited to no special character support. This is where Unicode and `NVARCHAR` come into play. Unicode supports storing character strings using two bytes instead of the ASCII one byte. Therefore, to support some languages, you need to use Unicode. To gain some hands-on experience, complete Exercise 5.9.

EXERCISE 5.9

Encode and Decode Data

1. Log in to the Azure portal at `https://portal.azure.com` ➢ navigate to the Azure Synapse Analytics workspace you created in Exercise 3.3 ➢ on the Overview blade, click the Open link in the Open Synapse Studio tile ➢ navigate to the Manage hub ➢ start your dedicated SQL pool ➢ navigate to the Develop hub ➢ create a new SQL script ➢ and then execute the following SQL statement:

```
SELECT DATABASEPROPERTYEX(DB_NAME(), 'Collation') AS Collation
```

The output is `SQL_Latin1_General_CP1_CI_AS`, which is the default (refer to Figure 3.28).

2. Execute the following SQL syntax:

```
CREATE TABLE [dbo].[ENCODE] (
    [ENCODE_ID]        INT              NOT NULL,
    [ENCODE]           VARCHAR (1)      NOT NULL
)
```

EXERCISE 5.9 *(continued)*

```
GO
INSERT INTO [dbo].[ENCODE] ([ENCODE_ID], [ENCODE]) VALUES (1, '殺')
INSERT INTO [dbo].[ENCODE] ([ENCODE_ID], [ENCODE]) VALUES (2, 'Ž')
INSERT INTO [dbo].[ENCODE] ([ENCODE_ID], [ENCODE]) VALUES (3, 'ß')
INSERT INTO [dbo].[ENCODE] ([ENCODE_ID], [ENCODE]) VALUES (4, '€')
INSERT INTO [dbo].[ENCODE] ([ENCODE_ID], [ENCODE]) VALUES (5, '陽')
```

3. Execute the following SQL statement. The output is similar to Figure 5.25.

```
SELECT * FROM [dbo].[ENCODE] ORDER BY [ENCODE_ID]
```

FIGURE 5.25 Encoding and decoding data—VARCHAR

Results Messages

View Table Chart ↦ Export results

Search

ENCODE_ID	ENCODE
1	?
2	Ž
3	ß
4	€
5	?

00:00:00 Query executed successfully.

4. Execute the following SQL statement:

```
CREATE TABLE [dbo].[ENCODEN] (
    [ENCODE_ID]      INT              NOT NULL,
    [ENCODE]         NVARCHAR (1)     NOT NULL
)
INSERT INTO [dbo].[ENCODEN] ([ENCODE_ID], [ENCODE]) VALUES (1, N'殺')
INSERT INTO [dbo].[ENCODEN] ([ENCODE_ID], [ENCODE]) VALUES (2, 'Ž')
INSERT INTO [dbo].[ENCODEN] ([ENCODE_ID], [ENCODE]) VALUES (3, 'ß')
INSERT INTO [dbo].[ENCODEN] ([ENCODE_ID], [ENCODE]) VALUES (4, '€')
INSERT INTO [dbo].[ENCODEN] ([ENCODE_ID], [ENCODE]) VALUES (5, N'陽')
```

5. **Execute the following SQL statement. The output is similar to Figure 5.26.**

```
SELECT * FROM [dbo].[ENCODEN] ORDER BY [ENCODE_ID]
```

FIGURE 5.26 Encoding and decoding data—NVARCHAR

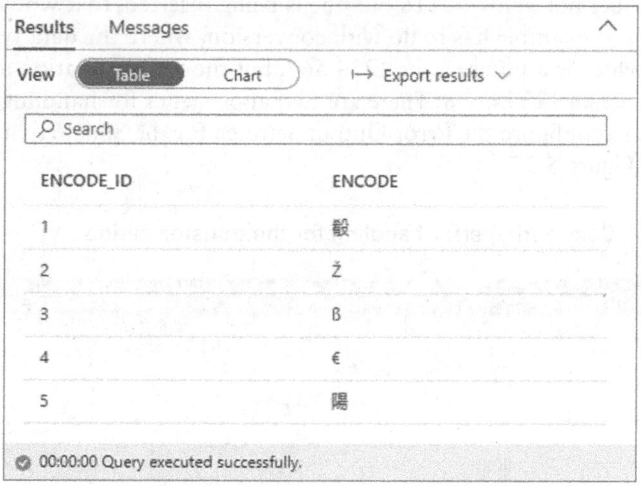

Results Messages

View Table Chart ↦ Export results

Search

ENCODE_ID	ENCODE
1	骰
2	Ž
3	ß
4	€
5	陽

00:00:00 Query executed successfully.

6. **Rename (for example, `Ch05Ex09`) and commit the SQL script to your integrated source code repository, as configured in Exercise 3.6, and then pause (shut down) the dedicated SQL pool. You can find the SQL script for this exercise in the `Chapter05/Ch05Ex09` directory on GitHub.**

The first action in Exercise 5.9 was to create, populate, and select the `[dbo].[ENCODE]` table. Notice that the data type for `[ENCODE]` was `VARCHAR`. When you store a character that does not fit into a single byte, then it cannot be correctly decoded. You can see this in Figure 5.25, when running the `SELECT` statement that results in a question mark (?) being rendered instead of the expected value. Using `NVARCHAR` as the data type for column `[ENCODE]` on the `[dbo].[ENCODEN]` table means the data stored in the column can be two bytes. Using `NVARCHAR` in combination with the `N` prefix on the data contained in the `INSERT` statement results in the data being stored correctly. Therefore, when the `SELECT` is performed on that table, as shown in Figure 5.26, the characters are decoded as expected and desired.

Configure Error Handling for the Transformation

As you transform data using Azure Synapse Analytics, there may be some failures when writing to the sink. The failures might happen due to data truncation, such as when the data type is defined as `VARCHAR(50)` but the value attempting to be inserted is 51 characters long. If a column does not allow `nulls` but one is being inserted, that would throw an error as well. The last example has to do with conversion, where the data type is defined as `decimal(7,3)`, which is a number like 1234.567, but the transformation logic is attempting to insert a value like 12345.678. There are two approaches for handling these kinds of errors. The first is to configure the Error Output Settings for the Sink activity in the data flow, as shown in Figure 5.27.

FIGURE 5.27 Configuring error handling for the transformation

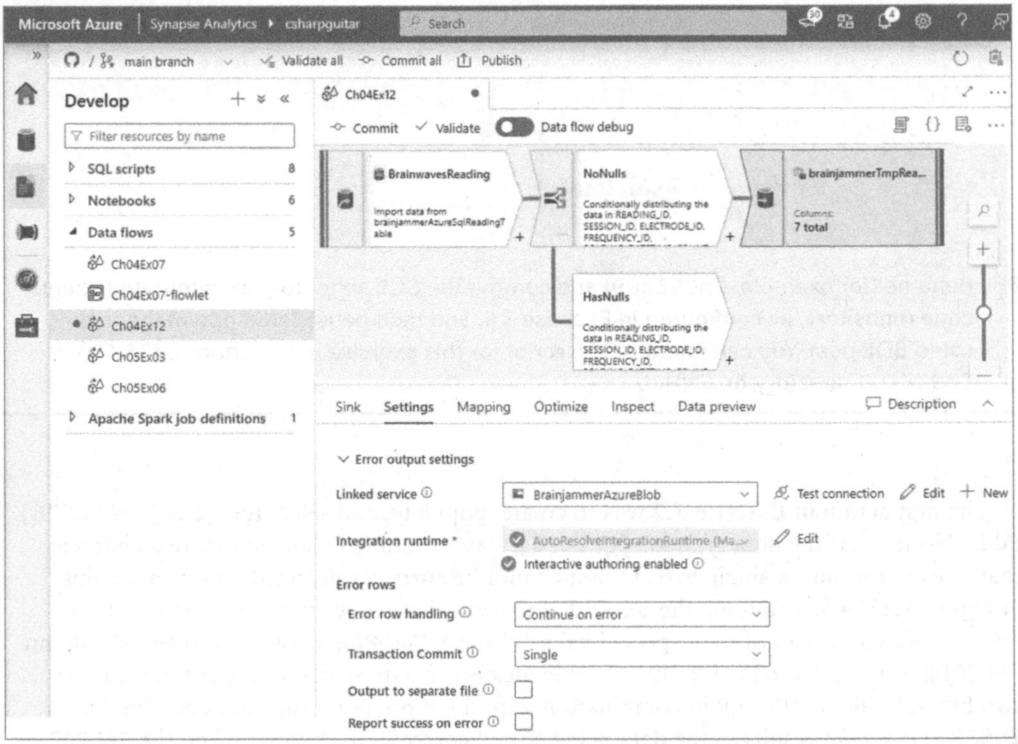

The configuration requires a linked service that is the location where the error log file will be written. An integration runtime is the compute power used to perform the writing of the log. The Error Rows section includes an Error Row Handling drop-down list box. The default value is Stop on First Error (Default). When the default value is selected, an error occurs. It means that the data flow will stop, which will cause the pipeline to stop as well.

This may or may not be desired. The alternative is to select the Continue on Error option, as shown in Figure 5.27, which does what its name implies. The Transaction Commit dropdown has values of either Single or Batch, which determine whether the error log is written after each transaction or at the end when the transformation completes. Single has better performance but is not the most optimal for large datasets; if you do have a large dataset, you should then consider Batch as the Transaction Commit setting. By default, the Output to a Separate File check box is disabled, which means the error file is appended to during each run. This contrasts with when the setting is enabled, in which case a new file is created for each run. The Report Success on Error check box is also disabled by default. This means that the pipeline will show as errored, but it will complete with an error log for review. If the check box is enabled, the pipeline will show as being successful, even though some errors happened but were handled due to this error handling configuration.

Figure 5.27 also shows the other option for handling errors: an additional activity, NoNulls, that checks for `nulls`. If no `null` is found, then the row is passed on to the sink for transformation and storage. If there is a `nulls`, then the data will not flow to the sink and is abandoned. This is more of a preventative action versus responding to an error, i.e., data cleaning. However, it is an option you might consider when implementing some kind of error handling solution.

Normalize and Denormalize Values

Normalization and denormalization can be approached in two contexts. The first context has to do with the deduplication of data and query speed on database tables in a relational database. The other context has to do with the normalization of data values in a machine learning scenario. Starting with the first context, begin with a review of the following descriptions of different database normal form rules which are used to normalize data. There are many normalization rules, but the most common are 0NF, 1NF, 2NF, and 3NF. 0NF does not qualify as one since it is considered to have no normalization.

Database Tables

0NF

This level of normal form is not considered normalized at all. It is not efficient for querying or searching, and the structure is not flexible.

```
BRAINWAVE

+---------+------+--------------+------------+------------+------------+
| MODE_ID | MODE | SCENARIO     | ELECTRODE1 | ELECTRODE2 | ELECTRODE3 | ...
+---------+------+--------------+------------+------------+------------+ ...
| 1       | EEG  | MetalMusic   | AF3        | AF4        | T7         | ...
| 2       | POW  | Meditation   | AF3        | AF4        | T7         | ...
+---------+------+--------------+------------+------------+------------+
```

Notice that some columns have similar, repeating names. Having attributes that repeat, like `ELECTRODE1`, `ELECTRODE2`, etc., is poor design in that it lacks flexibility.

1NF

The objective for the first normal form is to remove any repeating groups, such as the columns `ELECTRODE1`, `ELECTRODE2`, `ELECTRODE3`, etc. The data in this normal form is two dimensional because a `MODE` has multiple `ELECTRODE`s. The repeating columns can be replaced with a new `ELECTRODE` table, as follows:

```
BRAINWAVE
+---------+------+-------------+--------------+------------------+
| MODE_ID | MODE | SCENARIO    | ELECTRODE_ID | SESSION_DATETIME |
+---------+------+-------------+--------------+------------------+
| 1       | EEG  | MetalMusic  | 1            | 2022-05-05 13:49 |
| 1       | EEG  | MetalMusic  | 2            | 2022-05-05 13:49 |
| 1       | EEG  | MetalMusic  | 3            | 2022-05-05 13:49 |
| 1       | EEG  | MetalMusic  | 4            | 2022-05-05 13:49 |
| 1       | EEG  | MetalMusic  | 5            | 2022-05-05 13:49 |
| 2       | POW  | Meditation  | 1            | 2022-05-05 14:11 |
| 2       | POW  | Meditation  | 2            | 2022-05-05 14:11 |
| 2       | POW  | Meditation  | 3            | 2022-05-05 14:11 |
| 2       | POW  | Meditation  | 4            | 2022-05-05 14:11 |
| 2       | POW  | Meditation  | 5            | 2022-05-05 14:11 |
+---------+------+-------------+--------------+------------------+
```

By adding the following `ELECTRODE` dimension table, you resolve the issue caused by having repeating column names:

```
ELECTRODE
+--------------+-----------+
| ELECTRODE_ID | ELECTRODE |
+--------------+-----------+
| 1            | AF3       |
| 2            | AF4       |
| 3            | T7        |
| 4            | T8        |
| 5            | Pz        |
+--------------+-----------+
```

You might be able to visualize why 1NF is easier to search when compared to 0NF. Think about a piece of information you would want to retrieve from the `BRAINWAVE` table. For example, which `SCENARIO`s are related to `ELECTRODE_ID = 5`? In 1NF you can use the `ELECTRODE` table and a `JOIN` to find the sought after piece of information. In 0NF, you would need to write a query that checks each column, to determine which column contains Pz. That is not very efficient. From a flexibility perspective, what happens if you want to add a new electrode? If the table is in 0NF, it requires a new column, but 1NF requires only an additional row of data in the ELECTRODE table.

2NF

The objective of the second normal form is to remove redundant data and to ensure that the BRAINWAVE table contains an entity with a primary key comprising only one attribute. In this example the duplicated data is removed from the BRAINWAVE table by adding the ModeElectrode table with a key of MODE_ID + ELECTRODE_ID. ELECTRODE_ID is removed from the BRAINWAVE table and placed into the ModeElectrode table, which contains the relationship between MODE and ELECTRODE. An entity is in 2NF if it has achieved 1NF and the additional requirements. The following tables represent the 2NF requirements. Notice that the duplication is removed.

```
BRAINWAVE
+---------+------+-------------+------------------+
| MODE_ID | MODE | SCENARIO    | SESSION_DATETIME |
+---------+------+-------------+------------------+
| 1       | EEG  | MetalMusic  | 2022-05-05 13:49 |
| 2       | POW  | Meditation  | 2022-05-05 14:11 |
+---------+------+-------------+------------------+
```

The ModeElectrode table identifies and maintains the relationship between MODE and ELECTRODE. This results in the deduplication of data in the BRAINWAVE table.

```
ModeElectrode
+---------+--------------+
| MODE_ID | ELECTRODE_ID |
+---------+--------------+
| 1       | 1            |
| 1       | 2            |
| 1       | 3            |
| 1       | 4            |
| 1       | 5            |
| 2       | 1            |
| 2       | 2            |
| 2       | 3            |
| 2       | 4            |
| 2       | 5            |
+---------+--------------+
```

The ELECTRODE table remains the same in this scenario, as it is required to comply with and achieve 1NF.

```
ELECTRODE
+--------------+-----------+
| ELECTRODE_ID | ELECTRODE |
+--------------+-----------+
| 1            | AF3       |
| 2            | AF4       |
| 3            | T7        |
| 4            | T8        |
| 5            | Pz        |
+--------------+-----------+
```

The ELECTRODE table is useful in JOINs, which will provide the name of the ELECTRODE and its link to the MODE.

3NF

An entity or table is in 3NF if it is 2NF and all its attributes are not totally dependent on the primary key in the BRAINWAVE table. For example, the SESSION_DATETIME in the SESSION table is transitively dependent on SCENARIO.

```
SCENARIO
+-------------+------------+------------------+
| SCENARIO_ID | SCENARIO   | SESSION_DATETIME |
+-------------+------------+------------------+
| 4           | MetalMusic | 2022-05-05 13:49 |
| 3           | Meditation | 2022-05-05 14:11 |
+-------------+------------+------------------+
```

A new SCENARIO table must be created in order to enable the removal of the SESSION_DATETIME column attribute from the BRAINWAVE table.

```
BRAINWAVE
+---------+------+-------------+
| MODE_ID | MODE | SCENARIO_ID |
+---------+------+-------------+
| 1       | EEG  | 4           |
| 2       | POW  | 3           |
+---------+------+-------------+
```

In order for both the ModeElectrode and ELECTRODE tables to achieve 3NF, they must comply with 2NF requirements also. To be considered 3NF, the entity must also be 2NF-compliant.

```
ModeElectrode
+---------+--------------+
| MODE_ID | ELECTRODE_ID |
+---------+--------------+
| 1       | 1            |
| 1       | 2            |
| 1       | 3            |
| 1       | 4            |
| 1       | 5            |
| 2       | 1            |
| 2       | 2            |
| 2       | 3            |
| 2       | 4            |
| 2       | 5            |
+---------+--------------+
ELECTRODE
+--------------+-----------+
| ELECTRODE_ID | ELECTRODE |
+--------------+-----------+
| 1            | AF3       |
| 2            | AF4       |
| 3            | T7        |
| 4            | T8        |
| 5            | Pz        |
+--------------+-----------+
```

The reverse of what you just read concerning normalization rules is what you would call denormalization. The reason you would denormalize data is to reduce the number of JOINs required to retrieve a desired dataset. A JOIN is a high-impact command. Running a SQL statement that contains many JOINs on large datasets will likely be more latent when compared to queries with fewer JOINs. Consider some of the previous exercises in this chapter in which you transformed data. An aspect of that was the denormalization of the data. An example is with the data that was pulled from a relational Azure SQL database with the structure illustrated in Figure 5.28, which is 3NF. The transformation employed JOINs over numerous reference tables. The resulting dataset was a single compact table that contained all the information necessary for exploratory analysis that requires no JOINs. The boxes show the connections between the tables.

The next bit of content enters the realm of machine learning, which is not something you would likely encounter on the DP-203 exam. However, as you progress into exploratory data analysis, the normalization of data values can help you visualize data in a more consumable manner.

FIGURE 5.28 Normalizing and denormalizing brainjammer values

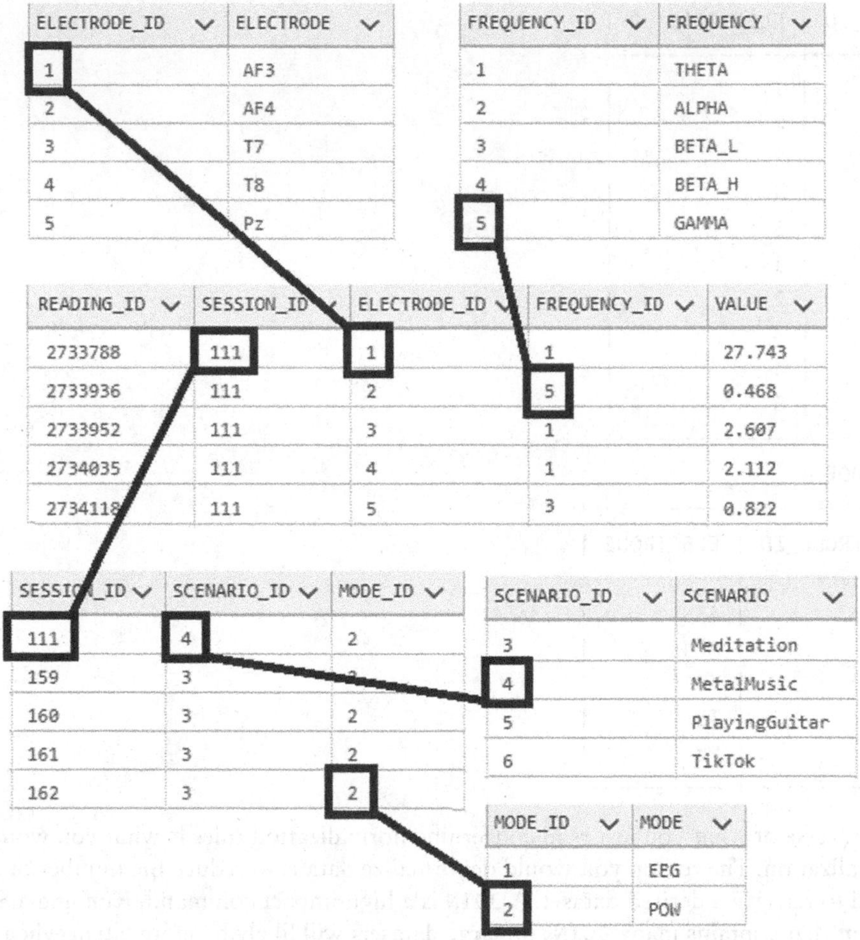

ELECTRODE_ID	ELECTRODE
1	AF3
2	AF4
3	T7
4	T8
5	Pz

FREQUENCY_ID	FREQUENCY
1	THETA
2	ALPHA
3	BETA_L
4	BETA_H
5	GAMMA

READING_ID	SESSION_ID	ELECTRODE_ID	FREQUENCY_ID	VALUE
2733788	111	1	1	27.743
2733936	111	2	5	0.468
2733952	111	3	1	2.607
2734035	111	4	1	2.112
2734118	111	5	3	0.822

SESSION_ID	SCENARIO_ID	MODE_ID
111	4	2
159	3	2
160	3	2
161	3	2
162	3	2

SCENARIO_ID	SCENARIO
3	Meditation
4	MetalMusic
5	PlayingGuitar
6	TikTok

MODE_ID	MODE
1	EEG
2	POW

Machine Learning

There are many techniques to consider when you want to better format data values for machine learning—or learning in general. Having data optimally organized increases the machine learning algorithm's ability to efficiently predict and train the data model. Two techniques, normalization and denormalizaton, are discussed here in more detail. Fundamentally, the concept of the normalization of data value has to do with changing the scale of the data without distorting the differences in ranges.

Normalization

Normalization is a technique that is often applied when preparing data for machine learning. The goal of normalization is to change the values of numeric columns in the dataset to use a common scale, without distorting differences in the ranges of values or losing information. Consider a query that performs some exploratory analysis using aggregate, analytic, and mathematical T-SQL functions of brain wave reading values by scenarios and frequency. The result of such a query may be something similar to the following.

```
+----------+-----------+---------+-------------+----------+--------+----------+
| SCENARIO | FREQUENCY | AVERAGE | STARNDARDEV | VARIANCE | MEDIAN | SQUARED  |
+----------+-----------+---------+-------------+----------+--------+----------+
| TikTok   | ALPHA     | 8.03769 | 28.50230488 | 812.3813 | 2.374  | 5.635876 |
| TikTok   | BETA_H    | 4.15734 | 15.90465451 | 252.9580 | 1.387  | 1.923769 |
| TikTok   | BETA_L    | 5.61691 | 23.43532764 | 549.2145 | 1.847  | 3.411409 |
| TikTok   | GAMMA     | 2.25973 | 8.469464626 | 71.73183 | 0.898  | 0.806404 |
| TikTok   | THETA     | 18.7486 | 39.01921699 | 1522.496 | 3.54   | 12.5316  |
+----------+-----------+---------+-------------+----------+--------+----------+
```

Notice the significant range of numbers in the output, where the smallest number is 0.806404 and the largest is 1522.496. If you attempted to visualize such a set of numbers, as shown in Figure 5.29, it might not be insightful.

FIGURE 5.29 Not normalized brain waves data

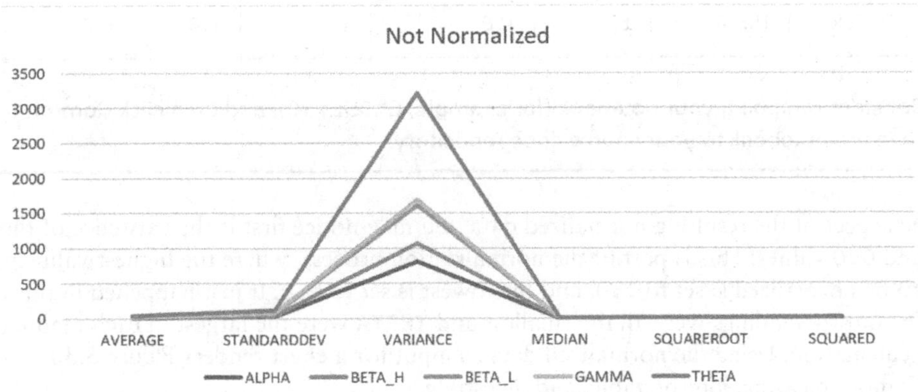

Perform Exercise 5.10 to normalize that data so that it renders more value when illustrated.

EXERCISE 5.10

Normalize and Denormalize Values

1. Log in to the Azure portal at `https://portal.azure.com` ➢ navigate to the Azure Synapse Analytics workspace you created in Exercise 3.3 ➢ on the Overview blade, click the Open link in the Open Synapse Studio tile ➢ navigate to the Develop hub ➢ create a new notebook ➢ select PySpark (Python) from the Language drop-down list box ➢ open the file `normalizeData.txt` on GitHub at `https://github.com/benperk/ADE` in the `Chapter05/Ch05Ex10` directory ➢ and then copy the contents into the notebook.

   Notice that the input for normalization is the same as the data shown in the previous data table.

2. Select your Spark pool from the Attach To drop-down list box ➢ click the Run Cell button ➢ wait for the session to start ➢ and then review the results, which should resemble the following:

```
+----------+-----------+---------+--------------+----------+--------+----------+
| SCENARIO | FREQUENCY | AVERAGE | STARNDARDEV | VARIANCE | MEDIAN | SQUARED |
+----------+-----------+---------+--------------+----------+--------+----------+
| TikTok   | ALPHA     | 0.35    | 0.656        | 0.511    | 0.635  | 0.412    |
| TikTok   | BETA_H    | 0.115   | 0.243        | 0.125    | 0.246  | 0.095    |
| TikTok   | BETA_L    | 0.204   | 0.49         | 0.329    | 0.441  | 0.222    |
| TikTok   | GAMMA     | 0.0     | 0.0          | 0.0      | 0.0    | 0.0      |
| TikTok   | THETA     | 1.0     | 1.0          | 1.0      | 1.0    | 1.0      |
+----------+-----------+---------+--------------+----------+--------+----------+
```

3. Consider renaming your notebook (for example, `Ch05Ex10`), and then click Commit to save the notebook to your source code repository.

The aspect of the resulting normalized data you may notice first is the existence of the `1.0` and `0.0` values. This is part of the normalization process, where the highest value in the data to be normalized is set to `1.0`, and the lowest is set to `0.0`. It just happened in this case that the `GAMMA` readings were all the smallest and `THETA` were the largest in each reading value calculation. Using the normalized data as input for a chart renders Figure 5.30, which is a bit more pleasing, interpretable, and digestible.

The classes and methods necessary to perform this normalization come from the `pyspark.ml.feature` namespace, which is part of the Apache Spark MLlib machine learning library. The first portion of the PySpark code that performs the normalization manually loads data into a DataFrame.

```
df = spark \
 .createDataFrame(
```

```
[
 ('TikTok',AlPHA',8.037698,28.50230489,812.381384,2.374,1.540779024,5.635876),
 ('TikTok', 'BETA_H',4.157344,15.90465452,252.9580353,1.387,1.177709642,1.923769),
 ('TikTok', 'BETA_L',5.616911,23.43532765,549.2145819,1.847,1.359043781,3.411409),
 ('TikTok', 'GAMMA',2.259732,8.469464627,71.73183106,0.898,0.947628619,0.806404),
 ('TikTok', 'THETA',18.7486,39.01921698,1522.499294,3.54,1.881488772,12.5316)],
["SCENA...", "FREQUE...","AVERA...","STANDA...", "VARIA...", "MEDIAN", "SQUARE...",
  "SQUAR..."])
```

FIGURE 5.30 Normalized brain waves data

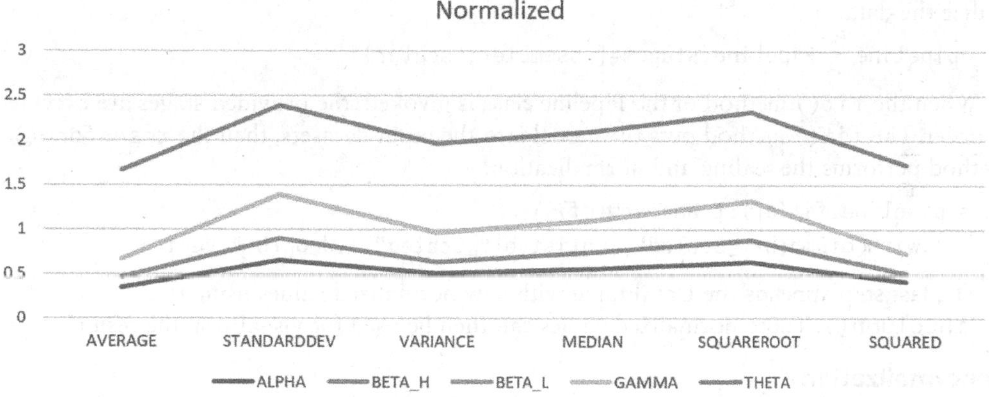

The next line of code defines a loop, which will iterate through the provided columns to be normalized.

```
for b in ["AVERAGE", "STANDARDDEV", "VARIANCE", "MEDIAN", "SQUAREROOT",
  "SQUARED"]:
```

The `VectorAssembler` transformation class merges multiple columns into a vector column. The code instantiates an instance of the class by passing the input data columns to the class's constructor. The result of the merge is stored into the `outputCol` variable, which includes column names appended with `_Vect`. A reference to the class instance and the result are loaded into a variable named `assembler`, which is a `Transformer` abstract class. The transformer is often referred to as the model, which is a common machine learning term.

```
assembler = VectorAssembler(inputCols=[b],outputCol=b+"_Vect")
```

The `MinMaxScaler` class performs linear scaling, aka normalization, or rescaling within the range of 0 and 1, using an algorithm similar to the following:

```
z = x - min(x) / max(x) - min(x)
```

The line of code that prepares the data for min-max normalization is presented here. The code first instantiates an instance of the class and passes the data columns to the constructor with an appended `_Vect` value. The result of the normalization will be stored into the `outputCol` variable with an appended `_Scaled` value on the end of its column name. A reference to the class instance and the result is loaded into a variable named `scaler` which is an `Estimator` abstract class.

```
scaler = MinMaxScaler(inputCol=b+"_Vect", outputCol=b+"_Scaled")
```

The pipeline in this scenario is the same as you have learned from the context of an Azure Synapse Analytics pipeline, in that it manages a set of activities from beginning to end. In this case, instead of calling the steps that progress through the pipeline "activities," they are called "stages." In this case, you want to merge the columns into a vector table and then normalize the data.

```
pipeline = Pipeline(stages=[assembler, scaler])
```

When the `fit()` method of the Pipeline class is invoked, the provided stages are executed in order. The `fit()` method puts the model into the input datasets, then the `transform()` method performs the scaling and normalization.

```
df = pipeline.fit(df).transform(df) \
    .withColumn(b+"_Scaled", unlist(b+"_Scaled")).drop(b+"_Vect")
```

The last step appends the DataFrame with new normalized values using the `.withColumn()`. Those normalized values can then be used for visualizing the result.

Denormalization

The inverse of normalization is denormalization. Denormalization is used in scenarios where you have an array of normalized data and you want to convert the data back to its original values. This is achieved by using the following code syntax, which can be run in a notebook in your Azure Synapse Analytics workspace. The code is available in the `denormalizeData.txt` file, in the `Chapter05/Ch05Ex10` directory on GitHub. The first snippet performs the normalization of the `AVERAGE` column found in the previous data table.

```
%%pyspark
import numpy as np
data = np.array([8.03769,4.15734,5.61691,2.25973,18.7486])
data_min = min(data)
data_max = max(data)
normalized = (data - data_min) / (data_max - data_min)
normalized

array([0.35041577,0.1150843,0.20360279,0,1])
```

To convert the normalized values back to their original values you perform denormalization, which is an inverse of the normalization algorithm.

```
denormalized = (normalized * (data_max - data_min) + data_min)
denormalized

array([8.03769,4.15734,5.61691,2.25973,18.7486])
```

You might be about the usefulness of this, as you already know what the original values are. In this case there is no need to denormalize them. Denormalization is very beneficial in testing machine learning algorithms. Machine learning involves predicting an outcome based on a model that is fed data—normalized data. The ability to denormalize normalized data enables you to test or predict the accuracy of the model. This is done by denormalizing the outcome and comparing it to the original values. The closer the match, the better your prediction and model.

Transform Data by Using Scala

In Exercise 5.4 you used the Scala language to perform data transformation. You received a data file in Parquet format, transformed it to a more queryable form, and stored it in a delta lake. If you were to briefly look over the language, you might find it difficult to differentiate the Scala language from PySpark, at least in the beginning. Consider the following example; the first line is Scala, and the second is PySpark:

```
var df = spark.read.parquet('/FileStore/business-data/2022/04/30')
df = spark.read.parquet('/FileStore/business-data/2022/04/30')
```

The only difference you can see is with the declaration of the `df` variable. The significant differences between the two will only be realized when you begin programming and coding large enterprise applications. Scala, an acronym for "scalable language," is an object-oriented programming language that runs in a *Java virtual machine (JVM)*. The JVM is a runtime host that is responsible for executing code, which also provides interoperability with Java code and libraries. PySpark is an API that provides an entry point into Apache Spark using Python. PySpark is considered a tool, not a programming language, that is useful for performing data science activities, but it is not necessarily the most preferred for creating high-scale applications. Consider the following pseudo-Scala code.

```
case class Mode(id: Int, name: String)
case class Scenario(id: Int, name: String)
case class Session(mode: Mode, scenario: Scenario)

val mode1 = new Mode(1, "POW")
val scenario1 = new Scenario(3, "Meditation")
val scenario2 = new Scenario(4, "MetalMusic")
```

```
val session1 = new Session(model, scenario1)

val scenariosSeq = Seq(scenario1, scenario2)
val df = scenariosSeq.toDF()
display(df)

+----+------------+
| id | session    |
+----+------------+
| 3  | Meditation |
+----+------------+
| 4  | MetalMusic |
+----+------------+
```

To achieve a similar outcome using PySpark, you would use the following code snippets. This example uses the Row class from Spark SQL, which requires the inclusion of the import statement.

```
from pyspark.sql import *

model = Row(id='1', name='POW')
scenario1 = Row(id='3', name='Meditation')
scenario2 = Row(id='4', name='MetalMusic')
scenarios = Row(mode=model, scenario=[scenario1, scenario2])
scenariosSeq = [scenario1, scenario2]
df = spark.createDataFrame(scenariosSeq)
df.show()

+----+------------+
| id | session    |
+----+------------+
| 3  | Meditation |
+----+------------+
| 4  | MetalMusic |
+----+------------+
```

It is not difficult to see the difference, and most of what you can do using Scala can also be done using PySpark. If you are most comfortable with the Python language, then it makes sense for you to use PySpark as the syntax; the methodology for PySpark is like that found in Python. However, Scala provides some benefits that do not exist in PySpark. For example, it is type-safe, compiles time exceptions, and offers an IDE named IntelliJ. Notice in the previous Scala code snippet that when you are defining the class, you also need to define the data type for the value, which is not required in the PySpark example. This can avoid unexpected exceptions in the execution of your code. If your code is expecting an integer and receives a string, there will be an exception; however, if your class does not allow the string to be entered into the class at all, then the runtime exception can be avoided. This leads to the second example: compile time. Because the `id` in the Scala code snippet is typed as an `Int`, if a subsequent line of code attempted to load a string into that variable, there would be a compile time exception. That means the code would not run until the value being loaded into that variable matched the type, which prevents an exception from happening by not compiling. Finally, there is an IDE named IntelliJ, which is targeted toward Java developers. IntelliJ is a very useful software tool for coding and troubleshooting Java code, which can then be simply converted into Scala.

Perform Exploratory Data Analysis

Exploratory data analysis (EDA) is a process of performing preliminary investigation on data. Ideally, when performing EDA, you would detect patterns or discover anomalies that produce previously unknown insights into the data source, such as the most common day and hour that Microsoft stock increases, or that the range of `THETA` frequency brain wave reading values are very high in the `PlayingGuitar` scenario versus other scenarios. Additionally, EDA is a useful activity to check assumptions and test hypotheses, for example, that `BETA` frequency brain wave reading values should not be low in a work scenario. A low `BETA` reading is linked to daydreaming and therefore isn't something you should be doing while working.

Before proceeding with the EDA exercise in Exercise 5.11, consider the following dataset, which provides some insights into the data you are about to analyze. The `statisticalSummary.txt` file in the `Chapter05` directory on GitHub contains the query to render this output. The data being analyzed is the brainjammer brain wave reading value, grouped by the scenario in which the value was generated.

```
+-----------+--------+--------+--------+-------+-------+-------+-------+----------+
| SCENARIO  | COUNT  | MEAN   | STD    | MIN   | 25%   | 50%   | 75%   | MAX      |
+-----------+--------+--------+--------+-------+-------+-------+-------+----------+
| Classic...| 506125 | 29.787 | 276.99 | 0.051 | 0.872 | 1.627 | 3.625 | 9986.869 |
| FlipCha...| 580237 | 46.643 | 358.27 | 0.068 | 1.053 | 1.904 | 4.043 | 9979.206 |
| Meditat...| 634740 | 29.620 | 294.67 | 0.065 | 0.88  | 1.924 | 4.526 | 9994.849 |
| MetalMu...| 521134 | 34.959 | 305.42 | 0.031 | 0.83  | 1.671 | 4.351 | 9992.889 |
| Playing...| 685650 | 39.931 | 313.32 | 0.088 | 2.414 | 3.807 | 6.798 | 9987.880 |
| TikTok    | 635986 | 15.406 | 165.33 | 0.051 | 0.976 | 1.692 | 3.482 | 9985.135 |
| WorkMee...| 253320 | 10.797 | 60.661 | 0.079 | 0.895 | 1.734 | 3.789 | 9782.769 |
| WorkNoE...| 720159 | 10.363 | 116.18 | 0.022 | 1.029 | 1.861 | 3.64  | 9985.042 |
+-----------+--------+--------+--------+-------+-------+-------+-------+----------+
```

There are two important findings to call out in the summarized statistical information. The first is the great distance between the `MIN` and `MAX` brainjammer brain wave reading values, which will have a big impact on the `MEAN` value. Also, the difference between the `MEAN`, which is `AVERAGE`, and the three distributions (`25%`, `50%`, and `75%`) has major gaps between them. This means there are some extreme values, aka outliers, in the dataset. None of this is expected or desired; therefore, some action needs to be taken to ignore or remove these values from the dataset used for EDA. To avoid this skewing of the data, approximately 2 percent of the data on either end will be removed in steps 2–4 of Exercise 5.11. Note that you must complete Exercise 5.1 before you can complete Exercise 5.11; the brain waves data that exists in the [brainwaves].[FactREADING] table is required.

EXERCISE 5.11

Perform Exploratory Data Analysis—Transform

1. Log in to the Azure portal at https://portal.azure.com ➢ navigate to the Azure Synapse Analytics workspace you created in Exercise 3.3 ➢ on the Overview blade, click the Open link in the Open Synapse Studio tile ➢ navigate to the Manage hub ➢ start your dedicated SQL pool ➢ navigate to the Develop hub ➢ create a new SQL script ➢ and then execute the following SQL statement:

```
SELECT COUNT(*) FROM brainwaves.FactREADING

4539223
```

2. Execute the following SQL syntax:

```
SELECT COUNT(*)
FROM brainwaves.FactREADING
WHERE [VALUE] < 0.274 OR [VALUE] > 392

99278
```

3. Execute the following SQL syntax:

```
SELECT * INTO brainwaves.FactREADINGHighLow
FROM brainwaves.FactREADING
WHERE [VALUE] < 0.274 OR [VALUE] > 392
SELECT COUNT(*) FROM brainwaves.FactREADINGHighLow

99278
```

4. Execute the following SQL syntax:

```
DELETE FROM brainwaves.FactREADING WHERE [VALUE] < 0.274
DELETE FROM brainwaves.FactREADING WHERE [VALUE] > 392
SELECT COUNT(*) FROM brainwaves.FactREADING

4438073
```

5. Execute the SQL syntax to calculate the statistical summary again, which renders results similar to the following:

```
+--------------+--------+--------+--------+-------+-------+-------+-------+---------+
| SCENARIO     | COUNT  | MEAN   | STD    | MIN   | 25%   | 50%   | 75%   | MAX     |
+--------------+--------+--------+--------+-------+-------+-------+-------+---------+
| Classical... | 492799 | 9.1424 | 29.76  | 0.274 | 0.892 | 1.634 | 3.539 | 391.850 |
| FlipChart    | 565591 | 9.4456 | 33.42  | 0.274 | 1.046 | 1.866 | 3.783 | 391.916 |
| Meditatio... | 611939 | 7.6830 | 27.526 | 0.274 | 0.928 | 1.959 | 4.468 | 391.992 |
| MetalMusi... | 504595 | 10.151 | 31.754 | 0.274 | 0.855 | 1.679 | 4.19  | 391.845 |
| PlayingGu... | 673387 | 11.187 | 31.741 | 0.274 | 2.395 | 3.753 | 6.501 | 391.958 |
| TikTok       | 628941 | 7.7538 | 25.975 | 0.274 | 0.984 | 1.693 | 3.447 | 391.945 |
| WorkMeeti... | 248777 | 10.008 | 28.172 | 0.274 | 0.931 | 1.769 | 3.854 | 391.381 |
| WorkNoEma... | 712044 | 6.8522 | 22.656 | 0.274 | 1.047 | 1.876 | 3.648 | 391.934 |
+--------------+--------+--------+--------+-------+-------+-------+-------+---------+
```

The previous queries are in the `preliminaryEDA.sql` file in the `Chapter05/Ch05Ex11` folder, on GitHub at `https://github.com/benperk/ADE`.

6. Execute the following SQL syntax. Consider adding a `WHERE` clause to the `SELECT` statement that projects only values for `SCENARIO = 'TikTok'`. The results are shown and match those in the "Normalization" section.

```
CREATE TABLE [brainwaves].[SCENARIO_FREQUENCY]
WITH
(
  CLUSTERED COLUMNSTORE INDEX,
  DISTRIBUTION = REPLICATE
)
AS
SELECT DISTINCT SCENARIO, FREQUENCY,
       AVG([VALUE]) OVER (partition by SCENARIO, FREQUENCY) as AVERAGE,
       STDEV([VALUE]) OVER (partition by SCENARIO, FREQUENCY) as STANDARDDEV,
       VAR([VALUE]) OVER (partition by SCENARIO, FREQUENCY) as VARIANCE,
       PERCENTILE_CONT(0.5) WITHIN GROUP (ORDER BY [VALUE])
         OVER (partition by SCENARIO, FREQUENCY) as MEDIAN,
       SQRT(PERCENTILE_CONT(0.5) WITHIN GROUP (ORDER BY [VALUE])
         OVER (partition by SCENARIO, FREQUENCY)) AS SQUAREROOT,
       SQUARE(PERCENTILE_CONT(0.5) WITHIN GROUP (ORDER BY [VALUE])
         OVER (partition by SCENARIO, FREQUENCY)) AS SQUARED
FROM brainwaves.FactREADING
GO
```

EXERCISE 5.11 ***(continued)***

```
SELECT * FROM [brainwaves].[SCENARIO_FREQUENCY] ORDER BY SCENARIO, FREQUENCY

+----------+-----------+---------+-------------+-----------+--------+----------+
| SCENARIO | FREQUENCY | AVERAGE | STARNDARDEV | VARIANCE  | MEDIAN | SQUARED  |
+----------+-----------+---------+-------------+-----------+--------+----------+
| TikTok   | ALPHA     | 8.03769 | 28.50230488 | 812.3813  | 2.374  | 5.635876 |
| TikTok   | BETA_H    | 4.15734 | 15.90465451 | 252.9580  | 1.387  | 1.923769 |
| TikTok   | BETA_L    | 5.61691 | 23.43532764 | 549.2145  | 1.847  | 3.411409 |
| TikTok   | GAMMA     | 2.25973 | 8.469464626 | 71.73183  | 0.898  | 0.806404 |
| TikTok   | THETA     | 18.7486 | 39.01921699 | 1522.496  | 3.54   | 12.5316  |
+----------+-----------+---------+-------------+-----------+--------+----------+
```

The previous queries are in the `preliminaryEDA.sql` file in the `Chapter05/Ch05Ex11` folder, on GitHub at `https://github.com/benperk/ADE`.

7. Select the Export Results drop-down menu item on the Results tab, and then select CSV, as shown in Figure 5.31. Note where the file is stored, as you will use this in Exercise 5.12.

FIGURE 5.31 Performing exploratory data analysis—visualizing data in Power BI

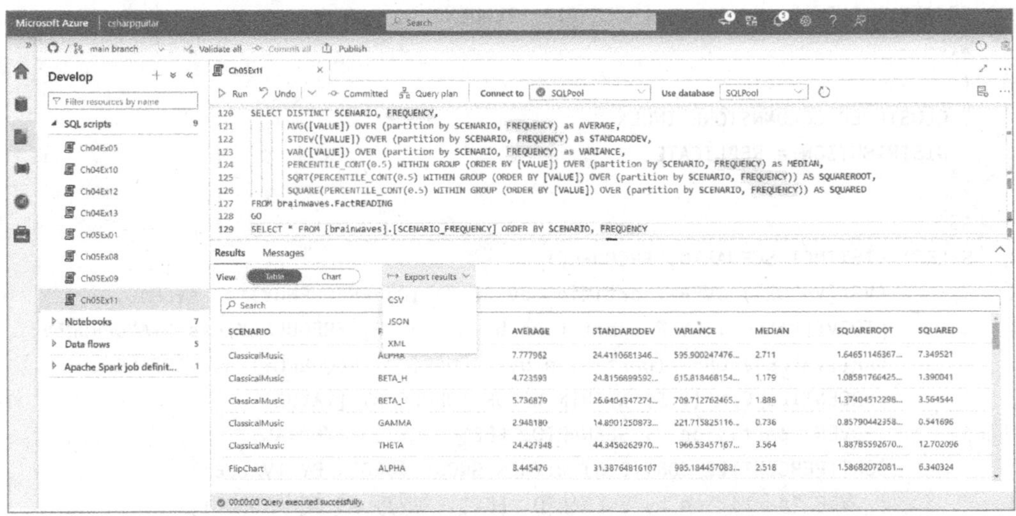

8. Consider renaming your SQL script (for example, `Ch05Ex11`), and then click the Commit button to save the notebook to your source code repository.

As you look over the output of the EDA data you created in step 6, it is hard to gain insights from that. This is why tools like Power BI and other graphing tools exist: to illustrate those numbers in a more consumable format. This is done in Exercise 5.12, but first a few points need to be discussed concerning Exercise 5.11. The approach used for the removal of outlying brain waves reading values was to remove 1 percent of the values from the bottom and top ranges, which is about 50,000 rows each. Through trial and error, it was determined that there were about 50,000 rows below a brain wave reading value of 0.274 and above 392. These constraints were then used to form the following SQL query and corresponding `DELETE` statements:

```
SELECT COUNT(*)
FROM brainwaves.FactREADING
WHERE [VALUE] < 0.274 OR [VALUE] > 392
DELETE FROM brainwaves.FactREADING WHERE [VALUE] < 0.274
DELETE FROM brainwaves.FactREADING WHERE [VALUE] > 392
```

Once the outliers were removed, the query to calculate the statical summary was re-executed. The resulting brain reading values for `MEAN`, `MIN`, 25%, 50%, 75%, and `MAX` fell into a more expected range. For ease of reference, both tables are provided here again for side-by-side review.

SCENARIO	COUNT	MEAN	STD	MIN	25%	50%	75%	MAX
Classic...	506125	29.787	276.99	0.051	0.872	1.627	3.625	9986.869
FlipCha...	580237	46.643	358.27	0.068	1.053	1.904	4.043	9979.206
Meditat...	634740	29.620	294.67	0.065	0.88	1.924	4.526	9994.849
MetalMu...	521134	34.959	305.42	0.031	0.83	1.671	4.351	9992.889
Playing...	685650	39.931	313.32	0.088	2.414	3.807	6.798	9987.880
TikTok	635986	15.406	165.33	0.051	0.976	1.692	3.482	9985.135
WorkMee...	253320	10.797	60.661	0.079	0.895	1.734	3.789	9782.769
WorkNoE...	720159	10.363	116.18	0.022	1.029	1.861	3.64	9985.042

SCENARIO	COUNT	MEAN	STD	MIN	25%	50%	75%	MAX
Classic...	492799	9.1424	29.76	0.274	0.892	1.634	3.539	391.850
FlipCha	565591	9.4456	33.42	0.274	1.046	1.866	3.783	391.916
Meditat...	611939	7.6830	27.526	0.274	0.928	1.959	4.468	391.992
MetalMu...	504595	10.151	31.754	0.274	0.855	1.679	4.19	391.845
Playing...	673387	11.187	31.741	0.274	2.395	3.753	6.501	391.958
TikTok	628941	7.7538	25.975	0.274	0.984	1.693	3.447	391.945
WorkMee...	248777	10.008	28.172	0.274	0.931	1.769	3.854	391.381
WorkNoE...	712044	6.8522	22.656	0.274	1.047	1.876	3.648	391.934

The query used to perform EDA on the brain wave reading values was simply a step into the unknown. Perhaps this is why it is considered exploratory. The word *exploratory* itself implies some kind of an adventure into the unknown, where new experiences, discoveries, and insights can be realized. From this point there is no textbook path to finding or discovering something; it is now based on your creativity, training, and experience in data analysis and with the context in which the data has been collected. One approach taken for further analysis here is based on the following query, which was executed in step 6 of Exercise 5.11:

```
SELECT * FROM [brainwaves].[SCENARIO_FREQUENCY] ORDER BY SCENARIO, FREQUENCY
```

As you learned at the end of Chapter 2, each brain frequency is linked to a trait. Here is the list again:

- `ALPHA` = Relaxation
- `BETA_H` = Concentration
- `BETA_L` = Problem-solving
- `GAMMA` = Learning
- `THETA` = Creativity

A hypothesis you might consider is that `ALPHA` values should be high while meditating and `GAMMA` values should be low while watching TikTok. Can you determine this when looking at the output of the `SELECT` statement from step 6?

SCENARIO	FREQUENCY	AVERAGE	STDEV	VARIANCE	MEDIAN	SQUARERT	SQUARED
Classic...	ALPHA	7.77796	24.41	595.9002	2.711	1.64651	7.34952
Classic...	BETA_H	4.72359	24.81	615.8184	1.179	1.08581	1.39004
Classic...	BETA_L	5.73687	26.64	709.7127	1.888	1.37404	3.56454
Classic...	GAMMA	2.94818	14.89	221.7158	0.736	0.85790	0.54169
Classic...	THETA	24.4273	44.34	1966.534	3.564	1.88785	12.7020
FlipCha...	ALPHA	8.44547	31.38	985.1844	2.518	1.58682	6.34032
FlipCha...	BETA_H	7.91475	35.10	1232.025	1.522	1.23369	2.31648
FlipCha...	BETA_L	8.39679	35.60	1267.615	2.171	1.47343	4.71324
FlipCha...	GAMMA	5.80837	25.45	648.0378	0.852	0.92303	0.72590
FlipCha...	THETA	16.8735	37.27	1389.521	3.547	1.88334	12.5812
Meditat...	ALPHA	10.6711	28.50	812.5112	4.688	2.16517	21.9773
Meditat...	BETA_H	5.33838	25.45	647.8040	1.203	1.09681	1.44720
Meditat...	BETA_L	6.92482	26.76	716.5744	2.05	1.43178	4.2025
Meditat...	GAMMA	3.49165	18.04	325.6560	0.564	0.75099	0.31809
Meditat...	THETA	11.6660	34.71	1204.922	3.318	1.82153	11.0091
MetalMu...	ALPHA	9.65091	29.62	877.7687	2.804	1.67451	7.86241

```
| MetalMu... | BETA_H   | 5.61864 | 26.93 | 725.7568 | 1.155 | 1.07470 | 1.33402 |
| MetalMu... | BETA_L   | 6.93686 | 28.15 | 792.9845 | 1.872 | 1.36821 | 3.50438 |
| MetalMu... | GAMMA    | 3.65391 | 18.65 | 348.0886 | 0.641 | 0.80062 | 0.41088 |
| MetalMu... | THETA    | 24.8180 | 44.66 | 1995.347 | 4.26  | 2.06397 | 18.1476 |
| Playing... | ALPHA    | 11.1915 | 31.60 | 998.6364 | 4.948 | 2.22441 | 24.4827 |
| Playing... | BETA_H   | 8.28999 | 29.35 | 861.9142 | 3.428 | 1.85148 | 11.7511 |
| Playing... | BETA_L   | 9.30315 | 29.97 | 898.2781 | 3.955 | 1.98871 | 15.6420 |
| Playing... | GAMMA    | 6.50749 | 23.09 | 533.5194 | 3.03  | 1.74068 | 9.1809  |
| Playing... | THETA    | 20.9508 | 40.49 | 1639.646 | 4.838 | 2.19954 | 23.4064 |
| TikTok     | ALPHA    | 8.03769 | 28.50 | 812.3813 | 2.374 | 1.54077 | 5.63587 |
| TikTok     | BETA_H   | 4.15734 | 15.90 | 252.9580 | 1.387 | 1.17770 | 1.92376 |
| TikTok     | BETA_L   | 5.61691 | 23.43 | 549.2145 | 1.847 | 1.35904 | 3.41140 |
| TikTok     | GAMMA    | 2.25973 | 8.469 | 71.73183 | 0.898 | 0.94762 | 0.80640 |
| TikTok     | THETA    | 18.7486 | 39.01 | 1522.499 | 3.54  | 1.88148 | 12.5316 |
| WorkMee... | ALPHA    | 8.60130 | 20.40 | 416.4155 | 2.488 | 1.57733 | 6.19014 |
| WorkMee... | BETA_H   | 2.92737 | 8.049 | 64.78699 | 1.277 | 1.13004 | 1.63072 |
| WorkMee... | BETA_L   | 4.78124 | 13.70 | 187.9109 | 1.934 | 1.39068 | 3.74035 |
| WorkMee... | GAMMA    | 2.21660 | 5.564 | 30.95878 | 0.693 | 0.83246 | 0.48024 |
| WorkMee... | THETA    | 30.9504 | 51.37 | 2639.236 | 3.557 | 1.88600 | 12.6522 |
| WorkNoE... | ALPHA    | 6.74185 | 18.26 | 333.4624 | 2.587 | 1.60841 | 6.69256 |
| WorkNoE... | BETA_H   | 2.48217 | 7.473 | 55.85412 | 1.491 | 1.22106 | 2.22308 |
| WorkNoE... | BETA_L   | 3.98338 | 12.70 | 161.4544 | 2.159 | 1.46935 | 4.66128 |
| WorkNoE... | GAMMA    | 1.70539 | 5.135 | 26.36919 | 0.92  | 0.95916 | 0.8464  |
| WorkNoE... | THETA    | 19.2447 | 42.11 | 1773.789 | 3.36  | 1.83303 | 11.2896 |
+------------+----------+---------+-------+----------+-------+---------+---------+
```

To create a visual representation of this data, complete Exercise 5.12. Once completed, use the visualization to determine whether the aforementioned hypothesis is true or false.

EXERCISE 5.12

Perform Exploratory Data Analysis—Visualize

This exercise requires a Power BI Premium subscription, which can be acquired at `https://powerbi.microsoft.com`.

1. Log in to your Power BI account > select Workspaces from the navigation bar > click the Create a Workspace button > enter a workspace name > enter a description (see Figure 5.32) > and then click Save.

EXERCISE 5.12 *(continued)*

FIGURE 5.32 Performing exploratory data analysis—visualizing data in Power BI (2)

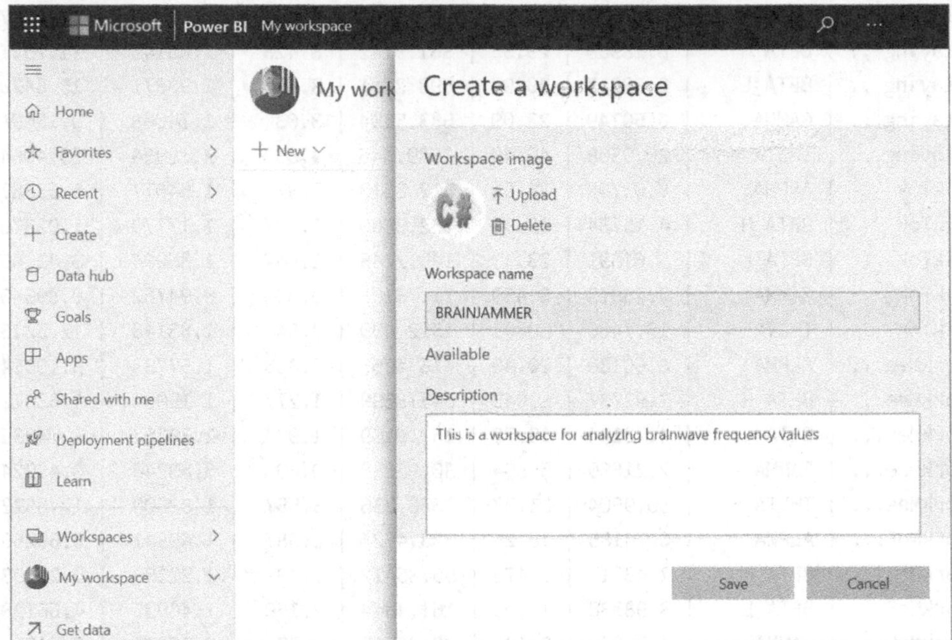

2. Once the Power BI workspace is provisioned, select the + New drop-down menu item ➤ select Upload a File ➤ and then upload the CSV file from step 7 in Exercise 5.11. The file, `Analysis.csv` is available on GitHub, in the `Chapter05/Ch05Ex12` directory. Once the file is uploaded, you will see it in the workspace, as shown in Figure 5.33.

FIGURE 5.33 Performing exploratory data analysis—Power BI workspace

Microsoft
Power BI
BRAINJAMMER
Goals
Apps
Shared with me
Deployment pipelines
Learn
Workspaces
BRAINJAMMER
Get data
BRAINJAMMER
Create app
New
Create a pipeline
View
Filters
Settings
Access
Search
All
Content
Datasets + dataflows
Datamarts (Preview)

Name	Type	Owner	Refreshed	Next refresh
Analysis	Dataset	BRAINJAMMER	5/17/22, 1:15:40 PM	N/A

3. Hover over the file with your mouse ➢ click the three vertical dots ➢ select Create Report from the popup menu ➢ expand Analysis in the Fields pane ➢ drag `FREQUENCY` into the Axis text box in the Visualizations pane ➢ drag `SCENARIO` into the Legend text box ➢ drag `MEDIAN` into the Values text box ➢ and then select the Stacked bar chart icon. The chart resembles Figure 5.34.

FIGURE 5.34 Performing exploratory data analysis—visualizing brain waves in Power BI

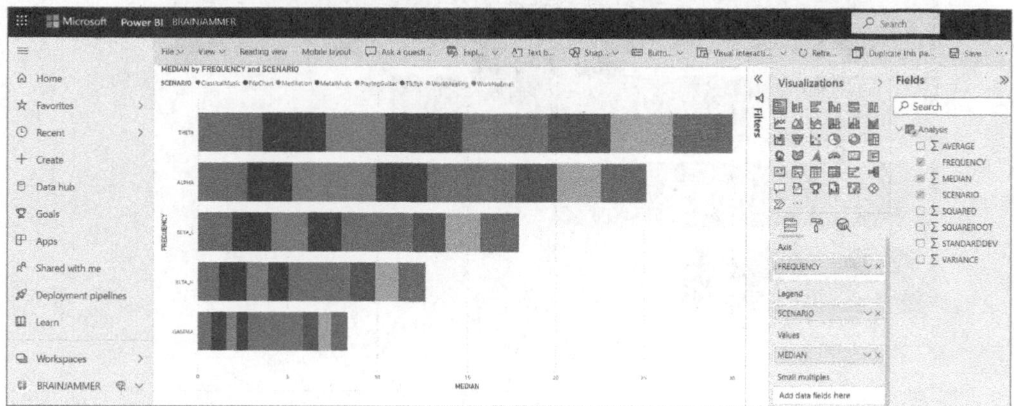

4. Select the Save menu item ➢ enter a name for the report ➢ and then Save.

The hypothesis of `ALPHA` being high while meditating turns out to be true, as shown in Figure 5.35. The meditation scenario has the highest `ALPHA` median value of all scenarios. It makes sense that while meditating the subject would be in a relaxed state.

Figure 5.36 shows a low brain wave reading value for `GAMMA`. The result is inconclusive because `GAMMA` readings for all scenarios are smaller in general than the other frequencies. In this case, more analysis is required to prove the hypothesis as to whether the test subject is learning or in a creative mindset while watching TikTok.

You now have a taste of what it is like to perform EDA and how to make some conclusions from it. You can use many other tables and perspectives to approach the analysis of this data. The findings and insights you can uncover are vast.

FIGURE 5.35 Performing exploratory data analysis—visualizing brain waves alpha meditation

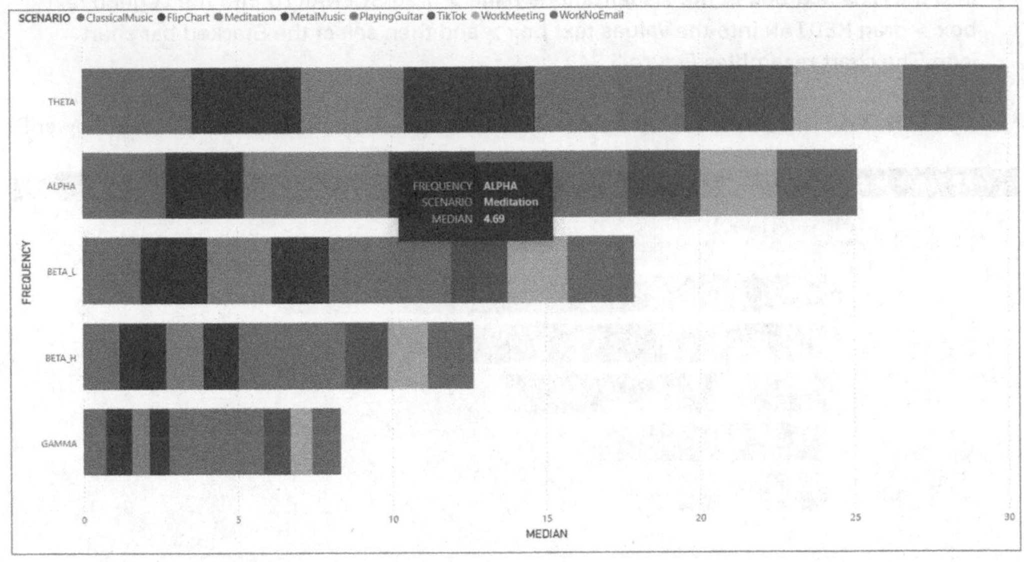

FIGURE 5.36 Performing exploratory data analysis—visualizing brain waves gamma TikTok

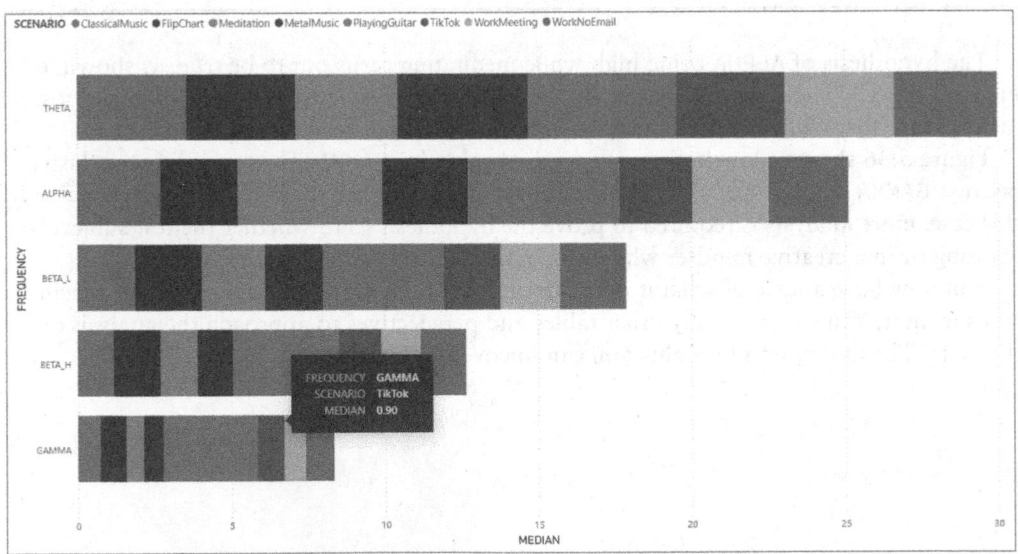

Transformation and Data Management Concepts

Now that you have performed some data transformation exercises, it is a good time to read about some applicable transformation and data management concepts.

Transformation

As you progressed through the exercises that transformed the brainjammer brain wave data, the first action you took was to learn something about the data. This phase is often called *data discovery*. To transform data, you need to know its structure and its characteristics, like data types and relationships. Upon discovering the shape and purpose of your data, you can then begin a phase called *data mapping*. This phase is where you consider the current state of the data and decide what you want the end state to be. You will need to identify each piece of data and map it to a final state. This includes identifying activities such as aggregation, filtering, joining, or modifying that will transform the data in some way. Next, you would create the code that will perform the transformation. Languages such as PySpark, Scala, C#, and T-SQL are commonly used in a Big Data context. The execution of the code against the raw data and the review of the outcome completes the final two steps. Figure 5.37 is a visual representation of the data transformation process.

FIGURE 5.37 The data transformation process

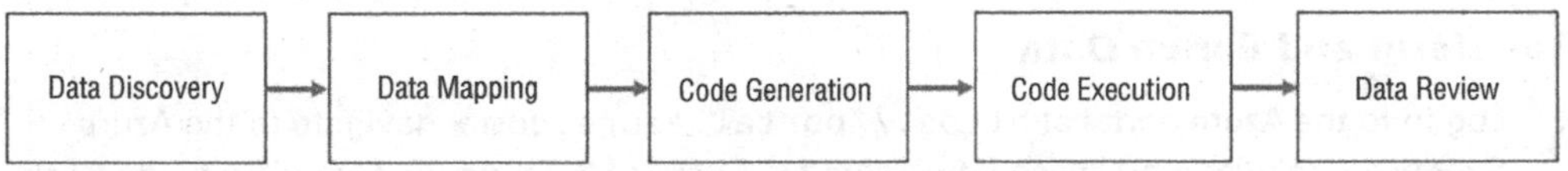

The data review phase does not necessarily mean that the data transformation process is complete. There can be numerous iterations of this process. As you experienced while performing the exercises in this chapter, a transformation process includes the conversion of data existing on an Azure SQL database to a Parquet file. Another transformation referenced dimension tables to create a version of all available brainjammer brain wave readings that was easier to use. A common phase in the process that happens after a data review is data enrichment.

Enrichment

Each time you iterate through the data transformation process, you expect the data to get better. That is called enrichment. Removing `null` values, normalizing the data, or removing data outliers are all types of data enrichment that improve usability, accuracy, and understanding. In Exercise 5.13 you will perform data enrichment to aggregate and normalize data using Azure Synapse pipeline activities and data flow transformations. The completed Azure Synapse pipeline will look something like Figure 5.38.

FIGURE 5.38 Transforming and enriching the data pipeline

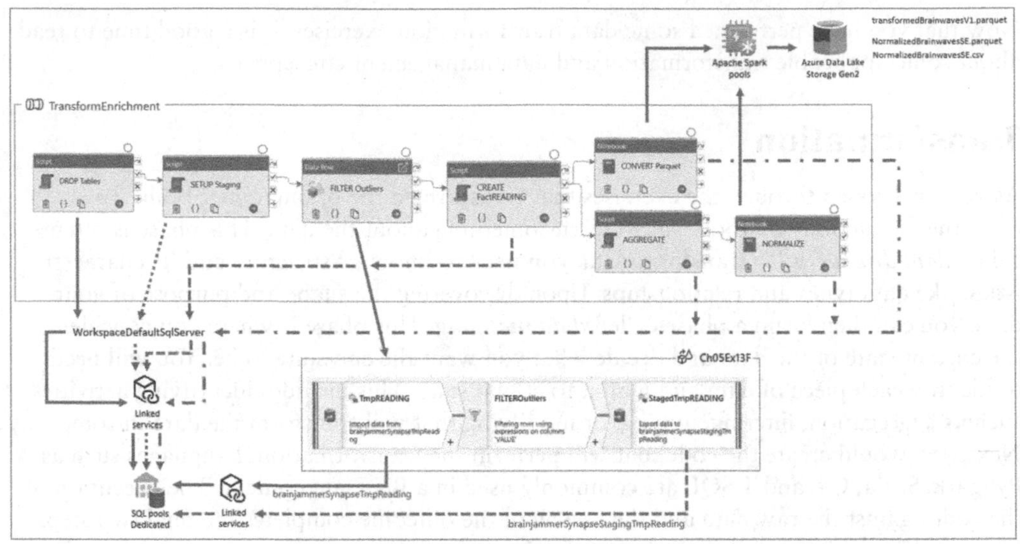

EXERCISE 5.13

Transform and Enrich Data

1. Log in to the Azure portal at `https://portal.azure.com` ➢ navigate to the Azure Synapse Analytics workspace you created in Exercise 3.3 ➢ on the Overview blade, click the Open link in the Open Synapse Studio tile ➢ select the Manage hub ➢ select SQL Pools from the menu list ➢ and then start the dedicated SQL pool.
2. Select the Integrate hub ➢ create a new pipeline ➢ rename the pipeline (I used **TransformEnrichment**) ➢ expand the General group within the Activities pane ➢ drag and drop a Script activity to the canvas ➢ enter a name (I used **DROP Tables**) ➢ select the Settings tab ➢ select the `WorkspaceDefaultSqlServer` from the Linked Service drop-down list box ➢ add your SQL pool name as the value of `DBName` (I used **SQLPool**) ➢ select the `NonQuery` radio button in the Script section ➢ and then enter the following into the Script multiline text box. Figure 5.39 represents the configuration.

```
IF OBJECT_ID (N'brainwaves.FactREADING', N'U') IS NOT NULL
 DROP TABLE [brainwaves].[FactREADING]
IF OBJECT_ID (N'brainwaves.SCENARIO_FREQUENCY', N'U') IS NOT NULL
 DROP TABLE [brainwaves].[SCENARIO_FREQUENCY]
```

FIGURE 5.39 Transforming and enriching data—pipeline drop script

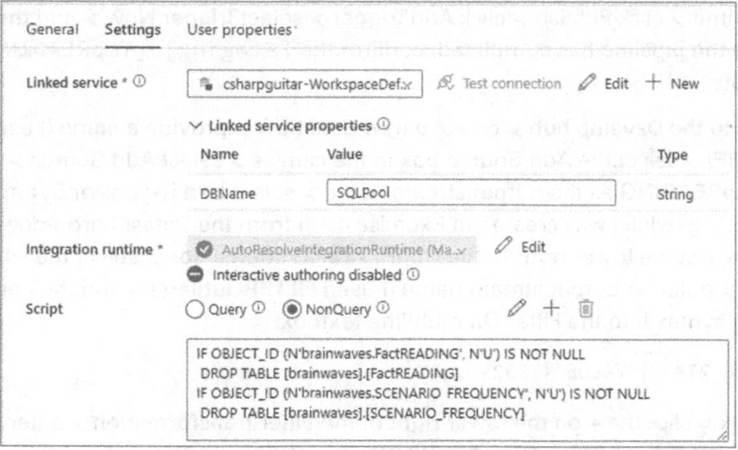

3. Add a Script activity to the pipeline ➢ enter a name (I used **SETUP Staging**) ➢ select the `WorkspaceDefaultSqlServer` linked service from the drop-down list box ➢ enter your dedicated SQL pool name as the DBName property value (I used **SQLPool**) ➢ select the NonQuery radio button ➢ and then add the following to the Script multiline textbox. The script is the `TransformEnrichmentPipeline.txt` file on GitHub, in the folder `Chapter05/Ch05Ex13`.

```
IF OBJECT_ID (N'staging.TmpREADING', N'U') IS NOT NULL
 DELETE FROM [staging].[TmpREADING]
ELSE
  CREATE TABLE [staging].[TmpREADING]
  (
    [READING_ID] [int]  NOT NULL,
    [SESSION_ID] [int]  NOT NULL,
    [ELECTRODE_ID] [int]  NOT NULL,
    [FREQUENCY_ID] [int]  NOT NULL,
    [READING_DATETIME] [datetime]  NOT NULL,
    [COUNT] [int]  NOT NULL,
    [VALUE] [decimal](8,3)  NOT NULL
  )
  WITH
  (
     DISTRIBUTION = ROUND_ROBIN,
     CLUSTERED COLUMNSTORE INDEX
  )
```

EXERCISE 5.13 ***(continued)***

4. Click Commit > click Publish > click Add Trigger > select Trigger Now > and then click OK. Once the pipeline has completed, confirm the `[staging].[TmpREADING]` table exists.

5. Navigate to the Develop hub > create a new data flow > provide a name (I used **Ch05Ex13F**) > select the Add Source box in the canvas > select Add Source > enter **TmpREADING** as the output stream name > select `brainjammerSynapse TmpReading` (which was created in Exercise 4.13) from the Dataset drop-down list box > click the + at the lower right of the TmpREADING source box > select the Filter Row modifier > enter an output stream name (I used **FILTEROutliers**) > and then enter the following syntax into the Filter On multiline textbox:

```
VALUE > 0.274 || VALUE < 392
```

6. Add a sink > click the + on the lower right of the Filter transformation > enter an output stream name (I used **StagedTmpREADING**) > create a new dataset by clicking the + New button to the right of the Dataset drop-down text box > target the `[staging] .[TmpREADING]` table you just created > and then click Commit.

7. Add the data flow from step 6 into your pipeline > expand the Move & Transform group > drag and drop a Data Flow activity to the canvas > enter a name (I used **FILTER Outliers**) > select the Settings tab > select the data flow from the Data Flow drop-down text box (for example, `Ch05Ex13F`) > configure staging storage like you did in step 8 of Exercise 4.13 > link the SETUP Staging activity to the data flow (for example, `FILTER Outliers`) > and then click Commit. Figure 5.40 shows the configuration.

FIGURE 5.40 Transforming and enriching data —filter transformation data flow

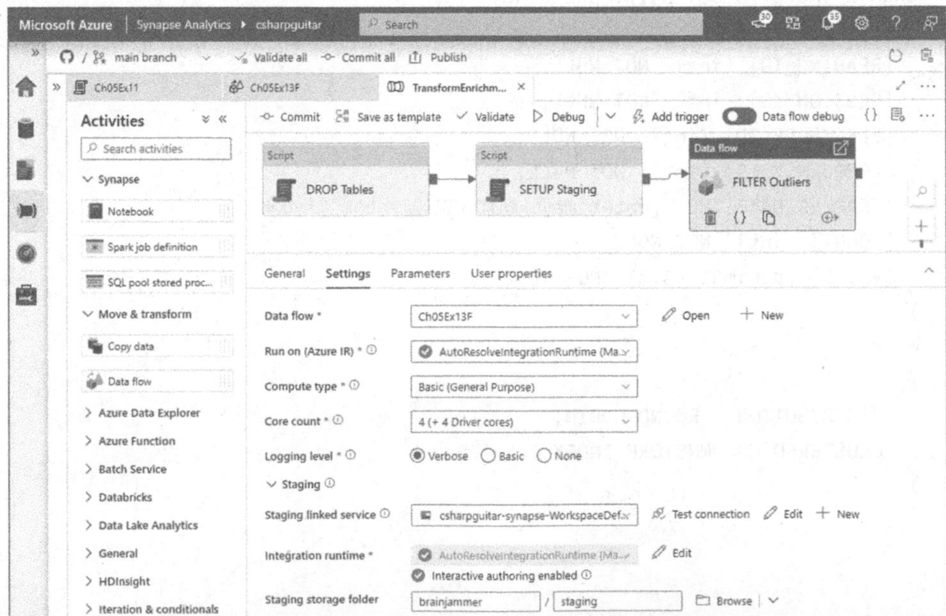

8. Add a Script activity to the pipeline ➢ enter a name (I used **CREATE FactREADING**) ➢ select the same linked service from the drop-down list box as you did earlier (for example, `csharpguitar-WorkspaceDefaultSqlServer`) ➢ enter your dedicated SQL pool name into the DBName property value (for example, `SQLPool`) ➢ select the NonQuery radio button ➢ and then add the following to the Script multiline textbox:

```
CREATE TABLE [brainwaves].[FactREADING]
  WITH
  (
    CLUSTERED COLUMNSTORE INDEX,
    DISTRIBUTION = HASH ([FREQUENCY])
  )
    AS
    SELECT  se.SESSION_DATETIME, r.READING_DATETIME,
            s.SCENARIO, e.ELECTRODE, f.FREQUENCY, r.[VALUE]
    FROM    [brainwaves].[DimSESSION] se, [staging].[TmpREADING] r,
            [brainwaves].[DimSCENARIO] s, [brainwaves].[DimELECTRODE] e,
            [brainwaves].[DimFREQUENCY] f
    WHERE   r.SESSION_ID = se.SESSION_ID AND se.SCENARIO_ID = s.SCENARIO_ID
            AND r.ELECTRODE_ID = e.ELECTRODE_ID AND r.FREQUENCY_ID =
              f.FREQUENCY_ID
```

9. Navigate to the Develop hub ➢ create a new notebook ➢ rename the notebook (I used **Ch05Ex13TB**) ➢ and then enter the following syntax:

```
%%spark
val df = spark.read.sqlanalytics("SQLPool.brainwaves.FactREADING")
df.write.mode("overwrite").option("header", "true").parquet("abfss://
brainjammer@csharpguitar.dfs.core.windows.net/EMEA/brainjammer/
in/2022/05/19/14/transformedBrainwavesV1.parquet")
```

10. Click the Commit button ➢ add a Notebook activity to your pipeline from the Synapse group ➢ enter a name (I used **CONVERT Parquet**) ➢ select the Settings tab ➢ select the notebook you just created ➢ select your Spark pool (for example, `SparkPool`) ➢ link the `CREATE FactREADING` Script activity to the notebook ➢ and then click Commit.

11. Add a Script activity to the pipeline ➢ enter a name (I used **AGGREGATE**) ➢ on the Settings tab select the same linked service from the drop-down list box as you did earlier (for example, `csharpguitar-WorkspaceDefaultSqlServer`) ➢ enter your dedicated SQL pool name into the DBName property value (I used **SQLPool**) ➢ select the NonQuery radio button ➢ and then add the following to the Script multiline textbox:

EXERCISE 5.13 *(continued)*

```
IF OBJECT_ID (N'brainwaves.SCENARIO_FREQUENCY', N'U') IS NOT NULL
 DROP TABLE [SCENARIO_FREQUENCY].[SCENARIO_FREQUENCY]

CREATE TABLE [brainwaves].[SCENARIO_FREQUENCY]
WITH
(
  CLUSTERED COLUMNSTORE INDEX,
  DISTRIBUTION = REPLICATE
)
AS
SELECT DISTINCT SCENARIO, FREQUENCY,
       AVG([VALUE]) OVER (partition by SCENARIO, FREQUENCY) as AVERAGE,
       STDEV([VALUE]) OVER (partition by SCENARIO, FREQUENCY) as STANDARDDEV,
       VAR([VALUE]) OVER (partition by SCENARIO, FREQUENCY) as VARIANCE,
       PERCENTILE_CONT(0.5) WITHIN GROUP (ORDER BY [VALUE])
          OVER (partition by SCENARIO, FREQUENCY) as MEDIAN,
       SQRT(PERCENTILE_CONT(0.5) WITHIN GROUP (ORDER BY [VALUE])
          OVER (partition by SCENARIO, FREQUENCY)) AS SQUAREROOT,
       SQUARE(PERCENTILE_CONT(0.5) WITHIN GROUP (ORDER BY [VALUE])
          OVER (partition by SCENARIO, FREQUENCY)) AS SQUARED
FROM brainwaves.FactREADING
```

12. Link the CREATE FactREADING Script activity to the AGGREGATE Script activity ➢ click the Commit button ➢ navigate to the Develop hub ➢ create a new notebook ➢ rename the notebook (I used **Ch05Ex13N**) ➢ and then enter the following syntax:

```
%%spark
val df = spark.read.sqlanalytics("SQLPool.brainwaves.SCENARIO_FREQUENCY")
df.createOrReplaceTempView("NormalizedBrainwavesSE")
```

13. Add another cell to the notebook ➢ click the + Code button below the first cell ➢ enter the code located in the Normalize.txt file in the Chapter05/Ch05Ex13 directory on GitHub (the code snippet is like that from Exercise 5.10) ➢ click the Commit button ➢ add a Notebook activity to your pipeline from the Synapse group ➢ enter a name (I used **NORMALIZE**) ➢ select the Settings tab ➢ select the notebook you just created (in my example, Ch05Ex13N) ➢ select your Spark pool (SparkPool) ➢ and then link the AGGREGATE Script activity to the NORMALIZE notebook.

14. Click the Commit button to save the pipeline to your source code repository ➢ click the Publish button ➢ review the changes ➢ click the OK button ➢ click the Add Trigger button➢ select Trigger Now ➢ and then click OK.

You might have noticed that the steps in Exercise 5.13 were a culmination of pieces of previous exercises. This is how you learn and ultimately improve your data analytics solution. It is improved by iterating through numerous versions of your solution. First, you needed to get the data into a friendly format and structure, then you performed some transformations using aggregate functions, and then performed some normalization and EDA. In Exercise 5.13 you pulled it all together into a single pipeline that retrieves the data from a source and ends with ready-to-use Parquet files. The following content discusses each step of the pipeline and what the outcome was, beginning with the `DROP Tables` Script activity.

The loading of the data from the Azure SQL database into the `[brainwaves].[TmpREADING]` table took place in Exercise 4.13. It is expected that the data already exists in that table.

The design of the `TransformEnrichment` pipeline included scripts that will create the `FactREADING` and `SCENARIO_FREQUENCY` tables. Therefore, the first activity was to make sure they did not exist and, if they did, they were dropped. This was done to avoid an exception when trying to create a table that already exists. The next activity, `SETUP Staging`, either deleted data in the `[staging].[TmpREADING]` table or created it. This staging table is intended to temporarily hold the filtered data from the `FILTER Outliers` activity. It was determined through some previous EDA that some brainjammer brain wave reading values were a great distance from the mean. The Filter activity removed those values and placed them into the staging table, which resulted in 4,437,221 rows of data remaining. The `CREATE FactREADING` Script activity pulled the data from the staging table and used the dimension reference tables to build the dataset for the `[brainwaves].[FactREADING]` table, which was created using the CTAS approach. Validation using a `SELECT COUNT(*)` statement was performed on both the staging and brain wave table to confirm that the count on each matched.

The `CONVERT Parquet` notebook used Scala code to retrieve the data stored on the dedicated SQL table and load it into a DataFrame. Then, the data in the DataFrame was written to a Parquet file and placed into the data lake. In this case, the data lake was an ADLS container. The `AGGREGATE` Script activity performed a CTAS that executed `AVG`, `STDEV`, `VAR`, `PERCENTILE_CONT`, `SQRT`, and `SQUARE` functions on the `VALUE` column in the just populated `[brainwaves].[FactREADING]` table. The aggerated and transformed data was then stored on the `[brainwaves].[SCENARIO_FREQUENCY]` table. Finally, the `NORMALIZE` notebook contained two cells. The first cell contained Scala code that loaded data into a DataFrame retrieved from a dedicated SQL pool table. The data loaded into the DataFrame was then written to a temporary Apache Hive table. The next cell that used the PySpark MLlib features selected the data from the Hive table and performed normalization on the brain wave reading aggregated values. The results were written to the data lake in both CSV and Parquet form. CSV is a valid format for running EDA and visualizing the output in Power BI, whereas Parquet is useful for Azure Databricks and Apache Spark.

Data Management

Data management can be described in many ways. It is a set of disciplines that pertain to the supervision of your enterprise data landscape. The topics covered in a data management scenario can be different and unique, depending on the industry. Figure 5.41 illustrates some of the more common disciplines.

FIGURE 5.41 Data management disciplines

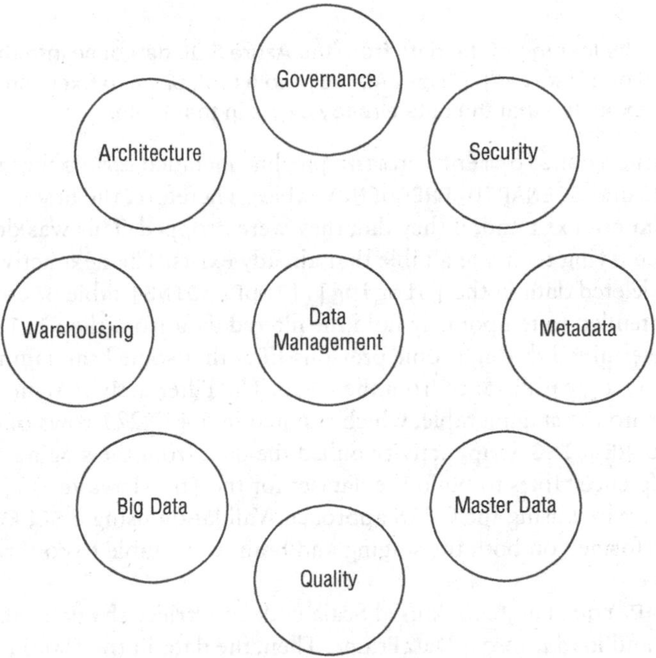

Governance is concerned with privacy, access control, and the retention of your data. Chapter 8 covers this in much more detail and explains which tools the Azure platform provides for implementing a governance and compliance solution. Security has to do with not only controlling access, such as reads, writes, and deletes, but also protecting the physical data at its stored location. This is also covered in more detail in Chapter 8. The management and usefulness of metadata was covered in Chapter 4, but in summary, metadata is information that exists for the purpose of explaining what the data is. It is critical for discovering and identifying the purpose of the data. Managing master data has to do with the storage of data in its originally ingested and stored form. Data is used for many reasons, and over time random updates or deletes can corrupt the data source, rendering it useless. Having a single version of the truth that is protected and managed is critical to the success of data management, which leads to the aspect of data quality. It does not take many actions to reduce the value of a dataset or database. Maintaining the quality should be a regular checking of access and permissions to help keep the data in a useful state. Running a Big Data solution also needs to be managed and is a common part of a data management solution. In many cases the processing of large datasets takes place in the cloud, which means you need to take special care when transferring the data, for example, if the data is of a sensitive nature. As your data progresses from the single version of the truth, aka the master version, through a Big Data solution, it needs a place to be stored, typically a data lake or a data warehouse. The data warehouse location needs policies and protective procedures, just like any other component of the data management solution. Finally, the architecture discipline can cover a hybrid scenario in which some data is stored on-premises and processing and temporary storage are performed in the cloud. It is important to know what data is stored where and how it flows through the system architecture.

Azure Databricks

Azure Databricks offers some nice charting capabilities, along with a few helpful basic EDA commands. Perform Exercise 5.14 to practice some of those commands and generate a chart or two.

When performing Exercise 5.14, if you receive the error "Failure to initialize configuration. Invalid configuration value detected for `fs.azure.account.key`," it means you are trying to access an ADLS container instead of the blob container. Review step 2 of Exercise 5.4 to remind yourself why this happens.

Before you begin Exercise 5.14, place the two Parquet files you created in Exercise 5.13 in an Azure Storage blob container. The two files, `NormalizedBrainwavesSE.parquet` and `transformedBrainwavesV1.parquet`, are available on GitHub in the `Chapter05/Ch05Ex14` directory.

EXERCISE 5.14

Transform Data by Using Apache Spark—Azure Databricks

1. Log in to the Azure portal at `https://portal.azure.com` > navigate to the Azure Databricks workspace you created in Exercise 3.14 > click the Launch Workspace button in the middle of the Overview blade > select the Compute menu item > select the cluster you also created in Exercise 3.14 > click the Start button > select the + Create menu item > select Notebook > enter a name (I used **brainjammer-eda**) > select Python from the Default Language drop-down list box > select the cluster you just started from the drop-down list box > and then click Create.

EXERCISE 5.14 *(continued)*

2. Enter the following syntax into the first cell, and then run the code:

```
import pandas as pd
df = spark.read.option("header", "true").parquet(
    "wasbs://<container>@<endpoint>/transformedBrainwavesV1.parquet")
pdf = df.select(df.SCENARIO, df.ELECTRODE, df.FREQUENCY,
                df.VALUE.cast('float')).toPandas()
print(pdf.head())
print(pdf.tail())
```

```
       SCENARIO ELECTRODE FREQUENCY  VALUE
0   WorkNoEmail       AF4    BETA_L  3.024
1   WorkNoEmail       AF4    BETA_L  1.725
2   WorkNoEmail       AF4    BETA_L  2.933
3   WorkNoEmail       AF4    BETA_L  1.318
4   WorkNoEmail       AF4    BETA_L  1.019
              SCENARIO ELECTRODE FREQUENCY  VALUE
4437216  PlayingGuitar        Pz     GAMMA  3.594
4437217  PlayingGuitar        Pz     GAMMA  8.314
4437218  PlayingGuitar        Pz     GAMMA  7.578
4437219  PlayingGuitar        Pz     GAMMA  7.220
4437220  PlayingGuitar        Pz     GAMMA  2.084
```

3. Hover your mouse over the lower middle of the previous cell ➢ click the + to add a new cell ➢ enter the following syntax ➢ and then run the code in the cell.

```
pdf.shape
```

```
(4437221, 4)
```

4. Add another cell ➢ enter the following syntax ➢ and then run the code.

```
pdf.info()
```

```
RangeIndex: 4437221 entries, 0 to 4437220
Data columns (total 4 columns):
 #   Column     Dtype
---  ------     -----
 0   SCENARIO   object
```

```
 1  ELECTRODE  object
 2  FREQUENCY  object
 3  VALUE      float32
dtypes: float32(1), object(3)
memory usage: 118.5+ MB
```

5. Add another cell ➢ enter then following syntax ➢ and then run the code.

```
pdf.describe()

    VALUE
count 4.437221e+06
mean 8.890862e+00
std 2.894011e+01
min 2.750000e-01
25% 1.065000e+00
50% 2.058000e+00
75% 4.395000e+00
max 3.919920e+02
```

6. Add another cell ➢ enter the following syntax ➢ run the code ➢ select the chart button group expander below the cell results ➢ select Box Plot ➢ select the Plot Options button ➢ configure the chart as shown in Figure 5.42 ➢ and then click Apply.

```
df = spark.read.option("header", "true").parquet(
     "wasbs://<container>@<endpoint>/NormalizedBrainwavesSE.parquet")
display(df)
```

FIGURE 5.42 Azure Databricks—configuring a box plot chart

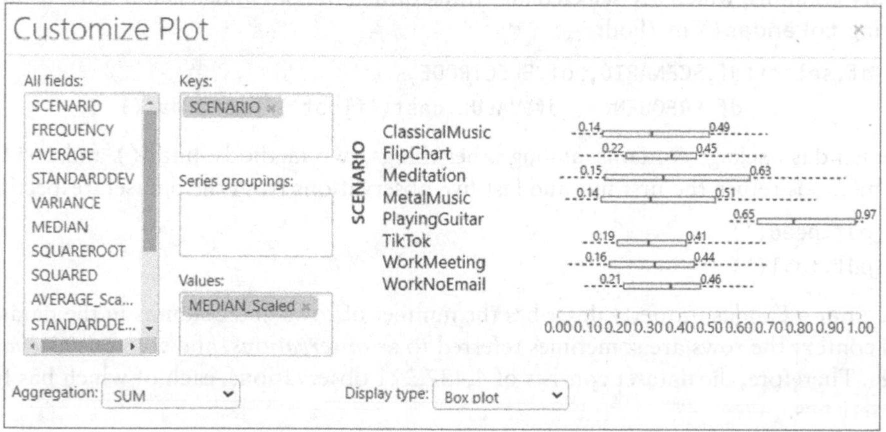

EXERCISE 5.14 *(continued)*

When you expand out the box plot, you should see the chart illustrated in Figure 5.43.

FIGURE 5.43 Azure Databricks—configuring a box plot chart (2)

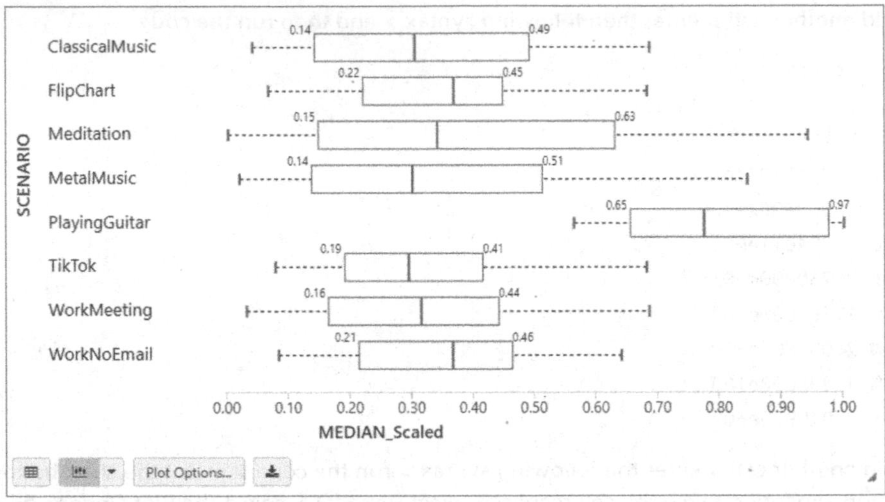

Exercise 5.14 uses a package named Pandas, which is one of the most popular libraries for working with data structures. You can find complete information about this package at `https://pandas.pydata.org`. The cell imports the package that is preinstalled on an Azure Databricks node by default. No action is required on your part to use this package, other than importing it. The next line of code loads the transformed brainjammer brain waves into an Apache Spark DataFrame. Then, the data is projected to store only the necessary columns, which are selected and transformed into a Pandas DataFrame using the following `toPandas()` method:

```
pdf = df.select(df.SCENARIO, df.ELECTRODE,
                df.FREQUENCY, df.VALUE.cast('float')).toPandas()
```

The Pandas package contains, among other things, two methods: `head()` and `tail()`. These methods return the first five and last five observations from the dataset, respectively.

```
print(pdf.head())
print(pdf.tail())
```

The `shape` Pandas property describes the number of rows and columns in the dataset. In this context the rows are sometimes referred to as *observations*, and columns as *characteristics*. Therefore, the dataset consists of 4,437,221 observations, each of which has four characteristics.

```
pdf.shape
(4437221, 4)
```

The `info()` method returns information about the data types (aka column values) attributed to the characteristics. When the `df.select()` method was performed to populate the dataset, there was a `cast()` performed on the `VALUE` characteristic. Therefore, you can see that `DType` has a `VALUE` of `float32` in the result set.

```
pdf.info()
```

The `describe()` method is useful for retrieving a summary of various statistical outputs. The mean, standard deviation, percentiles, and minimum and maximum values are all calculated and rendered with executions of a single method.

```
pdf.describe()
```

Finally, passing a DataFrame as a parameter to the `display()` method enables charting features. Selecting the charting button below the cell provides some basic capabilities for visualizing your data. Many third-party open-source libraries are available for data visualization, for example, Seaborn, Bokeh, Matplotlib, and Plotly. And Azure Databricks offers many options for charts and exploratory data analysis. If you have some ideas or take this any further, please leave a message on GitHub. The notebook used in the code samples in Exercise 5.14 has been exported as a Jupyter notebook and placed on GitHub.

Data Modeling and Usage

Data modeling is focused on uncomplicating data by reorganizing it into a state where business decisions and insights can be gained. Consider, for example, how the brainjammer brain wave data looked in its initial state. At first glance there is little to no value to be gained from data in such format.

```
+------------+------------+--------------+--------------+------+-------+--------+
| READING_ID | SESSION_ID | ELECTRODE_ID | FREQUENCY_ID | DATE | COUNT | VALUE  |
+------------+------------+--------------+--------------+------+-------+--------+
| 1          | 1          | 1            | 1            | ...  | 0     | 44.254 |
| 2          | 1          | 1            | 2            | ...  | 0     | 5.479  |
| 3          | 1          | 1            | 3            | ...  | 0     | 1.911  |
| 4          | 1          | 1            | 4            | ...  | 0     | 1.688  |
| 5          | 1          | 1            | 5            | ...  | 0     | 0.259  |
+------------+------------+--------------+--------------+------+-------+--------+
```

Performing some transformation on the data provided some opportunity to gain value. Viewing the data after its initial transformation provides a better understanding of what the data is meant to represent.

```
+----------------+-----------+-----------+--------+
| SCENARIO       | ELECTRODE | FREQUENCY | VALUE  |
+----------------+-----------+-----------+--------+
| ClassicalMucis | AF3       | THETA     | 44.254 |
| ClassicalMucis | AF3       | ALPHA     | 5.479  |
| ClassicalMucis | AF3       | BETA_L    | 1.911  |
| ClassicalMucis | AF3       | BETA_H    | 1.688  |
| ClassicalMucis | AF3       | GAMMA     | 0.259  |
+----------------+-----------+-----------+--------+
```

Next, you performed some exploratory data analysis on the data to determine any insights or traits that the data produces. This data does provide some insights but is best consumed visually and in relation to data with similar characteristics. In this case comparing the statistical frequency values to other scenarios can induce some conclusions and introduce more questions.

```
+----------------+-----------+-------+--------+---------+--------+--------+-------+
| SCEANRIO       | FREQUENCY | MEAN  | STD    | VAR     | MEDIAN | SQROOT | SQR   |
+----------------+-----------+-------+--------+---------+--------+--------+-------+
| ClassicalMusic | ALPHA     | 7.777 | 24.411 | 595.900 | 2.711  | 1.646  | 7.349 |
| ClassicalMusic | BETA_H    | 4.723 | 24.815 | 615.818 | 1.179  | 1.085  | 1.390 |
| ClassicalMusic | BETA_L    | 5.736 | 26.640 | 709.712 | 1.888  | 1.374  | 3.564 |
| ClassicalMusic | GAMMA     | 2.948 | 14.890 | 221.715 | 0.736  | 0.857  | 0.541 |
+----------------+-----------+-------+--------+---------+--------+--------+-------+
```

What is next? Data modeling also has linkages into the machine learning context. Remember that one objective of the insights learned from the brainjammer brain wave data is to find a trend or pattern in the data. Then, you can use that pattern to analyze brain wave readings, in real time or near real time, to distinguish what scenario the individual is performing. If you study Figure 5.43, you might be able to make some educated conclusions concerning brain wave reading ranges using the median value. There is significant overlap, which may hinder your ability to precisely predict the scenario. *Azure Machine Learning (AML)* provides some advanced capabilities for providing more precise results.

Data Modeling with Machine Learning

Machine learning is a very interesting emerging area. You shouldn't expect many questions concerning AML on the exam, but as a data engineer you should know something about how to use it and what you can expect from it. Complete Exercise 5.15, where you will gain both of those aspects. Before you begin, however, please note that, as of this writing, in order to run an *Automated Machine Learning (AutoML)* job from Azure Synapse Analytics, your Spark pool must be version 2.4. The pool you created in Exercise 3.4 targeted version 3.1. Therefore, you need to create a second Spark pool that targets version 2.4 to complete this exercise. This requirement might change in the future, but this is the case for now.

EXERCISE 5.15

Predict Data Using Azure Machine Learning

1. Log in to the Azure portal at `https://portal.azure.com` ➢ enter **Azure Machine Learning** into the Search box ➢ select Azure Machine Learning from the drop down ➢ select the + Create menu item ➢ enter a subscription ➢ enter a resource group ➢ enter a workspace name (I used **brainjammer**) ➢ choose an appropriate region ➢ click the Review + Create button ➢ and then click Create.
2. Once provisioned, the resource from step 1 navigate to the AML Overview blade ➢ select the Access Control (AIM) link from the navigation menu ➢ select the + Add menu item ➢ select Add Role Assignment from the drop-down menu ➢ select Contributor ➢ click Next ➢ select + Select Members ➢ search for the Azure Synapse Analytics workspace you created in Exercise 3.3 (in my case, `csharpguitar`) ➢ select it from the search results ➢ and then click the Select button. The configuration should resemble Figure 5.44.

FIGURE 5.44 Azure Machine Learning—brainjammer contributor access

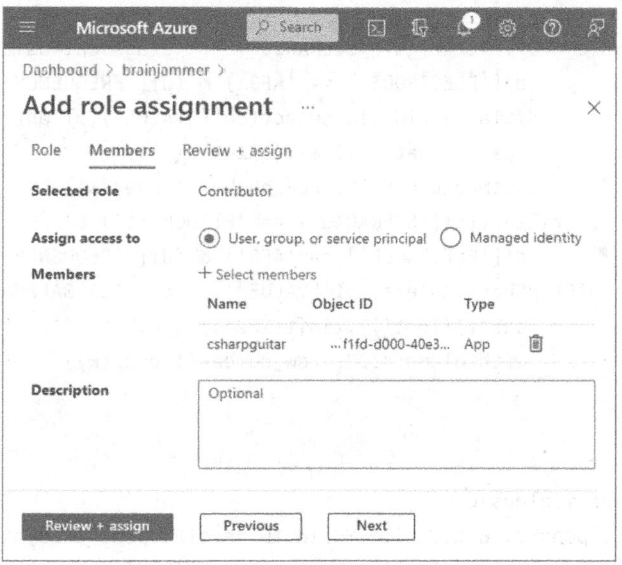

3. Click the Review + Assign button twice ➢ navigate to the Azure Synapse Analytics workspace you created in Exercise 3.3 ➢ on the Overview blade, click the Open link in the Open Synapse Studio tile ➢ select the Manage hub ➢ select Linked Service ➢ select the + New item ➢ select the Azure Machine Learning tile ➢ click the Continue button ➢ enter a name (I used **BrainjammerAML**) ➢ select the AML workspace you just provisioned ➢ and then click Commit.

EXERCISE 5.15 *(continued)*

4. Select the Develop hub ➢ create a new notebook ➢ select the version 2.4 Spark pool from the Attach To drop-down list box ➢ and then enter the following syntax:

```
df = spark.read.option("header","true") \
    .parquet('abfss://...@...dfs.core.windows.net/.../transformedBrainwavesV1
      .parquet')
df = df.select(df.SCENARIO, df.ELECTRODE, df.FREQUENCY, df.VALUE
.cast('float'))
```

5. Add a new cell ➢ click the + Code button at the lower center of the current cell ➢ and then enter the following code snippet. The code is available in the `AzureML Brainwaves.txt` file, in the `Chapter05/Ch05Ex15` directory, on GitHub. The code snippet shown here is a summary; copy all the code from GitHub.

```
From pyspark.sql.functions import col, lit, row_number
from pyspark.sql.window import Window
w = Window().partitionBy(lit('VALUE')).orderBy(lit('VALUE'))

dfClassicalMusic = df.filter((df['SCENARIO'] == 'ClassicalMusic') &
                   (df['ELECTRODE'] == 'AF3') & (df['FREQUENCY'] == 'ALPHA'))
dfClassicalMusic = dfClassicalMusic.select(col("VALUE").alias("CMAF3ALPHA") \
                   .cast('float')).limit(20246) \
                   .withColumn("ID", row_number().over(w))
dfFlipChart = df.filter((df['SCENARIO'] == 'FlipChart') &
                   (df['ELECTRODE'] == 'AF3') & (df['FREQUENCY'] == 'ALPHA'))
dfFlipChart = dfFlipChart.select(col("VALUE").alias("FCAF3ALPHA") \
                   .cast('float')).limit(20246) \
                   .withColumn("ID", row_number().over(w))
...
...

dffull = dfClassicalMusic \
    .join(dfFlipChart, dfClassicalMusic.ID == dfFlipChart.ID) \
    .join(dfMeditation, dfClassicalMusic.ID == dfMeditation.ID) \
    .join(dfMetalMusic, dfClassicalMusic.ID == dfMetalMusic.ID) \
    .join(dfPlayingGuitar, dfClassicalMusic.ID == dfPlayingGuitar.ID) \
    .join(dfTikTok, dfClassicalMusic.ID == dfTikTok.ID) \
    .join(dfWorkNoEmail, dfClassicalMusic.ID == dfWorkNoEmail.ID)

dfMerged = dffull \
```

```
    .select(dffull.CMAF3ALPHA, dffull.FCAF3ALPHA, dffull.MEDAF3ALPHA, \
     dffull.METAF3ALPHA, dffull.PGAF3ALPHA, dffull.TTAF3ALPHA, dffull
        .WNEAF3ALPHA)

dfMerged.write.mode("overwrite").saveAsTable("brainjammeraml")
```

6. Execute the code in both cells > after completion, select the Data hub > select the Workspace tab > and then navigate to the table just created, as illustrated in Figure 5.45.

FIGURE 5.45 Azure Machine Learning—brainjammer table

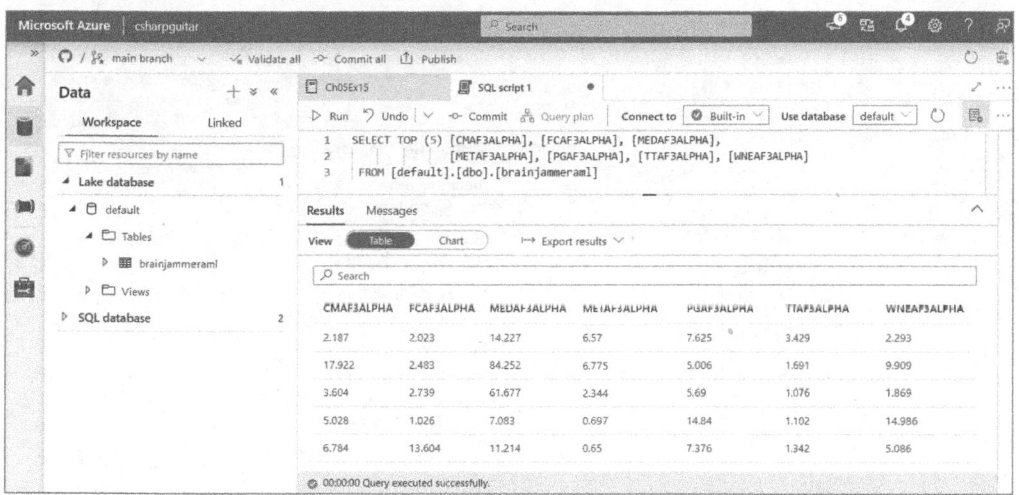

CMAF3ALPHA	FCAF3ALPHA	MEDAF3ALPHA	METAF3ALPHA	PGAF3ALPHA	TTAF3ALPHA	WNEAF3ALPHA
2.187	2.023	14.227	6.57	7.625	3.429	2.293
17.922	2.483	84.252	6.775	5.006	1.691	9.909
3.604	2.739	61.677	2.344	5.69	1.076	1.869
5.028	1.026	7.083	0.697	14.84	1.102	14.986
6.784	13.604	11.214	0.65	7.376	1.342	5.086

7. Consider renaming the notebook (for example, `Ch05Ex15`) > click the Commit button > click the Publish button > right-click the table > select Machine Learning > select Train a New Model > select Regression > click Continue > select the Azure Machine Learning Workspace from the drop-down (for example, `BrainjammerAML`) > select `MEDAF3ALPHA` from the Target Column drop-down list box > select your version 2.4 Spark pool > click Continue > leave the defaults > and then click Create Run.

   This will take up to the 3 hours.

8. Navigate to the AML workspace created in step 1 > select Jobs from the navigation pane > and then select the job you just submitted via Azure Synapse Analytics. Once completed, the page should resemble Figure 5.46.

EXERCISE 5.15 *(continued)*

FIGURE 5.46 Azure Machine Learning—brainjammer job

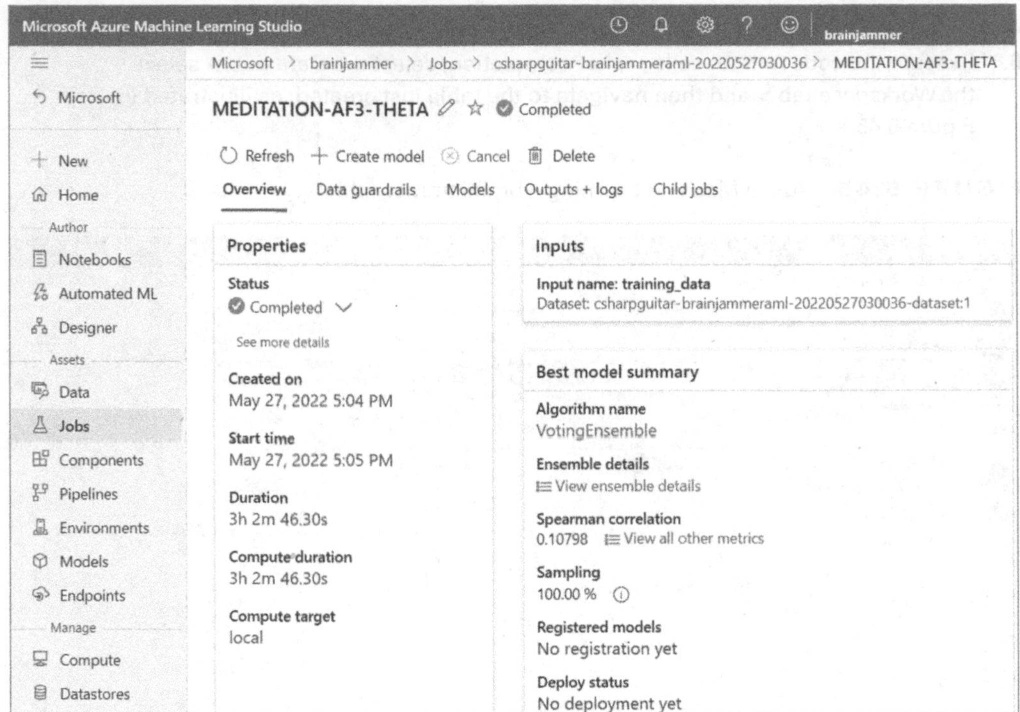

9. Review the job results, and then select the Models tab to see the Spearman correlation results.

After you provisioned the AML workspace, you granted Contributor access to your Azure Synapse Analytics managed identity. Figure 5.47 shows how this might look. Note that the Azure Synapse identity can be assigned to more than a single role. In this case it is assigned to both Contributor and Owner.

The next step was to create a linked service for the AML that you just provisioned. You have done this many times now, so it shouldn't have been a problem. It is important to note that the linked service must be committed and published before you can submit the AutoML run to AML for modeling. This is mentioned in step 7, but as this wasn't the case for the numerous other linked services created so far, it needs to be called out again. The next action was to create a new notebook and attach it to the v2.4 Spark pool. You have seen the first snippet of code in the first cell numerous times. The code loads the brainjammer brain wave data created in Exercise 5.15 into a DataFrame and selects the desired columns.

```
df = spark.read.option("header","true") \
     .parquet('abfss://...@...dfs.core.windows.net/.../transformedBrainwavesV1
         .parquet')
df = df.select(df.SCENARIO, df.ELECTRODE, df.FREQUENCY, df.VALUE
.cast('float'))
```

FIGURE 5.47 Azure Machine Learning—Access Control (IAM)

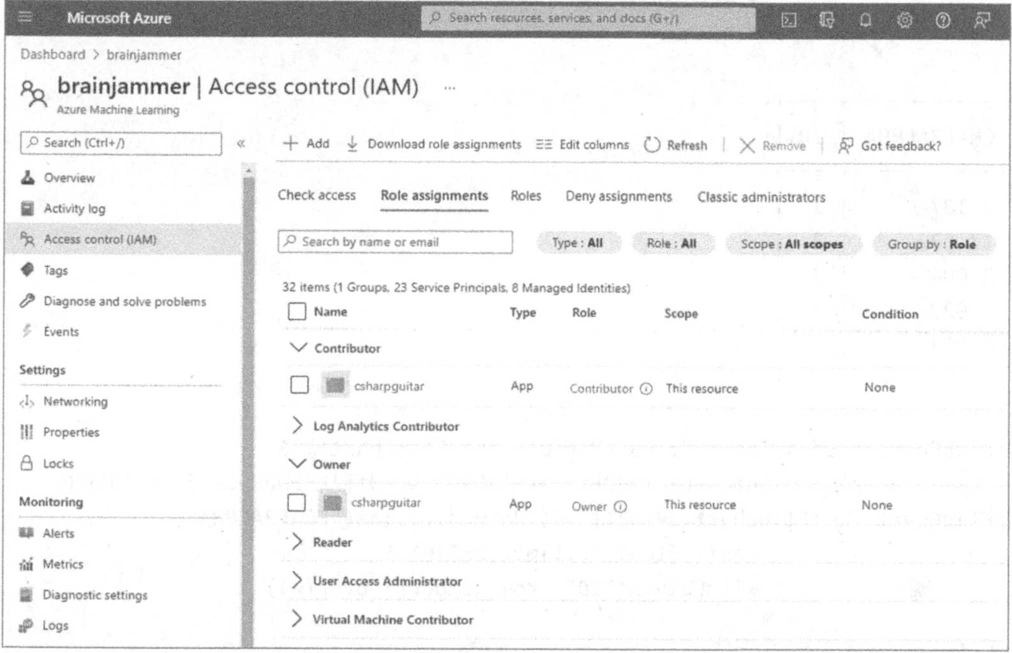

The next bit of code imports the `col()`, `lit()`, and `row_number()` methods and instantiates a `Window()` object partitioned and ordered by the `VALUE` column.

```
from pyspark.sql.functions import col, lit, row_number
from pyspark.sql.window import Window
w = Window().partitionBy(lit('VALUE')).orderBy(lit('VALUE'))
```

Be sure to download all the source code in the `Chapter05/Ch05Ex15` directory from GitHub at `https://github.com/benperk/ADE`. Only a portion of the code is provided in Exercise 5.15, as it is repetitive for every brain wave scenario. The first line of code uses the `filter()` method to project the data down to a specific scenario, electrode, and frequency.

The next line of code gives this column a name, which can be used to identify the scenario, electrode, and frequency. The column is cast to a float data type and limited to 20,246 rows of data. The limiting of the data here has to do with ensuring that the number of rows for all scenarios are the same. Finally, an `ID` column is added to the dataset using the value generated from the `row_number()` method.

```
dfClassicalMusic = df.filter((df['SCENARIO'] == 'ClassicalMusic') &
                   (df['ELECTRODE'] == 'AF3') & (df['FREQUENCY'] == 'ALPHA'))
dfClassicalMusic = dfClassicalMusic.select(col("VALUE").alias("CMAF3ALPHA") \
                   .cast('float')).limit(20246) \
                   .withColumn("ID", row_number().over(w))
dfClassicalMusic.show(5)

+------------+----+
| CMAF3ALPHA | ID |
+------------+----+
| 2.187      | 1  |
| 17.922     | 2  |
| 3.604      | 3  |
| 5.028      | 4  |
| 6.784      | 5  |
+------------+----+

dfFlipChart = df.filter((df['SCENARIO'] == 'FlipChart') &
                   (df['ELECTRODE'] == 'AF3') & (df['FREQUENCY'] == 'ALPHA'))
dfFlipChart = dfFlipChart.select(col("VALUE").alias("FCAF3ALPHA") \
                   .cast('float')).limit(20246) \
                   .withColumn("ID", row_number().over(w))
...
```

The reason for generating the new column name has to do with the following code snippet, which joins together all the columns into a single DataFrame. It uses the `ID` column generated by the `row_number()` method to join the DataFrames together. Because the number of rows is the same for all DataFrames, all the data has a match.

```
dffull = dfClassicalMusic \
    .join(dfFlipChart, dfClassicalMusic.ID == dfFlipChart.ID) \
    .join(dfMeditation, dfClassicalMusic.ID == dfMeditation.ID) \
    .join(dfMetalMusic, dfClassicalMusic.ID == dfMetalMusic.ID) \
    .join(dfPlayingGuitar, dfClassicalMusic.ID == dfPlayingGuitar.ID) \
    .join(dfTikTok, dfClassicalMusic.ID == dfTikTok.ID) \
    .join(dfWorkNoEmail, dfClassicalMusic.ID == dfWorkNoEmail.ID)
```

```
dffull.show(5)

+------------+----+------------+----+--------------+----+-------------+
| CMAF3ALPHA | ID | FCAF3ALPHA | ID | MEDAF3ALPHA  | ID | METAF3ALPHA | ...
+------------+----+------------+----+--------------+----+-------------+
| 2.187      | 1  | 2.023      | 1  | 14.227       | 1  | ...
| 17.922     | 2  | 2.483      | 2  | 84.252       | 2  | ...
| 3.604      | 3  | 2.739      | 3  | 61.677       | 3  | ...
| 5.028      | 4  | 1.026      | 4  | 7.083        | 4  | ...
| 6.784      | 5  | 13.604     | 5  | 11.214       | ...
+------------+----+------------+----+--------------+
```

From the dffull DataFrame, the desired and completely transformed dataset is finally realized. The columns containing the brainjammer brain wave readings per scenario, electrode, and frequency are loaded into the DataFrame, ignoring the ID column, as that data is not needed. The contents of the DataFrame are then loaded into the table shown in Figure 5.45.

```
dfMerged = dffull \
    .select(dffull.CMAF3ALPHA, dffull.FCAF3ALPHA, dffull.MEDAF3ALPHA, \
     dffull.METAF3ALPHA, dffull.PGAF3ALPHA, dffull.TTAF3ALPHA, dffull
        .WNEAF3ALPHA)
dfMerged.write.mode("overwrite").saveAsTable("brainjammeraml")
```

The data that is submitted to an AutoML job for modeling must be in a format that supports the type of modeling you want to perform. The mapping of those data format requirements to the modeling algorithm is outside the scope of this book. However, note that all the effort to transform the data in Exercise 5.15 was required to perform a linear regression AML model type. Transforming data in such a way to meet the requirements without losing the intent and the value of the data, as you experienced, requires just as much hands-on experience as it does having the technical skillset. As you may have noticed in step 7, in addition to a regression model, there were two other models, classification and time series forecasting. These models are summarized here:

- **Classification:** Predicts the likelihood that a specific outcome will be achieved (binary classification) or detects the category an attribute belongs to (multiclass classification). Example: foresee if a customer will renew or cancel their subscription.
- **Regression:** Approximates a numeric value based on input variables. Example: predict stock prices based on the weather.
- **Time series forecasting:** Assesses values and trends based on historical data. Example: predict interest rate developments over the next year.

After selecting the regression model and progressing to the next window, you were prompted to enter the AML workspace and the linked service that pointed to it. The column you selected as the target column was MEDAF3ALPHA. The expectation was that the results of the AML modeling would provide some information about how the meditation brain wave values related to the other values in the table. Finally, you selected the v2.4 Spark pool, which provides the compute for running the modeling. On the next window you left the default value in the Primary metric, which was the Spearman correlation. The Spearman correlation ranking is useful for assessing how strongly a relationship exists between given variables. It is a statistical dependency computation and quite complicated in its description. The other options are Normalized Root Mean Squared Error, R2 Score, and Normalized Mean Absolute Error. Again, these are very scientific concepts; if they interest you, you can pursue them further using other resources.

The next section is rather important, as you want to control the amount of time allowed for the modeling to run. This process can take a lot of resources and a lot of time, and because you are charged for both, it is wise to control them. A reason for the reduction of the data that targeted a specific scenario, electrode, and frequency was to reduce the time required to complete the modeling. After the regression modeling has been completed, many results should be available for review on the Model tab. Potentially thousands of algorithms are performed, and the results rendered.

Usage

You might now be asking yourself how you can then use the results of the Spearman correlation linear regression modeling AutoML job. The answer is actually provided in Figure 5.46. The Best Model Summary section includes the algorithm name that was found to be most relevant. In this case the best model is VotingEnsemble, which had a Spearman correlation value of 0.10798. That value means there is a very weak correlation between the meditation brain wave reading values and the other scenario values in the modeled dataset. If you select the Models tab, you will notice that the VotingEnsemble algorithm is at the top of the list, which also signifies it as the most relevant model. You can also see an overview of all the algorithm models, their associated values, and the opportunity to explore other results. Selecting the VotingEnsemble algorithm link and then the Metrics tab results in the output illustrated in Figure 5.48.

To create the AML model using the VotingEnsemble algorithm job, select the + Create Model menu option, which walks you through a wizard. Once the model is created, notice the Deploy drop-down from Figure 5.48. The Deploy drop-down provides two options, Deploy to Real-time Endpoint and Deploy to Web Service, both of which results in the provisioning of an HTTPS-accessible endpoint that can be used to invoke the model. After successful deployment, it is possible to send data in JSON format to the model. The result would be a prediction of a possible future value based on the input provided. The response would be fast, as the model is already trained and will simply parse the data, process it using the modeled algorithm, and return a result for consumption. Other options to predict and score your data using the deployed model endpoint are to use the Azure CLI or any client that can send a request to a REST API—for example, `curl`, as shown here:

```
curl --request POST "$ENDPOINT-URL" --data @endpoint/online/model/
  brainwaves.json
```

FIGURE 5.48 Azure Machine Learning—VotingEnsemble algorithm

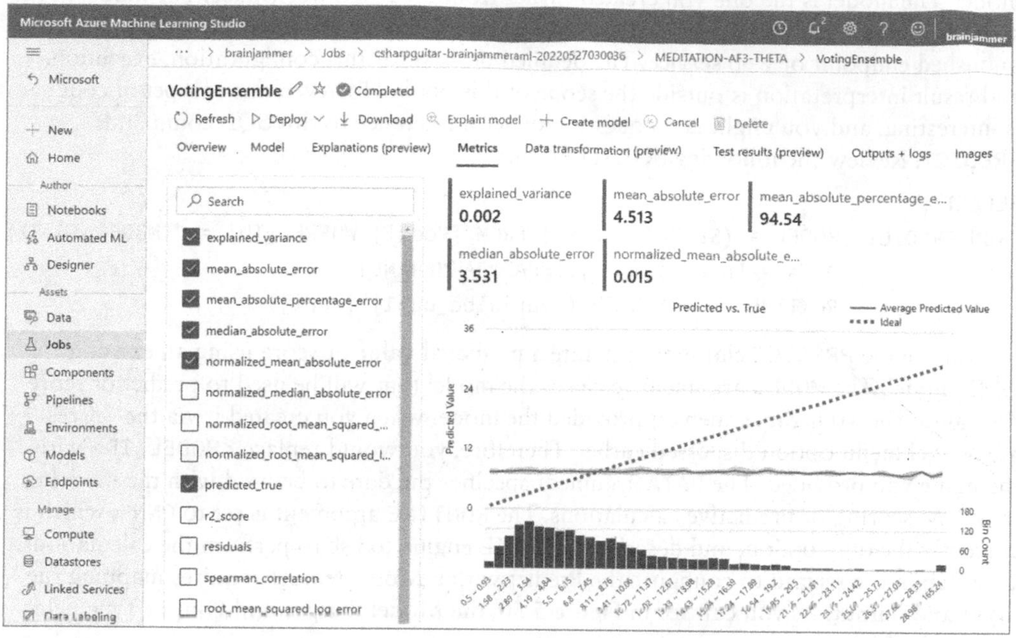

Another option for consuming an AML model is from a table hosted in a dedicated SQL pool running in Azure Synapse Analytics. Hover the mouse over a table and click the ellipse (. . .) to render the menu options, as shown in Figure 5.49.

FIGURE 5.49 Azure Machine Learning—usage prediction with a model workspace

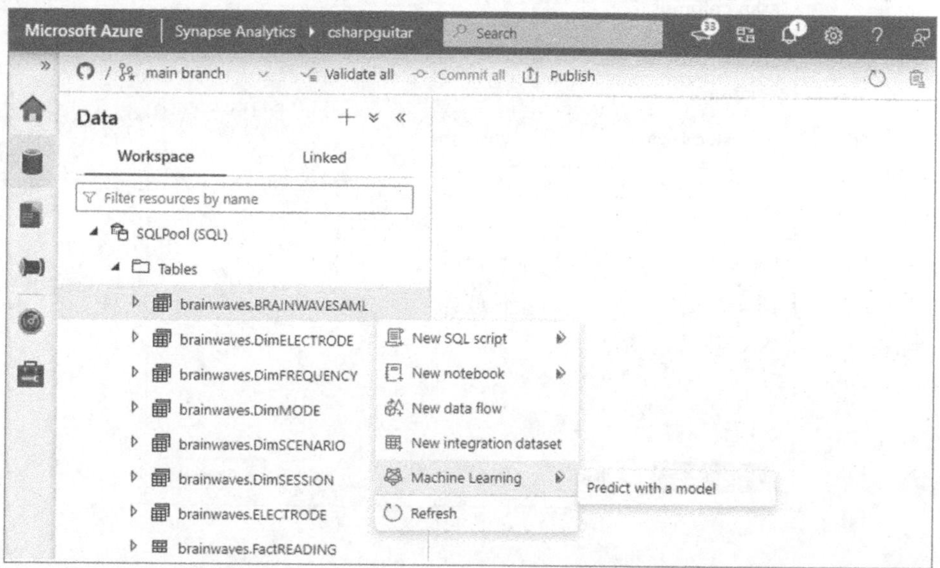

The wizard walks you through the steps to configure the prediction feature for the chosen model. The model is the one you created earlier from the AML workspace. The model in the scenario is accessible using the AML linked service you created in Exercise 5.15, versus the published endpoint or web service. The detailed process for this configuration, execution, and result interpretation is outside the scope of this book. However, one snippet of code is interesting, and you might get a question or see a reference to this SQL command: `PREDICT`. Review the following SQL statement:

```
SELECT *
FROM PREDICT (MODEL = (SELECT [model] FROM [Model] WHERE [ID] = "<MODEL_ID>"))
              DATA = [brainjammer].[BRAINJAMMERAML],
              RUNTIME = ONNX WITH ([varialbe_out1] [real])
```

You use the `PREDICT` clause to generate a predicted value or score using an existing AML model. The `MODEL` argument retrieves the model that will be used to predict or score the value. The `ID` is the name you provided the model when you created it via the + Create Model menu option discussed earlier. Therefore, you would replace `<MODEL_ID>` with the name you provided. The `DATA` argument specifies the date to be used with the model to make the scoring or predictive calculations. The `RUNTIME` argument is set to `ONNX`, which is currently the only option, and describes the AML engine to use to perform the calculations. One step in the wizard to configure the Predict with a Model feature requires mapping the input and output. As you can see in Figure 5.50, the Model Output and Output Type fields are required.

FIGURE 5.50 Azure Machine Learning Usage—predict with a model

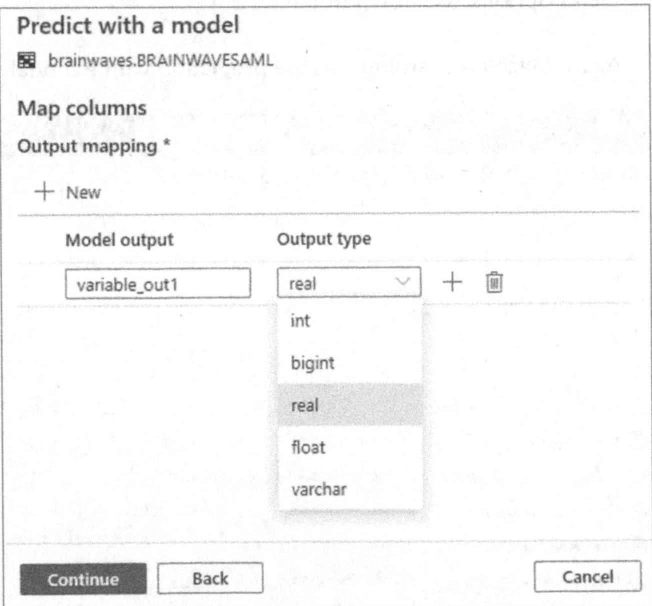

`variable_out1` is the name provided when you configure the output mappings and is queryable after the model scoring or prediction algorithm has run successfully.

Azure Stream Analytics

Azure Stream Analytics is not a direct consumer of the information provided by AML or from EDA. It is, however, the primary indirect recipient of the findings and the reason that this analysis was done. The objective has been to find some numbers that are unique per brain wave scenario. You can use those discovered unique values, or perhaps a range of values that uniquely represents the scenario, and compare them to a stream of brain wave values in real time. Then you can attempt to determine the scenario or activity an individual is doing based on the brain wave values. Table 5.2 represents those findings, which will be used later to attempt and hopefully achieve this objective.

TABLE 5.2 Brainjammer brain wave values

Session	Frequency	Value range
ClassicalMusic	ALPHA	> 3.8431 <= 4.3924
	BETA_H	> 1,2008 <= 1.2259
	BETA_L	> 1.9012 <= 1.9363
	GAMMA	> 0.8502 <= 0.8675
	THETA	> 14.6206 <= 16.8396
FlipChart	ALPHA	> 2.8132 <= 2.9904
	BETA_H	> 1.5539 <= 2.5029
	BETA_L	> 2.206 <= 3.075
	GAMMA	> 1.0568 <= 2.0608
	THETA	> 6.849 <= 8.6702
Meditation	ALPHA	> 4.3924 <= 5.0287
	BETA_H	> 1.2994 <= 1.38
	BETA_L	> 2.0487 <= 2.1775
	GAMMA	> 0.8675 <= 0.9364

TABLE 5.2 Brainjammer brain wave values *(continued)*

Session	Frequency	Value range
	THETA	> 2.344 <= 5.1052
MetalMusic	ALPHA	> 3.493 <= 3.8431
	BETA_H	> 1.2259 <= 1.2994
	BETA_L	> 1.9363 <= 2.0487
	GAMMA	> 0.8378 <= 0.8502
	THETA	> 11.9715 <= 14.6206
PlayingGuitar	ALPHA	> 5.0287 <= 5.4611
	BETA_H	> 2.5023 <= 4.2886
	BETA_L	> 3.075 <= 4.8075
	GAMMA	> 2.0608 <= 4.0281
	THETA	> 8.6702 <= 10.28
TikTok	ALPHA	> 2.9904 <= 3.1755
	BETA_H	> 1.38 <= 1.4488
	BETA_L	> 1.8497 <= 1.9012
	GAMMA	> 0.9364 <= 1.0155
	THETA	> 10.28 <= 11.9715
WorkNoEmail	ALPHA	> 3.1755 <= 3.493
	BETA_H	> 1.4488 <= 1.5539
	BETA_L	> 2.1775 <= 2.206
	GAMMA	> 1.0155 <= 1.0568
	THETA	> 5.1052 <= 6.849

The ranges were calculated using the following pseudocode logic:

```
AverageMedian = (SUM(MeanReadingValue) by SCENARIO, FREQUENCY) / 5)
AverageMedian.orderBy().asc
Midpoint = (AverageMedian1 + AverageMedian2) / 2
Startpoint = (AverageMedian1 - Midpoint) + AverageMedian1
```

The first line adds up all the MEAN brainjammer brain waves values per frequency, per scenario. That sum is then divided by five, because there are five electrodes (AF3, AF4, T7, T8, Pz). The result is ordered from smallest to largest, as follows:

```
+----------------+---------------+
| Scenario       | AverageMedian |
+----------------|---------------|
| FlipChart      | 2.9018        |
| TikTok         | 3.0789        |
| WorkNoEmail    | 3.2721        |
| MetalMusic     | 3.7139        |
| ClassicalMusic | 3.9722        |
| Meditation     | 4.8125        |
| PlayingGuitar  | 5.2449        |
+----------------+---------------+
```

Consider the first two scenarios in the preceding table, which are ALPHA frequency brain wave values from all five electrodes. Compare the smaller FlipChart.ALPHA reading value with the larger TikTok.ALPHA value. Adding those two values together and dividing them by two results in the Midpoint between those readings.

```
2.9904 = (2.9018 + 3.0789) / 2
```

The Midpoint is the end range for the FlipChart.ALPHA reading and the beginning range of the TikTok.ALPHA value. Subtracting the value, i.e., Midpoint, from the FlipChart.ALPHA value returns a negative number. Adding it to the FlipChart.ALPHA gives you the starting point for identifying a FlipChart scenario based on an ALPHA frequency.

```
2.8132 = (2.9018 - 2.9904) + 2.9018
0.0886 = 2.9904 - 2.9018
0.0886 = 2.9018 - 2.8132
```

The result is that the distance between the starting range and stopping range for the given scenario is the same.

Summary

In this chapter you learned about data transformation. Exactly what is considered data transformation is relative and can be any activity that changes the shape or format of the data. Pulling some data from an Azure SQL database and saving it to a Parquet file is a form of data transformation, as is converting numeric foreign keys to more readable data using dimension table references. Each iteration of transformation takes it closer and closer to the end objective of rendering business data from which valuable insights can be gathered. Those insights are then used to make decisions about gaining further data insights, driving business operations, or predicting future performance.

You can use numerous tools on Azure to perform data transformation. Azure Synapse Analytics is the recommended tool for those moving new or existing midsized data analytics work streams to the cloud. Azure Databricks and Azure HDInsight also provide data transformations for those who already have those products on-premises and want to move the workloads to the cloud. Transformation activities like cleansing and splitting data, shredding JSON, encoding, and decoding, and normalizing data are all possible on the Azure platform.

Once you have data transformed into a state that is ready for analysis, you perform exploratory data analysis (EDA), which requires creativity, at least one hypothesis, and a good understanding of your data. Use Azure Machine Learning (AML) predictions to estimate a numeric value based on a group of input variables. The model in AML that is helpful for this is called regression, but there are other types of modeling capabilities in AML. Once you find what you are looking for, you can use charting tools in Azure Databricks or Power BI to show the results in a way that is easy to consume visually.

Exam Essentials

The *T* in ETL. After data is ingested (extracted), it needs to be molded into a format and structure that can then flow through the remaining steps of your pipeline. This molding and formatting activity is called transformation. It is the most critical part of the ETL process, as it organizes data in many shapes and forms into a standard structure ready for loading and analysis.

Jupyter notebooks. Sharing your source code and business logic can be a challenge when working in small, medium, and large teams. Having a standard format in which your project dependencies are stored makes sharing code easier. Jupyter notebooks can be exported and imported between Azure HDInsight, Azure Databricks, and Azure Synapse Analytics, which enables great flexibility and many opportunities to gain the advantages each product offers.

Encoding data. If you are running your data analytics in English, you likely will not need to worry too much about encoding and decoding the data. If this is not the case, however, then you need to take actions to ensure that data that contains non-English characters (also called special characters) is handled, selected, and rendered as expected.

Data normalization. Normalizing your data has more than a single meaning and depends on the context. In a RDBMS it has to do with a concept called normal form. Normal form is intended to reduce duplication and improve query performance. Another meaning has to do with the visualization of data points. When data is normalized in this context, all plotted data is converted into values between 0 and 1 so that it all fits nicely in a chart, reducing outliers.

Data modeling with machine learning. Changing your data from a raw form into an uncomplicated structure reads like the definition of transformation. That is true, but in this context it refers to Azure machine learning data models like classification, regression, and time series forecasting.

Review Questions

Many questions can have more than a single answer. Please select all choices that are true.

1. Which of the following are examples of data transformation?
   - **A.** Converting data in CSV format to Parquet
   - **B.** Loading relational data from Azure SQL into a DataFrame
   - **C.** Casting a timestamp data type to a date data type
   - **D.** Removing rows that contain a `null` from a dataset

2. In which of the following scenarios would you use data encoding?
   - **A.** To cast a date from MM-DD-YYYY to YYYY-MM-DD
   - **B.** To properly render special characters on a computer screen
   - **C.** To reduce query latency
   - **D.** When working with a language that has more than 256 characters

3. When creating a chart to illustrate your data, what benefits would you get from normalizing the data?
   - **A.** The numerical data points are converted into values between 0 and 100.
   - **B.** The numerical data points are converted into values between 0 and 1.
   - **C.** The conversion of data into a static range improves the understanding when charted because it is more restricted to a given range.
   - **D.** Data is normalized by removing data—such as `nulls`, special characters, or date ranges—that does not meet the configured parameters.

4. Which of the following is Scala syntax?
   - **A.** `var df = spark.read.parquet()`
   - **B.** `df = spark.read.parquet()`
   - **C.** `case class Scenario(id: Int, name: String)`
   - **D.** `scenario = [scenario1, scenario2]`

5. A Jupyter notebook is supported in which of the following Azure products?
   - **A.** Azure Synapse Analytics
   - **B.** Azure Databricks
   - **C.** Azure Stream Analytics
   - **D.** Azure Data Studio

6. Which of the following describe a data flow?
    A. It pulls data from a source.
    B. It writes data to a source.
    C. It writes data to a sink.
    D. It writes converted data back to the source.
7. Which of the following statements about an Azure Synapse Analytics pipeline are true?
    A. It performs all activities serially; running pipeline activities in parallel is not supported.
    B. It can contain only a single data flow.
    C. It can only be triggered manually.
    D. It can contain more than one data flow.
8. What effect does dividing code snippets into multiple cells in a notebook have?
    A. A DataFrame instantiated and loaded in one cell cannot be accessed from another.
    B. It improves the debugging experience.
    C. It improves performance tuning.
    D. It helps you grasp the overall purpose of the code easier.
9. Which of the following are components of data management?
    A. Security
    B. Governance
    C. Cost projection
    D. All of the above
10. Which one of the following SQL operators is used primarily with Azure Machine Learning models?
    A. `UNION`
    B. `PREDICT`
    C. `OPENJSON`
    D. `^=`

Chapter 6

Create and Manage Batch Processing and Pipelines

EXAM DP-203 OBJECTIVES COVERED IN THIS CHAPTER:

- ✓ Design and develop a batch processing solution
- ✓ Manage batches and pipelines

Having programs run on a reoccurring schedule is a very common scenario, especially when working with data. These programs are usually referred to as batch jobs and target repetitive long-running tasks or tasks that operate on large datasets. A batch job consists of some source code that connects to a database or accesses a data file, then moves the data or manipulates it in some way. After the transfer and/or manipulation is complete, the output is stored in a location for consumption. In large enterprises a team of people can be responsible for managing many interdependent batch jobs. If a job fails or runs out of sequence, the result can have serious consequences on the integrity of the data. Batch job scheduling software is available to avoid such scenarios. The category of such software is known as workload automation. Some of the more common products are Tidal, cron, and Windows Task Scheduler. The need for managing and triggering batch jobs remains, but the tools have changed. Figure 6.1 illustrates the toolsets available on Azure.

FIGURE 6.1 The role of Azure Batch processing in a data analytics solution

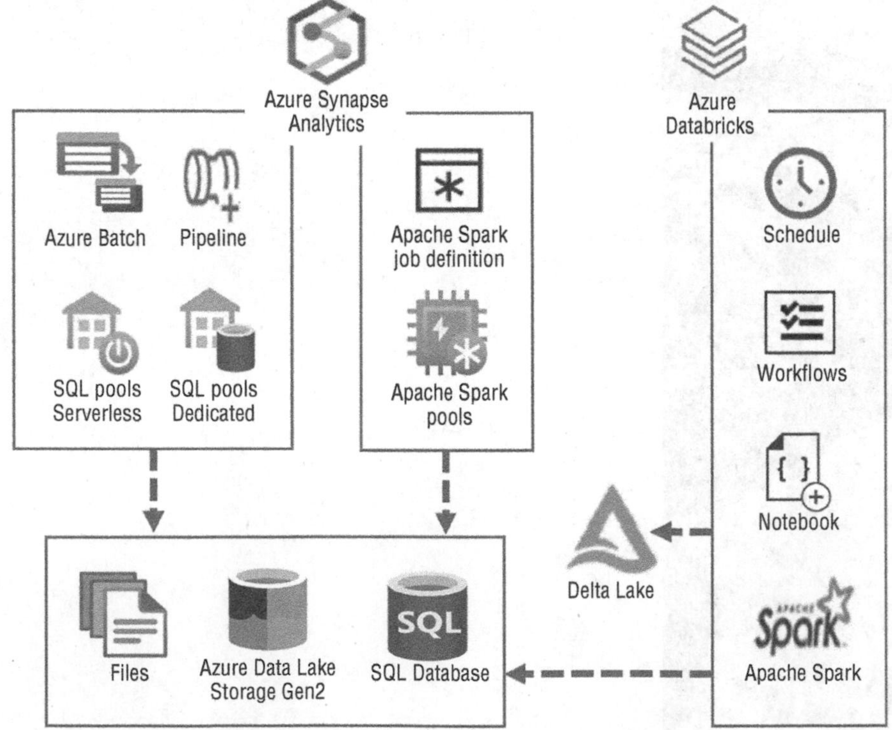

Azure Batch, which was briefly introduced in Chapter 1, "Gaining the Azure Data Engineer Associate Certification," provides the configuration and management of batch processing solutions. As shown in Figure 6.1, Azure Batch can be integrated with an Azure Synapse Analytics pipeline as an activity. The code run from that batch job can access data in your data lake, process it, and store it on your ADLS container, in Azure Synapse Analytics, or in any other place your workspace has access to. There are two places where you can run Apache Spark jobs. The first option is in Azure Synapse Analytics via an Apache Spark job definition, as introduced in Chapter 4, "The Storage of Data." The second option is to schedule jobs in Azure Databricks, as introduced in Chapter 3, "Data Sources and Ingestion." This option enables you to schedule workflows to run the code in a notebook at a given interval. The output can be retrieved from your data lake and written to your delta lake or any other accessible and supported data storage product. There are numerous other products and possibilities, but for the context of this book, only these are covered. The following topics are necessary to comprehend as you prepare for the DP-203 exam.

Design and Develop a Batch Processing Solution

From a general batch processing perspective, you need to consider the following concepts when designing a solution:

- Using compute resources efficiently
- I/O management
- Scheduling and dependencies
- User interaction

When thinking about the compute resources necessary for running your batch solution, you should consider two factors. The first factor is the code you or a developer will write to extract, transform, and load data from your data lake. In other words, the way a connection is made to the data source, the manner the data is retrieved, the kind of logic written to transform the data, and the way the resulting dataset is stored all require attention. The most important point—and the one that will have the most impact on compute resources—is the code that transforms the data. A very common scenario for processing data is to retrieve a dataset and then program a loop that analyzes each row of the dataset and performs an action on it. The following is a pseudocode example of such a loop:

```
do
{
  Match(aLargeAmountOfText, "\"(([^\\\\"]*)(\\\\.)?)*\"")
  response = requests.get("https://fqdn/api/brainjammer")
  dataset.MoveNext()
}
while (dataset.EOF == false)
```

Some activities are known to cause latency and/or high CPU consumption. An example of an activity that consumes a lot of CPU is searching large strings for keywords. The loading of that much data into memory can be slow, and, depending on how the text in memory is searched, the CPU can become overloaded and processing can grind to a halt. Specifically, running a poorly written regular expression is known to have such an effect on a CPU. An example of a regular expression that will cause 100 percent CPU consumption is shown as the parameter passed to the `Match()` method. Don't use anything like this. Another cause of latency has to do with I/O operations, which require thread context switching for reading/writing to disk or accessing a resource located on another computer. Depending on the type of local disk, reading and writing to a physical disk can be slow. Therefore, perform as much transformation in memory in order to avoid the need to read or write to disk. Additionally, as shown in the previous code example, if you call, for example, a REST API within a loop, the job is vulnerable to latency. The job can be latent not only due to the I/O context switch but also due to the current load on that server that hosts the REST API. In general, that would be bad practice, but it does happen and sometimes may be your only option.

Some latencies are expected, however, when running batch jobs, sometimes taking hours. The amount of data being processed can be very large, and that in itself is a cause for them to take a longer time to complete the data processing. There are a few options to mitigate some of the resource consumption problems you might encounter when running batch jobs. A rather simple solution is to schedule the job to run at a time when users or other applications are not competing for the same resources. For example, if the batch job needs to pull data from an OLTP data source and you know there is less activity on that data source after 23:00 at night, then run the batch job after that. This contrasts with attempting to extract data at 10:00 in the morning on a business day. Simply put, avoid prime business hours when scheduling batch jobs.

Scaling is a means for managing latency, for example, adding more CPUs and memory or structuring the data so that the batch takes certain pieces of the data. This way, you might have six batch jobs running in parallel, each with instructions to process different datasets from the same data source. Remember that the more quickly your jobs run and the transformation is completed, the faster your business can gain insights from it. Some jobs may be time sensitive; therefore, monitoring latency and improving performance is an important aspect here, as it is in most areas of IT. Finally, note that when you run your batch solutions on the Azure platform, most of these compute resource scenarios are managed by Microsoft so that you can instead focus on your project details. However, it is good to know and to have been exposed to these points in the event you need to design or manage an on-premises or hybrid batch solution.

The second factor has to do with managing dependencies. Figure 6.2 shows three scenarios: one-to-one, one-to-many, and a range.

Batching solutions can be very complex, not only because of the actions they perform but also because of the interrelated dependencies they can have with other batch jobs. It is not uncommon to have many hundreds of batch jobs supporting a large enterprise organization. Many of those jobs depend on the output from another batch job that has already been completed successfully. For example, consider that you have a batch job that converts a CSV file to Parquet so that a downstream job that requires data in that format can consume it. If for some reason the file cannot be converted or experiences an error during the process, then the next batch job in the sequence should not proceed. You can manage this kind of scenario by creating relationships between batch jobs. In a one-to-one relationship, as shown in Figure 6.2, if the batch job named `batchA` does not complete successfully, `batchB` will not be scheduled for execution. A one-to-many scenario means that a batch job—in this scenario, `batchC`—can be executed only if both `batchA` and `batchB` complete as expected. Finally, a range or large number of batch jobs must be completed before triggering `batchD`. In this case a set of 10 batch jobs must be completed before proceeding to `batchD`. You can also create many-to-many relationships between batch jobs, as shown in Figure 6.3.

FIGURE 6.2 Azure Batch processing—dependencies

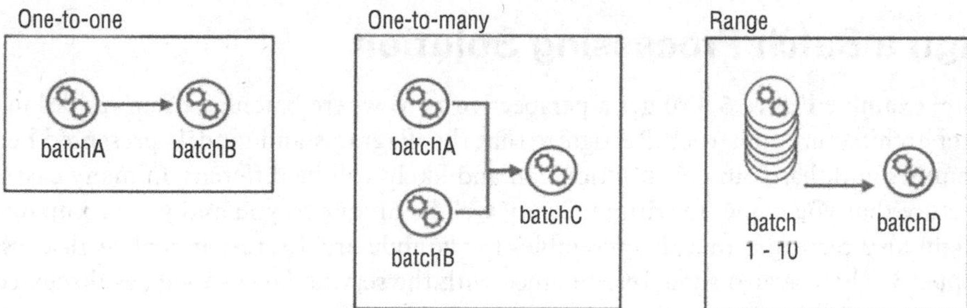

FIGURE 6.3 Azure Batch processing—many-to-many dependency

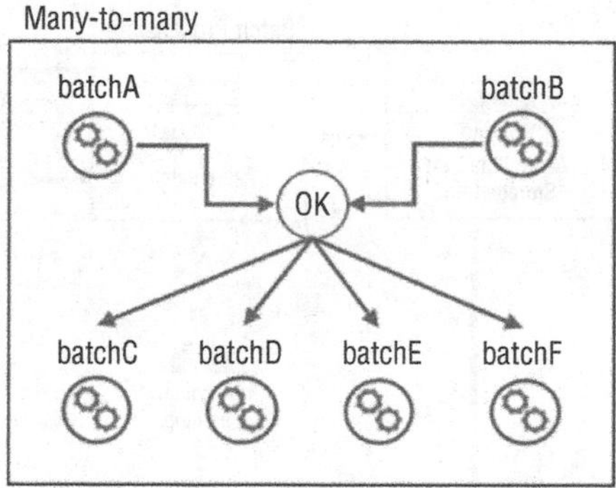

This scenario requires that both `batchA` and `batchB`, which constitute many batch jobs, complete successfully before continuing. If both `batchA` and `batchB` are successful, only then are the dependent downstream batch jobs executed. A useful tactic to recognize here is that the unrelated and independent downstream batch jobs can run in parallel. This can decrease the duration of the batch job solution. The last concept to discuss has to do with user interactions with batch job processing. Many problems that happen in any IT solution are caused by human error. Manually executing a SQL query that drops a database or table or wrongly updating a large amount of data can have a significant impact on your business. Recovering from such an event has a lot to do with the precautions you or your company have taken to recuperate from such scenarios. The best way to avoid such a scenario is to use automation to remove the frequency with which humans interact with your data. Performing as much as possible through automation, very often by using batch job solutions, achieves such an objective. If you know your batch jobs are performing as expected, there is rarely a need to intervene. The lack of intervention can also improve data quality, as the same code will produce the same output when run on the same data and would not deviate from that, unlike humans sometimes might. Now that you know some basics about batch jobs, read on to learn more about using batch jobs in the Big Data paradigm.

Design a Batch Processing Solution

To begin, examine Figure 6.4 to get a perspective as to where batching often resides in a Big Data architecture construct. Recognize that the diagrams and models presented here are examples and that your end solution can and likely will be different. In many cases, the architecture that you come up with may very well be unique to you and your company. You might also recognize that this resembles the lambda architecture model, as discussed in Chapter 3. There is also some resemblance with the serving layer model, as discussed in Chapter 4.

FIGURE 6.4 Batch processing in Big Data architecture

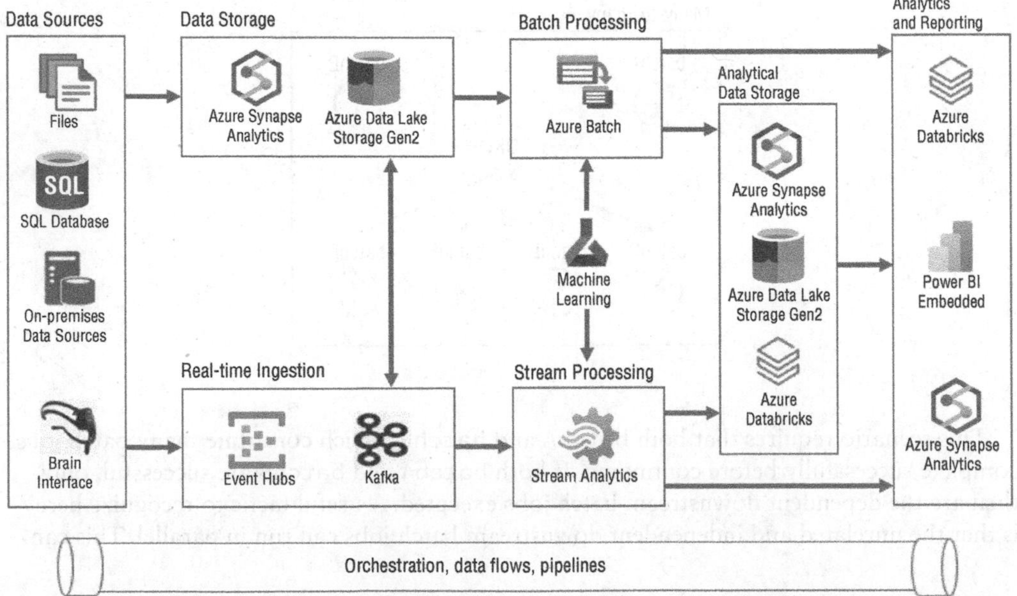

You might be able to conclude from Figure 6.4 that batch processing is utilized for scenarios where the stream of data is noncontinuous, especially when compared to the real-time ingestion stream. An ingestion phase or step usually happens before the batching procedures are performed. The ingestion is performed to copy, move, or collect data from numerous locations and store it in a data lake hosted on Azure. This ingestion, as you have learned, provides the opportunity to store the data in a single location close to the compute resources you will use to perform data analytics. Additionally, ingestion is the phase where you logically structure and host the data in directory structures like the following:

```
{Region}/{SubjectMatter}/in/{yyyy}/{mm}/{dd}/{hh}/
{Region}/{SubjectMatter}/out/{yyyy}/{mm}/{dd}/{hh}/
EMEA/brainjammer/in/2022/06/10/14
```

If the data is contained in files or in a SQL pool inside Azure Synapse Analytics, the most logical place to store this data is in an ADLS container. You may need to perform some kind of transformation prior to running a batch process on it. Having the data on the Azure platform in the recommended directory structure provides you an opportunity to do that. After the data is in your Azure data lake and in a format ready for processing, then you can perform your batch processing. Ultimately, the data is processed and progressed through the numerous DLZs, as shown here—first into the out directory and then through the necessary transformations:

```
EMEA/brainjammer/out/2022/06/10/17
EMEA/brainjammer/bronze/2022/06/11/10
EMEA/brainjammer/silver/2022/06/11/14
EMEA/brainjammer/gold/2022/06/12/23
```

If you are working with relational data, then you would use a series of temporary, staging, dimensional, and fact tables to perform the same progression through the Big Data pipeline phases. Batch processing is used to perform specific activities, typically in the transformation phase of the Big Data pipeline. Figure 6.4 attempts to show this position, but there is another model that can illustrate where batch processing is employed in data analytical solutions: the lambda architecture.

Lambda Architecture

This architecture model was detailed extensively in the sections that covered the design (Chapter 3) and implementation (Chapter 4) of the serving layer. Like the serving layer, the batch layer is a component of the lambda architecture. The final component is the speed layer, which is covered in Chapter 7, "Design and Implement a Data Stream Processing Solution." The batch layer is responsible for incrementally loading noncontinuous data from your data lake into the serving layer. The data flow takes place along the cold path and, as a result, takes a bit longer to become available to consumers and reporting. A reason for the delay has to do with the large volume of data on which the batch job is likely executing. Another is that before the data is placed onto the serving layer for consumption, it needs to be in an efficient querying format. The complexity, variety, and quantity of the data on which the batch process runs has a great impact on the time required to transform the data to this level of quality. This is a reason why numerous models are based on lambda but do not mirror it exactly.

Refer to the illustration of the lambda architecture in Figure 3.13 to view this batching position and responsibility. You might also be able to transpose the serving layer on top of the Analytical Data Storage component in Figure 6.4. Figure 6.4 mimics many elements of the lambda architecture, but an additional layer provides an opportunity to perform additional transformation before exposing the results of the batch processing to consumers and reporting resources.

Develop Batch Processing Solutions

There are many Azure products that can be used to develop a batch processing solution. As you have read, historically, a batch process was defined as a program hosted on a batch server that was triggered on a regular basis. There is no limitation to what a batch job is allowed to do, but in most cases it would access a data source, retrieve data, transform data, and output the result. Or the batch job might simply update some data on a table and be done with it. The point is that it is currently difficult to describe from an implementation perspective what a batch process is. Does it mean that you must use a product that contains the word batch in it? Consider that the data flow transformation feature can perform actions that are very similar to what has historically been done with what was commonly called a batch job. Recognize this ambiguity and don't get caught up in semantics; the objective is to manage your data and get it transformed as quickly, securely, and with the highest degree of quality as possible. The following are examples of some batch processing solutions. Some use products that include the word batch, and some do not. As you work through the examples, learn them, and then take what you've learned and apply it to the context you are working in. Because you will be exposed to numerous products and features, you can choose the one that works best for you based on your requirements.

Azure Synapse Pipelines

At this point you are no beginner when it comes to pipelines. You have configured quite a few in previous exercises. You have not, however, used the Batch Service Azure Synapse Analytics pipeline activity. The Batch Service activity uses an Azure Batch account to employ the aspects of batch processing.

Azure Batch

Azure Batch provides customers with compute resources commonly referred to as nodes for executing large-scale software-based workloads. These workloads, or tasks, are custom-coded programs that perform custom actions. In a *high-performance computing (HPC)* environment, these programs can benefit from massive scaling capabilities that provide parallel processing capabilities. An HPC environment offers an extraordinary amount of CPU or memory, commonly used for 3D imaging, financial simulations, or Big Data processing, for example. If a batch solution has tasks that can run independently from each other, Azure

Batch can be configured to run those jobs in parallel using resources from a pool of nodes, aka a node pool. Figure 6.5 represents a possible Azure Batch workload.

FIGURE 6.5 An Azure Batch workflow

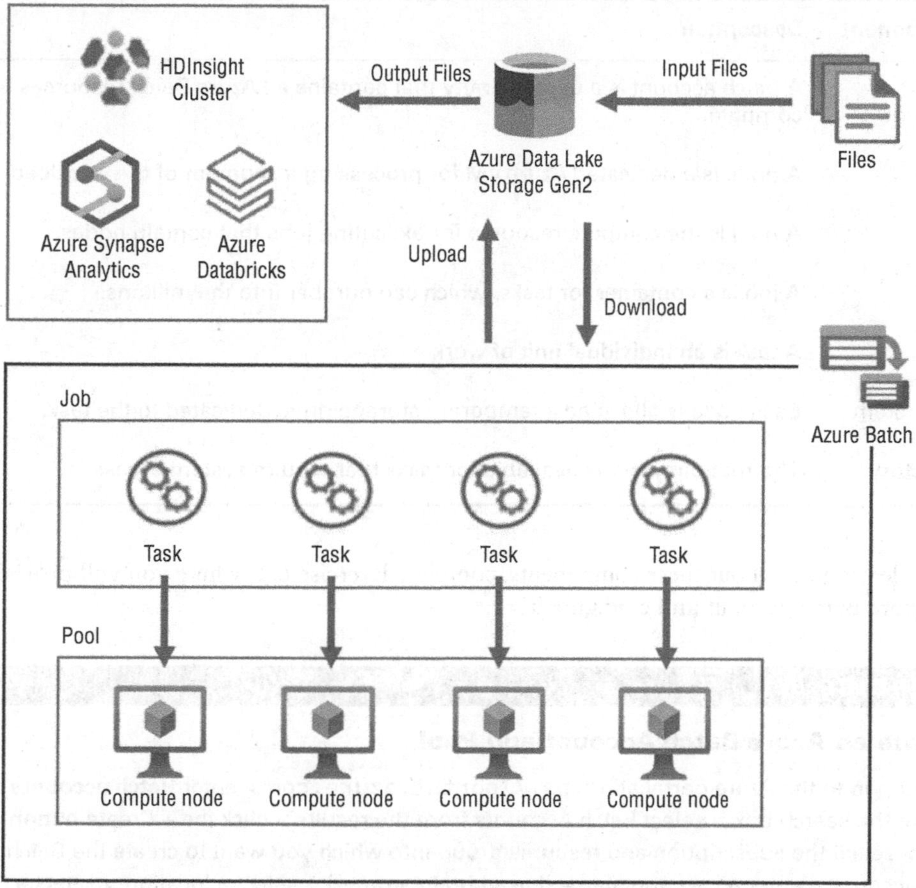

As illustrated on the right of Figure 6.5, files are generated from some data producer and ingested by numerous means into an ADLS container. A job is scheduled to run at predefined intervals or on-demand and contains one or more tasks. Those tasks download data from the data source and begin performing their action on the data. If the tasks are unrelated and can be run in parallel, then multiple tasks are triggered simultaneously for execution. Executing code requires a compute resource—in this case, an Azure virtual machine. The VM is allocated from the pool, the code is executed, and then the output is uploaded to a datastore and made available to consumers. In this case, the consumers can be HDInsight, Azure

Synapse Analytics, or Azure Databricks, or the data might be ready for reporting and rendering to Power BI. Table 6.1 provides a brief summary of the Azure Batch components.

TABLE 6.1 Azure Batch resource components

Component	Description
Batch account	A batch account is a unique entity that contains all Azure Batch resources and compute.
Node	A node is a dedicated Azure VM for processing a segment of the workload.
Pool	A pool is the compute resource for executing jobs that contain nodes.
Job	A job is a container for tasks, which can number into the millions.
Task	A task is an individual unit of work.
Filesystem	Each node is allocated a temporary storage drive dedicated to the task.
Directory	The root directory is available for tasks that require system access.

To learn more about these components, complete Exercise 6.1, where you will provision an Azure Batch account and configure it.

EXERCISE 6.1

Create an Azure Batch Account and Pool

1. Log in to the Azure portal at `https://portal.azure.com` ➢ enter **Batch accounts** in the search box ➢ select Batch Accounts from the results ➢ click the + Create button ➢ select the subscription and resource group into which you want to create the Batch account ➢ enter an account name (I used **brainjammer**) ➢ select a location ➢ select a storage account (consider using the one from Exercise 3.1) ➢ click the Review + Create button ➢ and then click Create.
2. Once the resource is provisioned, navigate to the Azure Batch blade ➢ select Pools from the navigation menu ➢ click the + Add button ➢ enter a pool ID (I used **brainwaves**) ➢ select `microsoftwindowsserver` from the Publisher drop-down ➢ select `windowsserver` from the Offer drop-down ➢ select `2022-datacenter-core-smalldisk` from the Sku drop-down ➢ select `Standard A1_v2` from the VM Size drop-down ➢ enter **2** in the Targeted Dedicated Nodes text box ➢ leave all other options as default ➢ and then click OK. Figure 6.6 illustrates an example of the configuration.

FIGURE 6.6 Azure Batch account and pool configuration

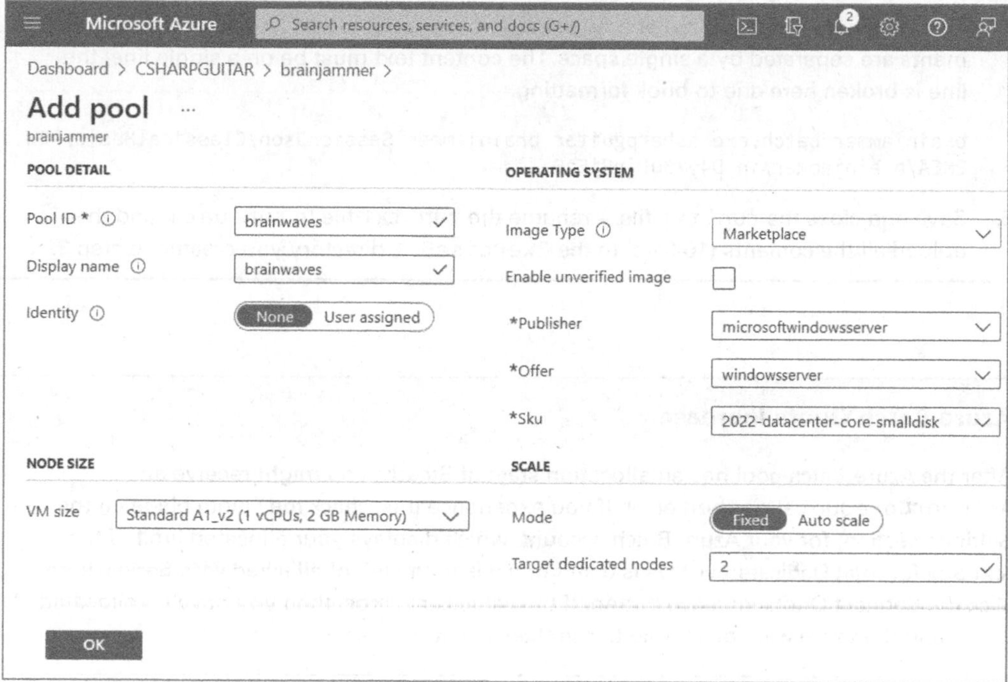

3. Navigate to the configured storage account from step 1 ➢ select the ADLS container (I used **brainjammer**) ➢ click the + Add Directory button ➢ enter **BatchJobs** as the name ➢ click Save ➢ select the `BatchJobs` folder ➢ click the + Add Directory button ➢ enter **Exercise6.1** as the name ➢ click Save ➢ download the `brainjammer-batch.zip` file from the `Chapter06/Ch06Ex01` folder on GitHub at `https://github.com/benperk/ADE` ➢ extract the contents on your local machine ➢ edit the `run.txt` file (notice that the `run.txt` file runs the `brainjammer-batch.exe`) ➢ and then update the five arguments passed to it.
   - Replace <StorageAccountName> with the Azure Storage Account you created in Exercise 3.1.
   - Replace <containerName> with the ADLS container you created in Exercise 3.1.
   - Replace <inputLocation> with the path to the JSON brain wave files you want to process.
   - Replace <outputLocation> with the path into which you want to store the batch job output files.
   - Replace <accountKey> with your storage account access key from the storage account you created in Exercise 3.1.

EXERCISE 6.1 ***(continued)***

4. The following is an example of how the arguments might look. Note that the arguments are separated by a single space. The content text must be on a single line; the line is broken here due to book formatting.

```
brainjammer-batch.exe csharpguitar brainjammer SessionJson/ClassicalMusic/POW
EMEA/brainjammer/in D4yx3uLjpPjEa0...==
```

5. Save and close the `run.txt` file > rename the `run.txt` file to `run.bat` > and then upload all the contents (16 files) to the `Exercise6.1` directory you created in step 3.

Azure Batch Quota Increase

After the Azure Batch pool has an allocation state of Steady, you might receive an `AccountCoreQuotaReached` error. If you experience this, check the Quota blade, in the Settings section, for your Azure Batch account, which displays your allocated limit. If the text box for Total Dedicated vCPUs is 0 and/or a 0 is to the left of all listed VMs Series, then click the Request Quota Increase button. If the values are zeros, then you have no allocated quota and therefore will not be able to run the batch job.

The code run in the `brainjammer-batch.exe` is available on GitHub in the `Chapter06/Ch06Ex01` folder. The code is C# and is in the `Program.cs` file. The first action the code takes is to capture the command-line arguments. The arguments you configured in the `run.bat` file provide the storage account name and container where the brainjammer brain wave JSON files are stored and where the output is written to once processed. The current year, month, day, and hour are dynamically appended to the end of the provided `outputLocation` value and will create the directory on the storage account, if it does not already exist. The `accountKey` is accessible on the Access Keys blade for the Azure storage account you configured in step 1 of Exercise 6.1. Click the Show Keys button to copy and paste the access key into the `run.bat` file. This is not the most secure means for granting access to your storage account, but until you learn more about managed identities and service accounts in Chapter 8, "Keeping Data Safe and Secure," this is the method used. It is secure, and the connection uses a secure protocol (HTTPS); it is just not as secure as the other approaches just mentioned.

The program then loads all the brainjammer brain wave JSON formatted sessions in the provided `inputLocation` argument. In this case the value is `SessionJson/ClassicalMusic/POW`, which analyzes all `ClassicalMusic` sessions. The code calculates the median value for each frequency for the entire session. Most sessions contain approximately 1,000 readings. The following is an example of the output. The output is the median frequency reading value for a single given brainjammer brain wave `ClassicalMusic` session. The values are expected to fall into the ranges that were identified through the EDA performed in Chapter 5, "Transform, Manage, and Prepare Data," and provided in Table 5.2.

```
{
  "ALPHA":  3.9184,
  "BETA_H": 1.237,
  "BETA_L": 1.911,
  "GAMMA":  0.8926,
  "THETA":  15.7086
}
```

To configure and trigger the Azure Batch job from Azure Synapse Analytics, perform Exercise 6.2. Note that both a job and task are created when the Batch Service activity is run, which is why you did not create them in Exercise 6.1. You will experience this as you work through Exercise 6.2.

EXERCISE 6.2

Develop a Batch Processing Solution Using an Azure Synapse Analytics Pipeline

1. Log in to the Azure portal at `https://portal.azure.com` ➢ navigate to the Azure Synapse Analytics workspace you created in Exercise 3.3 ➢ select the Open link in the Open Synapse Studio tile on the Overview blade ➢ select the Manage hub ➢ select Linked Services from the menu list ➢ click the + New button ➢ search for **Batch** ➢ select Azure Batch ➢ and then click Continue.

2. Enter a name (I used **BrainjammerAzureBatch**) ➢ enable interactive authoring ➢ enter the Azure Batch access key (located in the Primary Access Key text box on the Keys blade for the Azure Batch account created in Exercise 6.1) ➢ enter the account name (I used **brainjammer**) ➢ enter the batch URL (also available on the Keys blade for the Azure Batch account called Account Endpoint) ➢ enter the pool name you created in Exercise 6.1 (I used **brainwaves**) ➢ select + New from the Storage Linked Service Name drop-down ➢ create a linked service to the storage account you placed the batch code (`brainjammer-batch.exe`) onto in step 3 of Exercise 6.1 ➢ and then click Test Connection. The configuration should resemble Figure 6.7.

EXERCISE 6.2 *(continued)*

FIGURE 6.7 Azure Batch linked service configuration

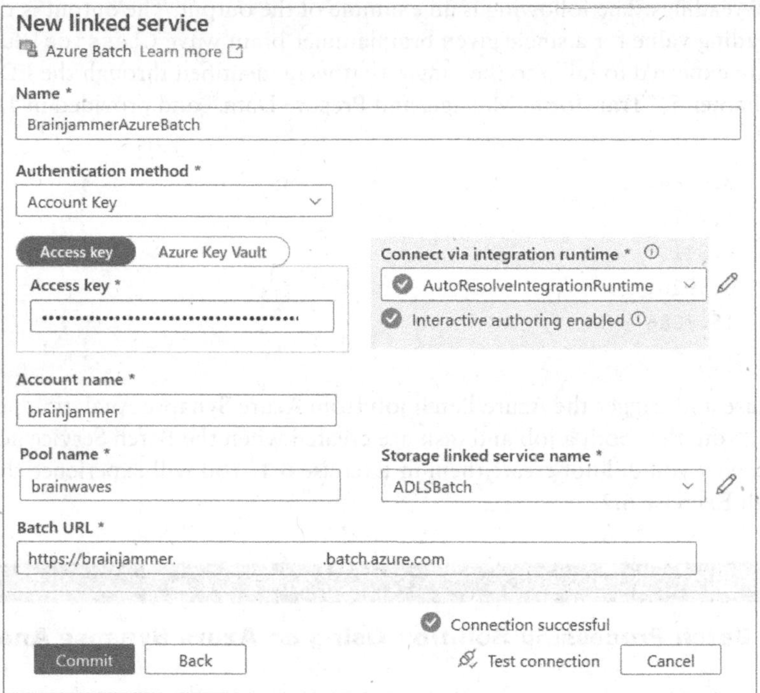

3. Click the Commit button ➢ select the Publish menu item ➢ navigate to the Integrate hub ➢ create a new pipeline ➢ rename the pipeline (I used **TransformSessionFrequencyToMedian**) ➢ expand the Batch Service group in the Activities rame ➢ drag the Custom activity to the editor canvas ➢ rename the activity (I used **Calculate Frequency Median**) ➢ select the Azure Batch tab ➢ select the Azure Batch linked service you created in step 2 from the drop-down (for example, `BrainjammerAzureBatch`) ➢ enable interactive authoring ➢ select the Settings tab ➢ enter **run.bat** in the Command text box ➢ select the Azure Storage linked service you created in step 2 from the Resource Linked Service drop-down ➢ click the Browse Storage button next to the Folder Path text box ➢ navigate to the `Exercise6.1` directory, which contains the `run.bat` file that you uploaded in Exercise 6.1 ➢ click OK ➢ and then click Commit. The configuration should resemble Figure 6.8.

FIGURE 6.8 Azure Batch Custom pipeline activity

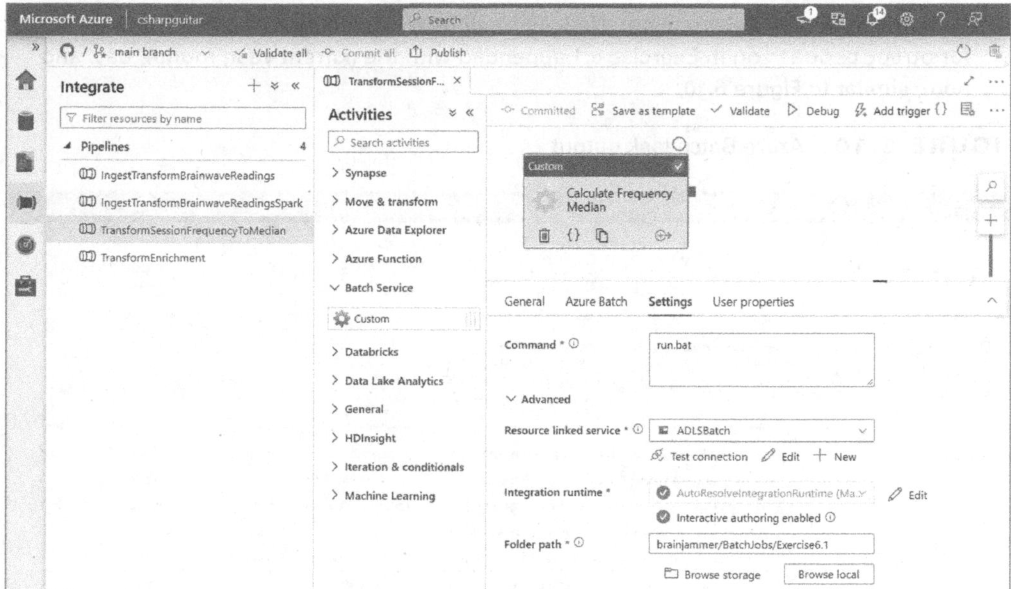

4. Click the Validate button ➢ click the Debug button, to test the batch job ➢ exit the Azure Synapse Analytics workspace and navigate to the Azure Batch Overview blade ➢ select Jobs from the navigation menu ➢ select the Job ID link (for example, `adfv2-brainwaves`) ➢ and then click the task. It will resemble a GUID. After the batch job is complete, you will see something like Figure 6.9.

FIGURE 6.9 Azure Batch task details

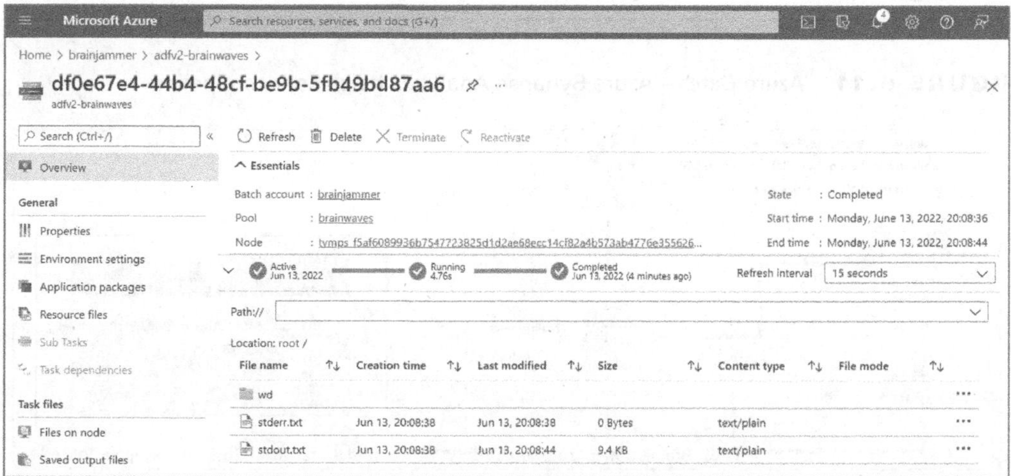

EXERCISE 6.2 ***(continued)***

5. Navigate to your ADLS container. New files will be rendered into the path you provided for `outputLocation` in Exercise 6.1 appended with the current year, month, day, and hour, similar to Figure 6.10.

FIGURE 6.10 Azure Batch task output

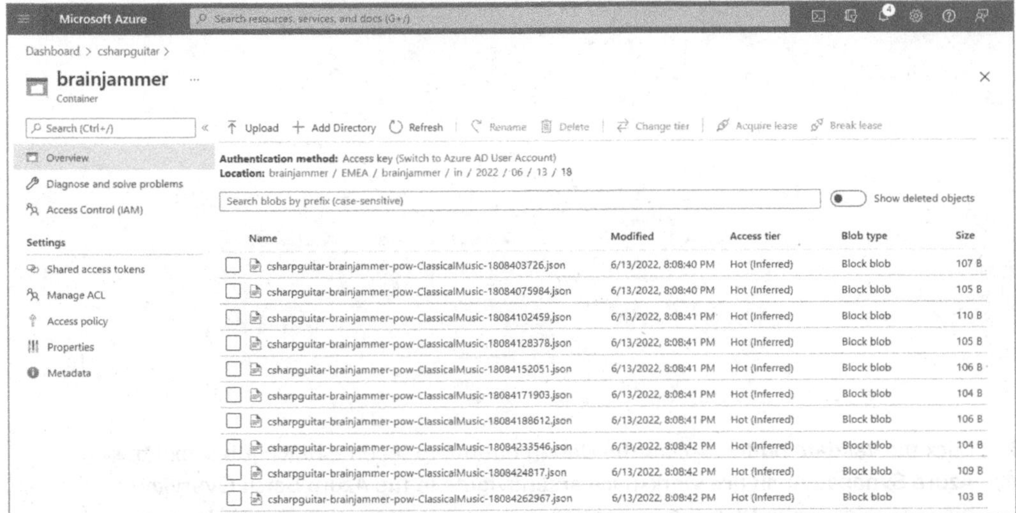

6. Navigate back to the Azure Synapse Analytics workspace, and then select the Publish menu item.

   Figure 6.11 illustrates the configuration.

FIGURE 6.11 Azure Batch—Azure Synapse Analytics batch service pipeline

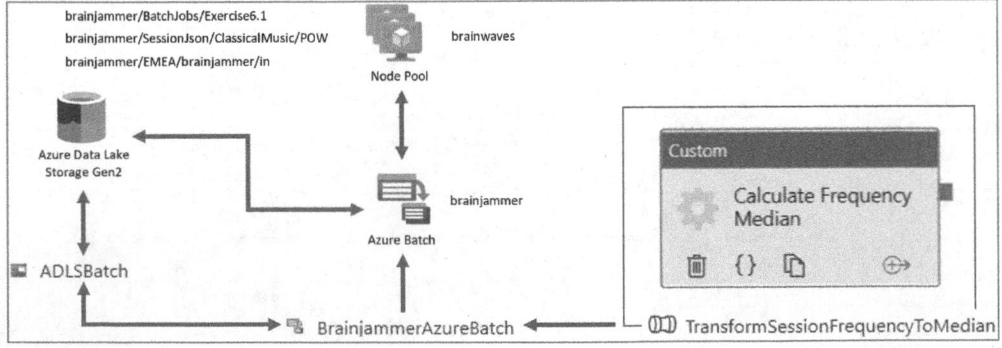

Note that all of the data being retrieved and stored by all the products configured uses the same ADLS container. This isn't always the case, but it makes managing the solution architecture easier. There are two points to watch out for. First, as much as possible, make sure the storage account is in the same region as the resources that use the data. This might not always be possible, but realize that you are charged for data ingress/egress when data is moved between Azure regions. Second, there are storage limitations, as shown in Table 6.2. These limits are large, but it is often the case that if you need more, you can contact Microsoft support, and they will increase the limit if there is justification. These limits are often in place to protect the customer from having a runaway rogue process that consumes resources indefinitely, at least up until the bill comes at the end of the month.

TABLE 6.2 Azure Storage limits

Resource	Limit per storage account
Maximum storage capacity	5 PB
Maximum requests per second	20,000

Recall Table 6.1, which summarizes the filesystem and directory components. Figure 6.9 shows an illustration of both. Notice the `root/` directory next to the Location label, which symbolizes where the focus is set on the filesystem. Also notice the `wd` directory folder, which represents the working directory. A task has read, write, update, create, and delete permissions on the `wd` directory, and any content in the directory is removed after 7 days. There is a task property named `RetentionTime`, which has a default of 30 days and can be updated on a task-by-task-basis, as required, meaning that each task can have its own retention setting. Finally, two log files are written to the `root/` directory: `stderr.txt` and `stdout.txt`. If the code throws an exception, the exception message and some details will be logged to the `stderr.txt` file. Therefore, if you are debugging a task and nothing is happening, you should look into this file. The `stdout.txt` file is where you can write application logs to. For example, notice in the `Program.cs` file, which performs the analysis on the brainjammer brain waves, that there are strategically placed `WriteLine()` methods that contain text details. Python logging code like `logging.debug()` would also be written to this file, if you had used Python instead of C#.

Apache Spark

Azure Spark job definitions were briefly introduced in Chapter 4, where you read about archiving data using a Python script. Complete Exercise 6.3 to gain hands-on experience with this feature. You will create and configure an Azure Spark job definition that converts JSON files to AVRO files, which are the most optimal format for batch processing. Then you will add the job to the pipeline you created in Exercise 6.2.

EXERCISE 6.3

Develop a Batch Processing Solution Using an Azure Synapse Analytics Apache Spark

1. Log in to the Azure portal at `https://portal.azure.com` ➢ navigate to the ADLS container you created in Exercise 3.1 ➢ create a directory named `ToAvro` in the `BatchJobs` directory ➢ download the `ToAvro.py` file from the `Chapter06/Ch06Ex03` directory on GitHub ➢ place the `ToAvro.py` file into the `BatchJobs/ToAvro` directory.
2. Navigate to the Azure Synapse Analytics workspace you created in Exercise 3.3 ➢ select the Open link in the Open Synapse Studio tile on the Overview blade ➢ select the Manage hub ➢ select Apache Spark pools ➢ click the + New button ➢ create a new Apache Spark pool (for example, `SparkPoolBatch`).
3. Navigate to the Develop hub ➢ click the + to the right of Develop ➢ select Apache Spark Job Definition from the pop-up menu ➢ select PySpark (Python) from the Language drop-down ➢ rename the job (I used **To Avro**) ➢ and then add the following to the Main Definition File text box:

```
abfss://<container>@<account>.dfs.core.windows.net/BatchJobs/ToAvro/ToAvro.py
```

4. Add the following to the Command Line Arguments text box (manually update the second argument with the path to the JSON files created in Exercise 6.2):

```
ClassicalMusic EMEA/brainjammer/in/2022/06/15/08 <container>@<account>
```

5. Click the Commit button, and then click the Publish button. The configuration should resemble Figure 6.12.

FIGURE 6.12 Azure Synapse Analytics—Apache Spark job definition

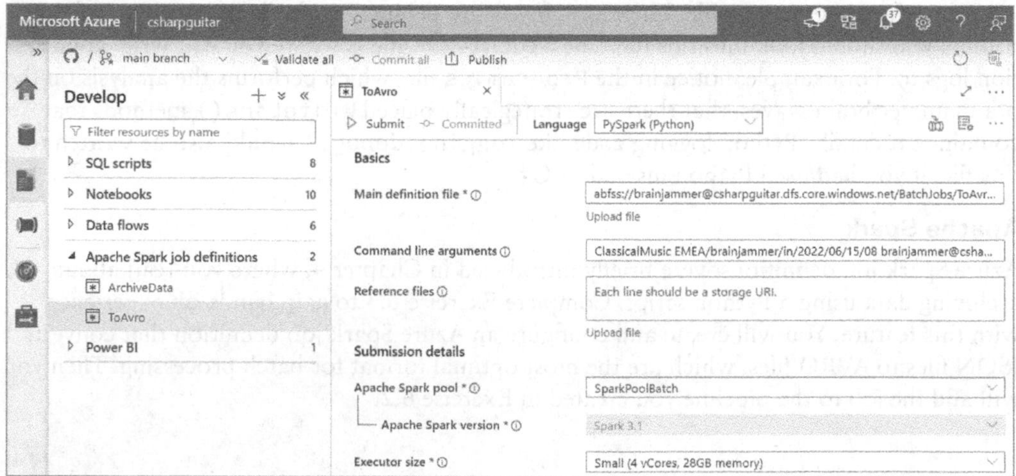

6. Click the Submit button. Once complete, navigate to the directory where the AVRO files are written to view the results. The following is an example directory path:

   `/EMEA/brainjammer/out/YYYY/MM/DD/HH`

7. Click the pipeline icon on the right side of the blade ➢ select Existing Pipeline ➢ select the pipeline created in Exercise 6.2 (for example, `TransformSessionFrequencyToMedian`) ➢ click the Add button ➢ connect the two activities by dragging the green box connector from the `Calculate Frequency Median` activity to the `To Arvo` activity ➢ select the Spark Job Definition activity in the editor canvas ➢ select the Settings tab ➢ enter the same value into the Main Definition File text box as from step 3 ➢ click the + New button to the right of Command Line Arguments ➢ enter the first argument ➢ click the + New button ➢ enter the second argument ➢ repeat the same steps for the third argument ➢ select the Apache Spark pool from the drop-down (for example, `SparkPoolBatch`) ➢ select Small from the Executor Size drop-down ➢ click the Disabled radio button to set the dynamically allocate executors ➢ enter **1** in the Executors text box ➢ click Commit ➢ click Publish ➢ and then click Debug. The output after successfully running all scenarios is shown in Figure 6.13.

FIGURE 6.13 Azure Synapse Analytics—Apache Spark job scenario result

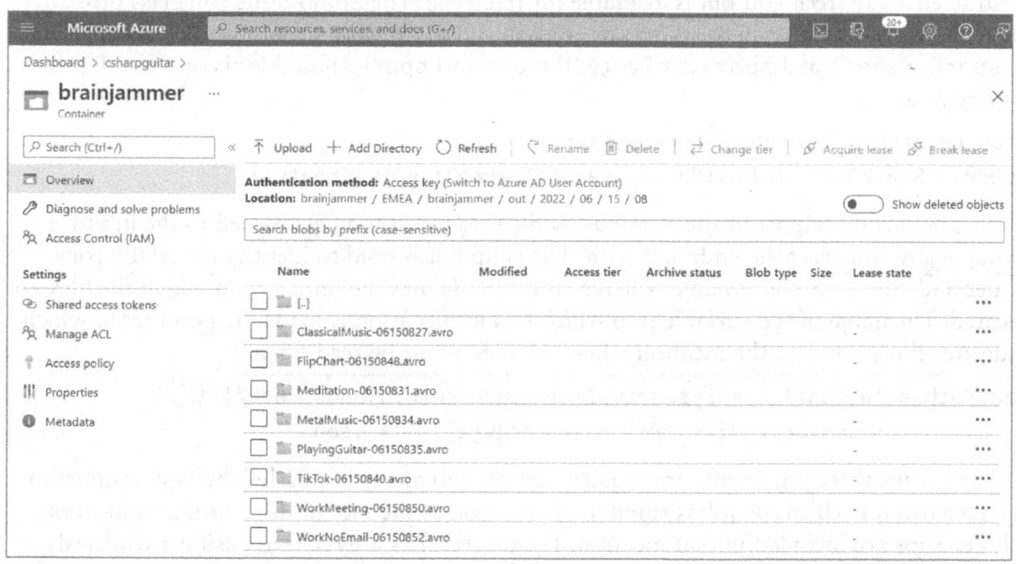

In Exercise 6.3 you created a new Apache Spark pool (`SparkPoolBatch`) that is dedicated to running this job. The decision to provision a new Apache Spark pool versus running on the same as the one which has been selected to run notebooks, for example, was made for two simple reasons. The first reason has to do with the potential for the overconsumption of resources. If all the compute resources in a pool get consumed, then performance will become latent. In a scenario where you are working in a team and numerous people are testing at the same time, you may experience performance contention between team members trying to do their work. Second, from a usage and architecture management perspective, it makes sense to separate and organize nodes by function. In some scenarios there may be packages and configurations that are required in one functional area while not in another. It is not optimal in all scenarios to attempt to have identical configurations companywide. Especially when it comes to startup scripts that have credentials to other services, you want to isolate those to only those nodes that need it. Therefore, performance, better organization, and security are good reasons for functionally organizing your Apache Spark pools. Computer programming includes a concept called the *separation of concerns (SoC)*, which can also be applied to architecture. SoC, in the context of architecture, as you can infer from the name, has to do with isolating the architecture elements away from those that might impact another. This is exactly what was adhered to by creating this new Apache Spark pool.

The first snippet of code in the `ToAvro.py` file initializes a `SparkSession`. It is necessary to instantiate a `SparkSession` when running an Apache Spark job, because the code runs inside a `pyspark-shell`, which is not the identical case when running PySpark in a notebook. When you are running PySpark code using a notebook, the `SparkSession` is created for you. The creation of the `SparkSession` and any exposure to the `pyspark-shell` is abstracted away from you but is available for reference. The `SparkSession` class provides the entry point for PySpark to access all the methods within the class. For example, in `spark.read()` and `spark.write()`, the keyword `spark` should look very familiar to you by now.

```
from pyspark.sql import SparkSession
spark = SparkSession.builder.appName("ToAvro").getOrCreate()
```

The next code snippet in the `ToAvro.py` file uses the arguments passed to the job to dynamically construct the endpoint path. The endpoint is used to identify the ADLS container and storage account name, whereas the path defines the directory in which the files are located. The name of the variable into which this information is loaded is `readPath`, which indicates this is, in fact, the location where the files are to be read from.

```
readPath = 'abfss://' + sys.argv[3] + '.dfs.core.windows.net/' \
           + sys.argv[2] + '/*' + sys.argv[1] + '*.json'
```

For clarity, three arguments are required for the job to run properly. The first argument is the scenario for which the job is running. If you look at the files in the `readPath` location, all scenarios are included in that location. The correct files are retrieved using a wildcard search. The following is an example of the wildcard pattern and how the files are named. If `ClassicalMusic` were passed as the first argument, then that file, and any file with `ClassicalMusic` in it, would be returned.

```
'/*' + sys.argv[1] + '*.json
csharpguitar-brainjammer-pow-ClassicalMusic-1808403726.json
```

The second argument is the path to the JSON files. In this case the value is `EMEA/brainjammer/in/2022/06/15/08`, which is where the Azure Batch job from Exercise 6.2 placed the JSON files with the calculated frequency median per scenario. Finally, the third argument is the ADLS container and storage account name, separated by the @ sign.

Then the next line of code reads (loads) the JSON files matching the wildcard pattern into a DataFrame.

```
df = spark.read.option("multiline","true").json(readPath)
```

The following code snippet constructs the `writePath`, which is the location where the AVRO files are to be written. The path uses the year, month, day, and hour from the `datetime.now()` method to produce the value for the `timeWritePath` variable. Finally, the third argument contains the ADLS container, and the storage account name is concatenated with the `timeWritePath` variable to produce the location where the AVRO files will be stored. Notice that there is some partial hard-coding of the path. You need to change this if you want to store the files elsewhere. If the directory does not exist, it will be created, which is much better than throwing a `DirectoryNotFound` exception.

```
import datetime
dt = datetime.datetime.now()
timeWritePath = str(dt.year) + '/' + str('%02d' % dt.month) + \
                '/' + str('%02d' % dt.day) + '/' + dt.strftime("%H") + '/'
writePath = 'abfss://' + sys.argv[3] + \
            '.dfs.core.windows.net/EMEA/brainjammer/out/' + timeWritePath
```

The final three lines of code are provided here. The first line dynamically generates the file name using the first argument, which is the brainjammer brain wave scenario, followed by some date information. The date values are used in an attempt to make it unique. The next line uses the `write()` method to save the AVRO file, then the `read()`method of the `SparkSession` class loads the AVRO file. The `show()` method results in the output being written to the Apache Spark job log file.

```
fileName = sys.argv[1] + '-' + str('%02d' % dt.month) + \
           str('%02d' % dt.day) + dt.strftime("%H") + str(dt.minute) + '.avro'
df.write.mode('overwrite').format("avro").save(writePath + fileName)
spark.read.format("avro").load(writePath + fileName).show()
```

You might have noticed that throughout the code numerous `print()` methods are called. The `print()` method includes a message; sometimes it includes a variable, which results in the value of that variable being written to the log file. Figure 6.14 illustrates the Apache Spark Applications blade located on the Monitor hub. The Monitor hub is discussed in detail in Chapter 9, "Monitoring Azure Data Storage and Processing." After you add the Apache Spark definition to the `TransformSessionFrequencyToMedian` pipeline and run it, you will see the output in the monitor logs. The logs are also gathered when you click the Submit button from the Apache Spark job definition.

FIGURE 6.14 Azure Synapse Analytics—Apache Spark job diagnostics and Monitor hub

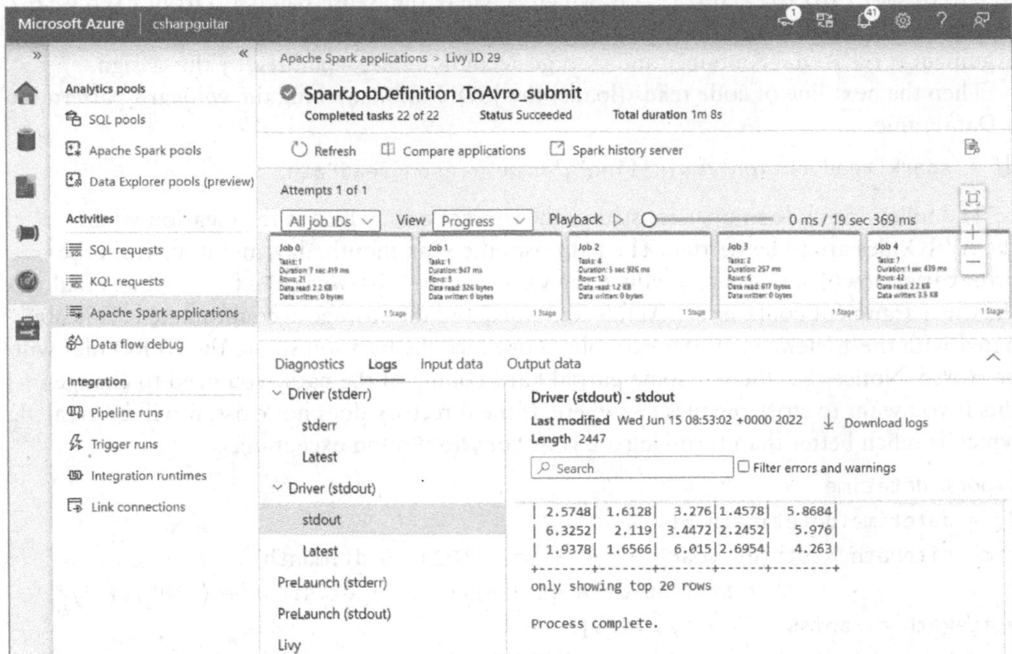

Notice the `stdout` option in the Logs tab. This is where the output of the `print()` method is stored. This is a very useful tool for debugging and troubleshooting your job. The `stderr` log is also useful for finding exceptions happening on the node. Figure 6.15 illustrates how the `TransformSessionFrequencyToMedian` pipeline is now configured.

Numerous other products for batch processing are available on the Azure platform. Read on to learn about a few more.

Azure Databricks

When performing batch processing in Azure Databricks, you need to know the terms workflows and jobs. When you are in the Azure Databrick workspace and select Workflows from the navigation menu and then click the Create Job button, a window like the one illustrated in Figure 6.16 is rendered. The options available in the Type drop-down are Notebook, Jar, and Python.

Once the job is created, you can schedule to run it at given time intervals, as you would expect. Notice in Figure 6.16 the cluster named `Shared_job_cluster`, which will be used for compute power to run your jobs. Azure Databricks offers two kinds of clusters. The aforementioned cluster, which will run your jobs, is a job cluster, also called an automated cluster. As the name implies, automated clusters are recommended for scheduled computerized jobs. When the Azure Databricks job scheduler is triggered, it will configure and provision a new job cluster to run your job on. The scheduler will also decommission the job cluster when the job is completed. The other type of cluster is referred to as interactive. When you create a notebook, this is the kind of cluster you choose. An interactive cluster is most useful for development and testing. This architectural division of concerns is similar to the one discussed in the last section, in that it is important to perform collaborative development and testing on interactive clusters and perform your production batch operations on automated clusters.

FIGURE 6.15 Azure Batch—Azure Synapse Analytics batch service pipeline with Apache Spark job definition

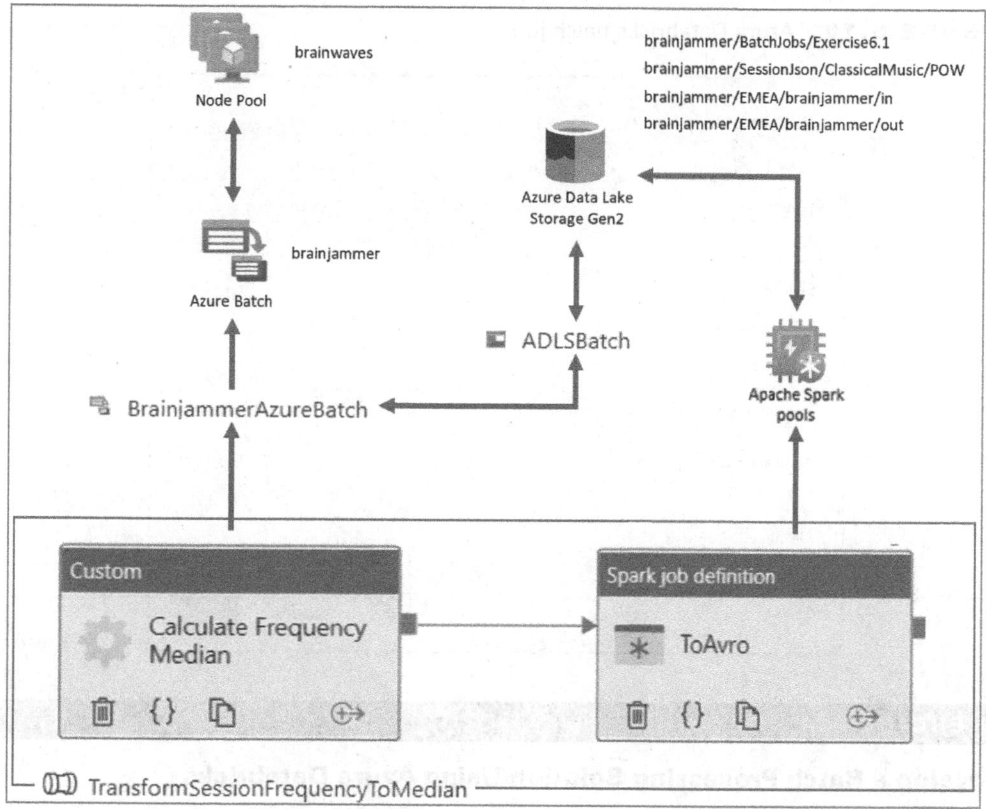

As stated, it is possible and often the case that your batch processing solution runs totally within the realm of Azure Databricks. It has all the features and capabilities one would expect for creating and managing an enterprise-level batch processing solution. However, this may not always be the case in every scenario. Consider Exercise 6.4, where you will add a Notebook activity to an Azure Synapse Analytics pipeline, which will trigger the batch job running in Azure Databricks. There is no specific reason to perform this action in this scenario. All the capabilities to perform what is required exist in both of these products.

The point you might take away from this is that you can mix and match, share and transfer data between all these systems, and use the best features available within them, as required. If there were ever a scenario where the Apache Spark version required to perform your task only currently existed on Azure Databricks and not on Azure Synapse Analytics, then you would have an option to progress your work forward. In many scenarios developers and data engineers have a very aggressive timeline to complete a project, so knowing more viable options can help them meet the deadline. Complete Exercise 6.4, where you will make the configurations required to run code on an Azure Databricks Apache Spark cluster, but the activity is triggered from an Azure Synapse Analytics pipeline.

FIGURE 6.16 Azure Databricks batch job

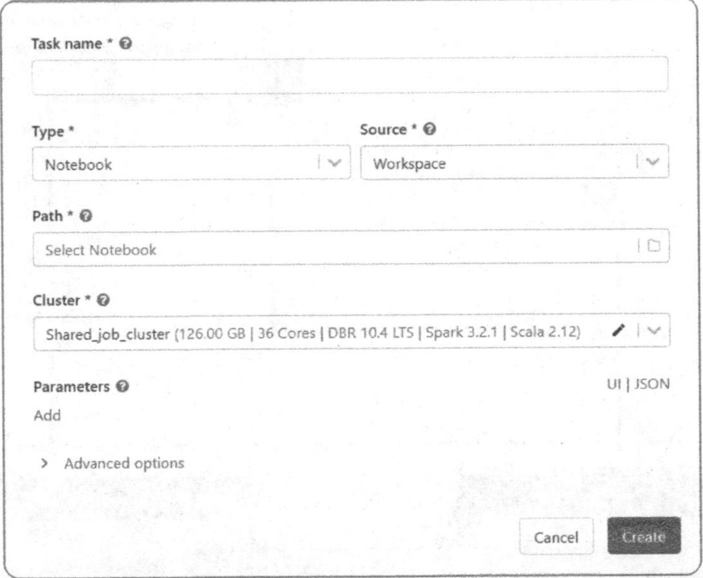

EXERCISE 6.4

Develop a Batch Processing Solution Using Azure Databricks

1. Log in to the Azure portal at `https://portal.azure.com` ➢ navigate to the Azure Databricks workspace you created in Exercise 3.14 ➢ click the Launch Workspace button on the Overview blade ➢ select Compute from the Azure Databricks Workspace navigation menu ➢ start a compute cluster ➢ select Workspace from the Azure Databricks Workspace navigation menu ➢ select Users ➢ select your account ID ➢ select

the drop-down arrow from the pop-out menu next to your account ID ➢ select Create ➢ select Notebook and provide a name (I used **IdentifyBrainwaveScenario**) ➢ select Python from the Default Language drop-down ➢ select the Apache Spark cluster you started earlier from the Cluster drop-down ➢ and then click Create.

2. Enter the following code into the first cell. The Jupyter/IPython file named `IdentifyBrainwaveScenario.ipynb` is in the `Chapter06/Ch06Ex04` directory on GitHub at `https://github.com/benperk/ADE`. Edit the `readPath` value to the path where the files were outputted to in Exercise 6.3.

```
from pyspark.sql.functions import lit, current_date
import datetime
scenario = 'ClassicalMusic'
readPath = "wasbs://<container>@<account>.blob.core.windows.net/*.avro"
df = spark.read.format("avro").load(readPath)
df = df[(df['ALPHA'].between(3.8431, 4.3924)) | \
        (df['BETA_H'].between(1.2008, 1.2259)) | \
        (df['BETA_L'].between(1.9012, 1.9363)) | \
        (df['GAMMA'].between(0.8502, 0.8675))  | \
        (df['THETA'].between(14.6206, 16.8396))]
df.select(lit(scenario).alias("SCENARIO"), "*",
          lit(current_date()).alias("TIMESTAMP")).show()
```

3. Create a new cell and enter the following code:

```
df.write.format("delta").mode("overwrite") \
     .saveAsTable("default.identifiedAs" + scenario)
display(spark.sql("SELECT * FROM default.identifiedAs" + scenario))
```

4. Return to the Azure portal at `https://portal.azure.com` ➢ navigate to the Azure Synapse Analytics workspace you created in Exercise 3.3 ➢ click the Open link in the Open Synapse Studio tile on the Overview blade ➢ select the Integrate hub ➢ select the pipeline you created in Exercise 6.2 (for example, `TransformSessionFrequencyToMedian`) ➢ expand the Databricks Activity group ➢ drag and drop a Notebook activity onto the editor canvas ➢ enter a name (I used **Identify Brainwave Scenario**) ➢ drag the green box connector from the To Avro activity to the Notebook activity ➢ select the Azure Databricks tab ➢ select + New to the right of the Databricks Linked Service drop-down list box ➢ enter a name (I used **BrainjammerAzureDatabricks**) ➢ enable interactive authoring ➢ select the Azure subscription, then the Databricks workspace you created in Exercise 3.14 and/or the one you worked with in step 1 of this exercise ➢ and then ensure the New Job Cluster radio button is selected.

EXERCISE 6.4 *(continued)*

5. Return to your Azure Databricks workspace ➢ select Settings ➢ select User Settings ➢ click Generate New Token ➢ enter a comment ➢ click Generate ➢ copy the token ➢ click Done ➢ after loading completes, paste the token into the Access Token text box of the Azure Databricks linked service you are creating in Azure Synapse Analytics ➢ select version 10.2 or 11.3 from the Cluster Version drop-down ➢ select Standard_F4 from the Cluster Node Type drop-down ➢ select 3 from the Python Version drop-down ➢ expand the Additional Cluster Settings group ➢ and then add your data information into the Name and Value fields in the Additional Cluster Settings section. (You did something similar previously in Exercise 5.4). The configuration should resemble Figure 6.17.

```
Name:  fs.azure.account.key.<blobAccount>.blob.core.windows.net
Value: F98yw7on7......==
```

FIGURE 6.17 Linked service configuration for the Azure Databricks batch job

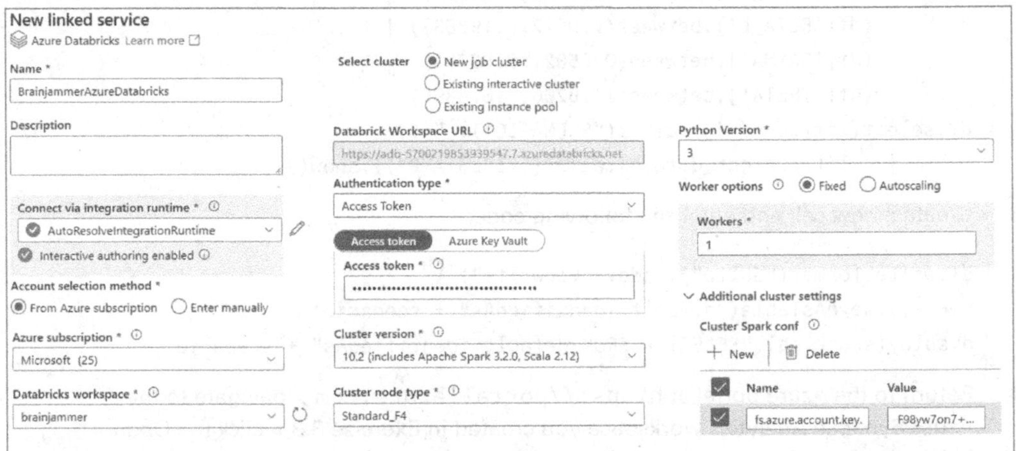

6. Click the Commit button ➢ select the Test Connection link on the Azure Databricks tab ➢ select the Settings tab ➢ click the Browse button to the right of the Notebook Path text box ➢ select Users ➢ select your account ID ➢ select the notebook you created in step 2 (for example, `IdentifyBrainwaveScenario`) ➢ click OK ➢ click the Commit button for the pipeline (for example, `TransformSessionFrequencyToMedian`) ➢ click

Validate > click Publish > and then click Debug. Figure 6.18 illustrates how the `TransformSessionFrequencyToMedian` pipeline is now configured.

FIGURE 6.18 Azure Databricks batch job pipeline configuration

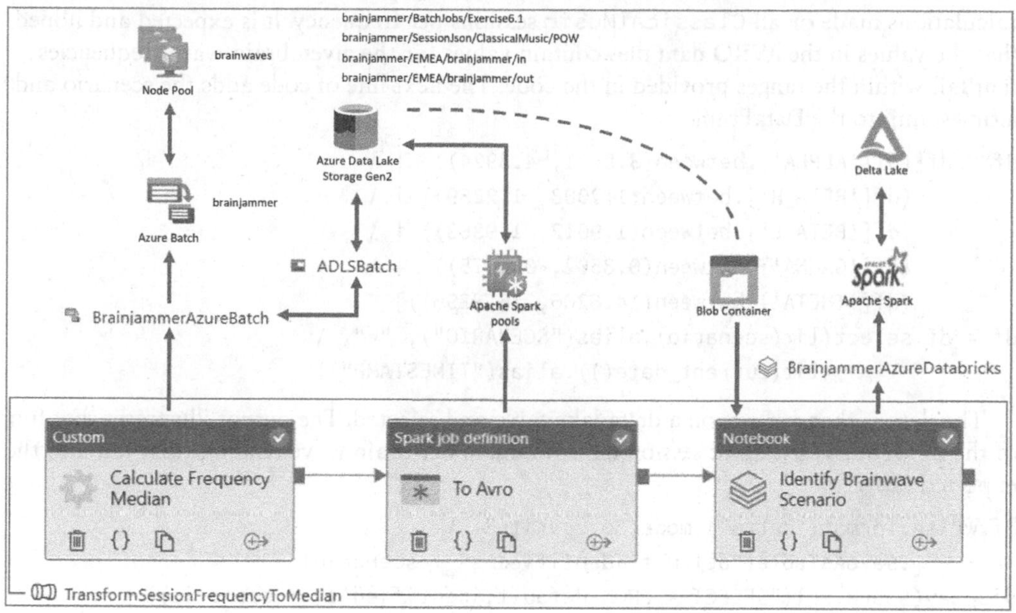

The configuration of this pipeline is growing in complexity as you progress through these lessons. You might take this that creating a visual diagram is something you should do. Imagine that you need to maintain or make a change to an element in a pipeline. An illustration will be helpful to identify all the dependencies and to locate where a change should take place. The first action in Exercise 6.4 is to create a notebook. Notice that in this case you choose an interactive cluster. You do so because you are about to test and develop some Python code. Later, when you configure the Notebook activity in Azure Synapse Analytics, you will instruct the scheduler to provision an automated job cluster. Then you add the first portion of the code into a cell. As the illustration in Figure 6.18 implies, the AVRO files are retrieved from an Azure Blob storage container instead of the ADLS container. This will be the case until you learn more about security, managed identities, and Azure Key Vault in Chapter 8. You can see that the protocol used to access the files is `wasbs`, which is most commonly used to access a blob container, instead of `abfss`, which is the common protocol for ADLS containers. The `readPath` variable uses a wildcard character to retrieve all the AVRO files from that container and load them into a DataFrame.

```
from pyspark.sql.functions import lit, current_date
import datetime
```

```
scenario = 'ClassicalMusic'
readPath = "wasbs://<container>@<account>.blob.core.windows.net/*.avro"
df = spark.read.format("avro").load(readPath)
```

The following code uses the results of the EDA found in Table 5.2 to validate the median calculations made on all ClassicalMusic sessions per frequency. It is expected and hoped that the values in the AVRO data files contain values for the given brain wave frequencies that fall within the ranges provided in the code. The next line of code adds the scenario and a timestamp to the DataFrame.

```
df = df[(df['ALPHA'].between(3.8431, 4.3924))  | \
        (df['BETA_H'].between(1.2008, 1.2259)) | \
        (df['BETA_L'].between(1.9012, 1.9363)) | \
        (df['GAMMA'].between(0.8502, 0.8675))  | \
        (df['THETA'].between(14.6206, 16.8396))]
df = df.select(lit(scenario).alias("SCENARIO"), "*", \
               lit(current_date()).alias("TIMESTAMP"))
```

The data is then written on a delta lake table and selected. The output illustrates that four of the 20 ClassicalMusic session have brainjammer brain wave readings that fall into the expected range.

```
df.write.format("delta").mode("overwrite") \
        .saveAsTable("default.identifiedAs" + scenario)
display(spark.sql("SELECT * FROM default.identifiedAs" + scenario))
+--------------+------+------+------+------+-------+----------+
|      SCENARIO| ALPHA|BETA_H|BETA_L| GAMMA|  THETA| TIMESTAMP|
+--------------+------+------+------+------+-------+----------+
|ClassicalMusic|4.1116| 1.237|1.4998|0.5494|66.4356|2022-06-16|
|ClassicalMusic|4.0828|1.5808| 3.994|0.3582|10.7822|2022-06-16|
|ClassicalMusic|3.9184|2.1326|2.6084|1.9516| 11.298|2022-06-16|
|ClassicalMusic|2.5872|0.8004| 1.911| 0.766|15.7086|2022-06-16|
+--------------+------+------+------+------+-------+----------+
```

When you return your focus to the TransformSessionFrequencyToMedian pipeline in Azure Synapse Analytics and the configured Azure Databricks linked service, you might have noticed something. One of the configuration requirements is the selection of the New Job Cluster radio button, as shown in the upper middle of Figure 6.17. This is the configuration where you instruct the scheduler to provision an automated cluster. The other option is for provisioning an interactive cluster, which you know isn't the correct one in this scenario because you are running a batch process. The other option is for provisioning nodes that you have configured in a pool via Azure Databricks.

When you configured a compute cluster in Azure Databricks, on many occasions you needed to modify the Spark configuration file. This is the place where you set up the blob storage endpoint and access key so that the connectivity to the blob storage account is authenticated successfully. The same is required when you want to perform the same action on a job cluster. This is achieved via the Cluster Spark Conf section of the Azure Databricks linked service configuration, as shown in the lower right of Figure 6.17.

```
fs.azure.account.key.<account>.blob.core.windows.net
```

When you run the pipeline and it gets to the activity that executes the Azure Databricks Notebook batch job, you can see the provisioning, status, and usage of the job cluster in the Azure Databricks workspace. By selecting the Compute navigation menu item, then the Job Clusters tab, you see what is illustrated in Figure 6.19.

FIGURE 6.19 Azure Databricks batch job pipeline status

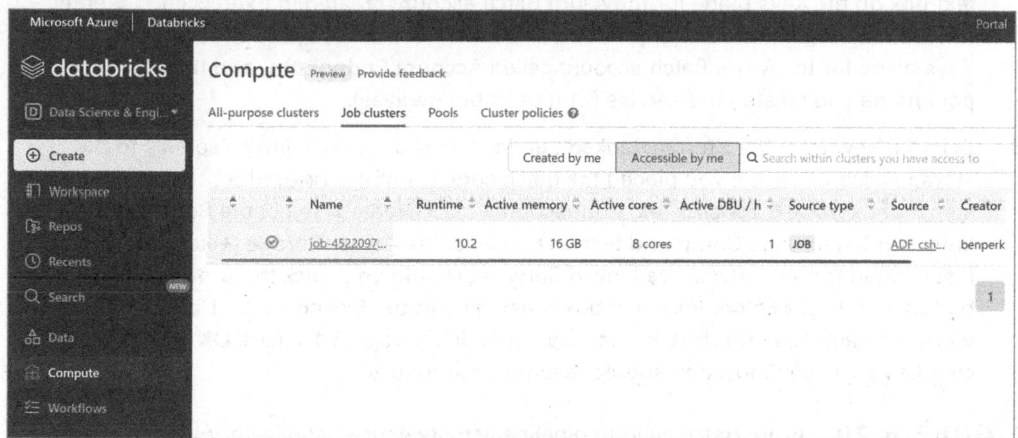

When you select the link in the Name column, you get access to configuration and event logs. To see the output and performance information, select the Workflows navigation menu item, then the Job Runs tab, and then the Job link.

Azure Data Factory

The batch processing capabilities of Azure Data Factory are almost identical to those of Azure Synapse Analytics. Regardless, you might get some questions on the exam about this tool, and you may find yourself in a position where you need to know about it; therefore, complete Exercise 6.5, which is the same as Exercise 6.2 but has been updated to target Azure Data Factory. As in Exercise 6.2, you need to have completed Exercise 6.1, where you provisioned an Azure Batch account, before starting Exercise 6.5.

EXERCISE 6.5

Develop a Batch Processing Solution Using an Azure Data Factory Pipeline

1. Log in to the Azure portal at `https://portal.azure.com` ➢ navigate to the Azure Data Factory workspace you created in Exercise 3.10 ➢ click the Open link in the Open Azure Data Factory Studio tile on the Overview blade ➢ select the Author hub ➢ select the + to the right of the search box ➢ select Pipeline from the pop-out menu ➢ select the pipeline ➢ expand Batch Service from the Activities pane ➢ and then drag and drop a Custom activity to the editor canvas.
2. Enter a name for the Custom activity (I used **Calculate Frequency Median**) ➢ select the Azure Batch tab ➢ select the + New link to the right of the Azure Batch Linked Service drop-down list box ➢ enter a name (I used **BrainjammerAzureBatch**) ➢ enable interactive authoring ➢ enter the Azure Batch Access key (located in the Primary Access Key text box on the Keys blade for the Azure Batch account created in Exercise 6.1) ➢ enter the account name (I used **brainjammer**) ➢ enter the Batch URL (also available on the Keys blade for the Azure Batch account called Account Endpoint) ➢ and then enter the pool name you created in Exercise 6.1 (I used **brainwaves**).
3. Select + New from the Storage Linked Service Name ➢ create a linked service to the storage account where you placed the batch code (`brainjammer-batch.exe`) in step 3 of Exercise 6.1 ➢ click Test Connection ➢ click Create ➢ select the Settings tab ➢ enter **run.bat** into the Command text box ➢ select the Azure Storage linked service you just created from the Resource Linked Service drop-down ➢ click the Browse Storage button next to the Folder Path text box ➢ navigate to the `Exercise6.1` directory, which contains the `run.bat` file you uploaded in Exercise 6.1 ➢ click OK ➢ and then click Save. The configuration should resemble Figure 6.20.

FIGURE 6.20 Azure Batch custom pipeline activity Azure Data Factory

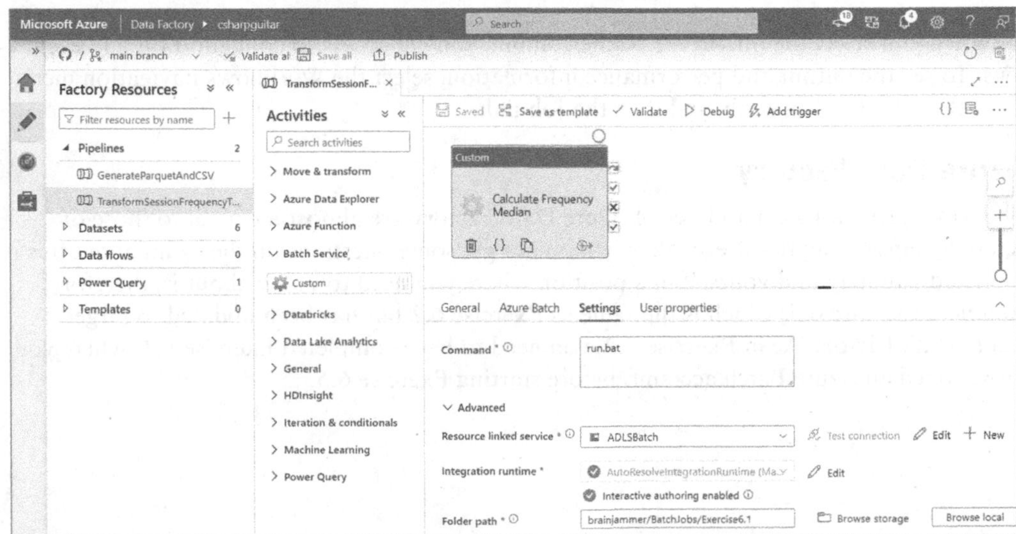

4. Click the Validate button ➢ click the Debug button, to test the batch job ➢ and then navigate to your ADLS container. New files will be rendered into the path that you provided for `outputLocation` in Exercise 6.1, appended with the current year, month, day, and hour. Navigate back to the Azure Data Factory workspace ➢ rename the pipeline (I used **TransformSessionFrequencyToMedian**) ➢ and then click Publish.

You can use a client application, Azure Batch Explorer, to view some usage and performance metrics for Azure Batch.

Azure Batch Explorer

As shown in Figure 6.21, Azure Batch Explorer provides a nice overview of the status of your Azure Batch account. You can download Azure Batch Explorer from `https://azure.github.io/BatchExplorer`.

FIGURE 6.21 Azure Batch Explorer

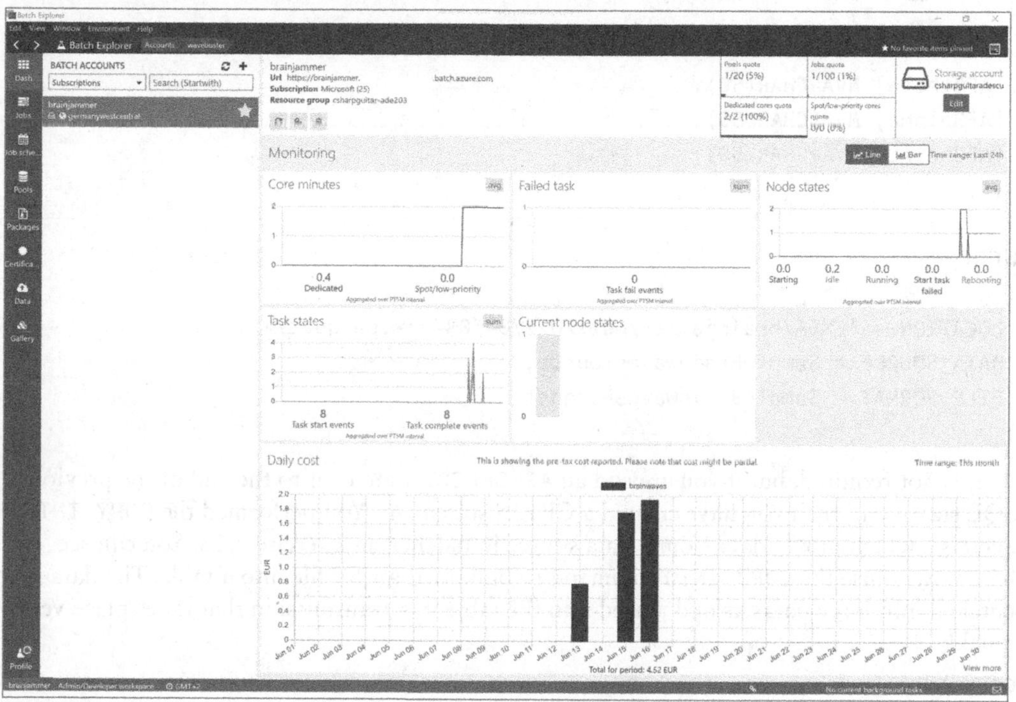

PolyBase

Batching is related to your current context. The examples you have read about up to now have to do with running batch jobs, which are small snippets of code that typically manipulate or move large amounts of data. PolyBase does perform something called batching, but it is different from a batch job. PolyBase is a technology that exists between a file and the ability to run T-SQL commands on that file. PolyBase is commonly implemented using external tables. Another feature of PolyBase is the batch loading of data, for example, while bulk loading data with the `COPY INTO` command. Why is this batching? The reason `COPY INTO` and PolyBase are considered batching models is due to the fact that when you are using this approach, data is not copied from the data source row by row. Instead, PolyBase batch loads the data in bulk, many rows at a time, which significantly reduces load times.

In Exercise 4.11 you created an external table using the following sequential steps:

- `CREATE DATABASE`
- `CREATE EXTERNAL DATA SOURCE`
- `CREATE EXTERNAL FILE FORMAT`

After creating those three references, you used them with the `CREATE EXTERNAL TABLE` statement, which creates the external table. The following is an example of that statement. You can see it in practice in Figure 4.33.

```
CREATE EXTERNAL TABLE SampleBrainwaves
(
 [Timestamp] NVARCHAR(50),
 [AF3theta] NVARCHAR(50),
 [AF3alpha] NVARCHAR(50),
 [AF3betaL] NVARCHAR(50),
 ...
)
WITH
(
 LOCATION = 'EMEA/brainjammer/out/2022/04/03/*/*.parquet/*',
 DATA_SOURCE = SampleBrainwavesSource,
 FILE_FORMAT = SampleBrainwavesParquet
)
```

It is not required, but if you append an `AS SELECT` statement to the end of the previous SQL statement, then you have created a CETAS statement. You performed the `COPY INTO` exercise, which moves data from a data source in batches, in Exercise 4.13. You can see here how to use the `COPY INTO` command to bulk load a CSV file into a table. The data is batched into large datasets and placed into the table in a transmission that takes place very quickly.

```
COPY INTO [brainwaves].[DimMODE]
FROM 'https://*.blob.core.windows.net/brainjammer/Tables/MODE.csv'
WITH (
    FILE_TYPE='CSV',
    FIRSTROW = 2
)
```

In both scenarios, i.e., the external table and `COPY INTO`, the existence of PolyBase is not intuitive. Unless you knew of its existence, you might think something like changing data in files in an ADLS container using SQL queries natively works. However, it does not. PolyBase performs its magic a few layers of abstraction below the interface, and magic it is—PolyBase is a very powerful tool.

HDInsight

If you were to run batch processing on HDInsight, you would likely choose either Hive or Pig to write and then execute the script. Hive is a SQL-like language that includes common SQL commands like `SELECT`, `INSERT`, `UPDATE`, and `DELETE`. The scripting also supports statements that can calculate the median of a given set of measurements, like the following:

```
hive> select percentile(cast(AF3THETA as DOUBLE, 0.5) from brainwaves
```

Pig is a declarative language, which is more like programming. Consider the following brainjammer brain wave readings:

```
x = (ALPHA:3.9184, BETA_H:1.237, BETA_L:1.911, GAMMA:0.8926, THETA:15.7086)
```

You can execute some Pig code like the following syntax, which will calculate the median:

```
y = FOREACH x GENERATE MEDIAN(ALPHA, BETA_H, BETA_L, GAMMA, THETA);
```

You can also run and schedule these scripts from an Azure Synapse Analytics pipeline, as shown in Figure 6.22.

FIGURE 6.22 Azure HDInsight batch processing

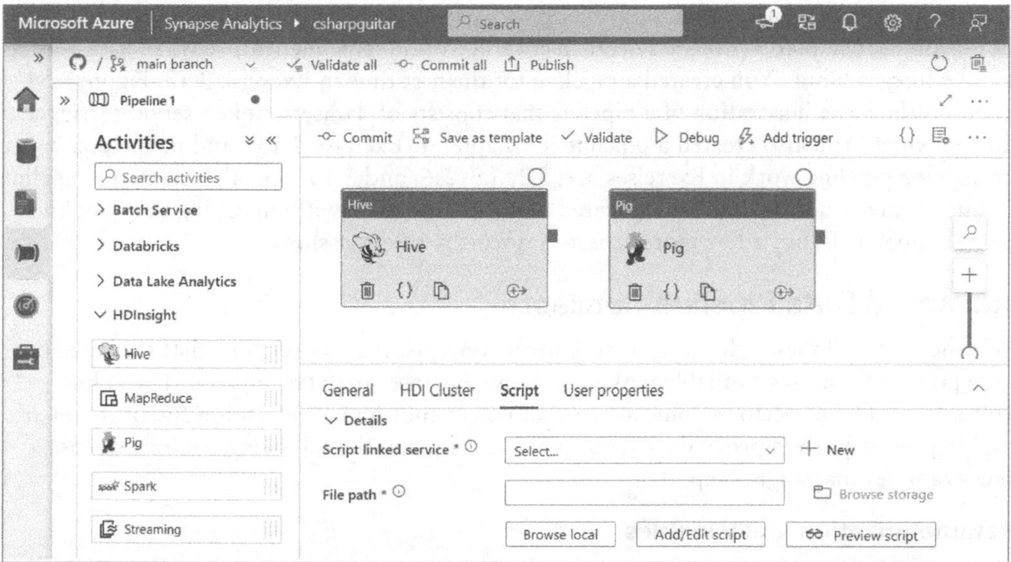

The HDInsight tab is where you select the HDInsight linked service that connects to your Azure HDInsight cluster. The attributes on the Script tab might look familiar. This is because the Script linked service points to an Azure storage account the batch file is hosted on. This is the same approach you took when executing a batch process using Azure Batch and an Azure Databricks Apache Spark cluster. The file you target via the File Path attribute could be a BAT file that contains the code examples you need to run. Performing batch processing on Azure HDInsight is a valid approach if you already have existing procedures on-premises and you want to move to the Azure platform. The administration and management requirements for running HDInsight batch processing are greater when compared to other Azure products that provide the same functionality.

Azure Data Lake Analytics

As mentioned in Chapter 1, Azure Data Lake Analytics is currently supported only by Azure Data Lake Storage Gen1. ADLS Gen1 is scheduled to retire on February 29th, 2024, and there is no plan to support ADLS Gen2 in Azure Data Lake Analytics. Therefore, Azure Data Lake Analytics will be deprecated on the same day. You can read the official announcement at `https://github.com/azure-deprecation/dashboard/issues/209`.

Create Data Pipelines

Your first exposure to an Azure Synapse Analytics pipeline in this book was in Chapter 2, "CREATE DATABASE dbName; GO," Figure 2.31, which may seem a long time ago. If you have persevered and read all the content and completed all the exercises since then, then you are in a good position concerning data pipelines. As a summary, consider that after the first introduction to pipelines, numerous other places exposed you to information about them. For example, Chapter 3 provided detailed coverage of the pipeline feature when accessed via the Integrate hub. You created a pipeline for the first time in Exercise 3.13. Figure 3.51 contains the basic illustration of a pipeline that consists of datasets, linked services, triggers, and activities. You also created a pipeline in Chapter 4 (Exercise 4.13), and in Chapter 5 you performed pipeline work in Exercises 5.1, 5.2, 5.3, 5.6, and 5.13. You also created a pipeline in this chapter—and a rather complicated one at that. It goes without saying that you know what a pipeline is, but a few more aspects are worthy of discussion.

Advanced Data Pipeline Concepts

Whether you call these advanced or additional concepts, the fact remains that they are some very powerful features available within an Azure Synapse Analytics pipeline. If you find yourself needing to perform some action that you cannot find as an option for, or if you are looking for ways to improve the overall pipeline run, then the following sections discuss a few examples that might help.

Parameterization and Variables

If you look back at Exercise 6.1 you might recall the hard-coding of some of the arguments that are stored in the `run.bat` file. When you think about batch processing, one of the benefits is hands-off automation. That means once you have completed the configuration and deployment of a batch job, you schedule it and let it run without any intervention. However, the values placed into the `run.bat` file do not really render such an experience. One approach to replace the arguments in the batch file is by using parameters. After selecting the pipeline you created in Exercise 6.2 (`TransformSessionFrequencyToMedian`), select the Parameters tab. Adding the arguments as parameters might resemble that shown in Figure 6.23.

FIGURE 6.23 Azure Synapse Analytics parameters

Parameters Variables Settings Output

+ New Delete

Name	Type	Default value
storageAccountName	String	csharpguitar
storageAccountContainerNa	String	brainjammer
inputLocation	String	SessionJson/ClassicalMusic/I
outputLocation	String	EMEA/brainjammer/in
accountKey	String	D4yx3uLjpPjEa0vyzHs6bclLK

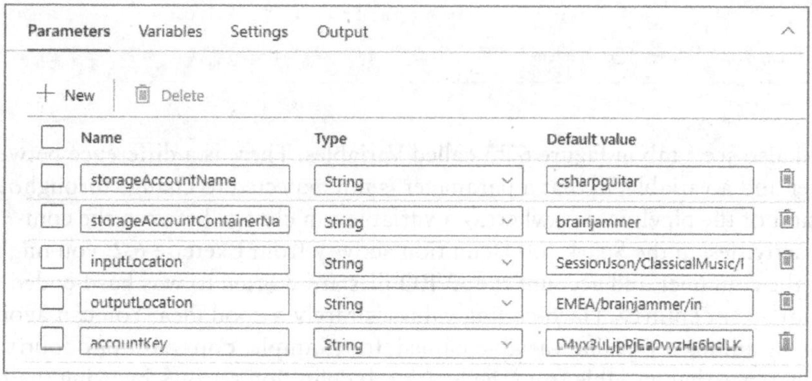

Click the Custom activity (`Calculate Frequency Median`) that executes the `run.bat` file, and then click the Settings tab. It is then possible to set the arguments within the Command multiline text box with the following syntax, as shown in Figure 6.24:

```
@concat('brainjammer-batch.exe ',
pipeline().parameters.storageAccountName, ' ',
pipeline().parameters.storageAccountContainerName, ' ',
pipeline().parameters.inputLocation, ' ',
pipeline().parameters.outputLocation, ' ',
pipeline().parameters.accountKey)
```

FIGURE 6.24 Azure Synapse Analytics parameters as command arguments

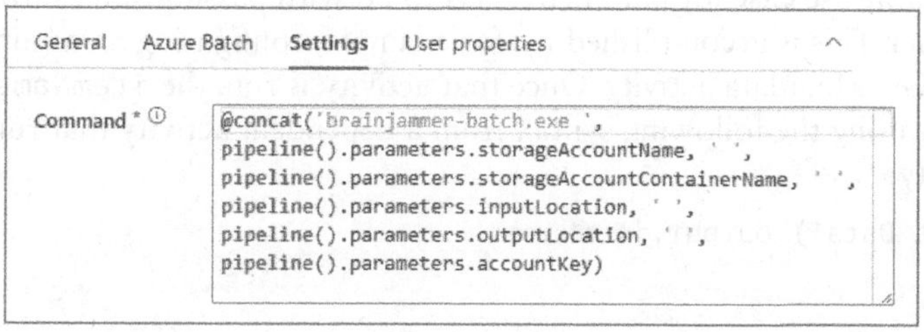

General Azure Batch Settings User properties

Command *

```
@concat('brainjammer-batch.exe ',
pipeline().parameters.storageAccountName, ' ',
pipeline().parameters.storageAccountContainerName, ' ',
pipeline().parameters.inputLocation, ' ',
pipeline().parameters.outputLocation, ' ',
pipeline().parameters.accountKey)
```

When the batch job is complete and the pipeline has been run, you can click either the input or output links by hovering over the Run status line on the Output tab to view the parameters, as shown in Figure 6.25.

FIGURE 6.25 Azure Synapse Analytics parameter input and output run details

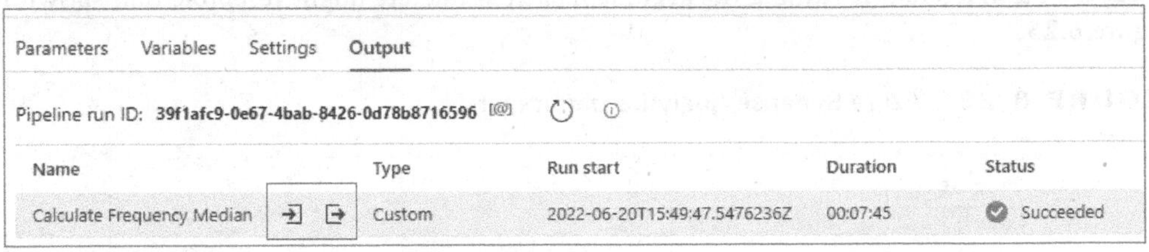

Parameters Variables Settings **Output**

Pipeline run ID: **39f1afc9-0e67-4bab-8426-0d78b8716596**

Name	Type	Run start	Duration	Status
Calculate Frequency Median	Custom	2022-06-20T15:49:47.5476236Z	00:07:45	Succeeded

You will also see a tab in Figure 6.23 called Variables. There is a difference between a parameter and a variable, in that a parameter is not expected to change throughout the execution of the pipeline run, whereas a variable can change between the completion of activities. In the Spark Job Definition activity from Exercise 6.2, you might recall that the container and account the AVRO files are written to was hard-coded to `<container>@<account>`. Hard-coding values is rarely a good idea. You can avoid hard-coding this by adding a pipeline variable named, for example, `containerAccount`. You can then reference that variable from the Spark job definition settings by using the following syntax:

```
@varialbes('containerAccount')
```

All that you read here will be performed in Exercise 6.6. Consider this content as a preface to that exercise.

The `containerAccount` variable can be set by using the `concat()` method to combine a parameter named `storageAccountContainerName` with a parameter named `storageAccountName`, with an `@` (at) sign between them—for example:

```
@concat(pipeline().parameters.storageAccountContainerName, '@',
        pipeline().parameters.storageAccountName)
```

Another valuable use case for parameters has to do with passing values from one activity to another. This is accomplished by, for example, configuring an argument named `itemName` in a Get Metadata activity. Once that activity is run, the `itemName` variable can be referenced by using the following syntax from a dependent activity that runs after the Get Metadata activity:

```
@activity('Get Data').output.itemName
```

Figure 6.26 illustrates this in more detail so that you can visualize how to add dynamic content to an argument or value.

FIGURE 6.26 Azure Synapse Analytics passing parameter between pipeline activities

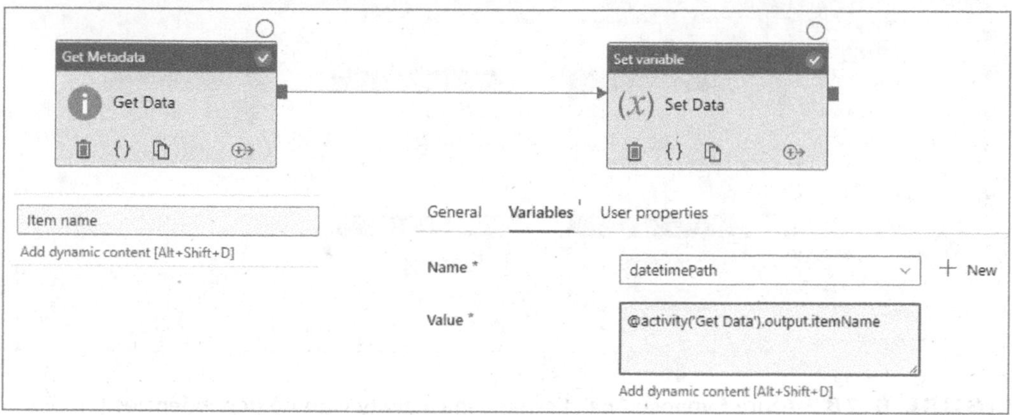

When you set focus to a value or argument text box that supports dynamic content, the link for Add Dynamic Content (Alt+Shift+D) is rendered. Clicking the link or pressing the keyboard combination opens an expression panel for you to add the script that delivers your expected value dynamically.

Parallelism

The opposite of parallel is serial. If you run activities in a pipeline serially, then the time required to complete the pipeline run is equal to the time each activity takes. For example, if you have five activities, each one takes 30 seconds to complete and they run serially, then the pipeline run will take three and a half minutes. However, if you run those same activities in parallel, the pipeline run will complete in 30 seconds. The caveat to consider when running activities in parallel has to do with dependencies. Figure 6.27 represents a pipeline that contains activities with no dependencies between them.

Notice that no lines connect the five activities together. The absence of those connecting lines signifies that there is no dependency between the activities. When you trigger the pipeline, all activities will run in parallel and complete faster than if they had been run in parallel. Up to this point the dependencies you have created between activities have been based on the successful completion of the activity. However, there are other conditions, such as failed, skipped, and completed. You can add different conditions by selecting the Add Activity On button located on the activity, as shown in Figure 6.28.

FIGURE 6.27 Azure Synapse Analytics pipeline activity with no dependencies

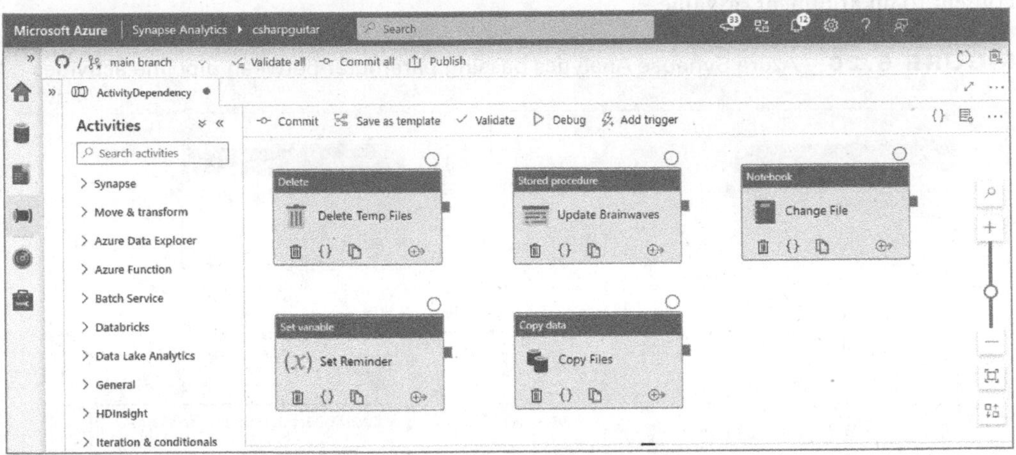

FIGURE 6.28 Azure Synapse Analytics pipeline activity with no dependencies (2)

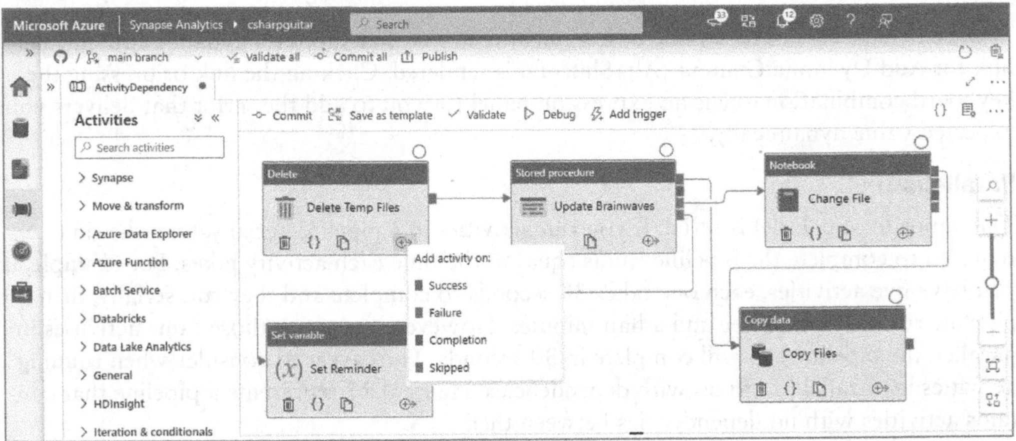

You see many dependencies now in Figure 6.28. For example, the Stored Procedure activity will not run until the Delete activity has completed successfully. When the Stored Procedure activity is skipped, then the Set Variable activity is performed, and the pipeline run terminates. If the Stored Procedure activity succeeded and the Notebook activity is skipped, then the Copy Data activity is executed, and the pipeline run completes. Since Skipped is also an option under Add Activity On, this is a bit hard to follow, as there is actually no skipped dependency on the notebook. If the stored procedure is successful, the Copy Data activity is executed. However, if the stored procedure fails, the Notebook activity is triggered. When it successfully runs, the Copy Data activity is executed, and the pipeline ends. You can see how complicated dependencies can become with large pipelines. This is a similar scenario to batch processing solutions that have a lot of dependencies. The reason highly skilled technical people are so much in demand is because they can manage all these complexities and produce results.

Pipeline JSON

When you configure a pipeline that includes activities with include numerous dependencies, all those settings are stored in JSON format. If configured to do so, this JSON file is what is placed into your source code repository like GitHub or Azure DevOps when you click the Commit button in the Azure Synapse Analytics workspace. You can also view it when you select the braces ({ }) in the upper right of the pipeline canvas. A pipeline JSON configuration file with nothing other than an annotation configured in it resembles the following:

```
{
 "name": "TransformSessionFrequencyToMedian",
 "properties": {
        "annotations": [
              "Exercise 6.6"
        ]
 }
}
```

In a real case the pipeline configuration would hold complete details of each activity that exists in the pipeline and the dependencies between them. The `Calculate Frequency Median` activity would have the command parameters like the following:

```
"command": {
  "value": "@concat('brainjammer-batch.exe ',
          \npipeline().parameters.storageAccountName, ' ',
          \npipeline().parameters.storageAccountContainerName, ' ',
          \npipeline().parameters.inputLocation, ' ',
          \npipeline().parameters.outputLocation, ' ',
          \npipeline().parameters.accountKey)",
  "type": "Expression"
}
```

In addition to the activities, the name and types of linked services are also present, as follows:

```
"resourceLinkedService": {
  "referenceName": "ADLSBatch",
                "type": "LinkedServiceReference"
}

"linkedServiceName": {
  "referenceName": "BrainjammerAzureBatch",
                "type": "LinkedServiceReference"
}
```

The pipeline JSON configuration file for `TransformSessionFrequencyToMedian` is in the `Chapter06` directory on GitHub. To conclude this section, complete Exercise 6.6, where you will implement the advanced pipeline concepts you just read about.

EXERCISE 6.6

Create Data Pipelines—Advanced

1. Log in to the Azure portal at `https://portal.azure.com` ➢ navigate to the Azure Synapse Analytics workspace you created in Exercise 3.3 ➢ click the Open link in the Open Synapse Studio tile on the Overview blade ➢ select the Integrate hub ➢ select the `TransformSessionFrequencyToMedian` pipeline from the Pipelines list ➢ with no activity selected, select the Parameters tab ➢ add the parameters as provided in Table 6.3 (refer to Figure 6.23) ➢ and then replace the default value with your unique values.

TABLE 6.3 Exercise 6.6 pipeline parameters

Name	Type	Default value
storageAccountName	String	<storageAccountName>
storageAccountContainerName	String	<ADLS containerName>
inputLocation	String	<Path to files for processing>
outputLocation	String	<Path to place files after processing>
accountKey	String	<storageAccountKey>

2. Select the `Calculate Frequency Median` activity ➢ select the Settings tab ➢ click the multiline text box that currently contains `run.bat` ➢ click the Add Dynamic Content link that is rendered ➢ place the following syntax (available in the `Chapter06/Ch06Ex06` directory on GitHub) into the dynamic content editor ➢ and then click OK.

```
@concat('brainjammer-batch.exe ',
pipeline().parameters.storageAccountName, ' ',
pipeline().parameters.storageAccountContainerName, ' ',
pipeline().parameters.inputLocation, ' ',
pipeline().parameters.outputLocation, ' ',
pipeline().parameters.accountKey)
```

3. With no activity selected, open the Variables tab ➢ add variables named `containerAccount` and `datetimePath` of type String with no default value ➢ drag and drop two Set Variable activities from the General group ➢ and then place both activities between the `Calculate Frequency Median` and the `To Avro` activity, as shown in Figure 6.29.

FIGURE 6.29 Azure Synapse Analytics pipeline variables

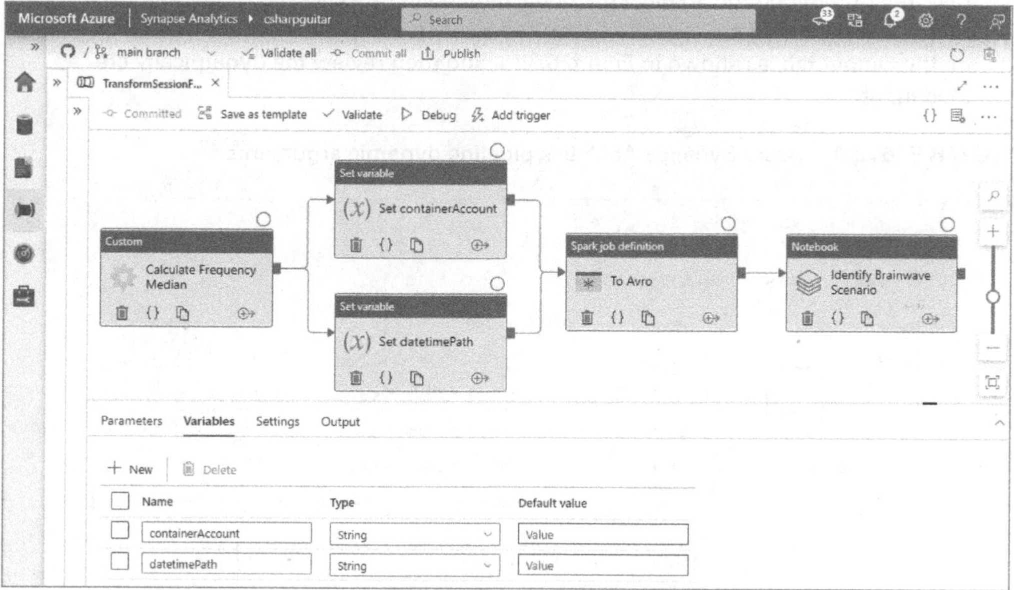

4. On the Variables tab of the `Set containerAccount` activity, select `containerAccount` from the drop-down list box ➢ set the focus to the Value multiline text box ➢ click the Add Dynamic Content link ➢ enter the following syntax into the dynamic editor ➢ and then click OK.

```
@concat(pipeline().parameters.storageAccountContainerName, '@', pipeline()
.parameters.storageAccountName)
```

5. Add the following syntax to the `Set datetimePath` activity using the same procedure as described in step 4:

```
@concat(utcnow('yyyy'), '/', utcnow('MM'), '/', utcnow('dd'), '/', utcnow('HH'))
```

6. On the Settings tab for the `To Avro` activity, click the third argument, which contains the `<container>@<accountName>` ➢ click the Add Dynamic Content link ➢ enter the following syntax into the dynamic editor ➢ and then click OK.

```
@variables('containerAccount')
```

EXERCISE 6.6 ***(continued)***

7. Replace the second argument, which was hard-coded, to, for example, `EMEA/brainjammer/in/2022/06/15/08` ➢ and then replace it with the following syntax using the same procedure described in step 6.

```
@concat('EMEA/brainjammer/in/', variables('datetimePath'))
```

8. Click the Commit button ➢ select the Publish menu item ➢ click the Debug button ➢ review the parameters ➢ click the OK button ➢ when complete, click the Input icon on the Output tab, as shown in Figure 6.30 ➢ and then review the dynamically created input.

FIGURE 6.30 Azure Synapse Analytics pipeline dynamic arguments

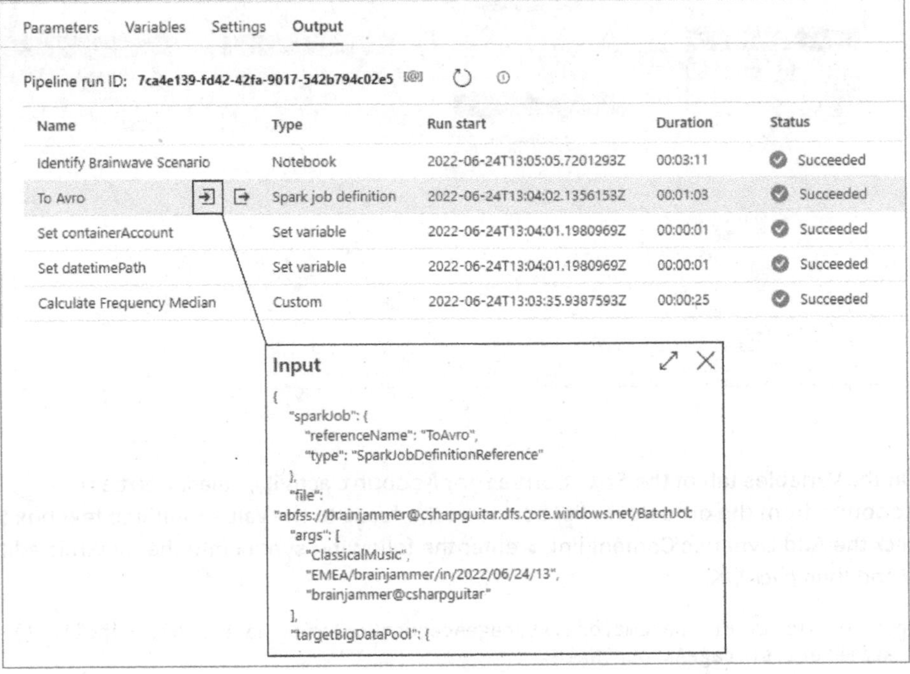

You might agree that being able to set parameters and variables dynamically is a very useful feature. It is important to avoid hard-coding values that your batch, pipeline, and activities use to process data. Those values tend to change, and when they do, there are exceptions and failures. In a lot of cases, it is not intuitively obvious that the issue lies with a parameter being used that is no longer valid. It is best to make your solutions as flexible as possible.

Triggers and Scheduling

The technique you have been using to run pipelines up to now has been to click either the Debug button or the Trigger Now item from the Add Trigger menu. Figure 6.31 shows both options.

FIGURE 6.31 Running an Azure Synapse Analytics pipeline

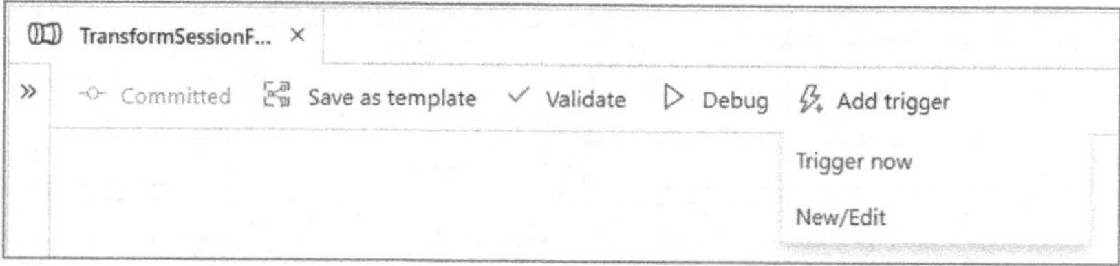

Each approach, Debug or Trigger Now, requires manual intervention, which is all right for testing and for performing the occasional unique pipeline activity. However, you know that doing work manually over and over again is not optimal and that any work that can be automated should be. So instead of manually triggering your batch process or pipeline execution, you can schedule it. The alternative to Trigger Now, as shown in Figure 6.31 is New/Edit. The experience when the New/Edit menu item is selected is the same for both Azure Synapse Analytics and Azure Data Factory. The following section describes that experience in detail.

Azure Synapse Analytics and Azure Data Factory

When you select New/Edit from the Add Trigger menu, an Add Triggers pop-out window that lists the existing triggers opens. Click the drop-down text box under the Add Triggers and select + New option. Figure 6.32 represents the window that is rendered.

The Start Date field is intuitive, in that the value is when you want the pipeline to be triggered. That value is usually in the future and is the first time it will run when the Start Trigger on Creation check box is selected. Notice also that you can select the time zone in which you want to run trigger the pipeline. If you are running a global Big Data program that has pieces scattered out in different countries, then it might be a good idea to choose UTC. This way you can avoid needing to calculate what time it is in the CST time zone when you are running the pipeline that is located in the CET time zone. Instead, you can always think in terms of UTC, which is a universal time, and use it for all your scheduling. However, if you are working within a single time zone, then it might be a good idea to use your local time zone, to keep things simpler.

FIGURE 6.32 Azure Synapse Analytics New/Edit trigger

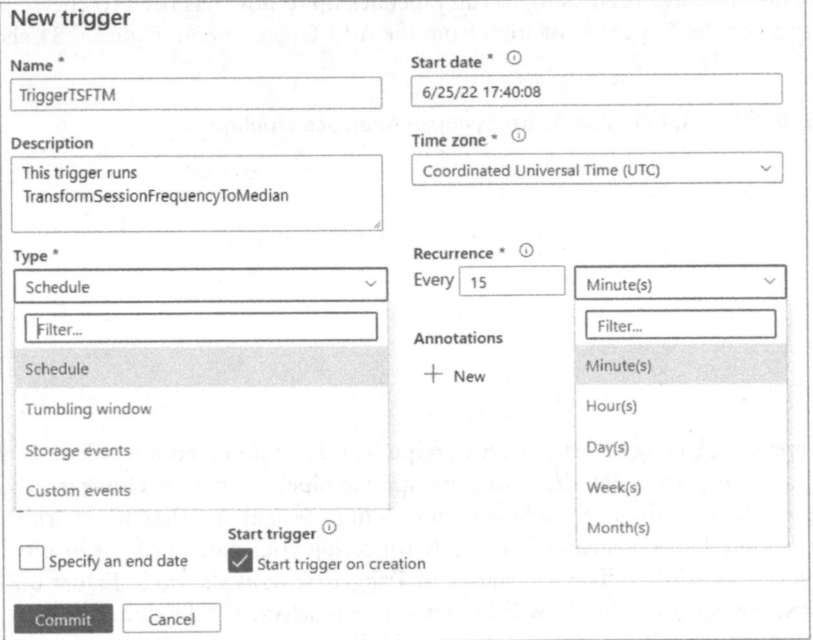

The Specify an End Date check box gives you the opportunity to define when the job will stop being triggered. The Recurrence option is how often or the frequency in which you want the pipeline to be triggered. The options are Minute(s), Hour(s), Day(s), Week(s), or Month(s). If you enter 4 in the Every text box and choose Hour(s) from the drop-down text box, then the trigger will run every 4 hours, or 6 times per day. It will run from the time you selected in the Start Date text box. The last option you need to select before committing the new trigger is the type of trigger you need. Table 6.4 summarizes the options.

TABLE 6.4 Types of pipeline triggers

Type	Relationship	Description
Scheduled	Many-to-many	Specify a start date, recurrence, and an end date.
Tumbling window	One-to-one	Like a scheduled trigger but with retry, concurrency, and other additional capabilities.
Storage event	One-to-one	Triggered when a file that resides on an Azure Storage container is created or deleted.
Custom event	One-to-one	Azure Event Grid triggers the pipeline on a received event.

Each of these trigger types has some uniqueness, but they are varied enough to provide all the features you need for any requirement. More details about each trigger type are provided in the following subsections.

SCHEDULED TRIGGERS

Scheduled triggers are useful when you want to run a pipeline regularly at a specific time. The default values for a scheduled trigger are to run every 15 minutes, which equates to 96 executions per day. One point to mention when running jobs with short intervals has to do with overlapping executions. You need to make sure that the actions being taken for a given run can be completed before the next scheduled runtime. If there is overlap, meaning you have two instances of the same pipeline running simultaneously, then data can be corrupted, so be sure to make the duration long enough to complete in all scenarios. Another option is to run the pipeline hourly, with the frequency defined by the number in the first text box that defaulted to 15. If the value is 15, it means the job will run every 15 hours, which is a little less than twice per day. A scenario for this would be when you expect to have new data arriving on or around a 15-hour interval that needs to be ingested, transformed, and made available for consumption.

A daily scheduled trigger provides the option to run the job every day at a given time. The default time is the 1 set in the Start Date text box on the New Trigger window. As shown in Figure 6.33, you can change the schedule execution time from the default value.

FIGURE 6.33 Azure Synapse Analytics daily scheduled trigger

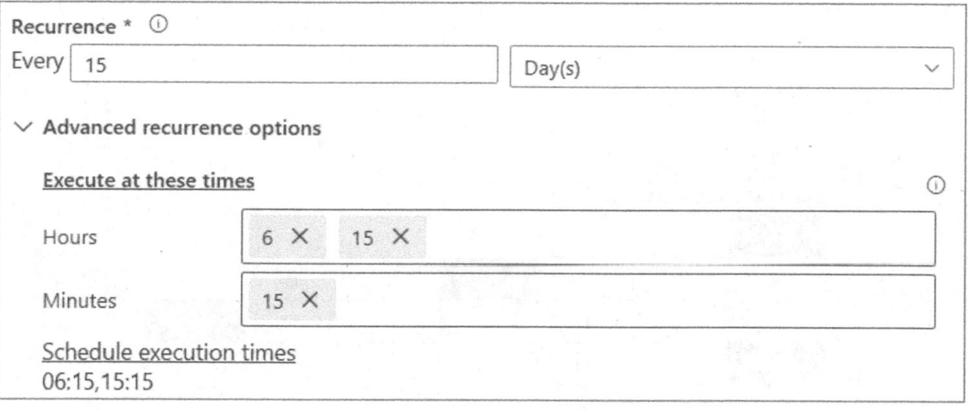

This is achieved by expanding the Advanced Recurrence options group and adding values for hours and minutes. When you select the weekly schedule, you are given the option to select the days you want the job to run. You can select every day of the week or just a few days, as shown in Figure 6.34.

FIGURE 6.34 Azure Synapse Analytics weekly scheduled trigger

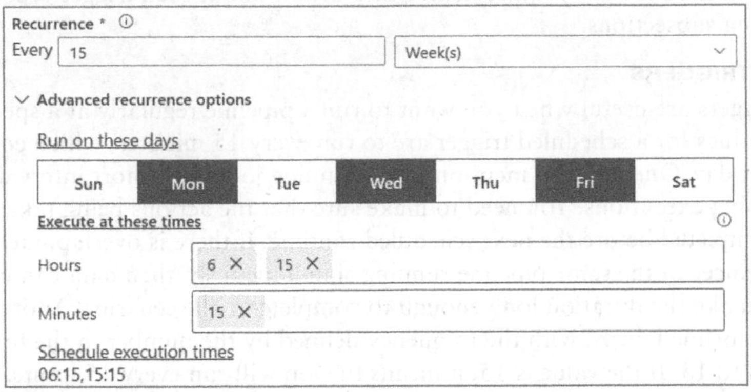

Recurrence *
Every 15 Week(s)
Advanced recurrence options
Run on these days
Sun Mon Tue Wed Thu Fri Sat
Execute at these times
Hours 6 × 15 ×
Minutes 15 ×
Schedule execution times
06:15,15:15

The configuration shown in Figure 6.34 will run twice per day: once at 06:15 and again at 15:15 on Monday, Wednesday, and Friday. The last option for configuring a scheduled trigger is monthly. As shown in Figure 6.35, you can select which days of the month the pipeline should run. In this scenario the job will run at 06:15 and 15:15 on the 1st, 11th, 21st, and the 22nd day of the month.

FIGURE 6.35 Azure Synapse Analytics monthly scheduled trigger

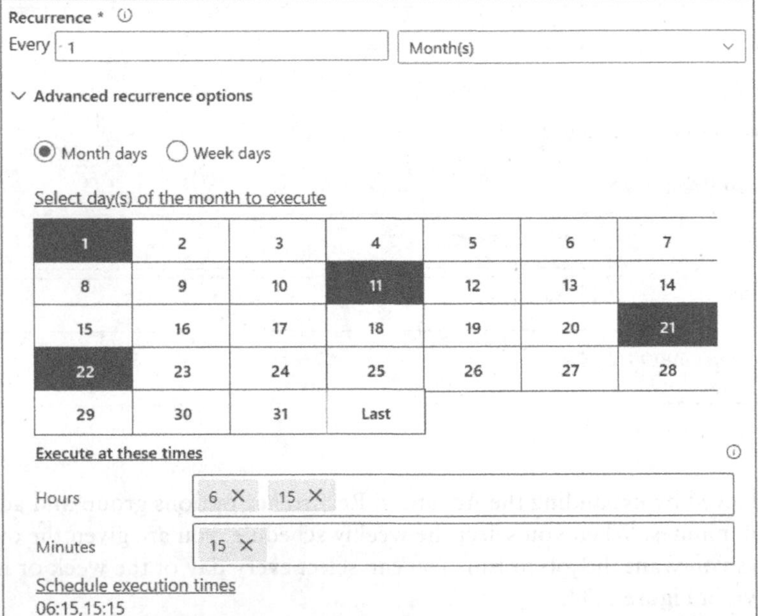

When you select the Week Days radio button, you are given two options: the iteration and the week day. The iteration values are First, Second, Third, Fourth, Fifth, and Last. The week day values are Sunday through Saturday. This means you can trigger the pipeline the first Monday of every month, the last Tuesday, or the third Friday, for example. You can also add multiple configurations, meaning you can trigger the pipeline to run on the fourth Wednesday and the second Saturday—almost any combination you need can be achieved.

The last scenario to cover regarding scheduled triggers is the many-to-many relationship they can have with pipelines. This means that a single schedule can trigger multiple pipelines, and pipelines can be triggered by multiple scheduled triggers. Figure 6.36 shows a way to achieve this.

FIGURE 6.36 Azure Synapse Analytics many-to-many scheduled trigger

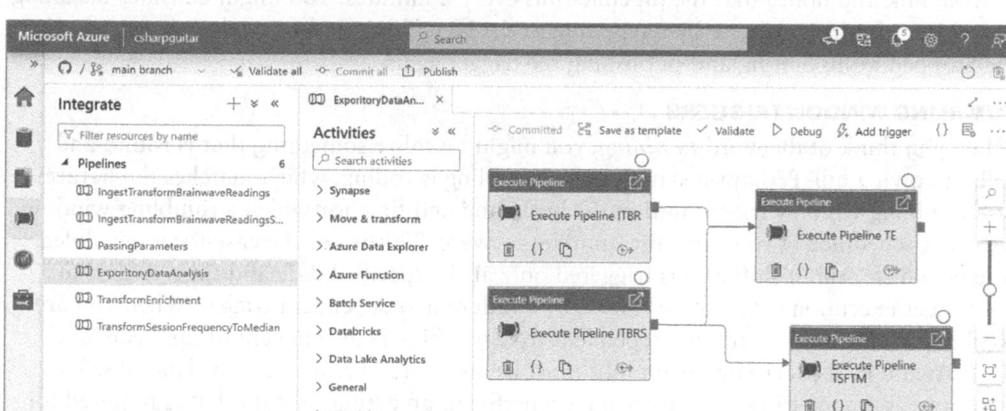

An Execute Pipeline activity is located within the General group. As in all pipelines, there can be many activities, and, in this case, all the activities are pipelines themselves. When this pipeline is triggered, it will run two pipelines in parallel. The Execute Pipeline activity named `Execute Pipeline TE` has a dependency on two parent pipelines and will run only after both are complete. However, Execute Pipeline TransformSessionFrequencyToMedian is dependent only on a single parent pipeline and will run after it is completed. To create a scheduled trigger, complete Exercise 6.7.

EXERCISE 6.7

Create a Scheduled Trigger

1. Log in to the Azure portal at `https://portal.azure.com` ➢ navigate to the Azure Synapse Analytics workspace you created in Exercise 3.3 ➢ click the Open link in the Open Synapse Studio tile on the Overview blade ➢ select the Integrate hub ➢ select any of the pipelines you have created so far ➢ select the Trigger drop-down menu ➢ select New/Edit ➢ and then select + New from the Choose Triggers drop-down text box.

EXERCISE 6.7 *(continued)*

2. Enter a name ➢ select Schedule from the Type drop-down text box ➢ enter **2** in the Every text box in the Recurrence section ➢ select Minute(s) from the drop-down ➢ check the Start Trigger on Creation check box ➢ click the Commit button ➢ click the Save button ➢ select the Publish menu item ➢ and then click OK.
3. Navigate to the Monitor hub ➢ click the Pipeline Runs link ➢ wait 2 minutes ➢ and then view the pipeline run details.

Each time the trigger fires, the pipeline you selected will run. After some minutes, click the Refresh link and notice that the pipeline runs every 2 minutes. You might consider disabling the trigger after this exercise by navigating to the New/Edit window of the trigger, selecting the Stopped radio button, and publishing the trigger again.

TUMBLING WINDOW TRIGGERS

When you think of the word *tumbling*, you might visualize something that is round and rolling down a hill. Perhaps a synonym for tumbling is rolling, which matches the nature of a tumbling window trigger in that the begin and end time for which a tumbling window trigger is scheduled to run can shift (tumble) forward. This is not the case for a scheduled trigger, which cannot shift and is triggered only at the specified date and time. A shift in the trigger execution time can be caused by a failure in a dependent trigger. When you are working in a scenario with interdependent triggers, there is the concept of upstream and downstream jobs, where upstream jobs must be completed before downstream jobs. That is because, in many cases, the upstream job performs an action on data that is required for the downstream job to work correctly. It has historically been very complicated to build a dependency graph between jobs. In some cases, the logic required to manage the dependencies between these tasks is more complicated than the logic that performs the transformation of the data itself. This complication is what makes tumbling window triggers so useful, because it exposes a simple interface for creating a dependency between jobs.

You might be wondering why a dependent tumbling window trigger's execution time can shift forward. A reason can be due to a failure of an upstream job that, for example, could load some data into a table. If that load fails, you would want to retry, reschedule, or abandon the triggering of the downstream job. Figure 6.37 represents the configuration options available specifically for a tumbling window trigger named `DailyBrainwaveIngestion`, which triggers a pipeline that pulls data from a data source and loads it into a table in an Azure SQL pool in an Azure Synapse Analytics workspace.

FIGURE 6.37 Azure Synapse Analytics tumbling window trigger

Look first at the Recurrence setting. Placing a 1 in the Every text box and selecting Hour(s) from the drop-down text box results in the triggering of the associated pipeline every hour from the entry in the Start Date field. The available options are Minute(s), Hour(s), and Month(s). Below the Recurrence option is an option to Specify an End Date if you need to stop the job at some time in the future. If this option is not selected, the trigger will run indefinitely. Next, setting the Delay value to 5 minutes means that when the Start Date is 00:00:00, the pipeline execution will begin at 00:05:00. The Delay value is the amount of time between the firing of the trigger and the execution of the pipeline run for the given time window. The Max Concurrency setting represents how many trigger runs can occur simultaneously. Assume that for some reason your trigger was not able to fire for the previous 12 hours. Because this trigger is scheduled to run hourly, there are 12 time windows the trigger needs to back fill. Having a Max Concurrency value of 6 means that the trigger will fire six times simultaneously. Assuming the failures happened between 00:00 and 12:00, the job will be triggered first for the first time windows of 00:00–01:00 and 06:00–07:00, and then the second time for the next 6 hours of 07:00–08:00 and 12:00–13:00. The Retry

Policy: Count value is the number of times the pipeline can run unsuccessfully before the run status is set to Failed. If you want to wait some time between a retry, you can set the Retry Policy: Interval in Seconds option to a value, for example, 90 seconds. With this setting, if the pipeline run is not successful, it will wait a minute and a half before running again. This is actually a good practice to follow, because it gives the platform some time to recover from the execution. If there is an exception in the process, it might take some time to write exception logs or perhaps even restart itself. So, consider building in some time for recovery if you decide to retry failed pipeline runs.

The capability to create dependencies to other triggers exists within the Advanced grouping. When you expand that group, you will see the option to add trigger dependencies. To create a dependency between the `DailyBrainwaveIngestion` trigger and other tumbling window triggers, such as `DailyElectLoad` and `DailyFreqLoad`, you select them from the Trigger drop-down text box. You will see only tumbling triggers in the list box; the other types of triggers are not supported. The two triggers illustrated in Figure 6.37 are `DailyElectLoad` and `DailyFreqLoad`. Since the initial load of the brainjammer brain wave data happens via the `DailyBrainwaveIngestion` trigger, it needs to happen before jobs that will pull electrode and frequency data from that Azure SQL pool table.

Next to the Trigger option are two additional options, Offset and Window Size. In general terms, an offset is the positive or negative value difference between two points. In this case, consider that the start time for this tumbling window trigger is 00:00, and the offset is zero. This means that these dependent triggers will fire after the upstream pipeline run completes. Had the value been 30 minutes, then the downstream trigger would be fired 30 minutes after completion of this upstream dependent job. If you want to increase or decrease the time window in which this dependent job can run, place that value in the Window Size text box. Consider that the `DailyBrainwaveIngestion` trigger is scheduled to run every hour if you need to reduce the time window for the `DailyElectLoad` trigger to run due to further dependencies, then you can configure that restriction. As mentioned previously, the management of interdependencies of jobs is very complicated. Making changes to them is very risky and, in many cases, it is not possible to test completely the impact of a change. Therefore, if you experience some issue, for example, with the `DailyElectLoad` trigger because another process locks the table at 45 after the hour, you can change the Window Size down to avoid that locking at 45 after the hour. Especially if you are certain the trigger completes within that timeframe, it is better to do this than to try to reschedule jobs. Rescheduling jobs can cause a domino effect, and you end up potentially changing the behavior of a large number of jobs, which can have a major negative impact.

Another point to make about a tumbling window trigger is that you can have a maximum of five dependencies. That means one tumbling window trigger can have five tumbling window triggers in the drop-down list boxes in the Advanced section. The amount of time a dependent trigger will wait for an upstream job to finish is 7 days. After 7 days, the downstream dependencies will time out and have a status of Failed. Finally, a tumbling window trigger has a one-to-one relationship with a pipeline. A tumbling window trigger cannot trigger more than a single pipeline.

STORAGE EVENT TRIGGERS

In the previous two trigger type scenarios, the data scheduled to be processed is expected to be in a specified location before the pipeline is triggered. An alternative to that is to notify the trigger when the data has been placed into a specific location. When the notification is sent and received, the trigger is fired, and the pipeline activities can access data and perform the necessary ingestion or transformation. If this is a desired scenario, and the data is placed into a storage account, then you can use the storage event trigger type. Figure 6.38 represents the configuration options for this kind of trigger.

FIGURE 6.38 Azure Synapse Analytics storage event trigger

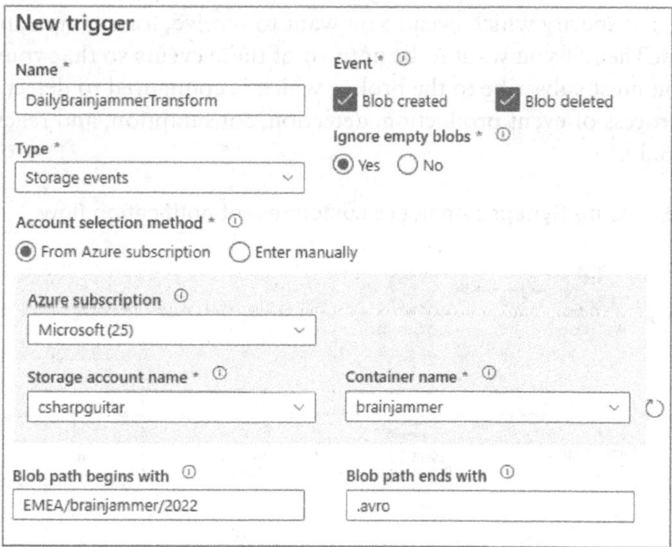

Notice that you can choose to have the event sent to the trigger based on the Blob Created or Blob Deleted event. This means that when a file is placed into the container on the identified storage account, the trigger is fired and the pipeline executed. The same would be true when a file is deleted from the container and account, in that the pipeline run would be executed. If you expect to receive files that can be empty, and those empty files cause some problem with the pipeline run, you can ignore them by selecting the Yes radio button under the Ignore Empty Blobs header. You can also filter which blobs result in a trigger event by adding values to either the Blob Path Begins With and/or the Blob Path Ends With parameters. In Figure 6.38 you see that the Blob Path Begins With value is `EMEA\brainjammer\2022`, which means that an event will be triggered when the blob exists in the `2022` folder. Additionally, since there is also a value of `.avro` in the Blob Path Ends With text box, blobs in the `2022` folder must also end with that file extension. Files that end with a different extension in that same directory will not trigger an event, and no pipeline will be run.

CUSTOM EVENT TRIGGERS

Event-driven architecture (EDA) is a software model that encompasses the production, reaction, detection, and consumption of events. Event producers can be, for example, an ADLS container, and an event consumer could be an Azure Synapse Analytics pipeline trigger. Therefore, it would be possible to wire up a blob created event to a trigger that executes a pipeline run. Note that it is also possible to create similar functionality with custom events using Event Grid. An event can come in many forms. The Blob Created event is one that happens when a new file is placed onto an ADLS container within an Azure storage account. Similarly, when a blob is deleted, a Blob Deleted event is generated. A consumer plugs into the producer by subscribing to a broker that manages the delivery of events. When you create the broker that will detect these events, you configure the source of the events, i.e., an ADLS container, and specify which events you want to receive, for example, `BlobCreated` or `BlobDeleted`. Then, if you want to be notified of these events so that your trigger can react to them, you must subscribe to the broker, which is configured to detect them from the producer. That process of event production, detection, consumption, and reaction is illustrated in Figure 6.39.

FIGURE 6.39 Azure Synapse Analytics custom event notification flow

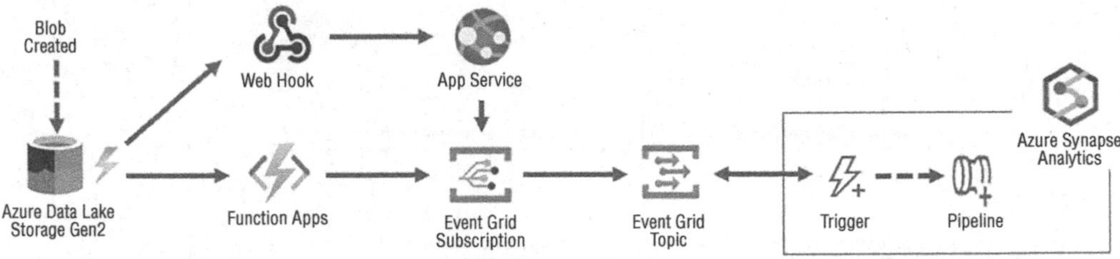

Azure Event Grid, first introduced in Chapter 3, is the broker used for this kind of behavior. The EDA process begins with the addition of a new file, which was placed into an ADLS container. Once the writing of that file is complete, a Blob Created event is generated. Any subscriber that has signed up to receive this notification will receive metadata that resembles the following:


```
[
  {
    "topic": "/subscriptions/<id>/.../Microsoft.Storage/.../<accountName>",
    "subject": "brainjammer/<path to the file>",
    "id": "<eventId>",
    "eventType": "Microsoft.Storage.BlobCreated",
    "eventTime": "2022-07-03T08:28:02",
    "data":{
      "api": "PutBlockList",
      "eTag": "0x8D4BLLC2E4835BN0",
      "contentType": "application/octet-stream",
```

```
            "contentLength": 893071,
            "blobType": "BlockBlob",
        },
        "dataVersion": "",
        "metadataVersion": "1"
    }
]
```


The format of the event notification sent to the subscribers is in JSON. This means that the service that receives the notification must be able to receive and parse the JSON data. There are numerous sources that can handle these event notifications. As shown in Figure 6.39, two sources are an Azure function and a webhook. An Azure function is a serverless compute offering designed to provide quick access to compute, on demand, to process small snippets of code. Therefore, an Azure function is a very good option for implementing this kind of process. A webhook basically provides the ability to route the event data to any endpoint that supports HTTPS. This can be an Azure App Service or an on-premises application.

An Event Grid subscription is a management utility that can contain multiple Azure Event Grid topics. Consider that the Event Grid topic is the actual endpoint with which subscribers bind to receive events. When you have numerous EDA solutions that contain many event notification flows, an Event Grid subscription is used to manage all your Event Grid topics. You use the features available from an Event Grid subscription to manage all your EDA services. Once you have an Event Grid topic, you add it to an Event Grid subscription. Then, from the service that wants the event notification, you add the service to the Event Grid topic. To bind the Event Grid topic to an Azure Synapse Analytics pipeline, you create a custom event and select Custom Events from the Type drop-down text box. You add the Event Grid topic into the Event Grid Topic Name text box, as shown in Figure 6.40.

FIGURE 6.40 Azure Synapse Analytics custom event trigger

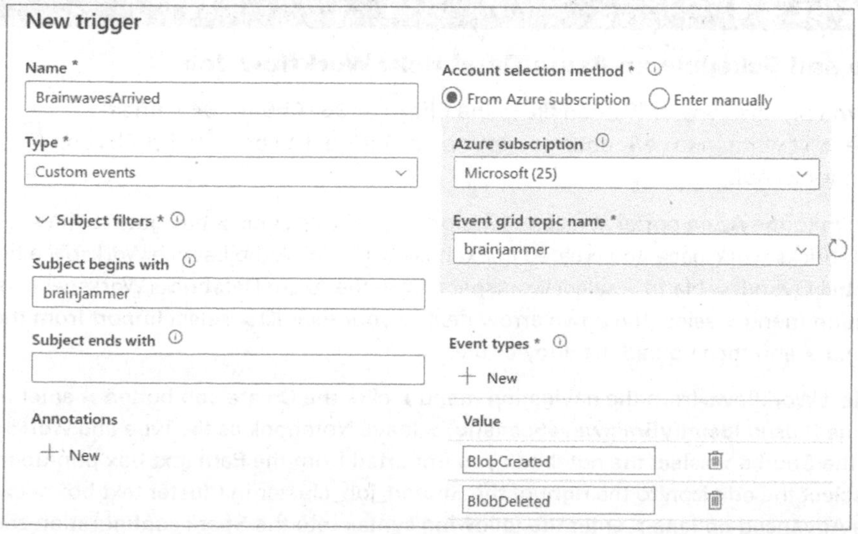

The configuration of the custom event also gives you the option to filter the events based on the subject and the event type. If you look at the JSON example provided previously, you will see an attribute named `subject`. If the `subject` contained in the event metadata includes, for example, `brainjammer`, then the pipeline will be triggered, so long as the event type matches as well. In addition to the `subject` attribute, there is also an `eventType` attribute in the JSON event metadata. The configuration limits the triggering of the pipeline to event types of either `BlobCreated` or `BlobDeleted`. Only when both the `subject` and `eventType` are matched will the trigger fire and the pipeline run. The filter on `subject` is optional; however, you must add at least one event type.

Azure Databricks

When you perform data analytics in Azure Databricks, it means you are using an Apache Spark cluster. It is possible to use Apache Spark pools in Azure Synapse Analytics, as you did in Exercise 6.3, where you created and ran a Spark Job Definition activity. In Exercise 6.4 you created a notebook named `IdentifyBrainwaveScenario` using an Azure Databricks workspace that imported some brain waves in AVFO format from a blob container. The file contained brain wave readings that were filtered by predetermined frequency ranges for a given session, like `ClassicalMusic`. The data was converted to delta and the results rendered as output to the output window. This notebook, like the Spark job, was then triggered manually from an Azure Synapse Analytics pipeline. You now know that it is possible to trigger the notebook that exists and runs on an Azure Databricks Apache Spark cluster. The available trigger types when triggered from Azure Synapse Analytics are scheduled, tumbling window, and custom event. Azure Databricks does include some scheduling capabilities, but they are not as sophisticated as those in Azure Synapse Analytics. You have read a bit about these capabilities and have seen some of the features in Figure 6.16 and Figure 6.19. In all cases, however, the execution of the notebook was manual. There also exist some scheduling capabilities. Complete Exercise 6.8, where you will schedule the execution of an Azure Databricks notebook using a workflow job. To successfully complete this exercise, you must have already completed Exercise 6.4.

EXERCISE 6.8

Create and Schedule an Azure Databricks Workflow Job

1. Download the Jupyter/IPython file in the `Chapter06/Ch06Ex04` named `IdentifyBrainwaveScenario.ipynb` on GitHub: `https://github.com/benperk/ADE`.
2. Log in to the Azure portal at `https://portal.azure.com` ➢ navigate to the Azure Databricks workspace you created in Exercise 3.14 ➢ click the Launch Workspace button on the Overview blade ➢ select Workspace from the Azure Databricks Workspace navigation menu ➢ select the down arrow next to your user ID ➢ select Import from the menu ➢ and then upload the Jupyter file.
3. Select Workflows from the navigation menu ➢ click the Create Job button ➢ enter a task name (I used **IdentifyBrainwaveScenario**) ➢ leave Notebook as the Type and Workspace as the Source ➢ select the notebook you imported from the Path text box pop-up menu ➢ select the edit icon to the right of the Shared_job_cluster in Cluster text box ➢ expand the Advanced options ➢ enter the following syntax into the Spark configuration section

> and then change the access key to your Azure blob storage account, like you did in Exercise 6.4.

```
fs.azure.account.key.csharpguitaradeblob.blob.core.windows.net F98yw7+Y.....D4jDb9b8
```

4. Consider reducing the cluster size and number of instances to save costs > click Confirm > and then click Create.

5. Click the Add Schedule button > select the Scheduled radio button from the Trigger Type section > check the Show Cron Syntax check box > and then enter the following syntax. Figure 6.41 shows the configuration.

```
0 0/2 * 1/1 * ? *
```

FIGURE 6.41 Azure Databricks scheduled trigger

Schedule
Schedule Type
Manual (Paused)
Scheduled
Schedule
0 0/2 * 1/1 * ? *
(UTC+00:00) UTC
Show cron syntax
Cancel
Save

6. Click the Save button > select Workflows from the navigation menu > and then select the job you just created. After a few minutes, you will see something similar to Figure 6.42.

FIGURE 6.42 Azure Databricks scheduled trigger log

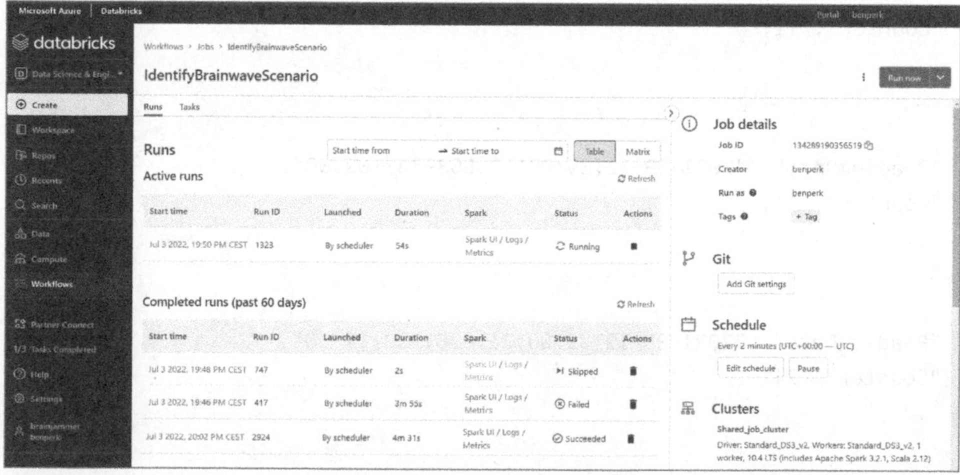

7. Click the Pause button to stop the job.

As mentioned, the capabilities for scheduling jobs in Azure Databricks are basic; only scheduled and manual jobs are supported. If you need more sophisticated scheduling capabilities, you can trigger an Azure Databricks job from an Azure Synapse Analytics pipeline.

Handle Duplicate Data

The impact of having multiple rows of identical data in your table and database depends on your requirements. In most cases, however, having a duplication of a row is not desired. When you are running aggregations that use `SUM`, `AVG`, `COUNT`, etc., having a duplicate can result in rendering the wrong measurement. Therefore, you do want to remove them at some phase in your data transformation pipeline. If you can get them removed before ingestion, that would be even better, but that is not always achievable. A very important requirement for managing and removing duplicate data is ensuring that there is a way to identify a duplication. Consider the following brain waves–reading JSON file, for example:

```
[
  {
    "ReadingDate": "2021-09-12T09:00:19.1072902+02:00",
    "Counter": 5,
    ...
  },
  {
    "ReadingDate": "2021-09-12T09:00:19.1072902+02:00",
    "Counter": 5,
    ...
  },
  {
    "ReadingDate": "2021-09-12T09:00:18.5589578+02:00",
    "Counter": 11,
    ...
  },
  {
    "ReadingDate": "2021-09-12T09:00:19.8539383+02:00",
    "Counter": 11,
    ...
  },
  {
    "ReadingDate": "2021-09-12T09:00:21.0961533+02:00",
    "Counter": 21,
    ...
  },
```

```
  {
    "ReadingDate": "2021-09-12T09:00:21.0961533+02:00",
    "Counter": 21,
    ...
  }
]
```

The data provides a few opportunities for identifying whether a row is duplicated. There is very precise `ReadingDate` that should not exist more than a single time in the file. A `Counter` that attempts to uniquely identify a reading is also included. Notice that the JSON data includes two entries with a different `ReadingDate` that have the same `Counter` value of `11`. Another two readings share an identical `ReadingDate` and `Counter`. Using both of these attributes together enables you to filter out duplicates, whereas using one or the other individually may not. Should the reading with a different `ReadingDate` be included or excluded from the ingestion? Whether these are duplicates is a decision made by a data expert, someone who understands how the data is collected. Once you are able to make the functional decision on what constitutes a duplicate, you can then write the query or create the transformation instructions to exclude or include it. There are numerous approaches for removing duplicates, some of which are discussed here.

Azure Synapse Analytics

When you load data into an Azure Synapse Analytics dedicated SQL pool table, you will realize the support for primary keys is missing. If primary keys were supported, then when you enforce such a constraint and a process attempts to enter a duplicate row, the insertion would fail. Having and enforcing primary keys and unique constraints would prevent duplicate data from being inserted into a dedicated SQL pool table. It was determined that extract, transfer, and load (ETL) use cases for dedicated SQL pool tables very often had a duplication of data. Throwing an error is very impactful on performance and throughput, so it was decided to avoid that, which means you need to take preventative actions if the existence of duplicate data impacts your data analytics pipeline and insights gathering. There are many methods for removing or preventing duplicates, for example, the `MERGE` SQL command, which was introduced in Chapter 3. Using the `MERGE` command with the `MATCHED` keyword results in duplicates not being inserted but updated. Another approach is to use other SQL commands like `JOIN` or `UNION`. In both of those scenarios, it is required to have multiple tables, for example, a fact table and a temporary table. You could then `JOIN` or `UNION` the two tables to find data duplicates, and then remove the duplicates. Another approach to avoiding duplicates that is available as a feature in both Azure Synapse Analytics and Azure Data Factory is to use a data flow. Capabilities within a data flow can prevent the duplicate from being ingested at all, which would negate the need to use `MERGE`, `JOIN`, or `UNION` to remove data.

Data Flows

There have been quite a few exercises in this book concerning data flows. What a data flow is should no longer be in question. So, jump right in with Exercise 6.9, where you will create a data flow that handles the duplication of data.

EXERCISE 6.9

Handle Duplicate Data with a Data Flow

1. Download the `csharpguitar-brainjammer-pow-0902-duplicates.json` file from the `Chapter06/Ch06Ex09` directory on GitHub at `https://github.com/benperk/ADE` ➢ and then upload the file to the ADLS container you created in Exercise 3.1.
2. Log in to the Azure portal at `https://portal.azure.com` ➢ navigate to the Azure Synapse Analytics workspace you created in Exercise 3.3 ➢ click the Open link in the Open Synapse Studio tile on the Overview blade ➢ select the Develop hub ➢ hover over the Data Flows section ➢ click the ellipse (`...`) ➢ select New Data Flow from the pop-up menu ➢ and then enter a name (I used **Ch06Ex09**).
3. Enable Data Flow Debug ➢ select the down arrow in the Add Source box ➢ select Add Source from the pop-up menu ➢ enter an output stream name (I used **DuplicateBrainwaves**) ➢ create a new dataset that points to the file uploaded in step 1 ➢ click the + New button to the right of the Dataset drop-down ➢ select Azure Data Lake Storage Gen2 from the Data Store window ➢ click Continue ➢ select JSON from the Format window ➢ click Continue ➢ enter a name (I used **BrainjammerDuplicatesJson**) ➢ select the ADLS container where you placed the file from step 1 ➢ enable interactive authoring ➢ select the file from step 1 by selecting the folder to the right of the File Path text boxes ➢ leave the remaining option as default ➢ and then click OK.
4. Expand the JSON Settings group on the Source Options tab ➢ select the Array of Documents radio button as the Document Form ➢ select the Data Preview tab ➢ click the Refresh button, if required ➢ and then view the data. Notice that there are 30 readings in the JSON file, as shown in Figure 6.43.

FIGURE 6.43 Handle duplicate data—data flow source

Source settings | Source options | Projection | Optimize | Inspect | Data preview ● | Description

Number of rows + INSERT 30 | * UPDATE 0 | × DELETE 0 | UPSERT 0 | LOOKUP 0 | ERROR 0 | TOTAL 30

Refresh | Typecast | Modify | Map drifted | Statistics | Remove | Export to CSV

	ReadingDate abc	Counter 123	THETA 1.2	ALPHA 1.2	BETA_L 1.2	BETA_H 1.2	GAMMA 1.2
+	2021-09-12T...	0	15.585	5.892	3.415	1.195	0.836
+	2021-09-12T...	1	26.864	5.871	3.56	1.331	0.799
+	2021-09-12T...	2	47.282	6.969	3.61	1.479	0.749
+	2021-09-12T...	3	75.78	9.287	3.58	1.624	0.7

5. Add an Aggregate transformation ➢ select the + sign on the lower right of the Source box ➢ select Aggregate from the Schema Modifier section ➢ enter an output stream name (I used **IdentifyDuplicates**) ➢ select the Group By navigation slider from the Aggregate Settings tab ➢ and then select and add each column in the order shown in Figure 6.44. Note that the order is important.

FIGURE 6.44 Handle duplicate data—data flow aggregate group by

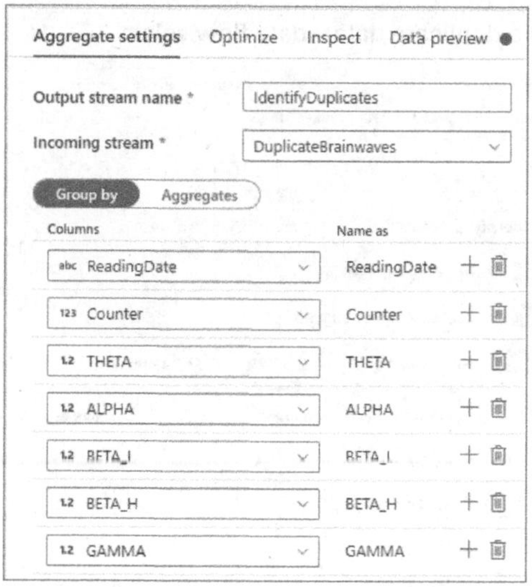

6. Select the Aggregates navigation button ➢ enter a new column named `Readings` ➢ and then enter the following associated expression (see Figure 6.45):

```
count(ReadingDate)
```

FIGURE 6.45 Handle duplicate data—data flow aggregate

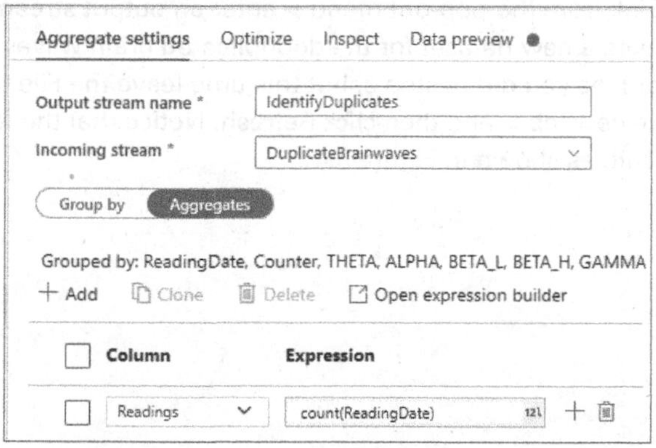

EXERCISE 6.9 *(continued)*

7. Select the Data Preview tab ➢ select Refresh ➢ view the results ➢ notice that duplicates are identified when the value in the `Readings` column is greater than `1` ➢ add a Select transformation ➢ select the + sign in the lower right of the Aggregate transformation ➢ enter an output stream name (I used **NoDuplicates**) ➢ and then remove the Reading column from the Input Columns section, as shown in Figure 6.46.

FIGURE 6.46 Handle duplicate data—data flow select

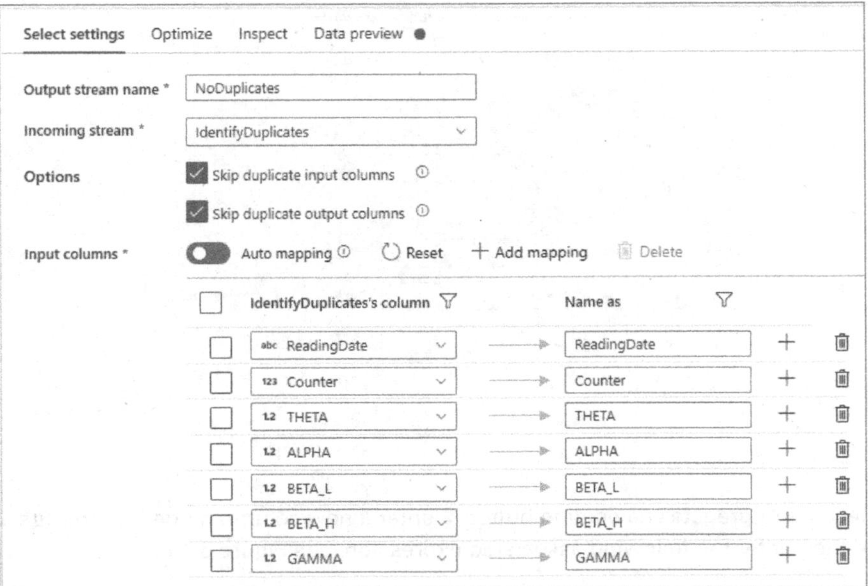

8. Add a sink destination by selecting the + sign in the lower right of the Select transformation ➢ select Sink from the pop-out menu ➢ enter an output stream name (I used **Brainwaves**) ➢ create a new dataset for the deduplicated brain waves (for example, `BrainwavesJson`), as you did in step 3, but this time leave the File text box empty ➢ select the Data Preview tab ➢ and then click Refresh. Notice that the four duplicates are not part of the result, as shown in Figure 6.47.

FIGURE 6.47 Handle duplicate data—data flow sink

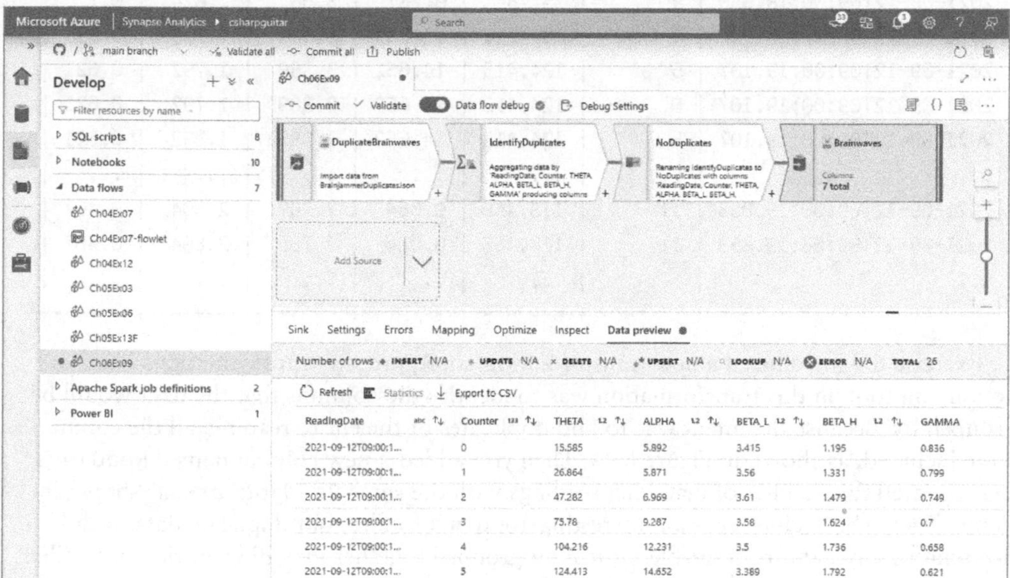

9. Click the Commit button, and then click the Publish button.

The first change you may have noticed in Exercise 6.9 versus some of the others has to do with the data. In order to get this ingestion to flow into the tool, the data needed to be in a different structure. For this example, the data was changed manually. In the real world you could have performed some data transformation to evolve from the JSON file format you have seen up to now to the one used in Exercise 6.9. Either way, the point is that you will likely receive data in many different formats, and you will likely need to format it into a structure that aligns with the requirements of the feature you want to use.

In Exercise 6.9 you used some transformations that have not yet been covered. You have already been exposed to Source and Sink, so there is no need to cover them in detail, other than reaffirming that the source is where the data is ingested from, and the sink is where you want to write the transformed data to. The Data Preview tab from the source, as shown in Figure 6.43, resembles the following:

```
+-------------------------+---------+---------+--------+--------+--------+-------+
| ReadingDate             | Counter | THETA   | ALPHA  | BETA_L | BETA_H | GAMMA |
+-------------------------+---------+---------+--------+--------+--------+-------+
| 2021-09-12T09:00:18.492 | 0       | 15.585  | 5.892  | 3.415  | 1.195  | 0.836 |
| 2021-09-12T09:00:18.558 | 1       | 26.864  | 5.871  | 3.56   | 1.331  | 0.799 |
```

```
| 2021-09-12T09:00:18.735 | 2       | 47.282  | 6.969  | 3.61   | 1.479  | 0.749 |
| 2021-09-12T09:00:18.850 | 3       | 75.78   | 9.287  | 3.58   | 1.624  | 0.7   |
| 2021-09-12T09:00:18.984 | 4       | 104.216 | 12.231 | 3.5    | 1.736  | 0.658 |
| 2021-09-12T09:00:19.107 | 5       | 124.413 | 14.652 | 3.389  | 1.792  | 0.621 |
| 2021-09-12T09:00:19.107 | 5       | 124.413 | 14.652 | 3.389  | 1.792  | 0.621 |
| 2021-09-12T09:00:19.107 | 5       | 124.413 | 14.652 | 3.389  | 1.792  | 0.621 |
| ...                     | ...     | ...     | ...    | ...    | ...    | ...   |
| 2021-09-12T09:00:19.853 | 11      | 118.456 | 9.084  | 2.709  | 2.804  | 0.467 |
| 2021-09-12T09:00:19.853 | 11      | 118.456 | 9.084  | 2.709  | 2.804  | 0.467 |
| ...                     | ...     | ...     | ...    | ...    | ...    | ...   |
+-------------------------+---------+---------+--------+--------+--------+-------+
```

Exercise 6.9 introduced a new transformation: an Aggregate transformation. The action you took in this transformation was to identify the columns that the data would be grouped by. Because the intent was to find duplicates of the entire reading, all the columns were included, as shown in Figure 6.44. Then you added a new column named `Readings` that counted the number of matching readings with the same `ReadingDate`, as shown in Figure 6.45. This technique is an interesting approach to filter out duplicate data. It did not remove any data from the file; instead, it grouped together matching entries and added a column that contained the count of matching readings. The Data Preview tab of the Aggregate transformation resembles the following. Notice that instead of having three rows for the reading with a counter of `5`, there exists only a single row. Similar for readings with counter `11` and `21`. Note that some of the data had to be modified to fit on the page, but you should get the point.

```
+---------------------+------+-------+-------+--------+--------+-------+----------+
| ReadingDate         | Cntr | THETA | ALPHA | BETA_L | BETA_H | GAMMA | Readings |
+---------------------+------+-------+-------+--------+--------+-------+----------+
| 2021-09-12T09:00:18.4 | 0  | 15.58 | 5.892 | 3.415  | 1.195  | 0.836 | 1        |
| 2021-09-12T09:00:18.5 | 1  | 26.86 | 5.871 | 3.56   | 1.331  | 0.799 | 1        |
| ...                 | ...  | ...   | ...   | ...    | ...    | ...   | ...      |
| 2021-09-12T09:00:19.1 | 5  | 124.4 | 14.65 | 3.389  | 1.792  | 0.621 | 3        |
| ...                 | ...  | ...   | ...   | ...    | ...    | ...   | ...      |
| 2021-09-12T09:00:19.8 | 11 | 118.4 | 9.084 | 2.709  | 2.804  | 0.467 | 2        |
| ...                 | ...  | ...   | ...   | ...    | ...    | ...   | ...      |
| 2021-09-12T09:00:21.0 | 21 | 35.37 | 8.319 | 5.014  | 0.816  | 0.83  | 2        |
| 2021-09-12T09:00:21.2 | 22 | 67.93 | 14.29 | 6.146  | 0.744  | 0.757 | 1        |
| ...                 | ...  | ...   | ...   | ...    | ...    | ...   | ...      |
+---------------------+------+-------+-------+--------+--------+-------+----------+
```

Then, in the next transformation, the Select transformation, you selected only those rows in the group by output, without the count that resulted in only 26 rows being selected from the 30. Recall that the output of the Aggregate transformation's Data Preview tab had only 26 rows, with an extra column that contained the number of duplicates, but still only one row of that specific duplicated data. So, when the Select transformation was run, you received only those 26 deduplicated rows, as summerized here.

ReadingDate	Counter	THETA	ALPHA	BETA_L	BETA_H	GAMMA
...	...	...	...	...	...	...
2021-09-12T09:00:18.850	3	75.78	9.287	3.58	1.624	0.7
2021-09-12T09:00:18.984	4	104.216	12.231	3.5	1.736	0.658
2021-09-12T09:00:19.107	5	124.413	14.652	3.389	1.792	0.621
...	...	...	...	...	...	...
2021-09-12T09:00:19.853	11	118.456	9.084	2.709	2.804	0.467
...	...	...	...	...	...	...
2021-09-12T09:00:21.096	21	35.378	8.319	5.014	0.816	0.83
2021-09-12T09:00:21.261	22	67.934	14.291	6.146	0.744	0.757
...	...	...	...	...	...	...

This is a very interesting technique and one that can be applied in other places in your data analytics processes.

Streaming

In addition to handling duplications in data that is being ingested and stored into your data lake for scheduled processing, you may need to handle duplications while streaming data. Data can be streamed into either Azure Stream Analytics or Azure Databricks, each of which has some concepts for managing data duplication.

Azure Stream Analytics

In order to manage the duplication of data streaming into an Azure Stream Analytics endpoint, you need to use a tumbling window. A required parameter for a tumbling window is the timeframe. The tumbling window concept for Azure Stream Analytics was introduced in Chapter 3 (refer to Figure 3.84). Take a look back over that for more clarity, if required. The query to manage data duplicates may resemble the following:

```
with readings as
(
  select count(distinct ReadingDate) AS date,
         count(distinct Counter) AS count,
         count(distinct THETA) AS theta,
         count(distinct ALPHA) AS alpha,
         count(distinct BETA_L) AS beta_l,
```

```
        count(distinct BETA_H) AS beta_h,
        count(distinct GAMMA) AS gamma
  from  brainwaves
  group by date, count, theta, alpha, beta_l,
        beta_h, gamma, TumblingWindow(minute, 5)
)
select date, counter, theta, alpha, beta_l, beta_h, gamma from readings
group by TumblingWindow(minute, 5)
```

You might recognize the same approach here as you experienced in Exercise 6.9. The first step is to select the distinct data for a tumbling time window of 5 minutes. The `group by` command binds together duplicate rows into a single row with a counter, but only a single row of data is stored in that given timeframe in the `readings` object. Then the rows of data are selected from `readings`, which results in only a single row being retrieved for a given reading, regardless of duplicates. The deduplicated data can then be passed into the destination output storage service. This approach only works for the timeframe given in the configured tumbling window. You will need to tune that value to find the one that works best for your scenario. It might also be necessary to take some additional steps to deduplicate the data as it flows along the cold path.

Azure Databricks

When attempting to handle duplicate data in an Azure Databricks stream, you need to know about the `OutputMode()` method. This method provides the interface to set the way in which data is written to the sink. The options are `Append` (default), `Update`, and `Complete`. When rows are appended to a table, they are added to the end of it. As the stream continues to receive data, the data on the table increases. The `Update` mode requires an aggregate, for example, the number of distinct occurrences. If there is no aggregate, the `Update` mode acts just like the `Append` mode. The aggregate in the following table is the count of distinct `Readings`, which represents the data output of a stream:

```
+-------------------------+---------+----------+
| ReadingDate             | Counter | Readings |
+-------------------------+---------+----------+
| 2021-09-12T09:00:18.924 | 0       | 1        |
| 2021-09-12T09:00:18.558 | 1       | 1        |
| ...                     | ...     | ...      |
| 2021-09-12T09:00:19.107 | 5       | 3        |
+-------------------------+---------+----------+
```

When the next stream of data is received, notice that the data from the first stream is not included in the second.

```
+-------------------------+---------+----------+
| ReadingDate             | Counter | Readings |
+-------------------------+---------+----------+
| 2021-09-12T09:00:19.853 | 11      | 2        |
| ...                     | ...     | ...      |
| 2021-09-12T09:00:21.096 | 21      | 2        |
| 2021-09-12T09:00:21.261 | 22      | 1        |
+-------------------------+---------+----------+
```

The reason for this is that there were no matches for `Readings` in the first stream that did exist in the second. When the `OutputMode` is `Update`, the stream will read the Kafka data, perform the aggregation, and output only the updated data. When you set the `OutputMode` to `Complete`, the output data is not updated; instead, it is overwritten. Therefore, you receive an output of the stream like the following with the processing of each stream:

```
+-------------------------+---------+----------+
| ReadingDate             | Counter | Readings |
+-------------------------+---------+----------+
| 2021-09-12T09:00:18.924 | 0       | 1        |
| 2021-09-12T09:00:18.558 | 1       | 1        |
| ...                     | ...     | ...      |
| 2021-09-12T09:00:19.107 | 5       | 3        |
| ...                     | ...     | ...      |
| 2021-09-12T09:00:19.853 | 11      | 2        |
| ...                     | ...     | ...      |
| 2021-09-12T09:00:21.096 | 21      | 2        |
| 2021-09-12T09:00:21.261 | 22      | 1        |
+-------------------------+---------+----------+
```

You use `Complete`, with an aggregate, when you need to overwrite all the data streams that have been received, duplicates included. `Append` and `Update` can result in duplicates, whereas `Complete` does not, because it overwrites the output of other data streams.

Handle Missing Data

In Exercise 5.5 you worked with a CSV file that contained `null` values. The action in that exercise to avoid the `null` values was to remove the record from the dataset. Depending on the data you are processing for finding business insights, this removal of the data can have an impact on the data processing outcome. A very important step to take before deciding how to handle missing data is to determine why the data is missing. This can be determined using the following three principles:

- *Missing at random (MAR)*: The missing data can be accounted for using other variables—for example, a disruption during a meditation session or the readjustment of the BCI on the head.

- *Missing completely at random (MCAR)*: The missing data is not related to the observation being studied—for example, the BCI ran low on battery and missed or wrongly logged some readings.
- *Missing not at random (MNAR)*: The missing data is caused by an unwillingness or inability to provide—for example, a test subject does not want their brain waves captured.

Missing data that falls into the MNAR category is the most problematic. MNAR data scenarios are an issue because the missing data can produce bias in the model if the entire reading is deleted. The following table contains some readings with missing data. Assume they are missing due to an MNAR scenario—for example, the subject moved the electrode to scratch their head for a brief moment.

ReadingDate	Counter	THETA	ALPHA	BETA_L	BETA_H	GAMMA
2021-09-12T09:00:18.492	0		5.892	3.415	1.195	0.836
2021-09-12T09:00:18.558	1	26.864	5.871	3.56	1.331	0.799
2021-09-12T09:00:18.735	2	47.282		3.61	1.479	
2021-09-12T09:00:18.850	3	75.78	9.287	3.58	1.624	
2021-09-12T09:00:18.984	4	104.216			1.736	0.658
2021-09-12T09:00:19.107	5	124.413	14.652	3.389	1.792	0.621
2021-09-12T09:00:19.245	6		15.983	3.259	1.805	0.587
2021-09-12T09:00:19.475	8	122.445	14.598	2.928		0.518
2021-09-12T09:00:19.602	9	118.611	12.675	2.782	2.114	0.493
2021-09-12T09:00:20.106	13	95.66	6.178	2.747	3.041	0.449

When missing data falls into the MAR and MCAR scenarios, it is okay to delete the reading because the reason for the missing data is identifiable. However, in the case of MNAR, the approach to handle this missing data is referred to as *imputation*. Imputation means that instead of removing the data, you replace it with a substitute value. There are many approaches for acquiring this missing data, from taking an educated guess to linear interpolation, which is a very sophisticated approach. A method that falls into the middle range of complexity is to use the mean, median, or mode to calculate a value for the missing measurement. Using any of those statistical assessments has the advantage of not changing the mean aggregate value of the session. The median value per reading and frequency have been added to the table and will not have an impactful effect on the final outcome.

ReadingDate	Counter	THETA	ALPHA	BETA_L	BETA_H	GAMMA
2021-09-12T09:00:18.492	0	**99.938**	5.892	3.415	1.195	0.836
2021-09-12T09:00:18.558	1	26.864	5.871	3.56	1.331	0.799

```
| 2021-09-12T09:00:18.735 | 2  | 47.282  | 10.981 | 3.61  | 1.479 | 0.604 |
| 2021-09-12T09:00:18.850 | 3  | 75.78   | 9.287  | 3.58  | 1.624 | 0.604 |
| 2021-09-12T09:00:18.984 | 4  | 104.216 | 10.981 | 3.389 | 1.736 | 0.658 |
| 2021-09-12T09:00:19.107 | 5  | 124.413 | 14.652 | 3.389 | 1.792 | 0.621 |
| 2021-09-12T09:00:19.245 | 6  | 99.938  | 15.983 | 3.259 | 1.805 | 0.587 |
| 2021-09-12T09:00:19.475 | 8  | 122.445 | 14.598 | 2.928 | 1.736 | 0.518 |
| 2021-09-12T09:00:19.602 | 9  | 118.611 | 12.675 | 2.782 | 2.114 | 0.493 |
| 2021-09-12T09:00:20.106 | 13 | 95.66   | 6.178  | 2.747 | 3.041 | 0.449 |
+-------------------------+----+---------+--------+-------+-------+-------+
```

Note that if you had removed the row where the two `ALPHA` readings were missing, it would have impacted `THETA` considerably. Removing those two rows would result in the median for `THETA` changing from `99.938` to `107.136`.

Handle Late-Arriving Data

There are many reasons why data might arrive late into your ADLS container, or data warehouse, including issues like network bandwidth, which can slow the throughput of data; not enough processing power to complete the upstream job in a timely manner; or the failure of the upstream job. In the cloud environment, a throttle could have been enforced due to an unexpected increase in consumption. Because there are so many reasons why data can arrive late, there are also many approaches for managing that scenario. Two scenarios are discussed here, but, as you would expect, the solution depends on your situation.

Delay a Pipeline Trigger

When you have a pipeline that is scheduled to run at a specific time and the data it should be processing arrives after the scheduled time, the data will not be processed. If the expected data is not present, the pipeline might fail and stop. If you do not plan for late-arriving data, code may run and perform unexpected and unwanted changes to your data. A method for handling late-arriving data in Azure Synapse Analytics is to set the delay time found within a tumbling window trigger. You can see the Delay property in Figure 6.37. Setting this property to 5 minutes means that the trigger will load data that arrives up to 5 minutes after the trigger's start date. How to come up with the amount of time to wait is based on your knowledge of delays that can occur to dependent upstream jobs. The frequency of the trigger is also useful for determining delay. If the trigger recurrence is hourly, then waiting anything longer than 30 minutes may or may not be a good idea. It depends on how long the pipeline runs and whether there is a possibility of overlapping the next start time. But it really depends on your current requirements and trigger settings.

Fact and Dimension Tables

You were first introduced to fact and dimension tables when they appeared in a star schema in Chapter 3. Table 3.5 listed the different slowly changing dimension (SDC) types, which range from one to six. In Exercise 4.9 and Exercise 4.10, you created dimension tables, and you used them in Exercise 5.1. In Exercise 5.1 you created a stored procedure that used the content in the dimension tables to create the data on the fact table. That scenario was a relatively simple example, because there were not any changes to the dimension tables between Exercise 4.10 and Exercise 5.1; therefore, the validity date on the dimension tables remained static. Imagine a scenario where the generation of the fact table data occurred before the arrival of an update on the dimensional table. And assume that the reason for the late arrival was due to the upstream being delayed.

Late-arriving fact table data is not as vexing as dimensional data because, as you learned in Exercise 5.1, dimensional tables are used for enriching the fact data. Therefore, it is imperative that dimension tables always be processed successfully before fact tables. There are a few approaches for managing this scenario. The first one is simply to create dependencies between the pipelines that load the fact and dimension tables, ensuring that all the work that needs to be done on the dimension tables is complete before performing the fact table transaction load. Another technique might be to use an approach that was covered in the last section, where a default or calculated value is used when data in the dimensional table is not available. For example, if you are using SDC Type 6 and the start date or end date is missing, your code can use the current date or a hard-coded date. If you know the default or hard-coded value, then you can come back at a later time, use that value as a filter, and update the fact table data with the new value, if required. Lastly, you can detect whether the fact table has arrived early. Early arrival can be just as impactful as late arrival, especially if the pipeline trigger is one that runs based on a storage event or customer event.

Data Streaming

For managing delays in a data streaming scenario, there is a concept known as a watermark. The details are covered in detail in Chapter 7, but as the context here is applicable, it seems like a good place to introduce it. A *watermark* is a marker that specifies the point at which the ingestion of the stream is located. As the data enters the stream processor, it is given a watermark. If the difference between the watermark and the clock time is greater than zero, there is a perceived delay in the stream processing. Chapter 7 covers the impact of this and how to fix it.

Upsert Data

The act of upserting is useful in scenarios where you are not certain if the data you are ingesting exists on the target sink. As you learned in Chapter 3, the `MERGE` command is a method for performing an upsert, where an upsert will insert the data into a table if the data does not already exist or update the row if it does. The pseudocode for a `MERGE` command resembles the following:

```
MERGE INTO TmpReading
USING updates
ON TmpReading.READING_ID = updates.READING_ID
WHEN MATCHED THEN
```

```
  UPDATE SET ...
WHEN NOT MATCHED THEN
  INSERT ...
```

If the `TmpReading.READING_ID` matches a `READING_ID` from the `updates` data injection source, it means the row already exists. When this is the case, the `UPDATE` statement under the `WHEN MATCHED THEN` condition is executed. If the `updates.READING_ID` is not matched, then the data is inserted onto the `TmpReading` table. In addition to the approach using the `MERGE` method, you can use an Alter Row transformation in a data flow. In Exercise 6.10 you will use the Alter Row transformation to perform upserts to data residing in an Azure Synapse Analytics dedicated SQL pool. The data flow is shown in Figure 6.48.

FIGURE 6.48 Upsert data, batching flow diagram

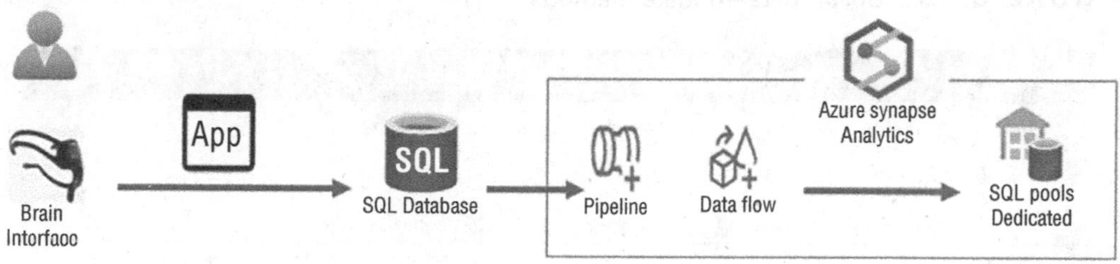

Figure 6.48 illustrates the data being captured from a BCI using a program that stores the data on an Azure SQL database—the one you created in Exercise 2.1. When the pipeline you created in Exercise 5.1 is run, the data flow you will update in Exercise 6.10 will perform the upserts into the SQL dedicated pool you created just before Exercise 3.7.

EXERCISE 6.10

Upsert Data

1. Log in to the Azure portal at `https://portal.azure.com` ➢ navigate to the Azure Synapse Analytics workspace you created in Exercise 3.3 ➢ click the Open link in the Open Synapse Studio tile on the Overview blade ➢ select the Develop hub ➢ expand the Data Flows section ➢ hover over the `Ch04Ex12` data flow ➢ click the ellipse (`...`) ➢ select Clone from the pop-up menu ➢ and then update the name (I used **Ch06Ex10**).
2. Enable the Data Flow Debug toggle switch ➢ using, for example, Azure Data Studio, execute the following `INSERT` and `UPDATE` statements on the Azure SQL database you created in Exercise 2.1. The syntax is available in the `UpsertData.sql` file located in the `Chapter06/Ch06Ex10` directory on GitHub.

```
INSERT INTO [dbo].[READING]
    ([SESSION_ID], [ELECTRODE_ID], [FREQUENCY_ID], [READING_DATETIME],
```

EXERCISE 6.10 *(continued)*

```
    [COUNT], [VALUE]) VALUES (1, 1, 1, '20220710 04:37:35.394 PM', 5, 22.454)
INSERT INTO [dbo].[READING]
   ([SESSION_ID], [ELECTRODE_ID], [FREQUENCY_ID], [READING_DATETIME],
    [COUNT], [VALUE]) VALUES (1, 1, 2, '20220710 04:37:35.394 PM', 6, 4.849)
UPDATE [dbo].[READING] SET VALUE = 4.4254 WHERE READING_ID = 1 --44.254
UPDATE [dbo].[READING] SET VALUE = 15.440 WHERE READING_ID = 9 --1.544
```

3. Select the Sink transformation in the data flow ➢ select the Settings tab ➢ deselect Allow Insert ➢ select the Allow Upsert check box (as shown in Figure 6.49) ➢ and then click the Add Alter Row button.

FIGURE 6.49 Upsert data—update methods

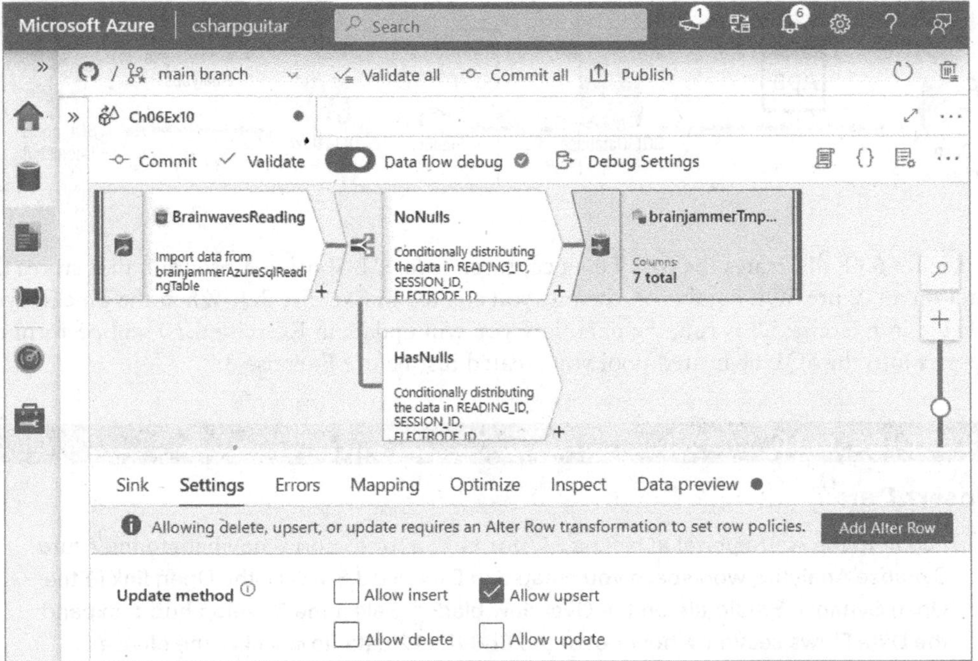

4. Name the Alter Row transformation (I used **UpdateBrainwaves**) ➢ select Upsert If from the Alter Row Conditions drop-down list box ➢ enter **true()** in the Condition text box ➢ select the Data Preview tab ➢ click the Refresh button ➢ and then view the results of the `true()` condition.

5. Select the Sink transformation ➢ select the Settings tab ➢ select the List of Columns radio button in the Key Columns section ➢ select READING_ID from the first drop-down text box ➢ click the + next to the drop-down text box ➢ select VALUE from the drop-down text box ➢ select the Data Preview tab ➢ and then click Refresh. The result will be something like Figure 6.50.

FIGURE 6.50 Upsert data—sink data preview

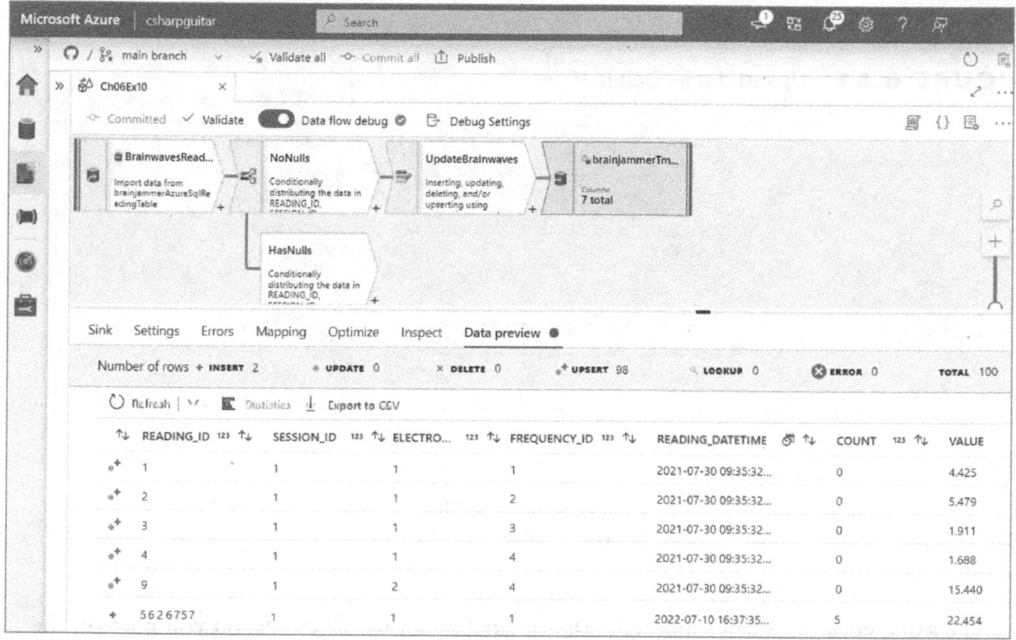

6. Click the Commit button, and then select the Publish menu item.

The Clone feature mentioned in step 1 can be very useful. Instead of needing to re-create and reconfigure the entire data flow from scratch, you cloned it and made the necessary modifications. This saves valuable time. When you selected the Settings tab for the Sink transformation in step 3, because the sink was a database, you were given the option to perform upserts. Had the sink been a file, for example, the option for upsert would not have been rendered. The available options, as shown in Figure 6.49, are as follows:

- Allow Insert
- Allow Delete

- Allow Upsert
- Allow Update

In Exercise 6.10 you disabled Allow Insert. This was to prevent the data that exists in the source from being reinserted and duplicated into the sink. If you needed to delete some data from the sink, then checking the Allow Delete check box would allow this to happen. You would then need to include a Delete If condition, perhaps like that shown in Figure 6.51. The condition of `isNull(VALUE)` will result in rows with no reading number in the `VALUE` column being deleted.

FIGURE 6.51 Upsert data—Delete If

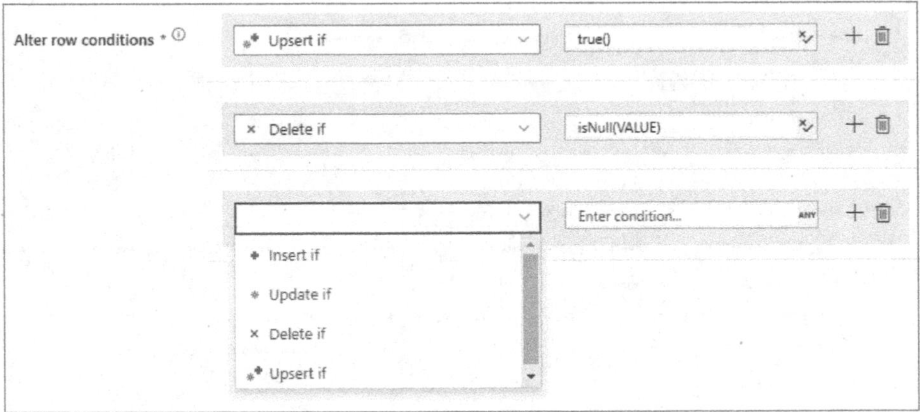

The same goes for Allow Update, in that regardless of which condition you place in the condition text box, if the result is true, then the sink will update that row. Regarding Allow Upsert, recall that the condition was set to `true()`. This means that all the rows are sent to the sink for processing. Because the Allow Upsert check box is checked, Azure Synapse Analytics handles the logistics around whether to update or insert the row. The selection of `READING_ID` and `VALUE` on the Settings tab of the sink provides the instructions to determine which rows are updated or inserted. If a row matches both the `READING_ID` and the `VALUE`, then the row is updated; otherwise, the row is inserted. If you wanted to then run the data flow from the `IngestTransformBrainwaveReadings` pipeline you created in Exercise 5.1, you could clone it and then update the `MoveToTmpReading` Data Flow activity to target the `Ch06Ex10` data flow instead of `Ch04Ex12`. The cloned pipeline must be successfully published prior to execution. Once the pipeline is executed, you will see the two rows updated and two new rows inserted, as per the update and insert statements you executed in step 2.

Hashed Column

Another interesting approach for implementing upsert logic is to use what is called a row hash. A very popular hashing algorithm is MD5. This algorithm is no longer secure, but it is useful in this scenario because the focus here is upserting, not security. MD5 cryptography is useful here because it will always return the same hashed value when provided the same input. The implementation begins with identifying which columns you want to hash. Consider that you want to hash the `READING_DATETIME` and the `VALUE` columns. The following represents the hashed value of the two identified columns, with the `MD5_Hash` column containing the hashed value:

```
+------------+--------------------------+--------+-----------------------------------+
| READING_ID | READING_DATETIME         | VALUE  | MD5_Hash                          |
+------------+--------------------------+--------+-----------------------------------+
| 5626757    | 20220710 04:37:35.394 PM | 22.454 | 356fe576d2766a01bd3737722750... |
+------------+--------------------------+--------+-----------------------------------+
```

If one of the column values on the data changes and an MD5 hash is created, it will be different from the one on the sink. So, part of the logic to determine if the row being ingested requires an update is by comparing the hash values. You can use a Derived Column transformation to add a column to the dataset named `columns_hash` with a conditional statement like the following:

```
md5(byNames(split($Columns, ',')))
```

The value passed to the `$Columns` comes from a data flow parameter named `Columns`, which is an array of the columns to hash, as shown in Figure 6.52.

FIGURE 6.52 Upsert data—MD5 Derived Column row hash

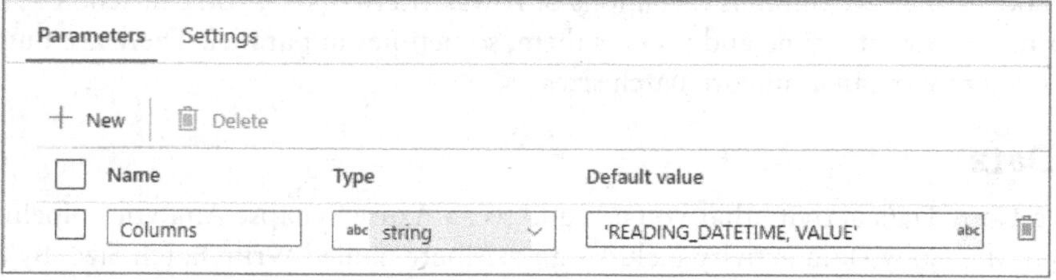

Then you add an Exists transformation to check if the `columns_hash` column on the source and sink match, as shown in Figure 6.53.

If there is a match, the row needs to be updated. If there is no match, the row is new and will be inserted.

FIGURE 6.53 Upsert data—MD5 Exists row hash

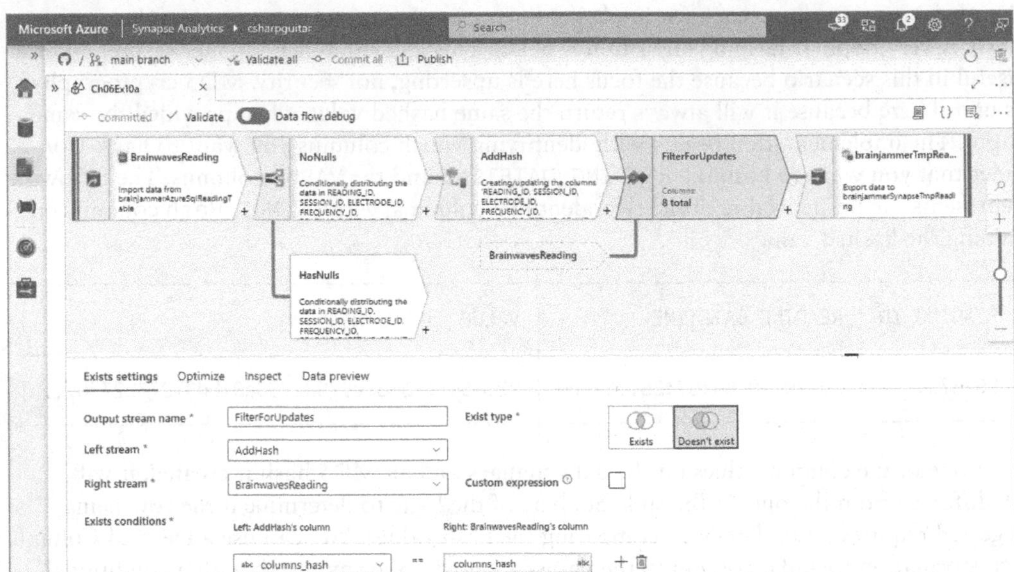

Configure the Batch Size

Combining multiple tasks together and running them has a reputation of making the completion of those tasks happen faster. If you instead perform one task at a time, one after the other, it inherently takes a bit longer. It is the same when working with data. If you send one row at a time from the data source to your data lake, you can imagine the amount of time it could take if there are millions or billions of rows. Alternatively, you can send or retrieve 1,000 or more rows at a time and process them, sometimes in parallel. There are numerous locations where you can configure batch sizes.

Copy Data

There is a Copy Data activity that you can add to an Azure Synapse Analytics pipeline. The Sink tab of the Copy Data activity includes an attribute named Write Batch Size. By default, the platform logic estimates the most appropriate batch size. The default value is based on the size of the row, which is calculated by combining all the columns together on a single row and measuring the total number of consumed bytes. In a majority of cases, using the default setting for Write Batch Size will result in the best performance. However, there may be a scenario that requires some customization and tuning. If you decide to give a specific value for the Write Batch Size attribute, you should also consider modifying the Degree of Copy Parallelism attribute on the Settings tab. By default, the value for the Degree of Copy Parallelism attribute is calculated by the platform logic. This attribute determines how many threads you want the Copy Data activity to read data from the source and copy to the sink in parallel. If optimal performance is not realized by the default algorithm, you can modify and tune these two attributes to find the perfect balance.

Sink

The Settings tab of a sink in a data flow includes an attribute named Batch Size. This setting is valid in the context of columnar storage and caching, which falls into the realm of Parquet structured files. The Batch Size default value is provided by platform logic, so unless there is a need to modify it, leave it empty. The value sets the amount of data that is loaded into memory in advance of the writing to the destination datastore. This improves performance because accessing data from memory is faster than loading it from disk. Do take some caution concerning the size and consider the amount of memory you have available, because if the value is larger than the available memory, you will get *out of memory (OOM)* exceptions. Those exceptions will cause the data flow and/or pipeline to fail.

Bulk Loading

Chapter 2 introduced the `BULK` command statement, which looks something like the following:

```
BULK INSERT [dbo].[READINGCSV]
FROM 'csharpguitar-brainjammer-pow-PlayingGuitar-0911.csv'
WITH (DATA_SOURCE = 'PlayingGuitarPOW',
      FIRSTROW = 2,
      FIELDTERMINATOR = ',',
      ROWTERMINATOR = '0x0a',
      BATCHSIZE = 1000);
```

What you did not see in Chapter 2 was the `BATCHSIZE` argument. If the value is not set, then it is assumed to be zero and means the entire file is sent to the destination in one transaction. For file size, performance, or network throttling reasons, you may want or need to change this behavior. If the value is changed to, for example, `1000`, then that many rows will be sent to the destination as a batch. The transmission will continue in batches of 1,000 rows until there is no more data to send.

Source Code

There are also techniques for batching database transactions in code. If you recall from Chapter 2, JSON brainjammer brain wave files were loaded into the Azure SQL database. The source code is located in the `Chapter02/Source Code` directory on GitHub; the file name is `JSONToAzureSQL.cs`. The code snippet used sent an `INSERT` statement to Azure SQL for each reading, like the following:

```
foreach (var reading in brainwaves.Session.POWReading)
{
 using (SqlCommand cmd = new SqlCommand(sql, connection))
 {
```

```
    cmd.Parameters.Add("@SESSION_ID", SqlDbType.Int).Value = sessionId;
    cmd.Parameters
       .Add("@READING_DATETIME", SqlDbType.DateTime).Value = reading
          .ReadingDate;
    cmd.Parameters.Add("@COUNT", SqlDbType.Int).Value = reading.Counter;
    cmd.Parameters.Add("@ELECTRODE_ID", SqlDbType.Int).Value =
       GetElectrode("AF3");
    cmd.Parameters
       .Add("@FREQUENCY_ID", SqlDbType.Int).Value = GetFrequency("THETA");
    cmd.Parameters.Add("@VALUE", SqlDbType.Decimal).Value = reading
       .AF3[0].THETA;
    cmd.ExecuteNonQuery();
  }
  ...
}
```

This code snippet would be enhanced by including a transaction. Placing a begin transaction object before the `foreach` loop and then committing the transaction outside of the loop would reduce latency. This is because when you are performing about 25 individual inserts, using a transaction would send all the inserts at once to the database and process them all at that time. This is better than sending about 25 individual `INSERT` statements to Azure SQL sequentially, which is the behavior without using a transaction.

```
SqlTransaction transaction = conn.BeginTransaction();
foreach (var reading in brainwaves.Session.POWReading)
{
 using (SqlCommand cmd = new SqlCommand(sqlList, connection, transaction))
 {
    cmd.Parameters.Add("@SESSION_ID", SqlDbType.Int).Value = sessionId;
    cmd.Parameters
       .Add("@READING_DATETIME", SqlDbType.DateTime).Value = reading
          .ReadingDate;
    cmd.Parameters.Add("@COUNT", SqlDbType.Int).Value = reading.Counter;
    cmd.Parameters.Add("@ELECTRODE_ID", SqlDbType.Int).Value =
       GetElectrode("AF3");
    cmd.Parameters
       .Add("@FREQUENCY_ID", SqlDbType.Int).Value = GetFrequency("THETA");
    cmd.Parameters.Add("@VALUE", SqlDbType.Decimal).Value = reading
       .AF3[0].THETA;
    cmd.ExecuteNonQuery();
 }
 ...
}
transaction.Commit()
```

This is a valid and useful form of batching together SQL statements that decreases both latency and network traffic.

Configure Batch Retention

In Exercise 6.2 you added a Custom activity to an Azure Synapse Analytics pipeline that triggered an Azure Batch job. The Settings tab for the Custom activity includes a property named Retention Time in Days. As you may recall, each time a batch job is triggered, the application package (the source code that performs the work on your data) is copied to the node. In addition to the application package, `stderr.txt` and `stdout.txt` log files are written and stored on the node. By default, those files persist on the node for 30 days. Depending on the change frequency and what the code in the application package does, the number of files and the amount of space the data needs on the node can be great. Figure 6.54 shows how the files can be viewed via the Azure portal.

FIGURE 6.54 Configure batch retention

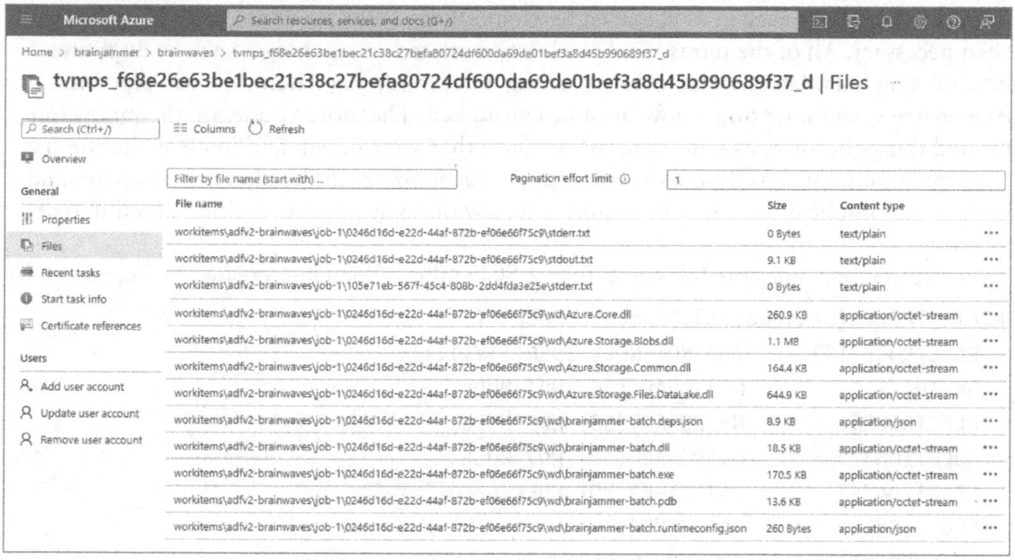

If the space runs out, then the batch job can fail. Therefore, if you need to decrease the retention period of the files to provide the necessary space, you can change this. Setting the Retention Time in Days property (aka `retentionTimeInDays`) to a value less than the default results in space being made available sooner. The opposite is also true: When you need to store the data for longer periods due to governance requirements, you can increase the retention period.

Design and Develop Slowly Changing Dimensions

The design of an SCD table was discussed in detail in Chapter 3, in the section "Design the Serving Layer." The notion of a star schema was also introduced in this same context, which is where you most often find dimension tables. Refer to Figure 3.14 for an illustration of what a star schema often looks like, and refer to Table 3.5 for an overview of the different SCD types. The building, development, and implementation of an SCD table was performed in Chapter 4, specifically in Exercise 4.10 and the section "Implement Logical Data Structures." Refer to Table 4.6 for a reference to the figures in this book that represent each SCD type. There is also a reference to SCDs in the "Handle Late-Arriving Data" section in this chapter. You need to know the internals and use cases of SCD types for the DP-203 exam.

This section falls into the parent section of "Design and Develop a Batch Processing Solution." This means there needs to be some kind of content around anything unique or different when compared to the serving layer or logical data structures. However, there are no unique design considerations in the context of batching when compared to logical structures or the serving layer. The implementation, however, would be different. In Exercise 4.10 you manually updated a Type 2 SCD dimension table; however, in a batch scenario you would include that query in a scheduled batch job that checks for changes and applies them when necessary. All of the terms you have learned related to batching—such as duplicate data, missing data, late-arriving data, upserting data, triggering batch jobs and pipelines, dependencies, and retention—now must be considered. The more you learn, the more complicated things become, as you begin to recognize that your design and implementation has many decision points. Additionally, you begin to recognize each decision has upstream and downstream implications that can require a review on their impact resulting in a different decision.

As a review, consider the following Type 2 SCD table, which you created in Exercise 4.10:

```
CREATE TABLE [brainwaves].[DimELECTRODE] (
  [ELECTRODE_ID]      INT NOT NULL IDENTITY(1,1),
  [SK_ID]             NVARCHAR (50) NOT NULL,
  [ELECTRODE]         NVARCHAR (50) NOT NULL,
  [LOCATION]          NVARCHAR (50) NOT NULL,
  [START_DATE]        DATETIME2 NOT NULL,
  [END_DATE]          DATETIME2,
  [IS_CURRENT]        INT NOT NULL
)
```

A Type 2 SCD table has the capability to provide versioning. With the existence of the `START_DATE` and `END_DATE`, along with the `SK_ID` and `IS_CURRENT` flag, it is possible to know which row is current and when previous rows were valid. Remember that dimension tables hold reference data used by the fact tables to transform itself into data that is useful for finding business insights. If dimension table data changes but you want to transform data using a previous version of the reference data on the dimension table, you can use a Type 2 SCD table. Finally, the `SK_ID` is a surrogate key that is helpful in the unique identification of a row. There is also the concept of a business key that could be used instead of a surrogate key, where a business key is something like an identification number used only within your company for the purpose of uniqueness.

Design and Implement Incremental Data Loads

The design part of incremental loading was covered in Chapter 3, in the section "Design for Incremental Loading." As shown in Figure 3.3, the serving layer is part of the lambda architecture. This section discusses the batch layer, which provides data to the serving layer along the cold path. As a quick refresher, remember that in all cases you want to make your data loading, movement, and transformation as efficient as possible. With that in mind, you can relate that it is not the most optimal approach to load all the data from a data source to a data analytics datastore on a regular basis. Instead, you would want to transfer only the newly added or modified data—a process known as incrementally loading data.

Why is an incremental data load more efficient and optimal when compared to a complete transfer of all source data? There are a few reasons, the first being that the speed and performance of the incremental load would be consistent over time. The more data you need to migrate, the longer it takes and a greater amount of compute resources are required. As time progresses the amount of data will increase; every day you will get new data, which requires longer transfers. However, transferring the bulk once, and then only the new and modified data after that initial load, results in a consistent amount of data being regularly transferred. Another reason is that the job will run faster, which makes sense because the less data you move, the less time it takes. Lastly, touching less data reduces the possibility of error. If you are moving all your data each time and there is an exception that causes the transfer to fail, there can be significant downstream impacts. If you instead load the changes, the impact of a failed or partial run would be more manageable because the time to repair and the amount of data required to retransmit would be much less when data is loaded incrementally. As discussed in the following sections, numerous approaches are useful for performing incremental loads along the cold path.

Watermarks

A watermark is a column in a source table that contains an identifier used to determine the current location/state/status of incremental data movement. The watermark value is commonly a datetime stamp but can also be an incrementing key. There are a few implementation methods you might consider concerning watermarks. The first is similar to the hashed column approach discussed previously. In that scenario each row has an additional column that is used to determine if the row has been updated since the previous run. Instead of using a hash value, you might consider making the column contain a datetime. The datetime can be either when it was inserted or updated. If the datetime in that column is greater than the last time in which the job ran, you can conclude it needs to be part of the incremental load. If your source data is a relational database that has an incremental primary key, then that can be used as a watermark. When your batch job is run, the first step in the code can be to access a reference table that stores the primary key of the last row used in the most recent job execution. For example, the value retrieved at the beginning of the batch run might be something like `1110`. Then, any row having a primary key greater than that number would be included in the incremental load. The primary key of the last row, for example, `2323`, would be inserted into the reference table and used as the start +1 the next time the batch job is triggered. In Exercise 6.10 you inserted the following two rows into the `READING` table:

```
+------------+-----------------------------+--------+
| READING_ID | READING_DATETIME            | VALUE  |
+------------+-----------------------------+--------+
| 5626757    | 20220710 04:37:35.394 PM | 22.454 |
| 5626758    | 20220710 04:37:35.445 PM | 4.849  |
+------------+-----------------------------+--------+
```

In this example, both scenarios mentioned previously would work. There is a datetime that can be compared to the batch runtime to determine if the row should be included. There is also a `READING_ID` that is an incremental primary key on the `READING` table. This can also be used to determine whether or not the row should be included.

Last Modified Date

A very useful piece of metadata that files expose is the date when they were last modified. You can access this metadata and use it to determine if the file was modified or created since the last time the batch job ran. To achieve that, complete Exercise 6.11.

EXERCISE 6.11

Implement Incremental Data Loads

1. Log in to the Azure portal at `https://portal.azure.com` ➢ navigate to the Azure Synapse Analytics workspace you created in Exercise 3.3 ➢ select the Open link in the Open Synapse Studio tile on the Overview blade ➢ select the Integrate hub ➢ hover over the Pipelines group ➢ select the ellipse (`...`) ➢ click New Pipeline from the pop-up menu ➢ and then provide a name (I used **IncrementalTransformSessionFrequencyToMedian**).
2. Drag and drop a Get Metadata activity from the General group ➢ change the name of the activity (I used **Get Brainwaves**) ➢ on the Settings tab for the Get Metadata activity ➢ create a new dataset ➢ click the + New button to the right of the Dataset drop-down list box ➢ select Azure Data Lake Storage Gen2 from the New Integration Dataset window ➢ click Continue ➢ select JSON from the Select Format window ➢ click Continue ➢ enter a name (I used **IncrementalBrainwavesJson**) ➢ select the default storage workspace (for example, `workspaceName-WorkspaceDefaultStorage`) from the Linked Service drop-down ➢ enable interactive authoring ➢ select the folder image to the right of the File Path text boxes ➢ navigate to the `inputLocation` where the files that require processing were stored from Exercise 6.1 (for example, `brainjammer/`

`SessionJson/ClassicalMusic/POW`) ➢ leave the File text box blank (do not select a JSON file) ➢ click OK ➢ and then OK again to complete the configuration of this dataset.

3. Make a small update to two or more of the brainjammer brain wave JSON files so that they get a new modified date ➢ and then upload those modified files to your ADLS container in the `inputLocation` directory (the same location as specified in step 2). The JSON files are in the `BrainwaveData/SessionJson` directory on GitHub at `https://github.com/benperk/ADE`.

4. Select the Settings tab for the Get Metadata activity ➢ click + New to the right of the Field list ➢ select Child Items from the drop-down list box ➢ set focus to the Start Time (UTC) text box in the Filter by Last Modified section ➢ select the Add Dynamic Content link ➢ and then add the following code snippet. The configuration should resemble Figure 6.55.

```
@getPastTime(1, 'Day')
```

FIGURE 6.55 Incremental data loads—Get Metadata activity

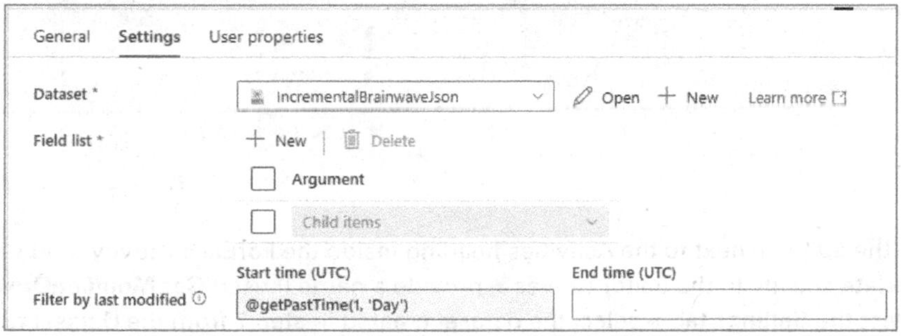

5. Click OK ➢ click Commit ➢ and then click Debug. Once complete, the Get Metadata activity output should resemble the following. You can view the output on the pipeline Output tab, as shown in Figure 6.30 and Figure 6.58.

```
{
    "childItems": [
        {
            "name": "csharpguitar-brainjammer-pow-2327.json",
            "type": "File"
        },
        {
            "name": "csharpguitar-brainjammer-pow-2328.json",
            "type": "File"
        }
    ],...}
}
```

EXERCISE 6.11 *(continued)*

6. Drag and drop a ForEach activity from the Iteration & Conditions activities group onto the editor canvas ➢ connect the Get Metadata activity to the ForEach activity ➢ click the connection box on the right side middle of the Get Metadata activity and drag it to the ForEach activity ➢ provide the ForEach activity a name (I used **ForEachBrainwaveFile**) ➢ select the Settings tab for the ForEach activity ➢ set the focus to the Items text box ➢ click the Add Dynamic Content link ➢ enter the following code snippet ➢ and then click OK; see Figure 6.56.

```
@activity('Get Brainwaves').output.childItems
```

FIGURE 6.56 Incremental data loads—ForEach activity

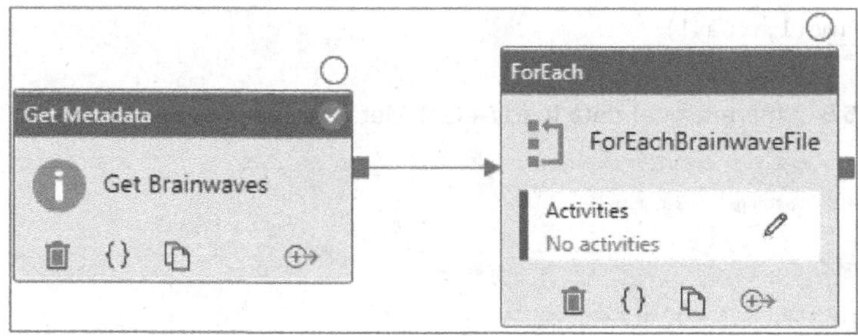

7. Click the edit pen next to the Activities heading inside the ForEach activity ➢ add a Get Metadata activity to the editor canvas ➢ provide a name (I used **Get ModifiedOrNew**) ➢ select the Settings tab ➢ select the dataset created in step 2 from the Dataset drop-down ➢ click the + New button next to the Field list ➢ select Add Dynamic Content from the drop-down ➢ enter the following syntax ➢ and then click OK.

```
@item()
```

8. Add an Execute Pipeline activity from the General group ➢ connect the Get Metadata activity to the Execute Pipeline activity ➢ enter a name for the Execute Pipeline activity (I used **Execute Incremental Brainwave Load**) ➢ select the Settings tab ➢ select the pipeline created in Exercise 6.2 (for example, `TransformSessionFrequencyToMedian`) ➢ click the Open button next to the Invoke Pipeline attribute ➢ add a new parameter ➢ enter **FileName** as the name ➢ select `string` from the Type drop-down ➢ leave the Default value blank➢ and then click Commit.

9. Navigate back to the ForEach editor canvas. The Parameter you just added to the `TransformSessionFrequencyToMedian` pipeline is rendered. Add the following syntax into the Value column, as shown in Figure 6.57:

```
@item()
```

FIGURE 6.57 Incremental data loads—Execute Pipeline activity

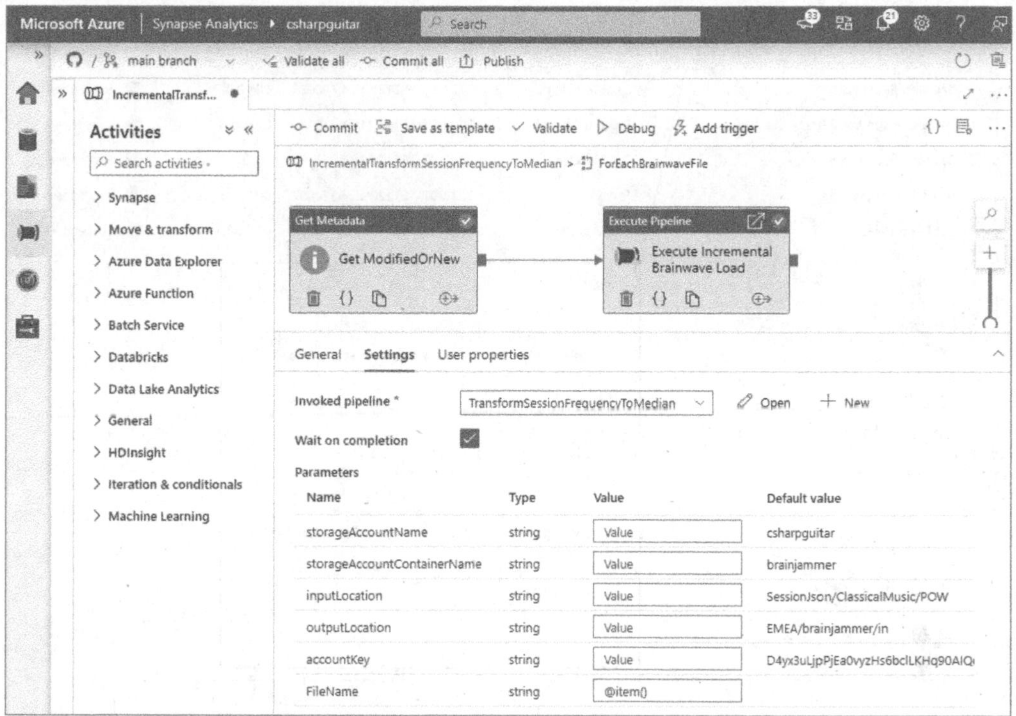

10. Click Commit > click Debug > and then view the pipeline output, as shown in Figure 6.58.

EXERCISE 6.11 *(continued)*

FIGURE 6.58 Incremental data loads—pipeline output

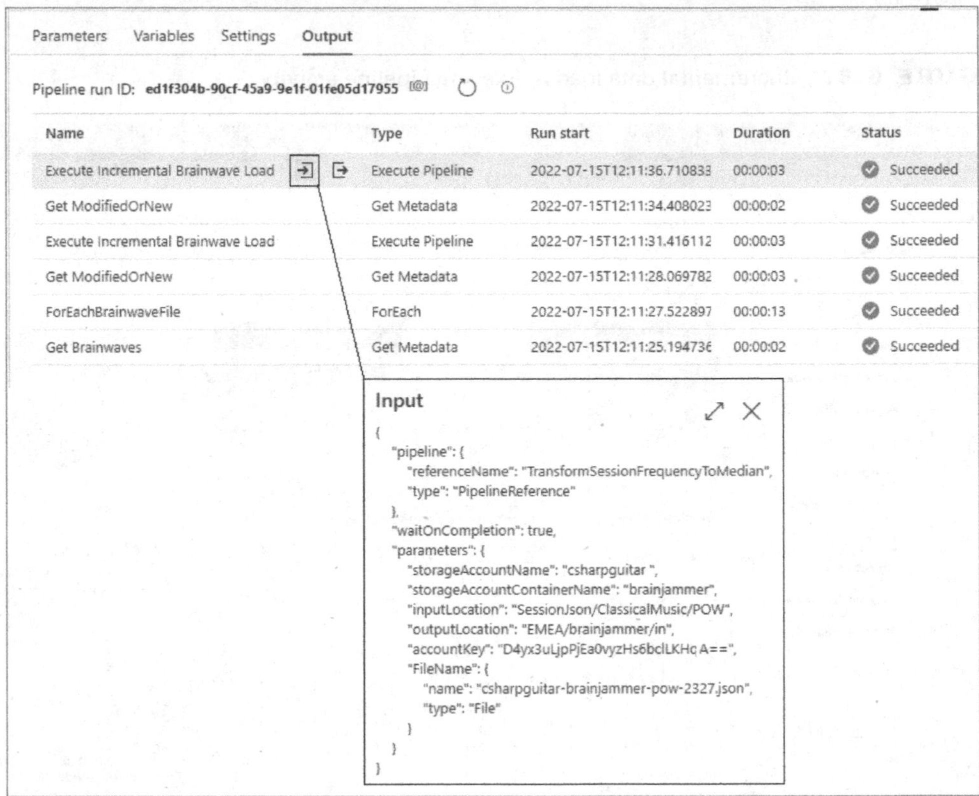

11. Click Publish.

That was a rather long exercise, but the principal flow is easily recognizable, in that the Get Metadata activity gathers a list of all files in the instructed location that have a last modified date of one day ago. The code snippet that generated the timeframe, `@getPastTime(1, 'Day')`, is dynamic. The list of files, aka child items, gathered by the Get Metadata activity is passed to the ForEach activity. Access to the output of the Get Metadata activity is referenced from the ForEach Items property using the syntax `@activity('Get Brainwaves').output.childItems`. The Get Metadata (`Get Brainwaves`) activity returned two files, which results in two iterations of the activities contained within the ForEach activity. Therefore, the two activities within the ForEach activity were executed twice, once per file, which is evident in the pipeline output in Figure 6.58. The ForEach activity contains a Get Metadata activity that receives and passes the `@item()` object to the Execute Pipeline activity. The object contains the name of a file that needs processing, which can then be concatenated with the `InputLocation` fed to the `brainjammer-batch.exe` batch job.

You might have noticed on the Settings tab of the ForEach activity the Sequential check box and the Batch Count text box, as shown in Figure 6.59.

FIGURE 6.59 Incremental data loads—ForEach activity settings

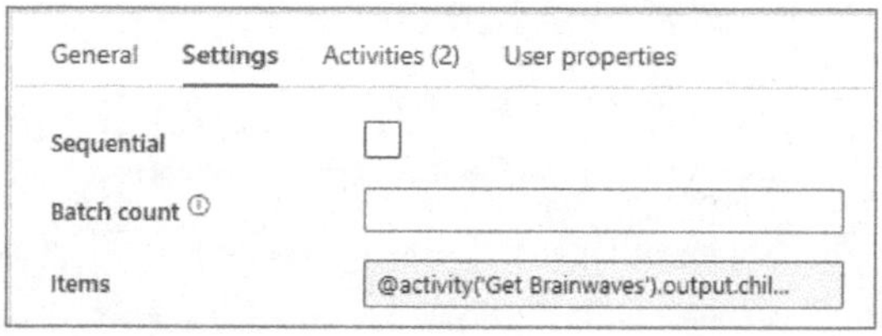

General	**Settings**	Activities (2)	User properties
Sequential	☐		
Batch count ⓘ			
Items	@activity('Get Brainwaves').output.chil...		

When you run the pipeline in debug mode, all the activities within the ForEach activity will run sequentially. The next iteration of the ForEach loop will not happen until all activities have completed. When you require that type of execution when running the pipeline via a trigger, check the Sequential check box. Doing so will result in each iteration running one after the other. If you want to instead run multiple iterations of the activities in parallel, leave the Sequential check box unchecked and provide a value of concurrency into the Batch Count text box. If no value is added, the default is 20 and the maximum is 50.

Directory Structure

The following directory structure should not be something new to you at this point. And perhaps you can already visualize how this directory can be used for the incremental loading of data.

```
{location}/{subject}/{direction}/{yyyy}/{mm}/{dd}/{hh}/*
```

Here are some specific examples:

```
EMEA/brainjammer/in/2022/07/15/09/
NA/brainjammer/out/2022/07/15/10/
```

A valid option for this approach is to use the Copy Data activity, as shown in Figure 6.60. The content of the `Wildcard` folder path could be something like the following code snippet:

```
@concat(variables('outputLocation'), '/',
        utcnow('yyyy'), '/',
        utcnow('MM'), '/',
        utcnow('dd'), '/',
        utcnow('HH'), '/')
```

FIGURE 6.60 Incremental data loads—Copy Data activity

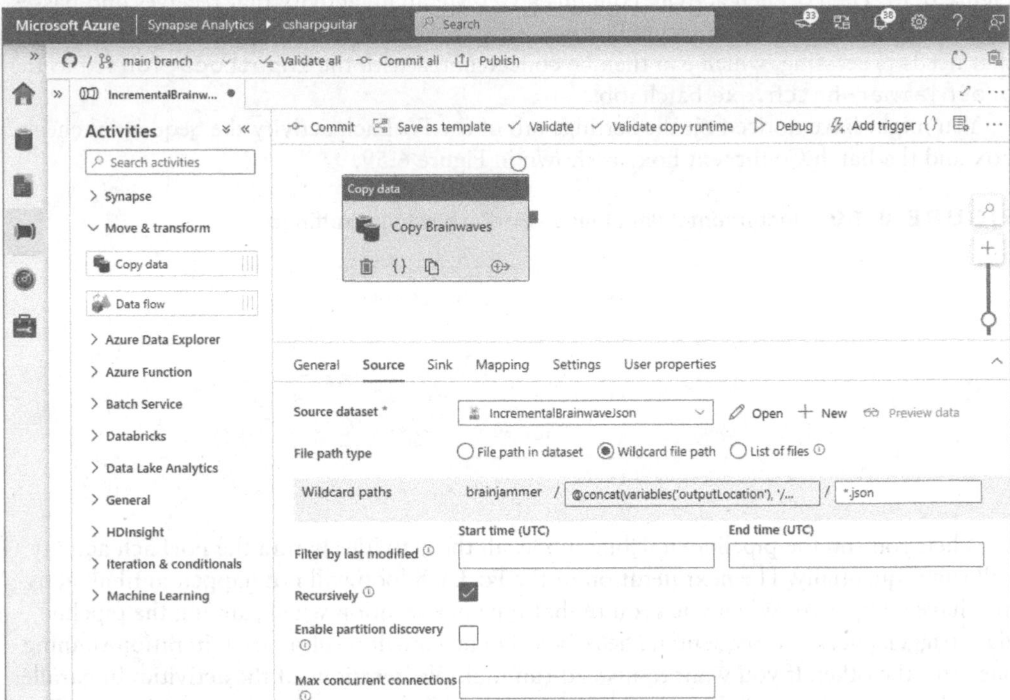

This approach can check for newly arriving files on an hourly basis and then copy them from the source to the sink. After the copy, you can perform any transformation using a batch job, notebook, or Spark job.

Integrate Jupyter/IPython Notebooks into a Data Pipeline

Your first exposure to a Jupyter notebook in this book was in Chapter 4. You learned that the Develop hub includes an Import feature that allows you to upload existing Jupyter notebooks, which have the file extension of `.ipynb`. Chapter 5 covered how to use a Jupyter notebook in Azure Synapse Analytics, Azure Databricks, Azure HDInsight, and Azure Data Studio. Chapter 5 also included two exercises that used Jupyter notebooks, Exercise 5.3 and Exercise 5.4. An example Jupyter notebook named `Ch05Ex03.ipynb` is in the `Chapter05` directory on GitHub. Building on all that, in this chapter you imported and executed an existing Jupyter notebook into an Azure Databricks workspace in Exercise 6.4. Later in that same exercise, you integrated that Jupyter notebook, which converted AVRO files to a delta table in the `TransformSessionFrequencyToMedian` Azure Synapse Analytics pipeline.

The Jupyter notebook for Exercise 6.4, `IdentifyBrainwaveScenario.ipynb`, is in the `Chapter06/Ch06Ex04` directory on GitHub. Finally, in Exercise 6.8 you scheduled a workflow job in Azure Databricks using that same Jupyter notebook. It should go without saying that you know a thing or two about Jupyter notebooks now.

Revert Data to a Previous State

As mentioned numerous times in this book, batch jobs and pipelines fail. Sometimes a failure has no impact on the data in your data lake, but in some cases the failure can cause serious problems. For example, if the parameters for a `DELETE` command are wrong, if the insertion of data only partially completes, or if the creation of a delta table fails due to a type mismatch, your data can be seriously corrupted, for a number of reasons. As you learned in Chapter 4, Exercise 4.4, point-in-time restore (PITR) depends on a snapshot for creating a restore point. For dedicated SQL pools, the creation of restore points happens automatically. Therefore, if your pipeline runs result in the corruption of data, you can follow the steps described in Exercise 4.4 to recover from the most recent backup. Another important concept to remember from Chapter 4 is the recovery point objective (RPO), which defines the length of time between failure and expected recovery. The final concept to call out, which was introduced in Chapter 4 and pertains to regressions, is a soft delete in the context of an ADLS container. This is a built-in data protection feature that prevents data loss when files or folders are unintentionally deleted.

In Exercise 3.15 you created an Azure Databricks delta lake. A delta lake has numerous beneficial capabilities. For example, ACID transactions and time travel are both relevant features when it comes to preventing regressions or recovering from them. When a database transition is considered ACID, the transaction is guaranteed to either be completed successfully or be rolled back successfully, in both of which cases there is no possibility of corrupting data. The time travel feature uses the `versionAsOf` option as a pointer to previous versions of delta tables. These versions are useful for determining the impact of failed activities run on the tables and provide the option to restore from a previous version. This book has discussed recovering data and rolling back data, which is synonymous with regressing to a previous state, but what happens if you cannot roll back but instead need to repair the data that requires the cleansing?

Data Cleansing

Cleansing data means removing or modifying content in your data lake that exists in unwanted data states. Duplicates, format issues, spelling errors, corrupted data, or old or irrelevant data are all examples of data you would not want in your data lake. How does this data end up in your data lake? There can be many reasons, such as human error, malicious exploits, or being entered from an upstream data source. Another common scenario of data corruption can be caused by exceptions somewhere along your batch job solution path. When your batch job solution begins to fail, a big problem can be created, especially if you only realize these failures after a few days or weeks. If the batch jobs have downstream dependencies and the job runs multiple times per day, then you likely have a very big problem, with a lot of corrupted data. Fixing that problem will require some serious time, effort, diligence, and patience.

How you resolve this is very dependent on the data, but recall something you learned in the "Handle Missing Data" section. You learned about MAR, MCAR, and MNAR. In scenarios in which the data falls into the categories of MAR and MCAR, it is safe to delete without having significant impact on your business insights and EDA. However, if your data is MNAR, then the approach you learned about called imputation is helpful. If that approach does not meet the requirements, there are some other approaches, but it all depends on you knowing what the data should look like. If you do not know the target you are working towards, then it is highly improbable that you will hit it. Begin by creating some queries or a file that contains the data in the form you expect. You can take that query and run the inverse of it, so that the data you do not want is returned. After you review the dataset, you can use that query to either delete or manipulate the dataset to cleanse it, which makes it useful. Data quality is one of the core data management disciplines discussed in Chapter 5 (refer to Figure 5.41). There is no quick and simple solution to cleanse your data. The amount of data in the Big Data industry is so huge that cleansing data manually is not realistic. If your organization can afford and utilize tools that specialize in this activity, you should use them; otherwise, you might find yourself in a frustrating, no-win situation.

Handle Security and Compliance Requirements

The in-depth coverage of security-related concepts is coming in Chapter 8, "Keeping Data Safe and Secure." The different aspects of security are vast, but here you will get a short introduction to the following topics:

- Networking
- Endpoint security
- Backup and recovery

While provisioning your Azure Batch account in Exercise 6.1, you may have noticed the Networking tab. You were instructed to leave the default value of All Networks. The other two options, Selected Networks and Disabled, provide some additional security features. For example, the Azure Batch endpoint you can use to trigger and configure your nodes and jobs is by default globally discoverable. The endpoint is not publicly accessible, rather only discoverable, which means you need an access key or some other form of authentication to configure nodes and manually trigger batch jobs. Had you chosen Disabled, the endpoint would be removed from the public DNS, which removes access from the public. Even if you had an access key, you could not access the endpoint publicly. Disabling the public endpoint and making it private is a feature of endpoint security. The other option, Selected Networks, can be used to restrict access by IP address ranges of machines that can access the Azure Batch account endpoint. The restriction is typically placed on VMs within a shared VNet or VMs in another peered VNet.

When creating backups, keep in mind that they contain the exact same data as the production data on your live database. The backups need to be protected just like access to your database. Backups are stored in an Azure storage account that can be restricted by RBAC controls. Additionally, backups are encrypted in transit and at rest, so even if a backup leaks out to the public, it is very unlikely that anyone would be able to decrypt and consume the data. There are many aspects to security, many of which will be covered in Chapter 8 in the context of Microsoft Defender for Cloud.

Design and Create Tests for Data Pipelines

As your pipelines become more complex and the data analytics solution you created becomes more critical to your company, testing will also become critical. Testing should be focused not only on newly created pipelines and data flows but also on changes to existing capabilities. When testing a new pipeline, you must consider performance, latency, and whether the results of the data ingestion and transformation meet the expectations. Those three aspects should take place without any unexpected programming logic exceptions. Exceptions can and often do happen, but you need to have recovery paths in place to protect your data. When you are making updates to existing pipelines, the previous points remain valid. In addition, though, you might have built in upstream and downstream dependencies. Each of those scenarios must be tested to ensure that no issues can cause data corruption or delay the processing and delivery of data to the consumers. Later chapters provide an in-depth look at monitoring, troubleshooting, and optimizing your data analytics processing on Azure—specifically, Chapter 9, "Monitoring Azure Data Storage and Processing," and Chapter 10, "Troubleshoot Data Storage Processing."

Scale Resources

Chapter 10 focuses on optimizing the compute and availability of your data workloads running on Azure. Remember that when you provisioned the nodes that will run the batch job, you selected the VM size on which the job will run. You also selected how many nodes you wanted and the number of vCPUs. With some configuration, you can create an autoscale formula that increases the number of nodes when required and decreases them when not. This saves you money by only using the compute resources required. You can use attributes like CPU percentage and utilized memory, as well as the number of running tasks and inbound network traffic, to determine scale up or scale down logic. In addition to scaling Azure Batch nodes, you can also scale both SQL and Spark pools in Azure Synapse Analytics automatically. Again, there is more to come about this in Chapter 10.

Design and Configure Exception Handling

You can handle exceptions in source code like Python, Java, Scala, or C# by including your code within `try{...} catch{...}` blocks. When something unexpected happens in your code, the `catch` portion of your code is written specifically to handle that exception. You can decide to either retry the transaction or stop the code path execution completely. There is the same concept in T-SQL commands that can handle and respond to exceptions. Keep in mind that if you do not place your code within these code blocks, the exception is considered unhandled and can crash the process and place the operating system or container into a bad state from which it cannot recover. This is known as a *hung server* and can result in schedules failing until the server is identified as being unhealthy, which results in a reboot, failover, or reconfiguration. From a pipeline perspective you have learned about linking pipeline activities (refer to Figure 6.20 and Figure 6.28). That you can link activities based on failure enables you to handle the fact that something unexpectedly went wrong. You may want to stop further activities from running if a failure is reached. Or, in some cases, the failure is expected, and the activity that runs due to the failure contains the logic to correct it. Chapter 9 and Chapter 10 include most of the details and Exercises about these topics.

Debug Spark Jobs Using the Spark UI

As you saw in Figure 6.42 and experienced in Exercise 6.8, there are some very nice features for managing and viewing the status of Spark jobs. There are also techniques for debugging and troubleshooting them. The details of these features are discussed in Chapter 10. There is also some related content later in this chapter, in the section "Manage Spark Jobs in a Pipeline."

Implement Azure Synapse Link and Query the Replicated Data

Chapter 2 briefly introduced data processing types such as OLTP, OLAP, and HTAP, and Chapter 10 covered them in a bit more detail. The overlying principle with these data processing types has to do with the impact that data analytics typically performed on an OLAP datastore has on a real-time transactional database, i.e., OLTP. For example, reporting on the average value of brain waves captured on the Pz electrode on the real-time database can cause latency on that database due to the size of the result set. It is common practice to place a copy of the dataset in near real time onto an OLAP database for performing reporting and exploratory analysis on so that any impact to the live ingestion of data can be avoided. HTAP is a hybrid data processing type that exposes a solution for performing real-time ingestion of data and the reporting of it on the database. An Azure Synapse Link provides an HTAP-like data processing capability for linking your operational databases, for example, OLTP like Azure SQL DB and SQL Server 2022, with your analytics workloads running in your Azure Synapse Analytics workspace.

The HTAP-like feature in Azure SQL and SQL Server is provided using a concept called change data capture (CDC). To enable CDC, you would execute the following SQL snippet for each real-time transactional table you want to perform data analytics on, also in real time:

```
EXEC sys.sp_cdc_enable_table
@source_schema = N'schema',
@source_name = N'TableName',
```

```
@role_name = N'role',
@filegroup_name = N'FilegroupName',
@supports_net_changes = 1
```

The successful execution of this SQL query on the Azure SQL or SQL Server database generates change logs that capture DML changes like `INSERT`, `UPDATE`, and `DELETE`. Those change logs are replicated to the change tables that reside on a dedicated SQL pool in Azure Synapse Analytics for use in your pipeline transformations and analysis. At the time of writing this book, your Azure SQL DB must be in Premium tier and have more than 100 eDTUs and more than one vCore. Creating the Azure Synapse Link is performed on the Integrate hub in the Azure Synapse Analytics workspace. The Link Connection wizard walks you through the configuration, which uses a linked service that is configured to your Azure SQL database (refer to Exercise 3.4). Once the linked service is configured, you can execute queries on the target change tables on the dedicated SQL pool via the Data hub, just like you would any other table in this context.

Use PolyBase to Load Data to a SQL Pool

PolyBase is a very powerful technology that works behind the scenes to enable the execution of SQL queries on data files, where the data files are, for example, in CSV format. In the Azure Synapse Analytics context, you use the PolyBase technology on serverless SQL pools that host external tables (refer to Table 3.7). Chapter 2 explained CETAS, which is the approach for creating external data tables. Refer to Figure 2.12 and Exercise 4.11, where you created an external table named `SampleBrainwaves` on the built-in serverless SQL pool that targeted a Parquet file. Figure 4.33 illustrates how this looks in Azure Synapse Analytics and the result of the query that utilized PolyBase to render the result set.

Read from and Write to a Delta Table

As mentioned in Chapter 3, a delta lake is a storage and management software layer that provides numerous benefits, including ACID transactions, time travel, and upserts. It is within your delta lake that you find delta tables, which benefit from the delta lake software layer. In Exercise 3.15 and Exercise 5.4, you created, populated, and queried delta tables. You achieve this by executing Python code similar to the following snippet:

```
df = spark.read \
 .option("header","true").csv("/FileStore/tables/brainwavesMeditation.csv")
df.write.mode("overwrite").format("delta").save("/FileStore/data/2022/03/14")
brainwaves = spark.read.format("delta").load("/FileStore/data/2022/03/14")
display(brainwaves)
print(brainwaves.count())
```

The code first reads from a CSV file stored locally on a Spark cluster, and then writes the data in delta format into a dataframe. The `format()` method passing the parameter of delta instructs the platform to organize the data correctly. Once the file is written in delta format, you can use the following code snippet to load the data contained in the file into a delta table:

```
display(spark \
 .sql("CREATE TABLE BRAINWAVES USING DELTA LOCATION '/FileStore/data/2022/
   03/14'"))
display(spark.table("BRAINWAVES").select("*").show(10))
print(spark.table("BRAINWAVES").select("*").count())
```

The SQL utilizes the `USING` SQL clause along with the `DELTA` keyword to instruct the creation of the table in delta form. You can then select and manipulate the data using standard SQL commands and queries.

Manage Batches and Pipelines

As you work through the Exercises in this book, you might have trouble remembering what exactly each pipeline or activity does. This is not uncommon and is why good documentation and processes to support the management of your batch jobs and pipelines are necessary to keep your data analytics solution healthy. Figures 6.11, 6.15, 6.18, and images in general, were created to provide a reference to what is happening in the pipeline and how it all links together. Writing pseudocode or the sequential steps a batch job performed is a useful technique for helping other team members understand what is happening. For example, the `brainjammer-batch.exe` batch job does the following:

1. Retrieves input from the command line
2. Builds the connection object for the ADLS container
3. Connects to the ADLS container and retrieve files
4. Loops through each brainjammer brain wave session file
5. Calculates a single median frequency value for each electrode
6. Uploads a new JSON file

These six steps will take you less time to read than looking over the source code to get an idea about what is going on in the executable. The source code is the `Program.cs` file in the `Chapter06/Ch06Ex01` directory. Managing your data analytics solution requires, in many respects, more effort than building and designing it. Therefore, it behooves you to build management capabilities into your solution. The following sections discuss some additional techniques for managing your batches and pipelines.

Trigger Batches

Earlier in this chapter you learned a great deal about triggering pipelines. You can trigger pipelines manually, or you can create numerous different Azure Synapse Analytics trigger types that run your pipeline for specific circumstances. Getting some details and an overview of the triggers you have in your workspace would be helpful. Knowing what you have is the minimum amount of information required to effectively manage them. You can find a list of all your triggers in the Manage hub by selecting Triggers from the navigation menu. The information there is informative, but you can also create a report using the Azure CLI. Running the following syntax from a PowerShell or command window results in the output shown in Figure 6.61:

```
$triggerQuery = "[].{Name: name, Type: properties.type, StartTime: " + `
           "properties.recurrence.startTime, Frequency: " + `
           "properties.frequency, State: properties.runtimeState, " + `
           " Scope: properties.scope}"
az synapse trigger list --workspace-name "csharpguitar-synapse" `
                        --query $triggerQuery -o table
```

FIGURE 6.61 Managing batches and pipelines' triggers

```
PS C:\> $triggerQuery = "[].{Name: name, Type: properties.type, StartTime: properties.recurrence.startTime,
                        Frequency: properties.frequency, State: properties.runtimeState, Scope: properties.scope}"

PS C:\> az synapse trigger list --workspace-name "csharpguitar" --query $triggerQuery -o table

Name                Type                    StartTime            State    Frequency   Scope
------------------  ----------------------  -------------------  -------  ----------  ----------------------------------------------------
TriggerTSFTH        ScheduleTrigger         2022-06-25T18:20:00  Stopped
TriggerITBR         ScheduleTrigger         2022-06-26T05:52:00  Stopped
Trigger Europe      ScheduleTrigger         2022-06-26T12:42:00  Stopped
Trigger NA          ScheduleTrigger         2022-06-26T12:47:00  Stopped
Trigger TP1         ScheduleTrigger         2022-06-26T12:47:00  Stopped
Trigger EDA         ScheduleTrigger         2022-06-26T12:48:00  Stopped
DailyEurope         TumblingWindowTrigger                        Stopped  Minute
DailyNorthAmerica   TumblingWindowTrigger                        Stopped  Minute
DailyFreqLoad       TumblingWindowTrigger                        Stopped  Minute
DailyElectLoad      TumblingWindowTrigger                        Stopped  Minute
BrainwaveArrival    CustomEventsTrigger                          Started              /subscriptions/ /resourceGroups/
                                                                                      /providers/Microsoft.EventGrid/topics/brainjammer
```

The result from the Azure CLI provides a bit more detail than you see in the browser. The Azure CLI provides all the details for all the configurations of all features in the workspace. You simply need to write the proper syntax to report out the information you want and need.

Schedule Data Pipelines

Scheduling pipelines that contain batch jobs, and scheduling pipelines in general, has been the overriding theme of this chapter. Refer to Table 6.4 for a brief description of all the different types of triggers available for a pipeline. You can use a scheduled trigger to specify a start date, a recurrence, and an end date. The "Create Data Pipelines" section includes significant information about scheduling triggers. For example, you created a scheduled trigger to run a pipeline in Exercise 6.7. Additionally, Figures 6.33, Figure 6.34, and Figure 6.35 illustrate what the different kinds of scheduled triggers look like while being configured. Finally, in Exercise 6.8, you scheduled a workflow job in Azure Databricks, with Figures 6.41 and 6.42 illustrating the experience. After reading this chapter, you should understand how to trigger pipelines and batch jobs.

Validate Batch Loads

As your pipeline progresses through the multitude of activities existing within it, it might be prudent to validate the data after each step, but it also might be unnecessary to validate after each and every step. Therefore, it is up to you to determine if validation is necessary based on what the activity does and how critical it is. You can use the following activities to validate data consistency during a pipeline run:

- Copy Data
- Validation
- Lookup
- Get Metadata

The behavior of each activity is focused on a similar data aspect: checking and validating the properties of the data that is about to be ingested or transformed—for example, whether the data or file exists, what the size is, what the name is, and where the file is located. All these aspects can be validated based on what you expect the outcome of upstream activities to be or what you believe is the proper structure of the data both before and after a pipeline or an activity is executed. Remember that in this context you are not concerned about missing, late, duplicated, or corrupted data. All the methods required to manage those scenarios have already been covered and require other approaches for correction. In this case, again, the focus is on making sure the incoming and outgoing data that is flowing through the pipeline is in the format, structure, and location that match your expected thresholds.

Enable Copy Activity Data Consistency Verification

The Copy Data activity is a very powerful and convenient way to ingest data to your data lake. Exercise 3.13 was your first exposure to the Copy Data activity. You used a Copy Data activity to convert and transform data in an Excel spreadsheet to Parquet format. In Exercise 5.2 you used a Copy Data activity in Azure Data Factory to copy and transform data (refer to Figure 5.8). The "Copy Data" section covers the Copy Data activity in a bit more detail. Refer also to Figure 6.60. To enable Data Consistency Verification on a Copy Data activity, click the Settings tab and check the Data Consistency Verification check box, as shown in Figure 6.62.

FIGURE 6.62 Validate batch loads with the Copy Data activity

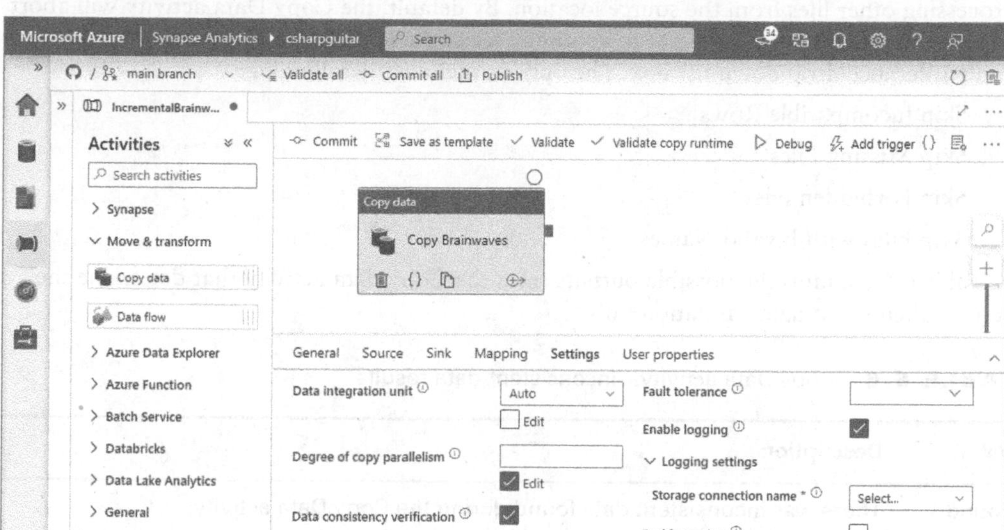

When this feature is enabled, the Copy Data activity will perform validations between the source and sink after the data has been copied. Validations like checksum, row count, and file size are performed. One additional step to configure Data Consistency Validation is to identify where the output log files are to be written. As shown in Figure 6.62, the Logging Settings group includes a Storage Connection Name drop-down list box. It requires an Azure Blob Storage or ADLS linked service as the location for storage. The log file is written in JSON format and contains information about the Copy Data activity, including the verification result and whether inconsistent data was found. Table 6.5 provides the possible values and descriptions of the verification results.

TABLE 6.5 Copy Data activity—verification results

Value	Description
Verified	The data is consistent between the source and the sink.
Not Verified	Data consistency validation is not enabled for this Copy Data activity.
Unsupported	Not supported on this copy pair.
Warning	The data is not consistent between the source and the sink.

If the data validation fails, you can choose to abort the Copy Data activity or continue processing other files from the source location. By default, the Copy Data activity will abort when validation fails. If you want to continue, select the level of fault tolerance from the Fault Tolerance drop-down list box. The options include the following:

- Skip Incompatible Rows
- Skip Missing Files
- Skip Forbidden Files
- Skip Files with Invalid Names

Table 6.6 contains the possible outputs from the Copy data activity that determine the action taken when data validation fails.

TABLE 6.6 Copy Data activity—inconsistent data results

Value	Description
Found	There was inconsistent data found during the Copy Data activity.
Skipped	Inconsistent data was found during the Copy Data activity and was skipped.
None	No inconsistent data was found, likely due to the validation not being enabled.

The log file contains also a timestamp, the name of the file that was processed, the verification result, the inconsistent data result, and a message why the file being considered is inconsistent.

Validation Pipeline Activity

Before the activities in your pipeline attempt to process data files, it might be prudent to confirm their existence. The Validation activity provides the capabilities to do this. Complete Exercise 6.12, where you will implement a Validation activity into an Azure Synapse Analytics pipeline.

EXERCISE 6.12

Validate Batch Loads by Using a Validation Activity

1. Log in to the Azure portal at `https://portal.azure.com` > navigate to the Azure Synapse Analytics workspace you created in Exercise 3.3 > click the Open link in the Open Synapse Studio tile on the Overview blade > select the Integrate hub > expand the Pipelines group > and then select the pipeline created in Exercise 6.2 (for example, `TransformSessionFrequencyToMedian`).

2. Drag and drop a Validation activity from the General group ➢ change the name of the activity (I used **Validate Brainwaves**) ➢ on the Settings tab for the Validation activity ➢ select the dataset used in Exercise 6.9 (for example, `BrainwavesJson`) ➢ select the True radio button to the right of Child Items ➢ connect the Validation activity to the Custom activity ➢ and then click Commit. The result should resemble Figure 6.63.

FIGURE 6.63 Validate batch loads with the Validation activity

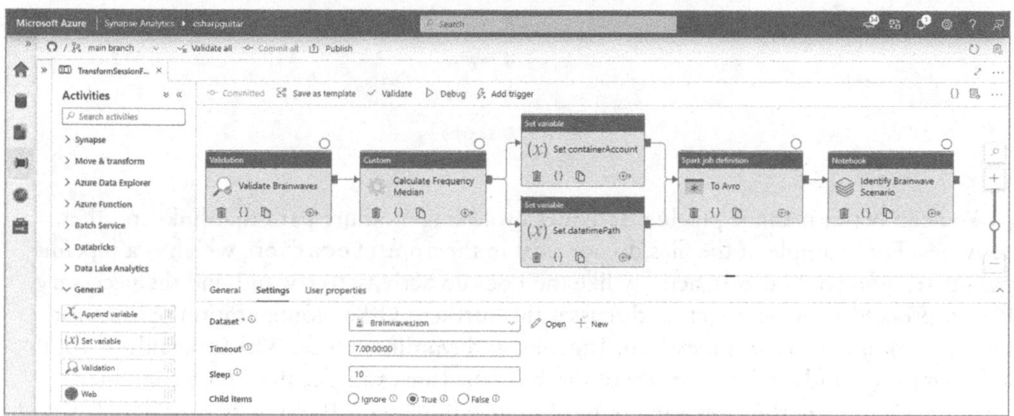

3. Select the Publish menu item ➢ click the Add Trigger button ➢ select Trigger Now ➢ and then click OK.

The dataset from Exercise 6.9 that you chose as the location to perform the validation on is the same location as the `inputLocation` parameter sent to the Custom activity. The following is the specific location:

`brainjammer/SessionJson/ClassicalMusic/POW`

This is desired because the purpose of the Validation activity is to confirm the existence of files within the targeted location. Selecting the True radio button, which is a property of Child Items, instructs the Validation activity to check for files in the targeted directory. Selecting Ignore checks for the existence of the folder only. Selecting False results in the confirmation that the folder exists but is empty. As there are indeed files in the target location defined by the dataset, the result of the validation is successful, which means the pipeline run will continue. Had the validation failed, the pipeline run would have stopped and not proceeded to the Custom activity, which is next. However, as shown in Figure 6.64, you can perform some activities if the validation results in a failure.

FIGURE 6.64 Validate batch loads with Validation activity failure

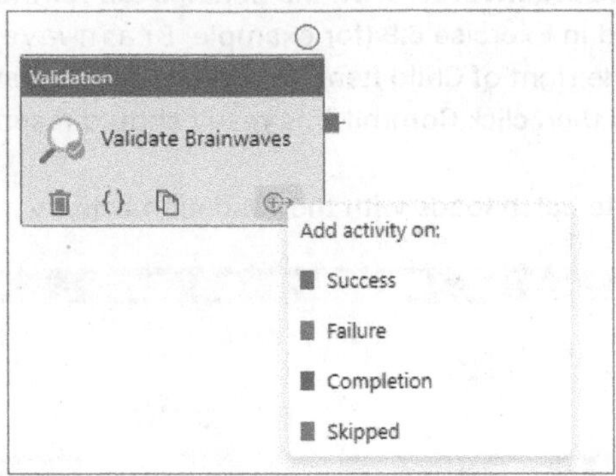

You can better manage pipeline activities by adding a failure path that links to other activities. For example, if the files do not exist in the `inputLocation`, which is a pipeline parameter, you could use an activity like the Lookup activity to try and find the necessary files to process. (The next section discusses this further.) Other configuration options for the Validation activity include Sleep, Timeout, and Minimum Size. With a default of 10, if an attempt to validate the existence of the files fails (for example, the ADLS container is not accessible), then the next attempt to validate will happen 10 seconds later. The Timeout value, which has a default of 12 hours, is the timeframe after which the Validation activity will stop trying to perform its task. Finally, for CSV files, there is an additional option that is not provided for JSON or Parquet files: Minimum Size. As you might have guessed, you can set this value to ensure that the file to be ingested or transformed is larger than a specific size. The default is zero bytes.

Lookup Pipeline Activity

The Lookup pipeline activity is used to retrieve content from a configuration file or table. This capability can be helpful in scenarios like those mentioned in the previous section where a Validation activity failed and you want to recover. To recover, you might consider providing other options in a configuration file for progressing the pipeline run forward. To get an idea of how to achieve this, complete Exercise 6.13.

EXERCISE 6.13

Validate Batch Loads by Using a Lookup Activity

1. Download file `brainjammerLookUp.json` from GitHub located in directory `Chapter06/Ch06Ex13` ➢ and then upload the file to the ADLS container you created in Exercise 3.1.
2. Log in to the Azure portal at `https://portal.azure.com` ➢ navigate to the Azure Synapse Analytics workspace you created in Exercise 3.3 ➢ click the Open link in the

Open Synapse Studio tile on the Overview blade ➢ select the Integrate hub ➢ expand the Pipelines group ➢ and then select the pipeline created in Exercise 6.2 (for example, `TransformSessionFrequencyToMedian`).

3. Drag and drop a Lookup activity from the General group ➢ change the name of the activity (I used **Lookup Brainwaves**) ➢ on the Settings tab for the Lookup activity ➢ click the + New button on the Settings tab next to the Source Dataset heading ➢ select Azure Data Lake Storage Gen2 ➢ click the Continue button ➢ select JSON ➢ click the Continue button ➢ enter a name (I used **AlternativeBrainwaveLocationsJson**) ➢ select the linked service that is bound to the ADLS container from step 1 ➢ enable interactive authoring ➢ wait until interactive authoring is enabled ➢ click the folder image to the right of the File Path text boxes ➢ navigate to the location where you placed the `brainjammerLookUp.json` file from step 1 ➢ select `brainjammerLookUp.json` ➢ click the OK button ➢ and then click the OK button again.
4. Connect the Validation activity to the Lookup activity along the failure path ➢ connect the Lookup activity to the Custom activity ➢ and then click Commit. The result should resemble Figure 6.65.

FIGURE 6.65 Validate batch loads with the Lookup activity

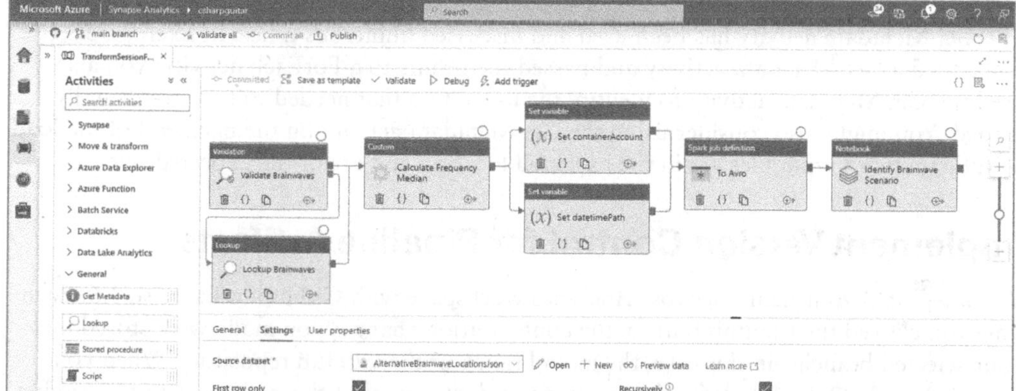

5. To make the Validation activity fail, navigate to the Settings tab of the Validation activity ➢ set the Child Items radio button to False ➢ set the Timeout to 0.00:03:00 ➢ click the Commit button ➢ select the Publish menu item ➢ click the Add Trigger button ➢ select Trigger Now ➢ and then click OK.

When the pipeline is completed, check the output of the Lookup activity. You should see something like the following, which is the first row of the contents of the `brainjammerLookUp.json` file. Retrieving the first row is the default, as you can see by the First Row Only check box in Figure 6.65.

```
{
   "firstRow": {
      "Id": "1",
      "inputLocation": "SessionJson/Meditation/POW",
      "storageAccountContainerName": "brainjammer"
   },...
```

That output is passed into whichever activity comes after the Lookup activity—in this case, the Custom activity that runs an Azure Batch job. The `inputLocation` value contained in the `brainjammerLookUp.json` file is accessible using the following syntax:

```
@{activity('Lookup Brainwaves').output.firstRow.inputLocation}
```

You could conceivably use that syntax to reset the `inputLocation` parameter, or you could change the logic of the Custom activity to use this value.

Get Metadata Pipeline Activity

The Get Metadata activity has been used and discussed numerous times. In Exercise 6.11 you added a Get Metadata activity and passed the results to a ForEach activity; you also used the Get Metadata activity to identify the list of files that needed to be incrementally loaded. You might also consider using the Get Metadata activity on the back end of the load to validate that output files are in the expected location and are of the expected size.

Implement Version Control for Pipeline Artifacts

You integrated your Azure Synapse Analytics workspace with GitHub in Exercise 3.6. Each time you clicked the Commit button, the configuration changes you made were stored into your selected branch—in this case, the main branch of the GitHub repository. When you then clicked the Publish button, the result was a deployment of those changes to the production workspace. If multiple users or developers are working on the same workspace, changes made by a commit will not be available to all users on that workspace until a publish is performed. This may not have been obvious, you have most likely been working through all these examples as an individual, not as a team. In Exercise 3.6 you configured the GitHub repository so that your changes were applied to the main branch, similar to Figure 6.66.

FIGURE 6.66 Implementing version control for pipeline artifacts

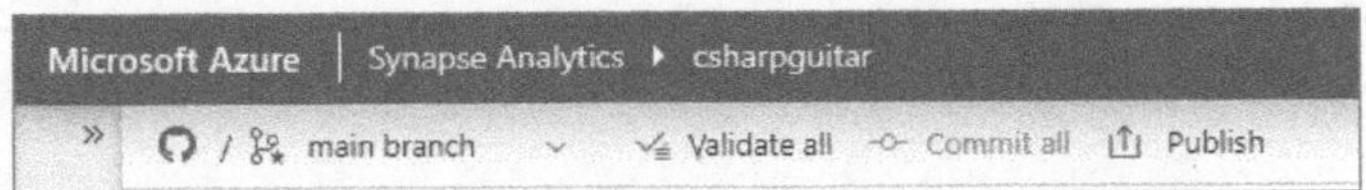

In general, that is not good practice, because you are effectively committing changes and deploying them directly into the production environment. Instead, you need to consider having numerous branches to host your changes that flow through your release process. A release process typically consists of a development, *user acceptance testing (UAT)*, and a production environment. A development environment changes often, and new features or bug fixes are initially created. Once the change is in an acceptable state, the code can be merged with the main branch, which is then deployed to the UAT environment. The environment is much more stable and is often referred to as a preproduction environment. It is the place where your user acceptance and regression testing take place. Once all the changes are approved, the changes can be applied to a branch that is destined for the production environment. CI/CD tools like GitHub Actions or Azure DevOps pipelines are commonly used to perform the release management and deployments through the release management processes.

You now have some experience with GitHub, so Azure DevOps will become the focus. Azure DevOps was introduced in Chapter 1 and briefly touched on in both Chapter 2 and Chapter 3. Azure DevOps provides the same capabilities you find when using GitHub. The choice is mostly a matter of the skill set of the team responsible for release management. Table 6.7 describes the components available in Azure DevOps.

TABLE 6.7 Azure DevOps components

Name	Description
Azure Boards	Tracks work items, new features, code defects, and their status
Azure Repos	A source code version control system (Git and TFVC)
Azure Pipelines	Automated build, test, and deployment service, enabled CI/CD
Azure Test Plans	Browser-based test management solution
Azure Artifacts	Stores and shares dependent packages, libraries, and dependencies

Figure 6.67 illustrates how each of the Azure DevOps components work together to form a release management process that includes CI/CD. The first component is Azure Boards, which you can use to track, log, and assign work to the developers or data engineers on your team. A term commonly used in this context is *work item*. A work item can be a new feature, a bug fix, a documentation request, or pretty much anything that needs to be done to support your data solution. Once the work item is assigned, the individual performing the work will test this on a nonproduction Azure Synapse Analytics workspace. After the changes are tested locally and published, that development workspace will be configured to write changes to a development code branch.

FIGURE 6.67 Implementing version control for pipeline artifacts, Azure DevOps release flow

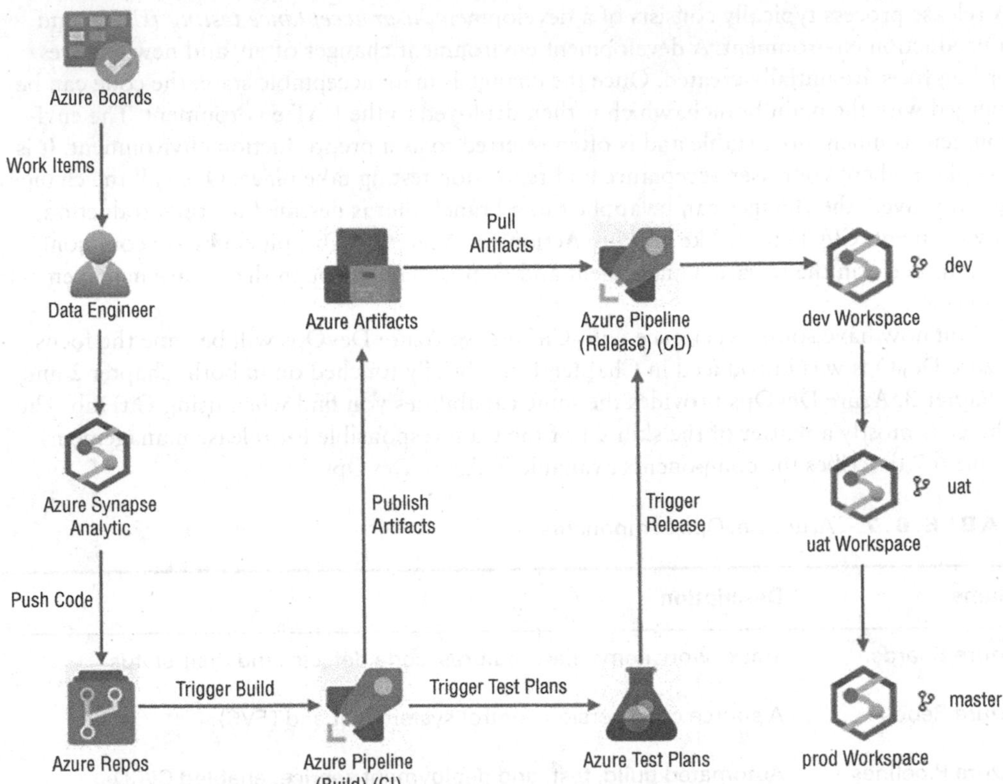

The code and/or configuration changes are pushed to Azure Repos, which is where the production code and configuration are stored. When you first create your Azure DevOps project and Azure repo, there exists only a single branch, typically called the main or master branch. It is common and recommended to have more than a single branch so that multiple individuals can work on the same code for different project deliverables in parallel. Once they both finish, a pull request is made, the code is merged, and it flows through the remainder of the CI/CD process. When the code is committed to the Azure repo branch, it automatically triggers an Azure pipeline, which builds the application. If the build requires the compilation of source code into an executable, for example, this is where that happens. If the application has a dependency on, for example, NuGet packages, npm packages, or some other assembly, Azure Artifacts is referenced to acquire them. It is possible to pull packages directly from the source; however, if you want to make sure each build uses the same exact package or binary, then they can be stored in and retrieved from Azure Artifacts.

Test-driven development (TDD) and basic functional testing should be performed before publishing to both the development and UAT environments. Azure Test Plans is a great tool for managing the status of tests, as well as for signing off on changes that will be deployed into the production environment. Each stage of the release deployment, from development to UAT to production, should require some form of review and approval prior to performing the release to the different environments. If automated testing scenarios are successful, that result can be regarded as an agreement to deploy into the targeted environment. When you have a fully automated process starting from a pull request to change a code, to publish, to development that flows through the other environments, then to production in a matter of minutes or hours, then you have achieved a true CI/CD release process.

Manage Data Pipelines

When you attempt to manage something, you must first know in some detail what it is you are managing. In this context, you need to manage a pipeline in Azure Synapse Analytics. Annotations can help you get a quick overview of what your pipelines do. If you open one of the pipelines you have created and select the Properties icon, as shown in Figure 6.68, in addition to the description, you can add an annotation, which links a searchable keyword to the pipeline.

FIGURE 6.68 Manage data pipeline annotations

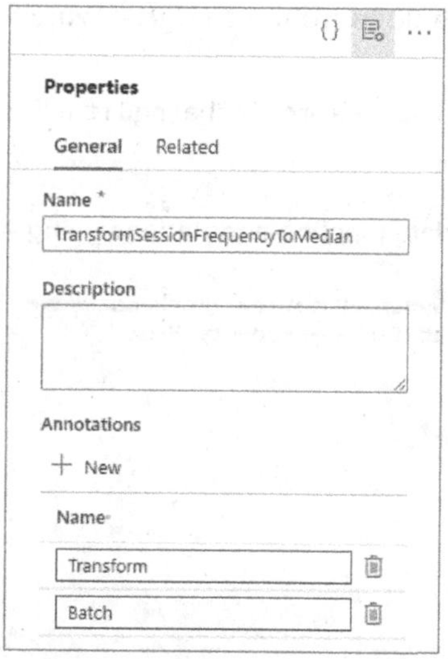

You can add annotations to pipelines, datasets, linked services, and triggers. You use annotations to search and filter resources. Annotations are similar to tags, which you read about earlier. You can view annotations via the Pipeline Runs page in the Monitor hub, which is covered in Chapter 9. You can also see annotations by using Azure PowerShell with the following snippet. Figure 6.69 shows the result.

```
Get-AzSynapsePipeline -WorkspaceName "csharpguitar" |
Format-Table -Property Name, Activities, Annotations
```

FIGURE 6.69 Managing data pipeline annotations using Azure PowerShell

```
PS C:\> Get-AzSynapsePipeline -WorkspaceName "csharpguitar" | Format-Table -Property Name, Activities, Annotations

Name                                     Activities                                                                Annotations
----                                     ----------                                                                -----------
IngestTransformBrainwaveReadings         {MoveToTmpReading, CreatePopulateFactReading}                             {Ingest}
IngestTransformBrainwaveReadingsSpark    {MoveToTmpReading, TranformReadingsParquet}                               {Transform, Parquet}
TransformEnrichment                      {DROP Tables, SETUP Staging, FILTER Outliers, CREATE FactREADING...}      {Transform, Enrich}
TransformSessionFrequencyToMedian        {Calculate Frequency Median, To Avro, Identify Brainwave Scenario,...}    {Transform, Batch}
ExporitoryDataAnalysis                   {Execute Pipeline ITBR, Execute Pipeline ITBRS, Execute Pipeline...}      {Explore}
IncrementalTransformSessionFrequencyT... {Get Brainwaves, ForEachBrainwaveFile}                                    {Ingest}
IncrementalBrainwaveCopy                 {Copy Brainwaves}                                                         {Ingest}
```

Using that Azure PowerShell cmdlet not only provides the annotations for each pipeline, but you can also get a list of all the activities that run within it, which leads nicely to a good approach to take when you need to manage a pipeline. When managing a pipeline, it is helpful to break it down into smaller pieces, and then determine what needs to be monitored for them to work as expected. You can break a pipeline into activities (see Figure 6.69), data flows, notebooks, SQL scripts, compute pools, etc. Here are some Azure PowerShell cmdlets that can help get better insights into the different components of your pipeline. The following snippet retrieves all the data flows from the targets Azure Synapse Analytics workspace, as illustrated in Figure 6.70.

```
Get-AzSynapseDataFlow -WorkspaceName "csharpguitar" |
Format-Table -Property Name
```

FIGURE 6.70 Managing data pipeline annotations using Azure PowerShell data flow

```
PS C:\> Get-AzSynapseDataFlow -WorkspaceName "csharpguitar"
      | Format-Table -Property Name

Name
----
Ch04Ex07-flowlet
Ch04Ex07
Ch04Ex12
Ch05Ex03
Ch05Ex06
Ch05Ex13F
Ch06Ex09
Ch06Ex10
Ch06Ex10a
```

The following code provides a list of all the notebooks, followed by the cmdlet for listing out the SQL scripts and Spark pools. Figure 6.71 shows the results of the Get-AzSynapseSparkPool cmdlet which displays the spark pools in the given workspace.

```
Get-AzSynapseNotebook -WorkspaceName "csharpguitar"
| Format-Table -Property Name

Get-AzSynapseSqlScript -workspaceName "csharpguitar"
| Format-Table -Property Name

Get-AzSynapseSparkPool -WorkspaceName "csharpguitar"
| Format-Table -Property Name, SparkVersion, NodeSize, NodeSizeFamily
```

FIGURE 6.71 Managing data pipeline annotations using Azure PowerShell Spark pool

```
PS C:\> Get-AzSynapseSparkPool -WorkspaceName "csharpguitar"
        | Format-Table -Property Name, SparkVersion, NodeSize, NodeSizeFamily

Name           SparkVersion NodeSize NodeSizeFamily
----           ------------ -------- --------------
SparkPool      3.1          Small    MemoryOptimized
SparkPoolv2    2.4          Medium   MemoryOptimized
SparkpoolXLv2  2.4          XLarge   MemoryOptimized
SparkPoolBatch 3.1          Small    MemoryOptimized
```

There also exists the option to list datasets, linked services, SQL pools, and all other resources necessary to effectively manage your pipeline.

Manage Spark Jobs in a Pipeline

The following Azure PowerShell cmdlets provide an overview of the Spark job definition activities you have on your workspace:

```
$pool = Get-AzSynapseSparkPool -WorkspaceName "csharpguitar" `
                               -SparkPoolName SparkPoolBatch
$pool | Get-AzSynapseSparkJob

$ws = Get-AzSynapseWorkspace -Name "csharpguitar"
$ws | Get-AzSynapseSparkJobDefinition -Name ToAvro
```

Each cmdlet provides the details about the configuration and existence of Spark jobs in the targeted workspace. The information is available using a browser; however, you need to look at each one individually. If there are many of them, that is not optimal. Instead, you can create a nice report that displays all the information you need. Generally, a Spark job definition activity targets a main definition file, which is typically hosted on an ADLS container. In case of exceptions or pipeline run failures due to this activity, you would first want to make sure this location and the file are where they should be. The cmdlet which retrives the job definition file provided previously is helpful with doing that. The arguments passed to the file and the Apache Spark pool that the job will run on are also important components of managing a Spark job. Chapter 9 discusses monitoring and managing pipelines in more detail.

Handle Failed Batch Loads

Monitoring and troubleshooting pipelines that contain batch loads is covered in more detail in Chapter 9 and Chapter 10. An option for handling a failed batch load is to add a Fail activity to the pipeline. To execute a batch job as part of a pipeline, you know that it runs within a Custom activity. When the Custom activity completes, it produces output that can be referenced using syntax like the following:

```
@activity('<Activity Name>').output.exitcode
```

If you connect the Fail activity to the failure path from the Custom activity, you can capture some information about the failure. Figure 6.72 illustrates how this looks.

FIGURE 6.72 Handling failed batch loads

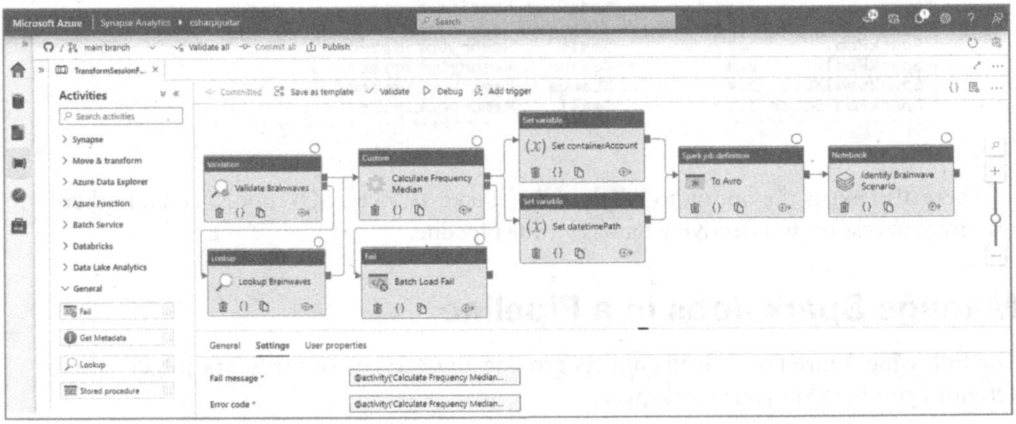

The `exitcode` provides a starting point to further determine the cause of the failure. Using this information can help determine which actions need to be taken. The output of the Custom activity also provides links to the `stdout.txt` and `stderr.txt` files, which can be very helpful as well. There is an additional complexity that has to do with data corruption. It is one thing to be alerted about a failed batch load, but where and when in the code path execution did it fail? Did it partially transform data, or did it go rogue and enter some bad data that will cause problems downstream? You have learned a bit about how to manage that situation in this chapter. So, regardless of the complexity, you should have the skill set that helps you respond to this kind of situation.

Summary

This chapter focused on designing and developing a batch processing solution. Your memory was refreshed about the batch layer portion of the lambda architecture and how it is responsible for incrementally loading the data along the cold path into the serving layer. Batch processing, when implemented in an Azure Synapse Analytics pipeline, runs within a Custom activity. The Custom activity is bound to an Azure Batch account that provides the nodes for executing the data transformation logic. There also exists the capability for running batch jobs in Azure Databricks using workflows, jobs, and notebooks. There are numerous approaches for scheduling the execution of batch jobs. Both Azure Synapse Analytics pipelines and Azure Databricks support triggering based on a schedule that uses date, time, and recurrence. Other triggering options, such as tumbling windows, storage events, and custom events, are found only with Azure Synapse Analytics and Azure Data Factory pipelines.

Batch job solutions are notoriously complicated due to the many upstream and downstream dependencies. In addition, handling missing data, duplicate data, and late-arriving data scenarios requires some special knowledge and procedures. Determining the significance of the missing or duplicate data is an important step in the decision process of whether to delete or correct the data. Using upsert capabilities and incremental loading of data are essential parts of correcting such scenarios.

Validating batch loads using the Validation and Lookup activities is very helpful in determining if the batch process ran as expected. Checking whether the files to be processed exist before processing and that the output files are expected are part of this validation. Managing the batch loads using Azure PowerShell or the Azure CLI provides a quick and simple overview of all your pipelines, datasets, activities, linked services, etc., in a single report. Finally, you learned about Azure DevOps, its many components, and how they all work together to implement CI/CD.

Exam Essentials

Azure Batch. Azure Batch is a high-performance computing product that offers nodes capable of processing the largest amounts of datasets that exist. When you run batch jobs in an Azure Synapse Analytics pipeline, the data processing takes place on an Azure Batch node. The nodes are highly scalable and can process tasks concurrently and in parallel.

Tumbling window. A pipeline that is scheduled using a tumbling window trigger is done so due to upstream dependencies. Therefore, if the upstream batch job the current batch job depends on is delayed, the batch job will wait and delay its execution until the upstream job is completed.

Event Grid. When a custom event trigger is created and bound to a pipeline, the event that triggers the batch job will come from an Event Grid event. A consumer like a pipeline can sign up to be notified about an event by hooking into an Event Grid topic, while an Event Grid subscription is where the event producer sends the event when it happens.

Upserting data. Upsert capabilities are built into the sink element contained in a Data Flow activity. Once the sink is configured, it is up to the platform to determine if an `INSERT` or `UPDATE` statement is necessary to load the data row into the target. You can also manually implement the `MERGE` SQL command to perform upsert activities.

Incremental data load. You should apply changes only after the initial load of source data into your data lake, which typically contains a large amount of data. This decreases costs, and the amount of data being copied is less, so it happens faster. You can use the last modified date of the file or a watermark to determine which files or data rows need to be included in the incremental load.

Review Questions

Many questions can have more than a single answer. Please select all choices which are true.

1. Which of the following pipeline activities would you use to validate a batch load?
   - A. Fail
   - B. Validation
   - C. Lookup
   - D. Notebook
2. The lambda architecture consists of which of the following layers?
   - A. Servicing
   - B. Batch
   - C. Enriched
   - D. Speed
3. Which Azure Synapse Analytics pipeline activity is used for running batch jobs?
   - A. Copy Data
   - B. U-SQL
   - C. Execute Pipeline
   - D. Custom
4. Which of the following trigger types will run only after an upstream dependent trigger has successfully completed?
   - A. Schedule
   - B. Storage event
   - C. Tumbling window
   - D. Custom event
5. Which of the following trigger types will trigger an Azure Synapse Analytics pipeline when a file is added to an Azure Blob Storage container?
   - A. Schedule
   - B. Storage event
   - C. Tumbling window
   - D. Custom event
6. Which of the following are useful for upserting data?
   - A. The `MERGE` SQL command
   - B. Watermarks
   - C. File metadata
   - D. Directory structures that include a date

7. What is an incremental data load?
   - **A.** Copying source data to a data lake
   - **B.** Copying changes from a data source to a data lake
   - **C.** Moving source data to a data lake
   - **D.** Moving changes from a data source to a data lake
8. Which of the following can you use to mark your Azure Synapse Analytics pipeline with a flag that is searchable and filterable?
   - **A.** An annotation
   - **B.** A tag
   - **C.** A pipeline variable
   - **D.** A pipeline global parameter
9. Which data flow transformation is useful for filtering out duplicates during data ingestion?
   - **A.** Select
   - **B.** Aggregate
   - **C.** Flatten
   - **D.** Filter
10. Which of the following are important security and compliance topics of interest?
    - **A.** Networking
    - **B.** .NET version
    - **C.** Endpoint security
    - **D.** Backup and recovery

Design and Implement a Data Stream Processing Solution

EXAM DP-203 OBJECTIVES COVERED IN THIS CHAPTER:

- ✓ Develop a stream processing solution
- ✓ Ingest and transform data
- ✓ Monitor data storage and data processing

Data streaming has become widespread through the implementation of LTE, 4G, and 5G devices and the ever-increasing sophistication of IoT sensors. Devices connected to LTE, 4G, or 5G networks can stream data constantly due to the high availability of network endpoints. Prior to the LTE, 4G, and 5G protocols, devices depended on Wi-Fi or Ethernet network connections based on IEEE 802 standards, which were not as widely accessible. The ease of access to globally connected networks has increased the volume and velocity of streamable data. This ease of network access has driven the necessity to create products and solutions that can ingest these high-velocity and high-volume data streams. Figure 7.1 illustrates a streaming solution using Azure products and services that consume, process, store, and present streamed data.

FIGURE 7.1 Azure stream processing

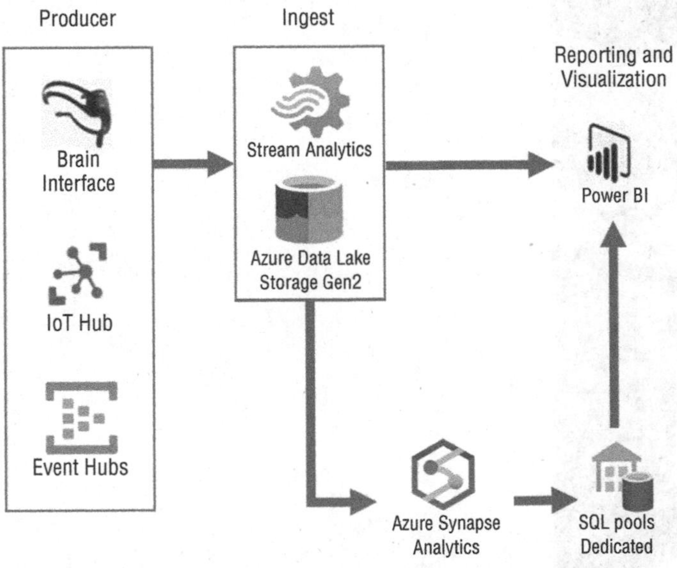

Both Azure IoT Hub and Azure Event Hubs are highly scalable and designed for ingesting very large amounts of data with high availability and low latency. The Basic tier for these products supports 1,000 events per second, while the Dedicated tier has no limit. As the data streams ingest into these endpoints, the data can be stored into your data lake for near real-time processing or processed in real time using Azure Stream Analytics. Analytic processes that require a bit more transformation can pass through Azure Synapse Analytics and get stored into a dedicated SQL pool. But for insights that need quick visualization and/or alerting, the data can flow directly to a product like Power BI for immediate consumption.

The Azure platform also includes the support for non-Microsoft products for the ingestion, storage, and processing of streamed data. Customers who already have a streaming solution based on these products and wish to gain the benefits of the cloud can migrate them to the Azure platform. Apache Kafka, which is a message ingestion endpoint, is readily available and supported with the Azure platform. Kafka is available as a cluster type with HDInsight. Storm in HDInsight 3.6, Apache Spark, and Hive are also available with HDInsight, providing stream processing and data storage capabilities. As an alternative to migrating your entire HDInsight solution to Azure, you can send Kafka event messages to Event Hubs. Then you can use, for example, Azure Stream Analytics to process the event messages and pass them along to the consumers. This would avoid the added burden of provisioning and managing the administrative overhead of HDInsight.

Develop a Stream Processing Solution

There are many reasons companies or individuals would want to analyze data streams. The overriding theme in this book is the analysis of brain wave measurements collected through a BCI while performing different activities, referred to as scenarios. The primary objective is to use exploratory data analysis (EDA) to find patterns that are specific to each scenario, then use those patterns to identify a scenario based on brain wave patterns in real time. In addition to that objective, the collected data is useful for additional purposes like testing new devices to determine if the reading is recorded the same. For example, in a meditation scenario, the `ALPHA` reading should be somewhere between 4.3924 and 5.0287. If this is not the case on a different device or when a software version on the current device is updated, then that would be a problem. That would mean that once the device changes or is updated, the data collected is not really useful for determining the scenario in real time anymore, since the BCI captures the wavelengths differently. Anomaly detection is another scenario where the collection, real-time streaming, and analysis of data are beneficial. From a brain wave perspective, after enough EDA is performed to find measurements that define a healthy brain, when readings fall outside that range, it might highlight some damage. Learning this might result in some actions taken to get the brain back into an expected state. Monitoring stock price or network traffic are also areas where real-time anomaly detection can be worthwhile. The former may earn some money, and the latter may identify and halt malicious activities.

Regardless of which scenario your data stream processing solution is expected to perform, there are some common considerations that apply. The considerations are common because the requirements of a data stream processing solution are mostly the same. In every scenario you need an ingestion point specifically designed to handle a high velocity level of incoming data. You require a tool to transform, filter, and aggregate that data in real time. Finally, you need a place to store and view the insights found from the data stream. The following section provides the details required to design and develop such a solution. In addition, there are some explanations of concepts that apply specifically to data streaming solutions that can help you better ingest, transform, analyze, and deliver the data for consumption.

Design a Stream Processing Solution

Before you begin piecing together the different Azure products for your data stream processing solution, you should first spend some time identifying your requirements. Choosing the products for running your data stream processing solution comes toward the end of your design phase. After identifying the constraints for your solution, the list of pertinent products will be much smaller. Also, by defining these constraints, you may uncover other products you might not have considered but which turn out to be a better fit. For example, Azure Functions, Azure Service Bus, or Azure App Service WebJobs have not come into the discussion in the data streaming context but do provide some streaming capabilities.

Data Stream Processing Considerations

The following sections discuss many of the decision points and considerations that will enable you to choose the product that best fits your requirements. For a quick overview of capabilities per product-oriented solution, see Table 7.1.

TABLE 7.1 Streaming product capabilities

Feature	Azure Stream Analytics	Azure Databricks	HDInsight with Spark Streaming	HDInsight 3.6 with Storm
Temporal / Windowing	Yes	Yes	Yes	Yes
Data Format	AVRO, JSON, or CSV	Any	Any	Any
Paradigm	Declarative	Both	Both	Imperative
Language	SQL, JavaScript	C#/F#, Scala, R, Python, Java	C#/F#, Scala, R, Python, Java	C#, Java
Pricing	Stream units	Databricks unit	Cluster hour	Cluster hour

In addition to the features in Table 7.1, a more detailed description of real-time vs. near real-time streaming, interoperability, and scaling are discussed. Each of those factors will have some influence on the products you choose to design and develop your data stream solution with.

Real-Time and Near Real-Time

Figure 7.1 illustrates a general architectural data streaming design, in that there is an ingestion, a transformation, and a presentation component. Splitting Figure 7.1 into a more granular solution so that it can distinctly demonstrate the difference between real-time and near real-time data streaming processing is warranted. Figure 7.2 illustrates how a real-time data stream processing solution could look. In a later exercise, Exercise 7.1, you will create a real-time data streaming solution similar to that shown in Figure 7.2. A solution like this is also often referred to as live streaming.

FIGURE 7.2 Azure real-time stream processing

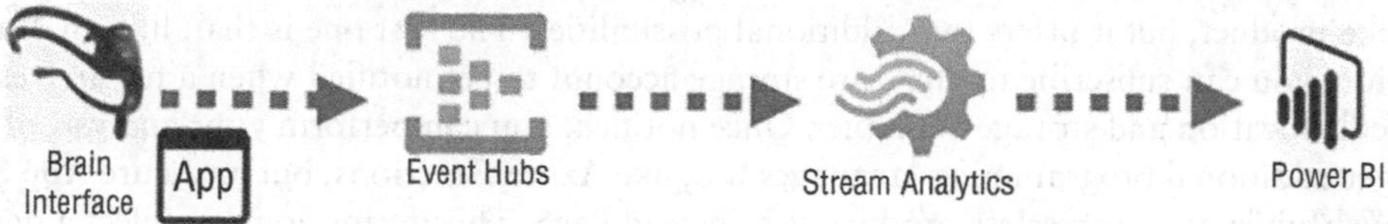

The data stream is being generated from an IoT device or an application that is sent directly to the Event Hub namespace. An Azure Stream Analytics job that has that Event Hub namespace configured as an input receives the data stream immediately upon arrival into the event hub. Remember that you provisioned the Event Hub namespace in Exercise 3.16 and provisioned and configured an Azure Stream Analytics job in Exercise 3.17. Finally, the output of the results is streamed, also in real time, to a Power BI workspace for visualization. As shown in Figure 7.3, instead of being streamed directly into the Azure Stream Analytics job, the data can be persisted on an ADLS container.

FIGURE 7.3 Azure near real-time stream processing

Once the data is stored on the ADLS container, you can decide when to process the data. This near real-time or on-demand approach can result in lower costs, as you can decide when to process the data and make the batch sizes smaller, which requires less compute power. If the data stream is not time-critical and you can wait some minutes or tens of minutes before it becomes available, then this method is much more cost efficient. An Azure

Stream Analytics job does support an Azure Blob Storage container as an input stream, in addition to IoT and Event Hubs. Therefore, in this scenario, as shown in Figure 7.3, instead of Event Hubs being configured as the input stream, the Azure Blob Container (i.e., the ADLS container) is configured. Once the data in the blob file in the ADLS container is processed, it becomes visible via a Power BI workspace. Alternatives to using Azure Stream Analytics in a near real-time scenario are Azure Functions and Azure App Service WebJobs, both of which were introduced in Chapter 1, "Gaining the Azure Data Engineer Associate Certification." Azure Functions supports subscribing to events that happen on an Azure Blob container, for example, when a file is written to it. Therefore, an Azure function can be used to process the persisted file, the same as Azure Stream Analytics. Azure Functions has no built-in interface with Power BI, which means you would need to manually build support for that. As shown in Table 7.1, you can use SQL and JavaScript in Azure Stream Analytics. An Azure function supports most programming languages; therefore, most solutions you design can be achieved with custom code. An Azure App Service WebJob can be viewed as a batch job–like product, but it offers two additional possibilities. The first one is that, like an Azure function, you can subscribe to an Azure storage account to get notified when a file arrives at a specific location and storage container. Once notified, you can perform your analysis of it. You get additional programming languages too, like Azure Functions, but an Azure App Service WebJob is not a serverless product; it is instead PaaS. This means you can select a dedicated amount of compute power to execute your processing that is always online and ready to process. Additionally, you can run other App Service Web Apps on the same host to share compute power and reduce costs. Table 7.2 provides a structured view of Azure Functions and Azure App Service WebJobs.

TABLE 7.2 Additional streaming product capabilities

Feature	Azure Functions	WebJobs
Temporal/Windowing	No	No
Data Format	Any	Any
Paradigm	Imperative	Imperative
Languages	C#, F#, Java, Node.js, Python	C#, Java, Node.js, PHP, Python
Pricing	Per execution	Per plan hour

Note that for certain scenarios, as previously stated, Azure Functions and WebJobs are valid product choices for near real-time data streaming solutions.

Temporal Windows

Chapter 3, "Data Sources and Ingestion," introduced the temporal concept, which focuses on data that is valid at a specific moment in time or in a given time frame. A temporal table, also referred to as a history table, can be seen in Figure 3.20. The meaning is the same in the context of a data stream processing solution. The primary difference is the time frame. In the serving layer context, the time frame could be years, months, weeks, or days, whereas in the data stream processing context, seconds and perhaps minutes are used most often. Chapter 3 includes detailed coverage of temporal windows available in Azure Stream Analytics. As you might recall, they are hopping, session, sliding, snapshot, and tumbling. The following code snippet is an example of a query that stores the result in a temporal tumbling window:

```
SELECT
    System.TimeStamp() AS IngestionTime,
    PERCENTILE_CONT(0.5) OVER (ORDER BY brainwaves.ALPHA) AS medianAPLHA,
    PERCENTILE_CONT(0.5) OVER (ORDER BY brainwaves.BETA_H) AS medianBETA_H,
    PERCENTILE_CONT(0.5) OVER (ORDER BY brainwaves.BETA_L) AS medianBETA_L,
    PERCENTILE_CONT(0.5) OVER (ORDER BY brainwaves.GAMMA) AS medianGAMMA,
    PERCENTILE_CONT(0.5) OVER (ORDER BY brainwaves.THETA) AS medianTHETA
INTO powerBI
FROM brainwaves
GROUP BY IngestionTime, TumblingWindow(second, 5)
```

Each brain wave reading sent to Azure Stream Analytics over a 5-second time frame is bundled together into a window. The data is received from the input named `brainwaves`, which you created and configured in Exercise 3.17. Then the `SELECT` statement, which calculates median values per frequency, is performed on the data that was received in that 5-second window. The median values are then sent to output named `powerBI` for consumption and visualization.

Data Format

As you saw in Table 7.1, the only stream product that does not support all standard data formats is Azure Stream Analytics, which currently supports only UTF-8, JSON, CSV, and AVRO; Azure Stream Analytics does not support the Parquet, XML, and ORC file types. If your streaming solution requires those file types, then you need to find another streaming product, such as Azure Databricks or HDInsight. Chapter 2, "CREATE DATABASE dbName; GO," discussed the most common file types used for data analytics, and Chapter 3 provided some additional information about the data formats and file types that have to do specifically with designing an Azure Data Lake solution.

Programming Paradigm

As shown in Table 7.1, Azure Stream Analytics supports only the declarative programming paradigm. The database querying language T-SQL is one of the most common declarative programming languages. Since the Stream Analytics query language is a subset of T-SQL Azure Stream Analytics, it is clearly declarative. A few differences between declarative and imperative programming have to do with control flow and idempotency. Control flow is what distinguishes declarative from imperative, in that control flow is not described in the declarative paradigm. That means that in the declarative programming paradigm, your approach is to define what you want the code to do, but you do not control exactly how it gets done. The example SQL statement in the "Temporal Windows" section illustrates this. The SQL statement is clear on what you want but does not dictate how to perform the computation. If the SQL statement ran procedurally, it would run the `INTO` command before the `FROM` command, which might result in placing the data into the output before it knows where to get the input from. The order (the control flow) is not relevant in the declarative paradigm. Consider the following Python HDInsight 3.6 Storm code snippet, which is imperative:

```
import storm
def process(self, tup):
    words = tup.values[0].split()
    for word in words:
        storm.logInfo("Emitting %s" % word)
        count = self._counter[word] +=1
        storm.emit([word, count])
```

An imperative program comprises commands the computer will perform. The code snippet describes how the program operates, step-by-step. Objects, like `words`, are instantiated, and assignments are made to both `words` and `word`, which are further traits of the imperative programming paradigm. The other difference between these two paradigms has to do with idempotency. Idempotency, in computer terms, means that a method or code snippet that is run multiple times returns the same expected results. An idempotent algorithm does not have to keep track of whether the operation has been triggered before. The Python code snippet provided earlier is not idempotent, because the emitted value would contain an unexpected `count` value, meaning the result of the method invocation would not be the same when run multiple times. If your data analytics require a lot of control over how the data should be processed, then you would need to choose a streaming product other than Azure Stream Analytics. Alternatively, if you need to only define what you want and let the underlying technology decide the best means for providing you that, then you can use one of the other declarative streaming products available on Azure.

Programming Language

The decision which programming language to use for streaming involves a few items. First, you need to know the skill sets of the people who will develop the code. It would be prudent to avoid a programming language that requires your current development staff to be retrained. If your staff is skilled with C#, you should lean heavily toward that language, but if Python is more in use, then you should use it. Another item that influences your choice of programming languages is based on what you saw in Table 7.1. The question is whether the product you want to use to implement your streaming solution supports that language. And, finally, it would make sense to keep the programming language the same across the entire data analytics solution. For example, the code written to send messages to Azure Event Hubs, the streaming product that analyzes the messages in near real time or real time, and any additional processing or presentation that happens after that, should all be created using the same language. There are many products that require programming, so you need to have a high-level overview of them all and try to keep the variety of programming languages to a minimum.

Interoperability

One of the more challenging aspects of creating an end-to-end IT solution is determining which systems and technologies can work together. One of the decision points discussed in the previous section had to do with choosing a programming language. As mentioned, you should attempt to select a language that works across the numerous products that make up your data analytics architecture. However, you first need to determine which products can be used with each other. Figure 7.4 illustrates the input interoperability between Azure products. For example, Event Hubs, IoT Hub, and Blob Storage can be used to send data to Azure Stream Analytics. If you need to send data from an Azure Service Bus or a Cosmos DB, you could not use Azure Stream Analytics and would instead likely choose an Azure WebJob.

FIGURE 7.4 Input interoperability in Azure products

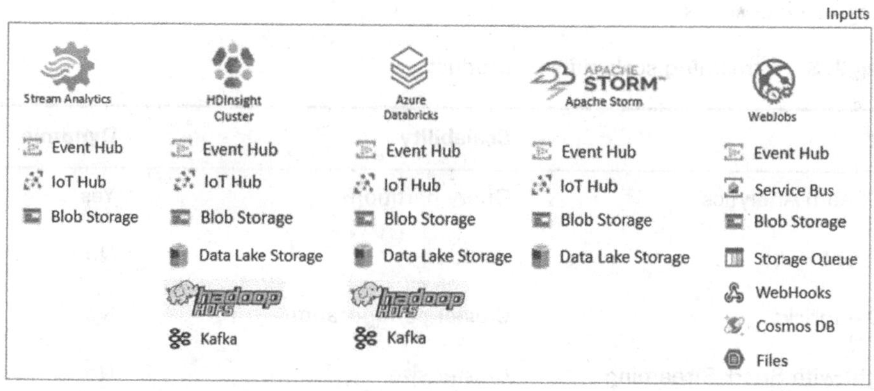

Input interoperability is not your only concern. Both the input and the sink (output) that your solution requires must be supported. Figure 7.5 illustrates the sink interoperability between Azure products.

FIGURE 7.5 Sink interoperability in Azure products

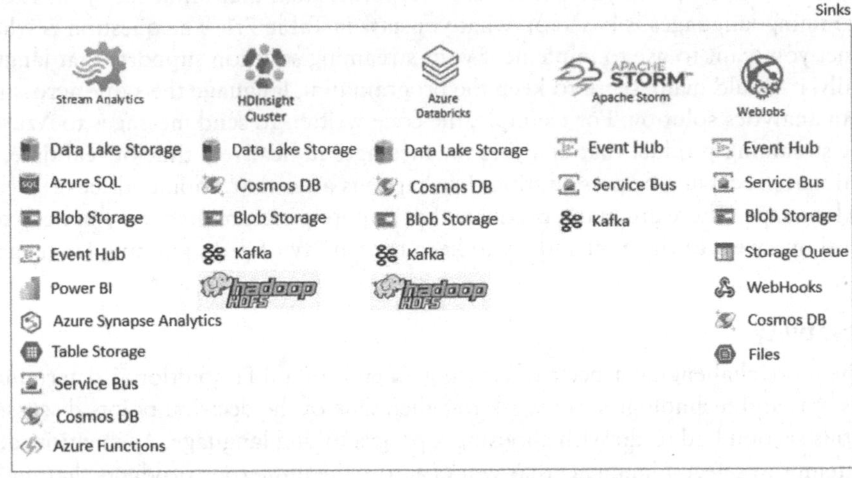

If your input is an event hub and your sink is an Azure storage queue, then, again, you cannot use Azure Stream Analytics. An Azure WebJob could fulfill this requirement as well.

Scaling

Chapter 10, "Troubleshoot Data Storage Processing," discusses performance and scaling techniques, but this is an appropriate place to introduce these concepts in the context of streaming products. It is important to know how each product scales when an unexpected burst of data is sent to it. Table 7.3 provides some information about how each Azure streaming product scales.

TABLE 7.3 Streaming scalability by product

Product	Scalability	Dynamic
Azure Stream Analytics	Query partition	Yes
Azure Event Hubs	Partition	No
Azure Databricks	Cluster configuration	No
HDInsight with Spark Streaming	Cluster size	No
HDInsight 3.6 with Storm	Cluster size	No
Azure Functions	Up to 200 parallel instances	Yes
Azure WebJobs	Up to 100 parallel instances	Yes

Scaling basically identifies how additional compute power is allocated to the Azure product when more is required. If the CPUs are maxing out at 100 percent or memory is being consumed, a queue can form, slowing down the ingestion of the stream. Adding another machine to the resource pool could help get the incoming data back under control. Azure Stream Analytics scales based on partitions. If you remember back in Exercise 3.17 when you added the Event Hub input named `brainwaves` to a Azure Stream Analytics job, there was a property named Partition Key. If the data being streamed is partitioned by a key, then you would gain some scaling efficiencies had you added a value there. Something like `electrodeId` or `frequencyId` are examples that could be applicable here. Then, as shown in Figure 7.6, you can scale out to a static or dynamic number of *streaming units (SU)* that can process data bound to the configured partition. A SU is a combination of CPU and memory allocated for processing streamed data.

FIGURE 7.6 Azure Stream Analytics scaling

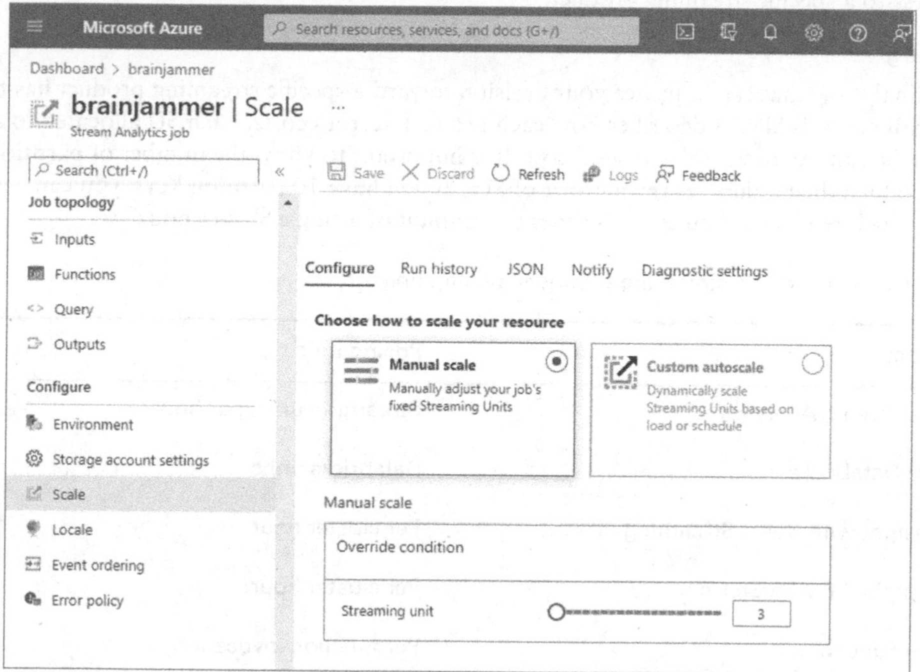

In Exercise 3.14 you provisioned and configured an Azure Databricks cluster. As shown in Figure 3.65, you set the Worker Type option to identify the amount of memory and the number of cores. You also set the Min Workers and Max Workers options to represent the available capacity. The platform will manage the execution of tasks on those workers; however, it will not increase or decrease them any more or less than what they are configured to be. For HDInsight, refer to Figure 3.86, where you learned that a similar configuration option can be used for each HDInsight node type, in that you can configure the node size and number of nodes for each node type running inside your HDInsight cluster. This configuration represents the maximum amount of compute capacity allocated to the cluster for performing data ingestion and transformation. Finally, Azure Functions and Azure WebJobs scale out to a maximum number of instances, where an instance is a dedicated one-, two-, or four-core VM. When a dedicated scale out happens, an exact replica of the VM running your code is configured and added to the compute farm to perform the programed computations. The maximum number of instances is provided in Table 7.3, but you can ask Microsoft to allocate more. Which kind of scaling meets the needs of your data analytics solution? The variety of node sizes is much greater when it comes to HDInsight and Azure Databricks; however, they will only scale out to the maximum number you have configured. While Azure Stream Analytics, Azure Functions, and Azure WebJobs have fewer types of VM SKUs, they will scale out to a very large number of them. Knowing if you need a fixed number of very powerful machines or a flexible number of strong machines can drive your decision-making process to a specific streaming product.

Pricing

The final topic that can influence your decision toward a specific streaming product has to do with price. Table 7.4 describes how each product accrues costs. Each SU allocated to an Azure Stream Analytics job carries a cost. It is important to know the number of partition keys, which then influences the number of SUs. If you have 10 partition keys, you can get 10 SUs, which renders a change of 10 times the amount of a single SU per hour.

TABLE 7.4 Azure streaming products' pricing units

Product	Pricing unit
Azure Stream Analytics	Streaming units per hour
Azure Databricks	Databricks units
HDInsight with Spark Streaming	Per cluster hour
HDInsight 3.6 with Storm	Per cluster hour
Azure Functions	Per function invocation
Azure WebJobs	Per app service hour

A *Databrick Unit (DBU)* is similar to a SU in that it represents the consumed CPU and memory over a given time period—in this case, an hour. For HDInsight, you may have noticed that the cost is estimated during its provisioning. Depending on the size and number of nodes, the cost is calculated per hour of consumption. An Azure function is charged based on the number of times it is executed, which makes it very cost effective. Azure WebJobs are charged in the same way as an Azure App Service, in that it depends on the size of the VM on which the Azure WebJob is placed, and are charged by the hour of consumption. There is no charge when the Azure WebJob is not running. Finding the most optimal cost for running your data analytics workloads is a very important factor when choosing not only an Azure streaming product, but any product you will use on the Azure platform.

Lambda Architecture

The last remaining layer of the lambda architecture to be covered in this book is the speed layer. Figure 3.13 illustrates all three lambda architecture layers. The serving layer was introduced in Chapter 3 and implemented in Chapter 4, "The Storage of Data." In Chapter 6, "Create and Manage Batch Processing and Pipelines," you implemented the batch layer, which completed the Data Flow through the cold path. The speed layer is the layer that ingests and transforms data through the hot path and most commonly is ingested using a streaming solution. The speed layer typically receives data generated by IoT devices sent through some kind of message ingestion endpoint. Those endpoints are, for example, Event Hubs, IoT Hub, or Kafka. Then any of the products described in Table 7.1 and 7.2 can be used to perform transformation to the streamed data. As shown in Figure 3.13, the output of the streaming product (such as Power BI) can be transmitted in real time to a consumer for visualization. The streamed data can also be placed on the serving layer for near real-time consumption. A summarized illustration of this is shown in Figure 7.7.

FIGURE 7.7 Lambda architecture speed layer, near real-time processing

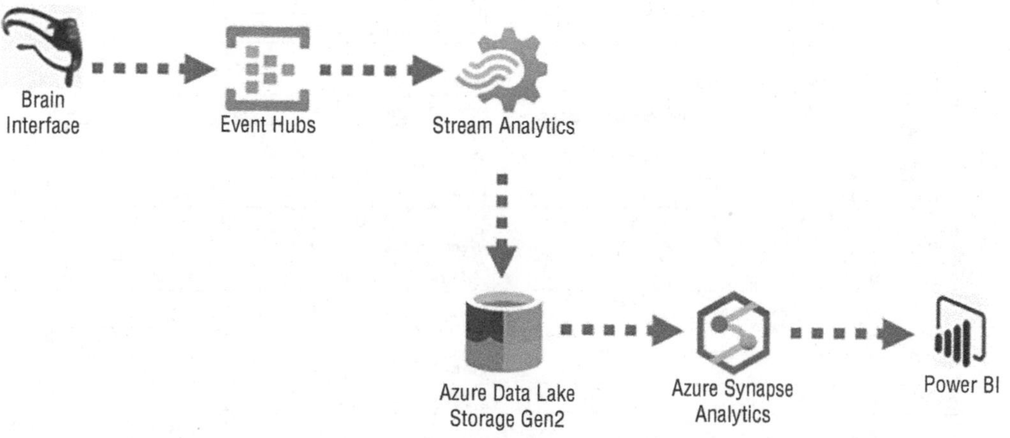

Figure 7.7 illustrates data being streamed from a BCI to an Event Hubs namespace. The data stream is then ingested by an Azure Stream Analytics job, transformed, and stored on an ADLS container. Additional transformations can be performed via an Azure Synapse Analytics pipeline to add any late arriving data, perform upserts, and find additional business insights. Once the pipeline runs, the data can then be consumed and visualized, for example, by Power BI. Complete Exercise 7.1, where you will configure Azure Stream Analytics to store a data stream on an ADLS container.

EXERCISE 7.1

Add an Output ADLS Container to an Azure Stream Analytics Job

1. Log in to the Azure portal at `https://portal.azure.com` ➢ navigate to the Azure Stream Analytics job you created in Exercise 3.17 ➢ select Outputs from the navigation menu on the Outputs blade ➢ select the + Add drop-down menu ➢ and then select Blob Storage.
2. Enter a name (I used **ADLS**) ➢ select the Select Blob Storage/ADLS Gen2 from the Your Subscription radio button ➢ select the subscription ➢ select the Azure storage account you created in Exercise 3.1 ➢ select the Use Existing radio button in the Container section ➢ select the ADLS container you want to store the data in (I used **brainjammer**) ➢ select Connection String from the Authentication Mode drop-down list ➢ and then enter the following into the Path Pattern text box:

   `EMEA/brainjammer/in/{date}/{time}`
3. Set the Date Format field to `YYYY/MM/DD`, and then set the Time Format field to HH. Figure 7.8 shows how the configuration should look.

FIGURE 7.8 Azure Stream Analytics ADLS output

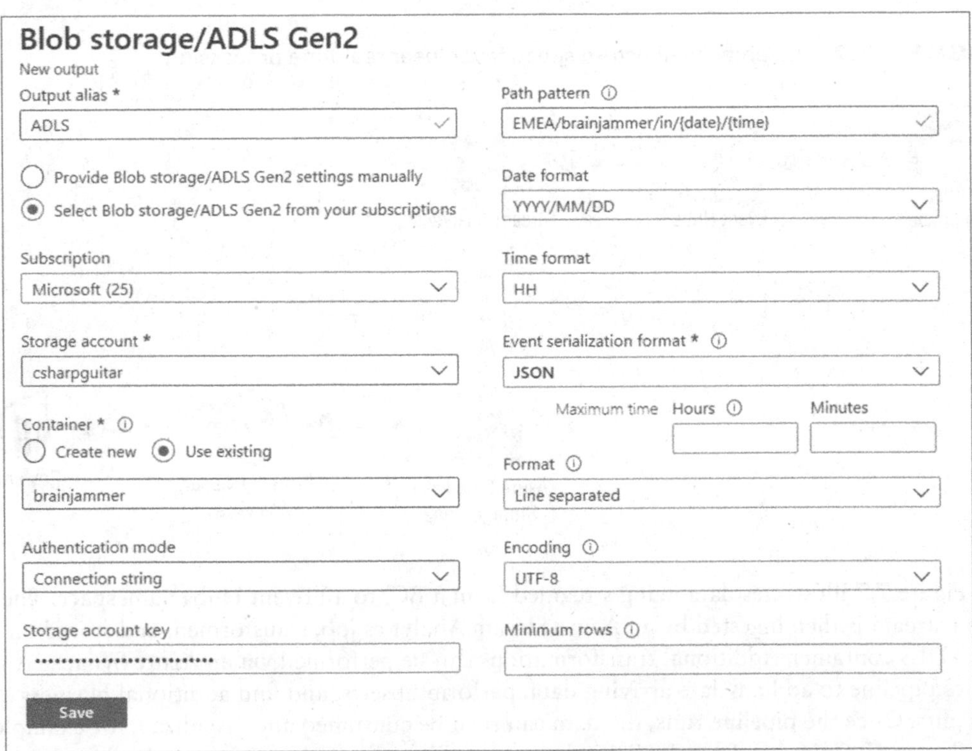

4. Click Save.

The data selected by the query that runs on the streamed data in Azure Stream Analytics and stored into the ADLS output should resemble Figure 7.9.

FIGURE 7.9 Azure Stream Analytics ADLS container path and file

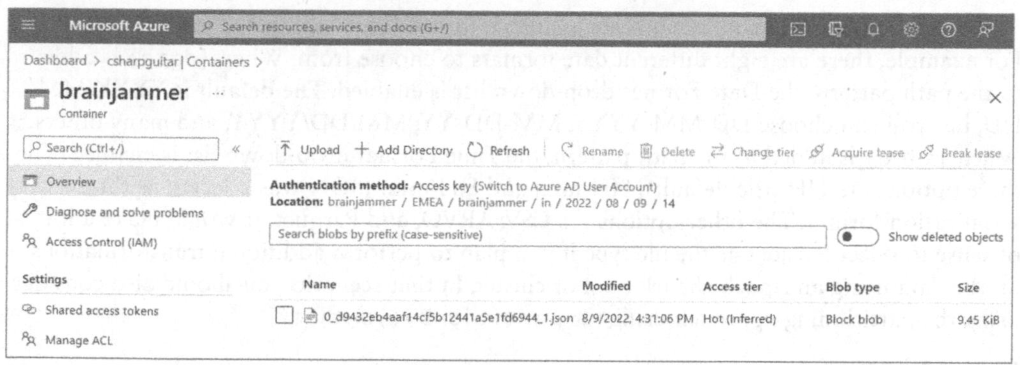

The file added to this container could then be used by any Azure data analytics product to perform more transformation and EDA to find business insights. An interesting option you might have noticed while configuring this output is the path pattern. The path pattern has been discussed in many places throughout this book for good reason. The options supported by the path pattern are flexible, which allows for some very powerful scenarios, starting with the prepended directory path of `EMEA/brainjammer/in` with the year, month, day, and hour appended to it. This pattern has been shown throughout the book and is an optimal directory structure for the ingestion of streamed data. You might instead want to implement the DLZ pattern and use something like `EMEA/brainjammer/cleansed-data` as the directory path to store your data. Another option is to use one of the columns from the `SELECT` statement as a value for the storge directory. For example, if the brain wave readings being sent to Azure Stream Analytics included a column named `scenario`, it could be used as a column name. If the scenario is `MetalMusic`, then you could use the following example to access the `scenario` value, which is used as the folder name:

```
EMEA/brainjammer/cleansed-data/{scenario}
```

In Exercise 4.2 you implemented partitioning in Azure Synapse Analytics using an Apache Spark pool. You used a DataFrame and the `partitionBy()`method, which looks something similar to the following code snippet. The output of that code resulted in a folder structure like the one shown in Figure 4.3.

```
df.write \
 .partitionBy('SCENARIO').mode('overwrite').csv('/path/ScenarioPartitions')
```

The result illustrated in Figure 4.3 can be queried by using the following path pattern example:

```
{path}/SCENARIO={scenario}
```

Having the data partitioned in such a way is optimal for running PySpark code on an Apache Spark pool or cluster. The code snippet to perform the query using the partition is provided here as a reminder.

```
spark.read.csv('path/SCENARIO=MetalMusic').show()
```

A few other configurable options are available for this blob storage/ADLS Gen2 output. For example, there are eight different date formats to choose from. When `{date}` is added to the path pattern, the Date Format drop-down list is enabled. The default is YYYY/MM/DD, but you can choose DD-MM-YYYY, MM-DD-YY, MM/DD/YYYY, and many others. When `{time}` is added to the path pattern, the Time Format drop-down list is enabled. The three options are HH (the default), HH-mm, and HH/mm. JSON was selected as the event serialization format. The other options are CSV, ARVO, and Parquet. It would make a lot of sense to select Parquet as the file type if you plan to perform additional transformations on the data using an Apache Spark pool or cluster. In that scenario you should also consider using the partitioning approach using the `partitionBy()` method.

Kappa Architecture

Much of the interest in the kappa architecture has to do with code duplication. The code that transforms data along the cold path is often duplicated on the hot path. If you look back at the code in the `brainjammer_batch.exe` located in the `Program.cs` file in the `Chapter06/Ch06Ex01` directory on GitHub, you might see some duplication. The objective of the batch layer code that processes the brain waves is to find the median brain wave reading values per frequency for a given session. The Azure Stream Analytics code snippet you saw in the "Temporal Windows" section does the same thing. In the batching scenario the median is calculated using the `Math.Round()` method, while in the Azure Stream Analytics scenario the median value is calculated using the `PERCENTILE_CONT()` T-SQL function. This scenario does prove the point, but like all similar situations the decision is based on the requirements. It is more cost effective to reduce the amount of data and the complexities of your code and architecture. However, not all data analytics solutions require a speed layer.

Create a Stream Processing Solution

The content in this section uses the concepts and technologies discussed in the previous design-oriented context. The objective of the stream processing solution is to identify the scenario in which brain waves are being read and then ingested, in real time. The temporal windowing function that will be utilized is tumbling, and the data format sent to the Azure Event Hub is in JSON format, resembling the following:

```
{
    "ALPHA" : 4.4116,
    "BETA_H" : 1.237,
    "BETA_L": 1.4998,
```

```
    "GAMMA": 0.8494,
    "THETA": 6.4356
}
```


Complete Exercise 7.2, where you will test that JSON file against an Azure Stream Analytics query. The testing will ensure that the query output meets the requirements to obtain the real-time visualization via a Power BI output. You will perform that configuration in Exercise 7.5.

EXERCISE 7.2

Develop a Stream Processing Solution with Azure Stream Analytics—Testing the Data

1. Log in to the Azure portal at `https://portal.azure.com` ➢ navigate to the Azure Stream Analytics job you created in Exercise 3.17 ➢ select Query from the Navigation menu ➢ select the Input Preview blade under the query window on the Query blade ➢ select the Upload Sample Input link ➢ upload the `meditation.json` file, which is located in the `Chapter07/Ch07Ex02` directory on GitHub ➢ and then click OK. Figure 7.10 shows how the data should look after the upload.

FIGURE 7.10 Test sample data upload in Azure Stream Analytics

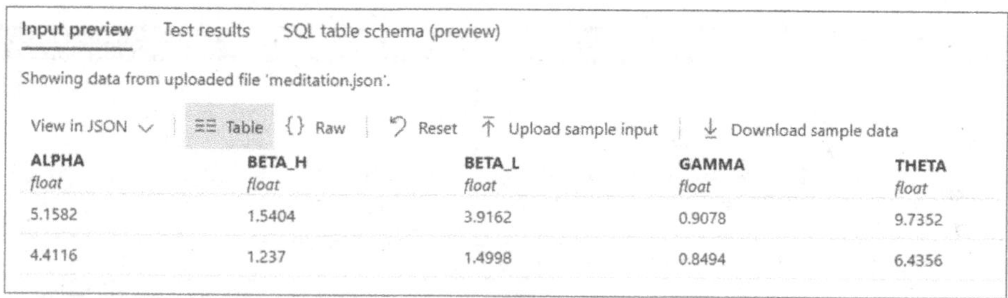

ALPHA float	BETA_H float	BETA_L float	GAMMA float	THETA float
5.1582	1.5404	3.9162	0.9078	9.7352
4.4116	1.237	1.4998	0.8494	6.4356

2. Enter the following Azure Stream Analytics query into the query window; the query is in the `StreamAnalyticsQuery.txt` file on GitHub.

```
WITH BrainwaveResults AS (
SELECT
    System.TimeStamp() AS IngestionTime,
    PERCENTILE_CONT(0.5) OVER (ORDER BY brainwaves.ALPHA) AS medianAPLHA,
    PERCENTILE_CONT(0.5) OVER (ORDER BY brainwaves.BETA_H) AS medianBETA_H,
    PERCENTILE_CONT(0.5) OVER (ORDER BY brainwaves.BETA_L) AS medianBETA_L,
    PERCENTILE_CONT(0.5) OVER (ORDER BY brainwaves.GAMMA) AS medianGAMMA,
```

EXERCISE 7.2 *(continued)*

```
    PERCENTILE_CONT(0.5) OVER (ORDER BY brainwaves.THETA) AS medianTHETA
FROM brainwaves
GROUP BY IngestionTime, TumblingWindow(second, 5))

SELECT medianAPLHA, medianBETA_H, medianBETA_L, medianGAMMA, medianTHETA,
CASE
    WHEN medianAPLHA > 4.3924 AND medianAPLHA <= 5.0287 THEN 'Meditation'
    WHEN medianBETA_H > 1.2994 AND medianBETA_H <= 1.38 THEN 'Meditation'
    WHEN medianBETA_L > 2.0487 AND medianBETA_L <= 2.1775 THEN 'Meditation'
    WHEN medianGAMMA > 0.8675 AND medianGAMMA <= 0.9364 THEN 'Meditation'
    WHEN medianTHETA > 2.344 AND medianTHETA <= 5.1052 THEN 'Meditation'
    ELSE 'Unknown'
END Scenario
INTO ADLS
FROM BrainwaveResults
```

3. Click the Test Query button. The result should resemble Figure 7.11.

FIGURE 7.11 The result of test data uploaded in Azure Stream Analytics

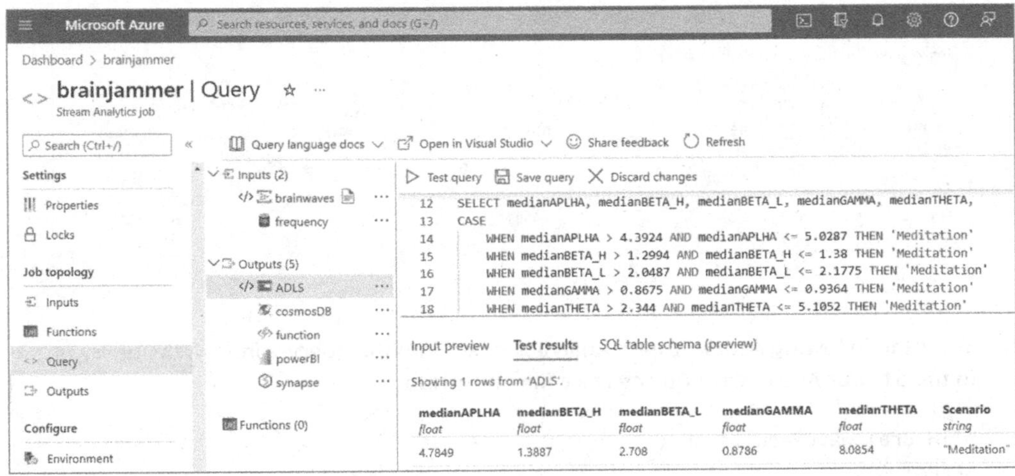

4. Click the Save Query button.

In Exercise 7.2 you received a working query; however, it took some time to create the query to produce the desired output. This is a very useful approach for creating your streaming solution. The query selects the five frequency values from the input file, along with a timestamp. The timestamp is used with the `GROUP BY` clause along with the tumbling window with a 5-second time interval. Placing the `SELECT` query, which calculates the median values of the brain wave input file over a 5-second time frame, within the `WITH` clause creates the interface to access the results from another associated `SELECT` query. The results of the query are used to determine if the median brain wave value per frequency matches the ranges identified through the EDA in previous chapters. The EDA results are in Table 5.2. The logic to determine the brain wave scenario uses `CASE WHEN` T-SQL statements, which are similar to if `()`, then `{}`, and else `{}` statements used in common programming languages like C#, Python, and Java. If any of the brain wave readings fall within the ranges identified as being from a meditation scenario, then "Meditation" is added as the value for the resulting `Scenario` column; otherwise, the value is "Unknown."

Notice that the query code used here is T-SQL and therefore abides by the declarative programming paradigm. Now that the input and output of the streamed data expected to flow through Azure Stream Analytics is clear, you will learn a bit more about Azure Event Hubs, implement the final solution in Azure Stream Analytics, and then configure Power BI to view the result of a meditation session in real time.

Azure Event Hubs

In Exercise 3.16 you provisioned a Basic tier Event Hubs namespace, and in Exercise 3.17 you configured it as an Azure Stream Analytics input. An important aspect of Azure Event Hubs has to do with partitioning (refer to Figure 3.77) and the partition count chosen when provisioning the event hub. The number of partitions that are allocated to an event hub is what dictates the amount of data it can handle. How partitioning works, the limitations, and many other features are based on the Events Hub namespace tier that was chosen during provisioning. In most cases, the features like the number of partitions cannot be changed once provisioned, so it is important to know the constraints and options before you provision for your production event hub. Table 7.5 compares the most important features so that you can choose the one that fits your current and future stream ingestion requirements.

TABLE 7.5 Azure Event Hubs tiers

Feature	Basic	Standard	Premium	Dedicated
Dynamic partition scale out	No	No	Yes	Yes
Maximum number of partitions	32	32	100	1,024
Multitenant	Yes	Yes	Isolated	No
Private link	No	Yes	Yes	Yes
Maximum message size	256 KB	1 MB	1 MB	1 MB

It is important to mention that once you create an event hub, you cannot change the partition count in the Basic or Standard tier. Both Premium and Dedicated tiers can be configured to scale based on load, which nullifies the situation of being bound to a fixed number of partitions. This flexibility comes at a higher price, as the higher tiers offer more features and throughput capacity. Every tier has a maximum number of partitions. In Exercise 3.16 you left the default of two partitions for the event hub, which cannot be changed. If you needed to change the number of partitions, you would need to provision another event hub and repoint your data producers and consumers to it. Multitenancy is a common cloud model. It does not mean that you share the same VM with other customers; it means that the grouping of the unit of compute resources is shared by multiple customers. For example, there is no network hardware separating the customers doing their work in a given tenant. If you have a requirement to isolate your workloads from other customers, you can provision a Premium tier Event Hubs namespace, which would separate your partitions from other customers using networking features like NSGs and firewalls. Or you can provision an entire tenant that is completely independent from all other cloud customers, but this is costly. If you do not want the Event Hubs namespace to exist in a public DNS, then you would want a tier that supports a private link. Otherwise, your Event Hubs endpoint will be globally discoverable. Clients must be authorized to access the endpoint; it is not usable anonymously. Lastly, notice the maximum allowed message sizes. The supported message sizes are large enough, when you consider the massive scale in which the Event Hubs endpoint is capable of managing.

Azure Stream Analytics

The work you have performed thus far in this book has been building up to the next few exercises. You have ingested brain wave data, transformed it into many formats, used many Azure data analytics products and features, and performed some very sophisticated exploratory data analysis. Now it is time to use the insights in a real-world application. Complete Exercise 7.3, where you will analyze brain waves readings in real time using Azure Stream Analytics.

EXERCISE 7.3

Develop a Stream Processing Solution with Azure Stream Analytics

1. Log in to the Azure portal at `https://portal.azure.com` ➢ navigate to the Azure Stream Analytics job you created in Exercise 3.17 ➢ select the Inputs link on the navigation menu ➢ select the Event Hub input (for example, `brainwaves`) ➢ and then click the Test button to confirm the connection is active.
2. Select the Query link and confirm the query is the one from Exercise 7.2.
3. Navigate to the Azure Synapse Analytics workspace you created in Exercise 3.3 ➢ start the SQL pool ➢ and then create the `BrainwaveMedians` table using the following SQL:

```
CREATE TABLE [brainwaves].[BrainwaveMedians] (
    [BRAINWAVE_ID]  INT NOT NULL IDENTITY(1,1),
    [medianAPLHA]              DECIMAL(20,3)  NOT NULL,
    [medianBETA_H]             DECIMAL(20,3)  NOT NULL,
    [medianBETA_L]             DECIMAL(20,3)  NOT NULL,
    [medianGAMMA]              DECIMAL(20,3)  NOT NULL,
    [medianTHETA]              DECIMAL(20,3)  NOT NULL,
    [Scenario]         NVARCHAR (100) NOT NULL
)
```

4. Select the Outputs link from the navigation menu of your Azure Stream Analytics job ➢ click the + Add drop-down ➢ select Azure Synapse Analytics ➢ enter a name (I used **synapse**) ➢ select the Select SQL Database from Your Subscription radio button ➢ select the subscription where your Azure Synapse Analytics SQL pool and table created in step 3 exist from the Subscription drop-down ➢ select the SQL pool ➢ select Connection String from the Authentication Mode drop-down ➢ enter the user ID (I used **sqladminuser**) of the SQL pool database ➢ enter the SQL pool database password ➢ and then enter **brainwaves.BrainwaveMedians** in the Table text box. Figure 7.12 shows the configuration.

FIGURE 7.12 Develop a stream processing solution Azure Stream Analytics output type Azure Synapse Analytics.

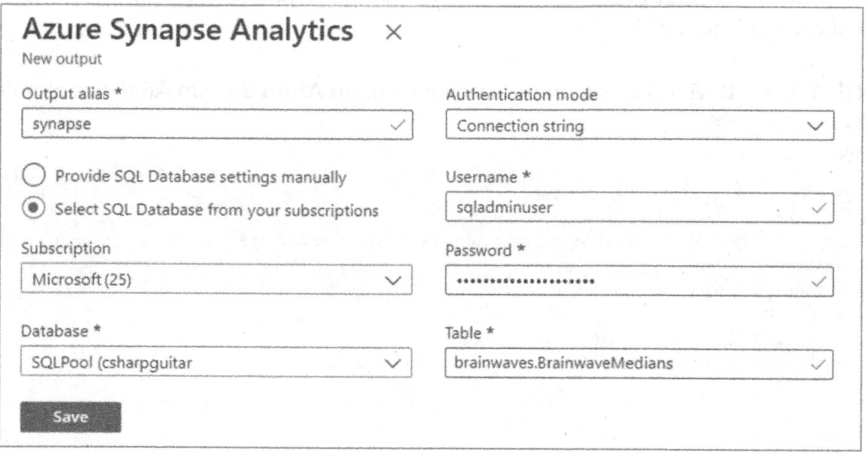

EXERCISE 7.3 ***(continued)***

5. Click the Save button (the connection must be successful) ➢ click the Query link on the navigation pane ➢ and then add the following query (located in the `StreamAnalyticsQuery.txt` file on GitHub) to the end of the existing query:

```
SELECT medianAPLHA, medianBETA_H, medianBETA_L, medianGAMMA, medianTHETA,
CASE
    WHEN medianAPLHA > 4.3924 AND medianAPLHA <= 5.0287 THEN 'Meditation'
    WHEN medianBETA_H > 1.2994 AND medianBETA_H <= 1.38 THEN 'Meditation'
    WHEN medianBETA_L > 2.0487 AND medianBETA_L <= 2.1775 THEN 'Meditation'
    WHEN medianGAMMA > 0.8675 AND medianGAMMA <= 0.9364 THEN 'Meditation'
    WHEN medianTHETA > 2.344 AND medianTHETA <= 5.1052 THEN 'Meditation'
    ELSE 'Unknown'
END Scenario
INTO synapse
FROM BrainwaveResults
```

6. Click the Save Query button ➢ click the Overview link ➢ click the Start button ➢ download `brainjammer.zip` from the `Chapter07/Ch07Ex03` directory on GitHub ➢ extract the files ➢ view the `brainjammer.exe` source code in the `Program.cs` and `Session.cs` files, also in the `Chapter07/Ch07Ex03` directory ➢ run the `brainjammer.exe` application ➢ and then enter the required information, similar to that shown in Figure 7.13.

FIGURE 7.13 Develop a stream processing solution Azure Stream Analytics simulate streamed brain waves.

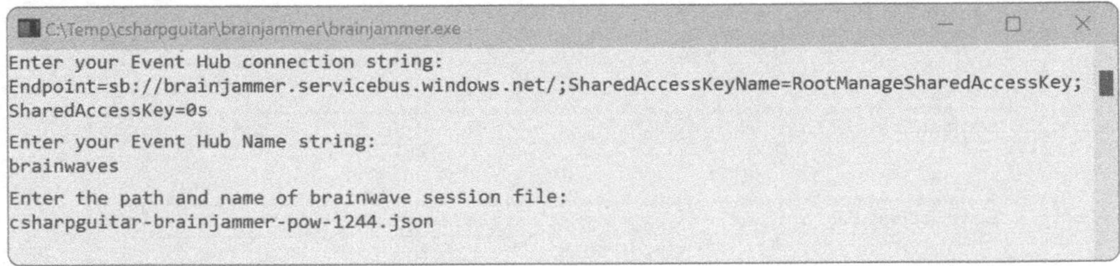

7. After the stream of brain waves finishes, look through the output of the stream in ADLS and Azure Synapse Analytics ➢ pause the SQL pool ➢ and then stop the Azure Stream Analytics job.

The data sent to your ADLS container will be the same as what you saw previously in Figure 7.9. The only difference is that the year, month, and hour will be different. Execute the following query on your Azure Synapse Analytics SQL pool:

```
SELECT TOP (100) [BRAINWAVE_ID], [medianAPLHA], [medianBETA_H],
                 [medianBETA_L], [medianGAMMA] ,[medianTHETA], [Scenario]
FROM [brainwaves].[BrainwaveMedians]
```

The query results will be similar to that shown in Figure 7.14. The most interesting value is the one stored in the Scenario column.

FIGURE 7.14 Develop a stream processing solution Azure Stream Analytics sent to Azure Synapse Analytics.

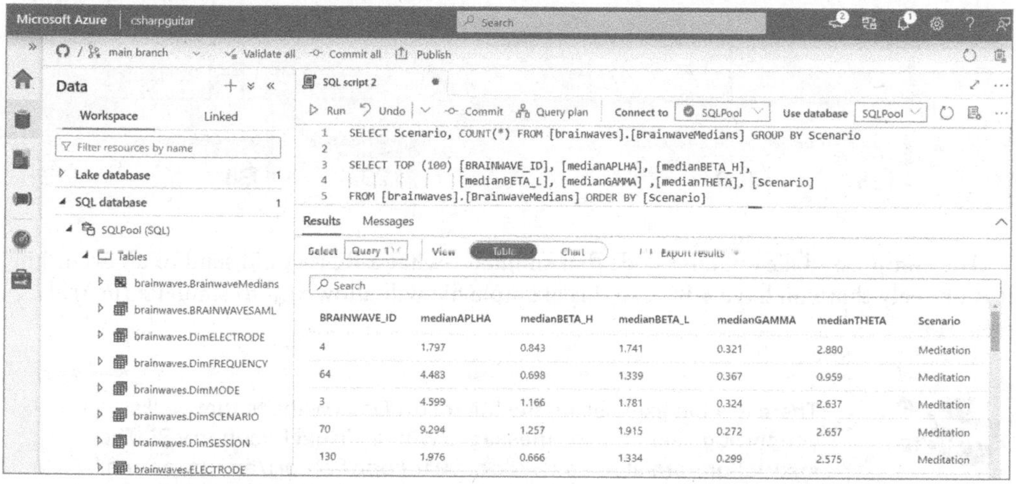

To confirm the messages passed through Event Hubs and the Azure Stream Analytics job, navigate to the Overview blades of each product and view the consumption metrics. You will see something similar to Figure 7.15.

The first action you took in Exercise 7.3 was to confirm that the input Event Hubs connection from the Azure Stream Analytics job created in Exercise 3.17 is still working. Next, you started your SQL pool in the Azure Synapse Analytics workspace you created in Exercise 3.3 and created a table named `[brainwaves].[BrainwaveMedians]` to store the data streamed from your Azure Stream Analytics job. Then, you created the output connection between the two named `synapse`. In Exercise 7.1 you created an output connection to an ADLS container, which means the Azure Stream Analytics job is configured to send output to both an ADLS container and an Azure Synapse Analytic dedicated SQL pool. This is accomplished by adding an additional T-SQL query that contains an `INTO` statement that points to `synapse`. The query that contains the `INTO` statement for the ADLS container remains as well. After saving the query, starting the Azure Stream Analytics job, configuring the event hub, and confirming that the SQL pool is running, you can send the data stream for processing. Note that the Azure Stream Analytics job must be stopped in order for you to modify the query.

FIGURE 7.15 Develop a stream processing solution Azure Stream Analytics sent to Event Hub and Azure Stream Analytics.

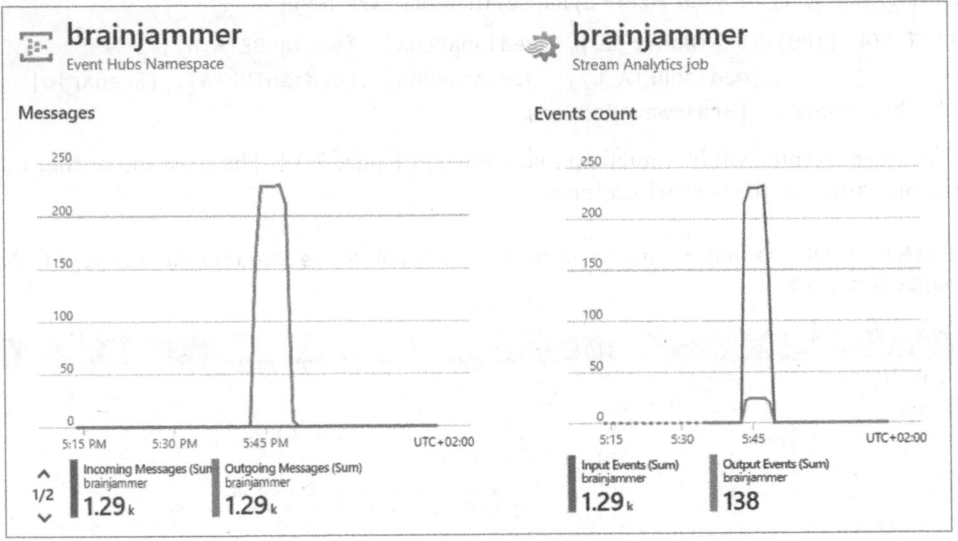

The compressed file contains code that simulates what a BCI would send to an event hub. It is unlikely that you have a BCI, so this example file will allow you to simulate the real scenario.

There is a fun exercise on the Microsoft Docs website that walks you through sending IoT messages with a virtual Raspberry Pi. The instructions are at `https://docs.microsoft.com/en-us/azure/stream-analytics/quick-create-visual-studio-code#run-the-iot-simulator`, and the link is in the `Chapter07` directory on GitHub.

Two brainjammer brain wave session files are included in the ZIP file that you downloaded from GitHub: `csharpguitar-brainjammer-pow-1244.json` is a meditation scenario, and `csharpguitar-brainjammer-pow-0904.json` is a metal music scenario. Either file can be used with the `brainjammer.exe` application. However, any file in the `BrainwaveData/SessionJson/*/POW` directory on GitHub (`https://github.com/benperk/ADE`) can be used with the application. You need to enter the event hub connection string, which is accessible on the Shared Access Policies blade of the event hub. The name of the event hub (not the Event Hubs namespace name) and the brainjammer brain wave session filename and location make up the event hub connection string.

Once the complete brain wave stream has passed though the Azure Stream Analytics job and into the Azure Synapse Analytics SQL pool, you can view the results. The following query and the results tell an interesting story:

```
SELECT Scenario, COUNT(*) FROM [brainwaves].[BrainwaveMedians] GROUP BY
Scenario
+-----------+-------+
| Scenario  | Count |
+-----------+-------+
| Unknown   | 40    |
| Meditation | 29   |
+-----------+-------+
```

The number of readings in the streamed brain wave session file was 1,286. The time frame of the windowing function was 5 seconds, as per the value in the following query:

```
TumblingWindow(second, 5)
```

The query run against the `[brainwaves].[BrainwaveMedians]` table returned 69 rows. This means the aggregate functions that calculated the median ran on 1286 / 69 = 18.6 readings. Additional EDA or a change in the time frame might result in a more desired outcome. This is something that will be done outside the context of this book. However, it is something that you can also pursue, because you now have the skills and experience to progress this forward. It might be that every scenario requires its own time window configuration, which would make the Azure Stream Analytics query very complex. There are many approaches for taking this forward to a working solution, which explains the point about the complexities and challenges of finding insights of data and then using them. Before progressing onto the Power BI portion of the solution, one additional topic that relates to Azure Stream Analytics needs to be covered: accessing and using reference data from an Azure Stream Analytics query.

Reference Data

Reference data is a set of numeric data that is used to look up a human-readable value. The numeric value is commonly a primary or foreign key. Reference data or reference tables are very common in the relational database model. You will also see this kind of reference data in the context of slowly changing dimensional tables, which have been covered in much detail throughout this book. Consider the following table, for example, which is not very helpful or comprehensible:

```
+--------------+-------+---------------------+
| FREQUENCY_ID | VALUE | READING_DATETIME    |
+--------------+-------+---------------------+
| 5            | 0.259 | 2022-08-12 08:46:32 |
+--------------+-------+---------------------+
```

If you had a reference table that contained a mapping between the numeric ID number and a human-readable value, the result of a query like the following would be much easier to understand:

```
SELECT FREQUENCY.FREQUENCY, READING.VALUE, READING.READING_DATETIME
FROM READING
JOIN FREQUENCY ON READING.FREQUENCY_ID = FREQUENCY.FREQUENCY_ID
```

The result of the query would be something like the following:

```
+--------------+-------+---------------------+
| FREQUENCY    | VALUE | READING_DATETIME    |
+--------------+-------+---------------------+
| GAMMA        | 0.259 | 2022-08-12 08:46:32 |
+--------------+-------+---------------------+
```

Using reference data from an Azure Stream Analytics query is possible. You can either use a file that contains the reference data, which is stored in either an Azure Blob Storage or an ADLS container, or create a reference table in an Azure SQL database. To reference data stored in an ADLS container, complete Exercise 7.4.

EXERCISE 7.4

Use Reference Data with Azure Stream Analytics

1. Log in to the Azure portal at `https://portal.azure.com` ➢ navigate to the ADLS container you created in Exercise 3.1 ➢ create a directory named `ReferenceData` ➢ and then upload `frequency.json` file to the `ReferenceData` directory. The `frequency.json` file is in the `Chapter07/Ch07Ex04` directory on GitHub.
2. Navigate to the Azure Stream Analytics job you created in Exercise 3.17 ➢ select the Inputs link on the navigation menu ➢ click the + Add Reference Input drop-down menu ➢ select Blob Storage ➢ enter a name (I used **frequency**) ➢ select the Select Blob Storage/ADLS Gen2 from the Your Subscription radio button ➢ select the storage account where you placed the reference file in step 1 ➢ select the container ➢ select Connection String from the Authentication Mode drop-down list ➢ and then enter **ReferenceData/frequency.json** in the Path Pattern text box. The configuration should resemble Figure 7.16.

FIGURE 7.16 Configure reference data for Azure Stream Analytics use.

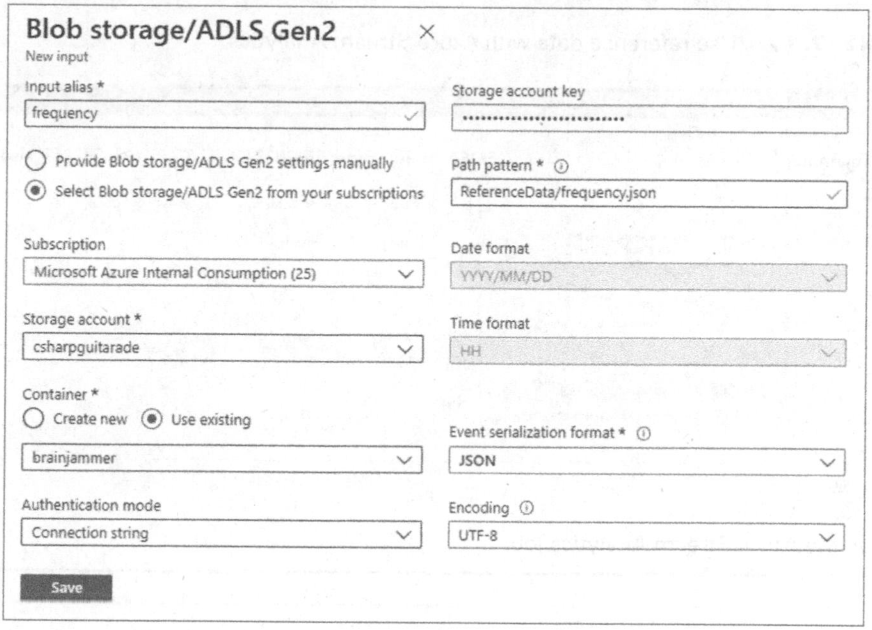

3. Click the Save button ➢ select the Query link on the navigation pane ➢ and then enter the following query into the query window; the query is in the `StreamAnalyticsQuery.txt` file in the `Chapter07/Ch07Ex04` directory on GitHub.

```
SELECT frequency.FREQUENCY, brainwaves.VALUE, brainwaves.READING_DATETIME
INTO ADLS
FROM brainwaves
JOIN frequency ON brainwaves.FREQUENCY_ID = frequency.FREQUENCY_ID
```

4. Start the Azure Stream Analytics job ➢ download and run the `brainjammer.exe` file located in the `brainjammer-refData.zip` file in the `Chapter07/Ch07Ex04` directory on GitHub; the source code is contained in the same directory in the file named `Program.cs` ➢ navigate to the ADLS Output container and path ➢ and then view the output, which should resemble Figure 7.17.

EXERCISE 7.4 *(continued)*

FIGURE 7.17 Use reference data with Azure Stream Analytics.

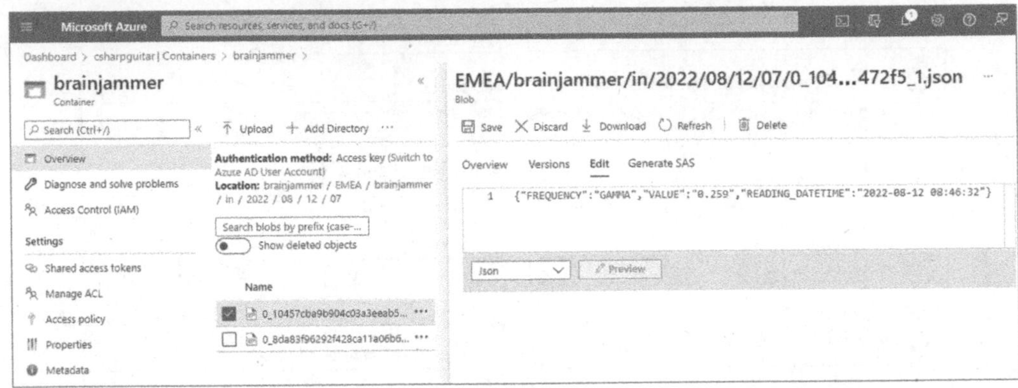

5. Stop the Azure Stream Analytics job.

In Exercise 7.4 you uploaded a reference file in JSON format that resembled the following:

```
{FREQUENCY_ID: 1, FREQUENCY:"THETA"}
{FREQUENCY_ID: 2, FREQUENCY:"ALPHA"}
{FREQUENCY_ID: 3, FREQUENCY:"BETA_L"}
{FREQUENCY_ID: 4, FREQUENCY:"BETA_H"}
{FREQUENCY_ID: 5, FREQUENCY:"GAMMA"}
```

You then created a reference input alias that provided access to the reference data from the Azure Stream Analytics query. The Azure Stream Analytics job needs to be running in order to access the reference data. Once the job was started, you used the `brainjammer.exe` application to send a simple JSON document, similar to the following, to your event hub, which flowed into Azure Stream Analytics for analysis and transformation:

```
{"FREQUENCY_ID":5,"VALUE":"0.259","READING_DATETIME":"2022-08-12 08:46:32"}
```

The query converted the `FREQUENCY_ID` of `5` to the `FREQUENCY` name using the reference data. The transformed data was stored into the output sink named `ADLS` that you configured in Exercise 7.1. The output was stored in JSON format and resembled the following:

```
{"FREQUENCY":"GAMMA","VALUE":"0.259","READING_DATETIME":"2022-08-12 08:46:32"}
```

The data can then be used by any other data analytics product that has access to the container.

Event Delivery Guarantees

Imagine that you have a real-time streaming solution that receives the same data more than once. In the brain wave reading scenario, this might not be very significant, but in some other scenarios, it could be. For example, in financial transactions, medical patient conditions, or airplane altitudes, receiving data more than once could have serious consequences. There are three concepts relevant in the event delivery context:

- Exactly once delivery
- Exactly once processing
- Duplicate records

The concepts are relatively self-explanatory. A guaranteed one-time delivery of an event means that the event is passed to the output sink once and only once. Azure Stream Analytics guarantees delivery at least once, which means that the output sink could conceivably receive the same event more than once. If the possibility of receiving a duplicate event is an issue for your solution, then there are some methods you can implement on the output sink. For example, if the sink supports upserts, or if the stream contains a primary key that is then enforced on the sink, then if Azure Stream Analytics sends the same event more than once, it can be managed at the destination. The second concept is a guarantee that the event is processed only once. Azure Stream Analytics does guarantee exactly once processing, which means that multiple events sent to an input will always return the same result. This is important in the event of a restart, which could result in the input receiving a duplicate event. You would expect the same result both times when the same event is processed. If the same event is processed more than once in the same transaction, the value would not be the same as if it had been processed only once.

There are a few scenarios in which an event would be duplicated, such as platform upgrades, a platform outage, or when the Azure Stream Analytics job is started using the When Last Stopped option, as shown in Figure 7.18.

FIGURE 7.18 Use reference data with Azure Stream Analytics.

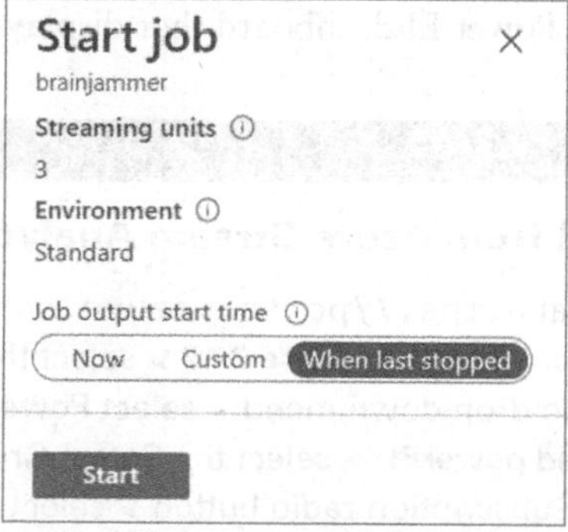

Platform upgrades like operating system, source code libraries, or product upgrades happen. In many scenarios the administrator of the Azure subscription is sent an email about this activity. The action you take in this scenario depends on the criticality of the data being streamed to your company. Although very rare, outages do happen. When they do, you need to determine the impact and take action, which could be anything from creating a support case with Microsoft to implementing your company's BDR process. When you start an Azure Stream Analytics job, you most likely start it with the Now option. But, as shown in Figure 7.18, there are two other options: Custom and When Last Stopped. Starting the job using the Now option means the starting point of the output stream is the current date and time. When the Azure Stream Analytics job is not running, it does not mean that the data producers have also stopped sending data to the inputs. In the exercises you have configured a temporal operator to manage the data the query is executed on. The temporal operator is a 5-second tumbling window. When the Now option is chosen, Azure Stream Analytics will look back 5 seconds into the input, process that data, and send it to the output. If the tumbling window were set to 5 minutes, then the look-back time frame would be 5 minutes. Setting the option to Custom means you can set the start time yourself. The behavior is the same as with Now, in that if you are using a temporal operator, Azure Stream Analytics will seek data from the time frame equal to or greater than the current time frame. If your job was stopped manually or failed and you want to restart it, then choose the When Last Stopped option. When you select this option, the last time the data was sent to the output sink is used to identify the data that needs to be included at start up.

Power BI

Looking through a dataset that contains text, even if it is business- or gold-quality data, is not optimal, especially when you are attempting to gather predictive insights. In such scenarios, and when viewing data in real time, a graphical representation of the data helps you to gain a better understanding of the data's meaning. Numerous tools are available for viewing a graphical visualization of data. For example, Microsoft Excel is a widely used spreadsheet, but it also has some useful data visualization features. However, if you need enterprise-level data visualization, the tool you should choose is Power BI. In Exercise 7.5 you will stream brainjammer brain waves to a Power BI dashboard that displays the scenario they belong to.

EXERCISE 7.5

Stream Data to Power BI from Azure Stream Analytics

1. Log in to the Azure portal at `https://portal.azure.com` ➢ navigate to the Azure Stream Analytics job you created in Exercise 3.17 ➢ select the Outputs link on the navigation menu ➢ select + Add drop-down menu ➢ select Power BI from the menu ➢ enter an output sink name (I used **powerBI**) ➢ select the Select Group (or Select Power BI) workspace from the Your Subscription radio button ➢ select the workspace you created in Exercise 5.12 from the Group Workspace drop-down list ➢ select User Token from the Authentication Mode drop-down list box ➢ enter a dataset name (I used **brainjammer**) ➢ enter a table name (I used **brainwaves**) ➢ click the Authorize button ➢ and then click Save. The configuration should resemble Figure 7.19.

FIGURE 7.19 Power BI Azure Stream Analytics output configuration

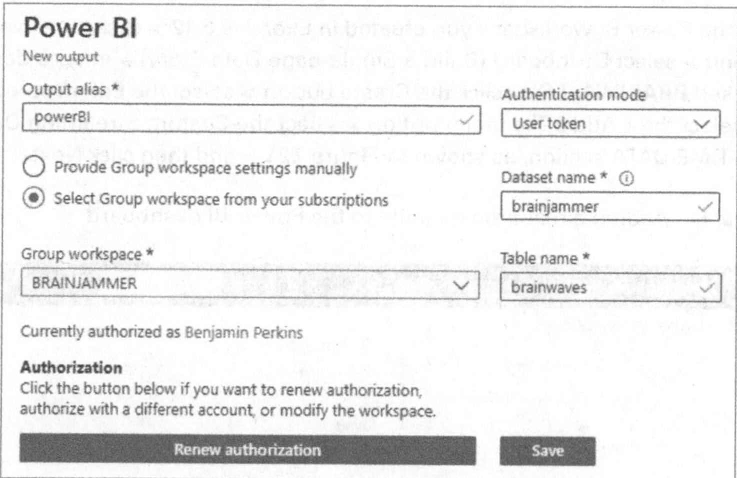

2. Select the Query link on the navigation menu ➢ enter the query located in `StreamAnalyticsQuery.txt` file found in the `Chapter07/Ch07Ex05` directory on GitHub ➢ click the Save Query button ➢ and then start the Azure Stream Analytics job.
3. Download, uncompress, and use the `brainjammer.exe` file located in the `brainjammer.zip` file from the `Chapter07/Ch07Ex03` directory on GitHub ➢ and then perform the same action as performed in step 6 of Exercise 7.3 (see Figure 7.13), which will create the dataset in Power BI, as shown in Figure 7.20.

FIGURE 7.20 The brainjammer streaming dataset in Power BI

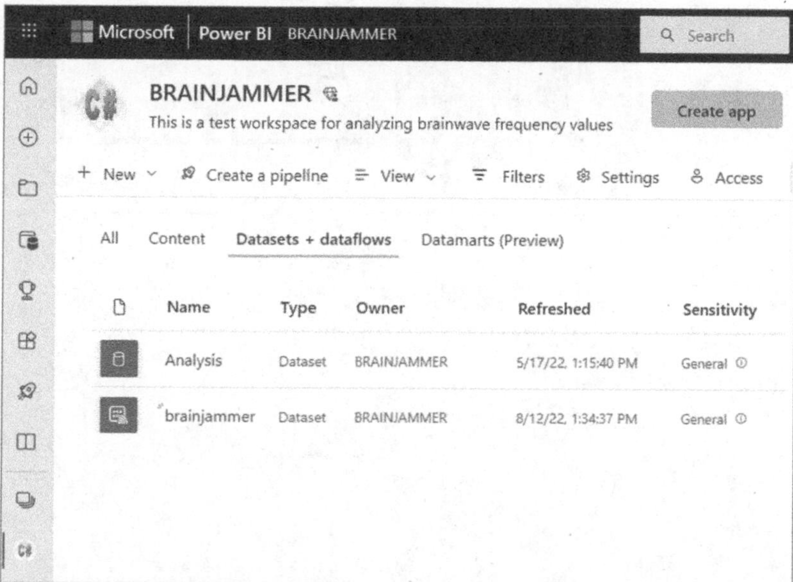

EXERCISE 7.5 *(continued)*

4. Log in to the Power BI workspace you created in Exercise 5.12 ➢ click the + New drop-down menu ➢ select Dashboard (Build a Single-page Data Story) ➢ enter a dashboard name (I used **BRAINWAVES**) ➢ click the Create button ➢ select the Edit drop-down menu ➢ select the + Add a Tile menu option ➢ select the Custom Streaming Data tile in the REAL-TIME DATA section, as shown in Figure 7.21 ➢ and then click Next.

FIGURE 7.21 Adding a real-time data tile to the Power BI dashboard

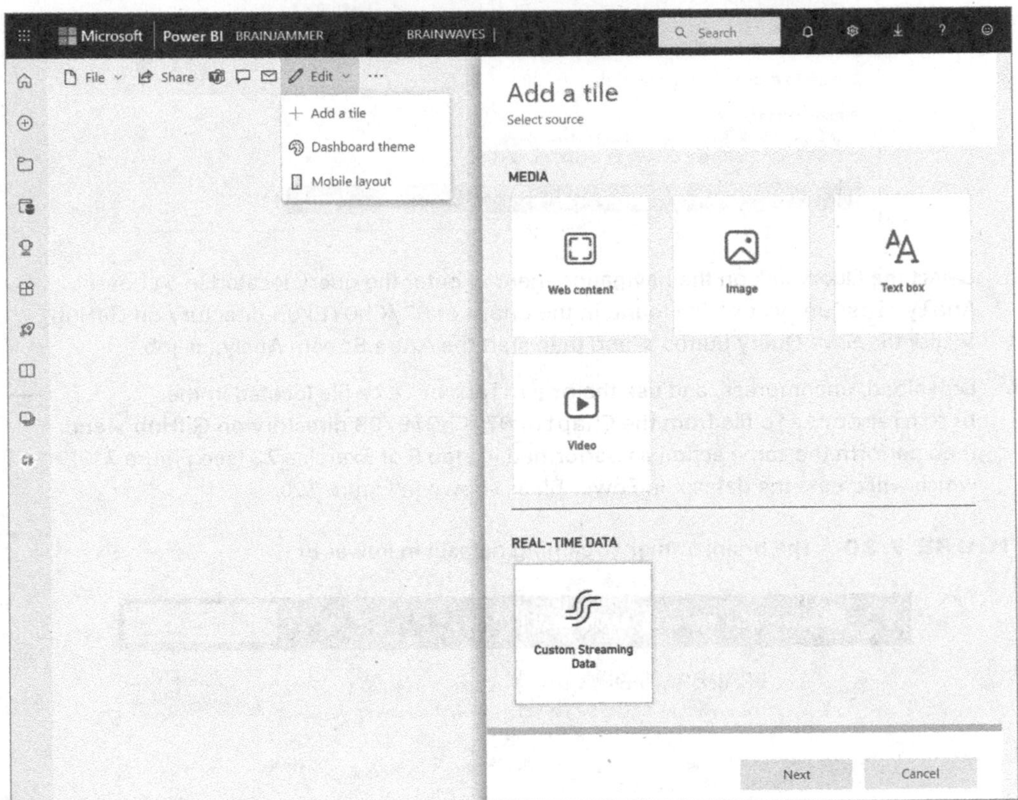

5. Select the dataset you configured in Azure Stream Analytics in step 1 of this exercise, shown previously in Figure 7.20 (for example, `brainjammer`) ➤ click Next ➤ select Clustered Bar Chart from the Visualization Type drop-down list box ➤ select Scenario from the Axis drop-down list box ➤ select each of the values from the Values drop-down list box, as shown in Figure 7.22 ➤ configure the Time Window to Display setting to 5 seconds.

FIGURE 7.22 Configuring a real-time data tile to the Power BI dashboard

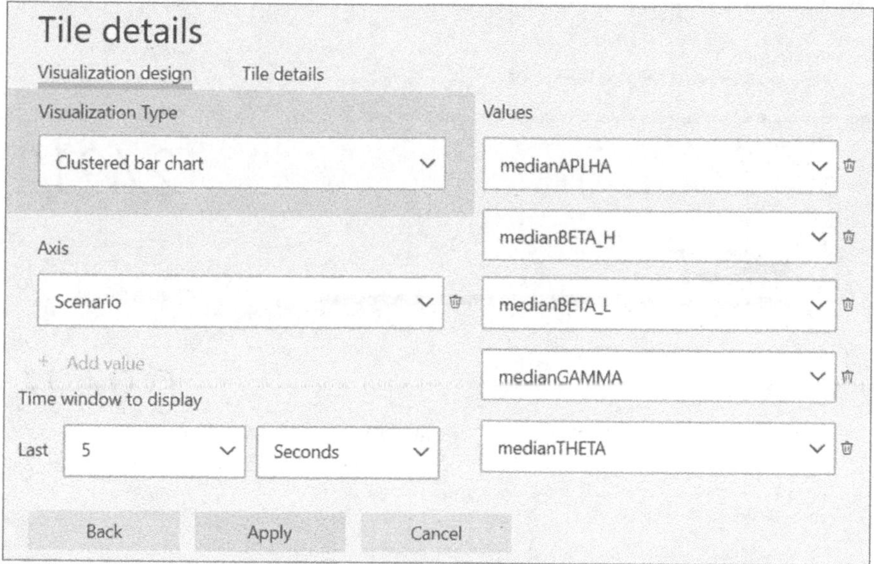

6. Click the Next button ➤ enter a title (I used **Brainwaves**) ➤ enter a subtitle (I used **Real-time brainwaves from the brainjammer**) ➤ and then click Apply.

7. Perform the same actions you performed in step 6 of Exercise 7.3 (see Figure 7.13) and in step 3 in this exercise, and then view the real-time brain wave stream flowing into the Power BI dashboard that you created in step 4 and 5 of this exercise, which should resemble Figure 7.23.

EXERCISE 7.5 ***(continued)***

FIGURE 7.23 Viewing a real-time data tile to the Power BI dashboard

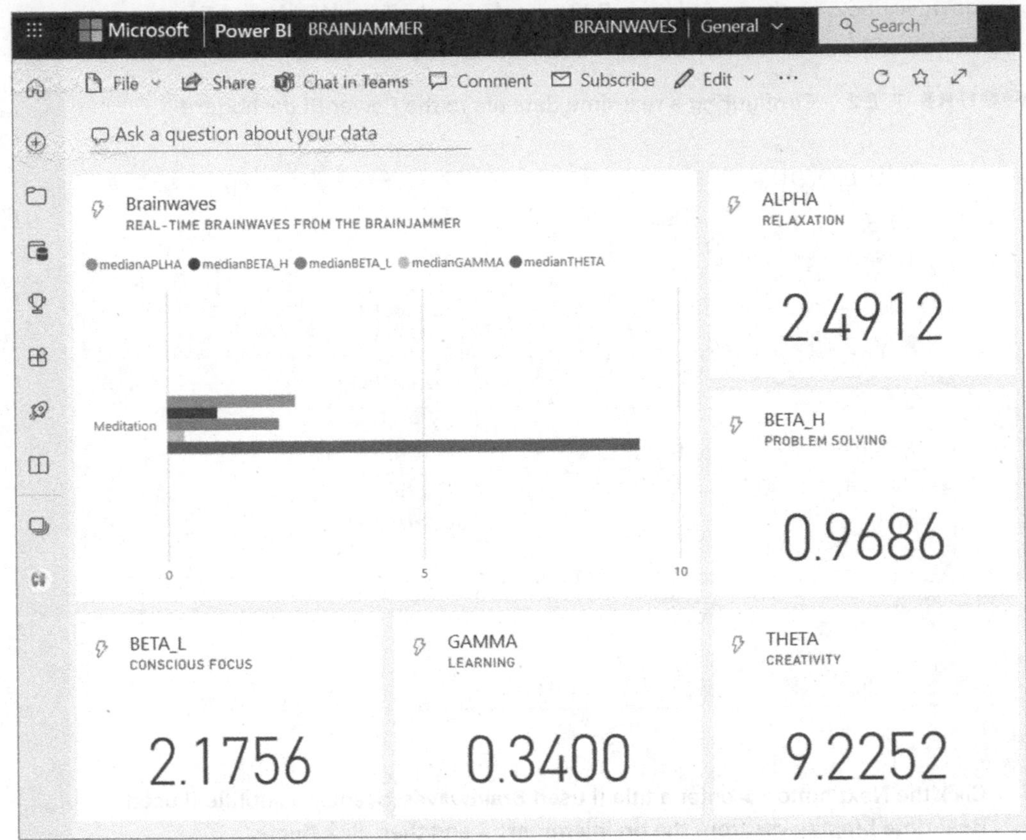

8. Stop the Azure Stream Analytics job.

The creation of Azure Stream Analytics inputs and outputs and what they are should now be very clear to you. It makes sense that you would need to create an output for Power BI to send the transformed streamed data to it. The input, as shown in the top portion of the query in Exercise 7.5, is the location from which the data is streamed to the Azure Stream Analytics job. The input is named `brainwaves`, which is the event hub you sent the brain wave readings to; it is referenced using the `FROM` clause.

```
WITH BrainwaveResults AS (
SELECT
```

```
    System.TimeStamp() AS IngestionTime,
    PERCENTILE_CONT(0.5) OVER (ORDER BY brainwaves.ALPHA) AS medianAPLHA,
    PERCENTILE_CONT(0.5) OVER (ORDER BY brainwaves.BETA_H) AS medianBETA_H,
    PERCENTILE_CONT(0.5) OVER (ORDER BY brainwaves.BETA_L) AS medianBETA_L,
    PERCENTILE_CONT(0.5) OVER (ORDER BY brainwaves.GAMMA) AS medianGAMMA,
    PERCENTILE_CONT(0.5) OVER (ORDER BY brainwaves.THETA) AS medianTHETA
FROM brainwaves
GROUP BY IngestionTime, TumblingWindow(second, 5)),
```

The query uses a tumbling window function with an interval of 5 seconds. This means the stream of brain wave readings are stored into memory for 5 seconds before the logic in the `SELECT` statement is performed. Once the first portion of the query is performed, the next portion is executed. Notice that the result of the first portion of the query is stored into a variable named `BrainwaveResults`, which is then used in the following query as the source of the data, accessed using the `FROM` clause:

```
ScenarioDetection AS (
SELECT medianAPLHA, medianBETA_H, medianBETA_L, medianGAMMA, medianTHETA,
CASE
    WHEN medianAPLHA > 4.3924 AND medianAPLHA <= 5.0287 THEN 'Meditation'
    WHEN medianBETA_H > 1.2994 AND medianBETA_H <= 1.38 THEN 'Meditation'
    WHEN medianBETA_L > 2.0487 AND medianBETA_L <= 2.1775 THEN 'Meditation'
    WHEN medianGAMMA > 0.8675 AND medianGAMMA <= 0.9364 THEN 'Meditation'
    WHEN medianTHETA > 2.344 AND medianTHETA <= 5.1052 THEN 'Meditation'
    ELSE 'Unknown'
END AS Scenario
FROM BrainwaveResults)
```

This portion of the query checks whether the median values calculated in the previous portion fall within the ranges expected of the meditation scenario. If they do, `Meditation` is stored into the `Scenario` column; if not, `Unknown` is placed into it. Finally, the data sent to the Power BI workspace is selected from the output of the second portion of the query from the `ScenarioDetection` variable and placed into the `powerBI` output sink.

```
SELECT Scenario, medianAPLHA, medianBETA_H, medianBETA_L, medianGAMMA, median
  THETA
INTO powerBI
FROM ScenarioDetection
```

The first time you run the `brainjammer.exe` application to send data to the Power BI workspace, you need to create the dataset into which the stream will flow. Without a dataset, you cannot add a tile to the dashboard. The `csharpguitar-brainjammer-pow-50.json` file in the `Chapter07/Ch07Ex05` directory contains fewer brain wave readings. Only one needs to be sent to Power BI to create the dataset. Once the dataset is created, you can access the Power BI workspace and create the dashboard and add the Custom Streaming Data tile.

The value selected for the Time Window to Display setting matched the tumbling window time frame of 5 seconds. You could make it 1 second, but that would not be prudent because data is sent to the dashboard only every 5 seconds. It does make sense to update the dashboard stream values with a time frame that matches the time frame in which the stream source sends the data. You might have noticed the additional card tiles in Figure 7.23. These tiles represent the median brain wave reading value placed into the dataset and presented in the dashboard. There is one card tile for each of the five frequencies. There are other types of tiles you might find interesting. Feel free to explore the additional features available in Power BI. Finally, be sure to stop the Azure Stream Analytics job once you complete Exercise 7.5, as it incurs cost even when not used.

Azure Databricks

An alternative to using Azure Stream Analytics for real-time or near real-time stream processing is Azure Databricks. If your current streaming solution uses Kafka and your team's primary programming language is Java, then Azure Databricks would be a good choice. Figure 7.24 illustrates how you can use Kafka to send event messages to Event Hubs that would then get consumed by an Apache Spark cluster in Azure Databricks.

FIGURE 7.24 Azure Databricks stream processing

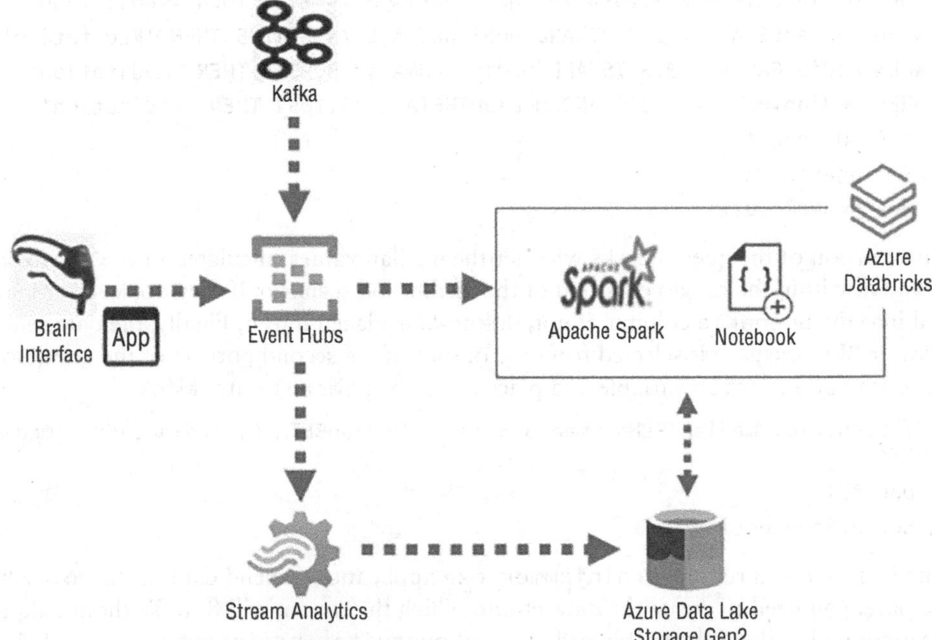

The reason you might choose to send Kafka messages to Event Hubs is to use Azure Stream Analytics, which exposes built-in ingestion capabilities—for example, all the output sinks shown in Figure 7.5. It is possible that your data analytics solution does not require ingestion and transformation products other than what is offered in the Azure Databricks product. If this is the case, you can consume Kafka event messages directly from an Apache Spark cluster. Read on to learn a bit more about the streaming capabilities available in Azure Databricks. Keep in mind that there will be a tendency to include Microsoft products when working with products on the Azure platform.

Kafka

Kafka was introduced in Chapter 2, where the concept of Spark streaming was first discussed, and covered again in detail in Chapter 3, in the context of Azure HDInsight and the comparison with Event Hubs. This section compares some programming logic between the Event Hubs and Kafka client data producers. Beginning with Event Hubs, you can see in the `Program.cs` file, in the directory `Chapter07/Ch07Ex03`, the library that contains the message producer. The following code builds the client and then sends the message data to Event Hubs:

```
using Azure.Messaging.EventHubs.Producer;

EventHubProducerClient producerClient = new
   EventHubProducerClient(EventHubConnectionString, EventHubName);
await producerClient.SendAsync(eventBatch);
```

The approach is similar when you are producing messages and streaming them to Kafka, in that you first include the library, then instantiate the client, and, finally, send the message.

```
package com.kafka.client;
import org.apache.kafka.clients.producer.KafkaProducer;
KafkaProducer producer = new KafkaProducer(properties);
producer.send(rec);
```

In both scenarios the details that define the endpoint to which the message is sent are part of the client building. That is the place where you decide if the messages are sent to Event Hubs or directly to an Apache Spark cluster that is listening for the arrival of the data.

readStream and writeStream

The producers of data use client libraries to package the message and send the data to an ingestion point. The location where the messages are ingested and processed is typically called server-side. The server, in this scenario, is a machine that has been configured to receive these messages, perform data transformation, and then store the data. Instead of storing the data, the code on the server could stream the messages for instant consumption. You have already learned how this is done using Azure Stream Analytics, and in Exercise 7.6 you will learn how to do this in Azure Databricks.

When data is streamed into the Spark Structured Streaming pipeline, it is first stored on an input table. This table is unbounded and will grow as large as necessary to store all streamed data as it arrives. The queries and operations you perform against the data stream are done against the data in the input table. The output of those queries and operations is stored in a table referred to as the results table. Figure 7.25 represents this flow. The results table is where data is taken from to be stored on external data sources like ADLS or an Azure Synapse Analytics Spark pool.

FIGURE 7.25 Azure Databricks Spark Structured Streaming

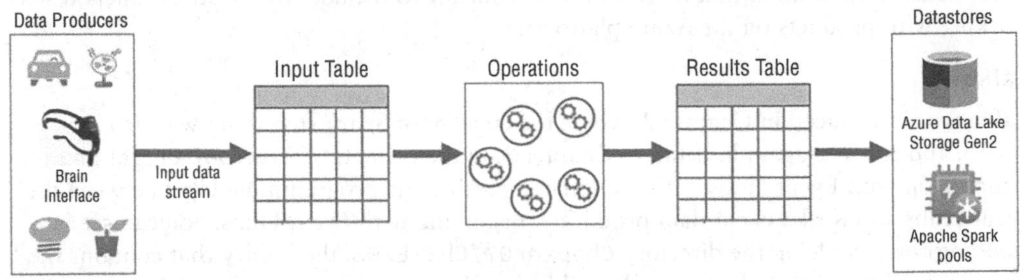

Two primary methods are used to work with data streams passing through an Apache Spark cluster, `readStream()` and `writeStream()`, both of which are part of the Spark stream processing engine. Configuring the server-side consumer of messages requires that you subscribe to the endpoint that notifies your code when a message arrives. When a message notification arrives, the `readStream()` method is triggered to then pull the message from the message ingestion point. Once the message is received from either a socket or event hub, the data can be transformed and written to a console, to a delta table, to an ADLS container, or to any supported datastore. The write process is achieved by using the `writeStream()` method.

Windowing Functions

This concept is not new. Windowing functions are temporal windows that let you capture streamed data for a given time frame, group, or partition, and then run aggregate functions on that data. Windowing in Spark is achieved using the `Window` class, `groupBy()`, `window()`, or `partitionBy()` methods. Consider the following example, which groups data in 10-second windows, updated every 5 seconds, and which would be run against the input table:

```
val messageCount = incomingStream.
    groupBy(window($"timestamp", "10 seconds", "5 seconds"), $"Body").count()
```

Aggregate functions such as `AVG`, `SUM`, `MIN`, and `MAX` are all supported and can be used to produce the output required for your solution. To get some hands-on experience with streaming data to an Apache Spark cluster in Azure Databricks, complete Exercise 7.6.

EXERCISE 7.6

Stream Data with Azure Databricks

1. Log in to the Azure portal at `https://portal.azure.com` ➢ navigate to the Azure Databricks workspace you created in Exercise 3.14 ➢ select the Launch Workspace button in the Overview blade ➢ select Compute menu item from the navigation pane ➢ select the cluster you created in Exercise 3.14 ➢ start the cluster ➢ select the Libraries tab ➢ click the Install New button ➢ select Maven from the Library Source section ➢ and then enter the following into the Coordinates text box. Figure 7.26 illustrates the configuration.

```
com.microsoft.azure:azure-eventhubs-spark_2.12:2.3.22
```

FIGURE 7.26 Installing the Event Hubs library on an Azure Databricks cluster

Install library ×
Library Source
Upload | DBFS/ADLS | PyPI | Maven | CRAN | Workspace
Coordinates
com.microsoft.azure:azure-eventhubs-spark_2.12:2.3.22
Search Packages
Cancel | Install

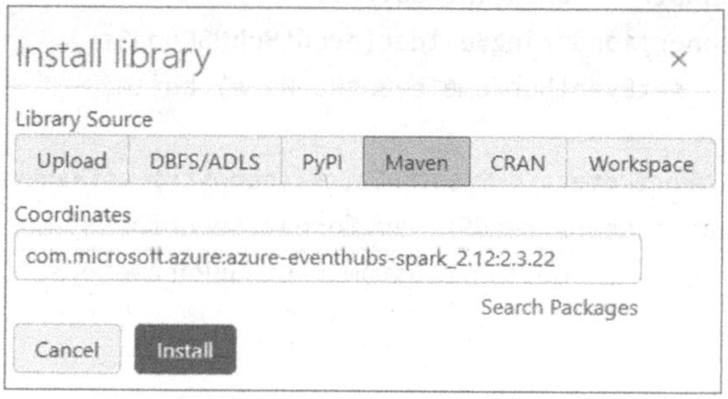

2. Click the Install button. Once the Status for the Event Hubs library is Installed, as shown in Figure 7.27, select the + Create item from the navigation menu.

FIGURE 7.27 The installed Event Hubs library on an Azure Databricks cluster

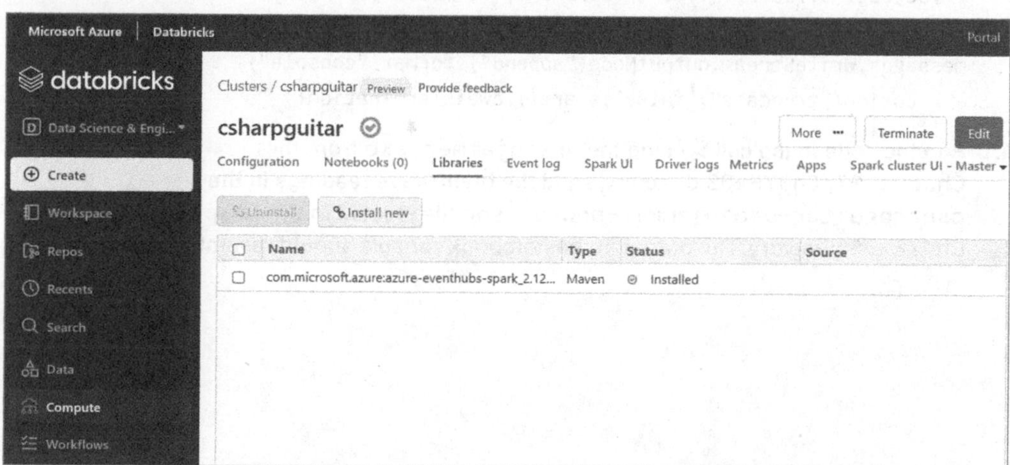

EXERCISE 7.6 *(continued)*

3. Select Notebook from the pop-out menu ➢ enter a name (I used **ReadBrainwavesFromEventHub**) ➢ select Scala from the Default Language drop-down list box ➢ select the Cluster where you just installed the Event Hubs library from the Cluster drop-down list box ➢ click the Create button ➢ and then enter the following code into the notebook cell. The code is in the `ReadBrainwavesFromEventHub.scala` file in the `Chapter07/Ch07Ex06` directory on GitHub.

```
import org.apache.spark.eventhubs.{ConnectionStringBuilder, EventHubsConf}
import org.apache.spark.sql.types.LongType

val eventHubName = "..."
val eventHubNSConnStr = "Endpoint=sb://..."
val connStr = ConnectionStringBuilder(eventHubNSConnStr).
                  setEventHubName(eventHubName).build

val customEventhubParameters = EventHubsConf(connStr).setMaxEventsPerTrigger(5)
val incomingStream = spark.readStream.format("eventhubs").
                          options(customEventhubParameters.toMap).load()

val messages =
  incomingStream
  .withColumn("Offset", $"offset".cast(LongType))
  .withColumn("Time (readable)", $"enqueuedTime".cast(TimestampType))
  .withColumn("Timestamp", $"enqueuedTime".cast(LongType))
  .withColumn("Body", $"body".cast(StringType))
  .select("Offset", "Time (readable)", "Timestamp", "Body")

messages.writeStream.outputMode("append").format("console").
    option("truncate", false).start().awaitTermination()
```

4. Run the code in the cell ➢ using the `brainjammer.exe` from the `Chapter07/Ch07Ex03` directory, send the brain wave readings in the `csharpguitar-brainjammer-pow-5.json` file located in the `Chapter07/Ch07Ex06` directory. The output in the notebook console should resemble Figure 7.28.

FIGURE 7.28 Streamed Event Hubs messages displayed in the Azure Databricks notebook console

```
-------------------------------------------
Batch: 0
-------------------------------------------
+------+--------------------+----------+------------------------------------------------------------------------------------------------+
|Offset|Time (readable)     |Timestamp |Body                                                                                            |
+------+--------------------+----------+------------------------------------------------------------------------------------------------+
|750008|2022-08-13 17:17:37.31 |1660411057|{ "ALPHA": 6.5852,"BETA_H": 1.3246,"BETA_L": 4.6202,"GAMMA": 0.403,"THETA": 28.0412 } |
|750240|2022-08-13 17:17:38.261|1660411058|{"ALPHA": 15.8164,"BETA_H": 2.7158,"BETA_L": 8.0866, "GAMMA": 0.694,"THETA": 10.8514 } |
|750416|2022-08-13 17:20:18.578|1660411218|{ "ALPHA": 5.0066, "BETA_H": 0.9966,"BETA_L": 3.7892,"GAMMA": 0.3544, "THETA": 41.1066 } |
|750592|2022-08-13 17:20:19.172|1660411219|{ "ALPHA": 9.4424, "BETA_H": 1.7814, "BETA_L": 5.783, "GAMMA": 0.492, "THETA": 17.639  } |
|750536|2022-08-13 17:20:19.441|1660411219|{"ALPHA": 12.9088,"BETA_H": 2.2852,"BETA_L": 7.0646, "GAMMA": 0.597,"THETA": 12.1018 } |
+------+--------------------+----------+------------------------------------------------------------------------------------------------+
```

5. Click the Stop Execution button, which stops the cluster.

The first action you took in Exercise 7.6 was to install the library required to make a connection to an Event Hubs endpoint. The `com.microsoft.azure:azure-eventhubs-spark_2.12:2.3.22` library contains methods to create the connection string and configure the Event Hubs listener. You then created a notebook that would eventually contain the code to receive and write the message data sent to your event hub. The first few lines of code, as shown here, import the specific classes from the event hub's library and then use the provided event hub name and endpoint address to build the connection string.

```
import org.apache.spark.eventhubs.{ConnectionStringBuilder, EventHubsConf}

val eventHubName = "brainwaves"
val eventHubNSConnStr = "Endpoint=sb://..."
val connStr = ConnectionStringBuilder(eventHubNSConnStr).
                     setEventHubName(eventHubName).build
```

The connection string is then passed as a parameter to the `EventHubsConf` class, which is used to make the connection with the Event Hubs namespace and hub. Notice that in addition to the connection string being used with the `EventHubsConf` class constructor, there is a method named `setMaxEventsPerTrigger`, which is passed a value of 5. This method sets the maximum number of events to be processed at one time.

```
val customEventhubParameters = EventHubsConf(connStr).setMaxEventsPerTrigger(5)
```

An instance of the `EventHubsConf` class named `customEventhubParameters` is then passed as a parameter to the `options()` method as part of the `spark.readStream()` method. When messages are sent to the event hub from a producer, the messages are then pulled into the `incomingStream` variable. The message is then formatted into a human-readable format and stored in `message`.

```
val incomingStream = spark.readStream.format("eventhubs").
                           options(customEventhubParameters.toMap).load()
val messages =
  incomingStream
  .withColumn("Offset", $"offset".cast(LongType))
  .withColumn("Time (readable)", $"enqueuedTime".cast(TimestampType))
```

```
.withColumn("Timestamp", $"enqueuedTime".cast(LongType))
.withColumn("Body", $"body".cast(StringType))
.select("Offset", "Time (readable)", "Timestamp", "Body")
```

The message is then written to the console using the following syntax:

```
messages.writeStream.outputMode("append").format("console").
   option("truncate", false).start().awaitTermination()
```

Chapter 6 introduced the `outputMode()` method. As you may remember, the different output mode types are `Append`, `Complete`, and `Update`. You might consider doing some additional work using Exercise 7.6 in order to gain a better understanding of how these different output modes affect the rows in the results table. `Append` mode adds new rows to the table since the last trigger, whereas `Complete` mode generates the entire table after every trigger, which minimizes the risk of duplication. `Update` mode adds the rows that were updated since the last event messages were added to the results table. When you set `truncate` to `false`, none of the data rendered in the console will be trimmed. This means you will see all the data returned; otherwise, you would see only the first 20 characters. The `start()` method is what keeps the program listening for event notifications from Event Hubs, which it will continue to do until it is manually stopped or the cluster is shut down. The `awaitTermination()` method enforces this behavior.

In Exercise 7.6 you did not do the full transformation of the data into median values nor compare them to the ranges per brain wave scenario. This is all completely possible; you just need to write the code to do it. An easy—rather, easier—approach might be to write the messages to an ADLS container that is an input for the Azure Stream Analytics job you already have. The query you have already written could then be used to perform the final stages of the ingestion, transformation, and streaming of the results to Power BI. You could use the following code snippet to store the results into an ADLS container instead of to the console:

```
val reading = incomingStream.
                    withColumn("Body", $"body".cast(StringType)).select("Body")
reading.writeStream.format("json").save("abfss://*@*.dfs.core.windows.net/...")
```

The format is set to JSON because the Azure Stream Analytics job is expecting that format. However, keep in mind that whenever possible you should use the Parquet format, as it is the most efficient format when consumed by Azure Databricks or PolyBase via Azure Synapse Analytics.

Finally, note that in Exercise 7.6 you used an interactive Apache Spark cluster. This means that you had to manually start the code that read and processed the event message in the notebook. If you wanted to run such a solution in a production scenario, you would need to provision an automated Apache Spark cluster. You might recall the introduction of automated Apache Spark clusters in Chapter 6, in the context of batch jobs. You will need to perform the same action in this context to make sure your streaming solution is running as required. To get the most availability and throughput of your structured streaming solution on the Azure platform, you might consider using Apache Hadoop YARN. Apache Hadoop YARN is available through the Azure HDInsight product offering, which is where you will achieve fault tolerance and seamless integration with other open-source big data products, features, and tools.

Process Time Series Data

The streaming of data from an IoT device, like a BCI, is an ideal fit for time series analysis. The data in this context is ideal because the data includes a timestamp and is received in order, both of which are time series data characteristics. Figure 7.29 shows a time series line chart that represents a chronological series of brain wave readings that were ingested.

FIGURE 7.29 A brain wave time series chart

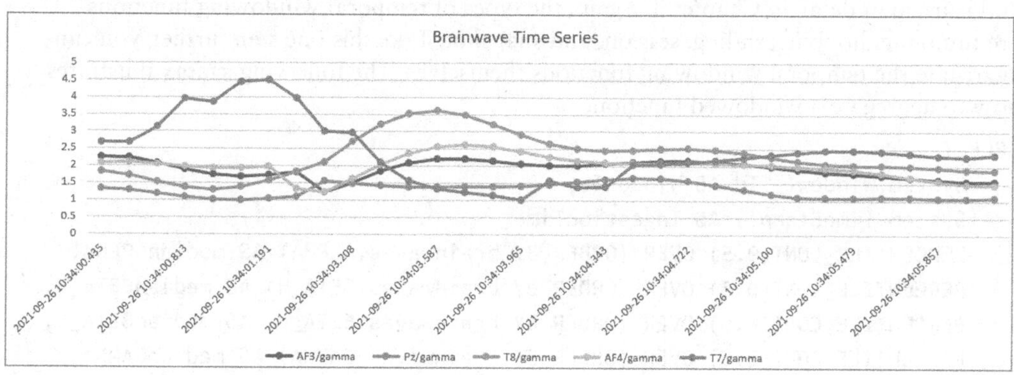

The more data you consume and store, the greater your ability to discover trends and spot anomalies. This kind of data is also very useful for predictive analysis. In Chapter 5, "Transform, Manage, and Prepare Data," you used this data to discover the median ranges of frequencies of brain wave readings per frequency. You then used those values in Exercise 7.5 to predict which brainjammer brain wave scenario is taking place in real time.

Another characteristic when working with time series data is the storage folder structures based on date and time, as follows:

```
{Region}/{SubjectMatter}/out/{yyyy}/{mm}/{dd}/{hh}/
EMEA/brainjammer/in/2022/08/17/17
```

You have seen this pattern in many places in this book. Structuring your data in this manner helps PolyBase and DataFrame queries perform better. They perform better because the amount of data in each directory would be smaller when compared to storing data for an entire day or week in a single file. Finding an optimal partition for your data is very important if you want a healthy, non-latent data solution. It is possible to take this naming convention to the file level, as follows:

```
filename_YYYY_MM_DD_HH_mm.parquet
brainwaves_2022_08_17_17_22.parquet
```

This means the queries can be optimized to run on data files down to the minute time frame, which might be the optimal design for a data analytics solution. If the ingestion frequency is once per minute, then you have attained equilibrium with the law of 60 once again.

Design and Create Windowed Aggregates

When you think about streaming aggregate functions, the functions in Table 3.20 should come to mind, for example, AVG, COUNT, MAX, and MIN. When you use the PERCENTILE_CONT and PERCENTILE_DISC aggregate functions in the streaming context, you restrict the execution of those aggregates to a set of data in a prescribed time frame, for example, running the AVG function on all received data within the last 5 seconds. The configuration of that time window is achieved using temporal windows, which you read about in this chapter and learned in detail in Chapter 3. Again, the types of temporal windowing functions are tumbling, hopping, sliding, session, and snapshot. Take this one step further, you can aggregate the temporal windowing functions themselves. The following syntax illustrates how to aggregate a windowed function:

```
SELECT
    System.Window().Id AS WindowId,
    System.TimeStamp() AS IngestionTime,
    PERCENTILE_CONT(0.5) OVER (ORDER BY brainwaves.ALPHA) AS medianAPLHA,
    PERCENTILE_CONT(0.5) OVER (ORDER BY brainwaves.BETA_H) AS medianBETA_H,
    PERCENTILE_CONT(0.5) OVER (ORDER BY brainwaves.BETA_L) AS medianBETA_L,
    PERCENTILE_CONT(0.5) OVER (ORDER BY brainwaves.GAMMA) AS medianGAMMA,
    PERCENTILE_CONT(0.5) OVER (ORDER BY brainwaves.THETA) AS medianTHETA
FROM brainwaves
GROUP BY WindowId, IngestionTime,
         Windows(
             Window('10s Tumble', TumblingWindow(second, 10)),
             Window('10s Hop', HoppingWindow(second, 10, 5)),
             Window('30s Session', SessionWindow(second, 30, 60)),
             Window('30s Sliding', SlidingWindow(second, 30)))
```

The Windows() function provides the technology to implement windowed aggregates. As you can see, the Windows() function accepts parameters of multiple window definitions, like tumbling, hopping, session, and sliding. The window Id is the first parameter of the Window() function and is referenced in the SELECT statement using the following code snippet:

```
System.Window().Id
```

To learn more about implementing windowed aggregates, complete Exercise 7.7. Note that you must have completed Exercise 7.3 in order to successfully complete this exercise, as it includes some resources you need to update.

EXERCISE 7.7

Develop and Create Windowed Aggregates

1. Log in to the Azure portal at https://portal.azure.com ➢ navigate to the Azure Synapse Analytics workspace you created in Exercise 3.3 ➢ select the Manage hub ➢ start the SQL pool (the same one you used in Exercise 7.3) ➢ select the Data hub ➢

and then create a new table named `BrainwaveWindowMedians`. The syntax is in the `BrainwaveWindowMedians.sql` file in the `Chapter07/Ch07Ex07` directory on GitHub.

2. Navigate to the Azure Stream Analytics job you created in Exercise 3.17 ➢ select Outputs from the navigation menu ➢ select the synapse alias you created in Exercise 7.3 ➢ change the value in Table to the following ➢ and then click Save.

```
brainwaves.BrainwaveWindowMedians
```

3. Select Query from the navigation menu ➢ add the query in the file `StreamAnalytics Query.txt`, which is located in the `Chapter07/Ch07Ex07` directory on GitHub ➢ click the Save Query button ➢ and then start the Azure Stream Analytics job.
4. Download, uncompress, and use the `brainjammer.exe` located in the `brainjammer.zip` file in the `Chapter07/Ch07Ex03` directory on GitHub ➢ perform the same action as performed in step 6 of Exercise 7.3 (see Figure 7.13).
5. Once the brain wave streaming is complete, navigate to the Azure Synapse Analytics workspace you created in Exercise 3.3 and view the newly added rows on the `[brainwaves].[BrainwaveWindowMedians]` table. Use the following query, for example:

```
SELECT medianAPLHA, medianBETA_H, medianBETA_L, medianGAMMA, medianTHETA
FROM [brainwaves].[BrainwaveWindowMedians]
WHERE WindowId = '10s Tumble'
ORDER BY IngestionTime
```

6. Stop the Azure Stream Analytics job, and then stop the Azure Synapse Analytics SQL pool.

The first action in Exercise 7.7 was to create a new table to store the stream of brain wave data readings. In addition to the frequency columns, there are columns named `WindowId` and `IngestionTime`. When you implement windowed aggregates, each window is allocated an identifier. They can be any string value, such as "20 Seconds," "20S," or "twenty." A valid `WindowId` should be one that is helpful toward identifying the type of aggregated window. The value stored in the `IngestionTime` column is the output of the `System.TimeStamp()` method. The method returns the date and time the brain wave reading was enqueued into Event Hubs. (There is more on this in the "Configure Checkpoints/Watermarking During Processing" section.)

Next, you updated the synapse output alias so that the result of the Azure Stream Analytics query would write the data into the table you just created. The first portion of the query should be quite familiar to you now.

```
WITH BrainwaveWindowResults AS
(
```

```
SELECT
    System.Window().Id AS WindowId,
    System.TimeStamp() AS IngestionTime,
    PERCENTILE_CONT(0.5) OVER (ORDER BY brainwaves.ALPHA) AS medianAPLHA,
    PERCENTILE_CONT(0.5) OVER (ORDER BY brainwaves.BETA_H) AS medianBETA_H,
    PERCENTILE_CONT(0.5) OVER (ORDER BY brainwaves.BETA_L) AS medianBETA_L,
    PERCENTILE_CONT(0.5) OVER (ORDER BY brainwaves.GAMMA) AS medianGAMMA,
    PERCENTILE_CONT(0.5) OVER (ORDER BY brainwaves.THETA) AS medianTHETA
FROM brainwaves
```

The statement is contained within a `WITH` clause so that the desired portions of the output can be referenced from a later `SELECT` statement. The only difference from the previous versions of this query is the addition of the two new columns just discussed. The next portion of the query is where the windowed aggregation is implemented. It performs a `GROUP BY` command that begins with the new columns, followed by the `Window()` method. The method takes an `n` number of `Window()` methods that contain parameters `WindowId` and the type of and configuration of each temporal window.

```
GROUP BY WindowId, IngestionTime,
    Windows(
        Window('10s Tumble', TumblingWindow(second, 10)),
        Window('10s Hop', HoppingWindow(second, 10, 5)),
        Window('30s Session', SessionWindow(second, 30, 60)),
        Window('30s Sliding', SlidingWindow(second, 30))
)
```

The query contains four different types of windowing functions, which is interesting because you might be able to use this technique to find the one that works best. One example is in the real-time brain wave scenario detection program, although there were many results from the tumbling window function that did not result in a match to the scenario being streamed. In addition to performing more EDA, you might consider changing the window function types and their durations to see if any result in higher matching. The approach of using many different types at the same time can help expedite the exploratory data analysis process. In this example the tumbling window will store the incoming brain wave readings for 10 seconds and then run the `SELECT` statement captured on that collected data. The hopping window will also store the incoming data for 10 seconds before executing the `SELECT` statement; however, there will be a 5-second overlap in those 10 seconds. Refer to Figure 3.80 as a reminder of how this looks in practice. The session window captures incoming brain wave readings for at least 30 seconds and a maximum duration of 60 seconds before executing the `SELECT` statement. Finally, the sliding window that is commonly used with the `HAVING` statement will execute the `SELECT` statements on windows of every 30 seconds that match the `HAVING` pattern, something like the following:

```
HAVING COUNT(*) > 10
```

Once the streaming is complete, you can view the query results in the SQL pool. A sample query was provided and results in the output are shown in Figure 7.30.

FIGURE 7.30 Windowed aggregates output

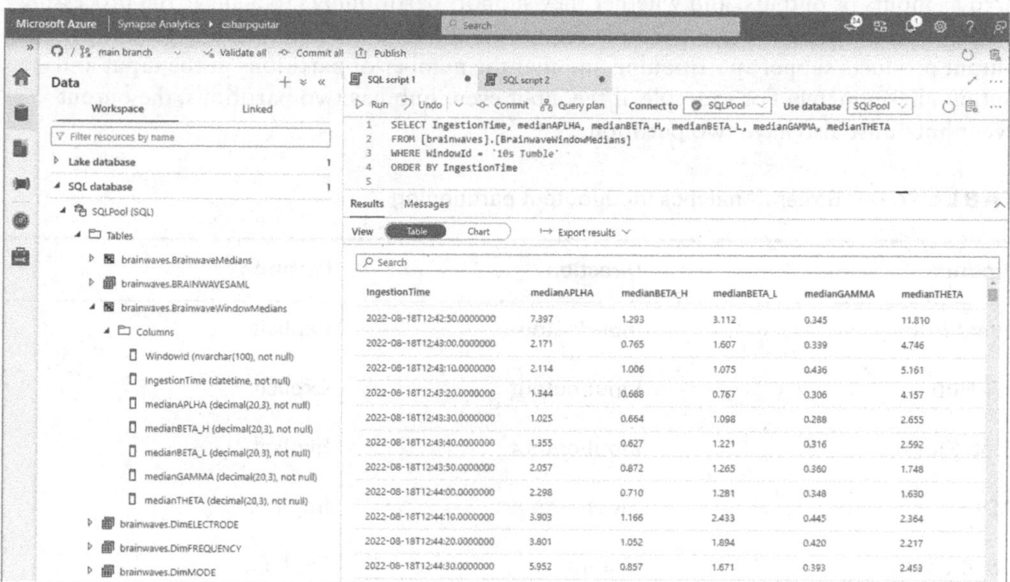

The output of the query represents the tumbling window results, which are calculated and output into the SQL pool table every 10 seconds. You could then conceivably use the scenario frequency ranges from Table 5.2 on each `WindowId` and determine which configuration results in the greatest match.

Process Data Within One Partition

Partitioning has been covered in many different scenarios and contexts. For example, in Exercise 2.2 you provisioned an Azure Cosmos DB and changed the partition key to `/pk`, and in Exercise 3.16 you provisioned an event hub with two partitions. The purpose and benefits of partitioning should be clear. To summarize: partitioning is the grouping together of similar data in close physical proximity in order to gain more efficient storage and query execution speed. Both efficiency and speed of execution are attained when data with matching partition keys is stored and retrieved from a single node. Data queries that pull data from remote datastores or different partition keys, or data that is located on more than a single node, takes longer to complete. The reason is due to the additional I/O reads necessary to retrieve all the data from potentially numerous remote locations. Recall from Table 7.3 that both Azure Stream Analytics and Azure Event Hubs use the concept of partitions for scalability; in this context, however, a partition is synonymous with a node rather than data structuring.

To achieve optimal processing of streamed data, you need to understand the different meanings of partitioning and how to implement them in each context. Table 7.6 summarizes which Azure products can be used with Azure Stream Analytics, whether they can be configured as inputs or outputs, and whether they support partitioning. To achieve the processing of data streams using a single partition requires that both Azure Stream Analytics input and output products support partitioning and that the number of partitions in the input and output aliases match. For example, if the input event hub has two partitions, the output event hub must also have two partitions.

TABLE 7.6 Stream Analytics input/output partitioning

Product	Direction	Partition
Event Hubs	Input/output	Explicit
IoT Hub	Input/output	Explicit
Blob Storage	Input/output	Explicit
ADLS	Input/output	Implicit
Cosmos DB	Output	Explicit
Service Bus	Output	Implicit
Synapse Analytics	Output	Implicit
Power BI	Output	Not supported

The Partition column in Table 7.6 may need more explanation. The "Implicit" value means that a partition key is provided as part of the default metadata, which is sent along with the streamed data, whereas the "Explicit" value means the partition key must be provided from the client as part of the data stream. Take a look in the `Program.cs` file located on GitHub in the `Chapter07/Ch07Ex03` directory. You will not find a partition key. To explicitly provide a partition key to the event hub from the client, which can then be used by the Azure Stream Analytics job, you update the code to something similar to the following code snippet:

```
IEnumerable<EventData> eventDataList = new List<EventData>()
  { eventData };
CancellationToken cancellationToken = new CancellationToken();
SendEventOptions eventOptions = new SendEventOptions()
  { PartitionKey = "pkBrainwavesPOW" };
await producerClient.SendAsync(eventDataList, eventOptions, cancellation
   Token);
```

When running in compatibility level 1.2 (the default) or greater, Azure Stream Analytics will automatically use the provided partition key to create a subset of your data. Older compatibility levels of Azure Stream Analytics require that you use PARTITION BY, as in the following example:

```
SELECT *
INTO Output
FROM Input PARTITION BY pkBrainwavesPOW
```

When a partition key is explicitly or implicitly provided, the subset of data with matching partition keys is processed on the same Azure Stream Analytics partition. Consider a scenario where you have many clients streaming data to your Azure Stream Analytics job, each one having a unique partition key. In this case, Azure Stream Analytics will process the data streams with different partition keys on different partitioned nodes in parallel, as illustrated in Figure 7.31.

FIGURE 7.31 Partition key mapping to Azure Stream Analytics partitions

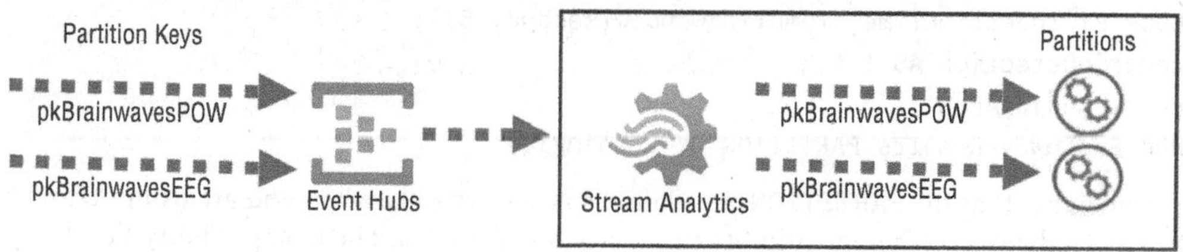

Without a partition key, the numerous BCIs that produce either POW or EEG brain waves and stream them to the same Event Hubs endpoint would not be grouped together. This would result in a random partition being selected to process the data stream, not in parallel. Using a partition key is much more efficient than processing the variety of data across all nodes sequentially. Finally, notice in Table 7.6 that Power BI does not support partitions, which means that optimal throughput of data streams through Azure Stream Analytics cannot be attained. This doesn't mean performance or throughput is inadequate; it means that when compared to an implementation that can use partition keys for input and output that support partitioning, performance would be slower for products that don't support partition keys.

Process Data Across Partitions

Streaming scenarios often do not meet the requirements necessary to achieve the parallelization achieved by partitioning. The most obvious example is related to the brainjammer brain wave solution implemented in this chapter. Partitioning cannot be utilized because the output type used for the data stream is Power BI, which does not support partitioning. Other reasons that prevent parallelized execution are mismatched partition counts and multistep queries. As mentioned briefly in the previous section, in order to achieve maximum parallel execution into, within, and out of the Azure Stream Analytics jobs, the number of partitions existing on the input type and output type must be the same. The other scenario that results in reduced parallelization efficiency has to do with multistep queries with different `PARTITION BY` values. A multistep query is similar to the one used in Exercise 7.5, where there exists more than a single `SELECT` statement, each of which could contain a `PARTITION BY` clause that uses different values for creating the partition. The first step could use both the `PartitionId` and a `ReadingId`, and the second use only the `ReadingId`. An example of this is shown in the following pseudo query:

```
WITH BrainwaveResults AS (
SELECT
    System.TimeStamp() AS IngestionTime,
    PERCENTILE_CONT(0.5) OVER (ORDER BY brainwaves.ALPHA) AS medianAPLHA,
    brainwaves.ReadingId,
    PartitiionId
FROM brainwaves PARTITION BY PartitionId, ReadingId
GROUP BY IngestionTime, TumblingWindow(second, 5)),
ScenarioDetection AS (
SELECT medianAPLHA
FROM BrainwaveResults PARTITION BY ReadingId)
```

Remember that the `PARTITION BY` clause is necessary only when you are using Azure Stream Analytics with a compatibility version of less than 1.2. The Compatibility Level blade for the Azure Stream Analytics job shows the current setting, which you can change if required. Figure 7.32 illustrates the blade in the Azure portal.

FIGURE 7.32 The Azure Stream Analytics Compatibility Level blade

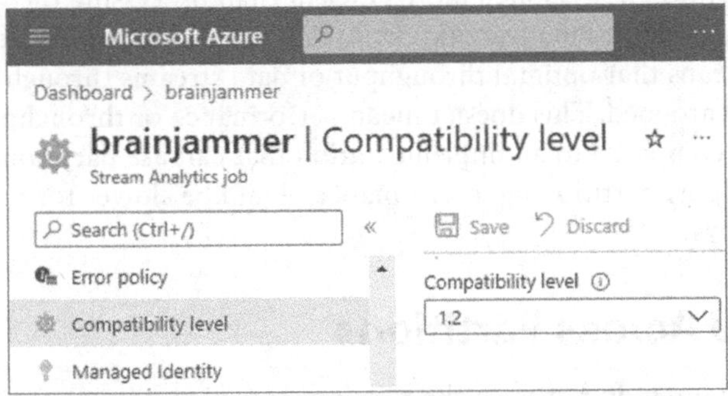

There is one more point to call out here regarding parallelization in a scenario where your solution doesn't meet the requirements for end-to-end partitioning. It was stated that

in order to achieve maximum parallelization, your solution must meet the requirements, and that just because all requirements are not met, it doesn't mean you can gain some parallelization. Some parallelization is better than none. Even though using a nonpartitioned output type like Power BI means that a portion of the data stream would flow more slowly, there still can be gains made using the input type and Azure Stream Analytics itself. For example, without including a partition key with the data stream sent to the Event Hubs endpoint, the data is load balanced across all partitions. In a scenario where there are only two and the volume and velocity are relatively low, this can still work fine. However, when you have, for example, between 100,000 and 1,000,000 events per minute spread across the maximum of 32 partitions, it is feasible that some kind of shuffling happens to order to put the data into a queryable form. By passing a partition key to Event Hubs, all events with the same partition key will flow into the same Event Hubs partition, which means that no shuffling is required and a single Azure Stream Analytics partition (i.e., a node) will perform the coded analytics on that subset of windowed data.

Upsert Data

An upsert in the stream processing context is the same as in other data analytics scenarios, such as batch or pipeline transformation processing. The action performed when executing an upsert is either an update or an insert. If the data currently being processed already exists in the datastore, an update is performed on that dataset. If the data does not already exist, then it is inserted into the datastore. The questions are, when in the stream processing pipeline can data be upserted, and where is the data stored so that the upsert can be performed? The answer to those questions, like in most cases, depends on the requirements for the stream processing solution. Consider the lambda architecture hot path, which feeds data to a speed layer and serving layer (refer to Figure 3.13). Data flowing along the speed layer that is consumed in real time has a very short window in which it can be upserted. Consider Figure 7.25, where an input table persists data in memory. You can use the processing that happens between that input table and the results table to perform the logic required to execute an upsert. Because the data is persisted into a datastore like Azure Cosmos DB, ADLS, or an Azure Synapse Analytics SQP pool along the serving layer, performing an upsert as the data arrives is possible prior to its consumption by downstream clients. The following sections discuss additional details about upserts specific to Azure Stream Analytics and Azure Databricks.

Azure Stream Analytics

The best solution for performing upserts using Azure Stream Analytics is to place them into a persisted datastore, perform the upsert there, and then make them available for consumption. This approach aligns best with the serving layer component of the lambda architecture. Numerous products can be used to persist the streamed data so that an upsert can be performed. A few of them are covered here.

Azure Synapse Analytics

There are numerous methods for performing upserts from an Azure Stream Analytics data stream in Azure Synapse Analytics. One approach is to replicate the pattern shown in Figure 7.25. Instead of placing the data directly into the final result table, you would place it first into an input table (i.e., a landing table or temporary table). As of this writing, the MERGE command in Azure Synapse Analytics is in preview, but it will be supported in the near term. Use the MERGE command between the two tables placed into a scheduled pipeline stored procedure activity. The following code snippet is an example of the command to create such a stored procedure:

```
CREATE PROC [brainwaves].[uspMergeBrainwaveMedians] AS
 MERGE INTO [brainwaves].[BrainwaveMedians] target
 USING [brainwaves].[BrainwaveMediansInput] AS i
 ON target.[ReadingDate] = i.[ReadingDate]
 WHEN MATCHED THEN
  UPDATE SET
   target.[medianALPHA] = i.[medianALPHA],
   target.[medianBETA_H] = i.[medianBETA_H],
   target.[medianBETA_L] = i.[medianBETA_L],
   target.[medianGAMMA] = i.[medianGAMMA],
   target.[medianTHETA] = i.[medianTHETA]
 WHEN NOT MATCHED BY target THEN
  INSERT
   (ReadingDate, medianALPHA, medianBETA_H, medianBETA_L, medianGAMMA,
     medianTHETA)
  VALUES
   (i.ReadingDate, i.medianALPHA, i.medianBETA_H,
    i.medianBETA_L, i.medianGAMMA, i.medianTHETA)
```

When the uspMergeBrainwaveMedians stored procedure is executed, it compares data on the target BrainwavesMedians table with the data on the input BrainwaveMediansInput table. If a match is found using a column named ReadingDate that exists on both tables, it means the row has been inserted once before. In this case the values on the target table (i.e., the results table) are updated with the values from the input table. If no match is found, it is concluded that the record is new and it is inserted into the target table. The text used to create the stored procedure is in the uspMergeBrainwaveMedians.sql file in the Chapter07 directory on GitHub at https://github.com/benperk/ADE.

In Exercise 5.1 you created a stored procedure named uspCreateAndPopulateFactReading and added it to the IngestTransform BrainwaveReadings Azure Synapse Analytics pipeline (refer to Figure 5.3). You performed that exercise before learning about triggers and scheduling, which were discussed in Chapter 6, so you were instructed to trigger the pipeline manually. However, now you can use what you learned in Chapter 6 about the different types of triggers to determine which kind to use. The Azure Stream Analytics query used in Exercise 7.5 created a tumbling window in 5-second intervals. Perhaps in this scenario either a scheduled or tumbling window trigger would be most appropriate. Considering that the data stream will flow through the serving layer, which is not real time, it might be prudent to trigger the pipeline using a schedule trigger. How frequently to run the pipeline depends on how urgently the data needs to be delivered along this path.

The other approach for performing upserts covered here is to use an Azure function. As shown in Figure 7.5, an Azure function can be used as an output with an Azure Stream Analytics job. The data is sent in JSON format to the Azure function from Azure Stream Analytics in the body of an HTTPS POST and resembles the following, depending on the Azure Stream Analytics query:

```
[{"Scenario": "Meditation",
  "ReadingDate": 2021-07-29T12:41:00,
  "medianAPLHA": 5.801,
  "medianBETA_H": 0.9892,
  "medianBETA_L": 2.6132,
  "medianGAMMA": 0.7368,
  "medianTHETA": 31.6376}]
```

To implement this solution, you would first deserialize the JSON content and format the data into the same `MERGE` statement used for the `uspMergeBrainwaveMedians` stored procedure, which may resemble the following:

```
MERGE INTO [brainwaves].[BrainwaveMedians] target
 ON target.[ReadingDate] = "2021-07-29T12:41:00"
 WHEN MATCHED THEN
  UPDATE SET
   target.[medianALPHA] = "5.801",
   target.[medianBETA_H] = "0.9892",
   target.[medianBETA_L] = "2.6132",
   target.[medianGAMMA] = "0.7368",
   target.[medianTHETA] = "31.6376"
 WHEN NOT MATCHED BY target THEN
  INSERT
   (ReadingDate, medianALPHA, medianBETA_H, medianBETA_L, medianGAMMA, median
      THETA)
  VALUES
   ("2021-07-29T12:41:00", "5.801", "0.9892", "2.6132", "0.7368", "31.6376")
```

It is possible to make a connection to your Azure Synapse Analytics SQL pool using a connection string from a remote source. In this case the remote source is an Azure function. You can find the connection string for your SQL pool on the Dedicated SQL Pool blade in the Azure portal, as shown in Figure 7.33.

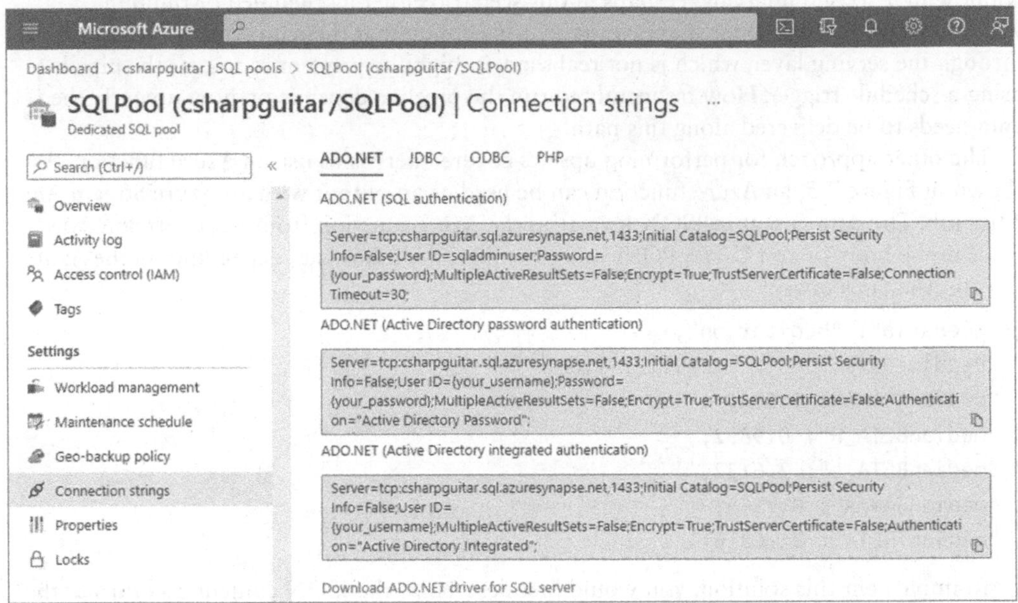

FIGURE 7.33 Upsert on streamed data using an Azure function, connection string

There are many approaches for executing an upsert on streaming data. They are limited only by your imagination and their support by the product you need to perform the action on.

Azure Cosmos DB

As you learned in the previous section, the output of the Azure Stream Analytics job is in JSON format. This means it is natively suited to flow directly into an Azure Cosmos DB. Figure 3.13 shows an Azure Cosmos DB as an example of a datastore in the serving layer of the lambda architecture. The upsert of data stored on an Azure Cosmos DB is built into the product itself when a compatibility level of 1.2 is set in your Azure Stream Analytics job. Azure Cosmos DB uses the document ID of the uploaded record to determine whether an insert or an update is required. As you would expect, when an existing document is found in the container that matches the document ID of the one received by Azure Cosmos DB, an update is performed to that document. Otherwise, when no document with the provided document ID exists in the container, the document is inserted. To get some experience and learn firsthand how this works, complete Exercise 7.8, where you will perform an upsert from Azure Stream Analytics on a document stored in an Azure Cosmos DB database container.

EXERCISE 7.8

Upsert Stream Processed Data in Azure Cosmos DB

1. Log in to the Azure portal at `https://portal.azure.com` ➢ navigate to the Azure Stream Analytics job you created in Exercise 3.17 ➢ select Outputs from the navigation menu ➢ select the + Add drop-down menu ➢ select Cosmos DB ➢ enter an output alias (I used **cosmosDB**) ➢ click the Select Cosmos DB from your subscription radio button ➢ choose the subscription ➢ select the Account ID ➢ select the database (consider using the Cosmos DB you created in Exercise 2.2, but it is not required) ➢ select the container name ➢ select Connection String from the Authentication Mode drop-down list box (if the Account Key field is greyed out, manually provide the settings) ➢ enter **ReadingDate** into the Document Id text box ➢ and then click Save. The configuration should resemble Figure 7.34.

FIGURE 7.34 Upserting streamed data on Azure Cosmos DB—configuring output

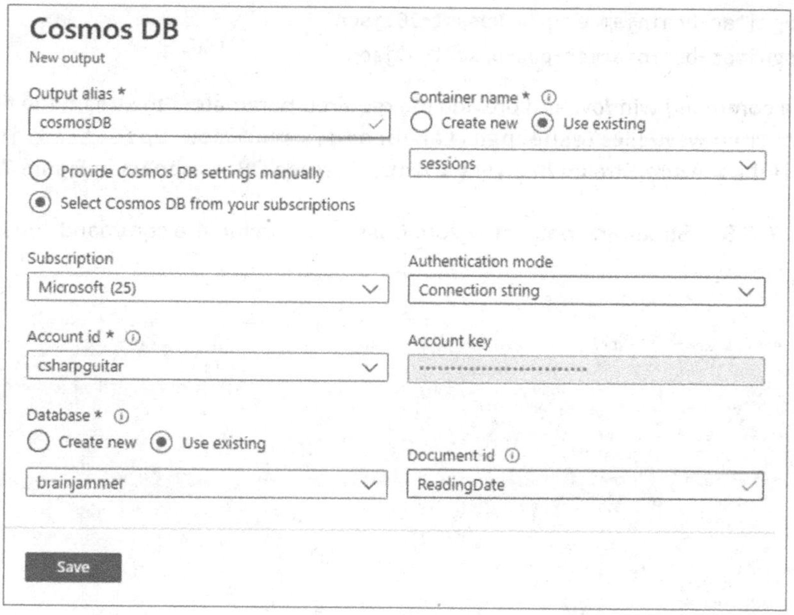

EXERCISE 7.8 *(continued)*

2. Select Query from the navigation menu ➢ enter the following query into the query window ➢ and then click Save Query. The query is available in the `StreamAnalyticsQuery.txt` file located in the `Chapter07/Ch07Ex08` directory on GitHub.

```
SELECT brainwaves.pk, brainwaves.ReadingDate, brainwaves.ALPHA, brainwaves
   .BETA_L,
       brainwaves.BETA_H, brainwaves.GAMMA, brainwaves.THETA
INTO cosmosDB
FROM brainwaves
```

3. Start the Azure Stream Analytics job ➢ download and extract the files located in the `brainjammer.zip` file in the `Chapter07/Ch07Ex08` directory on GitHub ➢ and then download the following JSON files from the GitHub location:

```
csharpguitar-brainjammer-pow-upsert-10.json
csharpguitar-brainjammer-pow-upsert-5.json
```

4. Open a command window and provide the required parameters to stream the first of the two brain wave files (`csharpguitar-brainjammer-pow-upsert-10.json`) to Event Hubs ➢ Azure Stream Analytics ➢ Azure Cosmos DB, as shown in Figure 7.35.

FIGURE 7.35 Streaming data into Azure Cosmos DB using the command console

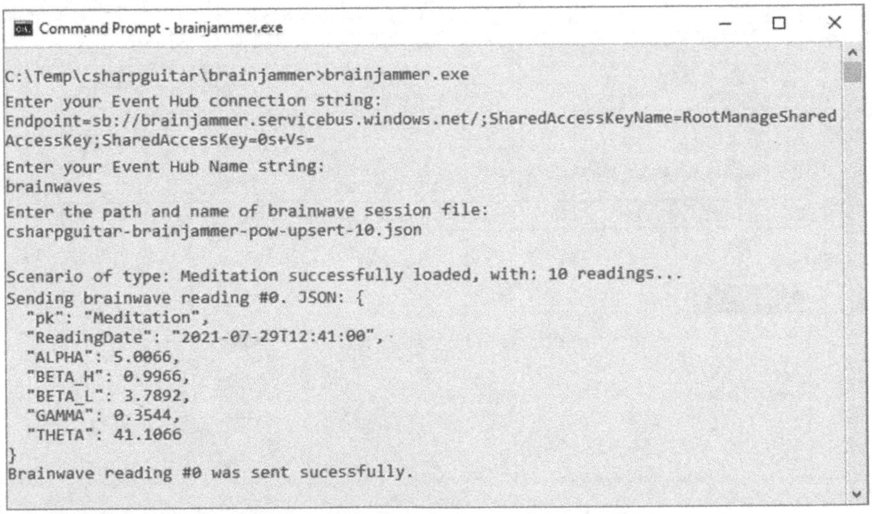

```
Command Prompt - brainjammer.exe

C:\Temp\csharpguitar\brainjammer>brainjammer.exe
Enter your Event Hub connection string:
Endpoint=sb://brainjammer.servicebus.windows.net/;SharedAccessKeyName=RootManageShared
AccessKey;SharedAccessKey=0s+Vs=
Enter your Event Hub Name string:
brainwaves
Enter the path and name of brainwave session file:
csharpguitar-brainjammer-pow-upsert-10.json

Scenario of type: Meditation successfully loaded, with: 10 readings...
Sending brainwave reading #0. JSON: {
  "pk": "Meditation",
  "ReadingDate": "2021-07-29T12:41:00",
  "ALPHA": 5.0066,
  "BETA_H": 0.9966,
  "BETA_L": 3.7892,
  "GAMMA": 0.3544,
  "THETA": 41.1066
}
Brainwave reading #0 was sent sucessfully.
```

5. Navigate to the Azure Cosmos DB that you provisioned in Exercise 2.2 and configured for the output alias in step 1 ➢ click the Data Explorer navigation item ➢ drill down to the Items collection ➢ and then select one of the streamed documents. Note that you might need to click the Refresh icon to the right of the /pk column. Figure 7.36 shows the result.

FIGURE 7.36 Inserting streamed data on Azure Cosmos DB, initial load

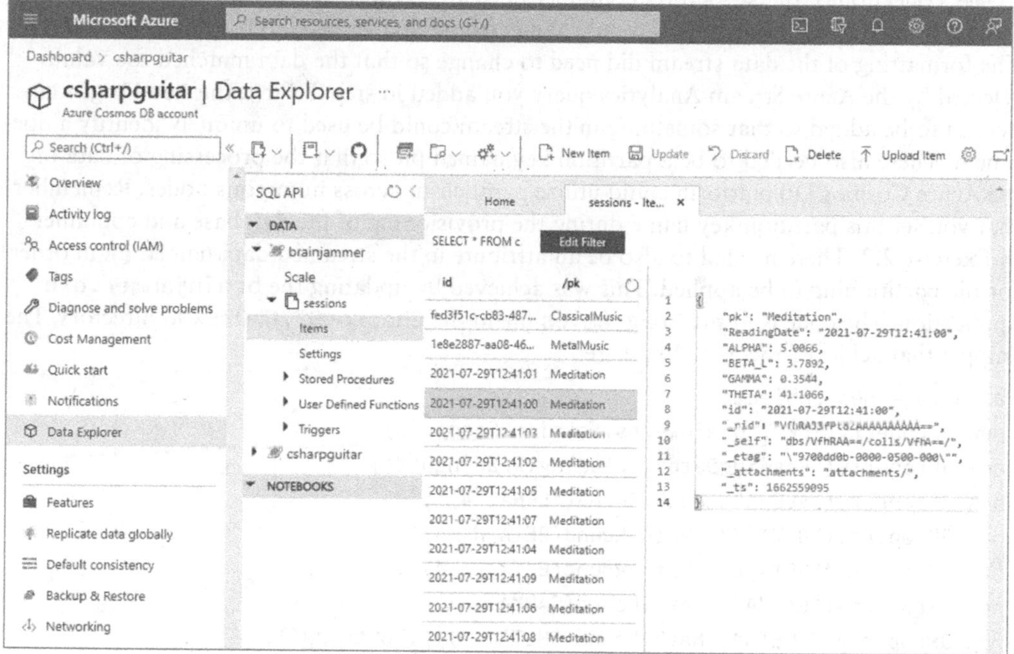

6. Click each streamed document and take special note of the THETA values for documents with the following IDs:

```
2021-07-29T12:41:00 "THETA": 41.1066
2021-07-29T12:41:01 "THETA": 28.0412
2021-07-29T12:41:02 "THETA": 17.639
```

7. Repeat step 4 using the `csharpguitar-brainjammer-pow-upsert-5.json` file ➢ view the documents again ➢ observe the differences ➢ and then stop the Azure Stream Analytics job.

The first action taken in Exercise 7.8 was to configure an output alias for an Azure Cosmos DB. You chose the connection string authentication mode that utilizes the accessible Azure Cosmos DB endpoint, which resembles the following: `https://csharpguitar.documents.azure.com`. Combining that endpoint with an access key, which is found on the Keys blade of the Azure Cosmos DB account, meets the requirements for making a connection to the database and container. You also added the value of `ReadingDate` to the Document Id text box, which results in the storage of the value into the `id` column in the `Items` collection of the `sessions` container in Azure Cosmos DB, as shown in Figure 7.36.

The format of the JSON files did not change from the ones used in previous examples. The formatting of the data stream did need to change so that the data matched the values selected by the Azure Stream Analytics query you added in step 2. First, the `ReadingDate` needed to be added so that something in the stream could be used to uniquely identify a document. There also needed to be a partition key named `pk` so that the processing of data on the Azure Cosmos DB platform could utilize parallelism across numerous nodes. Remember that you set this partition key name during the provisioning of the database and container in Exercise 2.2. There needed to also be an attribute in the streamed data named `pk` in order for the partitioning to be applied. This was achieved by updating the `brainjammer.exe` application. The code is in the `Program.cs` file in the `Chapter07/Ch07Ex08` directory. The snippet that achieved this is shown here:

```
var data = new JObject(
 new JProperty("pk", brainwaves.Session.Scenario),
 new JProperty("ReadingDate", reading.ReadingDate),
 new JProperty("ALPHA", Math.Round(ALPHA, 4)),
 new JProperty("BETA_H", Math.Round(BETA_H, 4)),
 new JProperty("BETA_L", Math.Round(BETA_L, 4)),
 new JProperty("GAMMA", Math.Round(GAMMA, 4)),
 new JProperty("THETA", Math.Round(THETA, 4))).ToString();
```

Notice that the Azure Stream Analytics query was updated to use the output alias of `cosmosDB` next to the `INTO` command. This is how the query is instructed to send the data stream to the Azure Cosmos DB. The input alias of `brainwaves` next to the `FROM` command remained the same as the data is streamed to the Event Hubs endpoints, as it has been for previous exercises.

The first file that was streamed, `csharpguitar-brainjammer-pow-upsert-10.json`, contains 10 brain wave readings. Because none of these readings currently exist in the container, all of them are inserted. Notice that 10 records are added to the container shown in Figure 7.36. The second file, `csharpguitar-brainjammer-pow-upsert-5.json`, contains three records with a `ReadingDate` that is equal to documents that currently exist in the container and two that do not have a match. This results in two new documents being added to the container, bringing the total up to 12, and the other three being updated. This is the example of an upsert at its finest. The first three upserted documents with the new THETA values and the two new documents are listed here.

```
2021-07-29T12:41:00 "THETA": 5.4866
2021-07-29T12:41:01 "THETA": 4.6612
2021-07-29T12:41:02 "THETA": 2.605
2021-07-29T12:42:03
2021-07-29T12:42:04
```

Lastly, you stopped the Azure Stream Analytics job to save costs, as it is no longer required.

Azure Databricks

In Exercise 7.6 you created a stream processing solution using Azure Databricks. That stream processing solution used the Append output mode and displayed the data stream in the console, as illustrated in Figure 7.28. This was achieved using the following Scala code snippet:

```
messages.writeStream.outputMode("append").format("console").
    option("truncate", false).start().awaitTermination()
```

As with Azure Stream Analytics, there are numerous ways in which upserting can be implemented. Two options are discussed in the following text, starting with a delta table solution. You would first need a delta table to store the incoming data stream, which can be achieved using the following code snippet, which is followed by code that loads the table into a reference object:

```
Seq.empty[(Long, Timestamp, Long, String)]
  .toDF("Offset", "Time", "Timestamp", "Body")
  .write.format("delta").mode("overwrite").saveAsTable("brainwaves")

var deltaTable = DeltaTable.forName("brainwaves")
```

Reading the data stream is the same as you implemented in Exercise 7.6.

```
val incomingStream = spark.readStream.format("eventhubs")
  .options(customEventhubParameters.toMap).load()
```

Writing the data stream is where you would implement the upsert logic. The first portion of the code notifies the runtime that the format of the data is to be structured in delta format. The `foreachBatch()` method iterates through all the streamed data for the given time window and attempts to merge it with the data on the existing data on the `brainwaves` delta table.

```
incomingStream.writeStream.format("delta").foreachBatch(
  deltaTable.as("bw").merge(messages.as("m"), "m.Time = bw.Time")
  .whenMatched().updateAll()
```

```
  .whenNotMatched().insertAll()
  .execute()
).outputMode("update").start()
```

The instantiation of the messages object is not displayed; however, it is the same as you performed in Exercise 7.6 and is shown in the sample source code on GitHub. The code for this example is in the Chapter07 directory in the brainwaveUpsert.scala Databricks notebook source file. The ID used to determine if a record already exists is within the Time column. If a match is found, the updateAll() method is called; otherwise, the insertAll() method is executed. Also notice the parameter value passed to the outputMode() method. Output mode was covered in detail in Chapter 6, where you learned that when Update is set as the Output mode, an aggregate is required; in this case, it is the value in the Time column. Instead of data being appended to the end of the table, an update is performed.

Another approach for implementing upserts in Azure Databricks is to use the MERGE SQL command. This is almost identical to the implementation you read about in the previous discussion concerning upserts Azure Stream Analytics to Azure Synapse Analytics.

```
messages.createOrReplaceTempView("updates")
messages.sql("""
  MERGE INTO brainwaves bw
  USING updates u
  ON u.Time = bw.Time
  WHEN MATCHED THEN UPDATE *
  WHEN NOT MATCHED THEN INSERT *
""")
```

The first line of code creates a temporary view that contains the current batch of streamed data. The next lines of code perform the MERGE SQL statement, which either updates matching records or inserts new ones.

Handle Schema Drift

Schema drift was introduced in Chapter 2, where you learned what a schema is and that schemas can, and often do, change. In Chapter 4 you learned about schema drift in the context of a Data Flow activity that exposes an option to allow schema drifting (refer to Figure 4.25). Consider the following JSON document, which is expected to be received from an IoT device like a BCI:

```
[{"Scenario": "Meditation",
  "ReadingDate": 2021-07-29T12:41:00,
  "APLHA": 5.801,
  "BETA_H": 0.9892,
```

```
  "BETA_L": 2.6132,
  "GAMMA": 0.7368,
  "THETA": 31.6376}]
```

The baseline schema definition for that document would resemble the following. Notice that the schema provides a description of the value and its expected data type.

```
{"Scenario": { "description": "The brainwave scenario", "type": "string" },
 "ReadingDate": {"description": "The brainwave reading date", "type":
   "datetime" },
 "ALPHA":  { "description": "ALPHA frequency reading",  "type": "float" },
 "BETA_H": { "description": "BETA_H frequency reading", "type": "float" },
 "BETA_L": { "description": "BETA_L frequency reading", "type": "float" },
 "GAMMA":  { "description": "GAMMA frequency reading",  "type": "float" },
 "THETA":  { "description": "THETA frequency reading",  "type": "float" }}
```

As time progresses and new devices and the software they use are updated, it is very possible that the format of the data being produced will deviate from the baseline. That deviation is referred to as *schema drift*. Consider that the newest version of the JSON document produced by the BCI now contains a value for `MODE` and modification to the `ReadingDate` data type. The newest document and schema would resemble the following:

```
[{"Scenario": "Meditation",
  "ReadingDate": 2021-07-29T12:41:00,
  "APLHA": 5.801,
  "BETA_H": 0.9892,
  "BETA_L": 2.6132,
  "GAMMA": 0.7368,
  "THETA": 31.6376,
  "MODE": "POW"}]

{"Scenario": { "description": "The brainwave scenario", "type": "string" },
 "ReadingDate": { "description": "The brainwave reading date", "type":
   "string" },
 "ALPHA":  { "description": "ALPHA frequency reading",  "type": "float" },
 "BETA_H": { "description": "BETA_H frequency reading", "type": "float" },
 "BETA_L": { "description": "BETA_L frequency reading", "type": "float" },
 "GAMMA":  { "description": "GAMMA frequency reading",  "type": "float" },
 "THETA":  { "description": "THETA frequency reading",  "type": "float" },
 "MODE":   { "description": "Either POW or EEG mode",   "type": "string" }}
```

The question is, how can you manage this schema drift in the context of a stream processing solution, as shown in Figure 7.37?

FIGURE 7.37 Handling schema drift in a stream processing solution

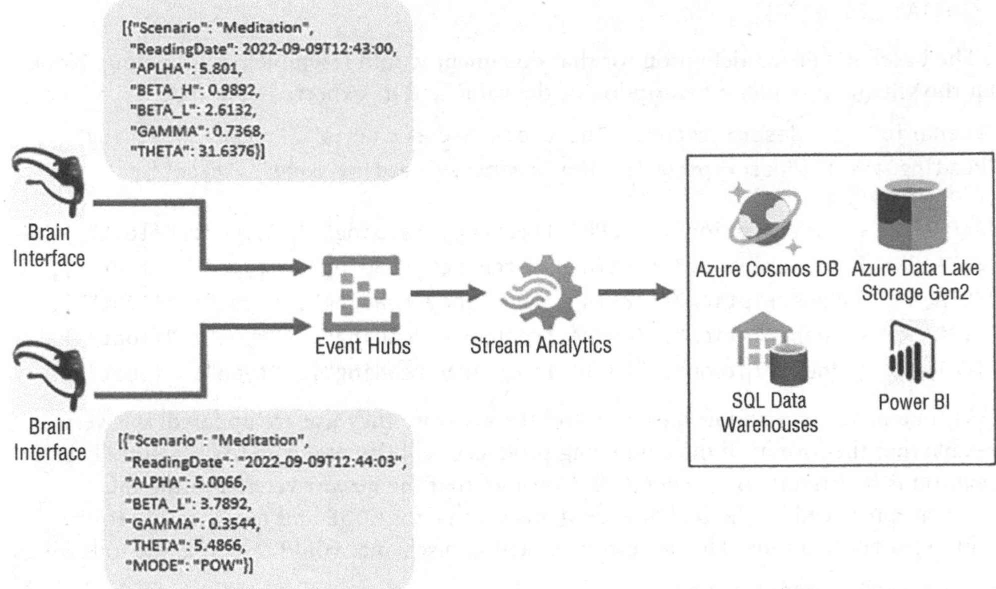

You would want to avoid creating new Event Hubs endpoints for every different kind of stream producer. You also would avoid that approach for each new software version of those data producers. The same goes for your Azure Stream Analytics job; it would not be optimal to have a job either for each data producer or for each schema variation produced. For any medium- to large-scale stream processing solution, that approach would be too costly, not only from a cloud consumption cost perspective but also from a maintenance and support perspective. You would end up with too many endpoints and too many jobs. An alternative would be to optimize the Azure Stream Analytics query, as you will do Exercise 7.9.

EXERCISE 7.9

Handle Schema Drift in Azure Stream Analytics

1. Log in to the Azure portal at `https://portal.azure.com` ➢ navigate to the Azure Stream Analytics job you created in Exercise 3.17 ➢ select Query from the navigation menu ➢ enter into the query window the query in the `StreamAnalyticsQuery.txt` file located in the `Chapter07/Ch07Ex09` directory on GitHub ➢ click the Save Query button ➢ and then start the job.

2. Download the `brainjammer-legacy.zip` file from the `Chapter07/Ch07Ex09` directory on GitHub ➢ extract and execute the `brainjammer.exe` application ➢ and then use the `csharpguitar-brainjammer-pow-legacy-schema-drift.json` file as input. Note that the stream was placed into the ADLS container, not into your

Azure Cosmos DB container; notice also there is no column for `MODE` in the output (see Figure 7.38).

FIGURE 7.38 Handling schema drift in a stream processing solution in ADLS

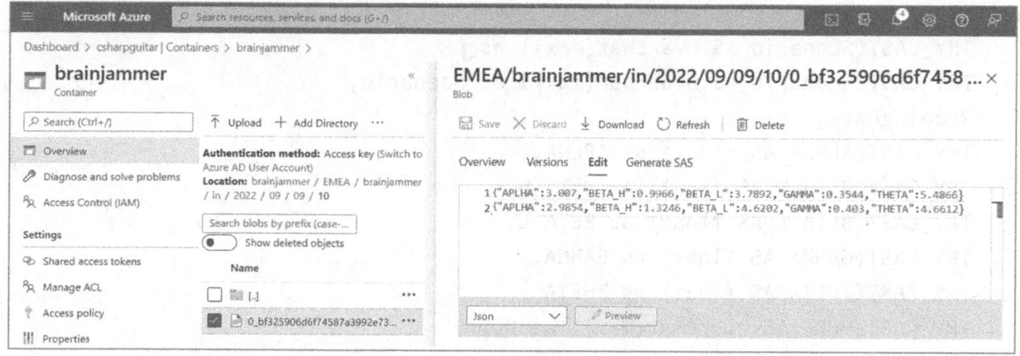

3. Download the `brainjammer-current.zip` file from the `Chapter07/Ch07Ex09` directory on GitHub ➢ extract and execute the `brainjammer.exe` application ➢ and then use the `csharpguitar-brainjammer-pow-current-schema-drift.json` file. Note that the stream was placed into the Azure Cosmos DB container, not into your ADLS container; notice also the `MODE` property and value exist in the output (see Figure 7.39).

FIGURE 7.39 Handling schema drift in a stream processing solution in Azure Cosmos DB

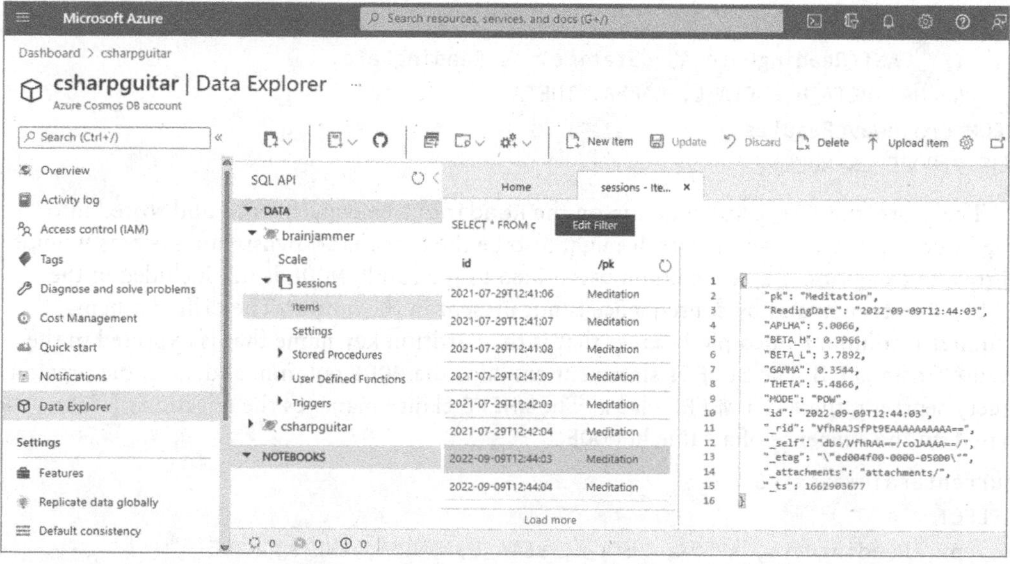

4. Stop the Azure Stream Analytics job.

The most critical part of Exercise 7.9 is the query. The first part resembles the following. Notice that the query includes the new addition of the schema, which includes `MODE`. However, `MODE` is neither selected nor provided by the devices that use the legacy schema.

```
WITH BrainwaveResults AS (
SELECT
    TRY_CAST(Scenario AS nvarchar(max)) as pk,
    TRY_CAST(Scenario AS nvarchar(max)) as Scenario,
    ReadingDate,
    TRY_CAST(ALPHA AS float) as APLHA,
    TRY_CAST(BETA_H AS float) as BETA_H,
    TRY_CAST(BETA_L AS float) as BETA_L,
    TRY_CAST(GAMMA AS float) as GAMMA,
    TRY_CAST(THETA AS float) as THETA,
    TRY_CAST(MODE AS nvarchar(max)) as MODE
FROM brainwaves),
```

A `TRY_CAST` function is not performed on `ReadingDate`, because it can be a data type of string or datetime. The next portion of the Azure Stream Analytics query uses the result in the `BrainwaveResults` dataset to format and capture the data in the necessary format. Notice that the original schema expected the data type of `ReadingDate` to be datetime. In the current schema that value will be a string. It is important to maintain that data type through this data stream, because downstream systems that use this data might break if for some reason the string value contained in `ReadingDate` does not cast to a datetime.

```
legacyBrainwaves AS (
SELECT
    Scenario,
    TRY_CAST(ReadingDate AS datetime) as ReadingDate,
    APLHA, BETA_H, BETA_L, GAMMA, THETA
FROM BrainwaveResults
WHERE MODE IS NULL),
```

Therefore, the `TRY_CAST` function on the `ReadingDate` is performed and stored into the `legacyBrainwaves` dataset. It might also be the case that downstream systems would throw an exception if a new column was added to the result. `MODE` is not included in the `SELECT` statement and by consequence is not present in the output. The drifted schema requires a column named `pk`, because that is the partition key name that is expected in the Azure Cosmos DB. The `SELECT` statement contains the `MODE` column, and, as in the previous query segment, there is a `WHERE` clause. The `WHERE` clause manages the selection of data based on the existence of a value in `MODE`.

```
currentBrainwaves AS (
SELECT
    pk, ReadingDate, APLHA, BETA_H, BETA_L, GAMMA, THETA, MODE
FROM BrainwaveResults
WHERE MODE IS NOT NULL)
```

If MODE is null, then the row is selected into the legacyBrainwaves dataset but not into the currentBrainwaves dataset, and vice versa, whereas when MODE is not null, the row is selected and stored into the currentBrainwaves dataset but not into the legacyBrainwaves dataset. The final two lines of the query resemble the following:

```
SELECT Scenario, ReadingDate, APLHA, BETA_H, BETA_L, GAMMA, THETA
  INTO ADLS FROM legacyBrainwaves

SELECT pk, ReadingDate, APLHA, BETA_H, BETA_L, GAMMA, THETA, MODE
  INTO cosmosDB FROM currentBrainwaves
```

Notice that the selected columns are slightly different and are each stored into a different output alias. As previously mentioned, when a schema is changed, it is important that downstream systems that use that data not be impacted. If there is a change that cannot be managed, then all systems that use the data would need to be tested with the new data. This is considered a breaking change. Those kinds of scenarios have a great impact, as a lot of testing is required. It would be easier to output the current version to a new location and have the option to use the new data, if necessary, instead of forcing them to be updated. Finally, notice that the values following the FROM clause reference the dataset populated from the two previous subqueries.

Note that the two brainjammer.exe applications simulate an upgrade to the device that produces data. The data streaming to your Event Hubs endpoint would now have an increase in data variety caused by a schema drift. Your Azure Stream Analytics job, the datastores, and the downstream consumers who use the data must be able to adjust to these changes. Exercise 7.9 is just one example of how that flexibility can be realized. Azure Stream Analytics does not need a schema definition for input data streams. The columns and datatypes are inferred dynamically and are implicitly cast when needed. This is a very powerful tool, but it comes with some caveats. While performing Exercise 7.9, you learned that Cosmos DB is not very supportive of the datetime datatype. When a TRY_CAST was performed on the ReadingDate into datetime format, the output failed to be stored into the Azure Cosmos DB container. The error was a format not expected or supported. The insertion was successful only when the ReadingDate was a string. Had the platform implicitly cast this value to datetime, it would not work when being stored in Azure Cosmos DB.

Finally, the source code for each brainjammer.exe is stored on GitHub in the Chapter07/Ch07Ex09 directory. The difference between each code snippet is the addition of a JProperty to contain MODE into the JObject class, as shown here:

```
new JProperty("MODE", brainwaves.Session.MODE)
```

The Session class into which the JSON files are deserialized required the addition of a MODE property, as shown here:

```
public class Session
{
  public string Scenario { get; set; }
  public string MODE { get; set; }
  public List<POWReading> POWReading { get; set; }
}
```

It is inevitable that content within data streams changes; therefore, it is very important to consider as many options as possible prior to developing your stream processing solution. Flexibility is paramount.

Configure Checkpoints/Watermarking During Processing

A checkpoint is a concept that identifies a point in time when your data is in a verifiable, production-ready state. For example, a checkpoint could be considered a backup of a set of data. This data could be used in recovery scenarios to get data that has been corrupted, deleted, or delayed back into a usable and unbroken state. In the context of Azure Stream Analytics, checkpointing is performed by the platform automatically. A checkpoint is performed on each node that is processing your data to perform streaming analytics every few minutes. If a platform upgrade happens or the node experiences a failure, the data checkpoint will be used to recover and restart the job on a new node. Two concepts you about learned in Chapter 4 are relevant here: point-in-time restore (PITR) and recovery point objective (RPO). PITR is dependent on a data snapshot taken at a given point in time, which is useful for restoring from data loss or data corruption. RPO defines the maximum amount of time it will take to recover the lost or corrupted data. Both concepts apply in the checkpointing capabilities offered with Azure Stream Analytics, which work behind the scenes without any action required from you.

A data stream, by definition, is continuously flowing; it never stops. Combining that fact with the need to monitor, replay, or repair data within the stream requires some capabilities to achieve. One such capability is a watermark. A *watermark* is an indicator that marks the point at which the event message has been ingressed by the stream processor. Figure 7.40 illustrates a data stream; each vertical line within the stream represents an event message.

FIGURE 7.40 A data stream with event messages and a watermark

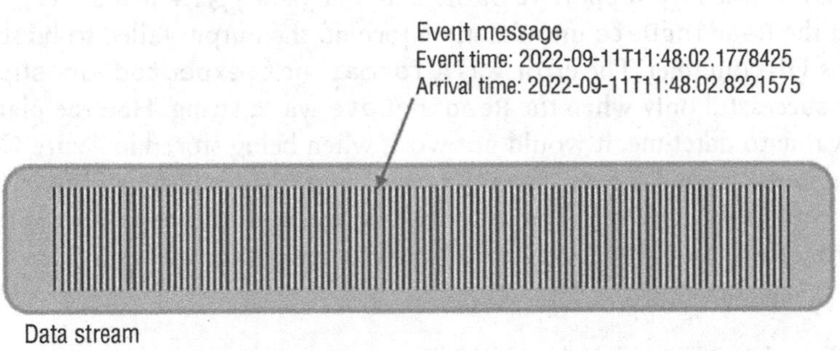

Each event message in the data stream has an event time and arrival time, which, as you can see, is a very precise datetime stamp. The event time is the timestamp that represents when the event message is generated by the data-producing device and is part of the event message payload. The arrival time is the timestamp that represents when the event message reached the ingestion endpoint, for example, an event hub. Each event message in the data stream is linked to a watermark that increases by the time frame windowing configuration for the given data stream. For example, the following window is defined as 5 seconds. The watermark will be the same for all event messages ingressed into the stream pipeline within that time window, as long as the event time and arrival time fall within the same 5-second period.

```
GROUP BY IngestionTime, TumblingWindow(second, 5)
```

The watermark is referenced for monitoring the performance of the data stream within that time window. The data stream can be replayed between two date timestamps or repaired when it is determined something unexpected happened during a given time frame. Keep in mind that this feature is managed by the platform and is abstracted away from you to a point where it is not easily observable. To better understand the watermarking concept, consider the data stream details shown in Table 7.7.

TABLE 7.7 Data stream illustration

Sequence	Arrival time	Event time	Watermark
0	10:00:00	10:00:01	10:00:00
1	10:00:02	10:00:02	10:00:00
2	10:00:04	10:00:04	10:00:00
3	10:00:06	10:00:06	10:00:05
4	10:00:09	10:00:09	10:00:05
5	10:00:11	10:00:10	10:00:10
6	10:00:11	10:00:05	10:00:10
7	10:00:13	10:00:13	10:00:10
8	10:00:15	10:00:15	10:00:15
9	10:00:17	10:00:16	10:00:15

The data points provided in Table 7.7 are visually represented in Figure 7.41. Notice that event messages that arrive within a 5-second window get the same watermark. For example, the event messages with sequence numbers between 0 and 2 all arrived between 10:00:00

and 10:00:05 and received the same watermark. You also will notice that the event message with sequence number six has an arrival time that is 6 seconds after its event time.

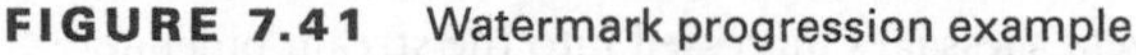

FIGURE 7.41 Watermark progression example

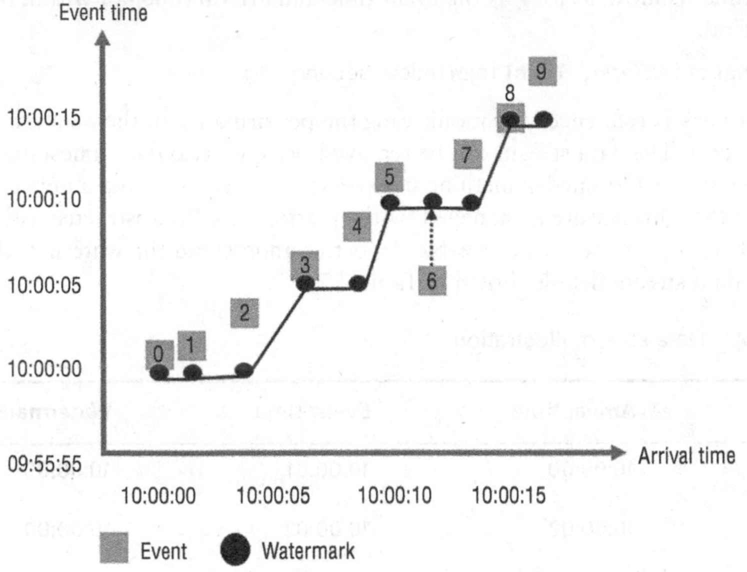

To understand what happens when event messages arrive outside a given time window and to learn about some other data streaming time progression concepts, it is important to understand time management.

In numerous places throughout this book, you have seen the data structure of a brain wave reading. This brain wave reading contains a column named `ReadingDate`. This can be considered the event time and is accessible using the `System.Timestamp()`, as shown in the following example query snippet, as well as through the column itself:

```
System.TimeStamp() AS IngestionTime
```

The ingestion point of the brain wave readings in all exercises has been via an event hub. Therefore, while working through this chapter's exercises, you may have noticed two columns on the Input Preview tab on the Query blade, such as those shown in Figure 7.42, `EventEnqueuedUtcTime` and `EventProcessedUtcTime`.

The `EventEnqueuedUtcTime` column is the timestamp in which the event message was received by the event hub for the Azure Stream Analytics job—in other words, the arrival time. The other column, `EventProcessedUtcTime`, is the date and time the Azure Stream Analytics job processed the event message. It makes sense then that the enqueued date timestamp is earlier than the processed date timestamp. Notice that the difference between the two date timestamps is about 14 seconds. To understand if 14 seconds is fast, slow, or expected, you first need to understand how Azure Stream Analytics manages time.

The variation in timestamps, like the ones shown in Table 7.7 and the one here, can be impacted for many reasons, such as clock skews between the data producer and the following five items: ingestion point availability, network bandwidth pressure, the stream processor, the unavailability of streaming data components, or latency on any of those streaming data components. Any kind of disruption can result in event messages arriving late, early, or out of order. To calculate whether an event message has arrived late, the platform compares the event time with the arrival time. If the difference between the two is greater than the time window, then the event message is considered late. Configuring the platform to handle such a scenario is done on the Event Ordering blade for the Azure Stream Analytics job, as shown in Figure 7.43.

FIGURE 7.42 The `EventEnqueuedUtcTime` and `EventProcessedUtcTime` columns on the Query blade

Input preview | Test results | SQL table schema (preview)

Showing sample events from 'brainwaves'.

Table | Raw | Refresh | Select time range | Upload sample input | Download sample data

ALPHA float	BETA_H float	BETA_L float	GAMMA float	THETA float	EventProcessedUtcTime datetime	PartitionId bigint	EventEnqueuedUtcTime datetime
15.8164	2.7158	8.0866	0.6946	10.8514	"2022-09-11T11:48:02.1778425Z"	0	"2022-09-11T11:47:48.7520000Z"
12.9088	2.2852	7.0646	0.597	12.1018	"2022-09-11T11:48:02.1778425Z"	1	"2022-09-11T11:47:48.4580000Z"
9.4424	1.7814	5.783	0.492	17.639	"2022-09-11T11:48:02.1778425Z"	0	"2022-09-11T11:47:48.2050000Z"
6.5852	1.3246	4.6202	0.403	28.0412	"2022-09-11T11:48:02.1622196Z"	1	"2022-09-11T11:47:47.9120000Z"
5.0066	0.9966	3.7892	0.3544	41.1066	"2022-09-11T11:48:02.1309911Z"	0	"2022-09-11T11:47:47.5800000Z"

FIGURE 7.43 Event ordering for a late-arriving streamed event message

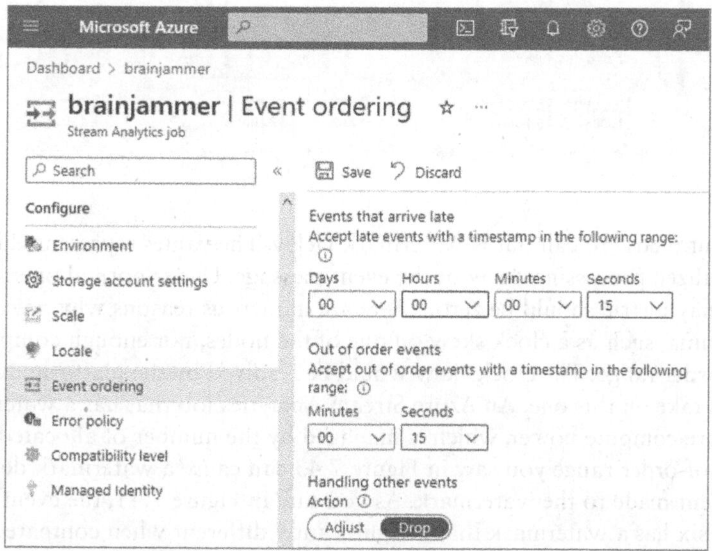

In this case, the range allows for event messages with an event time to be up to 15 seconds after the arrival time. Any event messages that fall outside of that range will be dropped. If the configuration had been less than 14 seconds, the readings shown in Figure 7.42 would have been ignored and not included in the Azure Stream Analytics output. Because the event time was within the range threshold, they were not dropped and received a timestamp stored in the `EventProcessedUtcTime` column that identifies when they were processed. If the event time had fallen outside of that range, you might have wondered why the event messages had not been processed. To gain some clues concerning why event messages are not processed, you can review the available Azure Stream Analytics job metrics. Some default metrics are viewable on the Overview blade for the Azure Stream Analytics job after you select the Monitoring tab (see Figure 7.44).

FIGURE 7.44 Azure Stream Analytics monitoring metrics

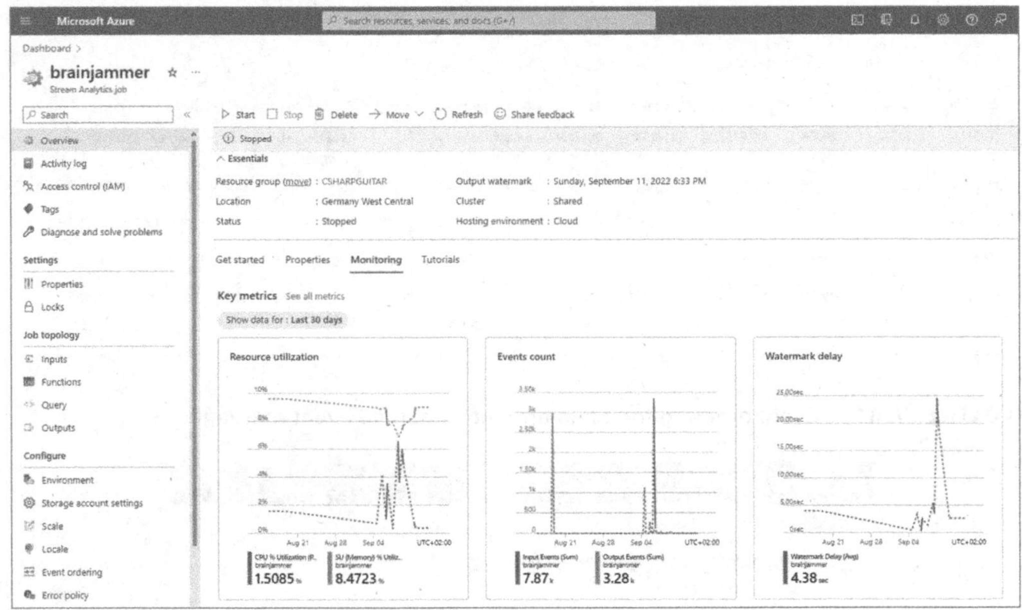

An important metric to call out is Watermark Delay. The values represented in the metric indicate the realized processing delay of the event message. Under normal operation the Watermark Delay metric should be zero. There are numerous reasons why a watermark delay is happening, such as a clock skew on one of the nodes, not enough compute resources, or the out-of-order range. The clock skew would be resolved by the platform, so there is no action you can take on this one. An Azure Stream Analytics job that has a watermark delay might need more compute power, which is managed by the number of allocated streaming units. The out-of-order range you saw in Figure 7.43 can cause a watermark delay because of the adjustment made to the watermark. As you saw in Figure 7.41, the event message with sequence six has a watermark that is significantly different when compared to the other event messages. Sequence six is considered a late-arriving message, but messages can also arrive early for many of the same reasons they arrive late. When messages arrive early, which means the event time is greater than the arrival time, it means the watermark will be older than the event time too. This is a problem if there is a restart of the Azure Stream Analytics job. Reasons for restarting were discussed earlier. One of the reasons is that you manually stopped the job and now want to start it again from the time it was last stopped (refer to Figure 7.18). To make sure no event messages are missed, messages are taken from the time of stoppage plus the configured time window. Since the early-arriving event messages will have a watermark greater than the time window, they will be dropped and won't be processed, but they will be incremented on the Early Input Events metric, which you can find by selecting the See All Metrics link next to the Key Metrics header in Figure 7.44.

Replay Archived Stream Data

When a disruption to your data stream processing occurs in Azure Stream Analytics, as you learned in the last section, the platform uses checkpoints and watermarks to recover. The recovery consists of processing any lost events and catching up to any queued event messages. There is currently no built-in archive of your data stream events. This means that, if you want it, you need to create it yourself. You might be surprised to read that an exercise you already completed in many ways created an archived set of data that can be used to replay the stream, if required. In Exercise 7.9, you wrote the output of your Azure Stream Analytics query to two different data storage products. The same approach is useful for writing an archive, as long as the data written can be used by an application to replay (resend) the data to the ingestion point. Consider Figure 7.45, which shows such an archival solution.

FIGURE 7.45 An archived data stream solution

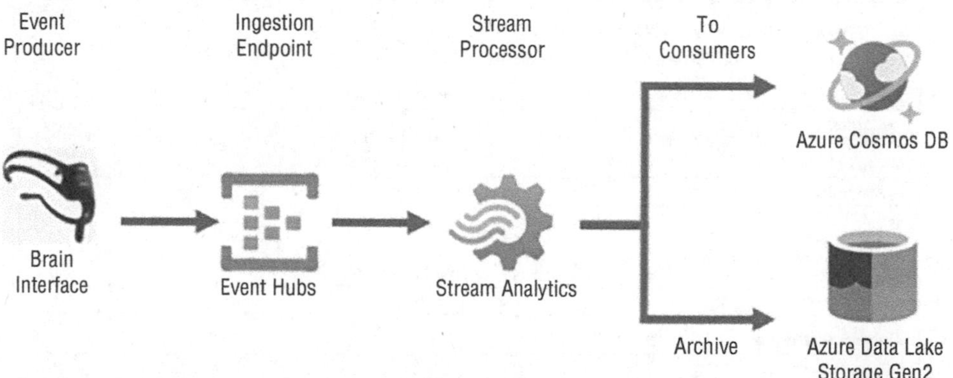

The solution begins with an event producer that sends data messages to an Azure Event Hubs endpoint. Azure Stream Analytics has subscribed to be notified of messages that are ingested into the endpoint message partition. The subscription was achieved by configuring Event Hubs as an input alias for the Azure Stream Analytics job. The data stream messages are retrieved from the Event Hubs partition and processed. Once the messages are processed, the data is stored in the data storage and configured as outputs used in the query's `INTO` statement. That scenario is exactly what you have achieved over the course of the exercises in this chapter. To replay a data stream using the data that was stored in your ADLS container, perform Exercise 7.10.

EXERCISE 7.10

Replay an Archived Stream Data in Azure Stream Analytics

1. Log in to the Azure portal at `https://portal.azure.com` ➢ navigate to the Azure Stream Analytics job you created in Exercise 3.17 ➢ select Input from the navigation menu ➢ select the + Add Stream Input drop-down menu ➢ select Blob Sorage/ADLS Gen2 ➢ provide an input alias name (I used **archive**) ➢ select Connection String from the Authentication Mode drop-down list box ➢ select the ADLS container where you stored the output in Exercise 7.9 ➢ and then enter the path to the file into the Path Pattern text box, perhaps like the following. Note that the filename is shortened for brevity and is not the actual filename of the output from Exercise 7.9.

   ```
   EMEA/brainjammer/in/2022/09/09/10/0_bf325906d_1.json
   ```

2. The configuration should resemble Figure 7.46. Click the Save button.

FIGURE 7.46 Configurating an archive input alias

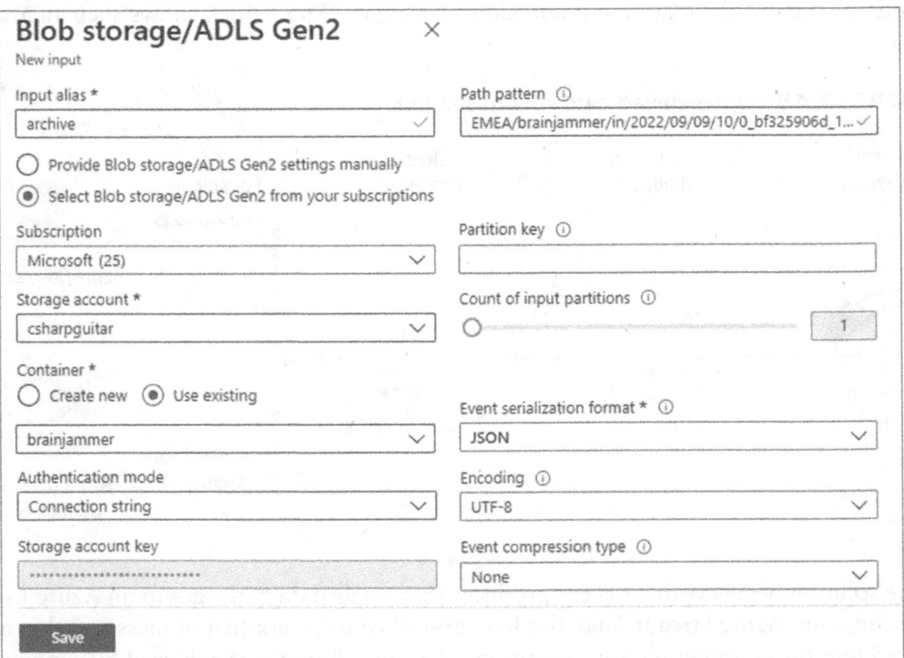

3. Select Query from the navigation menu ➤ enter the following query into the query window ➤ click the Save Query button ➤ and then start the job. The query is available in the `StreamAnalyticsQuery.txt` file located in the `Chapter07/Ch07Ex10` directory on GitHub.

```
SELECT Scenario, ReadingDate, ALPHA, BETA_H, BETA_L, GAMMA, THETA
INTO ADLS
FROM archive
```

4. Wait until the job has started ➤ navigate to the ADLS container and location you configured for the `archive` input alias in step 1 ➤ download the `0_bf325906d_1.json` file from the `Chapter07/Ch07Ex10` directory on GitHub ➤ upload that file to the ADLS container ➤ and then navigate to the location configured for your ADLS Output alias. A duplicate of the file is present, as shown in Figure 7.47.

FIGURE 7.47 Archive replay data result

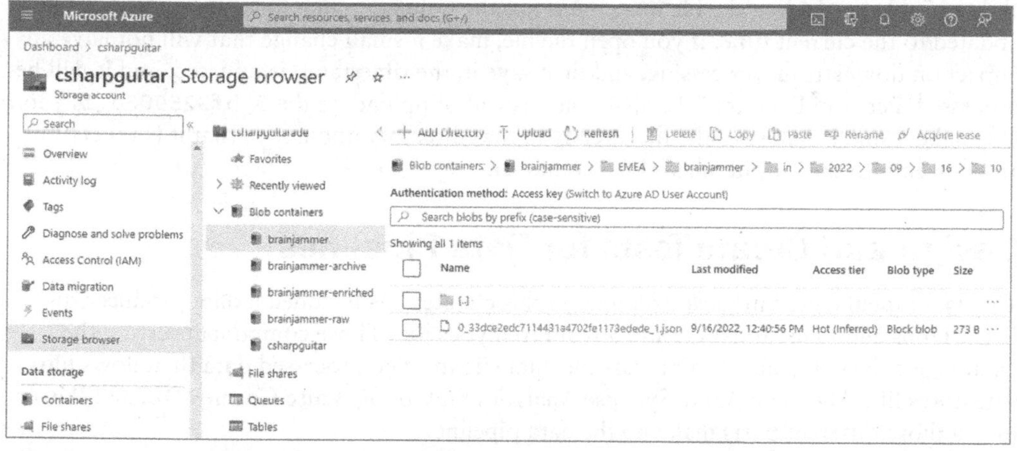

5. Stop the Azure Stream Analytics job.

Exercise 7.10 illustrates how a file generated by the output of a data stream can be replayed and stored on a targeted datastore. You may be wondering why something like this would be needed. Testing new features, populating testing environments with data, or taking a backup of the data are a few reasons for archiving and replaying data streams. One additional reason to replay data is due to downstream systems not receiving the output. The reason for missing data might be an outage on the downstream system or a timing issue. If an outage happened downstream and data was missing from that store, it is likely easy to understand why: the data is missing because the datastore was not available to receive the data.

The timing issue that can result in missing data can be caused by the timestamp assigned to the data file. The timestamp for a data file stored in an ADLS container is in an attribute named `BlobLastModifiedUtcTime`. Consider the action you took in step 4 of Exercise 7.10, where you uploaded a new file into the location you configured as the input for your Azure Stream Analytics job. Nothing happened when you initially started the job, for example, at 12:33 PM. This is because files that already exist in that location will not be processed, because their timestamp is earlier than the start time of the Azure Stream Analytics job. When you start a job with a Job Output Start Time of Now (refer to Figure 7.18), only files that arrive after the time are processed. Once you added the file with a timestamp after the job had already been started, for example, 12:40 PM, it got processed.

The same issue could exist for downstream systems, in that the data file could arrive at a datastore but the processor is experiencing an outage of some kind. When it starts back up and is online, it may be configured to start processing files only from the current time forward, which would mean the files received during the downtime will not be processed. In some cases, it might be better and safer to replay the data stream instead of reconfiguring and restarting all the downstream systems to process data received while having availability problems. Adding the file in step 4 is not the only approach for getting the timestamp updated to the current time. If you open the file, make a small change that will not have any impact on downstream processing, and then save it, the timestamp is updated, and it will be processed. Perform Exercise 7.10 again but instead of uploading the `0_bf325906d_1.json` file, make a small change to the file already in that directory and notice that it is processed and passed into the output alias ADLS container.

Design and Create Tests for Data Pipelines

The data pipeline used in most examples in this chapter has included a data producer, an Event Hubs endpoint, and an Azure Stream Analytics job. Those components create the data, ingest the data, and then process the data stream. The processed data then flows into datastores like ADLS, an Azure Synapse Analytics SQL pool, Azure Cosmos DB, and Power BI. All those different parts make up the data pipeline.

To design a test for the data pipeline, you must identity the different components, which were mentioned in the preceding paragraph. The next step is to analyze each component to determine exactly what the data input format is, what is used to process that data, and what the output should be. If you take the BCI that produces brain wave readings, for example, the input consists of analog vibrations originating from a brain. The BCI is connected to a computer via Bluetooth, and a program converts the analog reading to a numeric value, which is then formatted into a JSON document and streamed to an event hub. Therefore, changes to the code that captures, transforms, and streams the brain wave readings to the event bub must be tested through the entire pipeline. Data is not modified as it flows through the event hub, so the next step in the pipeline to analyze is the Azure Stream Analytics job query. If the format of the incoming data stream had been changed, a change to the query would be required. For example, the addition of a new column to the data event message would require a change to the query. The final step is to validate that the output of the stream processing had an expected result on all downstream datastores that receive the processed data content.

In most mid- to large-size projects, you would perform these tests in a testing environment that has an exact replica of the production data pipeline. As you learned in Chapter 6, you can use an Azure DevOps component named Azure Test Plans for more formal new features and regression testing capabilities. You will learn more about Azure Test Plans in Chapter 9, "Monitoring Azure Data Storage and Processing," and Chapter 10, "Troubleshoot Data Storage Processing."

Monitor for Performance and Functional Regressions

The "Configure Checkpoints/Watermarking During Processing" section discussed some metrics that are useful for monitoring performance, such as Watermark Delay, Resource Utilization, and Events Count (refer to Figure 7.44). Many other metrics are available. The following are a few of the more interesting metrics:

- Backlogged Input Events
- CPU % Utilization
- Data Conversion Errors
- Early Input Events
- Input Events
- Last Input Events
- Out of order Events
- Output Events
- Runtime errors
- SU (Memory) % Utilization

Each of these metrics can potentially help you find out the cause of issues your Azure Stream Analytics job is having. A regression means that a bug in your code that was previously fixed has been reintroduced into the application. From an Azure Stream Analytics perspective, this would happen in the query, or, if your job contains a function, the code may have been corrupted in that area of the processing logic. To help determine when this happened, you can review the Activity Log blade, which provides a list of changes made over a given time frame. If you have your queries and function code in a source code repository, then you could also take a look in the file history to see who changed and merged the code, when, and how.

Optimize Pipelines for Analytical or Transactional Purposes

There are numerous approaches for optimizing data stream pipelines. Two such approaches are parallelization and compute resource management. You have learned that setting a partition key in the date message results in the splitting of messages across multiple nodes.

By doing this your data streams are processed in parallel. You can see how this looks in Figure 7.31 and the discussion around it. Managing the compute resources available for processing the data stream will have a big impact on the speed and availability of your data to downstream consumers. As shown in Figure 7.48, the increase in the watermark delay was caused by the CPU utilization on the processor nodes reaching 100 percent.

FIGURE 7.48 Azure Stream Analytics job metrics, CPU at 99 percent utilization

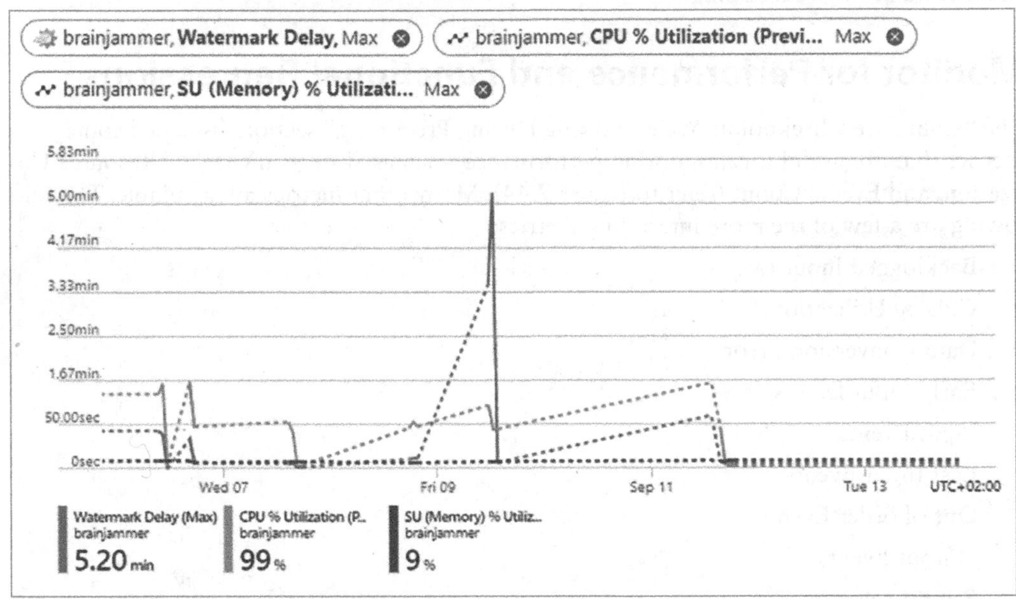

When the CPU is under such pressure, event messages get queued, which causes a delay in processing and providing output. Increasing the number of SUs allocated to the Azure Stream Analytics job will have a positive impact on the pipeline, making it more optimal for analytical and transactional purposes.

Scale Resources

As mentioned in the previous section, adding more resources to the Azure Stream Analytics Job will result in faster processing of the data stream. This assumes that you have noticed some processing delays and see that the current level of allocated resources is not sufficient. To increase the amount of compute power allocated to an Azure Stream Analytics job, select the Scale navigation link for the given job, as shown in Figure 7.49.

FIGURE 7.49 Azure Stream Analytics job scaling

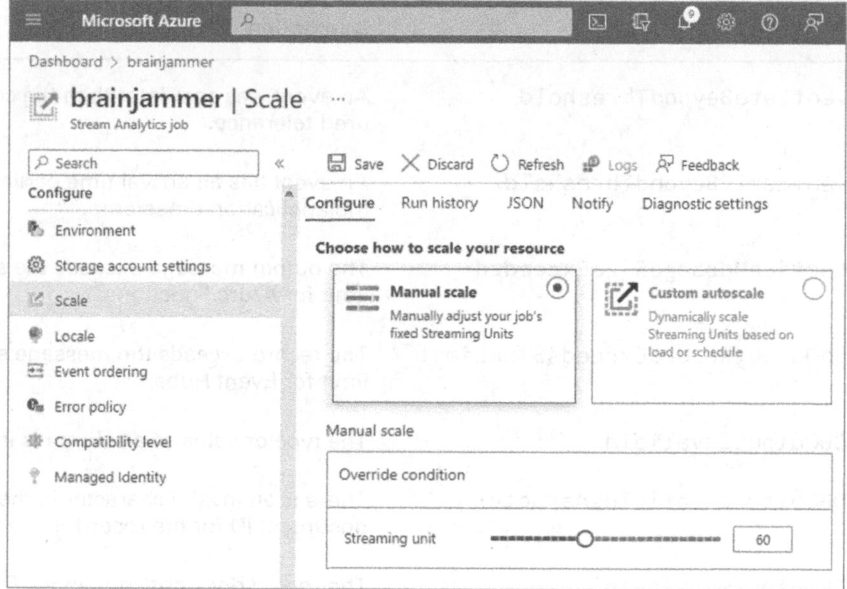

Once compute power is allocated, when you start the job, instead of seeing 3, as shown in Figure 7.18, you will see the number described in the Manual Scale Streaming Unit configuration. In this case, the number of SUs would be 60.

Design and Configure Exception Handling

An exception is an unexpected event that occurs in the execution of your program code or query. Exceptions do happen and need to be managed because, in most cases, unmanaged exceptions stop the execution of your code at that point. This can leave your data and your program in an undesirable state, which can result in further data corruption. You need to understand which kinds of known exceptions can happen in your Azure Stream Analytics processing. Table 7.8 provides a list of Azure Stream Analytics exceptions.

TABLE 7.8 Azure Stream Analytics exceptions

Exception	Description
`InputDeserializationError`	Unable to deserialize input data.
`InputEventTimestampNotFound`	Unable to retrieve a timestamp for a resource.
`InputEventTimestampByOverValueNotFound`	Cannot get the value of the `TIMESTAMP BY OVER COLUMN`.

TABLE 7.8 Azure Stream Analytics exceptions *(continued)*

Exception	Description
`InputEventLateBeyondThreshold`	An event was sent later than the configured tolerance.
`InputEventEarlyBeyondThreshold`	An event has an arrival time earlier than the application timestamp.
`AzureFunctionMessageSizeExceeded`	The output message exceeds the size limit for Azure Functions.
`EventHubOutputRecordExceedsSizeLimit`	The record exceeds the message size limit for Event Hubs.
`CosmosDBOutputInvalidId`	The type or value of a column is invalid.
`CosmosDBOutputInvalidIdCharacter`	There is an invalid character in the document ID for the record.
`CosmosDBOutputMissingId`	The record does not contain an ID to use as a primary key.
`CosmosDBOutputMissingIdColumn`	The record is missing a document ID property.
`CosmosDBOutputMissingPartitionKey`	The record is missing the partition key property.
`CosmosDBOutputSingleRecordTooLarge`	A single record is too large to write.
`SQLDatabaseOutputDataError`	Cannot write to Azure SQL Database due to data issues.

When you begin processing your data stream and nothing is happening, the reason is likely one of the exceptions listed in Table 7.8. There are numerous locations where you can view exceptions that get thrown during the stream processing. The first one is diagnostic logging, which is configurable from the Diagnostic Settings blade in the Azure portal. There is more on this feature in Chapter 9; however, look at Figure 7.50 to get an idea about what this looks like.

FIGURE 7.50 Azure Stream Analytics Diagnostics Setting

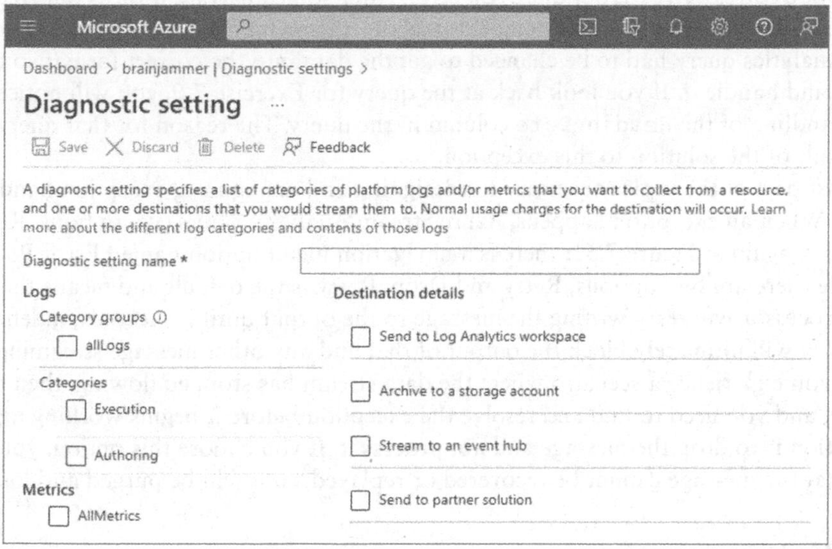

Microsoft Azure

Dashboard > brainjammer | Diagnostic settings >

Diagnostic setting ...

Save Discard Delete Feedback

A diagnostic setting specifies a list of categories of platform logs and/or metrics that you want to collect from a resource, and one or more destinations that you would stream them to. Normal usage charges for the destination will occur. Learn more about the different log categories and contents of those logs

Diagnostic setting name *

Logs

Category groups

allLogs

Categories

Execution

Authoring

Metrics

AllMetrics

Destination details

Send to Log Analytics workspace

Archive to a storage account

Stream to an event hub

Send to partner solution

Notice the different categories and that logging performance metrics are also possible. The locations where you can store the logs are listed in the Destination Details column. The options are a Log Analytics workspace, a storage account, an event hub, or a partner solution, which are endpoints provided by Microsoft Azure partners. The other location to view exceptions is on the Activity Log blade, as shown in Figure 7.51.

FIGURE 7.51 Azure Stream Analytics Activity log warnings and errors

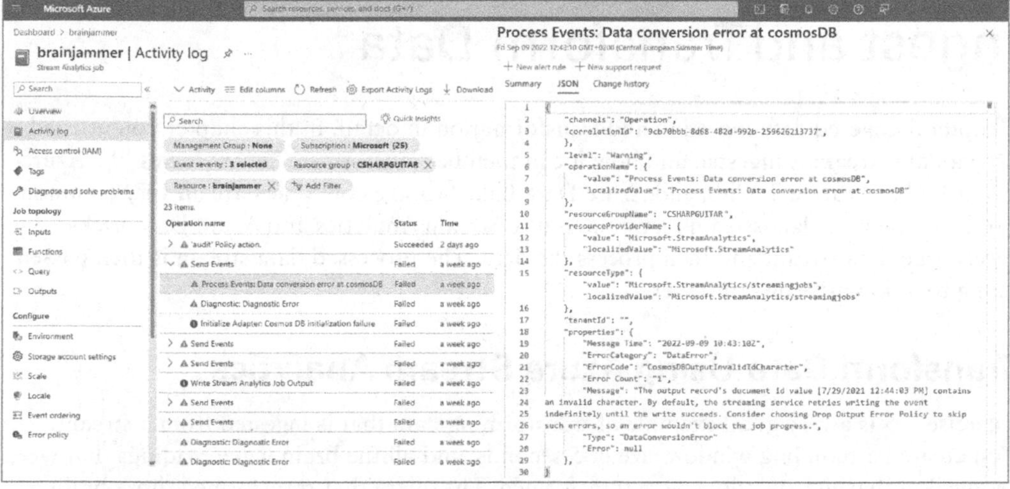

Line 21 of the Send Events operation warning message shows a `CosmosDBOutputInvalidIdCharacter` error. After some analysis, it turns out Azure Cosmos DB does not like the timestamp used as the document ID in that format. The Azure Stream Analytics query had to be changed to get the data into the correct format so that the output could handle it. If you look back at the query for Exercise 7.9, you will notice some special handling of the `ReadingDate` column in the query. The reason for that query pattern was a result of the solution to this exception.

The last part of the topics necessary for designing and configuring exception handling is just that. When an exception happens, Azure Stream Analytics offers two options, Retry and Drop. Look again at Figure 7.51; there is a navigation menu option named Error Policy. On that blade there are two options, Retry and Drop. Retry is the default and means the data stream processor will retry writing the message to the output until it succeeds, indefinitely. This setting will ultimately block the output of that and any other message streaming to that point. If you experience a scenario where the data stream has stopped flowing, then there is a blockage, and you need to find and resolve the exception before it begins working again. The other option is to drop the message and not process it. If you choose this option, you need to realize that the message cannot be recovered or replayed, so it will be purged and lost.

Handle Interruptions

As previously mentioned, the platform will handle data stream interruptions when caused by a node failure, an OS upgrade, or product upgrades. However, how can you handle an exception that starts happening unexpectedly? Look back at Figure 7.51 and notice an option named + New Alert Rule, just above the JSON tab. When you select that link, a page will render that walks you through the configuration of actions to be taken when an operation completes with a Failed status. This is covered in more detail in Chapter 10.

Ingest and Transform Data

Chapter 5 covered data ingestion and transformation in detail. In this chapter you learned how a data stream is ingested and how it can then be transformed. Technologies like Azure Event Hubs, Azure IoT Hub, and Azure Data Lake Storage containers are all very common products used for data stream ingestion. Azure Stream Analytics and Azure Databricks receive the data stream and then process the data. The processed data stream is then passed along to a downstream consumer.

Transform Data Using Azure Stream Analytics

Exercise 7.5 is a very good example of transforming data that is ingested from a stream. You created a tumbling window size of 5 seconds, and all the brain wave readings that were received in that time window were transformed. The query that transformed those brain wave readings calculated the median for each frequency. Once calculated, the median values were compared against estimated frequency values for the meditation scenario, and the result was then passed to Power BI for real-time visualization.

Monitor Data Storage and Data Processing

The monitoring capabilities concerning stream processing are covered in Chapter 9. This section is added to help you navigate through the book while referring to the official online DP-203 exam objectives/Exam Study Guide, currently accessible from `https://learn.microsoft.com/en-us/certifications/exams/dp-203`.

Monitor Stream Processing

You will find some initial information about monitoring stream processing in the "Monitor for Performance and Functional Regressions" section in this chapter. You will find a more complete discussion of this topic in Chapter 9, in the section with the same name, "Monitor for Performance and Functional Regressions."

Summary

This chapter focused on the design and development of a stream processing solution. You learned about data stream producers, which are commonly IoT devices that send event messages to an ingestion endpoint hosted in the cloud. You learned about stream processing products that read, transform, and write the data stream to a location for consumers to access. The location of the data storage depends on whether the data insights are required in real time or near real time. Both scenarios flow through the speed layer, where real-time insights flow directly into a consumer like Power BI and near real-time data streams flow into the serving layer. While the insights are in the serving layer, additional transformation can be performed by batch processing prior to consumption. In addition to the time demands on your streaming solution, other considerations, such as the data stream format, programming paradigm, programming language, and product interoperability, are all important when designing your data streaming solution.

Azure Stream Analytics has the capacity to process data streams in parallel. Performing work in parallel increases the speed in which the transformation is completed. The result is a faster gathering of business insights. This is achieved using partition keys. Partition keys provide the platform with information that is used to group together the data and process it on a dedicated partition. The concept of time is very important in data stream solutions. Arrival time, event time, checkpoints, and watermarks all play a very important role when interruptions to the data stream occur. You learned that when an OS upgrade, node exception, or product upgrade happens, the platform uses these time management properties to get your stream back on track without losing any of the data. The replaying of data streams is possible if you have created or stored the data required to replay them. There are no such data archival features on the data streaming platform to achieve this.

There are many metrics you can use to monitor the performance of your Azure Stream analytics job. For example, the Resource Utilization, Event Counts, and Watermark Delay metrics can help you determine why the stream results are not being processed as expected or at all. Diagnostic settings, alerts, and Activity logs can also help determine why your stream processing is not achieving the expected results. Once you determine the cause of the problem, you can increase the capacity by scaling, configuring the error policy, or changing the query to fix a bug.

Exam Essentials

Azure Event Hubs, Azure Stream Analytics, and Power BI. When you are designing your stream processing solution, one consideration is interoperability. Azure Event Hubs, Azure Stream Analytics, and Power BI are compatible with each other and can be used seamlessly to implement your data stream processing design. Other products are available on the Azure platform for streaming, such as HDInsight 3.6, Hadoop, Azure Databricks, Apache Storm, and WebJobs.

Windowed aggregates. Windowing is provided through temporal features like tumbling, hopping, sliding, session, and snapshot windows. Aggregate functions are methods that can calculate averages, maximums, minimums, and medians. Windowed aggregates enable you to aggregate temporal windows.

Partitions. Partitioning is the grouping of similar data together in close physical proximity in order to gain more efficient storage and query execution speed. Both efficiency and speed of execution are attained when data with matching partition keys is stored and retrieved from a single node. Data queries that pull data from remote datastores, different partition keys, or data that is located on more than a single node take longer to complete.

Time management. The tracking of the time when data is streaming into an ingestion point is crucial when it comes to recovering from a disruption. The timestamps linked to an event message, such as event time, arrival time, and the watermark, all help in this recovery. The event time identifies when the data message was created on the data-producing IoT device. The arrival time is the enqueued time and reflects when the event message arrived at the ingestion endpoint, like Event Hubs.

Watermark. As shown in Figure 7.41, the watermark is a time that reflects the temporal time frame in which the data was processed by the stream processor. If the time window is 5 seconds, all event messages processed within that time window will receive the same watermark.

Review Questions

Many questions can have more than a single answer. Please select all choices that are true.

1. Which layers of the lambda architecture does data streaming flow through?
   - **A.** Only the speed layer
   - **B.** The batch and serving layer
   - **C.** The speed layer and the serving layer
   - **D.** Both A and C
2. Which path does data streaming flow on, according to the lambda architecture?
   - **A.** The hot path
   - **B.** The cold path
   - **C.** The warm path
   - **D.** The archive path
3. Which of the following are considerations for the design of a stream processing solution?
   - **A.** Data format
   - **B.** Interoperability
   - **C.** Open-source availability
   - **D.** Pricing
4. What benefit do you gain from running on multiple Azure Stream Analytics partitions?
   - **A.** Better performance of multistep queries
   - **B.** Faster output of data to Power BI
   - **C.** Parallel execution
   - **D.** Faster throughput with input and output products having a different number of partitions
5. Which of the following products must explicitly provide a partition key?
   - **A.** Azure Event Hubs
   - **B.** Azure IoT Hub
   - **C.** Azure Blob Storage
   - **D.** Power BI
6. What is the purpose of a partition key?
   - **A.** To uniquely identify an event message
   - **B.** To provide the means for grouping similar data together
   - **C.** To index data once it is stored in a dedicated SQL pool
   - **D.** To perform upserts

7. Where can you perform an upsert on data ingested into a data streaming solution?
   A. In the serving layer
   B. In the Power BI data stream
   C. In an Azure Cosmos DB container
   D. In an Azure Stream Analytics job container

8. Which of the following describes an event message arrival time?
   A. `EventEnqueuedUtcTime`
   B. The time when an Azure Event Hub receives the event message
   C. The time the event message is created on the data producer
   D. When the arrival time is the same as the watermark

9. Which of the following are valid error policies for an Azure Stream Analytics job?
   A. Archive
   B. Complete
   C. Replay
   D. Drop

10. Which of the following metrics are useful for determining if there is enough compute resources to process your data stream?
   A. Events Count
   B. Watermark Delay
   C. Partition Count
   D. CPU Utilization

Secure, Monitor, and Optimize Data Storage and Data Processing

PART IV

Chapter 8

Keeping Data Safe and Secure

EXAM DP-203 OBJECTIVES COVERED IN THIS CHAPTER:

- ✓ Implement data security
- ✓ Develop a batch processing solution
- ✓ Design and implement the data exploration layer

Security is the most discussed topic in the IT industry. Once a computer is connected to a network, it becomes immediately vulnerable to all sorts of malicious activities. If the computer and the networking devices encompassing it have not been configured to prevent such activities, then any resource, document, or service on the computer is vulnerable. Depending on what is hosted on the computer, the loss of it, the tampering with it, or the publication of it can have catastrophic consequences for the data owner and the business they work for. Therefore, you must ensure that all necessary precautions are taken to secure your data, your computers, your networks, and the endpoints that are open for connectivity. As a data engineer, the most important aspect of security you should recognize is that you need to engage with experts when implementing the security component of your data analytics solution. The last thing you want to do is create a data security solution that results in unexpectedly exposing sensitive data.

This chapter discusses the most common concepts related to security, auditing, compliance, and governance on the Azure platform. Azure Active Directory (Azure AD) and role-based access control (RBAC) are both very important actors when it comes to securing your data solution. In most medium- and large-sized companies with frequently changing solution landscapes, before you can implement and manage security, you need to maintain an inventory of your resources. Microsoft Purview is helpful for managing, documenting, discovering, and auditing your Azure footprint. After identifying all your resources, you can use tools like Azure Policy and Azure Governance to make sure your solutions satisfy any industry or geographical compliance requirements.

Design Security for Data Policies and Standards

When you begin thinking about security, many of the requirements will be driven by the kind of data you have. Is the data personally identifiable information (PII), such as a name, email address, or physical address, that is stored, or does the data consist of historical THETA brain wave readings? In both scenarios you would want some form of protection from bad actors who could destroy or steal the data. The amount of protection you need should be identified by a *data security standard*. The popular Payment Card Industry (PCI) standard seeks to define the kinds of security mechanisms required for companies who want to transmit, process, and store payment information. There are numerous varieties of PCI that can be helpful as a baseline for defining your own data security standards based on the type of data your data analytics solution ingests, transforms, and exposes. For example, the standard might identify the minimum version of TLS that consumers must use when consuming your data. Further examples of data security standards are that all data columns must be associated with a sensitivity level, or that all data that contains PII must be purged after 120 days.

A *data security policy* contains the data security standards component along with numerous other sections that pertain to security. A data security policy can be used to identify security roles and responsibilities throughout your company so that it is clear who is responsible for what. For example, what aspects of data security does a certified Data Engineer Associate have? At what point does data security merge into the role of a Security Engineer? A data security policy also accounts for the procedures when there are security violations or incidents. How to classify data, how to manage access to data, the encryption of data, and the management and disposal of data are all components that make up a data security policy. Some basic security principals—such as that there be no access to customer data by default and to always grant the lowest level of privileges required to complete the task—are good policies to abide by. Most of these security aspects are covered in more detail later in this chapter. After completing this chapter, you will be able to contribute to the creation of a data security policy and strategy.

As you begin the effort to describe and design your data security model, consider approaching it from a layered perspective. Figure 8.1 represents a layered security model. The first layer focuses on network security. In this chapter you will learn about virtual networks (VNets), network security groups (NSGs), firewalls, and private endpoints, each of which provides security at the networking layer.

FIGURE 8.1 Layered security

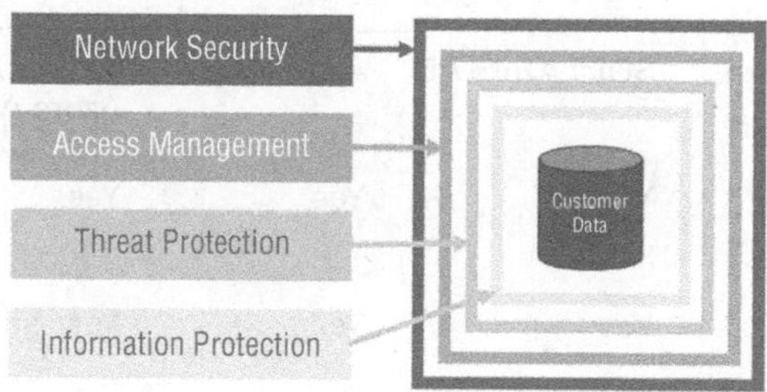

The next layer is the access management layer. This layer has to do with authentication and authorization, where the former confirms you are who you say and the latter validates that you are allowed to access the resource. Common tools on Azure to validate that a person is who they claim to be include Azure Active Directory (Azure AD), SQL authentication, and Windows Authentication (Kerberos), which is in preview at the time of writing. Managing access to resources after authentication is successful is implemented through role assignments. A common tool for this on Azure is role-based access control (RBAC). Many additional products, features, and concepts apply within this area, such as managed identities, Azure Key Vault, service principals, access control lists (ACLs), single sign-on (SSO), and the least privilege principle. Each of these will be described in more detail in the following sections.

The kind of business a company performs dictates the kind of data that is collected and stored. Companies that work with governments or financial institutions have a higher probability of attempted data theft than companies that measure brain waves, for example. So, the threat of a security breach is greater for companies with high-value data, which means they need to take greater actions to prevent most forms of malicious behaviors. To start with, performing vulnerability assessments and attack simulations would help find locations in your security that have known weaknesses. In parallel, enabling threat detection, virus scanners, logging used for performing audits, and traceability will reduce the likelihood of long-term and serious outages caused by exploitation. Microsoft Defender for Cloud can be used as the hub for viewing and analyzing your security logs.

The last layer of security, information protection, is applied to the data itself. This layer includes concepts such as data encryption, which is typically applied while the data is not being used (encryption-at-rest) and while the data is moving from one location to another (encryption-in-transit). Data masking, the labeling of sensitive information, and logging who is accessing the data and how often, are additional techniques for protecting your data at this layer.

Table 8.1 summarizes the security-related capabilities of various Azure products.

TABLE 8.1 Azure data product security support

Feature	Azure SQL Database	Azure Synapse Analytics	Azure Data Explorer	Azure Databricks	Azure Cosmos DB
Authentication	SQL / Azure AD	SQL / Azure AD	Azure AD	Tokens / Azure AD	DB users / Azure AD
Dynamic masking	Yes	Yes	Yes	Yes	Yes
Encryption-at-rest	Yes	Yes	Yes	Yes	Yes
Row-level security	Yes	Yes	No	Yes	No
Firewall	Yes	Yes	Yes	Yes	Yes

Azure data products enable you to configure each layer of the security model. The Azure platform provides many more features and capabilities to help monitor, manage, and maintain the security component of your data analytics solution. The remainder of this chapter provides details about these features and capabilities. But before you continue, complete Exercise 8.1, where you will provision an Azure Key Vault resource. Azure Key Vault is a solution that helps you securely store secrets, keys, and certificates. Azure Key Vault comes with two tiers, Standard and Premium, where the primary difference has to do with hardware security module (HSM) protected keys. HSM is a key protection method, which is a physical device dedicated to performing encryption, key management, authentication, and more. HSM is available in the Premium tier only. A software-based key protection method is employed when a Standard tier is utilized. HSM provides the highest level of security and performance and is often required to meet compliance regulations. This product plays a very significant role in security, so learning some details about it before you continue will increase your comprehension and broaden your perspective.

EXERCISE 8.1

Create an Azure Key Vault Resource

1. Log in to the Azure portal at `https://portal.azure.com` ➢ click the menu button on the upper left of the browser ➢ click + Create a Resource ➢ select Security from the Categories section ➢ select Key Vault ➢ select the subscription ➢ select the resource group ➢ enter a key vault name ➢ select a region ➢ and then select a pricing tier (I used Standard). Leave the remaining options as the defaults.

2. Click the Next button ➢ leave the defaults on the Access Policy tab ➢ select the check box next to your user identity in the Access Policies section ➢ click the Edit button ➢ observe the default Key, Secret, and Certificate default permissions ➢ click Next ➢ leave the defaults on the Networking tab ➢ click the Review + Create button ➢ and then click Create.

3. Once the key vault is provisioned, navigate to it ➢ select Keys from the navigation menu ➢ select the + Generate/import menu link ➢ and then enter a name (I used **brainjammerKey**). The configuration should resemble Figure 8.2. The Elliptic Curve Name radio buttons show the available algorithms.

EXERCISE 8.1 *(continued)*

FIGURE 8.2 Creating an Azure Key Vault key

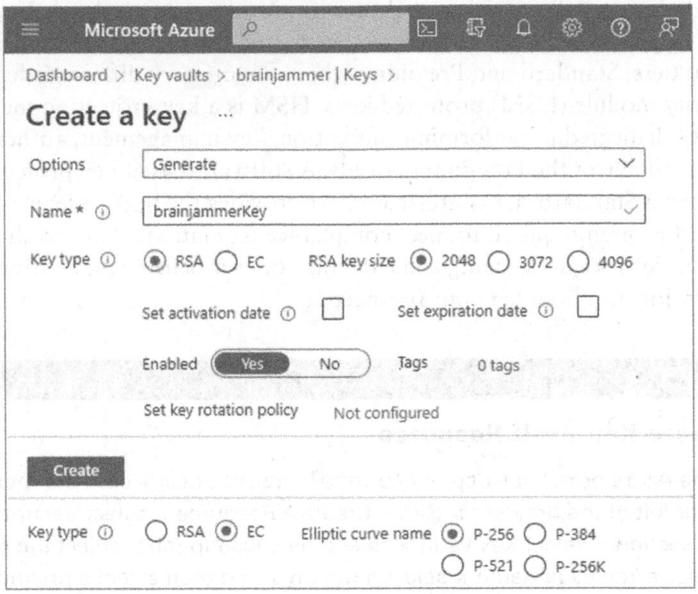

4. Click the Create button ➢ select the Secrets navigation item ➢ click the + Generate/Import menu option ➢ enter a name (I used **azureSynapseSQLPool**) ➢ and then enter a secret value (I used the password of my Azure Synapse Analytics dedicated SQL pool). The configuration should resemble Figure 8.3.

FIGURE 8.3 Creating an Azure Key Vault secret

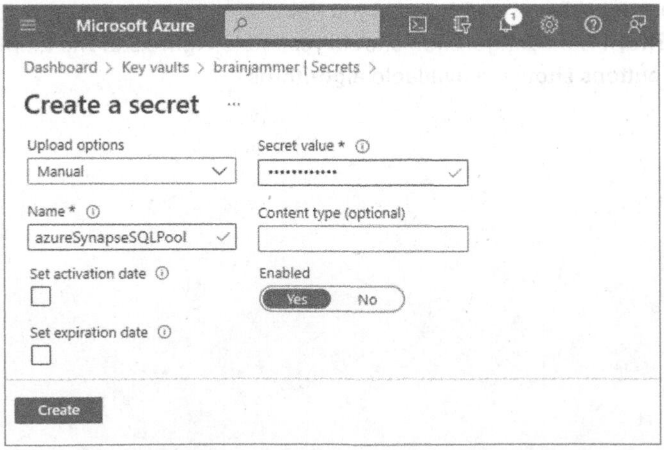

5. Click the Create button ➢ select the Certificates navigation item ➢ click the + Generate/Import menu option ➢ enter a certificate name (I used **brainjammerCertificate**) ➢ and then enter a subject value (I used **"CN=brainjammer.net"**). The configuration should resemble Figure 8.4.

FIGURE 8.4 Creating an Azure Key Vault certificate

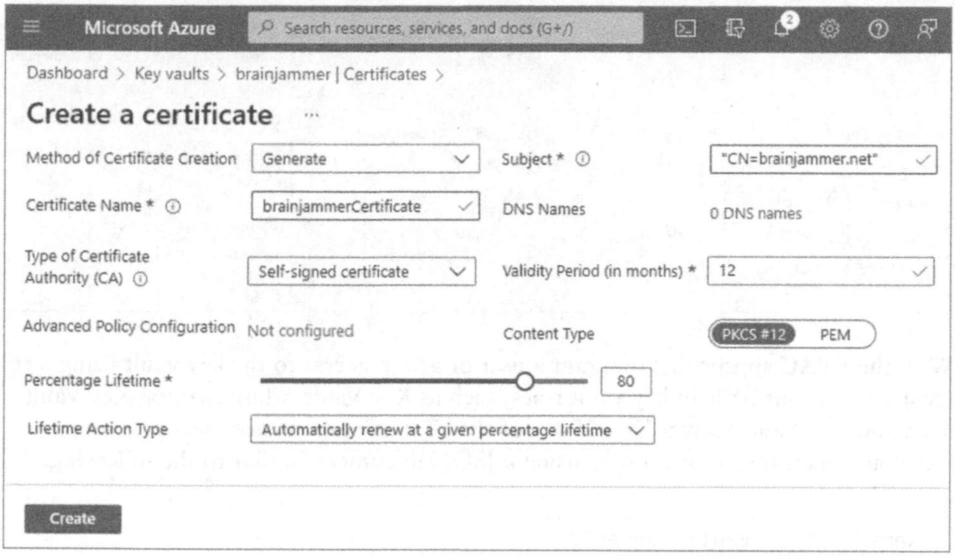

6. Click Create.

Exercise 8.1 is straightforward in that you should recognize most of the options and understand what they mean. A few features and concepts, however, are worthy of discussion. On the Access Policy tab, you likely noticed the option to manage access by either Key Vault access policy or Azure role-based access control (RBAC). The Key Vault access policy enables you to grant service principals, users, applications, or user groups access to specific operations on the keys, secrets, and certificates hosted in the key vault—for example, those shown in Figure 8.5. Figure 8.5 is similar to what you saw in step 2 of Exercise 8.1 when viewing the default permissions.

FIGURE 8.5 Vault access policy operations

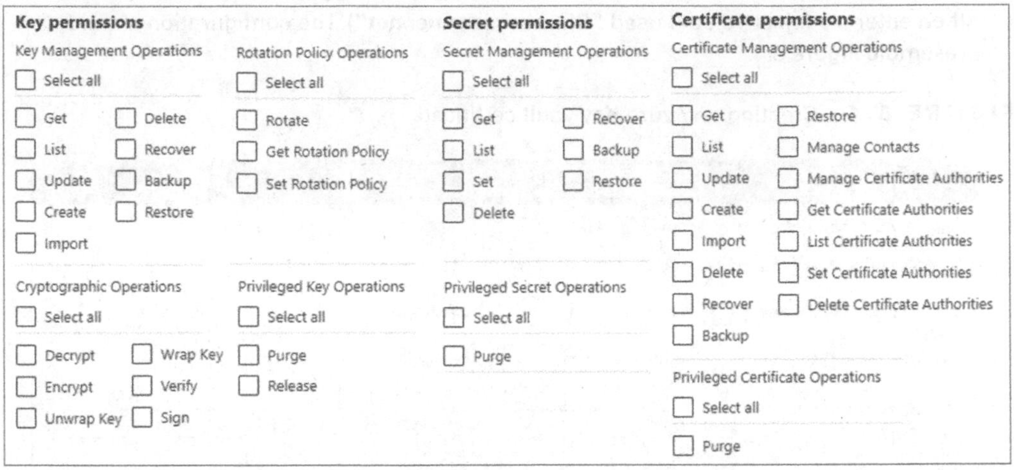

Key permissions

Key Management Operations

- Select all
- Get
- List
- Update
- Create
- Import
- Delete
- Recover
- Backup
- Restore

Rotation Policy Operations

- Select all
- Rotate
- Get Rotation Policy
- Set Rotation Policy

Cryptographic Operations

- Select all
- Decrypt
- Encrypt
- Unwrap Key
- Wrap Key
- Verify
- Sign

Privileged Key Operations

- Select all
- Purge
- Release

Secret permissions

Secret Management Operations

- Select all
- Get
- List
- Set
- Delete
- Recover
- Backup
- Restore

Privileged Secret Operations

- Select all
- Purge

Certificate permissions

Certificate Management Operations

- Select all
- Get
- List
- Update
- Create
- Import
- Delete
- Recover
- Backup
- Restore
- Manage Contacts
- Manage Certificate Authorities
- Get Certificate Authorities
- List Certificate Authorities
- Set Certificate Authorities
- Delete Certificate Authorities

Privileged Certificate Operations

- Select all
- Purge

With the RBAC approach, you grant a user or group access to the key vault using a role. There are numerous built-in key vault roles, such as Key Vault Administrator, Key Vault Reader, and Key Vault Secrets User. If any of the built-in roles do not meet your requirements, you can create a custom role, using a JSON document similar to the following:

```
{
   "Name":  "Key Vault Reader",
   "Id":  null,
   "IsCustom":  true,
   "Description":  "Read Azure Key Vault resources and create support cases",
   "Actions":  [
                  "Microsoft.KeyVault/vaults/*/read",
                  "Microsoft.KeyVault/operations/read",
                  "Microsoft.KeyVault/locations/*/read",
                  "Microsoft.KeyVault/checkNameAvailability/read",
                  "Microsoft.Support/*"
               ],
   "NotActions":  [ ],
   "DataActions":  [
                 "Microsoft.KeyVault/vaults/*/read",
                 "Microsoft.KeyVault/vaults/secrets/readMetadata/action"
               ],
```

```
    "NotDataActions": [ ],
    "AssignableScopes": [
                "/subscriptions/#######-####-####-####-#########"
    ]
}
```

The Networking tab enables you to configure a private endpoint or the binding to a virtual network (VNet). The provisioning and binding of Azure resources to a VNet and private endpoints are discussed and performed in a later section. After the provisioning the key vault, you created a key, secret, and a certificate. The keys in an Azure key vault refer to those used in asymmetric/public key cryptography. As shown in Figure 8.2, two types of keys are available with Standard tier: Rivest-Shamir-Adleman (RSA) and elliptic curve (EC). These keys are used to encrypt and decrypt data (i.e., public-key cryptography). Both keys are asymmetric, which means they both have a private and public key. The private key must be protected, as any client can use the public key to encrypt, but only the private key can decrypt it. Each of these keys has multiple options for the strength of encryption. For example, RSA has 2,048, 3,072, and 4,096 bits. The higher the number, the higher the level of security. High RSA numbers have caveats concerning speed and compatibility. The higher level of encryption requires more time to decrypt, and not all platforms can comply with such high levels of encryption. Therefore, you need to consider which level of security is best for your use case and security compliance requirements.

A secret is something like a password, connection string, or any text up to 25k bytes that needs protection. Connection strings and passwords commonly are stored in configuration files or hard coded into application code. This is not secure, because anyone who has access to the code or the server hosting the configuration file has access to the credentials and therefore the resources protected by them. Instead of that approach, applications can be coded to retrieve the secret from a key vault, then use it for making the required connections. In a production environment, the secret can be authenticated against a managed identity or service principal when requested. Secrets stored in a key vault are encrypted when added and decrypted when retrieved. The certificate support in Azure Key Vault provides the management of x509 certificates. If you have ever worked on an Internet application that uses the HTTP protocol, you have likely used an x509 certificate. When this type of certificate is applied to that protocol, it secures communication between the entities engaged in the conversation. To employ the certificate, you must use HTTPS, and this is commonly referred to as Transport Layer Security (TLS). In addition to securing communication over the Internet, certificates can also be used for authentication and for signing software. Consider the certificate you created in Exercise 8.1. When you click the certificate, you will notice it has a Certificate Version that resembles a GUID but without the dashes. Associated to that Certificate Version is a Certificate Identifier, which is a URL that gives you access to the certificate details. When you enter the following command using the Azure CLI, you will see information like the base-64–encoded certificate, the link to the private key, and the link to the public key, similar to that shown in Figure 8.6.

```
az keyvault certificate show `
--id https://<name>.vault.azure.net/certificates/<certificateName>/1a00fab90...
```

FIGURE 8.6 Azure Key Vault x509 certificate details

The link to the private key and public keys can be used to retrieve the details in a similar fashion. The first Azure CLI cmdlet retrieves the private key of the x509 certificate, which is identified by the `kid` attribute. The second retrieves the public key using the endpoint identified by the `sid` attribute.

```
Az keyvault secret show `
--id https://<name>.vault.azure.net/secrets/<certificateName>/1a00fab90...

az keyvault key show `
--id https://<name>.vault.azure.net/keys/<certificateName>/1a00fab90...
```

The ability to list, get, and use keys, secrets, and certificates is controlled by the permissions you set up while creating the key vault. Put some thought into who and what gets which kind of permissions to these resources.

Design a Data Auditing Strategy

When you take an audit of something, it means that you analyze it and gather data about the data from the results. Many times the findings result in actions necessary to resolve inefficient or incorrect scenarios. What you analyze, what you are looking for, and what kind of analysis you need to perform are based on the requirements of the object being audited. The data management perspective (refer to Figure 5.41) includes disciplines such as quality, governance, and security. Each of those are good examples of scenarios to approach when creating a data auditing strategy. From a data quality perspective, you have been exposed to cleansing, deduplicating, and handling missing data using the MAR, MCAR, and MNAR principles, as discussed in Chapter 5, "Transform, Manage, and Prepare Data," and Chapter 6, "Create and Manage Batch Processing and Pipelines." This chapter focuses on the governance and security of data and how you can learn to design and implement strategies around those topics.

Governance encompasses a wide range of scenarios. You can optimize the scope of governance by identifying what is important to you, your business, and your customers. The necessary aspects of data governance include maintaining an inventory of data storage, enforcing policies, and knowing who is accessing what data and how often. The Azure platform provides products to achieve these aspects of data governance (refer to Figure 1.10). Microsoft Purview, for example, is used to discover and catalog your cloud-based and estate-based data estate. Azure Policy provides administrators the ability to control who and how cloud resources are provisioned, with Azure Blueprints helping to enforce that compliance. Compliance is a significant area of focus concerning data privacy, especially when it comes to PII, its physical location, and how long it can be persisted before purging. In addition to those products, you can find auditing capabilities built into products like Azure Synapse Analytics and Azure Databricks. When auditing is enabled on those two products specifically, failed and successful login attempts, SQL queries, and stored procedures are logged by default. The audit logs are stored into Log Analytics workspace for analysis, and alerts can be configured in Azure Monitor when certain behaviors or activities are recognized. Auditing is applied across the entire workspace, when enabled, and can be extended to log any action performed that affects the workspace.

Microsoft Azure provides policy guidelines for many compliance standards, including ISO, GDPR, PCI DSS, SOX, HIPPA, and FISMA, to name just a few of the most common standards. From a security perspective, you have seen the layered approach (refer to Figure 8.1) and have learned about some of the information protection layer features, with details about other layers coming later. Data sensitivity levels, RBAC, data encryption, Log Analytics, and Azure Monitor are all tools for protecting, securing, and monitoring your data hosted on the Azure platform.

Microsoft Purview

Microsoft Purview is especially useful for automatically discovering, classifying, and mapping your data estate. You can use it to catalog your data across multiple cloud providers and on-premises datastores. You can also use it to discover, monitor, and enforce policies, and classify sensitive data types. Purview consists of four components: a data map, a data catalog, data estate insights, and data sharing. A data map graphically displays your datastores along with their relationships across your data estate. A data catalog provides the means for browsing your data assets, which is helpful with data discovery and classification. Data estate insights present an overview of all your data resources and are helpful for discovering where your data is and what kind of data you have. Finally, data sharing provides the necessary features to securely share your data internally and with business customers. To get some hands-on experience with Microsoft Purview, complete Exercise 8.2, where you will provision a Microsoft Purview account.

EXERCISE 8.2

Create a Microsoft Purview Account

1. Log in to the Azure portal at `https://portal.azure.com` ➢ enter **Purview** in the search box in the upper middle of the browser ➢ select Microsoft Purview account ➢ select the + Create menu option ➢ select the subscription ➢ select the resource group ➢ enter a Microsoft Purview account name (I used **brainjammer**) ➢ select a region ➢ leave the managed resources as the default ➢ navigate through the other tabs ➢ leave the defaults ➢ click the Review + Create button ➢ and then click Create.
2. Once provisioning is complete, navigate to the Microsoft Purview Overview blade ➢ select the Open link to open the Microsoft Purview Governance Portal ➢ select the Data Map hub ➢ select Collections ➢ and then select the Role Assignments tab, as shown in Figure 8.7. Make sure your account is within the Collection Admins group; if not, add it.

FIGURE 8.7 Microsoft Purview default root collection

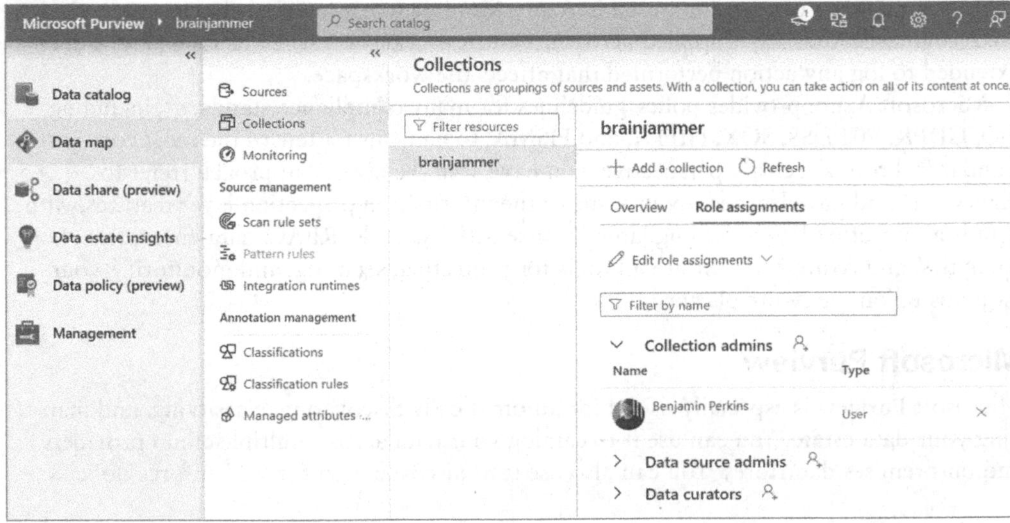

3. Click the + Add a Collection menu button > enter **Data Engineering** in the Display Name text box > enter your account into the Collection Admins group > click the Create button > and then select the root collection (for example, `brainjammer`) to do the same again, but this time enter **R&D** in the Display Name text box.
4. Select the Sources navigation link > click the Register menu button > select the Azure Data Lake Storage Gen2 resource > click Continue > enter a name (I used **ADLS-csharpguitar**) > select the subscription that contains the ADLS container you created in Exercise 3.1 > select the storage account name > select Data Engineering from the Select a Collection drop-down list > click the Register button > click the Register button again > select Azure Synapse Analytics > click Continue > enter a name (I used **ASA-csharpguitar**) > select the subscription that contains the Azure Synapse Analytics workspace you created in Exercise 3.3 > select R&D from the Select a Collection drop-down list > and then click Register. The result should resemble Figure 8.8.

FIGURE 8.8 Microsoft Purview Map view

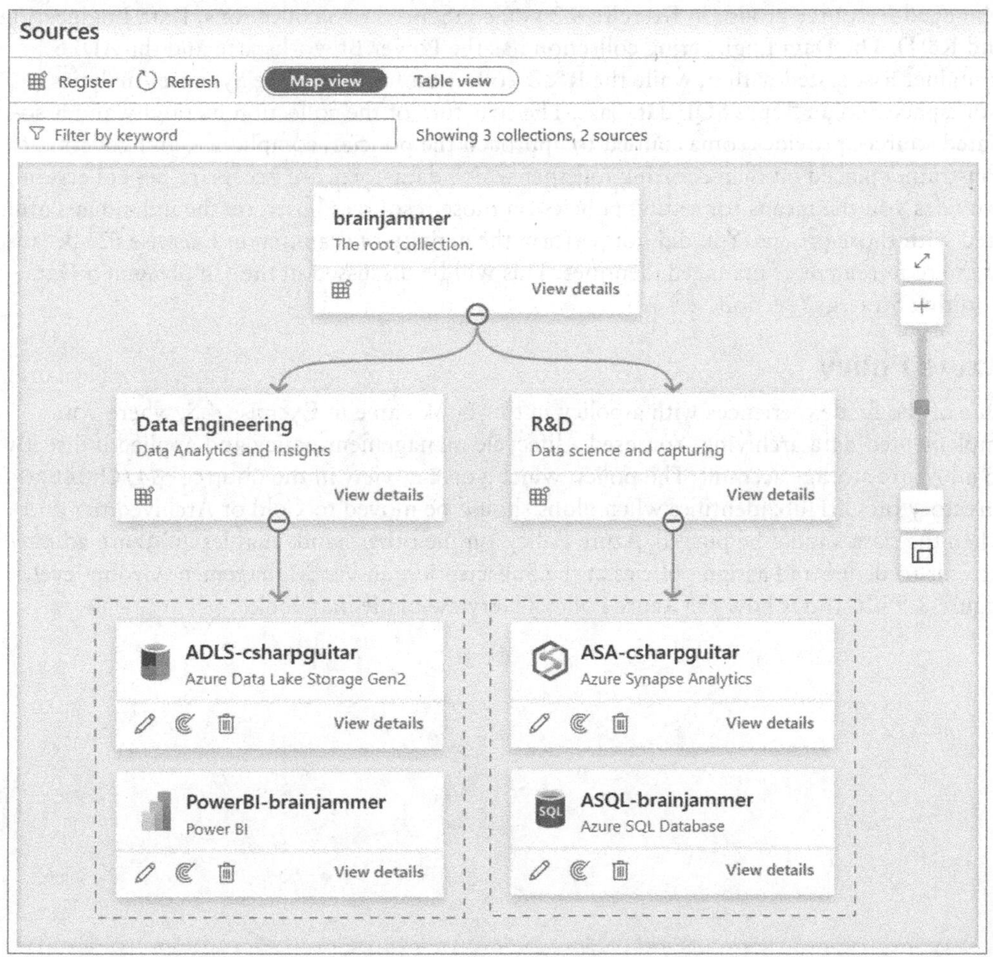

EXERCISE 8.2 *(continued)*

5. Navigate to the Azure Key Vault you created in Exercise 8.1 ➢ select Access Policies ➢ click the + Create menu button ➢ check the Get and List operations in the Secret permissions / Secret Management Operations section ➢ click Next ➢ search for and select the Microsoft Purview account name you just provisioned ➢ click the Next button twice ➢ and then click Create.

The additional registration of the Power BI workspace and an Azure SQL database are for effect only at this point. Feel free to register additional or different resources to your collections. The provisioning of the account was straightforward. You were again confronted by the concept of a Managed Resource group, which you experienced in Exercise 3.3. As a reminder, this resource group contains Azure products required by the provisioned resource. In this case, an Azure storage account is required and was stored in the provisioned Managed Resource group. In Exercise 8.2 you configured two collections, Data Engineering and R&D. The Data Engineering collection has the Power BI workspace and the ADLS container associated with it, while the R&D collection has the Azure Synapse Analytics workspace and an Azure SQL database. The structure of the collection hierarchy and associated sources provides some context to approach the policies, compliance, and governance constraints placed on them. Sorting together which datastores are necessary per collection provides you the means for setting policies on those resources based on the individuals affiliated with those groups. You did not perform the activity of scanning in Exercise 8.2 because of the requirement of managed identities. This will be discussed in the "Implement a Data Auditing Strategy" section.

Azure Policy

One of the first experiences with a policy in this book came in Exercise 4.5, where you implemented data archiving. You used a lifecycle management policy and applied it directly to an Azure storage account. The policy, which you can view in the `Chapter04/Ch04Ex04` directory on GitHub, identifies when blobs should be moved to Cold or Archived tier and when the data should be purged. Azure Policy, on the other hand, enables an Azure administrator to define and assign policies at the Subscription and/or Management Group level. Figure 8.9 illustrates how the Azure Policy Overview blade may look.

FIGURE 8.9 The Azure Policy Overview blade

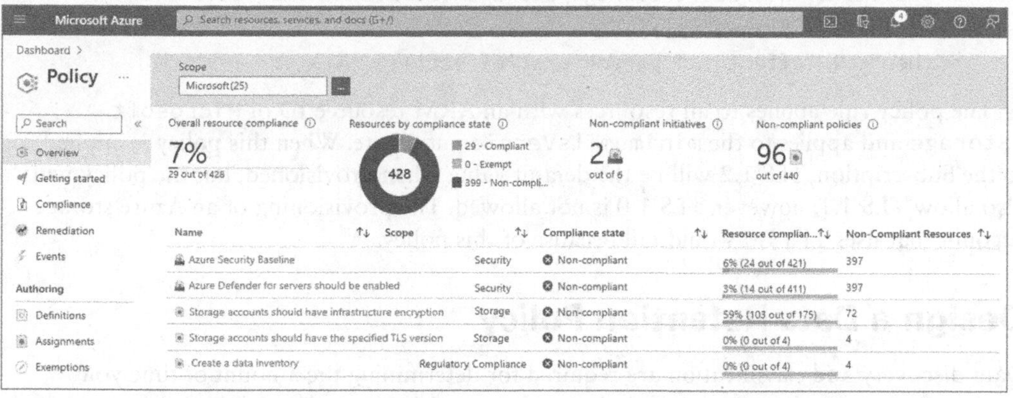

Each policy shown in Figure 8.9 links to the policy definition constructed using a JSON document, as follows. You can also assign the policy to the Subscription and a Resource group.

```
{ "properties": {
   "displayName": "Storage accounts should have the specified minimum TLS
      version",
    "allowedValues": [ "Audit", "Deny", "Disabled" ],
    "defaultValue": "Audit" },
    "minimumTlsVersion": {
     "type": "String",
     "metadata": { "displayName": "Minimum TLS Version" },
     "allowedValues": [ "TLS1_1", "TLS1_2" ],
        "defaultValue": "TLS1_2" }},
     "policyRule": {
      "if": { "allOf": [
      {
       "field": "type", "equals": "Microsoft.Storage/storageAccounts"
      },
      { "anyOf": [
        {
         "field": "Microsoft.Storage/storageAccounts/minimumTlsVersion",
         "notEquals": "[parameters('minimumTlsVersion')]"
        },
```

```
{
 "field": "Microsoft.Storage/storageAccounts/minimumTlsVersion",
 "exists": "false" }]}]},
"then": { "effect": "[parameters('effect')]" }}}}
```

The policy rule applies to all resources with an ARM resource ID of `Microsoft.Storage` and applies to the `minimumTlsVersion` attribute. When this policy is applied to the Subscription, TLS 1.2 will be the default value when provisioned, but the policy will also allow TLS 1.1; however, TLS 1.0 is not allowed. The provisioning of an Azure storage account that uses TLS 1.0 would fail because of this policy.

Design a Data Retention Policy

Data discovery and classification are required for determining the amount of time you need to retain your data. Some regulations require maximum and/or minimum data retention timelines, depending on the kind of data, which means you need to know what your data is before designing the retention policy. The policy needs to include not only your live, production-ready data but also backups, snapshots, and archived data. You can achieve this discovery and classification using what was covered in the previous few sections of this chapter. You might recall the mention of Exercise 4.5, where you created a lifecycle management policy that included data archiving logic. The concept and approach are the same here. The scenario in Exercise 4.5 covered the movement and deletion of a blob based on the number of days it was last accessed. However, in this scenario the context is the removal of data based on a retention period. Consider the following policy example, which applies to the blobs and snapshots stored in Azure storage account containers. The policy states that the data is to be deleted after 90 days from the date of creation. This represents a retention period of 90 days.

```
{ "enabled": true,
  "name": "deleteAfter90Days",
  "type": "Lifecycle",
  "definition": { "actions": { "baseBlob": {
     "delete": { "daysAfterCreationGreaterThan": 90 }},
   "snapshot": {
     "delete": { "daysAfterCreationGreaterThan": 90 }}},
   "filters": { "blobTypes": [ "blockBlob" ]}}}
```

When it comes to defining retention periods in relational databases like Azure SQL and Azure Synapse Analytics SQL pools, there are numerous creative approaches. One approach might be to add a column to each data row that contains a timestamp that identifies its creation date. You then can run a stored procedure executed from a cron scheduler or triggered using a Pipeline activity. As this additional information can be substantial when your datasets are large, you need to apply it only to datasets that are required to adhere to such policies. It is common to perform backups of relation databases, so remember that the backups, snapshots, and restore points need to be managed and bound to retention periods, as required. In the context of Azure Databricks, you are most commonly working with files or delta tables. Files contain metadata that identifies the creation and last modified date, which can be referenced and used for managing their retention. Delta tables can also include a column for the data's creation date; this column is used for the management of data retention. When working with delta tables, you can use a *vacuum* to remove backed up data files. Any data retention policy you require in that workspace should include the execution of the vacuum command.

A final subject that should be covered in the context of data retention is something called time-based retention policies for immutable blob data. "Immutable" means that once a blob is created, it can be read but not modified or deleted. This is often referred to as a write once, read many (WORM) tactic. The use case for such a feature is to store critical data and protect it against removal or modification. Numerous regulatory and compliance laws require documents to be stored for a given amount of time in their original state.

Design for Data Privacy

Keeping data private depends primarily on two factors. The first factor is the implementation of a security model, like the layered approach illustrated in Figure 8.1. Implementing a security model has the greatest probability of preventing malicious behaviors and bad actors from having an impact on your data and your IT solution in general. The tools and features that can help prevent those scenarios include VNets, private endpoints, Azure Active Directory, RBAC, and Azure threat protection functionality. The second factor has to do with the classification and labelling of the data, which needs to be kept private and requires an additional level of protection. A very helpful tool is linked to your SQL pools and other Azure SQL products: Data Discovery & Classification. As shown in Figure 8.10, when Data Discovery & Classification. is selected, the database is analyzed for content that might benefit with some additional form of classification and sensitivity labeling.

FIGURE 8.10 Data Discovery & Classification

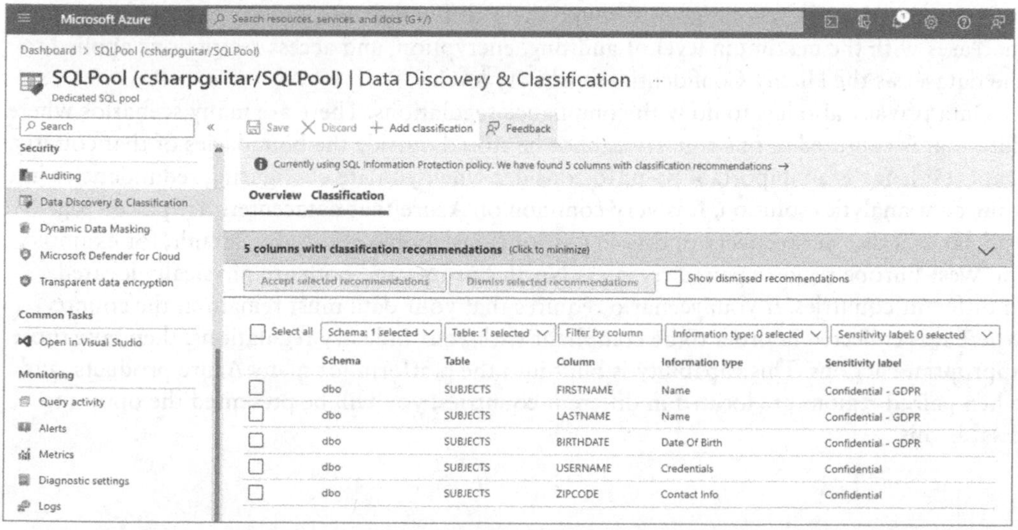

Notice that selecting the Data Discovery & Classification navigation menu item resulted in a scanning of the dbo schema on the Azure Synapse Analytics dedicated SQL Pool. A table named SUBJECTS was discovered to potentially contain PII data, and the tool recommended the sensitivity label and the classification of the data in the Information Type column. The SUBJECTS schema is located on GitHub in the Chapter08 directory. Recognize that you are the expert when it comes to the data hosted on your database. Information stored in columns may be named in a way that results in it not being recognized as requiring additional protection. For this scenario, you can use the + Add Classification menu button to add both the classification and sensitivity label. When you select the + Add Classification menu button, the pop-up window in Figure 8.11 is rendered.

FIGURE 8.11 Data Discovery & Classification, Add Classification window

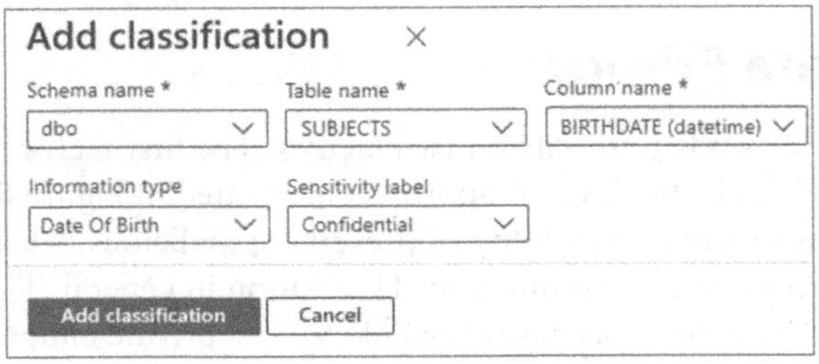

This feature exposes all the schemas, tables, and columns that exist on the database. After selecting add classification, you can then set the classification and sensitivity labels. In this case, the SUBJECTS table contains the column named BIRTHDATE and is classified as Date Of Birth related. The Sensitivity Label drop-down is set to Confidential, which means that some kind of protective measure should be taken to control who can access the data. The other sensitivity levels are Public, General, and Highly Confidential. Reading through those examples, you can conclude that a sensitivity level of Public would likely not need any masking or encryption. As you progress through those different levels, the amount of security also increases with the maximum level of auditing, encryption, and access restrictions applied to the dataset as the Highly Confidential sensitivity level.

Data privacy also has to do with compliance regulations. There are many scenarios where data that is captured in one country cannot be stored outside the boundaries of that country. Data residency is an important point to consider when you are configuring redundancies into your data analytics solution. It is very common on Azure that datacenters are paired together and act as a disaster recovery option in case of catastrophic events. By default, for example, the West Europe region's paired region is North Europe, and both are physically located in different countries. If your scenario requires that your data must remain in the country where it is collected in order to be compliant with your industry regulations, then take those appropriate actions. This capability is built into the platform for many Azure products, and when paired regions are located in different countries, you will be presented the option to disable this.

Design to Purge Data Based on Business Requirements

The primary difference between purging and deleting has to do with whether or not the data is gone for good. When you purge data, it means there is no way to recover it. If something called a soft delete is enabled, it means that the data can be recovered during a preconfigured timeframe. After that timeframe, the data will be purged. Soft-deleted data continues to consume storage space in your database or on your datastore, like an Azure storage container. The storage consumption is only freed when the data is purged. Like all scenarios related to retention and data deletion discussed up to now, you need to first decide which data has a sensitivity level that must adhere to a retention policy. Once you determine which data must be deleted, you need to determine at what age the data should be removed. After identifying those two pieces of information, you might consider deleting the data from your database using the DELETE SQL command. The following command removes all the data from the SUBJECTS table where the CREATE_DATE value is 3 months old from the current date:

```
DELETE FROM SUBJECTS WHERE CREATE_DATE < DATEADD(month, -3, GETDATE())
```

When the amount of data is large, this kind of query can have a significant impact on performance. The impact can result in latency experienced by other data clients inserting, updating, or reading data from the same database. A very fast procedure for removing data is to place the data onto a partition that is defined by the column that defines the lifecycle of the data, for example, using the CREATE_DATE in the SUBJECTS table as the basis for a partition. When the data on that partition has breached the retention threshold, remove the partition, and the data is removed. Another approach is to select the data you want to keep, use the result to insert it into another table, and then switch the tables. This is achieved using CTAS, which was introduced in Chapter 2, "CREATE DATABASE dbName; GO," along with the partitioning concept mentioned previously. The following SQL snippet is an example of how to achieve the purging of data without using the DELETE SQL command:

```
SELECT * INTO SUBJECTS_NEW FROM SUBJECTS
WHERE CREATE_DATE > DATEADD(month, -3, GETDATE())
RENAME OBJECT SUBJECTS TO SUBJECTS_OLD
RENAME OBJECT SUBJECTS_NEW TO SUBJECTS
DROP TABLE SUBJECTS_OLD
```

The SELECT statement retrieves the data with a creation date that is not older than 3 months and places the data into a new table. The existing primary table named SUBJECTS is renamed by appending _OLD to the end. Then the newly populated table that was appended with _NEW is renamed to the primary table name of SUBJECTS. Lastly, the table containing data that is older than 3 months is dropped, resulting in its deletion.

Design Data Encryption for Data at Rest and in Transit

Encryption is a very scientific, mathematics-heavy concept. The internals are outside the scope of this book, but in simple terms when data is encrypted, it looks like a bunch of scrambled letters and numbers that are of no value. The following is an example of the word `csharpguitar` using the key created in Exercise 8.1:


```
p0syrFCPufrCr+9dN7krpFe7wuwIeVwQNFtySX0qaX3UcqzlRifuNdnaxiTu1XgZoKwKmeu6LTfrH
rGQHq4lDClbo/KoqjgSm+0d0Ap/y2HR34TFgoxTeN0KVCoVKAtu35jZ52xeZgj1eYZ9dww2n6psGG
nMRlux/z3ZDvm4qlvrv55eAoSawbCGWOql3mhdfHFZZxLBCN2eZzvBpaTSNaramME54ELMr6ScIJI
ITq6XJYTFH8BGvPaqhfTTO4MbizwenpijIFZvdn3bzQGbnPElht0j+EQ7aLvWOOyzJjlKcR8MN4jO
oYNULCZTBi/BVvlhYpUsKxxN+YW27POMAw==
```


There is no realistic method for anyone or any computer to revert that set of characters back into the original word. That is the power of encryption implemented using public and private keys. Only by having access to the private key can one make sense of that character sequence. The only means for decryption is to use the `az keyvault key decrypt` Azure CLI cmdlet or a REST API that has access to the private key. This leads well into two very important security concepts that pertain greatly to the storage of data on Azure: encryption-at-rest and encryption-in-transit.

Data stored in an Azure storage account is encrypted by default. No action is required by you to encrypt your data that is stored in a container. It is encrypted even if it is not used, which is where the name encryption-at-rest comes from. The data is simply stored, idle, doing nothing, but is secured by encryption. This kind of protection is intended to defend against a bad actor getting access to the physical hard drive that contains data. When the bad actor attempts to access the data, they will see only the scrambled characters. If they do not have the associated keys, which should only be accessible in a key vault, there is no chance of decrypting the data. Therefore, your data is safe, even when it is resting and not being used. Back in Exercise 3.1 where you created an Azure storage account and an ADLS container, there was a tab named Encryption. That tab includes two radio buttons, as shown in Figure 8.12. The default was to use a Microsoft-Managed Key (MMK) for the encryption-at-rest operation; the other optiom is named Customer-Managed Key (CMK). If you select CMK, then you can reference a key you have created in an Azure Key Vault to use as a default encryption key.

Storage account encryption is available for customers who need the maximum amount of security due to compliance or regulations. Also notice the Enable Infrastructure Encryption check box. When this box is selected, the data stored in the account is doubly encrypted. Double encryption is available for both data at rest and data in transit. Instead of being encrypted with just one key, the data is encrypted with two separate keys, the second key being implemented at the infrastructure level. This is done for scenarios where one of the encryption keys or algorithms is compromised. When Enable Infrastructure Encryption is selected and one of the encryption keys is compromised, your data is still encrypted with 256-bit AES encryption by the other key. The data remains safe in this scenario. Another common encryption technology on the Azure platform that is targeted towards databases is Transparent Data Encryption (TDE). TDE protects data at rest on SQL Azure databases, Azure SQL data warehouses, and Azure Synapse Analytics SQL pools. The entire database, data files, and database backups are encrypted using an AES encryption algorithm by default, but like Azure Storage, the encryption key can be managed by the customer or by Microsoft and stored in an Azure key vault.

FIGURE 8.12 Azure storage account encryption type

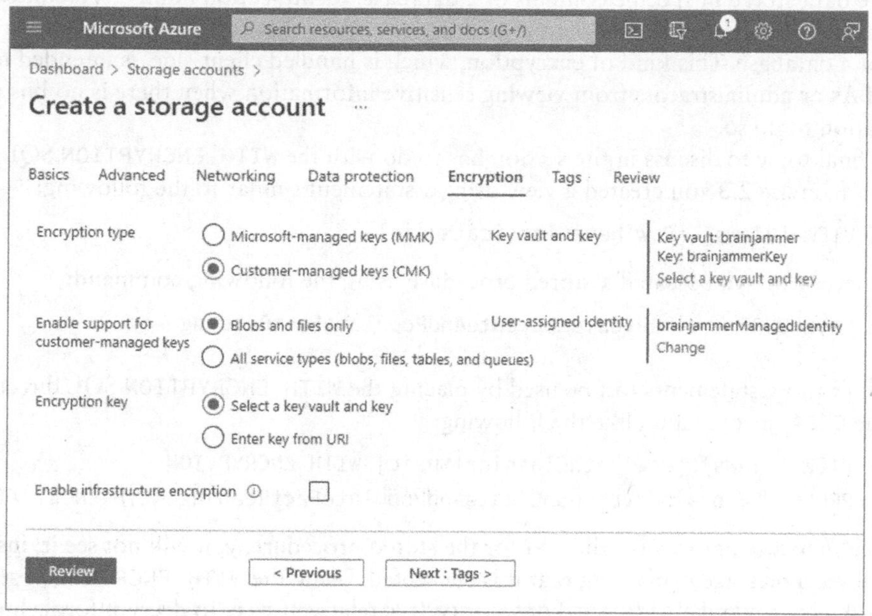

The opposite of resting is active, which can be inferred to data being retrieved from some remote consumer. As the data moves from the location where it is stored to the consumer, the data can be vulnerable to traffic capture. This is where the concept of encryption-in-transit comes into scope. You encrypt data in transit by using TLS 1.2, which is currently the most secure and widely supported version. As previously mentioned, TLS is achieved by using an x509 certificate in combination with the HTTP protocol. Consider the following common Azure product endpoints:

- `https://accountName.blob.core.windows.net/container`
- `https://accountName.dfs.core.windows.net`
- `https://web.azuresynapse.net`
- `https://workspaceName.dev.azuresynapse.net`
- `https://accountName.documents.azure.com:443`
- `https://vaultName.vault.azure.net`
- `https://adbEndpoint.azuredatabricks.net`

In all cases, the transfer of data happens using HTTPS, meaning the data is encrypted while in transit between the service that hosts it and the consumer who has authorization to retrieve it. When working with Linux, the protocol to use is secure shell (SSH), which ensures the encryption of data in transit; HTTPS is also a supported protocol. An additional encryption concept should be mentioned here: encryption-in-use. This concept is implemented using a feature named Always Encrypted and is focused on the protection of sensitive data stored in specific columns of a database. Identification numbers, credit card numbers, PII, and need-to-know data are examples of data that typically resides in the columns of a database. This kind of encryption, which is handled client-side, is intended to prevent DBAs or administrators from viewing sensitive information when there is no business justification to do so.

The final topic to discuss in the section has to do with the `WITH ENCRYPTION` SQL statement. In Exercise 2.3 you created a view using a statement similar to the following:

```
CREATE VIEW [views].[PowThetaClassicalMusic]
```

In Exercise 5.1 you created a stored procedure using the following command:

```
CREATE PROCEDURE brainwaves.uspCreateAndPopulateFactReading
```

Each of those statements can be used by placing the `WITH ENCRYPTION` SQL directory after the `CREATE` command, like the following:

```
CREATE VIEW [views].[PowThetaClassicalMusic] WITH ENCRYPTION
CREATE PROCEDURE brainwaves.uspCreateAndPopulateFactReading WITH ENCRYPTION
```

If you then attempt to view the text for the stored procedure, you will not see it; instead, you will see a message explaining that it is encrypted. Using the `WITH ENCRYPTION` statement provides a relatively low level of security. It is relatively easy to decrypt for technically savvy individuals; however, it is quick and simple to implement, making it worthy of consideration.

Design Row-Level and Column-Level Security

In a relational database, a table is made up of rows of data. Each row can have many columns. Once your data has been ingested and transformed and is ready for consumption, you may need to apply some additional security at the row or column level. Row-level security (RLS) is very similar to a filter commonly implemented using the `WHERE` clause. This works fine as long as no one has direct access to the data and can run queries that circumvent this level of projection. In this case, if you need to restrict access on a row level, and you have clients that connect directly to your database, then you need to apply RLS. Implementing RLS requires what is called a `FILTER PREDICATE`, which is applied using the `CREATE SECURITY POLICY` statement. Consider a scenario where you have implemented a global brain wave repository that allows anyone to upload their brain wave readings to your datastore for processing and data analytics. Consider taking it one step further and provide the option for those individuals to perform analytics on their scenarios. As the platform owner, you would want to see all readings from all those who have uploaded data; however, you would want to restrict individuals' access to only their data. RLS is a means for achieving just that. Consider the following SQL statement:

```
CREATE SECURITY POLICY BrainwavesFilter_ext
ADD FILTER PREDICATE Security.fn_securitypredicate(brainwaveProducer)
ON dbo.Brainwaves_ext
WITH (STATE = ON);
```

The statement creates a policy named BrainwavesFilter_ext and adds a predicate based on a value stored on a table named Brainwave_ext. The value in column brainwaveProducer is the user account ID of the person who uploaded brain waves. When CRUD queries are executed against the Brainwave_ext table, the policy uses the predicate to filter, change, remove, insert, and/or deliver the data for the user who uploaded it.

Another feature that you can apply to the data is called column-level security. Recall from the SUBJECTS table a few columns are worthy of a Confidential sensitivity level. Columns like USERNAME, ZIPCODE, EMAIL, and BIRTHDATE contain data that should not be accessible to the public or generally available. If you have a user in your Azure Synapse Analytics dedicated SQL pool named brainjammer and do not want that user to have access to these columns, you can execute the following command to exclude the columns from the list:

```
GRANT SELECT ON SUBJECTS
  (ID, FIRSTNAME, LASTNAME, EMAIL, COUNTRY, CREATE_DATE) TO brainjammer;
```

If that user then attempts the following SELECT statement, an error would be rendered stating that access is denied:

```
SELECT * FROM SUBJECTS
```

In the Implement Row-Level and Column-Level Security section you will perform an exercise and experience column level security firsthand.

Design a Data Masking Strategy

A mask is an object that partially conceals what is behind it. From a data perspective, a mask would conceal a particular piece of the data but not all of it. Consider, for example, email addresses, names, credit card numbers, and telephone numbers. Those classifications of data can be helpful if there is ever a need to validate a person's identity. However, you would not want all of the data rendered in a query; instead, you can show only the last four digits of the credit card number or the first letter of an email address and the top level domain value like .com, .net, or .org, like the following:

```
bXXXXX@XXXXXX.net
```

There is a built-in capability for this masking in the Azure portal related to an Azure Synapse Analytics dedicated SQL pool. As shown in Figure 8.13 navigating to the Dynamic Data Masking blade renders masking capabilities.

The feature will automatically scan your tables and find columns that may contain data that would benefit from masking. You apply the mask by selecting the Add Mask button, selecting the mask, and saving it. Then, when a user who is not in the excluded list, as shown in Figure 8.13, accesses the data, the mask is applied to the resulting dataset. Finally, the primary objective of masking is to conceal enough of the data in a column so that it can be used but not exploited. That partial data visibility demonstrates the difference between masking and encryption. When data in a column is encrypted, none of it is readable, whereas a mask can be configured to allow partial data recognition.

FIGURE 8.13 Dynamic Data Masking dedicated SQL pool

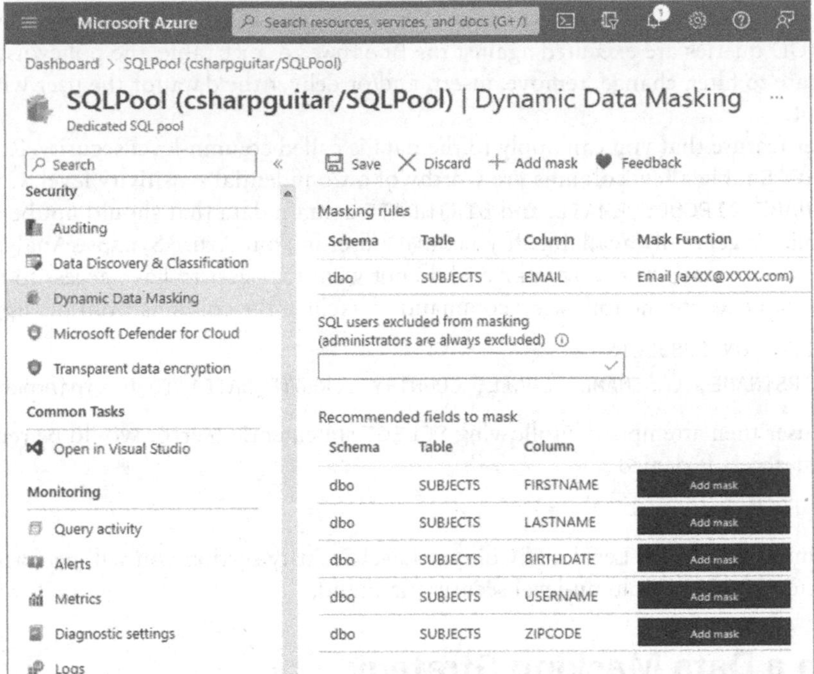

Design Access Control for Azure Data Lake Storage Gen2

There are four authorization methods for Azure storage accounts. The method you have been using in most scenarios up to now has been through access keys. An access key resembles the following:

```
4jRwk0Ho7LB+si85ax...yuZP+AKrr1FbWbQ==
```

The access key is used in combination with the protocol and storage account name to build the connection string. Clients can then use this to access the storage account and the data within it. The connections string resembles the following:

```
DefaultEndpointsProtocol=https;AccountName=<name>;AccountKey=<account-key>
```

On numerous occasions you have created linked services in the Azure Synapse Analytics workspace. When configuring a linked service for an Azure storage account, you might remember seeing that shown in Figure 8.14, which requests the information required to build the Azure storage account connection string.

FIGURE 8.14 ADLS access control access keys

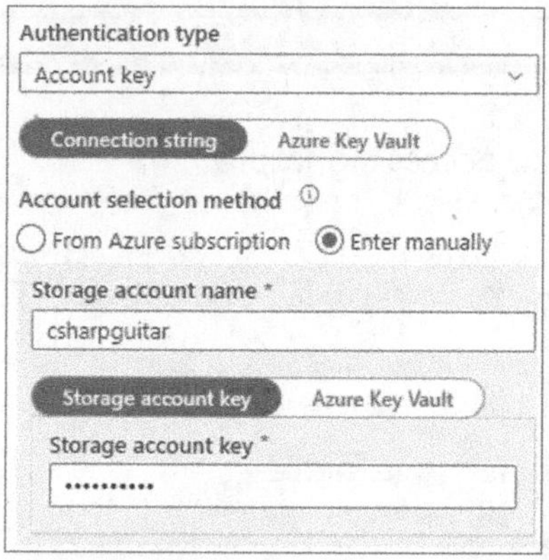

Notice that the options request the authentication type, which is set to access key, sometimes also referred to as an account key, to be used as part of a connection string, followed by the storage account name and the storage account key. Those values are enough for the client—in this case, an Azure Synapse Analytics linked service—to successfully make the connection to the storage account. HTTPS is used as default, which enforces data encryption-in-transit; therefore, an authentication type is not requested. Another authorization method similar to access keys is called shared access signature (SAS) authorization. This authorization method gives you a bit more control over what services, resources, and actions a client can access on the data stored in the account. Figure 8.15 shows the Shared Access Signature blade in the Azure portal for Azure storage accounts.

When you use either an access key or a SAS URL, any client with that token will get access to your storage account. There is no identity associated with either of those authorization methods; therefore, protecting that token key is very important. This is a reason that offering the retrieval of the account key from an Azure key vault is also an option, as you saw in Figure 8.14. Storing the access key and/or the SAS URL in an Azure key vault would remove the need to store the key within the realm of an Azure Synapse Analytics workspace. Although this is safe, reducing the number of clients who have possession of your authorization keys is a good design. Any entity that needs these keys can be granted access to the Azure key vault and the keys for making the connection to your storage account. The other two remaining authorization methods are RBAC and ACL, which are covered in the following sections. As an introduction to those sections, Table 8.2 provides some details about both the Azure RBAC and ACL authorization methods.

TABLE 8.2 Azure storage account authorization methods

Method	Scope	Require an identity	Granularity level
Azure RBAC	Storage account, container	Yes	High
ACL	File, directory	Yes	Low

FIGURE 8.15 ADLS Access control shared access signature

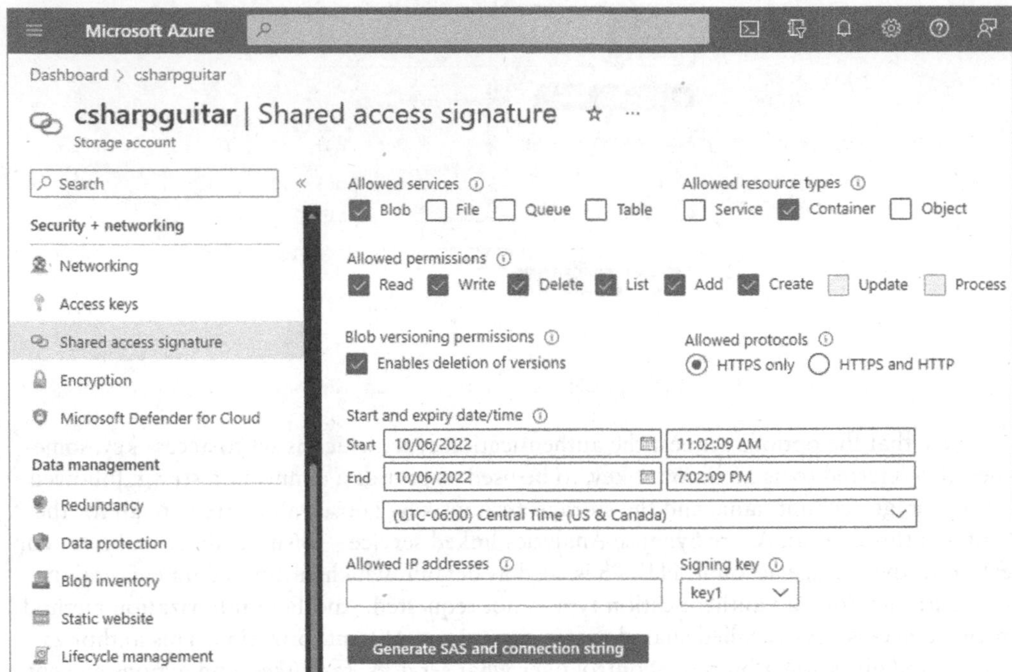

Authorization placed upon an Azure storage account using an RBAC is achieved using a role assignment at the storage account or container level. ACLs are implemented by assigning read, write, or delete permissions on a file or directory. As shown in Figure 8.16, if the identity of the person or service performing the operation is associated with an RBAC group with the assignment allowing file deletion, then that access is granted, regardless of the ACL permission.

However, if the identity associated with the group that is assigned RBAC permissions does not have the authorization to perform a delete but does have the ACL permission, then the file can be deleted. The following sections describe these authentication methods in more detail.

Azure Role-Based Access Control

RBAC has been discussed in Chapter 1, "Gaining the Azure Data Engineer Associate Certification," Chapter 3, "Data Sources and Ingestion," and Chapter 5. What RBAC is, its purpose, and how it achieves controlling access to Azure resources should be somewhat clear at this point. This section will go into a bit more detail in the context of an Azure storage account that includes an ADLS container. The implementation of RBAC assignments for a specific resource is performed on the Access Control (IAM) blade for the given resource, as you have seen previously in Figure 1.28 and Figure 5.47. Figure 8.17 provides an example of the permission related to an Azure storage account.

FIGURE 8.16 RBAC and ACL permission evaluation

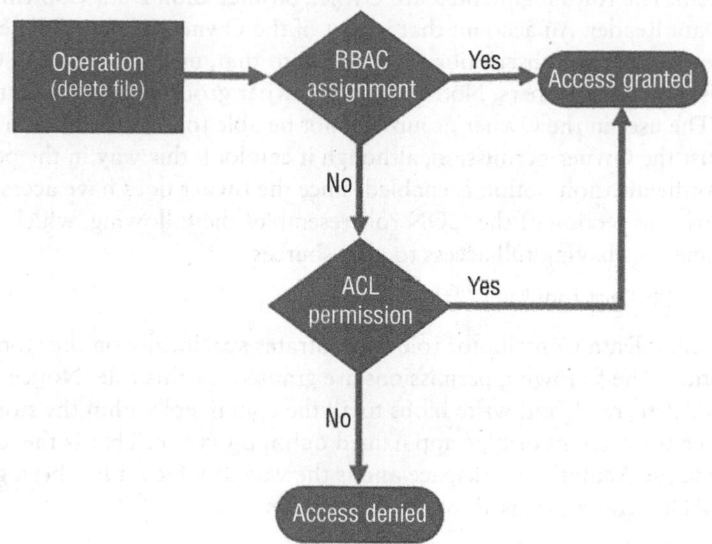

FIGURE 8.17 RBAC Access Control (IAM) Azure storage account

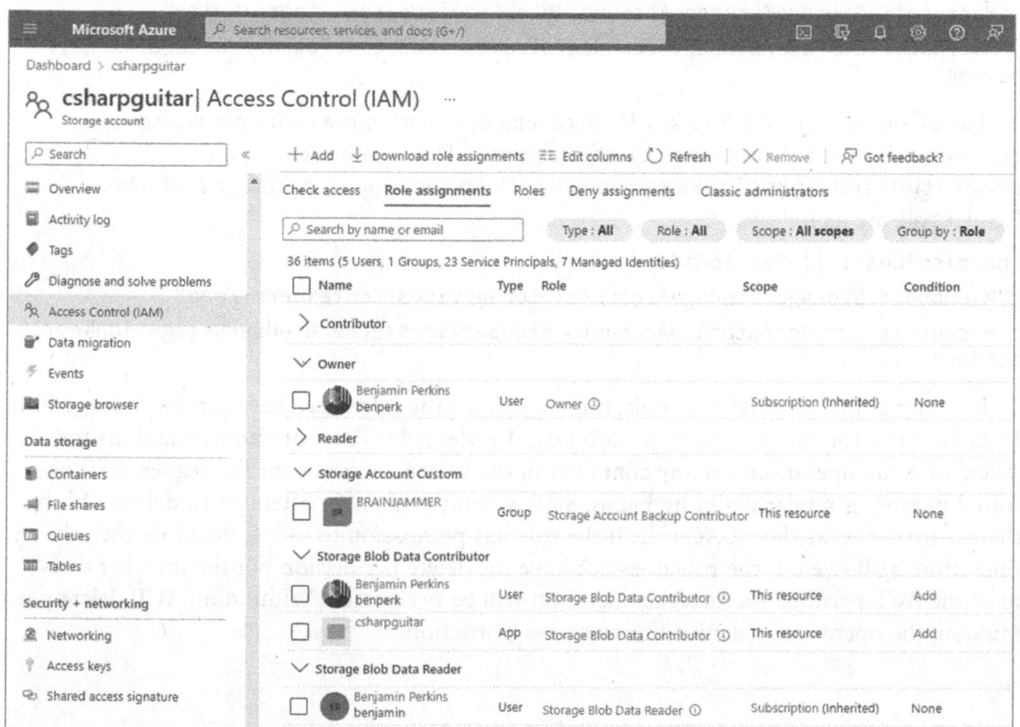

Notice that the Role Assignments tab is selected and that there are numerous roles and users within them. The roles highlighted are Owner, Storage Blob Data Contributor, and Storage Blob Data Reader. An account that is part of the Owner role has full access to manage all resources within the subscription. In addition to that, members with an Owner role can assign roles to other members. Notice that the Owner group does not grant access to the data layer. The user in the Owner group will not be able to read the data in the storage account with just the Owner permission, although it can look this way in the portal if the Account Key Authentication option is enabled, since the owner does have access to those keys. The permissions section of the JSON role resembles the following, which supports the preceding statement of having full access to all resources:

```
"permissions": [{ "actions": [ "*" ...]
```

The Storage Blob Data Contributor role concentrates specifically on the storage accounts in the subscription. The following permissions are granted for this role. Notice that members of this role can delete, read, and write blobs to all the containers within the storage account. You might notice the account of type app named `csharpguitar`. That is the identity linked to the Azure Synapse Analytics workspace and is the way in which it has been granted permission to the ADLS container used for the workspace.

```
"permissions": [{ "actions": [
 "Microsoft.Storage/storageAccounts/blobServices/containers/delete",
 "Microsoft.Storage/storageAccounts/blobServices/containers/read",
 "Microsoft.Storage/storageAccounts/blobServices/containers/write",
 "Microsoft.Storage/storageAccounts/blobServices/generateUserDelegationKey/
action" ...]
```

The ability to receive a SAS key for accessing data within the container is also granted to the Storage Blob Data Contributor role. This is achieved via the `generateUserDelegationKey` permission. The permissions for Storage Blob Data Reader role are as follows.

```
"permissions": [{ "actions": [
 "Microsoft.Storage/storageAccounts/blobServices/containers/read",
 "Microsoft.Storage/storageAccounts/blobServices/generateUserDelegationKey/
action" ...]
```

Looking at the permission details, it is easy to see the difference between the Storage Blob Data Contributor role and Storage Blob Data Reader role. There are no permissions for delete or write operations on any container in the storage account for the reader. As illustrated in more granular detail by Figure 8.18, when the member attempts to delete a blob, the platform checks the RBAC role. If the role has permission to delete the blob, then the operation is allowed. If the role does not have the delete permission but the member does have the ACL permission, then the operation will be performed. Without an ACL delete permission, the operation is denied due to access restriction.

FIGURE 8.18 RBAC role and ACL permission evaluation

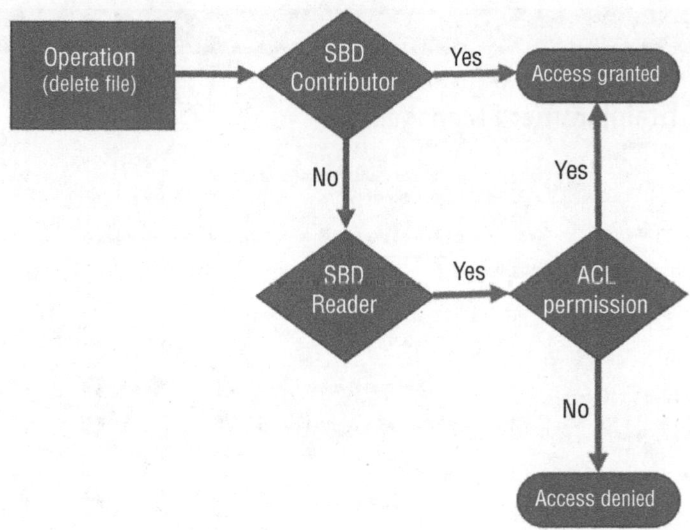

Remember that if a built-in RBAC role does not meet your requirements, you can create a custom RBAC role to include or exclude permissions. As shown in Figure 8.17, a group named `BRAINJAMMER` has been added to a custom RBAC role named Storage Account Custom. The group is an Azure Active Directory security group that contains members who are also part of the Azure Active Directory tenant. Those members receive the permissions associated with the RBAC custom permission list. As you know, adding individual members to RBAC roles at the resource level is the most inefficient approach. Instead, you should create groups that effectively describe the role, add members to it, and then add the group to the RBAC role. You will create this group in Exercise 8.12.

POSIX-like Access Control Lists

There was an extensive discussion about ACLs in Chapter 1. Two concepts need to be summarized again: the types of ACLs and the permission levels. The two kinds of ACLs are Access and Default, and the three permission levels are Execute (X), Read (I), and Write (W). Access ACLs control the access to both directories and files, as shown in Table 8.2. Default ACLs are templates that determine access ACLs for child items created below a directory with applied access ACLs. Files do not have default ACLs, and changing the ACL of a parent does not affect the default or access ACLs of the child items. The feature to configure and manage ACLs is available on the Manage ACL blade for a given ADLS container, as shown in Figure 8.19.

FIGURE 8.19 The Manage ACL blade

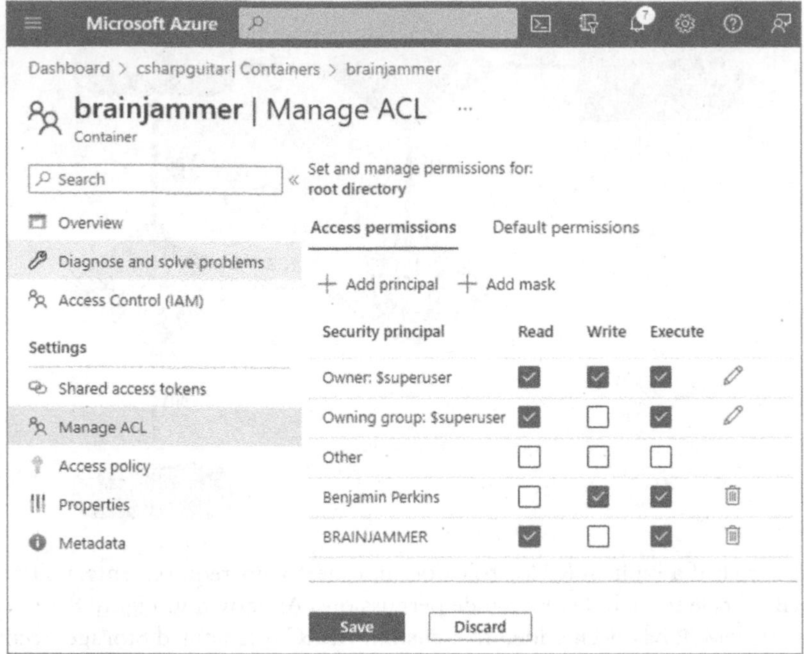

Figure 8.10 shows two tabs. The Access Permissions tab is in focus. The Azure AD security group `BRAINJAMMER` has been granted Access-Read and Access-Execute permissions, which means the content within the ADLS container directory can be listed. Listing the contents of a directory requires both Read (R) and Execute (X) permissions. The individual who was added to the Storage Blob Data Reader RBAC group shown in Figure 8.17 has been granted Access-Write and Access-Execute. Write (W) and Execute (X) ACL permissions are required to create items in the targeted directory. The other tab, Default Permissions, is where you can configure permissions that will be applied to the child items created below the root directory, which is the one in focus, as shown under the Set and Manage Permissions For heading. Now that you have some insights into data security concepts, features, and products, continue to the next section, where you will implement some of what you just learned.

Implement Data Security

Until your security objectives and requirements are finalized, you should not proceed with any form of implementation. You need to first know specifically what your goal is before you begin taking action. If your business model requires that your data complies with industry regulations, the requirements to meet those rules must be part of your design. Remember that Microsoft Purview and Azure Policy are helpful tools for guiding you through regulatory compliance. Those tools are also helpful for discovering your data sources and determining which sensitivity levels they require. Those sensitivity levels provide guidance into the level of security to apply to the dataset. After completing those steps, use something like the layered security diagram shown in Figure 8.1 as a guide for implementing security. The following sections cover the information protection, access management, and network security layers. The threat protection layer, which includes features like anomaly activity detection and malware detection, is best designed and implemented by security professionals. Note, however, that Microsoft Defender for Cloud is specifically designed for securing, detecting, alerting, and responding to bad actors and malicious activities preventing them from doing harm.

Implement a Data Auditing Strategy

Before you can design and implement a data security solution, you need to discover and classify your data. As you learned, Microsoft Purview has features for discovering, classifying, and proposing a sensitivity level. In Exercise 8.2 you provisioned a Microsoft Purview account, viewed the Collection Admins role assignments, and added a few collections. In Exercise 8.3 you will perform a scan that discovers data assets within the targeted collection and identifies whether they meet basic classification and sensitivity levels. Before you begin Exercise 8.3, it is important to call out three security actions you took in the previous two exercises that are required for Exercise 8.3 to work. Recall step 4 in Exercise 8.1, where you created an AKV secret named `azureSynapseSQLPool` that contains the password for your Azure Synapse Analytics dedicated SQL pool. You will configure Microsoft Purview to use this Azure Key Vault secret to access and analyze the assets within that dedicated SQL pool. In Exercise 8.2, step 2, you validated that your account was in the Collection Admins group on the Role Assignments tab for the root collection. Additionally, in step 5 of Exercise 8.2 you granted Get and List permissions to the Azure Key Vault secret to your Microsoft Purview account identity. As you will configure in Exercise 8.3, one more permission is required to make this work for your Azure Synapse Analytics dedicated SQL pool. The same Microsoft Purview account identity that you granted access to Azure Key Vault must be added to the Reader role via Access control (IAM) on your Azure Synapse Analytics workspace.

Note that each Azure product that you want to perform a scan on from Microsoft Purview will likely have its own set of permissions and role access requirements. You will need to find this out using online documentation on a product-by-product basis. Exercise 8.3 and previous exercises provide the instructions to perform a scan on an Azure Synapse Analytics dedicated SQL pool. Complete Exercise 8.3 to gain hands-on experience with this product and feature.

EXERCISE 8.3

Configure and Perform a Data Asset Scan Using Microsoft Purview

1. Log in to the Azure portal at `https://portal.azure.com` ➢ navigate to the Azure Synapse Analytics workspace you created in Exercise 3.3 ➢ select the Access Control (IAM) navigation menu item ➢ click the + Add menu button ➢ select Add Role Assignment from the drop-down list ➢ select Reader from the Role list ➢ click Next ➢ select the Managed Identity radio button ➢ click the + Select member link ➢ select Microsoft Purview Account from the Managed Identity drop-down list box ➢ select the Microsoft Purview account you created in Exercise 8.2 ➢ click the Select button ➢ click the Review + Assign button ➢ navigate to the Overview blade ➢ click the Open link in the Open Synapse Studio tile ➢ select the Manage hub ➢ select SQL Pools from the menu list ➢ and then start the dedicated SQL pool.
2. Select the Manage hub ➢ select the Microsoft Purview item in the External Connections section ➢ click the Connect to a Purview Account button ➢ select the Purview account created in Exercise 8.2 (for example, `brainjammer`) ➢ click Apply ➢ and then select the link to your Microsoft Purview account tab, as shown in Figure 8.20.

FIGURE 8.20 Connecting Microsoft Purview to Azure Synapse Analytics workspace

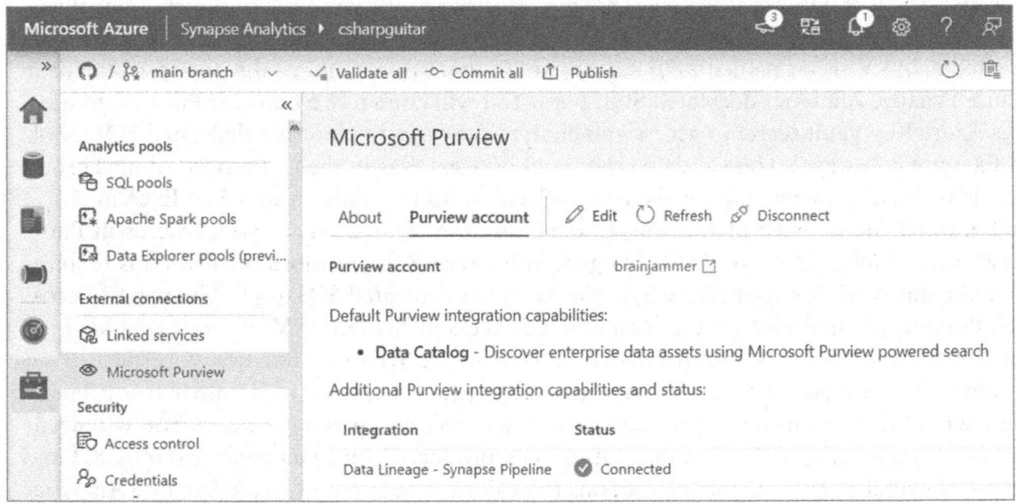

3. Select the Data Map hub ➢ select Sources from the navigation menu ➢ select the Register menu item ➢ select Azure Synapse Analytics from the Register Source window ➢ click Continue ➢ enter a name (I used **ASA-csharpguitar**) ➢ select the workspace you

configured in step 2 from the Workspace Name drop-down list box ➢ select the R&D collection from the Select a Collection drop-down list box ➢ and then click Register.

4. Select the View Details link on the just registered source in the Map view ➢ select the New Scan menu item ➢ enter a name (I used **ScanDedicatedSQLPool**) ➢ select + New from the Credential drop-down list box ➢ enter a name (I used **sqladminuser**) ➢ enter the user ID/name of your Azure Synapse Analytics dedicated SQL pool (I used **sqladminuser**) ➢ select the + New from the Key Vault Connection drop-down list box ➢ enter a name (I used **brainjammerKV**) ➢ select the Key Vault you created in Exercise 8.1 ➢ click Create ➢ enter the Azure Key Vault secret name that stores your Azure Synapse Analytics password (I used **azureSynapseSQLPool**) ➢ click Create ➢ select your dedicated SQL pool from the SQL Database drop-down list box ➢ select the Test Connection link ➢ and then click Continue. The configuration resembles Figure 8.21.

FIGURE 8.21 Configuring scanning in Microsoft Purview

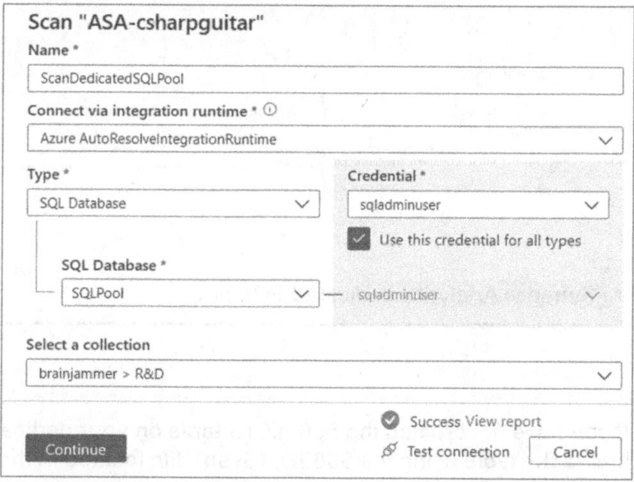

5. Click the Continue button to perform the scan using the default scan rule set ➢ select the Once radio button ➢ click Continue ➢ and then click the Save and Run button. When the scan is complete, you will see something like Figure 8.22.

EXERCISE 8.3 *(continued)*

FIGURE 8.22 The result of a Microsoft Purview scan

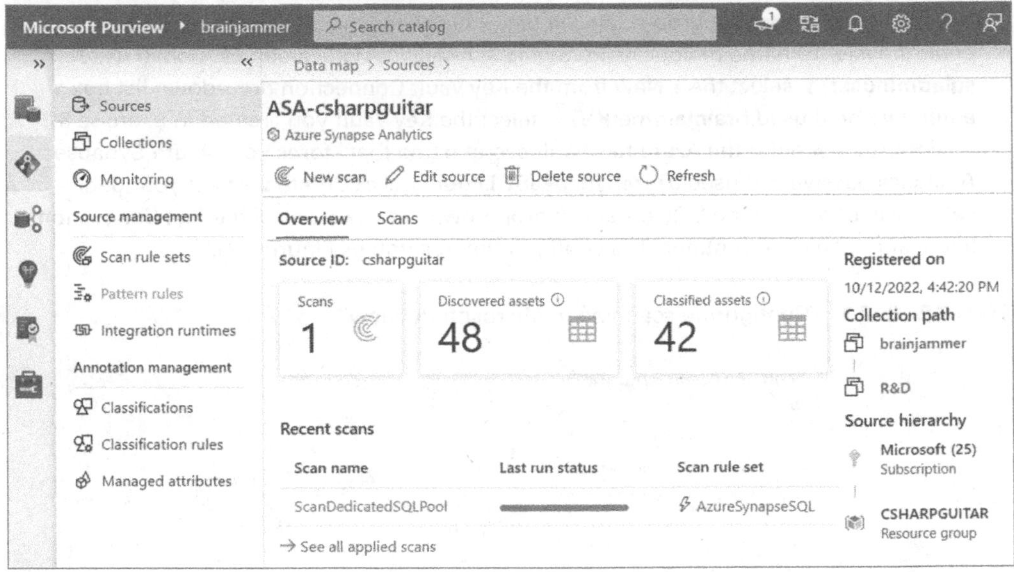

6. Stop your Azure Synapse Analytics dedicated SQL pool.

NOTE If you have not created the SUBJECTS table on your dedicated SQL pool, create the table using the SUBJECTS.sql file located in the Chapter08 directory on GitHub.

The first action you took after accessing the Azure portal was to add the Microsoft Purview account identity to the Reader role of the Azure Synapse Analytics workspace. Note that adding this role assignment at the workspace level results in the Reader permissions being granted to all resources that exist in the workspace. This is a good level of access for Microsoft Purview to perform proper governance and auditing activities. It is also possible to provide this level of access specifically to a SQL or Spark pool using the same approach via the Access control (IAM) role assignments feature while those analytics pools are in focus. Next, you navigated to the Manage hub on the Azure Synapse Analytics workspace and bound the Microsoft Purview account together with the workspace. This provided easy access to the Microsoft Purview Governance portal.

Until you configure the new credential, as shown in Figure 8.21, you may receive a `Failed to load serverless databases from Synapse workspace` error message. Once you select the new credential (for example, `sqladminuser`), the error will go away. In this example, the username and password are the same for both the serverless and dedicated SQL pools.

Once in the Microsoft Purview Governance portal, you registered a collection named `ASA-csharpguitar` into the R&D parent collection. After the collection that targeted your Azure Synapse Analytics workspace was completed, you began with the configuration of an asset scan. A credential that can access both the serverless and dedicated SQL pool is required at this point. Selecting the + New item from the Credential drop-down list box provided the option to do this. You added a connection to the Azure Key Vault connection that targets the secret created in Exercise 8.1. The secret contains the password of your dedicated SQL pool, which is, in this example, the same as the built-in serverless database SQL pool. Once configured and selected from the Credential drop-down list box, you were able to select the dedicated SQL pool as the target data source of the scan.

When you selected to use the System Default scan rule set, you chose to use all the supported classification rules. While configuring the scan, you might have noticed the View Details link below that value. Clicking the View Details link currently renders a list of 208 classification rules grouped together with names such as Government, Financial, Base, Personal, Security, and Miscellaneous. You also have the option to create a custom rule that allows you to include your own additional set of items to scan for. The Security scan checks for passwords that match common patterns; the Government scan checks for values that match an ID; and the Personal scan checks for birth dates, email addresses, and phone numbers, for example. If you didn't look at that, go back and check it out for the full set of attributes that are searched for when running an asset scan. The next window gives you the option to schedule the audit scan weekly or monthly. In a live scenario, where you have a lot of activity on your data sources, this would be a good idea. Lastly, you ran the scan, viewed the results shown in Figure 8.22, and then stopped the dedicated SQL pool. In Exercise 8.5 you will use those results to classify and curate the data existing in the `SUBJECTS` table.

Azure Synapse Analytics includes an Auditing feature for dedicated SQL pools. Complete Exercise 8.4 to configure and implement Auditing on an Azure Synapse Analytics dedicated SQL pool.

EXERCISE 8.4

Audit an Azure Synapse Analytics Dedicated SQL Pool

1. Log in to the Azure portal at `https://portal.azure.com` ➢ enter **Log Analytics Workspaces** in the Search box and select it from the drop-down ➢ click the + Create button ➢ select a subscription ➢ select a resource group ➢ enter a name (I used **brainjammer**) ➢ select a region ➢ click the Review + Create button ➢ and then click Create.

EXERCISE 8.4 *(continued)*

2. Navigate to the Azure Synapse Analytics workspace you created in Exercise 3.3 ➢ select the SQL Pools navigation menu item ➢ select your dedicated SQL pool ➢ start the dedicated SQL pool ➢ select the Auditing navigation menu item ➢ set the Enable Azure Auditing toggle switch to on ➢ select the Log Analytics check box ➢ select the subscription where you placed the Log Analytics workspace from step 1 ➢ select the workspace from the Log Analytics drop-down list box ➢ and then click Save. The configuration should resemble Figure 8.23.

FIGURE 8.23 Dedicated SQL pool auditing configuration

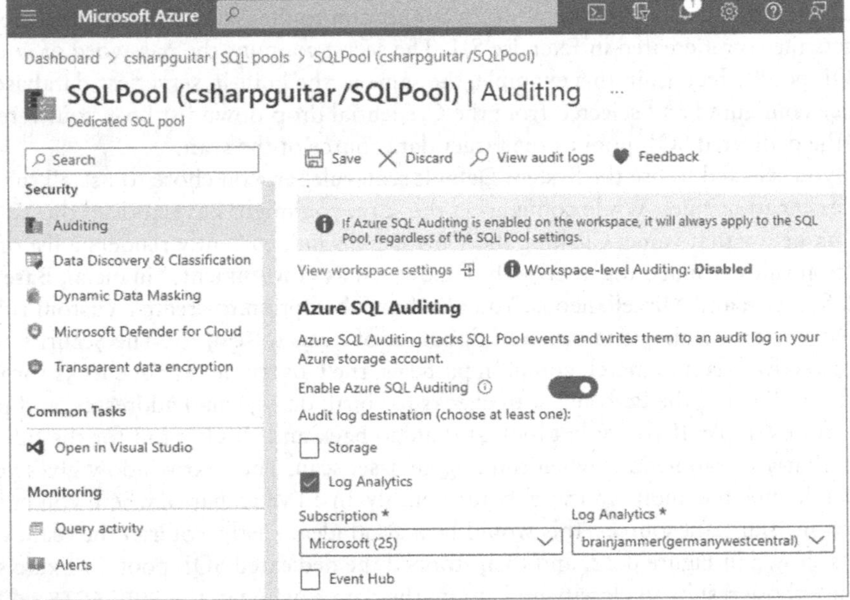

3. After some minutes, navigate to the Diagnostic Settings navigation menu item for the dedicated SQL pool ➢ notice the setting prefixed with `SQLSecurityAuditEvents_` ➢ click the Edit Setting link associated with that diagnostic setting ➢ check the Sql Requests check box ➢ and then click Save. The configuration should resemble Figure 8.24.

FIGURE 8.24 Dedicated SQL pool Diagnostic setting configuration

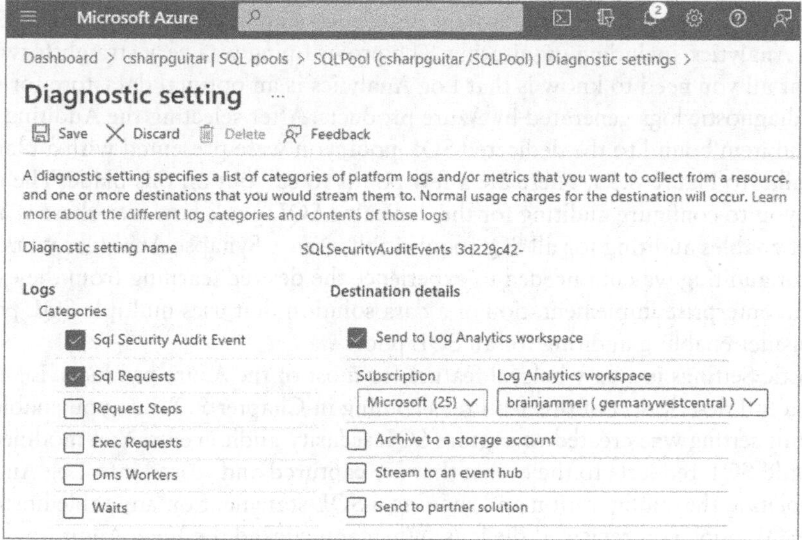

4. After some minutes, execute the following query on the dedicated SQL pool configured in the previous steps:

```
SELECT * FROM [dbo].[SUBJECTS]
```

5. After some minutes, select the View Audit Logs menu button (refer to Figure 8.23) ➢ click the Log Analytics menu button ➢ and then execute the default query. An example query is available on GitHub in the `Chapter08/Ch08Ex04` directory. The output should resemble Figure 8.25.

FIGURE 8.25 View dedicated SQL pool audit logs in Log Analytics.

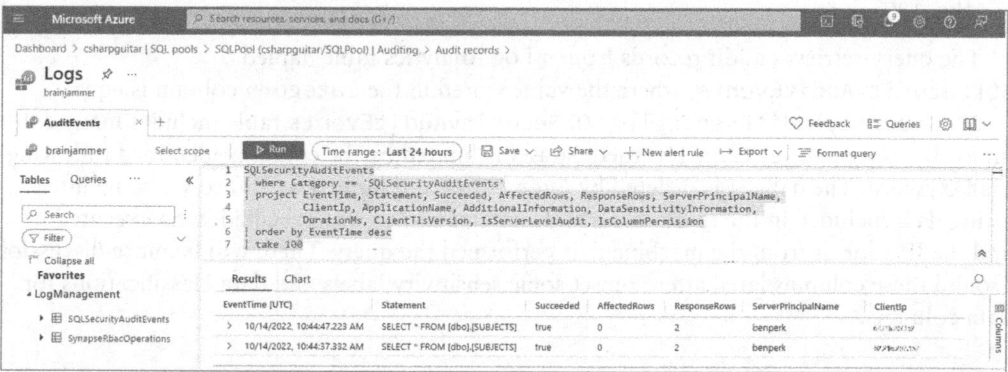

6. Stop the dedicated SQL pool.

The first step taken in Exercise 8.4 resulted in the provisioning of an Azure Log Analytics workspace. This is the recommended location to store, analyze, and manage audit logs. Chapter 9, "Monitoring Azure Data Storage and Processing," includes detailed coverage of Azure Log Analytics, including monitoring. The provisioning was very straightforward, so at this point all you need to know is that Log Analytics is an optimal datastore for storing audit and diagnostic logs generated by Azure products. After selecting the Auditing navigation menu item bound to the dedicated SQL pool, you were presented with a blade that looked similar to Figure 8.23. There are a few points to call out on this blade. The exercise instructed you to configure auditing for the dedicated SQL pool; however, there is another option that enables auditing for all SQL pools in the Azure Synapse Analytics workspace. This level of auditing was not needed to experience the desired learning from the exercise, but in a real enterprise implementation of a data solution that uses multiple SQL pools, you should consider enabling auditing for all SQL pools.

Diagnostic Settings is a very helpful feature for most of the Azure products. Like Log Analytics, a full description of this feature is coming in Chapter 9. When you enabled auditing, a default setting was created to capture SQL security audit events. You modified the setting to add SQL requests to the events that are captured and stored into Log Analytics. After completing the configuration and running a SQL statement on any table hosted in the dedicated SQL pool, you reviewed the logs. When you clicked the View Audit Logs menu button, as shown in Figure 8.23, you were navigated to the Log Analytics workspace. The Log Analytics query editor enabled you to execute queries against the audit data being stored into it. Exercise 8.4 used the following query:

```
SQLSecurityAuditEvents
| where Category == 'SQLSecurityAuditEvents'
| project EventTime, Statement, Succeeded, AffectedRows, ResponseRows,
          ServerPrincipalName, ClientIp, ApplicationName, AdditionalInformation,
          DataSensitivityInformation, DurationMs, ClientTlsVersion,
          IsServerLevelAudit, IsColumnPermission
| order by EventTime desc
| take 100
```

The query retrieves audit records from a Log Analytics table named `SQLSecurityAuditEvents`, where the value stored in the `Category` column is equal to `SQLSecurityAuditEvents`. The `SQLSecurityAuditEvents` table includes many columns. By using `project`, the returned dataset is limited by the columns identified following that keyword. The dataset is ordered by `EventTime` and limited to 100 rows. Some interesting data included in the result is the SQL statement that was executed, who executed it, and the IP address from the machine that performed the query. There will be more discussion around these columns later, after you set some sensitivity labels and data classifications for data columns.

Manage Sensitive Information

The tool capable of discovering and auditing your data is Microsoft Purview, which can search all your data real estate hosted on Azure, on-premises, and even on other cloud provider platforms. In Exercise 8.3, you used Microsoft Purview to scan a dedicated SQL pool to identify the assets within it. Figure 8.26 shows the result of that scan. The result is accessible on the Data Estate Insights hub within the Microsoft Purview Governance portal.

FIGURE 8.26 Scanning a dedicated SQL pool with Microsoft Purview

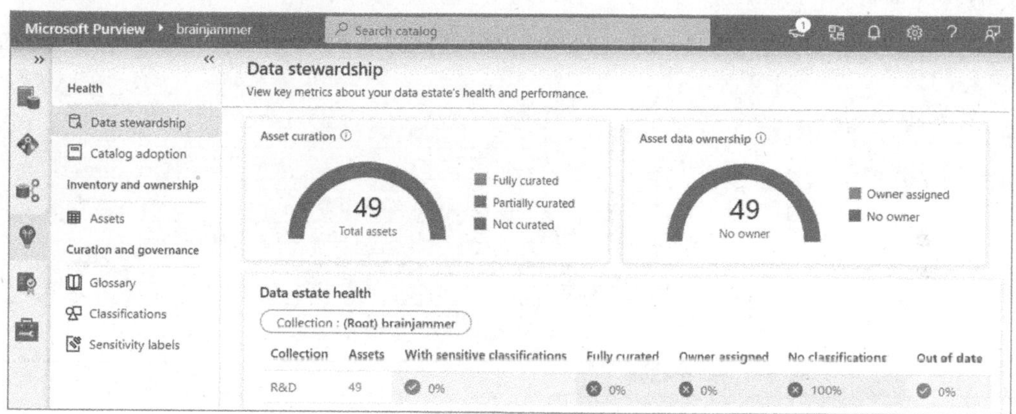

The scan found 49 total assets that have neither sensitivity labels nor classifications. This is because neither of those activities has been performed yet. Something like what you saw previously in Figure 8.11 needs to be carried out on the data. That example of data classification was illustrated from another tool for managing sensitive data, Data Discovery & Classification, which, when used in combination with Auditing, can be used to target dedicated SQL pools running in an Azure Synapse Analytics workspace. Complete Exercise 8.5, where you will apply sensitivity labels and data classifications.

EXERCISE 8.5

Apply Sensitivity Labels and Data Classifications Using Microsoft Purview and Data Discovery

1. Log in to the Azure portal at `https://portal.azure.com` ➢ navigate to the Microsoft Purview Governance Portal you provisioned in Exercise 8.2 ➢ select the Data Estate Insights hub ➢ select the link under the Assets heading on the Data Stewardship blade (the link is represented by the number 49 in Figure 8.26) ➢ scroll down and select the `SUBJECTS` table link ➢ select the Schema tab ➢ and then click the Edit button. The configuration should resemble Figure 8.27.

EXERCISE 8.5 *(continued)*

FIGURE 8.27 Microsoft Purview Data estate insights schema data classification

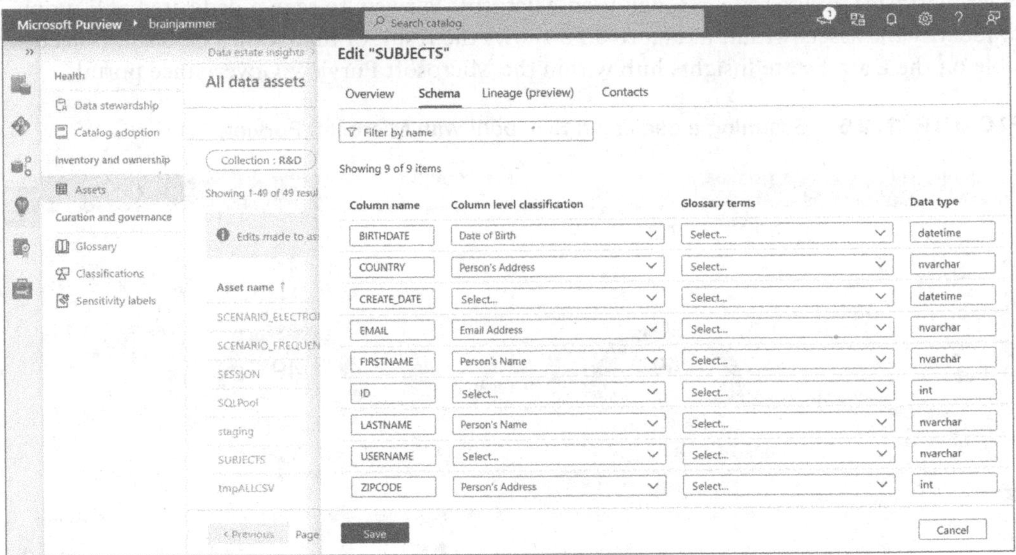

2. Click the Save button ➢ observe the results ➢ navigate to the Azure Synapse Analytics workspace you created in Exercise 3.3 ➢ select the SQL Pools navigation menu link ➢ select your dedicated SQL pool ➢ start the SQL pool ➢ and then select Data Discovery & Classification. The following message will appear at the top of the Data Discovery & Classification blade: "Currently using SQL Information Protection policy. We have found 6 columns with classification recommendations," as shown in Figure 8.28. Click that message. The six columns and the recommendations should resemble Figure 8.28.

FIGURE 8.28 SQL Information Protection policy classification recommendations

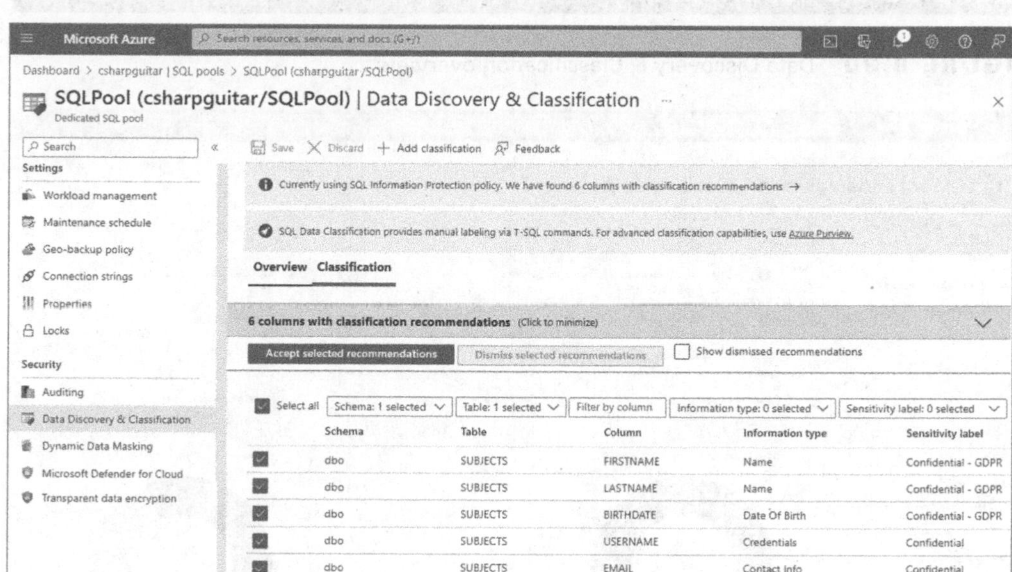

3. Click the + Add Classification menu button ➢ select dbo from the Schema Name drop-down ➢ select `SUBJECTS` from the Table Name drop-down ➢ select `COUNTRY` from the Column Name drop-down ➢ select `Contact Info` from the Information Type drop-down ➢ select `General` from the Sensitivity Label drop-down➢ and then click Add Classification. The configuration should resemble Figure 8.29.

FIGURE 8.29 Data Discovery & Classification, Add classification 2

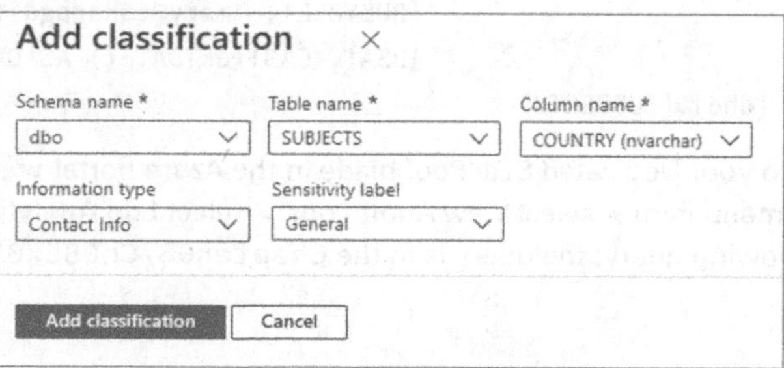

4. Select the Select All check box ➢ click the Accept Selected Recommendations button ➢ and then click Save. The Overview tab will display something similar to Figure 8.30.

EXERCISE 8.5 *(continued)*

FIGURE 8.30 Data Discovery & Classification overview

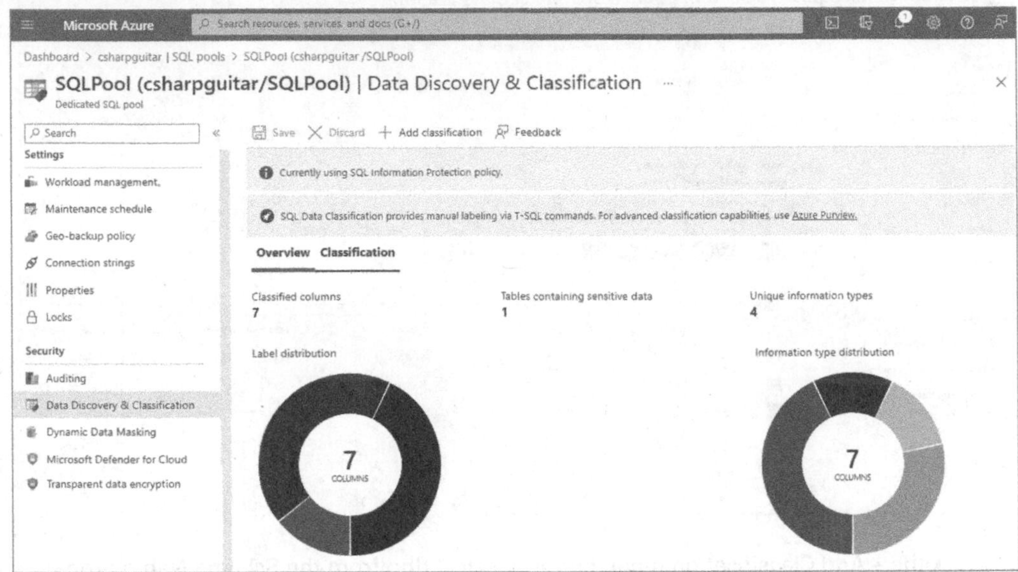

5. Execute the following two SQL statements on your dedicated SQL pool. The statements are in the `auditSubjects.sql` file in the `Chapter08/Ch08Ex05` directory on GitHub.

```
INSERT INTO [dbo].[SUBJECTS] SELECT 'MARY', 'PERKINS', '19900730 08:00:00 AM',
                                    'BUSYBEE', 'mary@csharpguitar.net', 70002,
                                    'USA', CAST(GETDATE() AS DATE)
SELECT * FROM [dbo].[SUBJECTS]
```

6. Navigate back to your Dedicated SQL Pool blade in the Azure portal ➢ select the Auditing navigation menu item ➢ select View Audit Logs ➢ select Log Analytics ➢ and then execute the following query; the query is in the `Chapter08/Ch08Ex05` directory on GitHub.

```
SQLSecurityAuditEvents
| where Category == 'SQLSecurityAuditEvents'
| where Statement has 'SUBJECTS'
| project EventTime, Statement, Succeeded, AffectedRows, ResponseRows,
          ServerPrincipalName, ClientIp, ApplicationName, AdditionalInformation,
```

```
        DataSensitivityInformation, DurationMs, ClientTlsVersion,
        IsServerLevelAudit, IsColumnPermission
    | order by EventTime desc
    | take 100
```

7. **Notice the contents added to the `DataSensitivityInformation` column. Consider stopping the dedicated SQL pool.**

Microsoft Purview is an extensive tool, and many of its capabilities are outside the scope of this book. A note in Figure 8.30 nicely summarizes Microsoft Purview: "For advanced classification capabilities, use Azure Purview." This is because Microsoft Purview can span a much greater scope of data sources when compared to the Auditing capabilities available for the dedicated SQL pool and an Azure Synapse Analytics workspace. The exercises that included Microsoft Purview are meant as an introduction to get you started. In step 1 of Exercise 8.5, you added column level classification values to the `SUBJECTS` table. In step 3, you added information type values (aka column-level classification values) and sensitivity labels to the `SUBJECTS` table again. You also added an additional classification on the `COUNTRY` column of the `SUBJECTS` table with a sensitivity label of General.

After these data labeling activities were completed, and because Auditing is enabled on this dedicated SQL pool, the `INSERT` and `SELECT` statements were logged. Navigating to your Log Analytics workspace and executing the query that searches the `SQLSecurityAuditEvents` table, you notice some new results being populated into the `DataSensitivityInformation` column. The following is a summary of the result. The full value from that column is in the `DataSensitivityInformation.xml` file in the `Chapter08/Ch08Ex05` directory on GitHub.

```
<sensitivity_attributes max_rank="20" max_rank_desc="Medium">
 <label="Confidential - GDPR" information_type="Name" rank="20" />
 <label="Confidential - GDPR" information_type="Date Of Birth" rank="20" />
 <label="Confidential" information_type="Credentials" rank="20" />
 <label="Confidential" information_type="Contact Info" rank="20" />
 <label="General" information_type="Contact Info" rank="10" rank_desc="Low" />
</sensitivity_attributes>
```

The information contained in the `DataSensitivityInformation` column describes the security label and type of information being retrieved by the `SELECT` statement. Remember that the `SELECT` statement is stored in the `Statement` column. Using the data in this table in combination with the user identity stored in the `ServerPrincipalName` column provides good information about who accessed what information and how often. There are many methods for adding sensitivity labels. Consider, for example, the following SQL statement, which sets the `CREATE_DATE` column on the `SUBJECTS` table to `Public`:

```
ADD SENSITIVITY CLASSIFICATION TO dbo.SUBJECTS.CREATE_DATE
    WITH ( LABEL='Public', INFORMATION_TYPE='Administrative', RANK=LOW )
```

The Azure CLI also provides many options for managing data classifications. To view the sensitivity label that was placed on the CREATE_DATE column by the SQL statement, execute the following Azure CLI cmdlet, which is followed by the output:

```
az synapse sql pool classification show --name sqlpool \
   --workspace-name csharpguitar --resource-group CSHARPGUITAR \
   --schema dbo --table SUBJECTS --column CREATE_DATE
```


```
{
  "columnName": "CREATE_DATE",
  "informationType": "Administrative",
  "isDisabled": null,
  "labelName": "Public",
  "name": "current",
  "rank": "Low",
  "resourceGroup": "CSHARPGUITAR",
  "schemaName": "dbo",
  "tableName": "SUBJECTS",
  "type": "Microsoft.Synapse/workspaces/sqlPools/sensitivityLabels"
}
```


You can also create sensitivity labels using Azure CLI cmdlets. The last topic to cover concerning managing sensitive information has to do with the management of files. Up to this point the context has been on tables within a relational database. However, while working on a data analytics solution, you will very likely come across the scenario of sensitive data sent and received within files.

On many occasions in this book, you have seen directory structures like the following:

```
EMEA\brainjammer\in\YYYY\MM\DD\HH
EMEA\brainjammer\out\YYYY\MM\DD\HH
EMEA\brainjammer\raw-files\YYYY\MM\DD\HH
EMEA\brainjammer\cleansed-data\YYYY\MM\DD
EMEA\brainjammer\business-data\YYYY\MM
```

To protect sensitive data, you can create directory structures like the following, which include a directory named Confidential, for example:

```
EMEA\brainjammer\raw-files\Confidential\YYYY\MM\DD\HH
EMEA\brainjammer\cleansed-data\Confidential\YYYY\MM\DD
EMEA\brainjammer\business-data\Confidential\YYYY\MM
```

Then, as shown in Figure 8.31, the directories are protected using ACLs.

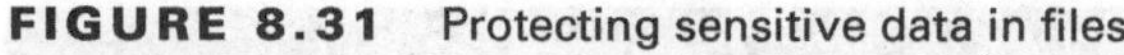

FIGURE 8.31 Protecting sensitive data in files

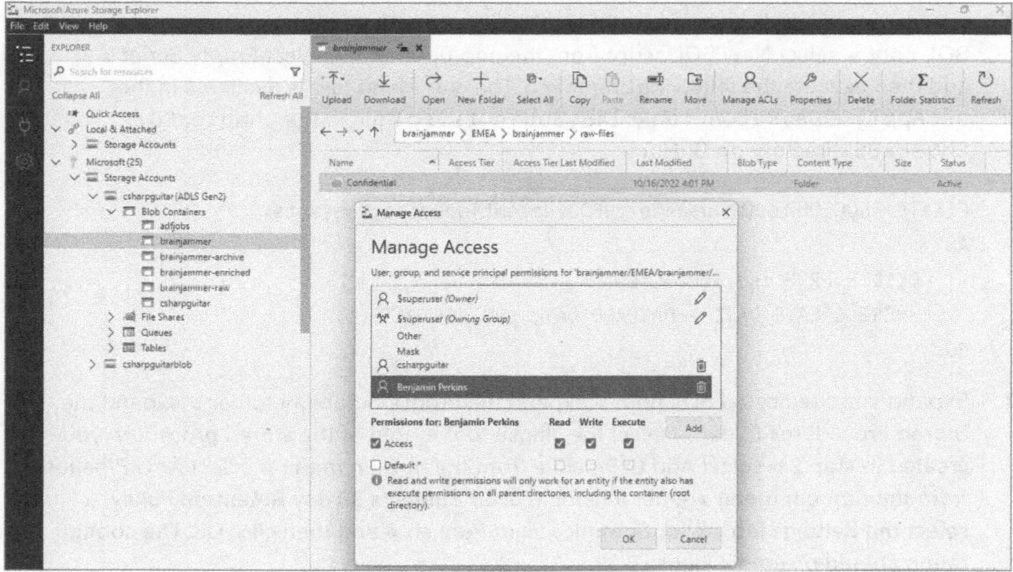

Figure 8.31 is taken from Microsoft Azure Storage Explorer and illustrates that one individual and the Azure Synapse Analytics service principal identity have ACL access to the Confidential directory. Consider creating a folder for each sensitivity label—for example, Public, General, Highly Confidential, and GDPR—and granting the necessary permissions to groups and service principals based on your business requirements.

Implement a Data Retention Policy

In Exercise 4.5, you implemented an Azure Storage account lifecycle management policy. By adding the `deleteAfter90Days` policy definition, as discussed previously, you would realize the implementation of a data retention policy in this context. To implement a data retention policy that applies to data stored on a relational database, for example, an Azure Synapse Analytics dedicated SQL pool, complete Exercise 8.6.

EXERCISE 8.6

Implement a Data Retention Policy

1. Log in to the Azure portal at `https://portal.azure.com` ➢ navigate to the Azure Synapse Analytics workspace you created in Exercise 3.3 ➢ select the SQL Pools navigation menu link ➢ select your dedicated SQL pool ➢ start the SQL pool ➢ select the Overview blade ➢ and then click the Open link in the Open Synapse Studio tile.

EXERCISE 8.6 *(continued)*

2. Navigate to the Data hub ➢ select the ellipse (. . .) to the right of your dedicated SQL pool ➢ select New SQL script from the pop-up menu ➢ select Empty Script ➢ and then execute the following command. The command text is available in the `uspApply90DayRetentionPolicySubjects.sql` file in the `Chapter08/Ch08Ex06` directory on GitHub.

```
CREATE PROCEDURE dbo.uspApply90DayRetentionPolicySubjects
AS
    DELETE FROM dbo.SUBJECTS
    WHERE CREATE_DATE > DATEADD(DAY, -90, GETDATE())
GO
```

3. Expand your dedicated SQL pool ➢ expand the Programmability folder ➢ expand the Stored Procedures folder ➢ select the ellipse to the right of the stored procedure you created in step 2 ➢ select Add to Pipeline from the pop-up menu ➢ select New Pipeline from the pop-out menu ➢ enter a name (I used **Subjects 90 day Retention Policy**) ➢ select the Settings tab ➢ click Commit ➢ click Publish ➢ and then click OK. The configuration should resemble Figure 8.32.

FIGURE 8.32 Implement a data retention policy in Azure Synapse Analytics.

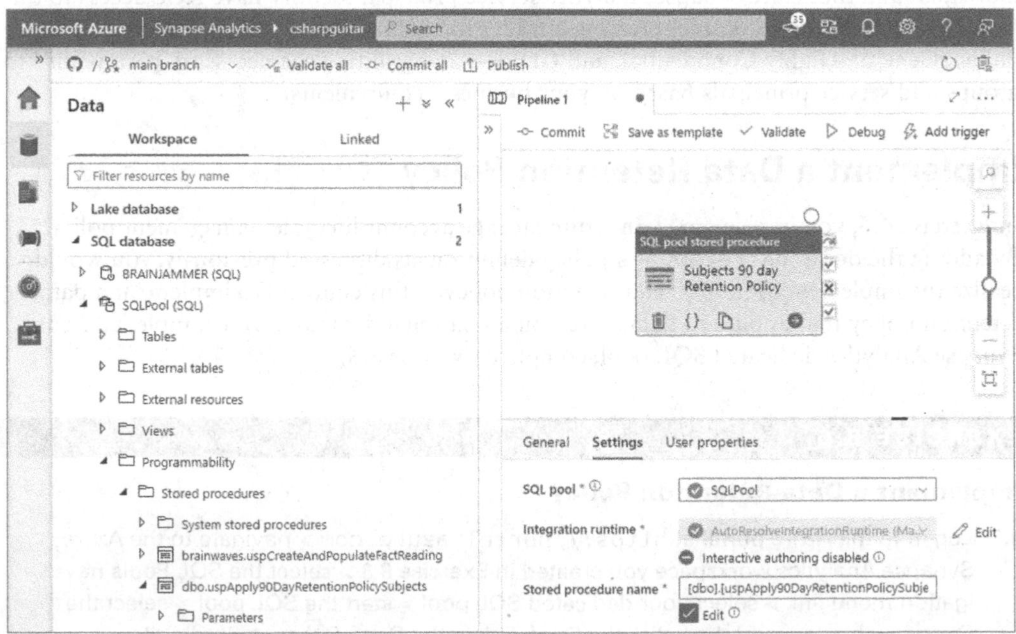

4. Click the Add Trigger button ➢ select New/Edit ➢ select + New from the Add Triggers drop-down list box ➢ configure the scheduled task to run on the first day of every month, similar to that shown in Figure 8.33 ➢ click the Commit button ➢ and then publish the trigger.

FIGURE 8.33 Implement a data retention policy schedule pipeline trigger.

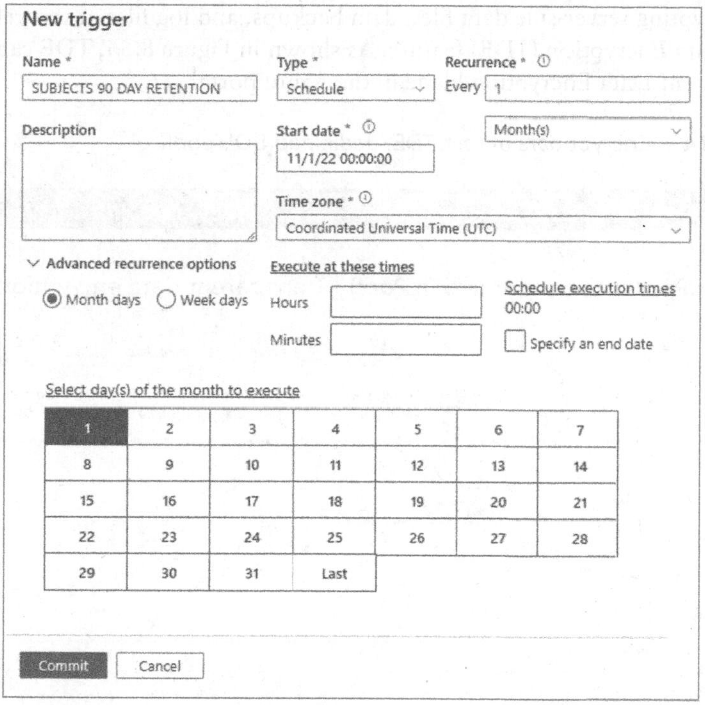

5. Stop the dedicated SQL pool.

Exercise 8.6 begins with the creation of a stored procedure that removes data from the `SUBJECTS` table. The `WHERE` clause checks if the date contained in the `CREATE_DATE` column is older than 90 days. If it is, then the row is deleted. You then added that stored procedure to an Azure Synapse Analytics pipeline using the SQL pool Stored Procedure activity. Once committed and published, you configured a schedule trigger to run the stored procedure once per month. This results in the deletion of data based on a 90-day retention. You might consider not committing and publishing the trigger, unless you really want to implement the retention policy.

Encrypt Data at Rest and in Motion

With very few exceptions, data stored on the Azure platform is encrypted at rest by default. This means that if a hard drive that contains your data is stolen or the server where your data is stored is unlawfully accessed, the data cannot be deciphered. Keep in mind that when you give a group, individual, or a service principal access to the data, the unencrypted data is available to them. From an Azure Synapse Analytics dedicated SQL pool perspective, the means for encrypting server-side data files, data backups, and log files at rest rely on the Transparent Data Encryption (TDE) feature. As shown in Figure 8.34, TDE can be enabled on the Transparent Data Encryption blade in the Azure portal.

FIGURE 8.34 Encrypt data at rest, TDE, dedicated SQL pool.

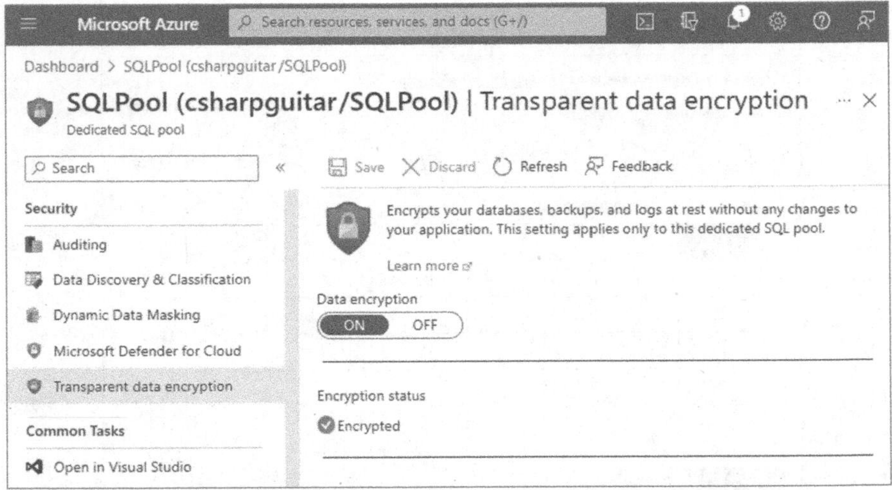

Encryption of data in motion is achieved by using the strongest possible version of TLS when accessing your data using the HTTP protocol. When HTTPS is utilized, a secure connection is made between the data consumer and the server. When the data is transferred through the network, it is encrypted using the strongest cypher that both the client and server support. If you want to make the network transmission even more secure, you might consider isolating the network communication channel using a virtual private network (VPN). This can be achieved by implementing the Azure VPN Gateway product or an Azure ExpressRoute. There are three common VPN models: point-to-point, point-to-site, and site-to-site. A point-to-point connection is restricted to a single connection between two machines, whereas a point-to-site connection means that a single machine has access to all the machines within a given site. A site in this context means an on-premises network. A site-to-site model would allow all machines contained in two networks to connect with each other. An ExpressRoute connection is a dedicated connection from Azure to your on-premises datacenter. It is configured with the help of an Internet service provider and is costly; however, it is the most secure means for transferring data, as the transmission does not traverse the Internet at all.

An additional concept, encryption-in-use, was explained earlier in the "Design Data Encryption for Data at Rest and in Transit" section. Recall that encryption-in-use is enabled using a product called Always Encrypted. As mentioned previously, TDE is used to encrypt data on the server-side; however, there may be a need to encrypt data client-side within an application. Always Encrypted is useful for encrypting data client-side, directly within an application, before storing it on the Azure platform. Encrypting data client-side ensures that individuals with highly privileged server-side credentials cannot view or decrypt the data without being specifically granted permission. This gives you complete control over your data, while allowing a third party, like Microsoft, to perform the database administration responsibilities.

Implement Row-Level and Column-Level Security

Row-level security (RLS) is implemented at the information protection level of the layered security model (refer to Figure 8.1). Row-level security restricts access to rows in a database table and is realized using the `CREATE SECURITY POLICY` command and predicates. Figure 8.35 illustrates row-level security.

FIGURE 8.35 Row-level security

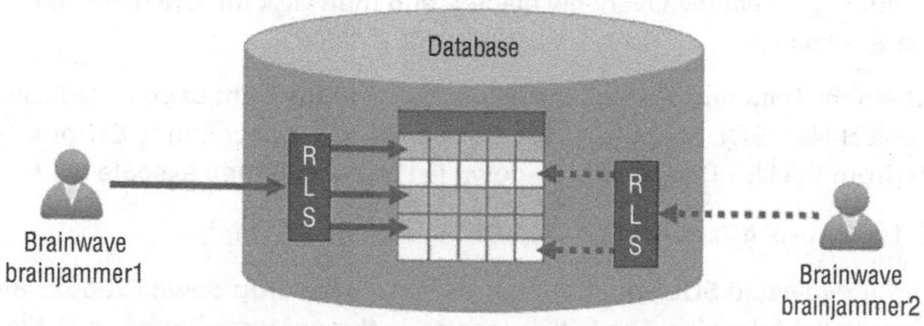

Using the `EXECUTE AS` statement prior to the `SELECT` statement, as follows, results in the result set being filtered based on the user permissions:

```
EXECUTE AS USER = 'BrainwaveBrainjammer1'
SELECT * FROM BRAINWAVES
```

Column-level security restricts access to specific columns on a database table, as illustrated in Figure 8.36.

To get hands-on experience implementing column-level security, complete Exercise 8.7.

FIGURE 8.36 Column-level security

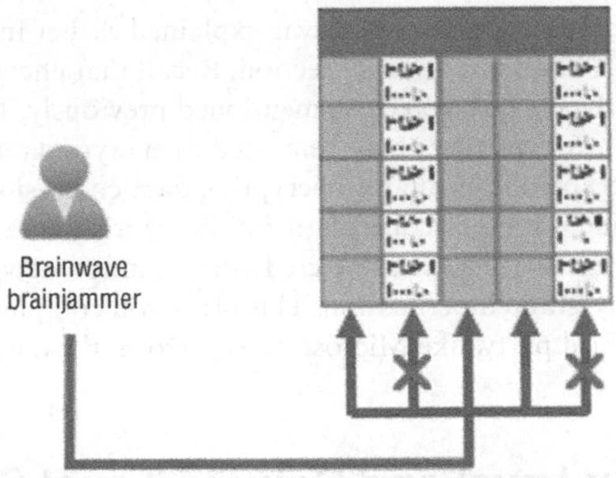

EXERCISE 8.7

Implement Column-level Security

1. Log in to the Azure portal at `https://portal.azure.com` ➢ navigate to the Azure Synapse Analytics workspace you created in Exercise 3.3 ➢ select the SQL Pools navigation menu link ➢ select your dedicated SQL pool ➢ start the SQL pool ➢ after the SQL pool is running, select the Overview blade ➢ and then click the Open link in the Open Synapse Studio tile.

2. Navigate to the Data hub ➢ select the ellipse (`...`) to the right of your dedicated SQL pool ➢ select New SQL Script from the pop-up menu ➢ select Empty Script ➢ select `master` from the Use Database drop-down list box ➢ and then execute the following:

```
CREATE LOGIN brainjammer WITH PASSWORD = 'csh@rpgu1tar'
```

3. Select your dedicated SQL pool from the Use Database drop-down list box, and then execute the following. The SQL is located in the `column-level.sql` file in the `Chapter08/Ch08Ex07` directory on GitHub.

```
CREATE USER brainjammer FROM LOGIN brainjammer WITH DEFAULT_SCHEMA = dbo
EXEC sp_addrolemember 'db_datareader', 'brainjammer'

DENY SELECT ON dbo.SUBJECTS TO brainjammer

GRANT SELECT ON SUBJECTS
 (ID, FIRSTNAME, LASTNAME, EMAIL, COUNTRY, CREATE_DATE) TO brainjammer
```

4. Log in to the dedicated SQL pool using Azure Data Studio; for example, executing the following with the user created in step 2 will give you the error shown in Figure 8.37.

```
SELECT * FROM [dbo].[SUBJECTS]
```

FIGURE 8.37 Column-level security enforcement exception

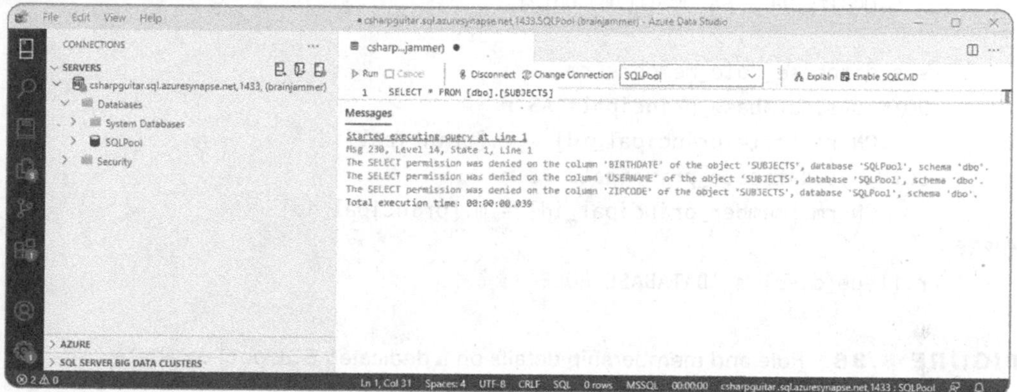

5. Stop the dedicated SQL pool.

Before you can create a user for a specific database, the login must first exist on the master database. Executing the following SQL command while targeting the `master` database hosted on your dedicated SQL pool accomplishes this:

```
CREATE LOGIN brainjammer WITH PASSWORD = 'csh@rpgu1tar'
```

Redirecting focus back to the `SQLPool` database, you then create a user who uses the login credentials created on the `master` database. You accomplished this with the following SQL statement. In addition to the user account creation, the default schema is set to `dbo`, which is where the `SUBJECTS` table is located.

```
CREATE USER brainjammer FROM LOGIN brainjammer WITH DEFAULT_SCHEMA = dbo
```

Adding the user account to a read-only group, as follows, provides read access permissions to all the tables on that database:

```
EXEC sp_addrolemember 'db_datareader', 'brainjammer'
```

To view all roles and the members of those roles, execute the following SQL command. This SQL text is located in the databaseRole.sql file in the Chapter08/Ch08Ex07 directory on GitHub. Figure 8.38 shows the result of the query.

```
SELECT
      r.[name] AS [Role], m.[name] AS [Member], m.Create_date AS [Created Date],
        m.modify_Date AS [Modified Date]
FROM
      sys.database_role_members rm
      JOIN sys.database_principals AS r
          ON rm.[role_principal_id] = r.[principal_id]
      JOIN sys.database_principals AS m
          ON rm.[member_principal_id] = m.[principal_id]
WHERE
      r.[type_desc] = 'DATABASE_ROLE'
```

FIGURE 8.38 Role and membership details on a dedicated SQL pool database

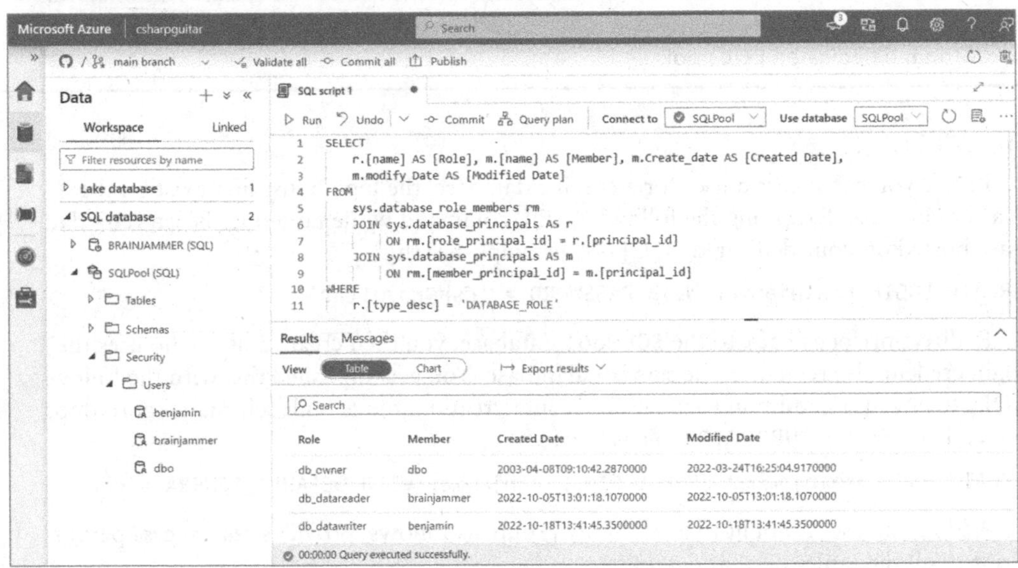

When the user is granted read access to the tables, it defaults to all the columns on that table. In order to remove access to all the columns for the SUBJECTS table, you first execute the following SQL statement, which removes SELECT access to the table:

```
DENY SELECT ON dbo.SUBJECTS TO brainjammer
```

Then you use the following SQL command to grant access only to the columns that the user should be permitted to retrieve:

```
GRANT SELECT ON SUBJECTS
 (ID, FIRSTNAME, LASTNAME, EMAIL, COUNTRY, CREATE_DATE) TO brainjammer
```

From that point on, when the user, brainjammer, accesses the SQLPool database and retrieves data from the SUBJECTS table, only the columns that have been granted permission can be retrieved. The following is the SQL query, followed by the output:

```
SELECT ID, FIRSTNAME, LASTNAME, EMAIL, COUNTRY, CREATE_DATE FROM dbo.SUBJECTS

+-----+-----------+----------+----------------------+-----+---------------------+
| ID  | FIRSTNAME | LASTNAME | EMAIL                |     | CREATE_DATE         |
+-----+-----------+----------+----------------------+-----+---------------------+
| 48  | MARY      | PERKINS  | mary@csharpguitar.net | USA | 2022-10-16 00:00:00 |
| 60  | BENJAMIN  | PERKINS  | ben@csharpguitar.net  | USA | 2022-10-12 00:00:00 |
| 120 | RUAL      | PERKINS  | rual@csharpguitar.net | USA | 2022-10-12 00:00:00 |
+-----+-----------+----------+----------------------+-----+---------------------+
```

Always shut down the dedicated SQL pool when not in use, to reduce costs.

Implement Data Masking

The primary difference between column-level security and dynamic data masking is that column-level security prevents the retrieval of the column completely. For example, if a user does not have permission on a column named BIRTHDATE and they attempt to retrieve it, a permission denied exception is rendered. Data masking, however, does allow the retrieval of the column data, although the data is partially concealed. Consider, for example, the EMAIL column from Exercise 8.7, which contains an individual's email address. This is not data you would want everyone to have access to, for numerous reasons. For example, someone writes a program that is intended to notify your customers of downtime or outage events. Consider that there are hundreds of thousands of customers in your database. During testing, the data is selected and emails sent to all your customers. Placing a mask on the EMAIL column would change the retrieved value from benjamin@csharpguitar.net to bXXXX@XXXX.com. Doing so would prevent sending all your customers an email on error. At the same time, however, you might want to see part of the column value for validation, perhaps the last four digits of a credit card number or identification number. Complete Exercise 8.8, where you will configure a dynamic data mask on the EMAIL column of the SUBJECTS table.

EXERCISE 8.8

Implement Data Masking

1. Log in to the Azure portal at `https://portal.azure.com` ➢ navigate to the Azure Synapse Analytics workspace you created in Exercise 3.3 ➢ select the SQL Pools navigation menu link ➢ select your dedicated SQL pool ➢ start the SQL pool ➢ after the SQL pool is running, select the Dynamic Data Masking blade ➢ select the + Add Mask menu item ➢ make the configurations as shown in Figure 8.39 ➢ and then click the Add button.

FIGURE 8.39 Implement data masking and masking rule.

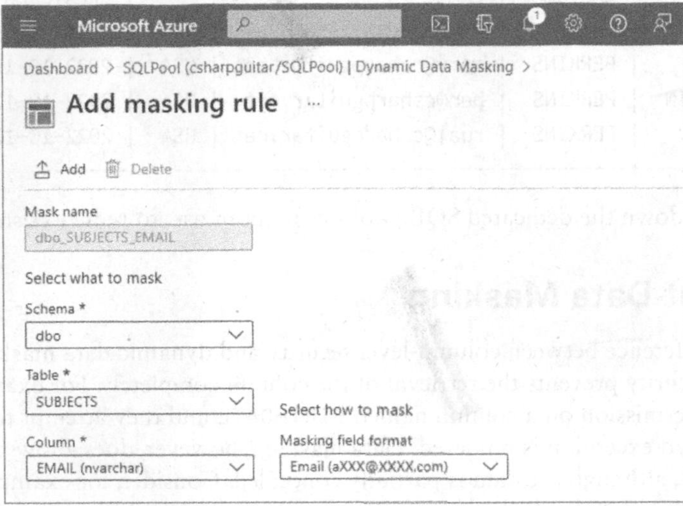

2. Click the Save button ➢ log in to the dedicated SQL pool using Azure Data Studio, with the credentials created in Exercise 8.7 ➢ and then execute the following:

```
SELECT ID, FIRSTNAME, LASTNAME, EMAIL, COUNTRY, CREATE_DATE FROM dbo.SUBJECTS
```

3. Notice that the data in the `EMAIL` column has the mask configured in step 1 and illustrated in Figure 8.39. Stop the dedicated SQL pool.

The following is the result of the SQL statement from step 2:

```
+-----+-----------+---------+--------------+--------+--------------------+
| ID  | FIRSTNAME | LASTNAME | EMAIL            | COUNTRY | CREATE_DATE         |
+-----+-----------+---------+--------------+--------+--------------------+
| 48  | MARY      | PERKINS | mXXX@XXXX.com | USA     | 2022-10-16 00:00:00 |
| 60  | BENJAMIN  | PERKINS | bXXX@XXXX.com | USA     | 2022-10-12 00:00:00 |
| 120 | RUAL      | PERKINS | rXXX@XXXX.com | USA     | 2022-10-12 00:00:00 |
+-----+-----------+---------+--------------+--------+--------------------+
```

It is possible to configure a custom mask instead of using the preconfigured masks. This requires that you provide the number of starting characters to show, followed by the padding string (something like `xxxxx.`), followed by the number of ending characters to display. Using a prefix and suffix value of three and the padding on the `EMAIL` column would result in `benxxxxx.net`, for example, which is a bit more useful than what is provided using the default.

Manage Identities, Keys, and Secrets Across Different Data Platform Technologies

Protecting credentials has historically been very challenging. Developers and data engineers need to access data, and that data is protected by an ID and password. As the complexity and size of your organization grows, it is easy to lose control over who has what credentials. Add that loss of control to the potential impact changing a password can have on a production environment. This scenario is commonly referred to as *credential leakage*. An initial solution to credential leakage was to store connection details in a managed credential store, something like Azure Key Vault. However, access to the credential store also requires credentials, so you are back in the same place as before the implementation of the credential store. The ultimate solution is to use a combination of Azure Key Vault and managed identities. Instead of using a credential to make a connection to a storage account or a database from application code, you instead reference the Azure Key Vault endpoint. An Azure Key Vault secret endpoint resembles the following:

```
https://<accountName>.vault.azure.net/secrets/<secretName>/5db1a9b5...
```

The code that uses that endpoint must implement the `DefaultAzureCredential` class from the Azure Identity library. The library works with all popular programming languages: .NET, Python, Go, Java, etc. Passing a new `DefaultAzureCredential` class to the `SecretClient` class results in the acquisition of the managed identity credential, which is a token. The `client` then stores all necessary attributes to perform the retrieval of a secret from the Azure Key Vault endpoint. The following C# code performs this activity:

```
var kvUri = "https://" + accountName + ".vault.azure.net";
var client = new SecretClient(new Uri(kvUri), new DefaultAzureCredential());
```

You can use the client to get a secret by using the following C# syntax:

```
var secret = await client.GetSecretAsync(secretName);
```

Now you know how a managed identity can avoid credential leakage, but you might be wondering what exactly are managed identities and what important aspects must you know in order to implement them safely and securely? Table 8.3 compares the two types of managed identities: system-assigned and user-assigned.

TABLE 8.3 Managed identity types

Characteristic	System-assigned managed identity	User-assigned managed identity
Provisioning	Azure resources receive an identity by default, where supported.	Created manually
Removal	The identity is deleted when the associated Azure resource is deleted.	Deleted manually
Sharing	The identity cannot be shared among Azure resources.	Can be shared

A system-assigned managed identity is created during the provisioning of the Azure resource. For example, an Azure Synapse Analytics workspace and a Microsoft Purview account both have a system-assigned identity by default. Azure products that are generally used to make connections to other Azure products or features have this managed identity created by default. In contrast, an Azure storage account receives data but does not commonly push data out to other systems, that would need an identity to do so. This is why you see no managed identities for Azure storage accounts. A system-assigned managed identity can be used only by the Azure resource to which it is bound, and it is deleted when the Azure resource is deleted. A user-assigned managed identity can be shared across Azure products and is a separate resource in itself and can have its own lifecycle. Perform Exercise 8.9, where you create a user-assigned managed identity.

EXERCISE 8.9

Create a User-assigned Managed Identity

1. Log in to the Azure portal at `https://portal.azure.com` ➢ enter **Managed Identities** in the Search text box ➢ select Managed Identities ➢ select the + Create menu item ➢ enter the subscription ➢ enter the resource group ➢ enter the region ➢ enter a name (I used **brainjammer**) ➢ click the Review + Create button ➢ and then click Create.

2. Navigate to the Azure Storage account you created in Exercise 3.1 ➢ select Access Control (IAM) from the navigation menu ➢ select the + Add menu item ➢ select Add Role Assignment ➢ select the Contributor Role ➢ click Next ➢ select the Managed Identity radio button ➢ click the + Select Members link ➢ select User-assigned Managed Identity from the Managed Identity drop-down ➢ select the managed identity created in step 1 ➢ click the Select button ➢ and then click the Review + Assign button.
3. On the Access Control (IAM) blade, select the Aole assignments tab. Notice the User-assigned Managed Identity is present in the Contributor role, as shown in Figure 8.40.

FIGURE 8.40 Creating and applying a user-assigned managed identity

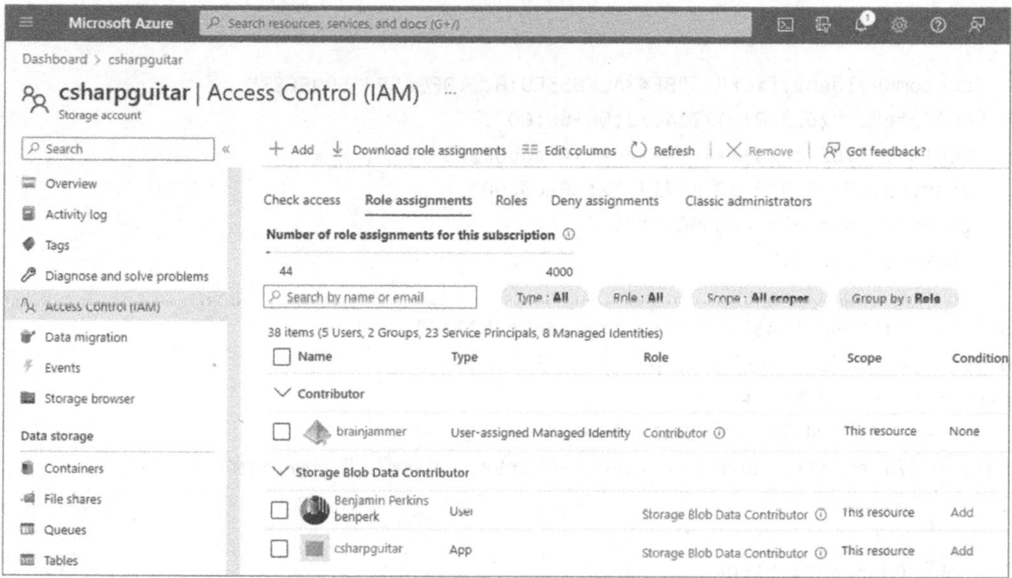

4. To show the details of the managed identity and any other identity within your subscription, use the following Azure CLI cmdlet:

```
az ad sp list --display-name <resourceName>
```

Creating a user-assigned managed identity is simple, as you just learned. Adding the identity to the Contributor role of your Azure storage account granted full access to manage all resources within the account. Any object you configure with this identity will have access to the Azure storage account and the ADLS containers within it. The Azure CLI cmdlet is helpful to identify not only user-assigned managed identities but also system-assigned. The use of the cmdlet using `brainjammer` as the value for `resourceName` results in the following summarized output:


```
{
 "accountEnabled": "True",
 "addIns": [],
 "alternativeNames": [
 "isExplicit=True",
 "/./././././Microsoft.ManagedIdentity/userAssignedIdentities/brainjammer"],
 "appId": "b48b4c9c-****-407b-****-7116b86ef07f",
 "displayName": "brainjammer",
 "keyCredentials": [
  {
   "customKeyIdentifier": "BE43ACEB55ED16...0F0C55055995683",
   "endDate": "2023-01-17T14:12:00+00:00",
   "keyId": "7024ca24-****-****-****-adbd0263****",
   "startDate": "2022-10-19T14:12:00+00:00",
   "type": "AsymmetricX509Cert",
   "usage": "Verify"
  },
"objectId": "89e3f948.***-***-***-134b8c4b2227",
"objectType": "ServicePrincipal",
"servicePrincipalNames": [
 "b48b4c9c-01d6-407b-a4ed-7116b86ef07f",
 "https://identity.azure.net/toyqBuBCbGrSr...WaKW+UJb3imrnfY9HrI="],
},
{
 "accountEnabled": "True",
 "addIns": [],
 "alternativeNames": [
 "isExplicit=False",
 "/./././providers/Microsoft.Purview/accounts/brainjammer"],
 "appId": "deb3f43e-****-4084-****-4caa3954e524",
 "displayName": "brainjammer",
 "keyCredentials": [
 {
  "customKeyIdentifier": "C2662B60FC4CEE0...B3D7C97DEE1715E62",
  "endDate": "2022-12-31T09:07:00+00:00",
  "keyId": "81d9f4a2-****-****-****-f60513678c41",
  "startDate": "2022-10-02T09:07:00+00:00",
  "type": "AsymmetricX509Cert",
```

```
    "usage": "Verify",
    "value": null
  }
"objectId": "0c54f2e1-***-***-***-4311a3094681",
"objectType": "ServicePrincipal",
"servicePrincipalNames": [
  "deb3f43e-cbeb-4084-b907-4caa3954e524",
  "https://identity.azure.net/LhvbDyhIXcBb...3jCA81LFEiqh94AKDltfW0="],
```

The Azure CLI cmdlet might be helpful in case you have numerous Azure products with the same name and need to find the specific one to grant permissions to. The `objectId` attribute uniquely identifies the managed identity. You can also see which Azure product it is associated with by looking in the ARM identifier, for example, `Microsoft.ManagedIdentity` or `Microsoft.Purview`. The `objectId` attribute is also often rendered on the Properties blade for the Azure resource, often referred to as the managed identity object ID. In general, it is recommended to use managed identities for authentication versus any other mechanism on Azure.

At the time of writing, Azure Databricks does not support outbound managed identities. You can use a few workarounds to make this work; however, none of them is officially supported or recommended. Instead, you are confined to a user, group, or service principal, but in most cases a service principal is, in essence, the same as a managed identity. The major difference is that a managed identity is always linked to an Azure resource, and no one knows its credentials because they are managed strictly by the platform. A service principal is linked to an app registration that is created in your Azure Active Directory and is given a user ID and password. The service principal identity can be assigned to RBAC roles for granting permissions to Azure resources. This is important to call out because of the work you did in Exercise 5.4, where you needed to access data hosted on a blob storage container using the following address and the `wasbs` protocol:

```
wasbs://<containerName>@<accountName>.blob.core.windows.net/*.parquet
```

This was necessary because at the time it was not possible to connect to an ADLS endpoint using a storage access key from an Apache Spark cluster. At that point you had not been exposed to Azure Key Vault, managed identities, IAM, or users, groups, and service principals. Using those authentication mechanisms allows connections to an ADLS container using the `abfss` protocol, as follows:

```
abfss://<containerName>@<accountName>.dfs.core.windows.net/*.parquet
```

Now that you know a bit about these products, features, and concepts, complete Exercise 8.10, where you will use the `abfss` protocol to grant access to an Azure Active Directory (Azure AD) user to execute Python logic.

EXERCISE 8.10

Connect to an ADLS Container from Azure Databricks Cluster Using ABFSS

1. Log in to the Azure portal at `https://portal.azure.com` ➢ navigate to the Azure Databricks workspace you created in Exercise 3.14 ➢ select the Admin Console link by expanding the drop-down list below your identity in the upper-right corner ➢ click the Add User button ➢ enter an email address of a user in your Azure Active Directory tenant ➢ and then click OK. The user should have Workspace and Databricks SQL access.
2. Select Compute from the navigation menu ➢ click the Create Cluster/Compute button ➢ and then configure the cluster as shown in Figure 8.41.

FIGURE 8.41 Creating a shared, credential passthrough spark cluster

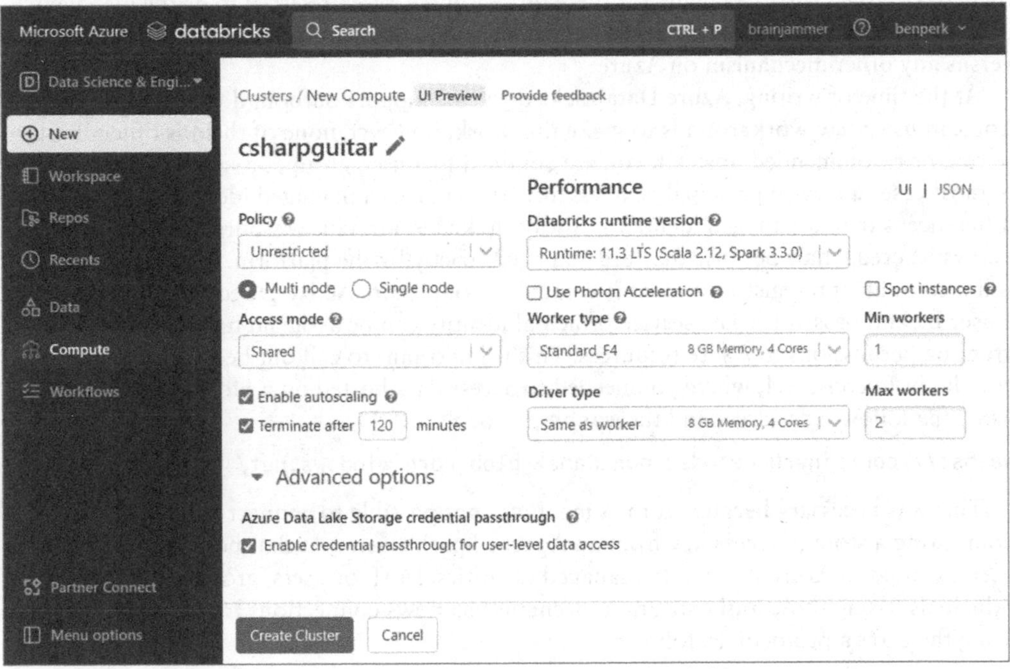

3. Click the Create Cluster button ➢ click the Cluster link on the Compute page ➢ click the More . . . button ➢ select Permissions from the drop-down list ➢ select the user from step 1 from the Select User, Group or Service Principal drop-down list ➢ set Can Manage as the permission ➢ click the + Add button ➢ and then click Save.

4. Download the `NormalizedBrainwavesSE.parquet` file from the `Chapter08/Ch08Ex10` directory on GitHub ➢ and then upload the file into the ADLS container you created in Exercise 3.1. Remember the location.
5. Navigate to the Azure Databricks workspace you created in Exercise 3.14 ➢ select Access Control (IAM) from the navigation menu ➢ select the + Add menu item ➢ select Add Role Assignment from the drop-down ➢ select the Contributor role ➢ click Next ➢ select the User, Groups, or Service Principal radio button ➢ select the + Select members link ➢ search for and select the user added in step 1 ➢ click the Select button ➢ and then click the Review + Assign button. The user will be added to the Contributor role, as shown in Figure 8.42.

FIGURE 8.42 Adding a user to an Azure Databricks workspace using RBAC

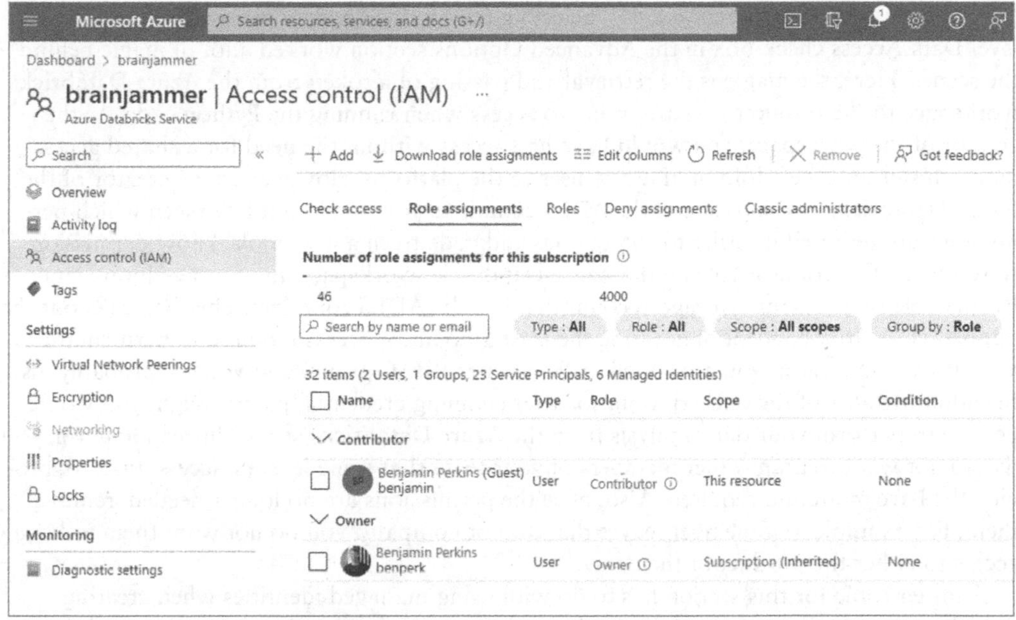

6. Add the same user from step 1 to the Storage Blob Data Reader RBAC role to the storage account created in Exercise 3.1 and the account you uploaded the Parquet file to in step 4, similar to that shown in Figure 8.17.
7. Access the Azure Databricks workspace using the URL provided on the Overview Azure Databricks blade, similar to the following. Use the credentials of the user from step 1.

```
https://<workspaceName>.azuredatabricks.net
```

EXERCISE 8.10 *(continued)*

8. Create a new notebook ➢ connect the notebook to the cluster created in step 2 ➢ execute the following Python code, which is available in the `brainjammer.ipynb` file in the `Chapter08/Ch08Ex10` on GitHub:

```
rawReadings = "abfss://<container>@<account>.dfs.core.windows.net/*.parquet"
rawReadingsDF = spark.read.option("header","true").parquet(rawReadings)
rawReadingsDF.createOrReplaceTempView("TmpREADING")
spark.sql("SELECT * FROM TmpREADING").limit(5).show()
```

The most critical part of Exercise 8.10 is the action you performed in step 2 when creating the cluster (refer to Figure 8.41). Selecting the Enable Credential Passthrough for User-level Data Access check box in the Advanced Options section worked a lot of magic behind the scenes. Here, the magic is the retrieval and passing of a token from the Azure Databricks workspace to the resource you are trying to access when running the Python code. As the creator of the workspace, you would have had access without the need for a shared access mode cluster and the addition of a new user to the platform. However, as the creator of the Azure Databricks workspace and the ADLS container, you would not have seen which permissions are required in order to run queries and code from a notebook. Those permissions were for the Contributor role on the Azure Databricks workspace and Storage Blob Data Reader role on the Azure storage account that has the ADLS container. This also calls out the important security concept of granting the least amount of access required to perform the activity. As the creator, you are added to the Owner RBAC group, and you are probably also the administrator of the Subscription; so, after enabling credential passthrough, you would be able to perform your data analysis from the Azure Databricks spark cluster. However, you would not want to grant other members of your team that same level of access. Instead, provide the bare minimum required. Also, once the permissions are no longer needed, remove them. For example, if a member leaves the team or company, you do not want them to have access to either the product or the data.

Another topic for this section has to do with using managed identities when creating linked services from Azure Synapse Analytics. In most of the exercises you performed that used a linked service, you set the authentication type to Account Key, which is then used as part of a connection string. This authentication approach is secure; however, a better approach would be to use a system- or user-assigned managed identity. To achieve that, you must add those managed identities to the RBAC role in the Azure product that the linked service is connecting to. Another option is storing the access key in an Azure key vault instead of using the connection string option. Complete Exercise 8.11, where you will configure a linked service to retrieve an authentication key from Azure Key vault.

EXERCISE 8.11

Use an Azure Key Vault Secret to Store an Authentication Key for a Linked Service

1. Log in to the Azure portal at `https://portal.azure.com` ➢ navigate to the access Azure key vault you created in Exercise 8.1 ➢ select Secrets from the navigation pane ➢ select the + Generate/Import menu item ➢ enter a name (I used **csharpguitarBLOB**) ➢ and then enter a connection string to an Azure storage account with a blob container (not an ADLS container) resembling the following, into the Secret Value text box:

```
DefaultEndpointsProtocol=https;AccountName=*;AccountKey=* ;EndpointSuffix=core
  .windows.net
```

2. Click the Create button ➢ navigate to the Azure Synapse Analytics workspace you created in Exercise 3.1 ➢ open the Manage hub ➢ select Linked Services ➢ select the + New menu item ➢ select an Azure Blob Storage service ➢ click Continue ➢ enter a name (I used **csharpguitarBlobWithAKS**) ➢ enable Interactive Authoring ➢ select Account Key from the Authentication Type drop-down ➢ select the Azure Key Value option ➢ select + New from the AKV Linked Service drop-down ➢ enter a name (I used **brainjammerAKV**) ➢ select the Subscription from the Azure Subscription drop-down ➢ select the Azure key vault name you created in Exercise 8.1 and added the secret to in step 1 ➢ select System Assigned Managed Identity from the Authentication Method drop-down ➢ select the To Secret radio button in the Test Connection section ➢ enter your secret name from step 1 (I used **csharpguitarBLOB**) ➢ and then select the Test Connection link. Figure 8.43 shows the outcome and configuration. The test connection failed to resolve the failure.

FIGURE 8.43 Access key in Key Vault from a blob linked service failure

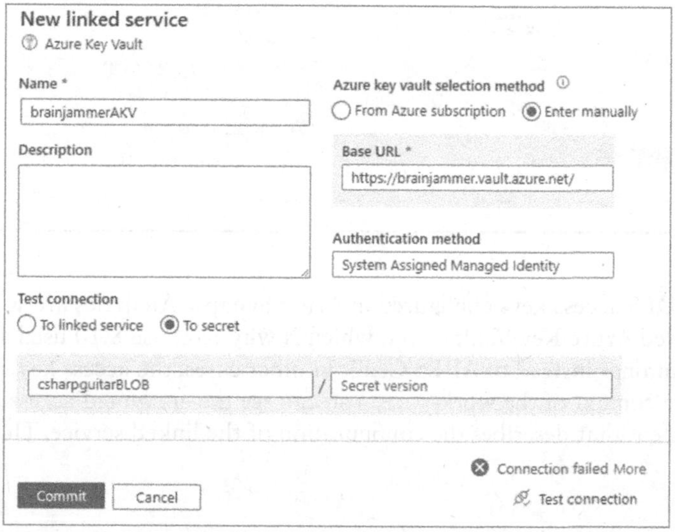

EXERCISE 8.11 ***(continued)***

3. Navigate back to the Azure key vault you created in Exercise 8.1 ➢ select Access Policies ➢ select the + Create menu item ➢ check Get and List from the Secret Permissions section ➢ click Next ➢ search for and add your Azure Synapse Analytics workspace system-managed identity as the principal ➢ click Next ➢ click Create ➢ test the connection again from the Azure Key Value linked service ➢ and then, when the connection is successful, click Commit.
4. On the New Linked Service window, select your secret name from step 1 (for example, `csharpguitarBLOB`) from the Secret Name drop-down ➢ select the Test Connection link ➢ and then, when the connection is successful, click Commit. The configuration should resemble Figure 8.44.

FIGURE 8.44 Access key from Key Vault to blob linked service failure

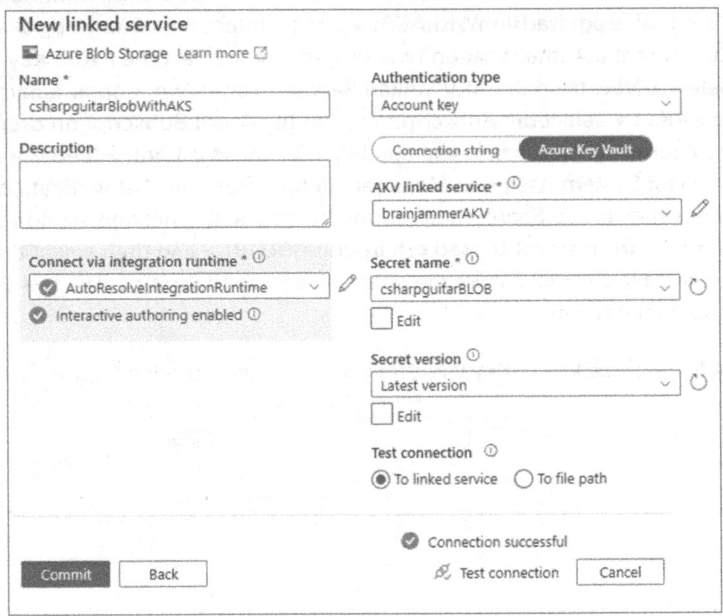

By default, ADLS access keys configured in Azure Synapse Analytics are stored in a platform-generated Azure Key Vault secret, which is why Exercise 8.10 used an Azure Storage Blob container instead of ADLS Gen2. In other cases, the access key is encrypted and stored within the context of the workspace. You can see the encrypted access key by viewing the JSON document that describes the configuration of the linked service. The first action in this Exercise 8.11 was to create a new secret in your Azure Key Vault account and store the connection string as the value. You then proceeded to create an Azure Blob Storage linked service that retrieves the access key from Azure Key Vault instead of storing the credentials locally. This required you to first create a linked service for an Azure key vault, and then target the secret for testing. That testing initially failed because there was no access policy for your Azure Synapse Analytics system-assigned managed identity on the Azure Key Vault account. Once you provided Get and List to the managed identity, the test worked successfully. Note that in Figure 8.43 you only provided the secret name, not the version. By default, if no version is provided, then the most current version of the secret is used. You can see this written out specifically in Figure 8.44 in the Secret Version drop-down list box. When you select Test Connection on the Azure Blob Storage linked service window, the platform pulls the connection string from Azure Key Vault and uses it to test the connection with the storage account. It is recommended in all cases from this point forward to use Azure Key Vault and managed identities when connections to Azure resources are required.

Implement Access Control for Azure Data Lake Storage Gen2

There are numerous methods for controlling access to an ADLS container. Connection strings, SAS tokens, RBAC, and ACLs are the most approaches. From a security layer perspective, as illustrated in Figure 8.1, this kind of security is applied at the access management layer. Although connection strings and SAS tokens are valid access control techniques, each requires an access key, which has a vulnerability due to credential leakage. The approach for solving that is to store those values in an Azure key vault and use managed identities to access and retrieve them when needed. When you are focused on controlling access at the level both a connection string and SAS token target, which is the storage account, the most secure and recommended approach is to use RBAC. As you may recall from Table 8.2, Azure RBAC has the scope of either the storage account or container, which is the same for a connection string and SAS token. If you require a more granular level of access control, all the way down to the data layer, down to the file level, then the optimal mechanism is to place ACLs on those files. In the case of both RBAC and ACLs, you apply either users, groups, or service principals to the control list.

Before moving onto the implementation of Azure RBAC and ACLs, you should know something about Microsoft Defender for Cloud (MDC). One of the components of MDC is Microsoft Defender for Storage, which can alert when a storage account is potentially being exploited or harmed. This feature targets the threat protection layer of the layered security model. As shown in Figure 8.45, to enable it, you must only set the Status toggle button to On for the storage plan.

FIGURE 8.45 Enabling Microsoft Defender for Storage

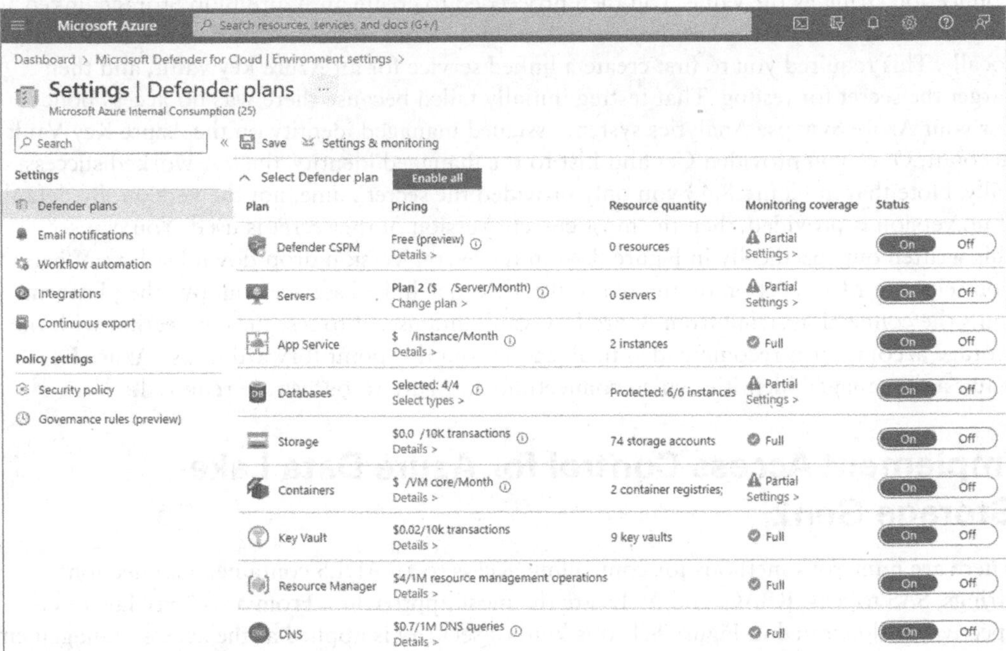

The Microsoft Defender for Storage threat protection feature applies to Azure Data Lake Storage Gen2, Azure Files, and Azure Blob Storage. There are also guidelines for investigating and mitigating activities like privilege abuse, compromised credentials, unauthenticated access, and social engineering attacks. The point is that in addition to setting these access controls, it is recommended to have a layer of protection that monitors and alerts when those access controls exhibit breached and unwanted behavioral patterns.

Implement Azure Role-Based Access Control

RBAC permissions are primarily used to restrict access to Azure resources. Some Azure products have expanded so that the security feature can be applied to the data that exists on the data source. The point here is to call out the difference between granting permission to an Azure resource and granting access to the data or services that reside within or on it. This section will be restricted to the understanding that an RBAC permission applies to the Azure resource. Figure 8.16 illustrated a flow chart that clarifies the operation flow when permissions are applied using RBAC. Figure 8.17 shows how this looks in the Azure portal. In Exercise 8.12 you will create a group named `BRAINJAMMER` in Azure Active Directory and add a separate account to the group. As you know, granting permissions to individuals is not efficient, especially when a large number of people need permissions. Therefore, the separate user account that is added to the Storage Blob Data Reader RBAC role on the

ADLS container, which is shown in Figure 8.17, will be removed and added to the group. Adding individuals to groups and then applying permissions to that group is a more efficient way to manage access permissions for resources. A note of caution here: do not completely remove your account from the RBAC groups on a product or feature, and especially not a subscription. If you do that, then you will lock yourself out of it and not be able to regain access.

EXERCISE 8.12

Implement Azure RBAC for ADLS

1. Log in to the Azure portal at `https://portal.azure.com` ➢ navigate to your Azure Active Directory ➢ select Groups from the navigation menu ➢ select the New Group menu item ➢ enter a name (I used **BRAINJAMMER**) ➢ set the Sensitivity level to General ➢ select the Member link ➢ add a user other than yourself ➢ select the identity ➢ click the Select button ➢ and then click Create. The configuration should be similar to Figure 8.46

FIGURE 8.46 Azure Active Directory created group

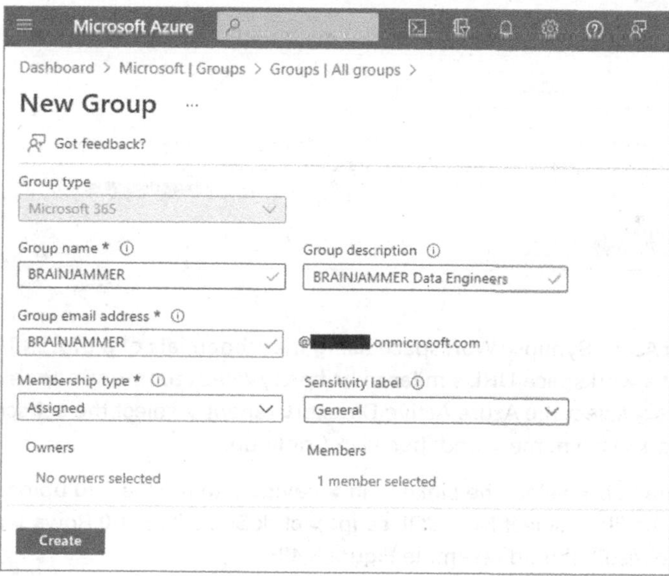

2. Navigate to your subscription ➢ select Access Control (IAM) from the navigation menu ➢ select + Add ➢ select Add Role Assignment ➢ and then add the group you created in step 1 to the Storage Blob Data Reader group.

EXERCISE 8.12 *(continued)*

3. Navigate to the ADLS container you created in Exercise 3.1 ➢ select the Access Control (IAM) navigation item ➢ select the Role Assignments tab ➢ notice that the group within the expected RBAC role exists ➢ create a directory path similar to the following ➢ and then upload the same file from Exercise 8.10, `NormalizedBrainwavesSE.parquet`, to the directory.

```
EMEA\brainjammer\business-data\Confidential\2022\10
```

4. Navigate to the Azure Synapse Analytics workspace you created in Exercise 3.3 ➢ navigate to Synapse Studio ➢ open the Manage hub ➢ select Access Control, located in the Security group ➢ click the + Add button on the Add Role Assignment window ➢ select Synapse Administrator ➢ select the Group you created in step 1, and then click Apply. The configuration should resemble Figure 8.47.

FIGURE 8.47 Add role assignment access control Synapse Contributor.

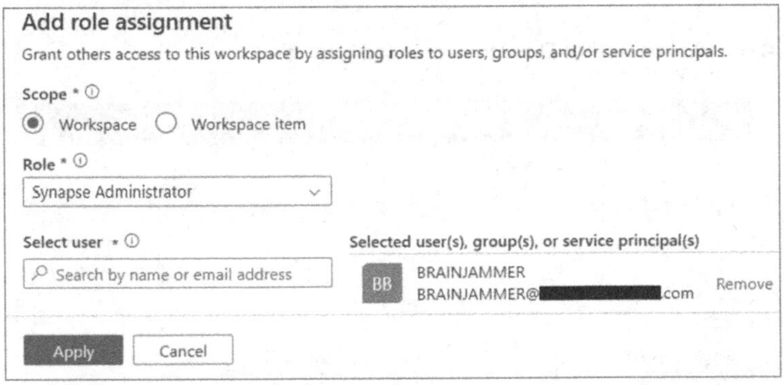

5. Log in to the Azure Synapse Workspace using the credentials of a `BRAINJAMMER` group member and a workspace URL similar to `https://web.azuresynapse.net/en/workspaces` ➢ select the Azure Active Directory tenant ➢ select the subscription ➢ select the workspace name ➢ and then click Continue.

6. Open the Data hub ➢ select the Linked tab ➢ navigate to the file you uploaded in step 2 ➢ right-click the file ➢ select New SQL script ➢ click Select Top 100 Rows ➢ and then click Run. The result should resemble Figure 8.48.

FIGURE 8.48 Add role assignment access control Synapse Contributor Parquet file.

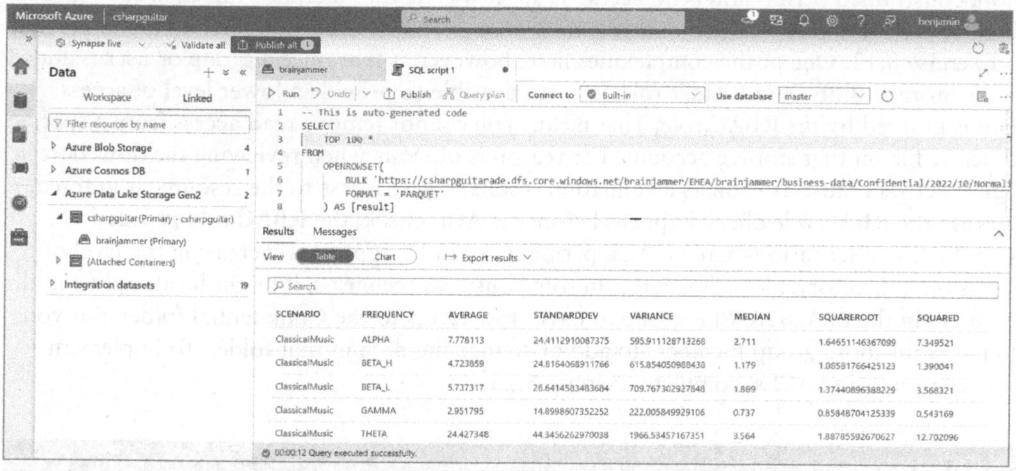

When groups and users are created, they are stored in the Azure Active Directory tenant. The tenant ID is typically a GUID that is bound to a primary domain. The primary domain is often your organization name appended to `.onmicrosoft.com`. While creating the Azure Active Directory group, you set a sensitivity label on it. It is good practice to begin placing sensitivity labels on all your resources from this point forward. After creating the group, you added a user to the group. It is important that you use a user account other than the one you used to provision all the resources from this book. This is because you, as the resource creator, will already have owner and/or admin access to them. Also keep in mind that if the user you add to the `BRAINJAMMER` group is a member in another group with a higher level of permissions, then those permissions will be applied instead of the limited set configured in Exercise 8.12.

You then created a folder structure on the ADLS container that included a confidential folder. This is a flag that should signal that additional attention needs to be given to the content within this folder. As you know from Figure 8.16, when access permissions are applied with RBAC, access to the resource and the content within it is granted as well. The final action was to grant the Azure AD group access to the Azure Synapse Analytics workspace using Access control (IAM). Because the workspace is bound to the same Azure Active Directory tenant, the same groups and users are accessible and addable from the access controls. The Role drop-down list box from Figure 8.47 contains all the Synapse RBAC roles you have been exposed to in some previous discussions. The `BRAINJAMMER` Azure AD group was added to the Synapse Administrator role because at this time it is required to perform operations on a serverless SQL pool. As you observed in Figure 8.46, the value in the Connect To drop-down list box is Built-in, which means the serverless SQL pool was used. Also, PolyBase is what managed to get the SQL query to run against a Parquet file and render as a table.

Implement POSIX-like Access Control Lists

One of the undesired side effects of adding the `BRAINJAMMER` group to the Storage Blob Data Reader role is that all the users within it have read access to all that data. Read access is the most limited amount of access one can be given to a data resource. The only other more constrained permission is no access at all. It was neither intended nor desired to give all those in the BRAINJAMMER group access to the files located in the Confidential folder created in Exercise 8.12. One of the complexities here, however, is that once a group or user is added to the Storage Blob Data Reader role, it is not possible to provide a lower level of access than is granted by the RBAC role. That means you cannot remove read access from a specific folder or file on that storage account. The reason is obvious when reviewing the flowchart in Figure 8.18, because as soon as a validation results in yes, access to the resource is granted. Because the RBAC role check happens before the ACL check, the RBAC role permission is applied. The scenario where an ACL permission can be applied is increasing the level of access on a directory, file, or resource. In some business scenarios, it might be all right for all the users in the BRAINJAMMER group to have read access to the Confidential folder. But you do not want those group members to add or change the data in that folder. To implement this scenario using ACLs, complete Exercise 8.13.

EXERCISE 8.13

Implement POSIX-like ACLs for ADLS

1. Log in to the Azure portal at https://portal.azure.com ➢ navigate to your Azure Active Directory ➢ create a new group named, for example, BRAINJAMMER-WRITERS (using the same instructions as in Exercise 8.12) ➢ add this group to the Storage Blob Data Reader role as well ➢ navigate to the ADLS container you created in Exercise 3.1 ➢ select the storage browser from the navigation pane ➢ and then navigate to the Confidential folder you created in step 3 of Exercise 8.12, similar to the location shown in Figure 8.49.

FIGURE 8.49 Managing ACLs for an ADLS folder

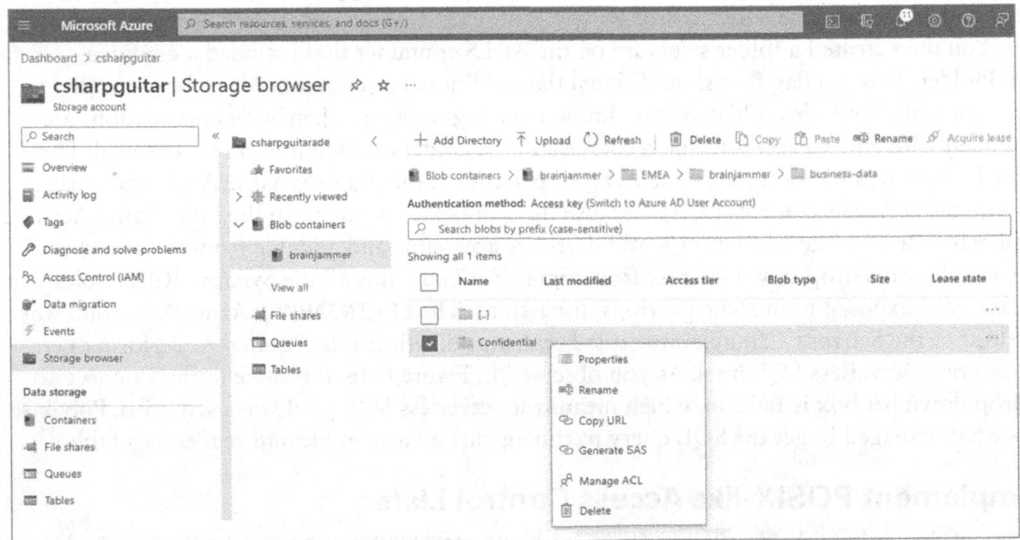

2. Right-click the Confidential folder ➢ select Manage ACL from the popup menu ➢ select the + Add Principal option ➢ add the BRAINJAMMER-WRITERS group ➢ grant Read, Write, and Execute permissions, as shown in Figure 8.50 ➢ and then click Save.

FIGURE 8.50 Adding an ACL to allow write access

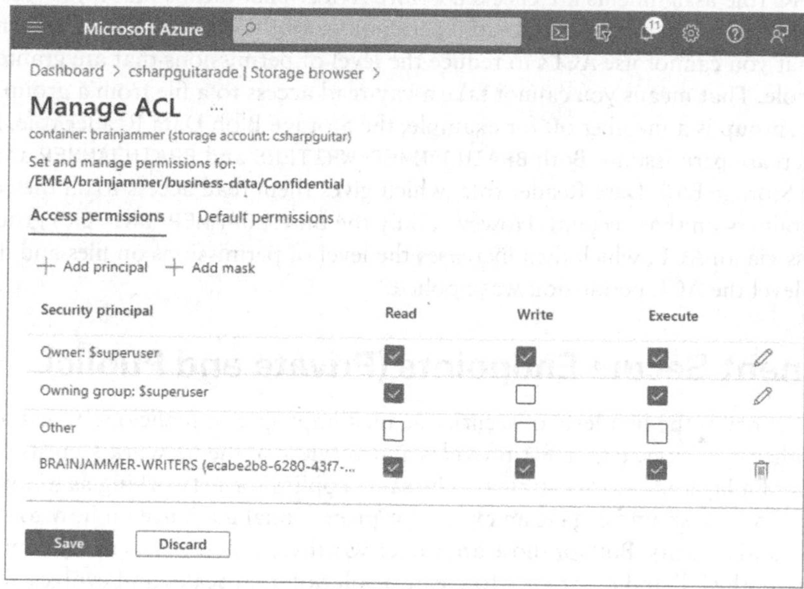

3. Log in to the Azure portal using the identity of someone in the BRAINJAMMER-WRITERS group ➢ navigate to the ADLS container created in Exercise 3.1 ➢ navigate one level below the Confidential folder ➢ and then upload and/or modify content within that directory successfully.
4. Log in to the Azure portal using the identity of someone in the BRAINJAMMER group ➢ navigate to the ADLS container created in Exercise 3.1 ➢ navigate one level below the Confidential folder ➢ and then upload and/or modify content within that directory unsuccessfully.

Setting up security can be challenging. Delays in the replication of permissions can cause some problems if either the security expert setting up the permissions or the individual needing the permission is impatient. For example, if a permission is granted, an unsuccessful test is performed moments later, and then you make another change, it is possible that the desired permission did not exist long enough to be experienced. Therefore, it is important to be patient, because the permission can take up to 5 to 10 minutes to be applied. The time lag and other challenges experienced setting up security are further justifications for using groups. By using groups, you can grant the permissions and complete the as expected once on that group, and then you add people to the group; you know exactly what permissions they have and that it works. Granting permissions on a case-by-case basis would be chaotic and stressful, and it would fail to scale.

Two valuable lessons should come from Exercise 8.12 and Exercise 8.13. The first lesson is that RBAC role assignments are checked before ACLs. That means that if the RBAC role has permissions greater than the ACLs, the permissions of the RBAC are applied. The second lesson is that you cannot use ACLs to reduce the level of permissions that are granted with an RBAC role. That means you cannot take away read access to a file from a group using an ACL if that group is a member of, for example, the Storage Blob Data Reader role. However, you can increase permissions. Both `BRAINJAMMER-WRITERS` and `BRAINJAMMER` are members of the Storage Blob Data Reader role, which gives them read access to all the content on the containers on that account. However, only the `BRAINJAMMER-WRITERS` group has write access via an ACL, which then increases the level of permissions on files and directories below the level the ACL permission was applied.

Implement Secure Endpoints (Private and Public)

Network security is the first level of security against improper or malicious access to your data and other resources. Figure 8.1 provides an overview of the network security layer in the context of a layered security strategy. The same applies for networking as it does for security, in that you should engage an expert for professional guidance on how to configure networking and security. Both of those are career worthy, as there exists many complexities that require both skill and experience to create a solution that scales and evolves along with your business. This chapter is intended to get you knowledgeable enough to know some details about security and networking, but not to the degree to design and implement an enterprise-wide solution. In this section, you will learn about virtual networks (VNets), network security groups (NSG), firewalls, and private and public endpoints.

When you provisioned the ADLS container in Exercise 3.1, you did not bind it to a VNet. Complete Exercise 8.14, where you will create a new Azure storage account and ADLS container that exists in a VNet.

EXERCISE 8.14

Create an Azure Storage Account and ADLS Container with a VNet

1. Log in to the Azure portal at `https://portal.azure.com` ➢ click the menu button in the upper left of the browser ➢ select + Create a Resource ➢ click Storage ➢ click Storage Account (if not found, search for **storage account**) ➢ select it ➢ and then click Create.

2. Select the Subscription and Resource group into which you want to create the storage account ➢ enter a storage account name (I used **csharpguitarvnet**) ➢ enter a location (which should be the same as the resource group location, but it is not required) ➢

choose Standard Performance ➢ and then select Locally Redundant Storage (LRS) from the Replication drop-down.

3. Click the Next: Advanced > button ➢ check the Enable Hierarchical Namespace check box in the Data Lake Storage Gen2 section ➢ check the Enable Network File System v3 check box in the Blob Storage section ➢ and then click the Next: Networking > button.

4. Select the Enable Public Access from Selected Virtual Networks and IP Addresses radio button ➢ select the Virtual Network Subscription ➢ select the Create Virtual Network link below the Virtual Network drop-down ➢ enter a name (I used **brainjammer-vnet**) ➢ select the default address ranges for both the VNet and the subnet, as shown in Figure 8.51 ➢ and then click OK.

FIGURE 8.51 Adding an Azure storage account with an ADLS container to a VNet

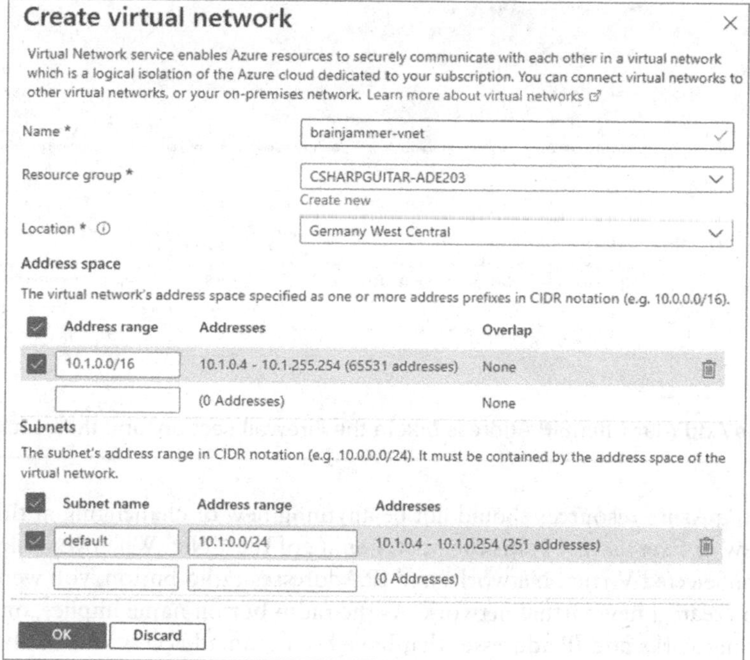

5. Click the Review button (feel free to navigate through the other tabs, but leave the defaults), and then click Create.

6. Once the provision is complete, navigate to the Overview blade of the storage account ➢ select the Data Lake Storage link on the Overview blade or Containers from the navigation menu ➢ click + Container ➢ enter a name (I used **brainjammer-vnet**) ➢ select Private (No Anonymous Access) from the Public Access Level drop-down list box ➢ and then click Create.

EXERCISE 8.14 *(continued)*

7. Select the Networking navigation link. The configuration should resemble Figure 8.52.

FIGURE 8.52 The Azure storage account VNet configuration

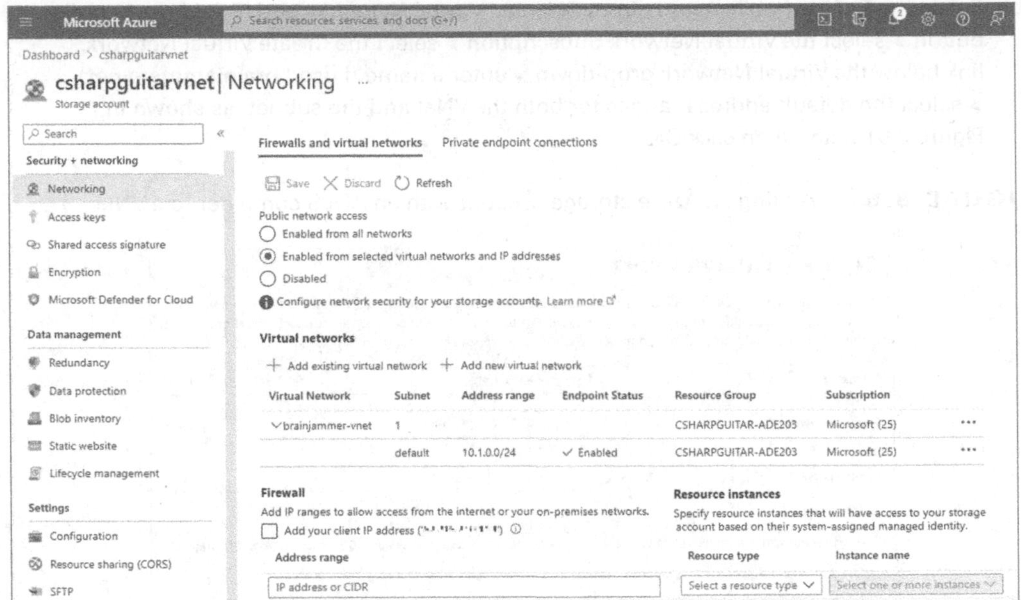

8. Check the Add Your Client IP Address box in the Firewall section, and then click Save.

Provisioning Azure resources should not be anything new or challenging at this point. What was new in Exercise 8.14 was the provisioning of the VNet. When you selected the Enabled from Selected Virtual Networks and IP Addresses radio button, you were provided the option to create a new virtual network. As the radio button name implies, once configured, only networks and IP addresses that have been granted access will be able to connect to this Azure storage account. While making the network configuration, you may have noticed a new term, CIDR notation. Classless Inter-Domain Routing (CIDR) is the method used to allocate IP addresses to a network's address space. The address space allocated to the VNet is from `10.1.0.0` to `10.1.255.254`, which means you can have up to approximately 65,531 devices connected to the VNet. The CIDR range is defined by the number that comes after the / (in this case, `16`). Notice in the subnet configuration portion that the range is defined by `/24`, which is a smaller number of IP addresses (251, for example). The smaller the number after the slash (/), the larger the number of IP addresses allocated to the network. The numbers range from `/0` through `/32`. It is also important to call out that when you are configuring a subnet, the CIDR range must reside within the VNet's address space.

Figure 8.52 includes two additional sections that should be discussed: Firewall and Resource Instances. Had you not added your client IP address to the list of allowed IP addresses, you would not be able to access any content within the containers. The same goes for any client or server from now on, in that, if the IP address is not in the allowed address range list or is not part of the VNet, then access will be denied, regardless of any RBAC or ACL permission. That makes sense because of where the network security layer exists. (It is the first layer in Figure 8.1.) That it fails so early means there is no chance to observe any Access Management or Information Protection permissions.

Another approach for granting access to the Azure storage account is by using resource instances. In Exercise 3.14 you added an IP range of `0.0.0.0` through `255.255.255.255`, which effectively allowed connectivity from everything through the network layer. This was done because it is inherently difficult to find IP addresses internal to Azure. For example, if you want to allow access from your Azure Synapse Analytics workspace to this Azure storage account, which IP address would you use? Although these lists do exist, a better approach might be to select `Microsoft.Synapse/workspaces` from the Resource Type drop-down list box and then select either a specific workspace or one of the other options—for example, all workspaces in the Azure AD tenant, in the current subscription, or in the current resource group. Doing so would avoid the requirement to find IP address ranges for all the datacenters in which your resources exist and the management required to apply and maintain them.

Now that you know more about VNets, perform Exercise 8.15, where you will provision another Azure Synapse Analytics workspace, bind it to the same VNet, and test connectivity.

EXERCISE 8.15

Create an Azure Synapse Analytics Workspace with a VNET

1. Log in to the Azure portal at `https://portal.azure.com` ➢ enter **Azure Synapse Analytics** in the search box ➢ click Azure Synapse Analytics ➢ click the + Create button ➢ select the subscription ➢ select or create a new resource group ➢ provide a workspace name (I used **csharpguitar-vnet**) ➢ select the region ➢ leave the From Subscription radio button enabled ➢ and then select the storage account and ADLS container that you provisioned in Exercise 18.15 (storage account example: `csharpguitarvnet`; ADLS container example: `brainjammer-vnet`).
2. Click the Next: Security > button ➢ enter a SQL password ➢ click the Next: Networking > button ➢ click the Review + Create button ➢ and then click Create.

On the Basics tab of the Azure Synapse Analytics workspace provision wizard, you may have noticed a message after selecting the ADLS account name. The message stated that the selected ADLS account must be used with a managed network and will be configured automatically. To view those configurations, navigate to the Networking blade of the storage account you selected in step 1 of Exercise 8.15 and created in Exercise 8.14. Notice that the

Azure Synapse Analytics workspace you just provisioned is added to the resource instances list. The Allow Network Access check box on the Security tab enables you to add the Synapse Analytics workspace to the resource instances list, which affects the SQL pool access to the storage account. The managed VNet configuration is not visible on the storage account side, but it can ensure that Spark pools and pipelines can access the storage account. However, it also requires that a managed private endpoint be created. As previously mentioned, the addition of the Azure Synapse Analytics workspace into this networking configuration avoids the need to find the set of workspace IP addresses for the firewall address range. You may have also noticed that the workspace is not bound to the VNet you created in Exercise 8.14. It is instead contained within a managed VNet. You may recall the managed VNet concept applied around an Azure Synapse Analytics workspace from Figure 3.41. In general, the managed VNet that is provisioned with a workspace simplifies the setup and configuration of the workspace networking component.

The other configuration performed on the storage account when the workspace is bound to the storage account protected by a VNet is a managed private endpoint. A managed service endpoint is created automatically when you choose the managed VNet configuration and needs to be approved on the storage account side. On the Networking blade, select the Private Endpoint Connections tab, select the Private Endpoint check box, and then click the Approve button. Figure 8.53 shows the configuration.

FIGURE 8.53 Azure storage account private endpoint configuration

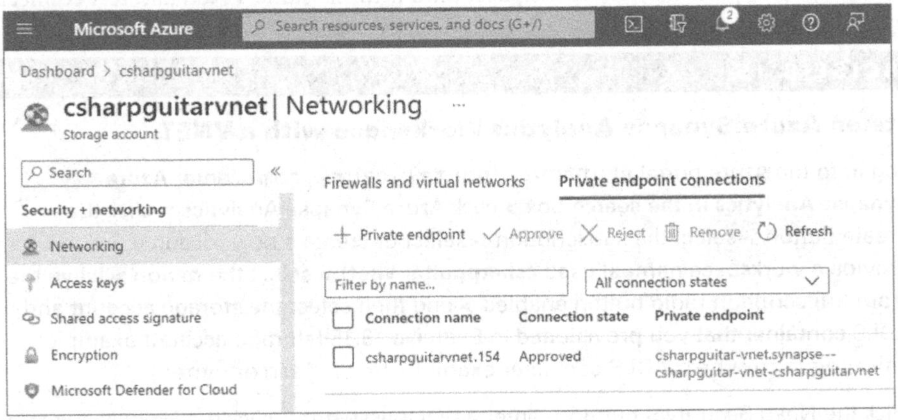

This changes the flow between the workspace and the ADLS container, as opposed to that shown in Figure 3.41, in that there is now an additional private endpoint. The added private endpoint is the new entry point to the storage account containing your ADLS container. You will find the same private endpoint in Synapse Studio on the Managed Private Endpoints blade, accessible via the Manage Hub. Private endpoints are a way to provide a public endpoint with a private IP address. When a private endpoint is created, it uses a private IP address from the VNet, adding an additional layer of security. Additional security is realized because when a private endpoint is added, you are effectively adding the resource into the VNet—in this case, the managed VNet. And, by default, only resources within that VNet have access to the resources within it.

Another networking security feature is a network security group (NSG). An NSG is provisioned by default when you create a VNet; you will find it in the same resource group that the VNet is in. As shown in Figure 8.54, NSGs can be applied to both inbound and outbound network traffic. You can also see that there is a rule named `AllowVnetInBound` that allows all port numbers and all protocols within the virtual network, which includes all subnets.

FIGURE 8.54 Network security group rules

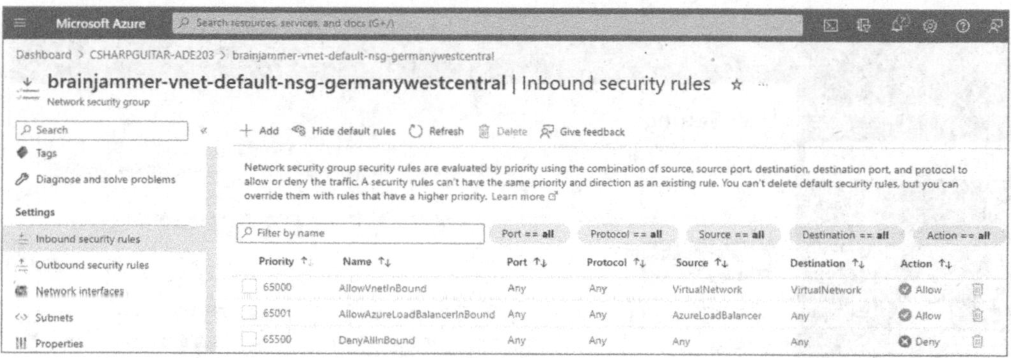

To add a security rule, click the + Add button. The resulting pop-out window provides the interface to configure all the attributes of a security rule. You can create a rule that targets a specific protocol, like HTTP, SSH, SMTP, and FTP, and identifies which ports are allowed or denied usage for inbound connectivity, for example, port 80 or port 25. These rules are helpful in locking down the network traffic flowing into and out of the VNet to only what you know should be happening. On the Outbound Security Rules blade, you will see a rule named `AllowInternetOutBound` with a destination value of `Internet`. If you want to deny all traffic to the Internet, you can change that so the action value is `Deny`. This is often done when a networking administrator wants to implement something called forced tunnelling.

The last networking security component to discuss is the firewall. A standalone Azure Firewall product provides access to lower level OSI layers than the ones you have seen previously. If, and only if, your security design requires security at those lower levels should you use Azure Firewall. Otherwise, the built-in firewall's access-restricting capabilities, as shown in Figure 8.52, will be enough. In this context, a firewall is a virtual device that allows or prohibits access to resources based on the IP address of the device requesting the resource. Using all the networking security concepts, such as private endpoints, firewalls, NSGs, and VNets, you can have a very secure networking security layer to protect your data.

Implement Resource Tokens in Azure Databricks

Chapter 3 provided an in-depth discussion of Azure Databricks, including access tokens. A token is a string value similar to the following, which, when used as part of an operation, validates that the operator is allowed to perform the task:

```
dapi570e6dffb9ee6b0966a4300c32a5c140-2
```

Personal access tokens are generated in the Azure Databricks workspace on the User Settings page, as shown in Figure 8.55. Clicking the Generate New Token button generates a pop-up window asking for a Comment and a Lifetime (Days) value.

FIGURE 8.55 Generating an access token

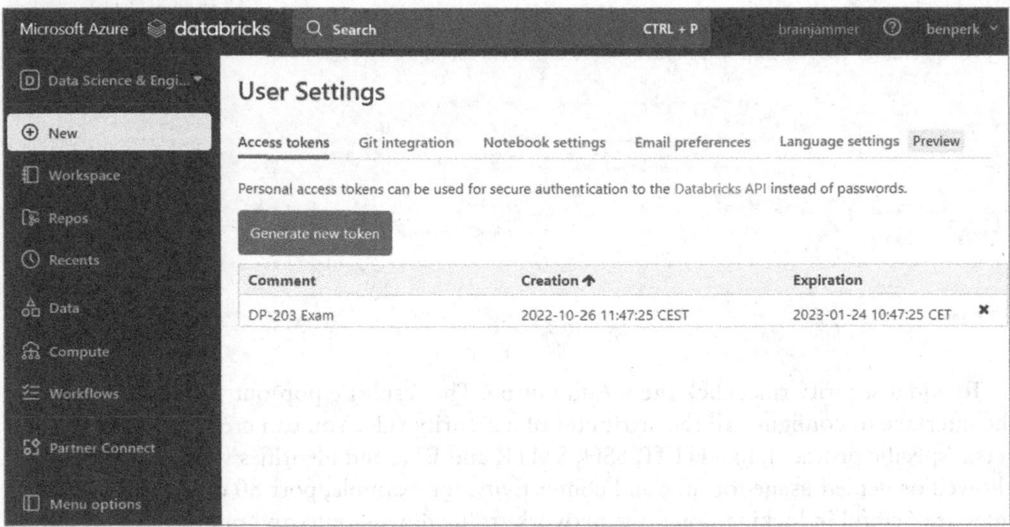

The Comment is a description of what the token is used for, and the Lifetime (Days) value is how long the token will be valid. After the time has elapsed, the token will no longer result in successful authentication. To use this token, it is normally passed as a parameter of a REST API. From a command console using `curl`, you can get a list of the clusters in your Azure Databricks workspace as follows:

```
set DATABRICKS_TOKEN= dapi570e6dffb9ee6b0966a4300c32a5c140-2
curl -X GET --header "Authorization: Bearer %DATABRICKS_TOKEN%" \
https://<workspace>.azuredatabricks.net/api/2.0/clusters/list
```

The result will render a JSON document with some cluster details similar to the following:

```
{
 "clusters":
 [{
```

```
"creator_user_name":"benperk",
"cluster_name":"csharpguitar",
"spark_version":"11.3.x-scala2.12",
"azure_attributes":{"first_on_demand":1,"availability":"ON_DEMAND_AZURE"},
"node_type_id":"Standard_F4",
"enable_local_disk_encryption":false,
"data_security_mode":"LEGACY_PASSTHROUGH",
"state":"TERMINATED",
"state_message":"Termination requested byenperk",
"termination_reason":
{
 "code":"USER_REQUEST",
 "type":"SUCCESS",
 "parameters": {"username":"benperk"}
}}]}
```


This information is helpful for getting an overview of the state of all the clusters for the given workspace. The type of cluster, the state, and the person who provisioned it are all included in the result from the REST API.

Load a DataFrame with Sensitive Information

When data is loaded from a file or table that contains sensitive data, you should mask that data prior to rendering it to the console. The following code places a mask on a column that contains an email address. The output of the `SUBJECTS.parquet` file, located in the `Chapter08` directory on GitHub, follows the code snippet.

```
%%pyspark
from pyspark.sql.functions import instr, expr
df = spark.read. \
    load('abfss://<container>@<account>.dfs.core.windows.net/SUBJECTS
      .parquet')
df = df.withColumn('pos_at', instr('EMAIL', '@')).withColumn('EMAIL_MASK',
   expr("""
    CONCAT(LEFT(EMAIL,{0}), REPEAT('*', pos_at-1-2*{0}), SUBSTR(EMAIL,
      pos_at-{0}))
    """.format(1)))
df.select(df.FIRSTNAME,df.LASTNAME,df.USERNAME,df.EMAIL_MASK)
   .show(truncate=False)
```

```
+-----------|----------|--------------+-----------------------------+
| FIRSTNAME | LASTNAME | USERNAME     | EMAIL_MASK                  |
+-----------|----------|--------------+-----------------------------+
| BENJAMIN  | PERKINS  | CSHARPGUITAR | b*******n@csharpguitar.net  |
| RUAL      | PERKINS  | DANCEMEISTER | r**l@csharpguitar.net       |
+-----------|----------|--------------+-----------------------------+
```

Masking data like government ID numbers, address details, phone numbers, and email addresses should be standard practice. No longer should you render any of these PII details to a console or application by default. Sensitivity labels, as you learned previously, should be applied in all cases and used for the basis of determining permissions for viewing unmasked data. A file named `mask.ipynb` containing the code snippet is in the `Chapter08` directory on GitHub.

Write Encrypted Data to Tables or Parquet Files

The previous section discussed masking data that is loaded in a DataFrame and then rendered to the console. Using that masking technique in combination with a following encryption feature would render a high level of data protection. You could effectively store the encrypted values of all PII data residing on your data tables or in your data files. Then, when the data is retrieved and the permissions justify the decryption, you can decrypt the data and apply the mask, again based on the permissions granted to the client retrieving the data. Numerous libraries and encryption algorithms can be used to encrypt data. One of the more popular libraries for use with Python is Fernet (`https://cryptography.io/en/latest/fernet`). The following code is an example of how to encrypt and decrypt a column contained within a Parquet file:

```
%%pyspark
from cryptography.fernet import Fernet
encryptionKey = Fernet.generate_key()
ek = Fernet(encryptionKey)
print(encryptionKey)
df = spark.read. \
    load('abfss://<container>@<account>.dfs.core.windows.net/SUBJECTS
      .parquet')
dfp = df.toPandas()
dfp['BIRTHDATE'] = dfp['BIRTHDATE'].apply(lambda x: ek.encrypt(bytes(x,
   'utf-8')))
dfp_encrypted = dfp[['FIRSTNAME', 'LASTNAME', 'BIRTHDATE', 'USERNAME',
   'EMAIL']]
display(dfp_encrypted)
dfp['BIRTHDATE'] = dfp['BIRTHDATE'].apply(lambda x: ek.decrypt(x))
dfp_decrypted = dfp[['FIRSTNAME', 'LASTNAME', 'BIRTHDATE', 'USERNAME',
   'EMAIL']]
display(dfp_decrypted)
```

The `SUBJECTS.parquet` file is located in the `Chapter08` directory on GitHub, as is a file named `encryptDecrypt.ipynb`, which includes the preceding code snippet. The first portion of the code imports the Fernet library and generates an encryption key. The encryption key resembles the following and is used for encrypting and decrypting the `BIRTHDATE` column:

```
MHfAzNysASlvESYfPumo4JiJmBRZm5Dpj2g8ovGGdMg=
```

Using that key, an encrypted value for the BIRTHDATE column resembles the following:

```
gAAAAABjWPLpmIlNVafUqkEKdipfevd4HL7ZO_F8xYvM40OLGvY8hg3ULB29ZYoBYNT7lIx1Y0ojvn
F9MOHZPZlbUMNFfuvi1g==
```

If you use the key directly on the encrypted column to decrypt it, like the following, you get the decrypted value:

```
dek = Fernet('MHfAzNysASlvESYfPumo4JiJmBRZm5Dpj2g8ovGGdMg=')
print(dek.decrypt(b'gAAAAABjWPLpmIlNVafUqkEKdipfevd4HL7ZO_
F8xYvM40OLGvY8hg3ULB29ZYoBYNT7lIx1Y0ojvnF9MOHZPZlbUMNFfuvi1g=='))
```

This is an important point regarding the initial code snippet, where the key is generated with each invocation of the code. If you encrypt the data and do not store the key, then you cannot decrypt it. If you want to encrypt the data prior to rendering it to the output without the intention of storing the encrypted values, then there is no need to store the key. However, if you do plan to store the data on a table using the saveAsTable() method or into a Parquet file, then you need to securely store the key and retrieve it when you want to decrypt the data. This is an example of a scenario where Azure Key Vault can be used to store the encryption key for later usage.

Develop a Batch Processing Solution

Chapter 6 covered all the aspects of designing a batch processing solution, excluding some security issues. At that point, you had not been exposed to an Azure key vault, managed identities, Access control (IAM), and RBAC; therefore, it was decided to not include those security aspects until this chapter. Chapter 6 called out three common topics that apply in this context: networking, endpoint security, and backup and recovery. The available networking capabilities for an Azure Batch account are the removal of public access to the public endpoint, for example, <accountName>.batch.azure.com, and the ability to restrict access using CIDR notation. As shown in Figure 8.56, you can access the option to remove public access on the Networking blade for the Azure Batch account.

The default option is All Networks, which means the endpoint is publicly accessible to all clients who have authorization to connect. The Selected Networks option provides the options shown in Figure 8.56, where you can configure IP addresses or IP ranges that are allowed to access the endpoint from the Internet and/or access a node directly. When you select the Disabled option, no access is allowed using the public endpoint; however, you can create a private endpoint. The Private Access tab provides the necessary options to configure a private endpoint for the Azure Batch account. Backups and log files containing results and details about job executions are stored on an Azure storage account chosen during provisioning. Having worked through the design and implementation of access control on ADLS containers, you should know the approaches not only for keeping that data secure but also for managing the permissions correctly so that only those who need access to such data are provided with it. A word of caution: if you have targeted the same storage account to store the backups and job logs as you used for your Azure Synapse Analytics workspace, then individuals who are in the Storage Blob Data Reader role will have read access to the batch data. This is not optimal, so you should consider having separate Azure storage accounts per Azure product.

FIGURE 8.56 Azure Batch networking restrictions

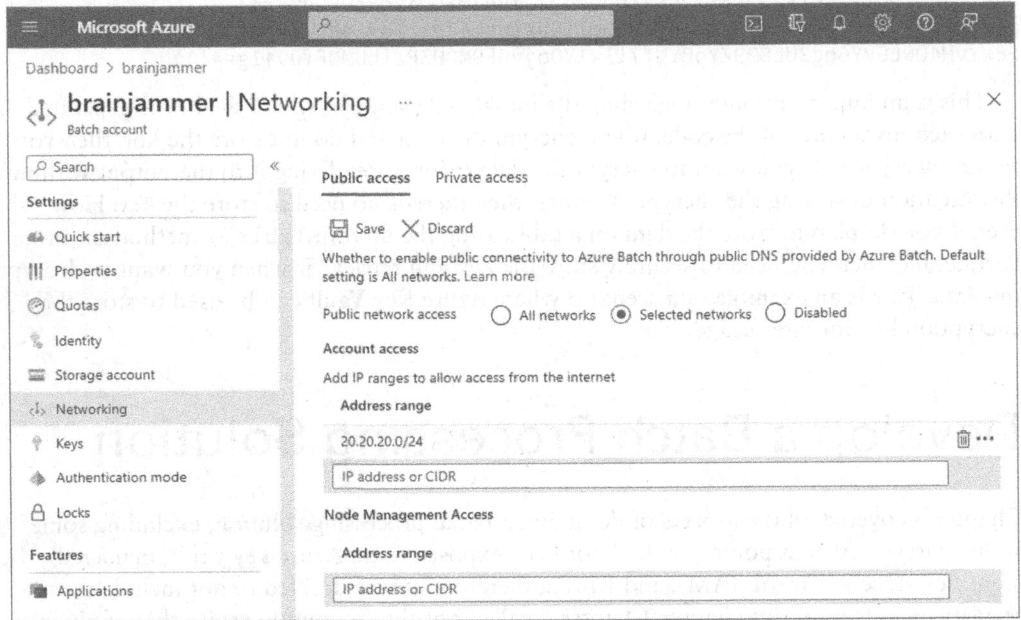

Handle Security and Compliance Requirements

From an Azure Batch security perspective, two areas are of utmost importance: the management console and the batch pools. The way you manage who can perform what activity on an Azure product or feature is through an RBAC role. If a built-in role does not meet your requirements, you can create a custom role. The most recent list of Azure built-in roles (`https://learn.microsoft.com/en-us/azure/role-based-access-control/built-in-roles`) does not include a role for Azure Batch with the associated ARM provider of `Microsoft.Batch`. Therefore, you might consider creating a custom RBAC role similar to the following:

```
{
    "Name":  "Azure Batch User",
    "Id":  null,
    "IsCustom":  true,
    "Description":  "Use Azure Batch resources",
```

```
    "Actions": [
                "Microsoft.Batch/batchAccounts/*/read",
                "Microsoft.Batch/batchAccounts/applications/write",
                "Microsoft.Batch/batchAccounts/pools/write",
                "Microsoft.Support/*"
            ],
    "NotActions": [ ],
    "NotDataActions": [ ],
    "AssignableScopes": [
                "/subscriptions/#######-####-####-####-#########"
    ]
}
```

After configuring the custom role, you can upload it using the Azure portal. From the Access Control (IAM) blade for your Azure subscription, click the + Add button, and then select the Add Custom Role menu item. A wizard will walk you through the creation and application of the custom RBAC role, as shown in Figure 8.57.

FIGURE 8.57 Configuring a custom Azure Batch RBAC role using the Azure portal

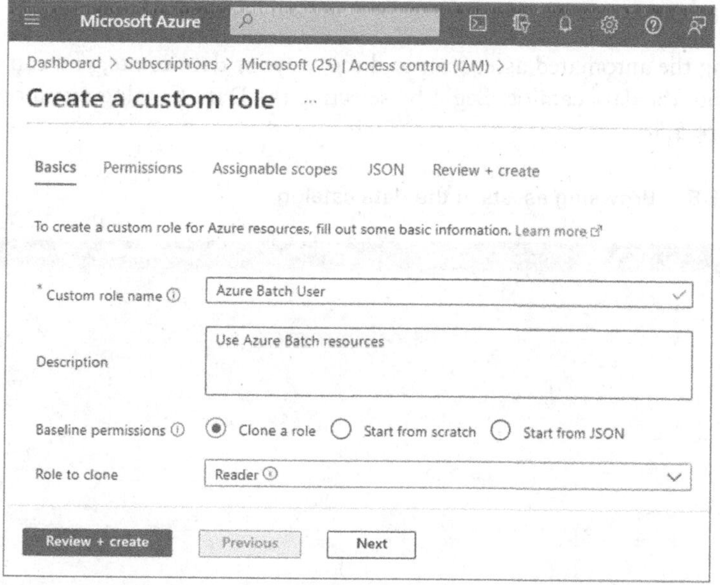

The other aspect of security regarding Azure Batch is managing the access to the batch pool that contains the nodes. Recall Exercise 6.1, where you provisioned the Azure Batch account and the batch pool. A detail named Identity was left at its default of None. The other option is User Assigned. You created a user-assigned managed identity in Exercise 8.9.

The identity is used to authenticate to cloud services and alleviates the need to store credentials in code or any place else. When you select User Assigned, you are given the option to be used to gain access to your Azure Batch pools and nodes.

Design and Implement the Data Exploration Layer

In Exercise 8.2 you provisioned a Microsoft Purview account where you also created collections and registered sources. Figure 8.8 shows the results of the collections and registrations. In Exercise 8.3 you performed an asset scan that searched through and discovered your Azure data estate for use with the execution of you audit strategy. Figure 8.22 shows the results. Microsoft Purview includes additional features that can help you gain a better understanding of the resources, products, and applications you have running on the Azure platform.

Browse and Search Metadata in Microsoft Purview Data Catalog

Instead of using the automated asset scan to discover your data estate, you can manually navigate through the data catalog. Begin by selecting the Data Catalog menu option, as shown in Figure 5.58.

FIGURE 8.58 Browsing assets in the data catalog

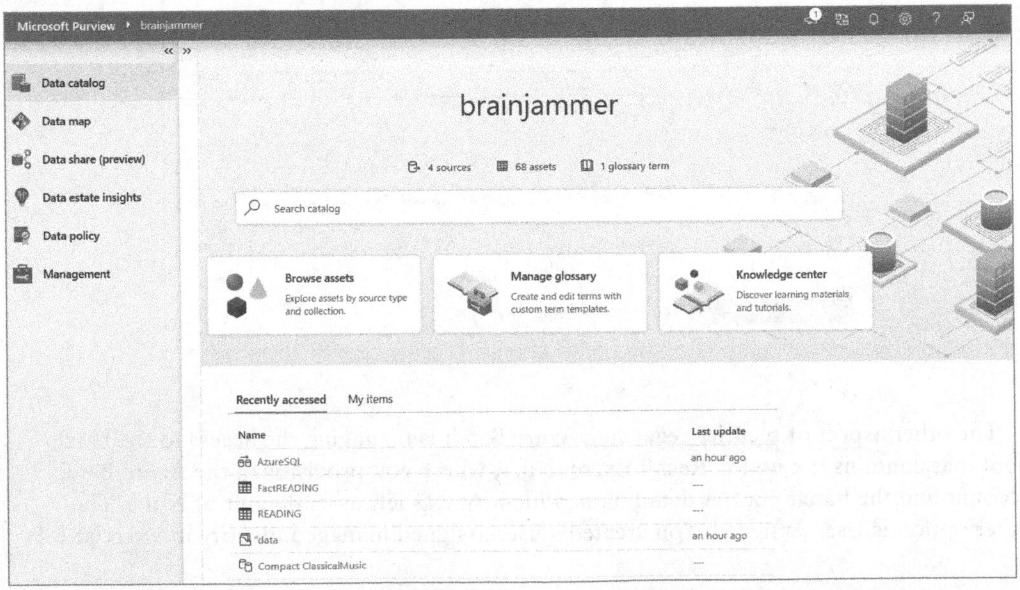

After selecting the Browse Assets tile, you are given the option to browse based on the collections or resource types you configured in Exercise 8.2 (see Figure 8.59).

FIGURE 8.59 Browsing assets based on source type

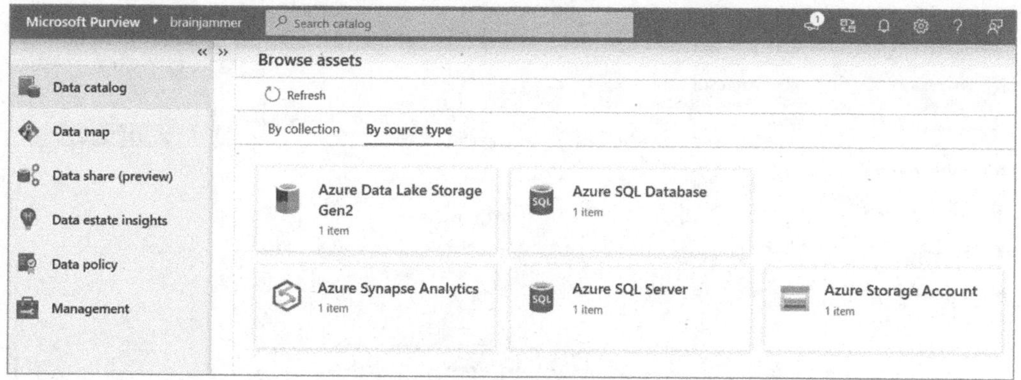

When you select the source type, for example, Azure Synapse Analytics, you are given a list of all workspaces. There is currently only one. Clicking that tile, then on a pipeline within that workspace, renders the page shown in Figure 8.60, which includes an overview of the database name, some of the discovered pipelines, and some additional details about the components contained within the pipeline.

FIGURE 8.60 Browsing assets based on source type

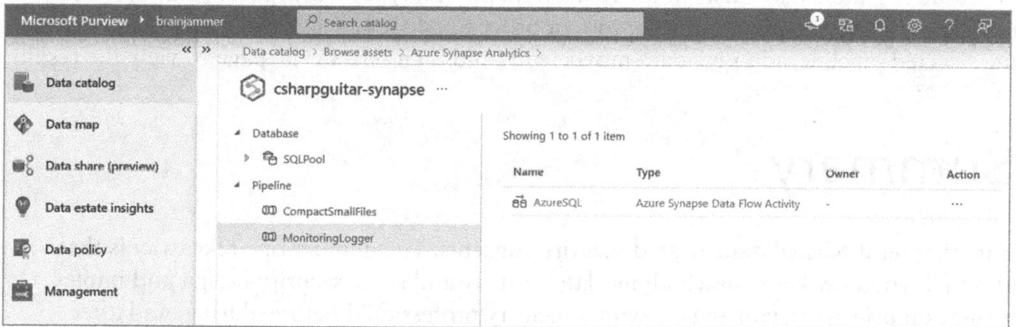

Push New or Updated Data Lineage to Microsoft Purview

The term *lineage* describes the flow of an object from its origin to its current state. In the data analytics context, the lineage of your data can be tracked from its source location to its current state. The flow is tracked, for example, from ingestion, through potentially multiple transformation iterations and the data's flow, into a visualization platform. You can view data lineage using Microsoft Purview by selecting the AzureSQL Data Flow activity (refer to Figure 8.60). Figure 8.61 shows the Lineage tab on the resulting page.

FIGURE 8.61 Viewing Microsoft Purview data lineage

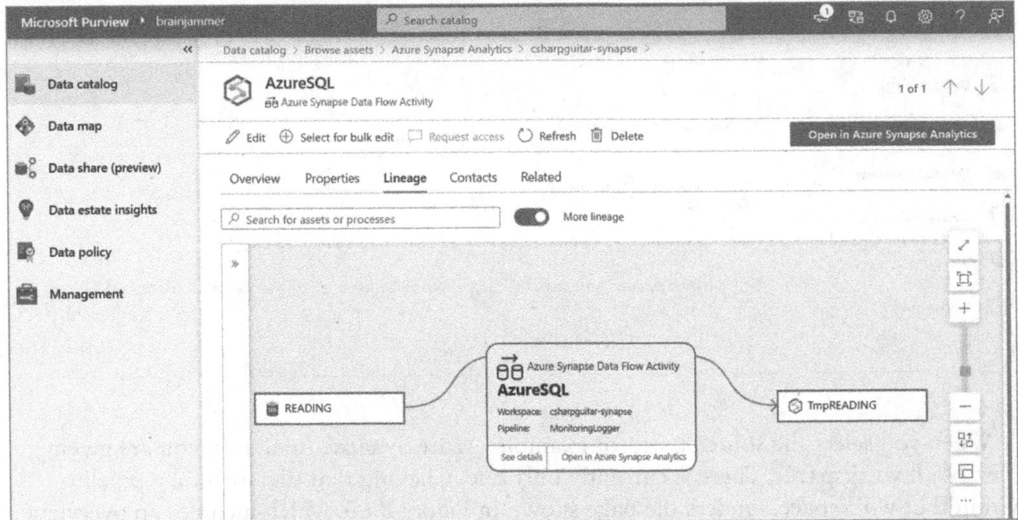

Notice that the origin of the data for that data flow is the `READING` table on an Azure SQL database. The data flow performs its transformations and places the data into the `TmpReading` table that exists in the Azure Synapse Analytics workspace. To update the lineage, click the Edit or Refresh button. In order to add a new lineage, you need to modify the selected pipeline, add new data movements, and then refresh the page to view the results.

Summary

This chapter discussed data-related security concepts. The number one takeaway is that although you now know much about data security and some security design and implementation principals, you engage with a security professional before, during, and after the design and implementation of your data security solution. Before beginning any data security design, you must perform an audit to find out what data sources you have and what data exists within them. The best tool for this is Microsoft Purview. Once you know what you have, you should identify and mark the data type and tag the data using sensitivity labels. Both encryption-at-rest and encryption-in-transit are required aspects of data protection. Encryption-at-rest is enabled by default for most Azure data products, whereas encryption-in-transit requires the use of TLS when the data transmission happens using

HTTP. Row-level security, column-level security, and data masking are useful methods for displaying data to a consumer in a privacy-compliant manner. Some rows may be viewable by the owner and not users, and certain columns on row, like an employee's salary, may have the similar viewability constraint, whereas some columns like an email address, government ID, or credit card can be masked, exposing only a few digits of the value.

This chapter also introduced Azure Key Vault and managed identities. You know that password leakage is an issue and that using Azure Key Vault and managed identities together is a way to stop it. Creating a group in Azure Active Directory and assigning permission to it is the recommended approach for granting permissions to users. Due to the complexities of implementing security, applying permissions to a group means it needs to happen only once. You can add someone who needs those permissions to the group, instead of granting permissions multiple times. Granting the group access to an Azure product is achieved using RBAC roles. An additional method for data protection is to use ACLs in an Azure data lake. VNets, NSGs, private endpoints, and firewalls are networking features that can be used to protect data on the networking layer. The chapter ended with some examples of masking and encrypting data in Parquet files using Python running an Apache Spark pool.

Exam Essentials

Data auditing. Microsoft Purview can review your Azure data real estate and provide a report on what exists. You can use the report to analyze the database columns in order to determine the type of data stored in them and what level of sensitivity label they require. Sensitivity labels range from Publicly Viewable to Highly Confidential. Azure Synapse Analytics dedicated SQL pools include a feature called Data Discovery & Classification that can be used to discover and classify your data. You should perform an audit of your data resources before beginning to design your data security solution. You need to know what you have before you begin creating something to protect it.

Encryption-at-rest and in-transit. Most of the data stored on the Azure platform is encrypted at rest. The data is encrypted by a Microsoft key, but it is possible to use your own key for the encryption. The encryption and decryption of the data happens by default on the platform; you do not need to do anything. The default encryption is helpful in the very unlikely scenario that a hard drive containing your data is stolen. If that happens, the data will be unusable because the data is encrypted. When data moves between two machines, it needs to be encrypted as well. Using TLS with HTTP is enough to implement data encryption-in-transit.

Managed identities. Many Azure products come with a default system-assigned identity. Only the platform has any knowledge of the credentials, which makes using them for granting permissions very secure. The other type is a user-assigned managed identity. The identity is provisioned manually, and instead of being managed by the platform and bound to an Azure product, it is a standalone credential, identical to a service principal. A user-assigned managed identity can be used to authenticate between products and applications in the same manner as system-assigned managed identity.

Azure Key Vault. Azure Key Vault stores keys, secrets, and certificates. When performing encryption and decryption, you can use Azure Key Vault to generate and store a key. You can also use Azure Key Vault to store passwords and tokens. When the password is needed, the credentials assigned to a system-assigned managed identity can be used to retrieve the password from Azure Key Vault and used in the application. Certificates for securing data transmissions or client certificate authentication can be stored and retrieved from Azure Key Vault.

RBAC and ACLs. RBAC roles enable you to grant access to Azure Active Directory groups for managing Azure products. Only a few RBAC roles grant access to data. Mostly, they grant access to the product or feature in Azure Data Lake. ACLs cannot be used to reduce the permission level granted by an RBAC role; however, they can increase the level. For example, an ACL can provide write access to an individual who is part of an RBAC role that has read-only permissions.

Review Questions

Many questions can have more than a single answer. Please select all choices which are true.

1. Which of the following are useful for data discovery and sensitivity levels?
   - **A.** Data Discovery & Sensitivity Labeling
   - **B.** Data Discovery & Classification
   - **C.** Microsoft Purview
   - **D.** Azure Blueprints
2. Which type of policy is most used in the context of data retention?
   - **A.** Azure retention policy
   - **B.** Lifecycle management policy
   - **C.** Azure Synapse Analytics data retention pool
   - **D.** Data purge policy
3. What is encryption-at-rest?
   - **A.** Data is encrypted when not being used.
   - **B.** Data is encrypted while being written.
   - **C.** Data is encrypted prior to deletion.
   - **D.** Data is not encrypted while in transit.
4. Which of the following can be used to implement encryption-in-transit?
   - **A.** TLS 1.1
   - **B.** SMTP
   - **C.** TCP/IP
   - **D.** TLS 1.2
5. Which of the following statements about column-level security are true?
   - **A.** If the consumer does not have permission to view the column value, the column value is encrypted and returned.
   - **B.** If the consumer does not have permission to view the column, an error is returned.
   - **C.** If the consumer has permission to view the column value, it is rendered to the client with a mask.
   - **D.** If the consumer does have access, the column value is returned.
6. Which of the following should permissions be applied to?
   - **A.** An Azure Active Directory group
   - **B.** An Azure Active Directory user
   - **C.** A user-assigned managed identity
   - **D.** An Azure RBAC role

7. Which of the following networking security options are highly useful for data security?
   - **A.** OSI level 4 Azure Firewall
   - **B.** Firewall settings
   - **C.** Private endpoints
   - **D.** Azure VPN Gateway
8. Which of the following statements about system-assigned managed identities are true?
   - **A.** Only the platform knows the credentials.
   - **B.** They are most often provisioned by default and bound to an Azure product.
   - **C.** They are most often provisioned by default but are not bound to an Azure product.
   - **D.** They are identical to a service principal.
9. Which three of the following can be stored in an Azure key vault?
   - **A.** Certificates
   - **B.** Secrets
   - **C.** Files
   - **D.** Keys
10. What is an Azure Databricks personal access token used for?
   - **A.** Passthrough authentication
   - **B.** The bearer token for REST API authentication
   - **C.** For gaining access to the Azure Databricks workspace
   - **D.** An authentication token that can be used with OAuth providers

Monitoring Azure Data Storage and Processing

EXAM DP-203 OBJECTIVES COVERED IN THIS CHAPTER:

- ✓ Monitor data storage and data processing
- ✓ Develop a batch processing solution
- ✓ Develop a stream processing solution

WHAT YOU WILL LEARN IN THIS CHAPTER:

- ✓ An overview of Azure monitoring

As you learned in Chapter 8, "Keeping Data Safe and Secure," before you can design a data security solution, you need to perform an audit. An audit discovers the data sources and analyzes the kind of data that resides within them. You need to know what you have before you can design a solution to protect it. Monitoring the Azure platform and the applications running on it is as necessary as an audit. The information you gather from monitoring is what you use to clarify the dependability of the platform, the applications running within it, or other application dependencies. Without any data that tracks the behavior of your application, it will not be possible to confirm any reported or unreported performance or availability issues. Furthermore, without application data captured from monitoring, you would not be able to perform any root cause analysis to find the reason for application issues. Finally, application data is what is most often used to determine which actions should be taken to improve any poorly behaving applications or specific areas within the applications.

Being proactive means taking action to prevent an inevitable event from happening before it does. You do not want to wait until a customer reports a problem before realizing that you need to enable monitoring. Historically, having a monitoring strategy and implementation plan was not a very high priority. Most of the focus was on developing new features, resolving any high impact bugs, and keeping the production system running. However, running your IT solutions in the cloud, on a third-party platform, is a reason to take monitoring more seriously. It is often very complicated to distinguish platform-related issues from application-related issues. And you must know that the cloud platform provider does not log any information about the applications running within it, due to privacy regulations. So, if you do not enable monitoring and your application fails, there will be no record of it. Therefore, you must enable monitoring, and you must create an end-to-end monitoring solution. That solution must incorporate the analysis of monitoring logs, which drives proactive actions to improve reliability and avoid problems before they happen.

The most used product on the Azure platform for implementing a monitoring strategy is Azure Monitor, which was introduced in Chapter 1, "Gaining the Azure Data Engineer Associate Certification," and shown in Figure 1.29. Azure Monitor consists of numerous technologies and features that will help you gain insights, visualize, analyze, and respond from the telemetry produced from the platform and your applications. This chapter covers monitoring capabilities on the Azure platform and Azure Monitor and includes details about implementing, retrieving, and interpreting monitoring logs.

Monitoring Data Storage and Data Processing

This section covers how to implement, configure, store, retrieve, and interpret monitoring logs. The logs discussed focus primarily on platform performance and availability. These logs do not track your application code or your custom configurations, but they do track and measure how your solution is functioning on the platform. However, determining why your solution behaves how it does requires a deeper level of logging. The next sections discuss how you can get the most out of the monitoring products and features available on the Azure platform.

Implement Logging Used by Azure Monitor

Azure Monitor is a management workspace that helps you integrate and create a monitoring solution. Most PaaS Azure products have many of the Azure Monitor features built in. That means that you can configure, store, and analyze performance data from the monitoring features bound to the product itself in the Azure portal. For a hybrid cloud solution with on-premises resources or IaaS products that you want to monitor with Azure Monitor, you need to have provisioned an Azure Monitor workspace. Perform Exercise 9.1, where you will create this workspace.

EXERCISE 9.1

Create an Azure Monitor Workspace

1. Log in to the Azure portal at `https://portal.azure.com` > enter **Azure Monitor workspace** into the Search box at the top middle of the web page > select it from the results > click the + Create menu button > enter a subscription > enter a resource group > enter a name (I used **brainjammer**) > enter a region > click the Review + Create button (note that Azure Monitor is not available in every region) > and then click Create.

Notice the two URLs on the Overview blade of the Azure Monitor workspace. One of them, the metric ingestion endpoint, is an ingestion endpoint for the metrics that your application generates. If you use the Azure Monitor SDK to send those logs to the Azure platform, this is where you send them. The other endpoint, the query endpoint, is used for querying the data. Again, using the Azure Monitor SDK, you can create an application that retrieves and renders the metric data to a console for viewing and analysis. The custom application that uses the Azure Monitor SDK would be something like Microsoft Intune or System Center, which is a product designed to capture application, networking, and operational data, and then send it for analysis to a data source like Azure Monitor. On-premises servers and Azure platform IaaS products like Azure Virtual Machines or Azure Kubernetes use this Azure Monitor workspace as the central hub for monitoring behaviors for those kinds of product scenarios.

It is important to call out the points in the previous paragraph because the concept of Azure Monitor is different when applied to Azure PaaS products. Azure Storage, Azure Synapse Analytics, Azure Stream Analytics, and many of the other products you have used have Azure Monitor logging capabilities built in. The products referred to in the following sentence are those found in the Azure portal in the Monitoring section. They are Alerts, Metrics, Diagnostic settings, and Logs. Keep in mind that when Azure Monitor is referred to in the context of Azure PaaS products, the meaning implies the monitoring features are contained in the Monitoring section of the Azure product. Monitoring data within these product-based monitoring features (i.e., metrics, diagnostics settings, and logs) remains for 45 days. If you require data to be available for longer, then you must use the endpoints from Exercise 9.1 to migrate and retrieve data for analysis. The following will take a closer look into each of these common Azure Monitor features, beginning with Logs. Keep in mind that the Azure Monitor workspace is currently in preview and contains only the managed Prometheus metrics, although in the future these will contain all Azure monitoring data.

When you select the Logs navigation from any Azure product, it might look similar to what you saw in Figure 8.25. The user interface rendered on the Logs blade is the same as what you saw in the Log Analytics workspace that you provisioned in Exercise 8.4. The user interface is built on top of Azure Data Explorer, so if you have ever worked with that product, you will notice a similarity. When you select the Logs navigation link from, for example, the Azure Synapse Analytics product, you will see something like Figure 9.1. Because the context in which you opened the Logs blade is in Azure Synapse Analytics, the scope is constrained to that. If you click the Select Scope link, you can target the Kusto queries to pull data from other Azure products in your subscription.

FIGURE 9.1 The Azure Synapse Analytics Logs blade

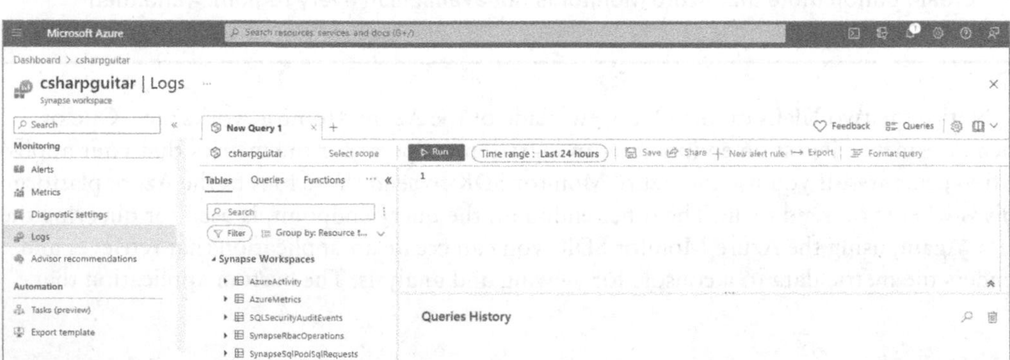

Metrics are very useful when you want to discover the amount of resources your application is consuming over a given time period, for example, how much memory or CPU, and, as shown in Figure 9.2, how many connections were made to a dedicated SQL pool. There exists a Metrics blade in the Azure portal for each product. Each product, as you might expect, will have a different set of metrics and aggregation in which they are displayed. You can use the information you gather from the metrics to determine how much the application is used.

FIGURE 9.2 Azure Synapse Analytics dedicated SQL pool metrics

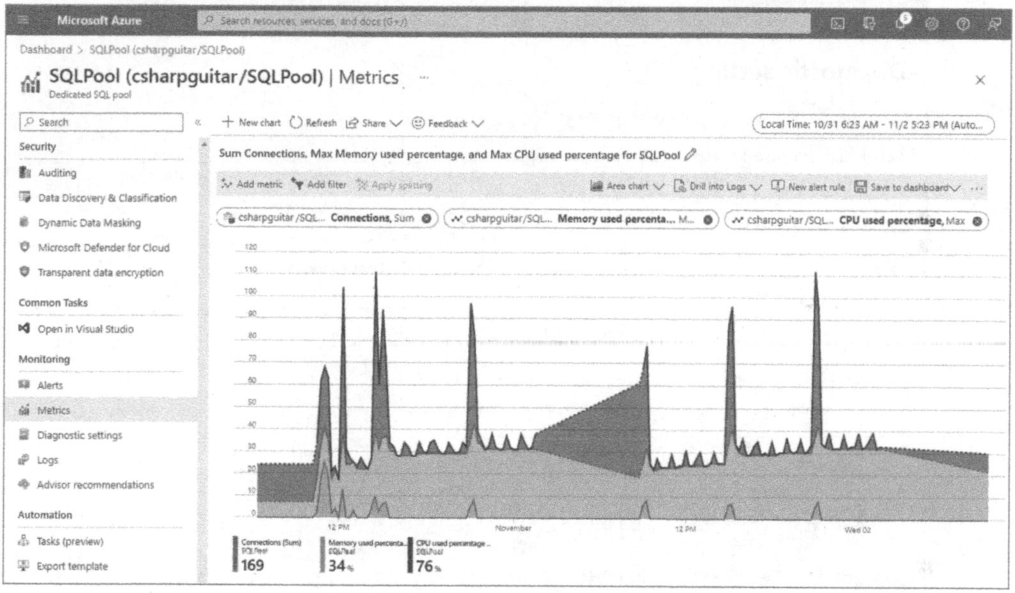

In Exercise 8.4, where you enabled auditing, you navigated to the Diagnostic Settings blade and saw the `SQLSecurityAuditEvents` setting that was generated automatically. You also noticed, as shown in Figure 8.24, additional log categories, including Sql Requests, Request Steps, Exec Requests, Dms Workers, and Waits. Those categories are all specific to a dedicated SQL pool. In addition to a Logs blade and Metrics blade, each Azure product also has a Diagnostic Settings blade. Figure 9.3 illustrates the Diagnostic Settings blade for an Azure Event Hub.

There are logs for monitoring incoming Kafka messages if you are using Azure Event Hubs for Kafka. Archive, Operational, Auto Scale, and Runtime logs are also available for storage into the configured destination datastore. Lastly, there is an option to store usage and performance metrics, which you saw in Figure 9.2, into a destination datastore for offline retrieval and analysis. The final monitoring feature that exists for Azure products is Alerts. As shown in Figure 9.1 and Figure 9.2, there exists an option named New Alert Rule.

This option is useful when you have a Kusto query in Log Analytics or a configured metric that you want to be notified about. For example, if the Kusto query only returns errors, if a row is returned from the query, you can be alerted to that. The similar is true regarding metrics. For example, when the CPU consumption or number of connections breaches a threshold value, then an alert can be sent. Perform Exercise 9.2 to configure an Azure Synapse Analytics alert.

FIGURE 9.3 Azure Event Hub diagnostic settings

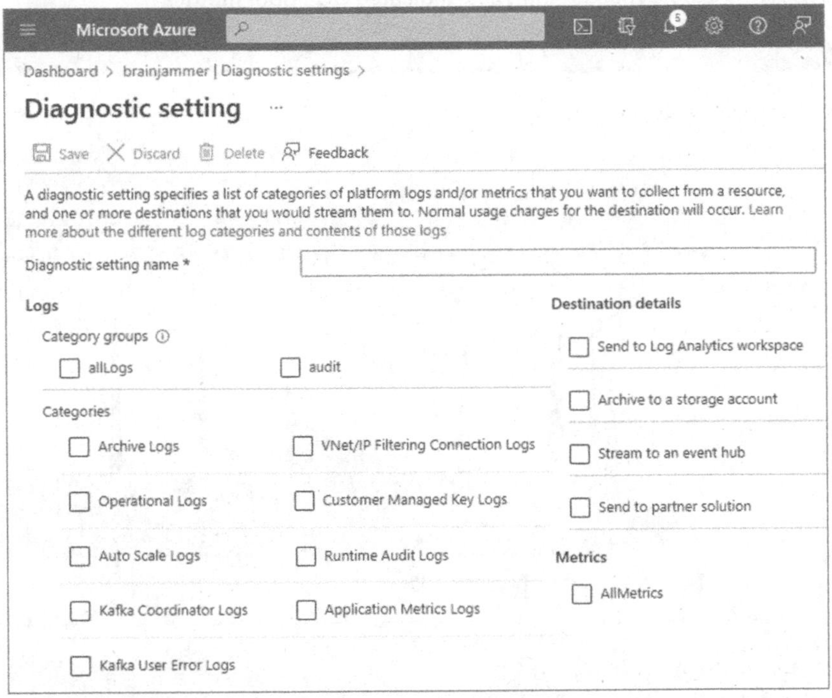

EXERCISE 9.2

Create an Azure Synapse Analytics Alert

1. Log in to the Azure portal at `https://portal.azure.com` > navigate to the Azure Synapse Analytics workspace you created in Exercise 3.3 > select Alerts from the Monitoring section on the navigation pane > select the + Create menu item > select Alert Rule from the drop-down menu > and then select Pipeline Runs Ended from the Select a Signal window.
2. From the Condition tab, set the Threshold to Static > select Total from the Aggregation Type drop-down list box > select Greater Than or Equal To from the Operator

drop-down list box and enter **1** into the Threshold value textbox ➢ select 1 hour from the Check Every drop-down list box ➢ and then select 6 hours from the Lookback Period drop-down list box. The configuration should resemble Figure 9.4.

FIGURE 9.4 Creating an Azure Synapse Analytics alert condition

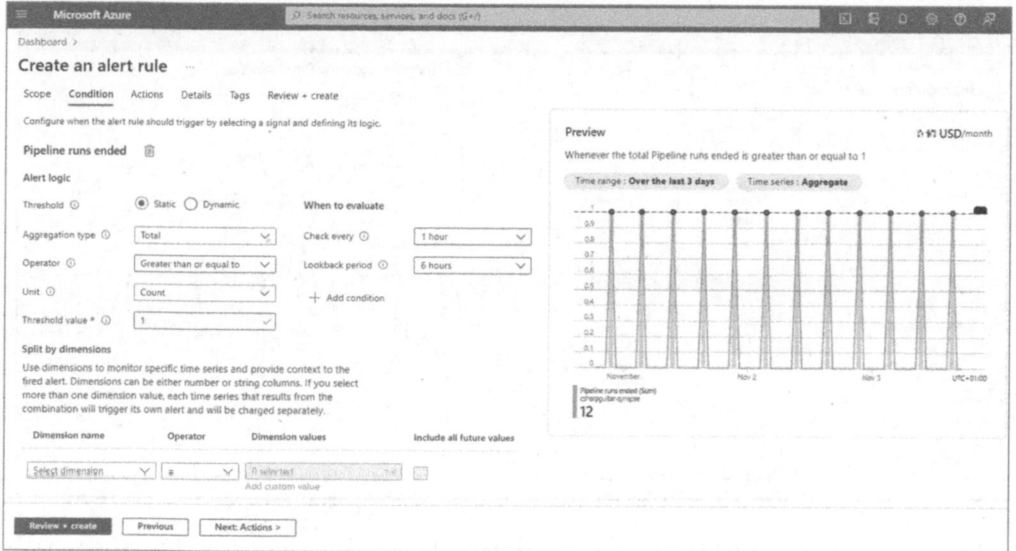

3. Click the Next: Actions > button ➢ click the + Create Action group button ➢ select the appropriate subscription resource group ➢ select a recommended region from the Region drop-down list box ➢ enter an Action group name (I used **brainjammer**) ➢ click the Next: Notifications > button ➢ select Email Azure Resource Manager Role from the Notification Type drop-down list box ➢ select Owner from the Azure Resource Manager Role on the Email Azure Resource Manager Role pop-up window ➢ toggle Enable the Common Alert Schema to Yes ➢ click OK ➢ enter a name (I used **brainjammer Owner**) ➢ click the Review + Create button ➢ and then click Create.
4. Select the Next: Details > button ➢ select the appropriate subscription and resource group ➢ select Informational from the Severity option ➢ enter an alert rule name (I used **brainjammerSynapsePipelineRun**) ➢ enter a description ➢ click the Review + Create button ➢ and then click Create. It might take a few moments to create the alert rule, so be patient.

EXERCISE 9.2 *(continued)*

5. After the alert rule has been created and executed, the Alerts blade for the Azure Synapse Analytics workspace should resemble Figure 9.5.

FIGURE 9.5 The Azure Synapse Analytics Alerts blade

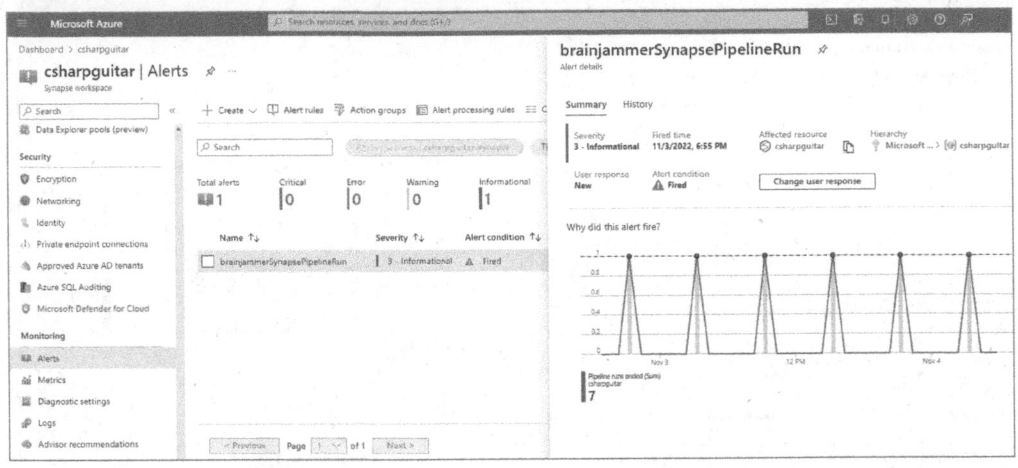

Three options are available on the + Create drop-down menu you selected in step 1: Alert Rule, Action Group, and Alert Processing Rules. In Exercise 9.2 you created both an alert rule and an action group. An alert rule is used to determine the circumstances in which an alert should be invoked. In Exercise 9.2 the condition was based on a single occurrence of the Pipeline Runs Ended event. The selected threshold was Static, which means you configured the Unit and Threshold values that will cause an alert to trigger. The other option, Dynamic, uses machine learning algorithms that create metrics considered normal for your targeted condition. If the metrics breach what is considered normal operating behaviors, an alert is triggered. Other options such as Check Every and Lookback Period enable you to configure how often the platform checks if the condition is met and determine if an alert notification should be sent. The lookback period is the timeframe in which the data is checked according to the entry in the Check Every drop-down.

The Details tab includes an important selection that pertains to all types of logging. The selection has to do with the verbosity and severity level of the alert. Table 9.1 provides a summary of each severity option.

TABLE 9.1 Logging verbosity and severity

Level	Alert type	Frequency
0	Critical	Very rare
1	Error	Rare

Level	Alert type	Frequency
2	Warning	Somewhat often
3	Informational	Often
4	Verbose	Always

When configuring this setting, you need to consider the expected frequency of the notification. Critical alerts should not happen very often and should therefore be configured to notify the most skilled members of the team who can quickly react and respond to the issue. Errors occur less often than critical alerts and would have less impact, but this type is still considered a rather high level of alert. Warnings can happen often and are usually not something that you would want to call someone outside of business hours to analyze and resolve. Informational and verbose alerts would trigger often and would not need to be acted upon with a high level of urgency. Those two severity and verbosity levels are for storing historical and performance logs used for learning the common behaviors of your application.

An alert group is where you configure the notification type and who receives the notification on the Notifications tab. The options are to email members of an Azure Resource Manager Role like Owner, Contributor, Reader, Monitoring Contributor, or Monitoring Reader. The other option is to send an email, SMS, mobile app notification, or a voice message to a phone number. Multiple notifications are supported, so you can send notifications to multiple ARM roles and to numerous phone numbers, or via text messages and emails. On the Basics tab, you select a region. In addition to the Global option, a few geographical recommendations are rendered based on the proximity of the resource group. Selecting one of the recommended regions means that redundancies are contained within a single geographic boundary. Selecting Global means that your alert redundancies span any geographic region. On the Actions tab you might have noticed that the notifications can be sent to some ingestion points or compute platforms, for example, Event Hubs, Logic App, Webhook, or an Azure Function. The alert is sent in JSON format and can be ingested or transformed using any of those technologies to store and gather insights from the data. An alert processing rule gives you a bit more control over what happens when an alert is invoked, for example, the ability to suppress notifications during times of planned maintenance and based on whether the issue is a onetime or reoccurring exception.

Configure Monitoring Services

As previously mentioned, Azure products include numerous built-in monitoring options—specifically, alerts, metrics, diagnostics settings, and logs. An additional feature is called the Azure Monitor activity log (see Figure 9.6).

FIGURE 9.6 The Azure Monitor activity log

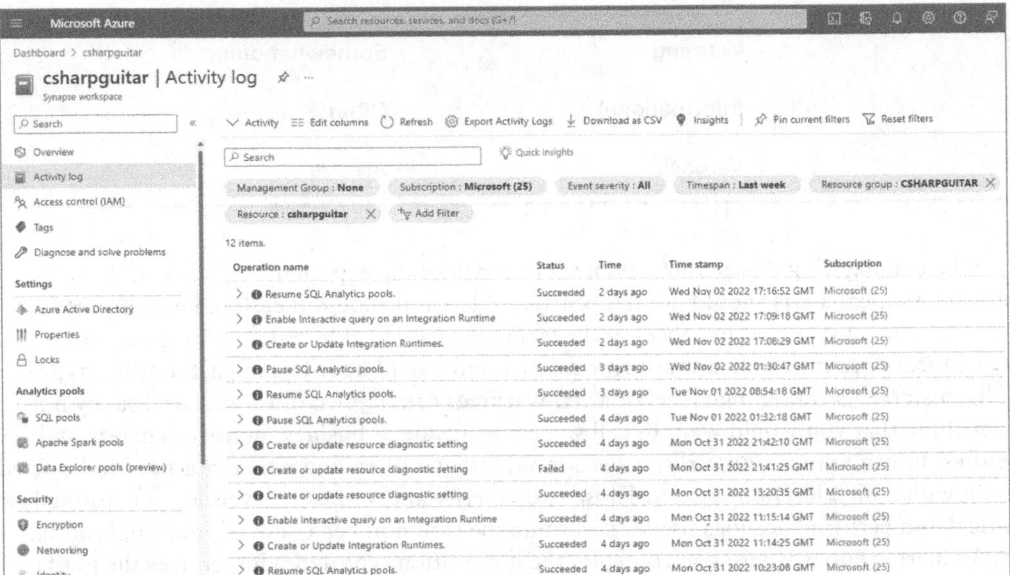

The activity log contains operations that have been performed against the product. It does not include information about any implementation of code or the execution of jobs, queries, or pipelines that run on the product. When you select one of the entries in the log, you are prompted with a summary and a JSON document that contains complete details about the operation. One window that displays the operational details includes a + New Alert Rule button that enables you to create an alert and receive a notification when that specific operation and status occur. The following sections discuss the distinctive capabilities available for specific Azure products.

Azure Storage and Azure Data Lake Storage

Two other monitoring features are available for an Azure storage account, in addition to the previous four already covered: Application Insights and Azure Workbooks. Application Insights is an SDK that can be included within the application code to help track down issues that happen there. The previously discussed monitoring features have been focused on the Azure platform and have targeted metrics like CPU, memory, concurrent connections, ingress, etc. The Azure Storage product is an application that executes source code to provide its service. Microsoft decided to include Application Insights in Azure Storage in order to log a more granular level of information. You can access this logging information by selecting the Insights navigation menu item, which includes the following tabs: Overview, Failures, Performance, Availability, and Capacity (see Figure 9.7).

FIGURE 9.7 The Azure Storage Account Insights Overview tab

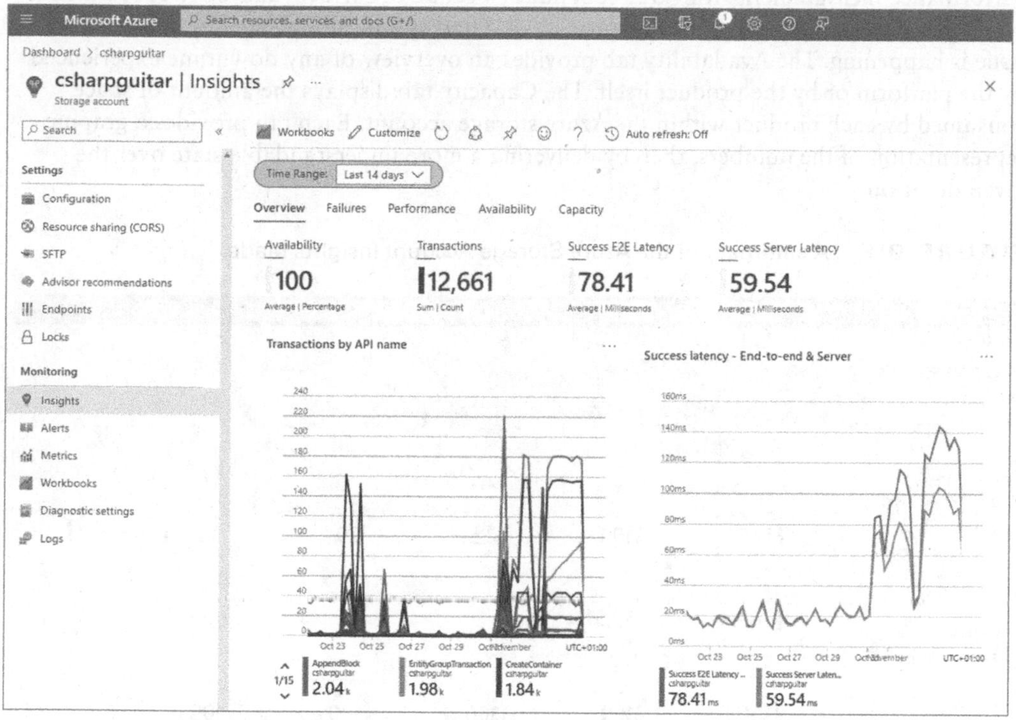

This is a very valuable feature for Azure storage accounts, because the metrics you are provided drive your knowledge deeper into the product. For example, you can see in the Transactions by API Name graph which APIs are being called the most—in this example, AppendBlock, EntityGroupTransaction, and CreateContainer. You can then research those APIs and how they may be impacting your solution. The data on the Insights blade provides just that: insights into how the Azure Storage application is being used, exposing some internals that bring you deeper into the product. The more you know about the product, the better you can then explain why certain symptoms are happening. Figure 9.8 shows a summary of the top-level metrics from the other tabs on the Insights blade.

The Failures tab provides insights into the total number of transactions over the given timeframe, as well as a breakdown of success versus different error types. The Performance tab provides an overview of end-to-end latency, which measures the transaction speed between the client and the server. The amount of time spent performing the transaction on the server side is also provided. This breakdown is helpful to determine if there is poor performance on the server-side processing or perhaps some network congestion is slowing down the operation. If you dig deeper into the Performance tab, you will find a breakdown per API name, which you learned about on the Overview tab. For example, there are performance measurements for `PutBlob`, `ReadFile`, `DeleteFile`, and `GetBlob`, which is very helpful to get very deep into the product and find specifically where any performance issue is happening. The Availability tab provides an overview of any downtime experienced by the platform or by the product itself. The Capacity tab displays the amount of space consumed by each product within the Azure storage account. Each tab provides a graphic representation of the numbers, thereby delivering a more understandable state over the given duration.

FIGURE 9.8 A summary of the Azure Storage Account Insights blade

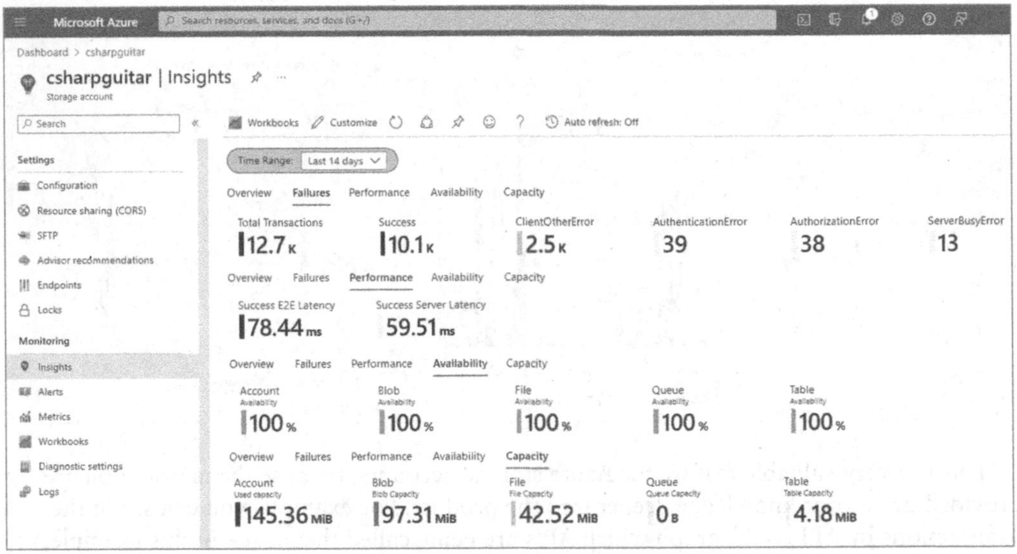

Another feature currently available to Azure storage accounts is something called Workbooks. As previously mentioned, Application Insights is an SDK that is coded into the product code, whereas the Workbooks capacity is an interface to configure the logging data published from within the Azure Storage product code. As shown in Figure 9.9, there are insights that match the tabs on the Insights blade and which you can customize to exactly what you need. You can also build a completely custom workbook that opens to a blank canvas, with options to add insights, queries, metrics, and much more.

The Alerts blade, in the context of an Azure storage account, provides access to conditions that are similar to the metrics shown in Figure 9.8—for example, availability, end-to-end latency, transactions, and used capacity. The Metrics blade renders options to target the storage account, blob, queue, files, or tables. The associated metrics are then grouped into two categories, capacity and transactions. Blob capacity, blob count, and blob container count are a few examples of available capacity metrics. The metrics available for the transactions category are the same as those on the Alerts blade and the Insights blade—specifically, availability, end-to-end latency, server latency, and transactions. Additionally, the Diagnostic Settings blade provides the option to target the account, blob, queue, table, or file feature directly. The Diagnostic Settings blade enables you to capture data from the `StorageRead`, `StorageWrite`, `StorageDelete`, and `Transaction` logs. When the diagnostic settings are configured, they are targeted to be stored in Log Analytics, and you can query those logs using Kusto queries in the Azure portal. Columns like `OperationName`, `StatusCode`, `StatusText`, `DurationMs`, `ServerLatencyMs`, `RequestBodySize`, and `Uri` are helpful to gather operational information about your solution.

FIGURE 9.9 Azure storage account Workbooks

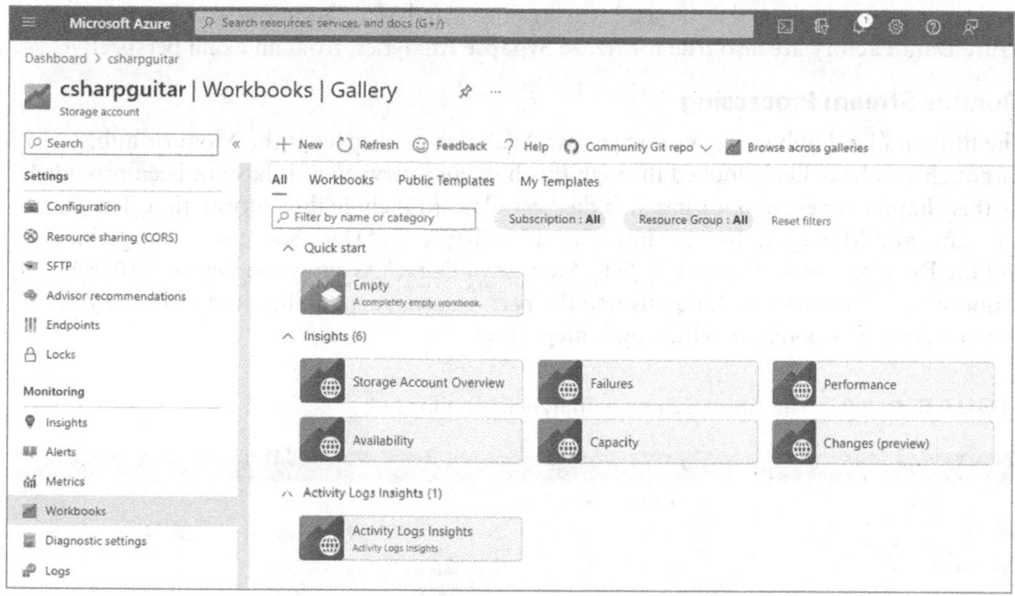

The following is example of a Kusto query that will retrieve 100 of the most recent Azure Storage blob logs:

```
StorageBlobLogs
| project TimeGenerated, OperationName, StatusCode, StatusText, DurationMs,
          ServerLatencyMs, RequestBodySize, Uri
| take 100
| order by TimeGenerated
```

The extracted data is also useful in case of errors or reliability issues, as the logs can be used to surface which operations failed, when, and what the operation was trying to do. (For more information about troubleshooting, see Chapter 10, "Troubleshoot Data Storage

Processing.") You do not need to directly navigate to the Log Analytics workspace you created in Exercise 8.4; instead, you can select the Logs link from the navigation menu while in the Azure storage account context. In this case, your scope is constrained to Azure Storage accounts. If you want to extract logs from different types of products using the same Log Analytics interface, then use the workspace you created in Exercise 8.4.

Azure Synapse Analytics

The DP-203 exam includes many questions that target Azure Data Factory. Currently, most new features are being deployed into the Azure Synapse Analytics workspace, and all of the capabilities that exist in Azure Data Factory are also present in Azure Synapse Analytics, unless otherwise stated. The following content, for the purpose of the DP-203 exam, can be used to answer questions that target Azure Synapse Analytics. Questions that are true for Azure Data Factory are also true for Azure Synapse Analytics, from an exam perspective.

Monitor Stream Processing

The fifth and final hub in the Azure Synapse Analytics workspace is the Monitor hub. Although you have likely looked through this hub, an overview of it has not been provided. As this chapter covers monitoring, it is the best place to include this information. The Data, Integrate, and Manage hubs were introduced in Chapter 3, "Data Sources and Ingestion," and the Develop hub in Chapter 4, "The Storage of Data." As shown in Figure 9.10, the Monitor hub provides logs for analyzing the performance, availability, and status of your Synapse Analytics pools, activities, and integration.

FIGURE 9.10 The Azure Synapse Analytics Monitor hub

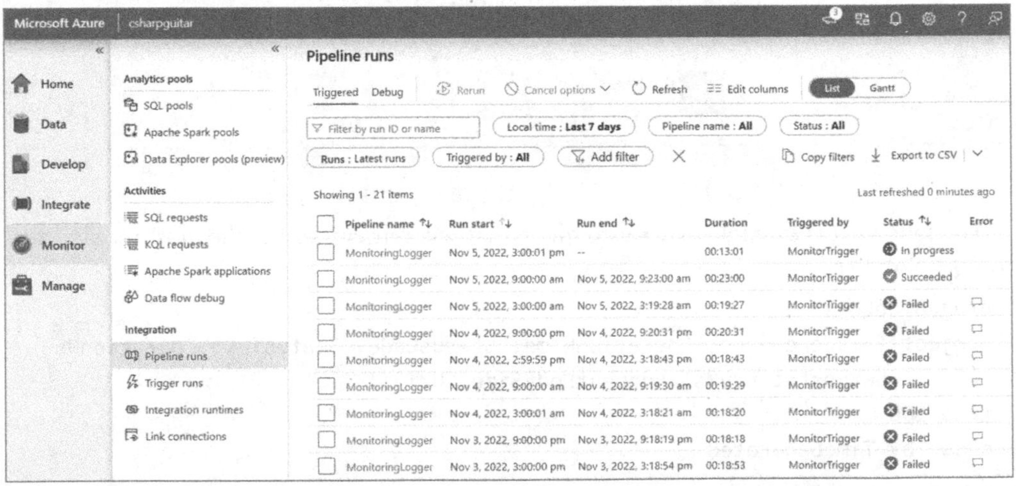

The following sections discuss the logging features on the Monitor hub in the Azure Synapse Analytics workspace.

ANALYTICS POOLS

The information in the Analytics Pools section targets the compute component of your workspace solution, including measurements such as CPU, memory, and compute size.

SQL POOLS

The SQL Pools section includes information about your built-in (aka serverless) SQL pool and your dedicated SQL pool(s), including the version, status, size, CPU utilization percentage, and memory utilization percentage. When you select a specific SQL pool, you are provided with a more granular peek at the SQL pool, for example, a historical view of DWU consumption and a line graph of active requests over a chosen timeframe.

APACHE SPARK POOLS

The same principle goes for Spark pools in that the initial page renders a report of all the Spark pools you have provisioned on the workspace. The Spark pool size, number of allocated vCores, and memory are also rendered on the main page per Spark pool. You can drill into additional history consumption and activity details of a specific Spark pool by selecting the desired Spark pool.

DATA EXPLORER POOLS

The Data Explorer Pools page, like the provisioning of a Data Explorer pool, is in preview. These pools are used for analyzing data stored on an Azure Data Explorer (ADE) cluster. Using KQL, you query, transform, and gather insights from the data. An overview of all Data Explorer pools is displayed on this page. Click a specific pool to see its details.

ACTIVITIES

The information in the Activities section provides some insights into the actions taking place on the analytics pools.

SQL REQUESTS

Queries run on your SQL pools are logged and can be viewed on the SQL Requests page. The page includes the SQL query itself, when it was run, how long it took, who submitted the query, and whether it was successfully executed. Sorting the output by status or duration can be a good starting point for troubleshooting any irregularities reported or experienced during a pipeline execution.

KQL REQUESTS

The KQL Request page provides the same content as the SQL Requests page.

APACHE SPARK APPLICATIONS

The Apache Spark Applications page was discussed in Chapter 6, "Create and Manage Batch Processing and Pipelines." Figure 6.14 illustrates the details of an invocation of a Spark notebook. The detail page provides a list of Spark sessions and batch jobs. The Spark session is the context in which the Spark notebook executes. You would expect to see the notebook name prepended to the invocation name. A batch job in this context is the platform feature that starts the Spark pool on demand. This is a great feature that saves costs because it removes the need to have your Spark pool running between pipeline runs. As a reminder, notebooks that run on Spark pools can be written in PySpark, Scala, .NET Spark (C#), Spark SQL and Spark R.

DATA FLOW DEBUG

The Data Flow Debug page renders details about active data flow debug sessions. Recall from Exercise 4.8, where you created your first data flow, the step to enable Data Flow Debug (refer to Figure 4.23). The details on this page identify who has created the debug session, how long the session will remain active, the compute type, number of allocated cores, and the bound integration runtime.

INTEGRATION

The Integration section contains information about items that typically have high concurrent connectivity with other products, features, and data sources operating in the workspace.

PIPELINE RUNS

The Pipeline Runs page (refer to Figure 9.10) is the default page when you access the Monitor hub. The page contains the name of the pipeline, the duration, what triggered it, its status, and any existing error details. This is a very helpful page to get an overview of how your pipelines are performing. When you select a pipeline run from the list, you will see details for each activity within the pipeline, for example, the activity name, type, when it started, duration, and status. If the pipeline execution is performing more slowly than expected, these details will be helpful to determine which specific activity is taking the most time.

TRIGGER RUNS

Triggers are what invoke a pipeline. In the example shown in Figure 9.10, the trigger name is `MonitorTrigger`, which triggers the pipeline named `MonitoringLogger`. Use the Trigger Runs page to gather details about the trigger type, the trigger status, and the number of pipelines it triggers for this and all the triggers on the workspace.

INTEGRATION RUNTIMES

An integration runtime (IR) is a compute resource that is used to help debug, run pipelines, manage data flow, test connectivity of linked services, and run SISS packages. The Integration Runtimes page lists all your IR. Additional details about an IR are available on the Details page. As shown in Figure 9.11, you also can find valuable information from the Activities page.

The pipeline name, activity name, activity type, duration, and status are all very valuable pieces of information when you are trying to discover how your data analytics solution is performing. Failures and long-running activities are good places to start when the solution is not running as expected.

FIGURE 9.11 Azure Synapse Analytics integration runtimes

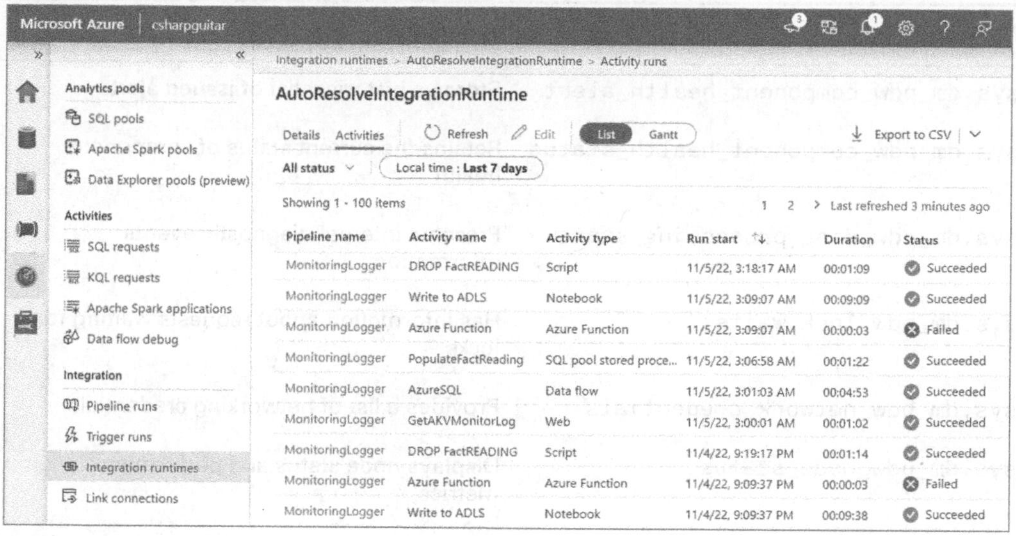

LINK CONNECTIONS

As of this writing, link connections are in preview. They are currently supported only with Azure SQL database and SQL server. When either of those datastores is linked with a dedicated SQL pool, the operational data from the source database is automatically replicated to the SQL pool. Once the operational data is in the Azure Synapse Analytics workspace, you can perform analytics on it and gather business insights from it.

System Dynamic Management Views

Chapter 2, "CREATE DATABASE dbName; GO," introduced Database Console Commands (DBCC), which have database-scoped dynamic management views (DMVs). Platform system dynamic management views (PDW) have a server scope, which, as the name implies, is focused on the health of the server the database is running on. Although PDWs and DMVs have different names and scope, their purpose is to provide useful information for tuning performance and diagnosing problems on dedicated SQL pools. There are many PDW and DMV functions, which are broken into categories such as Change Tracking, Database, Execution, I/O, and Transactions. The category most relevant in this context is Azure Synapse Analytics & Parallel Warehouse. Table 9.2 provides many of the PDW and DMV functions in this category, plus a few noteworthy functions for monitoring Azure Synapse Analytics workspace features.

TABLE 9.2 Synapse platform system dynamic management views

Name	Description
sys.dm_pdw_component_health_alert	Stores a historical list of issued alerts
sys.dm_pdw_component_health_status	Retains the current status of component health
sys.dm_pdw_diag_processing_stats	Presents internal diagnostic events information
sys.dm_pdw_lock_waits	Has information about requests waiting for locks
sys.dm_pdw_network_credentials	Provides a list of networking credentials
sys.dm_pdw_node_status	Displays node status and performance metrics
sys.dm_pdw_nodes	Renders a list of nodes in the workspace
sys.dm_pdw_os_event_logs	Contains Windows Event logs per node
sys.dm_pdw_os_performance_counters	Has Windows performance counters per node
sys.dm_pdw_os_threads	Shows a list of and details about threads per node
sys.dm_pdw_resource_waits	Lists wait information for workspace resources
sys.dm_pdw_sys_info	Presents application-level activity counters
sys.dm_pdw_wait_stats	Shows node wait states for queries and requests
sys.dm_pdw_waits	Lists wait states for queries, requests, and locks
sys.dm_tran_active_transactions	Displays SQL Server-level transaction details
sys.dm_tran_current_transaction	Returns transaction-specific details
sys.dm_tran_database_transactions	Displays database-level transaction details
sys.dm_tran_locks	Presents the active lock manager status

Name	Description
sys.dm_pdw_errors	Provides query or request execution error details
sys.dm_pdw_exec_requests	Provides current and recent request information
sys.dm_pdw_exec_sessions	Lists current and recently open sessions
sys.dm_pdw_request_steps	Lists steps that make up a request or query
sys.dm_pdw_sql_requests	Stores query distributions as part of SQL steps

Because they are based on internal and implementation specific data, these DMVs and functions change often. Therefore, you should not create any application dependency on them. Additionally, you must recognize that they depend directly on the software versions the product is running on, where "software versions" implies the entire stack, from the operating system to the source code library performing the operations. This means that you can expect a great variety of function availability and rendered output. To be successful in this area, you must be flexible and skilled at operational data interpretation and the configuration of DBMS management components. The following are a few examples of DMV output, beginning with `sys.dm_pdw_nodes`. These functions can be executed within a SQL script that targets a dedicated SQL pool within your Azure Synapse Analytics workspace. The output followed by the TSQL that generates it contains the node ID, type, name, and passive state:

```
SELECT TOP 10 * FROM sys.dm_pdw_nodes

+-------------+---------+-------+------------+
| pdw_node_id | type    | name  | is_passive |
+-------------+---------+-------+------------+
| 17          | CONTROL | DB.17 | False      |
| 17          | CONTROL | DB.17 | False      |
+-------------+---------+-------+------------+
```

The following DMV renders a list of current and recent threads per node:

```
SELECT TOP 10 * FROM sys.dm_pdw_os_threads

+-------------+-----------+------------+-------+--------------+----------------+
| pdw_node_id | thread_id | process_id | state | wait_reson   | processor_time |
+-------------+-----------+------------+-------+--------------+----------------+
| 17          | 66792     | 31384      | Wait  | EventPairLow | 16             |
| 17          | 49240     | 31384      | Wait  | EventPairLow | 94             |
```

```
| 17          | 44924    | 31384    | Wait  | UserRequest  | 266            |
| 17          | 50184    | 31384    | Wait  | UserRequest  | 16             |
| 17          | 53508    | 31384    | Wait  | UserRequest  | 719            |
+-------------+----------+----------+-------+--------------+----------------+
```

The following DMV renders information about what requests and queries wait on most during execution:

```
SELECT TOP 10 * FROM sys.dm_pdw_wait_stats

+-------------+------------------------+---------------+---------------+
| pdw_node_id | wait_name              | max_wait_time | request_count |
+-------------+------------------------+---------------+---------------+
| 17          | CLR_MANUAL_EVENT       | 5066          | 279920        |
| 17          | SLEEP_TASK             | 12015         | 47957         |
| 17          | MEMORY_ALLOCATION_EXT  | 19            | 25449         |
| 17          | SOS_WORK_DISPATCHER    | 1063756       | 13818         |
| 17          | CLR_TASK_START         | 81            | 7062          |
+-------------+------------------------+---------------+---------------+
```

The following DMV lists information about active, idle, and closed sessions:

```
SELECT TOP 10 * FROM sys.dm_pdw_exec_sessions

+------------+--------+------------+--------------+-------------+----------+
| session_id | status | request_id | login_name   | query_count | sql_spid |
+------------+--------+------------+--------------+-------------+----------+
| SID3715    | Idle   | (NULL)     | System       | 197         | 174      |
| SID3813    | Active | QID45537   | benperk      | 4           | 114      |
| SID3712    | Closed | (NULL)     | benperk      | 2           | 2262     |
| SID3809    | Idle   | (NULL)     | sqladminuser | 18          | 119      |
+------------+--------+------------+--------------+-------------+----------+
```

Using the `session_id` from the previous output, you can execute the following query to find the four queries that were executed:

```
SELECT * FROM sys.dm_pdw_exec_requests where session_id = 'SID3813'

+------------+-----------+-------------+-------+-----------------------------------+
| request_id | status    | elapse_time | db_id | command                           |
+------------+-----------+-------------+-------+-----------------------------------+
| QID45534   | Completed | 15          | 8     | SELECT TOP 10 * FROM sys.dm_pdw* |
| QID45535   | Completed | 31          | 8     | SELECT TOP 10 * FROM sys.dm_pdw* |
| QID45536   | Completed | 15          | 8     | SELECT TOP 10 * FROM sys.dm_pdw* |
| QID45537   | Completed | 62          | 8     | SELECT TOP 10 * FROM sys.dm_pdw* |
+------------+-----------+-------------+-------+-----------------------------------+
```

Using the request_id from the previous output, you can execute the following query and look through the steps that took place to execute the SQL statement:

```
SELECT * FROM sys.dm_pdw_sql_requests where request_id = 'QID45537'

+------------+------------+-------------+------+------------------+
| request_id | step_index | pdw_node_id | spid | command          |
+------------+------------+-------------+------+------------------+
| QID45537   | 0          | 17          | 114  | BEGIN TRY IF 0 ... |
| QID45537   | 1          | 17          | 114  | CREATE TABLE [ ... |
| QID45537   | 2          | 17          | 114  | SELECT [T1_1.[ ... |
| QID45537   | 3          | 17          | 114  | DROP TABLE [t. ... |
+------------+------------+-------------+------+------------------+
```

The previous DMV functions target the SQLPool database, which means they were focused on the database. The following functions target the master database on the dedicated SQL pool, which means the results will contain data related to all databases hosted on the targeted pool. A large set of performance counters can be accessed using the DMV function named sys.dm_os_performance_counters. Execute the following to get a list of available Windows performance counters:

```
SELECT DISTINCT counter_name
FROM sys.dm_os_performance_counters
ORDER BY counter_name
```

The last DMV function to be called out is useful for monitoring database transactions like rollback, commits, save points, status, and state:

```
SELECT TOP 10 * FROM sys.dm_tran_database_transactions
```

A column named database_transaction_state will contain a number that describes the state of the transaction. Table 9.3 describes the potential numbers.

TABLE 9.3 database_transaction_state column description

Value	Description
1	The transaction has not yet been initialized.
3	The transaction is initialized but has not generated logs.
4	The transaction has generated logs.
5	The transaction is prepared.
10	The transaction has been committed.
11	The transaction has been rolled back.
12	The transaction is being committed.

A lot of documentation about the meaning of the values in the columns returned by many of these functions is available online. You can find search for the functions at `https://learn.microsoft.com`. In-depth coverage of these functions and column values is outside the scope of this book, but you do not need to know much about them for the exam. In true operational use, not only do you need to know what these column values mean, but you must also know if they represent a scenario that is considered an anomaly, which you can learn only through hands-on experience with the application itself. There is a lot to learn in this area, requiring much experience, so keep learning and doing, starting with the Exercise 9.3. To attain insights from Exercise 9.3, there needs to be monitor log data to analyze. As you saw in Figure 9.10, the pipeline being monitored was named `MonitoringLogger`. This pipeline was pulled together using activities from many previous exercises and is illustrated in Figure 9.12.

FIGURE 9.12 An Azure Synapse Analytics sample pipeline to generate monitor logs

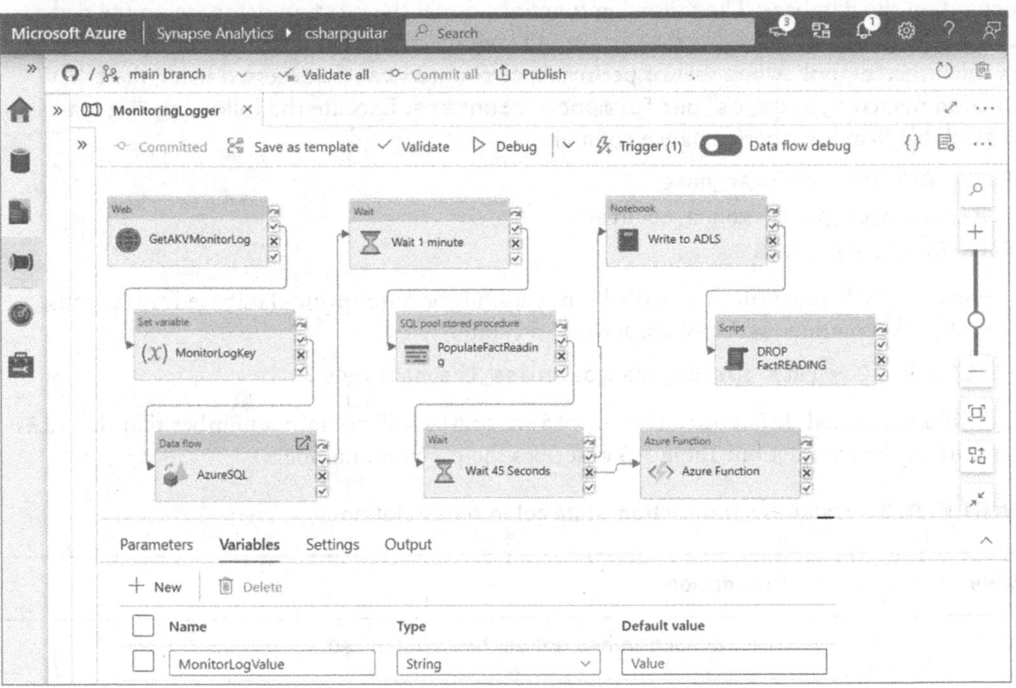

The export of the pipeline is in the `Chapter09` directory on GitHub, in the file `MonitoringLogger.json`. It is provided to give you some idea of what was used to generate the logs in this exercise. After about a week of running the pipeline 4 times per day, every 6 hours, there was enough data to find some operational insights. You might consider creating a sample pipeline and letting it run for some time before beginning this exercise, to ensure that you have some logs to look at.

EXERCISE 9.3

Monitor and Manage Azure Synapse Analytics Logs

1. Log in to the Azure portal at `https://portal.azure.com` > navigate to the Azure Synapse Analytics workspace you created in Exercise 3.3 > select the pipeline you created to generate usage logs > select the Properties icon (refer to Figure 6.68) > enter an annotation (I used **Monitoring**) > and then commit and publish the pipeline.
2. After numerous pipeline trigger invocations, navigate to the Monitor hub > select Pipeline Runs from the Integration section > choose the Edit Columns menu item > move the Annotations column to the second position > and then click OK.
3. Click the Add Filter button > select Annotations from the drop-down list box > and then select an annotation group filter for grouping your pipeline runs, as shown in Figure 9.13.

FIGURE 9.13 Azure Synapse Analytics pipeline runs filtered by annotations

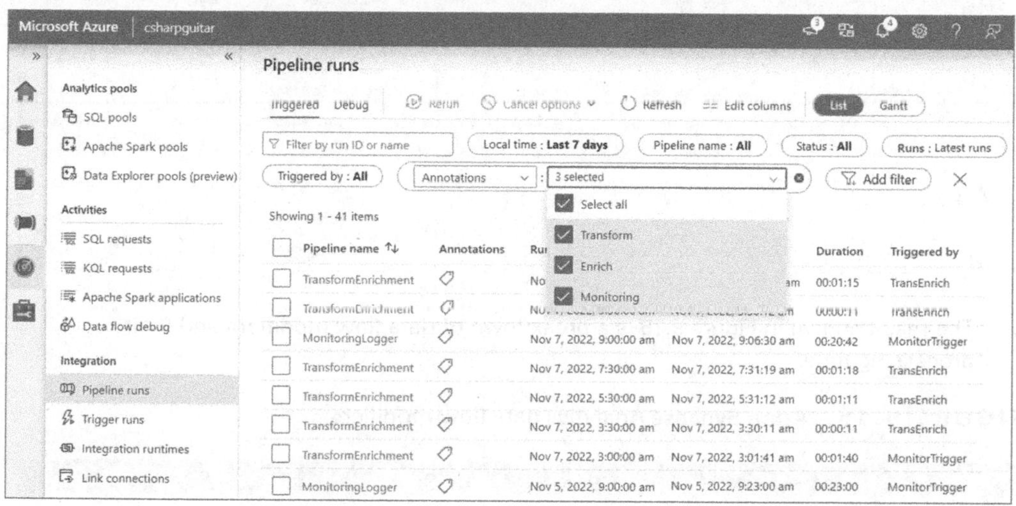

4. Select one of the pipeline runs from the list in the Activity Runs section. You will see a breakdown of the duration of each activity within the pipeline. If your pipeline has a Data Flow activity, hover over it and click the glasses, as shown in Figure 9.14.

EXERCISE 9.3 *(continued)*

FIGURE 9.14 Azure Synapse Analytics activity runs

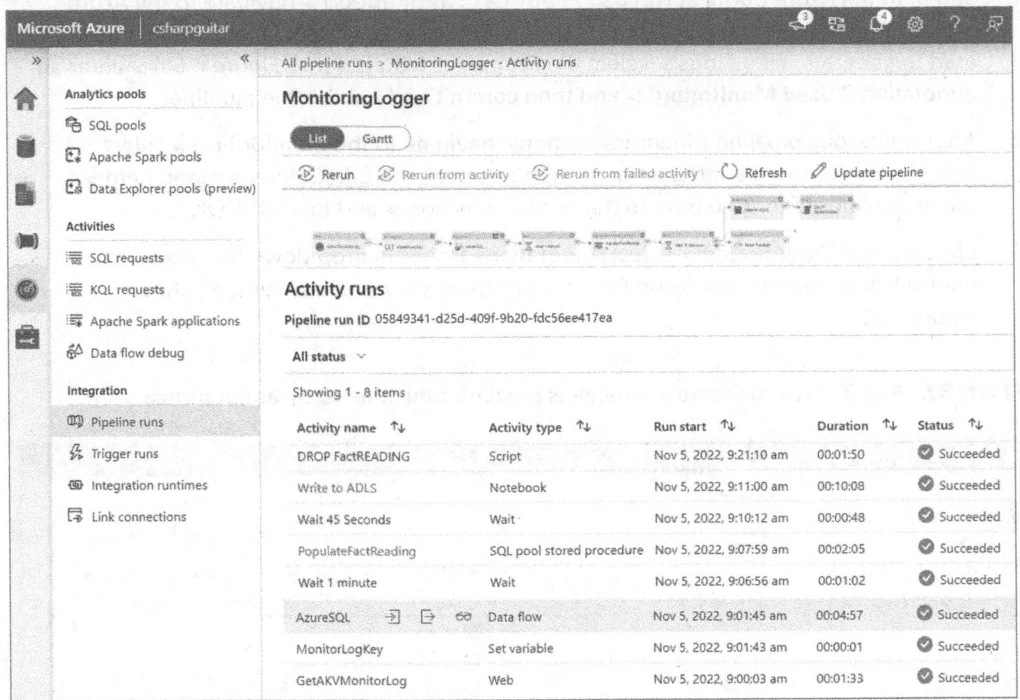

5. The result shown in Figure 9.15 is a breakdown of data flow modifiers and their processing time.

FIGURE 9.15 Azure Synapse Analytics data flow modifiers

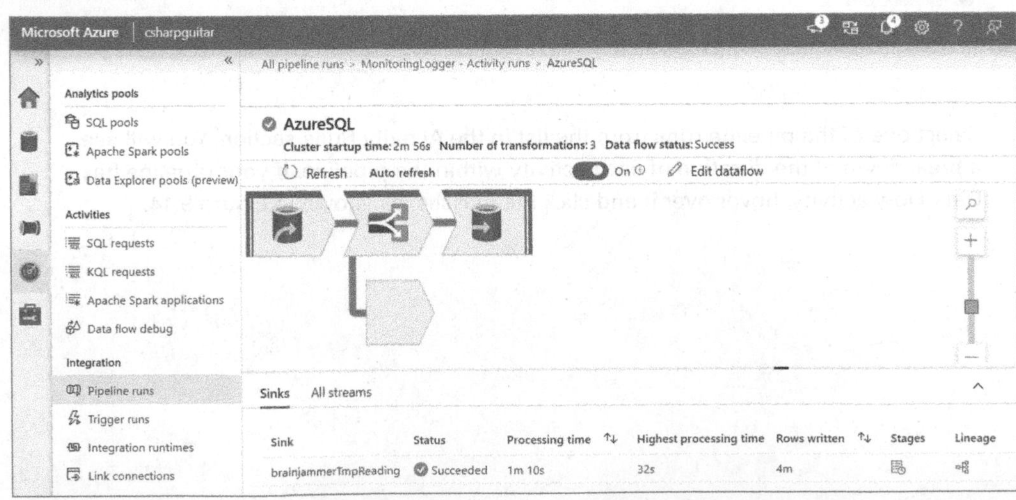

6. An activity in the pipeline executed a notebook on a Spark pool. As shown in Figure 9.14, the activity is named Write to ADLS. Click the activity name to view the log of that execution. You will see something similar to Figure 9.16.

FIGURE 9.16 Azure Synapse Analytics Apache Spark applications

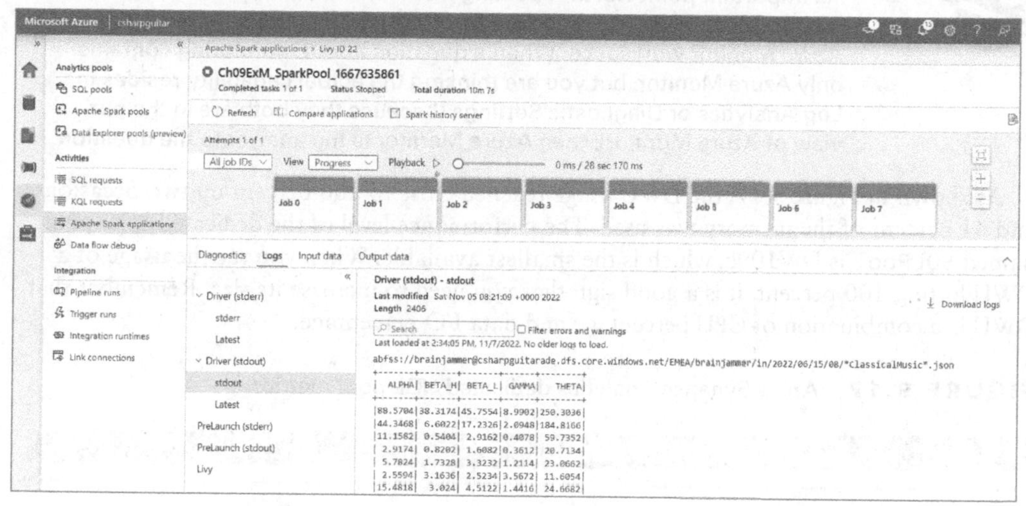

Exercise 9.3 is intended to provide you with steps to navigate through pipeline monitoring features available in the Azure Synapse Analytics workspace. The features depend on the pipeline and the activities that run within it; for example, you will see Data Flow and Notebook log details only if there are Data Flow and Notebook activities in the pipeline. The first step in the exercise was to add an annotation to a pipeline introduced in Chapter 6. Adding an annotation to your pipeline properties is a good habit, because it is a value that can be used to filter out or group together related runs on the Pipeline Runs page. You saw the duration value for each pipeline run, which represents the amount of time it took to complete all pipeline activities. When you select the pipeline name, you are presented with a more granular view of the activities within the pipeline and the duration on a per-activity basis. You can drill further into the Data Flow and Notebook activities to show the amount of time per modifier. From a notebook perspective, there are stderr logs, stdout logs, and job-by-job details, including duration.

In addition to the monitoring capabilities within the Azure Synapse Analytics workspace, there are the standard monitoring features in the Azure portal. You will recognize them as Alerts, Metrics, Diagnostics, and Logs. The Alerts feature, in the context of an Azure Synapse Analytics workspace, provides access to conditions like what you saw in Figure 9.5 and in Exercise 9.2. Additional examples include login attempts, activity runs ended, link connection events, link latency, and trigger runs ended. The Metrics feature at the Azure Synapse Analytics workspace level are categorized into groups concerning the serverless SQL pool, for example, the amount of processed data in bytes, pipeline, linked services, and streaming. You can find greater insights into dedicated SQL or Spark pools on the respective Metrics blade.

An important point worth repeating from an exam perspective is that all monitoring tools are approached from the context and perspective of the Azure Monitor workspace. When a question about monitoring contains only Azure Monitor, but you are thinking the actual capability resides in Log Analytics or Diagnostic Settings (because they both are in the purview of Azure Monitor), then Azure Monitor is the answer to the question.

As shown in Figure 9.17, the DWU usage reached close to 100 percent on two occasions, and 41 percent of the memory was used. The performance level of the dedicated SQL pool named `SQLPool` is DW100c, which is the smallest available. When you see the usage of a DWU hitting 100 percent, it is a good sign that you need to increase its size. Remember that DWU is a combination of CPU percentage and data I/O percentage.

FIGURE 9.17 Azure Synapse Analytics dedicated SQL pool metrics

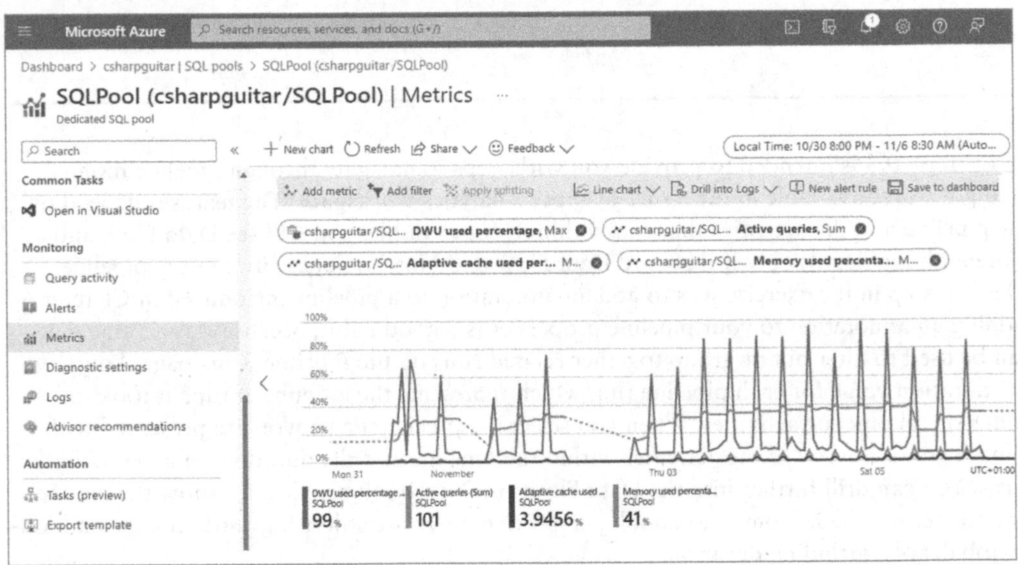

Another useful metric for measuring performance is the Adaptive Cache Used Percentage. When your data is cached in memory, a query does not need to access a data source or file, which is an I/O operation, to retrieve data. It is much faster to retrieve data from memory than from disk. Therefore, a cache hit value of 3.9 percent may not be optimal. If you need to improve performance, you can dig deeper into the active queries to determine if something can be done to improve caching. Apache Spark pools offer metrics on vCore and memory allocations. If you see that those values are nearing 100 percent, then an upgrade would be recommended. Refer to Table 9.3 for the different node sizes for Apache Spark pools. Some examples of data logged by the diagnostics settings targeting the Azure Synapse Analytics workspace include Synapse RBAC Operations, Built-in Pool Requests Ended, and Integration Pipeline, Activity, and Trigger Runs. Targeting the storage of these diagnostics settings to a Log Analytics cluster, you can query the data using a query similar to the following:

```
SynapseIntegrationPipelineRuns
| project TimeGenerated, PipelineName, Annotations, OperationName, Level,
   Status
| take 100
| order by TimeGenerated
```

The result of this query provides some insights into the status, result, and frequency of your pipeline runs. In isolation this data would provide a limited view of what is happening in your data analytics solution. Combining queries from multiple tables and across multiple products can result in great operational insights. For example, if a pipeline run fails, you can include data from the `SynapseIntegrationActivityRuns` table and the `StorageBlobLogs` table to see how the transaction flowed across products as well as tables.

The final topic for this section has to do with troubleshooting PolyBase issues. This is very often in the context of the serverless SQL pools and external tables. Numerous DMVs can be used and typically include the word *external*. A few of them are provided in Table 9.4.

TABLE 9.4 DMVs for troubleshooting PolyBase

Name	Description
`sys.dm_exec_external_work`	Lists communications with external sources
`sys.dm_exec_external_operations`	Lists operational details about PolyBase
`sys.external_tables`	Lists external tables in the database
`sys.external_data_sources`	Lists external data sources in the database
`sys.external_file_formats`	Lists each external file format
`sys.dm_exec_distributed_requests`	Lists details about both the current PolyBase query and recent queries

You can use the `sys.dm_exec_distributed_requests` DMV in a query to find the execution ID of the longest-running query, as follows:

```
SELECT execution_id, est.text, edr.total_elapsed_time
FROM sys.dm_exec_distributed_requests  edr
     cross apply sys.dm_exec_sql_text(sql_handle) est
ORDER BY total_elapsed_time DESC;
```

The result comes in handy if you are experiencing performance issues related to PolyBase and external tables. The result will provide the ID of the query that is taking the longest. Then you can perform more analysis to find the steps and commands that are being optimized and find ways to improve them.

Azure Stream Analytics

The same monitoring-related features exist for Azure Stream Analytics as for other Azure products: alert rules, metrics, diagnostic settings, and logs. In addition to those, Azure Stream Analytics has a feature you might want to know about called the *job diagram*. Although this feature is currently in preview, it can give you an overall perspective of your job. As shown in Figure 9.18, you can view the input, the objects into which data is stored within the query, and the outputs. You can view numerous metrics and activity logs for the job or any of the steps that make up the job by selecting the step from the drop-down list box that is currently set to Jobs.

FIGURE 9.18 Azure Stream Analytics job diagram

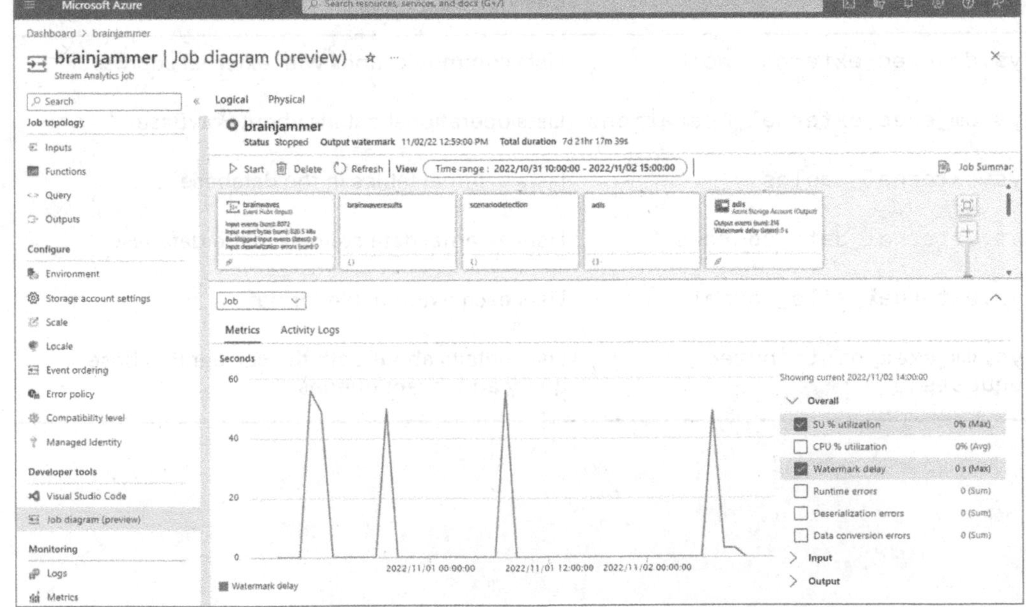

Alert rule conditions that target events for an Azure Stream Analytics job are plentiful, for example, function events, out of order events, early input events, input events, and late input events. Additionally, conditions can be triggered based on watermark delay or CPU and SU percent consumption, both of which are useful for determining if more capacity is needed. Metrics, as previously noted, provide a link directly to the Alert Rules blade, which will use the condition exposed in the configured metrics feature, as shown in Figure 9.19. Metrics are also helpful to learn how two or more metrics relate to each other. As shown in Figure 9.19, CPU % Utilization has a direct correlation with Watermark Delay.

FIGURE 9.19 The Azure Stream Analytics Metrics hub

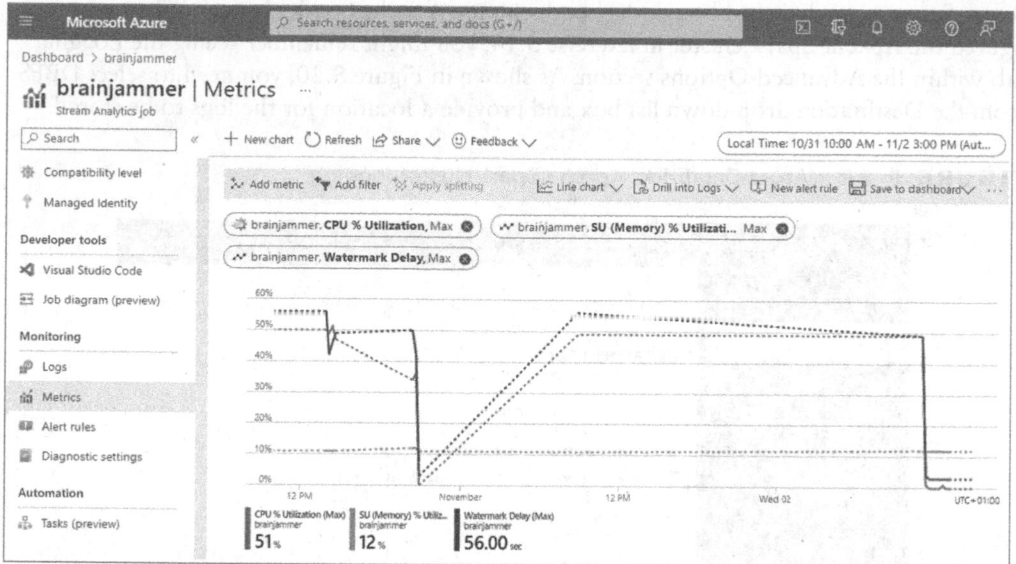

When diagnostic settings are configured, you can log execution, authoring, and metrics into a Log Analytics workspace, storage account, event hub, or a custom third-party solution. The storage options for diagnostic settings data are the same for all Azure products. When targeting a Log Analytics workspace, you can execute a Kusto query like the following to gather information about errors:

```
AzureActivity
| project TimeGenerated, CategoryValue, Level, OperationNameValue,
      ActivityStatusValue, Properties
| where Level == 'Error'
| take 100
| order by TimeGenerate
```

The result of this query is useful for troubleshooting any job or activity failures. Additionally, more complex queries can be run from the Log Analytics workspace directly and can be configured to span across all the products that make up your data analytics solution. If you are experiencing problems and cannot find an issue when targeting one specific product, then expanding the search to dependencies is the next step in debugging the issue.

Azure Databricks

The "Azure Synapse Analytics" section described the logging of the execution of a notebook on an Apache Spark cluster (refer to Figure 9.16). In Chapter 3, Exercise 3.14, you provisioned an Apache Spark cluster that runs in the context of Azure Databricks and not Azure Synapse Analytics, although they both can use Apache Spark clusters. When you configured the Apache Spark cluster in Exercise 3.14, you might remember seeing the Logging tab within the Advanced Options section. As shown in Figure 9.20, you need to select DBFS from the Destination drop-down list box and provide a location for the logs to be stored.

FIGURE 9.20 Azure Databricks Apache Spark cluster logging

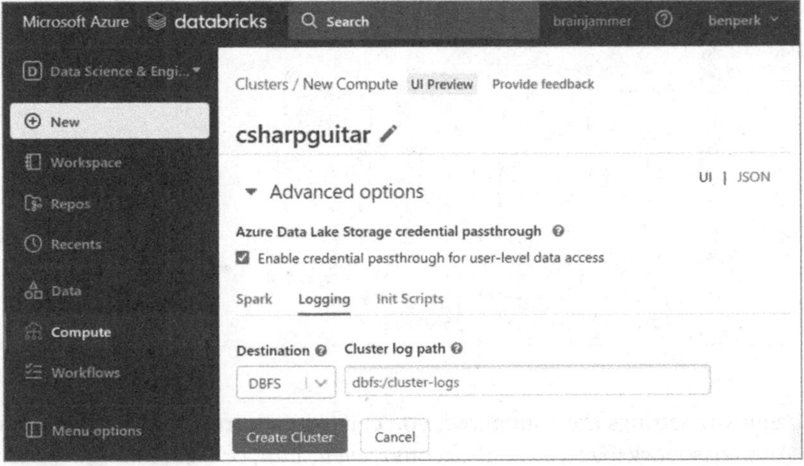

Alert rules, Metrics, and Log do not render on the Azure Databricks page in the Azure portal. The only available monitoring feature is Diagnostic settings. Currently, 25 different categories of logs can be stored, including DatabricksClusters, DatabricksJobs, DatabricksNotebooks, DatabricksWorkspace, DatabricksPools, and DatabricksPipelines. As there is no Logs navigation item currently for Azure Databricks, you will need to navigate to the Log Analytics workspace that you configured to store the Diagnostic settings log for. The following Kusto query will provide a list of notebook operations, along with their status:

```
DatabricksNotebook
| project TimeGenerated, OperationName, Category, ActionName, Response
| take 100
| order by TimeGenerated
```

There are a few open-source libraries you can configure to ingest Azure Databricks logs directly into Azure Monitor, for example, log4j, Azure Databricks Monitoring Library, and Dropwizard. However, the configuration and implementation of those solutions are outside the scope of this book. Finally, there is a metrics tab in the Azure Databricks workspace that resembles Figure 9.21.

FIGURE 9.21 Azure Databricks cluster metrics

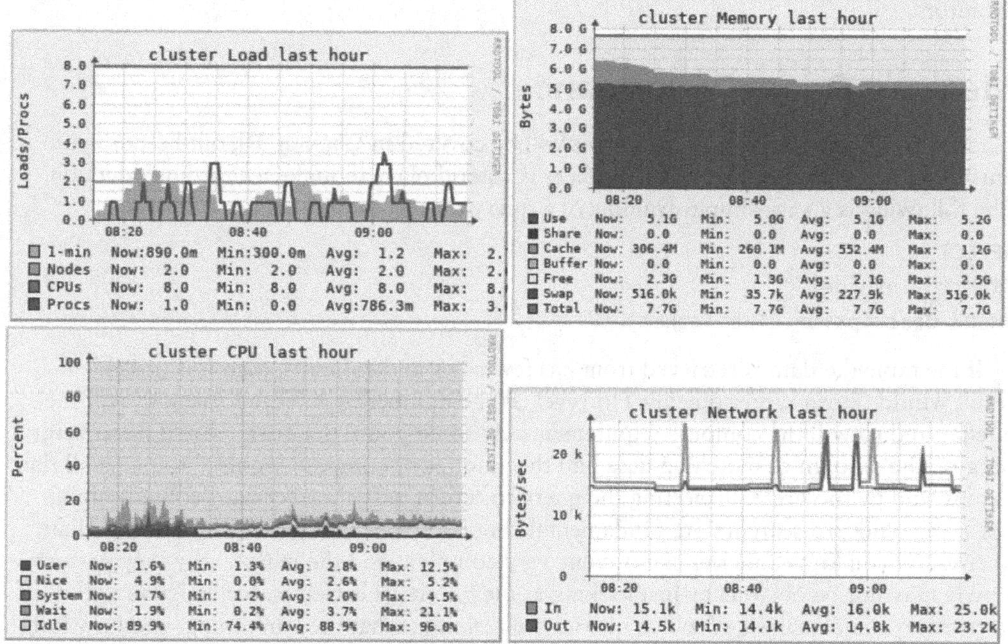

The metrics are helpful to determine the consumption of CPU and memory on the cluster. There is also a metric that shows network utilization.

Understand Custom Logging Options

As you now know, there are many built-in monitoring logs you can configure to feed into Azure Monitor using Log Analytics. All the categories within each Azure product's diagnostic settings and many of the metric values feed automatically into Azure Monitor once configured to do so. Many other logs are helpful when it comes to supporting and troubleshooting IT solutions, for example, IIS logs, Event Tracing for Windows (ETW), and Windows and Linux performance logs. In addition to those known monitor log types, your application may create custom logs that are unique. To ingest known monitor logs like IIS and ETW, you need to install an Azure Monitor extension onto the machine that generates the logs. This is like an agent, service, or listener that binds to the monitor event pipeline, captures the logs, and copies them in Azure Monitor for analysis through Log Analytics queries.

Custom logs require some configuration in the Azure portal. From the Log Analytics workspace where you want the custom log to be uploaded, you navigate to the Custom Logs blade. There is a wizard that walks you through the configuration of your sample log file. Part of the configuration requires that you identify where this file is hosted on the machine running the Azure Monitor extension so that the agent can access it and send it to Azure Monitor.

Measure Query Performance

Most of the performance-related content will be covered in Chapter 10, but because you must have logs and metrics to analyze, here is a good place to make a short introduction. The following is a very simple example of a query that would not be performant:

```
SELECT *
FROM theInternet
WHERE description LIKE '%the%'
```

If the table the data is retrieved from has few rows and columns, then it is possible a result would return rather quickly. However, as the number of rows increases, so will the latency and so will the compute requirements. At some point, the query would never return, because the amount of matching data and the amount of compute required to parse all the data would be too great. Projecting the query to return only the necessary columns and not using wildcard searches are fundamental characteristics that pertain to writing reliant queries. As you know, queries can become very complex, and the reason why they perform slowly may not be obvious by just looking at the queries themselves. Instead, you will need to perform some analysis of which queries are running, what they are doing, and how long they are taking. There are two areas to review when you need to determine how queries running on a dedicated SQL pool are performing: Azure Monitor metrics and DMVs.

Figure 9.17 showed dedicated SQL pool metrics that can have some impact on the performance of query execution: Adaptive Cache Used Percentage and Adaptive Cache Hit Percentage, which is also of value in this context. Each metric determines how optimally the workloads are using adaptive cache. Adaptive cache on dedicated SQL pools is stored on local SSDs, and the used percentage value represents the amount used across all nodes. The Adaptive Cache Hit Percentage pertains to the sum of all hits on clustered column store indexes across all nodes. As previously explained, pulling queried data from memory and/or SSDs is much more performant than from hard disk. That means if you can write queries in a way that uses data cached in memory, the queries will execute faster. Also, depending on where you execute the queries from, there may be a product that helps you customize caching behaviors of your data analytics solution. The other option for measuring query performance is from a feature already discussed: DMVs. For example, you can use the `sys.dm_pdw_exec_requests` DMV to identify the queries that might need some investigation. Once you find that list, you can use the `sys.dm_pdw_request_steps` DMV to identify the execution plan or steps that the query performs to complete the operation. Looking into each step will help you find the specific step or group of steps causing the most latency. Then you can take a deeper look into them and recommend some optimization activities. Finally, deadlocks or hangs might occur when you have multiple queries that share a resource or excessive queuing. The `sys.dm_pdw_waits` DMV enables you to identify which queries are impacted by either of those scenarios.

Monitor Data Pipeline Performance

There are numerous options for determining the performance of pipelines running on your Azure Synapse Analytics dedicated SQL pool. Two that are very useful are Metrics and the Monitor hub Pipeline Runs page. Metrics related to Azure Synapse Analytics are available both for the workspace and for each dedicated SQL pool. From a workspace perspective, viewing the metrics for pipeline runs and activity runs can give you insights into how used the workspace is. For a more granular look, you can view metrics like active queries, CPU used percentage, DWU used percentage, memory used percentage, and queued queries, from a dedicated SQL pool perspective. Figure 9.2 illustrates a few of the stated metrics. These metrics can help you determine if the currently allocated compute resources are nearing the level of overutilization.

In Figure 9.10, you can see a column named Duration. This column identifies the amount of time the pipeline took to execute from start to end. Whether or not that duration is acceptable depends on what it does. If the amount of time appears to take longer than what you expect, you can drill down into a pipeline to view its activities, as shown in Figure 9.14. The default presentation of the activities is a list that also has an associated Duration value, the sum of which should equal the pipeline duration. You can also view the numerical values in the Duration column in Gantt format, as shown in Figure 9.22.

FIGURE 9.22 Monitoring data pipeline performance Gantt chart

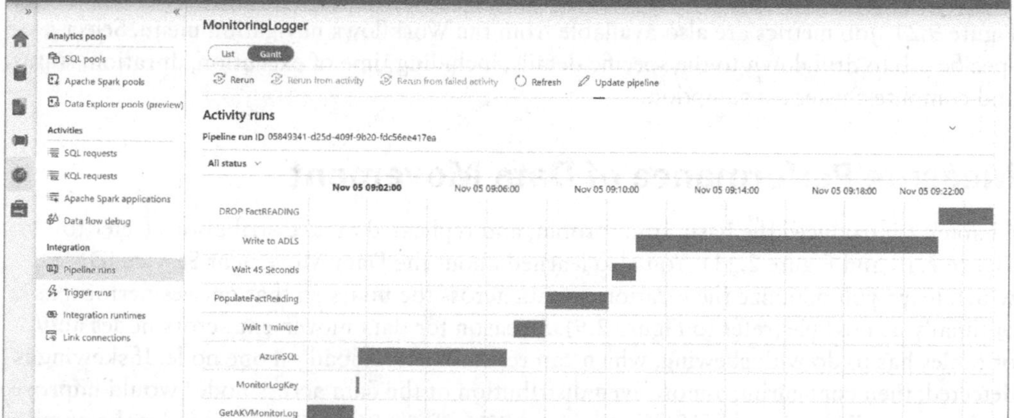

It is easy to recognize which activities take the longest by looking at the times, but the chart makes it much easier to determine where most of the time is spent. Consider the activity

named AzureSQL, for example. This is not the longest running activity, but perhaps it is expected to run much more quickly than it is. In Figure 9.15 you saw that you can drill into the data flow to see the different modifiers that are running within it. What you did not see is that you can also select each modifier to get even more details at that level. For example, that data flow is pulling all 4,537,353 rows of brain wave readings from an Azure SQL database hosted in the central US to a temporary dedicated SQL pool table hosted in central Germany. More analysis into that specifically would be required to determine if that is slow or fast.

Monitor Cluster Performance

When you see the word *cluster*, your mind should navigate to the Apache Spark context. When running your data analytics on the Azure platform, you then need to determine if you are in the Azure Synapse Analytics or Azure Databricks context, both of which give you access to running data analytics on Apache Spark clusters. In Figure 9.14, you saw a pipeline run that included a notebook, written in Scala, that ran on an Apache Spark cluster in Azure Synapse Analytics. It is also obvious in Figure 9.22 that this activity took the longest of all the activities in the pipeline. When you hover over the Write to ADLS activity, you will see glasses like you saw for the Azure SQL activity in Figure 9.14. Clicking them will open the notebook, allowing you to look at the Scala code and see what might be taking so long. Instead of clicking the glasses linked to Write to ADLS, when you select the activity name itself, the Apache Spark applications log for the job opens, as shown in Figure 9.16. When you select the Spark History Server menu item, you are provided some Apache Spark cluster environment metrics similar, but not identical, to that shown in Figure 9.21. Lastly, Apache Spark pools that run in the Azure Synapse Analytics workspace have the standard monitoring features like alerts, metrics, diagnostics settings, and logs.

To find cluster performance data, the recommended option is to use Azure Monitor Log Analytics from the Azure portal. Log Analytics can query data logged from your Diagnostics Settings configuration that focuses on the workspace, clusters, jobs, notebook, and metrics. You can find cluster performance metrics in the Azure Databricks workspace, as shown in Figure 9.21. Job metrics are also available from the Workflows navigation menu. Select a specific job to drill down to the specific details, including time of execution, duration, status, and compute cluster consumption.

Measure Performance of Data Movement

Chapter 2 introduced the hash, round-robin, and replicated table distributions (refer to Figure 2.10 and Figure 2.11). You also learned about the Data Movement Service (DMS), which helps you optimize the location of data across the nodes so that queries perform as optimally as possible (refer to Figure 2.9). A reason for data movement across nodes and/or tables has to do with skewing, which can result in excess load on one node. If skewing is detected, then configuring a more even distribution of the data across nodes would improve performance. Executing the DBCC command `PDW_SHOWSPACEUSED` will render the number of rows, reserved disk space, and disk space for all tables on a database or for a single table. For example, the following snippet would be helpful in gathering those insights from the `FactREADING` table:

```
DBCC PDW_SHOWSPACEUSED ('[SQLPool].[brainwaves].[FactREADING]');
```

Another DBCC command, `PDW_SHOWEXECUTIONPLAN`, will show the execution plan for a query on a specific dedicated SQL pool node. This can identify query performance details in general but is also helpful in identifying skewing. You can use that information, in combination with output from a DMV named `sys.dm_pdw_dms_workers`, to drill into data distributions and determine if one is working harder than another. Comparing the number of rows processed and the duration across the distributions on a node will identify the one or more that are suffering. For example, if one distribution is processing a factor of 10 more rows when compared to other distributions, some data needs to be redistributed. Also, if the same number of rows are queried but one distribution takes much longer than another, there needs to be a reconfiguration or redistribution of the data to resolve those pressure points.

Interpret Azure Monitor Metrics and Logs

Metrics and logs located in the Monitoring section of most Azure products in the Azure portal are within the purview of Azure Monitor. Figure 9.2 shows an example of metrics, and Figure 9.1 shows an example of logs. The discussion of what those features are and how to use them surrounds those figures. The descriptions of those metrics and logs will enable you to take action when either generates the need to do so. That is a general statement; however, metrics values and log statements are relevant to the platform configuration and application directly. It is only possible to make general statements, but a baseline understanding provides you a starting point to build upon so that you can gain application-specific metric thresholds and log interpretations. In this section you will learn about metrics and log details related to Azure Synapse Analytics workspaces, dedicated SQL pools, and Apache Spark pools. Table 9.5 details Azure Synapse Analytics workspace metrics.

TABLE 9.5 Azure Synapse Analytics workspace metrics

Name	Aggregate	Description
Activity Runs Ended	Count, Sum	Total number of activity runs
Link Connection Events	Sum	Total number of connections to linked services
Link Latency in Seconds	Avg, Max, Min	Realized latency through linked services
Link Processed Data	Sum	Processed linked service data by volume in bytes
Link Processed Rows	Sum	Total rows processed through a linked service
LinkTable Events	Sum	Generated table events from a linked service
Pipeline Runs Ended	Count, Sum	Number of ended pipeline runs
Trigger Runs Ended	Count, Sum	Number of ended trigger runs

The workspace Metrics blade also includes metrics for the built-in, serverless SQL pool: Data Processed (Bytes), Login Attempts, and Requests Ended. These metrics are helpful for determining how utilized the serverless SQL pool is. Table 9.6 provides the metrics available for dedicated SQL pools.

TABLE 9.6 Dedicated SQL pool metrics

Name	Aggregate	Description
Active Queries	Sum	Total number of active queries across all SQL pool nodes
Adaptive Cache Hit %	Avg, Max, Min	Identifies cache utilization
Adaptive Cache Used %	Avg, Max, Min	Identifies cache utilization
Connections	Sum	Number of SQL pool logins
Connections Blocked by Firewall	Sum	Number of blocked SQL pool logins by firewall rule
CPU Used %	Avg, Max, Min	CPU utilization across all SQL pool nodes
DWU Limit	Avg, Max, Min	Configured size of SQL pool
DWU Used	Avg, Max, Min	DWU limit multiplied by the DWU percentage
DWU Used %	Avg, Max, Min	Combination of CPU and I/O usage across all SQL pool nodes
Local tempdb Used %	Avg, Max, Min	tempdb utilization across all SQL pool nodes
Memory Used %	Avg, Max, Min	Memory utilization across all SQL pool nodes
Queued Queries	Sum	Cumulative count of queued queries

If the numbers returned from the adaptive cache metrics are low, it means that you should look to see if your dedicated SQL pool requires additional capacity. Another approach is to rerun your workloads so that the cache is loaded into memory on the node. What determines if the metrics value is low depends on the application and is drawn from your direct experience with it. Also, if you see numbers from the Queued Queries metric, it means that the concurrency limit was reached across your nodes. This is a clear indication that more capacity is needed for your pool or that queries are being blocked by some shared resource. Table 9.7 provides details about Apache Spark pools running in the Azure Synapse Analytics workspace.

TABLE 9.7 Apache Spark pool metrics

Name	Aggregate	Description
Active Apache Spark Applications	Avg, Max, Min	Number of active Apache pools
Enabled Apache Spark Applications	Sum	Number of enabled Apache pools
Memory Allocated (GB)	Avg, Max, Min	Allocated memory to an Apache pool
vCores Allocated	Avg, Max, Min	Allocated vCores to an Apache pool

From a logging perspective, you might have noticed that the selected categories from Diagnostic Settings is what instructs the platform to log that data into the selected locations. The examples in this chapter have been to target an Azure Monitor Log Analytics workspace, which is accessible directly or by selecting the Logs navigation menu item, which places you directly into the product scope. The tables into which logs can be stored for an Azure Synapse Analytics workspace are as follows:

- Synapse RBAC Operations
- Synapse Gateway Api Requests
- Built-in Sql Pool Requests Ended
- Integration Pipeline Runs
- Integration Trigger Runs
- Synapse Link Event

Each log is placed into a dedicated table with many columns. The details found in the columns are helpful for determining the specific command, query, or API used. In addition, the log can show whether the command was successful, and if not, the actual status and an error message, which can help you determine what caused the unsuccessful operation. Additionally, columns such as duration, number of rows, dataset sizes, and file sizes are also often present and are helpful in gaining an understanding of the behaviors your application displays during given scenarios. For example, how does your application behave when the number of retrieved rows is 100,000? Does it fail? Is it slow? Or does it fly like a jet plane? Using logged numerical values and timeframes in combination with the performance metrics can give you a good overview of the application and platform state and help drive decisions to improve its behavior. The following logs are available for dedicated SQL pools:

- Sql Requests (`sys.dm_pdw_sql_requests`)
- Request Steps (`sys.dm_pdw_request_steps`)
- Exec Requests (`sys.dm_pdw_exec_requests`)
- Dms Workers (`sys.dm_pdw_dms_workers`)
- Waits (`sys.dm_pdw_sql_requests`)

If the names of the log tables look familiar, you might be thinking of their related PDWs, which are provided as well. The content in the log tables is what you should expect to find from the resulting PDW executions. Apache Spark pool logs have one table, Big Data Pool Applications Ended. Each product has its own set of metrics, logs, and use cases. For the DP-203 exam, those concepts covered in this chapter are necessary for you to understand. However, consider expanding your scope of knowledge and find what each product offers, to see if you can link together all products that make up your data analytics solution.

Monitor and Update Statistics about Data Across a System

Optimized query statistics make the queries that run on your database perform faster. The query optimizer runs automatically, so in most cases the query plan, as shown in Figure 9.23, will already contain the most optimal plan. The statistics used to optimize queries are used during the compilation of the query prior to execution. When the same queries are executed multiple times, the same compiled query using the same statistics is used to complete the operation. If the standard interval between the automated update of statistics is not keeping up with the speed of change on the table or view, then you can manually update the statistics. When the query statistics are updated, whether manually or automatically, the queries must be recompiled to reuse the new statistics. This has an impact on performance, so try not to update too often.

To manually update the statistics used to build the query plan and statistics, you can use the `UPDATE STATISTICS` SQL command or a system stored procedure named `sp_updatestats`. The following example uses `UPDATE STATISTICS` to perform this update on the `[dbo].[READING]` table:

```
UPDATE STATISTICS dbo.READING;
GO
```

FIGURE 9.23 Monitoring and update statistics execution plan

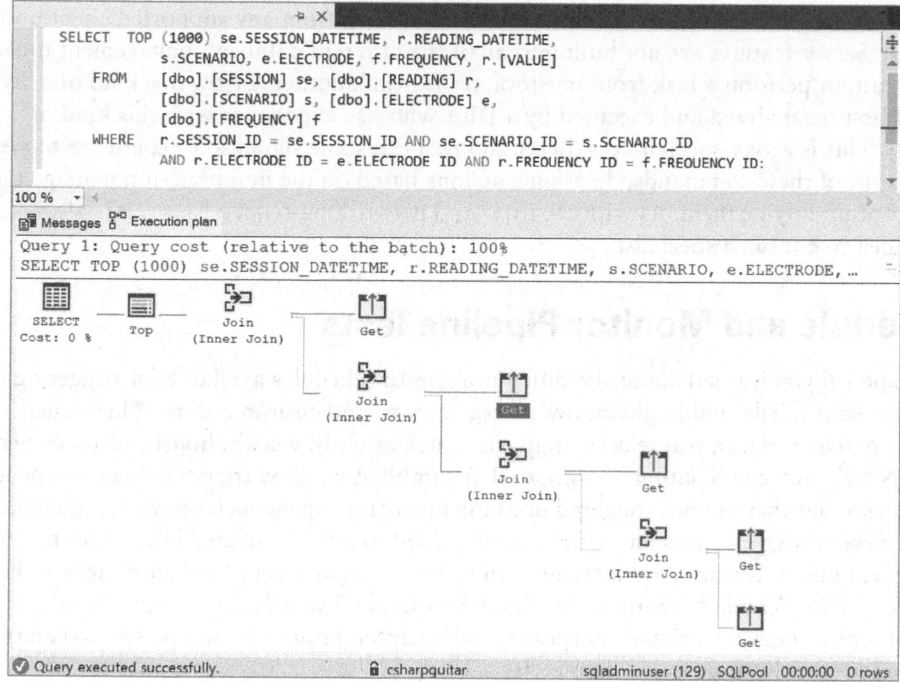

To view the statistics, you can use the following DBCC command:

```
DBCC SHOW_STATISTICS ("dbo.READING", _WA_Sys_00000004_671F4F74);
```

Figure 9.24 shows the results.

FIGURE 9.24 Monitoring and update statistics view statistics

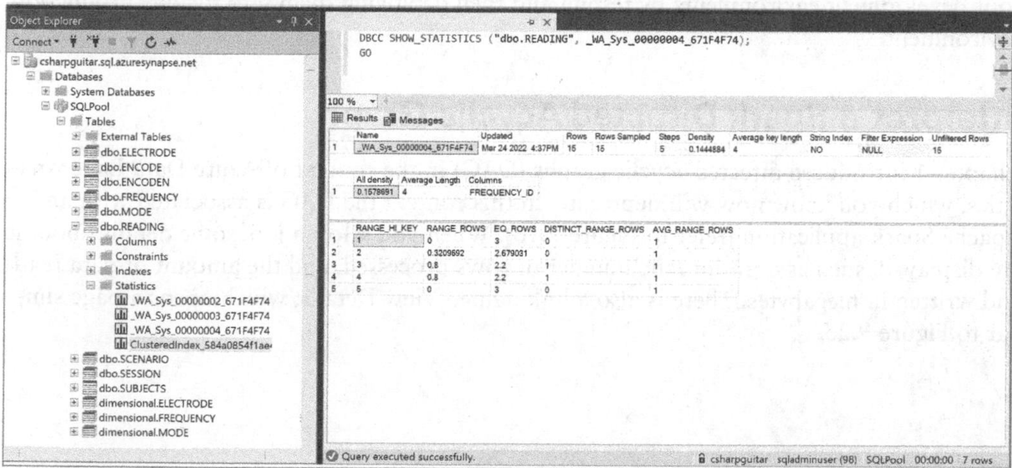

	Name	Updated	Rows	Rows Sampled	Steps	Density	Average key length	String Index	Filter Expression	Unfiltered Rows
1	_WA_Sys_00000004_671F4F74	Mar 24 2022 4:37PM	15	15	5	0.1444884	4	NO	NULL	15

	All density	Average Length	Columns
1	0.1578691	4	FREQUENCY_ID

	RANGE_HI_KEY	RANGE_ROWS	EQ_ROWS	DISTINCT_RANGE_ROWS	AVG_RANGE_ROWS
1	1	0	3	0	1
2	2	0.3209692	2.679031	0	1
3	3	0.8	2.2	1	1
4	4	0.8	2.2	1	1
5	5	0	3	0	1

Notice that both of these commands, `UPDATE` and `SHOW_STATISTICS`, were executed using Microsoft SQL Server Management Studio against the dedicated SQL pool. Keep in mind that the global endpoint is available for connection from any supported client utility. All SQL Server features are not built into all of the different database management tools, so if you cannot perform a task from one tool, try it from another. Lastly, this kind of activity would best be analyzed and executed by a DBA who has experience with this kind of activity. This is a very specialized skill set and requires some significant experience to view the output of these commands, determine actions based on the numbers, and manage the impact of modifying them. As with security- and networking-related issues, it is always a good idea to consult a specialist.

Schedule and Monitor Pipeline Tests

In Chapter 6 you learned about the different types of schedules available for triggering a pipeline: scheduled, tumbling window, storage events, and custom events. When scheduling a pipeline trigger, you select a frequency, such as daily, weekly, hourly, or twice per hour. Nearly any combination is supported. A tumbling window trigger manages dependent triggers so that they are not triggered until the upstream dependencies have completed. A storage event triggers a pipeline when a file is added to a folder in an ADLS container, for example. Finally, a custom event trigger can be bound to an Event Grid subscription that exposes the invocation to many endpoints, for example, Event Hubs. Monitoring the execution of a pipeline is the primary purpose of this chapter. From a testing perspective, most of the content for this topic is in Chapter 10.

You should not test changes to a pipeline in a production/live environment; rather, you should set up a replica environment that is identical to the live environment and test any changes to your logic against this environment. This will prevent any corruption or deletion of your production data. From a pipeline artifact perspective, you learned about implementing version control in Chapter 6. Each time you click the Commit button, the changes are uploaded to GitHub. You also learned about Azure DevOps, CI/CD, and TDD, which are useful products and techniques for managing code development and testing changes from your development environments by testing and then deploying them into the live production environment.

Interpret a Spark Directed Acyclic Graph

Chapter 1 introduced directed acyclic graphs (DAG) in the context of Azure Data Lake Analytics, which you know now will deprecate. In this context the DAG is associated with an Apache Spark application (refer to Figure 9.16). When you select a job, some details about it are displayed, such as duration, the number of rows processed, and the amount of data read and written in megabytes. There is also a link named View Details, which opens a page similar to Figure 9.25.

FIGURE 9.25 Apache Spark application details

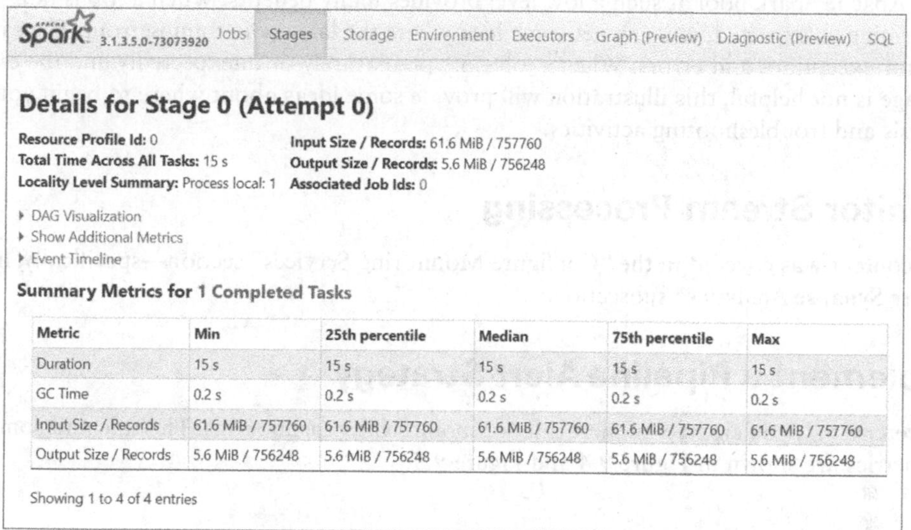

The default tab, Stages, contains an expandable grouping named DAG Visualization. Expanding this group results in a DAG diagram representing the different steps the application took as it progressed from invocation to completion. The job in this example is not complex, as shown in Figure 9.26. However, some applications can be very complex and have tens or hundreds of steps that are performed within the job. Consider this as being like a SQL execution plan, but for an Apache Spark application job.

FIGURE 9.26 DAG Visualization

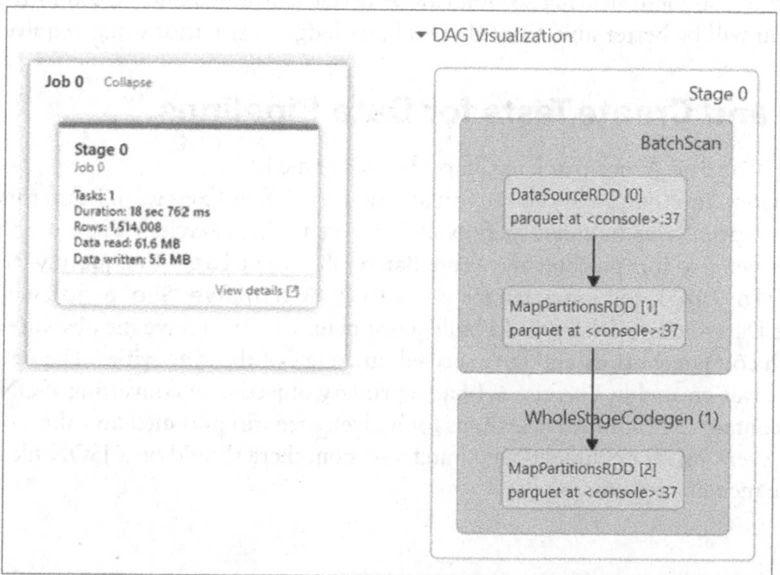

A graphical visualization of how a Scala notebook is running on an Azure Synapse Analytics Apache Spark pool at such a low level provides many benefits. When a job is not performing as expected, you can get some idea where the latency is coming from. The same goes for exceptions and errors. When a job exits prematurely or unexpectedly and the error message is not helpful, this illustration will provide some ideas about where to begin your analysis and troubleshooting activities.

Monitor Stream Processing

This content was covered in the "Configure Monitoring Services" section—specifically, in the "Azure Synapse Analytics" subsection.

Implement a Pipeline Alert Strategy

In Exercise 9.2, you created an alert rule for monitoring pipeline runs. The rule and some of the metrics are shown in Figure 9.4 and Figure 9.5.

Develop a Batch Processing Solution

Chapter 6 covered everything you need to know about designing and implementing batch processing from an Azure Synapse Analytics pipeline. In order to test and/or troubleshoot pipelines, you need to first know what kind of logs exist, how to configure them, how to retrieve them, and what they mean. This is why this section is here, in the chapter that covers monitoring, and is also why some additional information regarding troubleshooting will be provided in Chapter 10. You should now have significant insights into the monitoring capabilities in Azure, so the following section can be better consumed and placed into context. By doing so, you will be better able to apply this knowledge in situations that require it.

Design and Create Tests for Data Pipelines

The pipeline that used Azure Batch in Chapter 6 was named `TransformSessionFrequencyToMedian` and was created in Exercise 6.2. After its initial creation, the pipeline was modified and updated in seven other exercises. There are three different components to this pipeline: the Azure Batch job (`Calculate Frequency Median`), a Spark job (`To Avro`), and the notebook (`Identify Brainwave Scenario`), which runs in the Azure Databricks workspace. To build a test plan, you must have the absolute details of what each component does and the expected outcomes of those activities. The Azure Batch account that was created in Exercise 6.1 had a primary objective of converting JSON documents that contain full brain wave sessions for a given scenario into median values per frequency. For every JSON document containing a session, there should be a JSON file created with just the median frequencies.

In this case there are 20 sessions, so 20 output files are expected, with the content resembling the following:

```
{
  "ALPHA": 1.4492,
  "BETA_H": 0.7406,
  "BETA_L": 2.4036,
  "GAMMA": 0.4342,
  "THETA": 3.3934
}
```

The Azure Batch job achieved this by a program named `brainjammer-batch.exe`, which is in the `Chapter06\Ch06Ex01` directory on GitHub. You should check the following:

- Whether the Azure Batch job completed successfully
- Whether the number of files taken from the input directory is equal to the number of files in the output directory

The Spark job activity was added in Exercise 6.3 with the purpose of converting the JSON files into AVRO files, which is the most optimal file format for batch processing. The Python code for this activity is also on GitHub, in the `Chapter06\Ch06Ex03` directory. The output is a group of AVRO files placed into an output directory. You should check the following during testing:

- Whether the Spark job completed successfully
- Whether files are in the specified output directory

The final activity was created in Exercise 6.4 and executed on an Azure Databricks Apache Spark cluster. The notebook written in Python retrieves the AVRO files generated by the To Avro activity. The frequency values contained in the AVRO files are compared against the values in Table 5.2. The output is written to a Delta table and then retrieved. You should check the following during testing:

- Whether the notebook run completed successfully
- Whether there are rows on the Delta table

In total, six tests must be carried out after changes. The tests must be successful prior to publishing those changes to the production environment. There are numerous approaches to perform testing. The first decision to make is whether the tests should be carried out manually or automated. In this scenario, because you are working alone, there is only a single pipeline in scope. The pipeline is not very complex, so a manual testing approach would be the most optimal. Setting up an automated testing solution is a large undertaking, and, in the previous scenario, the effort required to set it up and manage it would outweigh its benefit. However, if you are working in a team environment, with many pipelines or relative complexity, and you perhaps want to implement CI/CD, then the effort to automate testing would be beneficial. You will learn why as the discussion progresses.

Once you decide to go the automated approach, and even to some extent, with manual testing, you need to determine the numerous types of testing. There are many, but five of the most common are summarized in Table 9.8.

TABLE 9.8 Different types of testing

Type	Description
Unit	Low level, test classes, methods, and functions in the source code
Integration	High level, cross-component testing, architecture, and code dependencies
Functional	Tests output against business requirements
Performance	Compares last version performance metrics with current version
Regression	Checks for old bugs reintroduced into the release pipeline

Which testing types you choose to implement depends on your requirements. Some form of unit testing is most often performed by the person who is writing the code. Once unit testing is completed, a TDD model can call out any new issues that have been introduced by the updates. In every case you should enforce this type of testing, for both manual and automated testing scenarios. Integration and functional testing can overlap somewhat, in that they both should take place in an environment that is not on a developer workstation or workspace. Instead, all changes should be installed into a completely different environment where all the code being released for a specific version is brought together. Integration testing confirms that the technical components work together, and functional testing confirms that the results of the testing still meet the business requirements. Performance testing makes sure there is no degradation of execution speeds. Lastly, regression testing checks for newly introduced bugs and for bugs that were fixed in a previous version being overwritten by a new change. This can happen if the developer took the wrong, older version of the pipeline from the source code repository that contains an old bug. The old bug was fixed in a newer version of the pipeline but will be overwritten when the new code changes are applied to the production branch.

Tools that can be used for automating testing include Azure DevOps, NUnit, and Azure PowerShell/CLI. Azure DevOps is by far the most sophisticated tool for managing automated test plans and for achieving CI/CD. Table 6.6 provided the different components of Azure DevOps, and Figure 6.67 showed a release workflow that included Azure Test Plans. Creating an Azure DevOps organization and projects requires many configurations that typically only Subscription administrators have access to. That (and the security-related complexities) is the reason you will only see the details of how Azure Test Plans looks instead of completing an exercise. Azure DevOps is located at a URL similar to the following:

```
https://dev.azure.com/<organizationName>/<projectName>
```

After replacing the `organizationName` and `projectName` with your unique values, you create an Azure test plan by clicking the + New Test Plan button on the Test Plans page, as shown in Figure 9.27.

FIGURE 9.27 Azure DevOps Azure Test Plans New Test Plan

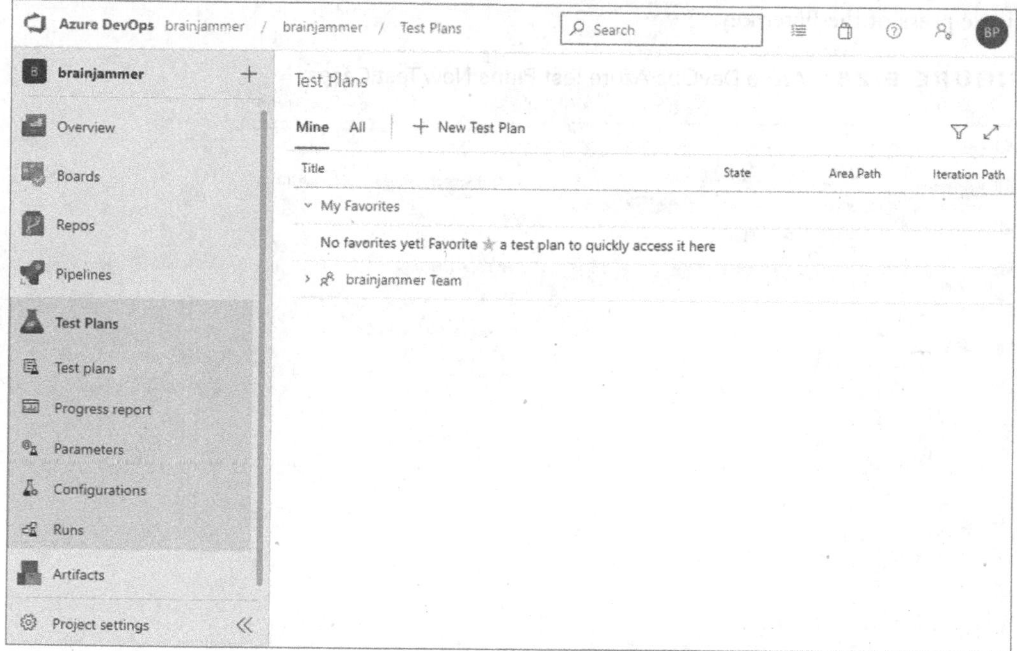

Once the test plan is created, you are offered the option to create test cases. In this context there are three test cases, one for each pipeline activity within the `TransformSessionFrequencyToMedian` pipeline. Each test case contains two steps. The test case resembles Figure 9.28.

When you select the Execute tab, the test cases are rendered to the page. Each step within the test cases is performed manually and their status recorded, as shown in Figure 9.29.

When a step within the test case fails, the outcome is set to a status of Failed and a textbox explains the reason. There is also a button to create a work item on the Azure DevOps Board so that the issue is documented and a developer or data engineer can look into it. The Chart tab enables you to create a visualization of the overall test plan status. This is very helpful for larger enterprise projects that have many team members testing many test cases.

If the endpoints of your Azure Synapse Analytics endpoints are not blocked by firewall rules or private endpoints, you can use an SDK or Azure PowerShell/CLI to test your pipelines. For example, you can use NUnit, a tool for testing code written within the Visual Studio IDE (`https://docs.nunit.org`). You can then write the code to trigger the pipeline, check the status of the pipeline, and check the storage account container for the expected results. Combining the code that performs the test with the NUnit framework can help you execute, monitor, and react to test plans from within Visual Studio. The endpoints called from the SDK are the same as those called using Azure PowerShell or Azure CLI. Therefore, the concept of their implementation is the same, in that you would call the ARM API from the related cmdlet to trigger a pipeline, check the status, and then check the output in the storage container for the expected results. This approach is a bit more manual; however, the entire test plan, like the one you create with an SDK, can be executed by a single press of the Enter key.

FIGURE 9.28 Azure DevOps Azure Test Plans New Test Cases

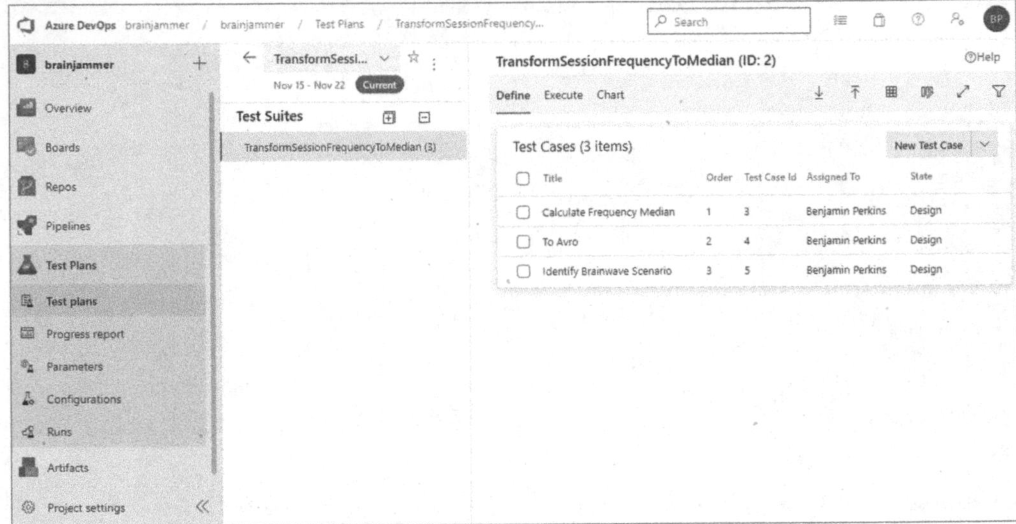

FIGURE 9.29 Azure DevOps Azure Test Plans Execute Test Cases

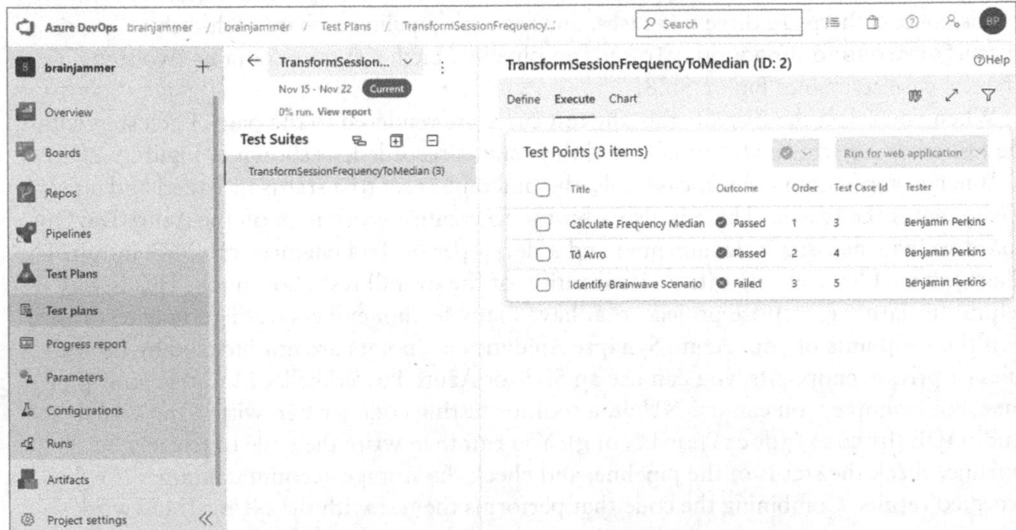

Develop a Stream Processing Solution

Chapter 7, "Design and Implement a Data Stream Processing Solution," covered stream processing in detail. The content in this chapter that pertains to data streaming needed context around logging and monitoring capabilities before covering them. At this point you should have a sophisticated understanding of what monitoring features exist specifically for Azure Stream Analytics.

Monitor for Performance and Functional Regressions

Most of what you need to know from this section's perspective is covered in the section "Configure Monitoring Services." Figure 9.18 and Figure 9.19 illustrate the job diagram and available metrics, respectively. This section provides a detailed look at the available Azure Stream Analytics metrics (see Table 9.9).

TABLE 9.9 Azure Stream Analytics metrics

Name	Description
Backlogged Input Events	The number of incoming event messages being queued, waiting to be processed
CPU % Utilization	The percentage of CPU utilized by the job
Data Conversion Errors	The number of data conversion errors (refer to Figure 7.51)
Early Input Events	Event messages with a timestamp earlier than their arrival time by 5 minutes
Failed Function Requests	The sum of failed Azure Machine Learning function calls
Function Events	The sum of events sent to an Azure Machine Learning function
Function Requests	The sum of calls to an Azure Machine Learning function
Input Deserialization Errors	The number of input messages that could not be deserialized
Input Event Bytes	The amount of data the job receives in bytes
Input Events	The sum of records deserialized from the input event
Input Sources Received	The number of messages the job receives

TABLE 9.9 Azure Stream Analytics metrics *(continued)*

Name	Description
Late Input Events	The events received outside the tolerance window (refer to Figure 7.43)
Out of order Events	The sum of events received out of order that occur outside the configured tolerance window (refer to Figure 4.43)
Output Events	The sum of event messages sent to output targets
Runtime Events	The sum of errors that occur during query processing
SU (Memory) % Utilization	The amount of memory used for processing the job
Watermark Delay	The Avg, Min, or Max watermark delay across all job outputs

Any number greater than zero for Backlogged Input Events means that your job cannot process the event quickly enough. The volume and frequency of incoming event messages are too great, and the job does not have enough compute power to process them all. If you notice this in your metrics, then you need to add more SUs to your job. The CPU % Utilization metric is not an indication that more SUs need to be added when the average value is over 90 percent. Use the CPU % Utilization metric in combination with the Backlogged Input Events and Watermark Delay metrics to determine if CPU is the bottle neck. The metrics for Early Input Events, Late Input Events, and Out of order Events are managed on the Event Ordering blade in the Azure portal for the given Azure Stream Analytics job (refer to Figure 7.43). The ordering of incoming event messages is discussed in Chapter 7, in the section "Configure Checkpoints/Watermarking During Processing," and illustrated in Figure 7.41. The Input Sources Received metric represents the number of event messages. As you learned in Chapter 7, an event hub message is sent within an `EventData` object. Each `EventData` object is counted as one received event message. If SU (Memory) % Utilization remains near or over 80 percent and both the Watermark Delay and the Backlogged Input Events are rising, you should consider increasing the number of SUs allocated to the job. As mentioned in Chapter 7, the Watermark Delay should be zero. Any average value other than zero means that there are delays in processing the event messages. When you see this metric consistently greater than zero, it is a good indication that more SUs are needed.

Design and Create Tests for Data Pipelines

The process for designing and creating tests for Azure Stream Analytics is the same from an Azure DevOps perspective as it is for batch processing, in that you create a test plan made of test cases that contain the steps required to complete the test case. The `brainjammer` Azure Stream Analytics job you created in Exercise 3.17 consists of three components: an input, a query, and an output. Breaking each of those components into what they are expected to do will provide the detail for each test case. The following is a breakdown of the expected outcomes from each component:

- Input: `brainwaves`
  - Capture the number of received brain wave readings on the Azure Event Hubs.
  - Capture the number of received brain wave readings on the Azure Stream Analytics job.
  - Are both numbers the same?
- Query
  - Are there any errors, backlogs, or watermark delays?
- Output: `powerBI`
  - Are the results of the query being streamed to Power BI?

The exercises regarding Azure Stream Analytics in Chapter 7 were all performed on the live job in the portal. You should not be making changes like that on a production job that is generating business insights, due to the disruption doing so would cause. Instead, you should create another, identical environment to perform your testing of any changes to the input, query, or output. After performing a test, you can use the steps in the preceding list to determine if the changes were successful. If they were successful, you would then commit the changes to your source code repository. Once code sets are merged and testing is signed off, the CI/CD process to move the changes into production is triggered.

To begin the integration of Azure Stream Analytics into a release pipeline, take a look at the Visual Studio Code blade in the Azure portal for your Azure Stream Analytics job. There are links to download Visual Studio Code and to manage a job from the IDE, and instructions on how to use `npm` package to set up the CI/CD pipeline. After your Azure DevOps project is set up, the next step of the release process is to install the Azure Stream Analytics Tools extension into the Visual Studio Code IDE. Figure 9.30 represents how this looks in the IDE, version 1.73.1.

Once integrated, you can export the job query locally, as shown in Figure 9.31, and make modifications to it.

Once the job query is local, you can make changes to it and perform testing against it. Once you are happy with the new changes, you commit the change to the Azure DevOps Repo, which triggers the CI/CD process. The provisioning, creation, and configuration of an end-to-end CI/CD process is outside the scope of this book. The complexities of creating such a procedure are worthy of their own book. The important points are that you should not modify your query that is running a live job and that you integrate Azure Stream Analytics jobs into a CI/CD pipeline using Visual Studio code and the mentioned extension.

FIGURE 9.30 Azure Stream Analytics Tools extension in the Visual Studio Code blade

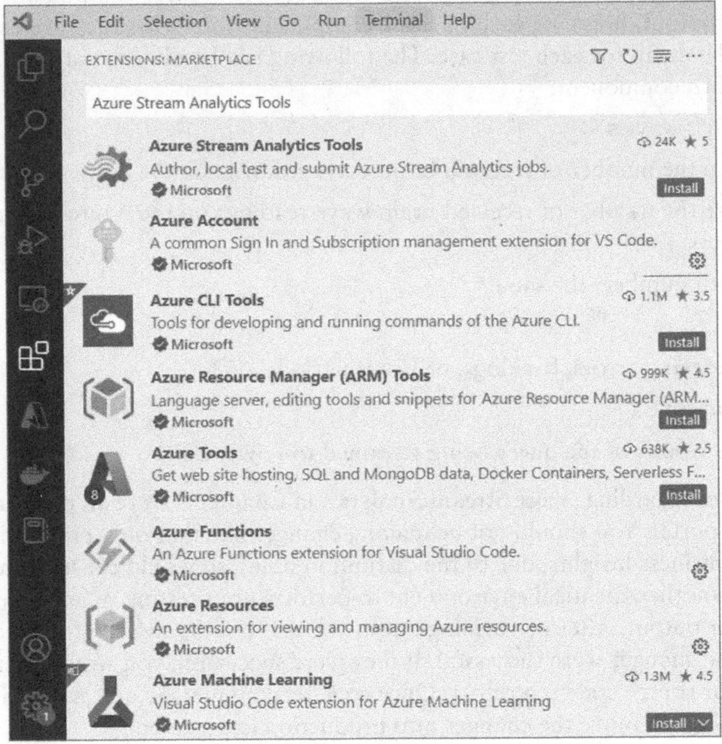

FIGURE 9.31 An Azure Stream Analytics job query in the Visual Studio Code blade

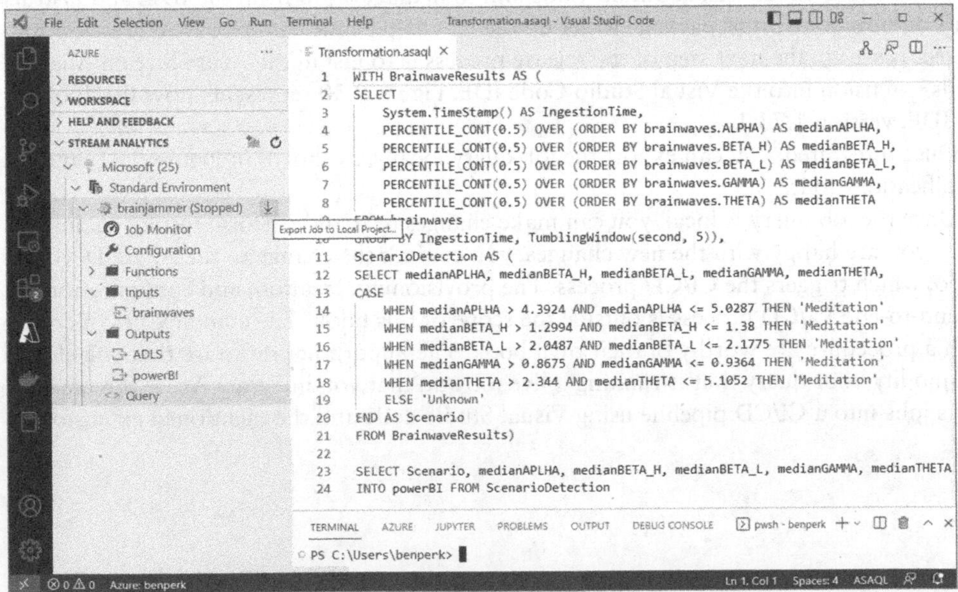

Azure Monitoring Overview

Every Azure product has some type of built-in monitoring capability. Most of them have alerts, metrics, diagnostics settings, and logs, which are components of Azure Monitor. This chapter provides a detailed look into those monitoring capabilities for ADLS, Azure Synapse Analytics, Azure Stream Analytics, and Azure Databricks. The following section provides a glimpse of those monitoring capabilities in some additional Azure products.

Azure Batch

Figure 9.32 shows the Metrics blade for an Azure Batch account. Notice the selected metrics of Dedicated Core Count, Job Start Events, Running Node Count, Task Start Events, and Task Complete Events.

FIGURE 9.32 The Azure Batch Metrics blade

The available categories of on the Diagnostic Settings blade are Service Logs, Audit Logs, and All Metrics. Adding a diagnostic setting to include these categories and target a Log Analytics workspace for storage enables you to query them using KQL. The metrics and logging available on this blade focus on pools, nodes, and tasks. For a deeper look at the execution details of a specific job, refer to Figure 6.9, which illustrates batch job–specific details and detailed log files like `stderr.txt` and `stdout.txt`. Additionally, Figure 6.21

illustrates the Batch Explorer, which provides a useful overview of the health of your Azure Batch account, pools, nodes, tasks, and jobs.

Azure Key Vault

The same monitoring capabilities exist in Azure Key Vault as in other Azure products. Figure 9.33 shows the Metrics blade.

FIGURE 9.33 The Azure Key Vault Metrics blade

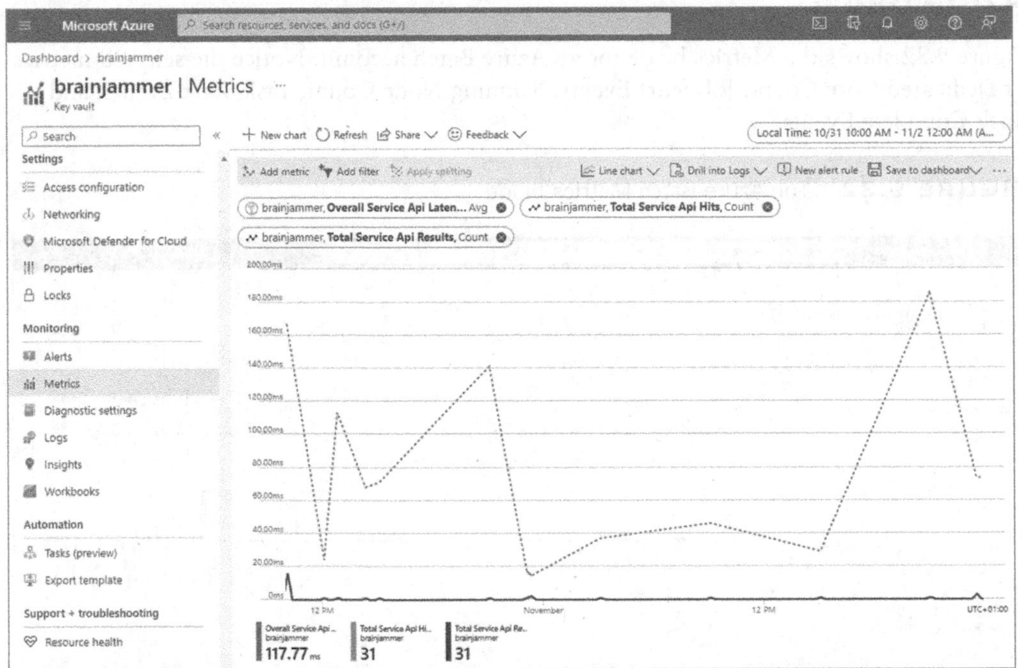

The configured metrics are Overall Service Api Latency, Total Service Api Hits, and Total Service Api Results. The latency value represents the speed at which the request for a key, secret, or certificate occurred, whereas the hits and results represent the number of requests and successful responses, respectively. Those three metrics provide a good overview of how Azure Key Vault performed over a historical timeframe. For Azure Key Vault, you see that it has the Insights blade, which gives you some extra capability to go deeper into the platform code. This is also the place where you can create workbooks, as discussed earlier in the ADLS section and shown in Figure 9.9. The Alerts, Logs, and Diagnostic Settings blades are also available for Azure Key Vault. Audit Logs, Azure Policy Evaluation Details, and All Metrics are the categories available for logging and analysis.

Azure SQL

The metrics available for an Azure SQL database are very similar to what you saw previously regarding a dedicated SQL pool. As shown in Figure 9.34, metrics include CPU Percentage, DTU Limit, DTU Percentage, DTU Used, Sessions Count, Successful Connections, and Workers Percentage, all of which are useful for gaining an overview of the resource health.

FIGURE 9.34 The Azure SQL Metrics blade

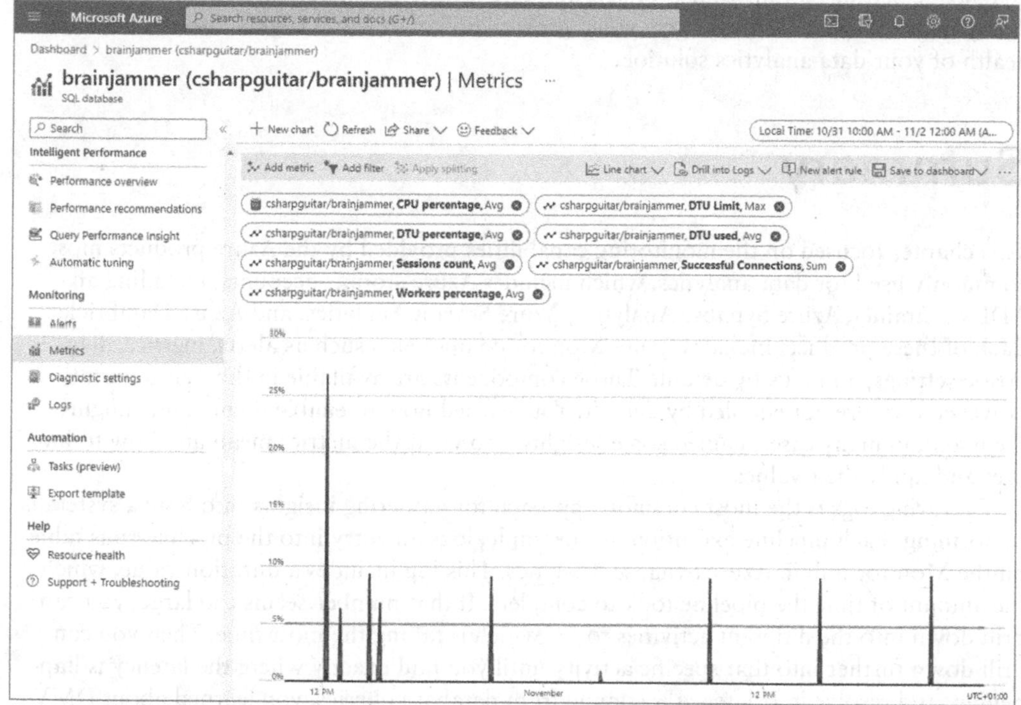

The Diagnostics Settings blade includes the following categories:

- SQL Insights
- Automatic Tuning
- Query Store Runtime Statistics
- Query Store Wait Statistics
- Errors
- Database Wait Statistics
- Timeouts

- Blocks
- Deadlocks
- Basic
- InstanceAndAppAdvanced
- WorkloadManagement

Each category, when configured to be stored into a Log Analytics workspace, represents a table with multiple columns. The columns typically contain performance and status information such as operation duration or error messages. In all cases, you should enable Diagnostic Settings for all your products and target their storage to an Azure Monitor Log Analytics workspace. This will give you a great platform to gain insights into the overall health of your data analytics solution.

Summary

This chapter focused on the monitoring capabilities provided by the Azure products most commonly used for data analytics, which includes Azure storage accounts, including an ADLS container, Azure Synapse Analytics, Azure Stream Analytics, and Azure Databricks. Each of these products includes Azure Monitor components such as alerts, metrics, diagnostic settings, and logs by default. Those components are available in the Azure portal; however, they are not enabled by default. You learned how to enable them and configure them and, in many cases, gained some insights into what the metrics mean and how to interpret and apply their values.

Capturing logs is the most common approach for gathering insights into how a system is performing. Each pipeline execution, for example, logs an entry into the pipeline runs table on the Monitor hub in Azure Synapse Analytics. This log includes a duration value, which is the amount of time the pipeline took to complete. If that number seems too large, you can drill down into the different activities to see which is taking the most time. Then you can drill down further into that specific activity until you find exactly where the latency is happening, and resolve it. If latency is coming from database queries, you learned about DMV, which can break the query into steps, while both `SHOW_STATISTICS` and an execution plan can illustrate the query execution process in a graphic. Finally, you learned about directed acyclic graphs (DAGs), which are similar to an execution plan but target the steps taken while running a notebook on an Apache Spark cluster.

Exam Essentials

Azure Monitor. Azure Monitor is like a container that encompasses many monitoring components. You can install it as an extension on an Azure VM and configure it to send performance and availability metrics to the workspace for storage. You can also install the extension on servers hosted in a private, on-premises datacenter. The features contained in the Monitoring section of Azure products in the Azure portal are part of Azure Monitor and include alerts, metrics, diagnostic settings, and logs.

Alerts. Any traceable event that takes place against your product or within the application can be captured and an alert sent to a group of individuals. Log Analytics queries, metric thresholds, or activity logs can all be monitored. When you create an alert, you set the frequency the evaluation is performed and the logic it uses to determine the event, and identify who receives the alert message and how.

Diagnostic settings. The data available for logging in this feature provides platform-specific information for the associated Azure product. The data can be stored in a Log Analytics workspace, a storage account, event hub, or a customized third-party solution. When configured to be stored in a Log Analytics workspace, the data is placed into a table that has the same name as the category, with columns for each part of the log. You can query the data using KQL for that given product via the Logs navigation item.

Monitor hub. The Monitor hub in the Azure Synapse Analytics workspace is where you gain insights into the performance and overall health of your resources. SQL, Apache Spark, and Data Explorer pool capacity and utilization metrics can be viewed within this hub. SQL and KQL request performance, Apache Spark jobs, and data flow logging are also viable logging options from the Monitor hub. Monitoring the pipelines that run on the workspace is likely the reason you will access this hub the most. Performance and other execution details about each pipeline run are stored here. Linked connections, integration runtimes, and trigger runs expose their execution logs here as well.

Directed acyclic graphs. Getting to the source of any technical problem is very complex and requires many years of training and experience. Many layers of stacked technologies must be drilled into to find the root cause. A directed acyclic graph (DAG) is useful for getting closer to the actual execution path of a job on an Apache Spark cluster. The illustration, as shown in Figure 9.26, breaks the job into stages and the steps that take place within them.

Review Questions

Many questions can have more than a single answer. Please select all choices which are true.

1. What is the purpose of adding an annotation to an Azure Synapse Analytics pipeline?
   A. It is used to pass parameters to the pipeline when triggered.
   B. It is used to manage exception messages.
   C. It is used to filter pipelines by ingest, transform, and enrich.
   D. It provides a summary of what the pipeline is for.

2. Which of the following are components of Azure Monitor?
   A. Alerts
   B. Metrics
   C. Diagnostics settings
   D. Logs

3. Which of the following are components of Azure Monitor?
   A. Activity logs
   B. Tags
   C. Logs
   D. Access control (IAM)

4. Which of the following SQL snippets would be latent when executed against large datasets?
   A. `SELECT *`
   B. `WHERE ID = 1`
   C. `SELECT NAME, AGE, BRAINWAVE`
   D. `WHERE description LIKE '%the%'`

5. Which of the following are not part of the Azure Test Plans module?
   A. Test plans
   B. Test cases
   C. Test regressions
   D. Test activities

6. Which of the following DMVs break down a SQL query into its numerous phases?
   A. `sys.dm_pdw_diag_processing_stats`
   B. `sys.dm_pdw_wait_stats`
   C. `sys.dm_pdw_request_steps`
   D. `sys.dm_tran_active_transactions`

7. Which of the following DMVs renders locked requests?
   - A. `sys.dm_pdw_lock_waits`
   - B. `sys.dm_pdw_waits_lock`
   - C. `sys.dm_pdw_resource_waits`
   - D. `sys.dm_pdw_node_status`
8. Which of the following Azure Stream Analytics metrics alone can identify a need to increase the number of allocated SUs?
   - A. Watermark Delay
   - B. CPU % Utilization
   - C. Backlogged Input Events
   - D. Out of Order Events
9. Which of the following options are not found on the Monitor hub in an Azure Synapse Analytic workspace?
   - A. Pipeline runs
   - B. Apache Spark jobs
   - C. Apache Spark applications
   - D. SQL requests
10. Which of the following can be configured to store logs in a Log Analytics workspace?
    - A. Azure storage accounts
    - B. Azure Synapse Analytics workspaces
    - C. Azure Stream Analytics jobs
    - D. Azure Databricks workspaces

Troubleshoot Data Storage Processing

EXAM DP-203 OBJECTIVES COVERED IN THIS CHAPTER:

- ✓ Optimize and troubleshoot data storage and data processing
- ✓ Develop a batch processing solution
- ✓ Manage batches and pipelines
- ✓ Develop a stream processing solution
- ✓ Monitor data storage and data processing

Chapter 9, "Monitoring Azure Data Storage and Processing," discussed the monitoring capabilities available on the Azure platform. The knowledge you gained will be helpful in the sections that discuss optimizations. You will learn which actions can be performed to improve the performance, resiliency, and availability of the in-scope Azure product. The log and metrics you now know how to configure, store, and collect can be used to set a performance baseline, to identify areas that experience latency, and to identify performance gains after optimizations have been applied. A performance baseline defines the duration and compute consumption for a given transaction. These values can be used to compare performance after optimizations meant to decrease latency are applied. Without a performance baseline to compare with current performance, it is not possible to determine if changes had the desired effect. With very complicated interdependent data analytics transactions, it can be challenging to identify where the bottleneck and latency are coming from. In this scenario, where your pipelines are complex, capturing and analyzing performance data can highlight the areas that should be analyzed. Analysis is certainly necessary if you see a sudden or gradual increase in duration, but in every case, you need a baseline to compare with the current performance metrics.

Not all performance optimizations need to wait until you notice the latency or question the duration. Throughout this book you have learned many recommended approaches for optimally configuring and storing your data, for example, partitioning, indexing, caching, and compression. Both partitioning and indexing have to do with optimizing query performance. Partitioning has to do with the grouping and placement of data so that queries can be performed on a single node as much as possible. This kind of partitioning is achieved with distribution models like hash, replicated, and round-robin, as introduced in Chapter 2, "CREATE DATABASE dbName; GO." Indexing is implemented by identifying columns in a table that can be used to uniquely identify a row. Queries execute faster when indexes exist, because the database engine has some additional instructions about where to find your data. Additionally, the effect of indexing results in the ordering of data on disk, which makes the data quicker to find, especially when compared to selecting randomly ordered table data. Caching helps performance by having commonly retrieved data loaded into memory. Reading from memory is much faster than reading from disk, which is an I/O operation that requires a thread switch. When loading or copying data files like CSV or JSON, you will not gain much performance by caching. Instead, making sure the data is compressed using `zip` or `tar` can result in a significant reduction in latency. It takes less time to copy a 100-megabyte file than a 1-gigabyte file.

This chapter also discusses scaling and troubleshooting. Scaling is one benefit (perhaps the most helpful) of running data analytics on the Azure platform. If your data procedures are allocated a specific amount of compute power but need more, they get more. If your application works fine when you have 100 files but you unexpectantly receive 1000, you can add additional compute capacity, in real time, to handle the additional workload, by scaling out or up. Scaling out means adding more identical nodes to the worker pool, and scaling up means increasing the number of CPUs and memory allocated to a single node.

Finally, troubleshooting failed operations is a very complicated activity, because most of what happens during the execution of your data analytics solution is abstracted away from the presentation layer. That means you cannot visually see what is happening and need to rely on operation logs and monitoring capabilities. If there are errors, the log files like `stdout` and `stderr` will typically contain some information about the cause of the issue or at least where the exception happened so that you can dig deeper into that specific component to find out more details. Monitoring capabilities will typically provide a status or a red flag when something unexpected has happened. In every case, though, you should anticipate errors or exceptions and take necessary steps to recover from them. This chapter covers how to achieve that.

Optimize and Troubleshoot Data Storage and Data Processing

In this section you will learn about compression, shuffling, partitioning, query and pipeline optimization, and troubleshooting. You have already been introduced to most of the content in this section and in this chapter, but not necessarily from an optimization or troubleshooting perspective. So, there is some new learning to gain from this content. Keep in mind as you read through this content that Azure Data Factory and Azure Synapse Analytics, from the perspective of the DP-203 exam, can be used interchangeably. This means if a question on the exam only includes the option of Azure Data Factory and the book highlights this feature in the context of Azure Synapse Analytics, you can select Azure Data Factory as the answer, with confidence. This is because all new data analytics features will be added to Azure Synapse Analytics, and at some point, only one of these products will exist after all features and customers have migrated to Azure Synapse Analytics.

An important aspect to optimizing and troubleshooting data analytics operations is to understand the different types of issues that occur. These issue types, often referred to as *antipatterns*, are summarized in Table 10.1.

TABLE 10.1 Performance and troubleshooting antipatterns

Antipattern	Description
Busy database	Too much data processing is happening on the database server.
Busy front end	Doing too much work asynchronously.
Chatty I/O	Continuous execution of small I/O requests.
Extraneous fetching	Retrieving too much data, not projecting effectively.

TABLE 10.1 Performance and troubleshooting antipatterns *(continued)*

Antipattern	Description
Improper instantiation	Destroying shared objects when reuse is possible.
Monolithic persistence	Using a single datastore that has different patterns of usage.
No caching	The lack of cached data.
Noisy neighbor	Shared resources are consumed by a single tenant.
Retry storm	Retrying failures too often.
Synchronous I/O	Blocking threads while I/O completes.

It is important to understand that the types of issues that can impact your data analytics solution are not infinite. The kinds of issue causing latency or errors are most likely caused by one or more of the antipatterns listed in Table 10.1. If you have offloaded much of the processing of data to the database server, for example, code running in a stored procedure, that processing can cause high utilization of the database compute resources. This can impact the ability of the database to retrieve data requested by other clients. Scaling up the server on which the database runs or relocating some of the data processing to the client can reduce the impact of the busy database antipattern. There is a term called *thread starvation*, which means that the kernel or the process is no longer able to allocate any threads to perform computations, i.e., processing. There are numerous types of threads, and each type of thread has a built-in limit on the total number that can be instantiated. A way to get around this limit is to better optimize the utilization of threads by running operations asynchronously. If you have a managed thread that needs to perform I/O, traditionally the managed thread would switch to an I/O thread, wait until the I/O operation has completed, and then return to the managed thread. This is not optimal, because the managed thread is idle, waiting for the I/O to complete. If the managed thread is asynchronous, it will not wait until the I/O operation is complete before returning the thread to the pool to be used for other executions. The busy front-end antipattern happens when too much work is happening on too many threads, which consumes all the resources on the server. Scaling to a larger machine might resolve the issue, but more investigation into the application code might also be justified to better manage threading.

Performing I/O is inherently latent, so when you do it, it needs to be worth the effort. If your application code is frequently writing very small bits of data to disk, retrieving a single row from a database, or sending small but frequent network messages, you might be experiencing the chatty I/O antipattern. The simple solution for this is to bundle together these single requests and send them all at once. You would need to look into your own application source code to determine this, but in any place you are writing files or data to disk or using the DISTINCT keyword in a query, you need to make sure this antipattern is not happening. You have learned that selecting all rows without a WHERE clause is not a pattern that represents projection. Projection means that you select only the data you need. Doing this reduces the amount of time required to retrieve the data from the database and the amount of time it takes to return the dataset to the client. When working with files, it is common to retrieve more than necessary in an effort to avoid additional or chatty I/O issues, but doing this results in the extraneous fetching antipattern. It is important to design the retrieval of data to be as precise as possible to avoid this pattern. When coding Scala or C#, it is common that you create an object to store data, for example, a DataFrame or an Event Hub client. Both of those classes are intended to be reused throughout the lifetime of the process. If you destroy them and then re-create them within the same process, then your application code will run more slowly because the instantiation of an object class carries a high overhead cost and should therefore be avoided when possible. Not reusing classes and their instantiated object results in the improper instantiation antipattern. Performing the instantiation at the class level in C#, versus within a specific method, would resolve this behavior.

In addition to storing relation data in an Azure SQL database, it is also possible to store documents in it as well. Doing so can result in a performant solution; however, you know that ADLS and Azure Cosmos DB are datastores designed specifically for storing documents. Having a single datastore to place your data into makes the solution architecture easier to understand and maintain; however, doing so may also result in poorer performance. If you identify that better performance can be attained by storing your blob documents in a datastore other than the one that contains your relational data, then you have just resolved the monolithic persistence antipattern. The benefits of caching data have been covered in much detail numerous times in this book. Chapter 9 discussed how to determine if the data is being retrieved from cache for a dedicated SQL pool (refer to Figure 9.17). The metric is Adaptive Cache Used Percentage. In all possible cases, it is highly recommended to implement data caching, as it greatly improves performance by avoiding high-cost I/O retrievals.

The noisy neighbor antipattern happens when an application on one server in a network consumes all available resources, impacting other servers and applications in that network. For example, take the limit of 2^{16} (65,536) ports on a Windows OS server. If one application consumes all those ports, then other servers cannot make connections outside that network. Additionally, networks have bandwidth capacities that can result in slow transmissions of data packets when consumed by other clients in the same network.

To avoid the retry storm antipattern, there is a coding pattern called *circuit breaker*. This pattern describes how you can determine if the error causing the failure will last some time, is expected to be resolved fast enough to retry immediately, or falls somewhere in between. The point is that you do not want to try to perform a failed request immediately, over and over again, if the resource you need to fulfill the request is not going to be back online for some time. Instead, implement the circuit breaker pattern to reduce the impact of failed requests, which is high, and retry the request within a timeframe that reflects the seriousness of the unavailable resource.

The opposite of an asynchronous thread is a synchronous thread. As previously mentioned, prior to the ability to manage the thread type in managed code, all threads executed synchronously, one after the other, and waited idly until the long-running actions on switch threads completed. I/O threads were, and still are, notorious for this, and you should avoid this kind of thread usage when possible. Knowing the kind of antipattern causing the unwanted or unexpected computational outcome helps you choose the right tools to troubleshoot and drives the discovery of the issue location. The location of the issue is more easily discoverable after the antipattern is identified because the location in which they occur is defined. For example, improper instantiation happens in application source code, whereas a noisy neighbor happens in the network.

Optimize Resource Management

As previously mentioned in this book, you should delete unneeded Azure products. Doing so will reduce costs and enable you to efficiently optimize and manage your Azure resources. Removing items that are no longer needed, especially when they generate a cost, is a rather intuitive action. Beyond that action, however, finding directions to further optimize and effectively manage your provisioned Azure resource might not be as easy. This is where a tool named Azure Advisor can help. Figure 10.1 illustrates some output of the Azure Advisor report from the Azure portal.

FIGURE 10.1 Azure Advisor score

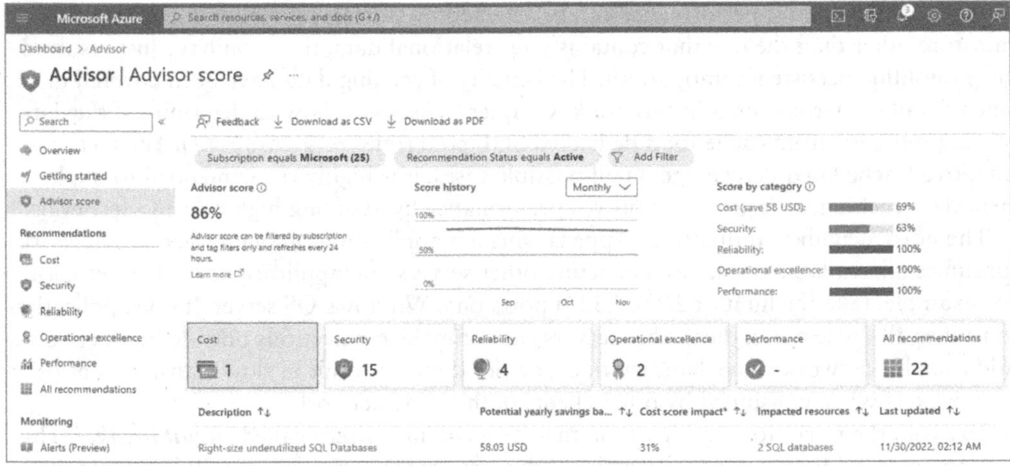

The first component of the report that you may notice is the Advisor score. An Advisor score of 100 percent means that all your assessed resources follow Azure recommended best practices. Azure best practice recommendations are broken into five categories, which are identified in tiles on the Azure Score blade with an associated number of unimplemented or missing recommendations. Each of the five components, often referred to as tenets or pillars, makes up a concept called the *Azure Well-Architected Framework*. The five categories are as follows:

- Cost optimization
- Security
- Reliability
- Operation excellence
- Performance efficiency

The default view on the Azure Score blade is the cost optimization pillar. As shown in Figure 10.1, there is an alert that states the size of database being used is perhaps too great. There is also an amount that might be saved if the right amount of compute power is selected. Handling cost is one of the most important aspects of optimizing and managing your Azure resources. In addition to the Azure Advisor recommendation, there is also a Cost Management feature on the Subscription blade in the Azure portal that can help. A breakdown of costs can be viewed based on service name, which is the kind of Azure product or feature, location, and resource group, as shown in Figure 10.2.

FIGURE 10.2 Azure Cost Management

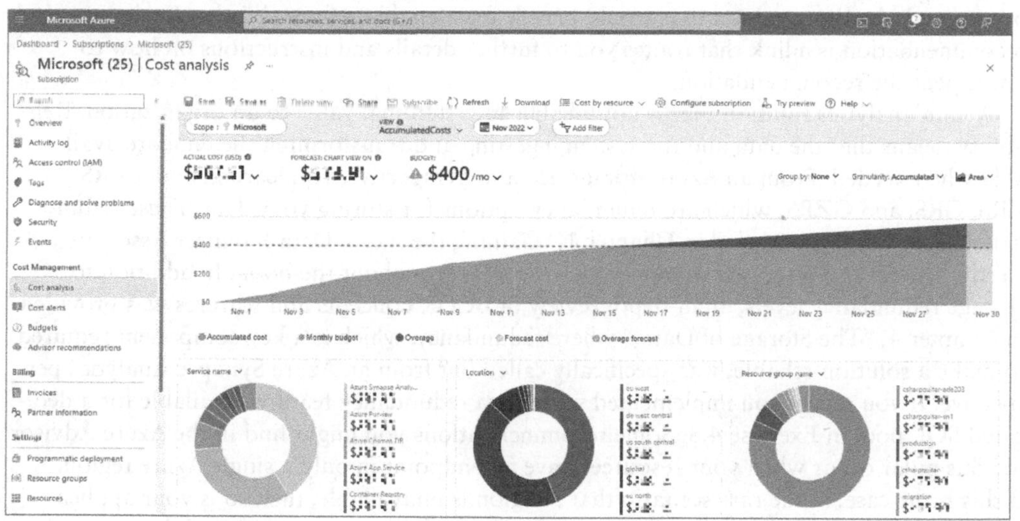

As you can see in the Cost Management section of the navigation menu, there are features for alerting and budgeting. Alerts can be configured to notify when a budget threshold is breached or nearing the threshold so that actions can be taken. There is also an option to alert based on usage anomalies. Using historical telemetry and sophisticated AI algorithms, you can be alerted when the consumption cost behaves in a way that is not deemed normal. For example, if a very expensive product is provisioned and consumed but has yet to be used, an alert will tell you of such actions and give you the opportunity to respond to it before massive costs are generated. Budgeting is an absolute necessity to prevent overspending and the undesired aftereffects of such occurrences. In cases where there is overspending, you have the option to suspend and/or delete the Azure products that are generating costs until the end of the budget period. In a production environment the result of doing this might have greater financial and customer impact than incurring the costs and reevaluating the budget constraint before the next cycle. The important point is that there is a budget that defines expected spending, and anything more than this should be justified via a formal review process.

Lastly, notice the Advisor Recommendations link in the Cost Management section. This link provides the same cost optimization report as found in Figure 10.1 for that Azure Well-Architected Framework pillar. In summary, from a cost optimization perspective, shut down or remove unused resources, choose the right size of machine to run your workloads, and set spending budgets to optimize resource utilization.

Even more important than managing costs is security. Security is the most important aspect to consider when running any data analytics solution. You learned a lot about this in Chapter 8, "Keeping Data Safe and Secure," which covered topics such as firewalls, private endpoints, and using Azure Key Vault to store secrets, keys, and certificates. Azure Advisor can provide results of vulnerability scans, identify Azure products with exposed public endpoints, and identify products that would benefit from enabling firewall rules. Each presented recommendation is a link that routes you to further details and instructions on how to implement the recommendation.

A data analytics solution that is not reliable adds minimal value to an organization. Reliability means that the data and the system ingesting and transforming the data are available when needed. From an Azure storage account perspective, you learned about LRS, ZRS, GRS, and GZRS, which are redundancy options for storing your data. These redundancy levels were introduced in Chapter 1, "Gaining the Azure Data Engineer Associate Certification," and discussed in numerous chapters throughout the book. In addition to storage redundancy levels, an in-depth review of BCDR concepts and features was provided in Chapter 4, "The Storage of Data," where redundancy, which is a key component required to make a solution reliable, was specifically called out from an Azure Synapse Analytics perspective. If you recall, you implemented some data redundancy features available for a dedicated SQL pool in Exercise 4.3. Some recommendations you might find in the Azure Advisor for this pillar occur when your resources have an endpoint in only a single Azure region. If this is the case, in the rare scenario that a region is unavailable, then so is your application. Having your mission-critical applications in multiple Azure regions is recommended to avoid that scenario. Additional common recommendations include enabling soft deletes and recovery points on the Azure products that support them and any kind of networking optimizations that apply to the provisioned Azure products.

Operational excellence recommendations have to do with automation, deployments, and monitoring, to name a few examples. Many Azure customers use a large number of Azure VMs and can therefore benefit from automation capabilities. Activities such as installing security patches, performing backups, or configuring a new VM can all be performed using scripts. These scripts typically contain JSON script that describes the configuration details for all dependent Azure resources required to build and configure the environment. These JSON-structured configuration files are often used when deploying new applications in a context known as ARM deployments. Deployments using this approach can provision and configure entire architectures including security, networking, compute, data storage, and application installation. These deployments can be very complex and require the name of the pillar in which it exists, i.e., operational excellence. Monitoring is another component of this pillar and was covered in detail in Chapter 9. From a monitoring perspective, the Azure Advisor report will identify which of your Azure products would benefit from enabling monitoring and configuring alerts based on defined performance thresholds.

Finally, performance efficiency has to do with the ability of your system to adapt to an increase or decrease of usage demand. This pillar has to do primarily with scalability, which includes not only the expectation to provide additional capacity when required but also to deallocate unneeded capacity when no longer needed. Not all Azure products can scale automatically and therefore some capacity planning and ongoing performance monitoring are necessary to maintain the optimal level of performance. There is more detail about scaling later in this chapter with regard to Azure Batch, Azure Stream Analytics, and Azure Synapse Analytics pipelines.

Compact Small Files

The "Design for Efficient Querying" section in Chapter 3, "Data Sources and Ingestion," discussed how the number of files can impact performance—specifically, that processing many small files can negatively impact performance. A reason for this is that an ADLS container is designed to work most optimally with larger files. Another reason is that loading files from disk requires an I/O operation. Each file retrieval could theoretically require an I/O operation that can result in creating a chatty I/O antipattern. To learn how to merge a group of small files into a single file, perform Exercise 10.1. This exercise merges all Classical Music brain wave CSV files located on GitHub, in the `BrainwaveData/SessionCSV/ClassicalMusic/POW` directory. These files have previously been copied to the ADLS container created in Exercise 3.1 and uploaded, as described in Exercise 3.2.

EXERCISE 10.1

Compact Small Files

1. Log in to the Azure portal at `https://portal.azure.com` > navigate to the Azure Synapse Analytics workspace you created in Exercise 3.3 > navigate to the Integrate hub > create a new pipeline > expand the Move & Transform group > drag and drop a Copy Data activity to the pipeline > and then select the Source tab.
2. Create a new ADLS Gen2 DelimitedText Source dataset that targets the Classical Music CSV brain wave files from Exercise 3.2. Leave the file name empty. The file path should resemble the following:

```
brainjammer/SessionCSV/ClassicalMusic/POW/
```

EXERCISE 10.1 ***(continued)***

3. Select the Wildcard File Path radio button as the File Path Type value, something similar to the following:

   ```
   brainjammer/SessionCSV/ClassicalMusic/POW/*
   ```

4. Select the Sink tab, and then create a new ADLS Gen2 Delimited Text Sink dataset to write the single merged CSV file into a directory in the ADLS container, perhaps like the following:

   ```
   brainjammer/EMEA/brainjammer/in/2022/11/30/14/
   ```

5. Select Merge Files from the Copy Behavior drop-down list box. Figure 10.2 shows a summarized view of the Source tab and Sink tab configurations.

FIGURE 10.3 Compacting small files—Source and Sink tabs

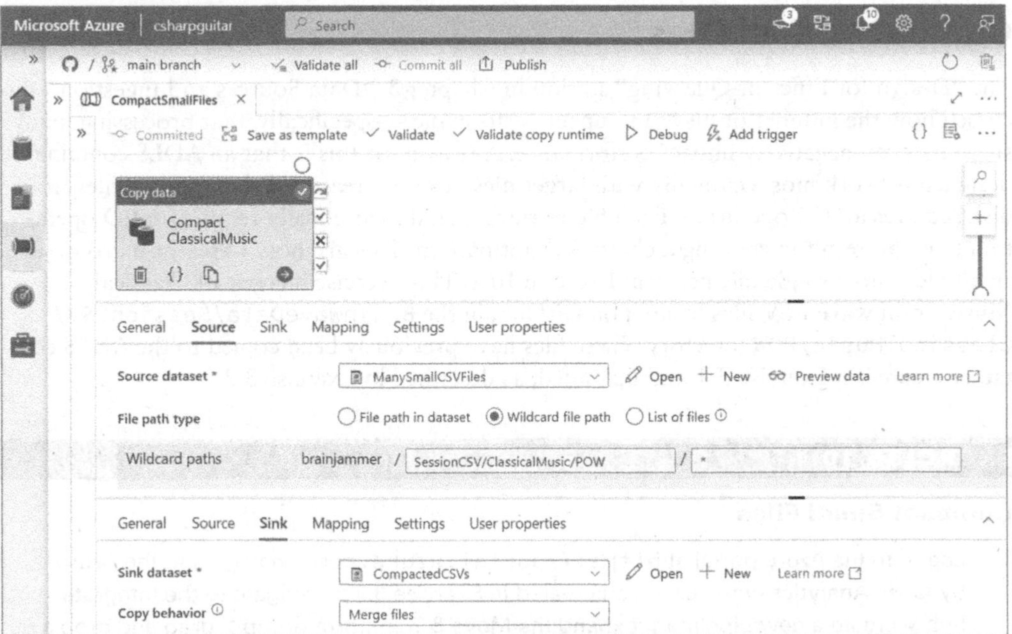

6. Click Commit ➢ click Commit All ➢ click Debug ➢ and then view the merged CSV file in the targeted sink location within the chosen ADLS container.

The pipeline and dataset JSON configuration files are located in the Chapter10/Ch10Ex01 directory on GitHub. These files will help you identify the specific configuration details if something is unclear or not working as expected. None of the steps performed in the Exercise 10.1 are new; you have already created a pipeline and datasets and configured a source and sink. The same is possible using Python code within a notebook running on an Apache Spark pool by using code similar to the following:

```
%%pyspark
df = spark.read \
  .load('abfss://container@account.dfs.core.windows.net/path/*.csv',
   format='csv', header=True)
df.write \
    .mode('overwrite').format('csv') \
    .save('abfss://container@account.dfs.core.windows.net/path/merged.csv')
```

The syntax should look familiar to you at this point, as you have performed similar activities in previous exercises. The code snippet loads all the CSV files in the provided path into a DataFrame and then writes the content of the DataFrame to a CSV file into the provided path.

To conclude this section, remember two points, the first concerning optimal file sizes. In Chapter 3 you learned that the optimal file size for dedicated SQL pools is between 100 MB and 10 GB. For Apache Spark pools, the optimal file size is between 256 MB and 100 GB. The second point to keep in mind is the law of 60 and the fact that queries will perform much better on tables with at least 1,000,000 rows. Details on both of those points are covered in Chapter 3, where the designing of a partitioning strategy is discussed.

Handle Skew in Data

Data skew, introduced in Chapter 2, is the uneven distribution of data across nodes. Refer to Figure 2.19 to visualize data skewing. As mentioned in Chapter 3, a large influx or purging of data that happens to be stored on a specific node due to the applied partition attributes can cause skewing. That event can cause shuffling, which is the platform's response to such an influx or purging of data. It is important, however, to proactively monitor your partitions so that the data distribution remains optimal as data scenarios change. One approach for monitoring data distribution and skewing is to execute the following code snippet, which was introduced in Chapter 9. An example output follows the code snippet.

```
DBCC PDW_SHOWSPACEUSED ('[SQLPool].[brainwaves].[FactREADING]');

+-------+------------------+------------+--------------+-----------------+
| ROWS  | RESERVED_SPACE | DATA_SPACE | UNUSED_SPACE | DISTRIBUTION_ID |
+-------+------------------+------------+--------------+-----------------+
| 72546 | 136472          | 136256     | 184          | 31              |
| 72524 | 98032           | 97792      | 208          | 37              |
```

```
| 72040 | 97276          | 98295          | 182            | 46              |
| 69311 | 98128          | 97920          | 176            | 17              |
| 35343 | 98160          | 97904          | 224            | 40              |
+-------+----------------+----------------+----------------+-----------------+
```

The result of PDW_SHOWSPACEUSED shows that data is in fact skewed across distributions. This is recognizable by the wide variety of data rows placed onto each node, which is identified by the value in the DISTRIBUTION_ID column. The goal is to have data spread evenly across all the distributions.

Another method for discovering and analyzing data skew is by executing the following PDW query, which is followed by a sampling of the results:

```
SELECT row_count, pdw_node_id, distribution_id
FROM sys.dm_pdw_nodes_db_partition_stats
ORDER BY row_count DESC
```

```
+-----------+-------------+-----------------+
| row_count | pdw_node_id | distribution_id |
+-----------+-------------+-----------------+
| 72546     | 9           | 31              |
| 72524     | 9           | 37              |
| 72040     | 9           | 46              |
| 69311     | 9           | 17              |
| 35343     | 9           | 40              |
+-----------+-------------+-----------------+
```

The output is similar to the DBCC command, with the addition of the node on which the distribution is hosted. Finally, recall from Chapter 5, "Transform, Manage, and Prepare Data," (Exercise 5.11) that you changed data in order to remove outlying data that was skewing the median and average calculations of brain wave scenarios. In addition to reconfiguring the partition parameters to improve skewing, the action you took in Exercise 5.11 is an example of how to approach solving this kind of issue.

Handle Data Spill

A data spill is the same as a data leak, which happens when protected data is transferred to an unauthorized person or stored in an unauthorized location. Data can be spilled by copying a protected file to a publicly accessible server or by mistakenly sending an email that contains confidential information to an unnecessarily wide email audience. A data spill is different from a data breach because there is no malice or malicious intent pertaining to a data spill. In this case, the response and the approach for handling a data spill would be different from that for a data breach. A significant difference between a spill and breach is the impact. The impact does depend heavily on the kind of information that was inadvertently shared with an unauthorized party, but once the event is discovered, retrieving the mishandled information is more likely. Whether the data spill was willful, inadvertent, or due to negligence, actions must be taken to handle the spill and to prevent future incidents.

Once a data spill has been detected, it is important to notify your security team, as they should have existing procedures to manage such events. From a forensics perspective, it is important that the person or procedure that discovers the spill takes no action to resolve it. The first step is to simply report the spill. The next step would be to contain the spill, to prevent the spread and exposure of the data to a wider audience. This can be done by disconnecting the server from the network, removing IP routing from the network for the server, or stopping any forwarding of the email that contains the spilled data. Next, the organization handling the spill should perform a damage or risk assessment based on the data content. If the data contained matters of national security, the risk of damage is much greater than a list of employee salaries. Actions to be taken after the assessment are greatly dependent on the kind of data and how widely it was spread. The last step is to clean up the data spill. Removing the file from a hard drive is not enough to consider the data removed, as it can be recovered if nothing has been written to the sectors where it was stored. Software designed for completely removing data from hard drives should be used in such cases. A reboot of the machine would also be recommended so that any remnants of the data are flushed from memory if there happened to be any stored there. Once the data is removed, the final step is to identify why the incident occurred and take the necessary corrective actions to prevent it from happening again.

Taking proactive measures to prevent data spills is preferred to a reactive approach. As you learned in Chapter 8, your data needs to be marked with sensitivity levels. Unless your data is marked with confidentiality or sensitivity levels, it is not realistic to expect that a spill is identifiable. Therefore, making sure this is implemented and enforced is the first step toward preventing data spills and securing your data. Intrusion detection, anomaly detection, and multifactor authentication (MFA) are some security controls that can protect your data from unauthorized parties. Data encryption, row and column level security, data masking, Azure Key Vault, RBAC, and ACLs, which were also covered in Chapter 8, are all options for securing your data. Finally, the staff who has access to confidential data needs to be regularly trained on how to handle and share this kind of information.

Another example of a data spill occurs in the Apache Spark context when the size of the data being processed exceeds the allocated memory for the given task. This is not an out of memory (OOM) exception but a heap memory issue, which does not leak into user or reserved memory space. Figure 10.4 illustrates a data spill in this context.

FIGURE 10.4 Handling data spill memory capacity

The impact of such a scenario is performance degradation caused by the overflowed data being written to disk. Writing to and reading data from disk is much slower than writing and reading from memory. Therefore, it is important to keep the datasets stored in partitions at a size that will fit into the task process, which hovers around a 4 GB limit. You can see the amount of data spill for a given job task by selecting the View Details link for the given task (refer to Figure 9.26). The Spill (Memory) and Spill (Disk) metrics represent the amount of data that exceeds the allocated memory. If values exist for these headings, your job partition is suffering from data spill.

Data skewing is one of the most common causes for data spills. If you determine there is significant skewing, fix that issue by either repartitioning to reduce the amount of data per partition or reshuffling the data. The intention behind reshuffling the data on a partition is to reduce its size so that it fits within the allocated memory. Another option is to increase the worker node size so that more memory is available for the task to perform its operation.

Find Shuffling in a Pipeline

Data shuffling was introduced in Chapter 2, where it was described as the movement of data from one node to another. When using the hash distribution model, remember that the distribution key provided to the `HASH` function determines how the data is organized across the compute nodes. Review Figure 2.10 to visualize this. It is common that datasets partitioned by the distribution key are so large that they must be spread across multiple nodes. Data shuffling is observed when a query is executed that must pull data from more than a single node. In other words, when a query is executed, the SQL statement is run on a single node. If the data required to gather and process that query completely exists on a partition on the same node as the one running the SQL statement, then no data shuffling is required. However, if only a portion of the data is on a partition where the SQL statement is running, then the platform, or the massively parallel processing (MPP) engine, must know where the other required data is hosted and retrieve it. Refer to Figure 2.9 to visualize the MPP engine. The amount of data shuffling depends on the amount of retrieved data, the distribution key, and the complexity of the SQL statement.

In addition to data shuffling, Chapter 2 introduced the DDL command `EXPLAIN`. Using the `EXPLAIN` command results in XML output, which mimics the visualization from Figure 9.23. Both the XML and its illustration are the location where you can find occurrences and details about data shuffling as it pertains to the specific SQL query. Figure 10.5 illustrates how the second `JOIN` in the SQL query is affected by a shuffle cost of 86 percent. This means that 86 percent of the data necessary to complete that join is located on a node other than the one executing the SQL statement.

The XML file includes additional details, including `operation_type=SHUFFLE_MOVE`. The `cost` value, which is rendered in Figure 10.5, is an estimated amount of time required to run the operation; `accumulative_cost` is the sum of all costs in the plan; `average_rowsize` is the estimated row size in bytes of retrieved rows during the operation; and `output_rows` is the number of rows retrieved during the operation. Comparing these values can give you some insights into the impact of data shuffling. Keep in mind that all data shuffling is not bad. When you see it happening, you need to review the impact and then determine if actions are required.

FIGURE 10.5 Finding shuffling in a pipeline—explain plan with shuffle cost

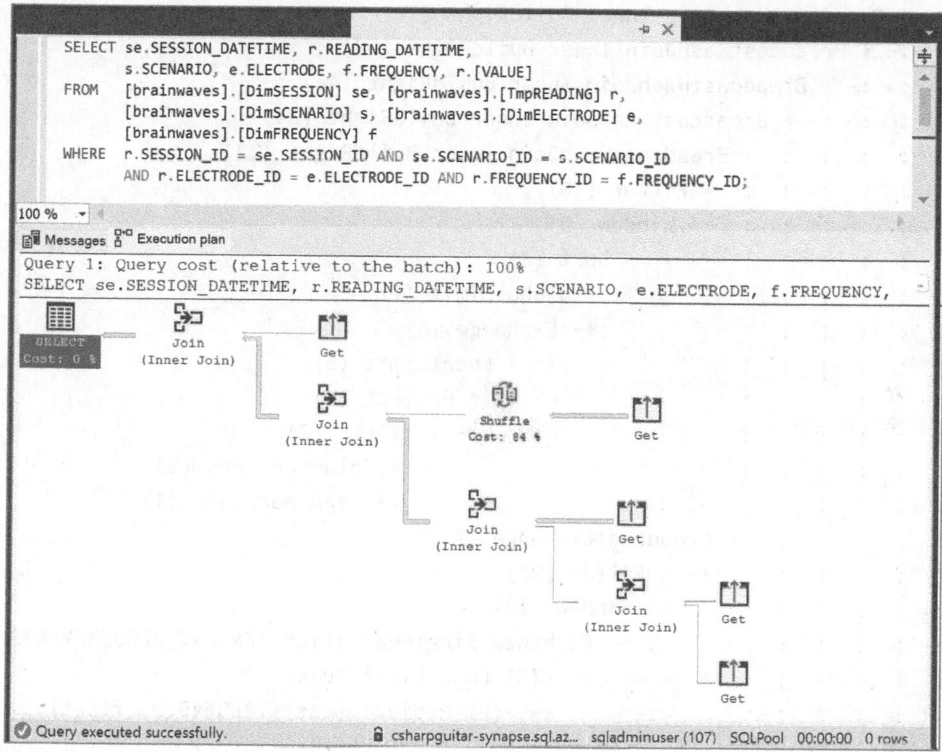

From a Spark pool perspective, there are two methods for identifying data shuffling. The first method is to use the `explain` method with syntax similar to the following, which you might recognize from Exercise 5.15:

```
dffull = dfClassicalMusic \
    .join(dfFlipChart, dfClassicalMusic.ID == dfFlipChart.ID) \
    .join(dfMeditation, dfClassicalMusic.ID == dfMeditation.ID) \
    .join(dfMetalMusic, dfClassicalMusic.ID == dfMetalMusic.ID) \
    .join(dfPlayingGuitar, dfClassicalMusic.ID == dfPlayingGuitar.ID) \
    .join(dfTikTok, dfClassicalMusic.ID == dfTikTok.ID) \
    .join(dfWorkNoEmail, dfClassicalMusic.ID == dfWorkNoEmail.ID)
dffull.explain(mode="formatted")
```

A summarized output of this query may resemble the following:

```
== Physical Plan ==
* Project (83)
+- * BroadcastHashJoin Inner BuildRight (82)
   :- * BroadcastHashJoin Inner BuildRight (70)
   :  :- * BroadcastHashJoin Inner BuildRight (58)
   :  :  :- * BroadcastHashJoin Inner BuildRight (46)
   :  :  :  :- * BroadcastHashJoin Inner BuildRight (34)
   :  :  :  :  :- * BroadcastHashJoin Inner BuildRight (22)
   :  :  :  :  :  :- * Filter (10)
   :  :  :  :  :  :  +- Window (9)
   :  :  :  :  :  :     +- * Sort (8)
   :  :  :  :  :  :        +- * GlobalLimit (7)
   :  :  :  :  :  :           +- Exchange (6)
   :  :  :  :  :  :              +- * LocalLimit (5)
   :  :  :  :  :  :                 +- * Project (4)
   :  :  :  :  :  :                    +- * Filter (3)
   :  :  :  :  :  :                       +- * ColumnarToRow (2)
   :  :  :  :  :  :                          +- Scan parquet  (1)
   :  :  :  :  :  +- BroadcastExchange (21)
   :  :  :  :  :     +- * Filter (20)
   :  :  :  :  :        +- Window (19)
   :  :  :  :  :           +- Exchange SinglePartition, ENSURE_REQUIREMENTS
   :  :  :  :  :              +- *(6) LocalLimit 20246
   :  :  :  :  :                 +- *(6) Project [cast(VALUE#5 as float)...
```

If there are remnants of data shuffling, they would be associated with the keyword `Exchange`. You can determine the impact by reviewing the associated details. The other method to find data shuffling is to view the directed acyclic graph (DAG), which was introduced in Chapter 9 and illustrated in Figure 9.26. When data shuffling is happening, you will also see an `Exchange` statement followed by a `Shuffle` statement.

Tune Shuffle Partitions

As you learned in the previous section, data shuffling occurs when the data required to successfully execute a SQL command must be retrieved from more than a single node. There are numerous reasons for this. One reason is skewing. When data is skewed, it means that there is an uneven distribution of data across the nodes. The results of either `PDW_SHOWSPACEUSED` or `sys.dm_pdw_nodes_db_partition_stats` are helpful to identify skewing. Using the results of skewing statistics and the results from the explain plan described in the previous section, you should be able to gain enough insights into whether your queries are suffering from shuffling. If you do find that there are examples of shuffles that are impacting the execution speed of your SQL queries, the following are some methods for improvement.

The first step is to identify the specific SQL query impacted by shuffling, and then compare it to the values in the `WITH` segment of the `CREATE TABLE` statement against which the SQL query executes. The `WITH` segment contains the index type, the distribution model, the distribution key, and the partition description, which can resemble the following:

```
WITH
(   CLUSTERED COLUMNSTORE INDEX,
    DISTRIBUTION = HASH([SCENARIO_ID]),
    PARTITION (
        [SCENARIO_ID] RANGE RIGHT FOR VALUES
                      (1, 2, 3, 4, 5, 6, 7, 8)));
);
```

The different types of indexes are as follows:

- Clustered columnstore index
- Heap
- Clustered index or nonclustered index

You can read about how these indexes operate in the "Data Concepts" section of Chapter 2. What may be obvious in the `WITH` clause is that `SCENARIO_ID` is used as the distribution key and the partition key. If the SQL query is optimized to select data that targets a single `SCENARIO_ID`, then you would not expect much shuffling. However, if the SQL query pulls data for multiple scenarios and those distributions are on different nodes, then shuffling will occur. Here are a few techniques that can be used to tune partition shuffling:

- Rewrite the SQL queries.
- Review `EXPLAIN` plan recommendations.
- Reshuffle/repartition.
- Optimize clustered columnstore tables.

Although this is a possible solution, it may not be practical in many scenarios. Building on the `SCENARIO_ID` example, consider the following SQL statement:

```
SELECT * FROM READING WHERE SCENARIO_ID IN (1, 2, 3, 4)
```

The SQL query requests all the data that matches four scenarios. Looking at the distribution and the partition settings, it should be obvious that there is a high probability of shuffling. Based on the configuration within the `WITH` clause, the data for each scenario is stored into different distributions and partitions. How to specifically optimize the SQL query depends greatly on which procedures are performed on the dataset after retrieval. You might realize faster performance by executing the query four times in parallel after projecting the SQL statement to a single scenario, like the following:

```
SELECT * FROM READING WHERE SCENARIO_ID = 1
SELECT * FROM READING WHERE SCENARIO_ID = 2
SELECT * FROM READING WHERE SCENARIO_ID = 3
SELECT * FROM READING WHERE SCENARIO_ID = 4
```

It would also make sense to identify the specific columns that are required from the READING table instead of using the wildcard character. This will reduce the size of the retrieved dataset and reduce latency. This action would not reduce shuffling, but it is simply good practice to make your data operations perform better. Some additional patterns to avoid data shuffling are using the CROSS JOIN type, using operators like IN or CONTAINS instead of equals (=), performing joins on columns that are different data types, and performing a join on a column, which is not part of the distribution key.

The next tuning technique to manage shuffling is to analyze the results of the explain plan for the given SQL query. As stated in the previous section, details about shuffling are available associated with the SHUFFLE_MOVE attribute in the XML file. There are cases when the database engine recognizes missing indexes that could benefit performance. Those and other recommendations are highlighted in the XML file as well as in the explain plan illustration in Figure 10.5. The database engine query optimizer uses statistics captured during the execution of queries as a basis for describing the explain plan and discovering inefficiencies and recommending solutions. You can improve performance by executing UPDATE STATISTICS or by running sp_updatestats more often than the database engine. There will be more detail later about these two approaches for maintaining statistics.

The third technique for tuning the effects of shuffling is to manually reshuffle or repartition the data. The objective here is to redistribute the data more evenly across the distributions and nodes, to avoid not only shuffling but skewing as well. A word of caution here: before you attempt either of these activities, recognize that they are considered expensive operations, which means they will be disruptive to the operational data activities happening while they are being applied and can affect data consumers after the change has been implemented. From a dedicated SQL pool perspective, you reshuffle and repartition your data by using CTAS. This specific example was provided in Chapter 2 from a copy perspective, but it is useful in this scenario as well. The process entails creating a table appended with _NEW, which has the new, optimized distribution and partition details contained in the WITH clause. Once the new table is created and populated with existing data, for example READING_NEW, you rename the existing table, as shown in the following syntax, rename the new table to the original name, and then drop the old table that contains the undesired distribution and partitions:

```
CREATE TABLE [dbo].[READING_NEW]
WITH
(
  CLUSTERED COLUMNSTORE INDEX,
  DISTRIBUTION = HASH([READING_DATETIME]),
```

```
  PARTITION ([READING_DATETIME] RANGE RIGHT FOR VALUES
     ('2022-10.01', '2022-11-01', '2022-12-01'))
)
AS
SELECT  *
FROM    [dbo].[READING];
RENAME OBJECT READING TO READING_OLD
RENAME OBJECT READING_NEW TO READING
DROP TABLE READING_OLD
```

For the Apache Spark pool perspective, refer to the "Design a Partition Strategy" section in Chapter 3. Methods like `spark.conf.set("spark.sql.shuffle.partitions", 200)` and `df.rdd.getNumPartitions()` provide insights and features for managing data partitions and shuffling. One final note concerning the number of partitions required for optimal performance. There is no absolute or standard recommendation for the number of partitions, because it depends greatly on the data and your specific scenario. You should have neither too few partitions nor too many. Too many partitions can decrease performance, as it reduces the effectiveness of the clustered columnstore indexes, whereas too few can cause skewing or large datasets with a wide variety of data. Using the information described so far for identifying shuffling should help you determine the best ratio over time and after implementing and testing these tuning techniques.

The last option discussed here for tuning for shuffling is to optimize clustered columnstore tables. There are two options: The first option is to avoid scenarios where a clustered columnstore is not optimal, and the other option is to push the data into a compressed columnstore segment. When you choose to use clustered columnstore indexes, you need to know which scenarios will not benefit from them. If your queries perform these actions more times than not, you should either rewrite the queries or use the other indexing varieties available for your dedicated SQL pool tables. Tables that store data that changes frequently will not benefit from a clustered columnstore; instead, consider heap or temporary tables. Data types such as `varchar(max)`, `varbinary(max)`, and `nvarchar(max)` will also not realize any benefits; instead, consider heap or a clustered index. The last scenario to avoid is using a clustered columnstore on tables with fewer than 60 million rows. The number 60 should trigger a term mentioned previously in this book, the law of 60, which leads well into the topic of pushing the data into compressed segments.

By default, a dedicated SQL pool allocates 60 distributions into which your database is divided. When you then partition the data, it is divided into even more segments. Each partition must contain 1 million rows in order to benefit from a clustered columnstore and compression. This is an example of how having too many partitions causes problems, in that if you partition so much that the number of rows within the partition is less than a million, then performance would be reduced—assuming that, prior to the partitioning, over a million rows of data existed.

As mentioned, there are some features helpful with determining the state of your partitions DBCC PDW_SHOWPARTITIONSTATS or sys.dm_db_partition_stats. You can also use the following algorithm to determine the number of partitions:

```
total number of rows / (1 million * 60) = number of partitions
```

Consider the previous example of provisioning that used the most common method of data type used for partitioning, which is date. There were three partitions: 2022-10-01, 2022-11-01, and 2022-12-01. Using 155 million as a hypothetical number to represent the total number of rows and plugging that into the equation results in the following:

```
155000000 / (1000000 * 60) = 2.58
```

The result identifies that the partitions have been overprovisioned. It would be prudent to repartition from three to two so that your queries can benefit from the performance gained by the clustered columnstore and compressed segments. The equation should also call attention to the point that unless your table contains at least 60 million rows, using a clustered columnstore or partitions is not justified for performance reasons. To determine the number of rows necessary to warrant the three partitions, use this formula. This is solved by multiplying both sides of the equation by 60 million.

```
x / (1000000 * 60) = 3
x = 180000000
```

The result is that the data that is to be stored into the table with these three partitions must be at least 180 million rows to gain any benefits.

One final point about partitioning is that partitions are applied onto each distribution. This means that because there are 60 by default, the provisioning of three results in 180 total partitions. The algorithm is interested only in the partitions in a single distribution; however, as this implementation is hard to visualize, it is worth stating here.

Before moving on to the next section, there is one final concept to discuss that can decrease shuffling: partition elimination. Partition elimination is implemented by optimizing the WHERE clause predicate so that the database engine can infer which data partitions contain the data. In the following SQL statement, notice that the WHERE clause specifically targets one of the three partitions created on the READING table:

```
SELECT VALUE
FROM   READING
WHERE  READING_DATETIME BETWEEN '2022-12-01' and '2022-12-31'
```

Structuring the SQL query in such a way results in the data server determining that access to a single partition is enough to fulfill the query request, meaning that all partitions do not require scanning before returning the requested data-saving time. Notice that the WITH clause, which created the three partitions based on date, also includes the keywords RANGE RIGHT FOR VALUES. The RANGE RIGHT keywords indicate that the associated values represent the lower value boundary. This is especially important when working with dates and partitions based on months. Without the RIGHT designation, data from midnight on the first day of the month would not be included in the same partition as the later values on the same day. Using RANGE with either LEFT or RIGHT makes partition elimination and your calculations based on a date range more performant and precise.

Table 10.2 provides some details about the partitioning tools discussed here.

Consider having a look back at other Parallel Data Warehouse Dynamic Management Views which were listed in Table 9.2. Ask yourself if they could be helpful in identifying or resolving shuffling or skewing, or optimizing data partitions.

TABLE 10.2 Database partition analysis features

Name	Description
sys.database_files	Identities how many files the database occupies
sys.dm_db_partition_stats	Renders the number of rows per partition
PDW_SHOWPARTITIONSTATS	Renders the size and number of rows for each partition
UPDATE_STATISTICS	Updates query optimization statistics (SQL query)
sp_updatestats	Updates query optimization statistics (stored procedure)

Tune Queries by Using Indexers

Indexes reduce query times by creating pointers to the location where data is stored in the database. Figure 10.6 illustrates how an index on a column named EF_ID is referenced and used by the SQL query to retrieve all the columns for the matching row from the FactREADING table.

Had the query been run directly against the table instead of the index, the entire table would be scanned, looking for the matching row identified by the contents of the WHERE clause. Consider that the search for the requested row begins from the first row in the table and proceeds downward until a match is made. It would have taken six rows before the match were made. This example shows only eight rows, but imagine if there were 1 billion rows. Imagine again that the row requested by the query is located in the last row. That query would take a lot of time to run. As covered in previous chapters, three types of indexes are available for a dedicated SQL pool: clustered columnstore, clustered/nonclustered, and heap. As a refresher, Table 10.3 summarizes these indexes.

FIGURE 10.6 Tuning queries by using indexer's indexes

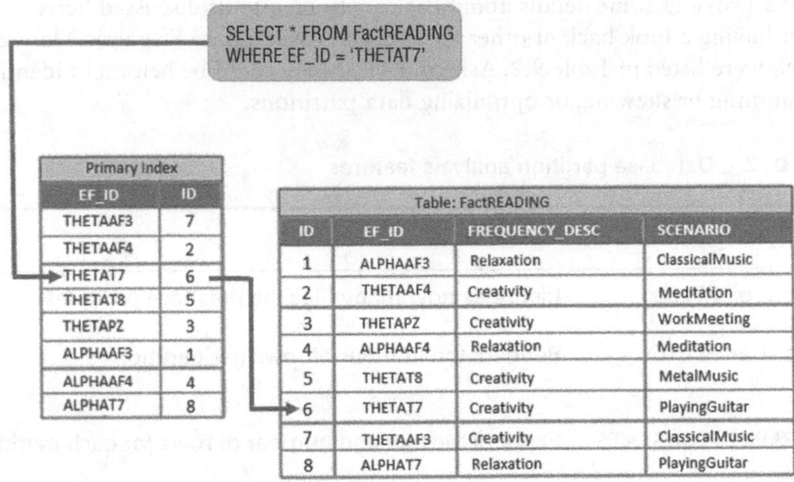

TABLE 10.3 Dedicated SQL pool indexes

Type	Benefit
Clustered columnstore	This offers the highest level of data compression and fastest read operations.
Clustered/ nonclustered	This is optimal when you are selecting a single row or a few rows using a lookup or filter.
Heap	Inserted data is not stored in order. This is used for very large staging tables that must insert quickly.

An important step to tuning your queries is to ensure that the queries you are running have the appropriate type of index. It basically comes down to knowing what the query does and then matching it to one of the three indexes in Table 10.3. In most big data scenarios with very large datasets, the index of choice is a clustered columnstore, which is the default when no index is provided when the table is created. However, performance is not gained from the columnstore index, because of the structure shown in Figure 10.6. Instead, the gain comes from the way the data is stored. Logically, columnstore data is structured as a table that contains rows and columns, but the data is physically stored in a column format. The structure of the physical manner in which the data is stored to disk is how performance gain is achieved from a clustered columnstore index. The type of index that applies to the illustration in Figure 10.6 has to do with clustered and nonclustered indexes. It is very often the case that you use a clustered index even when you are retrieving large datasets of up to 100 million rows. The point here is that when you need to query a lot of data, you will have better performance when using a columnstore index. Specifically, what is meant by "a lot" can be determined by remembering the law of 60 and noting that the threshold number of "a lot" is at least 60 million rows. If and when you decide to use a clustered index, consider the following SQL command, which creates one:

```
CREATE TABLE [dbo].[READING] (
    [READING_ID]          INT           NOT NULL IDENTITY(1,1),
    [SESSION_ID]          INT           NOT NULL,
    [ELECTRODE_ID]        INT           NOT NULL,
    [FREQUENCY_ID]        INT           NOT NULL,
    [READING_DATETIME]    DATETIME      NOT NULL,
    [COUNT]               INT           NOT NULL,
    [VALUE]               DECIMAL(7,3)  NOT NULL
)
WITH ( CLUSTERED INDEX ( READING_ID, SESSION_ID, ELECTRODE_ID, FREQUENCY_ID ));
```

A disadvantage of clustered indexes is that the only queries that benefit from them are those that filter the query in the way the index is created. This means that only queries that have those four IDs in the `WHERE` clause will utilize the index; other queries will result in a table scan. One way to determine which indexes are needed for your data analytics is by knowing about all the queries and the data they are retrieving. For smaller applications, this might be possible; however, it would not be feasible in an enterprise with numerous teams and many databases. One way you can find out which queries are being run against tables and if they would benefit from an index is by using an indexer. An indexer is the tool or process by which data is indexed. A tool called Query Store is useful for SQL databases and is supported on Azure Synapse Analytics. It is not enabled by default. To enable it, execute the following SQL statement, replacing `databaseName` with the name of the dedicated SQL pool where you want this feature enabled:

```
ALTER DATABASE [databaseName]
SET QUERY_STORE = ON;
```

The information you can find using the data logged by Query Store includes queries with long execution times, queries that perform the most I/O transactions, queries with the highest wait durations, and comparisons between like queries that highlight downward performance trends. This data is pulled from dynamic management views (DMV), which hold information useful for identifying which queries on the database are latent and which queries would benefit from an index. As shown in Table 10.4, there are DMVs that recommend columns in a table that should exist in an index, and much more.

TABLE 10.4 Index-related Dynamic Management Views

Name	View	Description
sys.query_store_query_text	Query Store	Stores the query command text
sys.query_store_query	Query Store	Stores the query command text and runtime execution statistics
sys.query_store_plan	Query Store	Links plans with queries
sys.query_store_runtime_stats	Query Store	Stores runtime statistics for queries
sys.query_store_wait_stats	Query Store	Contains query wait information
sys.dm_pdw_exec_requests	Execution	Lists all steps taken for recent or active queries
sys.dm_pdw_request_steps	Execution	Lists all steps taken for a given query
sys.dm_pdw_dms_workers	Execution	Contains information about workers that process DMS steps
sys.dm_pdw_sql_requests	Execution	Holds information about SQL queries
sys.indexes	Object	Lists the indexes on the database
sys.index_columns	Object	Lists indexed columns per index
sys.pdw_index_mappings	Synapse	Links the physical index name to the logical index used on Compute node
sys.dm_db_index_operational_stats	Index	Returns I/O, latching, access method, and locking activity
sys.dm_db_index_physical_stats	Index	Returns fragments and size information for indexes and data
sys.dm_db_index_usage_stats	Index	Lists the index types and usage frequency
sys.dm_db_missing_index_columns	Index	Identifies the columns that are missing an index
sys.dm_db_missing_index_details	Index	Renders details about missing indexes

The Query Store uses these DMVs behind the scenes and offers some built-in capabilities, which can be graphically viewed in SQL Server Management Studio (SSMS). Figure 10.7 illustrates the output of one such report named Top Resource Consuming Queries.

FIGURE 10.7 Tuning queries with the Top Resource Consuming Queries report

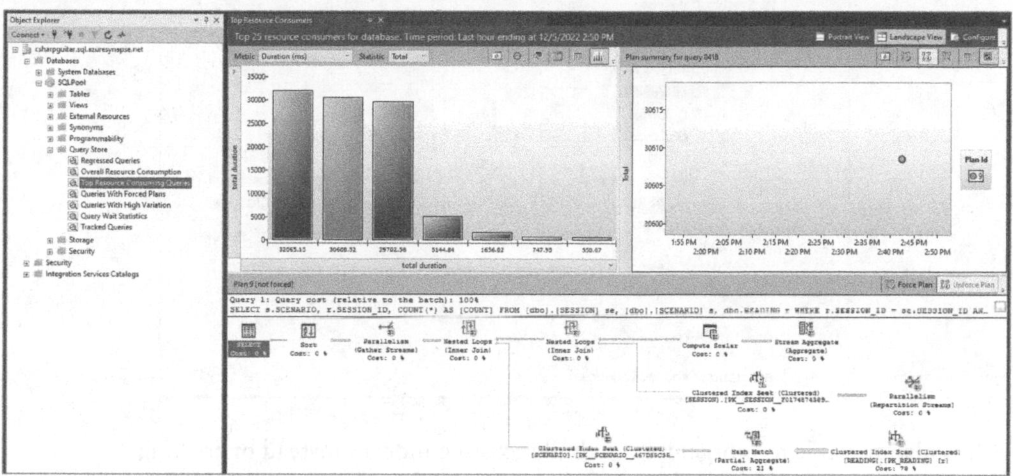

The default reports can give you insights into the areas in your data analytics solution that consume the most amount of CPU, memory, and/or time. Once you have the top problem queries identified, you can use the plethora of DMVs from Table 10.4 to dig deeper into the query execution and determine if there is a need to create additional indexes or even re-create the table with a clustered columnstore index. Performing the actual tuning depends on the queries you discovered from your analysis. Take the previous SQL query, which retrieves data from the `READING` table and has a clustered index like the following:

```
CLUSTERED INDEX ( READING_ID, SESSION_ID, ELECTRODE_ID, FREQUENCY_ID )
```

Then hypothetically consider that you found many queries that matched the following pattern:

```
SELECT READING_DATETIME, COUNT, VALUE
FROM   READING
WHERE ELECTRODE_ID = 2 AND FREQUENCY_ID = 4
```

In this scenario it would make sense to create a clustered index that contains those two fields, something like the following. The indexes on the dedicated SQL table can be seen in SSMS, as illustrated in Figure 10.8. For more information about indexes, refer to the "Data Concepts" section in Chapter 2 and the "Design and Implement the Data Exploration Layer" section in Chapter 4.

```
CREATE NONCLUSTERED INDEX IX_READING_ELECTRODE_FREQUENCY
ON dbo.READING( ELECTRODE_ID, FREQUENCY_ID )
```

FIGURE 10.8 Tuning queries with a nonclustered index

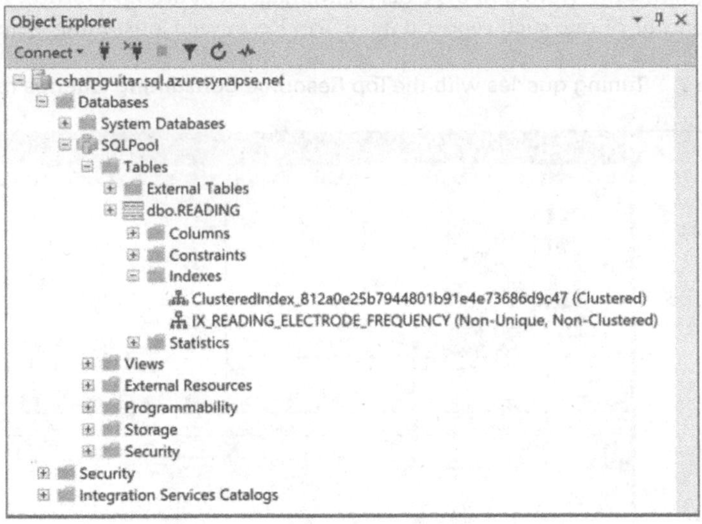

It is also possible to reorganize or rebuild existing indexes instead of creating new ones. You would do this if your analysis showed that the existing indexes are not used and you want to reduce the impact of such a change. SQL commands using `ALTER INDEX REORGANIZE` and `ALTER INDEX REBUILD` can be used for such activities. This rebuild and reorganization of the indexes used the `tempdb`, so make sure there is enough space to handle the indexing activity. Another option to tune your queries is to force a query to use a different query plan. There might be scenarios where the explain plan generated by the Query Optimizer is not the most optimal one, often due to changes in usage behaviors or frequent structural changes. You might also discover when running a query against `sys.query_store_plan` that there exist multiple plans for the given query, and it is using a nonoptimal one. By using the following SQL command, which executes a Query Store stored procedure, you force the query identified by a `query_id` to a specific plan identified by `plan_id`. (Figure 10.7 shows the values for the two parameters.) You would be able to find the same by using one or more of the DMVs in Table 10.4.

```
EXEC sp_query_store_force_plan @query_id = 8418, @plan_id = 9;
```

Contrary to the previous example, if you find that a query is forced to a specific explain plan, you can remove the binding by executing the unforce stored procedure using the following SQL command:

```
EXEC sp_query_store_unforce_plan @query_id = 8418, @plan_id = 9;
```

Note the Force Plan and Unforce Plan buttons in Figure 10.7, just above and to the right of the graphical illustration of the explain plan. The result of clicking those buttons is the same as that realized by running the stored procedures. As shown in Table 10.5, numerous Query Store stored procedures can be useful for tuning and managing your queries.

TABLE 10.5 Query Store stored procedures

Name	Description
`sp_query_store_clear_hints`	Removes query hints for a given `query_id`
`sp_query_store_flush_db`	Flushes Query Store in-memory data to disk
`sp_query_store_force_plan`	Forces Query Optimizer to use a specific plan for a given query
`sp_query_store_remove_plan`	Purges the plan from the Query Store
`sp_query_store_remove_query`	Removes the query and runtime stats from Query Store for the given query
`sp_query_store_reset_exec_stats`	Deletes the runtime states for the given plan from Query Store
`sp_query_store_unforce_plan`	Removes the forced plan bound to a query
`Sp_query_store_set_hints`	Updates or creates hints for a given `query_id`

These are rather advanced activities, so you should consult a DBA who has experience with the database and tables you want to change before changing them. You should consult with someone with experience on those specific tables and database prior to tuning them because, although the intent is to improve performance, these changes can cause a disruption as the explain plans are recalculated. The result could also be a degradation in performance, which might require a rollback, so you need to know how to roll back before you implement such changes. Lastly, don't forget about scaling, which entails increasing the performance level of your dedicated SQL pool. Refer to Table 3.8 for a list of dedicated SQL pool performance levels.

There are truly too many aspects of tuning to discuss here because of the vast variety of ways data analytics solutions can be implemented. This section provides some basic tips and will be helpful for the exam. One last tuning tip before proceeding has to do with materialized views that were introduced in Chapter 2. Remember that if your data analytics solution utilizes standard views and they appear latent, then you should consider converting them to materialized views. A materialized view will deliver better performance for the retrieval of complex queries in general and when compared to standard views, which you did in Exercise 2.3.

Tune Queries by Using Cache

The benefits of caching have been stated numerous times throughout this book and in this chapter. The fact is, retrieving data from memory is faster than retrieving it from disk, which is an I/O transaction. What has not been mentioned is the fact that dedicated SQL pools will cache repetitive query results with a feature, once enabled, called *result set caching*. Not only does that make queries return faster, but it also reduces the demand for computational resources, as the query does not have to be recompiled. To check if result set caching is enabled, execute the following SQL query, which is followed by sample results:

```
SELECT name, is_result_set_caching_on
FROM   sys.databases
```

```
+---------+--------------------------+
| name    | is_result_set_caching_on |
+---------+--------------------------+
| master  | False                    |
| SQLPool | False                    |
+---------+--------------------------+
```

Since the result renders a value of `False` for the database identified in the `name` column, execute the following SQL command to enable result set caching. The target database must be `master`, and you need to replace `databaseName` with your database. After the successful execution of this SQL command, the value for `is_result_set_caching_on` for the targeted database will be set to `True`.

```
ALTER DATABASE <databaseName> SET RESULT_SET_CACHING ON
```

Table 10.4 contains a DMV named `dm_pdw_exec_requests` that contains a column named `result_cache_hit`, which will identify if and how the query utilized caching. Execute the following query, which provides insights into whether or not a query is being retrieved from cache, and is followed by some sample results:

```
SELECT request_id, total_elapsed_time, command, result_cache_hit
FROM sys.dm_pdw_exec_requests
WHERE result_cache_hit IS NOT NULL
ORDER BY submit_time DESC
```

```
+------------+--------------------+------------------------------+------------------+
| request_id | total_elapsed_time | command                      | result_cache_hit |
+------------+--------------------+------------------------------+------------------+
| QID52464   | 46                 | SELECT FREQUENCY, ACTIVIT... | 1                |
| QID52455   | 125                | SELECT FREQUENCY, ACTIVIT... | 0                |
+------------+--------------------+------------------------------+------------------+
```

The first time a SQL query is executed, it is not cached in the result set cache. You can see this behavior in the table where the `result_cache_hit` is equal to `0`. Also note that the amount of time to perform the query is 125 ms, which is fast but three times slower than the same query run against the cache, which completed in 46 ms. The first line in the previous table was the second execution of the SQL query and was read from cache, as identified by the value of `1`. If this query were executed 100 million times per day, then at the end of the month that would be a significant time savings. There are also some Database Console Commands (DBCC) that are helpful with managing result set cache, for example, `SHOWRESULTCACHESPACEUSED` and `DROPRESULTSETCACHE`. As its name suggests, `SHOWRESULTCACHESPACEUSED` will show you information about the storage space used for caching for the database on which it is run. The following is an example of the `SHOWRESULTCACHESPACEUSED` output:

```
+----------------+------------+-------------+--------------+
| RESERVED_SPACE | DATA_SPACE | INDEX_SPACE | UNUSED_SPACE |
+----------------+------------+-------------+--------------+
| 5938704        | 5935848    | 1656        | 1200         |
+----------------+------------+-------------+--------------+
```

The `DROPRESULTSETCACHE` command does just as the name implies, in that executing it will remove all the cache entries from the database.

There is one other form of caching available for a dedicated SQL pool: adaptive cache. This was introduced in Chapter 9, illustrated in Figure 9.17, and described in Table 9.6. This caching method delivers performance gains by knowing where data needs to be located based on access frequency and patterns. The data is physically stored as close to the compute as possible using a combination of both a fast SDD cache layer and remote storage. The metrics to determine the success and impact of the adaptive cache are Adaptive Cache Hit Percentage and Adaptive Cache Used Percentage. Low numbers for those metrics can signify that your dedicated SQL pool needs additional capacity.

Optimize Pipelines for Analytical or Transactional Purposes

Much of the effort required to optimize and tune a pipeline lies in the discovery phase. That means trying to find where the slowness is coming from. Once you locate the general area, you can further debug by drilling down into the area details until you get to the actual piece of code or SQL query step that is causing the problem. That is no simple task. A majority of the content in Chapter 9 had to do with configuring, capturing, and analyzing performance and availability logs. Those logs are what you use to determine where the problem exists, if there is one, and how bad the issue is, and are useful to compare performance to after a change is made. Before delving into the specific performance aspects of optimizing a pipeline, first recall the terms OLTP, OLAP, and HTAP, which were introduced in Chapter 2.

From a transactional perspective, the term OLTP should come to mind. OLTP, which stands for online transactional processing, captures data in real time from activities like placing an order or ingesting a brain wave reading. OLTP tables need to be optimized for inserts.

Alternatively, OLAP, which stands for online analytical processing, is a database that stores historical data that is useful for analysis and business insights gathering. From an OLAP perspective, the database tables need to be optimized for reads. This means you would want to avoid a scenario in which you have an OLTP solution using the same database tables as the one OLAP does because of isolation levels (introduced in Chapter 3) and a potential overutilization of the table. For example, if you are handling a large volume of concurrent incoming data that needs to be inserted into a table, while at the same time a large report that queries heavily on the same table is requested, there would be contention. Not only would there be contention, but if the isolation level is read uncommitted, then the report might retrieve some data that has not yet been committed, which could be rolled back. That would render potentially incorrect results for the report. An approach for managing this common situation is to use HTAP, which stands for hybrid transaction/analytical processing.

A database that would benefit from HTAP is one that must handle both OLTP and OLAP operations. This means the database and tables within it need to handle both inserts, updates, and deletes while simultaneously providing performant data retrievals from select statements. You might be rightly thinking that dedicated SQL pools are not or have not been discussed in the context of OLTP. This is true, and you should feel confident in your learning that a dedicated SQL pool is not what you would want to use for OLTP transactions. This is due to the available performance level offerings, which currently do not offer tiers optimized for OLTP or HTAP implementation. Therefore, HTAP solutions apply more to Azure SQL and even Azure Cosmos DB products.

You implement an HTAP solution into an Azure SQL database by creating a nonclustered columnstore index, similar to the following:

```
CREATE NONCLUSTERED COLUMNSTORE INDEX NCCX_READING_ELECTRODE_FREQUENCY
ON dbo.READING( ELECTRODE_ID, FREQUENCY_ID )
```

This code results in the creation of an updatable columnstore index on which OLAP operations can operate. Additionally, memory will be allocated to handle OLTP transactions that get regularly ingested into the columnstore index. This has effectively separated the OLTP transactions and OLAP operations (see Figure 10.9). Keep in mind that this feature is only supported in the Business Critical or Hyperscale tiers of Azure SQL; it is not available in General Purpose.

If you experience unexpected behaviors when using HTAP on Azure SQL, there is a DMV that might lead your investigations in the right direction. The `sys.dm_db_xtp_nonclustered_index_stats` DMV is used to identify statistics on the in-memory nonclustered columnstore index. As mentioned, it is also possible to implement HTAP on an Azure Cosmos DB. From an Azure Cosmos DB perspective, you implement HTAP when you provision the container, which you did in Exercise 2.2. Turning on the analytical store resulted in something identical to that shown in Figure 10.9. Specifically, it resulted in the container containing both a transactional store and an analytical store, where data is inserted into the transactional store and auto syncs into the analytical store, also in near real time. Implementing HTAP, which separates your transactional data from the analytical one, is the most impactful action you can take to improve performance in this context. The other option is to copy the data from the transactional table to a table that is used for analytical purposes. You can certainly imagine the complexities surrounding that, especially if there are hundreds of millions of rows. It is an option, however, if you only copy changes or delta from the source table to the destination. This was covered in the "Design for Incremental Loading" section in Chapter 3.

FIGURE 10.9 Optimizing pipelines for analytics or transactional purposes

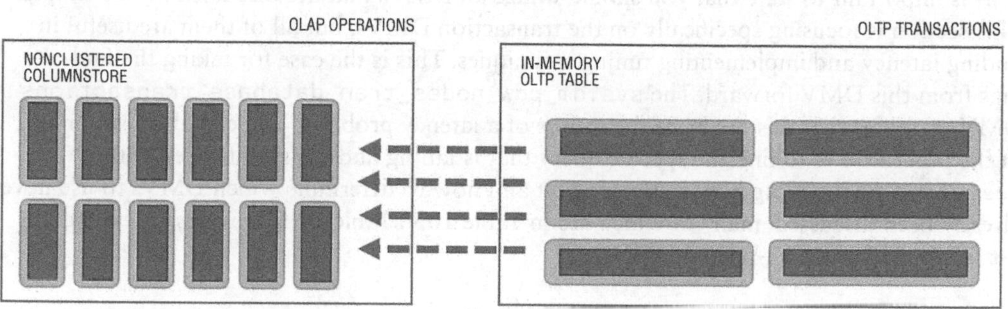

The remainder of this section discusses latency discovery and performance tuning in the context of DMVs, scaling, data flows, and some Spark specifics. From a DMV perspective, the focus here is on transactions, which are OLTP transactions. The relevant DMVs that concern transactions are summarized in Table 10.6, two of which are discussed in more detail, beginning with `sys.dm_pdw_nodes_tran_database_transactions`. Transactions typically comply with the ACID concept, which was introduced and discussed in Chapter 3. One aspect of the ACID concept is a mechanism called atomicity. This mechanism ensures that a transaction is successfully completed; if not, the transaction is rolled back. A rollback is an impactful event, and its occurrence will be visible in the form of failed queries or long execution durations. Both of those symptoms can have numerous root causes, but you can use the DMV to determine if the reason is due to transactions being rolled back. The following is a sample query that will identify if rollbacks are happening. The output of the query follows. The column value for rollback is `0`, implying there are no rollbacks. A value of `1`, however, would mean rollbacks are taking place.

```
SELECT
 SUM(CASE WHEN t.database_transaction_next_undo_lsn IS NOT NULL
        THEN 1 ELSE 0 END) AS [rollback], t.pdw_node_id,
        nod.[type]
FROM sys.dm_pdw_nodes_tran_database_transactions t
```

```
JOIN sys.dm_pdw_nodes nod ON t.pdw_node_id = nod.pdw_node_id
GROUP BY t.pdw_node_id, nod.[type]

+----------+-------------+---------+
| rollback | pdw_node_id | type    |
+----------+-------------+---------+
| 0        | 19          | COMPUTE |
| 0        | 19          | CONTROL |
+----------+-------------+---------+
```

It is important to state that you should utilize all DMVs that are discussed in this chapter. This section is focusing specifically on the transaction DMVs, but all of them are useful in finding latency and implementing tuning techniques. This is the case for taking the findings from this DMV forward. The `sys.dm_pdw_nodes_tran_database_transactions` DMV identifies that this might be the source of a latency problem. You can also use some of the other DMVs to find the specific query that is failing and the specific step within the query. Ideas surrounding how to pursue that and how to determine which DMVs to use have already been discussed, many of which are in Table 10.4. Table 10.6 provides an extended list of some transaction-related DMVs.

TABLE 10.6 Transaction and HTAP dynamic management views

Name	Description
`sys.dm_tran_commit_table`	Lists committed transactions per table
`sys.dm_db_xtp_transactions`	Lists active in-memory OLTP transactions
`sys.dm_tran_current_snapshot`	Displays a view of all active transactions
`sys.dm_tran_database_transactions` `sys.dm_pdw_nodes_tran_database_transactions`	Renders information about transactions
`sys.dm_tran_session_transactions`	Provides correlation information between sessions and transactions
`sys.dm_tran_active_transactions`	Returns information about transactions
`sys.dm_tran_current_transaction`	Lists information about a specific transaction
`sys.dm_tran_locks`	Lists locked transactions

Another DMV that is useful for monitoring transactions is `sys.dm_pdw_nodes_os_performance_counters`, which can provide the size of the transaction log file. This DMV was introduced in Table 9.2. Performing a select on that system table and checking the value in column `counter_value` will determine if the transaction log file size is too big, which means you should scale up to get more compute resources. In order to filter the query down a bit more, you would want to search for "log file(s)" in the `counter_name` column and "distribution" in the `instance_name` column. The size threshold for the transaction log file is around 160 GB; if you reach that, you should consider scaling up.

The concept of scaling, as discussed numerous times, has to do with adding compute resources to your workspace for running your data analytics processes. Scaling in the context just discussed has to do with the performance level of the dedicated SQL pool. The compute infrastructure responsible for running your data integration capabilities—such as your pipeline, triggers, linked services, access controls, and so on—is the integration runtime (IR). Chapter 3 discussed the capabilities of an IR, with Table 3.12 listing the different IR types and their provided compute resources. An IR does not provide the compute for the running of SQL queries on your dedicated SQL pools, Apache Spark pools, or batch processing, which is discussed later, nor does it provide the compute resource for a data flow, discussed next. Keep in mind that each datastore requires its own allocated amount of compute resources, and you need to keep an eye on which one specifically requires the scale.

The last point of discussion in this section has to do with an activity in a pipeline that can have a significant impact on performance: the Data Flow activity. An insight concerning Data Flow activities you should have gained from Exercises 4.7, 5.1, and 5.3 is that this is the activity that performs the heavy data ingestion and initial transformation work. Specifically, a data flow begins with a data source from which the data is pulled. The data is copied to the workspace, numerous transformations are performed on the data, and, finally, the transformed data result is inserted into a sink. Those three segments—source, transformation, and sink—are a good paradigm for compartmentalizing the areas to perform your optimization efforts. In Exercise 9.2 you learned how to determine the duration of a Data Flow activity that runs within your pipeline. If the duration is longer than expected, or if you just want to drill into the details of the data flow, that capability is available on the Monitor hub and shown in Figure 9.15. Clicking the icon in the Stages column for the data flow sink transformation, as shown in Figure 9.15, breaks that duration down into transformation and stages, like that shown in Figure 10.10.

You can also click each transformation in the data flow to view further diagnostic details, as shown in Figure 10.11.

Both data flow performance and diagnostic metric sources just presented help you determine where to start with your optimization effort. From both a source and sink perspective, recall the configurations available through their numerous tabs, for example, Projection and Optimize, as shown in Figure 5.21, Figure 4.26, and Figure 5.22. Tightening the columns of data you bring from the source onto the platform for transformation can increase performance. Projecting and tightening data means that you remove unnecessary columns from the query that retrieves the data, thus reducing the amount of data. If this is an option, then the Projection tab on the source is the place to perform that. For both the source and sink data, you are provided with an option to set partitioning. In each case, for both the source and sink, the data needs to be physically located in some datastore and in some format. In step 5 of Exercise 5.6, you selected the round-robin distribution model into which the sink data will be structured onto the node, and you left the default of Use Current Partitioning for the source. The other options for defining the structure of your transformed data are Hash, Dynamic Range, Fixed Range, and Key. As you've read in many examples in this book, the distribution model you choose depends on how your data is used.

FIGURE 10.10 Optimizing pipelines for analytics or transactional purposes: data flow sink transformation

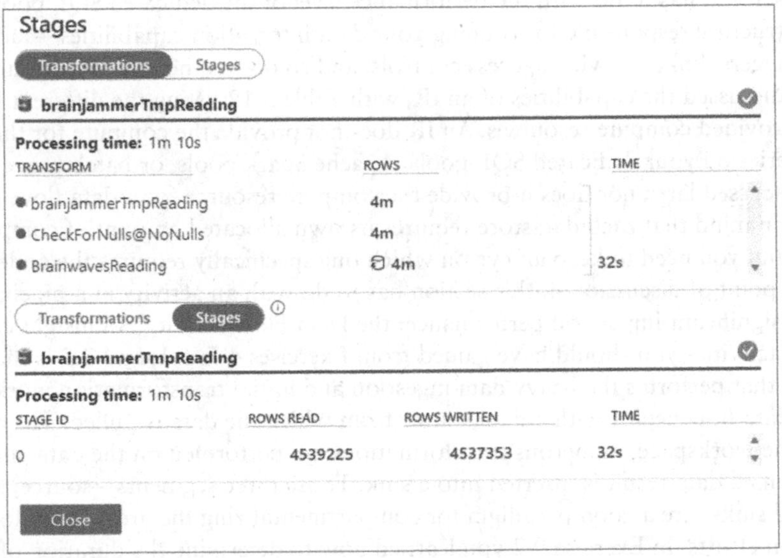

Stages

Transformations | Stages

brainjammerTmpReading

Processing time: 1m 10s

TRANSFORM	ROWS	TIME
brainjammerTmpReading	4m	
CheckForNulls@NoNulls	4m	
BrainwavesReading	4m	32s

Transformations | Stages

brainjammerTmpReading

Processing time: 1m 10s

STAGE ID	ROWS READ	ROWS WRITTEN	TIME
0	4539225	4537353	32s

Close

Another option for optimizing a sink is to disable indexes prior to loading the data into the sink. Indexes are a must-have when retrieving data from a data table; however, indexes slow insert operations. You can disable indexes by executing the following SQL commands:

```
ALTER INDEX ALL ON brainwaves.[TmpREADING] DISABLE
ALTER INDEX ALL ON brainwaves.[TmpREADING] REBUILD
```

Remember that part of the integration dataset configuration of a sink is to identify the location, which includes the table, into which the data will be written. That table is the one on which you disable and then reapply the indexes during the data flow execution. There are two multiline text boxes on the Settings tab of the data flow, as shown in Figure 10.12, where you can add Pre SQL scripts and Post SQL scripts. You can also see them in Figure 10.11, along with the duration each took.

FIGURE 10.11 Optimizing pipelines for analytics or transactional purposes: data flow transformations

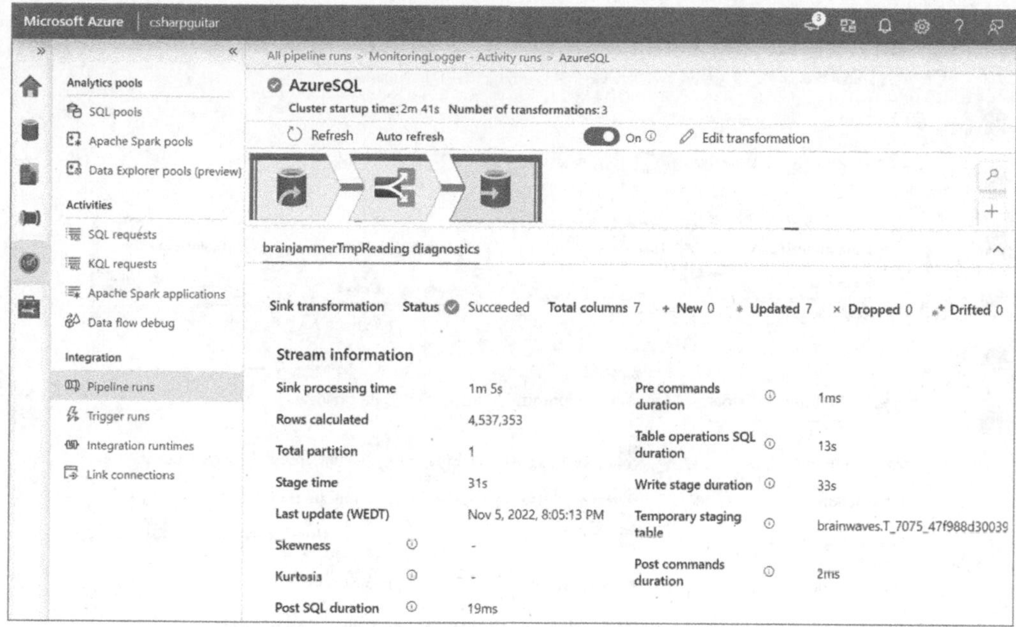

Configuring the pipeline to execute data flows in parallel is another option for improving sink performance. When you have multiple data flows within your pipeline that can run in parallel, then you can implement that by selecting the Run in Parallel check box for the given data flow, as shown in Figure 10.13.

The Compute Size, Compute Type, and Core Count drop-downs enable you to scale the resources allocated to a data flow. Table 10.7 shows the options in the Compute Size drop-down.

TABLE 10.7 Data Flow Compute size

Compute size	Compute type	Core count
Small	Basic (General Purpose)	4 (+ 4 Driver cores)
Medium	Basic (General Purpose)	8 (+ 8 Driver cores)
Large	Standard (Memory Optimized)	16 (+ 16 Driver cores)

FIGURE 10.12 Optimizing pipelines for analytics or transactional purposes: data flow pre and post SQL scripts

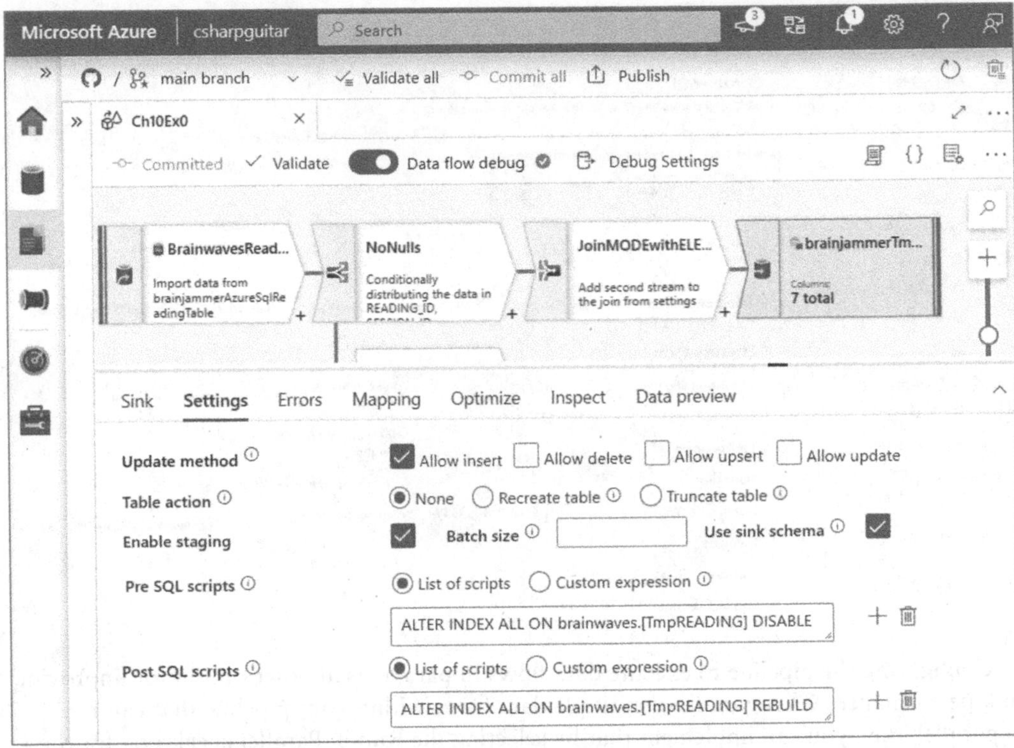

FIGURE 10.13 Optimizing pipelines for analytics or transactional purposes: data flow parallel execution

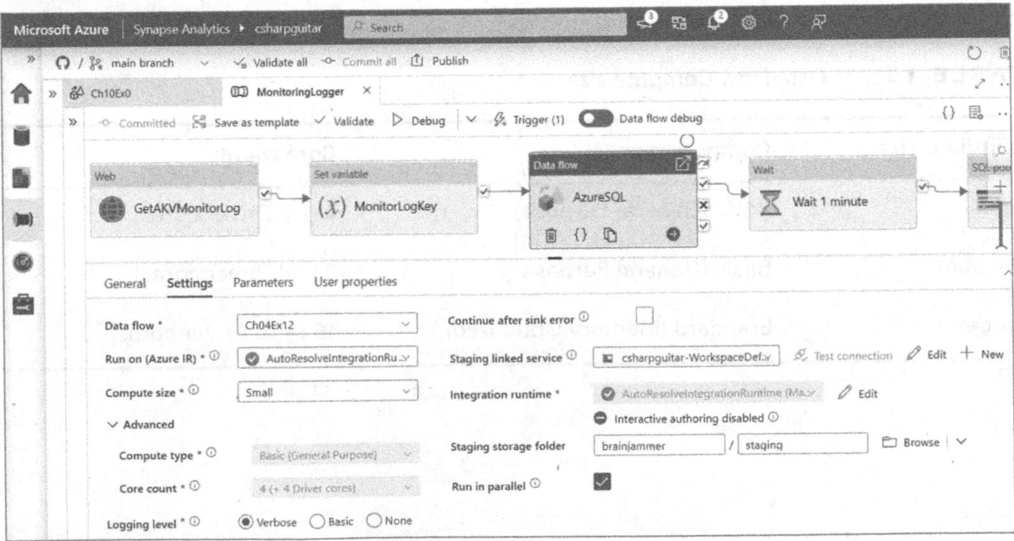

The other option in the Compute Size drop-down is Custom, which enables the Compute Type and Core Count boxes, allowing you to select up to 256 (+ 256 driver cores) for either Basic or Standard type. In addition to allowing you to select a greater core count, the Custom drop-down enables you to add dynamic content. This means you can write some logic that can be used to determine the compute type and/or the core count at runtime. Consider the following code snippet, for example:

```
@if(greater(activity('GetAKVMonitorLog').output.size, 1000000000), 128, 64)
```

This snippet checks the output of the `GetAKVMonitorLog` activity, which hypothetically provides the number of rows that need transformation for this run. If the size is greater than 1 GB, then set the core count to 128. If the `greater()` method returns `false`, meaning the number of rows is less than 1 GB, allocate 64 cores toward transforming the data. This is a very powerful approach for managing the amount of allocated compute resources at runtime.

The third segment of the data flow discussed in this section falls between the source and the sink, which is where the transformation of the data occurs. Many transformations can take place during the operation (refer to Table 4.4 and Table 4.5). For transformations like joins, exists, and lookups, there is a feature called *broadcasting*. If the data stream that either of those three transformations receives is small enough to fit inside the memory of the node on which the data flow executes, then the data can be loaded into memory instead of to disk, which is much faster because there is no I/O. Figure 10.14 shows the three options for configuring broadcasting: Auto, Fixed, and Off.

FIGURE 10.14 Optimizing pipelines for analytics or transactional purposes: data flow broadcasting

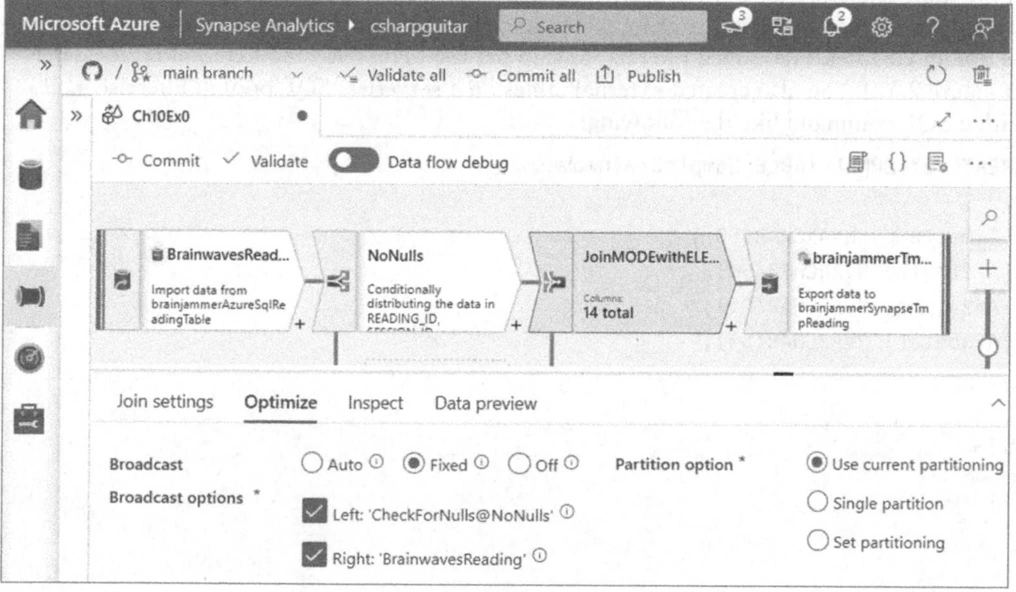

When the Auto option is selected, the data flow engine will decide if and when to broadcast. Setting the option to Off is recommended when you know in advance that the data stream, incoming (Left) or outgoing (Right), is too large to fit inside of the memory allocated to the data flow. Setting the option to Off disables the feature for the data flow engine, which results in a reduction in required compute resources. The compute resource is also reduced when the Broadcast option is set to Fixed, which not only disables the auto process but also enforces the storage of data into memory instead of disk.

Optimize Pipeline for Descriptive versus Analytical Workloads

The "Analytics Types" section in Chapter 2 described the numerous categories of data analytics—descriptive, diagnostic, predictive, preemptive, and prescriptive—each of which is an analytical workload. This is concluded by what you learned in the previous section: that OLTP operations are transactional, and OLAP operations are analytical. With the review of those five data analytics types, you should understand that none of them is transactional. Therefore, all optimization techniques that have been discussed that are applicable to OLAP operations apply here: the parallel execution and runtime scaling capabilities of data flows, the plethora of DMVs, indexing, caching, columnstores, execute plans, query execution statistics, partitions, distributions, and compacting files, to name some of the more impactful examples.

The data analytics pipelines you run in the analytical context means that you will be ingesting data a lot more often from numerous data sources. That statement is highly probable because of HTAP or combined OLTP/OLAP scenarios where the data remains in the same datastore for both transactional and analytical reasons. Therefore, it is prudent to discuss PolyBase, external tables, and the Copy activity. The External Table section in Chapter 2 described the relationship between PolyBase and external tables (refer to Figure 2.12). You also created external tables on a serverless SQL pool in Exercise 4.11, with a SQL command like the following:

```
CREATE EXTERNAL TABLE SampleBrainwaves
(
 [Timestamp] NVARCHAR(50),
 [AF3theta] NVARCHAR(50),
 [AF3alpha] NVARCHAR(50),
 [AF3betaL] NVARCHAR(50),
...
)
WITH
(
```

```
  LOCATION = 'EMEA/brainjammer/out/2022/04/03/*/*.parquet/*',
  DATA_SOURCE = SampleBrainwavesSource,
  FILE_FORMAT = SampleBrainwavesParquet
)
```

These two technologies, PolyBase and external tables, work together so that SQL queries, like the one here, can be run against data stored in files, commonly stored in an ADLS container. As shown in Figure 4.33, the following is the output of the preceding `CREATE EXTERNAL TABLE SampleBrainwaves` SQL query:

```
SELECT TOP 10 * FROM SampleBrainwaves
```

There are two optimization points to call out in the context of PolyBase and external tables. The first has to do with the number and size of files being loaded into the external table, and the other concerns querying the data existing on it. Your first thought when asked about number thresholds in the context of Azure Synapse Analytics is the number 60—the law of 60, in particular. The most optimal number of files to load into an external table is 60 or more, which maximizes the parallelism of your data load. To review why that is done, remember that in Exercise 5.6 you split a single large file of 391 MB into 60 files. Because there are 60 distributions on dedicated SQL pool external tables, the load of those files could happen on multiple nodes and would be more performant when compared to a single, large file due to the concurrent parallelism.

The other technique that can optimize performance has to do with querying the data on external tables. The magic of PolyBase is delivered with APIs that provide the capability to query files with SQL statements. Those files remain hosted on an Azure storage account, which is not backed by significant compute power. This means that each time a query is executed on an external table, the entire file is loaded into the `tempdb`. The query is executed against the data in the `tempdb` and not the file hosted in an ADLS container. You can image the impact on query performance if the file is big. If you find that the same query is run on an external table many times, then you might consider storing the dataset on a local table.

From a Copy activity perspective, you must consider that the data being ingested into the Azure Synapse Analytics workspace must traverse across the network. Therefore, the most important consideration is the physical location of the data that needs ingestion in proximity to the physical location of the nodes. You do not want data to be transmitted across an ocean but rather across the internal network inside a single datacenter. So, keep the datastore, and the nodes that will ingest and transform your data as close to each other as possible.

The other major influencer on copy (aka ingestion) performance is the size or amount of data being copied. If the data is in the form of a file then by all means use compression. Compression can reduce the size of a file being transferred over the network, which will greatly reduce the time required to do so. When ingesting from a relational database, copy data in bulk as opposed to line by line. If you move data line by line, each row is read at a time from the source datastore and then inserted at the same frequency into the destination. That is very slow. When you use `BULK INSERT` or a bulk copy program (BCP), as discussed in numerous chapters but introduced in Chapter 2, retrieving many rows at once and then inserting them concurrently drastically decreases the time required to copy data.

Troubleshoot a Failed Spark Job

It is inherently difficult to train or document how to troubleshoot technical problems because of the wide variety of symptoms one is exposed to. That means when an example is used to teach troubleshooting, it will most likely not be one that the person being trained will experience. Instead, there are two points to make concerning troubleshooting. The first one is that technical problems, from an application-level perspective, come in three forms: exceptions, slowness, and unavailability. You can troubleshoot each type of problem by using the information you learned in the Chapter 9. As shown in Figure 9.16, `stdout` logging is useful for observing the output of an Apache Spark job. As shown in Figure 10.15, you can use `stderr` logging to render exceptions that are generated within the job.

FIGURE 10.15 Troubleshooting a failed Spark job: `stderr`

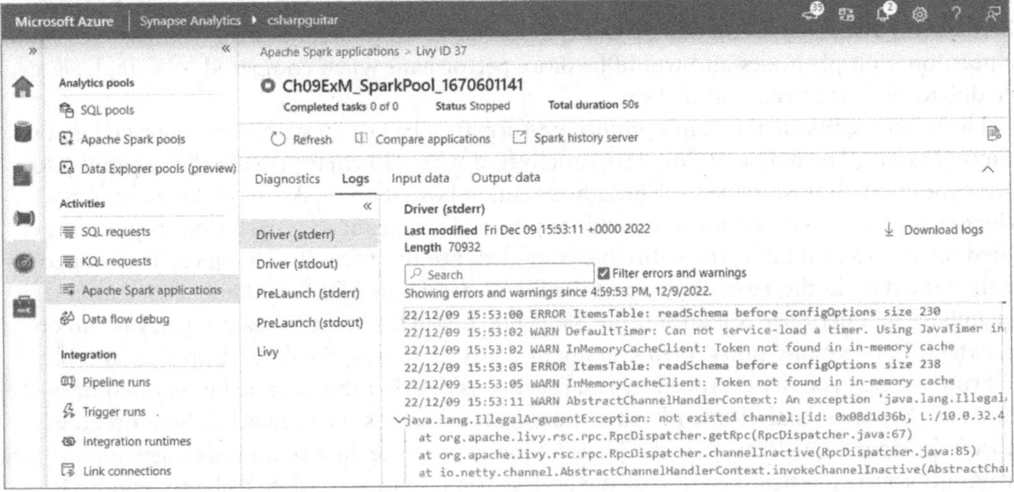

The exception message can be helpful to determine the reason for the exception and trigger some ideas for how to avoid and correct the issue. From a slowness perspective, there are two areas you need to analyze. The first area is the source code the job is executing. You need to determine if there are any bad coding patterns, such as recursion, imbedded loops (aka loops within loops), or any of the patterns stated in Table 10.1. There second area is the resource consumption of the Apache Spark cluster or pool that was consumed during the job execution, as shown in Figure 9.21, which illustrates network, CPU, and memory consumption for the Apache Spark cluster that ran the job. There is a similar set of metrics for the Apache Spark pool when the job is run from the Azure Synapse Analytics workspace, as discussed in the "Monitor Cluster Performance" section of Chapter 9. Both platforms, Azure Databricks and Azure Synapse Analytics, have autoscaling capabilities. When you created the Azure Databricks workflow in Exercise 6.8, you were instructed to set the number of workers to one and not enable autoscaling. This was done to reduce costs as you were testing and learning, and it is necessary to make sure compute is not consumed unnecessarily or accidentally. However, in a production scenario where you know that you may need extra capacity, you can enable autoscaling, as shown in Figure 10.16.

FIGURE 10.16 Troubleshooting a failed Spark job: scaling Apache Spark workflow cluster

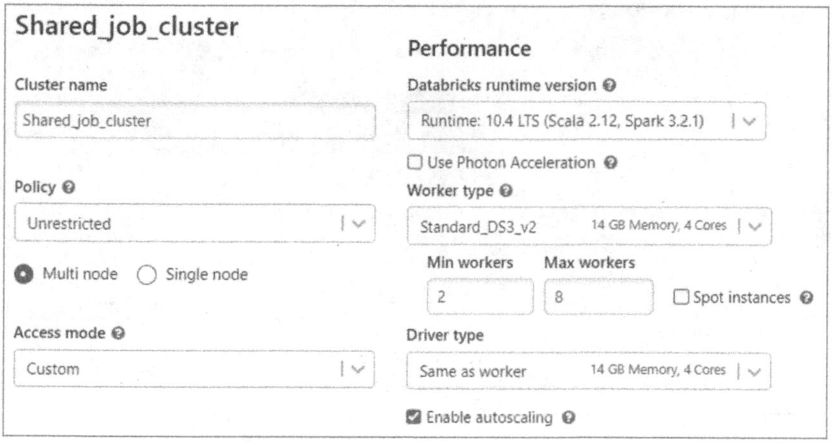

Checking the Enable Autoscaling check box increases the Min Workers value to 2 and the Max Workers value to 8. You can modify both values to allow an increase/decrease of the minimum workers and increase/decrease the maximum number of workers the cluster can be scaled to. Each node in the cluster will contain the compute resources identified in the Worker Type drop-down list box. Apache Spark pools in Azure Synapse Analytics have the same runtime capability for determining the worker size as they do for a data flow. The following expression sets the Executor Size value to Large when the `size` value from the `GetAKVMonitorLog` activity is greater than 100 MB; otherwise, set the Executor Size to Small. Figure 10.17 shows the configuration.

```
@if(greater(activity('GetAKVMonitorLog').output.size, 100000000), 'Large',
  'Small')
```

Also notice the Dynamically Allocate Executors option. When this option is enabled, the platform will add additional nodes with compute resources identified by the Execute Size value, as required.

The final technical issue has to do with availability. If one or more of the dependencies the job relies on is not online or has crashed, then the job will time out and fail. The reasons for this occurrence are many, such as a newly implemented firewall rule, a breach in the threshold of DTUs for a database, an unhandled exception in a system process, a power outage in the datacenter, or an update to the user ID and password. The fact that the job cannot access a dependent resource will result in an exception, and the exception will provide a message. From that point, you need to act based on the specific resource that is not accessible. The resolution could be as simple as a reboot.

FIGURE 10.17 Troubleshooting a failed Spark job: scaling Apache Spark pool job

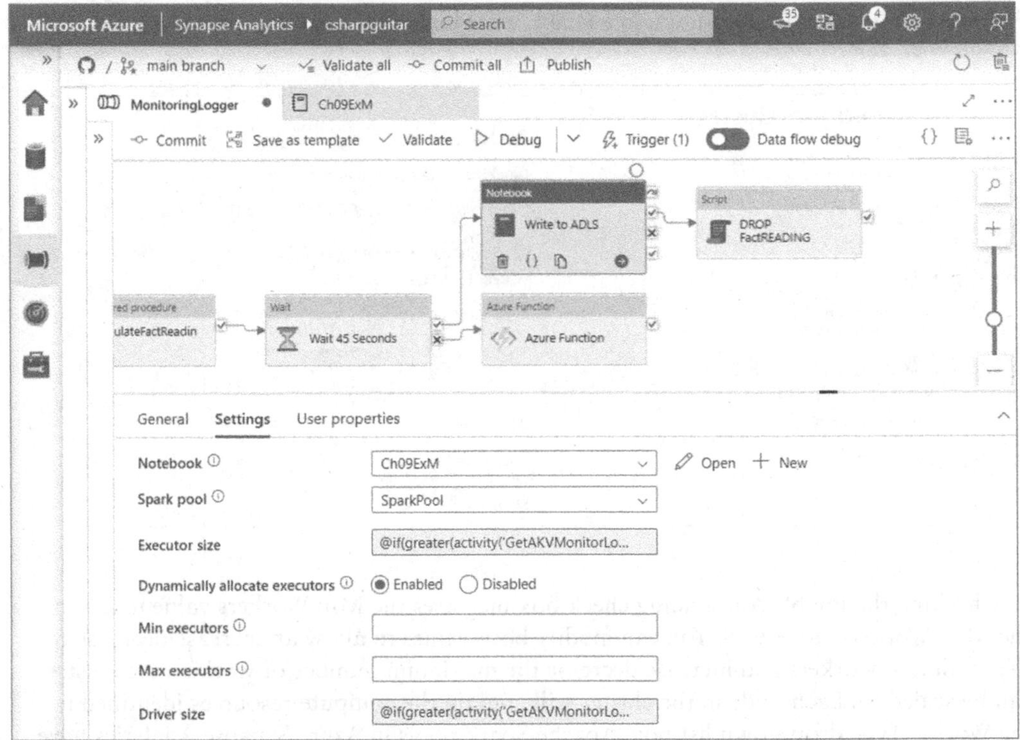

Troubleshoot a Failed Pipeline Run

It is almost certain that at some point while running your data analytics procedures, something unexpected will happen. When it does, you must gather information like the symptoms experienced and the log files that will help you get down to the reason for the behavior. Knowing what you read in the last section about the abundant variety of scenarios that lead to the complexity of provided relevant examples, you can rely on the stated forms of issues. Those forms are for exceptions, slowness, and availability.

The initial location to begin troubleshooting a failed pipeline run is on the Monitor hub on your Azure Synapse Analytics workspace. Recall from Figure 9.10 that you can view the status of recent pipeline runs. A run with a status of Failed is a good indicator of an issue. Additionally, you can look at Figure 9.11, which will render the specific activity in the pipeline that failed. The perspectives in Figure 9.11 and Figure 10.18 will give you cross-pipeline run visibility, which helps you find a single activity that is causing the problem. This is in contrast to looking at each pipeline run individually, as in Figure 9.10, and checking the activities from there.

FIGURE 10.18 Troubleshooting a failed pipeline run

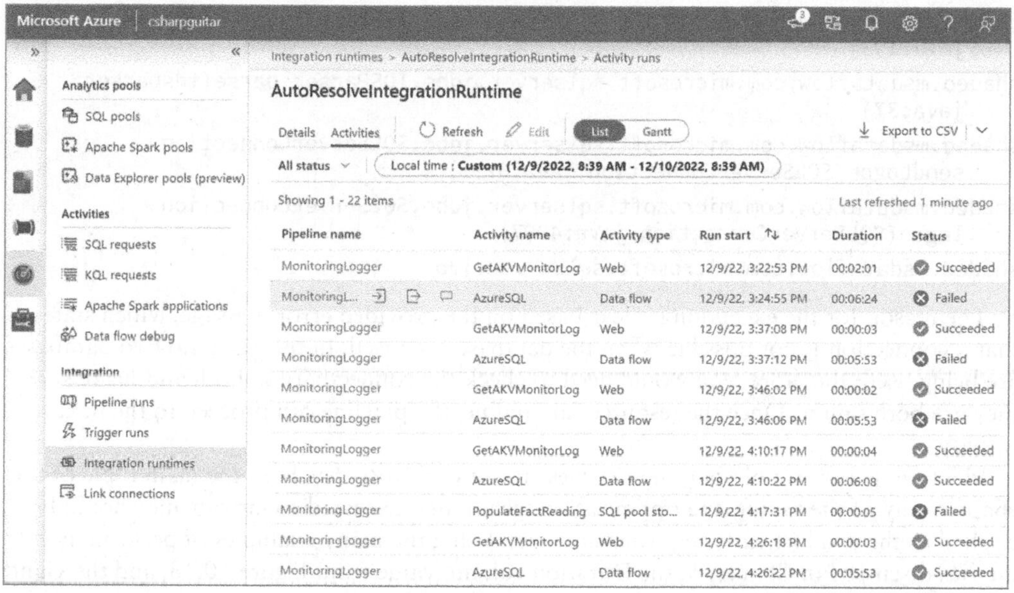

Pipeline name	Activity name	Activity type	Run start	Duration	Status
MonitoringLogger	GetAKVMonitorLog	Web	12/9/22, 3:22:53 PM	00:02:01	Succeeded
MonitoringL...	AzureSQL	Data flow	12/9/22, 3:24:55 PM	00:06:24	Failed
MonitoringLogger	GetAKVMonitorLog	Web	12/9/22, 3:37:08 PM	00:00:03	Succeeded
MonitoringLogger	AzureSQL	Data flow	12/9/22, 3:37:12 PM	00:05:53	Failed
MonitoringLogger	GetAKVMonitorLog	Web	12/9/22, 3:46:02 PM	00:00:02	Succeeded
MonitoringLogger	AzureSQL	Data flow	12/9/22, 3:46:06 PM	00:05:53	Failed
MonitoringLogger	GetAKVMonitorLog	Web	12/9/22, 4:10:17 PM	00:00:04	Succeeded
MonitoringLogger	AzureSQL	Data flow	12/9/22, 4:10:22 PM	00:06:08	Succeeded
MonitoringLogger	PopulateFactReading	SQL pool sto...	12/9/22, 4:17:31 PM	00:00:05	Failed
MonitoringLogger	GetAKVMonitorLog	Web	12/9/22, 4:26:18 PM	00:00:03	Succeeded
MonitoringLogger	AzureSQL	Data flow	12/9/22, 4:26:22 PM	00:05:53	Succeeded

Notice in Figure 10.18 that the issue with this pipeline has to do with the AzureSQL Data Flow activity. This pipeline was used in the Chapter 9 as an example, and you can see the AzureSQL activity in Figure 9.12. You can view the pipeline configuration file `MonitoringLogger.json` in the `Chapter09` folder on GitHub. The AzureSQL activity is the data flow that was created in Exercise 4.13 and resembles Figure 4.38. The activity it performs is the ingestion of brain wave reading from an Azure SQL database to a temporary table that exists in a dedicated SQL pool. To find out the exception causing the AzureSQL activity to fail, hover over the line showing the failure and select the comment icon, as shown in Figure 10.18. In this scenario, the exception error code is `DF-Synapse-DBNotExist`, with summarized details provided here:

```
Job failed due to reason: at Sink 'brainjammerTmpReading': Cannot
   connect to SQL database: 'jdbc:sqlserver://csharpguitar.sql.azuresynapse
   .net:1433;database={SQLPool}', 'Managed Identity (factory name):
   csharpguitar-synapse'.[SQL Exception]Error Code:40892, Error Message:
   Cannot connect to database when it is paused. ClientConnectionId:174263d3-
   d6da-427e-b146-5bd14cab0901, error stack:shaded.msdataflow.com.microsoft.
   sqlserver.jdbc.SQLServerException.makeFromDatabaseError(SQLServerException.
   java:265)
shaded.msdataflow.com.microsoft.sqlserver.jdbc.TDSTokenHandler
   .onEOF(tdsparser.java:300)
shaded.msdataflow.com.microsoft.sqlserver.jdbc.TDSParser.parse(tdsparser
   .java:133)
shaded.msdataflow.com.microsoft.sqlserver.jdbc.TDSParser.parse(tdsparser
   .java:37)
shaded.msdataflow.com.microsoft.sqlserver.jdbc.SQLServerConnection
   .sendLogon(SQLServerConnection.java:6295)
shaded.msdataflow.com.microsoft.sqlserver.jdbc.SQLServerConnection
   .logon(SQLServerConnection.java:4907)
shaded.msdataflow.com.microsoft.sqlserver.jdb
```

The reason for the exception is clear based on the provided error message, which states that a connection is not possible when the database is paused. In this scenario two databases are being used; therefore, you would need to check the connectivity to both and make sure they are both online. Once the resources are online, the pipeline can proceed to the next activity.

Identifying and troubleshooting slowness for optimization has been the main topic of this chapter. Any of the tuning and optimization techniques discussed so far can and should be applied to the product suffering from slowness. Using the many examples of performance metrics discussed in Chapter 9, the Duration column value from Figure 10.18, and the Gantt chart visualization of the pipeline run in Figure 9.22 will guide you to the point of slowness and contention. A point to call out here that was not mentioned in the previous section is that the level of logging that you have enabled can cause slowness. The higher the level of logging, the bigger impact on the performance of your pipeline. Figure 4.39 and Figure 5.40 show examples of a location to configure the logging level. The concept of verbosity was introduced in Chapter 3 and described in detail in Chapter 9 (refer to Table 9.1).

The last topic to mention in the context of slowness has to do with overutilized compute resources. This is one of the most common scenarios you will encounter. The metrics you configure to monitor the health of your data analytics pipeline should target this specifically. When those metrics show that compute resources are under pressure, the action to take is to increase the allocated amount by scaling. Scaling on Azure is very easy, as shown in Figure 10.19.

FIGURE 10.19 Troubleshooting a failed pipeline run: scaling a dedicated SQL pool

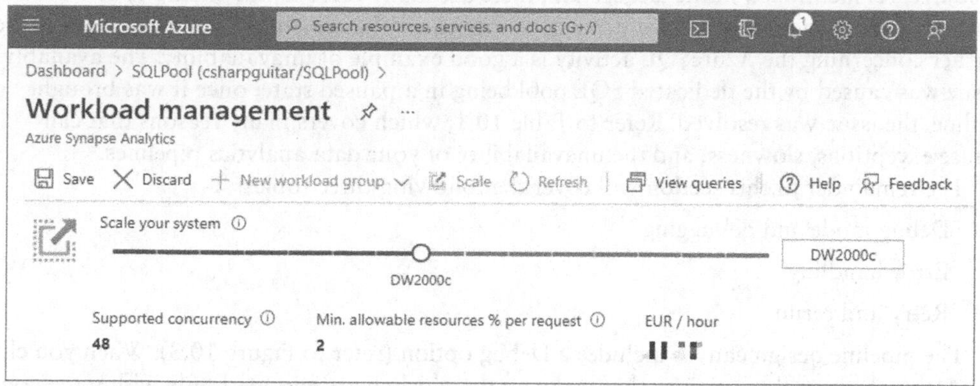

Making a few configurations on the additional amount to allocate and clicking the Save button is all it takes to add more compute to the dedicated SQL pool. It is just as easy with an Apache Spark pool, as shown in Figure 10.20.

FIGURE 10.20 Troubleshooting a failed pipeline run: scaling an Apache Spark cluster

Scale Settings
SparkPool
Configure the settings that best align with the workload on the Apache Spark pool.
Autoscale *
Enabled Disabled
Node size family
MemoryOptimized
Node size *
Small (4 vCores / 32 GB)
Number of nodes *
3
88
Estimated price
Est. cost per hour 1.53 to 44.88 EUR View pricing details
Allow session level packages
Enabled Disabled
Dynamically allocate executors
Enabled Disabled
Default number of executors
20
45
Intelligent cache size
50%
Apply
Cancel

Keep in mind that scaling will have some transient impact on your pipelines, so you should not perform a scale up or down while a pipeline or any other process is running. You might not be in a situation that allows the stoppage of all operations that run against your nodes, but you should try to avoid scaling procedures while the compute resources are being used.

The last form of troubleshooting has to do with the unavailability of a dependent resource. As mentioned in the last section, there are many reasons, for example, new firewall rules or a crash that rendered the dependent application inaccessible. The issue that was used earlier concerning the AzureSQL activity is a good example of unavailability. The availably issue was caused by the dedicated SQL pool being in a paused state; once it was brought online, the issue was resolved. Refer to Table 10.1, which covers many reasons that can cause exceptions, slowness, and the unavailability of your data analytics pipelines.

The remainder of this section will cover the following three topics:

- Debug mode and debugging
- Error handling
- Retry and rerun

The pipeline design canvas includes a Debug option (refer to Figure 10.3). When you click the Debug button, the activities that make up the pipeline are executed only within the context of your local session. This means the operations performed by the activities are visible only to you. After you are confident with the changes and are ready to move to the next phase of deployment, you can commit the changes to your source code repository and publish them. Once published, the changes you made will be visible to others and available for release into your production environment. You learned about testing and release processes in Chapter 9. The point here is that debugging is performed during the development phase against test data until the developer has met all the requirements. Use the Debug button to perform this testing during this phase of the project.

Now refer to Figure 10.13 and Figure 10.17. In addition to the Debug button, there is a toggle switch named Data Flow Debug. This toggle switch appears only when a Data Flow activity is in the pipeline. When the toggle switch is present and not yet enabled, select the Debug button or toggle the switch to the on position, which renders the pop-out window shown in Figure 10.21.

FIGURE 10.21 Troubleshooting a failed pipeline run: enabling Data Flow Debug

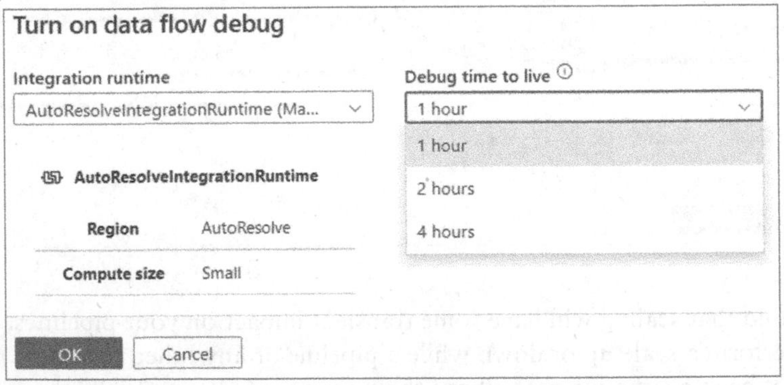

The pop-out window enables you to select the integration runtime to use for the pipeline execution. Data flows often perform very large ingestion and transformational activities, and this additional amount of compute power is required to process them. The default amount of time to keep the IR active is 1 hour, but if you need a longer TTL, you can configure it for up to 4 hours. Note that you are charged for the consumption of the node, which is configured for the IR—in this case, Small, which is 4 (+ 4 driver cores). Once the Data Flow Debug option is enabled, it can be debugged during the pipeline execution and monitored on the Debug tab of the Pipeline Runs monitor (refer to Figure 9.10). Notice in Figure 10.12 that Data Flow Debug is enabled. You will also notice the Debug Settings button. When you click it, a pop-out window appears (see Figure 10.22). The debug settings let you limit the number of rows to be returned, set parameters, and determine how the data is to be stored while debugging.

FIGURE 10.22 Troubleshooting a failed pipeline run: debug settings

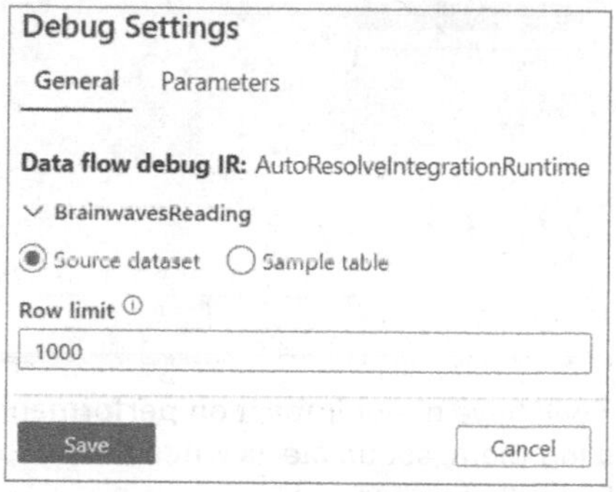

The next useful for debugging has to do with setting breakpoints. Breakpoints are flags, set at strategic locations along your pipeline, that instruct the pipeline execution engine to stop moving forward. This is a very useful tool, especially when you want to make sure the output of a previous activity is as expected before moving forward to perhaps a very long-running data flow. In most of the figures in this book that show selected activities within a pipeline, you will notice a circle on the top right. That is where and how you set a breakpoint. When you click the circle, it will become solid, as shown in Figure 10.23.

This option is also referred to as the Debug Until feature. When the circle is selected, the pipeline will be executed until the breakpoint is hit. The pipeline execution shown in Figure 10.23 will process up to the `PopulateFactReading` SQL pool stored procedure activity. That activity will be executed but will stop progressing from that point. During the development or debugging process, you might encounter a scenario that unavoidably has a probability of failure. Managing the possibility of errors in a pipeline requires some form of error handling. The reason for handling (aka managing) errors is to prevent the pipeline from halting execution before completion. If pipeline execution stops before completion, the data may be only partially processed, leaving it in an undesired or unexpected state. Data in an unexpected format or timeframe can cause problems when you try to correct the error by running the pipeline again, thus potentially causing even more errors. This is why it is prudent to handle errors: so that the need to perform data cleansing due to errors can be avoided in the first place.

FIGURE 10.23 Troubleshooting a failed pipeline run: breakpoints

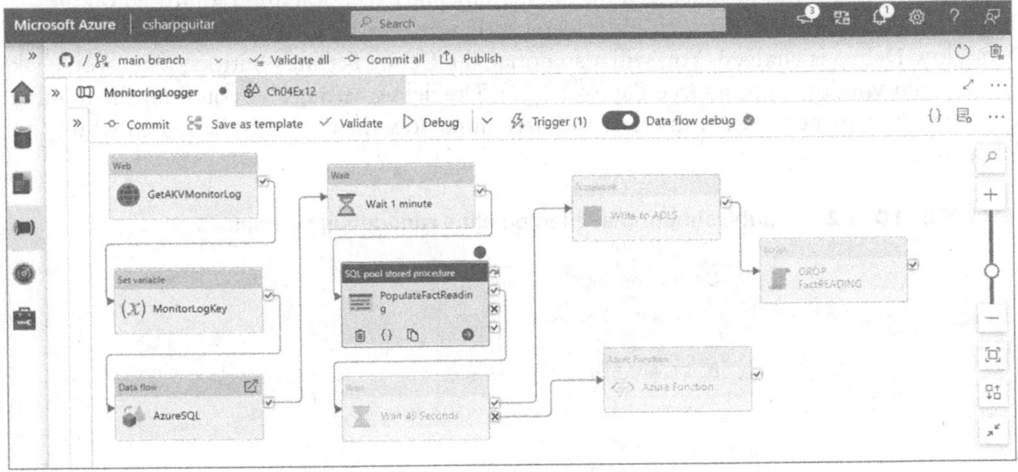

Exceptions will have major impact on performance, even if handled, so you should log them, set up alerts when they happen, and work toward avoiding them all together.

Chapter 6, "Create and Manage Batch Processing and Pipelines," introduced the different execution paths (aka conditions) that can be taken between pipeline activities. As shown in Figure 6.28, the four options are Success, Failure, Completion, and Skipped. You also saw the execution paths in Figure 6.64 and Figure 6.65, which were part of Exercise 6.13, and Figure 6.72. As a discussion point, note in Figure 10.24 the failure dependency between a data flow named AzureSQL and a Script activity named DROP FactReading. There is also a failure dependency between the SQL pool stored procedure activity named PopulateFact-Reading and the DROP FactReading Script activity.

The behavior is that if either AzureSQL or PopulateFactReading fail, then DROP FactReading will be executed. If that activity is completed successfully, then the pipeline will report a Success status. Alternatively, if there was no failure condition from either of those two activities and either of them failed, then the pipeline would report a Failed status. A failed pipeline execution should trigger an alarm that would engage humans to investigate and fix the problem. Getting a person to troubleshoot a failed pipeline is an expensive process. You could instead handle the error. Handling the error requires application knowledge. That means you would need to know what AzureSQL and PopulateFactReading do and what their dependencies are. AzureSQL basically copies brain wave data from an Azure

SQL database to a database on a dedicated SQL pool. If either of those databases is not available or the copy fails, then in this context you would not want any data analytics performed on the table named `FactREADING`. The PopulateFactReading activity executes the stored procedure named `uspCreateAndPopulateFactReading`, which you applied within Exercise 5.1. The code is in the `Chapter05/Ch05Ex01` directory on GitHub. The SQL in the stored procedure expects that the table named `FactREADING` does not exist. If the table does already exist, then the attempt to create it will fail, which is why there is a failure dependency with an activity that drops that table. Changing the code in the stored procedure might be a better option than implementing error handling; however, making changes to product code is risky and requires a lot of testing and approvals. The first of two benefits of the failure condition is that it prevents the pipeline from returning a Failed status, which triggers support. The second benefit is that it enables you to clean up data that might prevent the next run on the pipeline from completing successfully. You might be thinking, if this is implemented, then the pipeline could be failing but reporting successful, and no one would know. That would be true had you not learned about monitoring, logging, and alerting in the Chapter 9. You would want to be sending Error logs to an Azure Monitor Log Analytics cluster and alerting when errors are happening.

FIGURE 10.24 Troubleshooting a failed pipeline run: dependency conditions

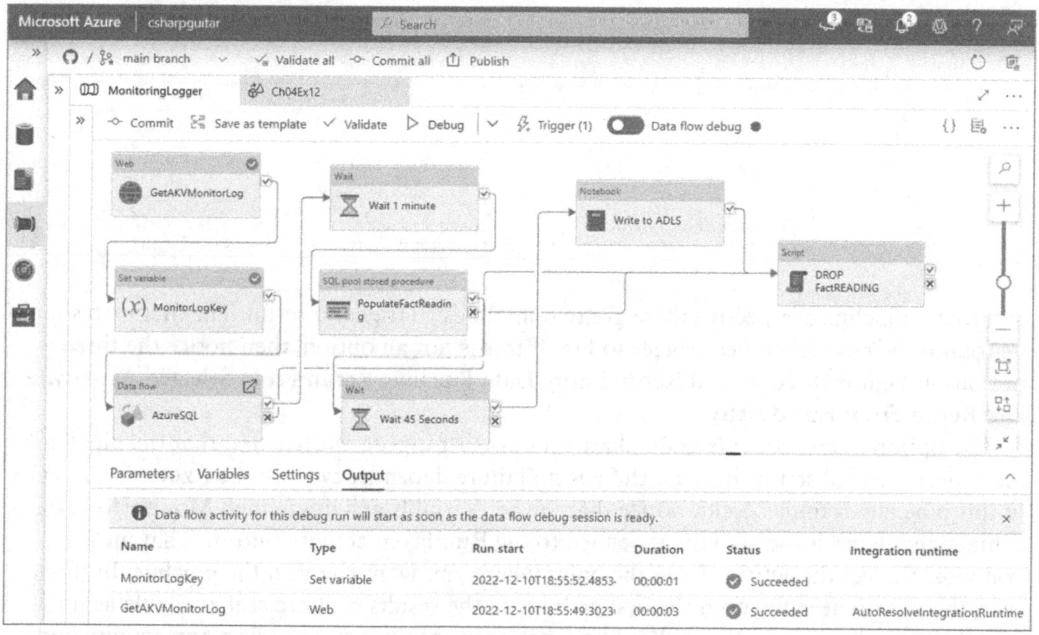

The final point has to do with retrying and rerunning data flows and pipelines. It is common to retry or rerun processes when there is an unexpected error, as previously

mentioned. The important point is that you need to make sure the data is in the expected state for further ingestion and transformation. If an error results in the stopping of a pipeline or Data Flow activity, then you need to check the data to make sure it was not corrupted, since the operation being run on it did not complete as expected. As shown in Figure 10.25, there are options that apply to a Data Flow activity to configure the number of retry attempts and the retry interval. A value of 5 for the Retry property instructs the data flow engine to attempt the execution of the activity five times before returning a status result of Failed to the pipeline. The value of 120 for Retry Interval causes the engine to wait 2 minutes between each retry.

FIGURE 10.25 Troubleshooting a failed pipeline run: retries

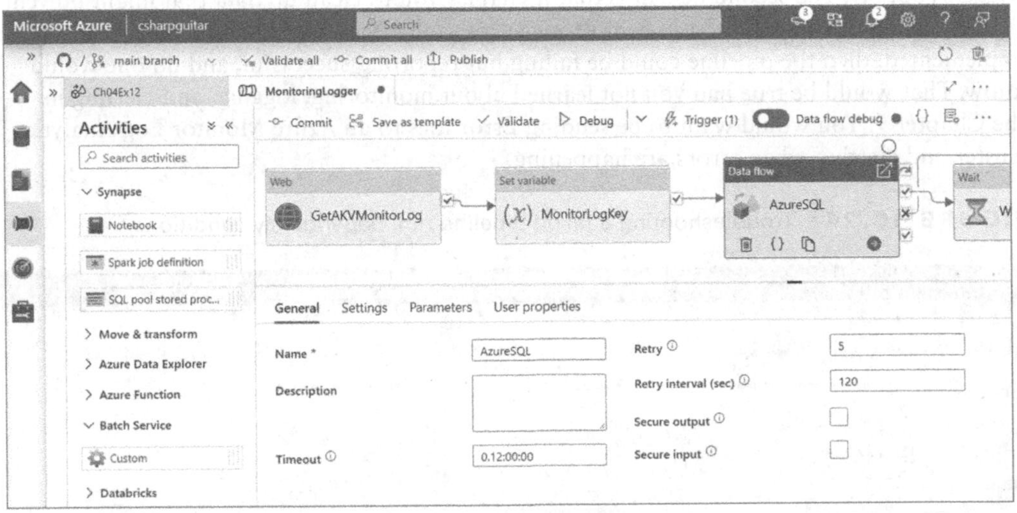

From a pipeline perspective there are two methods to trigger a rerun. The first is to simply wait until the next scheduled trigger to fire. If this is not an option, then notice the three options in Figure 10.26 named Rerun Entire Data Pipeline, Rerun From Selected Activity, and Rerun From Failed Activity.

The option names provide good clues about their purpose. Notice first that the pipeline did report a Failed status, because there is no failure dependency from the AzureSQL activity in this pipeline example. Next, notice that the Set Variable activity named MonitorKeyLog is highlighted and is the activity appended to the Run From activity button. That means you would select the activity from the point where you want to rerun the pipeline. In this case, there is no need to rerun the first activity, as the results of it are still available as input into the second activity, MonitorKeyLog. The other option is to not select any activity and rerun the pipeline from the point of failure—in this case, the Azure SQL activity.

FIGURE 10.26 Troubleshooting a failed pipeline run: reruns

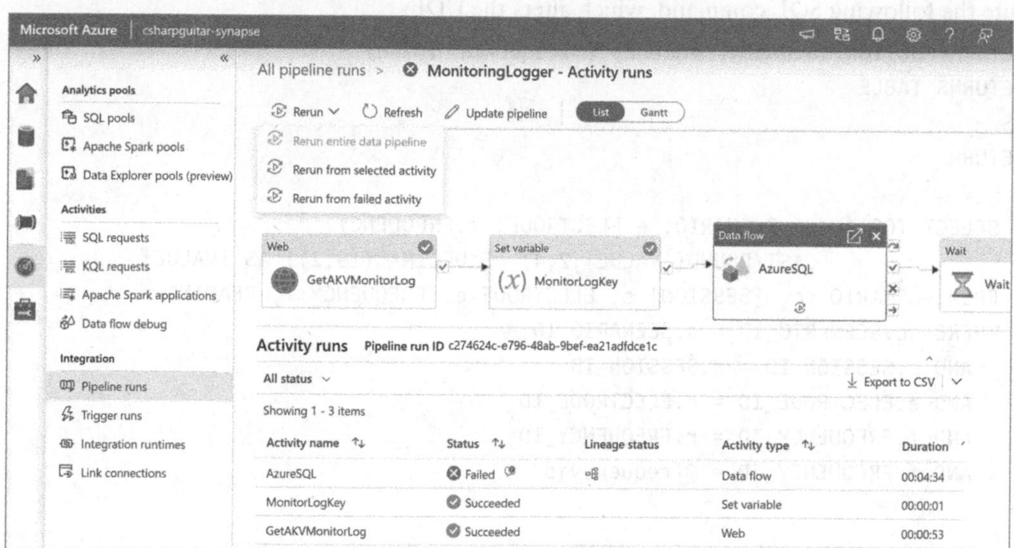

Rewrite User-Defined Functions

The description of user-defined functions (UDF) in Chapter 2 is very informative, so have a look back at it if you need a refresher. In general terms, a UDF is a code snippet that performs some action on your data. These code snippets are most commonly triggered using the method name from within either SQL queries or stored procedures. One benefit of a UDF is that it reduces the amount of written code necessary to perform actions. This was the example from Chapter 2. Another benefit is that you can validate or format data. The result of the SQL query from Chapter 2 displays the values with three decimal points, as follows:

```
SELECT * FROM ValuesByFrequency (1)

+------------------+------------+------------+------------+
| SCENARIO         | ELECTRODE  | FREQUENCY  | VALUE      |
+------------------+------------+------------+------------+
| ClassicalMusic   | AF3        | THETA      | 4144.103   |
| PlayingGuitar    | AF4        | THETA      | 26.250     |
| TikTok           | AF3        | THETA      | 9.681      |
| ...              | ...        | ...        | ...        |
+------------------+------------+------------+------------+
```

If you want to rewrite the UDF so that only two decimals are rendered, you would execute the following SQL command, which alters the UDF:

```
ALTER FUNCTION ValuesByFrequency (@frequencyid int)
RETURNS TABLE
AS
RETURN
(
  SELECT TOP 10 sc.SCENARIO, e.ELECTRODE, f.FREQUENCY,
              CAST(ROUND([VALUE],2,4) AS DECIMAL(19,2)) AS [VALUE]
  FROM SCENARIO sc, [SESSION] s, ELECTRODE e, FREQUENCY f, READING r
  WHERE sc.SCENARIO_ID = s.SCENARIO_ID
    AND s.SESSION_ID = r.SESSION_ID
    AND e.ELECTRODE_ID = r.ELECTRODE_ID
    AND f.FREQUENCY_ID = r.FREQUENCY_ID
    AND f.FREQUENCY_ID = @frequencyid
)
```

When you then use the rewritten UDF by executing the following SQL statements, the resulting data in the `VALUE` column will be rounded to two decimal places. The results of the query follow the snippet. The `ALTER` statement and the SQL query are in the `Chapter10` folder on GitHub, in a file named `alterUDF.sql`.

```
SELECT * FROM ValuesByFrequency (1)
```

```
+------------------+-------------+-------------+------------+
| SCENARIO         | ELECTRODE   | FREQUENCY   | VALUE      |
+------------------+-------------+-------------+------------+
| ClassicalMusic   | AF3         | THETA       | 4144.10    |
| PlayingGuitar    | AF4         | THETA       | 26.25      |
| TikTok           | AF3         | THETA       | 9.68       |
| ...              | ...         | ...         | ...        |
+------------------+-------------+-------------+------------+
```

In Chapter 3, you learned about functions with regard to Azure Stream Analytics. Specifically, you read about JavaScript UDFs with an example like the following, which returns the square root of the number passed as a parameter:

```
function squareRoot(n) {
  return Math.sqrt(n);
}
```

To change or rewrite this UDF, access it via the portal and make the change, similar to that shown in Figure 10.27.

FIGURE 10.27 Rewriting Azure Stream Analytics user-defined functions

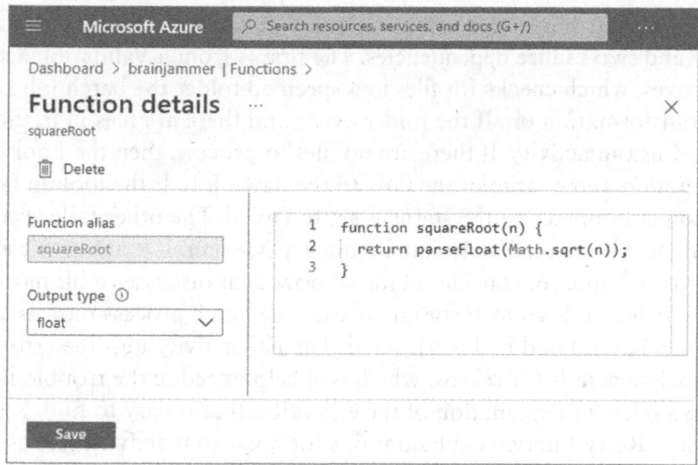

Making the change is not so complicated. Keep in mind that you would not want to make this change directly to your production data analytics pipeline. This would also require functional and regression testing prior to moving into a live environment. This also applies to the changes made to the SQL function, as it does to the following UDF contained in a notebook that runs on an Apache Spark cluster. In Exercise 5.10 you wrote the following UDF:

```
unlist = udf(lambda x: round(float(list(x)[0]),3), DoubleType())
```

The UDF helped in the process of normalizing brain wave data from the disbursement shown in Figure 5.29 to a more normalized form, as shown in Figure 5.30. Making a change to this is the same as proposed in the previous example. This is achieved by opening the notebook named `Ch05Ex10` and performing the update. Once you complete the local testing, make the commits and have the modification flow through your release management process.

Design and Develop a Batch Processing Solution

The processes discussed here were introduced in Chapter 6. A reason for introducing them there and following up here is that many of the concepts—such as logging, monitoring, and error handling—had not yet been covered. At this point, however, it is just a matter of connecting the dots and providing more detail within the context of each of these three sections.

Design and Configure Exception Handling

Refer to Figure 6.72, which is a representation of a pipeline that contains an Azure Batch Custom activity and two failure dependencies. The first is from a Validation activity named Validate Brainwaves, which checks for files in a specified folder the batch job is expected to perform its transformation on. If the folder exists and there are files in it, then the flow continues to the Custom activity. If there are no files to process, then the Lookup activity performs its operation and continues the flow to the batch job. If the lookup fails, then the pipeline execution is stopped and the status is set to Failed. The other failure condition is from the Custom activity named Calculate Frequency Median. If you haven't already looked at this section from Chapter 6, consider doing so now, as it discusses a bit more about error handling in the batch source code. If for any reason the batch process returns an error, the Fail activity named Batch Load Fail is triggered. The Fail activity logs the error message and code into the pipeline details for review, which will help expedite the troubleshooting efforts, as you will have a relevant explanation of the exception that is easy to find. Keep in mind there are Retry and Retry Interval configurations for a Custom activity, just as for a Data Flow activity. If failures are handled well in your batch code, then rerunning the job again after a short pause might result in a successful outcome.

Debug Spark Jobs by Using the Spark UI

When it comes to debugging all kinds of applications, much of the time and effort is spent trying to identify the component(s) that caused the issue. Once the component(s), like a Spark job, for example, is identified as a key contributor to the problem, the next step is to search for logs from that specific component. Those logs might hold information that explain in detail what took place. To get an overview of Spark jobs in Azure Databricks, refer to Figure 6.42, which illustrates the workflow dashboard, which is useful for getting an overall view of the job health. Drilling down into the job specifics will render more information to guide you further along the debugging process. Consider, for example, Figure 9.21, which renders resource utilization during the job run. Figure 9.25 is an illustration of the Spark UI, which shows very low-level information about the Spark job. Expanding the DAG visualization group renders Figure 9.26, which is a method-by-method execution path of the job. This is about as granular as you can get, and it should show you precisely where the issue is being experienced. After finding the specific location, you should discuss the issue with a developer to determine the course of action. Lastly, if the Spark job is being run from an Azure Synapse Analytics Spark pool, then in addition to the information provided, there also exist an illustration of the Spark application (see Figure 9.16) and direct access to the `stderr` and `stdout` logs.

Scale Resources

Figure 6.6 shows the select node size when you provisioned your Azure Batch pool. Notice that the Mode toggle switch is set to Fixed, with a targeted dedicated nodes value of 2.

This means the amount of compute capacity allocated to this pool is fixed and will not scale. If the utilization of the allocated resource reaches 100 percent, then the jobs will either screech to a halt or run very slowly. The alternative to Fixed mode is Auto Scale, which can be changed after the pool is provisioned. There is a Scale navigation item and a Scale menu link on the Overview blade in the Azure portal for the Azure Batch pool. Clicking the Scale button and then enabling the Auto Scale toggle switch renders the blade shown in Figure 10.28.

FIGURE 10.28 Scaling resources: Azure Batch pool

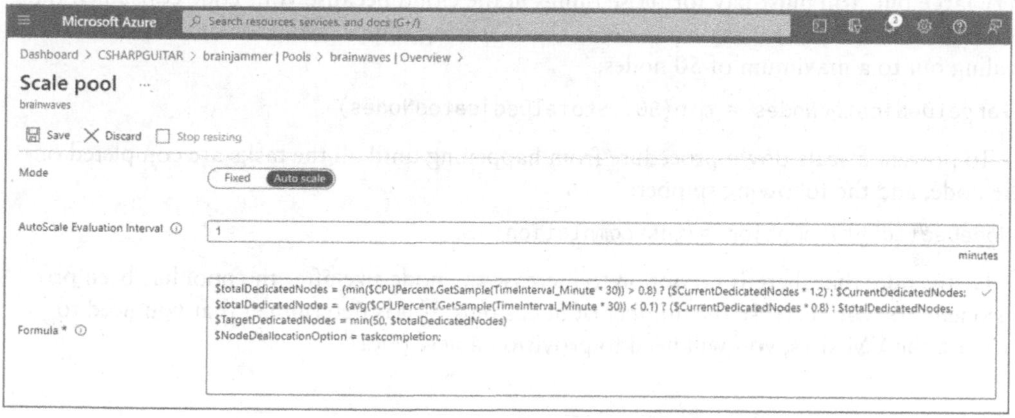

As shown in Figure 10.28, scaling is managed with an autoscale formula. The first snippet sets the number of nodes based on a sampling of CPU consumption. The CPU sample time frame is 30 minutes, which is 30 multiplied by the value of the AutoScale Evaluation Interval setting, which in this case is 1. If the CPU percentage is over 80 percent, increase the current number of nodes by 20 percent; otherwise, leave the current number of nodes as they currently are. The variable named `totalDedicatedNodes` is a service-defined variable, and making a change to it results in the platform taking an action on its change.

```
$totalDedicatedNodes =
    (min($CPUPercent.GetSample(TimeInterval_Minute * 30)) > 0.8) ?
    ($CurrentDedicatedNodes * 1.2) : $CurrentDedicatedNodes;
```

It is important to scale back down when capacity is no longer needed. When you scale up, those nodes will remain allocated and generate cost regardless of whether they are utilized or not. The platform does not make any conclusions about whether your batch job requires more or less compute capacity; you must manage this completely, scaling down as necessary. The following snippet checks the CPU percentage every 30 minutes. If the result is less than 10 percent CPU consumption, then the number of nodes will be scaled down by 80 percent. It is important to not scale down too quickly, and you need to keep the scale-up and scale-down thresholds as far apart as possible. There is a concept called *flapping*, where scale-up and scale-down rules overlap, which causes unexpected behaviors. It does take some time to get jobs running on a new node. If the scale-up and scale-down rules are too close together, a scale command could be triggered during this lag time and cause some issues.

```
$totalDedicatedNodes =
    (avg($CPUPercent.GetSample(TimeInterval_Minute * 30)) < 0.1) ?
    ($CurrentDedicatedNodes * 0.8) : $totalDedicatedNodes;
```

It is also good practice to manage the maximum number of nodes the platform will scale out to. If a rogue job gets started and consumes large amounts of CPU, you could receive a very large bill. You must pay for those things in the cloud because your code consumed the compute whether you meant it to or not. The following snippet will restrict the platform to scaling out to a maximum of 50 nodes:

```
$TargetDedicatedNodes = min(50, $totalDedicatedNodes)
```

To prevent a scale-down procedure from happening until all the tasks are completed on the node, add the following snippet:

```
$NodeDeallocationOption = taskcompletion;
```

Lastly, note that there is no option to increase the node size after the pool has been provisioned. You can increase the number of nodes only. If it is determined that you need to increase the VM sizes, you will need to provision a new pool.

Monitor Batches and Pipelines

This section is a follow-up to Chapter 6. It is placed here so that you can recall the content reading about logging, monitoring, optimizing, and troubleshooting techniques in this chapter and Chapter 9.

Handle Failed Batch Loads

There are many actions you can take within the Azure Batch job itself from a coding perspective. In every case, implement `try/catch()` statements around the source code that performs the data transformation. The other options are adding a Fail activity, which will result in good error messages to the support team, retrying the batch job execution, and/or adding failure dependencies to the Custom activity in an additional attempt to recover from the failed job. It is important to consider the implications of failed batch jobs that are responsible for loading data. Refer to the following sections in Chapter 6, which identify how to handle failed batch loads:

- "Handle Duplicate Data"
- "Handle Missing Data"
- "Handle Late-Arriving Data"

- "Regression to a Previous State"
- "Validate Batch Loads"

The way in which you handle a batch load failure depends greatly on what the load is doing and the downstream dependencies of the data.

Design and Develop a Stream Processing Solution

The following sections contain some additional optimization and troubleshooting techniques that build on top of the logging, monitoring, and debugging techniques discussed in this chapter and in Chapter 9.

Optimize Pipelines for Analytical or Transactional Purposes

This section builds on the content in Chapter 7, "Design and Implement a Data Stream Processing Solution," about scaling. In this chapter and in Chapter 9, you learned a bit more about monitoring, error handling, and troubleshooting capabilities. From an optimization perspective, the most effective way to achieve optimal performance with an Azure Stream Analytics job is by parallelization. Table 7.6 introduced the types of input and output partitioning, which are the key enablers for parallelization. The following sections in Chapter 7 explain how input and output partitioning work:

- "Process with One Partition"
- "Process Across Partitions"

To get maximum throughput, the number of partitions of the incoming stream must equal the number of partitions of the outgoing stream (refer to Figure 7.31). Remember that when your job is running in compatibility level 1.2 or greater, the platform automatically provides a partition key; otherwise, you should use the `PARTITION BY` clause in your query, similar to the following:

```
SELECT *
INTO Output
FROM Input PARTITION BY pkBrainwavesPOW
```

From a troubleshooting perspective, the first place to start is with performance and availability metrics. Chapter 7 introduced the available diagnostic settings, which, when configured, store metrics, execution, and authoring Azure Stream Analytics data into an Azure Monitor Log analytics cluster (refer to Figure 7.50). The data stored in the cluster can be queried using KQL to locate components of the job that are performing slowly or encountering errors. Once those points are identified, they can be analyzed further to find the reason for the problem. Then you can engage the team and come up with an approach to resolve it.

In addition to diagnostic settings, you learned about the activity logs, which can show failed operations (refer to Figure 7.51). Configuring an alert rule when operations return a status of Failed is good practice for maintaining the reliability of your solution. The option to create this alert rule is available directly on the Activity log blade, as shown in Figure 7.51. In Chapter 9, Table 9.9 exposed you to all the available Azure Stream Analytics metrics and their meanings. There was also a discussion around using numerous metrics together, which led to a better understanding of performance- or error-related issues. When used together, the Backlogged Input Events, Watermark Delay, and CPU % Utilization options are very helpful for determining if there is a compute capacity issue. Figure 9.18 and Figure 9.19 are examples of the metrics capability for an Azure Stream Analytics job. You can further optimize your Azure Stream Analytics job by handling interruptions and scaling resources.

Handle Interruptions

An interruption to the processing of your data stream flowing through your Azure Stream Analytics job can occur in many forms. One of the most catastrophic examples is caused by an event such as a storm or other event that results in the closure of all datacenters in a given Azure region. Although these events are considered extremely rare, some businesses run such critical business applications that continue to operate under extreme circumstances. For example, medical, police, communication, and transportation services must operate in emergencies and need their applications to continue to run.

Chapter 4 introduced BCDR, which is the recovery plan created ahead of time that should be followed when the situation dictates. The plan outlines the transfer of your operations from one region to another, for example, from West Europe to North Europe or from East US to West US, both of which represent paired Azure regions. Refer to Table 4.2 for more examples of paired Azure regions. When an entire region is offline, you will need to provision an identical replica of the environment you had in the offline region. Having this replica environment provisioned in advance and keeping it updated with your data will result in a faster recovery from an event like this. Recognize, however, that this can come with a significant cost. Having this standby environment is dependent on the degree of importance of that application and the impact should it be unavailable. If the impact is great, then the cost is justifiable. If not, an alternative may be to have the scripts ready to provision the infrastructure as a temporary solution. Then, once the primary production environment is back online, redirect users back to the original environment and move the data created during the outage.

Another type of interruption can occur when a single datacenter in the region goes offline. This form of interruption is resolved by availability zones, which are isolated datacenters in a region, as introduced in Chapter 1. Many Azure products, such as Azure Event Hubs, are automatically replicated into multiple datacenters to manage occurrences of this specific kind of scenario. If the situation arises that necessitates the redirection of traffic from one zone to the other, it will be managed for you. There would be some transient impact; however, that momentary disruption is much less than being totally offline for a longer period of time.

At the time of this writing, an Azure Stream Analytics job, as you created in Exercise 3.17, does not support availability zones. To gain zone replication for an Azure Stream Analytics job, you must provision your own cluster. Configuring and managing an Azure Stream Analytics cluster is not covered in this book. Briefly, that product provisions a dedicated amount of compute resources that can be used to run all your jobs. This contrasts with the job created in Exercise 3.17, where each job is on a multitenant cluster. To view or change this, navigate to the Environment blade in the Azure portal, change the configuration to Dedicated, and then provision the cluster, as shown in Figure 10.29.

FIGURE 10.29 Handling interruptions: dedicated Azure Stream Analytics cluster

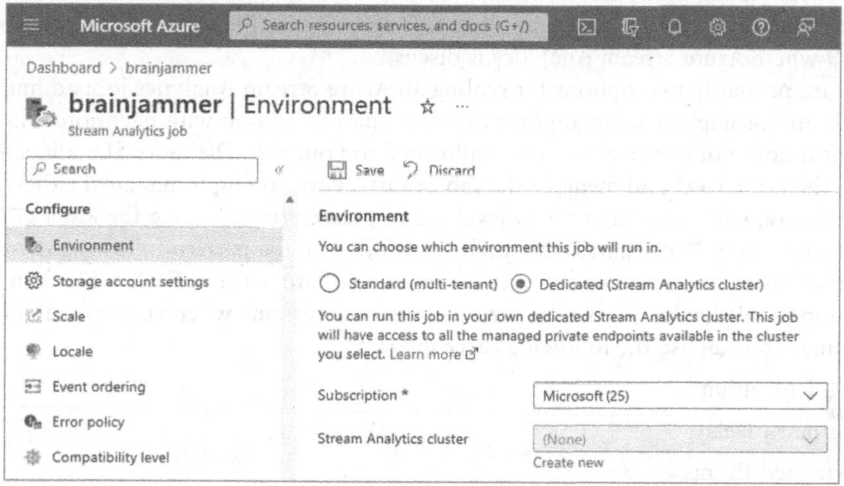

If you require zone replication, then you must provision an Azure Stream Analytics cluster; otherwise, you will need to have a BCDR plan that includes the provisioning of the job in a paired region. The other form of interruption was the one touched on in Chapter 7, which concerned node failure, OS updates, and product upgrades. If the node your job is running on is identified as being unhealthy, the platform will take an action to rehost your job on another instance. A massive amount of telemetry is generated and monitored on the Azure platform that is used for managing and taking actions when servers are identified as being unhealthy, so you do not need to worry much about that. The same goes for OS and product updates, especially when your job spans across availability zones. Upgrades of these kinds are rolled out strategically to avoid causing downtime. Consider a situation in which your job is in three zones and an OS patch needs to be applied. The platform will do its best to not install the upgrade onto nodes in the different zones that host the same job at the same time. This results in the endpoint being available to ingest, transform, and output data even when updates are being applied. The final form of interruptions is focused on the application itself, which has to do with bottlenecks and resource consumption. In that scenario, you might need to add additional compute resources to the job, as covered in the next section.

Scale Resources

Chapter 7 and Chapter 9 covered what you need to know for the exam concerning scaling. The intention of the content here is to summarize the three important concepts related to scaling. The first concept has to do with understanding the options you have regarding scaling an Azure Stream Analytics job. The second concept concerns the discovery and analysis of usage and performance metrics that identify when scaling is necessary. The last concept has to do with scaling itself, that is, how to scale specifically. Again, you should already have an idea about all three of these scaling aspects. If not, reread Chapter 7 and have a look over Chapter 9 where Azure Stream Analytics is discussed.

There are primarily two options for scaling an Azure Stream Analytics job: adding additional SUs and/or implementing and/or optimizing parallelization with partitions. An SU represents the amount of compute resources allocated to your job. The more SUs allocated to your job, the more CPU and memory the job can use. Partitioning is managed either by the platform, when in compatibility level 1.2 or greater, or by adding the `PARTITION BY` clause to your query. Every partition match resulting from the pattern following the `PARTITION BY` clause results in the data being divided into subsets. Each subset can be processed in parallel, which increases throughput. To determine when your job might benefit from scaling, you can use the following three metrics:

- SU % Utilization
- Watermark Delay
- Backlogged Events

When SU % Utilization exceeds 80 percent and you notice an increase in the Watermark Delay and Backlogged Events numbers, that is a sign that you should increase the number of SUs allocated to the job. Refer to Figure 7.48, Figure 9.18, and Figure 9.19, which provide an example of Azure Stream Analytics usage and performance metrics. After determining that your job will benefit from additional SUs, you can scale manually, as shown in Figure 7.49, which allocates a static amount of compute resources to your job. The other option is to configure a custom autoscale rule, as shown in Figure 10.30.

Notice that the rule is based on the metrics identified earlier as those that are useful for identifying the need for adding SUs to the job. The numbers for the Watermark Delay and Backlogged Events metrics would need to be calculated using usage behaviors of the job over a longer time period. There also exists a throttle, which limits the maximum number of SUs to allocate, which is helpful for managing costs. Finally, in addition to adding SUs, consider reevaluating the way in which your incoming data is partitioned. If there is a structural change that can be made on the data producers that results in the addition of a partition id, then parallelization throughput can be realized, for example, including the electrode ID with the data stream and adding it to the PARTITION BY clause.

FIGURE 10.30 Scaling resources: custom autoscale rule

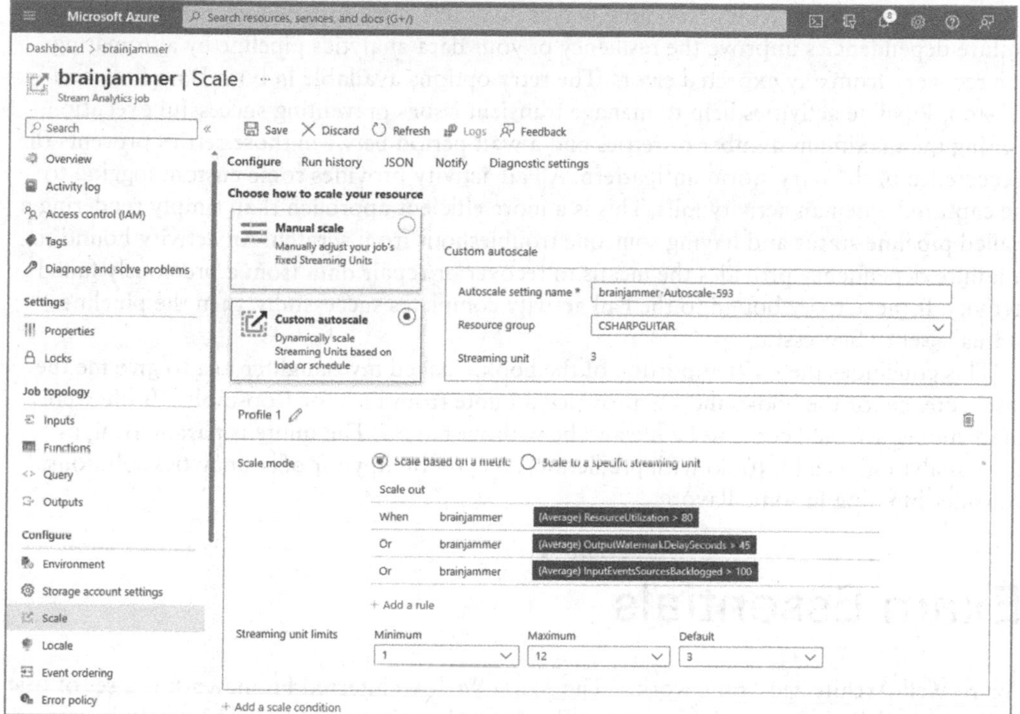

Summary

This chapter discussed numerous aspects for optimizing data storage, data processing, and pipelines. From a data storage perspective, you learned how data skewing, data spills, and shuffling have a negative impact on the storage and usability of your data. Using a command like PDW_SHOWSPACEUSED to show how data is stored across distribution is a way to determine if your data is skewed. Using an explain plan (i.e., query plan) can expose data shuffling, which causes latency due to the time required to retrieve data from the different nodes where the data is stored. You also learned that optimizing your partitions, enhancing table indexes, and making sure you are reading from cache all improve query performance.

Many data management views (DMV) are very useful for troubleshooting inefficient data storage and performance. They are specialized for indexes, transactions, queries, partitions, and everything else necessary for managing and optimizing a database. For example, the `sys.dm_pdw_request_steps` DMV lists all the steps taken for a given query. That means once you have narrowed down any latency to a specific query, you can break it down even further into the different steps the query must perform to complete.

Error handling and troubleshooting perspectives like retry capabilities, Fail activities, and failure dependencies improve the resiliency of your data analytics pipeline by automating the recovery from any expected errors. The retry options available in both Data flow and Custom Pipeline activities help to manage transient issues preventing successful execution. Setting the maximum number of retries and a wait period between those retries prevents the occurrence of the retry storm antipattern. A Fail activity provides some custom logging to be captured when an activity fails. This is a more efficient approach than simply rendering a Failed pipeline status and having someone troubleshoot from scratch. An activity bound to a failure dependency provides the means to recover or repair data from a previously failed activity. If the activity bound to the Fail activity completes successfully, then the pipeline status is set to Successful.

This concludes the written portion of the book. I asked my daughter Lea to give me the last sentence for the book, and she provided a quote from Eleanor Roosevelt: "If life were predictable, it would cease to be life and be without flavor." The quote is paradoxical, as data analytics has a lot to do with predictions. As you build your data analytics solutions, consider building in some flavor.

Exam Essentials

Azure Well-Architected Framework. The Azure Well-Architected Framework is a set of best practices to follow for running your workloads on the Azure platform. They include cost optimization, security, reliability, operation excellence, and performance efficiency.

Result set cache. When the same SQL queries are executed many times, performance can be improved by enabling the result set cache mechanism. The `result_cache_hit` column in the `sys.dm_pdw_exec_requests` table gives you insights about how often queries are using cache versus reading the data from disk.

I/O operations. When working with files or data that is stored on disk, the retrieval operations incur additional overhead, which increases execution time. The delay is caused by a thread switch from a procedural thread to an I/O thread and back. It is recommended to merge many small files into larger files to reduce the number of I/O operations. It is also recommended to enable cache, which reads data from memory instead of disk, which also avoids the I/O overhead cost.

Indexes. Columnstore indexes will be your most performant type of index when running on a dedicated SQL pool. Clustered indexes are identified by a sequence of columns that are to be used in the WHERE clause of a SQL query. When the WHERE clause matches the index, the data will be found faster because a scan of the table is not required; instead, the index points directly to the data on the table.

OLTP, OLAP, and HTAP. An OLTP database is a database users or customers send transactional data to in real time (for example, orders or brain wave readings). An OLAP is a data source where data is retrieved and used to gather business insights. Performing inserts and selects from the same datastore can cause contention issues. An HTAP is the solution to that scenario. When implemented, HTAP allows both inserts and selects to function on the same datastore without conflicting with each other.

Review Questions

Many questions can have more than a single answer. Please select all choices that are true.

1. Which components are part of the Azure Well-Architected Framework?
   - **A.** Cost optimization
   - **B.** Networking
   - **C.** Computing excellence
   - **D.** Security
2. What does the law of 60 have to do with?
   - **A.** The number of distributions on a dedicated SQL pool
   - **B.** A good number of files to process in parallel
   - **C.** The concept that 60 million rows of data on a table is optimal for gaining compression benefits
   - **D.** The optimal number of tables to have in an Azure Cosmos DB
3. Which algorithm can be used to determine the optimal number of partitions for a dedicated SQL pool?
   - **A.** Total number of rows = 60,000,000 * number of partitions.
   - **B.** Number of partitions / 60 = total number of tables.
   - **C.** Total number of nodes = number of partitions * 60.
   - **D.** Total number of rows / (1 million * 60) = number of partitions.
4. Why should you compact or merge small files?
   - **A.** ADLS is designed to work better with larger files.
   - **B.** Loading many files from disk is a latent I/O operation.
   - **C.** Merging together many small files reduces the number of I/O operations.
   - **D.** Only TAR compression is supported with dedicated SQL pools.
5. Which of the following can help to identify skewed data?
   - **A.** `DISTRIBUTION_ID`
   - **B.** An explain plan
   - **C.** `DBCC PDW_SHOWSPACEUSED`
   - **D.** `sys.dm_pdw_nodes_db_partition_stats`
6. Which tools are helpful for identifying data shuffling?
   - **A.** `SHOWRESULTCACHESPACEUSED`
   - **B.** `EXPLAIN`
   - **C.** `SHUFFLE_MOVE`
   - **D.** `df.explain(mode="formatted")`

7. Which of the following would produce data helpful for tuning data shuffling latency?
   - A. `sys.dm_pdw_nodes_db_partition_stats`
   - B. `PDW_SHOWSPACEUSED`
   - C. `UPDATE STATISTICS`
   - D. `df.shuffleOptimizer(true)`
8. Which of the following actions can be taken to resolve data shuffling?
   - A. Rewriting the SQL queries
   - B. Reviewing the explain plan recommendations
   - C. Reshuffling/repartitioning
   - D. Optimizing clustered columnstore tables
9. Which indexes are valid on a dedicated SQL pool?
   - A. Nonclustered columnstore
   - B. Clustered columnstore
   - C. Heap
   - D. Clustered/nonclustered
10. Which type of index is necessary to implement an HTAP solution on a dedicated SQL pool?
    - A. Nonclustered columnstore
    - B. Clustered columnstore
    - C. Heap
    - D. Clustered/nonclustered

ppendix

Answers to Review Questions

Chapter 1: Gaining the Azure Data Engineer Associate Certification

1. A, B. There is no such thing as Azure Cosmos DB or integration runtime pools. SQL and Spark pools are the only pools available in Azure Synapse Analytics.

2. A, B, C, D. All of the listed components are part of Azure Synapse Analytics.

3. C, D. A data lake is an ambiguous term that means all of the data that is useful for gathering and finding value in your data.

4. D. Azure HDInsight is best for customers who want to move existing on-premises HDInsight workloads to the cloud.

5. B. Azure Stream Analytics typically receives messages from Azure Event Hubs, analyzes them in real time, and takes some action on the content, such as streaming data from an automobile that has an unexpected GPS position that needs to be identified.

6. A, C, D. There is no product named SQL on Elastic Pools.

7. A, D. RBAC does not grant or deny access to data on a data source. Those credentials are specific to the provisioned product. RBAC only grants read, write, and delete of resources via the Azure portal. ABAC (preview) can be used to restrict based on sensitivity level, but not RBAC. RBAC is not that granular.

8. A, B, C. It is not a guest account; it is an account associated to a resource.

9. A, C. A subnets is a required part of a VNet and is the place where your connected resources are bound to. An NSG is a tool that lets you control inbound and outbound traffic based on port, IP, and protocol.

10. C. Azure Monitor is the tool you should use for gathering logs and for analyzing those logs.

Chapter 2: CREATE DATABASE dbName; GO

1. A, B, D. PHP is a programming language. A file with that extension would contain source code and not data. The other three file formats are valid.

2. A, B, C. There is no organizational data structure.

3. C. Replicated copies the data to all nodes in the cluster. There is no All type of distributed tables.

4. A. Store data on a dimension table when changes are not expected often.
5. C. PolyBase is a tool that works behind the scenes to give access and enforce compatibility between source and target data sources.
6. A. A view is a table that pulls data from other tables into a single, queryable table.
7. A, B, C. There is no function named `createOrReplaceTemporaryView()`—the correct name is `createOrReplaceTempView()`.
8. A, B, C, D. They are all aggregate SQL functions.
9. A, D. There is no SQL function, clause, or command named `PARSEJSON` or `CLOSEJSON`.
10. A. Don't confuse digest with ingest. Digest is not part of the big data analytics stages.

Chapter 3: Data Sources and Ingestion

1. B. A data lake is where all your data is stored. In most cases this is a central location. The data in a data lake is retrieved and transformed, usually from a raw state into business-ready report-quality data. Often it is stored back into the data lake after the cleaning, for example, eventually to the gold landing zone.
2. C. An EXE file is not a data file and therefore not supported on Azure Synapse Analytics.
3. D. Parquet files are the recommended format for performing file-based data analytics.
4. A, B. Using the `partitionBy()` method and placing files into logically named directory structures are valid partition strategies. The size of files impacts performance but does not contribute to partitioning.
5. A, B, C, D. All of the above. These are all reasons to perform some partitioning of data.
6. B, C. Data on dimension tables are like reference tables and do not change often. Fact tables are what you perform queries on. They contain the current data and therefore change often, due to updates.
7. C. A Type 3 SCD table provides only the previous value for data on the dimensional table. A Type 6 table is a combination of Types 1, 2, and 3.
8. A, B, C. A Type 6 SCD table combines all the capabilities from Type 1, 2, and 3.
9. B. False. For customers without current, or with small, in-house data analytics solutions, Azure Synapse Analytics is recommended. For customers who currently use open-source products like HDInsight or Databricks, Azure offers a version of those.
10. A, C, D. You cannot use HDInsight with Azure Stream Analytics. The other three options provide a portion of a streaming solution.

Chapter 4: The Storage of Data

1. A, C. A Parquet file is not a codec compressed file, and a TAR.JZ file doesn't exist. The other two, ZIP and TAR, are supported.

2. B, D. Partitioning improves performance and discoverability because you can better target your queries and the data is stored logically. Partitioning does not reduce costs, because the data, in its entirety, remains on the datastore.

3. B. The redundancy setting is for the Azure storage account and not on a container. Therefore, GRS configured on the Azure storage account is the correct option. Both LRS and ZRS remain in a single region.

4. A, B, D. There is no dedicated table distribution type.

5. D. Temporal tables are supported only on Azure SQL and/or on-premises SQL Server. When a temporal table is created, a sister table that contains CRUD data changes is also created, commonly referred to as a history table.

6. A, D. A Type 1 SCD table provides only the information necessary to know about a change. Finding out what the value was before the change is not possible using a Type 1 SCD table.

7. B. Only answer B is correct. A Type 3 SCD table stores not only the current value but also the value that previously existed in that column.

8. A, B, C. An external table utilizes PolyBase behind the scenes to load a file into a table, which can then be queried using SQL syntax.

9. C, D. Metadata is data that describes data. Answer D includes examples of the data that describes data.

10. A, B. The names of the DLZs that make up a big data analytics solution can be any logical sequence. Raw and bronze are common, while the others are not.

Chapter 5: Transform, Manage, and Prepare Data

1. A, B, C, D. All of the examples are forms of data transformation.

2. B, D. Encoding does not cast or change the format of date data types. That is a culture activity and does not improve the performance of queries.

3. B, C. The conversion of data points results in values between 0 and 1. The benefit of this is that outliers, which might skew the illustration, are scaled in. This makes the illustration more ingestible to the human eye.

4. A, C. Scala typically requires you to define and instantiate a variable before it can be used; otherwise, the code will not compile.

5. A, B, D. There is no support for notebooks—or any code that would run in a notebook—in Azure Stream Analytics. The other answers are correct.

6. A, C. A data flow pulls data from a source, converts it, and writes it to a sink. The sink is bound to a linked service that identifies the structure of the dataset and the product it is written to.

7. D. It is possible to run pipeline activities in parallel. You can have more than one data flow activity in a pipeline, and pipelines can be triggered by both a schedule and manually.

8. B, C, D. Objects instantiated in any cell before the one currently in focus can be accessed in later cells. Isolating code snippets into smaller pieces makes it easier to debug and performance tune, since the point of contention is confined to a smaller snippet of code. Looking at every line of code and trying to figure out what it all does is hard. Breaking the code down into smaller pieces improves comprehension.

9. A, B. Data management is not concerned with the direct management of the costs associated with data.

10. B. The `PREDICT` operator is used to identify the model in AML to be used with a given dataset for predicting future values. The other options can be used in more than AML scenarios.

Chapter 6. Create and Manage Batch Processing and Pipelines

1. B, C. The Validation activity will check if files exist and their size. The Lookup activity is useful for providing alternative paths to find files if there is a failure. The other two activities are not helpful in this scenario.

2. A, B, D. There is no enriched layer in the lambda architecture.

3. D. The Custom activity is used for running batch jobs. The other activities do not support running an Azure Batch job.

4. C. Only a tumbling window trigger provides this capability.

5. B, D. A storage event trigger is the easiest to configure, but you can also achieve the same using a custom event trigger.

6. A, B, C, D. All of the answers are true and helpful.

7. B, D. Both copying and moving only the changes made to a data source into your data lake are considered incremental data loads.

8. A. Only an annotation would result in linking a searchable or filterable word to a pipeline.

9. A, B. An Aggregate transformation lets you perform a `group by` query that results in duplicate rows being grouped together in a single row. Then, using the Select transformation, you can select the individual rows.

10. A, C, D. Many areas can concern security and compliance. The important ones from the possible options are networking, endpoint security and backup and recovery.

Chapter 7: Design and Implement a Data Stream Processing Solution

1. D. As shown in Figure 3.13, the data stream flows along the hot path into the speed layer. From there the data can flow into the serving layer for more transformation, or it can be directly consumed from the speed layer.

2. A. There is no warm or archive path. The cold path flows through the batch layer and the serving layer, whereas the hot path flows through the speed layer. Option A, the hot path, is the correct answer.

3. A, B, D. That a solution is open source is not a primary concern when it comes to the design of a stream processing solution. Each option in open-source or proprietary solutions offers features capable of providing a stream processing solution.

4. C. Options A, B, and D are reasons why stream processing cannot be performed on multiple partitions. Only option C is possible and therefore correct.

5. A, B, C. Power BI does not support partition keys, and the other three products must code the event message to include the partition key as part of the metadata.

6. B. A partition key is used to group data together so that it can be processed on a single partition, which results in faster execution.

7. A, C. A data stream is in constant motion and therefore cannot be upserted in real time. The data must be persisted on a datastore to achieve that. Those datastores exist in the serving layer. One datastore that can be configured at that layer is an Azure Cosmos DB container. It is not possible to upsert a live data stream in Power BI, and there is no Azure Stream Analytics job container.

8. A, B. The time in which the event message is generated on the data producer is the event time, and arrival time is not the same as a watermark. Both options A and B are correct.

9. C, D. Replay and Drop are the only valid error policies. Archive and Complete do not exist.

10. B, D. The number of incoming data events and partition counts will not tell you if you have enough compute resource to execute the processing of them. The Watermark Delay and CPU Utilization metrics will help.

Chapter 8: Keeping Data Safe and Secure

1. B, C. There is no product or feature named Data Discovery & Sensitivity Labeling, and Azure Blueprints is not useful for this purpose. Only options B and C are correct.
2. B. A lifecycle management policy is used to manage when data should be deleted from a datastore.
3. A. Encryption-at-rest is exactly as the name suggests; data is encrypted while not being used.
4. A, D. TLS is used with HTTP to encrypt data transmissions. All TLS versions can be used to implement encryption-in-transit.
5. B, D. Options A and C are not correct; only options B and D are correct.
6. A. Granting permissions can be complicated; therefore, you want to do it as few times as possible, which is why permissions should be granted to a group. Then, any user or identity who needs those permissions can be added to the group and get the permissions without hassle. Although the other options are possible, they are not recommended.
7. B, C. Azure Firewall is useful only if access to your data needs to be protected by an attribute only available at OSI level 4. This is very rare and therefore not considered a viable option. Azure VPN Gateway is useful for managing connectivity between on-premises networks and cloud networks when setting up a hybrid solutions. Only options B and C are viable.
8. A, B. Options A and B are true. Because option B is true, option C is false. A user-assigned managed identity, not a system-assigned identity, is identical to a service principal.
9. A, B, D. Files are not stored in an Azure key vault.
10. B. Only option B is correct. Azure Databricks passthrough authentication is used to grant the identity of the user in Azure Databricks to data hosted in Azure. The identity used with passthrough authentication must be in the Azure AD. The token cannot be used to gain access to the workspace and is not valid with OAuth providers in general.

Chapter 9: Monitoring Azure Data Storage and Processing

1. C. Only answer C is correct. Any value can be placed into an annotation and then filtered. The purpose of an annotation is to provide the ability to group your pipelines into categories, making it easier to see what is going on in heavily used workspaces.
2. A, B, C, D. Each component is considered part of the Azure Monitor portfolio of logging, monitoring, and alerting features.

3. C. Only logs are considered part of the Azure Monitor portfolio. All the other options are valid features but not part of Azure Monitor, and not all of them are for monitoring.

4. A, D. Retrieving all columns in a row, which would happen when `SELECT *` is executed, would be latent. Select only the columns necessary. Option D uses a wildcard and is a known latent pattern. Use this with caution, but try not to use it at all.

5. C, D. A test plan and a test case are both primary components of the Azure Test Plans component. Options C and D do not exist.

6. C. See Table 9.2 for a description of each DMV.

7. A. See Table 9.2 for a description of each DMV. Option B does not exist.

8. A, C. CPU % Utilization alone is not sufficient to determine if there is a capacity issue that can be resolved by adding SUs. Out of order events do not have anything to do with SUs. Both A and C can provide insights in isolation that warrant an increase in SU job allocation.

9. B. Apache Spark jobs are not on the Monitor Hub—or on any hub, for that matter.

10. A, B, C, D. Each product can use the diagnostic settings from within the Azure portal to store logs in a Log Analytics workspace.

Chapter 10: Troubleshoot Data Storage Processing

1. A, D. The Azure Well-Architected Framework comprises cost optimization, security, reliability, operation excellence, and performance efficiency.

2. A, B, C. The law of 60 is a guide for designing your data analytics storage on an Azure Synapse Analytics dedicated SQL pool. There is no optimization for the number of tables on either Azure Cosmos DB or on any datastore product on Azure.

3. A, D. Both options A and D will result in identifying the optimal number of partitions to provision. Options B and C will not, as the number of nodes or tables has nothing to do with implementing optimal partitioning.

4. A, B, C. Options A, B, and C are all true. A compressed file takes less time to be transmitted in a network. If there are many files, you should merge them into a single, larger file, which ADLS is optimized for.

5. A, C, D. If there are too many rows in a data distribution, as identified by a `DISTRIBUTION_ID`, then the data is considered skewed. Both options C and D also provide insights into skewing. Option B identifies query execution paths, not skewing.

6. B, C, D. Options B, C, and D all result in some helpful data that provides insights into shuffling. Option A is focused on caching statistics only.

7. A, B, C. There is no method named `shuffleOptimizer()`. The other options all provide insight into data shuffling, which can be used to design a fix.

8. A, B, C, D. Each option is a valid approach for resolving data shuffling that is causing latency. Keep in mind that shuffling will happen, but it only needs to be analyzed and reduced when it impacts performance.

9. A, B, C, D. Each of the index types are supported on a dedicated SQL pool.

10. A. A nonclustered columnstore index is required to implement an HTAP solution on a dedicated SQL pool.

Index

A

B

D

E

F

G

H

I

J

K

L

M

N

O

P

Q

R

T

U

V

W

X–Y–Z

V

W

X-Y-Z

Online Test Bank

To help you study for your MCA Azure Data Engineer certification exam, register to gain one year of FREE access after activation to the online interactive test bank—included with your purchase of this book! All of the practice questions in this book are included in the online test bank so you can study in a timed and graded setting.

Register and Access the Online Test Bank

To register your book and get access to the online test bank, follow these steps:

1. Go to `www.wiley.com/go/sybextestprep`. You'll see the **"How to Register Your Book for Online Access"** instructions.
2. Click "here to register" and then select your book from the list.
3. Complete the required registration information, including answering the security verification to prove book ownership. You will be emailed a pin code.
4. Follow the directions in the email or go to `www.wiley.com/go/sybextestprep`.
5. Find your book on that page and click the "Register or Login" link with it. Then enter the pin code you received and click the "Activate PIN" button.
6. On the Create an Account or Login page, enter your username and password, and click Login or, if you don't have an account already, create a new account.
7. At this point, you should be in the test bank site with your new test bank listed at the top of the page. If you do not see it there, please refresh the page or log out and log back in.